Louisville Slugger
TPX
B.A.T.S. Program
Baseball & Academic Targeting Service
48 States
$10 Million in Scholarships
1 Service...
The Baseball Factory
Your Link to the Colleges
Call for details:
1-800-641-HITS
Join Us at a Pro Park Near You!
Pro Evaluation
Touch 'em all!
Internet Exposure
Targeted Video
Showcase

With all the benefits the BCA provides,

it's hard to believe the membership fee is only *$30!*
But it is, and here's what you get:

Awards

- Players of the Year -- district and national
- all-America and all-district teams
- district and national Coaches of the Year
- district assistant Coaches of the Year
- district and national Grounds-keeper/Field of the Year

Recognition

- national team rankings in *BASEBALL AMERICA*
- Victory Club -- 50, 100, 150, etc., victory certificates
- 5, 10, 15, 20, 25, 30-year Coaching Service plaques
- continuous member plaque (after 5 years)

B C A

Publications

- **SCORECARD** -- quarterly newsletter
- **FROM THE DUGOUT** -- coaching ideas and strategy
- annual **MEMBERSHIP DIRECTORY**
- **EXTRA INNINGS** -- 10-issue newspaper with national coverage of high schools

Convention

- top speakers at clinic sessions
- special events: Awards Luncheon; state association meeting & more
- showcase of latest baseball products
- professional growth credit

Insurance

- $1,000,000 liability coverage — free to members

Upcoming Conventions:
1998: December 4-6, Tulsa, OK
1999: December 3-5, Tucson, AZ
2000: December 1-3, Knoxville, TN

Membership Application

NAME______________________________ TITLE______________
(Please Print or Type) Last First Middle Init. (Head, Assistant, etc.)

SCHOOL/
ORGANIZATION______________________________

SCHOOL/ORGANIZATION
LOCATION______________________________
Street/P.O. Box City State ZIP

PREFERRED MAILING
ADDRESS______________________________
(for all mailings throughout year) Street/P.O. Box City State ZIP

TELEPHONE: (School): ______________ (Home): ______________

(E-mail address): ______________________

The 1999 season will be my __________ year of coaching baseball.

Mail to:
BCA Membership
P.O. Box 5128
Bella Vista, AR 72714-0128

Dues enclosed: **US $30**
(in US funds) **Canada $35**
(in US funds) **Outside North America $50**
(Checks or money orders only)

OFFICIAL ATHLETIC COLLEGE GUIDE: BASEBALL

1999

TABLE OF CONTENTS

The editor has tried to ensure that both the academic and athletic information contained in this guide is up to date and accurate although subject to change. For that reason the reader should verify important information with the college or university admissions office or Baseball coach.

THE SPORT SOURCE, INC., 1845 Summit Avenue, Suite 402, Plano, TX 75074, call (800)862-3092, or e-mail sports@thesportsource.com, or visit THE SPORT SOURCE web site at **http://www.thesportsource.com**

PREFACE

THE SPORT SOURCE, INC. is pleased to present our *Sixth Edition* of the ***Official Athletic College Guide: BASEBALL***. With over ten years of assisting high school athletes in their pursuit of playing at the collegiate level, we continue to explore ways to improve our ***College Guides***. They have become the definitive publications in the sports of Baseball, Softball, and Soccer, functioning as both a reference handbook and self-promotional tool. Our commitment to providing the most current and comprehensive information available to our readers remains our No.1 priority!

The ***Official Athletic College Guide: BASEBALL*** was created, in part, to allow college Baseball coaches an effective medium for disseminating information about their programs to high school athletes, their parents, youth and high school coaches, and guidance counselors. The information they have provided is systematically organized and packaged in the ***College Guide*** to provide concise, accurate, and timely data for the prospective student-athlete and his family. If fully utilized, it will assist your son in making the best choice to meet specific academic interests while continuing his athletic career. In addition, this publication will supplement the numerous other handbooks that offer more complete information regarding academics, on-campus facilities, and student lifestyles - publications that are available directly from the various colleges and universities.

The ***College Guide*** is an important tool in the research, identification, and selection of schools that meet the student's athletic and academic program needs. We believe this publication to be the most comprehensive listing available, containing detailed information on more than 1400 colleges and universities. The data compiled in this book was gathered through phone inquiries and detailed questionnaires mailed to college and university Baseball coaches throughout the United States. The profiles are divided by state and listed in alphabetical order by school name within each geographic area.

We continue to learn from student-athletes enrolled in various colleges and universities who used the ***College Guide*** to assist them in choosing the particular school they are currently attending. It is sometimes difficult to evaluate one's own ability as a player, so in each profile, we will attempt to provide a barometer of that program. This book will allow student-athletes to assess not only a university's academic strengths, but also the competitiveness of its Baseball program. We have detailed each team's strengths based on its schedule, history, number of seniors, past achievements, and style of play.

Our previous editions of the ***Official Athletic College Guide: BASEBALL***, ***Official Athletic College Guide: SOFTBALL***, and ***Official Athletic College Guide: SOCCER*** have been well received by college coaches. For the prospective student-athlete, one of the keys to communicating effectively with a college coach is to be able to converse intelligently about their program - valuable knowledge that is contained within this book! Accordingly, we have been advised that prospective players who have used our publications are submitting resumes that are more professional and comprehensive, and cover letters that are more direct with interested student-athletes more capable of conversing about a college's respective program.

THE SPORT SOURCE™ ***Official Athletic College Guide: BASEBALL*** will be your definitive third-party reference handbook during the process of selecting a college Baseball program that's right for you. Our goal is to supply enough information so that you, the student athlete, can make an intelligent and informed decision on the continuation of your Baseball and academic career.

THE PUBLISHER

As founder of THE SPORT SOURCE, INC., **Charlie Kadupski** continues to annually compile, edit, and publish the ***Official Athletic College Guides: BASEBALL, SOFTBALL, and SOCCER*, and the *Official Club & Tournament Guide: SOCCER***. Mr. Kadupski is a former collegiate Soccer player having also played professionally with the San Jose Earthquakes, Houston Hurricanes, and Ft. Lauderdale Strikers of the North American Soccer League (NASL), the Los Angeles Lazers of the Major Indoor Soccer League (MISL), and the Dallas Americans of the American Soccer League (ASL). While at Hartwick College, he was an All-American selection in 1977 - the same year his college men's team won the NCAA Division I National Championship.

Charlie currently holds a USSF "A" License and serves on the United States Soccer Federation (USSF) National Coaching Staff and Editorial Board. He is also the full-time Coaching Director for the Storm Soccer Club in Plano, Texas.

ACKNOWLEDGMENTS

The *Sixth Edition* of the ***Official Athletic College Guide: BASEBALL*** is the tireless effort of our dedicated staff and the joint cooperation of college coaches and administrators throughout the United States. We would like to especially thank NCAA Division I head coach **Mike Martin** and assistant **Chip Baker** of **Florida State University,** and **Ron Polk**, Assistant Athletic Director and former head coach at **Mississippi State University,** for their contributing articles and shared vision for this publication in assisting young student-athletes in reaching their goals of participating in college athletics. With less than 10% of high school players receiving college athletic scholarships for Baseball, our goal is to assist both those gifted young athletes who qualify, and, more importantly, the other 90% who just want an opportunity to play and compete in the sport that has become their passion.

Sponsor Recognition: THE SPORT SOURCE would like to also thank the **NATIONAL ASSOCIATION OF INTERCOLLEGIATE ATHLETICS (NAIA)** for their continued commitment to higher education, collegiate athletics, and the growth and support of men's competitive Baseball in the United States.

Special thanks to:

Abbott Sparks
Lyman Memorial H.S., Lebanon, CT
Mitchell Jr. College, New London, CT
Hartwick College, Oneonta, NY

Special acknowledgment for their help each year with the production of the *Official Athletic College Guides: BASEBALL, SOFTBALL, and SOCCER* and the *Official Club & Tournament Guide: SOCCER.*

Editor & Publisher:
Charlie Kadupski

Edit Staff / Production:
Michael Calabria
Marevi Bishop
Mary Baumgartner

Support & Marketing:
Teresa Shuman
Filippo Costanzo
Becky Warlick
Lily Lima

Technical Advisors:
Rose & Bob Baker
Bob Estep
Frank Pyle
David Samuels

Cover Art / Ad Agency:
Coffee Black Advertising
1400 Turtle Creek Blvd.
Dallas, TX 75207

Design & Layout:
Dave Marshall

Cover Photography:
National Association of
Intercollegiate Athletics

Printing Company:
Brenda Cockrell
Dallas Offset, Inc.
2110 Panaromic Circle
Dallas, TX 75211

INTRODUCTION

Selecting the best college or university to meet your needs may seem like an enormous and intimidating task. The prospect of choosing one school from more than 800 may produce intense feelings of anxiety, panic, and even fear of making the wrong decision. But fear and panic are products of the unknown. There is no reason for this process to be overwhelming. By being organized and diligent, and surrounding yourself with the right resources and materials, you will be able to make an informed decision - a decision that you can truly feel good about!

Written by college coaches, former professional and college players, and college administrators, the ***Official Athletic College Guide: BASEBALL*** is your prime weapon against the anxiety associated with the college selection process. Every step is detailed by experts who describe the best methods to help you get noticed by college coaches. You will also learn what the coaches expect from you as a player, and what questions you should ask regarding their specific athletic program.

Most people travel from the known to the unknown. The known is that you are a junior or senior in high school with a certain GPA and test scores. The unknown is, "Where am I going to college?" The task is not impossible. You will simply need to identify a school that offers the academic programs that best suit your needs, and a Baseball program that is compatible with your athletic ability. You may have as many as 20 schools on your initial list., but only target those schools where the minimum test scores and required GPA fit your own.

Use the ***College Guide*** extensively, but don't make it your only resource. Consult other reference materials. Ask questions of your parents, guidance counselors, coaches and other administrators at the colleges that interest you. Gather your information carefully; then examine your options. With regard to your own athletic and academic career, this may be the single biggest decision you will make to this point in your life. While it requires careful consideration, the process itself should never be a stumbling block, but rather a fun and exciting time to share with your parents in planning for your future. It does require a focused and concerted effort, however, and a lack of follow-through may create roadblocks forcing you to make unnecessary compromises in the type of school or sports program you may be seeking.

The process of identifying your interests and selecting the appropriate colleges should begin early. Your freshman year in high school is not too soon to begin the process. Those especially talented players will have less to worry about - the college coaches will be pursuing them. However, it is the greater majority of student-athletes who need to be prepared. As a prospective college player, it is critical that you do your research, and are identified by college coaches as early as possible. Your high school varsity Baseball program and summer leagues are the best vehicles for college coaches to spot you as a prospective recruit. "All-Star" and college showcase events are also effective activities for personal recognition and identification by college coaches. Those student-athletes who make a conscious effort to evaluate college programs, and narrow those choices as they progress through their high school career, will have identified two to three solid choices by December of their senior year.

Most college coaches begin to identify student-athletes as high school juniors - your year to shine as both a player and a student. But even if you have delayed the process of selecting a college until your senior year, all hope is not lost. High school coaches who are well-connected will be able to pinpoint tournaments or showcase events in which college coaches will be present. (Please refer to the ***Tournament Directory*** located in the back of this book.) You must take the initiative to contact the coach at the school or schools that interest you by sending them your resume. Preface it with a personalized cover letter and be sure to mention your game schedule and the dates of any showcase events where you might be playing. In this situation, time is very critical - you will need to be seen quickly by college coaches in order for them to fairly evaluate your abilities before they make commitments to other players. (This topic is discussed further in the section titled **The Student Athlete's Role in Choosing a College**.)

Throughout the evaluation process, be advised that college coaches are *selling* their programs. They are going to tell you all the best things about their school and their team. Remember also, that college coaches are not just promoting their program to you, but to 25 or more other players as well. It is important to make sure the information you hear is accurate. If you do your homework, you won't overestimate your ability, or underestimate the competition for the position you wish to play. There may also be weaknesses and shortcomings in the program that you will be forced to identify on your own. If you make a mistake in your quest to join a high-profile program, you may end up riding the bench for four years or transferring to another school. This is the reason it is so very important to take an analytical approach to this process. Do your homework and be sure to do a thorough job.

As previously mentioned, one of the most critical steps in the recruitment process is your direct correspondence with the college coach. Because there are often coaching changes, it is highly recommended that you contact the college athletic department to verify the current coach and the correct spelling of the his name before mailing any correspondence. Compose your resume and address a personalized cover letter directly to the Baseball coach. Be sure to include specific information about the program - information contained in the academic and athletic profiles listed in this book. Typically, the 1400+ profiles will also include information on the number of All-District players, All-State players, and High School All-Americans participating in the Baseball program. If a team indicates that out of 20 players, they have 10 All-District players, 7 All-State players and 3 All-America players, then you can assume this to be a very strong program. Other colleges may list 7 or 8 "walk-ons" on their roster. Assess your interests and ability accordingly.

***

The first step in the identification and evaluation process is to thoroughly explore this handbook. It contains much of the information you will need to make an informed decision. Choosing the best avenue to continue your education and athletic development really is not as hard as it seems. We hope the ***Official Athletic College Guide: BASEBALL*** will assist you in making the right choice. We believe there is a program to fit everyone's needs. With proper research, you will find the program that is right for you.

Much success to you in the classroom *and* on the field of play!

Editor's Note: *The following sections, "THE COLLEGE IDENTIFICATION AND SELECTION PROCESS" and "THE STUDENT ATHLETE'S ROLE IN CHOOSING A COLLEGE", both have one goal; to prepare the prospective student athlete for college Baseball. Although similar in many ways, these methods have various distinctions that make them unique. They are all positive techniques. You are encouraged to examine them all and choose one or more methods that you feel will work for you.*

WHAT DOES IT TAKE TO PLAY COLLEGE BASEBALL?

MIKE MARTIN
HEAD BASEBALL COACH
FLORIDA STATE UNIVERSITY

The question of "what it takes for a student-athlete to compete at the collegiate level" is constantly brought before me in my travels across the country. The answer may be as broad and vague as the question. In this book you will find hundreds of Baseball programs. Is there a Baseball program right for you? Yes. Can you walk into any program and compete immediately? Probably not.

To compete successfully as a NCAA Division I player, a student-athlete must be focused, dedicated, and opportunistic. NCAA Division I is the most recognized and competitive level of college Baseball. The time commitment of a Division I player is likened to a full-time job as both players and coaches alike put in long hours all year long to insure success and team development. These hours (15-30 per week, depending on the team) are in addition to college classes, individual study, and social activities. Even so, these programs are so sought after that they attract literally thousands of applicants each year. To play college Baseball, however, you don't necessarily have to limit your search to Division I colleges and universities.

Speed, power, and arm strength are the primary components that distinguishes a Division I player from Division II, Division III, and NAIA. The technical speed and proficiency of a player to make plays with quickness and accuracy separates the top Division I player from all others. The tactical speed to read and anticipate rather than just reacting determines the speed of the game, and thus the level of play from Division I (tactically fastest) on down. If you are deficient in any of these key qualities, maybe you should look for a lower level of play where you can compete with more success.

College coaches receive hundreds of letters and phone calls every week from high school players, coaches, and parents claiming that they have a player that can play Division I Baseball. The college coach's first question is always, "Have you ever seen my team play?" and "Do you know what Division I competition is like?" Too often they don't. Having only seen youth and high school games, they are not aware of the intensity and speed of play at the college level. The same could be said of college coaches pushing their players to the professional level; we naturally think that our most talented players can excel even with the increased pressure which that level demands.

A quality Division I player typically has a clear repertoire of attributes to bring to a college team. Summer select camp programs can help you hone those skills and evaluate your own abilities with respect to other top players in your recruiting class. Our camp program is always a great place for us to evaluate young talent. Typically, I'm looking for real aggressive, assertive, quick paced, give 110% all the time type of players. But that's my style, and the style of play I demand here with my program. Other coaches will evaluate talent based on different criteria.

Here are examples of the capabilities of a typical Division I player:

<u>Pitchers</u>

- Leadership - instills confidence in teammates
- Exhibits speed, consistency, and control
- Diversity of pitches
- Ability to adjust to different hitters
- Excellent arm strength
- Handles pressure well

<u>Catchers</u>

- Leadership - controls the tempo of the game
- Reads hitters well
- Calls pitches with confidence
- Quick release with excellent arm strength
- Throws accurately to bases
- Displays mental and physical toughness

WHAT DOES IT TAKE TO PLAY COLLEGE BASEBALL?

Middle Infielders

Excellent footwork and range
Quick release with good arm strength
Throws with accuracy
Ability to consistently turn the double play
Vocal leader on the field

Infield Corners

Excellent instincts and quickness
Reacts quickly to line drives and ground balls down the base line
Ability to handle tough throws both in the air and in the dirt (1st Base)
Quick release with good arm strength (3rd Base)
Throws with accuracy

Outfielders

Excellent speed and quickness
Good judgment and instincts with fly balls and line drives
Ability to make strong accurate throws to bases and home plate

Hitters

Ability to make solid contact with the ball
Adjusts well to different pitches
Reads and reacts to coaches signs and puts the ball into play
Can hit with power
Excels in pressure situations

What does it take to play college Baseball? The answer is "What do you want from your college Baseball experience?" If you have the technical, tactical, and physical tools to play at the Division I level, do you have the time and dedication? If you would sit the bench for a Division I team, wouldn't you be happier playing for a Division II, III, or NAIA program?

The question of college choices can be comprehensively researched in the pages of this book. The answers to questions about your future as a collegiate Baseball athlete ultimately lie in your abilities and aspirations.

Mike Martin is the Head Baseball Coach at Florida State University. He is the fourth winningest active college Baseball coach, and ranks second nationally among active Division I Baseball coaches with a .744 winning percentage. Currently in his 20th season at FSU, Coach Martin has compiled an overall record of 1022-250 and was named ACC "Coach of the Year" in 1995 and 1998. Under his leadership, the Seminoles have made 19 straight NCAA post-season tournament appearances and advanced to the College World Series 9 times. In addition, Coach Martin has coached 38 All-Americans, 72 All-Conference Selections, 3 Golden Spikes Award winners, and has 88 former players who have signed professional contracts.

WHAT A COLLEGE COACH LOOKS FOR IN A PLAYER?

RON POLK
HEAD BASEBALL COACH
U.S.A. NATIONAL BASEBALL TEAM
ASSISTANT ATHLETIC DIRECTOR
FORMER HEAD BASEBALL COACH
MISSISSIPPI STATE UNIVERSITY

I am often asked: "What do you look for in a player?" My answer can vary from year to year depending on the recruiting needs of our program.

Position play may be a major characteristic in determining who we recruit, but it is only one of the many traits we consider. Each program has its own philosophy and personality and we try to identify potential student-athletes with a similar style. Not every outstanding player will match with every program. The ability to blend within a team is as important as being able to contribute on the field. We look for team-oriented players with a great passion for the game of Baseball.

To play college Baseball, a player needs technical and tactical skills coupled with certain physical and psychological attributes. Even the most skilled players may be deficient in one of these key areas. What we look for are players possessing a good balance of these qualities, and the desire and ability to develop.

It is critical to be exceptional in at least one area. If you are a top-level pitcher, you can make a contribution. If you are an exceptional hitter but have only an adequate arm, you can make a contribution. If you show strong leadership skills, but have average physical abilities, you can make a contribution. One of our key responsibilities as coaches is to be able to blend the strengths of individual players into a successful team.

The best players are outstanding in more than one area, and the truly elite players are extraordinary in all areas. I believe that strength in the "mental game" is most crucial. Ultimately, what often defines winners is their toughness and desire. Below are descriptions of the four areas that I feel are essential to the college game.

PSYCHOLOGICAL

This is your mental game. Your ability to deal with adversity. It is the intensity and confidence that you display in critical situations that sets you apart from the other athletes on the field. It's your ability to cope with the frustration that is innate in our sport. Remember, even a great hitter fails every 7 out of 10 at bats.

Your passion for the game also falls in this category. Passion is measured not only by your love for the game, but also by your determination, hustle, and desire. It makes an impression when you are the first person on the field, and the last person in the clubhouse at the end of practice. It's demonstrated by your tenacity in tough situations, your unwillingness to settle for second best. It's defined by the player who wants the bat in his hands with an 0-2 count, two outs in the bottom of the 9th inning, and his team one run down in a critical game.

PHYSICAL

Physical characteristics include height, body type, speed, arm strength, quickness, etc. You can further develop some of these traits (speed, strength, and quickness), but much of who you are is what you will be. Because you are short doesn't limit your opportunities as a pitcher, it just means you will need to work harder and be more efficient with your technique. Lack of running speed will limit a short game player, but it doesn't matter as much if you are a power hitter or can make up for your lack of speed with smart base-running.

College programs place much emphasis on strength training and speed enhancement. You will further develop your body and technical skills once you enter college. The best way to deal with a deficiency in a physical area is to be aware of it, and then to discover ways to minimize your limitation via better technique and more efficient movement.

WHAT A COLLEGE COACH LOOKS FOR IN A PLAYER?

TECHNICAL

Your ability to execute fundamental skills demonstrates your technical proficiency. The closer you are to perfection in your basic skills such as throwing, fielding, base-running, hitting, and bunting, the more likely you are to be recruited. Even advanced skills are noted by recruiters such as footwork, slap hitting, different types of slides, etc. We as coaches all believe in the old adage, "perfect practice makes perfect players," the more you practice the better you will be. Your performance in games always shows how much effort you put into practice.

TACTICAL

Understanding the strategy of Baseball is another area that is important. Knowing "what to do when" is critical to your ability to adjust to the college game. What base to throw to, when to take risk as a base-runner, what back-up responsibility you have as an outfielder all demonstrate your knowledge of the game of Baseball. Your college Baseball experience will continue to develop your technical and tactical skills and knowledge of the game, but you must have a solid foundation from the start.

ACADEMICS

Lastly, and equally important, if your academics are not in order, you will not be allowed the opportunity to play and compete. You can be sure that included in the initial information a college coach will request is a prospect's academic record. You must be a solid student with a college preparatory curriculum. The NCAA and NAIA have very specific guidelines regarding eligibility for student-athletes. Talk with your high school guidance counselor or coach for more information, and please don't underestimate the value of strong academic standing in the recruitment and admissions process.

Ron Polk is currently the head coach of the U.S.A. National Baseball Team, and Assistant Athletic Director and former head Baseball coach at NCAA Division I Mississippi State University. He has coached the Men's National Team during 7 international tours and in 1998 was named "National Coach of the Year" in Baseball by the United States Olympic Committee. In 22 years as head coach at MSU, Coach Polk compiled an overall record of 888-422 - currently the most wins by a head coach in Southeastern Conference history. During that time his Bulldog teams won 4 Southeastern Conference Championships and appeared in 5 College World Series. Throughout his career he has coached 27 All-Americans and 61 All-Southeastern Conference players. Coach Polk has also authored 2 textbooks - THE BASEBALL PLAYBOOK and THE BASEBALL-SOFTBALL PLAYBOOK - the leading textbooks used in teaching Baseball and Softball credit courses at the collegiate level.

SELECTING A COLLEGE

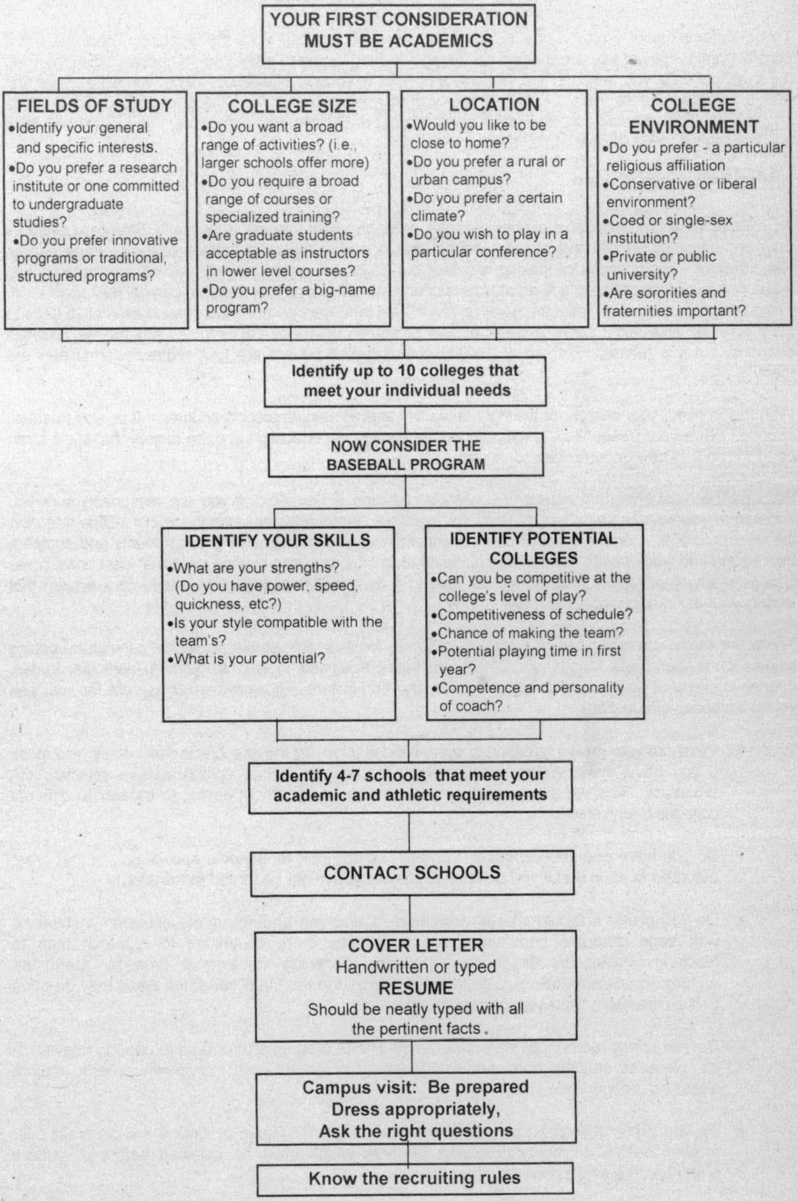

YOUR FIRST CONSIDERATION MUST BE ACADEMICS

FIELDS OF STUDY
- Identify your general and specific interests.
- Do you prefer a research institute or one committed to undergraduate studies?
- Do you prefer innovative programs or traditional, structured programs?

COLLEGE SIZE
- Do you want a broad range of activities? (i.e., larger schools offer more)
- Do you require a broad range of courses or specialized training?
- Are graduate students acceptable as instructors in lower level courses?
- Do you prefer a big-name program?

LOCATION
- Would you like to be close to home?
- Do you prefer a rural or urban campus?
- Do you prefer a certain climate?
- Do you wish to play in a particular conference?

COLLEGE ENVIRONMENT
- Do you prefer - a particular religious affiliation
- Conservative or liberal environment?
- Coed or single-sex institution?
- Private or public university?
- Are sororities and fraternities important?

Identify up to 10 colleges that meet your individual needs

NOW CONSIDER THE BASEBALL PROGRAM

IDENTIFY YOUR SKILLS
- What are your strengths? (Do you have power, speed, quickness, etc?)
- Is your style compatible with the team's?
- What is your potential?

IDENTIFY POTENTIAL COLLEGES
- Can you be competitive at the college's level of play?
- Competitiveness of schedule?
- Chance of making the team?
- Potential playing time in first year?
- Competence and personality of coach?

Identify 4-7 schools that meet your academic and athletic requirements

CONTACT SCHOOLS

COVER LETTER
Handwritten or typed
RESUME
Should be neatly typed with all the pertinent facts.

Campus visit: Be prepared
Dress appropriately,
Ask the right questions

Know the recruiting rules

THE COLLEGE IDENTIFICATION AND SELECTION PROCESS

This chapter provides hints on how to make the selection process more manageable. There are many possible options, but if you are methodical, organized, and willing to spend the necessary time reviewing the available data, you will soon find that only a handful of schools offer exactly what you want. Your first task is to determine the type of colleges you wish to attend. If you follow the guidelines outlined in this chapter, you should be able to eliminate a great number of choices. In many cases, this process will allow you to better define your own wants, needs, and goals.

COLLEGE ACADEMIC LIFE

As a Baseball player with proven skills, you are probably more interested in quality Baseball programs than any other aspect of university life. Indeed, that is one of the main themes of the ***College Guide***. Nevertheless, your chances of making a career out of your Baseball playing abilities are limited. Even those who eventually find a place on a professional roster often find their careers can be very short-lived. The average professional Baseball player retires in their late twenties and must rely on alternative skills to earn a living. This might seem a bleak picture to someone whose life revolves around the Baseball diamond, but it is realistic. Put simply: professional Baseball players are few; professional careers are many.

With this in mind, your search for the right university should revolve around education first, and Baseball second. While your Baseball skills will deteriorate with age, an education and the degree that seals it can open the door to new opportunities continually.

Perhaps the most important aspect of university selection is flexibility. If you are reasonably sure you know what you want to study (engineering, for example), thoroughly research those institutions that offer the best programs. Compile a list of colleges maintaining quality engineering departments and compare their strong and weak points. Remember, however, that most students change majors at least once; some change many times before finding the right field. So be mindful not to lock yourself into a system that inhibits your ability to change and grow.

There are many different types of programs. Some, for example, stress traditional curriculum, basing studies on a liberal arts foundation. Others are better equipped to train students in particular trades, offering courses of study as diverse as finance and horticulture. To decide which is right for you, ask yourself a series of questions:

- What are your main interests? In systematic fashion, list those subjects that interest you most. If you have many varied interests, look for schools with a comprehensive selection of programs. This will allow you to change majors freely without having to transfer to different colleges or universities.

- Do you have one specific interest or skill? If so, look for schools specializing in that area, but keep in mind that if you do change majors you might be forced to transfer.

- Do you prefer a faculty that is dedicated to teaching undergraduate courses? Institutions with large graduate populations are sometimes more committed to research than to teaching. Professors at those institutions generally have less time to spend on undergraduate activities outside the classroom. On the other hand, the ideas they do bring to the classroom represent current research.

- Do you prefer more innovative programs? These programs offer unique opportunities such as overseas studies, cooperative work/study programs, and individually created majors stressing independent study.

- Do you prefer a more structured, traditional program? These programs are generally built around certain university core requirements which must be satisfied before a student embarks on a single major.

THE COLLEGE IDENTIFICATION AND SELECTION PROCESS

UNIVERSITY SIZE

You can eliminate many colleges and universities by determining the environment in which you feel most comfortable. In other words, do you prosper in larger classes or in a smaller, more personal atmosphere? To pick a school based primarily on its size, you will undoubtedly have to make some trade-offs. Large institutions generally have large classes. This often means that instruction is less personal and interaction among students and professors is limited. On the other hand, larger institutions usually offer more extracurricular activities and broader educational possibilities. Conversely, at small universities, classes tend to be smaller allowing students to more readily exchange ideas with professors and other students during class discussions. There are potential drawbacks though. Because the enrollment is small, the student population may be less diverse than at a larger college or university.

Additionally, small schools do not have the resources necessary to offer a wide array of career options; therefore, the curriculum is usually more focused. If you do not know what you want to study, a small school might not be right for you. Ask yourself the following questions when determining the university size most appropriate for you:

- What kind of environment exists at your high school? Are you more comfortable in large or small classes? Do you want to experience a different kind of environment or do you prefer to stick to what you already know?

- Do you want to meet and interact with many of your classmates personally? This is more likely at a small school.

- Is a wide range of activities outside the classroom important? If you answer yes, then a larger university may better suit your needs.

- Would you like an academic program which offers specialized training in many fields, or one that focuses on a limited curriculum? Large universities obviously offer a wider range of courses. That, however, does not automatically ensure a better institution. Small universities can sometimes compensate for the lack of fields with more one-on-one instruction and better access to resources.

- Are you concerned with the expertise of the faculty? Though the size of an institution does not determine faculty qualifications, there are some things you should research and consider. For example, at large universities, graduate students sometimes teach lower level courses. Though generally well-qualified, they do not have the experience or knowledge most professors possess.

- Do you want to play Baseball at a big-name university? Or, would you do better to target a smaller school where your chances to play might be better?

UNIVERSITY LOCATION

Another way to narrow your prospective list of schools is to determine geographically where you may want to spend the next four years. Some questions you should try to answer include:

- Do you want to stay close to home or do you want the challenge of living far from your family in a distant environment?

- Would you rather experience a rural or an urban campus? If you grew up in a small town, it may be beneficial for you to experience life in a big city for several years. On the contrary, if you are from a large city, can you see yourself adapting to a rural environment?

- Do you prefer a particular climate? If you dislike cold weather, you might eliminate universities in the North and Northeast. On the other hand, you might want to consider those areas if you also enjoy winter recreational sports.

- As a Baseball player, do you prefer the competition a particular conference offers? Do the West Coast universities play a style more compatible with your skills? East Coast? North?

UNIVERSITY ENVIRONMENT

Each university or college offers a unique environment. Though hard to grasp from brochures and handbooks, each institution has distinct social, religious, and political attitudes. In order to better assess the information provided in printed materials, be sure to ask specific questions when speaking with college representatives.

- Do you want to attend an institution with a particular religious affiliation?

- Are you more comfortable in a conservative or liberal environment? You can gather insights about predominant political trends by reading campus newspapers, talking to university representatives, finding documentation written by faculty members, and asking questions of students when making campus visits.

- Do you want to attend a university that considers fraternities and sororities important aspects of social life? Many Baseball players consider their team an adequate substitute for organized social activities. Others might want a social life apart from their Baseball team.

- Do you prefer a coed or single sex institution?

- Would you like to attend a private school or a public institution? Though private schools are generally more expensive, cost alone should not deter you from pursuing the university of your choice. Financial aid is available for many qualified applicants.

COLLEGE BASEBALL

If you have followed the guidelines presented in this chapter, you should have compiled a preliminary list of schools based on academic, philosophical, social, and other prerequisites. Now you can start looking at college Baseball programs.

Does the school have special academic counseling for athletes? This is very important because academic counselors who deal specifically with athletes can give you a slight edge. He or she can help you select the right courses and the best professors to allow you the flexibility you will need for training, games, and travel. Along the same lines, does the college have tutors available to athletes? If tutors are available, ask if they are free, or if you are required to pay for their services. Depending on your financial situation, it may make a difference, particularly if you are a marginal student. Also, are there required study sessions for athletes? These study sessions can be helpful in making sure you are devoting enough time to your studies. Many freshmen simply do not know how to budget their time.

How many players from the program have graduated and earned degrees in the last five years? This may give you an indication of the amount of emphasis a school puts on academics. Check to see what percentage of athletes graduate, and then weigh that against the percentage who graduate from the entire student body. Keep in mind that not all schools are alike, so strict comparisons of these numbers may sometimes be misleading.

What is the total number of players on athletic scholarship? Consider what effect this will have on your chances for a scholarship and on your playing time. There are other important questions to ask with regard to scholarships. What will the complete financial aid package include? Depending on how much need-based aid for which you will qualify, you may find a variety of sources comprising your total financial aid package. Grants-in-aid, loans, work study and other aid programs can be combined with scholarship money to meet your needs. You will need to know how to renew the scholarship each year - there is no such thing as a four-year scholarship. It must be renewed every year. If you hear something about the renewal process you don't understand, ask for an explanation. You won't want to deal with surprises later on. Finally, you should determine what happens if you get injured and can't play for all, or part of a season.

THE COLLEGE IDENTIFICATION AND SELECTION PROCESS

How many games does a team play each year? You have to balance your desire to play as much Baseball as possible with the realization that you can't get in over your head academically. Is there a fall season. A fall season is a good way to get into shape and make a determination about how much playing time you might see during your freshman and sophomore years.

How successful has the school's program been in recent years? Obviously, everybody wants to play for a winner. But the more successful a program is, the stronger the competition will be for playing time. The school's conference and playoff record can give yet another indication of its success. Is there a current upswing that indicates the program has turned the corner, or a down trend, indicating a turn for the worse.

Are you being recruited for a specific position? If so, find out who is ahead of you at that position. This can help determine your chances for playing time. If there are two sophomores ahead of you, there's a better chance of you being in the middle of the bench than in the middle of the line-up. Or, you may be asked to switch positions. Ask yourself honestly if you'll be happy moving to another position.

What kind of athletic facilities does the school have? Sure you're going to be a student, but you're also going to be an athlete. It's best to find out where you will be playing and training. Poor facilities may contribute to injuries, stifle development, or adversely affect your mental approach to the game. On the other hand, don't let a shiny new stadium color your judgment if you are not comfortable with the coaching staff.

Find out also if they have indoor training facilities. Does the program have a weight room and strength coach? Your physical development will play a major role in your success as a college player, and proper training facilities and professional coaching can help elevate your game to the next level. Find out what kind of in-season and off-season conditioning program you can expect from each program.

Does the school offer a junior varsity Baseball program? If so, how many players are on the junior varsity and varsity teams? If a junior varsity program is offered, find out if it is used as a feeder for the varsity, and if there is any movement to and from each program.

Who comprises the coaching staff? It is important to know who you will be "working for" during your college career. Find out if one specific coach will be working with players at your position, or if it will be the head coach.

Now that you have identified some of the things you want out of a Baseball program, look at the list of schools you have already compiled for academic and other considerations. Try to find those schools among the university profiles listed in this guide. Are their Baseball programs also compatible? If so, these are the schools you definitely want to pursue. If not, you might have to make some trade-offs. For example, can you adapt to a new position if a particular coach says you may have to switch? If you are flexible, you can expand the list of schools that interest you. Remember, there are many quality schools with good Baseball programs. Everyone should be able to find a number of match-ups that qualify for their final list.

At this point, attempt to identify up to ten colleges or universities that really interest you. Focus on these schools. The chapters on *Admissions* and *Paying For College* describe how to prepare information that will assist you with college admission requirements. Economic factors generally prohibit visiting all the campuses. Nevertheless, if you can afford the cost, visit as many schools and talk to as many coaches as you can. The chapter on *The Importance of Campus Visits* explains what the coach may be looking for, and how you can prepare yourself for this important meeting.

SUMMARY

It is important to remember that your final selection of a college or university should be based primarily on your educational needs. The ***Official Athletic College Guide: BASEBALL*** does not describe individual academic programs in detail. For academic and other information, you should consult other handbooks devoted to that purpose by looking at individual college brochures, and consulting with parents, guidance counselors, current and former players, and college officials. Compile your list of schools from those resources. The Baseball profiles in the ***College Guide*** should assist you in reducing the number of universities on your list to a more manageable size. Together with the school's complete academic profile you will be able to determine the right college to meet both your academic and athletic needs.

THE STUDENT ATHLETE'S ROLE IN CHOOSING A COLLEGE

The diversity and abundance of opportunities for young men to participate in a college Baseball program is overwhelming when considering the full range of classifications from NCAA Division I, II, III, NAIA, and NJCAA. To date there are 1400+ colleges and universities that sponsor Men's Baseball programs.

Each of the these schools is unique in three key areas: academic programs, social and environmental factors, and athletic standards. The obvious result of any comprehensive search is that a positive match for the prepared and well-informed student-athlete does certainly exist.

The recommended process involves a focused effort in three areas. These are simply referred to as **THE THREE P's.**

I. **BE PROACTIVE:** Take a proactive approach to gathering information beginning the sophomore year. This should involve a system for prioritizing choices and a continuous evaluation of personal athletic and academic goals.

II. **BE PERSISTENT:** Once prioritized, be persistent in communicating your goals and personal interests to the program(s) of choice.

III. **BE PREPARED:** Prepare both athletically and academically to meet necessary eligibility and admission requirements.

THE WELL-INFORMED STUDENT ATHLETE

What are the variables to consider in selecting a college? The most frequent questions and discussion topics encountered may be generally categorized as *academic, social* and *athletic related.* Essentially, the student-athlete should be attempting to set a variety of immediate and long-term goals for their own personal growth in each of these key areas. Matching a college opportunity to these goals is a vital step in achieving them.

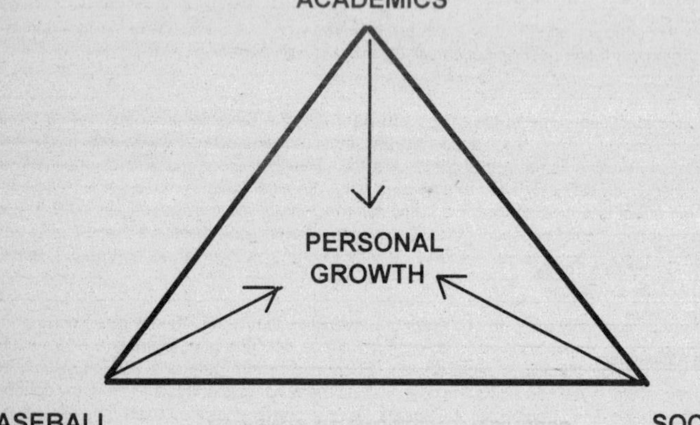

AN ORGANIZED APPROACH TO "THE COLLEGE CHOICE"

A simple but complete analysis is critical to filtering the information that the student-athlete will discover as you begin to look at each program. The diagram is intended to help rank each variable that may be valuable in the decision-making process. As you begin to gather information from a variety of sources you should assign a ranking - numerical value for that specific variable. Quantitatively, begin to rank your top six colleges (1 - 6) according to personal criteria with the top choice being a "6." (See following page.)

COLLEGE EVALUATION TABLE

SELECTION FACTORS	1	2	3	4	5	6
SCHOOL NAME						
ACADEMICS						
Academic Focus - Degree of Difficulty						
Academic Offering in Selected Major						
Size - Total Enrollment						
Athlete Tutoring						
Student-Athlete Support Services						
Quarter / Semester System						
Admissions - GPA Standard						
Admissions - SAT/ACT Standard						
Coaches Academic "Perspective"						
Requirements for Selected Major						
Tuition (In-State)						
Tuition (Non-resident)						
BASEBALL PROGRAM						
NCAA / NAIA Affiliation (i.e. Div I, II, III)						
Immediate Contribution/Playing Time						
Player Turnover (Number of Juniors / Seniors)						
Distribution of Scholarship Monies						
Coaching Staff Qualifications						
Total Staff & Time Commitment						
Competitive Schedule						
Athletic Department Commitment						
Facilities						
Training Schedule (NCAA Traditional Season)						
Training Schedule (Fall / Non-Traditional season)						
Coaches Interest In Me?						
Team Atmosphere (Player's Perspective)						
Travel Requirements						
Coach's Contacts to Higher Levels (All Star Teams)						
SOCIAL / ENVIRONMENTAL						
Metropolitan / City / Suburban / Rural						
Ethnic Diversity						
Cultural Environment						
Coed						
Fraternity / Sorority System						
Distance From Immediate Family						
Recreational Activities Available						
Campus Atmosphere						
Climate						
Team Social Atmosphere						

ESSENTIAL QUESTIONS TO CONSIDER

ACADEMICALLY... Will I have the desire, support, and ability to succeed here?

SOCIALLY... Will I be comfortable with my surroundings and able to grow as a person?

BASEBALL... Will I contribute and become a better player?

THE STUDENT ATHLETE'S ROLE IN CHOOSING A COLLEGE

ACADEMIC ELIGIBILITY & ADMISSION REQUIREMENTS

Each Division (I,II,III) of the NCAA has some variability in eligibility requirements. The NAIA and NJCAA are significantly different from the NCAA. As well, the admissions requirements for various colleges and universities may be unique and vary greatly from one to another. However, it is possible to generally view the following items as essential elements for admission criteria to most colleges.

KNOW THE RECRUITING RULES

A recruit should know a few basic NCAA rules:

- A college coach may not have off-campus contact with a recruit until July 5th after his junior year in high school.
- A recruit may not practice with an NCAA Division I college team on a campus visit.
- A player may not accept payments for playing for any club team.
- A recruit should not accept any financial rewards for attending an institution outside the formal scholarship opportunities.
- Recruitment must be by members of the institution's academic and athletic staff only.
- Rules for NAIA and junior college associations are different. Therefore, the recruit should always seek advice directly from the association's governing body if something that seems too good to be legal. Also, NCAA Division III rules vary from NCAA rules at other levels. If a recruit has questions, she should obtain a current copy of the ***NCAA Guide for the College-Bound Student-Athlete*** which is published annually by the NCAA.

Choosing a college or university is a big decision and should not be taken lightly. As a student-athlete you need to enhance your opportunities for recruitment by helping in the process. The more knowledgeable and organized you are, the better your chances will be. Obviously, this process doesn't take the place of pure athletic ability and hard work, but if you have the talent and dedication to play at the collegiate level you need to freely communicate this to the coaches.

ADMISSION STEPS

STANDARDIZED TEST RESULTS: (SAT or ACT) These standardized tests represent common admission criteria. It is recommended that as a student-athlete you take the preliminary (PSAT or PACT) exam as a junior for two very important reasons - most students improve their scores by repeated attempts at the exam, and secondly, the exam is a prerequisite to an official campus visit to NCAA Division I and Division II schools.

PHOTOCOPIES OF UNOFFICIAL HIGH SCHOOL TRANSCRIPTS: Once you have established an open dialogue with a coaching staff, you should provide a copy of your academic history. Many athletic departments have access to qualified people who will analyze these transcripts and assess the probability of admission to the school well in advance of the official notification.

THE ADMISSIONS APPLICATION: This step must be completed during the first few months of the senior year. College coaches are not the admissions officials - the final decision for admission lies with a college official outside of the athletic department. In this regard, the Baseball coaching staff is typically delighted when notified that a student-athlete has been responsible for completing the admission process on his own.

Be aware that in some cases an application may be "coded" by the athletic department in order to speed the process, or in some special cases to aid in the admission process. This is a specific question that should be asked of the coaching staff prior to making application.

COLLEGE ELIGIBILITY REQUIREMENTS FOR THE STUDENT-ATHLETE

ATHLETIC ELIGIBILITY REQUIREMENTS

This section is categorized separately because it is, in fact, a separate issue. While the athlete may be "admitted" to a college, this does not guarantee athletic eligibility - more rules to play by!

> The NCAA has established a National Clearinghouse from which all decisions regarding an athlete's initial eligibility at an institution will be determined. If the athlete is not registered and certified through the Clearinghouse he will not be able to participate in Division I or Division II Baseball.

The key steps:

Freshman through Senior Year: Academic Requirements

1. Earn a minimum GPA of 2.5 on a 4.0 scale

2. Credit in at least 13 core academic courses, including:
   4 years of English (3 years for Division II)
   2 years of Math
   2 years of Social Science
   2 years of Science (minimum 1 lab science)
   1 year additional English, Math Science
   2 years additional any of above or foreign language

3. NCAA - Division I & II:
   Earn a summary score of at least 68 on the ACT or a combined score of 820 on the SAT. (Note: these scores may be higher based upon a sliding scale relative to the student's cumulative GPA.)

GPA	SAT	ACT SUM
2.5	820	68
↓	↓	↓
2.0	1010	86

NCAA - Division III:
Based on eligibility requirements set by the member institution and the college's participating athletic conference.

NAIA: Qualification criteria is based on any 2 of the 3 requirements outlined below.
1. A minimum GPA of 2.0 on a 4.0 scale
2. A combined score for the SAT of 860 or ACT of 18
3. Rank in the top 50% of high school graduating class

Junior Year: Registration with Clearinghouse

Immediately after the completion of the second semester the student-athlete should register with the Clearinghouse. This is accomplished by requesting a Clearinghouse "Student Release Form" from the high school counselor's office. The student should provide two copies of the form to the high school counselor for processing.

Senior Year: Verification of Standardized Test Scores

Verify that the standardized test scores and official transcripts have been sent to the Clearinghouse.

Finally, there are other valuable reference materials to aid in the student-athlete's pursuit of college playing opportunities. These publications will provide additional specific information:

NCAA RULES ***NCAA Guide For The College-Bound Student-Athlete***

Write to:

National Collegiate Athletic Association
6201 College Blvd.
Overland Park, KS 66211-24
Phone (913) 339-1906
Website **http://www.ncaa.org**

NAIA RULES ***NAIA Guide For The College-Bound Student***

Write to:

NAIA Headquarters
6120 South Yale, Suite 1450
Tulsa, OK 74136
Phone (918) 494-8828
Website **http://www.naia.org**

NCAA CLEARINGHOUSE

Write to:

NCAA Clearinghouse
2255 North Dubuque Rd.
P.O. Box 4044
Iowa City, IA 52243-4044
Phone (319) 337-1492

ACADEMIC RATINGS OF COLLEGES

Gourman Report, Dr. Jack Gourman

COLLEGES & BASEBALL PROGRAM INFORMATION

Official Athletic College Guide: BASEBALL, Charlie Kadupski
THE SPORT SOURCE™
1845 Summit, Suite 402
Plano, TX 75074
Phone (800) 862-3092
Dallas Area (972) 509-5707
Fax (972) 516-1754
Website **http://wwwthesportsource.com**
E-mail **sports@thesportsource.com**

*Editor's Note: Please be aware that NCAA and NAIA rules and regulations regarding recruitment of high school athletes are under constant review. Annually request the current edition of the **NCAA Guide for the College-Bound Student-Athlete** and **NAIA Guide For The College-Bound Student,** but don't assume that you have definitive information - when in doubt, contact the NCAA or NAIA directly for clarification of any rules regarding recruiting practices.*

COMMUNICATING WITH COLLEGE COACHES

NARROWING YOUR FOCUS

Student athletes should contact only a limited number of colleges. There are many factors to be considered when choosing colleges: location, size, public or private, academic difficulty, courses of study, cost, availability of academic and/or athletic scholarships, and opportunities for need based financial aid. Added to these are factors regarding the Baseball program: level of play, competitiveness of the schedule, chance of making the team, and the competence and personality of the coach.

Once you have determined what your personal needs will be, some additional research is required. Obtain a reputable college reference guide from a book store or a local library to assist you in your evaluation. Realistically, student-athletes should not expect to find a college that is tailor-made for them, but rather one that provides a reasonable fit.

STEP I: WRITTEN COMMUNICATION

Having identified 7 - 10 schools of interest, entering your junior year of high school you should begin contacting the coaches for each program. Initially, this should be written communication that supplies the coaching staff with important information regarding you as a student-athlete.

CONTACTING THE BASEBALL COACH

Take the time to prepare your resume and write a letter to each college coach. A personal cover letter is more effective than a generic version for all coaches. The cover letter should explain your expectations in terms of education, the Baseball program, financial need, and scholarship requirements. Be sure to request literature about the college, and specifically, the Baseball program. The cover letter should also be typed (although more recently, college coaches have given special consideration to neat handwritten letters) and, of course, have correct spelling and proper grammar.

Remember that the resume should be one (1) typed page which presents only pertinent information. Coaches would rather read concise information about a player than page after page of trivia. If a player has a video tape it may be listed on the resume, but should be sent only at the request of the coach. The resume should be sent to all the selected colleges and contain the following sections:

- A personal section with name, address, phone number, date of birth, height, weight, social security number, and high school graduation year.
- An academic section with high school name, address and phone number; grade point average and/or class rank and standardized test information (SAT, PSAT, ACT scores).
- An athletic section with a list of all Baseball teams on which the student athlete currently plays (high school, club, league, etc.), positions played, coaches names and team records. List any Baseball honors that have been received. This section should include any other sports that the athlete plays and any honors in those sports. Baseball camps recently attended are also helpful.
- A reference section with the names of 3 or 4 people who can accurately gauge the player's character and ability. In other words, those who are knowledgeable of the game and the player as a person. References' addresses and phone numbers are necessary.

STEP II: TELEPHONE CONTACT

The single key variable that separates a single student-athlete from all of the other solicitation letters received by a college coach is regular follow-up. Be sure to call once or twice each month after sending your resume and cover letter. The majority of correspondence received by coaches are form letters mailed to numerous programs with the hope that some interest will be generated. A specific letter followed by a telephone call indicates a sincere interest in a given program.

COMMUNICATING WITH COLLEGE COACHES

The athlete should have a specific purpose in calling; most often it is to update the coaching staff on key games, tournaments, or other opportunities to see you compete. It is also an effective way to directly express interest in the program and to ask questions regarding information not readily available from published sources such as college brochures or the ***College Guide***. Most coaches will be happy to answer questions that aid in the decision process, but may be less enthusiastic regarding information that is readily available from other sources, i.e. school size, degree programs, and athletic conference. *Rememeber - Direct conversation allows the coach and the athlete to assess personalities and interest levels.*

The well-prepared student-athlete will have assembled this information *prior* to the telephone call. NCAA rules permit high school athletes to call the coach without restrictions. However, be aware that a college coach may *not* call the student including returning messages until after July 1st following the completion of your junior year in high school.

Editor's Note: Included on the following pages are examples of both a resume and cover letter. Yours, obviously, should be personalized, and include any information you believe to be pertinent. Remember, these are only examples. Yours should include anything you think will help a college coach evaluate your abilities, but do keep them brief.

SAMPLE RESUME

GEORGE MALSBURY
5535 McCommas
Dallas, TX 75206
(214)250-2103 / big-stick@baseballonline.com

Date of Birth: March 9, 1982 — Height: 5' 11"
SSN: 446-29-1999 — Weight: 195 lbs.

Academic

High School:	W.T. White High School 1244 Forest Ln. Dallas, TX 57228 (214) 385-5660
Graduation Date:	Class of 2000
GPA/Class Rank:	3.28 GPA (4.0) Top 25% in class Honors program - Math
SAT/ACT Scores:	610 Math, 560 Verbal: 1170 - SAT Total 11 Math, 12 Verbal: 23 - ACT Total

Athletic

High School Baseball:	W.T. White Longhorns Varsity team, 1996-98 All-District Honorable Mention - Sophomore All-District - Junior Position: Third Base Bats: Right Throws: Right
Baseball Club:	Dallas Mustangs Coach: Jim Turner / Bill Thacker 3-Time Regional All-Star

References

Coaches:	Kevin McGhee Head coach, W.T. White High School 12345 Inwood Rd. Dallas, TX 75228 (214) 827-9951
	Bob Suarez Former Coach, Mustangs (214) 696-9642
Personal:	Jennifer Cathey Counselor W.T. White High School

SAMPLE COVER LETTER

YOUR NAME
Address
City, State Zip
Home Telephone / E-mail Address

Date

Coach's Name
Men's Baseball Coach
Name of College
Address
City, State, Zip

Dear (Coach's Name):

Based on my research in preparation for choosing a college, (name of college) has both an excellent reputation, and the types of academic and athletic programs I hope to pursue after graduation from high school.

The enclosed resume details my academic standing and Baseball experience. I am currently a junior, with a GPA of ___ on a 4.0 scale, and taking college preparatory classes with an emphasis on (list core courses). The strength and variety of courses offered at (name of college) provide several degree plans of interest to me, although I have not yet decided on a specific major area of study.

More specifically, your Baseball program is of primary interest to me. I believe my skills and abilities would fit well into your program, and enable me to contribute to the success of the (team name) while continuing to develop my Baseball talents under your style of play.

I would like to pursue all available means for financial aid, and I believe my academic standing should qualify me for scholarship assistance.

Thank you for any consideration you can give me as a future (team name). Please send me information on your program, and any suggestions you may have on how best to prepare for attendance at (name of school) in the fall of (your graduation year).

Sincerely,

(Your Name)

Editor's Note: The sample cover letter is for illustration purposes only. Please be original and write your own letter. College coaches tell us they have seen this one a few times and are likely to file it in the trash!

THE IMPORTANCE OF CAMPUS VISITS

CONDUCTING CAMPUS VISITS

To get the best feel for a college, it is best to plan a minimum of two visits to the campus - an initial visit and a second or "paid" visit. If this were to occur, you should plan an initial visit sometime in your junior year. The second visit would then occur during your senior year. Sometimes, because of distance or a late start in the college search process, this is not possible and the visits will have to be combined.

The initial visit is a way for you to get acquainted with the college and for the coaches and players to get acquainted with you - their recruit. Many athletes schedule a number of college visits on the same trip, as each visit will take only a short time. The initial visit should include a tour of the campus, an admissions interview (if available) and a talk with the Baseball coach or a representative of the Baseball program. As a student-athlete, you will need to call ahead and arrange interview times with the admissions department and the Baseball coach.

Come prepared for both of these interviews, and be appropriately dressed since first impressions can mean a great deal. You should also have a list of specific questions to be asked of coaches, players, and college administrators. Coaches and admissions personnel are looking for individuals who have some substance. You should ask pertinent questions that fill in the gaps of your knowledge about the college and its Baseball program.

Sample questions to ask the Baseball coach:

- What is the status of the returning team, including eligibility of players at the same position as the recruit?
- What are your chances of making the team and/or significant playing time as a freshman, sophomore, etc.?
- What is the availability and chances for a scholarship?
- What is the general practice schedule?
- How much time does Baseball require? Does Baseball interfere with a player's ability to complete academic work?
- How does the red-shirt program work?
- What are the coaches' goals for the team in the next four years?
- What equipment is provided for each player?

Many admission's department personnel will ask difficult questions that will require you to give thoughtful, unprepared responses. Think through your answers and give serious intuitive answers. Most of these questions will be about personal experiences so no preparation is required. It is helpful, however, to gain experience in an interview situation.

Be completely up-front with the coach and ask questions that will help you better understand the level of commitment required for participation in the Baseball program. Most coaches will not bring up the subject of Baseball scholarships unless asked, so find out what is available and what your own chances might be. As a recruit be persistent, but táctful in seeking answers to all your questions.

The coach will want to get a feel for your personality - the type of player and competitor you are and may ask for your own assessment of personal strengths and weaknesses. The coach may also want to know where his program stands on the your list and information regarding other schools of interest. Be sure to answer these questions thoroughly and honestly.

The second visit, which can be a paid visit, should occur after you have narrowed your choices to a small number of schools. Paid visits can only be made after a student has started their senior year. Each student is allowed five paid visits by NCAA rules to different schools and only one paid visit per school. A visit would be considered "paid" if the Baseball program provides *anything* free for the recruit (i.e., meals, lodging, etc.) The college may pay for transportation to and from the school and any expenses incurred during normal living arrangements as long as these expenses are not excessive. Paid visits can last up to 48 hours.

On the second visit the recruit will probably be staying with a varsity Baseball team member. If this occurs, you are encouraged to go to class with the player to experience the full flavor of campus life, and get questions answered from a player's perspective. Be aware, however, that the coach will be observing you so,therefore, act accordingly. At NCAA institutions, a recruit may not practice with the team while on a paid visit.

Editor's Note: If the two visits have to be combined, be ready to evaluate the college on a one-shot basis. Do as much as possible in this visit. Remember, you will spend almost four years of your life at your chosen college. An insightful visit limits the chances of making a mistake.

THE INTERNET AND YOUR COLLEGE SEARCH

ADVANTAGES OF THE INTERNET

With the low cost of computers and ease of Internet access almost anyone can now get "online", whether it be from your high school, home, public library, or the workplace. What previously was a medium for use only by computer enthusiasts has now become a medium for the masses. A simple message can easily be viewed by millions of people - almost instantly. That's a "reach" more powerful than any television network or metro newspaper could ever have dreamed about even 5 years ago. And that message could be your message!

This rapidly-evolving medium continues to open the door of opportunity to both student-athletes and college coaches alike. Taking a proactive approach to the recruiting process in today's marketplace means using all the tools current technology has to offer. Your ability to promote yourself to college coaches should not be limited to a well-written resume and personal cover letter. E-mail and personal Web sites have become an effective and viable means of communicating with busy college coaches caught balancing games and training sessions, a hectic travel and recruiting schedule, and their personal life. With a laptop computer and Internet access a coach can literally take his office with him. The net effect has been to stretch recruiting budgets and provide alternate means of locating and tracking potential recruits. A quick e-mail to or from a college coach shows genuine interest and opens the door for future direct contact either by telephone or in person.

Through extensive recruiting budgets, and both academic and athletic scholarships, colleges commit significant funds annually to the students and athletes they attract. To minimize these costs and to attract both the top students and top athletes, colleges and sports information directors have jumped into the Internet with both feet making available vast resources - and they have only just begun to really explore the capacity of the Internet to help people learn and communicate about their programs. This new wealth of information has allowed student-athletes to explore how they match up with other scholarship candidates, and where playing opportunities may exist.

WHY YOU SHOULD HAVE YOUR OWN WEB SITE

As a result of recent technology developments, you can easily become part of this online community, have your own Web site, and explore the benefits of the Internet during the recruiting process. Your personal Web site will allow you to promote your abilities directly to coaches and college selection committees. Maintaining your site will provide a "fresh look" with new information and your accomplishments, including game highlights, honors, and personal stats. And you can manage this site on your own without depending on third party assistance - i.e. recruiting services or a Webmaster. You control the information being published and the timely release of updated information. Remember, the recruiting process represents a narrow window from your sophomore through senior year in high school. If playing college athletics remains your primary goal, you will want to create a chronological overview of your athletic career to assist college coaches in evaluating your abilities as both a player and student-athlete.

Your Web site can also be a powerful networking tool. Learn to use it effectively to interact with other people in your respective sport, such as your prep or club coach, and to assist you in creating your own online community. Having your information readily available will help others in promoting your abilities directly to various contacts at the collegiate level. To maximize your site's effectiveness, be sure to promote it through your personal e-mail account. (There are various providers who offer free e-mail accounts.) By building a private directory of your contacts, you can provide quick and effective notification of updates to your site.

Also encourage your team to build and maintain its own Web site. Information about the other players including the competitiveness and overall success of your team will all contribute to a college coach's evaluation of you as a player, and whether you are the "right fit" for his athletic program.

TIPS FOR DEVELOPING YOUR WEB SITE

Just like any good advertisement, your site must effectively convey your message to your target audience - in this case college coaches. Make it concise, well organized, and informative. Use your creativity to effectively communicate your message, and try to minimize the entertainment value associated with all the "gimmicky" shooting stars, fireballs, flashing signs, and scrolling message screens in more commercial sites.

Treat your Web site as print medium. Lay it out like a news magazine and use color highlights, font styles, photographs, and subtle graphics to dress your page and not to dominate it. The college coaches will appreciate being able to quickly get the information they need, and are more likely to thoroughly read the material you present, if they are not being bombarded by technical enhancements.

WHAT SHOULD APPEAR ON YOUR WEB SITE

When building your site, it is of primary importance for you to provide as much information about yourself both as an athlete and student without jeopardizing your own right to privacy. Remember, anyone with a computer and Internet access will be able to log-on and visit your Web site. Although you will want to include a resume of your accomplishments, do not include your home address, telephone number, and social security number which should not be a part of your biographical information on the Internet.

If you want to include a contact number, use your e-mail address or a third party telephone number such as a parent's work number or (with permission) that of your coach. While your most important personal contact will be directly with the college coach, if interested he / she will likely ask permission from your parents' before speaking with you, or leave a telephone number where you can call back. College coaches are recruiting you - not your parents, so be sure you take the time to speak with them personally and return their calls. As a quick overview your Web site should include the following:

- Your name, city of residence, e-mail address, third party contact number, high school and its address, graduation year, GPA, class rank, standardized test scores, a listing of your extra-curricular activities, religious preference (if pertinent to your college search), accomplishments - both academically and athletically, other sports you participate in, current coaches - high school and club teams, won-loss records on those teams, current game schedule, any tournaments or showcase events you know you will be participating in, and personal references (again with permission only).
- A current photograph - in your uniform works fine as long as your face is plainly visible!
- Team photograph and action shot of yourself
- In addition to the above, take time to describe some of your personal goals both on and off the field of play; possible degree plans; what you are looking for in a college environment - urban v. rural, larger v. smaller enrollment, on-campus v. off-campus housing, geographic location, climate, social aspects - fraternities/sororities, religious affiliation, etc.; and athletically - under what coaching style you best excel; your style of play; level of competition- NCAA Division I, II, III, NAIA, NCCAA, or NJCAA; and basically, anything a college coach and admissions department can use to evaluate you as a potential student-athlete for their college or university.

WHEN TO LAUNCH AND UPDATE YOUR WEB SITE

Your Web site is a personal snap shot of you as a student and potential college athlete. Much of the information you publish on your site will remain static (unchanged), however, any pertinent information including changes in your e-mail address and contact numbers, updated grades, standardized test scores, class rank, team and personal accomplishments, certain photographs, etc. should be updated at least semi-annually beginning your sophomore year, and as available beginning your junior year in high school.

PROMOTING YOURSELF AND YOUR WEB SITE

Identify the colleges you wish to target using one of the various student-athlete college handbooks currently available, or by directly visiting college Web sites on the Internet. Develop a Name & Address Book of college coaches capturing college Web sites and coaches e-mail addresses within the directory of your e-mail service. Prepare a more extensive resume with your home address, telephone numbers, birth date, and your Social Security Number along with a personal cover letter to be sent both e-mail and hard copy directly to college coaches beginning your sophomore year in high school. Be sure to include your Web address and do encourage the coaches to visit it periodically for updates. You will want to follow-up the initial distribution of resumes and cover letters with a personal phone call directly to the coach 7-10 days after it is sent. Remember, due to NCAA restrictions, college coaches may talk to you if they receive your call, but will not be able to *return* your telephone calls until after July 5th going into your senior year in high school.

Do not overlook the importance of hyper links to other Web sites. You will want to initiate link requests to your team or club for permission to link to their Web site. College coaches who are attracted to a particular team or club because of their reputation for competitiveness, or developing college level players in the past, may just "stumble" on your site. You will not want to miss-out on the opportunity to be "front and center" with your Web site if you fit their criteria as a player.

SUMMARY

From your site, coaches can view your player statistics, accomplishments, etc. and extend their recruiting efforts beyond the limits of their budgets. What does this mean to you as a student-athlete? With only limited resources invested, you can systematically identify college programs, evaluate scholarship opportunities based on your own individual profile, review college admission requirements, view the campuses, and create a personal profile to share with coaches both in the U.S. and around the world - all without ever leaving your desktop computer.

Editor's Note: These are merely guidelines and suggestions for using the Internet and building your own Web site. It is strongly recommended that any decision to build and maintain your own personal site be something that you discuss with your parents, coaches, and academic advisers. As well, you will need to refer to current collegiate recruiting guidelines regarding use of the Internet as outlined in the NCAA Guide For The College-Bound Student-Athlete - for more information call 913.339.1906, or visit their Web site at ***www.ncaa.org****. Also, please refer to the NAIA Guide For The College-Bound Student - for more information call 918.494.8828, or visit their Web site at* ***www.naia.org****.*

COLLEGE PLANNING CHECKLIST

High School Sophomore Year

"The College Identification & Selection Process"

	Activity	Planned	Scheduled	Completed	Notes
Jul Aug Sep	•Student meeting with counselor •Set academic plan for Junior Year •Check with counselor for PSAT & PACT registration deadlines •Purchase *Official Athletic College Guide: BASEBALL* •Obtain current *Guide for the College-Bound Student-Athlete* from NCAA •Complete a practice admission application •Set-up files - begin to assemble college information				
Oct Nov Dec	•Parent & Student meeting with counselor •Check with counselor for PSAT & PACT test dates •Use academic & CPN to write for admissions information on wide range of schools •Review progress with parents •Attend College Night at high school •Begin to identify 7-10 college programs				
Jan Feb Mar	•Review material in college file •Continue requesting information •Review progress with parents •Become familiar with financial aid publications from counselors •Update list of potential colleges				
Apr May Jun	•Parent/Student meet with counselor to review goals/progress/interest •Review progress with parents •Begin a college contact list •Review academic progress •Plan next year's academic program •Begin investigating sources for financial aid •Continue to update list of potential colleges				

COLLEGE PLANNING CHECKLIST
High School Junior Year

	Activities	Planned	Scheduled	Completed	Notes
Jul Aug Sep	•Student meeting with counselor •Check with counselor for Oct. & Nov. SAT/ACT registration deadlines •Develop more selective college contact list - begin writing to college coaches •College coaches may legally contact you & receive collect calls after July 1 of Junior year •Discuss Achievement Test results with counselor •Purchase updated edition of the *Official Athletic College Guide: BASEBALL* •Obtain current *Guide for the College-Bound Student-Athlete* from NCAA •Continue to review and update list of potential colleges				
Oct Nov Dec	•Review progress with parents •Explore opportunities for college / high school joint enrollment credit •Check with counselor for Oct & Nov SAT/ACT test dates •Check with counselor for Dec SAT registration deadline •Achievement Tests given in early Nov nationally •Review all material in college file •Visit College Nights/College Fairs •Complete at least 2 admission applications for practice only •Get Letters of Recommendation •Continue to review and update list of potential colleges				
Jan Feb Mar	•Visit local colleges of different types & sizes •Check with counselor for SAT/ACT registration deadlines and test dates •Discuss Achievement Test results with counselor •Develop your preference profile •Organize your personal portfolio •Arrange for spring/summer visits, interviews at colleges in which you have an interest •Continue researching financial aid sources •Continue to review and update list of potential colleges				
Apr May Jun	•Take SAT and ACT •Academic plan for senior year •Parent & student meeting with counselor •Achievement Tests given in early May •Review academic record, plan next year's program •Explore possibility of enrolling in AP courses during SR year for college credit •Review admissions applications questions & concerns with counselor •Register with NCAA National Clearinghouse				

COLLEGE PLANNING CHECKLIST
High School Senior Year

	Activity	Planned	Scheduled	Completed	Notes
Jul Aug Sep	•Finalize application essay topics •Continue writing college coaches/provide fall schedule •Arrange for college visits & interviews •Check with counselor for SAT/ACT retake registration and schedule •Discuss Achievement Tests results with counselor •Parent & student meeting with counselor •Purchase updated edition of the *Official Athletic College Guide: BASEBALL* •Obtain current *Guide for the College-Bound Student-Athlete* from NCAA				
Oct Nov Dec	•Show application essays to teachers/parents for proof & comments before finalizing •Request recommendation from teachers/faculty •Check with counselor for SAT/ACT registration and test schedule •If applying for early decision, complete and send application •Get tax records to prepare for financial aid forms •Obtain all financial aid forms (national & from schools) •Narrow list to 5 schools for possible application •Apply to at least 3 schools •Inform counselor of college applications (for transcripts to be sent) •National Letter of Intent Signing is November •Achievement Test given in early November nationally •Review material in college file with parents				
Jan Feb Mar	•File Financial Aid Forms ASAP after January 1 •Final visits to schools where applied •Make sure all applications have been sent •Parent & student meeting with counselor •Re-take SAT & ACT if necessary •Decision time - "Good Luck!" •National Letter of Intent Signing Day				
Apr May Jun	•Review progress with parents •AP Examinations given in May •Review acceptances and aid offers - choose college you wish to attend •If you are put on waiting lists, contact college admissions officer & speak with guidance counselor •Handle necessary deposits to college you have chosen •Inform all colleges to which you applied of the decision to attend or not attend that school •Achievement Tests given in May nationally •Notify counselor of your choice & have sent - final grades, proof of graduation, etc.				

COLLEGE PLANNING CHECKLIST

High School Senior Year (Continued)

	Activity	Planned	Scheduled	Completed	Notes
Jun Jul Aug	•Keep in shape (train, run, and play Baseball) •Find out who your roommate will be if you do not already know. •Check out living quarters and find out what you need to take. •Get ahead in your studies - take basic English or History courses at the local jr. college. •Visit the university to work out your freshman schedule. Baseball workouts and classes can become a heavy load for a freshman new to the college scene. •Be mentally and physically prepared for long hours.				

COLLEGE ADMISSIONS

APPLYING TO SELECTIVE COLLEGES: The Admissions Committee

What makes applying to selective colleges and universities more of a challenge is that they are in fact *selective*; that is to say, they have many applicants to choose from and have therefore established selection criteria to determine worthy candidates. Students are not chosen solely on the basis of academic credentials, but also based on what the college is looking for in terms of filling academic and athletic programs. As a Baseball player, you will not be evaluated like other candidates; your ability, as well as the needs of the team will be taken into careful consideration. Although the coach will have input, he will not have the authority to make the final decision regarding your admission request.

The matching approach to college admissions requires two basic steps: getting a realistic view of what is available, and an accurate assessment of your abilities. The number of selective colleges is small and can be defined easily by looking at any of the readily available guidebooks. Although definitions of "selective" may vary, most knowledgeable sources would say there are perhaps two hundred such institutions in the country. Of these, not all schools offer Baseball programs, or compete in NCAA Division I, or offer scholarships, or have strong winning traditions. The point is that by evaluating academic admission requirements and strength of the Baseball program, you can separate institutions into categories and place them in a simple matrix or grid. (See page 15.) The programs more suitable to your abilities will appear with the higher accumulated values.

You can, and should, undertake a similar exercise for yourself looking at your academic achievements and standardized test scores, and rank them along with your Baseball abilities. As an example, assign values for your SAT scores with a ranking from a high of 1600 = 10, to 1000 = 4 or a top 20% class ranking being worth an 8. Create similar values for playing on district or state level teams, all league and MVP honors, invitational opportunities, and so on through your senior year. You can then roughly determine where you stand. Keep in mind that there are relatively few institutions or individuals that score high in all areas. Just as it is very difficult to find institutions that have high academic standards and offer competitive Baseball with a strong winning tradition, it is very difficult to find "blue chip" athletes that are similarly "blue chip" scholars. In fact, college administrators concede that there are only a limited number of gifted Baseball players with superb academic credentials to fill the needs of their institutions. The resulting compromise is to balance academic standards with athletic abilities in order to find qualified student-athletes to fill college rosters. If your Baseball abilities are stronger than your academics, try to match-up with those schools that are stronger in Baseball than academics, and vice versa.

Once you have identified compatible colleges and universities, you can begin to eliminate schools from this list based on standard evaluation criteria - academic programs offered, distance from home, cost, and so on. This will further narrow your choices and give you an idea of where you might want to make initial contacts. Of course, while you are looking at colleges, coaches may be contacting you, which may continue to expand the number of colleges on your list.

Further elimination will occur by looking at particulars of your given situation - how much a college may want you to enroll, and whether your academic credentials deviate too far from their norm. In other words, are you as qualified as other applicants? If not, how far might an admissions committee be willing to compromise to get a talented Baseball athlete?

First, try to gauge your value to the Baseball program. Keep in mind that not all institutions apply the same standards with regard to the Baseball program. Look at your position - what is the depth of the team at that position, and what year are the starters? Is their skill level far greater than yours? In short, do they need help, and do they need it right away? If the answer is clearly yes, an admissions committee may be likely to compromise on the academic side. However, there is a limit to how far they will go, even for a marquee player!

This "flexibility" can only be estimated, and the only truly reliable way to know is to ask the players. The coach should be willing to give you their phone numbers. If you have any questions, do not hesitate to ask them about their credentials and their success academically on campus. Of course, be sure to ask how many hours they commit to their studies, so that you can fairly assess both their ability and willingness to work. If your credentials are well below key players, your chances are not good; if they are the same as average players, they are good; and if they are better than average players, your chances are excellent.

This should give you a pretty clear picture of your chances allowing you to direct your inquiries accordingly. Your chances for success will magnify where your academic credentials are close to current players, and your Baseball ability is within two years of making a contribution at your position. Be wary of long shots because they are just that and rarely pan out. Be aware, also, that any time you show a college both athletic and academic promise, you not only assure your chances of admission, but greatly increase your chances for a merit scholarship.

PRESENTING YOURSELF: The Application and Interview

How can you improve your chances at any selective institution? Present yourself well. It will not always *be* the difference, but it *does* make a difference and you want as much on your side as possible. You have only one, two, and possibly three bonafide opportunities to do this. The first, and most important, is the application itself; the second is a campus interview or visit that you initiate; the third is the campus visit that may be initiated by the athletic department, and for some selective schools, the fourth may be an interview with a review board. For all of these the basics are the same: you want to create the most positive impression that you can without giving up spontaneity or genuineness. Fake it and you will be found out - guaranteed!

The application should be organized, neat, complete, and returned early. The appearance cannot be over-emphasized. Admissions officers and committees will form an impression of you based on the application. Never send in anything that is not first rate in every respect with words correctly spelled, forms signed, grammar that befits an educated person -- no coffee stains or grease spots. Be sure to type it, and think of it as a professional resume.

The same rules apply for personal meetings or interviews. Dress appropriately, neatly, and with good taste, including your hair, face, and fingernails. Over-dressed is always better than under-dressed, and take into account the taste in clothes for the season and region of the country you will be visiting. Make your appointment well in advance and be on time; better yet, be slightly early. If you are unavoidably detained, call and let the person know you will be late. A good rule of thumb is to prepare yourself as though your interview is with a potential employer. Do your homework on the school you are visiting and master the basic information to minimize dialogue about programs the institution does not have.

Different individuals and institutions will conduct interviews in different ways, but most selective institutions are interested in some very basic things: What interests you? How do you invest your time? With what results? What have you gained from this? Have you pursued anything in depth and have you been recognized by others for this effort? Can you ask intelligent questions? Can you respond intelligently to intuitive questions? The outcome will be to discern excellence, dedication, motivation and enthusiasm. Or to put it another way, they are designed to find out if you are you as good in the classroom as you are on the field!

Above all, spend some time collecting your thoughts before the interview. Why are you interested in this particular college or university? What is important for your own personal growth? If you need to, write down your questions. Try to word them in a way that will reveal useful information. For example, ask how many of the classes your freshman year will have less than 25 students. Ask whether these classes are taught by tenured senior faculty. Ask how many Baseball players graduated in the top third of their class, what the grade point average is for the Baseball team. Be as particular and specific as possible. The more thorough you are, the more likely it is that you will be remembered in a positive way. And of course, keep in mind that although the interview will rarely get you crossed off the list; if done well, it will most certainly put you at or near the top.

IMPORTANT DIFFERENCES AMONG SELECTIVE INSTITUTIONS: The Six Categories

It is worthwhile to identify the various types of colleges and universities, and to learn more about their admissions criteria. The six types of institutions are private colleges and universities (including the Ivy League), and state or public universities, the U.S. Service Academies, state and private military academies, and junior colleges. While there are clearly differences among the various members within each group, understanding the common characteristics is beneficial to understanding the admissions process.

As a group, the *private selective colleges* including the Ivy League have the most freedom in pursuing any type of mission that they choose, and almost total freedom in choosing whatever students they wish to admit to achieve that mission. This freedom is occasionally curbed by athletic league affiliations, but more generally is curbed by faculty review of the admissions activities, usually by setting higher academic standards as a part of the admission policy. Although it is extremely rare for faculty to be involved in selecting candidates, it does happen in some instances, and you need to be aware of this in researching schools. Faculty members generally put more weight on academic indicators and objective test scores than admissions officers. Most admissions officers are very reluctant to admit athletes who are significantly less qualified academically than other candidates because of the negative opinion that will be formed. Be sure as well that your references including high school faculty can vouch for your character, integrity, and academic accomplishments.

The *Ivy League* is an association of private colleges comprising a specific athletic conference; it is the only athletic association founded on the premise that athletes should not be given scholarships. While this may be important if you are looking for an athletic scholarship, it has even more important ramifications for admissions. As an athletic conference, each member institution is required to report the academic qualifications of recruited athletes to other member institutions such that all athletes are within certain guidelines for the general population of admitted and enrolled students.

Of all selective institutions, state and public colleges and universities will typically have lower academic admission standards for residents of their state; however, they often have higher standards for those out-of-state applicants. Applying to a selective university in your state always makes good sense. Applying to a public college or university out-of-state should be carefully evaluated since private selectives may be more generous in terms of admissions standards and financial aid. One way to gauge this is to look at the geographic composition of the members of the Baseball team. If a large number of the players come from out-of-state you know that the admission committee has sufficient leeway to give you reasonable consideration; if the converse is true you may want to place your bets elsewhere. Remember, too, that the number of public selective institutions is rather small. This is due to the fact that, by their public nature, tuition and admission requirements must be affordable for residents, yet still attractive to qualified out-of-state applicants. For this reason your residence may be as much a factor in determining your chance for admission as your credentials. View this, of course, in light of the geographic composition of the athletic teams as indicated above.

The *U.S. Service Academies* differ from the other groups in several important respects, not the least of which is the fact that they are free to those student athlete's who gain appointment. While the Ivy League offers no merit scholarships although very generous with those demonstrating need, the service academies offer all appointees a merit scholarship. Of course, the hitch is that applicants must be sure they want the discipline and lifestyle that these institutions offer, and also willing to accept military service requirements after graduation. The other salient difference is that although these institutions are selective, they conduct their admissions business very differently from all the rest. Essentially, almost everyone who is admitted attends. As a result, the number of students admitted is very small compared to other institutions where (as a general rule) fewer than half of the admitted students will choose to enroll. Since the general admission procedures are readily available, there is no need to cover them here; be sure, however, that you understand the singular nature of these institutions, the unique environment and curriculum, and the difficulty of transferring to another college or university later if you find it's not for you.

State and Private Military Academies have the same characteristics as other state and private colleges and universities for admissions and available financial aid, but offer similar discipline and lifestyle as the U.S. Service Academies without the mandatory military service requirements after graduation.

JUNIOR COLLEGES

There are many paths to follow in your pursuit of higher education. A junior college is often a viable alternative to beginning a college education at a four-year school. A student-athlete may make a more comfortable transition to campus life in a smaller, friendlier and more familiar setting. The junior college also offers an Associate Degree for those who are seeking to gain employment after only two years of study.

Most junior colleges build a solid academic foundation for students who wish to move on to a four-year degree program and for those who have not fully applied themselves in previous settings. They allow students to acclimate themselves more slowly to the rigors of college life relieving some of the academic pressure by adding a personal touch that may not be found at larger universities. This does not mean, however, that they are less demanding than four-year institutions.

Junior colleges almost always offer a smaller student-instructor ratio than that of a larger state school. And, because building the "academic foundation" is paramount, the junior college normally excels in support services. Resource rooms, tutoring, labs, mentorship programs, and academic counseling are staples of a junior college education.

When selecting a college money may be a primary concern. Attending a nearby community college while living at home for the first year or two can significantly cut the cost of a four-year degree. The junior college offers a very affordable tuition that allows students and their parents some breathing room in the first two years. Moving away from home to attend a junior college offers the advantage of lower tuition, however housing, food and miscellaneous living expenses may match the costs for room and board while attending an in-state university.

Many junior college programs are serious about athletics, recognizing that they are valuable in the overall education of an individual. It is also widely recognized that through athletics an individual can increase his or her market value as a prospective student-athlete to a four-year school.

Junior college athletics are geared towards the continuation of skill development for an individual in a particular sport. Some athletes do not reach their full potential in high school. As in the academic areas, the junior college athletic program is also geared to improving the student's physical abilities. NJCAA intercollegiate athletic competition is very keen, with the various conference, district, regional and national play-offs and tournaments providing a great proving ground and barometer for student-athletes who want to pursue their sport at the NCAA Division I, II, and III levels, or in the NAIA.

Many student-athletes fall through the cracks of the recruiting process, while others are simply unable to make a decision about their future in education and athletics. For some, the financial situation is appealing; for others, the need to develop academically is a priority. These are all reasons that may best describe the cross section of student-athletes found in many junior colleges. Junior college affords them the opportunity to play Baseball at the collegiate level. For the most part, these student-athletes continue their education and playing careers at four-year schools. Many are recruited from the junior college setting, and many receive scholarships. These are success stories which cannot be ignored or discounted.

SUMMARY

Evaluate yourself and selective institutions on two dimensions - athletic and academic, then match yourself as closely as possible. Apply early and taking care to leave a good first impression both on the application and during interviews or visits. Understand the differences that exist among the general grouping of selective institutions, and use this information to your advantage as you attempt to choose the best match possible.

Above all, do not get caught up thinking this is a "life or death" decision, or that only one college could possibly be the "right" one for you. The fact is that if a college can provide the educational opportunities you want for your future and offer you an opportunity to play Baseball, it is really hard to see how you can lose!

COLLEGE PLANNING CHECKLIST & WORKSHEET

The following pages represent a checklist for the prospective college athlete. Along with your parents, use these guidelines in assembling your college selection criteria beginning with your sophomore year. By using these guidelines as a planning tool you will have a road map that will keep you pointed in the right direction throughout the selection process.

***** Parents, please insure that all high school records are sent by the school to the college admission office upon graduation. Player participation will not be allowed until his records are on file with the college or university. *****

PAYING FOR COLLEGE

GORDON PECK
FORMER ASSOCIATE DEAN OF ADMISSIONS AND FINANCIAL AID
DAVIDSON COLLEGE

As you begin the important process of selecting a college, you and your parents will probably be influenced by the stated cost of each institution. Please do not be! At least, not at first.

Too many students rule out a college that may be well suited to meet their needs because of that college's apparent high price. They assume that a student must be from a low-income family in order to qualify for financial aid. They are unaware of student employment opportunities, creative payment plans, and low interest loans. Some have not turned over enough stones in search of competitive scholarships and restricted grants. Others are simply bewildered by the perceived complexities of the financial aid application process.

In the pages that follow, we will attempt to dispel these misconceptions and to provide you with the information you need to plan the financing of the most important investment you may make in your lifetime: your college education. We will focus on three general areas of assistance:

- Need-Based Financial Aid
- Non Need-Based Aid Including Merit Scholarships
- Family Financial Planning

Need-based aid will receive the most attention because, as the foundation of most college financial aid programs, it provides the largest dollar volume of assistance. Before we guide you through the analysis, it is important that you accurately interpret the college price tag.

COLLEGE COSTS

No matter where you enroll, your expenses will include direct educational costs and living expenses. Financial aid assistance is generally determined by your school year budget using five categories:

- Tuition And Fees
- Room And Board
- Books And Supplies
- Personal Expenses (Clothing, Laundry, Medical, etc.)
- Transportation

Typically the first category represents fixed costs payable directly to the college.

Room and board will be set by the college in the case of resident (on campus) students, but expenses may vary greatly for students living off campus.

Books, supplies, and personal expenses will vary with the student's academic program and personal spending habits.

Transportation costs for resident students are generally estimated on the basis of two round-trips home during the academic year while commuting students must estimate gasoline, parking and other related costs.

To be certain that you are comparing oranges with oranges when determining estimated college costs, we suggest that you use a chart similar to **X1** (on the next page) to record actual and estimated costs in each category for each college you are considering. Be sure you are comparing costs for the same academic year. **College A** may be publishing 1998-99 costs while **College B** may be listing 1999-2000 costs.

PAYING FOR COLLEGE

X1 - ESTIMATING COLLEGE COSTS

Items of Expense	College A	College B	College C	College D
Tuition	______	______	______	______
Fees	______	______	______	______
Books/supplies	______	______	______	______
Room	______	______	______	______
Board	______	______	______	______
Personal expenses	______	______	______	______
Transportation	______	______	______	______
Other	______	______	______	______
TOTAL	______	______	______	______

Most colleges will provide estimates of costs in each category based on annual student surveys. Insist that the colleges you are considering provide these figures in updated form.

YOUR FAMILY CONTRIBUTION

Now that you have determined the estimated annual costs of your top choice of colleges, let us take a close look at how colleges determine your family's contribution toward college costs. *Remember*, do not rule out any college until you have analyzed all the possible means of reducing the real costs.

All colleges and government agencies expect you to pay something toward college expenses according to your family's financial strength. Most college financial aid offices will determine your family's ability to pay based on a standard financial aid "need analysis" system called Congressional Methodology. The analysis will examine your parents' income and assets as well as your own savings and summer earnings potential to determine an expected parent and student contribution toward annual college costs.

Through 1993-94, families have provided financial information to colleges on a Financial Aid Form (FAF), the Student Aid Application for California (SAAC) or the Family Financial Statement (FFS). The analysis of your family takes account much more than your parents annual income. You may assume that families with higher incomes will be expected to contribute more to college expenses, but the methodology also considers family assets (home equity, investments, savings) and family expenses. A family with six dependents and unusual medical expenses will be expected to contribute less than a family of three even though their annual income is similar.

In addition to the parent's contribution, you, the student, will be expected to contribute at least $700 towards your annual educational costs. The actual amount will depend on your earnings for the previous year and the savings you have been able to accumulate.

To the extent that each family's situation is unique, financial aid officers invite you to provide documentation which may substantiate unusual expenses or circumstances which cannot be adequately demonstrated on the FAF. Usually, high consumer debt may not be a legitimate basis for adjusting the results of the standard formula, but many other uncontrollable drains on income may be worth sharing with each aid office.

Okay, you still need a good estimate of what your parent's contribution might be. **Table X2** (below) provides an approximation of what many college, state, and private student aid programs will expect parents to pay at various income levels.

Figures on the chart are based on the following assumptions:

- One Child In College
- Only One Parent Working
- No Unusual Financial Circumstances

Your actual circumstances could lead to an increase or decrease. Please use the figures as a *general guide only*.

TABLE X2	**ESTIMATED PARENTS' CONTRIBUTION**															
This chart of typical expected family contributions derived from the Financial Aid Form (FAF).																
Net Assets	$20,000				$40,000				$60,000				$80,000			
Family Size	**3**	**4**	**5**	**6**	**3**	**4**	**5**	**6**	**3**	**4**	**5**	**6**	**3**	**4**	**5**	**6**
Income Before Taxes																
$ 8,000	$ 0	$ 0	$ 0	$ 0	$ 0	$ 0	$ 0	$ 0	$ 0	$ 0	$ 0	$ 0	$ 314	$ 0	$ 0	$ 0
12000	0	0	0	0	0	0	0	0	417	0	0	0	999	493	0	0
16000	266	0	0	0	562	72	0	0	1090	600	139	0	1618	1128	667	130
20000	916	398	0	0	1176	687	228	0	1706	1215	756	236	2316	1750	1284	784
24000	1567	1049	563	13	1804	1302	843	323	2430	1848	1371	851	3183	2481	1927	1379
28000	2296	1700	1214	663	2544	1947	1458	937	3317	2585	2025	1456	4265	3376	2686	2034
32000	3216	2471	1888	1314	3451	2709	2124	1552	4451	3517	2801	2133	5579	4533	3643	2813
36000	4388	3420	2688	2001	4636	3674	2935	2231	5764	4718	3800	2947	6892	5846	4866	3814
40000	5546	4616	3711	2824	5784	4864	3958	3081	6922	5992	5051	3972	8050	7120	6179	5068
44000	6621	5691	4827	3852	6869	5939	5076	4091	7997	7067	6204	5208	9125	8195	7332	6336
48000	7824	6895	6031	5035	8072	7143	6278	5283	9200	8271	7407	6411	10328	9399	8535	7539
52000	9027	8098	7,234	6238	9276	8346	7482	6487	10404	9474	8610	7615	11532	10602	9738	8743
56000	10180	9301	8437	7442	10428	9549	8685	7690	11556	10677	9813	8818	12684	11805	10941	9946
60000	11252	10384	9583	8645	11500	10633	9831	8893	12620	11761	10959	10021	13756	12889	12087	11149

Add a minimum student contribution of $700-$1000 to the parent contribution you derived from the table and you will have a rough estimate of the total family contribution you may be expected to pay at each of the colleges where you are accepted. Remember that the parents' contribution, as derived through the need analysis system, is a measure of the family's capacity to pay over time; it is not an amount that is expected to come solely from current income. While a few families may be able to provide the entire parent contribution from current income, most families use some combination of savings and borrowing to satisfy their share of the annual college costs. Supplemental loan programs, financing, and other options will be discussed later.

COLLEGE COST - FAMILY CONTRIBUTION = FINANCIAL AID ELIGIBILITY

Once your estimated family contribution has been determined, it should be subtracted from the total costs of the various colleges you are considering (remember, we are talking about need-base aid; "merit" aid is another matter). Because the majority of colleges will base their analysis on the same methodology, the expected family contribution will be about the same at each college.

Knowing the total college costs at the schools you are considering (**Table X1**) and knowing your estimated parents' contribution (**Table X2**), you are now able to begin the comparison of net costs of the colleges you are considering. For purposes of illustration, let us say that your family of six is supported on an income of $52,000 and that net assets are valued at $40,000. Using **Table X2**, you estimate that your parents' contribution would be $6,187. You then subtract that $6,187 and $1,000 (student contribution), a total family contribution of $7,187 from the total costs at colleges A, B, C and D as follows:

	COLLEGE A	COLLEGE B	COLLEGE C	COLLEGE D
Total Costs	$8,000	$12,000	$16,000	$20,000
Family Contribution	7,487	7,487	7,487	7,487
Aid Eligibility	513	4,513	8,513	12,813

As the various college financial aid offices use the standardized need analysis formula, family's annual contribution to your college costs should remain constant while your "need" or financial aid eligibility will vary with college costs. College D at $20,000 will be no less affordable than College A at $8,000 for the family used in this illustration. Knowing that the family contribution will be the same at Colleges A, B, C and D, this family can concentrate on important non-financial considerations in choosing the most appropriate college.

PACKAGING

After your financial aid eligibility is determined, the next task for the financial aid office is to determine which financial aid resources should be combined to form your financial aid "package". Packages may contain grants, scholarships, student loans, and campus employment. Sources of these may include federal and state funds, independent agencies, and college itself. Not all colleges are able to offer you a package that meets all of your financial need, and among those schools that do meet 100% of financial need, aid packages may vary greatly. To illustrate, look at three possible packages that might be offered to meet the $12,813 need of a student attending College D in the previous illustration.

	SHORTFALL PACKAGE	HIGH SELF-HELP	LOW SELF-HELP
Loan	$2,500	$3,000	$2,000
Job	1,500	1,500	800
State Grant	1,000	1,000	1,000
College Grant	1,000	7,313	9,013
Total	$6,000	$12,813	$12,813

The "shortfall package" provides $6,000 of financial aid but that amount falls $6,813 short of the calculated need. Most colleges will not offer you a package that falls so far short of your need unless your application materials arrive late or the institution simply has inadequate funds to provide full need for all its students. The "high self-help" package starts with a combination of loan and job (self-help) which totals $4,500 or 35% of the package. The "low self-help" package includes a total of $2,800 in self-help or 22% of the package, a more favorable package because the student's repayment and employment responsibilities are reduced. Both of these $12,813 packages meet 100% of the student's calculated need while holding the family contribution at $7,187.

You will be informed about your calculated need and the resulting financial aid package by way of an "award letter." Each college where you have been accepted for admission, applied for aid, and provided on-time financial aid application forms, will send you an "award letter" informing you of the amount and type of aid you will receive. This letter should reach you well before the deadline date for making your admissions deposit so that you will have time to compare packages and ask questions about your package.

NON-NEED BASED ASSISTANCE

In spite of our encouragement and your family's best efforts, the need analysis system may determine that you are not eligible for need-based financial aid, or perhaps your parents feel they cannot come up with all of the family contribution calculated by your top choice colleges. What then? There may still be hope in the form of grants-in-aid, merit scholarships, payment plans, alternative loan programs, and other creative financing options.

Grants and merit scholarships--As discussed earlier, many need-based financial aid packages will include grants or scholarships. Many colleges also offer gift aid (grants and scholarships) without regard to financial need to recognize outstanding accomplishments and potential in academics, performing arts, athletics, and other special talents. These special awards may be offered to no more than ten percent of the students at a particular college and may range in value from a hundred dollars to full cost.

Competition for these college-sponsored scholarships is keen and frequently requires a separate application. You should ask each college you are considering about the requirements and procedures that apply to merit scholarships at that institution. You should explore the possibility of scholarships and grants from private organizations. Your parents' employers, professional organizations, service organizations, churches, local PTA groups, veterans' organizations, charitable societies, and many other groups frequently provide aid for college-bound students. Begin your search for these private scholarships in your school's guidance library. Also check with the public library for such guides as **"The College Blue Book: Scholarships, Fellowships, Grants and Loans or Financial Aid for Higher Education," Oreon Keesler, Editor.**

Again, you might turn to individual college financial aid offices about outside sources of scholarships that have been used by their students in the past.

Alternative loan program--The loans referred to in our earlier discussion of packaging are subsidized student loans, available only to students who demonstrate need. These need-based loans are provided through the Perkins or Stafford loan programs, and they are generally included within a student's need-based package. In this section, we want to make you aware of educational loan options available to parents and students who may not qualify for need- based aid or who may need assistance meeting the family contribution expected by the financial aid office.

At the federal level, Congress has authorized two programs: Parent Loans for Undergraduate Students (PLUS) and Supplemental Loans for Students (SLS). PLUS loans are available for parents of dependent students, and SLS loans are for independent students. Unlike the Perkins and Stafford loan programs, there is no in-school interest subsidy and very limited opportunity to postpone payments until after college. However, the programs offer interest rates and repayment advantages over most consumer loans.

Several alternative loan programs have been developed in the private sector over the past few years. Some are supported by nonprofit organizations such as **The Education Resources Institute (TERI)** in Boston, and **Concern: Loans for Education in Washington, D.C.** These loans offer high annual limits (as much as $25,000 annually) to credit-worthy families, plus options for postponing principal repayment while the student remains in school. Loan programs are also sponsored by banks and other for-profit organizations. Some of these arrangements establish a line of credit which families may draw against as needed for educational costs. Other loan plans may be tied to tuition payment plans.

Tuition payment plans--Some colleges, plus a number of private financial institutions provide payment plans which allow families to spread the cost of attending college over the entire school year. Such plans provide a budget-wise option to the traditional lump sum payment at the beginning of each semester. Generally, the only charge for such programs is an application fee, unless the program is combined with an educational loan. Organizations such as Academic Management Services of Pawtucket, RI and the Knight Tuition Payment Plan of Boston work closely with several colleges in arranging individual payment plans for families.

Other options--A number of other creative options are being developed to help families better plan and manage the costs of higher education. Federal agencies, state governments, colleges, financial institutions, and various consortia are involved in the creation of savings plans, prepayment plans, tuition guarantee plans, and other alternatives too numerous to mention here. Our advice is to gather all the facts you can through your guidance office from publications such as **"The College Cost Book"** published by The College Board and Peterson's, **"The College Money Handbook,"** and especially from the financial aid offices at the colleges you are considering.

SCHEDULE FOR FINANCIAL AID APPLICANTS

Junior Year

As you investigate colleges, check each college's literature for financial aid application requirements, deadlines, and any special programs for which you may be eligible. When planning your college visits, try to set an appointment to see a financial aid officer. Be prepared with specific questions about application requirements, competitive scholarship programs, packaging policies, alternative loan programs, and other questions important to your family.

Senior Year

September - get a copy of **"Meeting College Costs,"** a publication of the College Scholarship Service, available in most guidance offices. Use the charts in this handy guide to estimate your family contribution and financial needs.

December - get the FAF (Financial Aid Form), the SAAC (Student Aid Application for California) or the FFS (Family Financial Statement) from the guidance office. The form may not be submitted before January 1, but you should familiarize yourself with requested information and begin to gather the financial records you will need to complete the form.

January / February - complete and submit the FAF (or SAAC or FFS). Make a copy for your records before sending them. Complete other financial aid application materials and send them to the colleges which you are applying. Make one last check for forms you may also need to submit to be considered for private scholarship programs or other outside aid. If you anticipate that you may not be eligible or receive enough need-based aid, you should complete your investigation of alternative loan programs and other sources of non-need based aid. Be sure to include college financial aid officers as you seek advice on these matters.

April / May - carefully compare the bottom line costs to your family from each of the colleges offering you financial aid. As you inform your first choice of colleges of your decision to attend, respond also to school's offer of financial aid. Be sure to let the other colleges know of your decision to attend the first choice college.

May / June - by now your family should have submitted copies of its federal tax returns, promissory notes for student loans and other required documents to the appropriate financial aid office. If suggested by your college, the Stafford loan application should be submitted at that time.

WHOM CAN I TRUST

While your high school coach and the college athletic recruiter may be very helpful and eager to assist you in the college search, it is important that you and your family maintain direct contact with the college financial aid offices. Do not send your financial aid application materials through the coach and do not rely on his or her interpretation of your eligibility for financial aid. Too many lost documents, missed deadlines, and misinterpreted financial aid packages have been attributed to well-meaning but unnecessary intercession by athletic recruiters.

While some high school officers may not have as much time or good information as you would like, they are still the best place to start when seeking financial aid advice. At a minimum, they can put valuable material into your hands and guide you to other people who can help. Financial aid officers at the college you are considering are probably in the best position to analyze your circumstances and lead you to the best sources of need-based and non need-based financial assistance.

Some of the publications referred to earlier can provide you with excellent guidance as you contemplate the serious matter of financing your education. We especially recommend:

The College Cost Book, 13th Edition, New York:
College Entrance Examination Board

Part I, Chapters 1-9 provide information about applying for aid and making the most of your own resources.

IF YOU HAVE MORE TIME

If college is still several years away for you, your family has the advantage of planning and saving for your college education. Remember, colleges will consider the student and her family as the first and primary source of funds for education, and the bulk of financial aid awards will continue to be awarded on the basis of financial need. Therefore, it behooves you to do all you can in advance to painlessly provide the calculated family contribution when the time comes.

Educational financial planning can be complicated, but it is not as cumbersome as paying for college when there has been no planning at all. Chapter Eight of **The College Cost Book** provides a valuable starting point for parents contemplating these matters. Read it and be encouraged. Start your savings plans knowing that college choices will be more numerous for those who have planned.

Publications and organizations that may be helpful in the search for financial aid:

1. **Federal Student Aid Information Center**
   PO Box 84, Washington DC 20044, (800) 433-3234, 9 am-5:30 pm EST
2. **How to Get into the College of Your Choice...and How to Finance It**
   William Morrow & Co., Inc., 105 Madison Avenue, New York, NY 10016
3. **Money Guide: Best College Buys**
   Time Inc. Magazine Co., PO Box 30626, Tampa, FL 33630-0626, (800) 633-9970
4. **Financial Aids for Higher Education: A Catalog for Undergraduates**
   William C. Brown Publishing, 2460 Kerper Blvd., Dubuque, IA 52001, (800) 553-4920
5. **Peterson's College Money Handbook**
   Peterson's Guides, PO Box 2123, Princeton, NJ 08643-2123, (800) 225-0261
6. **Winning Money for College: The High School Student's Guide to Scholarship Contests**
   Peterson's Guides, Box 2123, Princeton, NJ 08540, (800) 225-0261
7. **Lovejoy's Guide to Financial Aid**
   Simon & Schuster, One Gulf & Western Plaza, New York, NY 10023, (212) 333-5800
8. **The Student Guide: Financial Aid from the U.S. Dept. of Ed.: Grants, Loans & Work-Study**
   U.S. Gov't Printing Office, PO Box 37000, Washington, DC 20013, (800) 433-3234
9. **Computer Assisted Scholarships for Higher Education Program (Cashe)**
   The American Legion Process Ctr., 600 S. Frederick ., Gaithersburg, MD 20877 (301) 258-0717
10. **The Student Guide: Five Federal Financial Aid Programs;** (800) 433-3234
11. **U.S. Department of Education, Office of Student Financial Assistance;**
    Washington, DC 20202-5464
12. **The Scholarship Book** by Daniel J. Cassidy, Prentice Hall

FOREIGN STUDENTS

THE SPORT SOURCE, INC. *has learned through its first ten years of publications that many student-athletes outside of the U.S. are using this* ***College Guide****. Because of this, we continue to include a brief outline of the steps necessary for international students to apply to schools in the U.S.*

As an international applicant it is important to begin the process as early as possible. You should apply no later than 6 months prior to the semester in which you wish to begin your studies. You will need the extra time to obtain your official school records, arrange for the required examinations, forward bank verification of your financial resources, for your application to be reviewed, and to obtain your visa.

It is important to note that many U.S. colleges and universities require international students applying for undergraduate studies (bachelor's degree) to pay all expenses themselves. Many universities do not give scholarships or financial aid to international students seeking undergraduate studies.

REQUIREMENTS

International students usually are required to be proficient in the English language, and good students in their own countries before they will be considered for admission into a college in the U.S. Students usually should have 12 years of study in their own country, beginning at age six. The last four or five years should include the study of English, history, mathematics and science. Although each university may be different, this is a basic overview of what many universities require for application from international students:

An Application Form: Answer every question. Your principal or headmaster may also be asked to answer questions on the form. There may or may not be an application fee.
Financial Certification: The student or his/her parents must often submit proof that the family or sponsor can pay for the schooling. This amount can range anywhere from $14,000-$20,000 per year, including tuition, room, food, books, and other miscellaneous expenses. The university needs an official statement from a bank, employer, sponsor, or other official affidavit of support.
School Records: These are transcripts or certificates of satisfactory study. Records should include an English translation of the subjects the student has studied and grades the student has made in each subject. It is very important to explain the grading system of each school attended.
Test of English as a Foreign Language (TOEFL): This is usually required for all international students except those whose native language is English. Information about this test can be found at U.S. Embassies, Consulates, offices of the United States Information Services, or at schools in your home country.
Aptitude Tests (SAT/ACT): These tests, such as the Scholastic Aptitude Test (SAT) or American College Testing's (ACT) Assessment Program which measure verbal and mathematical ability are required for both international students and American students.

VISA

After you have been admitted and have submitted the financial certification information with bank statements, the university will send you a visa qualifying document. In most cases, you will be sent an I-20, a document which is used to get an F-I student visa. To get the visa you will need to go to your nearest American Embassy or Consulate and show the following three items:

- Your Passport
- Your I-20
- Your Current Financial Certification

Because you may be asked to prove your financial resources, you should retain certified copies of the original financial information that your sent to U. S. colleges when applying.

If you already are in the United States, you will not need to get a new visa; you will receive a transfer, which will extend your time to the dates of the appropriate academic program. An I-20 will be sent for you to do your transfer.

ALABAMA

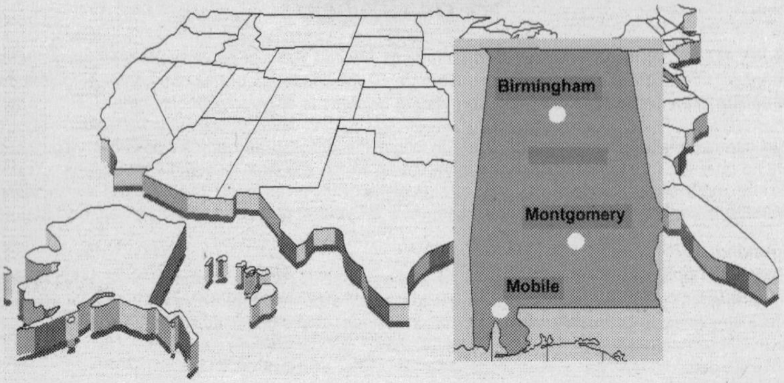

SCHOOL	CITY	AFFILIATION 99	PAGE
Alabama A & M University	Normal	NCAA II	45
Alabama Southern Community College	Monroeville	NJCAA	45
Alabama State University	Montgomery	NCAA I	45
Auburn University	Auburn	NCAA I	46
Auburn University - Montgomery	Montgomery	NAIA	46
Bevill State Community College - Fayette	Fayette	NJCAA	47
Birmingham Southern College	Birmingham	NAIA	47
Bishop State Community College	Mobile	NJCAA	48
Calhoun Community College	Decatur	NJCAA	48
Central Alabama Community College	Alexander City	NJCAA	49
Chattahoochee Valley State Community College	Phoenix City	NJCAA	49
Enterprise State Junior Community College	Enterprise	NJCAA	50
Faulkner State Community College	Bay Minette	NJCAA	50
Faulkner University	Montgomery	NAIA	51
Gadsden State Community College	Gadsden	NJCAA	51
Huntingdon College	Montgomery	NAIA	51
Jacksonville State University	Jacksonville	NCAA I	52
Jefferson Davis Community College	Brewton	NJCAA	53
Jefferson State Community College	Birmingham	NJCAA	53
Lurleen B. Wallace State J C	Andalusia	NJCAA	53
Miles College	Birmingham	NCAA II	54
Northwest Shoals-Phil Campbell	Phil Campbell	NJCAA	54
Samford University	Birmingham	NCAA I	55
Shelton State Community College	Tuscaloosa	NJCAA	55
Snead State Community College	Boaz	NJCAA	56
Southern Union State College	Wadley	NJCAA	56
Spring Hill College	Mobile	NAIA	57
Stillman College	Tuscaloosa	NCAA III	57
Talladega College	Talladega	NAIA	58
Troy State University	Troy	NCAA I	58
Tuskegee University	Tuskegee	NCAA II	59
University of Alabama	Tuscaloosa	NCAA I	59
University of Alabama - Birmingham	Birmingham	NCAA I	60
University of Alabama - Huntsville	Huntsville	NCAA II	61
University of Mobile	Mobile	NAIA	61
University of Montevallo	Montevallo	NCAA II	62
University of North Alabama	Florence	NCAA II	63
University of South Alabama	Mobile	NCAA I	63
University of West Alabama	Livingston	NCAA II	64
Wallace State Community C - Dothan	Dothan	NJCAA	65
Wallace State C - Hanceville	Hanceville	NJCAA	65

Alabama A & M University

4900 Meridian Street N.W.
Normal, AL 35762
Coach: Tom Wesley

NCAA II
Bulldogs/Maroon, White
Phone: (256) 858-4004
Fax: (256) 851-5369

ACADEMIC

Founded: 1875
Web-site: http://www.aamu.edu/
Student/Faculty Ratio: 17:1
Undergraduate Enrollment: 4,000
Scholarships/Academic: No **Athletic:** Yes
Total Expenses by: Year **In State:** $ 5,000

Type: 4 Yr., Public, Coed
SAT/ACT/GPA: 700/17 (sliding scale)
Male/Female Ratio: 48:52
Graduate Enrollment: 1,300
Fin Aid: Yes
Out of State: $ 6,700

Degrees Conferred: AA, AS, BA, MS, MBA, Med, PHD
Programs of Study: Accounting, Agriculture, Animal Science, Art Education, Biology, Business Administration, Chemistry, Computer Science, English, History, Marketing, Physical Education, Political Science, Preveterinary, Psychology Telecommunications, Zoology

ATHLELIC PROFILE

Conference Affiliation: Southern Intercollegiate Athletic Conference

Alabama Southern Community College

P.O. Box 2000
Monroeville, AL 36461
Coach: Michael Jeffcoat

NJCAA
Eagles/Royal, Black, White
Phone: (334) 575-3156
Fax: (334) 575-5356

ACADEMIC

Founded: 1965
SAT/ACT/GPA: 500/21
Student/Faculty Ratio: 18:1
Scholarships/Academic: Yes **Athletic:** Yes
Total Expenses by: Year **In State:** $ 1,200

Type: 2 Yr., Public, Jr. College, Coed
Graduate Enrollment: 1,850
Male/Female Ratio: 34:68
Fin Aid: Yes
Out of State: $ 1,900

Degrees Conferred: Associate
Programs of Study: Accounting, Art, Banking/Finance, Biological, Business, Chemistry, Computer, Education, Engineering, History, Insurance, Liberal Arts, Mathematics, Medical, Nursing, Occupational Therapy, Physical Respiration, Radiological, Science, Social Science

ATHLETIC PROFILE

Conference Affiliation: Alabama Junior & Community College Conference
Program Profile: Program is well funded, with a plan for summer of 1998 facility improvement. Will have a new dugout, backstop, bleachers, press box, concession stand and bathrooms. Has Bermuda grass, which is excellent playing surface.
History: The baseball program began in 1970.
Achievements: Second place finished in 1996 State Tournament; 1-2nd team All-American in 1996.
Style of Play: Aggressive bunt, steal, hit & run offense. Centered around solid pitching & defense.

Alabama State University

915 S Jackson St
Montgomery, AL 36101
Coach: Larry Watkins

NCAA I
Hornets/Black, Gold
Phone: (334) 229-4228
Fax: (334) 299-4992

ACADEMIC

Founded: 1874
Web-site: Not Available
Student/Faculty Ratio: 17:1
Undergraduate Enrollment: 4,500
Scholarships/Academic: Yes **Athletic:** Yes
Total Expenses by: Year **In State:** $ 3,500
Type: 4 Yr., Public, Coed
SAT/ACT/GPA: 700/17
Male/Female Ratio: 1:14
Graduate Enrollment: 400
Fin Aid: Yes
Out of State: $ 5,000
Degrees Conferred: AA, AS, BA, BS, MA
Programs of Study: Accounting, Banking/Finance, Biological Science, Business Administration, Computer Science, Criminal Justice, Education, Engineering, English, Fine Arts, History, Journalism, Marketing, Math, Physics, Political Science, Psychology, Social Science, Visual/Performing Arts

ATHLETIC PROFILE

Conference Affiliation: SWAC

Auburn University

PO Box 351
Auburn, AL 36831
Coach: Hal Baird
NCAA I
Tigers/Burnt Orange, Navy
Phone: (334) 844-9767
Fax: (334) 844-9778

ACADEMIC

Founded: 1856
Religion: Non-Affiliated
Web-site: Not Available
Student/Faculty Ratio: 15:1
Undergraduate Enrollment: 18,349
Scholarships/Academic: Yes **Athletic:** Yes
Total Expenses by: Year **In State:** $ 1,426
Type: 4 Yr., Public, Liberal Arts, Coed
Campus Housing: No
SAT/ACT/GPA: 1076/24
Male/Female Ratio: 1.2:1
Graduate Enrollment: 3,014
Fin Aid: Yes
Out of State: $ 2,926
Degrees Conferred: BS, BA, MA, MS
Programs of Study: 150 areas of baccalaureate study including Agriculture, Agronomy, Animal Science, Production, Entomology, Horticulture, Architecture, Business, Marketing, Management

ATHLETIC PROFILE

Conference Affiliation: SouthEastern (West) Conference
Program Profile: Play a NCAA 56 game schedule from February to May. Play at Plainsman Park in Auburn University campus in Auburn, AL. The new Plainsman Park is now open and is a state of the art facility modeled after Camden Yards in Baltimore, MD and seats 4,166. The stadium contains a 30' green wall in the left field reminiscent of "The Green Monster" at Boston's Fenway Park.
Achievements: College World Series Participant 1994. Auburn is one of only 2 schools to produce a Rookie of the Year (Greg Olsen), All-Star MVP (Bo Jackson), and a league MVP (Frank Thomas).
Coaching: Hal Baird, Head Coach (East Carolina 1971). Steve Renfroe, Assistant Head Coach (Auburn 1982). Tom Slater, Assistant Coach (VMI 1992).

Auburn University - Montgomery

7300 University Drive
Montgomery, AL 36117-3596
Coach: Q.V. Lowe
NAIA
Senators/Orange, White
Phone: (334) 244-3237
Fax: (334) 244-3886

ACADEMIC

Founded: 1967
Web-site: http://www.aum.edu/
Type: 4 Yr., Public, Liberal Arts, Coed
SAT/ACT/GPA: 860/18

Student/Faculty Ratio: 20:1
Male/Female Ratio: 40:60
Undergraduate Enrollment: 4,500
Graduate Enrollment: 1,700
Scholarships/Academic: Yes **Athletic:** Yes
Fin Aid: Yes
Total Expenses by: Year **In State:** $ 4,175
Out of State: $ 8,225
Degrees Conferred: BA, BS, MA, MS, PhD, EdD
Programs of Study: Accounting, Art, Biology, Business and Management, Chemistry, Communications, Computer Information Systems, Computer Science, Criminal Justice, Economics, Education, Environmental Biology, Finance, Graphic Art, Law Enforcement, Marine, Nursing, Social Science, Political Science, Psychology, Mathematics

ATHLETIC PROFILE

Conference Affiliation: Southern State Conference
Program Profile: The Senators baseball program is one of national prominence at the NAIA level. AUM plays in probably the toughest NAIA conference in the natiion, the Southern States. The AUM baseball complex, a natural grass facility, features a 40-locker clubhouse, seating for 500 and is a practice site for the NCAA Division II World Series.
History: AUM founded its program in 1987 and Q.B. Lowe guided the Senators to a second-in-the-nation finish in 1990. The Senators have a winning percentage of .592.
Achievements: 10 All-Americans (2B Scott Zepp - 1st team and LHP Jason Stamp - Honorable Mention in 1985). SSC Champs in 1987, 1990, & 1995 (tournament), 4 players drafted.
Coaching: Q.V. Lowe, Head Coach, was with the Cubs; Yankees Coach and Expos Organization; Coach of the Year in 1990.
Style of Play: Aggressive offense and deep pitching staff.

Bevill State Community College - Fayette

2631 Temple Avenue North
Fayette, AL 35555
Coach: Matt Bragga
NJCAA
Bears/Green, Royal, White
Phone: (205) 932-3221
Fax: (205) 932-3294

ACADEMIC

Type: 2 Yr., Public, Jr. College, Coed
Programs of Study: Contact school for programs of study.

ATHLETIC PROFILE

Conference Affiliation: NJCAA

Birmingham Southern College

BSC Box 549035
Birmingham, AL 35254
Coach: Brian Shoop
NAIA
Panthers/Black, Gold
Phone: (205) 226-4797
Fax: (205) 226-3059

ACADEMIC

Founded: 1856
Type: 4 Yr., Private, Liberal Arts, Coed
Religion: Methodist
Campus Housing: Yes
Web-site: http://www.bsc.edu/
SAT/ACT/GPA: 26
Student/Faculty Ratio: 15:1
Male/Female Ratio: 49:51
Undergraduate Enrollment: 1,087
Graduate Enrollment: 83
Scholarships/Academic: Yes **Athletic:** Yes
Fin Aid: Yes
Total Expenses by: Year **In State:** $ 20,886
Out of State: $ 20,886
Degrees Conferred: BA, BS, BF, BM, Med

Programs of Study: Accounting, Biology, Business, Chemistry, Computer, Economics, Education, English, Fine Arts, Graphic Design, Health, History, Information Science, International, Marketing, Math, Music, Philosophy, Political, Psychology, Social Science, Visual and Performing Arts

ATHLETIC PROFILE

Conference Affiliation: Tran South Conference
Program Profile: Play on Scoushy - Striplin Field, a natural grass. Stadium has seating capacity of 1,000; facilities include locker room and weight room.
History: The program had a record of 42-18 in 1996.
Achievements: 4 Conference Titles in 1990's; 6 All-Americans in 1990's & 15 went to pros in 1990's.
Coaching: Brian Shoop, Head Coach, nine years, compiled a record of 321-143. He was named Conference Coach of the Year 4 out of 6 years. Butch Thompson, Andy Ford, and Monte Marshall, Assistant Coaches.
Style of Play: Defense and situational hit, cut down on errors, likes to run.

Bishop State Community College

351 North Broad Street
Mobile, AL 36603
Coach: William Paterson

NJCAA
Wildcats/Gold, Green
Phone: (334) 690-6436

ACADEMIC

Founded: 1965
Type: 2 Yr., Public, Jr. College, Coed
Undergraduate Enrollment: 3,661
Campus Housing: No
Student/Faculty Ratio: 19:1
Male/Female Ratio: 36:64
Scholarships/Academic: No **Athletic:** Yes **Fin Aid:** Yes
Total Expenses by: Year **In State:** $ 1,200 **Out of State:** $ 2,400
Degrees Conferred: Associate
Programs of Study: Accounting, Business Administration, Computer Information Systems, Criminal Justice, Deaf Interpreter Training, Emergency Medical Technology, Liberal Arts, Nursing, Physical Education, Psychology, Respiratory Therapy

ATHLETIC PROFILE

Conference Affiliation: AJCCC

Calhoun Community College

PO Box 2216
Decatur, AL 35609-2216
Coach: Gary Redus

NJCAA
Warhawks/Royal, White
Phone: (256) 306-2854
Fax: (256) 306-2885

ACADEMIC

Founded: 1967
Type: 2 Yr., Public, Jr. College, Coed
Student/Faculty Ratio: 25:1
Campus Housing: No
Undergraduate Enrollment: 8,000
Graduate Enrollment: None
Total Expenses by: Year **In State:** $ 1,500 **Out of State:** $ 2,500
Degrees Conferred: AA, AS
Programs of Study: Automotive, Biological, Carpentry, Computer, Corrections, Cosmetology, Criminal Justice, Dental, Education, Medical Technology, Science, Therapy, Management, Real Estate, Theatre

ATHLETIC PROFILE

Conference Affiliation: NJCAA, Alabama Junior/Community College Conference
Program Profile: Excellent playing field with grass field and no lights (390' down lines, 430' centerfield), Fall and Spring season, 60 games, double headers.

History: Coach Fred Frickie started program in 1967 and has been the only coach (640-395). Several players in pros including Gary Redus with the Texas Rangers.
Achievements: 4 All-Americans, 5 state titles, 1 region championship, coach of the year 5 times, numerous draftees.
Style of Play: Aggressive and hard nosed.

Central Alabama Community College

PO Box 699
Alexander City, AL 35010
Coach: Larry Giangrosso

NJCAA
Trojans/Navy, Old Gold
Phone: (256) 234-6346
Fax: (256) 234-0384

ACADEMIC

Founded: 1965
Type: 2 Yr., Public, Jr. College, Coed
Undergraduate Enrollment: 2,100
Campus Housing: No
Student/Faculty Ratio: 15:1
Male/Female Ratio: 45:55
Scholarships/Academic: Yes **Athletic:** Yes **Fin Aid:** Yes
Total Expenses by: Year **In State:** $ 1,100 **Out of State:** $ 1,700
Degrees Conferred: Associate
Programs of Study: Agriculture, Banking/Finance, Business, Community Service, Computer, Criminal Justice, Drafting/Design, Education, Electrical/Electronics, Engineering and Applied Science, Environmental, Fire, Law, Liberal Arts, Music, Nursing

ATHLETIC PROFILE

Conference Affiliation: Alabama Junior/Community College Conference Div. I
Program Profile: We play a 56 game schedule in the spring season. We have a beautiful baseball field with a mini-stadium that holds 300 people. A pressbox with coaches offices, coaches and umpires dressing room, concession stands & bathrooms. The field is 330 down the lines, 385 in gaps and 400 in the center field. A lot of full territory. We also have a state of the art, weight room.
History: The program began in 1991. In the first seven years, there have been 3 Division Championships and a Runner-Up finish in the Division I State Tournament in 1995. From 1993 - 1996 CACC posted 40+ win seasons winning 44 in 1993, 43 in 1994, 40 in 1995 and 42 in 1996; CAEC has averaged 36 a season over 7 years.
Achievements: Every player that has stayed here two years has graduated. For 7 years, we have averaged over a 3.00 GPA .68 out of 79 players over the past 7 years have gone on to play at 4-year schools. 22 of these played at Division I level. We have had 3 All-Americans. Coach Giangrosso was Coach of the Year in 1992, 1993, & 1994. We have had 2 players drafted and several after they went on to a four-year schools.
Coaching: Larry Giangrosso, Head Coach, eight years. Started the program from the ground up beginning in 1991. The program didn't own baseball when he arrived. I seven short years, Giangrosso has built and restabilished Central Alabama as one of the top Division I junior college in the nation. Lee Hall, Assistant Coach, eight years.
Style of Play: Year in , year out, we will put a team on the field that plays extremely hard. We will run the bases, play good defense and have a very solid pitching staff. We will also mix in some players who hit with power.

Chattahoochee Valley State Community College

2602 College Drive
Phoenix City, AL 36869
Coach: B.R. Johnson

NJCAA
Pirates/Blue, Gold
Phone: (334) 291-4907
Fax: (334) 291-4980

ACADEMIC

Founded: 1974
Type: 2 Yr., Public, Jr. College, Coed
Undergraduate Enrollment: 2,010
Campus Housing: No

Student/Faculty Ratio: 21:1 **Male/Female Ratio:** 41:59
Scholarships/Academic: Yes **Athletic:** Yes **Fin Aid:** Yes
Total Expenses by: Year **In State:** $ 1,100 **Out of State:** $ 2,000
Degrees Conferred: Associate
Programs of Study: Accounting, Art, Agriculture, Banking/Finance, Biological Science, Business Administration, Chemistry, Computer Information Systems, Criminal Justice, Engineering, Forestry, Insurance, Medical Technology, Nursing, Occupational Therapy, Physical Education, Physics, Radio/Television, Retail Management, Theatre, Wildlife Management

Enterprise State Junior Community College

P.O. Box 1300
Enterprise, AL 36331
Coach: Tim Hulsey
NJCAA
Boll-Weevils/Green, White
Phone: (334) 347-2623
Fax: (334) 393-6223

ACADEMIC

Founded: 1965 **Type:** 2 Yr., Public, Jr. College, Coed
Undergraduate Enrollment: 1,897 **Campus Housing:** No
Student/Faculty Ratio: 25:1 **Male/Female Ratio:** 40:60
Scholarships/Academic: Yes **Athletic:** Yes **Fin Aid:** Yes
Total Expenses by: Year **In State:** $ 1,524 **Out of State:** $ 3,054
Degrees Conferred: AAS
Programs of Study: All areas including: Agriculture, Aircraft and Missile Maintenance, Automotive Technology, Aviation Technology, Banking/Finance, Communications, Computer Science, Criminal Justice, Education, Insurance, Journalism, Law Enforcement, Marketing, Medical Records

ATHLETIC PROFILE

Conference Affiliation: Alabama Junior and Community College Conference
Program Profile: Excellent academic program, opportunities for four year college scholarships, and professional exposure. Excellent field and stands.
History: Enjoys good reputation -- normally involved in state tournament. Excellent win/loss record.
Achievements: Jerome Walton - Cinncinatti. 1988-1989 Coach of the Year. State Champs in 1981 - 1982; State Runner-Up in 1994; Division Champs in 1989.
Coaching: Tim Hulsey, Head Coach, entering 25 years of coaching. BSEd from Auburn, MSEd from South Alabama, played baseball at both, 12 years high school coaching, 10 years ESJC.
Style of Play: Hit & run, bunt, aggressive base running, power in 3-4-5 hole.

Faulkner State Community College

1900 S Highway 31
Bay Minette, AL 36507
Coach: Wayne Larker
NJCAA
Sun Chiefs/Crimson, Navy
Phone: (334) 580-2135
Fax: (334) 580-2155

ACADEMIC

Founded: 1963 **Type:** 2 Yr., Public, Jr. College, Coed
Undergraduate Enrollment: 4,000 **Campus Housing:** No
Scholarships/Academic: Yes **Athletic:** Yes **Fin Aid:** Yes
Total Expenses by: Year **In State:** $ 4,225 **Out of State:** $ 4,225
Degrees Conferred: Associate
Programs of Study: All areas of study

ATHLETIC PROFILE

Conference Affiliation: AJCCC Division I

Program Profile: A full year baseball program. Play a 56 game spring season, a 20 game fall season with 25 squad games. Travel across the Southeast and to Florida, and take overnight trips. Trips are taken by two greyhound team buses. The home field is Stanley James Field, lighted for night games, capacity of 2,000.
History: 1969-1982 Stan James record of 319-160; 1983-1984 Julius Wilson record of 42-37; 1985 to present Wayne Larker 380-217. A total of 741-414 record.
Achievements: 5 State Championships, 3 State Runner-up, 5 District Runner-up, 13 Division Championships; many players in pro baseball, State Region champs 2 years, many players in Division I NCAA. Never a losing season.
Coaching: Wayne Larker, Head Coach since 1985, 13 years as head coach, Masters in Exercise Physiology, five league championships, two years playing Long Beach CC, CA; two years University of South Alabama, two years California Angels Minors. Blaine Larker, Assistant Coach, two years Long Beach CC, 2 years California State Fullerton, College World Series 1984 All-Tournament 3B.

Faulkner University

5345 Atlanta Highway
Montgomery, AL 36109-3398
Coach: Wynn Fletcher

NAIA
Eagles/Blue, Grey, White
Phone: (334) 260-6148
Fax: (334) 260-6277

ACADEMIC

Founded: 1942
Student/Faculty Ratio: 18:1
Undergraduate Enrollment: 750
Scholarships/Academic: Yes
Athletic: Yes
Total Expenses by: Year
In State: $ 10,400
Type: 4 Yr., Private, Liberal Arts, Coed
SAT/ACT/GPA: 860/18
Religion: Church of Christ
Fin Aid: Yes
Out of State: $ 10,400
Programs of Study: Biology, Business Administration, Education, English, General Studies, Liberal Arts, Optometry, Prelaw, Religion, Sports Management

ATHLETIC PROFILE

Conference Affiliation: Southern States Conference

Gadsden State Community College

PO Box 227
Gadsden, AL 35902-0227
Coach: Bill Lockridge

NJCAA
Cardinals/Cardinal, Silver
Phone: (256) 549-8445
Fax: (256) 549-8444

ACADEMIC

Founded: 1965
Undergraduate Enrollment: 4,000
Student/Faculty Ratio: 21:1
Scholarships/Academic: Yes
Athletic: Yes
Total Expenses by: Year
In State: $ 4,100
Type: 2 Yr., Public, Jr. College, Coed
Campus Housing: No
Male/Female Ratio: 47:53
Fin Aid: Yes
Out of State: $ 4,800
Degrees Conferred: Associates
Programs of Study: Broadcasting, Business Administration, Commerce, Carpentry, Civil Engineering Technology, Computer Science, Court Reporting, Criminal Justice, Legal Secretarial

Huntingdon College

1500 East Fairview Avenue
Montgomery, AL 36106
Coach: Scot Patterson
Email: spatterson@huntington.edu

NAIA
Hawks/Scarlet, Grey
Phone: (334) 833-4501
Fax: (334) 833-4486

ACADEMIC

Founded: 1854 **Type:** 4 Yr., Private, Liberal Arts, Coed
Religion: Methodist **Campus Housing:** Yes
Web-site: http://www.huntingdon.edu/ **SAT/ACT/GPA:** 1020/20/2.5
Student/Faculty Ratio: 9:1 **Male/Female Ratio:** 1:2
Undergraduate Enrollment: 750 **Graduate Enrollment:** None
Scholarships/Academic: Yes **Athletic:** No **Fin Aid:** Yes
Total Expenses by: Year **In State:** $ 16,000 **Out of State:** $ 16,000
Degrees Conferred: BS
Programs of Study: Accounting, Art, Biology, Business Administration, Chemistry, Computer Science, Computer Information Systems, Dance, Drama, Education, Health Science, Psychology, Social Science, Physical Education, Religion, Philosophy

ATHLETIC PROFILE

Conference Affiliation: Southeast Independent
History: The program began in 1963.
Achievements: 1987 NAIA National Tournament; Conference Champs in 1986, 1987 & 1989; 1997 Regionals; 1998 Independent Runner-up.
Coaching: Scot Patterson, Head Coach, started with the program since '90. D. Conville, Assistant.
Roster for 1998 team/In State: 24 **Percent of Graduation:** 90%
Freshmen Receiving Fin Aid/Athletic: 0 **Academic:** 16
Number of Fall Games: 5 **Number of Spring Games:** 50
Positions Needed for 1999/2000: Pitcher, Outfielders
Most Recent Record: 23 - 25 - 0
Schedule: Birmingham Southern, Auburn-Montgomery, Columbia College, Berry College, Montevallo, Union.

Jacksonville State University

700 Pelham Rd N
Jacksonville, AL 36265
Coach: Rudy Abbott

NCAA I
Gamecocks/Red, White
Phone: (256) 782-5367
Fax: (256) 782-5666

ACADEMIC

Founded: 1883 **Type:** 4 Yr., Public, Coed
Religion: Non-Affiliated **Campus Housing:** Yes
Web-site: Not Available **SAT/ACT/GPA:** 900/19
Student/Faculty Ratio: 26:1 **Male/Female Ratio:** 45:55
Undergraduate Enrollment: 6,600 **Graduate Enrollment:** 1,100
Scholarships/Academic: Yes **Athletic:** Yes **Fin Aid:** Yes
Total Expenses by: Year **In State:** $ 4,490 **Out of State:** $ 6,980
Degrees Conferred: BA, BS, BFA, BMU, MA, MS
Programs of Study: Accounting, Art, Biology, Chemistry, Computer, Corrections, Criminal, Dietetics, Drama, Ecology, Environmental, Finance, Merchandising, Military Science, Preprofessional Programs, Security, Technology

ATHLETIC PROFILE

Conference Affiliation: Trans American Athletic Conference
Program Profile: Jacksonville State now has a new playing field.
History: 1990-1991 Division II National Championship; seven College World Series appearances.
Achievements: 5 Conference titles, 11 Division titles, 7 Region titles, 7 World Series appearances, 2 World Series titles, 6-times Gulf South Conference and District Coach of the Year, 1 ACC Coach of the Year, 29 All-Americans, 65 players drafted (Todd Jones, Astros, and Tim Van Egmond, Boston).
Coaching: Rudy Abbott, Head Coach.
Style of Play: Hard-nosed, aggressive style of play.

Jefferson Davis Community College

220 Alco Drive
Brewton, AL 36427
Coach: Keith Griffin

NJCAA
Warhawks/Red, White, Blue
Phone: (334) 809-1563
Fax: (334) 809-1652

ACADEMIC

Founded: 1965
Type: 2 Yr., Public, Jr. College, Coed
Student/Faculty Ratio: 25:1
Campus Housing: No
Undergraduate Enrollment: 1,600
Graduate Enrollment: None
Scholarships/Academic: Yes **Athletic:** Yes **Fin Aid:** Yes
Total Expenses by: Year **In State:** $ 1,200 **Out of State:** $ 1,950
Degrees Conferred: Associates
Programs of Study: Applied Art, Art, Biology, Biological Science, Business Administration, Business Management, Education, Elementary Education, Finance/Banking, History, Law Enforcement, Police Science, Liberal Arts, General Studies, Marketing, Medical Assistance Technology, Music, Nursing, Physical Education, Political Science, Recreation and Leisure Service, Secretarial Studies, Office Management, Theatre, Arts/Drama

Jefferson State Community College

2601 Carson Road
Birmingham, AL 35215
Coach: Ben Short

NJCAA
Pioneers/Maroon, Grey
Phone: (205) 856-8523
Fax: (205) 856-8535

ACADEMIC

Founded: 1965
Type: 2 Yr., Public, Jr. College, Coed
Religion: Not-Affiliated
Campus Housing: No
Student/Faculty Ratio: 21:1
Male/Female Ratio: 39:61
Total Expenses by: Year **In State:** $ 1,200 **Out of State:** $ 2,400
Degrees Conferred: Associates
Programs of Study: Accounting, Agricultural Technology, Banking/Finance, Business Administration, Child Development/Psychology, Computer Programming, Criminal Justice, Engineering Technology, Fashion Merchandising, Fire Science, Insurance, Interior Design, Law Enforcement, Postal Management, Radiological Technology, Recreation/Leisure Services

ATHLETIC PROFILE

Conference Affiliation: AJCCC
Program Profile: Jefferson State is a Division II community college, with a 56 game spring schedule. We have a natural grass field. We have an indoor/outdoor batting cages. We have an indoor pool and weight room.
History: The program began in 1965.
Achievements: Won State and finished 3rd in the nation in 1997.
Coaching: Ben Short, Head Coach. Ab Argent, Assistant Coach.
Style of Play: Good defense; good pitching; aggressive on the base pads.

Lurleen B. Wallace State Junior College

PO Box 1418
Andalusia, AL 36420
Coach: Steve Helms

NJCAA
Saints/Blue, White
Phone: (334) 222-6591
Fax: (334) 222-6567

ACADEMIC

Founded: 1969
Type: 2 Yr., Public, Jr. College, Coed
Student/Faculty Ratio: 20:1
Campus Housing: No
Undergraduate Enrollment: 1,147
Graduate Enrollment: None
Scholarships/Academic: No **Athletic:** No **Fin Aid:** Yes
Total Expenses by: Year **In State:** $ 1,152 **Out of State:** $ 2,304
Degrees Conferred: Associate
Programs of Study: Business, Computer Programming, Computer Science, Forest Technology, Liberal Arts

ATHLETIC PROFILE

Conference Affiliation: Southern Division Conference
Program Profile: Baseball has been played in Miles for over 50 years, and during the past two years our team finished the season in fourth place. Our record in 1995 was 17-15, and in 1996 18-15. In 1996 we lead the nation as a team in hitting (400) average. We play on natural grass, and the stadium is named Willie Mays Field.
History: Program has over 50 years history.
Achievements: 3 All-Conference players, and Black College All-americans for three years in a row (1995, 1996 and 1997), 3 players drafted and two are being ranked at now.
Coaching: Steve Helms, Head Coach.

Miles College

5500 Myron Massey Boulevard
Birmingham, AL 35208
Coach: Willie Patterson

NCAA II
Golden Bears/Purple, Gold
Phone: (205) 929-1615
Fax: (205) 929-1616

ACADEMIC

Founded: 1905
Type: 4 Yr., Private, Coed
Undergraduate Enrollment: 1,050
Campus Housing: No
Student/Faculty Ratio: 22:2
Male/Female Ratio: 48:82
Scholarships/Academic: Yes **Athletic:** No **Fin Aid:** Yes
Total Expenses by: Year **In State:** $ 7,550 **Out of State:** $ 7,550
Degrees Conferred: AA, AB, BS
Programs of Study: Biology, Business Administration, Chemistry, Communications, Education, English, Math, Music, Natural Science, Political Science, Predentistry, Preengineering, Preveterinary Medicine, Social Science

ATHLETIC PROFILE

Conference Affiliation: SIAC (Southern Intercollegiate Athletic Conference)
Program Profile: Baseabll has been played for over 50 years and during the past two years our team finished the second season in 4th place. Our record last year (1996) was 17-15 and this year (1997) is 18-15. In 1996 we led the nation in stolen bases. In 1993 we led the nation in walks and in 1997 led the nation as a team in hitting (400) average. Play on a natural grass at Willie Mays Field.
History: History of program is over 50 years.
Achievements: 3 All-Conference players and Black College All-Americans for three years in a row (1995, 1996, and 1997); 3 players drafted and two are being asked now.
Coaching: Willie Patterson, Head Coach.

NorthWest Shoals-Phil Campbell

Rt 3 Box 77
Phil Campbell, AL 35581
Coach: Tommy Jackson

NJCAA
Vikings/Navy, Orange
Phone: (256) 331-5291

ACADEMIC

Founded: 1963
Type: 2 Yr., Public, Jr. College, Coed
Religion: Not-Affiliated
Campus Housing: No
Scholarships/Academic: Yes **Athletic:** Yes **Fin Aid:** Yes
Total Expenses by: Year **In State:** $ 3,000 **Out of State:** $ 4,000
Degrees Conferred: Associate
Programs of Study: All Majors

ATHLETIC PROFILE

Conference Affiliation: AJCCCA
Program Profile: NJCAA -- play 56 game spring schedule and 20 game fall schedule. Our new baseball facility opened in the Fall of 1995.
Style of Play: Aggressive, sound, fundamental baseball.

Samford University

800 Samford University
Birmingham, AL 35229
Coach: Tim Parenton

NCAA I
Bulldogs/Red, White, Blue
Phone: (205) 414-4095
Fax: (205) 870-2131

ACADEMIC

Founded: 1841
Type: 4 Yr., Private, Liberal Arts, Coed
Religion: Southern Baptist
Campus Housing: No
Web-site: Not Available
SAT/ACT/GPA: 1000/24
Student/Faculty Ratio: 14:1
Male/Female Ratio: 38:62
Undergraduate Enrollment: 3,200
Graduate Enrollment: 1,350
Scholarships/Academic: Yes **Athletic:** Yes **Fin Aid:** Yes
Total Expenses by: Year **In State:** $ 12,500 **Out of State:** $ 12,500
Degrees Conferred: BA, BGS, BM, BS, BSED, BSN, MBA, Mmus
Programs of Study: Accounting, Athletic Training, Art, Biology, Church Recreation, Computer Science, Dramatic Arts, Early Childhood Education, Engineering, Physics, Environmental Science, Fashion Merchandising, International Relations, Management, Languages, Journalism, Professional Programs, Speech, Theatre, Voice

ATHLETIC PROFILE

Conference Affiliation: Trans American Athletic Conference (TAAC)
Program Profile: Has a new stadium. Facilities include natural grass field. The playing surface is in superb condition. Have indoor and an outdoor batting cages.
History: Program began on Division I level in 1988; first winning season was in 1997.
Achievements: 1991 Western Division Champions (TAAC). Lee Gann named to All-South TAAC 2nd team in 1993. Wendall McGee (MVP) drafted by Phillies in 1994.
Coaching: Tim Parenton, Head Coach, entering his second year as a coach. Todd Buczek, Assistant Coach. Gerald Tuck, Assistant Coach.
Style of Play: We will be aggressive in all aspects.

Shelton State Community College

9500 Old Greensboro Road
Tuscaloosa, AL 35405
Coach: Bobby Sprowl

NJCAA
Buc's/Green, Gold
Phone: (205) 391-2206

ACADEMIC

Founded: 1979
Type: 2 Yr., Public, Jr. College, Coed
Undergraduate Enrollment: 5,167
Campus Housing: No

Total Expenses by: Year **In State:** $ 1,68 **Out of State:** $ 2,848
Degrees Conferred: Associate
Programs of Study: Art Education, Automotive Technologies, Biology, Biological Science, Business Administration, Business Education, Chemistry, Computer Science, Cosmetology, Data Processing, Drafting & Design, Early Childhood Education, Education Emergency, Emergency Medical Technology, Elementary Education, Home Economics, Medical Record Service, Music

ATHLETIC PROFILE

Conference Affiliation: NJCAA
History: The baseball program began in 1985.
Achievements: Russ Douts drafted by Seattle; 4 Conference Titles; 9 players drafted.
Coaching: Bobby Sprowls, Head Coach, started in 1986,1989 and 1995. Juan DeBrand - Assistant Coach, started in 1996 as an assistant coach.

Snead State Community College

PO Drawer D
Boaz, AL 35957
Coach: Gerry Ledbetter

NJCAA
Parsons/Royal, Gold
Phone: (256) 593-5120
Fax: (256) 593-7180

ACADEMIC

Founded: 1935
Type: 2 Yr., Public, Jr. College, Coed
Undergraduate Enrollment: 1,589
Campus Housing: No
Student/Faculty Ratio: 24:1
Male/Female Ratio: 43:57
Scholarships/Academic: Yes **Athletic:** Yes **Fin Aid:** Yes
Total Expenses by: Year **In State:** $ 2,200 **Out of State:** $ 3,200
Degrees Conferred: Associate
Programs of Study: Banking/Finance, Business, Criminal Justice, Data Processing, Electronics Engineering, Engineering Design, Fire Science, Law Enforcement, Liberal Arts, Office Management

ATHLETIC PROFILE

Conference Affiliation: Alabama Junior and Community College Conference (AJCCC)
Program Profile: The Snead baseball program and facilities have both steadily improved since Gerry Ledbetter became coach in 1992. The field is natural grass and is exceptionally well manicured. Regular season games begin in mid-February and end in late April.
History: Snead has been a junior college since 1935. At various times in the last 60 years has had a baseball team. In 1995, Snead just missed qualifying for the Alabama/Region XXII tournament.
Coaching: Gerry Ledbetter, Head Coach, has coached various sports at the high school level for 25 years and is beginning his 4th year at Snead. Jerry Hallmark , Pitching Coach.
Style of Play: Hit and run, good defense.

Southern Union State College

Roberts Street
Wadley, AL 36276
Coach: Joe Jordan

NJCAA
Bison/Blue, Gold
Phone: (256) 395-2211
Fax: (256) 395-2215

ACADEMIC

Founded: 1922
Type: 2 Yr., Public, Coed
Undergraduate Enrollment: 6,499
Campus Housing: No
Student/Faculty Ratio: 20:1
Male/Female Ratio: 41:59
Scholarships/Academic: Yes **Athletic:** Yes **Fin Aid:** Yes
Total Expenses by: Year **In State:** $ 1,200 **Out of State:** $ 2,400
Degrees Conferred: Associate

Programs of Study: Banking/Finance, Business Administration, Computer Information, Liberal Arts, Nursing, Office Management.

ATHLETIC PROFILE

Program Profile: Playing field is a natural grass.
History: Baseball program began in 1969.
Achievements: Conference Champs in 1989, 1990, 1991, 1993, & 1995; Region XXII in 1991, & 1995 Champs; Coach of the Year in 1991 and 1995; All-Americans were Ricky Collins, Muke Garner, Eben Wells, Garland Trimble, Tim Freeman, Clarence Prothro, Trey Breitbarth, Chris Tidwell; drafted players were Brian Moon, Rodney Stevenson, Franklin Anderson, Kyle Graham, Tim Vanegmond, Tony Locey, David Guthrie, and Jeff Andrews.
Coaching: Joe Jordan, Head Coach. Jon Hopper, Assistant; Jason Baglio, Student Assistant.
Style of Play: We try to be in better shape, work harder, and out hustle other teams. We try to be sound fundamentally.

Spring Hill College

4000 Dauphin Street
Mobile, AL 36608
Coach: Frank Sims

NAIA
Badgers/Purple, White
Phone: (334) 380-3486
Fax: (334) 460-2196

ACADEMIC

Founded: 1830
Religion: Catholic
Web-site: http://www.shc.edu/
Student/Faculty Ratio: 14:1
Undergraduate Enrollment: 1,050
Type: 4 Yr., Private, Liberal Arts, Coed
Campus Housing: Yes
SAT/ACT/GPA: 1050/ 24
Male/Female Ratio: 50:50
Graduate Enrollment: 75
Scholarships/Academic: Yes **Athletic:** Yes **Fin Aid:** Yes
Total Expenses by: Year **In State:** $ 17,300 **Out of State:** $ 17,300
Degrees Conferred: AS, BA, BS, MA, MS, MBA, Med
Programs of Study: Accounting, Advertising, Biology, Broadcasting, Business, Chemistry, Communications, Computer, Drama, Economics, Education, English, Environmental, Finance, Languages, General Science, History, Math, Preprofessional Programs, Religion, Theology

ATHLETIC PROFILE

Conference Affiliation: Gulf Coast Athletic Conference
Program Profile: Field Name: The Pit, natural grass, dimensions: 323' LF, 370' LCF, 403' CF, 367' RCF, 312' RF. Field Fact: The Pit is one of the oldest ,continuously used fields in the country, with games being played on the field dating back to the turn of the century.

Stillman College

2600 Stillman Boulevard
Tuscaloosa, AL 35401
Coach: Jimmy Rochelle

NCAA III
Tigers/Gold, Navy
Phone: (205) 366-8838
Fax: (205) 366-8996

ACADEMIC

Founded: 1876
Web-site: http://www.stillman.edu/
Student/Faculty Ratio: 13:1
Type: 4 Yr., Private, Liberal Arts, Coed
Undergraduate Enrollment: 950
Male/Female Ratio: 32:68
Scholarships/Academic: Yes **Athletic:** No **Fin Aid:** Yes
Total Expenses by: Year **In State:** $ 8,950 **Out of State:** $ 8,950
Degrees Conferred: BA, BS

Programs of Study: Biology, Business Administration, Chemistry, Communications, Computer Science, Education, English, History, Interdisciplinary Studies, International Studies, Management, Mathematics, Music, Philosophy, Physical Education, Physics, Religion, Sociology

Talladega College

627 West Battle Street
Talladega, AL 35160
Coach: Carlton Hardy

NAIA
Tornadoes/Crimson, California Blue
Phone: (256) 761-6239
Fax: (256) 761-6387

ACADEMIC

Founded: 1867
Type: 4 Yr., Private, Coed
Undergraduate Enrollment: 642
Campus Housing: No
Student/Faculty Ratio: 9:1
Male/Female Ratio: 43:57
Scholarships/Academic: Yes **Athletic:** Yes **Fin Aid:** Yes
Total Expenses by: Year **In State:** $ 9,048 **Out of State:** $ 9,048
Degrees Conferred: BA
Programs of Study: Biology, Business Administration, Chemistry, Computer Science, Education, English, Journalism, Management, Mathematics, Music, Physics, Social Science

ATHLETIC PROFILE

Conference Affiliation: Independent
Program Profile: Play on natural grass facilities.
History: Rich tradition of baseball. Great years as a perennial powerhouse in the Division II. Chase Riddle is a legendary coach with two national championships and numerous conference and regional championships in 1979-1990, and Division I in 1994-1997 seasons.
Achievements: Coach of the Year in 1978, 1980 & 1981 in the Sunshine State Conference; 1993 ABLA Regional Coach of the Year; Mid-Continent Conference Coach of the Year in 1996-1997; East Coast Conference of the Year in 1994; TSU East Coast Conference Champs in 1994; Mid-continent Champs in 1995 & 1997 in the Division I; Division Gulf South Champs in 1980, 1981, 1982, 1988, & 1987; Region Champs in 1980, 1981, 1984, 1985, 1986, & 1987; National Champs in 1986 & 1987; 32 All-Americans; Major Leagues: Danny Cox & Mike Perez.
Style of Play: Aggressive - dominated by hard working young men who believe that defense and pitching wins championships.

Troy State University

100 South George Wallace Dr
Troy, AL 36082
Coach: John Mayotte
Email: jhutto@troyst.edu

NCAA I
Trojans/Cardinal, Black, Silver
Phone: (334) 670-3489
Fax: (334) 670-3724

ACADEMIC

Founded: 1887
Type: 4 Yr., Public, Coed
Religion: Not-Affiliated
Campus Housing: Yes
Web-site: http://www.troyst.edu
SAT/ACT/GPA: 870+/18+
Student/Faculty Ratio: 22:1
Male/Female Ratio: 52:48
Undergraduate Enrollment: 5,100
Graduate Enrollment: 350
Scholarships/Academic: Yes **Athletic:** Yes **Fin Aid:** Yes
Total Expenses by: Year **In State:** $ 6,350 **Out of State:** $ 8,600
Degrees Conferred: Bachelors, Masters, Specialist
Programs of Study: Accounting, Marketing, Education (Elementary & Secondary), Athletic Training, Environmental Science, Sports Medicine, Sport & Fitness Management, Criminal Justice, Journalism (Broadcast & Print), Management, Art, Biology, Social Science, Chemistry, Sociology, Special Education, Physical Science, English, History, Finance, Economics

ATHLETIC PROFILE

Estimated Number of Baseball Scholarships: 11.7
Conference Affiliation: Trans America Athletic Conference
Program Profile: Five year Division I program; two National Championships in Division I NCAA Division I Regionals, two of the last four seasons. Lost in TAAC Tournament Finals in 1998. Natural turf with a seating capacity of 1,750. New stadium projected for 1999-2000 season.
History: Rich tradition of baseball - powerhouse in Division II under Chase Riddle. Division I under Coach Mayote the Trojans has been 176-96 with regional appearances in Tallahassee in 1995 and Tuscaloosa in 1997.
Achievements: South Region Coach of the Year in 1993; Conference Coach of the Year in 1978, 1980, 1981, 1994, 995, 1996 & 1997. TSU has had 32 All-Americans and Danny Cox and Mike Perez played in the major leagues. National Champs in 1986 & 1987.
Coaching: John Mayotte, Head Coach, compiled an overall record of 814-470 at TSU. Was an assistant coach at University of South Florida (1976-1977), Head Coach at Eckerd Florida from 1977-1990; Troy State from 1991-1997, CapeCod League Manager from 1983-1987. Rod McWhorter, Assistant Coach & Recruiting Coordinator, four year college player, Columbus College graduate. Jerry Martinez, Pitching, 6 years pro ball with Dodgers, 7 years Division I coaching.
Roster for 1998 team/In State: 10 **Out of State:** 23 **Out of Country:** 3
Total Number of Varsity/Jr. Varsity: 33 **Percent of Graduation:** 95%
Number of Seniors on 1998 Team: 11 **Number of Spring Games:** 56
Freshmen Receiving Fin Aid/Athletic: 3 **Most Recent Record:** 37 - 21 - 0
Positions Needed for 1999/2000: Pitchers 6-8; Catchers-2, 1st/2nd Base, 3-OF, SS
Schedule: Florida State, Florida, Alabama, Auburn, South Alabama, Ohio State
Style of Play: Varies with the physical abilities of players. Must be excellent in all phases of the game to compete with the great teams in the Southeast Region.

Tuskegee University

321 Chappie James Center
Tuskegee, AL 36088
Coach: Rod Randolp
NCAA II
Golden Tigers/Crimson, Gold
Phone: (334) 727-8902
Fax: (334) 727-8202

ACADEMIC

Founded: 1881
Type: 4 Yr., Private, Coed
SAT/ACT/GPA: 800/17
Campus Housing: Yes
Student/Faculty Ratio: 12:1
Male/Female Ratio: 47:53
Undergraduate Enrollment: 2,875
Graduate Enrollment: 190
Scholarships/Academic: Yes **Athletic:** Yes **Fin Aid:** Yes
Degrees Conferred: BA, BS, Barch, BSN, Med
Programs of Study: Aeronautical Engineering, Agriculture, Animal Science, Architectural Engineering, Banking/Finance, Business Administration, Chemistry, Construction Engineering, Economics, Education, Electrical Engineering, Horticulture, Marketing, Medical Technology

University of Alabama

PO Box 870393
Tuscaloosa, AL 35487
Coach: Jim Wells
NCAA I
Crimson Tide/Crimson, White
Phone: (205) 348-4029
Fax: (205) 348-9945

ACADEMIC

Founded: 1831
Type: 4 Yr., Public, Arts, Engineering
Religion: Non-Affiliated
Campus Housing: Yes
Web-site: http://www.ua.edu
SAT/ACT/GPA: 1010/20
Student/Faculty Ratio: 20:1
Male/Female Ratio: 1:1

Undergraduate Enrollment: 15,000 **Graduate Enrollment:** 4,000
Scholarships/Academic: Yes **Athletic:** Yes **Fin Aid:** Yes
Total Expenses by: Year **In State:** $ 7,420 **Out of State:** $ 11,300
Degrees Conferred: BA, BS, BM, MS, MBA, MD
Programs of Study: Accounting, Advertising, Athletic Training, Banking/Finance, Communications, Communication Disorders, Computer Science, Education, Engineering, English, Fashion Design, Foreign Languages, Journalism, Management, Marine Science, Marketing, Math, Medical

ATHLETIC PROFILE

Conference Affiliation: Southeastern Conference
Program Profile: The Crimson Tide plays its games at Sewell-Thomas Stadium which has a seating capacity of 4,500. Field is natural grass. Has approximately 35 home games. Facility includes 20 road locker rooms and has a typical SEC facility.
History: Program began in 1892. Has a .623% winning is second all time in SEC more SEC championships (Most in SEC). 1950, 1983, 1996, 1997 - Omaha; 16 All-Americans; 15 All-SEC, 56 Academic All-SEC.
Achievements: 1997 National Coach of the Year - Jim Wells; 96 SEC Coach of the Year - Jim Wells; 96 SEC Champs; 97 National Runner-Up; 96 Omaha; 95, 96, & 97 SEC Tournament Champs.
Coaching: Jim Wells, Head Coach, entering his fourth season, 1997 National Coach of the Year,1996 SEC Coach of the Year. Mitch Gasparo, Assistant Coach. Todd Butler, Assistant Coach. Kirk Blount, Adm. Assistant. Shayne Kelly, Volunteer Coach.
Style of Play: Good defense, aggressive pitching and power hitting.

University of Alabama - Birmingham

UAB Arena, 617 - 13th Street, S
Birmingham, AL 35294
Coach: Pete Rancont

NCAA I
Blazers/Black, Green, White
Phone: (205) 934-5181
Fax: (205) 934-7505

ACADEMIC

Founded: 1966 **Type:** 4 Yr., Public, Coed
Religion: Not-Affiliated **Campus Housing:** Yes
Web-site: http://www.uab.edu/ **SAT/ACT/GPA:** 840+/ 20
Student/Faculty Ratio: 17:1 **Male/Female Ratio:** 45:55
Undergraduate Enrollment: 10,805 **Graduate Enrollment:** 5,447
Scholarships/Academic: Yes **Athletic:** Yes **Fin Aid:** Yes
Total Expenses by: Year **In State:** $ 7,700 **Out of State:** $ 9,900
Degrees Conferred: BA, BS, BFA, MA, MS, MBA, Med, PhD, EdD, DDS, MD
Programs of Study: Allied Health, Business and Management, Engineering, Health Sciences, Life Sciences, Parks & Recreation, Protective Services, Public Affairs, Social Sciences

ATHLETIC PROFILE

Conference Affiliation: C-USA (New Conference)
Program Profile: Facilities are located on campus, which seats 1,000, has a natural surface, and great weather with plenty of night games. Play a 56 game Spring Schedule.
History: Program began in 1979. Began in the Sun Belt Conference and won the conference championship the last year as a member in 1991. Have been Conference Champions two out of three seasons in Great Midwest Conference. 1996 - 33-25, 13-11, plays in C-USA, fourth in conference, picked to finish fifth in pre-season.
Achievements: Conference Coach of the Year - Pete Rancot in 1992; Sun Belt Champs in 1991, Great Midwest Champs in 1992, 1994. Jay Cole named All-American in 1993.
Coaching: Pete Rancot, Head Coach, twelve years as a head coach, five years as an assistant coach (hitters and infielders). Steve Giuispie, Assistant Coach. Frank Walton, Assistant Coach.
Style of Play: Tough defensive unit up the middle, strong pitching, good speed with ability to steal bases and make teams work, good power - usually 60 - 70 HR a season as a team.

University of Alabama - Huntsville

205 Spragins Hall
Huntsville, AL 35805
Coach: Bobby Pierce

NCAA II
Chargers/Royal, Red, White
Phone: (256) 890-6144
Fax: (256) 890-7306

ACADEMIC

Founded: 1969
Type: 4 Yr., Public, Coed, Engineering
Religion: Non-Affiliated
Campus Housing: Yes
Web-site: http://www.uah.edu/
SAT/ACT/GPA: 990/ 19
Undergraduate Enrollment: 7,500
Graduate Enrollment: 2,500
Scholarships/Academic: Yes **Athletic:** Yes **Fin Aid:** Yes
Total Expenses by: Year **In State:** $ 7,500 **Out of State:** $ 7,500
Degrees Conferred: BA, BS, Master, MBA, PhD
Programs of Study: Engineering, Business, Art, Communications, Education, English, Foreign Languages, International Trade, History, Music, Philosophy, Political Science, Psychology, Sociology, Nursing, Biology, Chemistry, Computer Science, Math, Optics, Physics, Etc.

ATHLETIC PROFILE

Estimated Number of Baseball Scholarships: 7
Conference Affiliation: Gulf South Conference
Program Profile: Top 10 Division II program intent on competing for national championships every year. Practice field is called Mastin Lake Park. Playing season is in February through May which consists of 56 games and a post-season. The Davis Stadium playing field has a seating capacity of 10,000. AA pro stadium of Milwaukee Brewers which has measurements of LF-345, LC-375, CF-405, RC-370, and RF-330.
History: Program began in the 1995-1996 school year. Went 38-16 in first season & lost in OSC Championship game. Total record in 3 years is 117-44 with one east division title, 2 conference tournament bids, & one NCAA regional bid. Was ranked as high as #2 in the country in 1998.
Achievements: In three seasons won one Division Title, 1 NCAA Regional Bid, 3 All-Americans, 5 All-Region players, 10 All-Conference players, and 4 professional signees. Set NCAA record with five consecutive home runs in game in 1998.
Coaching: Bobby Pierce, Head Coach, All-SEC, was an outfielder at University of Alabama in 1980-1981; head coach at Chipola Junior College in 1982-1989. He compiled a record of 259-95; assistant coach at Alabama in 1989-1994; head coach at UAH in 1995 to the present with a record of 37-16. Jeff Crane , Assistant Coach, was an infielder at University of Alabama in 1991-1992, graduate assistant coach at Alabama in 1993-1994, associate scout for Pittsburg Pirates in 1994 and assistant coach at UAH in 1995 to the present.
Roster for 1998 team/In State: 20 **Out of State:** 12 **Out of Country:** 1
Total Number of Varsity/Jr. Varsity: 32 **Percent of Graduation:** 0
Number of Seniors on 1998 Team: 11 **Number of Spring Games:** 56
Freshmen Receiving Fin Aid/Athletic: 2 **Academic:** 5
Most Recent Record: 41 - 17 - 0 **Baseball Camp Dates:** June - July
Positions Needed for 1999/2000: SS, LHP, RHP, Catcher
Schedule: Kennesaw State University, University of North Alabama, Valdosta State University, Birmingham Southern, Auburn University-Montgomery, Delta State University
Style of Play: Fundamentally sound philosophy - strong pitching and depth with good defense at the middle; offensively, good team speed coupled with ability to handle the bat.

University of Mobile

P.O. Box 13220
Mobile, AL 36663
Coach: Mike Jacobs

NAIA
Rams/Marron, White
Phone: (205)675-5990
Fax: (205) 675-53322

ACADEMIC

Founded: 1964
Type: 4 Yr., Private, Liberal Arts, Coed
Religion: Southern Baptist Convention
Campus Housing: Yes
Web-site: http://www.umobile.edu/
SAT/ACT/GPA: 720
Student/Faculty Ratio: 15:1
Male/Female Ratio: 44:66
Undergraduate Enrollment: 2,000
Graduate Enrollment: 200
Scholarships/Academic: Yes **Athletic:** Yes **Fin Aid:** Yes
Total Expenses by: Year **In State:** $ 10,910 **Out of State:** $ 10,910
Degrees Conferred: AA, AS, BA, MA, MS, MBA, MSN, AND
Programs of Study: B.S.N. and A.D.N. Nursing Programs, Teacher Education Programs, Sports Medicine Programs, M.S. in Physical Therapy

ATHLETIC PROFILE

Conference Affiliation: Gulf Coast Conference

University of Montevallo

Station 6760
Montevallo, AL 35115
Coach: Bob Riesener
Email: peevyd@um.montevallo.edu
NCAA II
Falcons/Purple, Gold
Phone: (205) 665-6760
Fax: (205) 665-6586

ACADEMIC

Founded: 1896
Type: 4 Yr., Public, Liberal Arts, Coed
Religion: Not-Affiliated
Campus Housing: Yes
Web-site: http://www.montevallo.edu/
SAT/ACT/GPA: 850 / 18
Student/Faculty Ratio: 18:1
Male/Female Ratio: 1:2
Undergraduate Enrollment: 3,000
Graduate Enrollment: 500
Scholarships/Academic: Yes **Athletic:** Yes **Fin Aid:** Yes
Total Expenses by: Year **In State:** $ 4,980 **Out of State:** $ 7,480
Degrees Conferred: BA, BS, Med
Programs of Study: Accounting, Banking & Finance, Broadcasting, Chemistry, Communications, Education, English, Fine Arts, French, Government, Health Science, History, Management, Marketing, Mathematics, Medical Technology, Music, Optometry, Photography, Political Science, Predentistry, Premed, Prelaw, Public Health, Social Science, Psychology, Spanish, Speech Pathology, Visual and Performing Arts

ATHLETIC PROFILE

Estimated Number of Baseball Scholarships: 9
Conference Affiliation: Gulf South Conference
Program Profile: Play at Kermit A. Johnson Field which has a seating capacity of 1,500. It is a natural grass field with measurements of LF-325, CF-380, RF-330, with lights and a press box.
History: Baseball was the first intercollegiate athletic activity at Montevallo after the school became coed in 1956. The UM program began in 1958 under Dr. Frank Lightfoot, who coached from 1958-1967. The current head coach, Coach Bob Riesener, came in 1974 and has led the Falcons to 781 wins in 25 seasons (752-532).
Achievements: Coach Riesener has an overall record of 892-587 in 29 years of coaching. Current major league Rusty Greer (Texas) played at UM from 1988-1990 and was a 10th round draft picked after his junior season. Currently , Mick Field drafted in 1996 by the AA-New Britain, and Bernard Hutchison drafted in 1996 by the A-Asheville, are playing minor league ball.
Coaching: Bob Riesener, Head Coach, started in 1974 and compiled a record of 892-587. He was a Rutgers graduate in 1963. Phil Phillips, Assistant, started in 1994; graduate of Montevallo in '93.
Roster for 1998 team/In State: 20 **Out of State:** 5 **Out of Country:** 6
Total Number of Varsity/Jr. Varsity: 31
Percent of Graduation: 90%
Number of Seniors on 1998 Team: 12
Most Recent Record: 29 - 21 - 0
Freshmen Receiving Fin Aid/Athletic: 3
Positions Needed for 1999/2000: 12
Number of Fall Games: 2
Number of Spring Games: 53

Schedule: North Alabama, Alabama-Huntsville, West Georgia, Kennesaw State, Birmingham
Style of Play: A hit & run squad with power capabilities. We hit a team record .359 with 78 hours last season. Pitching depth should be our strong suit as we return the entire staff from 1998. Our defense should be sound comming off a .960 year.

University of North Alabama

Wesleyan Avenue
Florence, AL 35632
Coach: Mike Lane

NCAA II
Lions/Purple, Gold
Phone: (256) 765-4397
Fax: (256) 765-4685

ACADEMIC

Founded: 1830
Religion: Non-Affiliated
Web-site: http://www.una.edu/
Student/Faculty Ratio: 22:1
Undergraduate Enrollment: 4,698
Scholarships/Academic: Yes **Athletic:** Yes
Total Expenses by: Year **In State:** $ 5,500

Type: 4 Yr., Public, Coed
Campus Housing: Yes
SAT/ACT/GPA: 700 Min
Male/Female Ratio: 41:59
Graduate Enrollment: 523
Fin Aid: Yes
Out of State: $ 7,500

Degrees Conferred: BA, BS, BFA, BAM, BGS, BM, BMMEd, BSEd, BSM, BSN, MA, MBA
Programs of Study: Art, Accounting, Banking/Finance, Biology, Broadcasting, Chemistry, Communications, Computer, Criminal Justice, Economics, Education, English, Fine Arts, French, Geography, German, History, Information Science, Journalism, Management, Marketing, Math.

ATHLETIC PROFILE

Conference Affiliation: Gulf South Conference
Program Profile: A Division II national contender, with outstanding facility, natural surface, 759 capacity; a beatiiful campus and southern weather conditions; good instruction and strong player development.
History: The University of North Alabama baseball program began in 1932. There have been nine head coaches. The Lions have won three Gulf South Conference titles, all coming since 1984, and advanced to the NCAA Division II Regional playoff eight times.
Achievements: 3 Gulf South Conference titles (1984, 1989, 1993); 8 NCAA playoff appearances (1984-1985, 1987, 1989, 1991-1994); 10 All-Americans under Mike Lane since 1984; 19 former Lion players have played or currently play pro baseball.
Coaching: Mike Lane, Head Coach; overall coaching record of 438-182-8 in 12 seasons at UNA; eight NCAA Regionals under Lane's direction; chosen by the U.S . Baseball Federation to serve as one of three coaches for the South team in the U.S. Baseball Trials in 1992.
Style of Play: Offensively: very aggressive and speed oriented. Defensively: good pitching and strength up the middle.

University of South Alabama

HPELS 1107 University of South Alabama
Mobile, AL 36688
Coach: Steve Kittrell

NCAA I
Jaguars/Red, White, Blue
Phone: (334) 461-1397
Fax: (334) 414-8244

ACADEMIC

Founded: 1963
Web-site: http://www.usouthal.edu/
Student/Faculty Ratio: 14:1
Undergraduate Enrollment: 9,500
Scholarships/Academic: Yes **Athletic:** Yes
Total Expenses by: Year **In State:** $ 7,000

Type: 4 Yr., Public, Liberal Arts, Coed
SAT/ACT/GPA: 820/ 19
Male/Female Ratio: 43:57
Graduate Enrollment: 3,000
Fin Aid: Yes
Out of State: $ 8,900

Degrees Conferred: Bachelors to PhD
Programs of Study: College of Arts and Sciences, College of Business and Management Studies, College of Education, College of Engineering, School of Continuing Education

ATHLETIC PROFILE

Conference Affiliation: Sun Belt Conference
Program Profile: The Alabama Gulf Coast provides an excellent atmosphere for Jaguars baseball games in the spring. South Alabama recently built a beautiful baseball clubhouse that is adjacent to its home park, the 3,500 seats Eddie Stanky Field. The underrated program gains more recognition each year by playing one of the nation's toughest schedules. In early season, USA hosts annual Coca-Cola Classic, which attracts some of the nation's best teams.
History: Entering its 34th season (1965). The Jaguars have quietly built their program into one of the nation's finest. The Jaguars appear annually in the national polls and are a fixture in the NCAA Regionals. The Jags have made 16 NCAA appearances and achieved two #1 regular season rankings (1973 and 1975). Former Major League great Eddie Stanky coached the Jaguars for 14 seasons (1969-1983) and regularly attends the games.
Achievements: South Alabama was rated the 23rd best program of the 1900's. Nearly 100 players have signed with professional baseball organizations. USA has dominated the Sun Belt Conference over the years by winning 8 tournament titles. The Jags have come within one victory of reaching the College World Series 6 times. A few of the Jaguars' most notable major leaguers include Lance Johnson of the Chicago Cubs, Luis Gonzalez of the Houston Astros and Jon Lieber of Pittsburgh.
Coaching: Steve Kittrell, Head Coach, 16th year, graduate at USA in 1983. Ron Pelletier, Assistant Coach, 14th seasons as a Hitting Instructor. The South Alabama coaching staff has worked together for 13 seasons. Led by 15-year mentor Steve Kitrell, the Jaguars are one of the nation's luckiest programs having a staff with such experience. Ronnie Powell, Assistant Coach. They are all former South Alabama players that follow the philosophy of legendary Eddie Stanky.
Style of Play: South Alabama is traditionally known for its hit & run; aggressive base running style.

University of West Alabama

UWA Station 5
Livingston, AL 35470
Coach: Mark Smartt

NCAA II
Tigers/Red, White, Black
Phone: (205) 652-3485
Fax: (205) 652-3600

ACADEMIC

Founded: 1835
Type: 4 Yr., Public, Liberal Arts, Coed
Religion: Non-Affiliated
Campus Housing: No
Web-site: Not Available
SAT/ACT/GPA: 700 Min
Student/Faculty Ratio: 22:1
Male/Female Ratio: 50:50
Undergraduate Enrollment: 2,000
Graduate Enrollment: 300
Scholarships/Academic: Yes **Athletic:** Yes **Fin Aid:** Yes
Total Expenses by: Year **In State:** $ 4,500 **Out of State:** $ 4,500
Degrees Conferred: AS, BA, BS, BMEd, BT, MA, MEd
Programs of Study: Accounting, Athletic Training, Biology, Biological Science, Business Administration, Commerce, Management, Business Education, Chemistry, Computer Science, Early Childhood Education, English, Environmental Science, History, Industrial Arts, Marine Biology

ATHLETIC PROFILE

Estimated Number of Baseball Scholarships: 6
Conference Affiliation: Gulf South Conference
Program Profile: A highly competitive program that plays in a great conference. Has a great campus facility and good crowds.
History: The program record dates back to 1969 but has been in place for many years prior.
Achievements: 11 All-Americans; 31 All-Region players; 72 All-Conference players; 20 players in professional ball throughout progam's history.
Coaching: Mark Smartt, Head Coach, started from 1995 to the present and compiled a record of 107-109. Played on 1986-1987 Division II National Champs at Troy State. Shane Adams, Assistant.

Roster for 1998 team/In State: 20 **Out of State:** 10 **Out of Country:** 0
Total Number of Varsity/Jr. Varsity: 30 **Percent of Graduation:** 80%
Number of Seniors on 1998 Team: 12 **Most Recent Record:** 28 - 27 - 0
Freshmen Receiving Fin Aid/Athletic: 2 **Academic:** 2
Number of Fall Games: 0 **Number of Spring Games:** 56
Positions Needed for 1999/2000: Catcher, Infielder, Pitcher
Schedule: University of Alabama, West Georgia, North Alabama, Alabama-Huntsville, Valdosta
Style of Play: Aggressive offensive minded club that plays extremely hard everyday.

Wallace State Community College - Dothan

Rt. 6 Box 62
Dothan, AL 36303
Coach: Mackey Sasser

NJCAA
Governors/Red, Black, White
Phone: (334) 983-3521

ACADEMIC

Type: 2 Yr., Jr. College, Coed
Programs of Study: Contact school for programs of study.

ATHLETIC PROFILE

Conference Affiliation: Southern Conference
Program Profile: Has a brand new baseball diamond which is all grass. Playing season in the fall that consists of 20 games and in the spring that consist of 54 games. Also has new batting cages. Has an 8 foot fence in outfield, 320 left, 390 center, and 320 right; new dugouts with a buck wall behind the backstop.
History: Won 5 State Championships; produced 9 professional athletes.
Achievements: 9 professional athletes; won 5 State Championships
Coaching: Mackey Sasser, Head Coach, entering his 8th seasons in big leagues; 4 years in minor leagues. Dustin Rennspier, Assistant Coach, five years in minor leagues.
Style of Play: Good running game, good pitching, excellent fundamentals (very aggressive).

Wallace State College - Hanceville

PO Box 2000
Hanceville, AL 35077
Coach: Randy Putnam

NJCAA
Lions/Navy, White
Phone: (256) 352-8247
Fax: (256) 352-8228

ACADEMIC

Founded: 1966 **Type:** 2 Yr., Public, Coed
Undergraduate Enrollment: 5,200 **Campus Housing:** No
Student/Faculty Ratio: 19:1 **Male/Female Ratio:** 38:62
Scholarships/Academic: No **Athletic:** Yes **Fin Aid:** Yes
Total Expenses by: Year **In State:** $ 1,800 **Out of State:** $ 2,500
Programs of Study: Accounting, Agriculture, Automotive Technology, Banking/Finance, Business Administration, Computer Programming, Computer Science, Criminal Justice, Drafting/Design

ATHLETIC PROFILE

Conference Affiliation: AJCCC
Program Profile: Stadium has a seating capacity 1,000 (chair back and roof covers seats). Facilities include two club houses, indoor hitting area and two weight rooms.
History: NJCAA College World Series in 1992 and 1997. Average 40 wins per season.
Achievements: 1992 and 1997 Southeast Coach of the Year.
Coaching: Randy Putnam, Head Coach. Chuck Davis, Pitching Coach, played with Boston Red Sox. Greg McGraw, Infield and Outfield Coach, played on the 1992 World Series Club.
Style of Play: Aggressive and intense.

ARIZONA

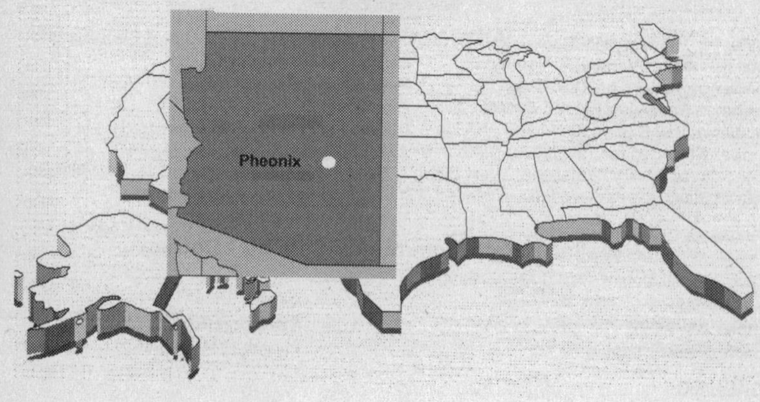

SCHOOL	CITY	AFFILIATION 99	PAGE
Arizona State University	Tempe	NCAA I	67
Arizona Western College	Yuma	NJCAA	67
Central Arizona College	Coolidge	NJCAA	68
Cochise College	Douglas	NJCAA	69
Glendale Community College	Glendale	NJCAA	69
Grand Canyon	Phoenix	NCAA I	70
Mesa Community College	Mesa	NJCAA	70
Phoenix College	Phoenix	NJCAA	71
Pima Community College	Tucson	NJCAA	71
Scottsdale Community College	Scottsdale	NJCAA	72
South Mountain Community College	Phoenix	NJCAA	72
University of Arizona	Tucson	NCAA I	72
Yavapai College	Prescott	NJCAA	73

Arizona State University

ICA Box 872505
Tempe, AZ 85287-2505
Coach: Pat Murphy

NCAA I
Sun Devils/Maroon, Gold
Phone: (602) 965-3677
Fax: (602) 965-9309

ACADEMIC

Founded: 1949
Religion: Non-Affiliated
Web-site: http://www.thesundevils.com
Student/Faculty Ratio: 20:1
Undergraduate Enrollment: 1,250
Scholarships/Academic: Yes **Athletic:** Yes
Total Expenses by: Year **In State:** $ 11,000
Type: 4 Yr., Public, Coed
Campus Housing: No
SAT/ACT/GPA: 930/22
Male/Female Ratio: 38:62
Graduate Enrollment: 100
Fin Aid: Yes
Out of State: $ 11,000
Degrees Conferred: BS, BS, BM, BGS, BSN, MA, MBA, Med
Programs of Study: Anthropology, Art, Broadcasting, Chemistry, Education, Music, Science, History, Geology, Economics, English, Geography, Humanities, Journalism, Math, Music, Philosophy, Political Science, Religious, Sociology

ATHLETIC PROFILE

Conference Affiliation: PAC-10 Southern Division
Program Profile: ASU boasts college baseball's greatest tradition. The Sun Devils play home games at picturesque Packard Stadium, a 7,875-seat facility with a natural grass playing field and state-of-the-art, new full practice fields, new covered and batting cages and bull pens. Also lounge behind dugout. Sun can be seen in Tempe about 310 days a year; season normally runs from January through June.
History: Arizona State baseball began as a varsity sport in 1959 and has had three coaches in its rich history. Bobby Winkles (1959-71), Dr. Jim Brock (1972-94) and Pat Murphy (1995-present). ASU has had 65 players go on to play in the major leagues, a total no other team can match. Among the names include, Rick Monday, Sal Bando, Reggie Jackson, and Floyd.
Achievements: Won 16 conference championships, 17 Regional and District championships, 17 College World Series appearances and won 5 titles; 48 All-Americans on 58 different occasions, 13 National Players of the Year; on 65 occasions, a player has garnered All-Conference acclaim; a player has been tabbed for All-College World Series team 51 times, and 5 MVPs; had 254 players drafted, 18 first round picks and 3 #1 selections, 68 players go on to play in the major leagues, adding Mike Deveraux to the list.
Coaching: Pat Murphy, Head Coach (Florida Atlantic, 1982, 481-235-3, 13th-year overall) third year. Doug Schreiber, Assistant Coach (recruiting coordinator, infielder), fourth year.
Style of Play: Aggressive under control. Attention to details - focused.

Arizona Western College

PO Box 929
Yuma, AZ 85366
Coach: John Stratton

NJCAA
Matadors/Seal Bown, Gold
Phone: (520) 726-1000
Fax: (520) 344-7537

ACADEMIC

Founded: 1963
Religion: Non-Affiliated
Student/Faculty Ratio: 20:1
Undergraduate Enrollment: 7,000
Scholarships/Academic: Yes **Athletic:** Yes
Total Expenses by: Year **In State:** $ 8,300
Type: 2 Yr., Public, Jr. College, Coed
Campus Housing: Yes
Male/Female Ratio: 50:50
Graduate Enrollment: None
Fin Aid: Yes
Out of State: $ 9,050
Degrees Conferred: AA, AAS, ASS, General Studies

Programs of Study: All primary areas: Administration of Justice, Art, Banking/Finance, Broadcasting, Business, CDA, Computer, Dietetics, English, Family Studies, General Business, Library, Languages, Nursing, Office, Paramedic, Science/Mathematics (13 areas)

ATHLETIC PROFILE

Estimated Number of Baseball Scholarships: 10+
Conference Affiliation: Arizona Community College Athletic Conference
Program Profile: Prime baseball country, perennial contender in one of the best leagues in the country; top notch facility with 3 batting tunnels, hybrid infielder, natural turf with a 5,000 capacity. Play all school year round.
History: Program has been in existence for thirty years.
Achievements: Won two times Coach of the Year, 2 Conference Titles, 2 Regional Titles; 1996 3rd place in National Tourney, 1 All-American, 30+ drafted players; 2 Big League; approximately 10 in the pro ball now.
Coaching: John Stratton, Head Coach, entering 15th year with the program, pitching coach for 11 years. He compiled a record of 400+ wins. National Champion NCAA Division I in 1980 and JUCO National Tourney. Alan Manifold, Assistant Coach.
Roster for 1998 team/In State: 15 **Out of State:** 7 **Out of Country:** 2
Total Number of Varsity/Jr. Varsity: 35 **Percent of Graduation:** 75%
Number of Seniors on 1998 Team: 12 **Number of Sophomores on 1998 Team:** 0
Freshmen Receiving Fin Aid/Athletic: 8 **Academic:** 2
Most Recent Record: 35 - 19 - 0 **Number of Spring Games:** 56
Positions Needed for 1999/2000: All-especially Outfielder, SS, Pitcher
Baseball Camp Dates: Christmas Break?
Schedule: Yavapai, South Mountain, University of Arizona, Howard, Odessa, New Mexico
Style of Play: We stress fundamentals. We play percentage baseball with a particular style that fits that year's make up.

Central Arizona College

8470 North Overfield Road
Coolidge, AZ 85228
Coach: Clint Myers

NJCAA
Vaqueros/Forest Green, Gold
Phone: (520) 426-4336
Fax: (520) 426-4466

ACADEMIC

Founded: 1961 **Type:** 2 Yr., Public, Jr. College, Coed
Religion: Non-Affiliated **Campus Housing:** No
Student/Faculty Ratio: 30:1 **Male/Female Ratio:** 50:50
Undergraduate Enrollment: 14,500+ **Graduate Enrollment:** None
Scholarships/Academic: Yes **Athletic:** Yes **Fin Aid:** Yes
Total Expenses by: Year **In State:** $ 3,700 **Out of State:** $ 8,000
Degrees Conferred: Associate
Programs of Study: Accounting, Agricultural Science, Agricultural Technologies, Automotive Technologies, Business Administration, Commerce, Management, Civil Engineering Technology, Computer Science, Construction Technology, Corrections, Criminal Justice, Early Childhood Education, Liberal Arts, General Studies, Mining Technology, Nursing

ATHLETIC PROFILE

Estimated Number of Baseball Scholarships: 24
Conference Affiliation: ACCAC
Program Profile: We play on one of the finest college fields in the state of Arizona. An all natural field with a dimensions of 345 down the lines to 412 in the center and 417 in the gaps. Facilities include 3 batting cage tunnels with an auxiliary infield and 8 pitchers mounds, one practice infield. The stadium size holds 500 people, concessions, picnic area. Playing season has 56 games, full fall schedule program teach the game.

History: Started in 1969; one national championship in 1976; current major leaguers include Doug Jones and Tom Paynozzi.
Achievements: Coach Meyer was inducted into NJCAA Hall of Fame; Conference Title in the last three years; 3 All-Americans in the last three years; 2 players drafted in the first round.
Coaching: Clint Myers, Head Coach, in his fourth year; played at Arizona State and with the St. Louis Cardinals. Jonh Wente, Assistant Coach, responsible with the pitchers and serve as a recruiting coordinator; played at Arizona State. Billy Aviles, Hitting Coach, played at Trevecca.
Roster for 1998 team/In State: 20 **Out of State:** 8 **Out of Country:** 4
Total Number of Varsity/Jr. Varsity: 32 **Percent of Graduation:** 98%
Number of Seniors on 1998 Team: 17 **Number of Sophomores on 1998 Team:** 0
Freshmen Receiving Fin Aid/Athletic: 7 **Academic:** 3
Number of Fall Games: 3 **Number of Spring Games:** 56
Schedule: South Mountain, Yavapai **Most Recent Record:** 31 - 21 - 0
Positions Needed for 1999/2000: Pitching, Outfielder, Hitting
Style of Play: Aggressive style of play with a certain understanding and knowledge of the game.

Cochise College

Rt 1, Box 100
Douglas, AZ 85607
Coach: Richard Hall

NJCAA
Apaches/Red, White
Phone: (520) 364-0295
Fax: (520) 364-0296

ACADEMIC

Founded: 1962 **Type:** 2 Yr., Public, Coed
Student/Faculty Ratio: 16:1 **Campus Housing:** No
Undergraduate Enrollment: 993 **Graduate Enrollment:** None
Scholarships/Academic: No **Athletic:** No **Fin Aid:** Yes
Total Expenses by: Year **In State:** $ 832 **Out of State:** $ 4,896
Degrees Conferred: Associate
Programs of Study: Agriculture, Aircraft and Missile Maintenance, Anthropology, Aviation, Behavioral, Biologial, Chemistry, Computer, Criminal, Education, English, Flight Training, Forestry, Health, History, Journalism, Law Political, Social Science

ATHLETIC PROFILE

Conference Affiliation: ACCAC
Program Profile: Home games are played at Apache Field.

Glendale Community College

6000 W Olive Avenue
Glendale, AZ 85302
Coach: Dave Grant

NJCAA
Gauchos/Red, Black
Phone: (602) 435-3046
Fax: (602) 435-3005

ACADEMIC

Type: 2 Yr., Jr. College, Coed
Programs of Study: Accounting, Advertising, Agriculture, Art, Automotive, Banking/Finance, Biological, Chemistry, Computer, Economics, Engineering, Forestry, Geology, Horticulture, Journalism, Law, Marketing, Pharmacy, Real Estate, Social Science

ATHLETIC PROFILE

Conference Affiliation: Arizona Community College Athletic Conference
Program Profile: Natural turf field with two batting cages, six bull pen mounds, 1 soft toss areas. Field dimensions is 340' down both lines, 370' to alleys, 405' to deal center. Has ten week fall practice season and 15 week spring season with a 56 games.

History: Began in 1967; NJCAA Champions in 1968; 3rd place in the NJCAA in 1991. Perennial playoff participant in Arizona Community College Athletic Conference.
Achievements: NJCAA Region 1 Coach of the Year in 1991 and 1994.
Coaching: Dave Grant, Head Coach, 18-year record at GCC is 513-429. Jeff Ludwig, Pitching Coach, played for 2 years in Cubs Organization. Seventh season as a pitching coach, eight pitchers drafted during that time. Corky Summers, Assistant Coach, coached on high school, Juco, and Division I levels. Handles hitters and outfielders.
Style of Play: Fundamentally sound - emphasis on control pitches who change speeds effectively. Aggressive offensive style, like to steal, bunt, hit and run.

Grand Canyon University

3300 West Camelback Road
Phoenix, AZ 85326
Coach: Gil Stafford

NCAA I
Antelopes/Purple, White
Phone: (602) 589-2805
Fax: (602) 589-2529

ACADEMIC

Founded: 1949
Type: 4 Yr., Private, Liberal Arts, Coed
Religion: Southern Baptist
Campus Housing: Yes
Web-site: http://www.grand-cayon.edu/
SAT/ACT/GPA: 930/22
Student/Faculty Ratio: 20:1
Male/Female Ratio: 38:62
Undergraduate Enrollment: 1,250
Graduate Enrollment: 100
Scholarships/Academic: Yes **Athletic:** Yes **Fin Aid:** Yes
Total Expenses by: Year **In State:** $ 11,000 **Out of State:** $ 11,000
Degrees Conferred: BA, BS, BM, BGS, BSN, MA, MBA, Med
Programs of Study: Accounting, Banking/Finance, Biology, Business, Chemistry, Communications, Criminal Justice, Economics, English, Graphic, History, International Business, Management

ATHLETIC PROFILE

Conference Affiliation: Western Athletic Conference
Program Profile: Excellent facility seats 2500, lights and practice facility. Division I program with excellent weather and a top-flight schedule; small school that treats baseball 'like football'.
History: Program began in 1953. Four-time NAIA Champion. Sixth year in NCAA Division I.
Achievements: 12 players in the major league including 1993 Rookie of the Year Tim Salmon. There have been 63 drafted in the last 16 years. NAIA National Champs in 1980 - 1982, and 1986.
Coaching: Gil Stafford, Head Coach, 18th year, compiled a record of 602 wins. Dave Stapleton, Pitching Coach, Big Leaguers with Brewers, pitched here National Champs in 1982. Ed Wolfe, Hitting Coach, two years pro ball, also has been an assistant coach at University of Texas - El Paso.
Style of Play: Aggressive, free swingers, play in a conference that is high scoring because of parks and altitude. We have the 'pitching' park and try to recruit a balance of players - we're mostly likely to fit our style to the players available.

Mesa Community College

1833 West Southern Avenue
Mesa, AZ 85202
Coach: Tony Cirelli

NJCAA
Thunderbirds/Scarlet, White
Phone: (602) 461-7562
Fax: (602) 461-7804

ACADEMIC

Founded: 1966
Type: 2 Yr., Public, Jr. College, Coed
Religion: Non-Affiliated
Campus Housing: None
Undergraduate Enrollment: 20,600
Graduate Enrollment: None
Scholarships/Academic: No **Athletic:** No **Fin Aid:** Yes
Total Expenses by: Hour **In State:** $ 34 p/h **Out of State:** $ 159 p/h
Degrees Conferred: Associate

Programs of Study: Accounting, Agriculture, Automotive, Banking/Finance, Biological, Business, Engineering, Manufacturing, Quality Control, Real Estate, Soil/Crop Science, Teacher Aide Studies, Interior Design, Insurance

ATHLETIC PROFILE

Conference Affiliation: Arizona Community College Athletic Conference
Program Profile: Beautiful playing field with turf infield, auxiliary infield, two batting cages. Play a 40 game in Fall, and 56 game in Spring.
History: The program began in 1966. NJCAA Champions 1970, 1971, 1972; ACCAC Champions nine-times 1969, 1970, 1971, 1972, 1973, 1980, 1982, 1993, 1996.
Achievements: 1996 Coach of the Year; first year won 40 games, only second year school has reached that plateau; 1 All-American in each of last two seasons, and 8 players drafted.
Coaching: Tony Cirelli, Head Coach, second season at Mesa. Zeke Zimmerman, Pitching Coach, for 16 years, also pitching coach for the California Angels Organization in the summer rookie league.
Style of Play: We run and put pressure on the defense. Set school record for stolen bases the last two seasons 1995 - 136 SB, 1996 - 167 SB.

Phoenix College

1202 W. Thomas Road
Phoenix, AZ 85013
Coach: Mike Poplin

NJCAA
Bears/Blue, Gold
Phone: (602) 285-7456
Fax: (602) 285-7333

ACADEMIC

Founded: 1920
Type: 4 Yr., Public, Coed
Religion: Non-Affiliated
Campus Housing: Yes
Web-site: http://www.azsoccer.org/
SAT/ACT/GPA: Recommend
Student/Faculty Ratio: 17:1
Male/Female Ratio: 3:5
Undergraduate Enrollment: 12,000
Graduate Enrollment: None
Scholarships/Academic: Yes **Athletic:** Yes **Fin Aid:** Yes
Total Expenses by: Semester **In State:** $ 1,000 **Out of State:** $ 3,500
Degrees Conferred: AA, AGS, AAS
Programs of Study: 202 Occupational/Educational Degree and Certificate Programs including: Accounting, Architecture, Banking/Finance, Behavioral, Business, Child Care, Construction, Dental, Medical, Marketing, Office, Paralegal, Real Estate, Travel/Tourism

Pima Community College

2202 W Anklam Road
Tucson, AZ 85709-0001
Coach: Roger Werbylo

NJCAA
Aztecs/Brown, Tennessee Orange
Phone: (520) 206-6056
Fax: (520) 884-6473

ACADEMIC

Founded: 1970
Type: 2 Yr., Public, Jr. College, Coed
Religion: Non-Affiliated
Campus Housing: No
Total Expenses by: Year **In State:** $ 4,200 **Out of State:** $ 7,200
Degrees Conferred: AA, AS
Programs of Study: 41 degrees in transfer programs including Business, Engineering, Liberal Arts

ATHLETIC PROFILE

Conference Affiliation: ACCAC
Program Profile: On the field year round, excellent facilities (stabilizer infield, carpeted hitting tunnels, extra practice infield, large weight room, locker and training rooms). Played in Regional tournaments 15 times and World Series 4 times.

History: 14 All-Americans, 30 professional players have come from Pima.
Coaching: Roger Werbylo, Head Coach. 3 full-time assistant coaches.

Scottsdale Community College

9000 East Chaparral Road
Scottsdale, AZ 85250
Coach: Larry Smith

NJCAA
Artichokes/Blue, White, Red
Phone: (602) 423-6617
Fax: (602) 423-6613

ACADEMIC

Founded: 1970
Type: 2 Yr., Public, Jr. College, Coed
SAT/ACT/GPA: High School Diploma
Undergraduate Enrollment: 7,000
Student/Faculty Ratio: 20:1
Male/Female Ratio: 50:50
Scholarships/Academic: No **Athletic:** Yes **Fin Aid:** Yes
Total Expenses by: Year **In State:** $ Varies **Out of State:** $ Varies
Degrees Conferred: AA
Programs of Study: General Studies

ATHLETIC PROFILE

Estimated Number of Baseball Scholarships: 15
Conference Affiliation: Arizona Community College Athletic Association
Program Profile: Excellent facilities - spring training site of Oakland A's. Weather permits outside play year-round. Fall starts September through November 15; spring season opens 56 games and starts February 1. Competes in tough JC Conference in the country.
History: Program began in 1972. Has made four trips to Junior College World Series; finished 3rd in 1997. In past nine years - 1 Regional Champs, 1 District Champs, 3 Regional Final Appearances.
Achievements: In the past nine years had 3 times Coach of the Year; 3 All-Americans; several players drafted, almost 100 percent placement of sophomore players continuing at a four-year university or college.
Coaching: Larry Smith - Head Coach, entering 23 years of coaching. He compiled a record of 658-422. Has 16 years on professional baseball as a pitching coach in Pittsburgh Pirates short season teams. Coached Switzerland's and Austria's national teams.
Schedule: All Conference Games
Style of Play: Make most of available talent. Definitely a development program for players to improve and advance.

South Mountain Community College

7050 South 24th Street
Phoenix, AZ 85040
Coach: George Lopez

NJCAA
Cougars/Royal, Silver
Phone: (602) 243-8236
Fax: (602) 243-8329

ACADEMIC

Type: 2 Yr., Jr. College, Coed
Programs of Study: Business Administration, Computer Information Systems, Liberal Arts, Office Management

University of Arizona

246 McKale Center
Tucson, AZ 85721
Coach: Jerry Stitt
Email: jstitt@u.arizona.edu

NCAA I
Wildcats/Red, Navy
Phone: (520) 621-4102
Fax: (520) 621-2681

ACADEMIC

Founded: 1885
Religion: Non-Affiliated
Web-site: Not Available
Student/Faculty Ratio: 19:1
Undergraduate Enrollment: 35,306
Scholarships/Academic: Yes **Athletic:** Yes
Total Expenses by: Year **In State:** $ 3,000
Type: 4 Yr., Public, Coed
Campus Housing: No
SAT/ACT/GPA: 23
Male/Female Ratio: 49:1
Graduate Enrollment: None
Fin Aid: Yes
Out of State: $ 8,600
Degrees Conferred: BA, BS, BFA, BM, MA, MBA, MFA, JD
Programs of Study: Accounting, Animal Science, Anthropology, Banking/Finance, Communications, Computer Engineering, Education, Horticulture, Languages, Journalism, Medical, Preprofessional Programs, Religion, Social Science, Speech

ATHLETIC PROFILE

Conference Affiliation: Pacific-10 (South) Conference
Program Profile: First class program with a top-notch facilities; excellent playing field which is a natural grass. Has a large stadium which has a seating capacity of 8,500, & has a quality press box.
History: Program began in 1904; three coaches ran the program from 1922-1996 (Pop McKale, Frank Sancet, and Jerry Kendall). Team has won three National Titles (1976, 1980 and 1986) and finished runner-up at CWS another three times (1956, 1959, and 1963); 14 CWS appearances, 28 post-season appearances; 4 WAC Titles; 3 PAC-10 South Titles; six All-time in CWS wins and games played and seventh in appeared; 140 players drafted; 1980 Golden Spikes Award Winner (Terry Francona); 1976 and 1980 Coach of the Year (Kendall).
Achievements: Jerry Kendall Coach of the Year in 1980; All-time record is 2082-1033-21; 48 straight winning seasons (1932-1982) 40 win seasons. Countless All-Americans & drafted players.
Coaching: Jerry Stitt, Head Coach, former assistant coach from 1979-1995. Started coaching as a head coach in 1996. He was All-American as a player at University of Arizona. Bill Kinneberg, Associate Coach and Pitching Coach. Victor Solis, Assistant Coach.
Roster for 1998 team/In State: 26 **Out of State:** 10 **Out of Country:** 0
Total Number of Varsity/Jr. Varsity: 36
Number of Seniors on 1998 Team: 2
Freshmen Receiving Fin Aid/Athletic: 7
Most Recent Record: 36 - 28 - 0
Percent of Graduation: 0
Number of Sophomores on 1998 Team: 8
Baseball Camp Dates: July 25 - August 6
Number of Spring Games: 56
Positions Needed for 1999/2000: Pitcher, Catcher, Outfielder, Infielder
Schedule: Stanford, USC, ASU, UCLA, California, Texas A&M
Style of Play: Aggressive at the plate and on the bases. Don't depend on three-run homer.

Yavapai College

1100 East Sheldan
Prescott, AZ 86301
Coach: Sky Smeltzer

NJCAA
Roughriders/Black Forest, Gold
Phone: (520) 776-2292
Fax: (520) 776-2293

ACADEMIC

Founded: 1969
Web-site: http://www.yavapai.cc.az.us/
Student/Faculty Ratio: 15:1
Undergraduate Enrollment: 3,600
Scholarships/Academic: Yes **Athletic:** Yes
Total Expenses by: Sem/Year **In State:** $ 4,400/yr
Type: 2 Yr., Public, Coed
Campus Housing: Yes
Male/Female Ratio: 2:3
Graduate Enrollment: None
Fin Aid: Yes
Out of State: $ 5,000/sem
Degrees Conferred: 64 Degrees
Programs of Study: Wide variety

ATHLETIC PROFILE

Estimated Number of Baseball Scholarships: 17
Conference Affiliation: ACCAC

ARIZONA

www.thesportsource.com
1-800-862-3092

Program Profile: Three National Championships. Play year around with excellent facilities. Numerous appearances at the College World Series.

History: Program won 3 National Championship in 1995, 1977 and 1993.

Achievements: 5-time Region 9 Coach of the Year, 12 players drafted, 7 All-Americans.

Coaching: Sky Smeltzer, Head Coach, compiled a record of 72-34 for two years. Todd Tylehart, Assistant Coach.

Roster for 1998 team/In State: 14 **Out of State:** 8 **Out of Country:** 2

Total Number of Varsity/Jr. Varsity: 24 **Percent of Graduation:** 92%

Number of Seniors on 1998 Team: **Number of Sophomores on 1998 Team:** 12

Freshmen Receiving Fin Aid/Athletic: 8 **Academic:** 1

Number of Fall Games: 10 **Number of Spring Games:** 56

Most Recent Record: 41 - 10 - 1 **Baseball Camp Dates:** August 2-7

Positions Needed for 1999/2000: Pitcher, Catcher

Schedule: Seminole, Seward County, Lassen

Style of Play: Power offense with running game.

ARKANSAS

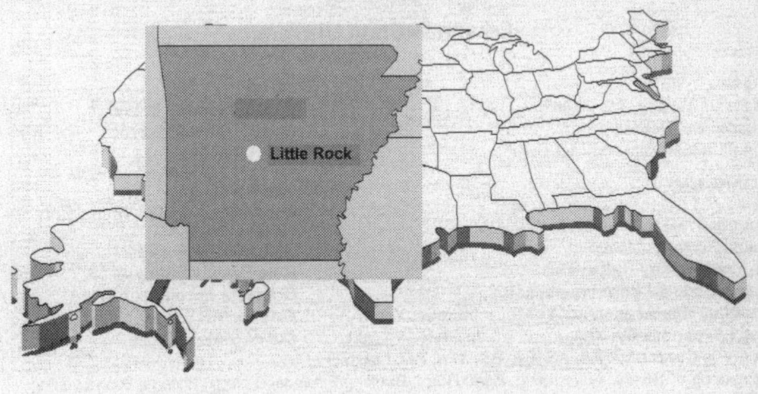

SCHOOL	CITY	AFFILIATION 99	PAGE
Arkansas State University	State University	NCAA I	76
Arkansas Tech University	Russellville	NCAA II	76
Harding University	Searcy	NCAA II	77
Henderson State Univ	Arkadelphia	NCAA II	77
Hendrix College	Conway	NCAA III	78
Lyon College	Batesville	NAIA	79
North Arkansas College - Technical College	Harrison	NJCAA	79
Ouachita Baptist University	Arkadelphia	NCAA II	80
Southern Arkansas University	Magnolia	NCAA II	80
University of Arkansas	Fayetteville	NCAA I	81
University of Arkansas - Little Rock	Little Rock	NCAA I	81
University of Arkansas - Monticello	Monticello	NCAA II	82
University of Central Arkansas	Conway	NCAA II	82
University of the Ozarks	Clarksville	NCAA III\NAIA	83
Westark Community College	Fort Smith	NJCAA	84
Williams Baptist College	Walnut Ridge	NAIA	84

Arkansas State University

PO Box 1000
State University, AR 72467
Coach: Bill Bethea
Email: asusid@inet.direct.com

NCAA I
Indians/Scarlet, Black
Phone: (870) 972-2700
Fax: (870) 972-2525

ACADEMIC

Founded: 1909
Religion: Not-Affiliated
Student/Faculty Ratio: 23:2
Undergraduate Enrollment: 8,762
Scholarships/Academic: Yes **Athletic:** Yes
Total Expenses by: Year **In State:** $ 1,950

Type: 4 Yr., Coed
SAT/ACT/GPA: 500/21
Male/Female Ratio: 44:56
Graduate Enrollment: None
Fin Aid: Yes
Out of State: $ 2,620

Degrees Conferred: AA, AS, BA, BS, BFA, BM, MA, MS
Programs of Study: Advertising, Agricultural, Banking/Finance, Biology, Botany, Broadcasting, Design, Economics, Geography, Journalism, Photography, Preprofessional Program, Real Estate, Wildlife, Zoology

ATHLETIC PROFILE

Conference Affiliation: Sun Belt Conference
Program Profile: Up and coming Division I program. Great facilities with new lights, a computerized scoreboard, an indoor hitting and a pitching facility.
History: The Arkansas State Baseball program was started in 1948, and after 50 seasons, the Indians have a total record of 761-977-8. However, under Coach Bill Bethea, ASU is 198-146 having won 30 or more games for the past five seasons. The team has made 4 appearances in NCAA Tourn. play including the latest in 1994, after winning the Sun Belt Conference Tournament Title.
Achievements: All-American-Wayne Pitcock in 1968; Dana Ryan in 1967; George Glenn in 1964-1966; Bill Bethea-SBC Coach of the Year in 1994; Rick Johnson-SLC Coach of the Year in 1982; ASC Coach of the Year in 1990; 1 SBC Tournament Championship in 1994; Matt Whiteside-currently play for Texas Rangers.
Coaching: Bill Bethea, Head Coach. Skip Blythe, Assistant Coach. David Grimes, Pitching.
Style of Play: Good fielding and good pitching along with a score timely hitting. Coach Bill Bethea's teams are very fundamentally sound and can get people out.

Arkansas Tech University

Tucker Coliseum, ATU
Russellville, AR 72801-2222
Coach: Billy Goss

NCAA II
Wonder Boys/Green, Gold
Phone: (501) 968-0648
Fax: (501) 964-0829

ACADEMIC

Founded: 1909
SAT/ACT/GPA: 800/17
Student/Faculty Ratio: 18:1
Undergraduate Enrollment: 4,166
Scholarships/Academic: Yes **Athletic:** Yes
Total Expenses by: Year **In State:** $ 1,902

Type: 4 Yr., Public, Coed
Campus Housing: Yes
Male/Female Ratio: 41:59
Graduate Enrollment: 190
Fin Aid: Yes
Out of State: $ 2,732

Degrees Conferred: AA, AS, BA, BS, BFA, M
Programs of Study: Accounting, Agricultre, Art, Biological Science, Business, Chemistry, Computer, Creative Writing, Economics, Engineering, Geology, Health, Journalism, Medical, Music, Natural Science, Parks/Recreation, Physical Science, Psychology, Social Science

ATHLETIC PROFILE

Estimated Number of Baseball Scholarships: 7.0

Conference Affiliation: AIC
Program Profile: All games played at Tech Field with a capacity of 500. Natural grass with a dimension's of 320-375-410-375-320.
History: Program began in 1912. All-time won/loss record is 709-623-9 (.558).
Achievements: 8 Conference/Division Championships, 16 seasons with 20 or more wins.
Coaching: Billy Goss, Head Coach, entering first season with the program. Brad Payton and Scott Mann, Assistant Coaches.
Roster for 1998 team/In State: 29 **Out of State:** 4 **Out of Country:** 0
Number of Seniors on 1998 Team: 2 **Most Recent Record:** 30- 16 - 1
Freshmen Receiving Fin Aid/Athletic: 19 **Academic:** 7
Number of Fall Games: 0 **Number of Spring Games:** 47
Positions Needed for 1999/2000: LH Pitcher, RH Pitcher, Center-fielder
Schedule: Delta State, Central Missouri, Central Oklahoma, SE Oklahoma, Southern Arkansas
Style of Play: Aggressive, hit and run, outstanding defense and great pitching.

Harding University

PO Box 2281
Searcy, AR 72149
Coach: Shane Fullerton

NCAA II
Bisons/Black, Gold
Phone: (501) 279-4344
Fax: (501) 279-4138

ACADEMIC

Founded: 1901 **Type:** 4 Yr., Private, Coed
SAT/ACT/GPA: 1000/24 **Campus Housing:** Yes
Student/Faculty Ratio: 16:1 **Male/Female Ratio:** 47:53
Undergraduate Enrollment: 3,540 **Graduate Enrollment:** 175
Scholarships/Academic: Yes **Athletic:** Yes **Fin Aid:** Yes
Total Expenses by: Year **In State:** $ 10,622 **Out of State:** $ 10,622
Degrees Conferred: AA, BA, BS, BFA, M
Programs of Study: Advertising, American, Art, Biblical, Biology, Business, Chemistry, Dietetics, Economics, Fashion, Finance, Journalism, Preprofessional Programs, Religious, Science, Speech, Special Education

ATHLETIC PROFILE

Conference Affiliation: Lone Star Conference
Program Profile: Team has been a consistent finisher in the top half of the old Arkansas Intercollegiate Conference. Facilities are good and improving. Indoor batting cage. All games played in the spring season. Field has natural grass with a sprinkler a system.
Achievements: Expect Senior, Pitcher - Tim Lacefield - to be drafted.
Coaching: Shane Fullerton, Head Coach, second year, served three years as assistant to Coach Bucy. Fullerton coached Blytheville, AR to district title. Randy Bostic, Assistant Coach, was a three year student assistant at David Lipscomb University.
Style of Play: Strong pitching and defense. Aggressive at the plate and at the bases.

Henderson State University

1100 Henderson St.
Arkadelphia, AR 71999-0001
Coach: Darren Preston

NCAA II
Reddies/Red, Grey
Phone: (870) 230-5071
Fax: (870) 230-5408

ACADEMIC

Founded: 1890 **Type:** 4 Yr., Public, Coed
SAT/ACT/GPA: 500/21 **Campus Housing:** Yes
Student/Faculty Ratio: 19:1 **Male/Female Ratio:** 45:55

Undergraduate Enrollment: 3,252 **Graduate Enrollment:** 290
Scholarships/Academic: Yes **Athletic:** Yes **Fin Aid:** Yes
Total Expenses by: Year **In State:** $ 1,860 **Out of State:** $ 2,270
Degrees Conferred: AA, BA, BFA, BS, BM, BME
Programs of Study: Accounting, Biological Science, Business, Chemistry, Communications, English, Pharmacy, Physics, Political, Preprofessional Programs, Recreation, Social Science, Speech Pathology

ATHLETIC PROFILE

Conference Affiliation: Gulf South Conference
Achievements: Phillip Taylor (former first baseman at HSU) plays Independent ball, as does former catcher Lanny Williams. Victor Martinez plays in Minor League.
Coaching: Darren Preston, Head Coach, 1990 graduate at Arkansas-Monticello, Masters from HSU in 1992, played college baseball at Louisiana Tech and Arkansas-Monticello.
Style of Play: We try to be aggressive.

Hendrix College

1600 Washington Avenue **NCAA III**
Conway, AR 72032 **Warriors/Black, Orange**
Coach: Jim Holland **Phone: (501) 450-1317**
Email: holland@hendrix.edu **Fax: (501) 450-3805**

ACADEMIC

Founded: 1876 **Type:** 4 Yr., Private, Liberal Arts, Coed
Religion: United Methodist **Campus Housing:** Yes
Web-site: http://www.hendrix.edu/ **Undergraduate Enrollment:** 1,000
Student/Faculty Ratio: 14:1 **Male/Female Ratio:** 4:5
Scholarships/Academic: Yes **Athletic:** No **Fin Aid:** Yes
Total Expenses by: Year **In State:** $ 15,105 **Out of State:** $ 15,105
Degrees Conferred: BA, two dozen major programs and Master in Accounting.
Programs of Study: Accounting, Biology, Chemistry, Dramatic Arts, Economics, Arts, Education, English, Fine Arts, French, German, History, International Relations, Mathematics, Music, Philosophy, Physics, Political Science, Predentistry, Preengineering, Prelaw, Premed, Prepharmacy, Psychology, Religion, Social Science

ATHLETIC PROFILE

Conference Affiliation: Southern Collegiate Athletic Conference
Program Profile: Seventh year of the program; record improved each year; natural grass playing field that has a 300 seat stadium that is considered one of the best in Arkansas; February - April is the playing season.
History: Began program in 1992 after 40 years of absence; record has improved each year; playing in very competitive conference; best finish so far has been a 3rd place finish (twice).
Achievements: 5 All-Conference players in 1997.
Coaching: Jim Holland, Head Coach, entering 23rd year at Hendrix College, graduate of University of Central Arkansas in 1966. Played at Westark Community College and University of Central Arkansas. Greg Baxendale, Assistant Coach.
Roster for 1998 team/In State: 70 **Out of State:** 30 **Out of Country:** 0
Total Number of Varsity/Jr. Varsity: 20 **Percent of Graduation:** 100%
Number of Seniors on 1998 Team: 2 **Baseball Camp Dates:** Early June
Number of Fall Games: 6 **Number of Spring Games:** 36
Positions Needed for 1999/2000: Pitcher, Catcher, Infielder
Schedule: University of Central Arkansas, Southwestern University, Pomona-Pitzer Colleges, University of Wisconsin-Oshkosh, St. Mary's University.
Style of Play: Emphasize fundamentals in all areas. New program has been weak in pitching so defense has been an emphasis; like to hit and run; aggressive on bases when speed is apparent in roster.

Lyon College

2400 Highland Drive
Batesville, AR 72501
Coach: Kirk Kelley

NAIA
Scots/Black, Red
Phone: (870) 698-4337
Fax: (870) 793-1763

ACADEMIC

Founded: 1872
Type: 4 Yr., Private, Liberal Arts, Coed
Religion: Presbyterian
Campus Housing: Yes
Web-site: http://www.lyon.edu/
SAT/ACT/GPA: 20+
Student/Faculty Ratio: 11:1
Male/Female Ratio: 1:2
Undergraduate Enrollment: 750
Graduate Enrollment: N/A
Scholarships/Academic: Yes **Athletic:** Yes **Fin Aid:** Yes
Total Expenses by: Year **In State:** $ 13,186 **Out of State:** $ 13,186
Degrees Conferred: BA, BS
Programs of Study: Art, Biology, Chemistry, Economics, English, History, Mathematics, Music, Politics, Psychology, Religion/Philosophy, Theatre

ATHLETIC PROFILE

Estimated Number of Baseball Scholarships: 6.25
Conference Affiliation: Tran South Conference
Program Profile: New facility opened in 1998, natural grass field with stadium that seats 500.
History: The program began in 1993. First year to be compete in the Tran South Conference.
Achievements: Has 3 players who have signed professional contracts; in 1997, finished 3rd in sectional; 1 1st team All-Conference player.
Coaching: Kirk Kelley, Head Coach, served as an Assistant Coach at Memphis State, Northwest Missouri, Allen County CC, compiled a record of 607 win 1997, (100th), was a scout for the Baltimore Orioles, summer collegiate coach in the Jayhawks Leagues. Mitch Mathis, Assistant Coach, 2nd player; played for Arkansas State University.
Roster for 1998 team/In State: 18 **Out of State:** 14 **Out of Country:** 0
Total Number of Varsity/Jr. Varsity: 32 **Percent of Graduation:** 100%
Number of Seniors on 1998 Team: 5 **Number of Sophomores on 1998 Team:** 0
Freshmen Receiving Fin Aid/Athletic: 12 **Academic:** 15
Number of Fall Games: 4 **Number of Spring Games:** 56
Most Recent Record: 27 - 29 - 0 **Baseball Camp Dates:** June
Positions Needed for 1999/2000: Middle Infielder, Catcher, 1st Base, Pitcher
Schedule: Arkansas State, Delta State, Birmingham Southern, Berry, Freed-Hardeman, Lipscomd, Union, Southern Arkansas, West Florida.
Style of Play: Very aggressive offensively.

North Arkansas College - Technical College

Pioneer Ridge
Harrison, AR 72601
Coach: Phil Wilson

NJCAA
Pioneers/Red, Grey
Phone: (870) 391-3282
Fax: (870) 391-3119

ACADEMIC

Type: 2 Yr., Jr. College, Coed
Degrees Conferred: Associates
Programs of Study: Agriculture, Automotive, Computer, Business, Criminal, Medical, Food Services, Hotel/Restaurant, Industrial/Heavy Equipment Maintenance, Liberal Arts, Machine/Tool Technology, Nursing, Welding

Ouachita Baptist University

410 Ouachita St
Arkadelphia, AR 71998-0001
Coach: Tom Murphree

NCAA II
Tigers/Purple, Gold
Phone: (870) 245-5296
Fax: (870) 245-5598

ACADEMIC

Founded: 1886
Type: 4 Yr., Private, Coed
SAT/ACT/GPA: 950/23
Campus Housing: Yes
Student/Faculty Ratio: 11:1
Male/Female Ratio: 48:52
Undergraduate Enrollment: 1,604
Graduate Enrollment: None
Scholarships/Academic: Yes **Athletic:** Yes **Fin Aid:** Yes
Total Expenses by: Year **In State:** $ 10,620 **Out of State:** $ 10,620
Degrees Conferred: BA, BS, BME, BM, M
Programs of Study: Accounting, Art, Biology, Business, Chemistry, Communications, Computer, Dietetics, Economics, Education, English, Languages, Health, History, Math, Medical, Preprofessional Programs, Speech

ATHLETIC PROFILE

Conference Affiliation: Lone Star Conference (NCAA), Independant (NAIA)
Program Profile: Rab Rodgers Field - Natural grass - seats 300.
Achievements: Arkansas Intercollegiate Conference Champions (NAIA Division I) - 1960, 1961-1967, 1968, 1969, 1970, 1971, 1972; NAIA All-Americans - Roger Patillo and Bubba Cope.

Southern Arkansas University

100 East University
Magnolia, AR 71753
Coach: Steve Goodheart

NCAA II
Muleriders/Blue, Gold
Phone: (870) 235-4127
Fax: (870) 235-5009

ACADEMIC

Founded: 1909
Type: 4 Yr., Public, Coed
Religion: Not-Affiliated
Campus Housing: Yes
Web-site: http://www.sau.mag.edu
SAT/ACT/GPA: 21
Student/Faculty Ratio: 18:1
Male/Female Ratio: 3:4
Undergraduate Enrollment: 2,408
Graduate Enrollment: 200
Scholarships/Academic: Yes **Athletic:** No **Fin Aid:** Yes
Total Expenses by: Year **In State:** $ 1,752 **Out of State:** $ 2,500
Degrees Conferred: AA, AS, BA, BS, BME, BSE, MED
Programs of Study: School of Business Administration, School of Liberal Arts and Performing Arts, General Studies, School of Science and Technology, School of Education, Master of Education

ATHLETIC PROFILE

Conference Affiliation: Gulf South Conference
Program Profile: Play on a natural grass field with measurements of LF-355, OF-410, RF-350. Field has no lights, has a seating capacity of 400, 3 turfed batting cages fo which one of them is lighted, season starts on February 14 and goes through May.
History: 1928 program in school started; NAIA affiliation untill 1996, then joined NCAA II; top 20 NAIA since 83; 10 Conference Champs & 3 World Series trips in 83, 87 and 91; 30 plus pro since 85.
Achievements: 9 Conference/District Coach of the Year titles; 1 Regional Coach of the Year; 1 National Coach of the Year in 1987 nomination; 17 All-Americans since 1983.

Coaching: Steve Goodheart, Head Coach, BS in Education, English major at South Arkansas in 1977, Master's from Arizona in 1980, graduate assistant at Arizona in 1979 and 1980 (NCAA champions in 1980). In 16 years at SAU, has 521-301-3 record (.634), best in school history. Won nine AIC championships in past 12 years, Coach of the Year seven times, Area Coach twice. Pete Southall - GA Pitchers, was an All-American - Arizona Diamondsbacks. Carlos Rivera, GA Hitters Scout. Steve Laughhaus, Infielders and Catchers, currently playing pro ball.
Style of Play: Adapt to talent of the players; 1998 - below average team' speed; 6 LH hitters. We will base hit, bunt and move runners. We like running ; but will do more bunting ,hitting and running, good defense and pitching.

University of Arkansas

PO Box 7777
Fayetteville, AR 72702
Coach: Norm DeBriyn

NCAA I
Razorbacks/Cardinal, White
Phone: (501) 575-3655
Fax: (501) 575-7481

ACADEMIC

Founded: 1871
Religion: Non-Affiliated
Web-site: http://www.uavk.edu
Student/Faculty Ratio: 18:1
Undergraduate Enrollment: 12,000
Scholarships/Academic: Yes **Athletic:** Yes
Total Expenses by: Year **In State:** $ 7,443

Type: 4 Yr., Public, Coed, Engineering
Campus Housing: No
SAT/ACT/GPA: 23/2.75
Male/Female Ratio: 55:45
Graduate Enrollment: 2,600
Fin Aid: No
Out of State: $ 11,391

Degrees Conferred: BA, MA, MS, BSA, BSCE
Programs of Study: Over 200 graduate and undergraduate degress in more than 150 fields of study in Agriculture, Food and Life Sciences, Arts and Sciences, Business, Education, Engineering, Architecture and Law

ATHLETIC PROFILE

Conference Affiliation: Southeastern Conference (SEC)
Program Profile: Based in the toughest collegiate baseball conference in the nation. Arkansas has consistently been among the top programs in the country where the completion of $8.8 million dollar baseball stadium. Arkansas has one of the top if not the top facility in the country. Major League accomodations include underground tunnels to dugouts, and a club house. Outfitted by Major League Tom Pagnozzi.
History: Arkansas first fielded a baseball team in 1897. Since then, Arkansas Baseball has been a model of excellence. The Razorbacks boast is an NCAA post-season appearance including 4 College World Series berths. The Hogs finished 2nd in the nation in 1978.
Achievements: Arkansas has boasted 20 All-Americans and 87 All-Conference Players. The Razorbacks have won 2 SWC titles and 5 NJCAA Regional Titles as well as 1 Conference Championship. In 1985 Jeff King of Arkansas was the #1 pick of the draft by the Pittsburgh Pirates.
Coaching: Norm DeBriyn, Head Coach, since 1970, compiled a record of 959-521-6; only five wins away from becoming the 17th coach in college baseball history to win 1,000 games. 6-time SWC Coach of the Year; 2 SWC Championships; longest served SEC Coach for 28 years. Doug Clark, Hitting Coach, entering his 21st season at Arkansas, All-Big 8 at Colorado as a player. Tim Montez, 1st year was 19-12 as pitcher at Pepperdine.
Style of Play: A team that utilizes the hit and run and kicks for power. Concentration is on pitching and defense.

University of Arkansas - Little Rock

2801 South University
Little Rock, AR 72204
Coach: Brian Rhees

NCAA I
Trojans/Maroon, White
Phone: (501) 663-8095
Fax: (501) 569-3030

ACADEMIC

Founded: 1927 | **Type:** 4 Yr., Public, Liberal Arts
Religion: Not-Affiliated | **Campus Housing:** Yes
Web-site: http://www.ualr.edu | **SAT/ACT/GPA:** 850+/21
Student/Faculty Ratio: 16:1 | **Male/Female Ratio:** 52:48
Undergraduate Enrollment: 9,000 | **Graduate Enrollment:** 2,000
Scholarships/Academic: Yes | **Athletic:** Yes | **Fin Aid:** Yes
Total Expenses by: Year | **In State:** $ 7,000 | **Out of State:** $ 11,500
Degrees Conferred: AA, AS, AAS, BA, BS, MA, MS, MBA, MD, JD
Programs of Study: Accounting, Advertising, Art, Biology, Business, Chemistry, Communicative Disorders, Computer, Construction, Criminal, Economics, Engineering, Finance, Geology, Health, Journalism, Science, Technology

ATHLETIC PROFILE

Conference Affiliation: Sun Belt Conference
Program Profile: The Trojans play in NCAA Division I with a season running from February through May. We play on a turf infield with grass outfield, seating for 120. Our fence is short, but the wall is 16 feet high.
History: Program first began in 1952 as Junior College and then moved to NAIA.
Style of Play: We do not feature any power and will depend on bunting people over; hit and run offense.

University of Arkansas - Monticello

Box 3066
Monticello, AR 71656-3066
Coach: Mike Martin
Email: martinmi@uamont.edu

NCAA II
Boll Weevils/Kelly Green, White
Phone: (870) 460-1258
Fax: (870) 460-1458

ACADEMIC

Founded: 1909 | **Type:** 4 Yr., Public, Coed
Religion: Not-Affiliated | **Campus Housing:** Yes
Student/Faculty Ratio: 20:1 | **Male/Female Ratio:** 45:55
Undergraduate Enrollment: 2,042 | **Graduate Enrollment:** 35
Scholarships/Academic: Yes | **Athletic:** Yes | **Fin Aid:** Yes
Total Expenses by: Year | **In State:** $ 1,906 | **Out of State:** $ 4,114
Degrees Conferred: AA, BA, BS, BMED
Programs of Study: Accounting, Agriculture, Biological Science, Business, Chemistry, Computer, Education, English, Forestry, History, Marketing, Mathematics, Music, Political Science, Preprofessional Programs, Psychology, Social Science, Special Education

ATHLETIC PROFILE

Conference Affiliation: Gulf South Conference

University of Central Arkansas

Bruce and Donaghey Streets
Conway, AR 72032
Coach: Toby White

NCAA II
Bears/Purple, White, Grey
Phone: (501) 450-3407
Fax: (501) 329-6717

ACADEMIC

Founded: 1907 | **Type:** 4 Yr., Public, Coed
Religion: Non-Affiliated | **Campus Housing:** Yes
Web-site: http://www.uca.edu/ | **SAT/ACT/GPA:** 890/19/3.0

Student/Faculty Ratio: 18:1
Male/Female Ratio: 40:60
Undergraduate Enrollment: 9,000
Graduate Enrollment: 1,024
Scholarships/Academic: Yes **Athletic:** Yes **Fin Aid:** Yes
Total Expenses by: Year **In State:** $ 6,212 **Out of State:** $ 8,432
Degrees Conferred: 17 Degrees with over 100 areas of study
Programs of Study: Business, Kinesiology, Education, Physical Therapy, Computer Science, Music, Journalism, Mass Communications, Nursing, Public Administration, Biology

ATHLETIC PROFILE

Conference Affiliation: Gulf South Conference
Program Profile: A very competitive NCAA Division II program, which will improve as scholarships become available. Facilities are adequate and improving each year. We play approximately 50 games per year. Our field has natural grass and our stadium seats about 500.
History: UCA baseball has always been very competitive in the NAIA, with a rich history of Arkansas Intercollegiate Conference Championships. Numerous players have gone on to play professional baseball. We will work hard to bring this same competitive spirit to the NCAA II conference.
Achievements: 10 Coach of the Year Honors; 18 Conference Titles; 3 NAIA All-Americans; 23 player to pro baseball.

University of the Ozarks

415N College Avenue
Clarksville, AR 72830
Coach: Bill Mueller
Email: wjmuelle@ozarks.edu

NCAA III\NAIA
Eagles/Purple, Gold
Phone: (501) 979-1409
Fax: (501) 979-1239

ACADEMIC

Founded: 1834
Type: 4 Yr., Private, Liberal Arts, Coed
Religion: Presbyterian
Campus Housing: Yes
Web-site: http://www.ozarks.edu/
SAT/ACT/GPA: 870/18/2.0
Student/Faculty Ratio: 11:1
Male/Female Ratio: 50:50
Undergraduate Enrollment: 600
Graduate Enrollment:
Scholarships/Academic: Yes **Athletic:** No **Fin Aid:** Yes
Total Expenses by: Year **In State:** $ 7,750 **Out of State:** $ 7,750
Degrees Conferred: BA, BS
Programs of Study: Accounting, Art, Business, Chemistry, General Studies, General Science, Education, English, Environmental Studies, History, Management, Marketing, Mathematics, Music, Physical Education, Physics, Psychology, Public Administration, Communications, Social Science, Theatre, Special Education, Prelaw, Premed, Kinesiology, Predentistry, Prepharmacy

ATHLETIC PROFILE

Conference Affiliation: American Southwest Conference
Program Profile: Hurie Field is the home of the Ozarks. It is a natural field with the lights sitting adjacent to the campus, plenty of parking, a press box, and a concessions stand. We also have a running track and weight room with both free & universal weights, located in the Mabee Hall (Gym).
History: Baseball at the University of the Ozarks dated back to the early 1900's but was dropped in the mid-1980's. Baseball was brought back five years ago by request of the students and is going stronger each year. In 1997 the team went to the playoffs and finished 3rd. We plan to build off a strong senior class this year (1997) and in the years to come.
Achievements: Bill Mueller first year head coach after being an assistant coach at Indiana University for five years. In the past three years we have had two Academic All-Americans and 5 All-Conference Selections.
Coaching: Bill Mueller, Head Coach, played and graduated from Indiana University. Played one year in St. Louis Cardinals Systems. Coached five years for Indiana University.
Style of Play: We like to run and have a good team speed. We have some players with a power but have success with a good team play. Our pitching is expanded and knows how to get people to hit the ball on the ground.

Westark Community College

5210 Grand Avenue
Fort Smith, AR 72913
Coach: Dale Harpenau
Email: dharpenau@systema.westark.edu

NJCAA
Lions/Royal Blue
Phone: (501) 788-7597
Fax: (501) 788-7601

ACADEMIC

Type: 2 Yr., , Jr. College, Coed
Web-site: http://www.westark.edu
Campus Housing: No
Programs of Study: Accounting, Automotive, Banking/Finance, Business, Computer, Drafting/Design, Education, Technologies

ATHLETIC PROFILE

Conference Affiliation: Bi - State Conference
Program Profile: Has a good fall and spring schedule. Play on a natural grass field which is well-lit. Good turf infield that has a seating capacity of 1,000.
History: Baseball became a serious program in 1965. Our program has a great tradition with several drafted players and some playing in the major leagues. Most two year players received scholarships to four year colleges & universities. Our program has a record of 983 wins since 1965.
Achievements: Bill Crowder, was one of Top 5 Coaches in the NJCAA striving for 1,000 wins in 1998. We had 10 All-Americans over 30 drafted and three played in the major league.
Style of Play: We try to be strong up the middle, starting with pitchers. We like speed using the bunting, hit and run Etc. Play percentage baseball while stressing all phases and work very hard on defense.

Williams Baptist College

60 W Fulbright
Walnut Ridge, AR 72476
Coach: Jim Smith

NAIA
Eagles/Blue, White
Phone: (870) 886-6741
Fax: (870) 886-3924

ACADEMIC

Founded: 1941
Type: 4 Yr., Private, Coed
Religion: Not-Affiliated
Campus Housing: No
Student/Faculty Ratio: 10:1
Male/Female Ratio: 43:57
Scholarships/Academic: Yes **Athletic:** Yes **Fin Aid:** Yes
Total Expenses by: Year **In State:** $ 4,800 **Out of State:** $ 4,800
Degrees Conferred: AA, BA, BSE
Programs of Study: Art, Bible Studies, Business and Management, Education, English, History, Music, Physical Education, Psychology, Theological Studies

ATHLETIC PROFILE

Conference Affiliation: Tran South Conference
Program Profile: The program has improved year after year. Season consists of 46 games. The home playing field is natural, with grass base lines.
History: Relatively new program, started in 1990.
Coaching: Jim Smith, Head Coach.
Style of Play: Team hitting is pretty consistant along with fairly strong defense. Pitching is the major weakness of this team.

CALIFORNIA

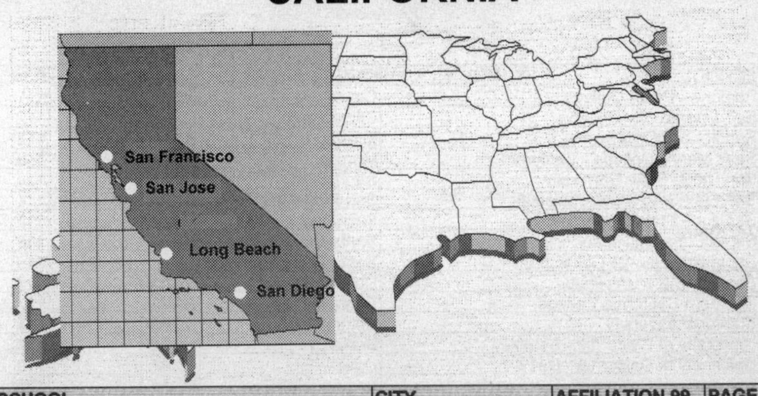

SCHOOL	CITY	AFFILIATION 99	PAGE
Allan Hancock College	Santa Maria	CCCCA	87
Antelope Valley Community College	Lancaster	CCCCA	87
Azusa Pacific University	Azusa	NAIA	87
Biola University	La Mirada	NAIA	88
Butte Community College	Oroville	NJCAA	89
California Baptist College	Riverside	NAIA	89
California Institute of Technology	Pasadena	NCAA III	90
California Lutheran University	Thousand Oaks	NCAA III	90
California State Poly Univ. - SLO	San Louis Obispo	NCAA I	91
California State Polytechnic Univ. - Pomona	Pomona	NCAA II	92
California State University - Chico	Chico	NCAA II	92
California State University - Dominguez Hills	Carson	NCAA II	93
California State University - Fresno	Fresno	NCAA I	93
California State University - Fullerton	Fullerton	NCAA I	94
California State University - Hayward	Hayward	NCAA II	95
California State University - Long Beach	Long Beach	NCAA I	95
California State University - Los Angeles	Los Angeles	NCAA II	96
California State University - Northridge	Northridge	NCAA I	97
California State University - Sacramento	Sacramento	NCAA I	98
California State University - San Bernardino	San Bernadino	NCAA II	98
California State University - Stanislaus	Turlock	NCAA II	98
Cañada College	Redwood City	CCC	99
Cerritos Community College	Norwalk	CCCCA	100
Chaffey College	Alta Loma	CCCCA	100
Chapman University	Orange	NCAA III	100
Citrus Community College	Glendora	CCCJC	101
Claremont - Mudds - Scrips College	Claremont	NCAA III	102
College of Marin	Kentfield	CCCCA	102
College of the Sequoias	Visalia	CCCCA	103
College of the Siskiyous	Weed	CJCAA	103
Concordia University - Irvine	Irvine	NAIA	104
Contra Costa College	San Pablo	CCCCA	104
Cypress College	Cypress	NJCAA	105
De Anza College	Cupertino	CCCCA	105
Lassen College	Susanville	CCC	106
Long Beach City College	Long Beach	CCCCA	106
Los Angeles Pierce College	Woodland Hills	CCCCA	106
Los Medanos College	Pittsburg	CCBA	107
Loyola Marymount University	Los Angeles	NCAA I	107
Master's College	Santa Clarita	NAIA	108
Menlo College	Atherton	NCAA III	109
Napa Valley College	Napa	CCAC	109
Occidental College	Los Angeles	NCAA III	110
Pepperdine University	Malibu	NCAA I	110
Point Loma Nazarene College	San Diego	NAIA	111

SCHOOL	CITY	AFFILIATION 99	PAGE
Pomona - Pitzer College	Claremont	NCAA III	111
Sacramento City College	Sacramento	CJUCO	112
Saddleback College	Mission Viejo	NJCAA	113
Saint Mary's College - California	Moraga	NCAA I	113
San Diego State University	San Diego	NCAA I	114
San Francisco State University	San Francisco	NCAA II	114
San Jose State University	San Jose	NCAA I	115
Santa Clara University	Santa Clara	NCAA I	116
Santa Rosa Junior College	Santa Rosa	CC	116
Sonoma State University	Rohnert Park	NCAA II	117
Southern California College	Costa Mesa	NAIA	117
Stanford University	Stanford	NCAA I	118
University of California - Berkeley	Berkeley	NCAA I	119
University of California - Davis	Davis	NCAA II	119
University of California - Los Angeles	Los Angeles	NCAA I	120
University of California - Riverside	Riverside	NCAA II	121
University of California - San Diego	La Jolla	NCAA III	121
University of California - Santa Barbara	Santa Barbara	NCAA I	122
University of La Verne	La Verne	NCAA III	123
University of Redlands	Redlands	NCAA III	123
University of San Diego	San Diego	NCAA I	124
University of San Francisco	San Francisco	NCAA I	125
University of Southern California	Los Angeles	NCAA I	125
University of the Pacific	Stockton	NCAA I	126
West Valley College	Saratoga	CCCCA	126
Westmont College	Santa Barbara	NAIA	127
Whittier College	Whittier	NCAA III	128

Allan Hancock College

800 S College Drive
Santa Maria, CA 93454
Coach: Doug Noce

CCCCA
Bulldogs/Royal Blue, Gold
Phone: (805) 922-6966x3227
Fax: (805) 349-8346

ACADEMIC

Founded: 1920
Religion: Non-Affiliated
Undergraduate Enrollment: 7,744
Scholarships/Academic: No **Athletic:** No
Total Expenses by: Year **In State:** $ 390

Type: 2 Yr., Public, Liberal Arts, Coed
Campus Housing: No
Student/Faculty Ratio: 18:1
Fin Aid: Yes
Out of State: $ 3,120

Degrees Conferred: Associate
Programs of Study: Accounting, Architecture, Art, Automotive, Biological, Business, Engineering, Computer, Cosmetology, Dental, Human Services, Industrial/Heavy Equipment Maintenance, International Law, Machine/Tool, Medical, Real Estate, Welding

ATHLETIC PROFILE

Conference Affiliation: Western States Conference
Program Profile: Field described as one of the nicest in California. Full year-round program. Players usally get 600 at-bats while in the program.
Achievements: WSC North Division Champions.
Coaching: Doug Noce, Head Coach, entering second year as a head coach. Grant Stephens, Assistant Coach. Bob Fystro, Assistant Coach.
Style of Play: "Bulldog" attitude. Aggressive at the plate and on the bases. We also want players who can play "little ball" (drag and push).

Antelope Valley Community College

3041 West Avenue K
Lancaster, CA 93536
Coach: Joe Watts

CCCCA
Marauders/Maroon, Silver, Gold
Phone: (805) 722-6440
Fax: (805) 722-6450

ACADEMIC

Founded: 1929
Student/Faculty Ratio: 9027/400
Total Expenses by: Year **In State:** $ Varies

Type: 2 Yr., Public, Jr. College, Coed
Undergraduate Enrollment: 9,027
Out of State: $ 3,510

Degrees Conferred: Associate
Programs of Study: Mathematics, Science, Business, Agricultural Science, Animal Science, Arts, Automotive Technologies, Psychology, Business Administration, Civil Engineering, Early Childhood Education, Computet Programming, Computer Science

Azusa Pacific University

901 E. Alosta
Azusa, CA 91702
Coach: Tony Barbone
Email: tbarbone@apu.edu

NAIA
Cougars/Orange, Black
Phone: (626) 812-3024
Fax: (626) 812-3034

ACADEMIC

Founded: 1899
Religion: Evangelical
Web-site: http://www.apu.edu/

Type: 4 Yr., Private, Liberal Arts, Coed
Campus Housing: Yes
SAT/ACT/GPA: 1000+

Student/Faculty Ratio: 17:1 **Male/Female Ratio:** 1:2
Undergraduate Enrollment: 2,400 **Graduate Enrollment:** 2,600
Scholarships/Academic: Yes **Athletic:** Yes **Fin Aid:** Yes
Total Expenses by: Year **In State:** $ 17,400 **Out of State:** $ 17,400
Degrees Conferred: BA, BS, Med, EdD
Programs of Study: More than 35 majors including Accounting, Applied Art, Art, Athletic Training, Biblical Studies, Biochemistry, Biology, Business, Communications, Marketing, Math, Ministries, Theology, Etc.

ATHLETIC PROFILE

Conference Affiliation: Golden State Atlantic Conference
Program Profile: Four year-2 tunnel cages, 4 bull pen mounds, lighted natural grass field.
History: The program began in 1965. The Cougars have had 19 30-win seasons including nine of the past ten years. Reached postseason play in 25 of 31 years playing baseball, winning the past 16 consecutive seasons.
Achievements: 17 consecutive playoff appearances; 7 out of 12 Conference Champs; 12 All-Americans.
Coaching: Tony Barbone, Head Coach, started coaching with the program in 1986, won 300th game in 1995, named 1996 GSCA Coach of the Year nine-time. Currently manager of Vermont Expos (New York-Penn League). Scott Winterborn and Paul Coppes, Assistant Coaches.
Roster for 1998 team/In State: 8 **Out of State:** 19 **Out of Country:** 0
Total Number of Varsity/Jr. Varsity: 27 **Percent of Graduation:** 92%
Number of Seniors on 1998 Team: **Number of Sophomores on 1998 Team:** 0
Freshmen Receiving Fin Aid/Athletic: 3 **Academic:** 4
Positions Needed for 1999/2000: Catcher, Pitchers, 1st Base, 3rd Base
Most Recent Record: 35- 11 - 0
Schedule: Lewis and Clark, Albertson, Cal Poly Pomona, Hasting, California State-San Bernadino.
Style of Play: Execution style of play. Pitching and defense; focus solid players who understand the game.

Biola University

13800 Biola Avenue **NAIA**
La Mirada, CA 90639 **Eagles/Red, White, Blue**
Coach: John Verhoeven **Phone: (562) 903-4886**
Fax: (562) 903-4890

ACADEMIC

Founded: 1908 **Type:** 4 Yr., Private, Coed
Religion: Non-Denominational **Campus Housing:** Yes
Web-site: http://www.biola.edu/ **SAT/ACT/GPA:** 1080
Student/Faculty Ratio: 16:1 **Male/Female Ratio:** 48:52
Undergraduate Enrollment: 2,200 **Graduate Enrollment:** 1,000
Scholarships/Academic: Yes **Athletic:** Yes **Fin Aid:** Submit FAF
Total Expenses by: Year **In State:** $ 18,986 **Out of State:** $ 18,986
Degrees Conferred: BA, BS, BM, Mdiv, ThM, Dmiss, PsyD, EdD, PhD, ThD
Programs of Study: Art, Biochemistry, Biological Science, Accounting, Computer Information Systems, Economics, Business Administration, Philosophy, Management, Marketing, Nursing, History, Humanities, Education, Sociology, Computer Science, Communications, Psychology

ATHLETIC PROFILE

Estimated Number of Baseball Scholarships: 5
Conference Affiliation: Golden State Athletic Conference
Program Profile: A budding program, nationally ranked all last season #1 ranked NAIA team in California.
History: 1959 program began; has produced 2 major leaguers - Todd Worrell and Tim Worrell.
Achievements: GSAC Conference Coach of the Year in '98; GSAC Conference Championsin 1998.

Coaching: John Venhoeven, Head Coach, former major league, pitcher with Angels, White Sox and Twins. Dave Castillo, Assistant Coach, played with the Tigers and Twins Organization. Mike Smith, Pitching Coach, former Cardinals , now pitching with Mission Veijo Vigilantes.
Roster for 1998 team/In State: 23 **Out of State:** 7 **Out of Country:** 0
Total Number of Varsity/Jr. Varsity: 25 **Percent of Graduation:** 75%
Number of Seniors on 1998 Team: 4 **Most Recent Record:** 34 - 16 - 0
Freshmen Receiving Fin Aid/Athletic: 6 **Academic:** 2
Number of Fall Games: 14 **Number of Spring Games:** 48
Positions Needed for 1999/2000: Pitcher
Schedule: California State Dominguez Hills, California State - Los Angeles, UNC-Riverside, California-Poly Pomona, California Pacific University.
Style of Play: Aggressive baserunning, strong bullpens, speed oriented, some bunting, fundamentally, round, play for the big inning; #1 players; have fun and win.

Butte Community College

3536 Butte Campus Drive
Oroville, CA 95965
Coach: Wendell Bolar

NJCAA
Roadrunners/Black, Gold, White
Phone: (530) 895-2521
Fax: (530) 895-2260

ACADEMIC

Founded: 1966 **Type:** 2 Yr., Public, Jr. College, Coed
Student/Faculty Ratio: 21:1 **Campus Housing:** No
Undergraduate Enrollment: 12,300 **Graduate Enrollment:** None
Total Expenses by: Year **In State:** $ Varies **Out of State:** $ 3,750
Degrees Conferred: Associate
Programs of Study: Accounting, Agricultural Business, Agricultural Economics, Agricultural Science, Animal Science, Applied Arts, Arts, Fine Arts, Automotive Technology, Construction Technology, Health Science, Home Economics, Practical Nursing, General Studies, Telecommunications, Natural Resources

California Baptist College

8432 Magnolia Avenue
Riverside, CA 92504-3297
Coach: Joe Szczepanski

NAIA
Lancers/Red, White, Blue
Phone: (909) 343-4318
Fax: (909) 689-4754

ACADEMIC

Founded: 1950 **Type:** 4 Yr., Private, Coed
Religion: Southern Baptist **Campus Housing:** Yes
Web-site: http://www.calbaptist.edu/ **SAT/ACT/GPA:** 870/ 20
Student/Faculty Ratio: 14:1 **Male/Female Ratio:** 50:50
Undergraduate Enrollment: 850 **Graduate Enrollment:** 45
Scholarships/Academic: Yes **Athletic:** Yes **Fin Aid:** Yes
Total Expenses by: Year **In State:** $ 13,000 **Out of State:** $ 13,000
Degrees Conferred: BA, BS, MS, BM
Programs of Study: Biology, Communications, Art, Business, Physical Education, Education, Liberal Arts, Religion, Premed, Prenursing, Predentistry, English, History, Psychology, Sociology

ATHLETIC PROFILE

Conference Affiliation: Golden State Athletic Conference
Program Profile: Games are played on campus at Lancer Field. At California Baptist, you have the opportunity to play for a conference, district, area, and national championship. We have a Fall program and Spring schedule that will challenge any small college in Southern California.

History: Program began in the 1950's. We had District play-off teams in 1988, 1990, 1991.
Achievements: 3 All-Americans and 3 players drafted since 1990
Style of Play: Strong offensive attack balanced with a good pitching and a good defense. Quick pace practice and games. We do not waste time. We want to succed in everything we do.

California Institute of Technology

1201 East California Boulevard
Pasadena, CA 91125
Coach: John D'Auria

NCAA III
Beavers/Navy, Orange, White
Phone: (626) 395-3263
Fax: (626) 584-0589

ACADEMIC

Founded: 1891
Religion: Not-Affiliated
Web-site: http://www.caltech.edu/
Student/Faculty Ratio: 3:1
Undergraduate Enrollment: 900
Type: 4 Yr., Private, Coed, Engineering
Campus Housing: No
SAT/ACT/GPA: 1320+
Male/Female Ratio: 70:30
Graduate Enrollment: 1,050
Scholarships/Academic: Yes **Athletic:** No **Fin Aid:** Yes
Total Expenses by: Year **In State:** $ 21,500 **Out of State:** $ 21,500
Degrees Conferred: BA, BS, MS, Phd
Programs of Study: Aeronautical Engineering, Astronomy, Biology, Chemical Engineering, Chemistry, Civil Engineering, Economics, Electrical Engineering, Engineering, Geochemistry, Geology, Geophysics, History, Literature, Mathematics, Mechanical Engineering, Physics, Planetary Science, Political Science, Seismology, Social Science, Space Science

ATHLETIC PROFILE

Conference Affiliation: Southern California Intercollegiate Athletics Conference

California Lutheran University

60 West Olsen Road
Thousand Oaks, CA 91360
Coach: Marty Slimak
Email: cludadm@clunet.edu

NCAA III
Kingsmen/Gold, Purple
Phone: (805) 493-3398
Fax: (805) 493-3860

ACADEMIC

Founded: 1959
Religion: ELCA
Web-site: http://www.callutheran.edu/
Student/Faculty Ratio: 14:1
Undergraduate Enrollment: 1,335
Type: 4 Yr., Private, Liberal Arts, Coed
Campus Housing: Yes
SAT/ACT/GPA: 900/2.5
Male/Female Ratio: 49:51
Graduate Enrollment: 600
Scholarships/Academic: Yes **Athletic:** No **Fin Aid:** Yes
Total Expenses by: Year **In State:** $ 20,000 **Out of State:** $ 20,000
Degrees Conferred: BA, BS, MA, MS
Programs of Study: Advertising, Art, Biochemistry, Business, Computer Science, Economics, Humanities, Religion, Social Sciences, Spanish, English, Speech, History, Dramatic Arts, Political Science, Philosophy

ATHLETIC PROFILE

Conference Affiliation: Southern California Intercollegiate Conference
Program Profile: North field has a capacity of 250; facilities are adjacent to field that include a practice infield, astro-turf batting cage, practice mounds, and a running trail. Southern California allows for an excellent climate to play in. Playing surface on infield is Bermuda grass.

History: Since the program began in 1962 as an NAIA member, CLU made 10 post-season appearances and captured the '90 NAIA District 3 Championships. Since joining NCAA Division III in '92, CLU has captured 6 out of 7 Southern California Intercollegiate Athletic Conference Championships, made 7 consecutive regional appearances, and been to four Div. III World Series, most recently in '98; National Runner-Ups in '92 and '96; 13 players signed pro contracts since '91.
Achievements: '90 NAIA District III Champions; '92, '93, '94, '96 SCIAC Champions, 11 NCAA All-Americans since '92; 2 Academic All-Americans in '91 and '92; 3 NAIA All-Americans in '81-'83.
Coaching: Marty Slimak, Head Coach, beginning his sixth year as a head coach, and 10th on staff. Current record is 150-63 (.704). He was named 1994 SCIAC Coach of the Year; 1998 NCAA Division III West Region Coach of the Year. Led the CLU into post-season play each of five years as a head coach. Played at UC-Santa Barbara where he earned bachelors degree. Masters from CLU. Milan Rasic, Assistant Coach, 1999 will be first year in CLU staff. Five years coaching experience at Sul Ross State University, NM Highlands University and College of the Southwest where he played and graduated from. He earned MED from Sul Ross State University. Jake Ganajian, Assistant Coach, '99 first year on staff. Played in 3 Division III World Series including '98 with CLU.
Roster for 1998 team/In State: 24 **Out of State:** 8 **Out of Country:** 0
Total Number of Varsity/Jr. Varsity: 32 **Percent of Graduation:** 91%
Number of Seniors on 1998 Team: 12 **Number of Sophomores on 1998 Team:** 5
Freshmen Receiving Fin Aid/Athletic: 0 **Academic:** 4
Most Recent Record: 28 - 15 - 0 **Number of Spring Games:** 40
Positions Needed for 1999/2000: Pitcher, Outfielder, Infielder Corners
Baseball Camp Dates: Summer 1999/call for dates
Schedule: University of Southern California, Chapman University, Montclair State University, University of Wisconsin - La Crosse, Eastern Connecticut State University
Style of Play: Play to win. Always among the national leaders in pitching and hitting. Aggressive, fundamental baseball.

California State Poly University - SLO

1 Grand Avenue
San Louis Obispo, CA 93407
Coach: Ritch Price

NCAA I
Mustangs/Green, Gold
Phone: (805) 756-1201
Fax: (805) 756-2650

ACADEMIC

Founded: 1901
Type: 4 Yr., Public, Liberal Arts, Coed
Religion: Non-Affiliated
Campus Housing: Yes
Web-site: http://www.calpoly.edu.
SAT/ACT/GPA: 1000
Student/Faculty Ratio: 19:1
Male/Female Ratio: 58:42
Undergraduate Enrollment: 15,540
Graduate Enrollment: 1,200
Scholarships/Academic: Yes **Athletic:** Yes **Fin Aid:** Yes
Total Expenses by: Year **In State:** $ 7,542 **Out of State:** $ Varies
Degrees Conferred: BA, BS, BLA, BAR, MA, MS, MBA, MCRP
Programs of Study: College of Agriculture (Business, Engineering, Systems Management, Science, Animal Science, Crop Science, Dairy/Food/Fruit Science, Forestry and Natural Resources, Nutritional, Horticulture, Plant Protection, Recreation, Soil Science), College of Architecture and Environmental Design (Engineering, Architecture, City and Regional Planning, Construction, Landscape), College of Business (Business Administration, Economics, Industrial Technology), College of Engineering (Aeronautical, Civil, Computer, Computer Science, Electrical, Engineering Science, Environmental, Industrial, Manufacturing, Materials, Mechanical), College of Liberal Arts (Applied Art and Design, English, Graphic Communication, History, Human Development, Journalism, Liberal Studies, Music, Philosophy, Political, Psychology, Social Science, Speech), College of Science and Mathematics (Biochemistry, Biological Sciences, Chemistry, Ecology and Systematic Biology, Math, Microbiology, Physical Education, Physical Science, Physics, Statistics)

ATHLETIC PROFILE

Conference Affiliation: Division I Conference

Program Profile: Play home games at San Luis Obispo stadium that seats 2,500 (with lights). New on-campus facility to be built in two years. Practice field is on campus. Play now at city park. San Luis Obispo is located five minutes from the beach between San Francisco and Los Angeles. It is a central coast college town with 38,000 population.
History: 1996 is the second year at Division I level. NCAA Division II National Champions 1989, third place 1992, second place 1993, five conference titles: 1989, 1992-1994.
Achievements: Mustangs in pros includes Ozzie Smith with the Cardinals, Mike Krukow with the Giants, John Orton with the Braves.
Coaching: Ritch Price, Head Coach, entering third year as a head coach, California Community College coached for eight years, four conference championships and six Coach of the Year awards - included is the 1996 Coach of the Year award for the WACC Conference.
Style of Play: Work and play hard hustle. Like the short game, and aggressive on the bases.

California State Poly University - Pomona

3801 West Temple Avenue
Pomona, CA 91768
Coach: Mike Ashman

NCAA II
Broncos/Green, Gold
Phone: (909) 869-2829
Fax: (909) 869-2814

ACADEMIC

Founded: 1938
Type: 4 Yr., Public, Coed, Engineering
Religion: Not-Affiliated
Campus Housing: Yes
Web-site: http://www.csupomona.edu/
SAT/ACT/GPA: Sliding Scale
Student/Faculty Ratio: 28:1
Male/Female Ratio: 57:43
Undergraduate Enrollment: 13,500
Graduate Enrollment: 3,000
Scholarships/Academic: Yes **Athletic:** Yes **Fin Aid:** Yes
Total Expenses by: Year **In State:** $ 10,188 **Out of State:** $ 12,996
Degrees Conferred: BA, BS, Barch, MA, MS, MBA
Programs of Study: Accounting, Aerospace Engineering, Agricultural Biology, Agricultural Business Management, Apparel Merchandising, Architecture, Chemistry, Behavorial Science, Construction Engineering, Computer Engineering, Industrial Engineering, Horticulture, Marketing Management

ATHLETIC PROFILE

Conference Affiliation: California Collegiate Athletic Association
Program Profile: NCAA Division II. Warm weather, beautiful facility (four full cages), schedule includes Division I powerhouses like Cal State Fullerton and Pepperdine. Only short 30 miles east of Los Angeles but in very rural setting with beautiful campus and surroundings.
History: Program began in 1960. Three Division II National Championships 1976, 1980, 1983. Regional Champions '79, '85. Conference Champions '76, '79, '80, '83, '85, '88, and '91.
Achievements: 22 All-Americans and over 120 players have gone into professional baseball.
Coaching: Mike Ashman, Head Coach, has 6 assistant coaches combined for a total of 66 years of coaching experience at Cal Poly under now retired coaching legend John Scolinos.
Style of Play: Depend upon personnel. Like players who play hard and practice hard all the time and who exhibit the 4-C's: Class, Character, Concern and Consistency.

California State University - Chico

First and Orange
Chico, CA 95929
Coach: Lindsay Meggs

NCAA II
Wildcats/Red, White
Phone: (530) 898-4636
Fax: (916) 898-4699

ACADEMIC

Founded: 1887
Type: 4 Yr., Public, Coed, Engineering
Religion: Non-Affiliated
Campus Housing: Yes

Web-site: http://www.csuchio.edu/
SAT/ACT/GPA: 820+
Student/Faculty Ratio: 20:1
Male/Female Ratio: 50:50
Undergraduate Enrollment: 13,200
Graduate Enrollment: None
Scholarships/Academic: Yes **Athletic:** No
Fin Aid: Yes
Total Expenses by: Year **In State:** $ 7,000
Out of State: $ 14,802
Degrees Conferred: BA, BS, BFA, MA, MS, MBA
Programs of Study: Business, Education, Communication, Science, Premed, Engineering, Art, Language, History, Accounting, Anthropology, Botany.

ATHLETIC PROFILE

Conference Affiliation: Northern California Athletic Conference

California State University - Dominguez Hills

1000 East Victoria Street
Carson, CA 90747
Coach: George Wing

NCAA II
Toros/Cardinal, Gold
Phone: (310) 243-3765
Fax: (310) 516-4488

ACADEMIC

Founded: 1960
Type: 4 Yr., Public, Liberal Arts, Coed
Religion: Non-Affiliated
Campus Housing: Yes
Web-site: http://www.csudh.edu/
SAT/ACT/GPA: 1200
Student/Faculty Ratio: 18:1
Male/Female Ratio: 1:2.3
Undergraduate Enrollment: 7,048
Graduate Enrollment: 2,929
Scholarships/Academic: Yes **Athletic:** Yes
Fin Aid: Yes
Total Expenses by: Year **In State:** $ 2,000
Out of State: $ 10,000
Degrees Conferred: BS, MA
Programs of Study: Anthropology, Biology, Business Administration, Chemistry, Clinical Science, Communication, Computer Science, Economics, English, Fine Arts, French, Geology, Health Science, History, Human Services, Mathematics, Nursing, Physical Education, Physics

ATHLETIC PROFILE

Conference Affiliation: California Collegiate Athletic Association
Program Profile: Our program is built around pitching and defense. Our park is very large, so offensively we play an action game.
History: We went to the College World Series in 1987 and moved recently to Western Regional in 1994. We have regularly been in the top 25 rankings and top 10 in pitching and defense.
Achievements: We currently have 6 players who are playing professionally. Greg Weebeck only in school. George Wing was named Coach of the Year in 1994.
Coaching: George Wing, Head Coach, also a pitching coach. Jeff Sears, Assistant Coach, Outfielder and catcher's coach. Darrell Couners, Assistant Coach, coaches the commers and hitters. Ron Keesten, Assistant Coach, coaches the middle infield and short game on offense.
Style of Play: Our program is built around pitching and defense. Action type offense. You must go to class!! Prepare for life beyond baseball.

California State University - Fresno

1620 E. Bulldog Lane
Fresno, CA 93740-7400
Coach: Bob Bennett
Email: bbennett@csufresno.edu

NCAA I
Bulldogs/Red, Blue
Phone: (559) 278-2178
Fax: (559) 278-7150

ACADEMIC

Founded: 1911
Type: 4 Yr., Public, Coed
Web-site: http://www.fresnostatebaseball.edu
Undergraduate Enrollment: 17,400

Scholarships/Academic: No **Athletic:** 9.9 **Fin Aid:** Available
Total Expenses by: Year **In State:** $ 7,500 **Out of State:** $ 14,000
Degrees Conferred: Numerous undergraduate and graduate
Programs of Study: Numerous. 56 different programs for undergraduate and 41 graduate.

ATHLETIC PROFILE

Estimated Number of Baseball Scholarships: 11.7
Conference Affiliation: Western Athletic Conference
Program Profile: Rated 6th facility in college baseball, natural grass with 7,000 seats, 4 hitting cages, and 6 pitching mounds. Top ten in attendance every year since 1985. Led nation in attendance twice in 1989 and 1990.
History: Program began in '22. Teams have won 28 conference champs; been to the College World Series three times (59, '88, '91). Home attendance has been ranked nationally in the top 5.
Achievements: 28 Conference Titles; 26 All-Americans; 131 players drafted in Bennett's ERA; 8 1st round draft choices; 31 former players have played major leagues, ten still active.
Coaching: Bob Bennett, Head Coach, compiled a record of 1,157-646; NCAA Coach of the Year in 1988 (sporting News); US National Team Coach in 1983 and 1986; 31st year as a head coach. Mike Rupcich, Assistant Coach, 23 years with the program. Steve Pearse, Assistant Coach.
Roster for 1998 team/In State: 27 **Out of State:** 3 **Out of Country:** 0
Total Number of Varsity/Jr. Varsity: 30 **Percent of Graduation:** 70%
Number of Seniors on 1998 Team: 6 **Number of Sophomores on 1998 Team:** 0
Freshmen Receiving Fin Aid/Athletic: 7 **Most Recent Record:** 33 - 29 - 0
Number of Fall Games: 0 **Number of Spring Games:** 65
Positions Needed for 1999/2000: Pitcher, Outfielder
Baseball Camp Dates: June 21-24; July 18-23; July 25-30
Schedule: Rice, Stanford, Fullerton State, North Carolina, Pepperdine, California
Style of Play: Fundamentally sound.

California State University - Fullerton

800 N. State College Boulevard **NCAA I**
Fullerton, CA 92634 **Titans/Navy, Orange**
Coach: George Horton **Phone: (714) 278-3789**
Email: ghorton@fullerton.edu **Fax: (714) 278-5396**

ACADEMIC

Founded: 1957 **Type:** 4 Yr., Public, Coed
Religion: Non-Affiliated **Campus Housing:** Yes
Web-site: http://www.fullerton.edu/ **SAT/ACT/GPA:** Sliding Scale
Student/Faculty Ratio: 19:1 **Male/Female Ratio:** 42:58
Undergraduate Enrollment: 20,000 **Graduate Enrollment:** 4,000
Scholarships/Academic: Yes **Athletic:** Yes **Fin Aid:** Yes
Total Expenses by: Year **In State:** $ 7,677 **Out of State:** $ 14,000
Degrees Conferred: BA, BS, BFA, BM, MA, MS, MFA
Programs of Study: Seven Schools - Arts, Business Education/Economics, Communications, Engineering/Computer Sciences, Human Development/ Community Services, Humanities/Social Sciences, Natural Sciences and Mathematics

ATHLETIC PROFILE

Conference Affiliation: Big West Conference
Program Profile: NCAA 56-game schedule from first week of February to middle of May. Play at Titan Field located in Southern California on CSF campus with state of the art message/scoreboard. Titan Field was opened in 1992 with CSF alum Kevin Costner throwing out the first pitch.
History: Division I play began in 1975. 1997 will mark 23rd season of CSF baseball. Titans have been to 16 Regional tournaments and 8 College World Series in 20 years. With new playing facilities, CSF hopes to host its first NCAA Regional Tournament.

Achievements: 1995 won NCAA College World Series, ranked #1 most of the year, won Big West Regular Season Title. 1994 Daunte Powell 1st round draft choice (SF Giants); 14 Conference Titles in 20 years, 18 players graduated to the major league; 1979 and 1984 NCAA Champions; 1992 Runner-UP; Phil Nevin won the Golden Spikes Awards, was a World Series MVP, drafted 1st by the Houston and played in the 1992 Summer Olympics in Barcelona.

California State University - Hayward

25800 Carlos Bee Boulevard
Hayward, CA 94542
Coach: Dirk Morrison
Email: dmorris@csuhayward.edu

NCAA II
Pioneers/Red, Black
Phone: (510) 885-3046
Fax: (510) 885-2282

ACADEMIC

Founded: 1957
Religion: Non-Affiliated
Web-site: http://www.csuhayward.edu/
Student/Faculty Ratio: 4:1
Undergraduate Enrollment: 9,800
Type: 4 Yr., Public, Liberal Arts, Coed
Campus Housing: Yes
SAT/ACT/GPA: 1300/30/2.0
Male/Female Ratio: 8:5
Graduate Enrollment: 2,700
Scholarships/Academic: Yes **Athletic:** No **Fin Aid:** Yes
Total Expenses by: Year **In State:** $ 3,500 **Out of State:** $ 6,000
Degrees Conferred: BA, BS, MA, MS, MBA
Programs of Study: Biology, Business, Chemistry, Communications, Computer, Criminal, Dramatic Art, Ecology, Economics, English, Environmental, Ethnic, Management, Math, Nursing, Philosophy, Physical, Recreation, Statistics, Taxation

ATHLETIC PROFILE

Conference Affiliation: Independent Conference
Program Profile: entering first year as a NCAA III Independent program. Play on excellent field with a new batting facility in progress. Team fieldhouse next to the field.
History: Presviously participated as a Division I freshmen from the State of California. Schedue includes Division I, II and III programs and a roster of no more than 22 players.
Achievements: 1987 Northern California Coach of the Year; John Toven 2nd Base was named All-Region in 1996; Kevin Clemens Pitcher was named All-Region in 1994.
Coaching: Dirk Morrison, Head Coach. Oscar Miller, Assistant Coach. Abel Alcantar, Assistant.
Roster for 1998 team/In State: 22 **Out of State:** 0 **Out of Country:** 0
Total Number of Varsity/Jr. Varsity: 22 **Percent of Graduation:** 90%
Number of Seniors on 1998 Team: 2 **Most Recent Record:** 18-28-0
Number of Fall Games: 5 **Number of Spring Games:** 40
Positions Needed for 1999/2000: Shortstop, Centerfield, Catcher, Left Handed Pitcher
Baseball Camp Dates: December Hitting Camp, March Skills Camp
Schedule: San Jose State, Sacramento State, Chico State, UC-Davis, Sonoma State, Georgetown
Style of Play: Pevent the big inning on offense and play for the big inning on defense. Situational and short game offense and keep double play in order on defense.

California State University - Long Beach

1250 Bellflower Blvd.
Long Beach, CA 90840
Coach: Dave Snow

NCAA I
49ers/Black, Gold
Phone: (562) 985-4661
Fax: (562) 985-8197

ACADEMIC

Founded: 1949
Religion: Non-Affiliated
Web-site: Not Available
Undergraduate Enrollment: 27,431
Type: 2 Yr., Public, Jr. College, Coed
Campus Housing: Yes
SAT/ACT/GPA: 820/2.5
Graduate Enrollment: None

Scholarships/Academic: Yes **Athletic:** Yes **Fin Aid:** Yes
Total Expenses by: Year **In State:** $ 7,625 **Out of State:** $ 11,761
Degrees Conferred: Associates
Programs of Study: Accounting, Anthropology, Banking/Finance, Biological Science, Botany, Business, Engineering, Design, Dietetics, Dramatics Arts, Geography, Geology, Industrial, Interdisciplinary, Religion, Vocational Science, Zoology

ATHLETIC PROFILE

Estimated Number of Baseball Scholarships: 11.7
Conference Affiliation: Big West Conference
Program Profile: The team plays on Blair Field which is grass and has a measurements of 348', 400', and 348'. Has a seating capacity of 3,600 and has lights.
History: The program began in 1989 to the present under Coach Dave Snow.
Achievements: NCAA consecutive Regional Appearance; Big West Champs in 1989, 1992, 1993, 1994, 1996, 1997, and 1998; College World Series in 1989, 1991, 1993, and 1998. Dave Snow was named NCAA Coach of the Year in 1986 and 1989.
Coaching: Dave Snow, Head Coach, started the program at Long Beach State University. He was named NCAA Coach of the Year in 1986 and 1989. He was an Olympic assistant coach in 1992 and 1996. Mike Weather, Assistant Coach, started coaching in 1993 to the present. Jim Yogi, Assistant Coach, began as an assistant in 1990 to the present. He is also the recruiting coordinator.
Roster for 1998 team/In State: 32 **Out of State:** 1 **Out of Country:** 0
Total Number of Varsity/Jr. Varsity: 33 **Percent of Graduation:** 40%
Number of Seniors on 1998 Team: 10 **Number of Sophomores on 1998 Team:** 6
Freshmen Receiving Fin Aid/Athletic: 8 **Number of Spring Games:** 56
Most Recent Record: 43 - 23 - 1 **Baseball Camp Dates:** Year-round
Positions Needed for 1999/2000: OF, Pitcher, 3rd Base
Schedule: USC, California-Fullerton, Miami, Wichita State, Arkansas, UCLA, Baylor
Style of Play: "Dirt Bags"

California State University - Los Angeles

5151 State University Drive
Los Angeles, CA 90032
Coach: John Herbold

NCAA II
Golden Eagles/Black, Gold
Phone: (213) 343-3080
Fax: (213) 343-3199

ACADEMIC

Founded: 1947 **Type:** 4 Yr., Public, Coed
Web-site: http://www.calstatela.edu/ **Campus Housing:** Yes
Student/Faculty Ratio: 20:1 **Male/Female Ratio:** 40:60
Undergraduate Enrollment: 16,000 **Graduate Enrollment:** 3,000
Scholarships/Academic: Yes **Athletic:** Yes **Fin Aid:** Yes
Total Expenses by: Year **In State:** $ 7,250 **Out of State:** $ 13,154
Degrees Conferred: BS, BA, MS, MA, PhD
Programs of Study: 50 Academic departments and divisions. Liberal Arts, Physical Sciences, Social Sciences, Business, Education, Physical Education

ATHLETIC PROFILE

Estimated Number of Baseball Scholarships: 5
Conference Affiliation: California Collegiate Athletic Conference
Program Profile: We are a Division II program which plays a great number of Division I games. We have lights and good weather.We are 23rd on the all-time draft list. We probably lead the nation in undrafted high school players coming here and signing as a juniors.
History: Began its baseball program in 1950 as an independent. Was a Division I program for many years. Tough league; we do not redshirt, emphasizing mainly local incoming high school seniors.
Achievements: Won league last two years; 7 players playing pro ball now; 3 players drafted last year - two of them junior (round two and 14); 1 senior signed - 8th round; 1 signed - was undrafted.

Coaching: John Herbold, Head Coach, 1984 to the present, ABCA Hall of Fame; member high school coach. Has 28 years coaching experience; 15 years at CSU-LA; over 100 players placed in pro-ball. Dave Soliz, Assistant Coach.
Roster for 1998 team/In State: 29 **Out of State:** 0 **Out of Country:** 0
Total Number of Varsity/Jr. Varsity: 27 **Percent of Graduation:** 80%
Number of Seniors on 1998 Team: 4 **Number of Sophomores on 1998 Team:** 11
Freshmen Receiving Fin Aid/Athletic: 3 **Academic:** 2
Most Recent Record: 20 - 29 - 0 **Number of Spring Games:** 56
Positions Needed for 1999/2000: 2 Pitchers, 2 Outfielders (maybe!)
Schedule: USC, Loyola, San Diego State, Lewis and Clark, Grand Canyon
Style of Play: We play pretty much a professional style of baseball - not much "little ball". We do not encourage transfer, and we rarely red-shirt if ever. Two years ago we faced five Division I All-American pitchers from USC, UCLA, and UOP.

California State University- Northridge

18111 Nordhoff Street
Northridge, CA 91330-8276
Coach: Mike Batesol

NCAA I
Matadors/Red, White, Black
Phone: (818) 677-7055
Fax: (818) 677-4762

ACADEMIC

Founded: 1958
Religion: Non-Affiliated
Web-site: http://www.csub.edu/
Student/Faculty Ratio: 24:1
Undergraduate Enrollment: 15,700
Type: 4 Yr., Public, Liberal Arts, Coed
Campus Housing: Yes
SAT/ACT/GPA: NCAA Minimum
Male/Female Ratio: 45:55
Graduate Enrollment: 11,500
Scholarships/Academic: Yes **Athletic:** Yes **Fin Aid:** Yes
Total Expenses by: Year **In State:** $ 7,000 **Out of State:** $ 12,500
Degrees Conferred: BA, BS, BM, MA, MS, MBA
Programs of Study: Accounting, Anthropology, Astrophysics, Banking/Finance, Biochemistry, Biology, Broadcasting, Business, Chemistry, Computer, Criminology, Dietetics, Earth Science, Economics, Engineering, Seismology, Religion, Etc.

ATHLETIC PROFILE

Conference Affiliation: Independent Conference
Program Profile: Cal State Northridge is an NCAA Division IA member who will compete as an independent in 1997. The Matadors won the Western Athletic Conference title in 1996, their final season as a member of the WAC. CS Northridge plays its home games at the 1,200 seat Matador Field. The field, which originally opened in 1961, had a brand new scoreboard installed prior to the 1996 season.
History: The Matador Baseball program is entering its 28th year in existence at CS Northridge. The school's all-time baseball record heading into 1997 is 1125-825-18 and Cal State Northridge has participated in NCAA postseason play 18 times. A program with a rich history of sending players on to the major league level, Cal State Northridge had five players taken in the 1996 major league draft.
Achievements: The 1996 UCS Northridge squad, the last to compete as a member of the Western Athletic Conference, had a year to remember as the Runner-Up at the NCAA West Regional at Stanford. The team was led by first year head coach Mike Batesole and WAC Co-Player of the Year-catcher Robert Fick.
Coaching: Mike Batesole, Head Coach, entering his third season as a head coach, posted a record of 52-18 in his first season and won a league championship. He is a 1990 graduate of Cal Fullerton.
Style of Play: A good power hitting team which also features speed through the line-up. The team hits to all fields for power. however they can score runs both with power and their heads up play on the basepaths.

California State University - Sacramento

6000 J. Street
Sacramento, CA 95819
Coach: John Smith

NCAA I
hornets/Green, Gold
Phone: (916) 278-7225
Fax: (916) 278-6481

ACADEMIC

Founded: 1947
Religion: Non-Affiliated
Web-site: http://www.csus.edu/
Student/Faculty Ratio: 8:1
Undergraduate Enrollment: 20,000
Scholarships/Academic: Yes **Athletic:** Yes
Total Expenses by: Year **In State:** $ 7,000
Degrees Conferred: BA, BS, MBA, MS

Type: 4 Yr., Public, Liberal Arts, Coed
Campus Housing: Yes
SAT/ACT/GPA: 820/ 18
Male/Female Ratio: 48:52
Graduate Enrollment: 4,000
Fin Aid: Yes
Out of State: $ 14,000

Programs of Study: Accounting, Anthropology, Art, Biochemistry, Biology, Business, Chemistry, Communication, Computer Science,Criminal Justice, Education, Finance, Engineering, Geography, Journalism, Nursing, Physics, Political Science, Prelaw, Philosophy, Microbiology

California State University - San Bernardino

5500 University Parkway
San Bernadino, CA 92407
Coach: Don Parnell

NCAA II
Coyotes/Lt. Blue, Brown
Phone: (909) 880-5021
Fax: (909) 880-5984

ACADEMIC

Founded: 1965
Religion: Non-Affiliated
Web-site: http://www.csusb.edu/
Student/Faculty Ratio: 18:1
Undergraduate Enrollment: 10,000
Scholarships/Academic: Yes **Athletic:** Yes
Total Expenses by: Year **In State:** $ 7,943
Degrees Conferred: Bachelors, Masters

Type: 4 Yr., Public, Coed
Campus Housing: Yes
SAT/ACT/GPA: 820+ varies w/GPA/
Male/Female Ratio: 40:60
Graduate Enrollment: 3,059
Fin Aid: Yes
Out of State: $ 13,847

Programs of Study: Accounting, Afro-American Studies, American Studies, Anthropology, Art, Biochemistry, Biological Science, Business Administration, Chemistry, Child Psychology, Communications, Computer Science, Creative Writing, Criminal Justice, Dietetics, Economics, English, Enviromental Studies, Finance, French, Geography, Geology, Graphic Art, Health Services Adminstration, Health Education, Health Science, History, Humanities, Human Development, Human Services, Information Science, Interdisciplinary Studies, Liberal Arts, Management, Management Information Systems, Marketing, Mathematics, Music, Natural Science, Nursing, Nutrition

ATHLETIC PROFILE

Conference Affiliation: California Collegiate Athletic Conference

California State University - Stanislaus

801 West Monte Vista Avenue
Turlock, CA 95382
Coach: Mark de la Motte
Email: mdelamot@toto.csu stani.edu

NCAA II
Warriors/Red, Gold
Phone: (209) 667-3272
Fax: (209) 667-3084

ACADEMIC

Founded: 1961
Type: 4 Yr., Public, Liberal Arts, Coed
Web-site: http://wwwlead.csustan.edu/
SAT/ACT/GPA: 820
Student/Faculty Ratio: 18:1
Male/Female Ratio: 40:60
Undergraduate Enrollment: 4,500
Graduate Enrollment: 1,500
Scholarships/Academic: Yes **Athletic:** No
Fin Aid: Yes
Total Expenses by: Year **In State:** $ 7,000 **Out of State:** $ 14,000
Degrees Conferred: BA, BS, MA, MS, MBA
Programs of Study: Accounting, Anthropology, Applied Mathematics, Art, Bilingual Education, Biology, Botony, Business, Chemistry, Communications, Computer Information Systems, Entomolgy, Criminal Justice, Environmental Studies, History, International Studies, Journalism, Liberal Arts, Physics, Prelaw, Premed, Prevet, Spanish, Statistics, Theatre, Urban Studies

ATHLETIC PROFILE

Conference Affiliation: CCAA
Program Profile: The team has a four weeks fall season and a 56 game schedule in the spring. Facilities include 3 full cages, machines, & grass field which has a measurements of 340 - 380 - 340.
History: Team began to play in 1965. In 1976 and 1977 won NCAA Division III National Champs.
Achievements: NCAA Division III National Champs; 18 All-Americans; 18 Players signed professional contracts.
Coaching: Mark de la Motte, Head Coach. Greg Wakefield, Assistant. Jason Pherson, Assistant.
Style of Play: Aggressive, hit and run; bunt.

Cañada College

4200 Farm Hill Boulevard
Redwood City, CA 94061
Coach: Mike Garcia
CCC
Colts/Forest Green, Gold, White
Phone: (650) 306-3275
Fax: (650) 306-3390

ACADEMIC

Founded: 1971
Type: 4 Yr., Public, Coed
Religion: Not-Affiliated
Campus Housing: Yes
Student/Faculty Ratio: 15:1
Male/Female Ratio: 50:50
Undergraduate Enrollment: 5,000
Graduate Enrollment: None
Scholarships/Academic: **Athletic:** No
Fin Aid: Yes
Degrees Conferred: AA
Programs of Study: Almost all areas of study available

ATHLETIC PROFILE

Conference Affiliation: Coast Conference
Program Profile: Colt's field is natural grass and has a seating capacity of 1,000. California Junior College playing season start on February 1and goes through May 29. Field has measurements of 320, 310, 400, 310, and 320.
History: Program began in 1970. In 1971 California State Champions; 8 Conference Championships (1971, 9175, 1979, 1989, 1991, 1994, 1996, and 1997. State Tournament Qualifiers in 1989, 1990, 1991, 1992, 1993, 1994, 1995, 1996, and 1997.
Achievements: Mike Garcia Conference Coach of the Year in 1996 and 1997; Felepe Alou, Jr., Moises Alou, Bobby Bonds, Jr., Ali Cepeda were All drafted out of Canada, and sons of former MLB player. Domingo/Gary Mota; current MLB are Kevin Jordan-2 Base - Phillies, Moises Alou-Outfielder - Marins, Rafael Bourngtl-Shosrtstop - A'S.
Coaching: Mike Garcia, Head Coach, started from 1985 to the present. He compiled a record of 301-152 (.664). JC All-American at Canada in 1976; team captain @ California State - Fullerton; NCAA Champions in 1979. He played five years of pro baseball with the Atlanta Braves in 1979-1984. Bob Freschi, Assistant Coach. Steve Buhaquias, Assistant Coach.
Style of Play: Play at a " High Speed" with a relaxed intensity.

Cerritos Community College

11110 Alondra Boulevard
Norwalk, CA 90650
Coach: Ken Gaylord

CCCCA
Falcons/Blue, White
Phone: (562) 860-2451x2890
Fax: (562) 467-5009

ACADEMIC

Founded: 1956
Type: 2 Yr., Public, Jr. College, Coed
Religion: Non-Affiliated
Campus Housing: No
Student/Faculty Ratio: 30:1
Undergraduate Enrollment: 20,717
Programs of Study: General Studies

Chaffey College

5885 Haven Avenue
Alta Loma, CA 91737
Coach: Chuck Deagle

CCCCA
Panthers/Red, Black
Phone: (909) 941-2345
Fax: (909) 466-2808

ACADEMIC

Founded: 1883
Type: 2 Yr., Public, Coed
Undergraduate Enrollment: 12,651
Campus Housing: No
Student/Faculty Ratio: 28:1
Male/Female Ratio: 39:61
Scholarships/Academic: No **Athletic:** No **Fin Aid:** Yes
Total Expenses by: Year **In State:** $ Varies **Out of State:** $ 3,600
Degrees Conferred: Associate
Programs of Study: Accounting, Anthropology, Art, Automotive, biological Science, Broadcasting, Business, Chemistry, Computer, Corrections, Drafting/Design, food, Geology, Gerontology, History, Marketing, Nursing, Philosophy, Photography, Religion, Telecommunications, Theatre

ATHLETIC PROFILE

Conference Affiliation: Foothill Conference
Program Profile: Campus Field has natural grass. Play from February 1 to May 5.
Achievements: Coach of the Year Honors - None; All-American.
Coaching: Chuck Deagle, Head Coach, Masters degree (Head and Assistant Coach), head and assistant coach - 28 years of coaching experience.
Style of Play: Bunt and run. Hit and run.

Chapman University

333 N. Glassell Street
Orange, CA 92866
Coach: Rex Peters

NCAA III
Panthers/Cardinal, Grey
Phone: (714) 997-6662
Fax: (714) 532-6010

ACADEMIC

Founded: 1864
Type: 4 Yr., Private, Liberal Arts, Coed
Religion: Disciples of Christ
Campus Housing: Yes
Web-site: http://www.chapman.edu/
SAT/ACT/GPA: 900/19/2.5
Student/Faculty Ratio: 11:1
Male/Female Ratio: 3:2
Undergraduate Enrollment: 2,299
Graduate Enrollment: 1,114
Scholarships/Academic: Yes **Athletic:** No **Fin Aid:** Yes
Total Expenses by: Year **In State:** $ 27,000 **Out of State:** $ 27,000
Degrees Conferred: BA, BS, BFA, BM, MA, MS, MBA, MFA

Programs of Study: Accounting, American Studies, Art, Biology, Business and Economics, Communication, Criminal Justice, Education, Liberal Studies, Music, Movement and Exercise Sciences, Languages, Philosophy, Psychology, Religion, Social Science

ATHLETIC PROFILE

Conference Affiliation: Independent Conference
Program Profile: The Chapman Baseball is a program on the rise. We are currently ranked nationally in Division III baseball. 1997 Western Regional Champions; Panthers' home field is called Hart Park in the City of Orange. It seats 300 people , has a natural grass playing surface and is equipped with lights.
History: The program began in 1939. National Champions 1966 and 1968. 20 All-Americans, 85 players have signed pro contracts, including CY Young winner Randy Jones.
Achievements: Coach Peters was named 1997 Western Region Coach of the Year; 1997 Western Regional Champions; Division III Cale Sheperd, Division III 2nd team All-American.
Coaching: Rex Peters, Head Coach, was named 1997 Western Region Coach of the Year. Fred Hoover, Assistant Coach, is in his 4th year as the pitching coach at Chapman. He was the head baseball coach at Golden West Junior College from 1966-1988 (7 championships). He was an assistant coach at University of California-Irvine and California Fullerton. Mitch Charles, Assistant Coach, is in his first year at Chapman. He coached at Golden West Junior College in 1997 and played at Cal Poly Pomona.
Style of Play: The Chapman baseball program play an aggressive style of baseball, including the little game. The main emphasis is on pitching and defense.

Citrus Community College

1000 West Foothill
Glendora, CA 91740
Coach: Skip Claprood

CCCJC
Fighting Owls/Royal, White
Phone: (626) 914-8656
Fax: (626) 914-8656

ACADEMIC

Founded: 1915
Type: 2 Yr., Public, Coed
Undergraduate Enrollment: 10,488
Student/Faculty Ratio: 22:1
Scholarships/Academic: No **Athletic:** No **Fin Aid:** Yes
Total Expenses by: Year **In State:** $ 400 **Out of State:** $ 3,600
Degrees Conferred: Association
Programs of Study: Automotive, Behavioral, Biological, Business, Computer, Cosmetology, Criminal Justice, Drafting/Design, Electrical/Electronics, English, Engineering, Journalism, Law, Modern Languages, Music, Natural Science, Photography, Real Estate, Water Resources

ATHLETIC PROFILE

Conference Affiliation: Foothill Conference
Program Profile: Sunken-diamond, concrete dug-outs, natural grass, scoreboard, four tunnels, two covered bull-pens, and 2 covered tunnels.
History: The program is one of the oldest in the nation , it began in 1927; won championships in every conference it has been a member; 16 championships since 1973; 6 in the last 8 years.
Achievements: Coach Claprood has received Coach of the Year honors eight times; 16 All-Americans; 130 dug-outs; 5 first round; 11 to the big league; lecturer on four continents.
Coaching: Skip Claprood, Head Coach, Coach of the Year honors 8 times. He compiled a record of 661-320; he served as a head coach at Chaffey College where he led them to Conference Titles in 1993 and 1995. Pat Woods, Assistant Coach, Oxnard College, reached playoffs three years, and one title. Sean Severns and Mike Salazar, Assistant Coach.
Roster for 1998 team/In State: 26 **Out of State:** 2 **Out of Country:** 0
Total Number of Varsity/Jr. Varsity: 28 **Percent of Graduation:** 85%
Number of Seniors on 1998 Team: 16 **Number of Sophomores on 1998 Team:** 0
Number of Fall Games: 30 **Number of Spring Games:** 42
Style of Play: Pressure oriented - executive. **Most Recent Record:** 32 - 12 - 0

Claremont - Mudds - Scrips College

500 East 9th Street
Claremont, CA 91711-6400
Coach: Randy Town

NCAA III
Stags/Cardinal, Gold, White
Phone: (909) 607-3796
Fax: (909) 621-8848

ACADEMIC

Founded: 1946
Type: 4 Yr., Private, Coed, Engineering
Religion: Non-Affiliated
Campus Housing: Yes
Web-site: http://www.mckenna.edu - www.scrippscol.edu
SAT/ACT/GPA: 1200/3.5
Student/Faculty Ratio: 10:1
Male/Female Ratio: 60:40
Undergraduate Enrollment: 2,000
Graduate Enrollment: N/A
Scholarships/Academic: Yes **Athletic:** No
Fin Aid: Yes
Total Expenses by: Year **In State:** $ 27,000 **Out of State:** $ 27,000
Degrees Conferred: BA, BS
Programs of Study: Business, Economics, English, Letters/Literature, Mathematics, Multi/Interdisciplinary Studies, Psychology, Social Sciences, Sciences

ATHLETIC PROFILE

Conference Affiliation: Southern California Intercollegiate Athletic Conference
Program Profile: Academic program devoted to baseball. Strong schedule (40 games), January - May, an outstanding. Playing surface (infield redone in 1998) with a seating capacity of 250.
History: Program was founded by Bill Arce in 1958 to the present. Strong winning tradition; 6 league championships. The first baseball coach and long time athletics director, nurtured the success and winning tradition of the program. We have had five head coaches: previous coach Pat Murphy (1986-1987) now pitches the Arizona State Team. We have had 16 All-Americans and 4 pro contracts, most formerly being Wes Packer.
Achievements: Randy Town was a Coach of the Year in 1996; had two All-Americans in 1996 (RHP and OF); & 1 first team All-American in 1997 (OF); last played to signed a pro contracts was in 1991.
Coaching: Randy Town, Head Coach, entering 12th season with the program; Coach of the Year in 1996. Has a ten years of coaching experience. He is a former right hand pitcher from the Cincinnati Reds Organization. Ray Eberle, Assistant Coach, entering his third season. Uman Vasquez, Assistant, entering his third season. Jack Helber, Assistant, former Legion Coach of Mark Maguire.
Roster for 1998 team/In State: 18 **Out of State:** 7 **Out of Country:** 0
Total Number of Varsity/Jr. Varsity: 26 **Percent of Graduation:** 100%
Number of Seniors on 1998 Team: 3 **Most Recent Record:** 17 - 21 - 1
Freshmen Receiving Fin Aid/Athletic: 0 **Academic:** 7
Number of Fall Games: 0 **Number of Spring Games:** 40
Positions Needed for 1999/2000: Pitcher, Outfielder
Baseball Camp Dates: Christmas; December 28-30; June
Schedule: Eastern Connecticut, Montclair, Linfield, Chapman, California Lutheran, Lewis and Clark
Style of Play: Aggressive, nature with the "put pressure on opponents; defense attitudes.

College of Marin

835 College Avenue
Kentfield, CA 94904
Coach: Tom Harrington

CCCCA
Mariners/Gold, Black
Phone: (415) 485-9589
Fax: (415) 453-4187

ACADEMIC

Founded: 1926
Type: 2 Yr., Public, Coed
Student/Faculty Ratio: 19:1
Male/Female Ratio: 38:62
Undergraduate Enrollment: 8,845
SAT/ACT/GPA: Open
Scholarships/Academic: No **Athletic:** No
Fin Aid: Yes

Total Expenses by: Year **In State:** $ 450 **Out of State:** $ 3,900
Degrees Conferred: Associate
Programs of Study: Accounting, Architecture, Art, Automotive, Behavioral Science, Biology, Business, Computer, Court Reporting, Dental, Ecology, Engineering, Geology, Humanities, Design, Landscape, Law, Marketing, Natural Science, Real Estate, Retail Sociology, Theatre

ATHLETIC PROFILE

Conference Affiliation: Bay Valley, Coast Conference

College of the Sequoias

915 South Mooney Blvd
Visalia, CA 93277
Coach: Jody Allen

CCCCA
Giants/Blue, Orange
Phone: (209) 730-3911
Fax: (209) 730-3894

ACADEMIC

Founded: 1925
Type: 2 Yr., Public, Coed
Undergraduate Enrollment: 9,500
Campus Housing: No
Student/Faculty Ratio: 20:1
Male/Female Ratio: 44:56
Scholarships/Academic: No **Athletic:** No **Fin Aid:** Yes
Total Expenses by: Year **In State:** $ 450 **Out of State:** $ 3,800
Programs of Study: Agriculture, Architecture, Art, Automotive, Business, Carpentry, Communications, Community Services, Construction, Criminal Justice, Deaf Interpreter Training, Engineering, English, History, Heating/Refrigeration/Air Conditioning, Horticulture, Law, Science

College of the Siskiyous

800 College Ave
Weed, CA 96094
Coach: Steve Neele

CJCAA
Hustlin' Eagles/Scarlet, White, Navy
Phone: (530) 938-5231
Fax: (530) 938-5228

ACADEMIC

Founded: 1960
Type: 2 Yr., Public, Coed
Religion: Not-Affiliated
Campus Housing: No
Student/Faculty Ratio: 10:1
Male/Female Ratio: 1:1
Undergraduate Enrollment: 3,000
Graduate Enrollment: None
Scholarships/Academic: No **Athletic:** No **Fin Aid:** Yes
Total Expenses by: Year **In State:** $ 3,390 **Out of State:** $ 5,500
Degrees Conferred: AS
Programs of Study: Fire Science, Criminal Justice, Physical Education, Nursing, General Education

ATHLETIC PROFILE

Conference Affiliation: Golden Valley Conference
Program Profile: One of the best on campus Junior College facilities that you can find. All grass field with dirt cutouts in box areas. Excellent hitting background - 'A Pitchers Park' (dimensions 340-380-400). Breathtaking view of Mount Shasta next to the field - Rival Part of California. Access to indoor tunnel. Year-round program with great weather Annual Arizona Spring break trip.
History: The program began in 1965. A program on the rise - good promise for 1997 season which includes an annual Arizona Spring Break trip.
Achievements: 2 players in major leagues: Mark Acre, Oakland A's (RHP); Dean Hatgraves, Atlanta Braves (LHP).

Concordia University - Irvine

1530 Concordia West
Irvine, CA 92715
Coach: Jackie Schniepp

NAIA
Eagles/Green, Black
Phone: (714) 854-8002
Fax: (714) 854-6771

ACADEMIC

Founded: 1972
Type: 4 Yr., Private, Liberal Arts, Coed
Religion: Lutheran
Campus Housing: Yes
Web-site: http://www.cui.edu/
SAT/ACT/GPA: 800/18/2.5
Student/Faculty Ratio: 15:1
Male/Female Ratio: 1:2
Undergraduate Enrollment: 800
Graduate Enrollment: 400
Scholarships/Academic: Yes **Athletic:** Yes **Fin Aid:** Yes
Total Expenses by: Year **In State:** $ 18,600 **Out of State:** $ 18,600
Degrees Conferred: BA, Masters
Programs of Study: Art, Behavioral Science, Biology, Business Administration, Communications, Elementary Education, English, History, Mathematics, Music, Liberal Studies, Prelaw, Humanities, Religion, Psychology, Sport Management

ATHLETIC PROFILE

Conference Affiliation: Golden State Athletic Conference
Program Profile: Play at level above NCAA Division II schools. Play on a natural surface, have full hitting facility. Weather allows for year-round practices.
History: First year of the program was in 1988.
Coaching: Jackie Schniepp, Head Coach, entering seventh season at the helm of the CU baseball program and after the team's 15th win in 1997, he has become Concordia's winningest baseball coach. He has successfully coached both the NCAA Division I and Division II levels and has led his teams to championships as a player. He is an insightful teacher and brings a sharp mind to the mental challenges and strategies of the game. Graduated from Westmont College in 1989 with a degree in Social Science and thus concluded and exceptional four-year playing career as a catcher. Tom Kelly, Assistant Coach, begins sixth season as the top assistant with the Eagles. He brings a deep commitment and dedication to the program and to the student-athletes. A former pitcher himself at Concordia, he is now solely responsible for the development of the pitching staff.
Style of Play: Our teams are characterized by good pitching, defense, and execution style offense, discipline approach.

Contra Costa College

2600 Mission Bell Drive
San Pablo, CA 94806
Coach: Marvin Webb

CCCCA
Comets/Blue, White
Phone: (510) 235-7800
Fax: (510) 234-1575

ACADEMIC

Founded: 1948
Type: 2 Yr., Public, Coed
Student/Faculty Ratio: 13:1
Campus Housing: No
Undergraduate Enrollment: 3,000
Graduate Enrollment: None
Total Expenses by: Year **In State:** $ Varies **Out of State:** $ 3,750+
Degrees Conferred: Associate
Programs of Study: Anthropology, Art, Fine Arts, Automotive Technology, Biology, Biological Science, Chemistry, Computer Programming, Computer Science, Criminal Jusitce, Culinary Arts, Emergency Medical Technology, Early Childhood Education, History, Home Economics, Engineering, Food Services Management, Human Services, Geography, Geology, Health Science, History, Hotel and Restaurant Mangement

Cypress College

9200 Valley View Street
Cypress, CA 90630
Coach: Scott Pickler

NJCAA
Chargers/Navy, Grey, White
Phone: (714) 821-7870
Fax: (714) 826-7620

ACADEMIC

Founded: 1966
Religion: Non-Affiliated
Undergraduate Enrollment: 14,600+
Total Expenses by: Year **In State:** $ 450
Degrees Conferred: Associate

Type: 2 Yr., Public, Coed
Campus Housing: No
Graduate Enrollment: None
Out of State: $ 4,000

Programs of Study: Anthropology, Arts, Fine Arts, Applied Art, Automotive Technology, Aviation Administration, Biology, Biological Science, Commerce, Management, Chemistry, Computer Science, Court Reporting, Dance, Data Processing, Dental Services, Economics, Engineering, Food Services Management, Human Services, Geography, Geology, Health Science, History, Hotel/Restaurant

ATHLETIC PROFILE

Conference Affiliation: Orange Empire Conference
Program Profile: Team has a clubhouse and three full cages for practice.
History: History of the program include the 1991 State Champions, 1994 State Champions, and the 1997 State Champions.
Achievements: Has 60 Drafted players in 13 years; has 88 scholarship to four years program in the past ten years.
Coaching: Scott Pickler, Head Coach. Bill Pinkham, Assistant Coach.
Style of Play: " Class "; aggressive.

De Anza College

21250 Stevens Creek Boulevard
Cupertino, CA 95014
Coach: Scott Hertler

CCCCA
Dons/Cardinal, Gold
Phone: (408) 864-8741
Fax: (408) 864-5419

ACADEMIC

Founded: 1967
Web-site: http://www.deanza.edu
Undergraduate Enrollment: 24,000
Scholarships/Academic: Yes **Athletic:** No
Total Expenses by: Year **In State:** $ Varies
Degrees Conferred: Associate Arts, Certificate programs

Type: 2 Yr., Public, Coed
Student/Faculty Ratio: 24:1
Male/Female Ratio: 48:52
Fin Aid: Yes
Out of State: $ Varies

Programs of Study: Administration of Justice, Advertising, Aero/Aviation, Afro-American Studies, Agricultural Sciences, Anthropology, Architecture, Art, Behavioral Sciences, Biochemistry, Botany, Business Adminsitration, Chemical Engineering, Chemistry, Chicano Studies, Child Development, Criminal Justice, Dentistry, Design, Development Studies, Ecology and Evolution, Economics, Engineering, Engineering Technology, English, Environmental Design, Environmental Studies, Enthic Studies, Forest Product, Forestry, French, Geography, Geology, Earth Science, German, Government, Home Economics, Industrial Arts, Law, Legal Studies, Italian, Mathematics, Liberal Studies, Microbiology, Music, Nursing, Physical Eduation, Philosophy, Physical Therapy, Political

ATHLETIC PROFILE

Conference Affiliation: Coast Conference

Lassen College

P.O. Box 3000
Susanville, CA 96130
Coach: Glen Yonan

CCC
Cougars/Black, Orange
Phone: (530) 251-8815
Fax: (530) 938-8964

ACADEMIC

Founded: 1925
Type: 2 Yr., Jr. College, Coed
Undergraduate Enrollment: 2,951
Student/Faculty Ratio: 15:1
Total Expenses by: Year **In State:** $ Varies **Out of State:** $ 3,990+
Programs of Study: Liberal Arts, Business, General Studies

ATHLETIC PROFILE

Conference Affiliation: Golden Valley Conference
Program Profile: Home games are played at Memorial Ballpark which has natural grass and measures 340-390-375-320. It has a seating capacity of 750.
History: Program exists for the last ten years ('88-'97). Made the playoffs for ten straight years, including seven conference titles and three runner-up. Advanced to a regional for the last five consecutive years including trips to the Final Four in 1994 and 1996.
Achievements: All Americans in from 1988 to 1997: Mike McCallum in 1988, Chad Debensky in 1990, Cliff Shanks in 1992, Jeff Leaman in 1993, Toby Larson in 1993, Chris Webb in 1994, Ryan Sheets in 1994, Scott Dewitt in 1995, Jim Fritz in 1995. Conference Titles in 1988, 1990, 1992, 1993, 1994, 1995, and 1995.
Coaching: Glen Yonan, Head Coach, 1990-1995 assistant coach at Lassen College; 1996-1997 Head Coach at Lassen College. John Deal - Assistant Coach, was an assistant coach for 13 years at Lassen College; Cort Cortez, Assistant Coach, was an assistant coach at Lassen College for five years; Bryan Neagle, Assistant Coach, was an assistant coach at College of the Redwoods, Eureka, CA for 2 years and three years at Lassen College; Carl Johnson, Assistant Coach, two years assistant at Lassen College; Casey Johnson - Assistant, one year coach at Lassen College.

Long Beach City College

4901 East Carson Street
Long Beach, CA 90808
Coach: Casey Crook

CCCCA
Vikings/Red, White, Black
Phone: (562) 938-4242
Fax: (562) 420-4638

ACADEMIC

Founded: 1927
Type: 4 Yr., Public, Coed
Undergraduate Enrollment: 25,100
Campus Housing: No
Student/Faculty Ratio: 32:1
Male/Female Ratio: 46:54
Scholarships/Academic: No **Athletic:** No **Fin Aid:** Yes
Total Expenses by: Year **In State:** $ 450+ **Out of State:** $ 3,600
Degrees Conferred: Associates
Programs of Study: Accounting, Advertising, Architectural, Art, Automotive, Aviation, Biology, Clothing/Textiles, Fashion Design/Technology, Flight Training, General Engineering, Horticulture, Insurance, Interior, Photography, Retail, Theatre, Travel/Tourism, Welding

Los Angeles Pierce College

6201 Winnetka Avenue
Woodland Hills, CA 91371
Coach: Bob Lofrano

CCCCA
Brahmas/Red, White
Phone: (818) 716-8850
Fax: (818) 710-4143

ACADEMIC

Founded: 1947
Web-site: http://www.lapc.cc.ca.us
Student/Faculty Ratio: 35:1
Undergraduate Enrollment: 18,212
Scholarships/Academic: No **Athletic:** No
Total Expenses by: Year **In State:** $ Varies
Degrees Conferred: Associate
Type: 2 Yr., Public, Coed
Campus Housing: No
Male/Female Ratio: 46:54
Graduate Enrollment: None
Fin Aid: Yes
Out of State: $ 4,100
Programs of Study: Accounting, Anthropology, Art, Behavioral Science, Business, Commercial Art, Computer, Construction, Deaf Interpreter, Engineering, Equestrian Studies, Illustration, Landscape, Natural Science, Photography, Theatre, Real Estate, Welding

Los Medanos College

2700 E Leland Road
Pittsburg, CA 94565
Coach: Mike Duitsman
CCBA
Mustangs/Cardinal, Gold
Phone: (925) 439-2185
Fax: (925) 427-1599

ACADEMIC

Founded: 1971
Religion: Not-Affiliated
Student/Faculty Ratio: 30:1
Scholarships/Academic: Yes **Athletic:** No
Total Expenses by: Year **In State:** 400+
Degrees Conferred: AA
Type: 2 Yr., Coed
Campus Housing: No
Male/Female Ratio: 42:58
Fin Aid: Yes
Out of State: $ 4,200
Programs of Study: Accounting, Anthropology, Art, Behavioral Science, Biological Science, Business Administration, Chemistry, Economics, Industrial, Music, Psychology, Real Estate, Recreation, Social Science

ATHLETIC PROFILE

Estimated Number of Baseball Scholarships: 1
Conference Affiliation: Bay Valley Conference
Program Profile: Year-round program with super facilities. Field is a natural grass.
History: 25 years program with a 5 Conference Championships and 1 State Championships.
Achievements: Conference champs 1980, 1983, 1987; State Championship
Coaching: Mike Duitsman, Head Coach, 7 years. Allan Beavers and Dan Bell, Assistant Coaches.
Roster for 1998 team/In State: 30 **Out of State:** 0 **Out of Country:** 0
Total Number of Varsity/Jr. Varsity: 30 **Percent of Graduation:** 90%
Number of Seniors on 1998 Team: 11 **Most Recent Record:** 19 - 17 - 0
Number of Fall Games: 27 **Number of Spring Games:** 44
Positions Needed for 1999/2000: Pitcher, Catcher
Schedule: Stanford, Chabot, Santa Rosa, Sacramento City, Orange Coast
Style of Play: Aggressive.

Loyola Marymount University

7101 W 80th Street
Los Angeles, CA 90045
Coach: Frank Cruz
NCAA I
Lions/Crimson, Air Force Blue
Phone: (310) 338-2949
Fax: (310) 338-5915

ACADEMIC

Founded: 1914
Religion: Jesuit - Catholic
Type: 4 Yr., Private, Liberal Arts, Coed
Campus Housing: Yes

Web-site: http://www.lmu.edu/
SAT/ACT/GPA: 1100/3.0
Student/Faculty Ratio: 14:1
Male/Female Ratio: 40:60
Undergraduate Enrollment: 4,100
Graduate Enrollment: 2,000
Scholarships/Academic: Yes **Athletic:** Yes **Fin Aid:** Yes
Total Expenses by: Year **In State:** $ 23, 441 **Out of State:** $ 23,441
Degrees Conferred: BA, BS, BBA, BSA, BSE, MA, MS, MBA, Med, Med, JD
Programs of Study: Accounting, Biochemistry, Biology, Business Administration, Civil Engineering, Communications, Dramatic Arts, Economics, Electrical Engineering, English, French, History, Humanities, Mathematics, Mechanical Engineering, Music, Philosophy, Physics, Political Science, Psychology, Religion, Social Science

ATHLETIC PROFILE

Conference Affiliation: West Coast Conference
Program Profile: Stadium seats 650, two cages, turfed, soft toss station, bunt station, team weight room. Season is late January through mid-May.
Achievements: Conference Titles in 1973, 1986 and 1990; College World Series in 1986; Regional Appearances in 1973, 1986, 1988-1990; Drafts in last three years were Mariners Andy Collett (13th), Collins Hind (18th), Shane Bowers (20th Twins), Jesse Ibarra (5th Giants).
Coaching: Frank Cruz , Head Coach.
Style of Play: Fundamentally sound emphasis on pitching and defense.

Master's College

21726 Palcerita Canyon Road
Santa Clarita, CA 91321-1200
Coach: Monte Brooks
NAIA
Mustangs/Royal Blue, White, Yellow
Phone: (805) 259-3540
Fax: (805) 254-6129

ACADEMIC

Founded: 1927
Type: 4 Yr., Private, Liberal Arts, Coed
Religion: Independent/Non-Denominational
Campus Housing: Yes
Web-site: http://www.masters.edu/
SAT/ACT/GPA: 1000/ 22
Student/Faculty Ratio: 17:1
Male/Female Ratio: 371/422
Undergraduate Enrollment: 793
Graduate Enrollment: 220
Scholarships/Academic: Yes **Athletic:** Yes **Fin Aid:** Yes
Total Expenses by: Year **In State:** $ 16,700 **Out of State:** $ 16,700
Degrees Conferred: BA, BS, MD in Biblical Counseling, Theology, Divinity
Programs of Study: Biblical Studies, Communication, English, History, Liberal Studies, Mathematics, Music, Natural Science, Physical Education, Political Studies, Biological Science, Business Administration, Home Economics

ATHLETIC PROFILE

Estimated Number of Baseball Scholarships: 4
Conference Affiliation: Independent Conference
Program Profile: Fabulous Climate, outstanding playing surface, natural field, 300 capacity, annual tournament host.
History: The program began in 1976.
Achievements: Went 34-10 in 1998; received Coach of the Year in Independent League; 7 All-Conference players; 1 All-American; 2 players drafted in 1998.
Coaching: Monte Brooks, Head Coach, 1997 was his first season, played five years professionally; coached at the high school, college and professional level, former assistant at The Master's College for 1995-1996. He compiled a record of 56-34; played for four years in San Diego Organization; played every position. He was a pitching coach of Florida Marlins for one year. Greg Morton, Assistant Coach.
Roster for 1998 team/In State: 13 **Out of State:** 10 **Out of Country:** 0
Total Number of Varsity/Jr. Varsity: 23 **Percent of Graduation:** 90+%
Number of Seniors on 1998 Team: 4 **Number of Sophomores on 1998 Team:** 10

Freshmen Receiving Fin Aid/Athletic: 2 **Academic:** 3
Number of Fall Games: 18 **Number of Spring Games:** 49
Positions Needed for 1999/2000: Pitcher, Catcher, Outfielder, Infielder
Most Recent Record: 34 - 10 - 0
Baseball Camp Dates: June 1-7; July 14-21; August 6-13
Schedule: Azusa Pacific, Biola, California State, California Poly-Pomona, Northwood
Style of Play: Aggressive on bases; put pressure on opposing team to make mistakes. Aggressive but under control at the plate; mix speed on the bump.

Menlo College

1000 El Camino Real
Atherton, CA 94027
Coach: Blair Neagle

NCAA III
Oaks/Blue, White
Phone: (650) 688-3775
Fax: (650) 324-4937

ACADEMIC

Founded: 1927
Type: 4 Yr., Private, Liberal Arts, Coed
Religion: Non-Affiliated
Campus Housing: Yes
Web-site: http://www.menlo.edu/
SAT/ACT/GPA: 800/ 24
Student/Faculty Ratio: 5:1
Male/Female Ratio: 6:1
Undergraduate Enrollment: 550
Graduate Enrollment: N/A
Scholarships/Academic: Yes **Athletic:** No **Fin Aid:** Yes
Total Expenses by: Year **In State:** $ 22,300 **Out of State:** $ 22,300
Degrees Conferred: BA, BS
Programs of Study: Business Communications, Computer Science, Humanities, Human Resources, Liberal Arts, Management, Psychology

ATHLETIC PROFILE

Conference Affiliation: Independent Conference
Coaching: Blair Neagle, Head Coach.
Style of Play: Quick and aggressive.

Napa Valley College

2277 Napa-Vallejo Highway
Napa, CA 94558
Coach: Nick Esposito

CCAC
Swamprats/Green, Gold
Phone: (707) 253-3220
Fax: (707) 253-3232

ACADEMIC

Founded: 1942
Type: 2 Yr., Public, Coed
Religion: Not-Affiliated
Campus Housing: No
Undergraduate Enrollment: 7,000
Student/Faculty Ratio: 23:1
Scholarships/Academic: No **Athletic:** No **Fin Aid:** Yes
Total Expenses by: Year **In State:** $ 2,500 **Out of State:** $ 6,000
Degrees Conferred: AA, AS
Programs of Study: General Education

ATHLETIC PROFILE

Conference Affiliation: Bay Valley Conference - Western Division, CACC
History: Conference Champions in 1990, 1993.
Achievements: 1 Conference titles 1990, 1993; 2 All-Americans, 6 All-Northern California, 4 players in professional baseball.
Style of Play: Aggressive, disciplined, team baseball.

Occidental College

1600 Campus Road
Los Angeles, CA 90041
Coach: Jeff Henderson

NCAA III
Tigers/Black, Orange
Phone: (323) 259-2683
Fax: (323) 341-4993

ACADEMIC

Founded: 1887
Type: 4 Yr., Private, Liberal Arts, Coed
Religion: Non-Affiliated
Campus Housing: No
Web-site: http://www.oxy.edu/
SAT/ACT/GPA: 1000
Student/Faculty Ratio: 12:1
Male/Female Ratio: 55%:45%
Undergraduate Enrollment: 1,585
Graduate Enrollment: 50
Scholarships/Academic: Yes **Athletic:** No **Fin Aid:** Yes
Total Expenses by: Year **In State:** $ 25,356 **Out of State:** $ 25,356
Degrees Conferred: BA, Graduate program: MA
Programs of Study: Anthropology, Art, Biology, Chemistry, Economics, Education, Engineering, Geology, History, International, Languages, Mathematics, Physical Fitness/Movement, Physics

ATHLETIC PROFILE

Conference Affiliation: Southern California Intercollegiate Athletic Conference

Pepperdine University

24255 Pacific Coast Hwy
Malibu, CA 90263
Coach: Frank Sanchez

NCAA I
Waves/Blue, Orange, White
Phone: (310) 456-4199
Fax: (310) 456-4322

ACADEMIC

Founded: 1937
Type: 4 Yr., Private, Coed
Religion: Not-Affiliated
Campus Housing: Yes
Web-site: http://www.pepperdine.edu
SAT/ACT/GPA: 1200/26/3.6
Student/Faculty Ratio: 13:1
Male/Female Ratio: 45:55
Undergraduate Enrollment: 2,816
Graduate Enrollment: None
Scholarships/Academic: Yes **Athletic:** Yes **Fin Aid:** Yes
Total Expenses by: Year **In State:** $ 30,000 **Out of State:** $ Varies
Degrees Conferred: BA, BS, MBA, MA, JD, MS, Mdiv
Programs of Study: Business and Management, Communications, Fine Arts, Health, Humanities, Letters, Literature, Natural Science, Religion, Social Science, Sports Medicine

ATHLETIC PROFILE

Conference Affiliation: West Coast Conference
Program Profile: Top - flight, highly competitive NCAA Division I program that plays excellent schedule. Home games are played at a 2,200-seat Eddy D. Field Stadium, a natural grass field that commands a spectacular view of the pacific ocean.
History: Program began in 1939. Perennial Top 25 ranked program and NCAA Championships participant. Team won the College World Series in 1992.
Achievements: Pepperdine has won 13 West Coast Conference Baseball titles and advanced to the NCAA Championships 17 times. Most notable former player is Mike Scott the 1996 CY Young Award Winner.
Coaching: Frank Sanchez , Head Coach, beginning second season, assistant coach the last ten years at USC. David Esquer, Assistant Coach. David Rhoades, Assistant Coach.
Style of Play: Aggressive, fundamental baseball with an emphasis on execution, sound pitching and solid team defense. Highly competitive national program.

Point Loma Nazarene College

3900 Lomaland Drive
San Diego, CA 92106-2899
Coach: Carroll Land
Email: pe@ptloma.edu

NAIA
Crusaders/Hunter Green, Gold
Phone: (619) 849-2266
Fax: (619) 849-2553

ACADEMIC

Founded: 1902
Religion: Nazarene
Web-site: http://www.ptloma.edu
Student/Faculty Ratio: 18:1
Undergraduate Enrollment: 2,000
Scholarships/Academic: Yes **Athletic:** Yes
Total Expenses by: Year **In State:** $ 17,000

Type: 4 Yr., Private, Liberal Arts, Coed
Campus Housing: Yes
SAT/ACT/GPA: None
Male/Female Ratio: 1:2
Graduate Enrollment: 400
Fin Aid: Yes
Out of State: $ 17,000

Degrees Conferred: BA, BSN, MA, MED, EDS
Programs of Study: Business and Management, Health Science, Home Economics, Letters/Literature, Multi/Interdisciplinary Studies, Social Science, Visual and Performing Arts

ATHLETIC PROFILE

Estimated Number of Baseball Scholarships: 20/20
Conference Affiliation: Golden State Athletic Conference
Program Profile: Established NAIA program with a veteran coach (38 seasons at the school). Picturesque ball park that overlooks the Pacific Ocean. Natural grass field with dimensions of 325, 355, 365, 330,325; superb stadium seating manicured grounds. Seasons starts February through May with off season work-outs.
History: The program began in 1948. Same coach since 1962; NAIA World Series in 1993 (third place) and 1994 (fifth place).
Achievements: Coach Land in ABCA Hall of Fame; past President of ABCA; NAIA Hall of Fame; 5 NAIA Academic All-American; 9 NAIA All-Americans; 15 players drafted by major league
Coaching: Carroll Land, Head Coach, past President of American Baseball Coaches Association. She was named ABCA Hall of Fame. Scott Sarver, Assistant Coach.
Roster for 1998 team/In State: 26 **Out of State:** 4 **Out of Country:** 0
Total Number of Varsity/Jr. Varsity: 30 **Percent of Graduation:** 0
Number of Seniors on 1998 Team: 9 **Number of Sophomores on 1998 Team:** 8
Freshmen Receiving Fin Aid/Athletic: 20 **Number of Spring Games:** 48
Positions Needed for 1999/2000: Pitchers, Catcher
Schedule: Master's College, Azusa Pacific, Bellevue, Birmingham Southern, Biola
Style of Play: Potent offense, average team speed, utilize entire pitching staff, manufacture runs when situation dictates it, fun-friendly, attractive product.

Pomona - Pitzer College

220 E. 6th Street
Claremont, CA 91711
Coach: Paul Svagdis
Email: psvagdi@pomona.edu

NCAA III
Sagehens/Blue, Orange
Phone: (909) 621-8422
Fax: (909) 621-8547

ACADEMIC

Founded: 1887
Religion: Non-Affiliated
Web-site: Not Available
Student/Faculty Ratio: 9:1
Undergraduate Enrollment: 1,450
Scholarships/Academic: No **Athletic:** No
Total Expenses by: Year **In State:** $ 28,000

Type: 4 Yr., Private, Liberal Arts, Coed
Campus Housing: Yes
SAT/ACT/GPA: 710
Male/Female Ratio: 50:50
Graduate Enrollment: None
Fin Aid: Yes
Out of State: $ 28,000

Degrees Conferred: BA, BS
Programs of Study: Economics, Psychology, Biology, English, Politics, Chemistry, International Relations, History, Neoroscience, Anthropology, American Studies, Art, Art History, Asian Studies, Black Studies, Classics, Computer Science, Geology, Mathematics, Media Studies, Music

ATHLETIC PROFILE

Conference Affiliation: Southern California Intercollegiate Athletic Conference
Program Profile: Four-year varsity program, no junior varsity at the current time. Has natural baseball field equipped with two outdoor batting cages and bullpens. Excellent facilities; has a seating capacity of 500.
History: Pomona College and Pitzer College entered into an Athletic Consortium in 1957.
Achievements: Emiliano Escanden drafted by the Cincinnati Red in 1994.
Coaching: Paul Svagdis, Head Coach, started in 1996, graduated from Tufts University in 1993, and in 1996 received his MA from Tufts in Education. He was a former assistant coach for both the baseball and football programs. He was recruitment coordinator and offensive coach for Tufts' strong baseball program. John Shelvey, Bill Swartz, Steve Vondran, Dale Litney, Frank Pericolrsi and Jamie Pinzino, Assistant Coaches
Style of Play: Aggressive with an emphasis on pitching and defense.

Sacramento City College

3835 Freeport Blvd
Sacramento, CA 95822
Coach: Jerry Weinstein
Email: weinsj@mail.scc.losrios.cc.ca.us

CJUCO
Panthers/Cardinal, Gold
Phone: (916) 558-2684
Fax: (916) 558-2022

ACADEMIC

Founded: 1916
Type: 2 Yr., Public, Liberal Arts, Coed
Religion: Non-Affiliated
Campus Housing: No
Student/Faculty Ratio: 30:1
Male/Female Ratio: 50:50
Undergraduate Enrollment: 25,000
Graduate Enrollment: None
Scholarships/Academic: Yes **Athletic:** No **Fin Aid:** Yes
Total Expenses by: Year **In State:** $ Varies **Out of State:** $ Varies
Degrees Conferred: AA
Programs of Study: General Education

ATHLETIC PROFILE

Conference Affiliation: Bay Valley Conference
Program Profile: Play in Union Stadium that has a seating capacity of 2,000. Facilities include Mellage Center, locker rooms, and indoor hitting turf, LF 315, CF 415, 2F 305. Bermuda infield, 10 batting cages; 4 indoor cages, 5 bullpens mounds, 3 practice diamonds, message center scoreboard.
History: League Champs - 18 for the last 19 years, State Champs 51/53/81, 250 players signed to Pro-Contract, 27 Big Leaguer, 6 current:
Achievements: Jerry Weinltein - 2-time Olympic coach, 19 Conference Champions; 20 major leaguers; 2 State Champions; 100 pro players.
Coaching: Jerry Weinstein, Head Coach; one of top coaches/teachers in baseball; former UCLA catcher; 1980-1982 minor league catching instructor, manager Expos (1989) and Cubs (1993/1994); scout for Orioles, Blue Jays, Brewers; 1992 and 1996 U.S. Olympic Team Coach; has developed 150+ pro players, over 200 players drafted, over 250 players signed pro contracts, and 23 players in major leagues. Paul Carmazzi - Associate Head Coach, 21st year, named to Sacramento Hall of Fame, Northern California JC Baseball Coach of the Year 1984. Top hitting coach on west coast. Andy McKay, Assistant Coach, entering sixth season with the program, Cape Cod League in 1993, University of Tampa Division II National Champs. Bob Cooper, Assistant Coach, entering first season with the program, former coach at Miami, Wake Forest and Tulane.
Roster for 1998 team/In State: 26 **Out of State:** 4 **Out of Country:** 0
Total Number of Varsity/Jr. Varsity: 40 **Percent of Graduation:** 90%

Number of Seniors on 1998 Team: 20
Number of Sophomores on 1998 Team: 0
Number of Fall Games: 120
Number of Spring Games: 50
Positions Needed for 1999/2000: All
Most Recent Record: 44 - 2 - 0
Schedule: Santa Ana, Fresno State, Chabot, American River, San Mateo, Delta
Style of Play: Emphasis on pitching and physical offense.

Saddleback College

28000 Marguerite Pkwy
Mission Viejo, CA 92692
Coach: Jack Hodges
Email: jhodges@saddleback.cc.ca.us

NJCAA
Gauchos/Cardinal, Gold
Phone: (949) 582-4642
Fax: (949) 347-9328

ACADEMIC

Founded: 1967
Type: 2 Yr., Public, Jr. College, Coed
Religion: Non-Affiliated
Campus Housing: No
Student/Faculty Ratio: 27:1
Male/Female Ratio: 45:55
Undergraduate Enrollment: 16,917
Graduate Enrollment: None
Scholarships/Academic: No **Athletic:** No **Fin Aid:** Yes
Total Expenses by: Year **In State:** $ 2,200 **Out of State:** $ 4,500
Degrees Conferred: Associates
Web-site: saddleback.cc.ca.us
Programs of Study: Accounting, American Studies, Anthropology, Astronomy, Automotive, Business, Child Development, Computer Engineering, Geography, Geology, Landscape, Legal, Literature, Manufacturing, Marine, Medical, Retail, Teacher Aide, Theatre, Travel/Tourism

ATHLETIC PROFILE

Conference Affiliation: Orange Empire Conference
Program Profile: Play a 50-game spring schedule in one of California's toughest community college conferences; play at Doug Fritz Field on the Saddleback campus.
History: First team was fielded in 1969; four conference championships. California Angels' Tim Wallach and Chicago Cubs' Mark Grace started their baseball careers at Saddleback.
Achievements: Saddleback has won 25 or more games the past 4 seasons; earned Southern California Regional berth each of those years; reached regional finals championship game 1995, 1996; 10 or more players continued their careers in each of past 4 seasons.
Coaching: Jack Hodges, Head Coach, played football and baseball at Stanford and baseball in Royals Organization; entering his nith year at Saddleback. 28 years of coaching baseball in Southern California; head coach of 1991 US Junior National team.Coach of the Year in 1996; compiled a record of 177-130. Ron Drake, Assistant Coach. Jeramy Gillen and Sommer McCartney, Assistant Coaches.
Style of Play: Aggressive, fundamental baseball.

Saint Mary's College - California

1928 Moraga Road
Moraga, CA 94575
Coach: John Baptista

NCAA I
Gaels/Red, Scarlet, White
Phone: (925) 631-4637
Fax: (925) 631-4405

ACADEMIC

Founded: 1863
Type: 4 Yr., Private, Liberal Arts, Coed
Religion: Catholic
Campus Housing: Yes
Web-site: http://www.stmarys-ca.edu/
SAT/ACT/GPA: 1115/24/3.3 avg
Student/Faculty Ratio: 20:2
Male/Female Ratio: 42:58
Undergraduate Enrollment: 2,500
Graduate Enrollment: 2,500
Scholarships/Academic: Yes **Athletic:** Yes **Fin Aid:** Yes
Total Expenses by: Year **In State:** $ 23,000 appr. **Out of State:** $ 23,000 appr.

Degrees Conferred: BA, BS, Nursing, MA, MS, MBA, Med
Programs of Study: Accounting, American, Anthropology, Art, Behavioral, Biology, Business, International, Chemistry, Communications, Economics, Engineering, Government, History, Math, Nursing, Philosophy, Psychology, Sociology

ATHLETIC PROFILE

Conference Affiliation: West Coast Conference
Program Profile: Play on a natural surface field with a measurements of L-340, LC-380, RC-380, and R-340. the stadium has a seating capacity of 3,500. Playing has a 56 game schedule which is a competitive schedule in Division I.
History: Program began in 1863. Baseball has been a major St. Mary's sport since 1872. SMC Phoenix played at the Oakland 'Brickpile' before campus moved to Moraga in 1928. A total of 49 SMC alums have gone on to the major leagues, so far. Teams have been called the 'Gaels' since mid 1990s. Tom Candiotti, Von Hayes, Broderick Perkins and James Mouton are SMC graduates.
Achievements: Major Leaguers are Tom Candiotti by the Dodgers, Joe Millette by the Phillies, James Mouton by the Astros, Von Hayes by the Phillies, Broderick Perkins by the Padres, Mike Young by the Orioles, Steve Senteney by the Toronto, Harry Hooper by the Boston Chicago, Hall of Fame, and Andy Cary by the Yankees; Brian Headley by the Brewers, Aaron Porter by the Angels, and Jason Weekley by the Dodgers.

San Diego State University

Athletic Department
San Diego, CA 92182
Coach: Jim Dietz

NCAA I
Aztecs/Scarlet, Black
Phone: (619) 594-6889
Fax: (619) 594-3019

ACADEMIC

Founded: 1897
Type: 4 Yr., Public, Coed
Religion: Non-Affiliated
Campus Housing: Yes
Web-site: http://www.sdsu.edu
SAT/ACT/GPA: 750+/ 18+
Student/Faculty Ratio: 12:1
Male/Female Ratio: 48:52
Undergraduate Enrollment: 24,000
Graduate Enrollment: 5,000
Scholarships/Academic: Yes **Athletic:** Yes **Fin Aid:** Yes
Total Expenses by: Year **In State:** $ 7,800 **Out of State:** $ 14,100
Degrees Conferred: BA, BS, MA, MS, MBA, MFA, PhD
Programs of Study: Business Management, Computer Sciences, Engineering, Telecommunication, Physical Therapy, Psychology, Mathematics, Education, Exercise and Nutritional Sciences

ATHLETIC PROFILE

Conference Affiliation: Western Athletic Conference
Program Profile: Great weather year round, lighted facility, seating for 1,000 (expect new stadium within two years), two indoor batting cages, indoor bullpen, natural turf, team clubhouse.
History: Program officially began in 1936, NAIA champs 1958, NCAA playoffs nine times, only three head coaches in program history.

San Francisco State University

1600 Holloway Avenue
San Francisco, CA 94132
Coach: Dave Nakama
Email: dnaks@sfu.edu

NCAA II
Gators/Purple, Gold
Phone: (415) 338-1226
Fax: (415) 339-1967

ACADEMIC

Founded: 1899
Type: 4 Yr., Public, Coed
Religion: Non-Affiliated
Campus Housing: Yes

Web-site: http://www.sfsu.edu/
SAT/ACT/GPA: 820+
Student/Faculty Ratio: 17:1
Male/Female Ratio: 1:3
Undergraduate Enrollment: 20,000
Graduate Enrollment: 7,000
Scholarships/Academic: Yes **Athletic:** Yes **Fin Aid:** Yes
Total Expenses by: Year **In State:** $ 7,000 **Out of State:** $ 16,000
Degrees Conferred: BA, BS, MA, MS, MBA
Programs of Study: Accounting, American Studies, Anthropology, Art, Biology, Chemistry, Broadcasting, Communications, Cinema, Engineering, Computer Science, Computer Information System, Dance, Creative Writing, Ecology, Economics, Education, Gerontology, Management, Marketing, Mathematics, Music, Nursing, Philosophy, Psychology, Political Science, Sociology, Social Science, Journalism, Physics, Astronomy

ATHLETIC PROFILE

Conference Affiliation: California Collegiate Athletic Association
Program Profile: The SFSU baseball program attracts many junior college transfer student-athletes. Therefore the team is always turning over new faces through the program. They play on Maloney Field (capacity is 100) which is natural field. The 1998 team played 56 games - conference high. Season begins in January and end the second week of May.
History: Baseball at SFSU began in 1950's. Over eleven coaches have coached. The SFSU winningest coach is Mike Simpson (1986-1997) with a 326-289-4 record.
Achievements: Conference Coach of the Year in 1986, 1989, and 1993.
Coaching: Dave Nakama, Head Coach, spent the last two seasons as an assistant coach at Stanford University. He comes to SFSU with a strong successful background. In two years at Stanford University, the team won two PAC 10 South Titles, advanced to the NCAA West Regional twice, recorded an 87-34-1. Prior to Stanford University, he was the head coach at Missouri Junior College from 1991-1996 and led his squad to the California State tournament.
Number of Fall Games: 0 **Number of Spring Games:** 56
Style of Play: Traditional style of play. **Most Recent Record:** 21 - 34 - 1

San Jose State University

One Washington Square
San Jose, CA 95192
Coach: Sam Piraro
NCAA I
Spartans/Blue, Gold, White, Black
Phone: (408) 924-1255
Fax: (408) 924-1301

ACADEMIC

Founded: 1865
Type: 4 Yr., Public, Coed, Engineering
Campus Housing: Yes
SAT/ACT/GPA: NCAA Requirements
Student/Faculty Ratio: 25:1
Male/Female Ratio: 52:48
Undergraduate Enrollment: 23,000
Graduate Enrollment: None
Scholarships/Academic: No **Athletic:** Yes **Fin Aid:** No
Total Expenses by: Year **In State:** $ 8,000 **Out of State:** $ 15,000
Degrees Conferred: BA, BS, BFA, MA, MS, MBA, MFA
Programs of Study: Business, Human Performance, Engineering, Communications, Administration of Justice

ATHLETIC PROFILE

Estimated Number of Baseball Scholarships: 10.5
Conference Affiliation: WAC
Program Profile: Play games at Class "A" pro field (mini stadium) with a seating capacity of 6,000.
History: The program began in 1908.
Achievements: 1997 WAC Coach of the Year; 1997 WAC Western Division Champions.
Coaching: Sam Piraro, Head Coach, considered winningest coach in school history. He compiled a record of 383-295 record since 1987. Doug Thurman, Assistant Coach.
Roster for 1998 team/In State: 28 **Out of State:** 0 **Out of Country:** 0
Total Number of Varsity/Jr. Varsity: 0 **Percent of Graduation:** 73%

Number of Seniors on 1998 Team: 7 **Most Recent Record:** 31 - 23 - 0
Freshmen Receiving Fin Aid/Athletic: 6 **Baseball Camp Dates:** July
Number of Fall Games: 15 **Number of Spring Games:** 56
Positions Needed for 1999/2000: Catcher, Middle Infielder, Pitcher
Schedule: Stanford, Rice, Fresno State, Washington State, Oregon State, BYU
Style of Play: Speed oriented, good defense, pitching.

Santa Clara University

Athletic Department
Santa Clara, CA 95053
Coach: Mike Cummins

NCAA I
Broncos/Maroon, White
Phone: (408) 554-4680
Fax: (408) 555-6942

ACADEMIC

Founded: 1851
Type: 4 Yr., Private, Coed, Engineering
Religion: Jesuit Catholic
Campus Housing: Yes
Web-site: http://www.scu.edu/
SAT/ACT/GPA: 1150/21
Student/Faculty Ratio: 13:1
Male/Female Ratio: 46:54
Undergraduate Enrollment: 4,000
Graduate Enrollment: 3,740
Scholarships/Academic: Yes **Athletic:** Yes **Fin Aid:** Yes
Total Expenses by: Year **In State:** $ 20,900 **Out of State:** $ 20,900
Degrees Conferred: BA, BS, MA, MS, MBA, PhD, JD
Programs of Study: Business and Management, Communications, Engineering, International, Letters/Literature, Multi/Interdisciplinary, Preprofessional Programs, Psychology, Social Sciences

ATHLETIC PROFILE

Conference Affiliation: West Coast Conference
Program Profile: Play at Buck Shaw Stadium, which has upgraded lights, natural turf, 6,800 seats. The season begins in late January and ends mid May.
History: Program has been successful since 1925. In 1996 League champs 40-22 record.
Achievements: Average 2-3 drafted players per year; 1988 and 1994 Regional League Champions; League Champions in 1996.

Santa Rosa Junior College

1501 Mendocino Avenue
Santa Rosa, CA 95401
Coach: Ron Myers

CC
Bear Cubs/Navy, Scarlet, White
Phone: (707) 527-4389
Fax: (707) 524-1752

ACADEMIC

Founded: 1918
Type: 2 Yr., Jr. College, Coed
Student/Faculty Ratio: 26:1
Male/Female Ratio: 42:58
Undergraduate Enrollment: 27,885
Graduate Enrollment: None
Scholarships/Academic: No **Athletic:** No **Fin Aid:** Yes
Total Expenses by: Year **In State:** $ Varies **Out of State:** $ Varies
Degrees Conferred: AA, AS, Vocational Certificate
Programs of Study: Agricultural, Animal Science, Art, Astronomy, Automotive, Aviation, Biology, Botany, Chemistry, Construction, Criminal, Justice, Dental, Economics, Medical, Forest, Geology, Humanities, Law, Math, Nutrition, Parks Management, Public, Sociology, Science, Theatre

ATHLETIC PROFILE

Conference Affiliation: Bay Valley, Western Division Conference

Program Profile: New natural turf playing surface. Finished 3-97. Season is in the fall that runs from August through December, & spring runs from January through May. Facility 's capacity is 400.
History: Baseball program has been at SRIC for over 50 years. SRIC has won a number of championships over the years.
Achievements: Coach of the Year in 1990 and 1995; Conference Titles in 1990 and 1995; All-American include: Bret Magnusson in 1988 (Player of the Year), Mike Switzer in 1988, Joe Dillon in 1995, and Jason Lene in 1997; numerous drafted players.
Coaching: Ron Myers, Head Coach, started coaching from 1982 to the present. He was named Coach of the Year in 1990 and 1995. Damon Neidlinger, Assistant Coach.
Style of Play: Play hard, very aggressive offensively.

Sonoma State University

1801 East Cotati Avenue
Rohnert Park, CA 94928
Coach: John Goelz

NCAA II
Cossacks/Columbia, White, Navy
Phone: (707) 664-2524
Fax: (707) 664-4104

ACADEMIC

Founded: 1960
Religion: Non-Affiliated
Web-site: http://www.sonoma.edu/
Student/Faculty Ratio: 16:1
Undergraduate Enrollment: 6,000
Scholarships/Academic: Yes **Athletic:** No
Total Expenses by: Year **In State:** $ 7,500

Type: 4 Yr., Public, Coed
Campus Housing: Yes
SAT/ACT/GPA: 820/ 18
Male/Female Ratio: 40:60
Graduate Enrollment: 1,000
Fin Aid: Yes
Out of State: $ 14,900

Degrees Conferred: BA, BS, BFA, MA, MS, MBA
Programs of Study: Accounting, Anthropology, Art, Banking/Finance, Biology, Botany, Cell Biology, Chemistry, Communications, Computer Science, Criminal Justice, Dance, Dramatic Arts, Economics, English, Geography, Geology, German, History, Marine Biology, Marketing, Math, Microbiology, Music, Nursing, Philosophy, Physics, Political Science, Psychology, Social Science

ATHLETIC PROFILE

Conference Affiliation: Northern California Athletic Conference
Program Profile: Play on a natural grass field which has dimensions of 325-368-390-357-320.
History: First of the program was in 1966. First winning season was in 1987; 3 conference titles in 1990's; nationally ranked 8 times in the last 12 years.
Achievements: NCAC Coach of the Year in 1990, 1991, and 1992; 40 players drafted or signed professionally since 1986; 4 All-Americans; over 25 All-Region players since 1986.
Coaching: John Goelz, Head Coach. Walter White, Infield Coach. Mark Domenichelli, Outfield Coach. Chad Bresater, Pitching Coach.
Style of Play: Winning style of play.

Southern California College

55 Fair Drive
Costa Mesa, CA 92626
Coach: Kevin Kasper

NAIA
Vanguards/Blue, White, Gold
Phone: (714) 556-3610
Fax: (714) 668-6144

ACADEMIC

Founded: 1920
Religion: Assembly of God
Web-site: http://www.sccu.edu/
Student/Faculty Ratio: 19:1
Undergraduate Enrollment: 970

Type: 4 Yr., Private, Liberal Arts, Coed
Campus Housing: Yes
SAT/ACT/GPA: 740+/ 18+
Male/Female Ratio: 45:55
Graduate Enrollment: 130

Scholarships/Academic: Yes **Athletic:** Yes **Fin Aid:** Yes
Total Expenses by: Year **In State:** $ 14,500 **Out of State:** $ 14,500
Degrees Conferred: BA, MA, MS, MTS
Programs of Study: Accounting, Biology, Anthropology, Broadcasting, Chemistry, Communications, Education, English, Finance, Humanities, Journalism, Management, Marketing, Mathematics, Physical Education, Prelaw, Premed, Social Science, Sociology, Theater

ATHLETIC PROFILE

Conference Affiliation: Golden State Athletic Conference
Program Profile: Successful program, 21 players signed pro contracts (draft - free agents), grass field, short left field porch. Play January through end of May. Stadium can seat up to 2,000 fans.
History: Won district championship three times. NAIA World Series appearances in 1985 taking fourth place in the nation. Have also been district runner-up two times.
Achievements: NAIA District III Champs in 1979; Golden State Athletic Conference Champs in 1985 & 1987; numerous All-Americans & 21 players drafted or signed as a free-agent in the last 6 years.
Style of Play: Young and aggressive. Good defense and exciting pitching. Timely hitting will win us a lot of ball games.

Stanford University

Baseball Office
Stanford, CA 94305
Coach: Mark Marquess

NCAA I
Cardinals/Cardinal, White
Phone: (650) 723-4528
Fax: (650) 725-2957

ACADEMIC

Founded: 1885
Type: 4 Yr., Private, Liberal Arts, Coed
Religion: Non-Affiliated
Campus Housing: Yes
Web-site: http://www.stanford.com
SAT/ACT/GPA: 1300+
Student/Faculty Ratio: 10:1
Male/Female Ratio: 55:45
Undergraduate Enrollment: 6,577
Graduate Enrollment: 6,610
Scholarships/Academic: Yes **Athletic:** Yes **Fin Aid:** Yes
Total Expenses by: Year **In State:** $ 31,833 **Out of State:** $ 31,833
Degrees Conferred: BA, BS, MA, MS, MBA, MFA, Med, PhD, EdD
Programs of Study: African - American Studies, Anthropology, Art, Asian Languages, Biological Sciences, Chemistry, Classics, Communication, Comparative Literature, Computer Science, Drama, Earth Science, East Asian Studies, Economics, Engineering, English, Feminist Studies, French, German Studies, History, Human Biology, International Relations, Italian, Latin American Studies, Linguistics, Math, Music, Philosophy, Physics, Political Science, Pyschology, Public Policy, Religion

ATHLETIC PROFILE

Conference Affiliation: Pacific - 10 Conference
Program Profile: The facilities for baseball at Stanford are without equal in terms of overall excellence. Often called the most beautiful college facility in the United States, Sunken Diamond is the home field of the Stanford Cardinals.
History: Program began in 1892 and carries an all-time record of 2,128-1,399-32 (.602 winning percentage). Has had just two losing seasons in the last 50 years.
Achievements: National Champions in 1987-1988; appeared in the NCAA Regional 16 of the last 18 years; made College World Series nine times in the last 15 years.
Coaching: Mark Marquess, Head Coach, 895-467-3 in 22 seasons, including two National Titles; led 1988 US Olympic team to the Gold Medal in Seoul; five-time PAC-Ten Southern Division Coach of the Year. Dean Stotz, Assistant Coach, has been rated as top recruiter in the country; has 22 years coaching experience. Tom Dunton, Assistant Coach, has 24 years of coaching experience, pitching coach, worked with Jack McDowell and Mike Massino.
Roster for 1998 team/In State: 19 **Out of State:** 16 **Out of Country:** 1
Total Number of Varsity/Jr. Varsity: 36 **Percent of Graduation:** 91%
Number of Seniors on 1998 Team: 2 **Number of Sophomores on 1998 Team:** 0

Baseball Camp Dates: June, July
Number of Spring Games: 56
Positions Needed for 1999/2000: All
Most Recent Record: 42 - 14 - 1
Schedule: USC, Arizona State, Washington, California State Fullerton, Texas, Fresno State
Style of Play: The basic philosophy of the Stanford baseball program is to recruit talented baseball players and make them play hard. We pride ourselves in the fact that no collegiate program works harder than we do. There is no short cut to success.

University of California - Berkeley

61 Harmony Gymnasium
Berkeley, CA 94724-422
Coach: Bob Milano

NCAA I
Golden Bears/Blue, Gold
Phone: (510) 643-6006
Fax: (510) 642-1765

ACADEMIC

Founded: 1868
Type: 4 Yr., Public, Coed
Religion: Non-Affiliated
Campus Housing: Yes
Web-site: http://www.berkeley.edu/
SAT/ACT/GPA: 900/ 22
Student/Faculty Ratio: 17:1
Male/Female Ratio: 54:46
Undergraduate Enrollment: 20,000
Graduate Enrollment: 10,000
Scholarships/Academic: Yes **Athletic:** Yes **Fin Aid:** Yes
Total Expenses by: Year **In State:** $ 12,000 **Out of State:** $ 20,000
Degrees Conferred: BA, BS, MA, MS, MBA, PhD, EdD, JD
Programs of Study: Anthropology, Art, Architure, Astronomy, Bioengineering, Biology, Business Administration, Chemistry, Communications,Computer Science, Earth Science, Economics, Engineering, Geology, Sociology, Political Science, Psychology, Physics

ATHLETIC PROFILE

Conference Affiliation: Pacific - 10 South Conference
Program Profile: Is considered one of the top two conferences in the nation. Evans Diamond was built it in 1933 . There are4000 seats and it has natural grass.
History: First team was in 1892 and 100 years later the Bears played in the College World Series. Cal won the first CWS in 1947 and the national title again in 1957. The Bears also have made regional appearances in 1980, 1985, 1988, 1991-92; World Series appearances in 1980 (3rd), 1988 and 1992 (tied for 7th).
Achievements: Current Coach Bob Milano, Pacific 10 South Co-Coach of the Year in 1980 and 1992; NCAA Titles in 1947 and 1957; 14 Conference Titles; 26 All-Americans; 67 players since 1978 (Milano's first season as a head coach) have been drafted and signed pro contracts.
Coaching: Bob Milano, Head Coach, is the winningest baseball coach in the history; was an assistant coach/business manager to the 1988 US Olympic Team.
Style of Play: Speed and an aggressive offensive approach. Pitching and defensively oriented. Goal every year is to make an appearance at the College World Series.

University of California - Davis

One Shields Avenue
Davis, CA 95616
Coach: Phil Swimley

NCAA II
Aggies/Yale Blue, Gold
Phone: (530) 752-7513
Fax: (530) 752-6681

ACADEMIC

Founded: 1908
Type: 4 Yr., Public, Liberal Arts, Coed
Religion: Non-Affiliated
Campus Housing: Yes
Web-site: http://www.ucdavis.edu/
SAT/ACT/GPA: None
Student/Faculty Ratio: 17:1
Male/Female Ratio: 49:51
Undergraduate Enrollment: 18,000
Graduate Enrollment: 2,500

Scholarships/Academic: Yes **Athletic:** Yes **Fin Aid:** Yes
Total Expenses by: Year **In State:** $ 4,099 **Out of State:** $ 11,798
Degrees Conferred: BA, BS, MA, MS, MBA, MFA, Med, PhD, EdD, MD, JD
Programs of Study: More than 100 undergraduate majors available

ATHLETIC PROFILE

Conference Affiliation: Northern California Athletic Conference
Program Profile: UC-Davis Community Stadium was built in 1987 with a seating capacity of 3,500 people. The all grass field is recognized as one of the best playing surfaces in Northern California. Facility includes lighted batting cages. Playing season begins February 14 with a regular season ending on May 4th.
History: Program began in the 1920's. Coach Swimley has been head coach for thirty years.
Achievements: Coach Phil Swimley was named NACB West Region Coach of the Year in 1995; 25 drafted players, 4 All-Americans; 8 Conference Titles.
Coaching: Phil Swimley, Head Coach, started from 1965 to the present, led six honors to Division II West Regional including 1995 World Series team. 1995 NABC West Region Coach of the Year. Played four years in Yankees Organization, compiled a record of 787-724. Matt Vaugh, Assistant Coach, entering seventh year, played for UCO as a pitcher from 1989 to 1992.
Most Recent Record: 24 - 20 - 1 **Number of Spring Games:** 54
Positions Needed for 1999/2000: RF, 3rd Base, Shortstop, Pitcher
Schedule: Grand Canyon, Chico State, UC-Riverside, Sacramento State, UC-Berkeley, California
Style of Play: Play smart, aggressive baseball. Run bases, play sound defense and win with your pitching.

University of California - Los Angeles

P.O. Box 24044 **NCAA I**
Los Angeles, CA 90024-004 **Bruins/Gold, Blue**
Coach: Gary Adams **Phone: (310) 794-8210**
Email: gadam@athletics.ucla.edu **Fax: (310) 825-8664**

ACADEMIC

Founded: 1919 **Type:** 4 Yr., Public, Coed
Religion: Not-Affiliated **Campus Housing:** No
Web-site: http://www.ucla.edu/ **SAT/ACT/GPA:** 1000/ 21
Student/Faculty Ratio: 21:1 **Male/Female Ratio:** 48:52
Undergraduate Enrollment: 23,914 **Graduate Enrollment:** 11,021
Scholarships/Academic: Yes **Athletic:** Yes **Fin Aid:** Yes
Total Expenses by: Year **In State:** $ 11,470 **Out of State:** $ 20,454
Degrees Conferred: BA, BS, MA, MS, MBA
Programs of Study: Anthropology, Art, Astrophysics, Biology, Classics, Compuer, Cybernetics, Earth Science, English, Languages, Geology, Geophysics, History, International, Meteorology, Nursing, Religion, Seismology

ATHLETIC PROFILE

Conference Affiliation: Pacific - 10 Southern Division I
Program Profile: Players train in the Acosta Athletic Center on campus. Home games are in Jackie Robinson Stadium 2 miles from campus. It is a natural grass field with a 330 feet down the lines, 365 in the gaps and 390 to the center. JRS seats is 1,250.
History: Baseball officially started at UCLA in 1920. Since the opening season the Bruins have competed in 9 post-season tournaments. Ranked in collegiate baseball's top 25 Final Season Poll 13 times. Ranked in the top 25 Baseball America Poll 7 times since 1986.
Achievements: 3 Conference Championships; 35 All-American Awards; 44 All-Tournament Selections; 73 All-PAC 10 Selections; 151 players drafted by Major League teams.
Coaching: Gary Adams, Head Coach, has won 797-643-7 games at UCLA and is UCLA's all-time winningest coach. Played second base for Bruins in 1959, 1960, 1962 (team captain, MVP). Vince Reringle, entering tenth season. Tim Leopard, Pitching Coach, entering third season.

Roster for 1998 team/In State: 35 **Out of State:** 5 **Out of Country:** 0
Total Number of Varsity/Jr. Varsity: 32 **Percent of Graduation:** 80%
Number of Seniors on 1998 Team: 2 **Number of Sophomores on 1998 Team:** 17
Most Recent Record: 24 - 33 - 0 **Number of Spring Games:** 57
Positions Needed for 1999/2000: Pitcher, Catcher
Baseball Camp Dates: June 21-24; June 28-7/ 11; 7/12-15; 7/19-22; Etc..
Schedule: Southern California, Washington, Arizona State, Georgia State, Stanford, California
Style of Play: The "Bruin way", players develop marked and physical skills. Players encouraged to "think on the fly". Catchers call all pitchers; aggressive hitting and baserunning. Players execute according to their own abilities coming together to form a team that prides itself on team play, hustle, and worth ethic.

University of California - Riverside

(New Program)

900 University Avenue
Riverside, CA 92521
Coach: Jack Smitheran
Email: jack.smitheran@ucr.edu

NCAA I
Highlanders/Blue, Gold
Phone: (909) 787-5441
Fax: (909) 787-3569

ACADEMIC

Founded: 1954 **Type:** 4 Yr., Public, Liberal Arts, Coed
Religion: Non-Affiliated **Campus Housing:** Yes
Web-site: Not Available **SAT/ACT/GPA:** 3.3
Student/Faculty Ratio: 12:1 **Male/Female Ratio:** 1:1
Undergraduate Enrollment: 9,000 **Graduate Enrollment:** 1,500
Scholarships/Academic: Yes **Athletic:** Yes **Fin Aid:** Yes
Total Expenses by: Year **In State:** $ 10,500 **Out of State:** $ 19,900
Degrees Conferred: BA, BS, MA, MS, MBA
Programs of Study: Anthropology, Biological Science, Botany, Business, Comparative Literature, Creative Writing, Engineering, Entomology, Geography, Geology, Languages, Law, Linguistics, Management, Philosophy, Religion, Seismology, Soil Science, Statistics, Women's Studies

ATHLETIC PROFILE

Estimated Number of Baseball Scholarships: 7
Conference Affiliation: California College Athletic Association
Program Profile: Stadium has a seating capacity of 2,500; facilities include lights, locker rooms and natural grass field which has 330-380-400-380-330 measurements.
History: The program began in 1958.
Achievements: 2 NCAA Division II Titles; 6 Regional Championships; 6 League Champions; 100 players drafted; 30 All-Americans; 10 Big Leaguers.
Coaching: Jack Smitheran, Head Coach, compiled a record of 914-620; NCAA II Coach of the Year; Area Coach of the Year five times; Conference Coach of the Year. Doug Smith, Assistant.
Roster for 1998 team/In State: 27 **Out of State:** 0 **Out of Country:** 0
Total Number of Varsity/Jr. Varsity: 30 **Percent of Graduation:** 94%
Number of Seniors on 1998 Team: 3 **Number of Sophomores on 1998 Team:** 5
Most Recent Record: 22 - 26 - 0 **Number of Spring Games:** 56
Positions Needed for 1999/2000: 3 Pitchers, 1-Outfielder, 2-Infielders
Schedule: CSU - Northridge, University of San Diego, Southern Utah, Louisiana State

University of California - San Diego

9500 Gilman Drive
La Jolla, CA 92093
Coach: Dan O'Brien

NCAA III
Tritons/Royal Blue, Gold
Phone: (619) 534-8162
Fax: (619) 534-8475

ACADEMIC

Founded: 1959
Type: 4 Yr., Public, Liberal Arts, Coed
Religion: Non-Affiliated
Campus Housing: Yes
Web-site: http://www.ucsd.edu
SAT/ACT/GPA: Required
Student/Faculty Ratio: 22:1
Male/Female Ratio: 51:49
Undergraduate Enrollment: 13,500
Graduate Enrollment: 3,500
Scholarships/Academic: Yes **Athletic:** No **Fin Aid:** Yes
Total Expenses by: Year **In State:** $ 1,629 **Out of State:** $ 4,426
Degrees Conferred: BA, BS,MA,MS, MFA, MD
Programs of Study: Anthropology, Art, Biochemistry, Biology, Biophysics, Communications, Computer Science, Dramatic Arts, Earth Science, Ecology, Engineering, English, Foreign Languages, Linguistics, Mathematics, Microbiology, Molecular Biology, Music, Philosophy, Physics, Physiology, Political Science, Psychology, Quantitive Methods, Religion, Social Science

ATHLETIC PROFILE

Conference Affiliation: Independent Conference
Program Profile: Division III program moving to Division II in fall of 2000. Has an outstanding campus and baseball field in La Jolla, California next to ocean. Building a stadium in 2000.
History: The program began in 1968 and has been ranked in the top ten several times in the past few years. In the last seven years, we have placed two players in to the major leagues.
Achievements: 1987 NCAA Division III West Region Coach of the Year; 4 Appearances in the Western Regionals since 1986; 8 All-Americans since 1986; 10 players drafted since 1985. Finished 3rd in 1994 in College World Series.
Coaching: Dan O'Brien, Head Coach, entering first season with the program. Jeff Waymire, position player coach and hitting instructor, entering first season with program. Brian Priebe, Pitching Coach/Director of Recruiting, entering first year with the program. John Titchern, Gradute Assistant, entering first year with the program.
Roster for 1998 team/In State: 27 **Out of State:** 4 **Out of Country:** 0
Total Number of Varsity/Jr. Varsity: 31 **Percent of Graduation:** 99%
Number of Seniors on 1998 Team: 5 **Number of Sophomores on 1998 Team:** 0
Number of Fall Games: 9 **Number of Spring Games:** 0
Baseball Camp Dates: 9/1-6; 9/8-13 **Most Recent Record:** 20 - 18 - 0
Schedule: University of California-Davis, University of California-Riverside, California State - Dominguez Hills, California State - Los Angeles, Eastern Connecticut State, Montclair State
Style of Play: Aggressive.

University of California - Santa Barbara

Intercollegiate Athletics
Santa Barbara, CA 93106
Coach: Bob Brontsema
NCAA I
Gauchos/Blue, Gold
Phone: (805) 893-3690
Fax: (805) 893-8640

ACADEMIC

Founded: 1989
Type: 4 Yr., Public, Coed
Religion: Non-Affiliated
Campus Housing: Yes
Web-site: http://www.ucsb.edu/
SAT/ACT/GPA: 1300/ 20
Student/Faculty Ratio: 19:1
Male/Female Ratio: 50:50
Scholarships/Academic: Yes **Athletic:** Yes **Fin Aid:** Yes
Total Expenses by: Year **In State:** $ 10,718 **Out of State:** $ 18,417
Degrees Conferred: BA, BS, BFA, MA, MS, MFA, PhD
Programs of Study: Art, Biology, Chemistry, Computer Science, Literature, Mathematics, Music Composition, Physics, Engineering, Anthropology, Art History, Biochemistry, Chemistry, Computer Science, Criminal Justice, Dance, Dramatic Art, Ecology and Evolution, Economics, Film Studies, French, Geography, History, Philosophy, Physics, Pharmacology, Physiology, Political Science, Psychology, Religion

ATHLETIC PROFILE

Conference Affiliation: Big West Conference
Program Profile: Play a 51-game schedule plus the conference tournament. The Gauchos play on natural grass in a new stadium equipped with luxury boxes and seats for 1,000.
History: Began in 1947. Joined Big West the first time in 1970, then again in 1985. Last won the Big West in 1986 going 45-19 (18-3 in BW) under Al Ferrer. Went to Regionals six times 1952, 1972, 1983, 1986, 1987, 1990.
Achievements: 1986 Big West Champs; 5 All-Americans; 2 players drafted in 1994 include Matt Bazzani (12th) and Matt Bokeneier (15th).
Coaching: Bob Brotsema, Head Coach, was an assistant at UCSB for ten years and former Gaucho
Style of Play: Aggressive, stresses solid defense and execution at the plate.

University of La Verne

1950 3rd Street
La Verne, CA 91750
Coach: Bobby Lee

NCAA III
Leos/Green, Orange
Phone: (909) 5933511x4265
Fax: (909) 392-2760

ACADEMIC

Founded: 1891
Religion: Church of the Brethren
Web-site: http://www.ulaverne.edu/
Student/Faculty Ratio: 14:1
Undergraduate Enrollment: 1,900
Scholarships/Academic: Yes **Athletic:** No
Total Expenses by: Year **In State:** $ 14,000

Type: 4 Yr., Private, Liberal Arts, Coed
Campus Housing: Yes
SAT/ACT/GPA: 900
Male/Female Ratio: 50:50
Graduate Enrollment: 900
Fin Aid: Yes
Out of State: $ 14,000

Degrees Conferred: BA, BS, MA, MS, MBA, EdD, JD
Programs of Study: Arts and Sciences, Athletic, Business, Management, Communications, Computer, Economics, Engineering, Law, Physical, Preprofessional, Social Sciences, Teacher Preparation, Visual and Performing Arts

ATHLETIC PROFILE

Conference Affiliation: Southern California Intercollegiate Conference
Program Profile: 1995 - New bleachers, infield turf, irrigation system. January to June season. No Fall practice. Lighted park. Great southern California climate. Pressbox, hitting cages.
History: Program began in 1923. 1995 Division III National Champions, 21-0 conference record. 13 conference titles in last 21 years. Pitching coach with Phillies for 12 years.
Achievements: 1984 Regional Coach of the Year; 1995 National Coach of the Year; National Champions; two All-Americans; 13 Conference Titles; 8 players drafted.

University of Redlands

P.O. Box 3080
Redlands, CA 92373-0999
Coach: Ken Miller
Email: kmiller@uor.edu

NCAA III
Bulldogs/Maroon, Grey
Phone: (909) 793-2121x2583
Fax: (909) 307-0936

ACADEMIC

Founded: 1907
Religion: Non-Affiliated
Web-site: http://www.redlands.edu/
Student/Faculty Ratio: 13:1
Undergraduate Enrollment: 1,500
Scholarships/Academic: Yes **Athletic:** No

Type: 4 Yr., Private, Liberal Arts, Coed
Campus Housing: Yes
SAT/ACT/GPA: 1100/ 19
Male/Female Ratio: 45:55
Graduate Enrollment: 500
Fin Aid: Yes

Total Expenses by: Year **In State:** $ 26,000 **Out of State:** $ 26,000
Degrees Conferred: BS, BA
Programs of Study: Art, Asian Studies, Biology, Business Administration and Accounting, Chemistry, Communicative Disorders, Computer Science, Economics, Education, History, Humanities, International Relations, Mathematics, Music, Philosophy, Physical Education and Athletics, Physics, Psychology, Race and Ethnic Studies, Religion, Sociology

ATHLETIC PROFILE

Conference Affiliation: Southern California Intercollegiate Athletic Conference
Program Profile: We play one of the toughest Division III schedules. Our field was just resurfaced last year, all grass, wonderful hitting backdrop.
History: The program began in 1921, playoffs in 1991 and 1993. Most highly tauted award a player can receive is the John Moore Memorial Award. Given each year to a senior who best exemplifies hustle, determination and sportmanship as exibited by the late John Moore ('65) during his career at the University of Redlands.
Achievements: Ken Miller was named SCIAC Coach of the Year in 1991, conference title in 1991, 4 players drafted in 1990's, average 1 All-West player per year.
Coaching: Ken Miller, Head Coach, entering 13th season as a head coach at his alma mater; Dickinson State in 1957. Cory Monroe, Assistant Coach, first year Division III, 2nd team west pitcher in 1998. Lance Hallberg, Assistant Coach, responsible with the infielder, entering third with the program. High School draftee, played Triple A Baseball for the Twins.
Roster for 1998 team/In State: 30 **Out of State:** 15 **Out of Country:** 0
Total Number of Varsity/Jr. Varsity: 45 **Percent of Graduation:** 100%
Number of Seniors on 1998 Team: 12 **Most Recent Record:** 23 - 15 - 0
Freshmen Receiving Fin Aid/Athletic: 0 **Academic:** 14
Number of Fall Games: 0 **Number of Spring Games:** 38
Schedule: University of California-Riverside, California Southern, Chapman Unviersiyt, Montclair State, University of Wisconsin - La Crosse, Point Loma Nazarene University
Style of Play: Hard working (school baseball) proud program.

University of San Diego

5998 Alcala Park
San Diego, CA 92110-2492
Coach: John Cunningham

NCAA I
Toreros/Col. Blue, Navy, White
Phone: (619) 260-8894
Fax: (619) 292-0388

ACADEMIC

Founded: 1949 **Type:** 4 Yr., Private, Liberal Arts, Coed
Religion: Roman Catholic **Campus Housing:** Yes
Web-site: http://www.acusd.edu/ **SAT/ACT/GPA:** Open
Student/Faculty Ratio: 18:1 **Male/Female Ratio:** 45:65
Undergraduate Enrollment: 5,000 **Graduate Enrollment:** 1,500
Scholarships/Academic: Yes **Athletic:** Yes **Fin Aid:** No
Total Expenses by: Year **In State:** $ 24,000 **Out of State:** $ 24,000
Degrees Conferred: BA, BS, MA, MS, MFA, Med, EdD, JD
Programs of Study: Business/Economics/Accounting, Communications, Computer, Education, Engineering, Letters/Literature, Marine Studies, Ocean Studies, Parks/Recreation, Protective Services, Psychology, Public, Social Science, Visual and Performing Arts

ATHLETIC PROFILE

Conference Affiliation: West Coast Conference
Program Profile: Play at our on campus stadium ,Cunningham Stadium ,with a natural grass and 1,200 seats, on-campus stadium, competing against the best teams in the west in the city with the best weather in the nation. The program belongs to a small school that has an enrollment of 6,400.
History: The program began in 1964. Coach Cunningham has been the only coach in the history of the program. Reached Division II World Series in 1971 and 1978 and moved to Division I in 1979.

Achievements: Cunningham was named WCC Co-Coach of the Year in 1993; 10 All-Americans; 43 pro-contracts signed.
Coaching: John Cunningham, Head Coach. Jake Molina and Glenn Goodwin, Assistant Coaches.

University of San Francisco

2130 Fulton Street
San Francisco, CA 94117
Coach: Nino Giarratano
Email: giarratano@usfra.edu

NCAA I
Dons/Green, Gold
Phone: (415) 422-2934
Fax: (415) 422-2510

ACADEMIC

Founded: 1855
Religion: Catholic
Web-site: http://www.usfca.edu/
Student/Faculty Ratio: 17:1
Undergraduate Enrollment: 5,000
Scholarships/Academic: Yes
Athletic: Yes
Total Expenses by: Year
In State: $ 22,500
Type: 4 Yr., Private, Liberal Art, Coed
Campus Housing: Yes
SAT/ACT/GPA: Yes
Male/Female Ratio: 40:60
Graduate Enrollment: 1,500
Fin Aid: Yes
Out of State: $ 22,500
Degrees Conferred: BS, MS, PhD
Programs of Study: Business, Sport Science, Psychology, English, Nursing, Law (MBA), Biology, Chemistry, Communications, Computer Science, Prephysical Therapy, Economics, Environmental Science, History

ATHLETIC PROFILE

Estimated Number of Baseball Scholarships: 7
Conference Affiliation: West Coast Conference
Program Profile: Excellent program. The Dons are Division I program on an up swing. They are becoming more competitive in resent years and finished 27-28 in 1996. USF has had recent players such as Jermaine Clark (2B, Third Team All-American) and Joe Nelson (RHP, fourth-round pick by Atlanta Braves).
History: The recorded history of the program began in 1968. The best season came with a 32-15-1 mark in 1971. USF had some lean years in the 1980's but are now on the upswing since the arrival of Head Coach Rich Hill. USF has won 20 or more games in each of the last three seasons.
Achievements: USF won school record in 34 games in 1998 and school record 18 WCC game. Finished in 3rd place in WCC for second straight year, USF has posted three straight winning seasons for the first time ever in the last three years.
Coaching: Nino Giarratano, Head Coach, former assistant coach for two years at Arizona State; 1998 College World Series Runner-Up. Eight years as a junior college coach at Trinidad State (6 years) and Yavapai College for 2 years. 5 JC College World Series appearance. Chad Konishi and Nate Rodriguez, Assistant Coaches.
Roster for 1998 team/In State: 25
Out of State: 13
Out of Country: 1
Total Number of Varsity/Jr. Varsity: 39
Most Recent Record: 34 - 24 - 0
Number of Seniors on 1998 Team: 9
Number of Sophomores on 1998 Team: 0
Number of Fall Games: 0
Number of Spring Games: 56
Schedule: Stanford, California, Washington, Pepperdine, Santa Clara, Loyola Marymount
Style of Play: USF is an aggressive offensive team that plays extremely hard baseball. The Dons are fundamentally sound on defense and are always in search of quality pitching. USF usually plays high-scoring and exciting ball games.

University of Southern California

Heritage Hall
Los Angeles, CA 90089-0601
Coach: Mike Gillespie

NCAA I
Trojans/Cardinal, Gold
Phone: (213) 740-8444
Fax: (213) 740-7584

ACADEMIC

Founded: 1880
Religion: Not-Affiliated
Web-site: http://www.usc.edu
Scholarships/Academic: Yes **Athletic:** Yes
Total Expenses by: Year **In State:** $ 30,126
Degrees Conferred: BA, BS, BFA, MA, MS, MFA

Type: 4 Yr., Private, Coed
Campus Housing: No
Undergraduate Enrollment: 14,470
Fin Aid: Yes
Out of State: $ Varies

Programs of Study: 197 Undergraduate Majors: 31 Graduate and Professional Programs, 110 Areas of Study including Business and Management, Communications, Engineering, Social Science, Visual and Performing Arts

ATHLETIC PROFILE

Conference Affiliation: Pacific 10

University of the Pacific

3601 Pacific Avenue
Stockton, CA 95211
Coach: Quincy Noble

NCAA I
Tigers/Orange, Black
Phone: (209) 946-2709
Fax: (209) 946-2731

ACADEMIC

Founded: 1851
Religion: Non-Affiliated
Web-site: http://www.oop.edu
Undergraduate Enrollment: 2,758
Scholarships/Academic: No **Athletic:** No
Total Expenses by: Year **In State:** $ 24,436
Degrees Conferred: BA, BS, BFA, MA, MS, PhD

Type: 4 Yr., Private, Coed, Engineering
Campus Housing: No
Student/Faculty Ratio: 15:1
Graduate Enrollment: 547
Fin Aid: Yes
Out of State: $ 24,436

Programs of Study: Accounting, Advertising, Athletic Training, Behavioral, Biology, Broadcasting, Business, Computer, Criminal, Engineering, Finance, Linguistics, Ministries, Natural Science

ATHLETIC PROFILE

Conference Affiliation: Big West Conference
Program Profile: Home games are played at Billy Hebert Field which seats 6,000. Voted "Best Field" in the California League. Program consists of a Varsity and Jr. Varsity team. Play in the Big West Conference, one of the most competitive leagues in the country.
History: Program will be 50 years old in 1997. Traditionally play in Best of the West Tournament.
Achievements: Dan Reichert (soph) - 1st player invited to the USA trials. Jason Flach - NAIA Player of the Year. Ranked 26th in the country in 1994. Recorded a team record of 36 wins and 22-game winning streak in 1994, the longest in NCAA Division I last year.
Coaching: Quincy Noble, Head Coach, 8 years at Pacific, 2nd winningest coach in the school's history. Assistant Coaches, Stan Stolte and Joe Moreno.
Style of Play: We have a strong pitching staff in 1996, but we need runs early to win.

West Valley College

14000 Fruitvale Avenue
Saratoga, CA 95070
Coach: Mike Perez
Email: mike_perez@westvalley.edu

CCCCA
Vikings/Navy, Orange
Phone: (408) 741-2176
Fax: (408) 867-1067

ACADEMIC

Founded: 1963
Religion: Non-Affiliated

Type: 2 Yr., Public, Coed
Campus Housing: No

Undergraduate Enrollment: 14,224 **Student/Faculty Ratio:** 26:1
Total Expenses by: Year **In State:** $ Varies **Out of State:** $ 3,600
Degrees Conferred: Associate
Programs of Study: General Studies

ATHLETIC PROFILE

Conference Affiliation: Coast

Westmont College

955 Lapaz Road
Santa Barbara, CA 93108
Coach: Bret Biegert
Email: bbiegert@westmont.edu
NAIA
Warriors/Maroon, White
Phone: (805) 565-6010
Fax: (805) 565-6221

ACADEMIC

Founded: 1940
Type: 4 Yr., Private, Liberal Arts, Coed
Religion: Non-Denominational
Campus Housing: Yes
Web-site: http:www.westmont.edu/
SAT/ACT/GPA: 1100
Student/Faculty Ratio: 1:20
Male/Female Ratio: 1/3:2/3
Undergraduate Enrollment: Yes
Graduate Enrollment: None
Scholarships/Academic: Yes **Athletic:** Yes **Fin Aid:** Yes
Total Expenses by: Year **In State:** $ 24,000 **Out of State:** $ 24,000
Degrees Conferred: BS, BA
Programs of Study: To implement an academic philosophy designed to meet the needs of individual students, Westmont offers a curriculum that includes a broad spectrum of disciplines. Students study under a high quality faculty deeply committed to research and scholarly activity as well as to personalized teaching. Within the framework of a strong liberal arts emphasis, Westmont provides opportunities for students to build a foundation for specialized education and to expand vocational horizons. They can form a basis for on the job training and move toward vocational goals suited to their personal abilities.

ATHLETIC PROFILE

Estimated Number of Baseball Scholarships: 2-3
Conference Affiliation: Golden State Athletic Conference
Program Profile: NAIA Division I program, natural playing surface with stadium capacity of 2,000, spectacular setting against Santa Yves Mountains overlooking Pacific Ocean in Santa Barbara, California.
History: The first year of the program was in 1960; GSAC charter member in 1987; 3 Conference Titles; 1 Sectional Title in 1997; 4 straight play-off appearances.
Achievements: GSAC Conference Champions in 1988, 1989 and 1994; NAIA Far West Sectional Champs in 1997; 24 pro's; 11 All-Americans.
Coaching: Bret Biegert, Head Coach, entering second year with the program. He was a 1994 graduate of Westmont, 1994 NAIA All-American Infielder, 1997 NAIA Farwest Sectional Champs.
Roster for 1998 team/In State: 20 **Out of State:** 4 **Out of Country:** 0
Total Number of Varsity/Jr. Varsity: 24 **Percent of Graduation:** 98%
Number of Seniors on 1998 Team: 4 **Number of Sophomores on 1998 Team:** 0
Freshmen Receiving Fin Aid/Athletic: 7 **Academic:** 11
Number of Fall Games: 2 **Number of Spring Games:** 50
Positions Needed for 1999/2000: Catcher, Pitcher, 1st Base, M-Infielder
Baseball Camp Dates: June 15-19; June 22-26
Schedule: University of California-Santa Barbara, California State - Dominguez, California State-Los Angeles, California Poly - San Louis Obispo
Style of Play: Extremely aggressive and hard-nosed, very spacious field lead to speed oriented offense with emphasis on pitching.

Whittier College

13406 Philadelphia Street
Whittier, CA 90601
Coach: Jim Pigott

NCAA III
Poets/Purple, Gold
Phone: (310) 907-4487
Fax: (310) 945-8024

ACADEMIC

Founded: 1887
Religion: Non-Affiliated
Web-site: http://www.whittier.edu/
Student/Faculty Ratio: 13:1
Undergraduate Enrollment: 1,300
Scholarships/Academic: Yes **Athletic:** No
Total Expenses by: Year **In State:** $ 26,096

Type: 4 Yr., Private, Liberal Arts, Coed
Campus Housing: Yes
SAT/ACT/GPA: 1100/21/3.0
Male/Female Ratio: 50:50
Graduate Enrollment: 100
Fin Aid: Yes
Out of State: $ Varies

Degrees Conferred: BA, BS, MA, MS, JD
Programs of Study: Anthropology, Art, Athletic Training, Biochemistry, Biology, Business and Management, Chemistry, Economics, Education, English, Fine Arts, French, Geology, History, International Studies, Liberal Arts, Literature, Mathematics, Modern Languages, Music, Philosophy, Physical Education, Physical Science, Physics, Political Science, Predentistry, Prelaw, Premed, Prevet, Psychology, Religion, Social Science, Spanish, Speech Pathology, Theatre

ATHLETIC PROFILE

Conference Affiliation: Southern California Intercollegiate Athletic Conference

COLORADO

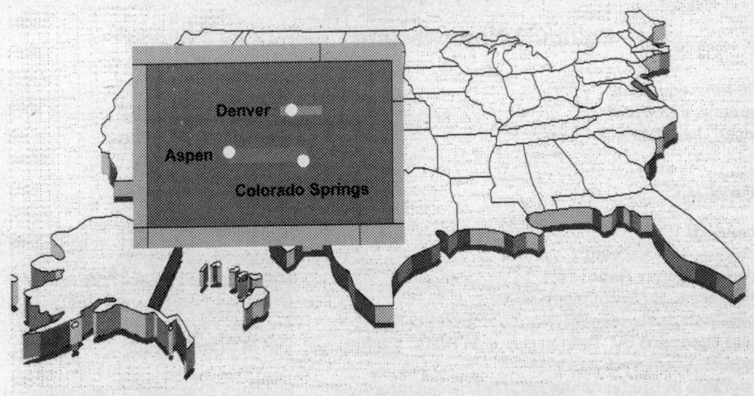

SCHOOL	CITY	AFFILIATION 99	PAGE
Colorado Northwestern Community	Rangely	NJCAA	130
Colorado School of Mines	Golden	NCAA II	130
Lamar Community College	Lamar	NJCAA	130
Mesa State College	Grand Junction	NCAA II	131
Metropolitan State College - Denver	Denver	NCAA II	132
Otero Junior College	La Junta	NJCAA	132
Regis University	Denver	NCAA II	133
Trinidad State Junior College	Trinidad	NJCAA	133
US Air Force Academy	US Air Force	NCAA I	134
University of Denver	Denver	NCAA I	134
University of Northern Colorado	Greeley	NCAA II	135
University of Southern Colorado	Pueblo	NCAA II	136

Colorado Northwestern Community College

500 Kennedy Drive
Rangely, CO 81648
Coach: Paul Conrad

NJCAA
Spartans/Red, White
Phone: (970) 675-3286
Fax: (970) 675-3330

ACADEMIC

Founded: 1962
Type: 2 Yr., Public, Jr. College, Coed
Religion: Not-Affiliated
Campus Housing: No
Student/Faculty Ratio: 14:1
Male/Female Ratio: 47:53
Undergraduate Enrollment: 560
Graduate Enrollment: None
Scholarships/Academic: No **Athletic:** Yes **Fin Aid:** Yes
Total Expenses by: Year **In State:** $ 3,900 **Out of State:** $ 7,000
Degrees Conferred: Associate
Programs of Study: Aircraft/Missile Maintenance, Aviation, Business, Computer, Criminal Justice, Dental Services, Farm/Ranch, Flight Training, Law, Liberal Arts, Medical Science

Colorado School of Mines

1500 Illinois Street
Golden, CO 80401
Coach: Mike Mulvaney

NCAA II
Orediggers/Blue, Silver
Phone: (303) 273-3367
Fax: (303) 273-3362

ACADEMIC

Founded: 1874
Type: 4 Yr., Public, Coed, Engineering
Religion: Non-Affiliated
Campus Housing: Yes
Web-site: http://www.gn.mines.colorado.edu/
SAT/ACT/GPA: None
Student/Faculty Ratio: 14:1
Male/Female Ratio: 75:25
Undergraduate Enrollment: 2,200
Graduate Enrollment: 900
Scholarships/Academic: Yes **Athletic:** Yes **Fin Aid:** Yes
Total Expenses by: Year **In State:** $ 10,840 **Out of State:** $ 18,740
Degrees Conferred: BS, MS, MEng, PhD
Programs of Study: Engineering (Chemical, Geological, Geophysical, Metallurgical/Materials, Mining, Petroleum), Chemistry, Economics, Mathematics, Physics

ATHLETIC PROFILE

Conference Affiliation: Rocky Mountain Athletic Conference
Program Profile: Member of NCAA II program. Field is natural grasss and located on campus.
History: First year of baseball program was in 1911; overall all-time record is 464-869.
Coaching: Mike Mulvaney, Head Coach, fifth year with the program. Drafted by Cincinnati Reds in 1988-1992; graduate of University of Wyoming in 1988. Dan McDermont, Assistant .
Style of Play: Good team speed; hit and run type of ball club. Rely on defense and pitching.

Lamar Community College

2401 S Main
Lamar, CO 81052
Coach: Scott Crampton

NJCAA
Runnin' Lopes/Black, Blue
Phone: (719) 336-2248
Fax: (719) 336-2448

ACADEMIC

Founded: 1937
Type: 2 Yr., Public, Jr. College, Coed,
Religion: Non-Affiliated
Campus Housing: Yes

Student/Faculty Ratio: 12:1
Male/Female Ratio: 50:50
Undergraduate Enrollment: 700
Graduate Enrollment: None
Scholarships/Academic: Yes **Athletic:** Yes **Fin Aid:** Yes
Total Expenses by: Year **In State:** $ 6,000 **Out of State:** $ 10,000
Degrees Conferred: Associate
Programs of Study: Agriculture and Business, Agronomy, Animal Science, Art, Biology, Business, Chemistry, Computer Science, Humanities, Mathematics, Physics, Preprofessional Programs, General Studies

ATHLETIC PROFILE

Estimated Number of Baseball Scholarships: 10
Conference Affiliation: Empire Conference
Program Profile: One of the best facilities in state of Colorado; 60' dugouts, 8 wooden wall, lights, and has a seating capcity of 3,000.
History: Has five straight winning seasons; last regional appearance was in 1995.
Achievements: Coach Crampton named 1995 Region IX Coach of the Year. 1995 Region IX Champions. 4 First Team All-Conference, 6 Second Team All-Conference, 3 All-Americans, several drafted players.
Coaching: Scott Crampton, Head Coach, entering fifth year with the program. He compiled record of 142-86 in four years. He played Division I and coached at Division I for six years. Greg Lasage, Assistant Coach.
Roster for 1998 team/In State: 10 **Out of State:** 15 **Out of Country:** 1
Total Number of Varsity/Jr. Varsity: 26 **Percent of Graduation:** 100%
Number of Seniors on 1998 Team: 8 **Most Recent Record:** 39 - 18 - 0
Freshmen Receiving Fin Aid/Athletic: 15 **Academic:** 3
Number of Fall Games: 30 **Number of Spring Games:** 56
Positions Needed for 1999/2000: Pitcher, All others
Schedule: Seward, Trinidad, Otero, Notheastern, Colby, Garden City
Style of Play: Blue collar, hard work ethic. First class on and off the field.

Mesa State College

PO Box 2647
Grand Junction, CO 81502
Coach: Chris Hanks

NCAA II
Mavericks/Maroon, White
Phone: (970) 248-1149
Fax: (970) 243-1980

ACADEMIC

Founded: 1972
Type: 4 Yr., Public, Coed
Religion: Non-Affiliated
Campus Housing: Yes
Web-site: http://www.mesastate.edu
SAT/ACT/GPA: 880/19/2.5
Student/Faculty Ratio: 28:1
Male/Female Ratio: 47:53
Undergraduate Enrollment: 4,500
Graduate Enrollment: 50
Scholarships/Academic: Yes **Athletic:** Yes **Fin Aid:** Yes
Total Expenses by: Year **In State:** $ 4,844 **Out of State:** $ 8,450
Degrees Conferred: Master's, Associates
Programs of Study: Accounting, Biological Science, Business, Communications, Computer, Criminal, Dramatic Arts, Economics, English, Fine Arts, Geology, History, Human Services, Management, Marketing, Parks/Recreation, Physics, Science, Social Science

ATHLETIC PROFILE

Conference Affiliation: Rocky Mountain Athletic Conference
Program Profile: The program is a member of NCAA Division II. One of top programs in the country. Amateur Field of the Year - twice in the past five years; Natural turf, stadium has a seating capacity of 10,000; Host for the NJCAA World Series. Facilities include lights in the stadium, press box, club house.

History: The program was a member of the NJCAA in 1925-1975; NAIA in 1975-1992; NCAA in 1993 to the present; over 25 Conference Championships; NCAA South West Coast Regional.
Achievements: One of the top 5 clubs in the country in drafted players; Coach of the Year three times; 12 Conference Championships in the past 20 years.

Metropolitan State College - Denver

Campus Box 9
Denver, CO 80217
Coach: Vince Porreco
Email: porresov@mscd.edu

NCAA II
Roadrunners/Navy, Cardinal
Phone: (303) 556-3301
Fax: (303) 556-2720

ACADEMIC

Founded: 1963
Religion: Not-Affiliated
Web-site: http://www.mscd.edu/
Student/Faculty Ratio: 22:1
Undergraduate Enrollment: 17,500
Scholarships/Academic: Yes
Athletic: Yes
Total Expenses by: Year
In State: $ 6,500
Degrees Conferred: BA, BS, BFA

Type: 4 Yr., Public, Coed
Campus Housing: No
SAT/ACT/GPA: 820/ 18
Male/Female Ratio: 1:1
Graduate Enrollment: None
Fin Aid: Yes
Out of State: $ 12,500

Programs of Study: Accounting, Anthropology, Art, Behavioral Science, Biology, Chemistry, Computer Information System, Computer Science, Criminalistics, Economics, English, Geography, Geology, Journalism, Land Use, Management, Marketing, Music, Philosophy, Physics, Political Science, Psychology, Public Administration, Social Work, Sociology, Spanish, Speech Communications, Theoretical Physics

ATHLETIC PROFILE

Estimated Number of Baseball Scholarships: 7
Conference Affiliation: Rocky Mountain Athletic Conference
Program Profile: NCAA Division II strong conference usually three teams in top 20. Growing program (new facilities, more scholarships, new logo).
History: 1979 baseball began; 2 coaches: Bill Helman coached for 14 years and Vince Porreco 6 years to the present.
Achievements: 1998 Coach of the Year; ranked 23th nationally; ranked 4th West Region; 8 drafted players; 14th nation team ERA.
Coaching: Vince Porreco, Head Coach. Kenny Leoneld, Pitching and Catching Coach, second in the nation in 1994. Chan Mayber, hitting and Infield Coach, drafted rockies in 1994; coached in 1997. Keith Kobold, Hitting and Infield Coach. Joe Schallmoser and Mark Sheley.
Roster for 1998 team/In State: 14
Out of State: 14
Out of Country: 0
Total Number of Varsity/Jr. Varsity: 0
Percent of Graduation: 90%
Number of Fall Games: 2
Number of Spring Games: 54
Baseball Camp Dates: 2/6,7,13,14; 6/14-18
Most Recent Record: 33 - 20 - 0
Positions Needed for 1999/2000: Pitcher, Middle Infielder, Catcher
Schedule: Ft. Hays State, University of Southern Colorado, Mesa State, Univ. of Northern Colorado
Style of Play: Aggressive baseball who focuses on pitching and defense. Emphasis towards dedication, commitment, responsibilty and loyalty.

Otero Junior College

1802 Colorado Avenue
La Junta, CO 81050
Coach: Gary Addington

NJCAA
Rattlers/Blue, White
Phone: (719) 384-6859
Fax: (719) 384-6933

ACADEMIC

Founded: 1941
Religion: Not-Affiliated
Undergraduate Enrollment: 1,000
Scholarships/Academic: No **Athletic:** No
Total Expenses by: Year **In State:** $ 5,000 **Out of State:** $ 7,700
Type: 2 Yr., Coed
Campus Housing: No
Student/Faculty Ratio: 18:1
Fin Aid: Yes
Degrees Conferred: Associate
Programs of Study: Agricultural, Architectural, Automotive, Biological Science, Education, History, Humanities, Literature, Mathematics, Medical, Nursing, Office, Physical Science, Psychology, Social Science, Theatre, Preprofessional Programs

Regis University

3333 Regis Boulevard
Denver, CO 80221-1099
Coach: Tom Dedin

NCAA II
Rangers/Blue, Gold
Phone: (303) 458-4070
Fax: (303) 964-5499

ACADEMIC

Founded: 1877
Religion: Jesuit
Web-site: http://www.regis.edu/
Student/Faculty Ratio: 16:1
Undergraduate Enrollment: 1,400
Scholarships/Academic: Yes **Athletic:** Yes
Type: 4 Yr., Private, Liberal Arts, Coed
Campus Housing: Yes
SAT/ACT/GPA: 1100/ 20
Male/Female Ratio: 50:50
Graduate Enrollment: 8,500
Fin Aid: Yes
Degrees Conferred: BA, BS, MBA, Nursing, Physical Therapy, MSL, MACL, MIS
Programs of Study: Business and Management, Communications, Life Sciences, Religion, Mathematics, Philosophy, Social Sciences, Theology

ATHLETIC PROFILE

Estimated Number of Baseball Scholarships: 6
Conference Affiliation: Rocky Mountain Athletic Conference
Program Profile: Regis Stadum seats 2,000 and has a 9' by 36' scoreboard. The field is in excellent condition and it includes ten batting cages with two bull pens. The field is one of the best in the region. The bleachers, scoreboard, and enclosure fences have been erected in recent years. Play Division I schools with a 56 game season.
History: Baseball at Regis began many, many years ago. Since Dedin's arrival (record 175-228-1 in his eight season), the field and program have both dramatically increased.
Coaching: Tom Dedin, Head Coach; former coach at University of Illinois where over 45 players were drafted; 4 players made it to the Big Leagues; 3 are there now; 1 All-American, Dedin coached team USA. Recently Rick Zimmerman (1991 draft by Braves), Tim Karns (1994 by the Orioles, Etc.. 6 former players played in majors. Dan McDermott, Assistant Coach.
Roster for 1998 team/In State: 15 **Out of State:** 15 **Out of Country:** 0
Total Number of Varsity/Jr. Varsity: 30 **Percent of Graduation:** 100%
Number of Seniors on 1998 Team: 7 **Number of Sophomores on 1998 Team:** 15
Freshmen Receiving Fin Aid/Athletic: 7 **Academic:** 7
Positions Needed for 1999/2000: Pitchers **Number of Spring Games:** 56
Style of Play: Aggressive and wide open. Strong hitting is taught, along with a fundamental defense and aggressive pitching.

Trinidad State Junior College

600 Prospect Street
Trinidad, CO 81082
Coach: Steve Ramharten

NJCAA
Trojans/Blue, Gold
Phone: (719) 846-5598
Fax: (719) 846-5667

ACADEMIC

Founded: 1925
Religion: Not-Affiliated
Undergraduate Enrollment: 2,281
Scholarships/Academic: No **Athletic:** No
Total Expenses by: Year **In State:** $ 4,500
Degrees Conferred: Associate
Type: 2 Yr., Public, Coed
Campus Housing: No
Student/Faculty Ratio: 17:1
Fin Aid: Yes
Out of State: $ 7,000
Programs of Study: Accounting, Agricultural, Automotive, Biological, Business, Computer, Corrections, Forestry, Engineering, Journalism, Landscape, Law, Mining, Natural Resources, Nursing, Office, Pharmacy, Psychology, Soil, Science, Conservation, Theatre, Veterinary

ATHLETIC PROFILE

Conference Affiliation: Empires Conference

US Air Force Academy

2169 Cadet Fieldhouse Drive
US Air Force Academy, CO 80840
Coach: Joe Giarrantano
NCAA I
Falcons/Blue, Silver
Phone: (719) 333-2057
Fax: (719) 333-2599

ACADEMIC

Founded: 1956
Religion: None
Web-site: http://www.usafa.af.mil/
Student/Faculty Ratio: 10:1
Undergraduate Enrollment: 4,000
Scholarships/Academic: Yes **Athletic:** Yes
Total Expenses by: Year **In State:** None
Degrees Conferred: BS
Type: 4 Yr., Public, Coed
Campus Housing: Yes
SAT/ACT/GPA: 1290/ 28
Male/Female Ratio: 3:1
Graduate Enrollment: None
Fin Aid: Yes
Out of State: None
Programs of Study: Business and Management, Engineering, Life Sciences, Psychology, Social Sciences, Letters/Literature, Parks/Recreation, Protective Services, Public Affairs

ATHLETIC PROFILE

Conference Affiliation: Western Athletic Conference
Program Profile: AFA enters its 17th season in the WAC. This season, the Falcons are part of the new WAC with 12 baseball members. AFA is in the central division with Utah, Brigham Young and affiliate member Grand Canyon. AFA plays at Falcon Field which has a seating capacity of 1,000, an astroturf infield and a grass outfield .
History: The Falcons first season was 1957, the Academy's first year in existence. Best record was 33-13 in 1979. Since joining the WAC, the team's best record was 28-22 in 1993. From 1993-1995, AFA posted three straight winning seasons for just the second time in school history.
Achievements: Had 5 All-Americans; seven Academic All-Americans; 26 All-WAC players.

University of Denver
(New Program)

2250 E. Jewell Avenue
Denver, CO 80208
Coach: Jack Rose
NCAA I
Pioneers/Red, Black
Phone: (303) 871-2275
Fax: (303) 871-3905

ACADEMIC

Founded: 1864
Web-site: http://www.du.edu
Type: 4 Yr., Private, Coed
Campus Housing: Yes

Student/Faculty Ratio: 13:1
Male/Female Ratio: 49:51
Undergraduate Enrollment: 2,736
Graduate Enrollment: 2,999
Scholarships/Academic: Yes **Athletic:** Yes **Fin Aid:** Yes
Total Expenses by: Year **In State:** $ 24,000 **Out of State:** $ Varies
Degrees Conferred: BA, BFA, BM, BSBA, MBA, MFA, MT
Programs of Study: Art, Art History, Education, English, Finance-Marketing, Finance-Real Estate, General Studies, Business, Hotel Restaurant and Tourism Management, Languages, History, Law, Marketing, Music, Philosophy, Religion

ATHLETIC PROFILE

Conference Affiliation: Independent

University of Northern Colorado

UNC Butler-Hancock # 208 P
Greeley, CO 80639
Coach: Terry Hensley
Email: thensley@athletics.unco.edu
NCAA II
Bears/Navy Blue, Gold
Phone: (970) 351-1714
Fax: (970) 351-2018

ACADEMIC

Founded: 1820
Type: 4 Yr., Public, Liberal Arts, Coed
Religion: Not-Affiliated
Campus Housing: Yes
Web-site: http://www.unco.edu/
SAT/ACT/GPA: Sliding Scale with GPA/
Student/Faculty Ratio: 21:1
Male/Female Ratio: Unknown
Undergraduate Enrollment: 5,500
Graduate Enrollment: 4,500
Scholarships/Academic: Yes **Athletic:** Yes **Fin Aid:** Yes
Total Expenses by: Year **In State:** $ 6,998 **Out of State:** $ 13,766
Degrees Conferred: MA, MS, PhD, EDD, BA, BS
Programs of Study: Biological, Business, Communication Disorders, Dietetics, Earth Science, Economics, English, Geography, Gerontology, Health, History, Human Rehabilitation, Services, Interdisciplinary, Journalism, Preprofessional Programs, Psychology, Recreation, Visual Arts

ATHLETIC PROFILE

Estimated Number of Baseball Scholarships: 6
Conference Affiliation: North Central Conference
Program Profile: We just spent $ 1.5 million to renovate our natural turf field which seats 3,500 people. We will be the summer home for the short team of the Colorado Rockies.
History: Early in 1990's; we were Division I until 1990. We have appeared in the Division I World Series more than eight times.
Achievements: 9 players play pro ball; we have 3 All-Americans; we won the NCC Title in 1997 and we got NCAA Coach of the Year.
Coaching: Terry Hensley, Head Coach is entering nine years with the program. He coached the catchers for four years, pitchers for another four years and weight, strength and conditioning for 1 year. He was 4-year letter winner at UNC and played professionally in the Netherlands. Dustin Neiman, Head Assistant Coach and Catcher Coach. Bruce Vaugh, Pitching Coach.
Roster for 1998 team/In State: 29 **Out of State:** 6 **Out of Country:** 0
Total Number of Varsity/Jr. Varsity: 55 **Percent of Graduation:** 74%
Number of Seniors on 1998 Team: 6 **Number of Sophomores on 1998 Team:** 10
Freshmen Receiving Fin Aid/Athletic: 6 **Academic:** 3
Number of Fall Games: 6 **Number of Spring Games:** 50
Positions Needed for 1999/2000: 1st Base, Centerfield, LHP, Dozen
Most Recent Record: 28 - 22 - 0
Baseball Camp Dates: June 8th-12th (Summer); December 20-23
Schedule: Mesa State, North Dakota, Fort Hays State, Pittsburg State, Colorado Rockies
Style of Play: Aggressive, in the top ten each year in many offensive stats.

University of Southern Colorado

2200 Bonforte Boulevard
Pueblo, CO 81001
Coach: Stan Sanchez

NCAA II
Thunderwolves/Red, White, Blue
Phone: (719) 549-2065
Fax: (719) 549-2570

ACADEMIC

Founded: 1969
Type: 4 Yr., Public, Coed
Religion: Non-Affiliated
Campus Housing: Yes
Web-site: http://www.uscolo.edu/
SAT/ACT/GPA: 820/17
Student/Faculty Ratio: 17:1
Male/Female Ratio: 46:54
Undergraduate Enrollment: 3,940
Graduate Enrollment: 130
Scholarships/Academic: Yes **Athletic:** Yes **Fin Aid:** Yes
Total Expenses by: Year **In State:** $ 6,944 **Out of State:** $ 13,188
Degrees Conferred: BA, BS, MS, MBA
Programs of Study: Accounting, Art, Automotive parts and service management, Biology, Business, Chemistry, Civil Engineering Technology, Computer Information Systems, Electrical Engineering, Electronic Engineering Technology, Computer Engineering, Elementary and Secondary Certification, English, Exercise Science, Athletic Training, Health Promotions, Foreign Languages, History, Industrial Engineering, Mass Communications, Mathematics, Mechanical Engineering, Music

ATHLETIC PROFILE

Conference Affiliation: Rocky Mountain Athletic Conference
Program Profile: 1996 NCAA II West Regional and RMAC Champions; Qualified for 1996 NCAA II College World Series. Our newly expanded stadium has a seating capacity of 4,000, 500 chairback box seats, and a natural playing surface. Play a Fall and Spring season.
History: Program reinstated in 1994 after an eight-year absence. Team has gone to NCAA II Regional tournament twice since the program was reinstated.
Achievements: 1996 RMC and NCAA II West Regional Champions; 5 All-americans in 3 years; 1996 NCAA II College World Series Participant; 2 Regional Players of the Year; Coach of the Year 2-times in three years.
Coaching: Stan Sanchez, Head Coach, former assistant at California State Northridge, over 20 years of college experience, two-times Conference Coach of the Year. Dave Lange, Assistant Coach. Bobby Applegate, Pitching Coach.
Style of Play: Aggressive, hard-nosed. Solid defense with a string pitching. Likes to run the bases and move runners around.

CONNECTICUT

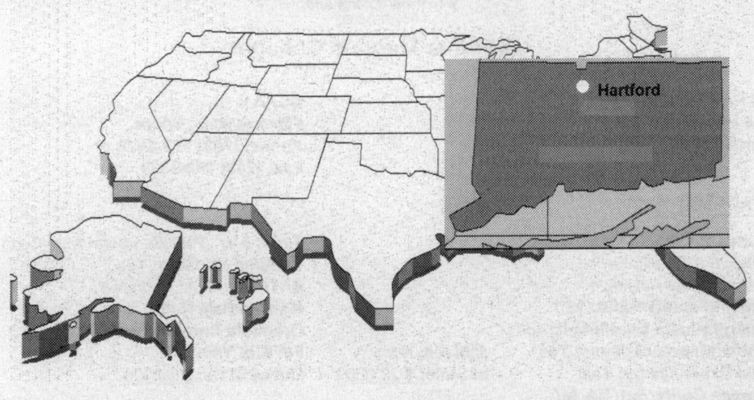

SCHOOL	CITY	AFFILIATION 99	PAGE
Albertus Magnus College	New Haven	NCAA III	138
Central Connecticut State University	New Britain	NCAA I	138
Eastern Connecticut State University	Willimantic	NCAA III	139
Fairfield University	Fairfield	NJCAA	139
Gateway College - Technical College	New Haven	NJCAA	140
Manchester College Technical College	Manchester	NJCAA	140
Mitchell College	New London	NJCAA	141
Naugatuck Valley Community Technical	Waterbury	NJCAA	141
Norwalk Community Technical College	Norwalk	NJCAA	142
Quinnipiac College	Hamden	NCAA II	142
Sacred Heart University	Fairfield	NCAA I	143
Southern Connecticut State University	New Haven	NCAA II	143
Teikyo Post University	Waterbury	NAIA	144
Trinity College - Connecticut	Hartford	NCAA III	144
US Coast Guard Academy	New London	NCAA III	145
University of Bridgeport	Bridgeport	NCAA II	145
University of Connecticut	Storrs	NCAA I	146
University of Connecticut - Avery Point	Groton	NJCAA	146
University of Hartford	West Hartford	NCAA I	147
University of New Haven	West Haven	NCAA II	147
Wesleyan University	Middletown	NCAA III	148
Western Connecticut State University	Danbury	NCAA III	148
Yale University	New Haven	NCAA I	149

Albertus Magnus College

700 Prospect Street
New Haven, CT 06511
Coach: Joe Tonelli

NCAA III
Falcons/Blue, White
Phone: (203) 773-8578
Fax: (203) 773-9539

ACADEMIC

Founded: 1925
Type: 4 Yr., Private, Lberal Arts, Coed
Religion: Catholic
Campus Housing: Yes
Web-site: Not Available
SAT/ACT/GPA: Required
Student/Faculty Ratio: 15:1
Male/Female Ratio: 3:1
Undergraduate Enrollment: 400+
Graduate Enrollment: 100+
Scholarships/Academic: Yes **Athletic:** No **Fin Aid:** Yes
Total Expenses by: Year **In State:** $ 20,000 **Out of State:** $ 20,000
Degrees Conferred: BA, MA
Programs of Study: Accounting, Biology, Business and Management, Communications, Economics, Management/Administration, English, Finance, Fine Arts, Mathematics, History, Human Services, Philosophy, Political Science, Prelaw, Premed, Psychology, Religion, Sociology

ATHLETIC PROFILE

Conference Affiliation: GNAC
Program Profile: We played home games at Quigley Stadium in West Haven, formerly a minor league park.
History: The program began in the 1992 season.
Style of Play: Hard working - well disciplined, aggressive baseball.

Central Connecticut State University

1615 Stanley Street
New Britain, CT 06050
Coach: George Redman

NCAA I
Blue Devils/Blue, White
Phone: (860) 832-3074
Fax: (860) 832-3084

ACADEMIC

Founded: 1849
Type: 4 Yr., Public, Liberal Arts, Coed
Religion: Non-Affiliated
Campus Housing: Yes
Web-site: http://www.ccsu.ctsateu.edu/
SAT/ACT/GPA: 930 combined SAT
Student/Faculty Ratio: 17:1
Male/Female Ratio: 45:55
Undergraduate Enrollment: 9,551
Graduate Enrollment: 2,495
Scholarships/Academic: Yes **Athletic:** Yes **Fin Aid:** Yes
Total Expenses by: Year **In State:** $ 4,457 **Out of State:** $ 7,196
Degrees Conferred: BS, BA, MA, MB, MS-Indutrial Technical Management, Sixth Year Certificate
Programs of Study: Accounting, American Studies, Actuarial Science, Anthropology, Archaeology, Astronomy, Art, Biology, Computer Science, Business, Chemistry, Communication, Engineering

ATHLETIC PROFILE

Conference Affiliation: Mid - Continent Conference
Program Profile: CCSU plays at Balf-Savin Field, which opened in 1994. Balf-Savin Field has a natural grass, and is located on campus.
History: The program began in 1935 and moved to Division I in 1986. Phillier All-Star pitcher Ricky Bottalico played here.
Achievements: In 1995, we swept state rivals University of Connecticut and Hartford University.
Style of Play: Speed and good pitching.

Eastern Connecticut State University

83 Windham Street
Willimantic, CT 06226
Coach: Bill Holloway

NCAA III
Warriors/Blue, White
Phone: (860) 465-5185
Fax: (860) 465-4696

ACADEMIC

Founded: 1889
Religion: Non-Affiliated
Web-site: http://www.ecsu.ctstateu.edu/
Student/Faculty Ratio: 17:1
Undergraduate Enrollment: 4,335
Scholarships/Academic: Yes **Athletic:** No
Total Expenses by: Year **In State:** $ 10,000

Type: 4 Yr., Public, Liberal Arts, Coed
Campus Housing: Yes
SAT/ACT/GPA: 900/2.5
Male/Female Ratio: 43:57
Graduate Enrollment: 297
Fin Aid: Yes
Out of State: $ 15,000

Degrees Conferred: AS, BA, BS, BGS, MS
Programs of Study: Accounting, Art, Biology, Business, Communications, Computer, Earth Science, Economics, Education, English, Environmental, History, Finance, Management, Microbiology, Sociology, Social Work

ATHLETIC PROFILE

Conference Affiliation: Little East Conference
Program Profile: Our new stadium opened for the 1997 season with 4,000 seats, lights, natural grass , hitting tunnels, practice infield, bullpens, a P.A. system and a scoreboard.
History: The program's inception was in 1949. We have had a postseason every year from 1969 to 1996, with exception of 1992. We got two National titles in 1982and 1990. Coach Holowaty is the winningest coach in New England Division III history with 800+ wins. 34 All-Americans, 24 have signed pro contracts since 1969.
Achievements: 2 National titles; 24 post-season appearances; 8 trips to the National Tournaments.
Coaching: Bill Holloway has been Head Coach for 29 years.
Style of Play: Aggressive offensively, solid fundamentally team concept.

Fairfield University

North Benson Road
Fairfield, CT 06430
Coach: John Slosar

NJCAA
Ravens/Navy, White
Phone: (203) 254-4000
Fax: (203) 254-4270

ACADEMIC

Founded: 1942
Religion: Jesuit
Web-site: http://www.fairfield.edu
Student/Faculty Ratio: 15:1
Undergraduate Enrollment: 3,000
Scholarships/Academic: Yes **Athletic:** Yes
Total Expenses by: Year **In State:** $ 24,160

Type: 4 Yr., Private, Liberal Arts, Coed
Campus Housing: Yes
SAT/ACT/GPA: 900+
Male/Female Ratio: 1:1
Graduate Enrollment: 800
Fin Aid: Yes
Out of State: $ 24,160

Degrees Conferred: BA, BS
Programs of Study: The College of Arts and Sciences, Preprofessional Programs, Applied Ethics minors available, The School of Business, Accounting minors available, The School of Nursing

ATHLETIC PROFILE

Conference Affiliation: ECAC, Patriot League
Program Profile: We have a competitive Division I program. We play games on a well-kept natural grass surface. Facilities include an outdoor batting tunnel, an outdoor workout area and a new locker/shower area adjacent to the field.

History: The program began in 1951. We are1995 MAAC South champions, runner-ups in conference tournaments and MAAC champions in 1983, 1991, 1993. We have had five 20-win seasons in the last six years, including a school record of 23 wins in 1992 and 1995.
Achievements: Slosar was named MAAC Coach of the Year in 1991. Our numerous individual honors are: MAAC South Player of the Year Mike Pike; MAAC South Rookie of the Year Jared DeCore; 2 All-MAAC selections and Pike was selected to ABCA's Division I Northeast Region All-Star team. Jim Manias was drafted in the 25th round by the Tampa Bay in 1996.
Coaching: John Slosar, Head Coach for the 14th season, graduated from the University of Connecticut and played professionally in the Mets Organization.
Style of Play: We evaluate the talent and adjust our style of play accordingly.

Gateway College - Technical College

60 Sargent Drive
New Haven, CT 06511
Coach: Steven Inverio

NJCAA
Ravens/Navy, White
Phone: (203) 789-6526
Fax: (203) 777-8415

ACADEMIC

Founded: 1968
Religion: Non-Affiliated
Student/Faculty Ratio: 22:1
Undergraduate Enrollment: 4,537
Scholarships/Academic: No **Athletic:** Yes
Total Expenses by: Year **In State:** $ 1,700

Type: 2 Yr., , Jr. College, Coed,
Campus Housing: No
Male/Female Ratio: 40:60
Graduate Enrollment: None
Fin Aid: Yes
Out of State: $ 4,700

Degrees Conferred: Associates
Programs of Study: Accounting, Automotive, Aviation, Biomedical, Business Administration, Computer, Dietetics, Drug/Alcohol/Substance Abuse Counseling, Education, Engineering, Food Services, Gerontology, Hospitality Services, Hotel/Restaurant, Radiological Recreation, Therapy, Retail Management

Manchester College Technical College

60 Bidwell Street
Manchester, CT 06045
Coach: John Susi
Email: ma-susi e mail.commnet.edu

NJCAA
Cougars/Royal Blue, White
Phone: (860) 647-6294
Fax: (860) 647-6267

ACADEMIC

Founded: 1963
Religion: Non-Affiliated
Student/Faculty Ratio: 26:1
Undergraduate Enrollment: 5,400
Total Expenses by: Year **In State:** $ 1,608

Type: 2 Yr., Jr. College, Coed
Campus Housing: No
Male/Female Ratio: Unknown
Graduate Enrollment: None
Out of State: $ 5,232

Degrees Conferred: Associated
Programs of Study: Accounting, Arts, Fine Arts, Business Administraion, Commerce, Management, Communications, Criminal Justice, Culinary Arts, Data Processing, Early Childhood Education, Food Services Mangement, Gerontology, Hotel and Restaurant Management, Human Services, Industrial Engineering Technology, Law Enforcement, Police Science, Legal Secretarial, Liberal Arts, Music, Occupational Therapy, Physical Education, Real Estate

ATHLETIC PROFILE

Conference Affiliation: NJCAA Region XXI (Divison III)

Program Profile: Our natural grass field is enclosed and measures 340' down lines, 380' in gaps, 400' dead center. Our field also has dugouts and bull pens.
History: Our baseball program is over 30 years old and turned NJCAA Division III in 1992. We were a National Runner-Up at World Series in 1993 and a World Series Particpant in 1994. We have qualified for every Regional Tournament (D III) since 1992. We also host a tournament every year.
Achievements: John susi - Regional and Districyt Coach of the Year in 1993 and 1994; Louisvile Slugger Award Winner in 1993 and 1994; Regional Champions in 1993 and 1994; Regional Runner-UP in 1996, National Runner-UP in 1993 (under Susi); 24 All-Region Players; and 5 All-Americans.
Coaching: John Susi, Head Coach. Chris Warken , Pitcher for MCIC in 1992 and 1993. He pitched at Methodist College, NC in 1994. He graduated from Methodist College, NC. Pitched in the NJCAA Division III World Series in 1993, American Legion World Series in 1991 and 1992. He pitched for Eastern Tides of New England College Baseball League in 1994 and 1995.
Style of Play: Sound fundamental, hard-nosed play. We play style according to what the team can or can't physically do. We not always go by "The Book". We like to let players "Go" a little and experience the game and all it's situations.

Mitchell College

437 Pequot Avenue
New London, CT 06320
Coach: Jeffrey Turner

NJCAA
Pequots/Red, White, Black
Phone: (860) 701-5047
Fax: (860) 701-5085

ACADEMIC

Founded: 1938
Religion: Non-Affiliated
Student/Faculty Ratio: 12:1
Undergraduate Enrollment: 528
Scholarships/Academic: No
Total Expenses by: Year

Athletic: Yes
In State: $16,000

Type: 2 Yr., Coed
Campus Housing: No
Male/Female Ratio: 52:48
Graduate Enrollment: None
Fin Aid: Yes
Out of State: $ 16,000

Degrees Conferred: Associates
Programs of Study: Accounting, Athletic Training, Biological Science, Business Administration, Computer, Criminal Justice, Ecology, Education, Environmental, Genral Engineering, Gerontology, Graphic Arts, Health Services/Science, Human Services, Liberal Arts, Marine Biology, Oceanography, Physical Education/Science, Recreational Services, Science, Sports Administration/Medicine

Naugatuck Valley Community Technical College

750 Chase Parkway
Waterbury, CT 06708
Coach: TBA

NJCAA
Vipers/Kelly, Navy
Phone: (203) 575-8072
Fax: (203) 575-8102

ACADEMIC

Founded: 1967
Religion: Non-Affiliated
Student/Faculty Ratio: 25:1
Undergraduate Enrollment: 5,239
Scholarships/Academic: No
Total Expenses by: Year

Athletic: Yes
In State: $ 1,550

Type: 2 Yr., Jr. College, Coed
Campus Housing: No
Male/Female Ratio: 45:55
Graduate Enrollment: None
Fin Aid: Yes
Out of State: $ 4,600

Degrees Conferred: Associate
Programs of Study: Accounting, Automotive, Banking/Finance, Business, Computer, Criminal Justice, Drafting/Design, Education, Engineering, Environmental, Food Services, Gerontology, Horticulture, Hotel/Restaurant, Human Services, Legal Studies, Liberal Arts, Manufacturing, Marketing, Mathematics, Natural Science, Nursing, Paralegal Studies, Sciences

Norwalk Community Technical College

188 Richards Ave
Norwalk, CT 06854
Coach: Mark Lambert

NJCAA
Panthers/Black, Red
Phone: (203) 857-7155
Fax: (203) 857-3346

ACADEMIC

Founded: 1961
Religion: Non-Affiliated
Student/Faculty Ratio: 15:1
Undergraduate Enrollment: 5,357
Scholarships/Academic: Yes **Athletic:** No
Total Expenses by: Year **In State:** $ 823
Degrees Conferred: Associates
Programs of Study: Contact school for program of study.

Type: 2 Yr., Jr. College, Coed
Campus Housing: No
Male/Female Ratio: 50:50
Graduate Enrollment: None
Fin Aid: Yes
Out of State: $ 823

ATHLETIC PROFILE

Conference Affiliation: CJCAA
Program Profile: The Panthers play a fall season and have taken spring trips to Texas, Maryland and Virginia. We play a 45-game spring season.
History: The baseball program began in the fall of 1993. The Panthers have made two trips to the Regionals in 1994 and 1995 and were the state champions in 1995 with a 37-7 record. The team was ranked seventh in the nation in 1994 and third in 1995 (57-11-0 total record).
Achievements: 5 All-Americans in 2 years.

Quinnipiac College

275 Mount Carmel Avenue
Hamden, CT 06518
Coach: Joe Mattei
Email: mattie@quinnipiac.edu

NCAA II
Braves/Navy, Gold
Phone: (203) 288-5251
Fax: (203) 281-8716

ACADEMIC

Founded: 1929
Religion: Non-Affiliated
Web-site: http://www.quinnipiac.edu/
Student/Faculty Ratio: 15:1
Undergraduate Enrollment: 3,200
Scholarships/Academic: Yes **Athletic:** Yes
Total Expenses by: Year **In State:** $ 13,800
Degrees Conferred: BA, BS, MS, MBA, MAT, PA
Programs of Study: Health Science (Physical Therapy, Occupational Therapy), Natural Science, Business, Computer Science, Liberal Arts, Mass Communications, Psychology

Type: 4 Yr., Private, Liberal Arts, Coed
Campus Housing: Yes
SAT/ACT/GPA: 1100/ 23
Male/Female Ratio: 1:5
Graduate Enrollment: 900
Fin Aid: Yes
Out of State: $ 13,800

ATHLETIC PROFILE

Estimated Number of Baseball Scholarships: 3
Conference Affiliation: Northeast - 10 Conference
Program Profile: The baseball program has an on-campus field called Braves Field, which is natural grass, has a seating capacity of 1,000 and has an indoor and outdoor hitting cage.
History: The program began in 1954. Our 45 year records are 674-464-11. The Northeast 10 record since 1988 is 137-68-2. We were Division II College World Series participants in 1983.
Achievements: Northeast 10 was Coach of the Year in 1997. We were Conference Champs in 1988, 1990, 1992, 1993, and 1997. Tim Belcher was named '97 All-American and Division II Northeast 10 Player of the Year.

Coaching: Joe Mattei, Head Coach, who is entering second year with the program, compiled a record of 42-29. Tim Belcher, Assistant Coach, was named Division II All-American in 1997.
Roster for 1998 team/In State: 13 **Out of State:** 12 **Out of Country:** 0
Total Number of Varsity/Jr. Varsity: 28 **Percent of Graduation:** 100%
Number of Seniors on 1998 Team: 2 **Number of Sophomores on 1998 Team:** 6
Freshmen Receiving Fin Aid/Athletic: 6 **Academic:** 8
Number of Fall Games: 14 **Number of Spring Games:** 42
Positions Needed for 1999/2000: Pitcher
Most Recent Record: 20 - 15 - 1
Schedule: Providence, Marist, Yale, St. Francis, Monmouth, LIU
Style of Play: Score as many runs as possible and keep the other team from scoring more than us.

Sacred Heart University

5151 Park Avenue
Fairfield, CT 06432
Coach: Nick Giaquinto
Email: giaquinton@sacredheart.edu

NCAA I
Pioneers/Scarlet, White
Phone: (203) 365-7632
Fax: (203) 365-7696

ACADEMIC

Founded: 1963
Religion: Catholic
Web-site: http://www.sacredheart.edu/
Student/Faculty Ratio: 14:1
Undergraduate Enrollment: 2,131
Scholarships/Academic: Yes **Athletic:** No
Total Expenses by: Year **In State:** $ 18,880

Type: 4 Yr., Private, Liberal Arts, Coed
Campus Housing: No
SAT/ACT/GPA: 530+
Male/Female Ratio: 50:50
Graduate Enrollment: None
Fin Aid: Yes
Out of State: $ 18,880

Degrees Conferred: AA, AS. BA, BS, MA, MS, MBA
Programs of Study: Business and Management, Business/Office and Marketing/Distribution, Communications, Computer Science, Health Sciences, Law, Letters/Literature, Social Sciences

ATHLETIC PROFILE

Conference Affiliation: New England Collegiate Conference
Program Profile: Our 18 million dollar practice and game field is off-campus. We have two on campus batting tunnels.
History: Our program began in 1966. In 1990-92 , we went to Division II regional tournament. In 1992, we played in Division II national championship tournament. In 1993 , we finished second in ECAC tournament.
Achievements: Nick Giaquinto was Northeast Region Division II Coach of the Year . We have14 pro-signees.
Coaching: Nick Giaquinto, Head Coach, is entering his 11th year with the program. He is Northwest Region Division II Coach of the Year. We have 14 pro-signees. Chris Petersen , Assistant Coach, is entering his fourth season with the program. Mark Caron, Graduate Assistant Coach, is entering his second year.
Style of Play: Aggressive - play hard every out - run out every battered ball, look to take extra base.

Southern Connecticut State University

501 Crescent Street
New Haven, CT 06515
Coach: Joe Bandiera

NCAA II
Owls/Blue, White
Phone: (392) 397-6021
Fax: (392) 397-4261

ACADEMIC

Founded: 1893
Religion: Non-Affiliated

Type: 4 Yr., Public, Liberal Arts, Coed
Campus Housing: Yes

Student/Faculty Ratio: 15:1
Male/Female Ratio: 1:5
Undergraduate Enrollment: 5,500
Graduate Enrollment: 2,500
Scholarships/Academic: Yes **Athletic:** Yes **Fin Aid:** Yes
Total Expenses by: Year **In State:** $ 10,000 **Out of State:** $ 15,000
Degrees Conferred: BA, BS
Programs of Study: Art Education, Art History, Biochemistry, Biology, Business Administration, Chemistry, Computer Science, Corporate Communication, Earth Science, Economics, Elementary Education, English, Geography, Journalism, Liberal Studies, Mathematics, Nursing, Philosophy, Physical Education, Physics, Political Science, Psychology, Public Health, Social Work, Sociology

ATHLETIC PROFILE

Conference Affiliation: NECC, ECAC
Program Profile: We play a 30/34-game schedule with a 10-game trip to a warmer climate. We play on a good-sized field with two batting cages and a bullpen mound. We have an expansive field house to practice indoors and conduct indoor scrimmages. Practice starts on February 15.
History: Our program began in 1867. We set a record for wins (21) in 1995. Coach Decker, in his seventh year, has improved the program by entering ECAC playoffs in his first two years as coach. We hosted ECAC Division III New England playoffs (#1 seed) in '92. We can particate in NCAA playoffs as of 1994.

Teikyo Post University

800 Country Club road
Waterbury, CT 06723-2540
Coach: Scott Oullette

NAIA
Eagles/Green, White
Phone: (203) 596-4531
Fax: (203) 596-4695

ACADEMIC

Founded: 1890
Type: 4 Yr., Private, Liberal Arts, Coed
Religion: Non-Affiliated
Campus Housing: Yes
Web-site: http://www.teikyopost.edu/
SAT/ACT/GPA: 860/ 18
Student/Faculty Ratio: 1.2:1
Male/Female Ratio: 30:70
Undergraduate Enrollment: 1,700
Graduate Enrollment: None
Scholarships/Academic: Yes **Athletic:** Yes **Fin Aid:** Yes
Total Expenses by: Year **In State:** $ 18,000 **Out of State:** $ 18,000
Degrees Conferred: BA, BS, AA, AS
Programs of Study: Accounting, Business Administration, Early Chidhood Education, English, Equesterian Studies, Fashion Merchandising, Finance, History, Hotel/Restaurant Management, Humanities, Interion Design, International Business, Liberal Arts, Marketing, Prelaw, Psychology

Trinity College - Connecticut

300 Summit Street
Hartford, CT 06512
Coach: Bill Decker

NCAA III
Bantams/Navy, Gold
Phone: (860) 297-2066
Fax: (860) 297-2492

ACADEMIC

Founded: 1823
Type: 4 Yr., Private, Liberal Arts, Coed
Religion: Non-Affiliated
Campus Housing: Yes
Web-site: http://www.trincoll.edu/
SAT/ACT/GPA: 1200
Student/Faculty Ratio: 11:1
Male/Female Ratio: 50:50
Undergraduate Enrollment: 1,750
Graduate Enrollment: 250
Scholarships/Academic: Yes **Athletic:** No **Fin Aid:** Yes
Total Expenses by: Year **In State:** $ 26,000 **Out of State:** $ 26,000
Degrees Conferred: BA, BS, MA, MS

Programs of Study: American Studies, Anthropology, Art, Biochemistry, Biology, Chemistry, Classics, Computer, Economics, Educational, Engineering, English, History, International, Mathematics, Modern Languages, Neuroscience, Religion, Women's Studies, Studio/Theater, Dance, Public Policy

ATHLETIC PROFILE

Conference Affiliation: New England Small College Athletic Conference

US Coast Guard Academy

15 Mohegan Avenue
New London, CT 06320
Coach: Don Pinhey

NCAA III
Bears/Blue, White, Orange
Phone: (860) 444-8600
Fax: (860) 444-8607

ACADEMIC

Founded: 1876
Religion: Non-Affiliated
Web-site: http://www.cga.edu/
Student/Faculty Ratio: 1:10
Undergraduate Enrollment: 825
Scholarships/Academic: No
Athletic: No
Total Expenses by: Year
In State: $ 4,158
Degrees Conferred: BS

Type: 4 Yr., Public, Coed
Campus Housing: Yes
SAT/ACT/GPA: None
Male/Female Ratio: 2:1
Graduate Enrollment: None
Fin Aid: No
Out of State: $ 12,676

Programs of Study: Business and Management, Computer Science, Engineering, Mathematics, Physical Sciences, Social Sciences

ATHLETIC PROFILE

Conference Affiliation: New England Women's and Men's Athletic Conference
Program Profile: In addition to outdoor facility, there is an indoor hitting cage and machine with 50' by 80' tartan surface for indoor practices and scrimmages. The season is in the Spring. We have a grass field on campus.
History: The program began in 1965. Don Pinhey is entering his 31st year as our head coach.
Achievements: We won two Conference Titles and have made two ECAC Tournament Appearances.
Coaching: Don Pinhey, Head Coach, is entering his 31st year as a head coach. He compiled an overall record of 356-477-5. Pete Barry, Assistant Coach.
Roster for 1998 team/In State: 3
Out of State: 19
Out of Country: 0
Total Number of Varsity/Jr. Varsity: 22
Percent of Graduation: 0
Number of Seniors on 1998 Team: 1
Most Recent Record: 10 - 20 - 0
Number of Fall Games: 5
Number of Spring Games: 30
Positions Needed for 1999/2000: Pitcher, 1st Base, Outfielder
Schedule: Babson, Wesleyan, Springfield, Wheaton, Trinity

University of Bridgeport

120 Waldemere Avenue
Bridgeport, CT 06604
Coach: Matt Reed

NCAA II
Purple Knights/Purple, White
Phone: (203) 576-4000
Fax: (203) 576-4057

ACADEMIC

Founded: 1927
Religion: Independent
Web-site: http://www.bridgeport.edu/

Type: 4 Yr., Private, Coed, Engineering
Campus Housing: Yes
SAT/ACT/GPA: 820/ 18

Student/Faculty Ratio: 11:1 **Male/Female Ratio:** 50%
Undergraduate Enrollment: 2,700 **Graduate Enrollment:** ?
Scholarships/Academic: Yes **Athletic:** Yes **Fin Aid:** Yes
Total Expenses by: Year **In State:** $ 21,605 **Out of State:** $ 21,605
Degrees Conferred: AA, AS, BA, BS, BFA, BM, MA, MS, MBA, DC
Programs of Study: Accounting, Biology, Business, Computer Engineering, Education, Human Resources, Arts, Humanities, Science, Social Sciences, Engineering, Dental Hygiene, Political Sciences, Journalism, Music, Etc.

ATHLETIC PROFILE

Conference Affiliation: ECAC, NECC

University of Connecticut

2095 Jillside Rd.
Storrs, CT 06269
Coach: Andrew Baylock

NCAA I
Huskies/National Flag Blue, White
Phone: (860) 486-2858
Fax: (860) 486-2197

ACADEMIC

Founded: 1881 **Type:** 4 Yr., Public, Coed
Religion: Non-Affiliated **Campus Housing:** Yes
Web-site: http://www.uconn.edu/ **SAT/ACT/GPA:** 940+
Student/Faculty Ratio: 14:1 **Male/Female Ratio:** 51:49
Undergraduate Enrollment: 10,629 **Graduate Enrollment:** 6,628
Scholarships/Academic: Yes **Athletic:** Yes **Fin Aid:** Yes
Total Expenses by: Year **In State:** $ 11,175 **Out of State:** $ 19,697
Degrees Conferred: BA, BS, MA, MS, MBA, PhD, DDS, MD, JD
Programs of Study: Business and Management, Communications, Engineering, Health Sciences, Home Economics, Letters/Literature, Multi/Interdisciplenary Studies, Psychology, Social Sciences

ATHLETIC PROFILE

Conference Affiliation: Big East Conference
Program Profile: We are a highly competitive member of an outstanding conference. J.O. Christian Field is natural grass with a permanent seating for 15,000. It has a press box, indoor cages next to the field, access to an Astroturf field and an indoor fieldhouse for winter practice.
History: We began in 1896. We had College World Series Appearances in 1957, 1959, 1965, 1972 & 1979.
Achievements: Coach Baylock was named ABCA Hall of Fame and was Pitching Coach with USA Baseball in 1985, 1988 and 1989. Our University became Big East Champions in 1990 and 1994. We had CWS Appearances in 1957, 1959, 1965, 1972 and 1979. Over 90 former Huskies were drafted or signed by pro clubs. We had 18 All-Americans.
Coaching: Andrew Baylock, Head Coach. Jim Penders and Jerry La Penta - Assistant Coaches.
Style of Play: Good pitching, sound defense and score a lot of runs.

University of Connecticut - Avery Point

1084 Shennecossett Rd
Groton, CT 06340
Coach: Roger Bidwell

NJCAA
Pointers/Blue, White
Phone: (860) 405-9183
Fax: (203) 445-3498

ACADEMIC

Type: 2 Yr., Jr. College, Coed
Programs of Study: Contact school for program of study.

University of Hartford

200 Bloomfield Avenue
West Hartford, CT 06117
Coach: Harvey Shapiro

NCAA I
Hawks/Scarlet, White
Phone: (860) 768-4656
Fax: (860) 768-5047

ACADEMIC

Founded: 1877
Religion: Non-Affiliated
Web-site: http://www.hartford.edu/
Student/Faculty Ratio: 11:1
Undergraduate Enrollment: 3,891
Scholarships/Academic: Yes
Athletic: Yes
Total Expenses by: Year
In State: $ 23,791

Type: 4 Yr., Private, Liberal Arts, Coed
Campus Housing: Yes
SAT/ACT/GPA: 850+
Male/Female Ratio: 52:48
Graduate Enrollment: 1,983
Fin Aid: Yes
Out of State: $ 23,791

Degrees Conferred: AA, AS, AAS, BA, BS, BFA, MA, MS, MBA, Med, D
Programs of Study: 70 Undergraduate programs and 50 graduate programs offered

ATHLETIC PROFILE

Conference Affiliation: America East Conference
Program Profile: Our home field is McKenna Field in East Hartford. The field is lighted, and seats 2,000. We play a four game Fall season and a fifty-two game Spring season. We take a Spring trip to NC, VA or CA. We play a twenty-eight game conference schedule and a fourteen game nonleague schedule. We play a 100% Division I schedule.
History: Our program began in 1958 and we entered Division I in 1985. We had an ECAC post season three of 7 years of membership. Only the top six teams go to the America East tournament.
Achievements: Jeff Bagwell (Astros) in 1991 NL Rookie of the Year; 1989 All-American; 1995 NL Most Valuable Player; 11 players drafted professionally in the last 8 years.

University of New Haven

300 Orange Avenue
West Haven, CT 06516
Coach: Frank Vieira

NCAA II
Chargers/Blue, Gold
Phone: (203) 932-7018
Fax: (203) 932-7470

ACADEMIC

Founded: 1920
Religion: Non-Affiliated
Web-site: http://www.newhaven.edu/
Student/Faculty Ratio: 14:1
Undergraduate Enrollment: 1,600
Scholarships/Academic: Yes
Athletic: Yes
Total Expenses by: Year
In State: $ 18,500

Type: 4 Yr., Private, Coed, Engineering
Campus Housing: Yes
SAT/ACT/GPA: 820/ 17
Male/Female Ratio: 7:5
Graduate Enrollment: 2,600
Fin Aid: Yes
Out of State: $ 18,500

Degrees Conferred: AS, BA, BS, MA, MS, MBA, PhD
Programs of Study: Business/Management, Communications, Computer Science, Criminal Justice, Engineering, Marketing and Distribution, Professional Studies, Pyschology, Social Sciences, Sport Management, Visual and Performing Arts

ATHLETIC PROFILE

Conference Affiliation: ECAC, NECC
Program Profile: The University of New Haven baseball is considered to be one of the top programs in the nation. Head Coach Frank Vieira is beginning his 35th year at the helm. New Haven has earned more than 20 NCAA tournament bids and won nearly 900 games. The team plays at Frank Vieira Field which features a new scoreboard, a two-tier press box and a graff field.

History: The program began in 1963 and will begin its 35th year of competition in 1997. New Haven has appeared in 22 NCAA tournaments and advanced to the Division II World Series 14 times. The program owns a 81% winning percentage with best in Division II. Also, 60 players have signed professional contracts from the program.
Achievements: Frank Vieira has eraned many Conference and Region Coach of the Year awards of which the most recent was in 1995. We won 12 Regional Championships during our history. More 30 of our players earned All-Americans status while 60 signed pro contracts. Seven of our players appeared in the major league including Steve Bedrosian, the 1987 CY Young Award Winner.
Style of Play: The team style of play consists of pitching and fielding. We led the country in pitching ERA and we came in fourth place fielding percentage in the country. Hitting (305) as a team was a low point of the season.

Wesleyan University

161 Cross Street
Middletown, CT 06459
Coach: Peter Kostacopoulos
Email: pkostacopoul@wesleyan.edu

NCAA III
Cardinals/Cardinal, Black
Phone: (860) 685-2924
Fax: (860) 685-2691

ACADEMIC

Founded: 1809
Type: 4 Yr., Private, Liberal Arts, Coed
Web-site: http://www.wesleyan.edu/
SAT/ACT/GPA: 1300
Student/Faculty Ratio: 9:1
Male/Female Ratio: 1:1
Undergraduate Enrollment: 650
Graduate Enrollment: 150
Scholarships/Academic: Yes **Athletic:** No **Fin Aid:** Yes
Total Expenses by: Year **In State:** $ 30,000 **Out of State:** $ 30,000
Degrees Conferred: BA, MA, PhD
Programs of Study: 960 courses offered in 50 Major Fields of Study ranging from Natural and Social Sciences to Fine Arts, Music, Theater, English, Foreign Languages

ATHLETIC PROFILE

Conference Affiliation: NESCAC, ECAC, Little Three Conference
Program Profile: The NCAA Division III program is very competitive. Our baseball field is located in the center of the campus. We have excellent fan support. We have a superior indoor practice facility which has measurements of 345' long fieldhouseand is completely netted for indoor games and practices. We have a batting cage and a natural surface on an outdoor playing field which runs from February 15 through March 5.
History: Baseball is the oldest sport in Wesleyan history. Began as an Agallian Baseball team in 1864. Ffirst varsity game was against Yale in 1865. In 121 seasons, overall record is 962-946-31.
Achievements: Our best season was in 1994 when we won the NCAA Regional and finished 2nd at the NCAA World Series. Our pitcher Craig Brewer was 2nd All-American. Peter Kostacopoulos was named Regional Coach of the Year for the 2nd time in his career. That year, the team had a 30-8 record. We posted 12 straight winning seasons from 1985-1996 with a .636 winning percentage.
Coaching: Peter Kostacopoulos, Head Coach, was named Regional Coach of the Year two times. He is entering his 26th year as the head coach. He compiled a record of 404-248-6 (.619), He was District I and Division III Coach of the Year. He graduated from University of Maine in 1957. Pete M. Kostacopulos, Assistant Coach, is responsible for the pitchers. He graduated from Trinity in 1992. Phil Guidrey, Infield Coach, graduated from Wesleyan in 1988.
Style of Play: Varies with the nature of the team. In general, work to advance runners while preserving opponents from doing the same.

Western Connecticut State University

181 White Street
Danbury, CT 06810
Coach: Moe Morhardt

NCAA III
Colonial/Blue, White
Phone: (203) 837-8608
Fax: (203) 837-9050

ACADEMIC

Founded: 1903
Web-site: http://www.ctstateu.edu/
Student/Faculty Ratio: 15:1
Undergraduate Enrollment: 3,500
Scholarships/Academic: Yes **Athletic:** No
Total Expenses by: Year **In State:** $ 7,000
Type: 4 Yr., Public, Liberal Arts, Coed
SAT/ACT/GPA: 900
Male/Female Ratio: 50:50
Graduate Enrollment: 1,000
Fin Aid: Yes
Out of State: $ 13,000
Degrees Conferred: AS, BA, BS, MA, MS, MBA
Programs of Study: Accounting, American Studies, Art, Biology, Chemistry, Communications, Computer, Contract Major, Dramatic Arts, Earth Science, Economics, Marketing, Meteorology, Law

ATHLETIC PROFILE

Conference Affiliation: Little East Conference
Program Profile: Financially based on financial aid and grants. We have a fully enclosed lighted field which is 322 down each lines, 376 to the left center field, 392 to the center field and 372 to the right center field. It seats 800 and has a new press box facility, a scoreboard, and an entirely new infield surface.
History: Our program began in 1949. The Ken Capodice era began in 1986. We have made five trips to FCAC. Our new coach for the 1997 season is Moe Morhardt.
Achievements: We had 7 players drafted including Jeff Bagwell-Nation's All-league Rookie of the Year and MVP and All-Star.
Coaching: Moe Morhardt, Head Coach, was with the Chicago Cubs from 1961-1962. Bill Walton, Assistant Coach, has 25 years of coaching experience and is also co-chairman of Communication Department. Daryl Morhardt, Assistant Coach, has three years of professional baseball experience as Division I coach. Anthony Reesich, Assistant Coach, came from Boston College.
Style of Play: We look for exceptional hitters and defensive players. We spend a great deal of time on defensive situations and base running. We like to score runs.

Yale University

P.O. Box 20816
New Haven, CT 06520
Coach: John Stuper
NCAA I
Bulldogs/Yale Blue, White
Phone: (203) 432-4747
Fax: (203) 432-7772

ACADEMIC

Founded: 1701
Religion: Non-Affiliated
Web-site: http://www.yale.edu/
Student/Faculty Ratio: 5:1
Undergraduate Enrollment: 5,200
Scholarships/Academic: No **Athletic:** No
Total Expenses by: Year **In State:** $ 28,800
Type: 4 Yr., Private, Liberal Arts, Coed
Campus Housing: Yes
SAT/ACT/GPA: Yes
Male/Female Ratio: 52:48
Graduate Enrollment: 5,200
Fin Aid: Yes
Out of State: $ 28,800
Degrees Conferred: BA, BS, MA, Doctorates, First Professional
Programs of Study: African and African -American Studies, Anthropology, Astronomy and Physics, Chemistry, Chinese, Classics, Comparitive Literature, Economics, Engineering, English, History, Judaic Studies, Latin American Studies, Mathematics, Organismal Biology, Philosophy, Physics

ATHLETIC PROFILE

Conference Affiliation: Ivy League, ECAC

DELAWARE

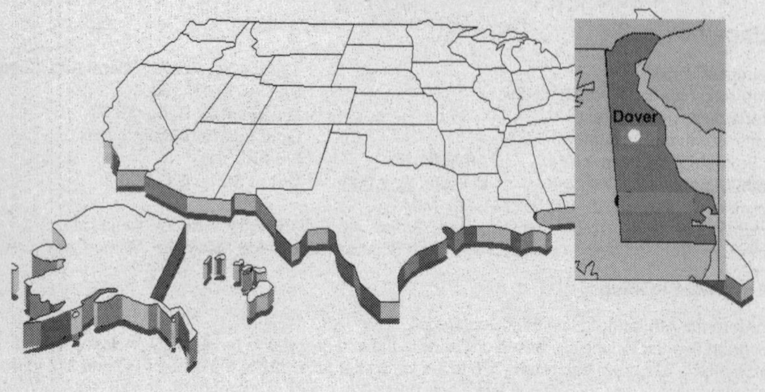

SCHOOL	CITY	AFFILIATION 99	PAGE
Delaware State University	Dover	NCAA I	151
Delaware Tech Owens Campus	Georgetown	NJCAA	151
University of Delaware	Newark	NCAA I	152
Wesley College	Dover	NCAA III	153
Wilmington College - Delaware	New Castle	NAIA	153

Delaware State University

1200 N Dupont Hwy
Dover, DE 19901-2277
Coach: Tripp Keister

NCAA I
Hornets/Red, Blue
Phone: (302) 736-2304
Fax: (302) 736-2200

ACADEMIC

Founded: 1891
Religion: Non-Affiliated
Web-site: Not-Available
Student/Faculty Ratio: 14:1
Undergraduate Enrollment: 3,030
Scholarships/Academic: Yes **Athletic:** Yes
Total Expenses by: Year **In State:** $ 5,776
Degrees Conferred: BA, BS, MA, MS, MBA, MSW, BT
Programs of Study: Accounting, Airway Science

Type: 4 Yr., Public, Coed
Campus Housing: Yes
SAT/ACT/GPA: 1000+
Male/Female Ratio: 47:53
Graduate Enrollment: 200
Fin Aid: Yes
Out of State: $ 8,808

ATHLETIC PROFILE

Estimated Number of Baseball Scholarships: 5
Conference Affiliation: Mid-Eastern Athletic Conference (MEAC), ECAC
Program Profile: We are a small Division I program with a 2,500 students. We have a 56 game Spring schedule and two trips to Florida (Spring break and conference championship). The conference winner goes to NCAA play-ins games. Our stadium has a natural grass playing field and holds approximately 200 people.
History: Records indicate that DSU baseball started in the early 1930's.
Achievements: We have MAEC Coach of the Year for 1989 and Conference Champions. We have the NCAA record for ten batting average of .396 set in 1989. The last player we had drafted is Pedro Swann in 1990. He is currently playing for the AAA Richmond Braves. We have a pitcher,Larry Burkindine, that may set drafted this June.
Coaching: Tripp Keister, Head Coach, is entering his first year with the program. Nate Goulet is Assistant Coach.
Roster for 1998 Team/In State: 12 **Out of State:** 10 **Out of Country:** 2
Total Number of Varsity/Jr. Varsity: 27 **Percent of Graduation:** 84%
Freshmen Receiving Fin Aid/Athletic: 5 **Academic:** 9
Most Recent Record: 8 - 36 - 0 **Number of Spring Games:** 56
Positions Needed for 1999/2000: Catcher, Pitcher, Infielder
Schedule: VCU, Old Dominion, University of Delaware
Style of Play: Aggressive.

Delaware Tech Owens Campus

PO Box 610 Rt 18
Georgetown, DE 19947
Coach: Curtis Brock

NJCAA
Roadrunners/Kelly, White
Phone: (302) 855-1636
Fax: (302) 856-5428

ACADEMIC

Founded: 1967
Religion: Non-Affiliated
Student/Faculty Ratio: 16:1
Undergraduate Enrollment: 1,944
Scholarships/Academic: No **Athletic:** Yes
Total Expenses by: Year **In State:** $ 1,200
Degrees Conferred: Associates

Type: 2 Yr., Jr. College, Coed
Campus Housing: No
Male/Female Ratio: 38:62
Graduate Enrollment: Unknown
Fin Aid: Yes
Out of State: $ 3,000

Programs of Study: Accounting, Agricultural Business, Architectural Technology, Automotive Technology, Business Administration, Commerce, Management, Carpentry, Civil Engineering Technology, Computer Programming, Construction Management, Criminal Justice, Drafting/Design, Data Processing, Journalism, Human Services, Medical Laboratoy Technology

ATHLETIC PROFILE

Conference Affiliation: Region 19
Program Profile: Delaware Tech Baseball team is a very aggressive unit. This is just their style of play. Most of the teams at Delaware Tech pass high team batting averages. The playing field is natural grass. The seating capacity is approximately 1,000.
History: Delaware baseball program started in 1989. The Roadrunner have been one of the top teams in the paths for the last four years. (high team rating, and also high team hitting).
Achievements: Coach of the Year in 1995; 1992 Runner-Up for Region 19; Region Title in 1985; 6 players drafted.
Coaching: Curtis Brock, Head Coach. John Jones and Chris Waldon, Assistant Coaches.
Style of Play: Very fundamental but aggressive on the basepath and at the plate.

University of Delaware

Bob Carpenter Center
Newark, DE 19716
Coach: Bob Hannah

NCAA I
Fightin' Blue Hens/Royal Blue, Gold
Phone: (302) 831-8596
Fax: (302) 831-4058

ACADEMIC

Founded: 1743
Religion: Non-Affiliated
Web-site: http://www.udel.edu/
Student/Faculty Ratio: 15:1
Undergraduate Enrollment: 15,359
Scholarships/Academic: Yes **Athletic:** Yes
Total Expenses by: Year **In State:** $ 9,000

Type: 4 Yr., Public, Coed, Engineering
Campus Housing: Yes
SAT/ACT/GPA: App. 1,000
Male/Female Ratio: 45:55
Graduate Enrollment: 3,200
Fin Aid: Yes
Out of State: $ 16,000

Degrees Conferred: BA, BS, BMAS, Engineering
Programs of Study: Over 110 Majors offered: Agricultural Sciences (Business Management, Economics, Education, Sciences, Engineering, Entomology, Etc.), Arts and Sciences (Anthropology, Art, Biochemistry, Biological, Biotechnology, Chemistry, Communication, Literature, Computer, Criminal Justice, Economics, English, Etc.), Business and Economics (Accounting, Finance, Management, Marketing), Education (Elementary), Engineering (Chemical, Civil, Electrical, Computer, Mechanical, Environmental), Human Resources (Apparel Design, Nutrition, Dietetics, Family and Consumer Services, Etc.), Textiles and Clothing (Merchandising), Nursing (Medical Technology, Nursing), Physical Education, Athletics and Recreation (Training, Health, Physical Education, Recreation/Park)

ATHLETIC PROFILE

Conference Affiliation: America East Conference
Program Profile: Delaware plays a highly competitive Division I schedule in the North Atlantic Conference. It plays about 50 games in Spring . The Fall season is dedicated to practices/intrasquad scrimmages. Ballpark has 2,000 seats and natural grass .Recent renovations at Delaware Diamond are: new seats and new pressbox . Lights are planned for the near future. UD plays some games at Wilmington Blue Rock Stadium which seats 6,000.
History: Play began in 1882. First (and oldest) intercollegiate game (entering its 107th season) played in 1892. The team has won 61.7% of its games since 1882 (1362) It is recognized as one of the top programs in the East and has produced 28 All-Americans, 50+ pro players, 32 draft picks and five ML. It has made nine NCAA tournament appearances (including 1996); advanced to the College World Series in 1970; and captured 19 Mid-Atlantic, East Coast and North Atlantic Conference regular season titles. All-time record is 1406-857-28 (.621).

Achievements: We have 4 ECC Coach of the Year honors including back-to-back in 1989 and 1990. Bob Hannah was named NCAA East Region Coach of the Year four times. Thirty-two of our players were drafted. We received 14 Conference Player of the Year Awards since 1976.
Coaching: Bob Hannah, Head Coach, was ECC Coach of the Year. He was NCAA East Region Coach of the Year four times. He is entering 34 years as a head coach. He is a member of the American Baseball Coaches Association Hall of Fame. He earned two straight East Coast Conference Coach of the Year awards in 1989 and 1990 and claimed the award a total of four times while Delaware was a member of the ECC from 1975 to 1991. He was named American East Coach of the Year three times.
Style of Play: Run and hit offense - aggressive defense.

Wesley College

120 North State State
Dover, DE 19990-1
Coach: Bob Reed

NCAA III
Wolverines/Navy, Columbia, White
Phone: (302) 736-2422
Fax: (302) 736-0345

ACADEMIC

Founded: 1873
Type: 4 Yr., Private, Liberal Arts, Coed
Religion: Methodist
Campus Housing: Yes
Web-site: http://www.wesley.edu/
SAT/ACT/GPA: 900
Student/Faculty Ratio: 15:1
Male/Female Ratio: 50:50
Undergraduate Enrollment: 800
Graduate Enrollment: 30
Scholarships/Academic: Yes **Athletic:** No **Fin Aid:** Yes
Total Expenses by: Year **In State:** $ 16,000 **Out of State:** $ 16,000
Degrees Conferred: Baccalaureates, some new Masters Programs
Programs of Study: Allied Health, Biology, Business and Management, Business/Office and Marketing/Distribution, Communications, Computer Sciences, Education, Environmental Science, Health Sciences, History, Law, Letters/Literature, Political Sciences

ATHLETIC PROFILE

Conference Affiliation: Independent Conference
Program Profile: We have a good Division III program. We have a very good playing field, with enclosed dugouts and field. There is also a double batting cage with polygrass floor. We have a Fall practice of 6 weeksand a competitive 36 game schedule.
History: We began playing Division III baseball in 1987. Our ten year record is 156-150-2. We won the ECAC South Region tournament in 1992.
Achievements: 1992 ECAC South Champions; Five of our players were named to All-Region.
Coaching: Bob Reed, Head Coach, has been head coach for 29 years.
Style of Play: Aggressive at the plate and on the bases, make the routine plays on defense and throw strikes.

Wilmington College - Delaware

320 N Du Pont Highway
New Castle, DE 19720
Coach: Matt Brainard

NAIA
Wildcats/Green, White
Phone: (302) 328-9401
Fax: (302) 328-8045

ACADEMIC

Founded: 1967
Type: 4 Yr., Coed
Religion: Non-Affiliated
Campus Housing: No
Student/Faculty Ratio: 22:1
Male/Female Ratio: 1:1.3
Undergraduate Enrollment: 5,500
Graduate Enrollment: Unknown
Scholarships/Academic: Yes **Athletic:** Yes **Fin Aid:** Yes

Total Expenses by: Year **In State:** $ 6,080+ **Out of State:** $ 6,008+
Degrees Conferred: Bachelors, Masters, Doctoral
Programs of Study: Accounting, Aircraft and Missile Maintenace, Air Traffic Control, Aviation Administration, Aviation Technology, Behavioral Science, Broadcasting, Business Administration, Commerce, Management, Communications, Criminal Justice, Early Childhood Education, Elementary Education, Finance/Banking, Human Resources, Liberal Arts, General Studies, Nursing, Sports Administration, Theatre Arts/Drama

ATHLETIC PROFILE

Conference Affiliation: Independent, Northeast Regional
Program Profile: We play on a natural surface field that seats approximately 1,200. We play a 45-50 game regular season schedule, which includes a trip to North Carolina during Spring break. Even though we are NAIA, we play what would be equal to a NCAA Division II schedule.
History: The program began in 1972. I was named coach in 1994, to become the fifth head coach in the program's history. We have made four trips to the NAIA World Series, with three of them coming in the 1990's. We have also won 17 conference or sectional championships, with four regional championship trophies.
Achievements: The program's highest finish nationally came in 1992, when we finished fifth in the nation. In 1993 we were pre-season Top 15. The program has had close to 30 players to receive some type of All-American status. There have been about eight players drafted or signed from the program, with the highest being a 25th round pick, and the last being a FA signee in 1994.
Coaching: Matt Brainard, Head Coach , has coached three seasons. In his first season, the Wildcats won the Northeast Region title. His team played at Wilmington and he was an HM All-American in 1992 and a second team All-American in 1993. He played two years with the Phillies before taking over at his Alma Mater.
Style of Play: Aggressive. Like to run, hit and run.

DISTRICT OF COLUMBIA

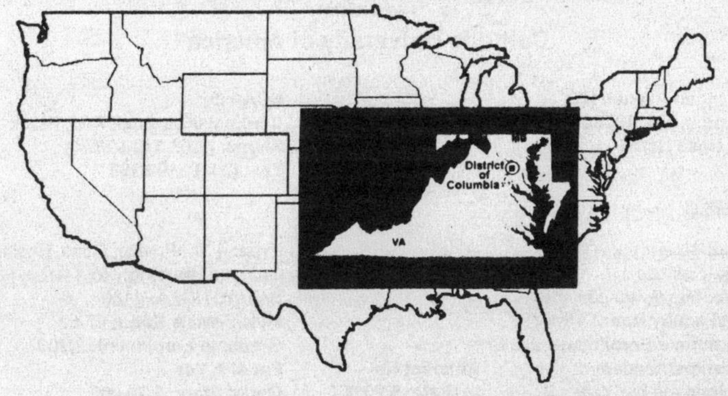

SCHOOL	CITY	AFFILIATION 99	PAGE
Catholic University of America	Washington	NCAA III	156
Gallaudet University	Washington	NCAA III	156
George Washington University	Washington	NCAA I	157
Georgetown University	Washington	NCAA I	158
Howard University	Washington	NCAA I	158

Catholic University of America

620 Michigan Avenue NE
Washington, DC 20064
Coach: Ross Natoli

NCAA III
Cardinals/Cardinal, Red, Black
Phone: (202) 319-5287
Fax: (202) 319-6199

ACADEMIC

Founded: 1887
Type: 4 Yr., Private, Coed, Engineering
Religion: Catholic
Campus Housing: No
Web-site: http://www.cua.edu/
SAT/ACT/GPA: 1100
Student/Faculty Ratio: 15:1
Male/Female Ratio: 47:53
Undergraduate Enrollment: 2,500
Graduate Enrollment: 3,700
Scholarships/Academic: Yes **Athletic:** No **Fin Aid:** Yes
Total Expenses by: Year **In State:** $ 20,000 **Out of State:** $ 20,000
Degrees Conferred: BA, BS, BArch, MA, MS, MFA, PhD, EdD, JD, Mdiv
Programs of Study: Architecture and Planning, Arts and Sciences, Engineering, Music, Nursing

ATHLETIC PROFILE

Conference Affiliation: Capital Athletic Conference
Program Profile: Compete in both fall and spring seasons and play a 45-game schedule against top Division III teams in the country and several Division I opponents including Georgetown, Navy, William and Mary and Mt. St. Mary's. We do a nine-day Spring trip to Cocoa Beach, Florida each year. Home games are played in a natural grass stadium. Indoor facilities include 5 batting cages, 5 portable pitching mounds, indoor track, nautilus and free weights and practice infield.
History: The program began in 1896. Wally Pipp attended architecture school from 1911-1913 before going on to star with NY Yankees. We played in Division I from 1974-1983. We advanced to the final game of the 1977 NCAA East Regional and participated in NCAA playoffs in 1979, 1981 and 1983. We moved to Division III in 1984. The Cardinals have averaged over 20 wins since 1991.
Achievements: We have 20+ wins season in 1992, 1993 and 1995;. Several of our players were named to the Capital Athletic Conference teams and NCAA Division III South Region teams. Our shortstop, John Douglas, was drafted by the Toronto Blue Jays in 1995.
Coaching: Ross Natoli, Head Coach, is on his 13th year at Catholic. He was a former player and coach at George, WA.
Style of Play: Emphasis is on pitching, defense and an aggressive offense. We are sound fundamentally and strive to make the routine plays on defense, manufacture runs offensively and capitalize on opponents mistakes and weakness.

Gallaudet University

800 Florida Avenue NE
Washington, DC 20002
Coach: Kris Gould
Email: @gallud.gallaudet.edu

NCAA III
Bison/Blue, Buff
Phone: (202) 651-5603
Fax: (202) 651-5274

ACADEMIC

Founded: 1857
Type: 4 Yr., Private, Liberal Arts, Coed
Web-site: http://www.gallaudet.edu/
Campus Housing: Yes
Student/Faculty Ratio: 5:1
Male/Female Ratio: 48:52
Undergraduate Enrollment: 1,339
Graduate Enrollment: 714
Scholarships/Academic: Yes **Athletic:** No **Fin Aid:** Yes
Total Expenses by: Year **In State:** $ 14,586 **Out of State:** $ 14,586
Degrees Conferred: AAS, BA, BS,MA, MS, MBA, MEd, PhD, EdD
Programs of Study: Accounting, Art History, Biochemistry, Biology, Business, Communications, Computer, Engineering, English, International Studies, Management, Math, Philosophy, Recreation, Religion, Social Science ***Contact school for more information

ATHLETIC PROFILE

Conference Affiliation: Capital Athletic Conference
Program Profile: We have a fall/spring baseball program. Our field is natural grass and has a 350 circumference fence. 35-40 games are normally scheduled every spring and 5-10 in fall. The weather in March is 56-65 degrees and in April 65-80 degrees. Training facilities include two weight rooms and two large indoor gymnasiums.
History: We have the only deaf college baseball team in the world. Gallaudet began its baseball program in spring 1895. Our 1995 team won a Gallaudet - best 13 game series versus all varsity college team competition. Gallaudet has fielded 68 teams between 1895 and 1995.
Achievements: 5 All-Conference players; 2 All-Region; 1995 team recorded 13 victories; 1993 team went to #2 NCAA III ranking in stolen bases.
Style of Play: Aggressive with improved pitching.

George Washington University

600 2nd Street NW
Washington, DC 20037
Coach: Tom Walter
Email: gwbsb@gwis2.circ.gwc.edu

NCAA I
Colonials/Buff, Blue
Phone: (202) 994-7399
Fax: (202) 994-6818

ACADEMIC

Founded: 1821
Type: 4 Yr., Private, Liberal Arts, Coed
Web-site: http://www.gwu.edu/
SAT/ACT/GPA: No required minimum
Student/Faculty Ratio: 14:1
Male/Female Ratio: 45:55
Undergraduate Enrollment: 6,581
Graduate Enrollment: 8,698
Scholarships/Academic: Yes **Athletic:** Yes **Fin Aid:** Yes
Total Expenses by: Year **In State:** $ 28,685 **Out of State:** $ 28,685
Degrees Conferred: 1184 Bachelors Degree conferred 1995-1996 foggy bottom campus.
Programs of Study: Accounting, Anthropology, Applied Mathematics, Archaelogy, Arts, Biology, Business, Chemistry, Computer Science, Criminal Justice, Economics, Engineering, Pschology

ATHLETIC PROFILE

Estimated Number of Baseball Scholarships: 11.7
Conference Affiliation: Atlantic 10 Conference
Program Profile: We are Teir I National level designation and fully-funded. We have3 paid full-time coaches. We are the only men's sport at the university to win an Atlantic 10 Championship NCAA Regional in 1979, 1989, 1992 in the past 8 years. We have yeilds and play in a natural grass, lighted field at Barcroft Park in Arlington, Virginia. It seats 1,200 and has a press box, bathrooms and batting cages. The field measures 325, 380, and 325.
History: The only data available is since 1953. Our record is approximately 778-727-11. We do, however, have some information on alums dating back as far as 1933.
Achievements: In 1998, Tom Walter was named Atlantic 10 Coach of the Year. Tom Boginski and Joe Beichert were 1st team All-Conference. Mike Roberts and Ryan Dacey were 2nd team All-Conference and Atlantic 10 West Division Champions. In 1998, 33-17 set a school record for wins.
Coaching: Tom Walter, Head Coach, graduated from Georgetown in 1991. He was named Atlantic 10 Coach of the Year in 1998. He compiled an overall record of 54-50. Joe Raccuia , Assistant Coach, graduated from Radford in 1994.
Roster for 1998 team/In State: 26 **Out of State:** 0 **Out of Country:** 0
Total Number of Varsity/Jr. Varsity: 26 **Percent of Graduation:** 97%
Freshmen Receiving Fin Aid/Athletic: 4 **Academic:** 2
Number of Seniors on 1998 Team: 6 **Number of Spring Games:** 56
Most Recent Record: 33 - 17 - 0 **Baseball Camp Dates:** June 22-25
Positions Needed for 1999/2000: Shortstop, 2 LHP, 1 RHP
Schedule: University of Washington, South Carolina, North Carolina-Greensboro, Coastal Carolina
Style of Play: We swing the bats - not much on the short game. Pitch and play defense.

Georgetown University

Athletics, Box 571121
Washington, DC 20057
Coach: Kirk Mason

NCAA I
Hoyas/Blue, Grey
Phone: (202) 687-2462
Fax: (202) 687-3981

ACADEMIC

Founded: 1789
Religion: Catholic Jesuit
Web-site: http://www.georgetown.ecu/
Student/Faculty Ratio: 12:1
Undergraduate Enrollment: 6,000
Scholarships/Academic: No **Athletic:** No
Total Expenses by: Year **In State:** $ 31,000
Type: 4 Yr., Private, Liberal Arts, Coed
Campus Housing: Yes
SAT/ACT/GPA: 1100+
Male/Female Ratio: 49:51
Graduate Enrollment: 6,000
Fin Aid: Yes
Out of State: $ 31,000
Degrees Conferred: BA, BS, MA, MBA, PhD, MD, JD
Programs of Study: Accounting, Anthropology, Archeology, Arts, Biology, Business and Management, Communications, Computer Science, Criminal Justice, Geography, Engineering, Mathematics, Philosophy, Human Resources, Religion, Political Science, Medical Technology

ATHLETIC PROFILE

Conference Affiliation: Big East Conference
Program Profile: Home games are played on natural grass field.
History: Program began in 1869.
Achievements: Sean Maloney was drafted in 1993 by the Milwaukee Brewers.
Coaching: Kirk Mason, Head Coach. Pete Wilke, Assistant Coach.
Total Number of Varsity/Jr. Varsity: 30/
Number of Seniors on 1998 Team: 10
Freshmen Receiving Fin Aid/Athletic: 0
Most Recent Record: 22 - 34 - 0
Percent of Graduation: 100%
Number of Sophomores on 1998 Team: 0
Academic: 4
Number of Spring Games: 56
Positions Needed for 1999/2000: Shortstops, Centerfielders, Catchers, Pitcher
Schedule: Duke, Rutgers, Notre Dame, West Virginia, St. John's, Seton Hall
Style of Play: Aggressive.

Howard University

2400 6th Street NW
Washington, DC 20059
Coach: Chuck Hinton

NCAA I
Bison/Navy, White
Phone: (202) 806-5162
Fax: (202) 806-9090

ACADEMIC

Founded: 1867
Web-site: http://www.howard.edu/
Student/Faculty Ratio: Unknown
Undergraduate Enrollment: 7,650
Scholarships/Academic: Yes **Athletic:** Yes
Total Expenses by: Year **In State:** $ 12,000
Type: 4 Yr., Private, Coed, Engineering
SAT/ACT/GPA: 820/18
Male/Female Ratio: 40:60
Graduate Enrollment: 3,050
Fin Aid: Yes
Out of State: $ 12,000
Degrees Conferred: BA, BS, BFA, BArch, BBA, BFA, BSW, MA, MS, BA, MFA, MEd, PhD, JD
Programs of Study: Accounting, Acturial Science, Anthropology, Arabic, Architecture, Banking/Finance, Botany, Business Administration, Chemistry, Criminal Justice, Economics, Education, Engineering, History, Insurance, International Business and Relations, Marketing

ATHLETIC PROFILE

Conference Affiliation: Mid-Eastern Athletic Conference

FLORIDA

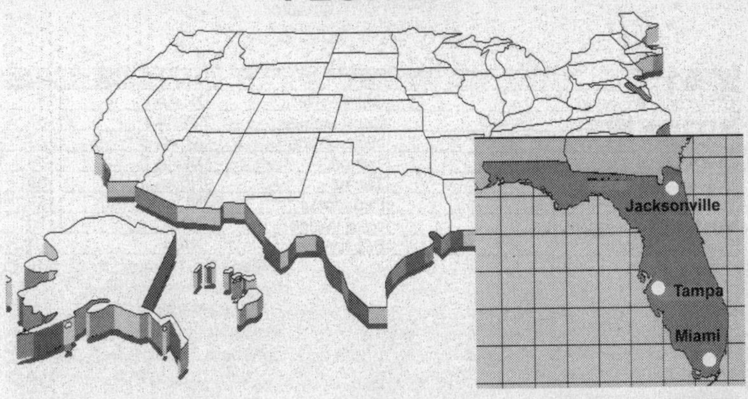

SCHOOL	CITY	AFFILIATION 99	PAGE
Barry University	Miami Shores	NCAA II	161
Bethune - Cookman College	Daytona Beach	NCAA I	161
Brevard Community College	Cocoa	NJCAA	162
Broward Community College	Ft Lauderdale	NJCAA	162
Central Florida Community College	Ocala	NJCAA	163
Chipola Junior College	Mariana	NJCAA	163
Eckerd College	St. Petersburg	NJCAA	164
Edward Waters College	Jacksonville	NAIA	165
Embry-Riddle Aeronautical	Daytona Beach	NAIA	165
Flagler College	St. Augustine	NAIA	166
Florida A & M University	Tallahassee	NCAA I	167
Florida Atlantic College	Boca Raton	NCAA I	167
Florida Community College - Jacksonville	Jacksonville	NJCAA	168
Florida Institute of Technology	Melbourne	NCAA II	169
Florida International University	Miami	NCAA I	169
Florida Memorial College	Miami	NAIA	170
Florida Southern College	Lakeland	NCAA II	170
Florida State University	Tallahassee	NCAA I	171
Gulf Coast Community College	Panama City	NJCAA	172
Hillsborough CC - Dale Campus	Tampa	NJCAA	173
Indian River Community College	Fort Pierce	NJCAA	173
Jacksonville University	Jacksonville	NCAA I	174
Lake City Community College	Lake City	NJCAA	174
Lynn University	Boca Raton	NCAA II/NAIA	175
Manatee Community College	Brandenton	NJCAA	175
Miami - Dade Community College	Miami	NJCAA	176
North Florida Junior College	Madison	NJCAA	176
Northwood University	West Palm Beach	NAIA	177
Nova Southeastern University	Fort Lauderdale	NAIA	177
Okaloosa - Walton Community College	Niceville	NJCAA	178
Palm Beach Atlantic College	West Palm Beach	NAIA	178
Palm Beach Community College	Lake Worth	NJCAA	179
Pasco Hernando Community College	New Port Richey	NJCAA	179
Pensacola Junior College	Pensacola	NJCAA	180
Polk Community College	Winter Haven	NJCAA	180
Rollins College	Winter Park	NCAA II	181
Saint John's River Community College	Palatka	NJCAA	181
Saint Leo College	Saint Leo	NCAA II	182
Saint Petersburg J C	St Petersburg	NJCAA	182
Saint Thomas University	Miami	NAIA	183
Santa Fe Community College	Gainesville	NJCAA	184
Seminole Community College	Sanford	NJCAA	184
Stetson University	Deland	NCAA I	184
Tallahassee Community College	Tallahassee	NJCAA	185
University of Central Florida	Orlando	NCAA I	186

SCHOOL	CITY	AFFILIATION 99	PAGE
University of Florida	Gainesville	NCAA I	187
University of Miami	Coral Gables	NCAA I	187
University of North Florida	Jacksonville	NCAA II	188
University of South Florida	Tampa	NCAA I	188
University of Tampa	Tampa	NCAA II	189
University of West Florida	Pensacola	NCAA II/NAIA	189
Warner Southern College	Lake Wales	NAIA	190
Webber College	Babson Park	NAIA	190

Barry University

11300 NE 2nd Avenue
Miami Shores, FL 33161
Coach: Chris Cafalone

NCAA II
Buccaneers/Red, Black, Silver
Phone: (305) 899-3558
Fax: (305) 899-3556

ACADEMIC

Founded: 1940
Religion: Catholic
Web-site: http://www.barry.edu/
Student/Faculty Ratio: 15:1
Undergraduate Enrollment: 1,575
Scholarships/Academic: Yes **Athletic:** Yes
Total Expenses by: Year **In State:** $ 18,000

Type: 4 Yr., Private, Liberal Arts, Coed
Campus Housing: Yes
SAT/ACT/GPA: 840+/18+
Male/Female Ratio: 40:60
Graduate Enrollment: 2,200
Fin Aid: Yes
Out of State: $ 18,000

Degrees Conferred: BA, BS, BFA, MA, MS, MBA, PhD, DPM
Programs of Study: Accounting, Art Administration, Athletic Training, Biology, Business and Management, Communications, Criminal Justice, Cytotechnology, Economics, Engineering Technology, International Business, Management Information Systems, Marine Science, Marketing, Mathematics, Nuclear Medical Technology, Philosophy, Physical Therapy, Pre-Professional Courses, Psychology, Sports Administration, Sports medicine, Theatre

ATHLETIC PROFILE

Conference Affiliation: Sunshine State Conference
Program Profile: We are a private School with 14 to 1 student teacher ratio. We have an excellent facility and a 56 game schedule with year round playing climate. We are in the toughest Division II conference in the nation.
History: Our program began in 1984. Our 1992-1993 year rated 18th in pre-season polls. We were ranked as high as 12th in the nation in 1992-93.
Achievements: 1 All-American candidate in 1993; 5 players drafted in 9 years.
Coaching: Chris Cafalone, Head Coach.
Style of Play: Aggressive but smart style of play - fundamentally sound approach to the game with a tremendous work ethic.

Bethune - Cookman College

640 Mary McLeon Bethune Blvd
Daytona Beach, FL 32114
Coach: Richard Skeel
Email: melendem@cookman.edu

NCAA I
Wildcats/Maroon, Gold
Phone: (904) 255-1401
Fax: (904) 253-4231

ACADEMIC

Founded: 1872
Religion: Methodist
Web-site: Not Available
Student/Faculty Ratio: 25:1
Undergraduate Enrollment: 2,335
Scholarships/Academic: Yes **Athletic:** Yes
Total Expenses by: Year **In State:** $ 13,469

Type: 4 Yr., Private, Liberal Arts, Coed
Campus Housing: Yes
SAT/ACT/GPA: 500/21/2.25
Male/Female Ratio: 47:53
Graduate Enrollment: None
Fin Aid: Yes
Out of State: $ 13,469

Degrees Conferred: Bachelors
Programs of Study: Church Music, English, History, International Studies, Liberal Studies, Mass Communications, Modern Languages, Music, Political Science, Religion and Philosophy, Social Science, Sociology, Accounting, Biology, Business Administration, Chemistry, Computer Science, Criminal Justice, Elementary Education, Gerontology, Mathematics, Nursing, Physics, Psychology, Special Learning Disabilities

ATHLETIC PROFILE

Estimated Number of Baseball Scholarships: 4
Conference Affiliation: Mideastern Athletic Conference
Program Profile: We play at Jackie Robinson ballpark which is also host of Daytona Cubs affiliated to the Chicago Cubs. The ballpark has natural grass and holds approximately 5,000 fans.
History: The record for 1995 was 29-19-0, the best record in the history of the program. We were 1996 and 1997 MEAC Conference Champions.
Achievements: 1996 and 1997 Conference Champions. In 1997, we had 2 players drafted with the Dodgers: Wayne Slater-Outfielder and Michael Rawls-LHP.
Coaching: Richard Skeel, Head Coach, started in 1997. Our overall record is 549-307 Coach Skeel was named Conference Coach of the Year in 1997. Mervyll Melendez, Assistant Coach.
Roster for 1998 team/In State: 10 **Out of State:** 10 **Out of Country:** 9
Total Number of Varsity/Jr. Varsity: 29 **Percent of Graduation:** 85%
Number of Seniors on 1998 Team: 4 **Number of Sophomores on 1998 Team:** 0
Freshmen Receiving Fin Aid/Athletic: 1 **Academic:** 3
Most Recent Record: 27 - 29 - 0 **Number of Spring Games:** 56
Positions Needed for 1999/2000: Pitchers, Centerfield
Schedule: Florida, Central Florida, Florida International, Jacksonville, Florida Atlantic, Stetson
Style of Play: We are a team that is going to hit the ball from gap to gap and steal bases. We'll play good defense and our pitchers will make hitters put the ball on the ground a lot.

Brevard Community College

1519 Clearlake Road
Cocoa, FL 32922
Coach: Ernie Rosseau

NJCAA
Titans/Royal, White
Phone: (407) 632-1111
Fax: (407) 633-4565

ACADEMIC

Founded: 1960 **Type:** 2 Yr., Jr. College, Coed
Religion: Non-Affiliated **Campus Housing:** No
Student/Faculty Ratio: 17:1 **Male/Female Ratio:** Unknown
Undergraduate Enrollment: 14,557 **Graduate Enrollment:** None
Total Expenses by: Year **In State:** $ 1,110+ **Out of State:** $ 4,050+
Degrees Conferred: Associates
Programs of Study: Accounting, Automotive Technology, Business Administration, Commerce, Management, Carpentry, Child Care/Child and Family Studies, Child Psychology, Child Development, Computer Information Systems, Computer Programming, Construction Technology, Corrections, Cosmetology, Early Childhood Development, Hotel and Restaurant Management, Fashion Merchandising, Fire Science, German International Business, Law Enforcement, Marketing, Retailing Merchadising, Real Estate

Broward Community College

225 East Las Olas Blvd
Ft Lauderdale, FL 33301-2298
Coach: Mike Hutch

NJCAA
Seahawks/Blue, White
Phone: (305) 475-7486
Fax: (305) 761-7514

ACADEMIC

Founded: 1959 **Type:** 2 Yr., Public, Coed
Web-site: http://www.broward.cc.dl.us/ **SAT/ACT/GPA:** None
Student/Faculty Ratio: 17:1 **Male/Female Ratio:** 60:40
Undergraduate Enrollment: 20,000 **Graduate Enrollment:** None
Scholarships/Academic: Yes **Athletic:** Yes **Fin Aid:** Yes
Total Expenses by: Year **In State:** $ 4,700 **Out of State:** $ 7,700

Degrees Conferred: Associates
Programs of Study: Accounting, Architectural Technologies, Automotive Technologies, Aviation Technology, Aviation Administration, Business administration, Commerce, Management, Child Care/Child and Family Studies, Civil Engineering Technology, Computer Information System, Construction Management, Corrections, Criminal Justice, Data processing, Dental Services, Early Childhood Education, Electrical and Electronics Technology, Electric Engineering Technology, Hotel and Restaurant Management, Insurance, Interior Design, Nursing, Paralegal, Mechanical Engineering, Physical Therapy, Pollution Control Technology, Respiratory Technology

Central Florida Community College

3001 SW College Road
Ocala, FL 34474
Coach: Marty Smith
Email: patriotbal@aol.com

NJCAA
Patriots/Royal White, Scarlet
Phone: (352) 854-2322
Fax: (352) 873-5884

ACADEMIC

Founded: 1958
Type: 2 Yr., Public, Jr. College, Coed
Undergraduate Enrollment: 8,000
Campus Housing: Yes
Web-site: members.aol.com/patriotbal
SAT/ACT/GPA: Placement Tests/MAPS
Student/Faculty Ratio: 22:1
Male/Female Ratio: 40:60
Scholarships/Academic: Yes **Athletic:** Yes **Fin Aid:** Yes
Total Expenses by: Year **In State:** $ 6,000 **Out of State:** $ 6,000
Degrees Conferred: Associate
Programs of Study: Accounting, Business Administration, Commerce, Management, Child Care/Child and Family Studies, Computer Programming, Criminal Justice, Dental Services, Drafting and Design, Education, Electronics Engineering Technology, Emergency Medical Technology, Environmental Sciences, Fire Science, Law Enforcement, Police Science, Legal Secretarial Studies, Liberal Arts, General Studies, Manufacturing Technology, Medical Secretarial, Ornamental Horticulture, Paralegal Studies, Physical Therapy, Secretarial Studies, Office Management

ATHLETIC PROFILE

Estimated Number of Baseball Scholarships: 10
Conference Affiliation: Mid Florida Conference
Program Profile: Our Junior College program in Florida has won the past two state championships in 1997 and 1998. We have a major league sized diamond..
History: State Tournament Appearances in 1980, 1988, 1991, 1994, 1996, 1997, and 1998,
Achievements: Coach of the Year for state in 1997-1998; mid-Florida Conference; Coach of the Year in 1996 and 1997; Gulf Patriot Coach of the Year in 1997 and 1998.
Coaching: Marty Smith, Head Coach, compiled a record of 147-76. Bob O'Brien, Assistant Coach.
Roster for 1998 team/In State: 20 **Out of State:** 5 **Out of Country:** 2
Total Number of Varsity/Jr. Varsity: 25 **Baseball Camp Dates:** June 4 sessions
Number of Seniors on 1998 Team: 0 **Number of Sophomores on 1998 Team:** 13
Freshmen Receiving Fin Aid/Athletic: 7 **Academic:** 1
Number of Fall Games: 20 **Number of Spring Games:** 56
Positions Needed for 1999/2000: All **Most Recent Record:** 41 - 16 - 0
Schedule: Indian River CC, Manatee CC, Florida CC, Miami Dade CC, Tallahassee CC, Santa Fe
Style of Play: Speed, aggressive, pressure on the defense style of offense. Solid pitching & defense.

Chipola Junior College

3094 Indian Circle
Mariana, FL 32446
Coach: Jeff Johnson
Email: johnsonj@chipola.cc.fl.us

NJCAA
Indians/Navy Blue, Gold
Phone: (850) 718-2237
Fax: (850) 718-2360

ACADEMIC

Founded: 1947
Type: 2 Yr., Jr. College, Coed
Religion: Non-Affiliated
Campus Housing: No
Web-site: Not-Available
SAT/ACT/GPA: 21+
Undergraduate Enrollment: 2,357
Student/Faculty Ratio: 22:1
Scholarships/Academic: No **Athletic:** Yes **Fin Aid:** Yes
Total Expenses by: Year **In State:** $ 2,100 **Out of State:** $ 5,000
Degrees Conferred: Associates
Programs of Study: Accounting, Agricultural Science, Agronomy, Banking/Finance, Business Administration, Communications, Computer Science, Crop Science, Education, Fine Arts, Liberal Arts, Medical Technology, Nursing, Preengineering, Science

ATHLETIC PROFILE

Estimated Number of Baseball Scholarships: 5
Conference Affiliation: Panhandle Conference
History: We have 18 scholarships, a great tradition and more state tourney appearance than any other Florida JUCO. We have 14 returning players from the 1997 team. Five of our top pitchers returniing.
Achievements: Conference Titles in 1983, 1985, 1986, 1987, 1991, 1992, and 1993. All-Americans were Raul Velez and Wendell Higginbotham. Since 1983, drafted players were Mark Higgins, Buck Watford, Mike Workman, Dennis Carter, Eric Yelding, Ed Gonzales, Bill Cunningham, Todd Englett, Jimmy Hitt, Kent Clement, Raul Velez, and Edwin Alisca, Pat Gervais, Joe Logan, Bill Madril, Raphael Perez, Ben Webb, Rolando Fernandez, Greg Hammond, Joel Smith, Keith Hines, Andy Dolson, Bobby Jones, Kevin Milligan, and a lot more.
Coaching: Jeff Johnson, Head Coach, has compiled a 73-39 record . Brent Shelton, Assistant Coach. John Foran, Assistant Coach.
Roster for 1998 team/In State: 10 **Out of State:** 11 **Out of Country:** 2
Total Number of Varsity/Jr. Varsity: 23 **Percent of Graduation:** 90%
Number of Seniors on 1998 Team: 6 **Number of Sophomores on 1998 Team:** 0
Number of Fall Games: 20 **Number of Spring Games:** 56
Positions Needed for 1999/2000: Outfielder **Most Recent Record:** 41 - 17 - 0
Schedule: Meridian, Central Florida, Okaloosa - Walton, Pasco Hernando, Middle Georgia
Style of Play: Pitching should be this year team's strength RHP. Phillip Sledge with University of Georgia, RHP Matt Steel signed with Georgia, LHP Brad Weis signed with Auburn, 36th draft pick Ben Saxon has yet to sign. Offensively we should be improved. Will have to depend on execution to score a lot of runs. Defensively we have to fill gaps in the middle that lost to graduation.

Eckerd College

4200 54th Street Avenue South
St. Petersburg, FL 33711
Coach: Bill Matthews

NJCAA
Tritons/Red, White, Black
Phone: (727) 864-8253
Fax: (727) 864-8968

ACADEMIC

Founded: 1958
Type: 4 Yr., Private, Liberal Arts, Coed
Religion: Presbyterian
Campus Housing: Yes
Web-site: http://www.eckerd.edu/
SAT/ACT/GPA: 1000
Student/Faculty Ratio: 14:1
Male/Female Ratio: 50:50
Undergraduate Enrollment: 1,400
Graduate Enrollment: None
Scholarships/Academic: Yes **Athletic:** Varies **Fin Aid:** Yes
Total Expenses by: Year **In State:** $ 22,000 **Out of State:** $ 22,000
Degrees Conferred: BA, BS
Programs of Study: All areas of study (except Physical Education and Engineering) including: Management, International Business, Marine Science/Biology, Political Science, Psychology, Human Resources Biology, Chemistry, Premed, Prelaw

ATHLETIC PROFILE

Conference Affiliation: Sunshine State Conference
History: Eckerd College has offered baseball for 33 years. We play a 50+ game schedule against some of the best teams in the country. Teams from the north and midwest travel annually to the 'Suncoast' to play Eckerd College. Several of our opponents are Div. I schools, (1990: 7-3; 1991: 4-3; 1992: 5-1; 1993: 5-2; 1994: 1-3).
Achievements: 3 Conference Titles; 8 Regional Tournament Berths; 1977 NCAA II National Runner-Up; 35 players drafted; 15 All-Americans.
Coaching: Bill Matthews, Head Coach, is on his 8th year as head coach.
Style of Play: Aggressive - take the extra bases. "Mental Toughes".

Edward Waters College

1658 Kings Road
Jacksonville, FL 32209
Coach: Carl Burden

NAIA
Tigers/Purple, Orange
Phone: (904) 366-2796
Fax: (904) 366-2706

ACADEMIC

Founded: 1866
Type: 4 Yr., Coed
Religion: Methodist Episcopal
Campus Housing: Yes
Student/Faculty Ratio: 13:1
Male/Female Ratio: Unknown
Scholarships/Academic: No **Athletic:** No **Fin Aid:** Yes
Total Expenses by: Year **In State:** $ 10,000 **Out of State:** $ 10,000
Degrees Conferred: Bachelors Degree
Programs of Study: Biology, Biological Science, Business Administration, Commerce, Management, Chemistry, Computer Information Systems, Criminal Justice, Early Childhood Education, Education, Elementary Education, English, History, Journalism, Mathematics, Physical Education, Psychology, Public Administrtion, Secondary Education, Social Science, Social Work

ATHLETIC PROFILE

Conference Affiliation: EIAC

Embry-Riddle Aeronautical

600 S Clyde-Morris Boulevard
Daytona Beach, FL 32114
Coach: Greg Guilliams
Email: guilliag@cts.erau.edu

NAIA
Eagles/Royal Blue, Gold
Phone: (904) 226-6553
Fax: (904) 226-6435

ACADEMIC

Founded: 1925
Type: 4 Yr., Private, Coed, Engineering
Religion: Non-Affiliated
Campus Housing: Yes
Web-site: http://www.db.erau.edu/
SAT/ACT/GPA: 900
Student/Faculty Ratio: 17:1
Male/Female Ratio: 4:1
Undergraduate Enrollment: 3,930
Graduate Enrollment: 205
Scholarships/Academic: Yes **Athletic:** Yes **Fin Aid:** Yes
Total Expenses by: Year **In State:** $ 12,000 **Out of State:** $ 13,700
Degrees Conferred: Associate, Baccalareate, Masters, AS, BS, MS
Programs of Study: Aircraft Maintenance, Airway Science, Aviation Business Administration, Aviation Maintenance Technology, Professional Aeronautics, Aerospace Engineering, Aerospace Studies, Aviatiom Computer Science, Civil Engineering, Electrical Engineering, Engineering Physics

ATHLETIC PROFILE

Estimated Number of Baseball Scholarships: 3

Conference Affiliation: Florida Sun Conference
Program Profile: Our home field is Jackie Robinson Stadium; also home to Class "A" Chicago Cubs. It seats 4,800, has lights, new clubhouse and beautiful natural grass playing surface. We play a full 67 game schedule that includes a 12 game Fall exhibition season ending in November. Our Spring season begins the last week of January and ends in May.
History: Our baseball program began in 1989. Since 1993, the baseball team has won at least 30 games each season and has been ranked in the top 20 every year beginning in 1994. In 1995 and 1996, the Eagles were regular season and then Tournament Champions. They finished one game away from the College World Series in 1996.
Achievements: Since 1994, Embry-Riddle has won two championships including three 30 wins seasons and two 40 wins seasons. Eight players have signed professional contracts and the Eagles have produced 8 All-Americans during this time, including the "Player of the Week" in 1996.
Coaching: Greg Guilliams, Head Coach, started at Embry-Riddle in the Fall of 1992. He played professionally in the Atlanta Braves Organization after being named to the All-American Squad his last three years in college. Named "Coach of the Year" in the Florida Sun Conference in 1995. Todd Guilliams, Assistant Coach.
Roster for 1998 team/In State: 20 **Out of State:** 7 **Out of Country:** 1
Total Number of Varsity/Jr. Varsity: 28 **Percent of Graduation:** 90%
Number of Seniors on 1998 Team: 5 **Number of Sophomores on 1998 Team:** 4
Freshmen Receiving Fin Aid/Athletic: 2 **Academic:** 2
Number of Fall Games: 12 **Number of Spring Games:** 52
Baseball Camp Dates: 12/20-24; 12/27-30 **Most Recent Record:** 41 - 11 - 0
Positions Needed for 1999/2000: Pitcher, Shortstop, 3rd Base
Schedule: University of North Florida, St. Thomas University, Brewton-Parker College, Auburn-Montgomery University, Rollins College, St. Leo College
Style of Play: Aggressive both offensively and defensively. Strong pitching and defense with good team speed. Believe that we will out work our opponents and achieve a level of excellence that will consistently put us on top. Our players are committed to our team goal of winning a national championship.

Flagler College

P.O. Box 1027
St. Augustine, FL 32085
Coach: Dave Barnett

NAIA
Saints/Cardinal, Gold
Phone: (904) 829-6481
Fax: (904) 826-0094

ACADEMIC

Founded: 1968 **Type:** 4 Yr., Private, Liberal Arts, Coed
Undergraduate Enrollment: 1,600 **Campus Housing:** Yes
Web-site: http://www.flagler.edu/ **SAT/ACT/GPA:** 1050/3.0
Student/Faculty Ratio: 20:1 **Male/Female Ratio:** 55:45
Scholarships/Academic: Yes **Athletic:** Yes **Fin Aid:** Yes
Total Expenses by: Year **In State:** $ 9,630 **Out of State:** $ 9,630
Degrees Conferred: BA
Programs of Study: Accounting, Art, Art Education, Business Communications, Deaf Education, Drama, Elementary Education, English, History, Literature, Mathematics, Philosophy, Psychology, Secondary Education, Social Sciences, Spanish, Sport Management

ATHLETIC PROFILE

Conference Affiliation: Florida Sun Conference
Program Profile: We are ranked as high as sixth in NAIA poll this season. We have an outstanding baseball facility. Our college is located in historic St. Augustine, FL, & is only 3 miles from the beach.
History: Our program started in 1978.
Achievements: 9 players drafted into professional baseball in the last 8 years.
Coaching: Dave Barnett, Head Coach, received his BA from Flagler College and his MA from Univ. of Iowa.
Style of Play: Fast, aggressive and smart.

Florida A and M University

1500 Wahnish Way
Tallahassee, FL 32307
Coach: Joe Durant

NCAA I
Rattlers/Orange, Green
Phone: (850) 599-3202
Fax: (850) 599-3206

ACADEMIC

Founded: 1887
Type: 4 Yr., Coed
Religion: Non-Affiliated
Campus Housing: Yes
Student/Faculty Ratio: 16:1
Male/Female Ratio: Unknown
Undergraduate Enrollment: 9,251
Graduate Enrollment: 1,197
Scholarships/Academic: No **Athletic:** No **Fin Aid:** Yes
Total Expenses by: Year **In State:** $ 1,863 **Out of State:** $ 7,108
Degrees Conferred: Bachelors, Masters
Programs of Study: Accounting, Actuarial Science, Agricultural Business, Agricultural Science, Animal Science, Architectural Technologies, Architecture, Art Education, Art/fine Arts, Biology, Biological Science, Business Administration, Commerce, Management, Business Education, Chemical Engineering, Chemistry, Civil Engineering Technology, Communications, Computer Information Technology, Construction Technology, Criminal Justice, Molecular Biology, Cell Biology, Music, Music Education, Mechanical Engineering, Occupational Therapy, Pest Control Technology

ATHLETIC PROFILE

Conference Affiliation: Mid-Eastern Athletic Conference
Program Profile: We are located just South of the Florida AandM University campus on Wahnish Way is Rattler Field, home of the Rattler Baseball Program since 1983. A new field was built at the present location with a self-contained sprinkler and drainage system in 1983. A fully-electronic scoreboard was added in 1984. The field also features two covered dugouts, a mini-fieldhouse which is topped by a 12-seat press box and contains restroom facilities and equipment storage areas. Aluminun bleachers arrayed behind home plate and along the baselines seat over 500 fans. There is a batting cage.
History: Our program began in 1899. It has a history perhaps as colorful as their leader brothers on the gridiron - a legacy replete with great teams and great players.
Achievements: Tournament Champions six times in the last nine years (1987, 1988, 1990, 1991, 1992, 1984, and 1986); Big South Conference winner in 1995.
Coaching: Joe Durant, Head Coach, was named head coach at his alma mater in the Summer of 1990. In five seasons at the helm, the intense, yet personable Durant has guided Florida AandM to three Mid-Eastern Athletic Conference title games (1994, 1992 and 1994) and to three consecutive MEAC Tournament title games (1994, 1995 and 1996). A graduate of Florida in 1976 where he received his master's degree in Health, Physical Education and Recreation. He was a catcher for the Rattlers. He is a member of the National Baseball Coaches' Association competition committee, which ranks Division I teams and select them for post-season play. Harry Sapp, Assistant Coach, begins his fourth season as an assistant coach. He served as an area scout for the Seatlle Mariners in 1989-1991. Also served as the President of the Tallahassee Branch of the National Adult Baseball Association in 1993-1994.
Style of Play: Speed and power; have added pitching in recent years (improved).

Florida Atlantic College

777 Glades Road
Boca Raton, FL 33413
Coach: Kevin Cooney

NCAA I
Blue Wave/Blue, Grey, Red
Phone: (561) 297-3710
Fax: (561) 297-3963

ACADEMIC

Founded: 1961
Type: 4 Yr., Public, Liberal Arts, Coed
Religion: Non-Affiliated
Campus Housing: Yes

Web-site: http://www.fau.edu/
SAT/ACT/GPA: Sliding Scale
Student/Faculty Ratio: 20:1
Male/Female Ratio: 2:5
Undergraduate Enrollment: 18,000
Graduate Enrollment: 2,000
Scholarships/Academic: Yes **Athletic:** Yes **Fin Aid:** Yes
Total Expenses by: Year **In State:** $ 7,500 **Out of State:** $ 12,500
Degrees Conferred: Bachelors, Masters, Specialist, Doctorate
Programs of Study: Schmidt College of Arts and Humanities (Art, Communication, English and Comparative Literature, History, Languages and Linguistics, Music, Philosophy, Theatre, Interdisciplinary Studies), Business (Accounting, Computing and Information Systems, Finance, International Business, Management, Marketing, Real Estate), Education (Elementary, Exceptional Student, Exercise Science/Wellness), Engineering (Computer, Computer Science, Electrical, Mechanical, Ocean), Liberal Arts (Biology, Economics, English, Geography, Geology, Graphic, Arts, History, Political Science, Psychology, Sociology), Nursing and Sciences (Biological Sciences including Marine Biology, Economics, Geography, Health Administration, Political Science, Social Psychology, Social Work, Sociology), Urban and Public Affairs (Public Management)

ATHLETIC PROFILE

Estimated Number of Baseball Scholarships: 10
Conference Affiliation: Trans America Athletic Conference
Program Profile: \we play on a natural grass, lighted field with 1,000 seat stadium plus hills with palm trees for additional seating. We start Fall in October and Spring in January . We have a 56 game schedule.
History: The program started in 1981 to the present, 6 post-season appearances NAIA to Division II; Division I since 1995.
Achievements: Coach Cooney has won four Regional Coach of the Year Awards and National Coach of the Year in 1987. His career record is 451-293-9. He coached 3 Major League pitchers and 3 and 5 AA pitchers who won the National Championship in '87. 9 players selected All-Americans; 30 drafted players; 6 players drafted in '96 including 3rd rounder; 2 Big Leaguers. The graduation rate is 75% for baseball.
Coaching: Kevin Cooney, Head Coach, is entering eleven years at FAU. He has 17 years college coaching experience. He is a former major league player. He handles pitching coach and has compiled a record of 451-293-9 for 17 years of coaching. He was named four times Regional Coach of the Year and National Coach of the Year. John McCormack, Recruiting Coordinator/Infielder and Catching; Steve Whitaker, Hitting and Outfield.
Roster for 1998 team/In State: 24 **Out of State:** 5 **Out of Country:** 0
Total Number of Varsity/Jr. Varsity: 30 **Percent of Graduation:** 75%
Number of Seniors on 1998 Team: 6 **Number of Sophomores on 1998 Team:** 0
Freshmen Receiving Fin Aid/Athletic: 2 **Academic:** 2
Number of Fall Games: 0 **Number of Spring Games:** 56
Baseball Camp Dates: December 19-23 **Most Recent Record:** 29 - 30 - 0
Positions Needed for 1999/2000: Pitcher, Shortstop, Catcher
Schedule: Miami, Kentucky, UCF, Stetson, Troy State, Rutgers
Style of Play: Aggressive offense; hit and run solid defense.

Florida Community College - Jacksonville

11901 Beach Blvd
Jacksonville, FL 32246-7625
Coach: Howard Roey

NJCAA
Stars/Red, White, Blue
Phone: (904) 646-2203
Fax: (904) 646-2204

ACADEMIC

Founded: 1963
Type: 2 Yr., Coed
Religion: Non-Affiliated
Campus Housing: No
Student/Faculty Ratio: 12:1
Male/Female Ratio: Unknown
Undergraduate Enrollment: 18,800
Graduate Enrollment: None
Total Expenses by: Year **In State:** $ 1,050 **Out of State:** $ 3,800
Degrees Conferred: Associate

Programs of Study: Architectural Technology, Automotive Technology, Aviation Administration and Technology, Biomedical Technology, Business Administration, Civil Engineering Technology, Construction Technology, Criminal Justice, Drafting and Design, Electronic Engineering Technology, Flight Training, Industrial Administration

ATHLETIC PROFILE

Conference Affiliation: NJCAA, FCCAA, Mid-Florida Conference

Florida Institute of Technology

Country Club Road
Melbourne, FL 32901
Coach: Les Hall

NCAA II
Panthers/Red, Grey
Phone: (407) 674-8193
Fax: (407) 984-8529

ACADEMIC

Founded: 1958
SAT/ACT/GPA: 1050+
Student/Faculty Ratio: 14:1
Undergraduate Enrollment: 3,865
Scholarships/Academic: Yes **Athletic:** Yes
Total Expenses by: Year **In State:** $ 18,500
Type: 4 Yr., Private, Coed, Engineering
Campus Housing: Yes
Male/Female Ratio: 67:33
Graduate Enrollment: 2,082
Fin Aid: Yes
Out of State: $ 18,500
Degrees Conferred: BA, BS, MS, MBA, MEd, PhD
Programs of Study: Accounting, Aeronautical Engineering, Aeronautical Science, Biochemistry, Biological Science, Business Administration, Computer Science, Economics, Electrical Engineering, Fisheries, Management, Marine Biology, Marketing, Mathematics, Mechanical Engineering, Microbiology, Physics, Pre-Proffesional Courses, Science Education, Technical & Business Writing

ATHLETIC PROFILE

Conference Affiliation: Sunshine State Conference

Florida International University

University Park Campus
Miami, FL 33199
Coach: Danny Price

NCAA I
Golden Panthers/Blue, Gold
Phone: (305) 348-2756
Fax: (305) 348-2963

ACADEMIC

Founded: 1972
Religion: Non-Affiliated
Web-site: http://www.fiu.edu/
Student/Faculty Ratio: 14:1
Undergraduate Enrollment: 23,417
Scholarships/Academic: Yes **Athletic:** Yes
Total Expenses by: Year **In State:** $ Varies
Type: 4 Yr., Public, Coed
Campus Housing: Yes
SAT/ACT/GPA: 1100
Male/Female Ratio: 43:57
Graduate Enrollment: 6,677
Fin Aid: Yes
Out of State: $ Varies
Degrees Conferred: BA, BS, MS, PhD
Programs of Study: Accounting, Arts and Sciences, Business Administration, Computer Science, Education, Engineering and Design, Health, Hospitality Management, Journalism and Mass Communications, Nursing, Public and Urban Affairs

ATHLETIC PROFILE

Estimated Number of Baseball Scholarships: 11.7
Conference Affiliation: Sun Belt Conference

Program Profile: We play 56 games February to May. All home games are played on campus at a baseball stadium that features a natural grass field, message board and all weather batting cages.
History: The program started in 1973 and joined Division I in 1983. The program has enjoyed winning seasons in 25 of 26 years and has recorded 40 or more wins 13 times and has gone to 3 NCAA tourneys in the last 4 years.
Achievements: Conference Championships in 1991, 1995, and 1998; 4 players from last year's team drafted professionally. Danny Price was named Conference Coach of the Year in 1998.
Coaching: Danny Price, Head Coach, started in 1980 and has won 751 career games. He was named Conference Coach of the Year in 1998. Rolando Casanova, Assistant Coach.
Roster for 1998 team/In State: 16 **Out of State:** 4 **Out of Country:** 6
Total Number of Varsity/Jr. Varsity: 26 **Percent of Graduation:** 0
Number of Seniors on 1998 Team: 6 **Freshmen Receiving Fin Aid/Athletic:** 8
Most Recent Record: 41 - 22 - 0 **Number of Spring Games:** 56
Positions Needed for 1999/2000: Pitcher, Catcher, Infielder, Outfielder
Baseball Camp Dates: Christmas, June, July
Schedule: Miami, Notre Dame, South Alabama, New Orleans, St. John's, Louisiana Tech
Style of Play: Pitching and defense, station to station with occasional long ball.

Florida Memorial College

15800 Northwest 42nd Avenue
Miami, FL 33054
Coach: Robert Smith

NAIA
Lions/Royal, Orange
Phone: (305) 626-3600
Fax: (305) 626-3691

ACADEMIC

Founded: 1879 **Type:** 4 Yr., Private, Coed
Undergraduate Enrollment: 1,600 **SAT/ACT/GPA:** 840/18
Student/Faculty Ratio: 15:1 **Male/Female Ratio:** 45:55
Scholarships/Academic: No **Athletic:** Yes **Fin Aid:** Yes
Total Expenses by: Year **In State:** $ 8,700 **Out of State:** $ 8,700
Programs of Study: Accounting, Air Traffic Control, Airway Computer Science, Airway Science Mangement, Aviation, Biological Business, Chemistry, Computer, Criminal Justice, Education, English, Fine Arts, Mangament, Philosophy, Public, Religion, Transportation Management

ATHLETIC PROFILE

Conference Affiliation: Florida Sun Conference
Program Profile: A competitive small college program, that participates in perhaps the toughest NAIA conference in America. A new facility is being built for the 1996-1997 season. We compete in the Fall (20 games) and Spring (50-55 games).
History: The program was started in 1977 by Coach Chico Arenas. I took over the program in 1981.
Achievements: Third place FSC 1992
Style of Play: Hit and run; aggressive play on offense.

Florida Southern College

111 Lake Hollingsworth Drive
Lakeland, FL 33801
Coach: Chuck Anderson

NCAA II
Moccasins/Red, White
Phone: (941) 680-4264
Fax: (941) 680-4122

ACADEMIC

Founded: 1885 **Type:** 4 Yr., Private, Liberal Arts, Coed
Religion: Methodist **Campus Housing:** Yes
Web-site: http://www.flsouthern.edu/ **SAT/ACT/GPA:** 1000/ 23
Student/Faculty Ratio: 17:1 **Male/Female Ratio:** 42:58

Undergraduate Enrollment: 1,600 **Graduate Enrollment:** None
Scholarships/Academic: Yes **Athletic:** Yes **Fin Aid:** Yes
Total Expenses by: Year **In State:** $ 16,000 **Out of State:** $ 16,000
Degrees Conferred: BA, BS, MBA, Nursing
Programs of Study: Accounting, Art, Biology, Business, Chemistry, Citrus/Horticulture, Communications, Criminology, Economics, Education, English, History, Mathematics, Music

ATHLETIC PROFILE

Estimated Number of Baseball Scholarships: 9
Conference Affiliation: Sunshine State Conference
Program Profile: We use the city facilities. It is home of Spring training of Detroit Tigers. We practice at Tigertown which has a four diamonds. The Mocs play all home games at Henley Field, a 1,000 seat ballpark. The stadium is 420' dead center, 375' in the alleys, and 330' down the lines.
History: We began in 1958 & won 8 NCAA DII titles. FSC has had 104 players sign with the pros.
Achievements: 31 NCAA post-season play; 107 players have signed pro contracts; 12th National Championships; 6 Coach of the Year and South Region Coach of the Year; 7 All-Americans; since 1980 to 1996 has All-Conference players. Numerous Most Valuable Player Awards.
Coaching: Chuck Anderson, Head Coach, was named head coach in 1983. In his 13 seasons he compiled a record of 607-169-1, which ranks him among the nation's leaders in winning percentage. He led the Southern Florida to their seventh NCAA National Championship. He was twice named Most Valuable Player for the Mocs. He was a member of the first ever Florida Southern team to participate in NCAA post-season. He is the president of the American Baseball Coaches Association. Russ McNickel, Assistant Coach, works with the Mocs infielders and hitters and is in-charge of recruiting for the program. He graduated from the University of South Alabama in 1988 with a bachelors degree in Health and Physical Education. Bob Gendron, Assistant Coach, is responsible with the pitchers. He earned All-American honors from Florida Southern in 1982. He played for San Francisco Giants.
Roster for 1998 team/In State: 20 **Out of State:** 12 **Out of Country:** 0
Total Number of Varsity/Jr. Varsity: 32 **Percent of Graduation:** 84%
Number of Seniors on 1998 Team: 14 **Number of Sophomores on 1998 Team:** 10
Freshmen Receiving Fin Aid/Athletic: 4 **Academic:** 4
Number of Fall Games: 20 **Number of Spring Games:** 56
Positions Needed for 1999/2000: All **Most Recent Record:** 37 - 17 - 0
Style of Play: Pitching, defense, and speed.

Florida State University

PO Drawer 2195
Tallahassee, FL 32316
Coach: Mike Martin

NCAA I
Seminoles/Garnet, Gold
Phone: (850) 644-1073
Fax: (850) 644-7213

ACADEMIC

Founded: 1857 **Type:** 4 Yr., Coed
SAT/ACT/GPA: 500/21 **Campus Housing:** Yes
Student/Faculty Ratio: 20:1 **Male/Female Ratio:** Unknown
Undergraduate Enrollment: 22,408 **Graduate Enrollment:** 7,856
Scholarships/Academic: No **Athletic:** No **Fin Aid:** Yes
Total Expenses by: Year **In State:** $ 1,882+ **Out of State:** $ 7,127+
Degrees Conferred: Bachelors and Masters
Programs of Study: Accounting, Actuarial Science, Advertising, American Studies, Anthropology, Applied Mathematics, Archaeology, Art Education, Art/Fine Arts, Art History, Biochemistry, Bioengineering, Civil Engineering, Cell Biology, Clinical Psychology, Communications, Comparative Literature, Computer Science, Corrections, Creative Writing, Criminal Justice, Criminology, Dance, Predentistry, Ecology, Economics, Education, Electrical Engineering Technology, Elementary Education, English, Environmental Engineering, Environmental Science, Environmental Studies, Fashion Design and Technology, Fashion Merchandising, Food Science, Health Education, History, Home Economics, Hotel and Restaurant Management, Humanities, Human Resources, Insurance

ATHLETIC PROFILE

Estimated Number of Baseball Scholarships: 11.7
Conference Affiliation: Atlantic Coast Conference
Program Profile: We have the premier program in the South . Our stadium has a seating capacity of 5,000 seat and a concrete grand stand. We have a big league style clubhouse, batting cages ,a natural grass field and a weight room.
History: The Florida State baseball program began in 1947. We had 21 consecutive NCAA Regional Appearances from 1978-1998. We hold 16 College World Series Appearances and 51 winning seasons.
Achievements: Atlantic Coast Conference Champions in 1995 and 1997; 62 All-Americans; 162 major league draft picks; 13 first round picks; 15 conference championships; 40 major leaguers; 3 Golden Spike Award winners.
Coaching: Mike Martin, Head Coach, is the fourth winningest active college coach in 20 seasons at FSU. He compiled a record of 1022-250 and was named ACC Coach of the Year in 1995 and 1998. Chip Baker, Assistant Coach, entering fifth year. Jaime Shouppe, Assistant Coach, entering tenth year with the program.
Roster for 1998 team/In State: 29 **Out of State:** 5 **Out of Country:** 0
Total Number of Varsity/Jr. Varsity: 34 **Percent of Graduation:** 80%
Number of Seniors on 1998 Team: 3 **Number of Sophomores on 1998 Team:** 8
Most Recent Record: 53 - 20 - 0 **Number of Spring Games:** 56
Baseball Camp Dates: June 20-25; July 11-16, 18-23; August 1-6, etc...
Schedule: Arizona State, Miami, Florida, Clemson, Georgia Tech, North Carolina State
Style of Play: Aggressive, baserunning, stressing sound pitching, defense and baserunning.

Gulf Coast Community College

5230 West Highway 98
Panama City, FL 32401
Coach: Darren Mazeroski

NJCAA
Commodores/Blue, Gold
Phone: (850) 872-3897
Fax: (850) 873-3530

ACADEMIC

Founded: 1957 **Type:** 2 Yr., Jr. College, Coed
Student/Faculty Ratio: 19:1 **Campus Housing:** No
Undergraduate Enrollment: 4,208 **Graduate Enrollment:** None
Scholarships/Academic: No **Athletic:** No **Fin Aid:** Yes
Total Expenses by: Year **In State:** $ 1,153+ **Out of State:** $ 4,325+
Degrees Conferred: Associates
Programs of Study: Accounting, Aviation Administration, Broadcasting, Business Administration, Commerce, Management, Child Psychology/Child Development, Civil Engineering Technology, Computer Programming, Construction Technology, Criminal Justice, Culinary Arts, Dental Services, Drafting and Design, Electronics Engineering Technology, Emergency Medical Technology, Fashion Merchandising, Finance/Banking, Fire Science, Flight Training, Hospitality Services, Human Services, Liberal Arts, General Studies, Marine Technology, Marketing, Retailing, Merchandising, Occupational Therapy, Paralegal Studies, Physical Therapy, Postal Management, Radio and Television, Radiological Technology, Real Estate, Respiratory Therapy, Office Management

ATHLETIC PROFILE

Estimated Number of Baseball Scholarships: 8
Conference Affiliation: Panhandle Conference
Program Profile: We play a total of 76 games, 20 in the Fall and 56 in the Spring.
Achievements: 11 major league players.
Coaching: Darren Mazeroski, Head Coach, is entering 6 years with the program and compiled a record of 257-102 in the last 6 years. He has an average of 42 wins per year. Kevin Humphrey, Assistant Coach.
Roster for 1998 team/In State: 10 **Out of State:** 12 **Out of Country:** 1
Total Number of Varsity/Jr. Varsity: 0 **Percent of Graduation:** 80%

Most Recent Record: 41 - 19 - 0
Number of Sophomores on 1998 Team: 13
Freshmen Receiving Fin Aid/Athletic: 6
Academic: 1
Number of Fall Games: 20
Number of Spring Games: 56
Positions Needed for 1999/2000: Pitcher, Catcher, Centerfielder
Schedule: DeKalb, Central Alabama, Meridian, Shelton State
Style of Play: Fundamental.

Hillsborough Community College - Dale Campus

PO Box 30030
Tampa, FL 33630-3030
Coach: Gary Calhoun

NJCAA
Hawks/Red, White, Blue
Phone: (813) 253-7446
Fax: (813) 253-7400

ACADEMIC

Founded: 1968
Type: 2 Yr., Jr. College, Coed
Religion: Non-Affiliated
Campus Housing: No
Student/Faculty Ratio: 26:1
Male/Female Ratio: Unknown
Undergraduate Enrollment: 18,307
Graduate Enrollment: None
Scholarships/Academic: No **Athletic:** No **Fin Aid:** Yes
Total Expenses by: Year **In State:** $ 1,124+ **Out of State:** $ 4,187+
Degrees Conferred: Associates
Programs of Study: Accounting, Architectural Technologies, Automotive Technologies, Biomedical Technology, Business Administration, Commerce, Management, Child Care/Child and Family Studies, Computer Information Systems, Computer Programming, Computer Technologies, Construction Technology, Corrections, Criminal Justice, Data Processing, Deaf Interpreter Training, Electronics Engineering Technology, Emergency Medical Technology, Finance/Banking, Fire Science, Hospitality Services, Hotel and Restaurant Managent, Human Services, Interior Design, Law Enforcement, Legal Studies, Liberal Arts, General Studies, Marketing, Retailing, Merchandising

Indian River Community College

3209 Virginia Avenue
Fort Pierce, FL 34981
Coach: Mike Easom

NJCAA
Pioneers/Royal, Gold
Phone: (561) 462-4772
Fax: (561) 462-4796

ACADEMIC

Founded: 1962
Type: 2 Yr., Jr. College, Coed
Student/Faculty Ratio: 8:1
Male/Female Ratio: 45:55
Undergraduate Enrollment: 6,890
Graduate Enrollment: None
Scholarships/Academic: No **Athletic:** Yes **Fin Aid:** Yes
Total Expenses by: Cr-Hr **In State:** $ 35/cr-hr **Out of State:** $ 135/cr-hr
Degrees Conferred: AA, AS
Programs of Study: Agricultural Business, Anthropology, Automotive Technology, Biological Science, Corrections, Criminal Justice, Dental Services, Electrical/Electronics Technology, Engineering Technology, Fire Science, General Engineering, human Services, Journalism, Law

ATHLETIC PROFILE

Conference Affiliation: Southern Conference
Program Profile: Home games are played at new Pioneer Field Complex which is a natural grass surface 340 to left, 375 allies and 335 to right.
History: Our program began in 1962. We won 4 Florida State Championships, 8 Southern Conference Championships and 90 players signed pro contracts in 22 years.
Achievements: 2 state championships, 1 regional championship, participated in NJCAA World Series 1993. Coach of the Year Honors for four years.

Coaching: Mike Easom, Head Coach. Charlie Frazier, Assistant Coach.
Style of Play: Aggressive offensively, good defense, above average pitching.

Jacksonville University

2800 University Boulevard N
Jacksonville, FL 32211-3384
Coach: Terry Alexander

NCAA I
Dolphins/Green, White
Phone: (904) 745-7412
Fax: (904) 743-0067

ACADEMIC

Founded: 1934
Type: 4 Yr., Private, Liberal Arts, Coed
Web-site: http://www.junix.ju.edu/
SAT/ACT/GPA: 1080/23
Student/Faculty Ratio: 14:1
Male/Female Ratio: 47:53
Undergraduate Enrollment: 2,064
Graduate Enrollment: 352
Scholarships/Academic: Yes **Athletic:** Yes **Fin Aid:** Yes
Total Expenses by: Year **In State:** $ 17,660 **Out of State:** $ 17,660
Degrees Conferred: BA, BS, MAT
Programs of Study: Accounting, Art, Aviation Administration, Biology, Business, Chemistry, Computer, Economics, English, Finance, International Business, Georgraphy, Management, Medical

ATHLETIC PROFILE

Conference Affiliation: Sun Belt Conference
Program Profile: Our 2,300 seat stadium continues to be updated, keeping it one of the finest facilities in the South. The playing surface is grass as weather is condusive to year-round play.
History: Since the program's inception in 1957, JU has compiled an overall record of 1081-807-7 (.572). The program has recorded four 40-win seasons in the 1990s, winning two Sun Belt Conference Championships. JU has appeared in six NCAA Regionals, including two of the last three years. Our program boasts 9 All-Americans and 67 drafted players.
Achievements: Terry Alexander has been named Sun Belt Conference Coach of the Year twice. JU was the SBC Champions in 1991 and 1995, advancing to an NCAA Regional in each of those years. We have been to 6 Regionals. 9 All-Americans; 67 players selected in the major league draft.
Coaching: Terry Alexander, Head Coach, is a 1977 Florida State graduate. He played two years at FSU and two years for the Pittsburgh Pirate Organization.
Style of Play: Aggressive, fundamental, strong team concept.

Lake City Community College

Rt 19, Box 1030
Lake City, FL 32025-8703
Coach: Tom Clark

NJCAA
Timberwolves/Green, White
Phone: (904) 752-1822
Fax: (904) 755-1521

ACADEMIC

Founded: 1962
Type: 2 Yr., Jr. College, Coed
Undergraduate Enrollment: 2,377
Campus Housing: Yes
Student/Faculty Ratio: 11:1
Male/Female Ratio: Unknown
Scholarships/Academic: No **Athletic:** No **Fin Aid:** Yes
Total Expenses by: Year **In State:** $ 4,442 **Out of State:** $ 7,547
Degrees Conferred: Associates
Programs of Study: Accounting, Business Administration, Commerce, Management, Computer Programming, Criminal Justice, Electronics engineering Technology, Emergency Medical Technology, Forest Technology, Landscape Architecture/Design, Law Enforcement, Police Science, Liberal Arts, General Studies, Marketing, Retailing, Merchandising, Medical Laboratory Technology, Nursing, Physical therapy, Practical Nursing, Secretarial Studies, Office Management

Lynn University

3601 N Military Trail
Boca Raton, FL 33431
Coach: Gregg Kilby

NCAA II/NAIA
Knights/Royal, White
Phone: (561) 994-0770
Fax: (561) 237-7283

ACADEMIC

Founded: 1962
Type: 4 Yr., Private, Liberal Arts, Coed
Web-site: Not-Available
SAT/ACT/GPA: 800/17
Student/Faculty Ratio: 10:1
Male/Female Ratio: 50:50
Undergraduate Enrollment: 1,500
Graduate Enrollment: 200
Scholarships/Academic: Yes **Athletic:** Yes **Fin Aid:** Yes
Total Expenses by: Year **In State:** $ 20,000 **Out of State:** $ 20,000
Degrees Conferred: AA, AS, BA, BS, MA, MPS
Programs of Study: Accounting, Aviation Management, Behavioral Science, Business and Management, Communications, Computer Science, Design, Education, Engineering, Fashion Marketing, Finance, Fine Arts, Health and Human Services, History, International Business, Management, Marketing, Parks/Recreation, Political Science, Protective Services, Psychology

ATHLETIC PROFILE

Program Profile: Lynn has a high-caliber Division II baseball program located in a hotbed for baseball. South Florida is one of the strongest regions in the nation. The Knights defeated six teams in the NCAA Division II Top 25 & 3 in the NAIA Top 25 in 1995, finishing second in the region.
History: The Knights have been an NAIA power for several years in the old district seven alignmemt. Lynn has moved up to the NCAA Division II ranks and expects to compete with the best teams at the highest level.
Achievements: 7 players All-Region honors and pitcher who was 7th nationally in ERA.
Coaching: Gregg Kilby, Head Coach.
Style of Play: Plays a very aggressive brand of baseball, always striving to use its team speed to score. A fundamentally sound team. The Knights steal, hit and run and move runners around the bases. The hitter/pitchers are aggressive and then the team is successful.

Manatee Community College

5840 - 26th Street West
Brandenton, FL 34207
Coach: Tim Hill

NJCAA
Lancers/Blue, Gold
Phone: (941) 755-1511
Fax: (941) 727-6182

ACADEMIC

Founded: 1957
Type: 2 Yr., Jr. College, Coed
Undergraduate Enrollment: 7,308
Campus Housing: No
Student/Faculty Ratio: 20:1
Male/Female Ratio: Unknown
Scholarships/Academic: No **Athletic:** No **Fin Aid:** Yes
Total Expenses by: Year **In State:** $ 1,123+ **Out of State:** $ 4,100+
Degrees Conferred: Associates
Programs of Study: Accounting, Architectural Technologies, Automotive Technology, Business Administration, Commerce, Management, Child Psychology/Child Development, Civil Engineering Technology, Commercial Art, Computer Information Systems, Computer Programming, Construction Technologies, Criminal Justice, Drafting and Design, Electrical Engineerig

ATHLETIC PROFILE

Conference Affiliation: NJCAA, FJCAA, Suncoast Region VII

Miami - Dade Community College

11380 NW 27th Ave
Miami, FL 33167
Coach: Steve Hertz

NJCAA
Falcons/Columbia Blue, Black, White
Phone: (305) 237-1362
Fax: (305) 237-1756

ACADEMIC

Founded: 1960
Type: 2 Yr., Jr. College, Coed
Student/Faculty Ratio: 24:1
Male/Female Ratio: Unknown
Undergraduate Enrollment: 5,1019
Graduate Enrollment: None
Scholarships/Academic: No **Athletic:** No **Fin Aid:** Yes
Total Expenses by: Year **In State:** $ 1,238+ **Out of State:** $ 4,350+
Degrees Conferred: Associates
Programs of Study: Accounting, Aerospace Sciences, Agricultural Science, American Studies, Anthropology, Architectural Technologies, Art Education, Art/Fine Arts, American Studies, Asian/Oriental Studies, Aviation, Business Administration, Commerce, Management, Commercial Art, Computer Programming, Computer Science, Communications, Commercial Art, Computer Graphics, Computer Information Systems, Drafting and Design, Education, Electrical and Electronics Technology, Electromechanical Technology, Emergency Medical Technology, Engineering Design, Film Studies, Forestry, Medical Assistant Technology, Natural Science, Music Education, Nursing

ATHLETIC PROFILE

Conference Affiliation: Florida-Southern Conference
Program Profile: Our program is two-year with basically a Fall season (exhibition) consisting of 20 games and a Spring (regular) season consisting of 50-55 games. Our field is natural turf with seating capacity of up to 2,000. Dimensions are 327' (lines), 390' (alleys) and 420' (center field).
History: The baseball program started in 1961 under ABA Hall of Fame member Dr. Demie Mainieri. A National Championship was attained in 1964 and many more accolades have been attained by the North Campus. Miami-Dade has put over 100 players into professional baseball. That puts the North Campus in company of the top college programs in the country.
Achievements: 195 players have been drafted form this program.

North Florida Junior College

1000 Turner Davis Drive
Madison, FL 32340
Coach: Lee Kuyrkendall

NJCAA
Sentinels/Scarlet, Silver
Phone: (850) 973-2288
Fax: (8504) 973-1696

ACADEMIC

Founded: 1958
Type: 2 Yr., Jr. College, Coed
Student/Faculty Ratio: 30:1
Male/Female Ratio: 1:2
Undergraduate Enrollment: 2,000
Graduate Enrollment: None
Scholarships/Academic: Yes **Athletic:** No **Fin Aid:** No
Total Expenses by: Year **In State:** $ 2,800 **Out of State:** $ 5,000
Degrees Conferred: AA
Programs of Study: Liberal Arts, General Studies

ATHLETIC PROFILE

Conference Affiliation: Panhandle Conference
Program Profile: We play a 56-game season. Our stadium seats 250 and has bathrooms, a pressbox, concession stands and natural turf.
History: Program began in 1986.
Achievements: 1993 All-American - Chris Pierce. Players drafted - Jay Noel, Steve Schneider, Jason Sullivan, Gorge Morales, Aaron Fultz, Paul Gomez, Stan Stewart, Tony Valdes

Northwood University

2600 North Military Trail
West Palm Beach, FL 33409
Coach: Joseph DiBenedetto

NAIA
Seahawks/Blue, White
Phone: (561) 478-5510
Fax: (561) 478-5593

ACADEMIC

Founded: 1982
Type: 4 Yr., Private, Coed
Undergraduate Enrollment: 760
Campus Housing: Yes
Student/Faculty Ratio: 17:1
Male/Female Ratio: Unknown
Scholarships/Academic: No **Athletic:** No **Fin Aid:** Yes
Total Expenses by: Year **In State:** $ 10,659 **Out of State:** $ 10,659
Degrees Conferred: Bachelors
Programs of Study: Accounting, Advertising, Business Administration, Commerce, Management, Computer Information Systems, Computer Management, Fashion Merchandising, Finance/Banking, Food Service Management, Hotel and Restaurant Management, International Business, Management information Systems, Marketing, Retailing, Merchandising

ATHLETIC PROFILE

Program Profile: Our program is young, but growing rapidly. We have a brand new baseball complex built in the Fall of 1993. We play a 50 game season in sunny, warm South Florida. NAIA District Seven is one of the toughest in the nation.
History: Our program began as a club in 1991. 1992 was the first season for intercollegiate play.
Achievements: Coach DiBenedetto was District Coach of the Yer in 1990 at Lynn University.
Coaching: Joseph DiBenedetto, Head Coach, is also Athletic Director and has 10 years of experience. Herb Triplett, Assistant Coach, is also Admissions Counselor and has 4 years of experience. Chris Applegate, Assistant Coach, has 2 years of experience.
Style of Play: Varies depending upon makeup of team. We stress pitching and defense as well as being fundamentally strong.

Nova SouthEastern University

3301 College Avenue
Fort Lauderdale, FL 33314
Coach: Sonny Hansley
Email: sonny@parris.nova.edu

NAIA
Knights/Navy, Gold
Phone: (954) 262-8259
Fax: (954) 262-3926

ACADEMIC

Founded: 1964
Type: 4 Yr., Private, Coed
Undergraduate Enrollment: 900
Campus Housing: Yes
Web-site: http://www.nova.edu/
SAT/ACT/GPA: 950
Student/Faculty Ratio: 11:1
Male/Female Ratio: 40:60
Scholarships/Academic: Yes **Athletic:** Yes **Fin Aid:** Yes
Total Expenses by: Year **In State:** $ 14,850 **Out of State:** $ 14,850
Degrees Conferred: BA, BS
Programs of Study: Accounting, Administrative Studies, Business Administration, Computer Information Systems, Computer Science, Elementary Education, Exceptional Education, Legal Studies (Prelaw), Liberal Arts, Life Sciences (Premedical), Ocean Studies, Psychology, Sports/Recreation and Exercise Studies

ATHLETIC PROFILE

Conference Affiliation: Florida Sun Conference
Program Profile: We have an outstanding grass playing facility with two lighted batting cages. We are a naturally ranked NAIA baseball team that plays in an extremely difficult baseball conference.

ATHLETIC PROFILE

Conference Affiliation: Florida Sun Conference
Program Profile: We have an outstanding grass playing facility with two lighted batting cages. We are a naturally ranked NAIA baseball team that plays in an extremely difficult baseball conference.
History: The baseball team began in the Spring of 1988 and had only one losing season in the past ten years. The baseball team has qualified for the SouthEast regional for 2 of the past three years.
Achievements: Coach of the Year in 1994 and 1997; Conference Champions in 1994 and 1997; All-Americans - Rich Palumbo in 1992 and Claude Love in 1995.
Coaching: Sonny Hansley, Head Coach, is entering his tenth year as head coach. Kevin Peyton, Assistant Coach, is entering his first season. Tom Hysell, Assistant Coach, is entering his first season. Robert Peper, Assistant Coach, is entering his first year.
Style of Play: We emphasize strong pitching and team defense. We will put pressure on the defense buy using our running game.

Okaloosa - Walton Community College

100 College Blvd
Niceville, FL 32578
Coach: David Garner

NJCAA
Raiders/Red, Silver
Phone: (850) 729-5268
Fax: (850) 729-6033

ACADEMIC

Founded: 1963
Type: 2 Yr., Jr. College, Coed
Web-site: http://www.owcc.net
Campus Housing: No
Student/Faculty Ratio: 20:1
Male/Female Ratio: 43:57
Undergraduate Enrollment: 5,820
Graduate Enrollment: None
Scholarships/Academic: No **Athletic:** Yes **Fin Aid:** Yes
Total Expenses by: Year **In State:** $ 900 **Out of State:** $ 3,500
Degrees Conferred: Associate
Programs of Study: Accounting, Art, Automotive, Aviation, Banking/Finance, Biological, Computer, Dietetics, Construction, Engineering, Fashion, Heating/Refrigeration/Air Conditioning, Hotel and Restaurant Management, Industrial, Meteorology, Ministries, Nutrition, Paralegal, Real Estate

ATHLETIC PROFILE

Conference Affiliation: Pan Handle Conference
Program Profile: Five year record of 193-91.
Achievements: Conference Champions 1996; State tournament appearances 1995, 1996.
Coaching: David Garner, Head Coach, is entering his fifth year at Okaloosa-Walton CC.

Palm Beach Atlantic College

901 S Flagler Drive
West Palm Beach, FL 33416
Coach: Kyle Forbes

NAIA
Sailfish/Blue, White
Phone: (561) 803-2523
Fax: (561) 803-2532

ACADEMIC

Founded: 1968
Type: 4 Yr., Private, Liberal Arts, Coed
Religion: Southern Baptist
Campus Housing: Yes
Web-site: http://www.pbac.edu/
SAT/ACT/GPA: 900/ 18
Student/Faculty Ratio: 18:1
Male/Female Ratio: 45:55
Undergraduate Enrollment: 2,000
Graduate Enrollment: 200
Scholarships/Academic: Yes **Athletic:** Yes **Fin Aid:** Yes
Total Expenses by: Year **In State:** $ 9,300 **Out of State:** $ 9,300
Degrees Conferred: BA, BS, BMA

ATHLETIC PROFILE

Conference Affiliation: Florida Sun Conference
Program Profile: We have a two months Fall season and a 4 months Spring season with a total of 56 games.
History: Our program began in 1984 and we joined NAIA in 1988.
Achievements: 4 All-Americans; most recent drafted player is Maney Leshay by the Milwaukee in 1996 - 16th round.
Coaching: Kyle Forbes, Head Coach, is entering his fifth season as a head coach. He compiled a record of 72-70. He was previously an assistant at Florida Atlantic. He led the Sailfish to a 29-17 season in 1997. He was formerly an assistant coach at Florida Atlantic University for two years. In both seasons, the Owls were ranked in the nation's Top 10. Keith Ambrose, Assistant Coach, is beginning his first season on the Sailfish coaching staff as the pitching coach. He graduated from Jupiter High School in 1993 then played for Palm Beach Community College.
Roster for 1998 team/In State: 15 **Out of State:** 15 **Out of Country:** 5
Total Number of Varsity/Jr. Varsity: 35 **Percent of Graduation:** 96%
Number of Seniors on 1998 Team: 4 **Most Recent Record:** 34 - 15 - 0
Number of Fall Games: 12 **Number of Spring Games:** 55
Style of Play: Emphasis on pitching and defense. 1997 and 1998 team has a good amount of power at the plate.

Palm Beach Community College

4200 S Congress Avenue
Lake Worth, FL 33461
Coach: Craig Gero

NJCAA
Panthers/Green, White
Phone: (561) 439-8188
Fax: (561) 439-8352

ACADEMIC

Founded: 1933 **Type:** 2 Yr., Jr. College, Coed
Student/Faculty Ratio: 24:1 **Male/Female Ratio:** Unknown
Undergraduate Enrollment: 16,016 **Graduate Enrollment:** None
Scholarships/Academic: No **Athletic:** No **Fin Aid:** Yes
Total Expenses by: Year **In State:** $ 1,100 **Out of State:** $ 4,000
Degrees Conferred: Associates
Programs of Study: Accounting, Banking, Finance, Biological Science, Botany, Chemistry, Communications, Data Processing, Education, Fire Science, Flight Training, history, Journalism, Law Enforcement, Mathematics, Nutrition, Office Management, Photography, Physical Education, Radiological Technology, Surveying Technology ***Contact Admission Office for more academic and admission information.

Pasco Hernando Community College

10230 Ridge Road
New Port Richey, FL 34654
Coach: Steve Winterling

NJCAA
Conquistadors/Black, Gold
Phone: (813) 847-2727
Fax: (813) 847-2727

ACADEMIC

Founded: 1972 **Type:** 2 Yr., Jr. College, Coed
Religion: Non-Affiliated **Campus Housing:** No
Student/Faculty Ratio: 25:1 **Male/Female Ratio:** Unknown
Undergraduate Enrollment: 5,808 **Graduate Enrollment:** None
Scholarships/Academic: No **Athletic:** No **Fin Aid:** Yes
Total Expenses by: Year **In State:** $ 1,100 **Out of State:** $ 4,100
Degrees Conferred: Associate

Programs of Study: Business, Computer Programming, Construction Technology, Criminal Justice, Dental Services, Emergency Medical Technology, Fire Science, Food Services, Hospitality Services, Human Services, Law Enforcement, Liberal Arts, Marketing, Nursing, Office Management, Welding Technology

ATHLETIC PROFILE

Conference Affiliation: Sun Coast

Pensacola Junior College

1000 College Blvd
Pensacola, FL 32504
Coach: Bill Hamilton

NJCAA
Pirates/Kelly Green, Navy Blue
Phone: (850) 484-1309
Fax: (850 484-1876

ACADEMIC

Founded: 1948
Type: 2 Yr., Jr. College, Coed
Student/Faculty Ratio: 14:1
Male/Female Ratio: Unknown
Undergraduate Enrollment: 12,000
Graduate Enrollment: None
Scholarships/Academic: No **Athletic:** Yes **Fin Aid:** Yes
Total Expenses by: Year **In State:** $ 6,000 **Out of State:** $ 9,000
Degrees Conferred: Associate
Programs of Study: Agricultural Business, Agricultural Science, Biomedical Technology, Civil Engineering, Communications Equipment Technology, Court Reporting, Drafting and Design, Electronics Engineering, Film and Fine Arts, Graphic Arts, Health Services, Law Enforcement, Liberal Arts, Medical Record Administration, Physical Education, Physical therapy, Respiratory Therapy ***Contact school Admission Office for more academic and admission information .

ATHLETIC PROFILE

Conference Affiliation: Panhandle/Florida Community College Activity Association
Program Profile: Our facilities include a natural grass, grass baselines, great lights, inning by inning scoreboard, three batting tunnels. The stadium has a seating capacity of a 500 people. We play a 20-game in the Fall and a 56-game in the Spring. We participated in 5 Fall tournaments and 2 Spring tournaments, which is great exposure.
History: We began over thirty years ago. Our current coach , Bill Hamilton, is in his 8th year. Our previous coach spent 21 years at PJC.
Achievements: Most recent conference title was in 1988; most recent playoff in 1991; 1995 Fla Juco Player of the Year; 1st team All-American - Brandon Black. Over 20 drafted players in the last seven years.
Coaching: Bill Hamilton, Head Coach. Jim Presley, Assistant Coach, is a former Mariner All-Star. Ryan Hepworth, Assistant Coach.
Style of Play: We have good hitting teams. We set all offensive records in the last seven years. The 1996 team was second in state in fielding percent. The 1998 team has at least 8 pitchers throwing 85mph or better.

Polk Community College

999 Avenue H, NE
Winter Haven, FL 33881
Coach: Johnny Wiggs

NJCAA
Vikings/Orange, Green
Phone: (941) 297-1007
Fax: (941) 297-1015

ACADEMIC

Founded: 1964
Type: 2 Yr., Jr. College, Coed
Student/Faculty Ratio: 27:1
Male/Female Ratio: 37:63
Undergraduate Enrollment: 6,000
Graduate Enrollment: None

Scholarships/Academic: No **Athletic:** Yes **Fin Aid:** Yes
Total Expenses by: Year **In State:** $ 1,150 **Out of State:** $ 4,125
Degrees Conferred: Associate
Programs of Study: Art, Art History, Astronomy, Biology, Botany, Broadcasting, Chemistry, Civil Engineering Technology, Communications, Corrections, Economics, Educational Media, Elementary Eduation, German, History, Literature, Medical Technology, Modern Languages, Music, Natural Science, Sociology, Spanish, Zoology

Rollins College

1000 Holt Avenue - 2730
Winter Park, FL 32789
Coach: Bob Rikeman
Email: rike27@iag.net

NCAA II
Tars/Blue, Gold
Phone: (407) 646-2328
Fax: (407) 646-1555

ACADEMIC

Founded: 1885
Religion: Non-Affiliated
Web-site: http://www.rollins.edu/
Student/Faculty Ratio: 10:1
Undergraduate Enrollment: 1,500

Type: 4 Yr., Private, Liberal Arts, Coed
Campus Housing: Yes
SAT/ACT/GPA: 1000
Male/Female Ratio: 40:60
Graduate Enrollment: 2,000

Scholarships/Academic: Yes **Athletic:** Yes **Fin Aid:** Yes
Total Expenses by: Year **In State:** $ 25,000 **Out of State:** $ 25,000
Degrees Conferred: Liberal Arts, Premed
Programs of Study: Art, Economics, Education, English, Environmental Studies, Foreign Language, History, International Studies, Mathematics, Pschology, Philosophy/Religion, Science, Sociology

ATHLETIC PROFILE

Conference Affiliation: Sunshine State Conference
Program Profile: We have a highly competitive Division I program which attracts Division I talent. Our playing season is 56 NCAA maximum with a full Fall season and off-season weights and plymetrics. We play at Harold Alford Stadium which has a seating capacity of 2,000 and is located at Rollins campus. The stadium has 419 Bermuda grass and is ranked in the top 5% of all college facilities, There are locker rooms, storage rooms and showers.
History: We started in 1895 and became a member of NCAA in 1947. We entered Division II in 1973. Rollins is the smallest school in college baseball history to play in the College World Series. We are the only school to advance to national championships in 3 different levels (NAIA, NCAA (all divisions in '54) and NCAA D-II).
Achievements: Over 80 drafted players including 8 current players drafted out of high school and junior college. Centry Club member for 100 career wins in three seasons. Several All-Americans.
Coaching: Bob Rikeman, Head Coach. Jim Harvath, Infield, Baserunning and Defense Coach. Jim Newin, Pitching Coach. Chuck Schall, Hitting and Catching Coach.
Style of Play: National League type offense . Great team speed, look to steal 100+ bases, bunt aggressively and move runners. Solid fundamentals, defense and great pitching.

Saint John's River Community College

5001 St Johns Avenue
Palatka, FL 32177-3897
Coach: Sam Rick

NJCAA
Vikings/Col Blue, White
Phone: (904) 312-4164
Fax: (904) 325-6627

ACADEMIC

Founded: 1958
Student/Faculty Ratio: 22:1
Undergraduate Enrollment: 3,400

Type: 2 Yr., Jr. College, Coed
Male/Female Ratio: 39:61
Graduate Enrollment: None

Scholarships/Academic: No **Athletic:** Yes **Fin Aid:** Yes
Total Expenses by: Year **In State:** $ 1,150 **Out of State:** $ 4,500
Degrees Conferred: Associate
Programs of Study: Appiled Art, Art, Business Administration, Commercial Art, Computer Programming, Criminal Justice, Electronics Engineering Technology, Liberal Arts, Marketing

Saint Leo College

MC 2038, P.O. Box 6665
Saint Leo, FL 33574
Coach: Ed Stabile
Email: athletic@saintleo.edu

NCAA II
Monarchs/Green, White
Phone: (352) 588-8506
Fax: (352) 588-8290

ACADEMIC

Founded: 1889
Web-site: http://www.saintleo.edu
Student/Faculty Ratio: 15:1
Undergraduate Enrollment: 900
Type: 4 Yr., Private, Liberal Arts, Coed
Religion: Catholic
Male/Female Ratio: Unknown
Graduate Enrollment: 200
Scholarships/Academic: Yes **Athletic:** Yes **Fin Aid:** Yes
Total Expenses by: Year **In State:** $ 17,240 **Out of State:** $ Varies
Degrees Conferred: BA, Masters
Programs of Study: Accounting, American Studies, Banking and Finance, Biology, Business Administration, Business, Law, Chemistry, Communications, Computer Science, Criminal Justice, Economics, Elementary Education, English, History, Human Resources, Management, Marketing, Political Science, Predentistry, Prelaw, Premed, Psychology, Public Administration, Religion, Social Science, Sport Administration

ATHLETIC PROFILE

Estimated Number of Baseball Scholarships: 9
Conference Affiliation: Sunshine State Conference
Program Profile: We have a very competitive Division II and we usually rank in the top 25. We have a natural beautiful grass field with dimensions of 315 right, 410 straight away center, 325 left. Left alley is 365 and right alley is 355.
History: Saint Leo Baseball began in 1966. In over 31 seasons, the program has an overall record of 820-612. Three teams have advanced to the NCAA Regional Tournament (1971, 1978, and 1996). Saint Leo has had eleven coaches.
Achievements: Two players were named All-Americans. Over 40 players have gone on to play professional baseball. Six players have made it to the major league including Bob Tewkebury and Jim Cuise.
Coaching: Ed Stabile, Head Coach, is entering his first season as a head coach. He was an assistant at Division I University of South Florida for 4 years. Mike Swenson, Assistant Coach.
Roster for 1998 team/In State: 13 **Out of State:** 15 **Out of Country:** 2
Number of Seniors on 1998 Team: 9 **Number of Sophomores on 1998 Team:** 5
Most Recent Record: 34 - 17 - 0 **Number of Spring Games:** 56
Schedule: Tampa, Florida Southern, Barry, University of Massachussetts, West Florida, Ithaca, Brewton-Parker, Florida Tech, Rollins, Lynn

Saint Petersburg J C

PO Box 13489
St Petersburg, FL 33733
Coach: Dave Pano

NJCAA
Trojans/Royal Blue, White
Phone: (813) 791-2662
Fax: (727) 791-2747

ACADEMIC

Founded: 1927
Student/Faculty Ratio: 19:1
Undergraduate Enrollment: 17,353
Scholarships/Academic: No **Athletic:** Yes
Total Expenses by: Year **In State:** $ 1,100
Degrees Conferred: Associate

Type: 2 Yr., Jr. College, Coed
Male/Female Ratio: 40:60
Graduate Enrollment: None
Fin Aid: Yes
Out of State: $ 4,000

Programs of Study: Anatomy, Anthropology, Astronomy, Banking, Biology, Building, Construction, Cooperative Education, Dance, Earth Science, Education, English as a Second Language, Funeral Services, Gerontology, History, Humanities, Interpreter Training, Legal Assisting, Logic *** Contact school admission office for more academic and admission information.

ATHLETIC PROFILE

Conference Affiliation: Suncoast Conference of FJCCA
Program Profile: Our home field is Joe DiMaggio Complex in Clearwater, Florida. The Trojans play in the Suncoast Conference, which is the strongest in the state of Florida and the nation. Five out of the last seven years our Suncoast Conference teams have won the State Championship.
History: 1961 to 1995 cumulative record 782-692-8. Coaches: Ralph Kern (1961-1965), George Brown (1967-1969), Ed Davis (1966, 1970-1995).
Achievements: Florida USBF/Topps Amateur Baseball Coach of the Year 1992. Four players in major leagues: Tim Teufel, Howard Johnson, Ben Hayes, Kurt Abbott. 25 minor league ball players.

Saint Thomas University

16400 32nd Avenue
Miami, FL 33054
Coach: Manny Mantrana

NAIA
Bobcats/Columbia Blue, Navy, White
Phone: (305) 628-6678
Fax: (305) 628-6790

ACADEMIC

Founded: 1961
Religion: Catholic
Web-site: http://www.stu.edu/
Student/Faculty Ratio: 15:1
Undergraduate Enrollment: 1,400
Scholarships/Academic: Yes **Athletic:** Yes
Total Expenses by: Year **In State:** $15,000
Degrees Conferred: BA, BS, MA, MS

Type: 4 Yr., Private, Liberal Arts, Coed
Campus Housing: Yes
SAT/ACT/GPA: 1000/20
Male/Female Ratio: 3:4
Graduate Enrollment: 500
Fin Aid: Yes
Out of State: $ 15,000

Programs of Study: Accounting, American Studies, Banking and Finance, Biology, Business Administration, Economics, Business Law, Chemistry, Communications, Computer Science, Criminal Justice, Elementary Education, History, Management, Marketing, Political Science, Predentistry, Prelaw, Premed, Psychology, Public Administration, Religion, Social Science, Sport Administration

ATHLETIC PROFILE

Estimated Number of Baseball Scholarships: 8
Conference Affiliation: Florida Sun Conference
Program Profile: The team is 131-46 under head coach Jim Pizzolatto in the last three years. We have been in the Southeast Regional tournament in two of the last three years. We play the toughest schedule possible including University of Miami.
History: Our program began in 1970 as an NCAA Division II school. In 1988, we moved to NAIA.
Achievements: Manny Mantrana - 1997 Fundraiser of the Year; 1998 FSC Coach of the Year; 1 player All-American; 2 second team; 2 Honorable Mention
Roster for 1998 team/In State: 22 **Out of State:** 3 **Out of Country:** 0
Total Number of Varsity/Jr. Varsity: 15 **Most Recent Record:** 54 - 14 - 0
Number of Seniors on 1998 Team: 2 **Number of Sophomores on 1998 Team:** 7
Freshmen Receiving Fin Aid/Athletic: 5 **Academic:** 7

Number of Fall Games: 15 **Number of Spring Games:** 55
Positions Needed for 1999/2000: Outfielders, Pitchers, Catchers
Schedule: University of Miami, University of Tampa, St. Leo College, Embry-Riddle, Auburn-Montgomery, Nova Southeastern
Style of Play: Smart hand and for full nine innings.

Santa Fe Community College

3000 NW 83rd Street
Gainesville, FL 32606
Coach: Harry Tholen

NJCAA
Saints/Col Blue, White
Phone: (352) 395-5540
Fax: (352) 395-5547

ACADEMIC

Founded: 1966
Type: 2 Yr., Jr. College, Coed
Student/Faculty Ratio: 22:1
Male/Female Ratio: Unknown
Undergraduate Enrollment: 11,800
Graduate Enrollment: None
Scholarships/Academic: No **Athletic:** Yes **Fin Aid:** Yes
Total Expenses by: Year **In State:** $ 1,400 **Out of State:** $ 4,300
Degrees Conferred: BBA, Associate
Programs of Study: Accounting, Agriculture, Anthropology, Biological Science, Botany, Chemistry, Corrections, Dental Services, Ecology, Education, English, Fire Science

Seminole Community College

100 Weldon Blvd
Sanford, FL 32773
Coach: Jack Pantelias

NJCAA
Raiders/Navy, Col Blue, White
Phone: (407) 328-2094
Fax: (407) 328-2193

ACADEMIC

Founded: 1966
Type: 2 Yr., Jr. College, Coed
Student/Faculty Ratio: 13:1
Male/Female Ratio: Unknown
Undergraduate Enrollment: 7,500
Graduate Enrollment: None
Scholarships/Academic: No **Athletic:** No **Fin Aid:** Yes
Total Expenses by: Year **In State:** $ 1,100 **Out of State:** $ 3,900
Degrees Conferred: Associate
Programs of Study: Accounting, Automotive Technology, Banking/Finance, Business, Civil Engineering Technology, Computer Informations System, Computer Programming, Computer Technology, Construction Technology, Criminal Justice, Data Processing, Drafting/Design, Electronics Engineering, Fire Science, Liberal Arts, Physical Therapy, Telecommunications

ATHLETIC PROFILE

Conference Affiliation: Mid Florida, NJCAA, FCCAA

Stetson University

421 N. Woodland Blvd.
Deland, FL 32720
Coach: Pete Dunn

NCAA I
Hatters/Green, White
Phone: (904) 822-8100
Fax: (904) 822-8148

ACADEMIC

Founded: 1883
Type: 4 Yr., Private, Liberal Arts, Coed
Web-site: http://www.stetson.edu/
SAT/ACT/GPA: 1020-1230/24-27/3.48

Student/Faculty Ratio: 11:1
Male/Female Ratio: 55:45
Undergraduate Enrollment: 2,200
Graduate Enrollment: 300
Scholarships/Academic: Yes **Athletic:** Yes **Fin Aid:** Yes
Total Expenses by: Year **In State:** $ 22,000 **Out of State:** $ 22,000
Degrees Conferred: BA, BS, BEd, BM, MA, MS, MBA, MEd, PhD
Programs of Study: Accounting, American Studies, Art, Biology, Business Administration, Chemistry, Communication Studies, Computer Science, Counseling, Economics, Education, English, Environmental Studies, Finance, Foreign Language, Geography, Geology, History, Humanities, Information Systems, Latin American Studies, Management, Marketing, Mathematics, Military Sciences, Philosophy, Physics, Political Science, Psychology, Religious Studies, Russian Studies, Sociology, Sports and Exercise Science, Sport Administration, Theatre

ATHLETIC PROFILE

Estimated Number of Baseball Scholarships: 11.7
Conference Affiliation: Trans America Athletic Conference
Program Profile: We have a highly competitive Division I program in Florida. We have a new $ 4.5 million stadium which will open on January 15, 1999 . It will have 2000 seats and a grass field. We have a full game schedule.
History: We are the oldest college baseball program in Florida. We started playing in 1895. We got full 56 NCAA Regionals in the last 16 years & became Division I in 1972. We joined TAAC in 1988.
Achievements: TAAC Champions in 1988, 1989 and 1990; NCAA at large bids in 1996 and 1007; 44 players signed professionally since 1980; 9 All-Americans since 1988 including consensus All-American first team in 1998.
Coaching: Pete Dunn, Head Coach, was TAAC Coach of the Year four times. Our first player drafted in 1970. Coach Dunn is an excellent teacher and has excellent strategies. He compiled a record of 696-422-2 since 1980. Tom Riginos, Recruiting Coordinator.
Roster for 1998 team/In State: 16 **Out of State:** 9 **Out of Country:** 2
Total Number of Varsity/Jr. Varsity: 27 **Number of Seniors on 1998 Team:** 3
Freshmen Receiving Fin Aid/Athletic: 6 **Academic:** 2
Most Recent Record: 30 - 31 - 1 **Number of Spring Games:** 61
Positions Needed for 1999/2000: LHP, Best Athlete
Schedule: Miami, Florida, Central Florida, South Florida, Jacksonville, Troy State
Style of Play: Aggressive, fundamental baseball, hit and run, steal bases, good pitching and defense; don't rely heavily on home run ball.

Tallahassee Community College

444 Appleyard Drive
Tallahassee, FL 32304
Coach: Mike McLeod

NJCAA
Eagles/Royal, Gold
Phone: (850) 922-0230
Fax: (850) 487-2265

ACADEMIC

Founded: 1966
Type: 2 Yr., Jr. College, Coed
Student/Faculty Ratio: 27:1
Male/Female Ratio: 46:54
Undergraduate Enrollment: 9,800
Graduate Enrollment: None
Scholarships/Academic: No **Athletic:** Yes **Fin Aid:** Yes
Total Expenses by: Year **In State:** $ 1,000 **Out of State:** $ 3,700
Degrees Conferred: Associate
Programs of Study: Business Administration, Civil Engineering Technology, Computer Programming, Criminal Justice, Dental Services, Emergency Medical Technology, Fire Science, Industrial Adminsitrations, Landscaping, Liberal Arts, Nursing, Office Management, Paralegal Studies, Postal Management, Radiological Technology, Respiratory Therapy

ATHLETIC PROFILE

Conference Affiliation: Panhandle Conference

Program Profile: Our NJCAA Division I program has 20 Fall scrimmages and 56 Spring games (25 Panhandle Conference). We have a natural grass field with lights and sunken dugouts. The stadium has 1,000 seats and a 42-ft. scoreboard.
History: The program began in 1991 and as gone 223-117-2 for a winning percentage of .652. Forty eight players have gone on to Division I programs . Nine players signed professional contracts straight from TCC.
Achievements: We won the Panhandle Conference in 1995 and received Coach of the Year Honors the same year. Thirty three drafted players have come through TCC with nine signing contracts. Forthy eight players have gone on to play Division I baseball.
Coaching: Mike McLeod, Head Coach. Mike Beasley, Assistant Coach. Allen Morlocke, Assistant Coach. Jim Hage, Assistant Coach.
Style of Play: Pitching and defense, and aggressive offensive play.

University of Central Florida

P.O Box 163555
Orlando, FL 32816
Coach: Jay Bergman

NCAA I
Golden Knights/Black, Gold
Phone: (407) 823-2256
Fax: (407) 823-5293

ACADEMIC

Founded: 1963
Type: 4 Yr., Public, Liberal Arts, Coed
Religion: Non-Affiliated
Campus Housing: Yes
Web-site: http://www.ucf.edu/
SAT/ACT/GPA: 900 sliding
Student/Faculty Ratio: 18:1
Male/Female Ratio: 50:50
Undergraduate Enrollment: 21,500
Graduate Enrollment: 5,000
Scholarships/Academic: Yes **Athletic:** Yes **Fin Aid:** Yes
Total Expenses by: Year **In State:** $ 1,800 **Out of State:** $ 7,000
Degrees Conferred: BA, BS, MS, MeD, PhD
Programs of Study: College of Arts and Sciences (Anthropology, Art, Biology, Chemistry, Communication, Computer, Economics, English, Languages, History, Humanities, Journalism, Liberal Arts, Math, Music, Philosophy, Physics, Political Science, Psychology, Radio/TV, Social Sciences, Sociology, Speech, Statistics, Theatre, Prelaw); College of Business Administration (Accounting, Economics, Finance, General Business, Hospitality, Management, Marketing); College of Education (Art, Business, Early Childhood, Elementary, English, Language, Math, Music, Physical, Science, Social Science, Vocational and Industry); College of Engineering (Aerospace, Civil, Computer, Electrical, Environmental, Industrial, Mechanical); College of Health and Public Affairs

ATHLETIC PROFILE

Conference Affiliation: Trans America Athletic Conference
Program Profile: A new baseball stadium is under construction and will be ready to play in the Spring of 1998. The seating capacity should be around 2,500.
History: The program began in 1973.
Achievements: Won 1993, 1995, and 1996 TAAC Titles; played in 1993, 1995, and 1996 NCAA Regionals; 4 players drafted in 1996; Coach Bergman 1995 Atlantic Region Coach of the Year.
Coaching: Jay Bergman, Head Coach, started in 1983 . He was head coach at Florida from 1976 to 1981. He is the 1995 Atlantic Region Coach of the Year with an overall record of 623-373-3 (.625). Greg Frady, Assistant Coach. Craig Cozark, Assistant Coach.
Roster for 1998 team/In State: 26 **Out of State:** 6 **Out of Country:** 0
Total Number of Varsity/Jr. Varsity: 32 **Percent of Graduation:** 90%
Number of Seniors on 1998 Team: 2 **Number of Sophomores on 1998 Team:** 8
Freshmen Receiving Fin Aid/Athletic: 5 **Academic:** 1
Most Recent Record: 41 - 21 - 0 **Number of Spring Games:** 57
Positions Needed for 1999/2000: Shortstop, LHP, 2 Base, OF
Baseball Camp Dates: Christmas
Schedule: Louisiana State, Rice, South Alabama, Florida, South Florida, Nicholls State, St. Johns
Style of Play: Pitching, defense and aggressive offensive style.

University of Florida

PO Box 14485
Gainesville, FL 32604
Coach: Andy Lopez

NCAA I
Gators/Orange, Blue
Phone: (352) 375-4683
Fax: (352) 375-7807

ACADEMIC

Founded: 1858
Religion: Non-Affiliated
Web-site: http://www.uaa.ufl.edu
Student/Faculty Ratio: 17:1
Undergraduate Enrollment: 30,000
Scholarships/Academic: Yes **Athletic:** Yes
Total Expenses by: Year **In State:** $ Varies

Type: 4 Yr., Public, Coed
Campus Housing: Yes
SAT/ACT/GPA: 970/20/2.0
Male/Female Ratio: 52:48
Graduate Enrollment: 10,000
Fin Aid: Yes
Out of State: $ Varies

Degrees Conferred: Bachelors, Masters, Doctoral
Programs of Study: Accounting, Advertising, Aerospace Engineering, Agricultural Business, Agricultural Economics, Agricultural Education, Agricultural Engineering, Agronomy, Soil and Crop Science, American Studies, Animal Science, Anthropology, Architecture, Art Education, Art/Fine Arts, Art History, Astronomy, Botany/Plant Science, Business Administration, Commerce, Management, Chemical Engineering, Chemistry, Civil Engineering, Classic, Computer Engineering, Computer Science, Conservation, Construction Management, Criminal Justice, Dairy Science, Dance, East Asian Studies, Ecology, Economics, Construction Management, English, Entomology, Health Science, Horticulture, Industrial Engineering, Insurance, Interior Design, Journalism, Management Information System, Mechanical Engineering, Microbiology, Music, Music Education, Natural Resources Management, Nuclear Engineering, Nursing, Nutrition, Occupational Therapy, Physician's Assistant Studies, Physics, Political Science, Psychology, Studio Art, Sociology

ATHLETIC PROFILE

Conference Affiliation: Southeastern Conference
Program Profile: We play in McVethan Stadium which has a seating capacity of 4,500. We were ranked in Top Ten in attendance in 1997. We play on natural grass. We attracted 5,000 spectators twice last season (1996) and averaged 2,500 per game.
History: Our program began in 1912. Won three College Wold Series appearances (1988, 1991 and 1996). We have eight SEC Championships.
Achievements: 37 Majors Leaguers, more than any other SEC school. Eight first round draft picks; 25 All-Americans; three Academic All-Americans.
Coaching: Andy Lopez, Head Coach, was a two-time National Coach of the Year selection. He coached Pepperdine University to the National Championship in 1992. He produced 38 players that signed pro contracts, 16 All-Americans and three Academic All-Americans. Gary Henderson, Assistant Coach. Steve Kling, Assistant Coach. Eric Ekstein, Assistant Coach.
Style of Play: Play hard.

University of Miami

#1 Hurricane Dr
Coral Gables, FL 33124
Coach: Jim Morris

NCAA I
Hurricanes/Green, Orange
Phone: (305) 284-4171
Fax: (305) 284-3227

ACADEMIC

Founded: 1925
Religion: Non-Affiliated
Web-site: http://www.miami.edu
Student/Faculty Ratio: 8:1
Undergraduate Enrollment: 8,350
Scholarships/Academic: Yes **Athletic:** Yes

Type: 4 Yr., Private, Coed
Campus Housing: Yes
SAT/ACT/GPA: 1000/24
Male/Female Ratio: 52:48
Graduate Enrollment: 5,200
Fin Aid: Yes

Total Expenses by: Year **In State:** $ 24,000 **Out of State:** $ 24,000
Degrees Conferred: BA, BS, MS, PhD, JD
Programs of Study: Aerospace Engineering, Afro-American Studies, American Studies, Anthropology, Audio Engineering, Biochemistry, Broadcasting, Caribbean Studies, Criminology, Foreign Languages, Latin American Studies, Photography, Real Estate, Renaissance Studies, *** Contact school admission office for more academic and adminssion information .

ATHLETIC PROFILE

Conference Affiliation: Independent
Program Profile: We play at Mark Light Stadium which has natural grass.
Achievements: 1995 - won Atlantic II Regional, placed third in College World Series, 10 players drafted. 1982, 1985 National Champions. 22 consecutive years in NCAA Regional - NCAA record.
Coaching: Jim Morris, Head Coach. Assistants, Turtle Thomas, Lazer Collazo, Johnny Rodriguez.
Style of Play: Hard, aggressive, pitching and defense with speed.

University of North Florida

4567 St. Johns Bluff Road South
Jacksonville, FL 32224
Coach: Dusty Rhodes

NCAA II
Osprey/Navy, Grey
Phone: (904) 646-2556
Fax: (904) 646-2836

ACADEMIC

Founded: 1972
Religion: Non-Affiliated
Web-site: http://www.unf.edu/
Student/Faculty Ratio: 30:1
Undergraduate Enrollment: 9,000
Type: 4 Yr., Public, Coed
Campus Housing: Yes
SAT/ACT/GPA: 1000/ 21
Male/Female Ratio: 57:43
Graduate Enrollment: 2,000
Scholarships/Academic: Yes **Athletic:** Yes **Fin Aid:** Yes
Total Expenses by: Year **In State:** $ 5,000 **Out of State:** $ 10,000
Degrees Conferred: BA, BFA, BS, BBA, BAE, MA, MS, MBA, MED, EdD
Programs of Study: College of Arts and Sciences, Business Administration, Computing Science and Engineering, College of Health, College of Education , Human Services

ATHLETIC PROFILE

Conference Affiliation: Sunshine State Conference
Program Profile: UNF's Harmon Stadium stands as one of college baseball's finest facilities. It has a superb lighting system, home and visitor locker rooms with showers, concession stand, press box, seating for 1,000 fans in chair back & bench back seats, and a picnic area. The field has one of the finest playing surfaces in the country (dimensions: 325' down lines, 365' power alleys, 400' center).
History: Our program began in 1988 and went to the NAIA World Series in 1989 and 1991 finishing third both times. The Ospreys are the only team in collegiate baseball to win 100 games in the first two years of a program's existence.
Achievements: 8 All-Americans; 17 players drafted into pros since 1989.
Coaching: Dusty Rhodes, Head Coach, was 8 years at UNFand worked as an assistant coach for USA Baseball Team in 1993 and 1994.
Style of Play: Aggressive fundamental baseball dependent upon the utmost desire to be dedicated and disciplined.

University of South Florida

4202 E Flower Avenue Sun 141
Tampa, FL 33620
Coach: Eddie Cardieri

NCAA I
Bulls/Green, Gold
Phone: (813) 974-3105
Fax: (813) 974-3068

ACADEMIC

Founded: 1956
Web-site: http://www.usf.edu/
Student/Faculty Ratio: 13:1
Undergraduate Enrollment: 26,000
Scholarships/Academic: Yes **Athletic:** Yes
Total Expenses by: Year **In State:** $ 5,800
Type: 4 Yr., Public, Coed
SAT/ACT/GPA: 910+
Male/Female Ratio: 44:56
Graduate Enrollment: 10,000
Fin Aid: Yes
Out of State: $ 9,400
Degrees Conferred: BA, BS, BFA, MA, MS, MBA, MFA, MEd, PhD, EdD, MD
Programs of Study: Accounting, Advertising, Anthropology, Biology, Botony, Broadcasting, Business, Communications, Criminal Justice, Economics, Education, Engineering, Finance, Geography, Geology, Gerontology, History, International Studies, Liberal Arts, Literature, Mathematics, Medical Technology, Microbiology, Natural Science, Philosophy, Physical Education, Physical Science, Physics, Political Science, Preprofessional Courses, Psychology, Religion, Science, Social Science, Special Education, Speech, Theatre, Zoology

ATHLETIC PROFILE

Conference Affiliation: Conference USA

University of Tampa

401 W Kennedy Boulevard
Tampa, FL 33601-490
Coach: Terry Rupp
NCAA II
Spartans/Scarlet, Black, Gold
Phone: (813) 253-6240
Fax: (813) 253-6288

ACADEMIC

Founded: 1931
SAT/ACT/GPA: 820/3.0
Student/Faculty Ratio: 5:1
Undergraduate Enrollment: 1,750
Scholarships/Academic: Yes **Athletic:** Yes
Total Expenses by: Year **In State:** $ 20,032
Type: 4 Yr., Private, Liberal Arts, Coed
Campus Housing: Yes
Male/Female Ratio: 3:1
Graduate Enrollment: 1,000
Fin Aid: Yes
Out of State: $ 20,032
Degrees Conferred: BA, BS, BFA, Bmus, MBA
Programs of Study: Accounting, Banking/Finance, Biological Science, Chemistry, Communications, Creative Writing, Criminal Justice, Economics, Education, Fine Arts, Marketing, Mathematics, Medical Laboratory Technology, Nursing, Philosophy, Physics, Psychology, Social Science, Political Science

ATHLETIC PROFILE

Conference Affiliation: Sunshine State Conference
History: 10th straight NCAA tournament appearances, National Champions 1992 and 1993.
Achievements: 10 straight NCAA Tournaments Appearances; National Champions in 1992 and 1993; Tino Matinez (Mariners), Sam Militeld (Yankees), Ozzie Timmons (Brewers), and Joe Vrso (Angels).
Coaching: Terry Rupp, Head Coach.
Style of Play: Aggressive.

University of West Florida

11000 University Parkway
Pensacola, FL 32514
Coach: Jim Spooner
NCAA II/NAIA
Argonauts/Blue, Green
Phone: (850) 474-2488
Fax: (850) 474-3342

ACADEMIC

Founded: 1967
Type: 4 Yr., Public, Liberal Arts, Coed
Undergraduate Enrollment: 8,000
Campus Housing: Yes
Web-site: http://www.uswf.edu/
SAT/ACT/GPA: 900/ 21
Student/Faculty Ratio: 26:1
Male/Female Ratio: 45:55
Scholarships/Academic: Yes **Athletic:** Yes **Fin Aid:** Yes
Total Expenses by: Year **In State:** $ 6,500 **Out of State:** $ 6,500
Degrees Conferred: AA, BA, BS, BFA, MA, MS, MBA
Programs of Study: Accounting, Advertising, Anthropology, Art, Biology, Broadcasting, Business, Chemistry, Communications, Computer Information System, Computer Science, Criminal Justice, Economics, Education, Engineering, English, Finance, French, History, Humanities, International Studies, Journalism, Marine Biology, Music, Natural Science, Physics, Political Science, Nursing, Physical Education, Physical Science, Religion, Social Science, Psychology

Warner Southern College

5301 Highway 27 South
Lake Wales, FL 33853
Coach: Jeff Sikes

NAIA
Royals/Royal Blue, Gold
Phone: (941) 638-7259
Fax: (941) 638-3776

ACADEMIC

Founded: 1968
Type: 4 Yr., Private, Coed
SAT/ACT/GPA: 840/18
Campus Housing: Yes
Student/Faculty Ratio: 14:1
Male/Female Ratio: 48:52
Scholarships/Academic: Yes **Athletic:** Yes **Fin Aid:** Yes
Total Expenses by: Year **In State:** $ 11,300 **Out of State:** $ 13,000
Degrees Conferred: AA, BA
Programs of Study: Accounting, Biblical, Business, Music, Communications, English, History, Education, Exercise Science, Psychology, Sociology, Sport and Leisure, Management

ATHLETIC PROFILE

Conference Affiliation: Florida Sun Conference
Program Profile: Playing season is in the Fall and in the Spring. The playing field is a natural grass. The stadium has a seating capacity of 200.
History: Our program began in 1976, joined NAIA in 1990. We had our first NAIA post season appearance in 1993. We were in the NCCAA National Tournament in 1992. We have taken four consecutive NAIA postseason trips since 1993.
Achievements: Has 2 drafted players; 5 free-agents; Florida Christian College Conference Champs 1984, 1986-1989, 8 Christian College All-Americans.
Coaching: Jeff Sikes, Head Coach, has a 218-186 record for 10 years. He graduated from Kentucky. Miguel Rivera, Assistant Coach.

Webber College

1201 Highway, 17 South
Babson Park, FL 33827
Coach: Brad Niethammer

NAIA
Warriors/Green, Gold
Phone: (941) 638-2951
Fax: (941) 638-2915

ACADEMIC

Founded: 1922
Type: 4 Yr., Private, Coed
Undergraduate Enrollment: 437
Campus Housing: Yes
Web-site: http://www.webber.edu/
SAT/ACT/GPA: 850/ 19
Student/Faculty Ratio: 17:1
Male/Female Ratio: 50:50

Scholarships/Academic: Yes **Athletic:** Yes **Fin Aid:** Yes
Total Expenses by: Year **In State:** $ 9,607 **Out of State:** $ 9,607
Degrees Conferred: AA, BA in Business Administration
Programs of Study: Management, Marketing, Finance, Accounting, International Travel and Tourism, Hotel and Restaurant Management, Sports and Club Management

ATHLETIC PROFILE

Estimated Number of Baseball Scholarships: 5
Conference Affiliation: Florida Sun Conference
Program Profile: We built a new baseball field in 1998 which is a natural turf.
History: The program began in Spring of 1994. Our record in 1994 was 17-31. It was 22-31 in 1995, 30-28 in 1996; 30-25 in 1997 and 22-26 in 1998. Our overall record is 121-141.
Achievements: We had two players in 1997 sign contracts with Independent Teams.
Coaching: Brad Niethammer, Head Coach, is entering his 6th season . He graduated from Appalachian State in 1990. Gary Garrett, Assistant Coach for 6 years, graduated from Livingston U.
Roster for 1998 team/In State: 20 **Out of State:** 10 **Out of Country:** 0
Total Number of Varsity/Jr. Varsity: 0 **Percent of Graduation:** 89%
Number of Seniors on 1998 Team: 5 **Number of Sophomores on 1998 Team:** 6
Freshmen Receiving Fin Aid/Athletic: 9 **Academic:** 7
Number of Fall Games: 10 **Number of Spring Games:** 55
Baseball Camp Dates: June - July; 4 weeks **Most Recent Record:** 22 - 26 - 0
Positions Needed for 1999/2000: 3 Pitchers, Shortstop, 3rd Base, Catcher, OF
Schedule: University of Tampa, Florida Southern, St. Thomas, Embry-Riddle, St. Leo
Style of Play: Aggressive and scrappy.

GEORGIA

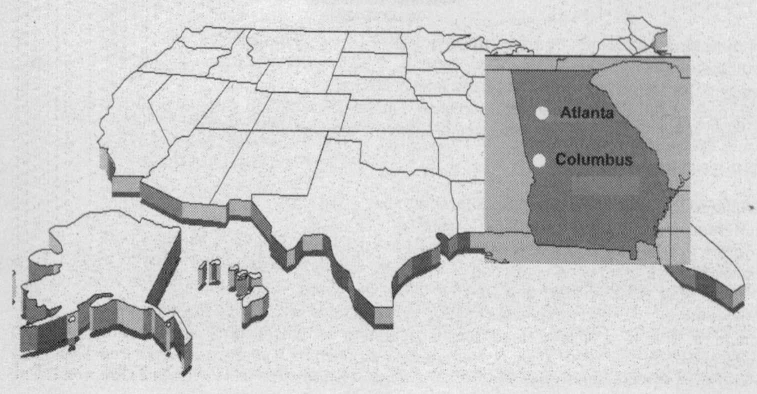

SCHOOL	CITY	AFFILIATION 99	PAGE
Abraham Baldwin College	Tifton	NJCAA	193
Albany State College	Albany	NCAA II	193
Andrew College	Cuthbert	NJCAA	193
Armstrong Atlantic State University	Savannah	NCAA II	194
Atlanta Christian College	East Point	NCCAA II	195
Augusta State University	Augusta	NCAA II	195
Berry College	Mount Berry	NAIA	196
Brewton - Parker College	Mount Vernon	NAIA	197
Clark Atlanta University	Atlanta	NCAA II	197
Columbus State University	Columbus	NCAA II	198
Emmanuel College	Franklin Springs	NAIA	198
Emory University	Atlanta	NCAA III	199
Georgia College	Milledgeville	NCAA II	199
Georgia Institute of Technology	Atlanta	NCAA I	200
Georgia Perimeter C (Former De Kalb C)	Dunwoody	NJCAA	201
Georgia Southern University	Statesboro	NCAA I	201
Georgia Southwestern State University	Americus	NAIA	202
Georgia State University	Atlanta	NCAA I	203
Gordon College	Barnesville	NJCAA	204
Kennesaw State College	Kennesaw	NCAA II	204
LaGrange College	La Grange	NAIA	205
Mercer University	Macon	NCAA I	205
Middle Georgia College	Cochran	NJCAA	206
Oglethorpe University	Atlanta	NCAA	207
Paine College	Augusta	NCAA II	207
Piedmont College	Democrest	NAIA	208
Savannah College of Arts & Design	Savannah	NCAA III	208
Savannah State College	Savannah	NCAA II	209
Shorter College	Rome	NAIA	209
State University of West Georgia	Carrollton	NCAA II	210
South Georgia College	Douglas	NJCAA	211
Southern College of Technology	Marietta	NAIA	211
Truett - McConnell College	Cleveland	NJCAA	212
University of Georgia	Athens	NCAA I	212
Valdosta State College	Valdosta	NCAA II	213
Young Harris College	Young Harris	NJCAA	214

Abraham Baldwin College

2802 Moore Hwy ABAC 41
Tifton, GA 31794-2601
Coach: Steve Janousek

NJCAA
Golden Stallions/Green, Gold
Phone: (912) 386-7217
Fax: (912) 386-7455

ACADEMIC

Founded: 1933
Student/Faculty Ratio: 25:1
Undergraduate Enrollment: 2,776
Scholarships/Academic: No **Athletic:** Yes
Total Expenses by: Year **In State:** $ 4,000
Type: 4 Yr., Public, Coed
Male/Female Ratio: 46:54
Graduate Enrollment: None
Fin Aid: Yes
Out of State: $ 6,000
Degrees Conferred: Associate
Programs of Study: Accounting, Agriculture, Animal Art, Biological Business, Chemistry, Computer

ATHLETIC PROFILE

Conference Affiliation: Georgia Junior College Athletic Association
Program Profile: ABAC offers a very competitive program, which is drill oriented. A 20 game Fall and 56 game Winter-Spring schedule includess other junior colleges from Alabama, Florida, and Georgia. ABAC offers one of the nicest natural playing fields in the region.
History: ABAC has a rich history in baseball dating back to the 1920's. There have been six past coaches. Tom Moody coached for 25 years before Craig Young took over the program in 1991. ABAC has a rich past of placing most of its players 4-year colleges with scholarships.
Achievements: ABAC's last conference title came in 1993. Several players were named to All-Conference and Tournament team. Coach Young received Coach of the Year Honors in 1993. ABAC has a total of 14 players over recent years who have signed professionally. Four of these players are currently still playing.

Albany State College

504 College Drive
Albany, GA 31705
Coach: Darryl Asberry

NCAA II
Golden Rams/Blue, Gold
Phone: (912) 430-4754
Fax: (912) 430-1774

ACADEMIC

Founded: 1903
Student/Faculty Ratio: 16:1
Undergraduate Enrollment: 350
Scholarships/Academic: Yes **Athletic:** Yes
Total Expenses by: Year **In State:** $ 500
Type: 4 Yr., Public, Coed
Male/Female Ratio: 50:50
Graduate Enrollment: None
Fin Aid: Yes
Out of State: $ 7,700
Degrees Conferred: AA, BA, BSW, BSN, MS, MBA
Programs of Study: Accounting, Arts, Fine Arts, Biology, Biological Science, Business Administration, Commerce, Management, Business Education, Chemistry, Computer Science

ATHLETIC PROFILE

Conference Affiliation: SIAC

Andrew College

413 College Street
Cuthbert, GA 31740-1395
Coach: Walter Banks

NJCAA
Tigers/Blue, Gold
Phone: (912) 732-2171x955
Fax: (912) 732-2176

ACADEMIC

Founded: 1854
Religion: Methodist
Student/Faculty Ratio: 12:1
Undergraduate Enrollment: 300
Scholarships/Academic: Yes
Total Expenses by: Year
Degrees Conferred: AA, AS, MA
Type: 2 Yr., Private, Liberal Arts, Coed
Campus Housing: Yes
SAT/ACT/GPA: Varies
Male/Female Ratio: 51:49
Athletic: Yes
Fin Aid: Yes
In State: $ 10,906
Out of State: $ 10,906

Programs of Study: Communication Arts, History, Humanities, International Studies, Language and Literature, Photographic Arts, Prelaw, Preministry, Teaching, Theatre Arts, Visual Art, Biological Sciences, Business Administration, Education, Exercise Science, Golf Management, Health and Physical Science, Medical Technology, Occupational Therapy, Physical Sciences, Physical Therapy, Physician's Assistant, Predentistry, Preforestry, Premedicine, Prenursing, Prepharmacy, Prevet

Armstrong Atlantic State University

11935 Abercorn Exit
Savannah, GA 31419
Coach: Joe Roberts
NCAA II
Pirates/Maroon, Gold
Phone: (912) 921-5686
Fax: (912) 921-5571

ACADEMIC

Founded: 1935
SAT/ACT/GPA: 700/17
Student/Faculty Ratio: 17:1
Undergraduate Enrollment: 5,600
Scholarships/Academic: Yes
Total Expenses by: Year
Degrees Conferred: AA, AS, AAS, BA, BS, BGS, BHS, MA,MS
Type: 4 Yr., Public, Coed
Campus Housing: Yes
Male/Female Ratio: 31:69
Graduate Enrollment: None
Athletic: Yes
Fin Aid: Yes
In State: $ 5,636
Out of State: $ 9, 515

Programs of Study: Art, Biological Science, Business, Chemistry, Computer, Criminal Justice, Dental Hygiene, Dramatic Arts, Education, English, Industiral Arts, Math, Music, Nursing, Political Science, Psychology, Secondary Education, Speech

ATHLETIC PROFILE

Estimated Number of Baseball Scholarships: 9.0
Conference Affiliation: Peach Belt Conference
Program Profile: We feel that the Peach Belt is the best Spring sports league in the NCAA II. We have 12 National titles and 9 National Runner-Ups in our five Spring sports over the past five years. We have a nice large field with Bermuda turf and MLB padded fences (340-380-390-380-340). We play the 56 game maximum beginning January 29 with 30 long games.
History: We are the second winningest NCAA II program since 1983 and the third winningest in just the 1990's. In the past eleven years, we have bids , 5 #1 seeds and 3 #2 seeds. We have 8 final top 20 Poll finishes and 35 All-Americans. We have had pro-signees in 16 years in a row.
Achievements: 3 NCAA II World Series; Coach Roberts was named South Atlantic Regional Coach of the Year on three different occasions.
Coaching: Joe Roberts, Head Coach, started with the program in1980 and compiled a record of 794-360 which is .688. He is the second winningest coach in NCAA II team since 1983. He is one of 3 NCAA II coaches to be in 8 of last 11 NCAA's. He has been to 3 NCAA II World Series and was selected three years as the South Atlantic Regional Coach of the Year. He is currently the National Poll Chairman. Calvain Culberson, Assistant coach, started with the program in 1996. He played four years at AASU, 8 years minors, and reached AAA. Tommy Thomson, Volunteer Hitting Instructor, started with the program in 1981.
Roster for 1998 team/In State: 9
Out of State: 14
Out of Country: 2
Total Number of Varsity/Jr. Varsity: 25
Percent of Graduation: 73%
Number of Seniors on 1998 Team: 7
Number of Sophomores on 1998 Team: 2
Freshmen Receiving Fin Aid/Athletic: 1
Academic: 4
Baseball Camp Dates: TBA
Number of Spring Games: 56

Positions Needed for 1999/2000: RHP, LHP, 2nd Base, SS, 3rd Base, OF, C
Most Recent Record: 38 - 21 - 0
Schedule: Kennesaw State, North Florida, Columbus State, Georgia College State, Valdosta State
Style of Play: In 1999 we will be another pitching and defense team with excellent power hitting potential and a very good defense with good speed in several spots. Our pitching depth and health along with hitting ability are our main concerns entering Fall practice and Christmas recruiting.

Atlanta Christian College

(New Program)

2605 Ben Hill Road
East Point, GA 30344
Coach: Alan Wilson

NCCAA II
Chargers/Royal, Gold
Phone: (404) 761-8861
Fax: (404) 669-2024

ACADEMIC

Founded: 1937
Religion: Christian
Web-site: http://www.acc.edu
Student/Faculty Ratio: 15:1
Undergraduate Enrollment: 350
Scholarships/Academic: Yes **Athletic:** No
Total Expenses by: Year **In State:** $ 10,500
Type: 4 Yr., Private, Coed
Campus Housing: Yes
SAT/ACT/GPA: 870/1.8
Male/Female Ratio: 1:2
Graduate Enrollment: None
Fin Aid: Yes
Out of State: $ 10,500
Degrees Conferred: Bachelors
Programs of Study: Business, Business Administration, Biblical Studies, Bachelor of Theology, Early Childhood Education, Humanities, Human Relations, Music

ATHLETIC PROFILE

Conference Affiliation: NCCAA
Program Profile: We play games on a grass previously used for practice by Olympic teams. We are a young program trying to build slowly with good young players.
Coaching: Alan Wilson, Head Coach, is on his 2nd year with the program. Shawn Lamb, Assistant.
Roster for 1998 team/In State: 12 **Out of State:** 4 **Out of Country:** 0
Total Number of Varsity/Jr. Varsity: 16 **Number of Seniors on 1998 Team:** 3
Freshmen Receiving Fin Aid/Athletic: 0 **Academic:** 14
Most Recent Record: 5 - 22 - 0 **Number of Spring Games:** 33
Positions Needed for 1999/2000: Pitchers, Catcher, 2nd/3rd Centerfielder
Schedule: West Georgia, Tennessee Temple, St. Norbert, Franklin, Clearwater, Southeastern

Augusta State University

2500 Walton Way
Augusta, GA 30910
Coach: Stan 'Skip' Fite
Email: sfite@aug.edu

NCAA II
Jaguars/Navy, White
Phone: (706) 731-7917
Fax: (706) 737-1628

ACADEMIC

Founded: 1925
Religion: Non-Affiliated
Web-site: http://www.aug.edu/
Student/Faculty Ratio: 25:1
Undergraduate Enrollment: 5,631
Scholarships/Academic: Yes **Athletic:** Yes
Total Expenses by: Year **In State:** $ 1,800
Type: 4 Yr., Public, Liberal Arts, Coed
Campus Housing: Yes
SAT/ACT/GPA: 820
Male/Female Ratio: 2291/386
Graduate Enrollment: 528
Fin Aid: Yes
Out of State: $ 5,679
Degrees Conferred: Associate, Bachelor, Master, Specialist

Programs of Study: Education, Business, Public Administration, Psychology, Art, Criminal Justice, Fine Arts, Music, Science, Nursing, Premed, International Studies, Spanish, French, German, Latin

ATHLETIC PROFILE

Estimated Number of Baseball Scholarships: 6.5
Conference Affiliation: Peach Belt Conference
Program Profile: We have a very competitive division II program. We play in one of the best Division II conferences in the nation. Our new facility has 335-lines, 390 center. We play 56 games in the Spring and have a 5 week workout in the Fall. The weather is excellent.
History: The program started in 1966 and was a Division I in 1985-1991. We have been Division II Peach Belt from 1992 to the present. We were Conference Champions in 1990 and 1991.
Achievements: We had 7 players drafted in the last five years. We got 2 All-American in the last five years. We got Coach of the Year in 1991 and 1992.
Coaching: Skip Fite, Head Coach, is entering his 14th year as head coach. He played at Chipola Junior, Valdosta State, Minnesota Twins, and Italy. Jamie Corr, Assistant Coach.
Roster for 1998 team/In State: 24 **Out of State:** 4 **Out of Country:** 1
Total Number of Varsity/Jr. Varsity: 29 **Percent of Graduation:** 87%
Number of Seniors on 1998 Team: 6 **Number of Sophomores on 1998 Team:** 7
Freshmen Receiving Fin Aid/Athletic: 7 **Academic:** 2
Most Recent Record: 28 - 23 - 0 **Number of Spring Games:** 56
Positions Needed for 1999/2000: LHP, Outfielder, 3rd Base
Baseball Camp Dates: Day camp only
Schedule: Kennesaw, Columbus, Valdosta, University of North Florida, West Georgia, Armstrong
Style of Play: Very aggressive, hit and run, steal; like speed - pitchers that throw strikes.

Berry College

2277 Martha Berry Highway
Mount Berry, GA 30149-5015
Coach: David Beasley
Email: pmarks@berry.edu

NAIA
Vikings/Navy, Silver
Phone: (706) 236-1721
Fax: (706) 236-1749

ACADEMIC

Founded: 1902
Type: 4 Yr., Private, Liberal Arts, Coed
Religion: Non-Denominational
Campus Housing: Yes
Web-site: http://www.berry.edu/
SAT/ACT/GPA: 1000
Student/Faculty Ratio: 14:1
Male/Female Ratio: 40:60
Undergraduate Enrollment: 1,800
Graduate Enrollment: 200
Scholarships/Academic: Yes **Athletic:** Yes **Fin Aid:** Yes
Total Expenses by: Year **In State:** $ 15,000 **Out of State:** $ 15,000
Degrees Conferred: BA, BS, MA, MBA
Programs of Study: Bachelor of Arts, Music, Science - Masters of Business Administration, Education, Education Specialist

ATHLETIC PROFILE

Conference Affiliation: Tran South Conference
Program Profile: We play on natural grass and our stadium seats 700.
History: Our program was reinstated in 1988 after a 12 year absence. We had baseball from 1949 to 1976 when our program was temporarily discontinued.
Achievements: Has 6 NAIA All-Americans; numerous MLB draftees; John Schaly was named Conference Coach of the Year in 1989; Conference Champions in 1989 and1997.
Coaching: David Beasley, Head Coach, compiled a record of 32-17 at Berry. His first season as a head coach was in 1997. Chad Parker and Kevin Ermind, Assistant Coaches.
Roster for 1998 team/In State: 19 **Out of State:** 10 **Out of Country:** 0
Total Number of Varsity/Jr. Varsity: 28 **Percent of Graduation:** 90%
Most Recent Record: 32 - 17 - 0 **Number of Spring Games:** 56
Positions Needed for 1999/2000: LHP, Centerfielder

Schedule: Columbus State, West Georgia University, Kennesaw State, Union University, Birmingham-Southern, Freed-Hardeman University
Style of Play: Pitching and defense, hit and run offense.

Brewton - Parker College

P.O. Box 2086
Mount Vernon, GA 30446
Coach: Mike Robins

NAIA
Wildcats/Navy, Orange
Phone: (912) 583-3274
Fax: (912) 583-4498

ACADEMIC

Founded: 1904
Religion: Baptist
Web-site: http://www.bpc.edu/
Student/Faculty Ratio: 12:1
Undergraduate Enrollment: 1,600
Scholarships/Academic: Yes **Athletic:** Yes
Total Expenses by: Year **In State:** $ 7,600

Type: 4 Yr., Private, Liberal Arts, Coed
Campus Housing: Yes
SAT/ACT/GPA: 860/ 18
Male/Female Ratio: 2:3
Graduate Enrollment: None
Fin Aid: Yes
Out of State: $ 7,600

Degrees Conferred: BA, BS, Associates
Programs of Study: Accounting, Agricultural Business, Applied Art, Art, Biology, Business and Management, Chemistry, Computer Information System, Dental Services, Economics, Education, English, Marketing, Mathematics, Medical Assistant Technology, Music, Nursing, Political Science, Ministries, Prepofessional, Psychology, Social Science, History, Physical Science

ATHLETIC PROFILE

Conference Affiliation: Georgia Athletic Conference
Program Profile: Brewton-Parker is one of the premier NAIA programs in the country. We have three recent Top Ten finishes. Our new stadium is second to none among small colleges and rivals that of the NCAA Division I ballparks.
History: Since early 1950's, we competed at the JUCO level. In 1989, we made the transition to a senior college.
Achievements: Coach of the Year in 1992, 1993, 1994, 1995 and 1996; Conference Champions in 1992, 1993, 1994, 1995, and 1996; 9 All-Americans since 1990 and 16 drafted players.
Style of Play: We are very offensive minded. We play for the big inning all the time.

Clark Atlanta University

James P Brawley Drive
Atlanta, GA 30314
Coach: Johnny Millen

NCAA II
Panthers/Red, Bleck, Gray
Phone: (404) 880-8123
Fax: (404) 880-8397

ACADEMIC

Founded: 1869
Web-site: http://www.cau.edu
Student/Faculty Ratio: 15:1
Undergraduate Enrollment: 2,392
Scholarships/Academic: Yes **Athletic:** Yes
Total Expenses by: Year **In State:** $ 12,252

Type: 4 Yr., Private, Coed
SAT/ACT/GPA: 900+
Male/Female Ratio: 31:69
Graduate Enrollment: 1,064
Fin Aid: Yes
Out of State: $ 12,252

Degrees Conferred: BA, BS, MA, MBA, PhD, EdD
Programs of Study: Philosophy, Psychology, Social Science, Math, Engineering, Business and Management, Communications, Computer Science, Languages

ATHLETIC PROFILE

Conference Affiliation: SIAC

Columbus State University

(Former Columbus College)

4225 University Avenue
Columbus, GA 31907
Coach: Greg Appleton

NCAA II
Cougars/Red, White, Blue
Phone: (706) 568-2444
Fax: (706) 569-3435

ACADEMIC

Founded: 1958
Type: 4 Yr., Coed
SAT/ACT/GPA: 500/21
Campus Housing: Yes
Student/Faculty Ratio: 24:1
Male/Female Ratio: 0
Undergraduate Enrollment: 4,766
Graduate Enrollment: 770
Scholarships/Academic: **Athletic:** **Fin Aid:** Yes
Total Expenses by: Year **In State:** $ 1,845+ **Out of State:** $ 9,549
Degrees Conferred: Bachelors, Masters
Programs of Study: Accounting, Art Education, Art/Fine Arts, Athletic Training, Biology, Biological Science, Business Administration, Commerce, Management, Computer Programming, Computer Science, Criminal Justice, Data Processing, Dental Services, Early Childhood Education, Education, Electrical and Electronics Technology, Electronics Engineering Technology, Elementary Education, English, Finance, Banking, Forestry, Geology, Health Science, History, Laboratory Technology, Liberal Arts, General Studies, Literature, Marketing, Retailing, Merchandising, Mathematics, Medical Laboratory Technology, Medical Records Services, Nursing, Parks Management

ATHLETIC PROFILE

Conference Affiliation: Peach Belt Athletic Conference (PBAC)
Program Profile: Our stadium has a seating capacity of 1,500. Cougar Field is a natural grass.
Coaching: Greg Appleton, Head Coach. Vince Massey, Assistant Coach.

Emmanuel College

P.O. Box 129
Franklin Springs, GA 30639-0129
Coach: Robbie Jones
Email: rjones@emmanuel-college.edu

NAIA
Lions/Navy, Gold
Phone: (706) 245-9721
Fax: (706) 245-4424

ACADEMIC

Founded: 1919
Type: 4 Yr., Private, Coed
Religion: Pentecostal
Campus Housing: Yes
Web-site: http://www.emmanuel.college.edu
SAT/ACT/GPA: 860/2.0
Student/Faculty Ratio: 14:1
Male/Female Ratio: 1:1
Undergraduate Enrollment: 1,000
Graduate Enrollment: None
Scholarships/Academic: Yes **Athletic:** Yes **Fin Aid:** Yes
Total Expenses by: Year **In State:** $ 10,000 **Out of State:** $ 10,000
Degrees Conferred: Bachelors
Programs of Study: Biblical Studies, Business Administration, Commerce, Management, Early Childhood Education, English, History, Interdisciplinary Studies, Liberal Arts, General Studies, Middle School Education, Ministries, Music, Pastoral Studies, Pharmacy, Psychology

ATHLETIC PROFILE

Estimated Number of Baseball Scholarships: 5
Conference Affiliation: Georgia Athletic Conference, NCAA District II
Program Profile: We have improved our facilities and have natural grass. Witter's Park seats 400. We have a Fall and Spring season.
History: Our program is only five years old and started in 1993. We made great strides in the last two years and in 1997 won 27 games in a tough conference.

Achievements: We had 2 players drafted in the last six years and 3 All-Americans in NCCAA.
Coaching: Robbie Jones, Head Coach, has led Emmanuel's program to a new level in the past three years earning post-season opportunities.
Roster for 1998 team/In State: 15 **Out of State:** 10 **Out of Country:** 0
Total Number of Varsity/Jr. Varsity: 25 /20 **Percent of Graduation:** 95%
Number of Seniors on 1998 Team: 13 **Most Recent Record:** 31 - 27 - 0
Number of Fall Games: 10 **Number of Spring Games:** 50
Positions Needed for 1999/2000: Catcher, 3 Base, Pitcher
Schedule: West Georgia University, Augusta State University, Brewton Parker, Georgia Southwestern, South Tech, Gardner-Webb University
Style of Play: Aggressive offensively, solid defensively.

Emory University

Woodruff PE Center
Atlanta, GA 30322
Coach: Kevin Howard
Email: khowa02@emory.edu

NCAA III
Eagles/Blue, Gold
Phone: (404) 727-0877
Fax: (404) 727-4989

ACADEMIC

Founded: 1836 **Type:** 4 Yr., Private, Coed
Religion: Methodist **Campus Housing:** Yes
Web-site: http://www.emory.edu/ **SAT/ACT/GPA:** 1200/25/3.5
Student/Faculty Ratio: 10:1 **Male/Female Ratio:** 50:50
Undergraduate Enrollment: 5,000 **Graduate Enrollment:** 5,000
Scholarships/Academic: Yes **Athletic:** No **Fin Aid:** Yes
Total Expenses by: Year **In State:** $ 31,100 **Out of State:** $ 31,100
Degrees Conferred: BA, BS, MA, MS, MBA, Med, PhD, MD, JD, Mdiv.
Programs of Study: Anthropology and Religion, Art History, Chemistry, Philosophy, Economics, History, Mathematics, Education, English, Creative Writing, Film Studies, Liberal Studies, Computer Studies, Music, Physics, Psychology, Political Science, Sociology, Theatre

ATHLETIC PROFILE

Conference Affiliation: University Athletic Association
Program Profile: We play on Chapell Park, site of practice for 1996 Summer Olympic Games. Our facilities are state of the art.
History: 1991 was the first year of baseball program at Emory. In 1995 we built a new stadium. We were 1996 and 1997 National Calibre Teams.
Achievements: 1994 UAA Champions; 1995 UAA Champions; 1996 NCAA Division III National Tournament; 1997 NCAA Division III National tournament; 1998 NCAA Division III National Tournament; 4 All-Americans; 3 players drafted; many All-Conference and All-Region Performers.
Coaching: Kevin Howard, Head Coach, compiled a record of 29-13 in 1994, 24-18-1 in 1995, 32-16 in 1996, 32-16 in 1997 and 31-13 in 1998. Matt Palm, Assistant Coach.
Roster for 1998 team/In State: 5 **Out of State:** 25 **Out of Country:** 0
Total Number of Varsity/Jr. Varsity: 30 **Percent of Graduation:** 100%
Number of Fall Games: 9 **Number of Spring Games:** 46
Positions Needed for 1999/2000: All **Most Recent Record:** 31 - 31 - 0
Style of Play: Hardworking, disciplined, fundamental, willing to pay the price to be the best you can be.

Georgia College

Baseball Office
Milledgeville, GA 31061
Coach: Steve Mrowka

NCAA II
Bobcats/Navy Blue, Hunter Green
Phone: (912) 445-5319
Fax: (912) 445-1790

ACADEMIC

Founded: 1889
Type: 4 Yr., Coed
Web-site: http://www.gac.edu
Campus Housing: Yes
Student/Faculty Ratio: 16:1
Male/Female Ratio: Unknown
Undergraduate Enrollment: 4,382
Graduate Enrollment: 1,152
Scholarships/Academic: Yes **Athletic:** Yes **Fin Aid:** Yes
Total Expenses by: Year **In State:** $ 5,268 **Out of State:** $ Varies
Degrees Conferred: Bachelors, Masters
Programs of Study: Aerospace Engineering, Applied Mathematics, Architecture, Atmospheric Science, Biology, Biological Science, Business Administration, Commerce, Management, Ceramic Engineering, Chemistry, Civil Engineering, Computer Engineering, Computewr Science, Construction

ATHLETIC PROFILE

Conference Affiliation: Peach Belt Athletic Conference
Program Profile: The weather is excellent. Our field is a natural grass and has an excellent surface. Our indoor facility includes locker rooms, showers, 2 batting cages, a study room and a video room.
History: We are a perennial power in NCAA II which finished ranked 7th in 1997, 30th in 1996, 2nd in 1995, and 12th in 1994.
Achievements: Steve Mrowka was named 1995 Region and Conference Coach of the Year and 1997 Conference Coach of the Year. 1997 All-Region drafted by Detroit Tigers - RHP Kevin Mobley. 1996 All-American - Outfielder Greg Winters.
Coaching: Steve Mrowka, Head Coach, is on his fourth year. He was Conference Coach of the Year in 1994. He was South Atlantic Region Coach of the Year in 1995. He was Manager Hyannis Mets of the Cape Cod baseball league. Don Norris, Assistant Coach. Wills Collins, Graduate Assistant.
Style of Play: Solid fundamentals and hustle.

Georgia Institute of Technology

150 Bobby Dodd Way NW
Atlanta, GA 30332-0455
Coach: Danny Hall

NCAA I
Yellow Jackets/Old Gold, White
Phone: (404) 894-5471
Fax: (404) 894-3445

ACADEMIC

Founded: 1885
Type: 2 Yr., Coed
SAT/ACT/GPA: 500
Campus Housing: Yes
Student/Faculty Ratio: 19:1
Male/Female Ratio: None
Undergraduate Enrollment: 9,469
Graduate Enrollment: 3,516
Scholarships/Academic: No **Athletic:** No **Fin Aid:** Yes
Total Expenses by: Year **In State:** $ 2,115 **Out of State:** $ 8,376
Degrees Conferred: Masters, Bachelors
Programs of Study: Aerospace Engineering, Applied Mathematics, Architecture, Athmospheric Science, Biology, biological science, Business administration, Commerce, Management, Ceramic Engineering, Computer Science, Construction Management, Construction Technologies, Earth Science, Economics, Electrical Engineering, Engineering Mechanics, Engineering Science, History of Science, Industrial Design, Industrial Technology, International Studies, Literature, Physics

ATHLETIC PROFILE

Conference Affiliation: Atlantic Coast Conference
Program Profile: Our home field, Russ Chandler Stadium, seats 2,500 and has a natural turf field. Our team holds Fall practice for four weeks and has no games against outside competition. We have a 56-game regular season in the Spring (week of practice and number of games set by NCAA rules).
History: History of Tech baseball dates back to the 1890's with a team fielded every year except 1936, 1944, and 1945. Tech has had 12 head coaches dating back to 1900. They include John Heisman and Bobby Dodd, who achieved Hall of Fame status as head football coaches at Tech, and Jim Morris, Tech's all-time winningest coach in any sport with 504 victories.

Achievements: Tech has been to the NCAA tournament 14 times, including the last 12 consecutive years. One College World Series appearance in 1994 in which Tech advanced to the championship game. Four Atlantic Coast Conference Championships (1985, 1986, 1987, 1988). 25 All-Americans, 10 players on USA teams, including three Olympians, 70 players drafted to the pros, 5 in majors.
Coaching: Danny Hall, Head Coach, started in 1994. He was head coach at Kent 1988-1993 and Division I assistant coach 1978-1987. Mike Trapasso, Assistant Coach, started in 1995. He was assistant coach at South Florida 1991-1994 and assistant coach at Missouri 1989-1991. Jeff Guy has been Assistant Coach since 1994. He was assistant coach at Columbus 1992-1993.
Style of Play: Premium placed on pitching, pitching depth, fundamentals on defense, speed on defense and on the basepaths. Tech traditionally has good power.

Georgia Perimeter College

(Former De Kalb College)

2101 Womack Road
Dunwoody, GA 30338
Coach: Tom Cantrell

NJCAA
Patriots/Red, White, Blue
Phone: (404) 299-4310
Fax: (770) 604-3791

ACADEMIC

Founded: 1964
Religion: Non-Affiliated
Undergraduate Enrollment: 16,073
Student/Faculty Ratio: 14:1
Scholarships/Academic: Yes
Athletic: Yes
Total Expenses by: Year
In State: $ Varies
Degrees Conferred: AA, AS
Programs of Study: Contact school for programs of study.

Type: 2 Yr., Public, Coed
Campus Housing: No
SAT/ACT/GPA: 640/14
Male/Female Ratio: 1:1.5
Fin Aid: Yes
Out of State: $ Varies

ATHLETIC PROFILE

Conference Affiliation: Georgia Junior College Athletic Association
Program Profile: Patriots Field has natural grass. There are dugouts, batting cages, 400 seats, coaches offices, new electronic score board, lighting for night games, and a press box. The Patriots play a 20-game Fall season and the regular season begins the second week in February. They are consistently ranked in the Top 20 Nationally.
History: Our first team was in 1969. We won the GJCAA championship in 1977,1980,1981and 1987. We finished second in the country in 1977. In the past 13 years, 30 players have been drafted by major league teams.
Achievements: 10 All-American selections, 4 players have made it to the major leagues; Greg Ward Coach of the Year 1980, 1981; Doug Casey Coach of the Year 1987; 90% of players have either received scholarships to 4-year schools or have been drafted. 1996 - 5 All-Region selections, ranked #29 by the NJCAA.
Coaching: Tom Cantrell, Head Coach, played at DeKalb 1984-1985. He played two years in the Atlanta Braves farm system. He was assistant coach at DeKalb since 1991. He was named head coach summer of 1995. Hal Gaalema, Assistant Coach/Pitching Coach, played at DeKalb and the University of South Carolina. He served two years as assistant coach at DeKalb from 1984-1985.
Style of Play: Aggressive style of play, hit and run, strong base stealing club. Outstanding hitting club, last season seven players hit over .300, aggressive on the base path. Strong pitching at number 1 and 2, outstanding short relief. Looks to out hustle the opposition.

Georgia Southern University

P.O. Box 8095
Statesboro, GA 30460
Coach: Jack Stallinas

NCAA I
Eagles/Navy, White
Phone: (912) 681-5187
Fax: (912) 871-1366

ACADEMIC

Founded: 1906
Type: 4 Yr., Public, Coed
Web-site: http://www.gasou.edu/
SAT/ACT/GPA: 850/2.2
Student/Faculty Ratio: 24:1
Male/Female Ratio: 48:52
Undergraduate Enrollment: 14,000
Graduate Enrollment: 1,000
Scholarships/Academic: Yes **Athletic:** Yes **Fin Aid:** Yes
Total Expenses by: Year **In State:** $ 7,200 **Out of State:** $ 11,500
Degrees Conferred: BA, BS, BBA, BSEd, MA, MS, Med, EdS, EdD
Programs of Study: Accounting, Biology, Broadcasting, Business, Chemistry, Civil Engineering, Commnucations, Computer Science, Counseling, Economics, Education, Electrical Engineering, English, Exercise Science, Food-Nutrition, Geology, German, Health, Physical Education, History, Industrial, Mathematics, International Studies, Journalism, Kinesiology, Journalism, Marketing, Math

ATHLETIC PROFILE

Estimated Number of Baseball Scholarships: 11
Conference Affiliation: Southern Conference
Program Profile: We are in NCAA Division I and a member of Southern Conference. We have a natural grass field that is lighted . It seats 2,000, and has a scoreboard with message center. The season is early February through May 20natural. There is a locker room and a baseball office building at stadium.
History: The program began in 1930. We were NAIA National Champions in 1962 and went to NCAA in 1969. 50 All-American players. 75+ signed professional . Current major leaguers -Joey Hamilton (Padres) and Todd Greene (Angels).
Achievements: Coach of the Year seven times; Conference Titles eight times.
Coaching: Jack Stallinas, Head Coach, has a record of 1,229 wins in 38 seasons and started in 1959. He is a member coaches of Hall of Fame. We made 3 trips to College World Series and 9 Regional Appearances. Scott Baker, Assistant Coach.
Roster for 1998 team/In State: 22 **Out of State:** 4 **Out of Country:** 0
Total Number of Varsity/Jr. Varsity: 26 **Percent of Graduation:** 90%
Number of Seniors on 1998 Team: 2 **Number of Sophomores on 1998 Team:** 6
Freshmen Receiving Fin Aid/Athletic: 12 **Academic:** 8
Most Recent Record: 22 - 28 - 0 **Number of Spring Games:** 56
Positions Needed for 1999/2000: Pitcher, Catcher, Middle Infield
Baseball Camp Dates: 6/21-25; 7/5-9; 7/12-16; 7/19-23; 7/26-30
Schedule: University of Miami, University of Georgia, Georgia Tech, East Carolina, Citadel
Style of Play: Hope for good pitching every year - adapt style of play to personnel.

Georgia Southwestern State University

800 Wheatley Street
Americus, GA 31709
Coach: Bill Haywood
NAIA
Hurricanes/Navy, Old Gold, Silver
Phone: (912) 931-2220
Fax: (912) 931-2143

ACADEMIC

Founded: 1906
Type: 4 Yr., Coed
Religion: Non-Affiliated
Campus Housing: Yes
Web-site: http://www.gsu.edu
SAT/ACT/GPA: 500/21
Student/Faculty Ratio: 15:1
Male/Female Ratio:
Undergraduate Enrollment: 2,066
Graduate Enrollment: 456
Scholarships/Academic: No **Athletic:** No **Fin Aid:** Yes
Total Expenses by: Year **In State:** $ 1,584 **Out of State:** $ 5,463
Degrees Conferred: Masters, Bachelors

Programs of Study: Accounting, Applied Art, Art Education, Art/Fine Arts, Automotive Technology, Aviation Technology, Behavioral Science, Biology, Biological Science, Botany Plant, Business Administration, Commerce, Management, Business Education, Ceramic Art and Design, Chemistry, Commercial Art, Computer Information System, Computer Programming, Computer Science, Computer Technology, Data Processing, Drafting and Design, Early Childhood Education, Earth Science, Education, Electrical and Electronics /Technology, Elementary Education, English, Environmental Technology, Marketing, Retailing, Merchandising, Mathematics, Middle School Education, Music, Music Education, Nursing, Painting, Drawing, Physical Education, Physical Sciences, Physics, Political Science,Psychology, Studio Art

ATHLETIC PROFILE

Conference Affiliation: Georgia Athletic Conference
Program Profile: Our facility was built by Works Project Authority in the 1930. It is 1/25 mile away from school. It has natural turf & has dimensions of 330' down lines, 405' Center, & 380' Power Alleys. It seats 5,000 & has a press box. The natural grass field is a historic site but has a new stadium.
History: Since 1958 we were a Junior College. We became a four-year school in 1964. Our program has always been competitive.
Achievements: Southern Conference Coach of the Year in 1981. Washington Senator in 1964-1968. All-American in 1964. Southern Conference Co-Cahmpions in 1981. Western Carolina University. Managered in 1969-1972 Washington Senator in minor league. Managered in 1973-1974 in Texas Region minor league. Managered in 1983 Seattle Mariners. 1982-1984 Coordinator of Instruction Seattle Mariners. 1985-1987 Director, player and personnel of Seattle Mariners.
Coaching: Bill Haywood, Head Coach, was a major league pitcher with the Washington Senators and a former Director of Player Development with the Seattle Mariners. He was Head Coach of Western Carolina 1968-1982. He was named 1981 Southern Conference Coach of the Year. Bryan McLain, Assistant Coach, was All-American in 1991 at West Georgia College. He was pre-season All-American in 1995 at West Georgia College. Tim Hill - Assistant Coach.
Style of Play: Pitching and defense.

Georgia State University

University Plaza
Atlanta, GA 30303
Coach: Percy Chris

NCAA I
Panthers/Royal Blue, Crimson, White
Phone: (404) 651-2772
Fax: (404) 651-0842

ACADEMIC

Founded: 1913
Religion: Non-Affiliated
Web-site: http://www.gsu.edu/
Student/Faculty Ratio: 14:1
Undergraduate Enrollment: 18,000
Scholarships/Academic: Yes
Total Expenses by: Year

Athletic: Yes
In State: $ 7,450

Type: 4 Yr., Public, Liberal Arts, Coed
Campus Housing: Yes
SAT/ACT/GPA: 900
Male/Female Ratio: 42:58
Graduate Enrollment: 5,000
Fin Aid: Yes
Out of State: $ 14,000

Degrees Conferred: AA, AS, BA, BBA, BFA, BIS, BM, BS, BSEd, BSW, MAS, MAEd, MA, MAT, MBA, MBEd, MEd, MFA, MHA, MHP, MLM, MM, MPA
Programs of Study: Arts, Business Administration, Fine Arts, Music, Science, Science in Education, Social Work, Interdisciplinary Studies

ATHLETIC PROFILE

Estimated Number of Baseball Scholarships: 10
Conference Affiliation: Trans America Athletic Conference
Program Profile: We play a very good conference and a full 56 game schedule. We have a natural grass playing surface. Our facility is being upgraded in all areas every year.
History: Our program resumed play in 1992 after a five year absence. Overall wins have increased each year. We won the TAAC Division Title in 1996.

Achievements: 2 TAAC Eastern Division Titles in 1996 and 1998; 13 All-Conference players since 1993, 2 All-Americans, 7 players signed professionally since 1995.
Roster for 1998 team/In State: 30 **Out of State:** 0 **Out of Country:** 0
Total Number of Varsity/Jr. Varsity: 30 **Percent of Graduation:** 95%
Number of Seniors on 1998 Team: 6 **Number of Sophomores on 1998 Team:** 6
Freshmen Receiving Fin Aid/Athletic: 3 **Academic:** 0
Most Recent Record: 23 - 29 - 0 **Number of Spring Games:** 56
Positions Needed for 1999/2000: Catcher, Outfielder, Pitcher
Schedule: Tennessee, Georgia Tech, Georgia, Central Florida, Stetson, Jacksonville

Gordon College

419 College Drive
Barnesville, GA 30204
Coach: Jerry Hand

NJCAA
Highlanders/Navy, Green, Gold, White
Phone: (770) 358-5000
Fax: (770) 358-4040

ACADEMIC

Founded: 1963 **Type:** 2 Yr., Public, Coed
Student/Faculty Ratio: 30:1 **Male/Female Ratio:** 39:61
Undergraduate Enrollment: 11,000 **Graduate Enrollment:** 1,250
Scholarships/Academic: No **Athletic:** Yes **Fin Aid:** Yes
Total Expenses by: Year **In State:** $ 3,500 **Out of State:** $ 5,500
Degrees Conferred: Associate
Programs of Study: Art, Behavioral Science, Business Administration, Computer Science, Education, English, Journalism, Liberal Arts, Matheamtics, Nursing, Physical Science, Pscyhology, Science, Theatre

Kennesaw State College

1000 Chastain Road
Kennesaw, GA 30144-5591
Coach: Mike Sansing

NCAA II
Owls/Black, Gold
Phone: (770) 423-6264
Fax: (770) 423-6665

ACADEMIC

Founded: 1963 **Type:** 4 Yr., Coed
Web-site: Not Available **SAT/ACT/GPA:** 500/21
Student/Faculty Ratio: 27:1 **Male/Female Ratio:** Unknown
Undergraduate Enrollment: 11,342 **Graduate Enrollment:** 1,195
Scholarships/Academic: Yes **Athletic:** Yes **Fin Aid:** Yes
Total Expenses by: Year **In State:** $ 1,584 **Out of State:** $ 5,463
Degrees Conferred: Bachelors, Masters
Programs of Study: Accounting, Art Education, Art/Fine Arts, Biology, Biological Science, Business Administration, Commerce

ATHLETIC PROFILE

Conference Affiliation: GIAC, Peach Belt
Coaching: Mike Sansing, Head Coach, has coached seven seasons. He has an overall record of 262-94 and a winning percentage of .736. He led the Kennesaw to a 48-14 overall mark, including : a second straight South Atlantic Regional Championships, the Peachbelt Athletic Conference regular season title and PBAC tournament crown. He was named the 1997 Regional Coach of the Year. Bob Roman , Assistant Coach, has coached seven seasons. He played an important part in making Kennesaw State one of the elite programs in all of college baseball. He has helped the team capture a pair of national championships at two different levels since becoming a part of KSU coaching staff. Brady Wiederhold, Assistant Coach.

LaGrange College

601 Broad Street
La Grange, GA 30240
Coach: Tommy Knight

NAIA
Panthers/Red, Black
Phone: (706) 812-7295
Fax: (706) 812-7350

ACADEMIC

Founded: 1831
Religion: Methodist
Web-site: http://www.lgc.peachnet.edu/
Student/Faculty Ratio: 15:1
Undergraduate Enrollment: 900
Scholarships/Academic: Yes **Athletic:** No
Total Expenses by: Year **In State:** $ 14,500

Type: 4 Yr., Private, Liberal Arts, Coed
Campus Housing: Yes
SAT/ACT/GPA: 860/16/2.0
Male/Female Ratio: 1:3
Graduate Enrollment: 100
Fin Aid: Yes
Out of State: $ 14,500

Degrees Conferred: AA, BA, BS, BBA. MBA, MEd
Programs of Study: Accounting, Arts, Biology, Business Administration, Chemistry, Computer Science, Criminal Justice, Economics, Education, English, History, International Business, Management, Mathematics, Nursing, Philosophy, Physical Education, Physical Science, Physics, Preprofessional Courses, Psychology, Radiological Technology, Religion, Social Work, Theatre

ATHLETIC PROFILE

Conference Affiliation: Georgia Athletic Conference
Program Profile: We are a member of NAIA and will be NCAA Division III in two years. Home games are played at Dunson Park which has an all grass infield. We will be building a new state of the art baseball facility. We play a Fall and Spring schedule.
History: The program began in 1983.
Achievements: Tommy Knight was named GAC Coach of the Year. Phil Williamson was named Conference Coach of the Year twice.
Coaching: Tommy Knight, Head Coach, started in 1997. He was named GAC Coach of the Year.
Roster for 1998 team/In State: 31 **Out of State:** 0 **Out of Country:** 0
Total Number of Varsity/Jr. Varsity: 0 **Percent of Graduation:** 98%
Number of Seniors on 1998 Team: 2 **Most Recent Record:** 12 - 37 - 0
Freshmen Receiving Fin Aid/Athletic: 0 **Academic:** 8
Number of Fall Games: 9 **Number of Spring Games:** 54
Positions Needed for 1999/2000: Pitchers **Baseball Camp Dates:** July 26-30
Schedule: Berry College, Birmingham Southern, Maryville College, Emory University, Brewton Parker College, Auburn Montgomery
Style of Play: Aggressive - defense.

Mercer University

1400 Coleman Avenue
Macon, GA 31207
Coach: Barry Myers

NCAA I
Bears/Orange, Black
Phone: (912) 752-2396
Fax: (912) 752-2061

ACADEMIC

Founded: 1833
Religion: Baptist
Web-site: http://www.mercer.peachnet.edu/
Student/Faculty Ratio: 12:1
Undergraduate Enrollment: 4,045
Scholarships/Academic: Yes **Athletic:** Yes
Total Expenses by: Year **In State:** $ 14,396

Type: 4 Yr., Private, Coed, Engineering
Campus Housing: Yes
SAT/ACT/GPA: 980/20
Male/Female Ratio: 2:1
Graduate Enrollment: 2,683
Fin Aid: Yes
Out of State: $ 14,396

Degrees Conferred: BA, BS, BBA, BSEng, BM, BMEd, MEd, MBA, MTM, MSEng, MSM, MD

Programs of Study: Accounting, African American Studies, Art, Biology, Business, Chemistry, Communications, Computer, Economics, Education, Industrial, Marketing, Medicine, Natural Science, Philosophy, Special Education

ATHLETIC PROFILE

Conference Affiliation: Trans America Athletic Conference
Program Profile: The baseball field will have lights beginning the 1997 season, making it the premiere facility in the conference.
History: The baseball program begins its 50th year of existence, and the Bears have had just two coaches during that time.
Achievements: Coach of the Year in TAAC in 1979, 1981, 1983, and 1994; TAAC Champs in 1979, 1981, 1983, and1994.
Coaching: Barry Myers, Head Coach.

Middle Georgia College

1100 Second St, SE
Cochran, GA 31014-1599
Coach: Craig Young
Email: cyoung@warrior.mgc.peach

NJCAA
Warriors/Red, Black
Phone: (912) 934-3044
Fax: (912) 934-3428

ACADEMIC

Founded: 1884
Religion: Non-Affiliated
Web-site: http://www.mgc.peachnet
Student/Faculty Ratio: 22:1
Scholarships/Academic: Yes **Athletic:** Yes
Total Expenses by: Year **In State:** $ 2,375
Degrees Conferred: Associate

Type: 2 Yr., Public, Liberal Arts, Coed
Campus Housing: Yes
Undergraduate Enrollment: 2,000
Male/Female Ratio: 1:2
Fin Aid: Yes
Out of State: $ 3,600

Programs of Study: Accounting, Agricultural Science, Aviation, Administration, Business, Chemistry, Criminal Justice, Data Processing, Education, English, Forestry, General Engineering, Geology, History, Military Science, Physical Education, Physics

ATHLETIC PROFILE

Estimated Number of Baseball Scholarships: 18
Conference Affiliation: NJCAA
Program Profile: We have a top quality Junior College program with a fieldhouse and stadium which seats close to 1,000. We have a 56 game schedule with a 20 game Fall season.
History: We have a rich tradition that started in the 1920's with a winning percentage of .800 over the last 31 years.
Achievements: MGC has won 14 Conference Titles; 15 Region Titles; 4 National Championships; 9 National Tournament Appearances; 13 All-Americans since 1977; 84 players drafted 3 currently in the majors.
Coaching: Craig Young, Head Coach, begins his second season at the helm. His 1998 team finished with a 47-13 mark. Chris Halliday, Assistant Coach.
Roster for 1998 team/In State: 22 **Out of State:** 0 **Out of Country:** 2
Total Number of Varsity/Jr. Varsity: 25 **Percent of Graduation:** 90%
Number of Seniors on 1998 Team: 12 **Most Recent Record:** 47 - 13 - 0
Freshmen Receiving Fin Aid/Athletic: 10 **Academic:** 7
Number of Fall Games: 20 **Number of Spring Games:** 56
Positions Needed for 1999/2000: Middle Infielder
Schedule: Okaloosa - Walton, Florida Community College, Chipola, DeKalb
Style of Play: Aggressive - will run but could adapt to my style. Solid defense and pitching are emphasized.

Oglethorpe University

4484 Peachtree Road NE
Atlanta, GA 30319
Coach: Bill Popp

NCAA
Stormy Petrels/Black, Old Gold
Phone: (404) 364-8417
Fax: (404) 364-8445

ACADEMIC

Founded: 1835
Type: 4 Yr., Private, Liberal Arts, Coed
Religion: Non-Affiliated
Campus Housing: Yes
Web-site: http://www.oglethorpe.edu/
SAT/ACT/GPA: 1050
Student/Faculty Ratio: 17:1
Male/Female Ratio: 1:2
Undergraduate Enrollment: 850
Graduate Enrollment: 125
Scholarships/Academic: Yrs **Athletic:** No **Fin Aid:** Yes
Total Expenses by: Year **In State:** $ 19,600 **Out of State:** $ 19,600
Degrees Conferred: BA, BS, MA, MBA
Programs of Study: Biology (Premed), Business Administration, Communications, Education, Enginnering, Political Science, Psychology, Social Sciences

ATHLETIC PROFILE

Conference Affiliation: Southern Collegiate Athletic Conference
Program Profile: We are in our 6th year of NCAA competition. We have a natural grass field with dimensions of 300, 360, 400, 360, & 315. Stadium seats 5,000. Season runs from January to April.
History: Baseball returned here in 1992, and the team's record over the past 5 seasons is 116-101. We are in a very competitive conference as well as South Region. We contend for a title every year.
Achievements: 1992, 1993, and 1994 Eastern Conference Champs; 2 Palyers of the Year in the conference; 5 named to All-Region team; 2 Academic All-Americans in 1997.
Coaching: Bill Popp, Head Coach, Kennesaw State 1992. Russ Russell, Assistant Coach, Georgia Souther 1994. Ward Jones, Assistant Coach, Oglethorpe 1995.
Style of Play: Hustle, desire to do whatever it takes to win, hit and run, bunt, steal and play hard.

Paine College

1235 - 15th Street
Augusta, GA 30901-8376
Coach: Stanley Stubbs

NCAA II
Lions/Purple, White
Phone: (706) 821-8228
Fax: (706) 821-8376

ACADEMIC

Founded: 1882
Type: 4 Yr., Private, Liberal Arts, Coed
Religion: CME Church Affiliated
Campus Housing: Yes
Web-site: http://www.painecollege.com
SAT/ACT/GPA: 700 avg/17 avg/2.0
Student/Faculty Ratio: 11:1
Male/Female Ratio: 33:67
Undergraduate Enrollment: 1,000
Graduate Enrollment: None
Scholarships/Academic: Yes **Athletic:** Yes **Fin Aid:** Yes
Total Expenses by: Year **In State:** $ 9,800 **Out of State:** $ 9,800
Degrees Conferred: BA, BS
Programs of Study: Accounting, Art, Biblical Studies, Biological Science, Business, Communicative Disorder, Computer, Criminal Justice, Drama, Economics, English, Finance, Geology, Health, History, Management, Marketing, Medical, Political Science, Recreation/Parks, Secondary Education, Sociology, Special Education, Speech

ATHLETIC PROFILE

Conference Affiliation: SIAC
Program Profile: We have an up an coming program, a nice recruiting area and on-campus facilities. Our stadium seats 300-350 and has natural grass.

Achievements: 1990 Conference Champions, 1998 Conference Runner-Up.
Coaching: Stanley Stubbs, Head Coach, is entering first year with the program. Dan Etter, Student Assistant Coach.
Roster for 1998 team/In State: 5 **Out of State:** 12 **Out of Country:** 0
Total Number of Varsity/Jr. Varsity: 20 **Percent of Graduation:** 75%
Number of Seniors on 1998 Team: 6 **Number of Sophomores on 1998 Team:** 8
Freshmen Receiving Fin Aid/Athletic: 4 **Academic:** 5
Most Recent Record: 30 - 19 - 0 **Number of Spring Games:** 60
Baseball Camp Dates: Not Listed as of yet
Schedule: Augusta State, Savannah State, Gannon, Albany State, Talladega College, Miles College
Style of Play: Speed, defense and hitting.

Piedmont College

P.O. Box 10
Democrest, GA 30535
Coach: Steve Hardwood

NAIA
Lions/Green, Gold
Phone: (706) 778-3000
Fax: (706) 776-2811

ACADEMIC

Founded: 1897 **Type:** 4 Yr., Private, Liberal Arts, Coed
Religion: Congregationalist **Campus Housing:** Yes
Web-site: http://www.piedmont.edu/ **SAT/ACT/GPA:** 850/ 21+
Student/Faculty Ratio: 15:1 **Male/Female Ratio:** 40:60
Undergraduate Enrollment: 700 **Graduate Enrollment:** None
Scholarships/Academic: Yes **Athletic:** Yes **Fin Aid:** Yes
Total Expenses by: Year **In State:** $ 9,800 **Out of State:** $ 9,800
Degrees Conferred: BA, BS
Programs of Study: Accounting, Art, Art Administration, Biology, Business Administration, Chemistry, Computer Information System, Economics, Education, English, History, Management, Mathematics, Music, Psychology, Social Science, Theater

ATHLETIC PROFILE

Conference Affiliation: Georgia Intercollegiate Conference

Savannah College of Arts and Design

342 Bull Street, P.O. Box 3146
Savannah, GA 31402
Coach: Luis Tiant
Email: info@scad.edu

NCAA III
Bees/Gold, White, Black
Phone: (912) 238-2401
Fax: (912) 231-2367

ACADEMIC

Founded: 1978 **Type:** 4 Yr., Private, Coed
Religion: Non-Affiliated **Campus Housing:** Yes
Web-site: http://www.scad.edu/ **SAT/ACT/GPA:** 500/20/2.0
Student/Faculty Ratio: 11:1 **Male/Female Ratio:** 57:43
Undergraduate Enrollment: 2,947 **Graduate Enrollment:** 517
Scholarships/Academic: Yes **Athletic:** No **Fin Aid:** Yes
Total Expenses by: Year **In State:** $ 13,500 **Out of State:** $ 13,500
Degrees Conferred: BFA, BArch, MArch, MFA, MA
Programs of Study: Architectural History, Architecture, Art History, Computer Art, Fashion, Fibers, Furniture, Graphic Design, Historic Preservation, Illustration, Industrial Design, Interior Design, Metal and Jewelry, Painting, Sequential Art, Photography, Video/Film

ATHLETIC PROFILE

Conference Affiliation: Independent Conference
Program Profile: The Bees have competed under the NCAA Division III since 1990. All home games are played at Savannah's Grayson Stadium (home of Minor League Sand Giants). It is a natural surface field with a stadium that holds 8,500 seats. Legendary Boston Red Sox pitcher, Luis Tiant, became SCAD's head coach in 1998. With Fall and Spring games, the athletes are required to condition all year long at SCDA's fitness center, while posting high academic marks. Players from all over the country and globe fill our roster. Since the program's inception in 1990, the Bees have posted two consecutive 20-win seasons, national statistical leaders in batting average, stolen bases, and ERA. We produced three All-Region players, and have competed in Texas, New York, Virginia and Tennessee, among many others places around the country. The Bees are steadily becoming a strong Division II force.
History: The program began in 1991 as NAIA school and gained NCAA Membership in 1993.
Coaching: Luis Tiant , Head Coach, is entering first year with the program.His has a Boston pitching fame (1971-1978) posting overall 229-172 record. He also played for the Yankees, Pirates, & Angels in Major Leagues. Ed Concepcion, Assistant Coach, is entering first year with the program.
Roster for 1998 team/In State: 1 **Out of State:** 24 **Out of Country:** 0
Total Number of Varsity/Jr. Varsity: 25 **Percent of Graduation:** 98%
Number of Seniors on 1998 Team: 8 **Number of Sophomores on 1998 Team:** 8
Freshmen Receiving Fin Aid/Athletic: 0 **Academic:** 6
Number of Fall Games: 15 **Number of Spring Games:** 36
Positions Needed for 1999/2000: All **Most Recent Record:** 14 - 22 - 0
Schedule: Methodist College, Emory University, University of Chicago, MIT, Bridgewater College, Maryville, Williams, Washington and Lee University, Southwestern, Nebraska Wesleyan University

Savannah State College

State College Branch
Savannah, GA 31404
Coach: Jamie Rigdon
NCAA II
Tigers/Blue, Orange
Phone: (912) 356-2801
Fax: (912) 353-3073

ACADEMIC

Founded: 1890 **Type:** 4 Yr., Public, Coed
Religion: Non-Affiliated **Campus Housing:** Yes
Undergraduate Enrollment: 1,750 **SAT/ACT/GPA:** 800/18
Student/Faculty Ratio: 19:1 **Male/Female Ratio:** 48:52
Scholarships/Academic: Yes **Athletic:** Yes **Fin Aid:** Yes
Total Expenses by: Year **In State:** $ 5,100 **Out of State:** $ 6,450
Degrees Conferred: AS, BA, BS, BBA, BSW
Programs of Study: Accounting, Biology, Business, Chemistry, Engineering, Computer, Criminal Justice, Economics, English, Languages/Literature, Environmental Science, Finance, History, Information Systems, Marine Biology, Marketing, Mathematics, Music

Shorter College

315 Shorter College
Rome, GA 30165
Coach: Ricci Lattanzi
NAIA
Hawks/Royal Blue, White
Phone: (706) 233-7347
Fax: (706) 236-1515

ACADEMIC

Founded: 1873 **Type:** 4 Yr., Private, Liberal Arts, Coed
Religion: Baptist **Campus Housing:** No
Web-site: http://www.shorter.edu **SAT/ACT/GPA:** 850/2.5
Student/Faculty Ratio: 28:1 **Male/Female Ratio:** 1:4

Undergraduate Enrollment: 2,000 **Graduate Enrollment:** 82%
Scholarships/Academic: Yes **Athletic:** Yes **Fin Aid:** Yes
Total Expenses by: Year **In State:** $ 13,500 **Out of State:** $ 13,500
Degrees Conferred: BA, BFA, BM, BS
Programs of Study: Accounting, Art, Banking/Finance, Biology, Broadcasting, Earth Science, Economics, Journalism, Management, Marketing, Math, Medical, Music, Parks/Recreation

ATHLETIC PROFILE

Estimated Number of Baseball Scholarships: 9
Conference Affiliation: Georgia Athletic Conference
Program Profile: Our program's philosophy revolves around recruiting talented student-athletes who are willing to commit themselves to developing each one's full potential on and off the field. A new field will be set in Spring of 1999. Our natural Bermuda playing season begins with pre-season Fall schedule. The Spring season schedule will begin mid-February through late May.
History: Our program began in the early 1970's which started the Hawks winning tradition of producing several players to the draft.
Achievements: 1998 Conference Champions; Coach Lattanzi was named Coach of the Year; Conference Titles: 1991 Conference Champs, Runner-Up 1989-1990, 1992 Runner-Up District 25, 1995 regular season GAC runner-up. All-Americans: Vaughn Robbins, Lamar Wright. Pro draft: Robert Long, Sacin Bagwell, Preston Cash, Scott Parrish, Troy Hooper, right fielder Marc Brzozoski in 29th round by Rockies.
Coaching: Ricci Lattanzi, Head Coach, starting his 8th year and is from Smyrma, GA. He was 5th at Shorter. He finished his playing career at Birmingham Southern. He was assistant at Birmingham Southern and MS at UA-Birmingham. He was head coach for 2 years at Truett McConnel and was named Coach of the Year. Matt Larry, Assist.
Roster for 1998 team/In State: 19 **Out of State:** 5 **Out of Country:** 0
Total Number of Varsity/Jr. Varsity: 24 **Percent of Graduation:** 98%
Number of Seniors on 1998 Team: 10 **Most Recent Record:** 32 - 22 - 0
Number of Fall Games: 8 **Number of Spring Games:** 51
Positions Needed for 1999/2000: Catcher, Pitcher, Outfielder, 3rd Base
Schedule: Kennesaw State University, Brewton Parker College, Columbus College, Berry College, Southern Tech, State University of West Georgia
Style of Play: Winning is most important only if it is done with integrity and class.

State University of West Georgia

1601 Maple Street
Carrollton, GA 30118
Coach: David 'Doc' Fowlkes

NCAA II
Braves/Red, Blue
Phone: (770) 836-6533
Fax: (770) 836-6792

ACADEMIC

Founded: 1933 **Type:** 4 Yr., Public, Coed
SAT/ACT/GPA: 850/20 **Campus Housing:** Yes
Student/Faculty Ratio: 20:1 **Male/Female Ratio:** 2:1
Undergraduate Enrollment: 6,000 **Graduate Enrollment:** 2,600
Scholarships/Academic: Yes **Athletic:** Yes **Fin Aid:** Yes
Total Expenses by: Year **In State:** $ 5,000 **Out of State:** $ 8,100
Degrees Conferred: AS, AAS, BA, BS, BFA, BBA, BM, BSN, MA, MS, MBA
Programs of Study: Accounting, Anthropology, Art, Banking/Finance, Biological, Business, Chemistry, Communications, Computer, Criminal justice, Earth Science, Management, Park/Recreation, Philosophy, Real Estate, Physics, Political Science, Social Science

ATHLETIC PROFILE

Conference Affiliation: Gulf South Conference
Program Profile: Cole Stadium seats 1,000 and has natural turf. We have Spring season only.
History: The program began in 1958.
Achievements: 10 All-Americans.

South Georgia College

100 West College Park Drive
Douglas, GA 31533
Coach: J. Scott Sims

NJCAA
Tigers/Navy Blue, Gold
Phone: (912) 389-4252
Fax: (912) 389-4258

ACADEMIC

Founded: 1906
Type: 2 Yr., Public, Coed
Undergraduate Enrollment: 1,500
Campus Housing: Yes
Student/Faculty Ratio: 15:1
Male/Female Ratio: 1:3
Scholarships/Academic: Yes **Athletic:** Yes **Fin Aid:** Yes
Total Expenses by: Year **In State:** $ 4,000 **Out of State:** $ 7,000
Degrees Conferred: AA, AS, AAS
Programs of Study: Accounting, Agriculture, Animal, Banking/Finance, Biological Science, Chemistry, Communications, Computer, Criminal justice, Economics, Education, English, French, History, Journalisn, Liberal Arts, Mathematics, Nursing, Office Management, Philosphy, Physical Education, Physics, Political Scinece, Psychology, Recreation

ATHLETIC PROFILE

Conference Affiliation: GJCAA
Program Profile: Our covered stadium has a seating capacity of a 1,000 and a Bermuda playing surface.
History: Our Tiger baseball program which started in the 1950's was very successful in the 1970's. Bobby Bowden football coach at FSU won a state championship here in baseball in 1958.
Achievements: SGC has had nine Academic All-Americans in the 1990's and currently has five players on the professional rosters as well as 12 players on the four-year school rosters
Coaching: J. Scott Simms, Head Coach, has coached seven years and compiled a record of 198-175. He coached nine years at Fitzgerald, GA High School. He graduated from Eastern Kentucky University. Andy Yanzetich, Assistant Coach.
Style of Play: Running win with a pitching and a defense.

Southern College of Technology

1100 South Marietta Parkway
Marietta, GA 30060
Coach: Eric Alexander

NAIA
Hornets/Green, White
Phone: (770) 528-5445
Fax: (404) 528-5515

ACADEMIC

Founded: 1933
Type: 4 Yr., Public, Coed
Religion: Non-Affiliated
Campus Housing: Yes
Undergraduate Enrollment: 6,000
SAT/ACT/GPA: 850/20
Student/Faculty Ratio: 20:1
Male/Female Ratio: 2:1
Scholarships/Academic: Yes **Athletic:** Yes **Fin Aid:** Yes
Total Expenses by: Year **In State:** $ 5,000 **Out of State:** $ 8,100
Degrees Conferred: AS, BA, MS
Programs of Study: Engineering, Architectrure, Computer, Construction, Environemental, Industrial Distribution, Management of Technonolgy, Manufacturing, Mathematics, Physics, Technical/Professional Communications, Textile

ATHLETIC PROFILE

Conference Affiliation: GIAC

Truett - McConnell College

100 Alumni Drive
Cleveland, GA 30528
Coach: Jim Waits
Email: jimw@truett.cc.ga.us

NJCAA
Danes/Blue, Grey, Red
Phone: (706) 865-2134
Fax: (706) 865-5135

ACADEMIC

Founded: 1947
Type: 2 Yr., Private, Liberal Arts, Coed
Religion: Baptist
Campus Housing: Yes
Undergraduate Enrollment: 400
SAT/ACT/GPA: 720/15/2.0
Student/Faculty Ratio: 15:1
Male/Female Ratio: 1:2
Scholarships/Academic: Yes **Athletic:** Yes **Fin Aid:** Yes
Total Expenses by: Year **In State:** $ 9,680 **Out of State:** $ Varies
Degrees Conferred: AA, AS, AB, MA
Programs of Study: Buisenss Administration, Liberal Arts, Music

ATHLETIC PROFILE

Estimated Number of Baseball Scholarships: 10
Conference Affiliation: Georgia Junior College Athletic Association
Program Profile: Johny Mize Field has added a new concrete wall backstop with netting from dugout. New dugouts have been completed along with a new press box. Seating capacity is approximately 1,000. Natural Bermuda turf field which has dimensions of 320', 390', 325'.
History: We began in 1986. We have participated in state playoffs for two years (1992 and 1994).
Achievements: Jeremy Loftice 1997 drafted by Los Angeles Dodgers and pre-season All-American; Joe Montelongo - 3rd team All-American 94 draft by Chicago Cubs; 1992 Region 17 Runner-Up.
Coaching: Jim Waits, Head Coach, has coached from 1994 to 1997. He was an assistant coach for four years in the Cape Cod Baseball League. He was assistant coach at DeKalb College, and Berry College. He was graduate assistant at Georgia Southern University. He compiled a record of 95-98 in four years. He played at DeKalb College and Western Carolina. Stewart Bailey, Assistant Coach.
Roster for 1998 team/In State: 25 **Out of State:** 5 **Out of Country:** 0
Total Number of Varsity/Jr. Varsity: 28 **Percent of Graduation:** 30%
Number of Seniors on 1998 Team: 15 **Positions Needed for 1999/2000:** All
Freshmen Receiving Fin Aid/Athletic: 7 **Academic:** 15
Schedule: Spartanburg Methodist, DeKalb, Middle Georgia, Gulf Coast, Chipola Junior
Style of Play: Pitching, defense and speed.

University of Georgia

1 Selig Cr, PO Box 1472
Athens, GA 30603
Coach: Robert Sapp

NCAA I
Bulldogs/Red, Black
Phone: (706) 542-7971
Fax: (706) 542-7984

ACADEMIC

Founded: 1785
Type: 4 Yr., Public, Coed
Web-site: http://www.sports.uga.edu
SAT/ACT/GPA: 1180/3.4
Student/Faculty Ratio: 20:1
Male/Female Ratio: 49:51
Undergraduate Enrollment: 30,000
Graduate Enrollment: 5,514
Scholarships/Academic: Yes **Athletic:** Yes **Fin Aid:** Yes
Total Expenses by: Year **In State:** $ 7,820 **Out of State:** $ 13,700
Degrees Conferred: AB to Doctorate
Programs of Study: Agricultural Environmental Science, Art and Science, Preprofessional Programs, Business Administration, Education, Environmental Design, Family and Consumer Sciences, Forest Resources, Journalism and Mass Communications, Pharmacy, Social work, Veterinary Medicine

ATHLETIC PROFILE

Conference Affiliation: Southeastern (Eastern Division)
Program Profile: Baseball has a rich tradition of success as the oldest sport on campus, dating back to 1886. Foley Field is ranked in the nation's top 10 baseball facilities. The natural grass stadium has a capacity for 3,200. It has indoor & an outdoor batting cages.
History: Baseball began in 1886 and is the oldest sport on campus. UGA appeared in the 1987 and 1990 College World Series, winning the national title in 1990 with a 52-19 record.
Achievements: Georgia has made other NCAA appearances in 1953, 1987, 1990 and 1992. It has participated in 14 SEC tournaments. UGA has had 18 players reach the major leagues, including 5 currently. First head coach was Hall of Fame Hugh Jennings who coached 1895-97. Jennings also coached the Detroit Tigers. 18 All-Americans.
Coaching: Robert Sapp, Head Coach, started June 5, 1996. He is the second winningest JUCO Coach witha mark of 890-181 (.831), four JUCO National titles, two Runner-Up in 20 years at Middle Georgia. Randy Mazey, Assistant Coach, is on his first year. He was Big South Conference Coach of the Year at Charleston Southern last three years. He is a former Clemson Standout/Assistant Coach. David Perno, Assistant Coach, is a former Bulldog.
Style of Play: Aggressive, hit and run, speed and power, avoid big inning when on the mound.

Valdosta State College

Blazer Fieldhouse
Valdosta, GA 31698
Coach: Tommy Thomas
Email: pemeyer@valdosta.edu

NCAA II
Blazers/Red, Black
Phone: (912) 259-5562
Fax: (912) 259-5561

ACADEMIC

Founded: 1906
SAT/ACT/GPA: 700
Student/Faculty Ratio: 24:1
Undergraduate Enrollment: 8,100
Scholarships/Academic: Yes **Athletic:** Yes
Total Expenses by: Year **In State:** $ 5,200
Type: 4 Yr., Public, Coed
Campus Housing: Yes
Male/Female Ratio: 41:59
Graduate Enrollment: 1,800
Fin Aid: Yes
Out of State: $ 8,200
Degrees Conferred: BA, BS, MA, MBA, MPA, MMEd
Programs of Study: Accounting, Anthropology, Art, Astronomy, Biology, Business, Chemistry, Communications, Computer, Criminal Justice, Economics, English, Finance, Geology, Management

ATHLETIC PROFILE

Estimated Number of Baseball Scholarships: 9
Conference Affiliation: Gulf South Conference
Program Profile: Our field is natural grass with a new state of the art fieldhouse and indoor practice facility. We have a beautiful field with first class ads on the fence. We have a 56 game schedule with many promotion games and two early season tournaments.
History: Our program began in 1954. We had over 21 post-season tournaments in the last 31 years, We had 8 national tournament appearances and were national champions in 1979.
Achievements: Tommy Thomas was named 7 Region Coach of the Year. We had one National Coach of the Year in 1979. We had many All-Americans and drafted players.
Coaching: Tommy Thomas, Head Coach, was National Coach of the Year. He has coached here for 31 years. He compiled an overall record of 1037-601 which is .633 percent. Shannon Jernigan, Assist.
Roster for 1998 team/In State: 13 **Out of State:** 10 **Out of Country:** 1
Total Number of Varsity/Jr. Varsity: 24 **Percent of Graduation:** 80%-90%
Number of Seniors on 1998 Team: 6 **Number of Sophomores on 1998 Team:** 4
Freshmen Receiving Fin Aid/Athletic: 3 **Baseball Camp Dates:** TBD
Most Recent Record: 31 - 19 - 0 **Number of Spring Games:** 56
Positions Needed for 1999/2000: 2-Infielders, 2-Outfielders, 2-Pitchers
Schedule: Tampa, Florida Southern, North Alabama, Alabama-Huntsville, St, Leo, West Georgia
Style of Play: Loves to run, hit and run, Etc.. Generally adapts to personnel.

Young Harris College

PO Box 37
Young Harris, GA 30582
Coach: Rick Robinson

NJCAA
Mountain Lions/Purple, White, Black
Phone: (706) 379-3111x5175
Fax: (706) 379-1673

ACADEMIC

Founded: 1886
Type: 2 Yr., Private, Coed
Student/Faculty Ratio: 15:1
Male/Female Ratio: 50:50
Undergraduate Enrollment: 540
Graduate Enrollment: None
Scholarships/Academic: No **Athletic:** Yes **Fin Aid:** Yes
Total Expenses by: Year **In State:** $ 9,500 **Out of State:** $ 9,500
Degrees Conferred: Associate
Programs of Study: Agriculture, Biological Science, Business Administration, Chemistry, Criminal Justice, Education, English, Geology, History, Journalism, Liberal Arts, Management, Mathematics, Medical, Music, Natural Science, Nursing, Physical Therapy, Physics, Political Science, Psychology, Recreation/Leisure Services, Religion, Science

ATHLETIC PROFILE

Estimated Number of Baseball Scholarships: 6
Conference Affiliation: Region 17
Program Profile: Our Fulton County Stadium which is the old Broncs Stadium will seat 500 with 200 seats out and has a grass playing surface. Fall practice is from August 31 to November 14. Spring practice is from January 12 to January 30.
History: The program began in 1994.
Achievements: 1 All-American; 3 drafted players, Region 17 Runner-Up in 1995.
Coaching: Rick Robinson, Head Coach, was high school head coach for five years. He was first assistant coach at Old Dominion University for 4 years. He was a major league scout for two years.
Roster for 1998 team/In State: 23 **Out of State:** 16 **Out of Country:** 1
Total Number of Varsity/Jr. Varsity: 30 **Percent of Graduation:** 92%
Most Recent Record: 31 - 22 - 0 **Number of Sophomores on 1998 Team:** 12
Freshmen Receiving Fin Aid/Athletic: 11 **Academic:** 7
Number of Fall Games: 20 **Number of Spring Games:** 56
Positions Needed for 1999/2000: LHP, RHP, Catcher, Shortstop
Baseball Camp Dates: TBA
Schedule: Gulf Coast CC, Bredard NC, Spartansburg, Michelle, DeKalb, Cleveland State
Style of Play: Aggressive but disciplined.

HAWAII

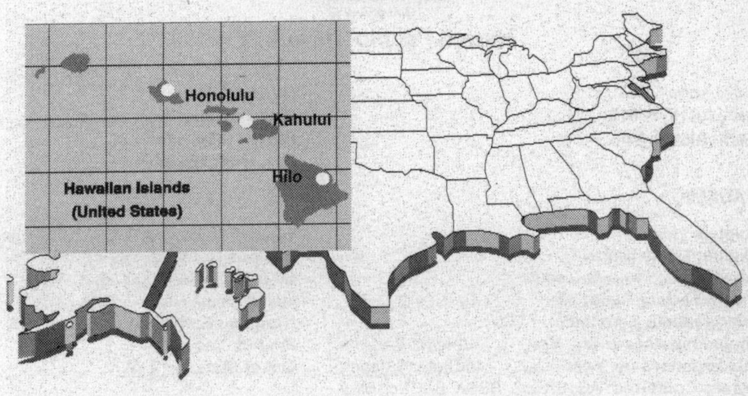

SCHOOL	CITY	AFFILIATION 99	PAGE
Hawaii Pacific University	Honolulu	NCAA II/NAIA	216
University of Hawaii - Hilo	Hilo	NCAA I	216
University of Hawaii - Manoa	Honolulu	NCAA I	217

Hawaii Pacific University

1060 Bishop Street, #PH
Honolulu, HI 96813
Coach: Allan Sato

NCAA II/NAIA
Blue Warriors/Blue, Green
Phone: (808) 544-0221
Fax: (808) 566-2405

ACADEMIC

Founded: 1965
Religion: Non-Affiliated
Web-site: http://www.hpu.edu/
Student/Faculty Ratio: 20:1
Undergraduate Enrollment: 7,000
Scholarships/Academic: Yes **Athletic:** Yes
Total Expenses by: Year **In State:** $ Varies

Type: 4 Yr., Private, Liberal Arts, Coed
Campus Housing: Yes
SAT/ACT/GPA: 1000/ 22
Male/Female Ratio: 55:45
Graduate Enrollment: 1,000
Fin Aid: Yes
Out of State: $ 12,800

Degrees Conferred: AS, BA, BS, BSBA, BSCSci, MBA
Programs of Study: Accounting, American Studies, Anthropology, Applied Mathematics, Business Administration, Communications, Computer Information System, Computer Science, Criminal Justice, Economics, English, History, Humanities, Human Development, Human Resources, Management, Marketing, Nursing, Political Science, Psychology, Social Science, Tourism

ATHLETIC PROFILE

Conference Affiliation: Far West Hawaii Independent Conference
Program Profile: We are an offensive minded club that plays on the best natural surface field in Hawaii.
History: The program began in 1983.
Achievements: NAIA Area I Regional Champs; 1991 NAIA World Series (Knocked out in 4th game).
Coaching: Allan Sato, Head Coach, played at HPU.
Style of Play: Aggressive style of play, emphasizing excellent short-game execution and fundamentals. Teams usually play an excellent and fundamentally sound defense.

University of Hawaii - Hilo

200 W Kawili Street
Hilo, HI 96720-4091
Coach: Joey Estrella, Jr.
Email: uhhadm@hawaii.edu

NCAA I
Vulcans/Red, White, Blue
Phone: (808) 974-7700
Fax: (808) 974-7711

ACADEMIC

Founded: 1947
Religion: Non-Affiliated
Web-site: http://www.uhh.hawaii.edu
Student/Faculty Ratio: 14:1
Undergraduate Enrollment: 2,600
Scholarships/Academic: Yes **Athletic:** Yes
Total Expenses by: Year **In State:** $ 6,446

Type: 4 Yr., Public, Liberal Arts, Coed
Campus Housing: Yes
SAT/ACT/GPA: 900/19/2.5
Male/Female Ratio: 40:60
Graduate Enrollment: 20
Fin Aid: Yes
Out of State: $ 12,034

Degrees Conferred: BA, BBA, BS, MA
Programs of Study: Agriculture, Anthropology, Art, Astronomy, Biology, Business Administration, Chemistry, Communications, Computer Science, Earth and Space Science, Economics, English, Geography, Geology, Hawaiian Languange and Literature, Hawaiian Studies, History, Japanese

ATHLETIC PROFILE

Estimated Number of Baseball Scholarships: 5-6
Conference Affiliation: Independent

Program Profile: We developing a Division I program after successfull NAIA affiliation. We have a natural grass, lighted facility on campus that currently seats 500. Our Spring season is January to May and we play the top twenty ranked teams.
History: We began Division I competition during the 1992 season. Schedule usually includes top ranked teams such as Arizona State, USC, UCLA, Arizona, Wichita State and San Diego State.
Achievements: Coach Estrella earned several NAIA District Coaching Honors along with two NAIA Area I Coach of the Year Honors in 1986 and 1989. We had 3 World Series Appearances.
Coaching: Joey Estrella, Head Coach, is on his 23rd season with the program. He earned NAIA Area I Coach of the Year Honors & NAIA District Coach honors several times. Kal Miyataki, Assist.
Roster for 1998 team/In State: 21 **Out of State:** 11 **Out of Country:** 0
Total Number of Varsity/Jr. Varsity: 32 **Percent of Graduation:** 70%-80%
Number of Seniors on 1998 Team: 6 **Number of Sophomores on 1998 Team:** 5
Freshmen Receiving Fin Aid/Athletic: 6 **Most Recent Record:** 16 - 31 - 0
Baseball Camp Dates: June **Number of Spring Games:** 48
Positions Needed for 1999/2000: Pitchers (RHP/LHP)
Schedule: Arizona State, Arizona, UCLA, Wichita State, San Diego State, Fresno State
Style of Play: Team's philosophy is to play strong defense with aggressive short game on defense.

University of Hawaii - Manoa

244 Dole Stree
Honolulu, HI 96822
Coach: Les Murakami

NCAA I
Rainbows/Green, White
Phone: (808) 956-6247
Fax: (808) 956-3543

ACADEMIC

Founded: 1907 **Type:** 4 Yr., Public, Coed
Web-site: http://www2.hawaii.edu/athletics/ **SAT/ACT/GPA:** 430/20
Student/Faculty Ratio: 14:1 **Male/Female Ratio:** 43:57
Undergraduate Enrollment: 13,000 **Graduate Enrollment:** 5,500
Scholarships/Academic: Yes **Athletic:** Yes **Fin Aid:** Yes
Total Expenses by: Year **In State:** $ 4,607 **Out of State:** $ 7,847
Degrees Conferred: Bachelors, Masters, Doctorate
Programs of Study: Accounting, Agricultural, Animal Anthropology, Architecture, Art, American Studies, Asian, Atmospheric, Biological, Botany, Business, Chemistry, Dental, Design, Economics

ATHLETIC PROFILE

Conference Affiliation: Western Athletic Conference
Program Profile: We are number one in baseball (college) stadiums in the nation. The field is Astroturf and seats 4,312. Usually first collegiate Division I game of the year is in Mid-January.
History: The program began in 1923. First year of NCAA was in 1971 when Coach Murakami took over the program. Prior to that, UH was a club team that played a handful of Division I teams.
Achievements: 1980 College World Series Runner-Up; Les Murakami was named 1986 NCAA District Coach of the Year; 1987 and 1991 WAS Coach of the Year; 6 WAC Titles; 17 All-Americans; 51 players drafted by Major League Baseball teams.
Coaching: Les Murakami, Head Coach, is on his 28th season with an overall record is 1,011-516-4 as of April 24, 1998. He entered the season with 10th wins (980) and 18th in winning percentage (.662) among active DI coaches. Among the NCAA all-time lists, he entered the season 18th wins and 51st in winning pct. He has led UH to 6 WAC Titles, 11 Regional Appearances and 2nd place finishes at the '80 College World Series. Carl Furutani, Dave Murakami & Les Nakama, Assistants.
Roster for 1998 team/In State: 21 **Out of State:** 15 **Out of Country:** 0
Total Number of Varsity/Jr. Varsity: 36 **Most Recent Record:** 31 - 16 - 0
Number of Seniors on 1998 Team: 3 **Number of Sophomores on 1998 Team:** 10
Baseball Camp Dates: 6/10-13; 6/15-18; 7/27-20; 8/3-6
Style of Play: Constant pressure on the defense by hit and run, stealing. Stresses fundamental of always trying to advance runners; outfield speed. A good blend of power and content hitters.

IDAHO

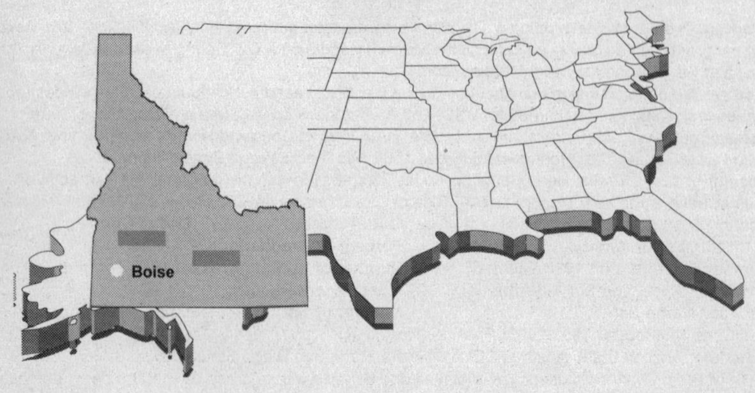

SCHOOL	CITY	AFFILIATION 99	PAGE
Albertson College	Caldwell	NAIA	219
College of Southern Idaho	Twin Falls	NJCAA I	219
Lewis-Clark State College	Lewiston	NCAA I	220
North Idaho College	Coeur D'Alene	NJCAA	221
Northwest Nazarene College	Nampa	NJCAA	222
Ricks College	Rexburg	NJCAA	222

Albertson College

2112 Cleveland Boulevard
Caldwell, ID 83605
Coach: Tim Mooney
Email: tmooney@acoti.edu

NAIA
Coyotes/Purple, Gold
Phone: (208) 459-5862
Fax: (208) 459-5854

ACADEMIC

Founded: 1891
Undergraduate Enrollment: 681
Web-site: http://www.acofi.edu/
Student/Faculty Ratio: 12:1
Scholarships/Academic: Yes
Total Expenses by: Year
Athletic: Yes
In State: $ 20,000
Type: 4 Yr., Private, Liberal Arts, Coed
Campus Housing: Yes
SAT/ACT/GPA: 510/21
Male/Female Ratio: 55:45
Fin Aid: Yes
Out of State: $ 14,100
Degrees Conferred: BA, BS
Programs of Study: Accounting, Anthropology, Art, Biological Science, Business Administration, Chemistry, Computer Science, Economics, Elementary Education, English, French, History, Mathematics, Music, Philosophy, Physical Education, Physical Fitness/Exercise Science, Physics, Political Science, Prelaw, Premed, Psychology, Religion, Science Education, Secondary Education

ATHLETIC PROFILE

Estimated Number of Baseball Scholarships: 5
Conference Affiliation: Cascade Conference
Program Profile: The program is one that was ranked in the top 25 in the last two seasons. Facilities include an outstanding indoor hitting cage for the winter off-season workout and an excellent weight room. Playing season consists of a 56 game schedule with a week long trip to Southern California. The field is natural grass with a seating of 4,000. We have a Fall season. Simplot Stadium has a seating capacity of 6,500.
History: Our program was reinstated in 1986 after having been dropped in the late 1970's. Albertson has qualified for the NAIA District 2 tournaments every year and is the only school in the district to have done so. Our best finish was runner-up (3 times). We have competed in the Post-season Tournament in 9 consecutive years.
Achievements: Defending National Champions in 1998; Conference Coach of the Year three times in a row; 2 All-Americans in 1998; 20 players in pro ball.
Coaching: Tim Mooney, Head Coach, has an overall record at Albertson of 423-231. His overall conference record is 140-26 with a percentage of .843. Shawn Humberger, Assistant Coach, works with the hitters and outfielders. He played at the College of Southern Idaho where he was a Junior College All-American. He played one year at UNLV and one year Coach Mooney at Albertson College. Gary White, Pitching Coach, played four years at UNLV and was an assistant coach at UNLV before coming to Albertson.
Roster for 1998 team/In State: 10
Out of State: 15
Out of Country: 3
Total Number of Varsity/Jr. Varsity: 30
Percent of Graduation: 80%
Number of Seniors on 1998 Team: 40
Number of Sophomores on 1998 Team: 60
Freshmen Receiving Fin Aid/Athletic: 4
Academic: 6
Most Recent Record: 55 - 8 - 0
Number of Spring Games: 55
Positions Needed for 1999/2000: Catcher, 3rd Base, Outfielder, Pitcher
Schedule: Cal State - Dominguez, Lewis and Clark, California Baptist, Southern California, Oregon
Style of Play: Aggressive; offensively sound. Fundamentally will use short game and pressure running offense.

College of Southern Idaho

315 Falls Avenue West
Twin Falls, ID 83303
Coach: Jim Walker

NJCAA I
Eagles/Gold, Black
Phone: (208) 733-9554
Fax: (208) 734-0245

ACADEMIC

Founded: 1968
Type: 2 Yr., Public, Coed
Religion: Non-Affiliated
Campus Housing: Yes
Web-site: http://www.csi.id.us
Undergraduate Enrollment: 4,200
Student/Faculty Ratio: 24:1
Male/Female Ratio: 1:3
Scholarships/Academic: Yes **Athletic:** Yes **Fin Aid:** Yes
Total Expenses by: Year **In State:** $ 2,715 **Out of State:** $ 3,115
Degrees Conferred: Associate
Programs of Study: Accounting, Agriculture, Anthropology, Art, Automotive, Banking/Finance, Behavioral Science

ATHLETIC PROFILE

Estimated Number of Baseball Scholarships: 5-full/8-partial
Conference Affiliation: Scenic West Conference
Program Profile: We are one of the most prolific baseball programs in the country. We have a beautiful natural grass field with outstanding playing surface, on -field clubhouse with shower, wash facilities, lockers , offices for coaches and a seating capacily of 750.
History: The program began in 1969. Head Coach Jim Walker came in 1974 and has compiled over 800 victories in his 24 career which includes nine trips to the Junior World Series.
Achievements: Jime Walker was named ten times District Coach of the Year and National Coach of the Year in 1984. This same year, CSI won the World Series. 10 Conference Titles; 13 All-Americans; 107 drafted players.
Coaching: Jim Walker, Head Coach, was with the Phillies. In his 24 years at CSI, he compiled a record of 842-312. Bob Maitia, Pitching Coach, was with the Blue Jays. He played at CSI and UNLV. He is entering his second year with the program. Boomer Walker, Defensive Coordinator and baserunning coach, played at CSI and Northeast Louisiana University. He is entering three years with the program.
Roster for 1998 team/In State: 4 **Out of State:** 20 **Out of Country:** 5
Total Number of Varsity/Jr. Varsity: 28 **Percent of Graduation:** 90%
Number of Seniors on 1998 Team: 14 **Most Recent Record:** 42 - 7 - 0
Freshmen Receiving Fin Aid/Athletic: 8 **Academic:** 3
Number of Fall Games: 16 **Number of Spring Games:** 54
Positions Needed for 1999/2000: Pitcher, Catcher, Infielders, Outfielders
Baseball Camp Dates: December 26-28; June 8-13
Schedule: Citrus, Utah Valley, Dixie, Walla Walla, Columbia Basin, Spokane Falls
Style of Play: A definite hitting school, we also hit for power but average over 150 stolen bases a year. Definitely known for its power hitting and power pitching.

Lewis-Clark State College

500 8th Avenue
Lewiston, ID 83501
Coach: Ed Cheff
NCAA I
Warriors/Red, White, Blue
Phone: (208) 799-2272
Fax: (208) 799-2801

ACADEMIC

Founded: 1893
Type: 4 Yr., Public, Coed
Undergraduate Enrollment: 8,200
Campus Housing: Yes
Student/Faculty Ratio: 17:1
Male/Female Ratio: 38:62
Scholarships/Academic: Yes **Athletic:** Yes **Fin Aid:** Yes
Total Expenses by: Year **In State:** $ 5,935 **Out of State:** $ 9,644
Degrees Conferred: AA, AS, AAS, BA, BS
Programs of Study: Accounting, Biological Science, Business Administration, Chemistry, Communications, Criminal Justice, Earth Science, Education, English, Geology, History, Liberal Arts, Management, Mathematics, Natural Science, Nursing, Personnel Management, Secondary Education, Social Science, Special Education

ATHLETIC PROFILE

Conference Affiliation: Pacific Northwest Athletic
Program Profile: Emphasizing the appropriate balance between academics and athletics, LCSC strives to assist student-athletes reach his/her maximum potential. Harris Field is one of the finest collegiate facilities in the country . It has a pro AAA lighting system, lighted outdoor batting cages and a 5,500-seat capacity. It has a leftfield line and a raised area behind LF fence and above both dugouts. It has a grass field.
History: We were NAIA National Champions 1984-85, 1987-92. We are regular partcipants in the Coca Cola Banana Belt, Paffile, Lewis-Clark Chevrolet and other tournaments. From 1982-1992 the Warriors played in the NAIA National Championship game all 11 years and won 8 times, including the last 6 in a row . This task was never accomplished in a team sport on any level of intercollegiate athletics. Our overall 18th year record under Cheff is 900-239. Our 1st team was in 1906.
Achievements: Our graduation rate higher than the campus average. 8 academic All-Americans since 1981; players actively involved in community charity fund raising & volunteer work; 35 All-Americans; 8 Academic All-Americans; 75 entering pro (5 currently on major league rosters).
Coaching: Ed Cheff, Head Coach, is on his 20th season. He was Coach of the Decade and a speaker at coaching clinics (national ABCA and state HS clinics). He was in the Hall of Fame in 1994. He was assistant coach of the USA Pan American team. Chad Miltenberger, Hitting/Head Assistant Coach, led to LCSC's 1st NAIAChampionship 1984 and All-American catcher. Gus Knickrehm, Pitching Coach/Recruiter, was starting pitcher in 1987 National Championship Team. Kekoa Kaluhiokalani, Assistant Coach. Paul Dean, Assistant Coach.
Style of Play: Teams consistently recognized as being well prepared and very aggressive. I really like the mentality this club will demonstrate on the field. Toughness, intensity and intelligence are qualities we have always hoped would define the type of players representing our program, and these guys fit that mold.

North Idaho College

1000 W Garden Avenue
Coeur D'Alene, ID 83814
Coach: Paul Manzardo
Email: paul_manzardo@nic.edu

NJCAA
Cardinals/Cardinal, White
Phone: (208) 769-3354
Fax: (208) 769-7779

ACADEMIC

Founded: 1933
Web-site: http://www.nic.edu
Undergraduate Enrollment: 3,600
Scholarships/Academic: Yes
Athletic: Yes
Total Expenses by: Year
In State: $ 4,500
Degrees Conferred: Associate
Programs of Study: General Studies

Type: 2 Yr., Private, Coed
Campus Housing: No
Student/Faculty Ratio: 16:1
Fin Aid: Yes
Out of State: $ 4,500

ATHLETIC PROFILE

Estimated Number of Baseball Scholarships: 18
Conference Affiliation: Region 18, Scenic West Athletic Conference, NJCAA
Program Profile: The Cardinals have an excellent on campus field with natural grass that seats 400. They play a 44-48-game schedule.
History: The program began in 1961.
Coaching: Paul Manzardo, Head Coach, is on his second year as a head coach. He played at Ferris State University in Big Rapids, Michigan. He was All-Conference second baseman in his junior and senior years. Tony Bevacqua and Lloyd Duman - Assistant Coaches.
Roster for 1998 team/In State: 13
Out of State: 6
Out of Country: 5
Total Number of Varsity/Jr. Varsity: 24
Percent of Graduation: 60%
Most Recent Record: 17 - 27 - 0
Number of Sophomores on 1998 Team: 9
Freshmen Receiving Fin Aid/Athletic: 11
Academic: 3
Number of Fall Games: 8
Number of Spring Games: 44
Positions Needed for 1999/2000: Pitcher
Schedule: CSI, Dixie, Utah Valley, Ricks, Treasure Valley, Columbia Basin
Style of Play: Quick, fundamental sound.

Northwest Nazarene College

623 Holly Street
Nampa, ID 83686
Coach: Brian Muir

NJCAA
Crusaders/Red, Black
Phone: (208) 467-8351
Fax: (208) 467-8396

ACADEMIC

Founded: 1913
Type: 4 Yr., Public, Liberal Arts, Coed
Religion: Nazarene
Campus Housing: Yes
Web-site: http://www.nnc.edu/
SAT/ACT/GPA: None
Student/Faculty Ratio: 14:1
Male/Female Ratio: 494/624
Undergraduate Enrollment: 1,101
Graduate Enrollment: 130
Scholarships/Academic: Yes **Athletic:** Yes **Fin Aid:** Yes
Total Expenses by: Year **In State:** $ 15,100 **Out of State:** $ 15,100
Degrees Conferred: 3 Associate of Arts, 119 Bachelor of Arts, 39 Masters
Programs of Study: Accounting, Biology, Business Administration, Chemistry, Communications, Computer Information Systems, Computer Science, Elementary Education, Engineering, English, Finance, Fine Arts, History, Humanities, International Relations, Mathematics, Music, Philosophy, Physical Education, Physics, Political Science, Predentistry, Prelaw, Premed, Prepharmacy, Psychology, Recreation, Social Science, Social Work, Sociology, Sport Medicine

ATHLETIC PROFILE

Conference Affiliation: Cascade Conference

Ricks College

Hart Bldg
Rexburg, ID 83460-0900
Coach: Jerry Schlegelmilch

NJCAA
Vikings/Royal, White
Phone: (208) 356-2127
Fax: (208) 356-2141

ACADEMIC

Founded: 1888
Type: 2 Yr., Private, Coed
Undergraduate Enrollment: 8,220
Campus Housing: Yes
Student/Faculty Ratio: 22:1
Male/Female Ratio: 43:57
Scholarships/Academic: No **Athletic:** Yes **Fin Aid:** Yes
Total Expenses by: Year **In State:** $ 3,700mbr **Out of State:** $ 4,500nonmbr
Degrees Conferred: Associate
Programs of Study: Accounting, Advertising, Agriculture, Animal Science, Architecture, Art, Automotive, Banking/Finance, Botany, Broadcasting/Design, Ecology, Engineering, Economics, Medical, Landscape, Journalism, Geology, Healht, Law, Military, Nutrition, Political Science, Recreation, Sport Medicine, Wildlife, Zoology

ILLINOIS

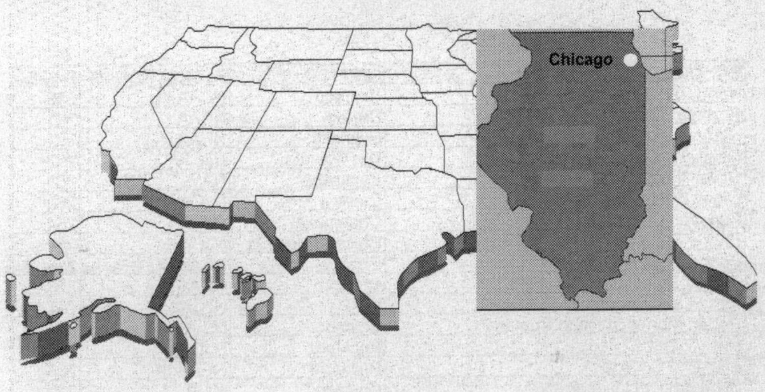

SCHOOL	CITY	AFFILIATION 99	PAGE
Augustana College	Rock Island	NCAA III	225
Aurora University	Aurora	NCAA III	225
Belleville Area College	Belleville	NJCAA	225
Benedictine University	Lisle	NCAA III	226
Black Hawk College	Moline	NJCAA	227
Blackburn College	Carlinville	NCAA III	227
Bradley University	Peoria	NCAA I	228
Carl Sandburg College	Galesburg	NCAA I	228
Chicago State University	Chicago	NCAA I	229
College of DuPage	Glen Ellyn	NJCAA	230
College of Lake County	Grayslake	NJCAA	230
Concordia University	River Forest	NCAA III	230
Eastern Illinois University	Charleston	NCAA I	231
Elgin Community College	Elgin	NJCAA	232
Elmhurst College	Elmhurst	NCAA III	232
Eureka College	Eureka	NCAA III	233
Greenville College	Greenville	NCAA III	233
Highland Community College	Freeport	NJCAA	234
Illinois Central College	East Peoria	NJCAA	234
Illinois College	Jacksonville	NCAA III	235
Illinois Institute of Technology	Chicago	NAIA	236
Illinois State University	Normal	NCAA I	236
Illinois Valley Community College	Oglesby	NJCAA	237
Illinois Wesleyan University	Bloomington	NCAA III	237
John A. Logan Community College	Carterville	NJCAA	238
John Wood Community College	Quincy	NJCAA	238
Joliet Junior College	Joliet	NJCAA	239
Judson College	Elgin	NAIA	240
Kankakee Community College	Kankakee	NJCAA	240
Kaskaskia College	Centralia	NCAA I	241
Kishwaukee College	Malta	NJCAA	241
Knox College	Galesburg	NCAA III	242
Lake Land College	Mattoon	NJCAA	243
Lewis and Clark Community College	Godfrey	NCAA II	243
Lewis University	Romeoville	NCAA II	244
Lincoln College	Lincoln	NJCAA	244
Lincoln Land Community College	Springfield	NJCAA	245
Lincoln Trail College	Robinson	NJCAA	245
MacMurray College	Jacksonville	NCAA III	246
McHenry County College	Crystal Lake	NJCAA	247
McKendree College	Lebanon	NAIA	247
Millikin University	Decatur	NCAA III	248
Monmouth College	Monmouth	NCAA III	249
Morton College	Cicero	NJCAA	249
North Central College	Naperville	NCAA III	250

SCHOOL	CITY	AFFILIATION 99	PAGE
North Park University	Chicago	NCAA III	250
Northern Illinois University	DeKalb	NCAA I	251
Northwestern University	Evanston	NCAA I	252
Oakton Community College	Des Plaines	NJCAA	252
Olivet Nazarene University	Kankakee	NAIA	253
Olney Central College	Olney	NJCAA	253
Parkland College	Champaign	NCAA I	254
Prairie State College	Chicago Heights	NJCAA	254
Principia College	Elsah	NCAA III	255
Quincy University	Quincy	NCAA II	256
Rend Lake Community College	Ina	NJCAA	257
Robert Morris-Chicago Campus	Chicago	NAIA	257
Rock Valley College	Rockford	NJCAA	257
Rockford College	Rockford	NCAA III	258
Saint Xavier University	Chicago	NAIA	259
Sauk Valley Community College	Dixon	NJCAA	259
Shawnee Community College	Ullin	NJCAA	259
South Suburban College	S Holland	NJCAA	260
Southeastern Illinois College	Harrisburg	NJCAA	261
Southern Illinois U - Carbondale	Carbondale	NCAA I	261
Southern Illinois U - Edwardsville	Edwardsville	NCAA II	262
Spoon River College	Canton	NCAA II	263
Trinity Christian College	Palos Heights	NAIA	263
Triton College	River Grove	NJCAA	264
University of Chicago	Chicago	NCAA III	264
University of Illinois - Chicago	Chicago	NCAA I	265
University of Illinois - Urbana/Champaign	Champaign	NCAA I	266
University of Saint Francis (St. Francis C)	Joliet	NAIA	267
Wabash Valley College	Mt. Carmel	NJCAA	267
Waubonsee Community College	Sugar Grove	NJCAA	268
Western Illinois University	Macomb	NCAA I	269
Wheaton College	Wheaton	NCAA III	269
William Rainey Harper College	Palatine	NJCAA	270

Augustana College

3500 Fifth Avenue
Rock Island, IL 61201
Coach: Greg Wallace

NCAA III
Vikings/Blue, Gold
Phone: (309) 794-7522
Fax: (309) 794-7525

ACADEMIC

Founded: 1860
Type: 4 Yr., Private, Liberal Arts, Coed
Religion: Evangelical Lutheran
Campus Housing: Yes
Web-site: http://www.augustana.edu/
SAT/ACT/GPA: 910+/24/3.0
Student/Faculty Ratio: 14:1
Male/Female Ratio: 47:53
Undergraduate Enrollment: 2,150
Graduate Enrollment: None
Scholarships/Academic: Yes **Athletic:** No **Fin Aid:** Yes
Total Expenses by: Year **In State:** $ 19,989 **Out of State:** $ 17,000
Degrees Conferred: BA
Programs of Study: Business and Management, Education, Health Science, Letters/Literature, Life Sciences, Psychology, Social Sciences

ATHLETIC PROFILE

Conference Affiliation: CCIW

Aurora University

347 South Gladstone Avenue
Aurora, IL 60506
Coach: Mark Walsh

NCAA III
Spartans/Royal, White
Phone: (708) 844-5111
Fax: (708) 844-7809

ACADEMIC

Founded: 1893
Type: 4 Yr., Private, Coed
Religion: Non-Denominational
Campus Housing: Yes
Web-site: http://www.aurora.edu/
SAT/ACT/GPA: 19
Student/Faculty Ratio: 14:1
Male/Female Ratio: 40:60
Undergraduate Enrollment: 1,300
Graduate Enrollment: 500
Scholarships/Academic: Yes **Athletic:** No **Fin Aid:** Yes
Total Expenses by: Year **In State:** $ 10,800 **Out of State:** $ 10,800
Degrees Conferred: BA, BSW, BS, BSN
Programs of Study: Accounting, Biology, Business Administration, Communications, Computer Science, Criminal Justice, Economics, Elementary Education, Education, Engineering Science, English, Environemental Science, History, Management, Marketing, Mathematics, Nursing, Physical Education, Political Science, Prelaw, Psychology, Social Work, Sociology

ATHLETIC PROFILE

Conference Affiliation: NIIC

Belleville Area College

2500 Carlyle Road
Belleville, IL 62221
Coach: Neil Fiala

NJCAA
Dutchmen/Blue, White
Phone: (618) 235-2700
Fax: (618) 235-1578

ACADEMIC

Founded: 1946
Type: 2 Yr., Public, Coed
Web-site: http://www.bacnet.edu/index.htm
Undergraduate Enrollment: 22,000
Student/Faculty Ratio: 30:1
Male/Female Ratio: 2:4
Scholarships/Academic: Yes **Athletic:** Yes **Fin Aid:** Yes
Total Expenses by: Semester **In State:** $ 1,500 **Out of State:** $ 4,600
Degrees Conferred: AA, AS, AAS
Programs of Study: Accounting, Agriculture, Aviation Technology, Business Administration, Computer Information System, Construction Management, Criminal Justice, Electrical, Engineering, Flight Enforcement, Marketing, Nursing, Physical Therapy

ATHLETIC PROFILE

Estimated Number of Baseball Scholarships: 8-10
Conference Affiliation: Great Rivers Athletic Conference
Program Profile: We play on a natural field with a manicured infield. The field measurements are: 325, 363, 377, 363, and 325. The on campus facility includes tarp. We have consistently been one of the top 20 programs in the past four seasons.
History: The program began in the early 1960's. We participated in the JC World Series in 1984. 16 Sectional Championships; 6 Region Championships; 4 Conference Championships.
Achievements: Coach Neil Fiala was named Conference Coach of the Year in 1996, 1997 and 1998. He was region Coach of the Year in 1996 and 1998. Fifty of his former players have signed contracts and nine have played major league. Our four year record is 204-83-4.
Coaching: Neil Fiala, Head Coach, is entering his fifth year as a head coach. He played in major leagues with St. Louis Cardinals and Cincinnati Reds. He was MVP of 1975 Junior College World Series. He also played in NCAA I World Series. He was an assistant coach at University of Illinois for three years from 1991 to 1993. Joe Bauer - Assistant Coach.
Roster for 1998 team/In State: 20 **Out of State:** 5 **Out of Country:** 0
Total Number of Varsity/Jr. Varsity: 25 **Percent of Graduation:** 75%
Number of Seniors on 1998 Team: 12 **Most Recent Record:** 45 - 15 - 2
Number of Fall Games: 20 **Number of Spring Games:** 56
Style of Play: Aggressive offensive style; conservative defensive style.

Benedictine University

5700 College Road
Lisle, IL 60532-0900
Coach: John Ostrowski
Email: jostrows@ben.edu
NCAA III
Eagles/Red, White
Phone: (630) 829-6147
Fax: (630) 960-0899

ACADEMIC

Founded: 1887
Type: 4 Yr., Private, Coed
Religion: Roman Catholic
Campus Housing: Yes
Web-site: http://www.ben.edu
SAT/ACT/GPA: 21/2.0
Student/Faculty Ratio: 10:1
Male/Female Ratio: 48:52
Undergraduate Enrollment: 1,750
Graduate Enrollment: 900
Scholarships/Academic: Yes **Athletic:** No **Fin Aid:** Yes
Total Expenses by: Year **In State:** $ 18,580 **Out of State:** $ 18,580
Degrees Conferred: 38 Undergraduates majors; 12 Graduate programs
Programs of Study: Accounting, Arts Administration, Biochemistry, Biology, Business and Economics, Chemistry, Clinical Laboratory Science, Communications Arts, Computer Science, Economics, Elementary Education, Engineering Science, English Languages and Literature, Environmental Science, Finance, Health Science, History, International Studies, Management and Organizational Behavior, Marketing, Mathematics, Molecular Biology, Music, Nutrition, Philosophy

ATHLETIC PROFILE

Conference Affiliation: Northern Illinois and Iowa Conference

Program Profile: We are one of the better Division III programs in the area. Have both varsity (45) and junior varsity (30) schedules. We have an excellent indoor (bubble batting cage) and outdoor (tarp) facilities. We fly to Ft. Meyers Florida for a ten day southern trip.
History: The program began in 1909 as St. Proepius College. The school went to coed and changed named in 1968 to Illinois Benedictine College. We became Benedictine University in 1996.
Achievements: Coach Ostrowski reached his 500th career victory at the age of 48. He is the fifth youngest coach to reach this milestone. His team has won 13 WIIC Conference Titles. He has had 2 players drafted in the last 5 years. They have received 4 NCAA Bids in the last 8 years and have had 2 first team All-Americans in the last 5 years.
Coaching: John Ostrowski , Head Coach, is entering his 27th season as a head coach. He has 571 wins and 473 losses. Dave Swanson - Assistant Coach.
Roster for 1998 team/In State: 80% **Out of State:** 8% **Out of Country:** 12%
Total Number of Varsity/Jr. Varsity: 22 /25 **Percent of Graduation:** 97.5%
Number of Seniors on 1998 Team: 3 **Most Recent Record:** 29 - 15 - 0
Freshmen Receiving Fin Aid/Athletic: 0 **Academic:** 70%
Positions Needed for 1999/2000: All **Number of Spring Games:** 40+
Schedule: Aurora University, Carthage, MacMurray, St. Francis, Wooster College, North Central
Style of Play: The Eagles are well drilled in the fundamentals. They are very aggressive offensively using both steals and hit/run.

Black Hawk College

6600 - 34th Avenue
Moline, IL 61265
Coach: Tim McChesney

NJCAA
Braves/Black, Gold
Phone: (309) 796-1311
Fax: (309) 792-5075

ACADEMIC

Founded: 1946 **Type:** 2 Yr., Public, Coed
Religion: 796-1311 **Campus Housing:** No
Undergraduate Enrollment: 6,335 **Student/Faculty Ratio:** 12:1
Total Expenses by: Year **In State:** $ 1,969+ **Out of State:** $ 7,296+
Degrees Conferred: Associate
Programs of Study: Accounting, Anthropology, Archaeology, Arts, Fine Arts, Automotive Technology, Biology, Biological Science, Broadcasting, Business Administration, Commerce, Management, Commercial Art, Computer Programming, Computer Science, Computer Technology, Earth Science, Economics, Education, Fashion/Design Technology, Real Estate, Practical Nursing

Blackburn College

700 College Avenue
Carlinville, IL 62626
Coach: Mike Neal
Email: mneal@mail-blackburn.edu

NCAA III
Beavers/Scarlet, Black
Phone: (217) 854-3231
Fax: (217) 854-3713

ACADEMIC

Founded: 1837 **Type:** 4 Yr., Private, Liberal Arts, Coed
Religion: Presbyterian **Campus Housing:** Yes
Undergraduate Enrollment: 561 **SAT/ACT/GPA:** 1000/21/3.0-4.0
Student/Faculty Ratio: 15:1 **Male/Female Ratio:** 1:1
Scholarships/Academic: Yes **Athletic:** No **Fin Aid:** Yes
Total Expenses by: Year **In State:** $ 11,120 **Out of State:** $ 11,120
Degrees Conferred: BA, BS in Engineering and Applied Science, Preprofessional Programs
Programs of Study: Accounting, Art, Biology, Business Administration and Management, Chemistry, Computer Science, Elementary Education, Political Science, Psychology, Spanish, Predentistry, Preengineering, Prelaw, Prenursing, Premedicine, Prephysical Therapy, Prevet

ATHLETIC PROFILE

Conference Affiliation: St. Louis Intercollegiate Athletic Conference
Program Profile: Our home field is Blackburn Athletic Field which has natural grass.
History: Our program began in 1983. In 1989, we finished with 18 wins (60% winning percentage), In 1990, we finished in 4th place in the NSCAA Tourn. In 1991, we broke school record with 20 wins.
Roster for 1998 team/In State: 13 **Out of State:** 5 **Out of Country:** 0
Total Number of Varsity/Jr. Varsity: 18 **Percent of Graduation:** 85%
Number of Seniors on 1998 Team: 5 **Most Recent Record:** 10 - 16 - 0
Number of Fall Games: 6 **Number of Spring Games:** 36
Positions Needed for 1999/2000: Pitcher, Outfielder, 1st Base, Middle Infielder
Schedule: Fontbonne, St. Scholastica, McMurray College, Augustana, Westminster, Wabash

Bradley University

1501 w. Bradley Avenue
Peoria, IL 61625
Coach: Dewey Kalmer
Email: ydog@bradley.bradley.edu

NCAA I
Braves/Red, White
Phone: (309) 677-2684
Fax: (309) 677-3626

ACADEMIC

Founded: 1897 **Type:** 4 Yr., Public, Coed
Web-site: http://www.bradley.edu/ **SAT/ACT/GPA:** 25
Student/Faculty Ratio: 15:1 **Male/Female Ratio:** 45:55
Undergraduate Enrollment: 5,000 **Graduate Enrollment:** 1,000
Scholarships/Academic: Varies **Athletic:** 6.5 **Fin Aid:** Varies
Total Expenses by: Year **In State:** $ 18,190 **Out of State:** $ 18,190
Degrees Conferred: BA, BS, MA, MS, MBA, MFA
Programs of Study: Business Administration, Communications and Fine Arts, Educational and Sciences, Engineering and Technology, Liberal Arts and Sciences

ATHLETIC PROFILE

Conference Affiliation: Missouri Valley Conference
Program Profile: Our program was ranked in the top 75 in the nation by collegiate baseball. We play in the MVC. We were ranked 7th in conference in the nation. Pete Vonachen Shelium at Meinou Field is one of the top facilities in the midwest,. It seats 6,200. It is a natural grass, lighted and also used by the St. Louis Cardinals Class A affiliation. Our Fall season is from September 1st to October 5th. Our Spring season is from February 22th to May 30th.
History: Our baseball program is the oldest sport in Bradley. Our first season was in 1898. Has had 72 winning seasons in its 97 years history & 2 appearances in the College World Series.
Achievements: Bradley has had 95 players signed professional contracts with 7 players reaching the Major Leagues. 3 first round picks since 1982; 1984 Olympic Team Member - Mike Dunne.
Coaching: Dewey Kalmer, Head Coach, graduated from Quincy College in 1966. He has 29 years of college coaching experience of which 18 were at BU. He is the all-time winningest coach at Bradley. 54 draft picks at Bradley; 7 Major League; top 30 active winningest coaches; top 50 winningest All-time Division coaches; .564 career winning percentage. John Young, Assistant Coach, graduated from Michigan in 1982. He is entering his 15th year in Division I. We have had 12 Major League players. Both of our coaches played professional baseball.
Style of Play: Bradley concentrates its recruiting efforts on pitching and normally relies on its pitching staff. Usually a solid defense club, we play a straight forward type of game on offense.

Carl Sandburg College

2232 South Lake Storey Road
Galesburg, IL 61401
Coach: Mike Bailey
Email: mbailey@csu.cc.il.us

NCAA I
Chargers/Red, White, Blue
Phone: (309) 341-5242
Fax: (309) 344-3526

ACADEMIC

Founded: 1967 **Type:** 2 Yr., Public, Coed
Web-site: htt://www.csu.edu **Campus Housing:** Yes
Student/Faculty Ratio: 12:1 **Male/Female Ratio:** ?
Undergraduate Enrollment: 3,200 **Graduate Enrollment:** 1,500
Scholarships/Academic: No **Athletic:** No **Fin Aid:** Yes
Total Expenses by: Year **In State:** $ 1,500 **Out of State:** $ 5,200
Programs of Study: Accounting, Agricultural, Automtotive, Business, Child Development, Cosmetology, Criminal Justice, Data Processing, Drafting/Design, Electrical/Electronics Technology, Fashion Merchadising, Law Enforcement, Liberal Arts, Marketing, Nursing, Office Management, Practical Nursing, Radiological Technology, Real Estate

ATHLETIC PROFILE

Program Profile: Our baseball field was rebuilt in the Fall of 1996 . It has a grass surface with 330' down lines, 385' power alleys, 400' center field and hitting tunnels. It seats 1,000 and has indoor and outdoor cages. Our playing season is fromm March through May (Fall schedule).
Achievements: Our most recent player drafted is Jason Hardebeck. He was drafted by the Pirates.
Coaching: Mike Bailey, Head Coach, compiled a record of 13-19 on his first year. He played Division I at Northern Iowa. Kent Brown , Assistant Coach, played Division I at Austin Peay class "A" -Padres Organization.
Roster for 1998 team/In State: 19 **Out of State:** 4 **Out of Country:** 0
Total Number of Varsity/Jr. Varsity: 23/ **Percent of Graduation:** 75%
Number of Seniors on 1998 Team: 14 **Most Recent Record:** 13- 19 - 0
Freshmen Receiving Fin Aid/Athletic: 8 **Academic:** ?
Number of Fall Games: 18 **Number of Spring Games:** 48
Positions Needed for 1999/2000: Pitcher, Outfielder
Schedule: Muscatine, Southeastern, Blackhawk, Kankakee, Lake Couty, Kishwaukee
Style of Play: Hard - trying to achieve consistency.

Chicago State University

9501 S King Dr. **NCAA I**
Chicago, IL 60628 **Cougars/White, Green**
Coach: Kevin McCray **Phone: (773) 995-3655**
Fax: (773) 995-3656

ACADEMIC

Founded: 1867 **Type:** 4 Yr., Public, Coed
SAT/ACT/GPA: 16 **Campus Housing:** Yes
Student/Faculty Ratio: 9:1 **Male/Female Ratio:** 5:1
Undergraduate Enrollment: 9,412 **Graduate Enrollment:** 2,436
Scholarships/Academic: Yes **Athletic:** Yes **Fin Aid:** Yes
Total Expenses by: Year **In State:** $ 6,508 **Out of State:** $ 8,476
Degrees Conferred: BA, BS, MA, MS, MED
Programs of Study: Accounting, Art, Banking/Finance, Biochemistry, Biological Science, Broadcasting, Business, Chemistry, Computer, Criminal Justice, Data Processing, Dietetics, Early Childhood Education, English, Geography, History, Hotel/Restaurant Management, Information Science, Management, Marketing, Mathematics, Medical, Music, Nursing, Occupation, Political Science, Psychology, Social Science, Preprofessional Programs

ATHLETIC PROFILE

Conference Affiliation: Mid-Continent Conference
Achievements: We are among the best defensive teams in nation and 6th in 1996.
Coaching: Kevin McCray, Head Coach, is in his seventh season. He played for Saint Xavier College in 1979 (fourth in Nation, NAIA).
Style of Play: We rely on fastball pitching and air tight defense. We manufacture runs on offense with speed, bunting, place hitting.

College of DuPage

22nd Street and Lambert Road
Glen Ellyn, IL 60137
Coach: Dan Kusinski

NJCAA
Chaparrals/Green, Gold
Phone: (630) 942-2734
Fax: (630) 858-5404

ACADEMIC

Founded: 1967
Type: 2 Yr., Public, Coed
Student/Faculty Ratio: 20:1
Male/Female Ratio: 41:59
Undergraduate Enrollment: 33,920
Graduate Enrollment: None
Scholarships/Academic: No **Athletic:** Yes **Fin Aid:** Yes
Total Expenses by: Year **In State:** $ 1,150 **Out of State:** $ 4,700
Degrees Conferred: AA, AS, AAS, AGS
Programs of Study: Accounting, Architectural, Automotive Technology, Business, Commercial Art, Communications, Computer, Corrections, Criminal, Culinary Arts, Drafting/Design, Drug/Alcohol/Substance Abuse Counseling, Medical, Fashion, Film, Video, Fire Science, Occupational Therapy, Office Management, Photography, Plastics, Radio/Television, Therapy

ATHLETIC PROFILE

Conference Affiliation: North Central Community College Conference
Program Profile: Over 100 athletes "tryout" for our squad with approximately 25 making the team. Our season begins in Arizona during our Spring Break. We fly (since 1985) with the school paying the majority of the costs. We have a 48 game season plus playoffs. The field is state of the art and has an underground sprinkler system.
History: Baseball started the first Spring in 1968. We have a winning record against every school in Illinois except one (44-1). 3 coaches total at DuPage; average 48 games per year.
Achievements: 1992 and 1993 NJCAA District "D" Coach of the Year. 1992 and 1993 ABCA Diamond Coach of the Year. 1992 Pitch and Hit Club of Chicago College Coach of the Year. 1986 and 1990 Conference Champs, 4 All-Americans. 1979 and 1992 5 players drafted, 2 in 1993.

College of Lake County

19351 West Washington Street
Grayslake, IL 60030
Coach: Gene Hanson

NJCAA
Lancers/Navy, Silver
Phone: (847) 543-2046
Fax: (847) 223-5691

ACADEMIC

Founded: 1967
Type: 2 Yr., Jr. College, Coed
Student/Faculty Ratio: 19:1
Male/Female Ratio: 42:58
Undergraduate Enrollment: 15,500
Graduate Enrollment: None
Scholarships/Academic: No **Athletic:** No **Fin Aid:** Yes
Total Expenses by: Year **In State:** $ 1,200 **Out of State:** $ 6,400
Degrees Conferred: Associate
Programs of Study: Accounting, Architectural, Automtoive, Business, Computer, Construction, Criminal Justice, Drafting/Design, Human Services, Industrial Administration, Industrial/Heavy Equipment Maintenance, Landscape, Library Science, Machine/Tool Technology, Marketing, Math

Concordia University

7400 Augusta Street
River Forest, IL 60305
Coach: Mike Palmer

NCAA III
Cougars/Maroon, Gold
Phone: (708) 209-3116
Fax: (708) 209-3176

ACADEMIC

Founded: 1864
Type: 4 Yr., Private, Coed
SAT/ACT/GPA:/22avg
Campus Housing: Yes
Student/Faculty Ratio: 16:1
Male/Female Ratio: 33:67
Undergraduate Enrollment: 1,300
Graduate Enrollment: 950
Scholarships/Academic: No **Athletic:** Yes **Fin Aid:** Yes
Total Expenses by: Year **In State:** $ 14,100 **Out of State:** $ 14,100
Degrees Conferred: BA, MA
Programs of Study: Biological Science, Business, Chemistry, Communications, Computer, Early Childhood Education, Earth Science, English, Geography, History, Management, Mathematics, Music, Nursing, Philosophy, Physical Fitness/Movement, Political Science, Preprofessional Programs, Psychology, Religion, Science Education, Secondary Education, Social Science

ATHLETIC PROFILE

Conference Affiliation: Northern Illinois Intercollegiate
Program Profile: We started with a new staff and a new direction in 1994. Our facility had $20,000 done in improvements. NIIC is a very competitive NCAA Division III program. It is a very disciplined program with professional instruction.
Achievements: In 1973 Lefty pitcher Steve Dorsch was first in the NCAA and the NAIA nationally with a .27 ERA. He had a 5-3 record including two 1-0 losses. Steve signed a pro contract and played with Pittsburg and Detroit in the minors.
Style of Play: Aggressive - fast - smart pitching.

Eastern Illinois University

Lantz Gym
Charleston, IL 61920-3099
Coach: Jim Schmitz
NCAA I
Panthers/Royal, Grey
Phone: (217) 581-2522
Fax: (217) 581-7001

ACADEMIC

Founded: 1895
Type: 4 Yr., Public, Liberal Arts, Coed
Religion: Non-Affiliated
Campus Housing: Yes
Web-site: http://www.eiu.edu/
SAT/ACT/GPA: 860/18
Student/Faculty Ratio: 18:1
Male/Female Ratio: 45:55
Undergraduate Enrollment: 9,000
Graduate Enrollment: 1,500
Scholarships/Academic: Yes **Athletic:** Yes **Fin Aid:** Yes
Total Expenses by: Year **In State:** $ 6,339 **Out of State:** $ 10,443
Degrees Conferred: BA, BS, BM, BSR, BSEd, MA, MS, MBA
Programs of Study: Accounting, Administrative Information Systems, African-Ameican Studies, Art, Biological Studies, Botany, Business Education, Career Occupations, Chemistry, Communication Disorders and Sciences, Computer Management

ATHLETIC PROFILE

Conference Affiliation: Ohio Valley Conference
Achievements: 1995 - won Mid-Continent Conference Division Champions; 4 players currently playing professionally.
Coaching: Jim Schmitz, Head Coach, is in his fifth year at Eastern Illinois. He was head coach at University of Cincinnati and spent four years coaching in the SEC.
Style of Play: Short game; steal, hit and run, move men over. Style is suited to scoring runs throughout the game.

Elgin Community College

1700 Spartan Drive
Elgin, IL 60123
Coach: Jay Bayler

NJCAA
Spartans/Royal, White
Phone: (847) 697-1000
Fax: (708) 888-7995

ACADEMIC

Founded: 1949
Type: 2 Yr., Jr. College, Coed
Student/Faculty Ratio: 21:1
Male/Female Ratio: 44:56
Undergraduate Enrollment: 9,500
Graduate Enrollment: None
Scholarships/Academic: No **Athletic:** Yes **Fin Aid:** Yes
Total Expenses by: Year **In State:** $ 1,300 **Out of State:** $ 5,000
Degrees Conferred: Associate
Programs of Study: Accounting, Art, Automotive, Banking/Finance, Business, Computer, Criminal Justice, Dental, Drafting/Design, Engineering, Fire Science, Food services, Gerontology, Graphic Arts, Horticulture, Human Services, Industrial Administration, Law, Mechanical/Tool Technology, Marketing, Materials, Nursing, Paralegal, Real Estate

ATHLETIC PROFILE

Conference Affiliation: Skyway Conference

Elmhurst College

190 S. Prospect Ave
Elmhurst, IL 60126-3296
Coach: Clark Jones

NCAA III
Bluejays/Blue, White
Phone: (630) 617-3143
Fax: (630) 617-3726

ACADEMIC

Founded: 1871
Type: 4 Yr., Private, Coed
SAT/ACT/GPA: 18avg
Campus Housing: Yes
Student/Faculty Ratio: 15:1
Male/Female Ratio: 1:2
Undergraduate Enrollment: 2,800
Graduate Enrollment: None
Scholarships/Academic: No **Athletic:** Yes **Fin Aid:** Yes
Total Expenses by: Year **In State:** $ 14,600 **Out of State:** $ 14,600
Degrees Conferred: BA, BS
Programs of Study: Art, Biology, Business and Economics, Chemistry, Communications Arts and Science, Computer Science and Information Systems, Education, English, Foreign Languages and Literature, Geography and Environmental Planning, History, Mathematics, Music, Nursing, Philosophy, Physical Education, Physics, Political Science, Psychology, Sociology, Theology and Religion, Urban Studies, Preprofessional Programs

ATHLETIC PROFILE

Conference Affiliation: College Conference of Illinois and Wisconsin
Program Profile: We have an indoor hitting cage. There is a practice area in our Physical Education Center. Butterfield Park is our home field & has been renovated with natural grass. Our playing season includes a Fall practice & a Spring competition starting in March & ending in May.
History: Baseball started the first Spring in 1968. We have a winning record against every school in Illinois except one (44-1). 3 coaches total at DuPage; average 48 games per year, awards , and 71 All-CCIW 2nd team honorees since 1975.
Achievements: 1997:CCIW Champion, CCIW Coach of the Year, 2 All-CCIW 1st team and 4 All-CCIW 2nd team honorees, 2 ABCA All-Central Region Honorees, 2 COSIDA/GTE Academic College Division All-District V honorees.
Coaching: Clark Jones, Head Coach, coached Ohio to a Mid-America Conference Championship in 1991. He has a BS in Pysical Education and a MA in Athletic Administration. He has 2 years HS

experience and 5 years college experience. Joe Niezoga, Assistant Coach, has 20+ years experience in HS and 6 years in college. Lance Marshall, Assistant Coach, has 3 years college experience.
Style of Play: Coach Jones favors speed on offense and defense.

Eureka College

300 E College Avenue
Eureka, IL 61530
Coach: Mike Walling

NCAA III
Red Devils/Maroon, Gold
Phone: (309) 467-6376
Fax: (309) 467-6402

ACADEMIC

Founded: 1855
Type: 4 Yr., Private, Coed
SAT/ACT/GPA: 21avg
Campus Housing: Yes
Student/Faculty Ratio: 12:1
Male/Female Ratio: 51:49
Undergraduate Enrollment: 500
Graduate Enrollment: None
Scholarships/Academic: No **Athletic:** Yes **Fin Aid:** Yes
Total Expenses by: Year **In State:** $ 16,000 **Out of State:** $ 16,000
Degrees Conferred: BA, BS
Programs of Study: Accounting, Biological, Business, Chemistry, Communications, Computer, Dramatics Arts, Economics, Education, English, Fine Arts, History, Management, Mathematics, Medical Music, Philosophy, Physical Education, Physical Science, Psychology, Religion, Science Education, Social Science, Speech

ATHLETIC PROFILE

Conference Affiliation: Northern Illinnois and Iowa Conference (NIIC)
Program Profile: We have a young program with a beautiful new all grass field that has in-ground watering and drainage systems.
History: Our program began in 1990-1991. All our games were played on the road while our new facility was being built. Slowly but surely the program is becoming competititve and consistent with stability in the coaching staff.
Achievements: On our third yeaar, we were invited to compete in the NAIA District. We had 20 playoffs even though they had a su.500 record. In 1996-1997, Jr. second baseman John DeCiceo was named NIIC All-Conference and second team All-Region.
Coaching: Mike Walling, Head Coach, started in 1996. His first year at Eureka he was head coach. He was an assistant coach at another school for four years. He was All-Conference and All-District Pitcher for Olivet Nazarene University. He was drafted by Atlanta Braves after Jr. Year and released two years later in "A" ball.
Style of Play: Aggressive on defense. Like to bunt and run, hit and run. Like to manufacture runs not wait for the three run and home runs.

Greenville College

315 E College Avenue
Greenville, IL 62246
Coach: Lynn Carlson

NCAA III
Panthers/Orange, Black
Phone: (618) 664-2800x4372
Fax: (618) 664-1060

ACADEMIC

Founded: 1892
Type: 4 Yr., Private, Liberal Arts, Coed
Religion: Free Methodist
Campus Housing: Yes
Web-site: http://www.greenville.edu/
Undergraduate Enrollment: 1,000
Student/Faculty Ratio: 17:1
Male/Female Ratio: 46:54
Scholarships/Academic: Yes **Athletic:** No **Fin Aid:** Yes
Total Expenses by: Year **In State:** $ 16,700 **Out of State:** $ 14,900

Degrees Conferred: BA, BS
Programs of Study: Education, Christian Contemporary Music, Premed, Business, Marketing, Management Information Systems, Computers, History, Political Science, Psychology, Sociology, Social Work, Etc.

ATHLETIC PROFILE

Conference Affiliation: St. Louis Intercollegiate Athletic Conference
Program Profile: Our field is R.E. Smith Field. We have an Indoor facility for hitting, infield, ct. and recreation center. We have an outstanding training program.
History: Intercollegiate baseball began in 1947. Twelve former Panthers have played professionally. We have a strong winning tradition.
Achievements: 4 past NAIA and NCAA District Coach of the Year winners in 1992, 1989, 1988, and 1984; 10 All-Americans; 5 District Champions; 8 NCAA World Series Appearances; 1995 NAIA playoff appearances.
Coaching: Lynn Carlson, Head Coach, is a former professional baseball player with the Pittsburgh Pirates Organization and former high school coach.
Style of Play: Aggressive, .340+ batting average; 4 players with a green light on bases, solid defense.

Highland Community College

2998 West Pearl City Road
Freeport, IL 61032
Coach: TBA

NJCAA
Cougars/Orange, White, Black
Phone: (815) 235-6121
Fax: (815) 235-6130

ACADEMIC

Founded: 1962
Type: 2 Yr., Jr. College, Coed
Web-site: http://www.highland.cc.ks.us
SAT/ACT/GPA: None
Student/Faculty Ratio: 18:1
Male/Female Ratio: 35:65
Undergraduate Enrollment: 2,825
Graduate Enrollment: None
Scholarships/Academic: No **Athletic:** Yes **Fin Aid:** Yes
Total Expenses by: Year **In State:** $ 1,100 **Out of State:** $ 3,700
Degrees Conferred: Associate
Programs of Study: Accounting, Agriculture, Arts, Automotive, Business, Chemistry, Computer, Criminal Justice, Drafting/Design, Education, Electrical/Electronics, Engineering, Food services, General Engineering, Food Services, General Engineering, Geology, History, Hospitality Service, Hotel/Restaurant Management, Human Services, Liberal Arts, Marketing, Math, Nursing, Physical Science, Political Science, Psychology, Real Estate, Social Science, Theatre

ATHLETIC PROFILE

Conference Affiliation: Arrowhead Conference
Program Profile: Our team plays a Spring season with a few games in the Fall.
History: The baseball program started in the early 1960's and continued through 1982. It was dropped due to funding and started in 1994.

Illinois Central College

One College Drive
East Peoria, IL 61635
Coach: Guy Goodman

NJCAA
Cougars/Royal Blue, Gold
Phone: (309) 694-5427
Fax: (309) 694-5579

ACADEMIC

Founded: 1966
Type: 2 Yr., Public, Coed
Religion: Non-Affiliated
Campus Housing: Yes

Student/Faculty Ratio: 20:1 **Male/Female Ratio:** Unknown
Undergraduate Enrollment: 11,750 **Graduate Enrollment:** None
Scholarships/Academic: Yes **Athletic:** Yes **Fin Aid:** Yes
Total Expenses by: Year **In State:** $ 1,500 **Out of State:** $ 4,000
Degrees Conferred: AA, AS
Programs of Study: Accounting, Agriculture, Architecture, Automotive, Banking/Finance, Business, Dental, Electrical/Electronics, Engineering, Fire, Graphic Arts, Health Services, Horticulture, Interior Design, Law, Liberal Arts, Library Science, Manufacturing, Marketing, Mechanical, Medical, Nursing, Occupational/Physical Therapy, Real Estate, Radiological, Respiratory, Robotics, Science

ATHLETIC PROFILE

Conference Affiliation: CCCI
Program Profile: Cougar Field has natural turf, 330 down each line, 387 down power alleys and 382 in center. It has a seating capacity of 500 people. It has indoor facilities.
History: We began in 1981 and were quasi-intramural for a number of years. Recently, (last 9) we have generally improved to be respectable. We won or shared conference titles in 3 of the last 4 years. In 1991, we awarded our first basefball scholarships.
Achievements: Conference title in 1992; shared title in 1994; All-Americans - Tony Hattan (Pitcher in 1994). Drafted players - Jim Thome (Cleveland Indians), now in the majors. Mark Smith - All-American in 1996.

Illinois College

1101 West College Avenue
Jacksonville, IL 62650
Coach: Ed Tuck

NCAA III
Blueboys/Blue, White
Phone: (217) 245-3381
Fax: (217) 245-3389

ACADEMIC

Founded: 1829 **Type:** 4 Yr., Private, Liberal Arts, Coed
Religion: Presbyterian and Church of Christ **Campus Housing:** Yes
Web-site: http://www.ic.edu/ **SAT/ACT/GPA:** 930/20
Student/Faculty Ratio: 15:1 **Male/Female Ratio:** 45:55
Undergraduate Enrollment: 950 **Graduate Enrollment:** None
Scholarships/Academic: Yes **Athletic:** No **Fin Aid:** Yes
Total Expenses by: Year **In State:** $ 13,700 **Out of State:** $ 13,700
Degrees Conferred: BA, BS
Programs of Study: 26 Majors plus 5 Preprofessional Programs including Humanities, Natural Science, and Social Science

ATHLETIC PROFILE

Conference Affiliation: Midwest Athletic Conference
Program Profile: The baseball program at Illinois College provides intercollegiate competition at the NCAA Division III level each Spring for a roster of approximately 26 players. The Blueboys perennially challenge for top honors in the competitive South Division of the Midwest Conference and have qualified for the league's championship playoffs the past three seasons (1994, 1995 and 1996). The team captured the Midwest Conference championship in 1995 and hosted the league tournaments in 1996. The typical season schedules is 15 games against the five other South Division teams and approximately 15 non-conference games. Each March, the team travels to Florida to compete in the Gene Cusic College Classic at Ft. Myers, FL.
History: Baseball has been a part of the intercollegiate athletic program at Illinois College for most of the 20th century. Few colleges and universities in Illinois have sponsored baseball teams longer than Illinois College. Prior to entering the Midwest Conference in 1984. Illinois College competed in the Prairie College Conference, the College Athletic Conference and the Little 19 Conference.

Illinois Institute of Technology

3040 S. Wabash
Chicago, IL 60616
Coach: Jim Darrah

NAIA
Scarlet Hawks/Scarlet, Grey
Phone: (312) 567-3298
Fax: (312) 567-7133

ACADEMIC

Founded: 1890
Type: 4 Yr., Private, Coed
SAT/ACT/GPA: 1100avg/25avg
Campus Housing: Yes
Student/Faculty Ratio: 12:1
Male/Female Ratio: 76:24
Undergraduate Enrollment: 2,550
Graduate Enrollment: 4,600
Scholarships/Academic: No **Athletic:** Yes **Fin Aid:** Yes
Total Expenses by: Year **In State:** $ 20,200 **Out of State:** $ 20,200
Degrees Conferred: BA, BS, MBA, MS, JD
Programs of Study: Aeronautical Engineering, Architecture, Chemical Engineering, Chemistry, Civil Engineering, Computer Engineering, Computer Scinece, Electrical Engineering, Civil Engineering, Computer Engineering, Computer Science, Electrical Engineering, Mathematics, Mechanical Engineering, Physics

ATHLETIC PROFILE

Conference Affiliation: Chicagoland Collegiate Athletic Conference
Program Profile: We have a Spring season and a Fall off-season. Most of our competition is local to Chicago except for our Spring break trip to Florida. We have a natural grass field . New grandstands and a press box were completed in 1996.
Achievements: Coach Darrah received Coach of the Year for the CCAC in 1992 and 1996. Jim Cannon received 1st team All-American and Academic All-American Honors in 1997.
Coaching: Jim Darrah, Head Coach, received Coach of the Year for the CCAC in 1992 and 1996. He has a won-lost record of 344-268 in 19 seasons at IIT. Rollie Wozniak, Assistant Coach. Wayne Porod, Assistant Coach.

Illinois State University

Campus Box 7130
Normal, IL 61790-7130
Coach: Jeff Stewart

NCAA I
Redbirds/Red, White
Phone: (309) 438-5151
Fax: (309) 438-3932

ACADEMIC

Founded: 1857
Type: 4 Yr., Public, Coed
Religion: Non-Affiliated
Campus Housing: Yes
Web-site: http://www.infosys.ilstu.edu/redbirds
SAT/ACT/GPA: NCAA Requirements/
Undergraduate Enrollment: 16,800
Graduate Enrollment: 2,700
Scholarships/Academic: Yes **Athletic:** Yes **Fin Aid:** Yes
Total Expenses by: Year **In State:** $ 8,225 **Out of State:** $ 13,925
Degrees Conferred: Associate
Programs of Study: Education, Biological Sciences, Communications, Psychology, Finance, Industrial Technology, Marketing, Mathematics, Music, Social Science, Social Work, Speech Pathology, Etc..

ATHLETIC PROFILE

Estimated Number of Baseball Scholarships: 11.7
Conference Affiliation: Missouri Valley Conference
Program Profile: We have a beautiful park with a grass playing field and newly remodeled hitting background in center. Our training facility is state of the art and it houses one of the best strength and conditioning programs in the country.

History: Our program started in 1890. Since then, Illinois State has compiled a 1,245-1,145-20 overall record and a 649-604-14 record since switching to Division I in 1971.
Achievements: The Illinois State baseball program has turned out 66 professionals during its storied history and this level of excellence has never been more evident than under the tenure of Jeff Stewart. In Stewart's ten seasons, 21 prospects have gone pro.
Coaching: Jeff Stewart, Head Coach, started at Illinois State in 1989 after serving as an assistant coach at Kansas State for two years and Mississippi State for two years. His overall coaching record is 404-38-1 and his record at ISU is 263-299. Tim Johnson - Assistant Coach.
Total Number of Varsity/Jr. Varsity: 33
Percent of Graduation: 85%
Number of Seniors on 1998 Team: 9
Number of Sophomores on 1998 Team: 9
Most Recent Record: 32 - 27 - 0
Baseball Camp Dates: 54
Positions Needed for 1999/2000: Pitcher, Catcher, Centerfield
Schedule: Wichita State, Illinois, Florida International, Northern Iowa, Seton Hall, Cincinnati
Style of Play: We have a team that is able to score a lot of runs in a hurry.

Illinois Valley Community College

815 N Orlando Smith Ave
Oglesby, IL 61348-9692
Coach: Bob Koopman

NJCAA
Apaches/Purple, Grey, Black
Phone: (815) 224-2720x505
Fax: (815) 224-3033

ACADEMIC

Founded: 1923
Type: 2 Yr., Jr. College, Coed
Student/Faculty Ratio: 22:1
Male/Female Ratio: Unknown
Undergraduate Enrollment: 4,281
Graduate Enrollment: None
Scholarships/Academic: Yes
Athletic: No
Fin Aid: Yes
Total Expenses by: Year
In State: $ 1,800
Out of State: $ 1,800
Degrees Conferred: AA, AS, AAS
Programs of Study: Art, Biology, Chemistry, Communications, Computer Scinece, Criminal justice, Dentistry, Education, Engineering, English, Foreign Languages, History, Law, Mathematics, Music, Philosophy, Political Science, Sociology, Theatre, Etc..

ATHLETIC PROFILE

Conference Affiliation: North Central Community College Conference (N4C)
Program Profile: IVCC's season begins with a practice season in the Fall. Practice begins in the gymnasium in January and the outdoor season begins in March. It runs through the beginning of May. IVCC has a refurbished grass field..
History: The IVCC baseball program had its best season in a decade in 1995 with a 18-12 record. The team's record dropped in 1996 to a record of 14-22.
Achievements: Todd Kein was second team All-Region IV. Kein received a baseball scholarship to the University of Illinois at Chicago.

Illinois Wesleyan University

Box 2900
Bloomington, IL 61702-2900
Coach: Dennis Martel

NCAA III
Titans/Green, White
Phone: (309) 556-3335
Fax: (309) 556-3484

ACADEMIC

Founded: 1850
Type: 4 Yr., Private, Liberal Arts, Coed
Religion: Methodist
Campus Housing: Yes
Web-site: http://www.iwu.edu/
SAT/ACT/GPA: 1050/23
Student/Faculty Ratio: 12:1
Male/Female Ratio: 46:54
Undergraduate Enrollment: 1,900
Graduate Enrollment: N/A

Scholarships/Academic: Yes **Athletic:** No **Fin Aid:** Yes
Total Expenses by: Year **In State:** $ 23,500 **Out of State:** $ 23,500
Degrees Conferred: BA, BS, BFA, BSCompSci
Programs of Study: Natural Sciences, Social Sciences, Preprofessional Sciences, Business, Fine Arts, Nursing

ATHLETIC PROFILE

Conference Affiliation: College Conference of illinois and Wisconsin
History: Since 1943 IWU teams have won 804 games with 630 losses. We are in the College Conference of Illinois and Wisconsin and have played since 1948. IWU is 447-283-1 for a .612 winning percentage with 17 championships and 12 second place finishes.

John A. Logan Community College

Baseball Office
Carterville, IL 62918
Coach: Jerry Halstead

NJCAA
Volunteers/Blue, Grey
Phone: (618) 985-3741
Fax: (618) 985-6610

ACADEMIC

Founded: 1967
Type: 2 Yr., Jr. College, Coed
Student/Faculty Ratio: 28:1
Male/Female Ratio: Unknown
Undergraduate Enrollment: 5,000
Graduate Enrollment: None
Scholarships/Academic: No **Athletic:** Yes **Fin Aid:** Yes
Total Expenses by: Year **In State:** $ 4,000 **Out of State:** $ 6,000
Degrees Conferred: Associate
Programs of Study: Accounting, Agricultural Science, Automtoive, banking/Finance, Criminal

ATHLETIC PROFILE

Conference Affiliation: Great Rivers Athletic Conference
Program Profile: We were ranked Top 10 from 1991 to1995 . We were third in the JUCO World Series of 1992. We play a 76 game schedule (20 Fall and 56 Spring) includingaa ten-day trip to Florida. We have outstanding facilities: double-wide artificial turf hitting cages, in-ground watering system, concrete dugouts, inning-by-inning scoreboard and drop-down cages in doors.
History: We began in 1967. We have won conference three years in a row 1992 to 1994. Top CC Player drafted in 1994 (John Ambrose-RHP) second round White Sox; Sectional Champs 1989, 1990, 1991, 1992, 1993, 1994, 1995.
Achievements: 5 All-Americans last 5 years; Coach of the Year 1992: National by Louisville Slugger and Diamond Sports; Conference Coach of the Year 1989, 1991 - 1993; Won 3 conference titles in a row, 4 of last 5; 10 drafted in the last 10 years.
Coaching: Jerry Halstead - Head Coach.
Style of Play: Very aggressive, hit and run, steal. Good pitching and defense.

John Wood Community College

150 South 48th Street
Quincy, IL 62301
Coach: Greg Wathen

NJCAA
Blazers/Black, Kelly
Phone: (217) 224-6500
Fax: (217) 224-4208

ACADEMIC

Founded: 1974
Type: 2 Yr., Jr. College, Coed
Student/Faculty Ratio: 20:1
Male/Female Ratio: 46:54
Scholarships/Academic: Yes **Athletic:** Yes **Fin Aid:** Yes
Total Expenses by: Year **In State:** $ 1,950+ **Out of State:** $ 1,950+
Degrees Conferred: Associates

Programs of Study: Accounting, Agricultural Business, Agricultural Science, Biology, Biological Science, Business Administration, Commerce, Management, Communications, Equipment Technology, Computer Information Systems, Computer Science, Cosmetology, Drafting/Design, Economics, Education, Fire Science, Food Services, French, German, Philosophy, Physical Education, Fire Science, Food Services, French, German, Philosophy, Physical Education

ATHLETIC PROFILE

Estimated Number of Baseball Scholarships: 9
Conference Affiliation: Collegiate Conference of Central Illinois
Program Profile: We have a year-round program with a 10 week Fall season and a Spring trip to Mississippi and Florida. We play half of our home schedule in a former minor league park.
History: Our first season was in 1993. We had a .500 record from our second year on.
Achievements: Wathen was 1994 Region 24/Division III Coach of the Year. He got All-American in both 1996 and 1997 and is currently catching in Mets Farm System.
Coaching: Greg Wathen, Head Coach, was Region and Division III Coach of the Year in 1994. He compiled a record of 101-126 in five years. Dave Simon - Assistant Coach.
Roster for 1998 team/In State: 18 **Out of State:** 6 **Out of Country:** 0
Total Number of Varsity/Jr. Varsity: 24 **Most Recent Record:** 20 - 22 - 0
Number of Seniors on 1998 Team: 6 **Number of Sophomores on 1998 Team:**
Freshmen Receiving Fin Aid/Athletic: 0 **Academic:** 9
Number of Fall Games: 28 **Number of Spring Games:** 50-60
Positions Needed for 1999/2000: Catcher, 1st, 2nd and 3rd Base, CF, Pitcher
Style of Play: Aggressive; running and thinking.

Joliet Junior College

1215 Houbolt Road
Joliet, IL 60431
Coach: Wayne King

NJCAA
Wolves/Purple, White
Phone: (815) 729-9020
Fax: (815) 280-6623

ACADEMIC

Founded: 1809 **Type:** 2 Yr., Jr. College, Coed
Student/Faculty Ratio: 20:1 **Male/Female Ratio:** Unknown
Undergraduate Enrollment: 10,000 **Graduate Enrollment:** None
Scholarships/Academic: Yes **Athletic: No** **Fin Aid: Yes**
Total Expenses by: Cr-Hr **In State:** $ 42/cr-hr **Out of State:** $ 42/cr-hr
Degrees Conferred: Associate
Programs of Study: Accounting, Agricultural Business, Agricultural Education, Art, Fine Arts, business Administration, Commerce, Management, Two-year Degrees

ATHLETIC PROFILE

Conference Affiliation: North Central Community College Conference
Program Profile: Best facility in the Northern Il for Junior Colleges. The playing surface at Joliet Junior College is natural surface. The Dimensions are 330 down left field line, 296 down right field line, 400 to center field and 375 to both power alleys.
History: Joliet Junior College is the nation's oldest two-year academic institution. We began in 1908. We started playing baseball in the early 1940s. We got National Champs Division III in1994. We were Runner-Up in 1995 and 3rd Place World Series in 1997.
Achievements: 1994 National Coach of the Year; 1993 to the present has 12 All-Americans.
Coaching: Wayne King, Head Coach, has compiled in eleven years of coaching a career record of 365-199. He was assistant coach for six years at Ohio University. Mark Smith, Pitching Coach, is entering his sixth year as an assistant coach.
Style of Play: Run the bases. Try to put the pressure on the defense.

Judson College

1151 N State Street
Elgin, IL 60123
Coach: Elliott Anderson

NAIA
Eagles/Blue, White
Phone: (847) 695-2500x2306
Fax: (847) 695-9252

ACADEMIC

Founded: 1963
Type: 4 Yr., Private, Liberal Arts, Coed
Religion: Baptist
Campus Housing: Yes
Web-site: Not Available
SAT/ACT/GPA: 860/18/2.0
Student/Faculty Ratio: 16:1
Male/Female Ratio: 45:55
Undergraduate Enrollment: 900
Graduate Enrollment: None
Scholarships/Academic: Yes **Athletic:** Yes **Fin Aid:** Yes
Total Expenses by: Year **In State:** $ 16,700 **Out of State:** $ 16,700
Degrees Conferred: BA, BS
Programs of Study: Accounting, Anthropology, Arts, Biblical Studies, Biology, Business and Management, Chemistry, Communications, Computer Information Systems, Computer Sciences, Education, Elementary Education, History, Linguistic, Literature, Mathematics, Philosophy, Physical Education, Physical Science, Preprofessional Programs, Psychology, Religion, Science, Social Science, Sociology, Speech, Theatre

ATHLETIC PROFILE

Conference Affiliation: Chicagoland Collegiate Athletic Conference (CCAC)
Program Profile: We are rebuilding a program which has only 2 seniors and 2 juniors. We have a respectable field. New dirt, sod, and drainage were added in 1995. We have a natural, beautiful setting overview of the Fox River and its sorroundings. We are a Chrisitian college that is serious about its faith and discipline.
History: Our program began in the 1970's. We used to be in the Northern Illinois Intercollegiate Conference. We only won 20 games one time. In the last fifteen years, we had 10 win season a few times. We are looking to truly become a baseball school within five years.
Achievements: First year coach - as a player - 3-time captain, 1 MVP, 2 All-District with a record of 85-89; .353 career BA.
Coaching: Elliott Anderson - Head Coach. John Hamann - Third Base Coach. Kevin Rahn - Outfielder Coach. Chris Wills - Strength and Conditioning Coach. Joey Flores - First Base Coach.
Style of Play: We are very young and inexperienced. We will be fundamentally sound and lose on talent base instead of mental and physical errors. We are rebuilding quickly and look to compete seriously in a year or two.

Kankakee Community College

Box 888 River Rd
Kankakee, IL 60901
Coach: Bruce Philips

NJCAA
Cavaliers/Navy, Red, White
Phone: (815) 933-0234
Fax: (815) 933-0217

ACADEMIC

Founded: 1966
Type: 2 Yr., Public, Jr. College, Coed
Student/Faculty Ratio: 18:1
Male/Female Ratio: 33:67
Undergraduate Enrollment: 3,400
Graduate Enrollment: None
Scholarships/Academic: Yes **Athletic:** Yes **Fin Aid:** Yes
Total Expenses by: Hour **In State:** $98/hr **Out of State:** In Dis-$35.5/hr
Degrees Conferred: AA, AS, Certificates
Programs of Study: Accounting, Agriculture, Art, Automotive, Business, Computer, Electrical/Electronics, Medical, Farm/Ranch, Heating/Refrigeration/AC, Law, Liberal Arts, Machine/Tool Technology, Marketing, Nursing, Radiological, Real Estate, Retail, Welding

ATHLETIC PROFILE

Estimated Number of Baseball Scholarships: 12
Conference Affiliation: Independent
Program Profile: We have a major quality field with underground water and drainage. It was professionally built to rule book specifications (335'-380'-405'-380'-335').
History: Our program began in 1970. We have 3 World Series Appearances, 5 Region Titles, 11 professional players and 7 All-Americans.
Achievements: Most recent record: 1997 and 1998 is 70-22 Division II World Series(ranked 4th in the country); 2 All-Americans; 35-10 in 1995 - Region Champs, 1 draft, 1 free-agent signing, 1 Academic; 7 NCAA Division I scholarships awarded to 1998 sophomore.
Coaching: Bruce Philips, Head Coach, has coached 1980-1987and 1993 to the present. He was Chicago Pro baseball College Coach of the Year in 1995 and 1997. He was Louisville Soccer Coach of the Year in 1995, 1997, and 1998. He was Diamond Sport Coach of the Year in 1997 and 1998. He was NJCAA Region III Coach of the Year in 1995, 1997 and 1998. He was NJCAA District Coach of the Year in 1997 and 1998. Todd Post - Assistant Coach.
Roster for 1998 team/In State: 12 **Out of State:** 8 **Out of Country:** 0
Total Number of Varsity/Jr. Varsity: 24 **Number of Seniors on 1998 Team:** 10
Freshmen Receiving Fin Aid/Athletic: 9 **Number of Spring Games:** 56
Positions Needed for 1999/2000: All **Most Recent Record:** 38 - 7 - 0
Schedule: Triton, Oak, South Suburban, Waubonsee, Joliet, Lincoln
Style of Play: Fundamentally sound and aggressive.

Kaskaskia College

27210 College Road
Centralia, IL 62801
Coach: Larry Smith

NCAA I
Blue Devils/Columbia Blue, White
Phone: (618) 532-1981x350
Fax: (618) 532-1990

ACADEMIC

Founded: 1966 **Type:** 2 Yr., Public, Coed
Student/Faculty Ratio: 14:1 **Male/Female Ratio:** 2,996
Scholarships/Academic: No **Athletic:** Yes **Fin Aid:** No
Total Expenses by: Year **In State:** $ 3,500 **Out of State:** $ 5,000
Degrees Conferred: AA, AS
Programs of Study: Accounting, Agricultural Business, Automotive Technology, Business Administration, Computer Information System, Law Enforcement, Liberal Arts, General studies, Nursing, Practical Nursing, Physical Therapy

ATHLETIC PROFILE

Conference Affiliation: Great Rivers Athletic Conference
Program Profile: The facilities are excellent . We host for the NJCAA Region tourney, HS Sectionals and Legion Division Tournaments. We have natural turf, 75' dugouts, artificial turf, cages/bullpens and a sprinkler system.
History: Our program started in 1966.
Achievements: Conference titles in 1968, 1973-74, 1979, 1981, 1988. Sectional champs 1975-76, 1985, 1989-1991. Regional champs 1991, 3rd in 1985, 4th in 1989.

Kishwaukee College

21193 Malta Road
Malta, IL 60150
Coach: Mike Davenport

NJCAA
Kougars/Dark Green, White, Black
Phone: (815) 825-2086
Fax: (815) 825-2072

ACADEMIC

Founded: 1968
Type: 2 Yr., Jr. College, Coed
Religion: Non-Affiliated
Campus Housing: No
Scholarships/Academic: Yes **Athletic:** Yes **Fin Aid:** Yes
Total Expenses by: Year **In State:** $ 5,500 **Out of State:** $ 5,500
Degrees Conferred: AA, AS, AAS
Programs of Study: Accounting, American Studies, Anthropology, Arts, Biology, Business, Chemistry, Classics, Computer, Economics, Education, English, French, German, History, Humanities, International Languages, Psychology, Social Science, Physics, Political Science, Preprofessional Programs, Social Science, Spanish, Studio Arts, Theatre

ATHLETIC PROFILE

Estimated Number of Baseball Scholarships: 8-tuitions
Conference Affiliation: Arrowhead Conference
Program Profile: We have a natural turf field on campus, and play in the Fall and Spring. Our program has been consistently strong.
History: Our program began in 1970 and has been consistently ranked nationally since 1984.
Achievements: Have had 57 drafted players in the last 15 years; have had 3 NJCAA All-Americans in the past wo years; including National Player of the Year in 1998; have won 12 of the last 15 conference championships; numerous NCAA Division I transfers
Coaching: Mike Davenport, Head Coach, started in 1995 to the present . His three year overall record is 96-60. Matt Ingram - Assistant Coach.
Roster for 1998 team/In State: 16 **Out of State:** 6 **Out of Country:** 0
Total Number of Varsity/Jr. Varsity: 22
Percent of Graduation: 75%
Number of Seniors on 1998 Team: 9
Most Recent Record: 34 - 24 - 0
Number of Fall Games: 20
Number of Spring Games: 56
Positions Needed for 1999/2000: Pitcher, Outfielder, Catcher
Schedule: Meridian, Mississippi Gulf Coast, MATC, Black Hawk, Kirwood, Copiah - Lincoln
Style of Play: Intense team baseball. Normally solid defensively and aggressive offensively.

Knox College

South Street
Galesburg, IL 61401
Coach: Shawn Dowds
NCAA III
Prairie Fire/Purple, Gold
Phone: (309) 341-7281
Fax: (309) 341-7806

ACADEMIC

Founded: 1837
Type: 4 Yr., Private, Liberal Arts, Coed
Web-site: http://www.knox.edu
Campus Housing: Yes
Student/Faculty Ratio: 12:1
Male/Female Ratio: 46:54
Undergraduate Enrollment: 1,195
Graduate Enrollment: None
Scholarships/Academic: Yes **Athletic:** No **Fin Aid:** Yes
Total Expenses by: Year **In State:** $ 24,150 **Out of State:** $ 24,150
Degrees Conferred: BA, Bachelors Degree
Programs of Study: Accounting, American Studies, Anthroplogy, Art, Biology, Business, Chemistry, Classic, Computer, Economics, Education, English, French, German, History, Humanities, International Languages, Literature, Psychology, Social Science, Physics, Preprofessional Programs, Social Science, Spanish, Studio Art, Theatre

ATHLETIC PROFILE

Conference Affiliation: Midwest Conference

Lake Land College

5001 Lake Land Blvd
Mattoon, IL 61938
Coach: Gene Creek

NJCAA
Lakers/Red, Black
Phone: (217) 234-5336
Fax: (217) 258-5460

ACADEMIC

Founded: 1966
Type: 2 Yr., Public, Coed
Undergraduate Enrollment: 4,760
Campus Housing: Yes
Student/Faculty Ratio: 15:1
Male/Female Ratio: 46:54
Scholarships/Academic: Yes **Athletic:** Yes **Fin Aid:** Yes
Total Expenses by: Year **In State:** $ 1,500 **Out of State:** $ 1,500
Degrees Conferred: Associate
Programs of Study: Accounting, Agriculture, Architecture, Automotive, Engineering, Business, Computer Science, Law, Physical Education, Electromechanical, Economics, Drafting/Design

ATHLETIC PROFILE

Conference Affiliation: Collegiate Conference of Central Illinois
History: Gary Gaelti played here in 1978.
Achievements: World Series in 1988.
Coaching: Gene Creek , Head Coach, has coached 28 years.He has 971 wins at Lake Land.

Lewis and Clark Community College

5800 Godfrey Road
Godfrey, IL 62035
Coach: Randy Martz

NCAA II
Trail Blazers/Royal Blue, White
Phone: (618) 466-3411
Fax: (618) 466-9271

ACADEMIC

Founded: 1970
Type: 2 Yr., Jr. College, Coed
Student/Faculty Ratio: 14:1
Male/Female Ratio: Unknown
Undergraduate Enrollment: 6,000
Graduate Enrollment: None
Scholarships/Academic: Yes **Athletic:** Yes **Fin Aid:** Yes
Total Expenses by: Year **In State:** $ 1,400 **Out of State:** $ 5,060
Degrees Conferred: Associate
Programs of Study: Accounting, Agriculture, Art, Automotive, Banking/Finance, Biological science, Broadcasting, Construction, Criminal Justice, Dental, Education, Law

ATHLETIC PROFILE

Conference Affiliation: MCCAC
Program Profile: Lewis and Clark's baseball program takes an annual Florida trip to Panama City Beach, Florida.
History: Division II junior college baseball began three years ago.
Achievements: Jason Isringhausen now playing with the Mets; Region 24 Champion 1996; Illinois-Midwest District C Sectional Champion 1996; Qualified for Junior College World Series - placed third out of eight teams invited to tournament.
Coaching: Randy Martz, Head Coach, was with the Chicago Cubs 1980-82. He received Coach of the Year Honors for District 'C'.
Style of Play: Solid defense, 3 to 4 man starting rotation, strong closer, strength in batting order 3-6.

Lewis University

Route 53
Romeoville, IL 60441
Coach: Irish O'Reilly

NCAA II
Flyers/Red, White
Phone: (815) 836-5255
Fax: (815) 836-5835

ACADEMIC

Founded: 1933
Type: 4 Yr., Private, Liberal Arts, Coed
Religion: Roman Catholic
Campus Housing: Yes
Web-site: http://www.lewisu.edu/
SAT/ACT/GPA: 700+/17+
Student/Faculty Ratio: 15:1
Male/Female Ratio: 50:50
Undergraduate Enrollment: 4,000
Graduate Enrollment: 1,000
Scholarships/Academic: Yes **Athletic:** Yes **Fin Aid:** Yes
Total Expenses by: Year **In State:** $ 16,000 **Out of State:** $ 16,000
Degrees Conferred: AA, AS, BA, BA, MA, MS
Programs of Study: Accounting, Airway Science, Applied Science, Art, Athletic Training, Avionics, Biology, Broadcasting, Business Administration, Chemistry, Communications, Computer Science, Criminal Justice, Economics, Education, English, Finance, History, Journalism, Liberal Arts, Marketing, Mathematics, Music, Nursing, Philosophy, Physics, Political Science, Psychology

ATHLETIC PROFILE

Conference Affiliation: Great Lakes Valley Conference
Program Profile: We have very good outdoor NCAA Division II playing facilities. There are 2 batting cages, 6 mounds and an outstanding well kept playing field. We play a 56 game schedule in Midwest weather. We usually play the most games in NCAA Division II. We have a forty-one year record of 1330-648-24 (.672).
History: We have one of the most successful programs in the Midwest. We won 3 NAIA National Championships 1974, 1975, 1976 and finished in NAIA Top six 10 times.We had 20 NAIA bids in 28 years and 9 NCAA bids in 13 years,. We finished NCAA Top five 4 times and won 23 Conference Championships in 41 years. In 1994, we won our 6th conference title and 3rd title in the last 5 years.
Achievements: Coach O'Reilly is the 8th winningest active coach in NCAA Division I Baseball. He got GLVC Coach of the Year 5 times. He got NCAA Regional Coach of the Year four times. He got NAIA Coach of the Year in 1980. He was NJCAA Coach of the Year in 1974. We were 1994 GLVC Champs and made 1994 NCAA National Championship Appearances. Three players were named ABCA All-american.
Style of Play: Very aggressive, championship quality, always in content for conference and NCAA bid. Winning program that graduates its players.

Lincoln College

300 Keokuk
Lincoln, IL 62656
Coach: Tony Thomas

NJCAA
Lynx/Purple, White
Phone: (217) 732-3155
Fax: (217) 735-5214

ACADEMIC

Founded: 1865
Type: 4 Yr., Private, Coed
SAT/ACT/GPA: Varies
Campus Housing: Yes
Student/Faculty Ratio: 13:1
Male/Female Ratio: 55:45
Undergraduate Enrollment: 550
Graduate Enrollment: None
Scholarships/Academic: Yes **Athletic:** Yes **Fin Aid:**
Total Expenses by: Year **In State:** $ 12,800 **Out of State:** $ 12,800
Degrees Conferred: Associate of arts
Programs of Study: Liberal Arts/General Studies

Lincoln Land Community College

5250 Shepherd Road
Springfield, IL 62704
Coach: Claude J. Kracik

NJCAA
Loggers/Columbia Blue, Scarlet
Phone: (217) 786-2426
Fax: (217) 786-2788

ACADEMIC

Founded: 1968
Type: 2 Yr., Public, Jr. College, Coed
Student/Faculty Ratio: 24:1
SAT/ACT/GPA: High School Diploma
Undergraduate Enrollment: 10,000
Graduate Enrollment: None
Scholarships/Academic: No **Athletic:** Yes **Fin Aid:** Yes
Total Expenses by: Year **In State:** $ 7,200 **Out of State:** $ 8,300
Degrees Conferred: AS, AA
Programs of Study: Accounting, Agricultural, Architecture, Automotive, Behavioral, Biological, Business, Criminal, Data Processing, Drafting/Design, Economics, Education, Humanities, Journalism, Law, Literature, Marketing, Mathematics, Music, Nursing, Office, Philosophy

ATHLETIC PROFILE

Estimated Number of Baseball Scholarships: 21
Conference Affiliation: Collegiate Conference of Central Illinois
Program Profile: We have a 56 game Spring schedule, a 20 game Fall scrimmage schedule and a Spring trip to Florida. The conference schedule has 20 games. Stadium distances are 327 down lines, 365 in gaps and 385 to center. We have a lighted, inning by inning scoreboard, 8 green wood board fence and natural grass.
History: Our program started Spring of 1969. We were region IV Champions in 1971 and 1987 and 2nd in 1979. We were Region XXIV Champions in 1993, 1994 and 1995. We were NJCAA Division II National Champions in 1994, 3rd in 1995 and 5th in 1993.
Achievements: Region Coach of the Year in 1991, 1987, 1993, 1994, and 1995; National Coach of the Year in 1994; Major League Performers include Pat Perry, Mark Clark, Jeff Fassero, Joe Sluarski. Sluarski pitched for Gold Medal Olympic Baseball Team 1988 USA; 12 All-Americans and 20 drafted players.
Coaching: Claude J. Kracik, Head Coach, started in the Fall of 1969. He has won over 770 games at LLCC. He has been a Trial Coach for the USA 1996 Jr. Olympic Team & 1997 USA Senior Olympic Team.
Roster for 1998 team/In State: 27 **Out of State:** 1 **Out of Country:** 0
Number of Sophomores on 1998 Team: 14 **Percent of Graduation:** 95%
Positions Needed for 1999/2000: Pitcher
Schedule: Hillsborough CC, Pasco - Hernando CC, St. Petersburg JC, John A. Logan, Lake Land, Parkland, North Florida, South Suburban, Illinois Central, Meramec
Style of Play: Aggressive offensively; fundamentally sound all around.

Lincoln Trail College

11220 State Hwy 1
Robinson, IL 62454
Coach: Tony Kestranek

NJCAA
Statesmen/Green, Orange
Phone: (618) 544-8657
Fax: (618) 544-3957

ACADEMIC

Founded: 1969
Type: 2 Yr., Public, Coed
Undergraduate Enrollment: 700
Student/Faculty Ratio: 15:1
Scholarships/Academic: Yes **Athletic:** Yes **Fin Aid:** Yes
Total Expenses by: Year **In State:** $ 864 **Out of State:** $ 3,510
Degrees Conferred: AA, AS, AAS
Programs of Study: General Degree for four-year studies and transfer to four-year programs.

Scholarships/Academic: Yes **Athletic:** Yes **Fin Aid:** Yes
Total Expenses by: Year **In State:** $ 864 **Out of State:** $ 3,510
Degrees Conferred: AA, AS, AAS
Programs of Study: General Degree for four-year studies and transfer to four-year programs.

ATHLETIC PROFILE

Conference Affiliation: Great Rivers Athletic Conference
Program Profile: Lincoln Trail plays a Fall season of 25 games and a Spring season of 55 games.
Achievements: 1992 Tucker Howard - Travis Hayes; 1994 All-Americans Jeremy Reeves - Seattle Mariners, Mike Eikenberry - Houston Astros.
Coaching: Tony Kestranek, Head Coach, played at Austin Peay State University. He was a graduate assistant at Lincoln Trail for two years. He is in his 3rd season and also serves as Athletic Director.
Style of Play: Fundamentally sound, aggressive, high energy baseball.

MacMurray College

447 E College Avenue
Jacksonville, IL 62650
Coach: Kris Doorey

NCAA III
Highlanders/Red, Blue, White
Phone: (217) 479-7143
Fax: (217) 479-7147

ACADEMIC

Founded: 1846
Religion: United Methodist
Web-site: http://www.mac.edu
Student/Faculty Ratio: 13:1
Undergraduate Enrollment: 648

Type: 4 Yr., Private, Liberal Arts, Coed
Campus Housing: Yes
SAT/ACT/GPA: 20
Male/Female Ratio: 287:361
Graduate Enrollment: N/A

Scholarships/Academic: Yes **Athletic:** No **Fin Aid:** Yes
Total Expenses by: Year **In State:** $ 16,205 **Out of State:** $ 16,205
Degrees Conferred: BA, BS
Programs of Study: Accounting, Art, Biology, Business Administration, Chemistry, Computer Electronics, Computer Science, Criminal Justice, Deaf Studies,Teacher Education, Elementary Education, English, French, History, International Studies, Journalism, Learning Disabilities and Social Emotional Disorders, Management Information Systems, Marketing, Mathematics, Music, Nursing, Premedicine, Preoccupational Therapy, Prephysical Therapy, Prevet, Psychology, Religion, Secondary Education, Social Work, Spanish, Sports Management

ATHLETIC PROFILE

Conference Affiliation: St. Louis Intercollegiate Athletic Conference
Program Profile: Our facilities include two indoor batting cages, two outdoor batting cages, weight room, field which is natural grass, fences, dugouts and scoreboard. The season consists of six weeks in the Fall and 40+ games in the Spring.
History: The program began in 1958. We accomplished 8 consecutive 20-win seasons, three NCAA post-season appearances and nationally ranked on our last three seasons.
Achievements: 1992-1997 six consecutive SLIAC Championships; 2 All-Americans; 8 players signed pro contracts.
Coaching: Kris Doorey, Head Coach, entering first season with the program. Former assistant coach for one year. He served as a head coach of the Stony Brook team in the Lon island Collegiate Wood Bat League in 1997. A 1991 graduate of Peru (NY) High School, he is a two-time Champion Valley Athletic Conference All-Star and earned All-New York State Honors.
Roster for 1998 team/In State: 27 **Out of State:** 8 **Out of Country:** 0
Total Number of Varsity/Jr. Varsity: 35 **Percent of Graduation:** 90%
Number of Seniors on 1998 Team: 9 **Most Recent Record:** 20 - 10 - 0
Freshmen Receiving Fin Aid/Athletic: 0 **Academic:** All
Number of Fall Games: 9 **Number of Spring Games:** 36
Positions Needed for 1999/2000: Pitcher, Shortstop, Outfielder, 1st Base
Schedule: Fontbonne, Illinois, Illinois Benedictine, Monmouth, Lakeland, Millikins, Washington
Style of Play: Aggressive, old fashioned baseball.

McHenry County College

8900 US Highway 14
Crystal Lake, IL 60012
Coach: Tom Kruse

NJCAA
Fighting Scots/Royal, Scarlet, White
Phone: (815) 455-8543
Fax: (815) 455-8899

ACADEMIC

Founded: 1967
Type: 2 Yr., Public, Coed
Web-site: http://www.mchenry.cc.il.us/
SAT/ACT/GPA: Minimal
Student/Faculty Ratio: 20:1
Male/Female Ratio: 1:1
Scholarships/Academic: Yes **Athletic:** Yes **Fin Aid:** Yes
Total Expenses by: Year **In State:** $ 400 **Out of State:** $ 1,000
Degrees Conferred: Associate
Programs of Study: Accounting, Agricultural Business, Automotive Technology, Business Administration, Computer Programming, Criminal Justice, Drafting/Design, Electrical/Electronics Technology, Horticulture, Industrial Engineering Technology, Liberal Arts, Marketing, Mechanical

ATHLETIC PROFILE

Estimated Number of Baseball Scholarships: 3 1/2
Conference Affiliation: Skyway Conference
Program Profile: Our field is natural turf and has a chain linked fence, water system, indoor batting cages and an outdoor batting cage. Our program is rebounding from a dismal season in 1997.
History: We started in 1990. We ranked # 6 nationally in a 1996 Final Poll. Our most wins were 40 in 1996.
Achievements: Conference Title in 1996; Regional Title in 1996; Kim Johnson Coach of the Year Region IV in 1996; Conference Region Champs in 1996; All-Americans were Tony Bakli, Jason Watts in 1996; Jon Byer in 1995; drafted players were Tony Bucci, Craig Strong, Mark Lechonice, Jason Faunt, Sean Busse and Jason Schulter.
Coaching: Tom Kruse, Head Coach, is entering his second year. Luis Encarnacion, Assist Coach and Pitching Coach, is entering his third year.
Number of Seniors on 1998 Team: 11 **Percent of Graduation:** 90%
Most Recent Record: 10 - 14 - 0
Schedule: Kishwaukee, Lake County, Kankakee, Illinois Central, Lincoln Land, Madison Area
Style of Play: Aggressive defensive and defensive style.

McKendree College

701 College Road
Lebanon, IL 62254
Coach: Jim Boehne

NAIA
Bearcats/Purple, White
Phone: (618) 537-6906
Fax: (618) 537-6876

ACADEMIC

Founded: 1828
Type: 4 Yr., Private, Liberal Arts, Coed
Religion: United Methodist
Campus Housing: Yes
SAT/ACT/GPA: 15 units of HS work/20/2.5
Web-site: http://www.mckendree.edu/
Student/Faculty Ratio: 14:1
Male/Female Ratio: 49:51
Undergraduate Enrollment: 2,100
Graduate Enrollment: None
Scholarships/Academic: Yes **Athletic:** Yes **Fin Aid:** Yes
Total Expenses by: Year **In State:** $ 15,850 **Out of State:** $ 15,850
Degrees Conferred: BA, BS, BBA, BFA, BSED, BSN
Programs of Study: Accounting, Art, Art Education, Biological Science, Botany, Business, Chemistry, Communications, Computer Science, Criminal Justice, Elementary Education, English, Fine Arts, International Relations, Management, Marketing, Mathematics, Microbiology, Physical Education, Political Science, Preprofessional Programs

ATHLETIC PROFILE

Estimated Number of Baseball Scholarships: 11-Full
Conference Affiliation: American MidWest Conference
Program Profile: Our field is resurfaced and has a drainage system It is highlighted as a backwards Fenway Park with a 30 ft. fence in rightfield.
History: Our program restarted with a first full-time baseball head coach in 1997-1998.
Achievements: Had two pitchers signed in June 1998: Corey Dagley by Phillies and Jeremy Book by Cardinals.
Coaching: Jim Boehne ,Head Coach, is entering his second season. He started with the program in 1997-1998 and a record of 27-17; AMC Co-Champs; Bernie Ysursa ,Assistant Coach, is the pitching coach and started in 1997-1998.
Roster for 1998 team/In State: 35 **Out of State:** 2 **Out of Country:** 0
Total Number of Varsity/Jr. Varsity: 40 **Most Recent Record:** 27 - 17 - 0
Number of Seniors on 1998 Team: 9 **Number of Sophomores on 1998 Team:** 0
Freshmen Receiving Fin Aid/Athletic: 13 **Academic:** 10
Number of Fall Games: 15 **Number of Spring Games:** 60
Positions Needed for 1999/2000: 9 **Baseball Camp Dates:** June
Schedule: SIU-Edwardsville, Missouri Baptist, SouthEast Missouri, St. Louis, Southern Indiana
Style of Play: No ground ball singles early in the count! Hit balls in the gap and out of the park!

Millikin University

1184 West Main
Decatur, IL 62522
Coach: Jeff Holm
Email: jholm@mail.millikin.edu

NCAA III
Big Blue/Blue, White
Phone: (800) 373-7733
Fax: (214) 420-6629

ACADEMIC

Founded: 1901 **Type:** 4 Yr., Private, Liberal Arts, Coed
Religion: Presbyterian **Campus Housing:** Yes
Web-site: http://www.millikin.edu **SAT/ACT/GPA:** 1100+/24
Student/Faculty Ratio: 14:1 **Male/Female Ratio:** 45:55
Undergraduate Enrollment: 2,000 **Graduate Enrollment:** None
Scholarships/Academic: Yes **Athletic:** No **Fin Aid:** Yes
Total Expenses by: Year **In State:** $ 20,000 **Out of State:** $ 20,000
Degrees Conferred: BA, BFA, BS, BSN, Bmus
Programs of Study: Accounting, Agricultural Business, Automotive Technologies, Business Administraton/Commerece/Management, Child Care, Criminal Justice, Drafting and Design

ATHLETIC PROFILE

Conference Affiliation: College Conference of Illinois and Wisconsin
Program Profile: The program has a 42 game regular Season and a Spring trip to Florida. Home field is called Sunnyside Park and is lighted. Our facilities include a cage, a pressbox, a concession stand,a grass field and an indoor large infield area with three indoor mounds.
History: We started in 1947 and have 8 conference titles. We have 8 players played professional baseball.
Achievements: 1975 Conference Champions; Rob Ruch was 1994 draft by Minnesota Twins; multiple All-Conference Performers.
Coaching: Jeff Holm - Head Coach, entering first year with the program.
Roster for 1998 team/In State: 45 **Out of State:** 5 **Out of Country:** 0
Total Number of Varsity/Jr. Varsity: 50 **Percent of Graduation:** High
Number of Seniors on 1998 Team: 8 **Number of Sophomores on 1998 Team:** 0
Freshmen Receiving Fin Aid/Athletic: 0 **Academic:** 96%

Number of Fall Games: 0 **Number of Spring Games:** 42
Positions Needed for 1999/2000: Infielder, Outfielder, Pitcher
Baseball Camp Dates: February - every Saturday
Schedule: Carthage, MacMurray, Lincoln University, Mississippi College, Belhaven College
Style of Play: Aggressive, hard work and have fun.

Monmouth College

700 E Broadway
Monmouth, IL 61462
Coach: Roger Sander

NCAA III
Figthing Scots/Red, White
Phone: (309) 457-2176
Fax: (309) 457-2168

ACADEMIC

Founded: 1853
Type: 4 Yr., Private, Liberal Arts, Coed
Religion: Presbyterian
Campus Housing: Yes
Web-site: http://www.pippin.monm.edu/
SAT/ACT/GPA: 18
Student/Faculty Ratio: 14:1
Male/Female Ratio: 48:52
Undergraduate Enrollment: 1,000
Graduate Enrollment: None
Scholarships/Academic: Yes **Athletic:** No **Fin Aid:** Yes
Total Expenses by: Year **In State:** $ 18,980 **Out of State:** $ 18,980
Degrees Conferred: BA
Programs of Study: 26 Undergraduate Majors leading to a BA Degree and a Further 14 Preprofessional Programs including: Accounting, Art, Biology, Business Administration, Chemistry, Classics, History, Computer Science, Economics, Education, Elementary Education, Learning Disabilities, Secondary Education, Bilingual Education, English, Environmental Science, Government, Topical, Mathematics, Modern Foreign Languages, Spanish, Music, Physical Education, Physics, Psychology, Religion and Philosophy, Sociology, Speech Communication and Theater Arts; Preprofessional Programs - Architecture, Dentistry, Engineering, Law, Library Science

ATHLETIC PROFILE

Conference Affiliation: Midwest Conference
Program Profile: We have a newly constructed natural grass field with dimensions of LFL 330', LPA 365', C 395', RPA 350' on a hill and RFL 320'. The infield is newly sodded. A new facility is being built for 1999.
History: Won 13 conference championships in last 24 years.
Achievements: Chris Wheat 1990 25th round draft; numerous free-agent signings; 5 Conference titles in the last 10 years.

Morton College

3801 South Central Avenue
Cicero, IL 60650
Coach: Mike Huber

NJCAA
Panthers/Navy, Orange
Phone: (708) 656-8000x371
Fax: (708) 656-3161

ACADEMIC

Founded: 1924
Type: 2 Yr., Public, Coed
Undergraduate Enrollment: 4,600
Student/Faculty Ratio: 20:1
Scholarships/Academic: No **Athletic:** Yes **Fin Aid:** Yes
Total Expenses by: Year **In State:** $ 1,400 **Out of State:** $ 4,600
Degrees Conferred: Associate
Programs of Study: Accounting, Automotive Technology, Banking/Finance, Business Administration, Data Processing, Dental Processing, Dental Services, Drafting/Design, Heating/Refrigeration/Air Conditioning, Law Enforcement, Liberal Arts, Marketing, Music, Nursing, Physical Therapy, Real Estate

North Central College

30 N Brainard St
Naperville, IL 60566-7063
Coach: Ed Mathey

NCAA III
Cardinals/Cardinal, White
Phone: (630) 637-5512
Fax: (630) 637-5521

ACADEMIC

Founded: 1861
Type: 4 Yr., Private, Liberal Arts, Coed
Religion: Methodist
Campus Housing: Yes
Web-site: Not Available
SAT/ACT/GPA: 820/20
Student/Faculty Ratio: 14:1
Male/Female Ratio: 52:48
Undergraduate Enrollment: 1,300
Graduate Enrollment: 1,200
Scholarships/Academic: Yes **Athletic:** No **Fin Aid:** Yes
Total Expenses by: Year **In State:** $ 16,326 **Out of State:** $ 16,326
Degrees Conferred: BA, BS, MA, MS, MBA
Programs of Study: 36 Academic Majors, 6 Graduate Degrees; Business Management, Communications, Computer Sciences, Physical Sciences, Psychology, Social Sciences

ATHLETIC PROFILE

Conference Affiliation: College Conference of Illinois and Wisconsin
Program Profile: Our field has natural grass and major league dimensions. We do an annual 10-day Florida trip. Our field has served as a site for conference and NCAA touranments. It is used for the Illinois Summer State tournament. Our program has consistently been ranked among the top 25 schools in NCAA Division III Defending College Conference of Illinois and Wisconsin champions.
History: Our college has produced seven conference champions and has made five NCAA Division III Regional Appearances since 1984, including the 1987 College World Series. Eleven players have been drafted or signed pro contracts since 1987. Currently we have one player in the Royals organization and one in the Yankees organization. Team members are ranked in the top 10 in 14 Division III statistical categories all-time.
Achievements: Won 6 of the last 11 CCIW Titles; 8 players drafted or signed professional contracts in the last 8 years; 15 consecutive seasons with 21 or more wins.
Coaching: Ed Mathey, Head Coach, was a Conference Coach of the Year in 1994 and 1996. He served as an advanced scout for the Cincinnati Reds & coached a club team in Melbourne, Australia.
Style of Play: Aggressive - fundamentally sound. Our philosphy is to incorporate as many players as possible into varsity scheme. In addition, North Central plays a 10-15 game junior varsity schedule so that as many players as possible have a chance to play.

North Park University

3225 W Foster Avenue
Chicago, IL 60625
Coach: Steve Vanderbranden

NCAA III
Vikings/Royal Blue, Gold
Phone: (773) 244-5675
Fax: (773) 244-4952

ACADEMIC

Founded: 1891
Type: 4 Yr., Private, Liberal Arts, Coed
Religion: Evangelical Covenent
Campus Housing: Yes
Web-site: http://www.northpark.com
SAT/ACT/GPA: 860/18/Upper 1/2
Student/Faculty Ratio: 15:1
Male/Female Ratio: 45:55
Undergraduate Enrollment: 1,700
Graduate Enrollment: 500
Scholarships/Academic: Yes **Athletic:** No **Fin Aid:** Yes
Total Expenses by: Year **In State:** $ 20,200 **Out of State:** $ Varies
Degrees Conferred: 35

Programs of Study: Accounting, Anthropology, Art, Biblical Studies, Biology, Business Administration, Chemistry, Clinical Laboratory, Science, Communication Arts, Constructed Majors, Economics, Education, English, Finance, General Science, History, International Business, Marketing, Math, Music, Nursing, Philosophy, PE, Physics, Politics and Government, Psychology, Social Studies, Sociology, Spanish, Sports Medicine, Swedish, Youth Ministry

ATHLETIC PROFILE

Conference Affiliation: College Conference of Illinois and Wisconsin
Program Profile: Play in one of the best conferences - CCIW. Play an excellent non-conference schedule.
History: Began playing in the CCIW in 1962 when North Park became a four-year school.
Achievements: 5 NCAA Division III Mideast Regular Appearances and 2 2nd place finishes; 5 have signed pro-contracts - Tim Naughton, Randy Rross, Jon Van Kempen, Peter Balis, Dan Casas.
Coaching: Steve Vandenbranden,Head Coach, compiled a record of 44-76 in three years. Chris Nelson - Assistant Coach.
Roster for 1998 team/In State: 22 **Out of State:** 7 **Out of Country:** 0
Total Number of Varsity/Jr. Varsity: 29 **Percent of Graduation:** 80%
Number of Seniors on 1998 Team: 2 **Number of Spring Games:** 42
Freshmen Receiving Fin Aid/Athletic: 0 **Academic:** 15
Positions Needed for 1999/2000: Pitcher, Catcher
Schedule: Carthage, Aurora, Benedictine, University of Illinois-Chico, North Central
Style of Play: Pitchers work ahead, minimize defensive mistakes, hit and run, take extra bases.

Northeastern Illinois University

(Program Discontinued)

Northern Illinois University

Baseball Office
DeKalb, IL 60115
Coach: Frank DelMedico

NCAA I
Huskies/Cardinal, Black
Phone: (815) 753-0147
Fax: (815) 753-9540

ACADEMIC

Founded: 1895 **Type:** 4 Yr., Public, Coed
Web-site: http://www.niu.edu/ **Campus Housing:** Yes
Student/Faculty Ratio: 17:1 **Male/Female Ratio:** 45:55
Undergraduate Enrollment: 15,800 **Graduate Enrollment:** 6,200
Scholarships/Academic: Yes **Athletic:** Yes **Fin Aid:** Yes
Total Expenses by: Year **In State:** $ 7,800 appr. **Out of State:** $ 12,500 appr.
Degrees Conferred: BA, BS, BSBA
Programs of Study: College of Business, College of Education, College of Engineering and Engineering Technology, College of Liberal Arts and Sciences, College of Professional Studies, College of Visual and Performing Arts

ATHLETIC PROFILE

Conference Affiliation: Mid-American Conference
Program Profile: We play a 17 week Spring schedule and a 5 week Fall schedule. Our indoor and outdoor training facilities have a beautiful grass surface, 1,500 capacity and a year-round conditioning program. The Huskies play a competitive schedule which traditionally includes many local rivals, plus several NCAA tournament qualifiers. Our 1997 campaign also includes 3 games at the Metrodome in Minneapolis.
History: NIU captured the Midwestern Collegiate Conference Championship in 1996, only the sixth year of the program. The Huskies won 27 games, the second straight year with 25 or more wins. Junior pitcher Paul Erschen earned second team Academic All-America status with nine victories,

while five regulars batted .300 or better in 1996. All five, however, graduated, leaving NIU to fill several holes in the lineup.
Achievements: Midwestern Collegiate Conference Champions in 1996; 2 players All-MCC; 5 repsentative on the All-Tournament squad.

Northwestern University

1501 Central Street
Evanston, IL 60208
Coach: Paul Stevens

NCAA I
Wildcats/Purple, Black
Phone: (847) 491-4652
Fax: (847) 491-8869

ACADEMIC

Founded: 1851
Type: 4 Yr., Private, Liberal Arts, Coed
Web-site: http://www.nusports.com
Campus Housing: Yes
Student/Faculty Ratio: 10:1
Male/Female Ratio: 49:51
Undergraduate Enrollment: 7,400
Graduate Enrollment: 5,000
Scholarships/Academic: No **Athletic:** Yes **Fin Aid:** Yes
Total Expenses by: Year **In State:** $ 18,108 **Out of State:** $ 18,108
Degrees Conferred: BA, BS, MS, MA, PhD
Programs of Study: African-American Studies, Anthropology, Applied Mathematics, Art, Art History, Asian Studies, Astronomy, Biological Science, Chemistry, Classic, English, Environmental Science, Computer Science, Dance, Economics, Engineering, Geography, Geological Science, History, International Studies, Italian, Journalism, Music, Music Education, Neuroscience, Philosophy, Physics, Political Science, Psychology, Religion, Secondary Education, Sociology, Theatre

ATHLETIC PROFILE

Conference Affiliation: Big 10 Conference
Program Profile: We play at Rocky Miller Park which is a natural grass with dimensions of 330-400-330. It has a seating capacity of 500, new locker rooms and a new indoor turf facility.
History: We began in 1871 and have an overall record of 1328-1481-30. Coach Steven compiled a record of 266-288-4.
Achievements: Paul Steven 2 times Coach of the Year Big Ten; All-American was Mark Loretta (Milwaukee Brewers); others in the Major League one of them is Joe Girandi.
Coaching: Paul Stevens, Head Coach, is entering his 11th year as head coach. He compiled a record of 266-288-4 at Northwestern University. He was named Big Ten Conference of the Year two-times. Tim Stoddaro, Ron Klein, and Joe Keewan - Assistant Coaches.
Style of Play: Aggressive and fundamental baseball.

Oakton Community College

1600 East Golf Road
Des Plaines, IL 60016
Coach: Rich Symonds

NJCAA
Raiders/Red, White, Blue
Phone: (847) 635-1921
Fax: (847) 635-1764

ACADEMIC

Founded: 1969
Type: 2 Yr., Jr. College, Coed
Student/Faculty Ratio: 23:1
Male/Female Ratio: 43:57
Undergraduate Enrollment: 11,254
Graduate Enrollment: None
Scholarships/Academic: No **Athletic:** No **Fin Aid:** Yes
Total Expenses by: Year **In State:** $ 1,000 **Out of State:** $ 3,900
Degrees Conferred: Associate

Programs of Study: Accounting, Architectural Technology, Automtoive Technology, Biomedical Technology, Business administration, Computer Programming, Data Processing, Fire Science, International Business, Law Enforcement, Machine/Tool Technology, Mechanical Design Technology, Medical Records Services, Real Estate

ATHLETIC PROFILE

Conference Affiliation: Skyway Conference

Olivet Nazarene University

P.O. Box 592
Kankakee, IL 60901
Coach: Rick Colling

NAIA
Tigers/Purple, White
Phone: (815) 939-5119
Fax: (815) 939-7933

ACADEMIC

Founded: 1938
Religion: Protestant - Nazarene
Web-site: http://www.olivet.edu/
Student/Faculty Ratio: 17:1
Undergraduate Enrollment: 1,582
Scholarships/Academic: Yes **Athletic:** Yes
Total Expenses by: Year **In State:** $ 16,424
Degrees Conferred: BA, BS, MBA

Type: 4 Yr., Private, Liberal Arts, Coed
Campus Housing: Yes
SAT/ACT/GPA: Open admission policy
Male/Female Ratio: 4:6
Graduate Enrollment: 412
Fin Aid: Yes
Out of State: $ 16,424

Programs of Study: Accounting, Art, Biblical Studies, Biology, Botany, Business Administration, Chemistry, Child Development, Christian Education, Church Music, Computer Science, Dietetics, Economics, Education, Engineering, Physics, English, Environmental Science, Geology, History

ATHLETIC PROFILE

Estimated Number of Baseball Scholarships: 8
Conference Affiliation: Chicago - Land Collegiate Athletic Conference
Program Profile: We have a four year varsity program with fine locker and field facilities. Spring season begins from March 15 through May 15. We have a natural grass field with a standard dimensions.
History: Program began in 1968 to the present. Has developed slowly, but is stranger over the past couple of years.
Achievements: Conference Runner-Up in 1998 (Chicagoland Collegiate Athletic Conference); 12 ONU players have been drafted in the past ten years.
Coaching: Rick Colling - Head Coach, PhD first year 1998-1999. Has coached at various levels for 12 years. Tracy Erickson - Assistant Coach.
Roster for 1998 team/In State: 16 **Out of State:** 8 **Out of Country:** 0
Total Number of Varsity/Jr. Varsity: 24 **Percent of Graduation:** 100%
Number of Seniors on 1998 Team: 6 **Number of Sophomores on 1998 Team:** 4
Freshmen Receiving Fin Aid/Athletic: 3 **Academic:** 7
Number of Fall Games: 9 **Number of Spring Games:** 42
Baseball Camp Dates: January 1999 **Most Recent Record:** 19 - 23 - 0
Positions Needed for 1999/2000: 6-positions, Pitcher, Shortstop, 2nd Base
Schedule: Lewis University, St. Joseph's, St. Xavier University, Bethel, University of St. Francis
Style of Play: Deliberate, but aggressive.

Olney Central College

305 N West Avenue
Olney, IL 62450
Coach: Dennis Conley

NJCAA
Blue Knights/Navy, White
Phone: (618) 395-4351
Fax: (618) 392-4824

ACADEMIC

Type: 2 Yr., Public, Coed
Degrees Conferred: Associate
Programs of Study: General Studies

ATHLETIC PROFILE

Conference Affiliation: Great River Athletic Conference
History: Olney Central's Baseball program began in 1970.
Coaching: Dennis Conley - Head Coach, 17 years. Josh Mathis - Assistant Coach, first year.
Style of Play: Aggressive, very hard nosed. Coach Conley likes a lot of hit and run.

Parkland College

2400 W Bradley Ave
Champaign, IL 61821
Coach: Jim Farr
Email: rodl@hotmail.com

NCAA I
Tribe/Green, Gold
Phone: (217) 351-2409
Fax: (217) 373-3897

ACADEMIC

Founded: 1965
Type: 2 Yr., Public, Coed
Undergraduate Enrollment: 9,000
Campus Housing: Yes
Student/Faculty Ratio: 20:1
Male/Female Ratio: 40:60
Scholarships/Academic: Yes **Athletic:** Yes **Fin Aid:** Yes
Total Expenses by: Year **In State:** $ 5,500 **Out of State:** $ 9,200
Degrees Conferred: AA, AS
Programs of Study: Agriculture, Business Administration, Communications, Criminal Justice, Education, Engineering, Liberal Arts, Life Sciences, Math, Physical Education, Physical Science, Preprofessional Medicine

ATHLETIC PROFILE

Conference Affiliation: Collegiate Conference of Central Illinois
Program Profile: By 1991,we will have a 1,200 seats lighted facility. Our games are played on natural grass field.
History: Our team has been ranked in NJCAA Division I. We have been in the top 20 during the 1990's while going 336-129 . We have a .715% over the past eight years.
Achievements: Freshman Brian Robens was named All-Americans in 1997. 1997 draft by TP Walgira (RHP); 1998 shortstop Ron Bush and RHP Andy Cook; Jim Farr was named Coach of the Year in 1993.
Coaching: Jim Farr, Head Coach, compiled a record of 149-148. He played at the major league level with Texas Rangers. John Cole and Marlin Ikenberry - Assistant Coaches.
Roster for 1998 team/In State: 12 **Out of State:** 16 **Out of Country:** 0
Total Number of Varsity/Jr. Varsity: 28 **Percent of Graduation:** 98%
Number of Seniors on 1998 Team: 4 **Most Recent Record:** 24 - 28 - 0
Freshmen Receiving Fin Aid/Athletic: 7 **Number of Spring Games:** 56
Positions Needed for 1999/2000: Shortstop, LHP, Outfielder
Schedule: North Carolina State, Penn State, Virginia State, Richmond, VCU, Liberty
Style of Play: Strong pitching and defense; need additional power and speed.

Prairie State College

202 S. Halsted St.
Chicago Heights, IL 60411
Coach: Mike Pohlman
Email: pohlman@ix.netcom.com

NJCAA
Pioneers/Purple, Forest Green, White
Phone: (708) 709-3620
Fax: (708) 755-2587

ACADEMIC

Founded: 1958
Type: 2 Yr., Coed
Student/Faculty Ratio: 19:1
Male/Female Ratio: 60:40
Undergraduate Enrollment: 5,500
Graduate Enrollment: None
Scholarships/Academic: Yes **Athletic:** Yes **Fin Aid:** Yes
Total Expenses by: Year **In State:** $ 1,770 **Out of State:** $ 5,460
Degrees Conferred: AAS, AAA
Programs of Study: Art Education, Arts, Fine Arts, Art History, Automotive Technology, Business Administration, Commerce, Management, Child Care, Child and Family Studies, Child Psychology, Commercial Art, Computer Information Systems, Computer Programming, Criminal Justice, Dental Services, Drafting/Design, Early Childhood Education, Education, Electrical and Electronics

ATHLETIC PROFILE

Conference Affiliation: Independent
Program Profile: We have a Junior College Division II program. Scholarships are available. We have an on campus baseball complex with a dimensions of 320 on lines, 375 allies, 395 center. Our facilities include batting tunnel, home plate cage, practice - protection screens and a pitching machine. We have Fall development practice and games,a Winter indoor training program, and a Spring season with a Florida trip.
History: Our sports were dropped by PSC in 1976. From 1978-1979 the programs were reinstated.
Achievements: Former Bloom High School (Chicago HS, IL) Coach with a record of 539-236; Lewis University Hitting Infield Coach - school record in team BA and HR International Baseball: Team Chicago has five International Tournament Championships, 2 AABC Wisconsin State Championships - Beloit Blues.
Coaching: Mike Pohlman - Head Coach. Jim Nohos - Pitching Coach. Carmi DeButch - Outfield and Hitting Coach.
Style of Play: Fundamentally sound in all phases of game. Use according to their abilities by the team development.

Principia College

1 Maybeck Place
Elsah, IL 62028
Coach: Larry Frank
Email: LAF@PRIN.EDU
NCAA III
Panthers/Blue, Gold
Phone: (618) 374-5036
Fax: (618) 374-5221

ACADEMIC

Founded: 1898
Type: 4 Yr., Private, Liberal Arts, Coed
Religion: Christian Science
Campus Housing: Yes
Web-site: http://www.prin.edu/
SAT/ACT/GPA: 800+
Student/Faculty Ratio: 8:1
Male/Female Ratio: 2:3
Undergraduate Enrollment: 550
Graduate Enrollment: None
Scholarships/Academic: Yes **Athletic:** No **Fin Aid:** Yes
Total Expenses by: Year **In State:** $ 12,000 **Out of State:** $ 12,000
Degrees Conferred: BA, BS
Programs of Study: Liberal Arts and Sciences, Business and Education, Computer Science, Communications, Earth Science, Economics, Education, Engineering Science, Environmental Studies, Mass Communications, Philosophy, Physics, Religion, Political Science

ATHLETIC PROFILE

Conference Affiliation: SLIAC
Program Profile: Principia College is an institution for christian scientists. Our season begins in late February and ends in late April. We take a Spring break trip to Florida annually.
History: We have fielded a baseball team since 1940's.
Achievements: Larry Frank received a Conference Coach of the Year Award in 1996.

Coaching: Larry Frank , Head Coach, started with the program in 1996 and has a record of 25-54-1. He played two years at Arizona State, currently batting practice pitcher for St. Louis Cardinals. Lee Ellis, Assistant Coach, started coaching the program in 1997. He played at East Carolina University and was named All-Conference shortstop at Fredonia State.
Roster for 1998 team/In State: 2 **Out of State:** 18 **Out of Country:** 0
Total Number of Varsity/Jr. Varsity: 20 **Percent of Graduation:** 90%
Number of Seniors on 1998 Team: 4 **Number of Sophomores on 1998 Team:** 0
Freshmen Receiving Fin Aid/Athletic: 0 **Academic:** 4
Most Recent Record: 5 - 20 - 0 **Number of Spring Games:** 30
Positions Needed for 1999/2000: Pitcher, 3rd Base, 1st Base, Outfielder
Schedule: Fontbonne, MacMurray, Westminster, Washington University, Millikin University, Hamline
Style of Play: Stress fundamentals, use hit and run stolen base.

Quincy University

1800 College Avenue
Quincy, IL 62301
Coach: Patrick Atwell

NCAA II
Hawks/Brown, White
Phone: (217) 222-8020
Fax: (217) 228-5257

ACADEMIC

Founded: 1860 **Type:** 4 Yr., Private, Liberal Arts, Coed
Religion: Roman Catholic **Campus Housing:** Yes
Web-site: http://www.quincy.edu/ **SAT/ACT/GPA:** 950/20/2.0
Student/Faculty Ratio: 12:1 **Male/Female Ratio:** 50:50
Undergraduate Enrollment: 1,200 **Graduate Enrollment:** 150
Scholarships/Academic: Yes **Athletic:** Yes **Fin Aid:** No
Total Expenses by: Year **In State:** $ 17,760 **Out of State:** $ 17,760
Degrees Conferred: BA, BS, MA
Programs of Study: Accounting, Art Biology, Business Administration, Chemistry, Communications, Computer Science, Education, English, Finance, History, Humanities, Human Resources, Information Science, International Studies, Management, Marketing, Mathematics, Medical Technology, Music, Music Business, Philosophy, Political Science, Psychology, Religious Education, Social Science, Special Education, Sports Management, Theology

ATHLETIC PROFILE

Estimated Number of Baseball Scholarships: 5
Conference Affiliation: Great Lakes Valley Conference
Program Profile: Our fully lighted stadium was built in 1930. It has a full field tarp and seats 3,000. We fo a Natural Fall baseball mostly intersquad and have a Full spring schedule.
History: We have 8 straight winning seasons that ended in 1998. Our school has had baseball since the 1940's.
Achievements: 1997 NCAA Regional Qualifier, Coach of the Year in 1997; Derek Hsilam was named Conference Coach of the Year in 1997; 2nd team All-American, Jason Braskies drafted 34th round by Padres. Bart Tuennies All-American in 1994.
Coaching: Patrick Atwell ,Head Coach, has been coach for 6 years at Quincy College. He has a record of 186-141-3 at Quincy. Brian Behrens - Assistant Coach.
Roster for 1998 team/In State: 26 **Out of State:** 15 **Out of Country:** 0
Total Number of Varsity/Jr. Varsity: 41 **Percent of Graduation:** 85%
Number of Seniors on 1998 Team: 13 **Number of Sophomores on 1998 Team:** 0
Freshmen Receiving Fin Aid/Athletic: 4 **Academic:** 7
Most Recent Record: 19 - 24 - 0 **Number of Spring Games:** 56
Positions Needed for 1999/2000: 3rd Base, Shortstop, 2nd Base, 1st Base, C-Field
Schedule: Alabama, SIU Edwardsville, Central Missouri, Central Oklahoma, Delta State
Style of Play: Depends on the personnel.

Rend Lake Community College

Rt 1
Ina, IL 62846
Coach: Rich Campbell

NJCAA
Warriors/Red, Black
Phone: (618) 437-5321
Fax: (618) 437-5536

ACADEMIC

Founded: 1967
Type: 2 Yr., Public, Coed
Student/Faculty Ratio: 16:1
Male/Female Ratio: 50:50
Undergraduate Enrollment: 4,000
Graduate Enrollment: None
Scholarships/Academic: Yes **Athletic:** Yes **Fin Aid:** Yes
Total Expenses by: Year **In State:** $ 4,500 **Out of State:** $ 5,300
Degrees Conferred: AA, AS, AAS
Programs of Study: Accounting, Agriculture, Art, Biology, Botany, Business, Chemistry, Computer Education, Early Childhood, Engineering, Finance

ATHLETIC PROFILE

Conference Affiliation: Great Rivers Athletic Conference
Program Profile: The Warriors have new cages (Turf). The field dimensions are 330, 390 and 410. There are new bleachers and a parking lot is being built.
History: We have 4 Conference Championships. We were 1 game shy of Division NJCAA World Series in 1997.
Achievements: Sectional champions 1982, 1986, 1988, 1992, 1993. Regional Runner-up 1992. Regional 3rd place 1993. 18 players have been drafted.
Coaching: Rich Campbell, Head Coach, is in his sixth year. Keith Schreiber - Assistant Coach.
Style of Play: We have a good combination of speed and power. We will need to score runs due to a very young pitching staff.

Robert Morris-Chicago Campus

180 N LaSalle Street
Chicago, IL 60601
Coach: Woody Urchak

NAIA
Colonials/Blue, White
Phone: (312) 836-4627
Fax: (412) 262-8557

ACADEMIC

Founded: 1913
Type: 4 Yr., Private, Coed
Web-site: http://www.RMCIL.EDU
SAT/ACT/GPA: 16
Student/Faculty Ratio: 12:1
Male/Female Ratio: 1:1.5
Scholarships/Academic: Yes **Athletic:** Yes **Fin Aid:** No
Total Expenses by: Year **In State:** $ 9,000 **Out of State:** $ 9,000
Degrees Conferred: BBA, AAS, Professional Diploma
Programs of Study: Business Administration, Accounting, Medical Assistant, Computer Science, Computer Aided Design, Sports Medicine

ATHLETIC PROFILE

Conference Affiliation: CCAC

Rock Valley College

3301 North Mulford Road
Rockford, IL 61114
Coach: Mike Armato

NJCAA
Trojans/Brown, Yellow
Phone: (815) 654-4430
Fax: (815) 654-4427

ACADEMIC

Founded: 1964
Type: 2 Yr., Public, Coed
Student/Faculty Ratio: 41:1
Male/Female Ratio: 45:55
Undergraduate Enrollment: 9,238
Graduate Enrollment: None
Scholarships/Academic: No **Athletic:** No **Fin Aid:** Yes
Total Expenses by: Year **In State:** $ 1,200 **Out of State:** $ 6,600
Degrees Conferred: Associate
Programs of Study: Accounting, Automotive, Aviation, Banking/Finance, Business, Computer, Constructions, Drafting/Design, Earth Science, Education, Engineering Technology, Industrial, International, Law, Library, Marketing, Pharmacy, Mechanical, Real Estate, Preprofessional Programs, Occupational, Quality Control, Retail

ATHLETIC PROFILE

Conference Affiliation: N4C

Rockford College

5050 East State Street
Rockford, IL 61020
Coach: Bill Langston
Email: regents@inwane.com
NCAA III
Regents/Purple, White
Phone: (815) 226-4085
Fax: (815) 226-4166

ACADEMIC

Founded: 1847
Type: 4 Yr., Private, Coed
Religion: Non-Affiliated
Campus Housing: Yes
Web-site: http://www.rockford.edu/
SAT/ACT/GPA: 20/2.5/4.0
Student/Faculty Ratio: 12:1
Male/Female Ratio: 1:2
Undergraduate Enrollment: 850
Graduate Enrollment: 650
Scholarships/Academic: Yes **Athletic:** No **Fin Aid:** Yes
Total Expenses by: Year **In State:** $ 20,600 **Out of State:** $ Varies
Degrees Conferred: BA, BS, BSN, BFA
Programs of Study: All Liberal Arts, All Preprofessional, Business Administration, Computer Science, Education, Nursing, Psychology

ATHLETIC PROFILE

Conference Affiliation: Northern Illinois and Iowa Conference
Program Profile: We have a full varsity and junior program. We play on natural grass stadium with ameasurements of 340', 390' and 340'. We have a Spring trip to Ft. Myers, Florida. We have a 6 week Fall program.
History: Our program began in 1963. We are a charter member of conference, formerly NAIA District 20.
Achievements: 4 NIIC Titles; 1 Coach of the Year; 3 All-Americans; 20 All-Regional players; 11 NAIA post-season appearances prior to 1984.
Coaching: Bill Langston ,Head Coach, compiled a record of 305-297 over 16 years of coaching. Chris Berry - Assistant Coach.
Roster for 1998 team/In State: 15 **Out of State:** 5 **Out of Country:** 0
Total Number of Varsity/Jr. Varsity: 20 **Percent of Graduation:** 90%
Number of Seniors on 1998 Team: 11 **Number of Sophomores on 1998 Team:** 4
Freshmen Receiving Fin Aid/Athletic: 0 **Academic:** 20
Number of Fall Games: 6 **Number of Spring Games:** 36
Positions Needed for 1999/2000: Middle Infielder, Outfielder, Pitcher
Baseball Camp Dates: June 15-28
Schedule: Carthage, Aurora, Benedictine, McMurray, Amherst, Albright, Fontbonne, Knox
Style of Play: Very aggressive running offense; solid defense - intelligent pitching.

Saint Xavier University

3700 West 103rd Street
Chicago, IL 60655
Coach: Mike Dooley

NAIA
Cougars/Red, Grey
Phone: (773) 298-3101
Fax: (773) 298-3111

ACADEMIC

Founded: 1846
Type: 4 Yr., Private, Liberal Arts, Coed
Religion: Roman Catholic
Campus Housing: No
Web-site: http://www.sxu.edu/
SAT/ACT/GPA: Required
Student/Faculty Ratio: 15:1
Male/Female Ratio: 25:75
Undergraduate Enrollment: 2,400
Graduate Enrollment: 1,400
Scholarships/Academic: Yes **Athletic:** Yes **Fin Aid:** Yes
Total Expenses by: Year **In State:** $ 15,000 **Out of State:** $15,000
Degrees Conferred: BA, BS, MA, MS, MBA
Programs of Study: Accounting, Aeronautical Engineering, Banking and Finance, Biology, Chemical Engineering, Chemistry, Communications, Computer Science, Criminal Justice, Education, English, Fine Arts, French, History, International Business, Management, Philosophy, Political Science, International Business, Mathematics, Predentistry, Premed, Prelaw, Prepharmacy, Religion Social Science, Spanish, Speech Pathology

ATHLETIC PROFILE

Conference Affiliation: CCAC

Sauk Valley Community College

173 Illinois, Rt 2
Dixon, IL 61021
Coach: Terry Cox

NJCAA
Redmen/Red, White
Phone: (815) 288-5511x372
Fax: (815) 288-5958

ACADEMIC

Founded: 1965
Type: 2 Yr., Jr. College, Coed
Student/Faculty Ratio: 19:1
Male/Female Ratio: 37:63
Undergraduate Enrollment: 2,800
Graduate Enrollment: None
Scholarships/Academic: No **Athletic: Yes** **Fin Aid:** Yes
Total Expenses by: Year **In State:** $ 1,300 **Out of State:** $ 4,000
Degrees Conferred: Associate
Programs of Study: Accounting, Anthropology, Biological Science, Chemistry, Corrections, Criminal Justice, Drafting/Design, Education, Electrical/Electronics Technology, Human Services, Liberal Arts, Marketing, Mechanical Design Technology, Philosophy, Physical Education, Radiological Technology, Social Science

ATHLETIC PROFILE

Conference Affiliation: Arrowhead Conference

Shawnee Community College

8364 Shawnee College Road
Ullin, IL 62992
Coach: Greg Sheppard

NJCAA
Saints/Maroon, Grey
Phone: (618) 634-2242
Fax: (618) 634-9028

ACADEMIC

Founded: 1967
Type: 2 Yr., Jr. College, Coed
Undergraduate Enrollment: 2,500
Campus Housing: No
Student/Faculty Ratio: 15:1
Male/Female Ratio: 40:60
Scholarships/Academic: Yes
Athletic: Yes
Fin Aid: Yes
Total Expenses by: Year
In State: $ 1,000
Out of State: $ 5,800
Degrees Conferred: Associate
Programs of Study: Applied Mathematics, Biology, Business Administration, Computer Science, Computer Technology, Dentistry, Humanities, Liberal Arts, Management, Medical Laboratory Technology, Natural Science, Occupational Therapy

ATHLETIC PROFILE

Conference Affiliation: Independent
Program Profile: Shawnee College plays its home games on the main campus in Ullin. Saint's field has a seats 400. Our baseball program has greatly benefitted from the completion of a new indoor practice facility, which allows for two hitting cages and indoor pitching space. Saint's field is a natural surface of Blue Grass/fesscue mix. We play 20 scrimmage games in the Fall against junior colleges and universities. A full 56 game schedule is played in the Spring.
History: Athletics at shawnee College began in 1970 and have grown to allow over 100 student-athletes to compete in six sports. Shawnee College baseball competed in the NJCAA Region 24 finishing in 4th place in the 1997 Region Tournament. Academics are a priority at Shawnee. This has been reflected in student-athlete performance. There were 9 student-atheltes from Shawnee who earned Academic All-Americans status in 1997 including 3 from the baseball program.
Achievements: Greg Sheppard was selected to coach the '90 Illinois NJCAA North/South All-Star game.
Coaching: Greg Sheppard, Head Coach, enters his second season as a head coach at Shawnee College in 1997-1998. He spent three years as a Pitching Coach at Southern Illinois College, where 7 of the 14 Pitchers he coached signed professional contracts. He was selected to coach in the 1990 Illinois NJCAA North/South All-Star game. For three years also, he was a head coach of the 1990 Harrisburg (IL) American Legion Baseball Program which produced 3 District Championships and a 77-33 (three years) record. Coach Sheppard was selected to represent the 25th Legion District in the 1989 All-Star game. Steve Vinyard ,Assistant Coach, joined the Saints for the 1997-1998 season. He spent three years as an assistant to Coach Sheppard for the Harrisburg (IL) American Legion Program. He will handle the Saints outfielders and will be in charge of baserunning, weight program and academic progress.
Style of Play: Aggressive with a high priority on fundamentals. Offense is geared to being able to handle the bat, including the hit and run, bunting using the whole field to hit. Pitchers are developed not only mechanically but mentally. The entire team maintains a year round training program which incorporates weights, plyometrics, agility and medicine ball. Shawnee athletics has an athletic trainer and medical support for all teams.

South Suburban College

15800 South State Street
S Holland, IL 60435
Coach: Steve Ruzich

NJCAA
Bulldogs/Blue, Grey
Phone: (708) 596-2000x2413
Fax: (708) 210-5733

ACADEMIC

Founded: 1927
Type: 2 Yr., Public, Coed
Student/Faculty Ratio: 24:1
Male/Female Ratio: 36:64
Undergraduate Enrollment: 7,700
Graduate Enrollment: None
Scholarships/Academic: No
Athletic: No
Fin Aid: Yes
Total Expenses by: Year
In State: $ 1,400
Out of State: $ 5,700
Degrees Conferred: Associate
Programs of Study: Accounting, Advertising, Art, Aviation, Banking/Finance, Engineering, Education, Technology, Sciences

ATHLETIC PROFILE

Conference Affiliation: Independent
Program Profile: We play on a natural grass field which has dimensions of 310 both down the lines, 375 gaps and 400 center. Our school was called Thornton Community and was changed in 1990 to South Suburban.
History: Our program began in 1972 and we went to the World Series in 1977. We went back in 1991 and finished 6th. Ron Mahay pitched for the Red Sox major league team and was 3-0; 2.70 era. He was one of the 9 players to be called up, sent back and make it back.
Achievements: Coach of the Year in 1991; Crawling, Midwest, hit-run, Region Juluios Matos All-American in 1994; playing minor league at Arizona; 8 players drafted; 75 players moved on to a four-year school; 1991 Region IV Champs; Midwest; 6th in the nation for 7 years (1992, 1993, 1994, 1995,1996, and 1997; Runner-up regional.
Coaching: Steve Ruzich, Head Coach, is entering 11 years as a head coach. He compiled a record of 395-224 and played professional with the White Sox. Al Medrano ,Assistant Coach, has coached 16 years and played in the Army. Jeff Struebing , Assistant Coach, coached 7 years and played at SSC and Chicago State. Matt Lyke,Assistant Coach, coached 1 year and was an assistant coach at Neosho Junior College.
Style of Play: Aggressive, hit and run; has 3 good pitchers. Should be better defensively.

Southeastern Illinois College

3575 College Road
Harrisburg, IL 62946-9477
Coach: Jay Burch

NJCAA
Falcons/Blue, Gold
Phone: (618) 252-5028
Fax: (618) 252-3156

ACADEMIC

Founded: 1960
Type: 2 Yr., Public, Coed
Student/Faculty Ratio: 20:1
Male/Female Ratio: Unknown
Undergraduate Enrollment: 2,964
Graduate Enrollment: None
Total Expenses by: Year **In State:** $ 1023+ **Out of State:** $ 5,538+
Degrees Conferred: Associate
Programs of Study: Accounting, Agricultural Business, Agricultural Economics, Arts, Fine Arts, Business Administration, Commerce, Business Management, Biology, Biological Science, Data Processing, Education, Electrical and Electronics Technology, Law Enforcement, Mining Technology, Music, Medical Laboratory

ATHLETIC PROFILE

Conference Affiliation: Great Rivers Conference

Southern Illinois University - Carbondale

Baseball Clubhouse
Carbondale, IL 62901-6702
Coach: Dan Callahan

NCAA I
Salukis/Maroon, White
Phone: (618) 453-2802
Fax: (618) 536-2152

ACADEMIC

Founded: 1869
Type: 4 Yr., Public, Coed
Religion: Non-Affiliated
Campus Housing: Yes
Web-site: http://www.siu.edu
SAT/ACT/GPA: 20 avg
Student/Faculty Ratio: 16:1
Male/Female Ratio: 40:60
Undergraduate Enrollment: 18,700
Graduate Enrollment: 4,4500
Scholarships/Academic: Yes **Athletic:** Yes **Fin Aid:** Yes
Total Expenses by: Year **In State:** $ 7,991 **Out of State:** $ 10,800

Degrees Conferred: AAS, BA, BS, BFA, MA, MS, MBA, MFA, MPA, MD, DBA, JD
Programs of Study: Accounting, Advertising, Agriculture, Animal Science, Anthropology, Architectural, Banking/Finance, Biological Science, Botany, Broadcasting, Business, Dental, Design, Dietetics, English, Forestry, Geology, Horticulture, Hotel/Restaurant, Journalism, Languages, Management, Optometry, Parks/Recreation, Paralegal, Photography, Preprofessional Programs

ATHLETIC PROFILE

Estimated Number of Baseball Scholarships: 11.7
Conference Affiliation: Missouri Valley Conference
Program Profile: We are mid to upper level Division I baseball. Last year our schedule strength was 47th in the nation. We have a recreation center for indoor Winter practice & a natural grass field. Abe Martin Field holds 1,800 spectators & the hill down the right field line accommodate 2,000.
History: Our first season was in 1923. Our field was named Abe Martin on April 30, 1972. It seats 2,000. The "OnThe Hill " surface grass (turf in front of the dugouts) seats 2,000 also. The field was named after Glenn "Abe" Martin who retired in 1971 after 33 years of service including 19 as head baseball coach.
Achievements: 14 trips to NCAA post-season in last 30 years; 5 trips to College World Series (twice in 1968 and 1971, National Runner-Up).
Coaching: Dan Callahan, Head Coach, is in his 3rd year. He has a 226-246 overall career record. He is a 1981 graduate of University of New Orleans. Ken Henderson, Assistant Coach, is a 1979 graduate of Missouri Southern. Derek Johnson, Assistant, is a 1994 graduate from Eastern Illinois.
Roster for 1998 team/In State: 21 **Out of State:** 9 **Out of Country:** 0
Total Number of Varsity/Jr. Varsity: 30 **Number of Spring Games:** 56
Number of Seniors on 1998 Team: 7 **Baseball Camp Dates:** June 7-11; June 15-18
Freshmen Receiving Fin Aid/Athletic: 2
Schedule: Wichita State, Notre Dame, New Orleans, Missouri, Stetson, Illinois
Style of Play: Aggressive base-running, tight defense, take extra bases, try to get pitchers into 7th, go with good bullpen.

Southern Illinois University - Edwardsville

Campus Box 1129
Edwardsville, IL 62026-1129
Coach: Gary Collins
Email: gcollins@siue.edu

NCAA II
Cougars/Red, White
Phone: (618) 650-2871
Fax: (618) 650-3369

ACADEMIC

Founded: 1957
Type: 4 Yr., Public, Coed
Web-site: http;//www.siue.edu/
Campus Housing: Yes
Student/Faculty Ratio: 15:1
Male/Female Ratio: 43:75
Undergraduate Enrollment: 8,700
Graduate Enrollment: 2,300
Scholarships/Academic: Yes **Athletic:** Yes **Fin Aid:** Yes
Total Expenses by: Year **In State:** $ 6,625 **Out of State:** $ 8,625
Degrees Conferred: Baccalaureate, Masters, Specialist, Doctoral
Programs of Study: Over 40 majors which includes Baccalaurette in Nursing.

ATHLETIC PROFILE

Estimated Number of Baseball Scholarships: 7
Conference Affiliation: Great Lakes Valley Conference
Program Profile: The program has been operating for 28 years. SIUE plays only a Spring season. Their home field is Roy E. Lee Field with a capacity of 2,000. The stadium has natural grass.
History: The program began in 1968 with Roy E. Lee was head coach through 1978. He compiled a record of 237-144-4. Collins took over as head coach in 1979 to the present. Collins has compiled a career record of 556-363-5 at SIUE. The baseball program's overall record is 793-507-9.
Achievements: 14 All-Americans; 28 Cougars in pro ranks; 17 appearances in NCAA II tournaments; 6 Appearances in NCAA II World Series.

Coaching: Gary Collins, Head Coach, is entering his 21st season as the winningest coach in SUIE history. He was drafted in 1969 with the St. Louis Cardinals Organization. Began his coaching career as an assistant at SUIE, then moved to Lewis and Clark. Later, he came back to SUIE as head coach.

Roster for 1998 team/In State: 24 **Out of State:** 3 **Out of Country:** 0
Total Number of Varsity/Jr. Varsity: 27 **Percent of Graduation:** 75%
Number of Seniors on 1998 Team: 10 **Number of Sophomores on 1998 Team:** 3
Freshmen Receiving Fin Aid/Athletic: 2 **Positions Needed for 1999/2000:** All
Number of Fall Games: 0 **Number of Spring Games:** 56
Style of Play: No particular style - depends on team's overall skills.

Spoon River College

23235 N County 22
Canton, IL 61520
Coach: Mike Mason

NCAA II
Crusaders/Red, Black, Blue
Phone: (309) 647-6303
Fax: (309) 647-6235

ACADEMIC

Founded: 1969 **Type:** 2 Yr., Public, Coed
Student/Faculty Ratio: 14:1 **Male/Female Ratio:** 1:4
Undergraduate Enrollment: 1,922 **Graduate Enrollment:** None
Scholarships/Academic: No **Athletic:** Yes **Fin Aid:** Yes
Total Expenses by: Hour **In State:** $ 44cr/hr **Out of State:** $ 66cr/hr
Degrees Conferred: Associate
Programs of Study: Accounting, Agriculture, Automotive Technology, Biological Science, Botany, Business Administration, Communications, Criminal Justice, Health Science, Law Enforcement, Liberal Arts, Manufacturing Technology, Political Science, Psychology

ATHLETIC PROFILE

Conference Affiliation: Independent
Program Profile: We are now in the processof building. The field is lighted. Pitchers park is 340 RF, 380 C and 340 LF. We do a 20-game Fall season, a 56-game Spring season and a Florid trip to Orlando. We have 10 full scholaraships that can be divided into halves.
History: Program began in 1970s
Achievements: 1 player signed by the Cubs.

Trinity Christian College

6601 West College Drive
Palos Heights, IL 60463
Coach: Bob Schaaf

NAIA
Trolls/Blue, White
Phone: (708) 597-3000
Fax: (708) 396-7460

ACADEMIC

Founded: 1959 **Type:** 4 Yr., Private, Liberal Arts, Coed
Web-site: http://www.trnty.edu/ **SAT/ACT/GPA:** 21+
Student/Faculty Ratio: 14:1 **Male/Female Ratio:** 45:55
Undergraduate Enrollment: 600 **Graduate Enrollment:** None
Scholarships/Academic: Yes **Athletic:** Yes **Fin Aid:** Yes
Total Expenses by: Year **In State:** $ 13,800 **Out of State:** $ 13,800
Degrees Conferred: BA, BS
Programs of Study: Accounting, Banking and Finance, Biology, Chemistry, Communications, Computer Science, Education, English, Fine Arts, History, Marketing, Music, Nursing, Philosophy, Predentistry, Prelaw, Premed, Psychology, Religion, Social Science, Special Education

Triton College

2000 North Fifth Avenue
River Grove, IL 60171
Coach: Bob Symonds

NJCAA
Trojans/Cardinal Red, Gold
Phone: (708) 456-0300
Fax: (708) 583-3778

ACADEMIC

Founded: 1964
Type: 2 Yr., Public, Coed
Student/Faculty Ratio: 30:1
Male/Female Ratio: 46:54
Undergraduate Enrollment: 12,000
Graduate Enrollment: None
Scholarships/Academic: Yes **Athletic:** No **Fin Aid:** Yes
Total Expenses by: Year **In State:** $ 4,500 **Out of State:** $ 6,500
Degrees Conferred: AA, AS
Programs of Study: Accounting, Advertising, Architectural Technology, Automotive Technology, Carpentry, Construction Management, Construction Technology **Contact school admission office for more information on academic and admission

ATHLETIC PROFILE

Conference Affiliation: North Central Community College Conference (N4C)
Program Profile: Due to conference rules, there is no Fall baseball season at Triton. However, Triton enrolls its players in a PE course so that they practice year around. Generally, Triton begins its games in March and plays about 25 double-headers. Our field is one of the nation's best. Its dimensions are 330' down the lines, 360' center field (20' high fence) and 375' in the power alley.
History: Triton began its program in 1969. There has been only 1 losing season in that span (1969 = 7-13). Overall, Triton's record is 1,081-331-1 (27 years). Since joining the conference in 1973, Triton has won it every year except twice. Triton has also advanced to the NJCAA World Series 10 times, including the last 4 years. Triton finished second in 1993 and 1994.
Achievements: In 26 years, coach Bob Symonds has a 1,061-312 record. He has had 19 All-Americans and 82 players sign pro contracts and 6 have made it to the Major Leagues. He has been named Conference Coach of the Year 14 times and Region Coach of the Year 14 times. He was also chosen as the Diamond/ABCA Coach of the Year twice. In 1992, he became the only one ever to be inducted into the NJCAA Coaches Hall of Fame. He is also a member of the Illinois High School Hall of Fame.
Coaching: Bob Symond ,Head Coach, helped coach a Team USA for Junior College Players. He was coach for the US Sports Festival 1983. Tom Doyle ,Pitching Coach, was All-American at Triton 1975. He finished his college career at Eastern Illinois.
Style of Play: Coach Symonds is aggressive. He likes speed on the base paths. He hits and runs often, as well as steals. Spends a lot of time in practice on the fundamentals. ***Symond's former players to get to the Majors are Kirby Puckett, Lance Johnson, Jeff Reboulet, Jarvis Brown, Steve Decker and Jerry Kutzler.

Truman College

(Former City College of Chicago)
(Program Discontinued)

University of Chicago

5640 S University Avenue
Chicago, IL 60637
Coach: Brian J. Baldea
Email: bbaldea@midway.uchicago.edu

NCAA III
Maroons/Maroon, White
Phone: (773) 702-4643
Fax: (773) 702-6517

ACADEMIC

Founded: 1892
Type: 4 Yr., Private, Coed
Religion: Non-Affiliated
Campus Housing: Yes

Web-site: http://www.uchicago.edu/
SAT/ACT/GPA: Selective
Student/Faculty Ratio: 6:1
Male/Female Ratio: 54:46
Undergraduate Enrollment: 3,600
Graduate Enrollment: 8,400
Scholarships/Academic: Yes **Athletic:** No **Fin Aid:** Yes
Total Expenses by: Year **In State:** $ 31,075 **Out of State:** $ 31,074
Degrees Conferred: BA, BS, MA, MS, MBA, MFA, PhD, MD, JD
Programs of Study: Premed, Prelaw, Economics, Life Sciences, Physical Sciences, Social Sciences, Languages, Letters/Literature, Multi/Interdisciplinary Studies

ATHLETIC PROFILE

Conference Affiliation: University Athletic Association
Program Profile: Our home field is called J. Kyle Anderson field and is a natural grass facility on campus. Our indoor practice site is Henry Crown Field House. We do annual trips to Ft. Myers and Tampa, Florida.
History: The program began in 1892.. Each of the last two seasons have set all-time university record for wins.
Achievements: 1997: National ranking in team winning percentage, home runs and scoring. NCAA III National Statistical Leader in 4 categories (home runs, RBI, runs, slugging percentage). Major league draft selection, All-American, Academic All-American, All-Region: Arthur Ashe, Jr., Scholar-Athlete Award Recipient.
Coaching: Brian Baldea,Head Coach, has coached collegiate baseball for 14 years. He was at Illinois State University for 7 years. His Chicago teams have rewritten all university records, including wins. David Grewer, Assistant Coach, is entering his first year with the program.
Roster for 1998 team/In State: 8 **Out of State:** 14 **Out of Country:** 0
Total Number of Varsity/Jr. Varsity: 22 **Percent of Graduation:** 100%
Number of Seniors on 1998 Team: 7 **Number of Sophomores on 1998 Team:** 0
Most Recent Record: 22 - 8 - 0 **Number of Spring Games:** 40
Positions Needed for 1999/2000: Pitchers, Catcher, M-Infielder
Schedule: Notre Dame, Southern Maine, Washington, Trinity, Aurora University, Benedictine
Style of Play: Smart and aggressive.

University of Illinois - Chicago

901 W Roosevelt Road
Chicago, IL 60608-1516
Coach: Michael Dee

NCAA I
Flames/Scarlet, Navy
Phone: (312) 996-8645
Fax: (312) 996-8349

ACADEMIC

Founded: 1896
Type: 4 Yr., Public, Coed, Engineering
Web-site: http://www.uic.edu/depts/sports
Campus Housing: Yes
SAT/ACT/GPA: Satisfactory combination of test scores and class rank/
Student/Faculty Ratio: 11:1
Male/Female Ratio: 50:50
Undergraduate Enrollment: 16,190
Graduate Enrollment: 8,393
Scholarships/Academic: Yes **Athletic:** Yes **Fin Aid:** Yes
Total Expenses by: Year **In State:** $ 11,250 **Out of State:** $ 16,950
Degrees Conferred: BA, BS, MA, MS, Phd
Programs of Study: Accounting, Anthropology, Applied Art, Architecture, Arts, Biochemistry, Biology, Business Administration, Chemistry, Classics, Communications, Computer Information Systems, Computer Science, Criminal Justice, Economics, Education, Engineering, English, French, Geography, Geology, German, History, Industrial Design, Information Science, Interdisciplinary Studies, Italian, Latin, Liberal Arts, Literature, Management, Materials Science, Mathematics, Medical Laboratory Technology, Music, Nursing, Occupational Therapy, Philosophy, Physical Education, Physical Fitness and Movement, Physical Therapy, Physics, Political Science, Predentistry, Prelaw, Psychology, Russian, Social Scienc ,Spanish, Statistics, Theatre

ATHLETIC PROFILE

Conference Affiliation: Midwestern Collegiate Conference
Program Profile: Our Division I schedule and conference is a 5-6 week Fall practice and games. Spring season begins in March with one or two mini weekend trips followed by a Spring break trip. Within 10-12 days we finish the regular season. Our natural field-brand new stadium has a seating capacity of 1,500 and a lighted field. The old field is still available and also has lights This field has a beautiful Chicago Skyline as a backdrop.
History: We began in 1946 as a two-year branch of the University of Illinois. Our program and school became four-year in 1965. In 1983, the entire program went to Division. In 1985, UIC was a member of the mid-conference (2 Championships). In 1994, UIC became a member of the Midwestern Collegiate Conference.
Achievements: 1990-1993 Mid-Continent Champions in 1991-1992 Divisional Champs; 1990-1993 Coach of the Year; in the last two years alone 6 players drafted: Jason Henry 2nd round by the New York Yankees in 1996 and Tom Szyborski byt he San Diego Padres in 1995 in 5th round.

University of Illinois - Urbana/Champaign

1700 South Fourth St
Champaign, IL 61820
Coach: Richard 'Itch' Jones

NCAA I
Fighting Illini/Orange, Blue
Phone: (217) 333-8605
Fax: (217) 244-9759

ACADEMIC

Founded: 1867
Type: 4 Yr., Public, Coed
SAT/ACT/GPA: 1150avg/26avg
Campus Housing: Yes
Student/Faculty Ratio: 12:1
Male/Female Ratio: 56:44
Undergraduate Enrollment: 27,000+
Graduate Enrollment: 9,000
Scholarships/Academic: Yes **Athletic:** Yes
Fin Aid: Yes
Total Expenses by: Year **In State:** $ 9,419
Out of State: $ 14,581
Degrees Conferred: BA, BS, BM, BFA, BA, MA, MS, MFA
Programs of Study: Accounting, Anthropology, Applied Art, Architecture, Arts, Biochemistry, Biology, Business Administration, Chemistry, Classics, Communications, Computer Information Systems, Computer Science, Interdisciplinary Studies, Italian, Latin, Liberal Arts, Literature, Management, Material Science, Mathematics, Medical Laboratory, Physical Education, Physical Fitness, Physical Therapy, Physics, Political Science, Predentistry, Prelaw, Psychology, Russian, Social Science, Statistics, Theatre

ATHLETIC PROFILE

Conference Affiliation: Big 10 Conference
Program Profile: Our top program is in the Big 10. We have outstanding facilities. There is an indoor bubble and a natural grass stadium that holds 1,500 seats.
History: We won the Big 10 Tournament in 1996 and 1997.
Achievements: Lou Boudreau (retired), John Ericks (Pirates), Jeff Innoz(Mets), Dareel Fletcher (Expos), Scott Spezio (A's); in minors: Mark Dalesandro (Cubs), Sean Mulligan (Indians), Bulba Smith (Rangers), Sean Lawrence (Pirates), Larry Sutton (KC), Forreg Wells (Colorado), Brian McClure San Diego) Josh Klineck (Brewers) Matt Arrandale (St. Louis).
Coaching: Richard 'Itch' Jones, Head Coach, joined UI in 1991 and coached 15 major leaguers. He was 20 years at Southern Illinois. He got his BS in 1960 and his MS in 1965 from Southern Illinois. He earned many honors as a collegiate player. He had a short playing career in Orioles minor league system. Dan Hartleb ,Pitching Coach, has coached six years. Todd Murphy ,Restricted Earnings Coach, has two years at Illinois and assisted at Princeton one year and at Butler two years.
Style of Play: Depends on the talent of each team.

University of Saint Francis

(Former College of St. Francis)

500 Wilcox Street
Joliet, IL 60435
Coach: Tony Delgado
Email: dlake@stfrancis.edu

NAIA
Fighting Saints/Brown, Gold
Phone: (815) 740-3464
Fax: (815) 740-3841

ACADEMIC

Founded: 1920
Type: 4 Yr., Private, Liberal Arts, Coed
Religion: Catholic
Campus Housing: Yes
Web-site: http://www.stfrancis.edu
SAT/ACT/GPA: 950/20/2.5
Student/Faculty Ratio: 11:1
Male/Female Ratio: 1:1
Undergraduate Enrollment: 1,300
Graduate Enrollment: 1,700
Scholarships/Academic: Yes **Athletic:** Yes **Fin Aid:** Yes
Total Expenses by: Year **In State:** $ 17,840 **Out of State:** $ 17,840
Degrees Conferred: BA, BS, BSN, MS, MBA
Programs of Study: Actuarial Science, American Politics, Art, Biology, History, Liberal Studies, Literature, Chemistry, Elementary Education, English, Environmental Science, Mathematics, Music, Natural Science, Philosophy, Political Science, Predental, Premedical, Prepharmacy, Social Work, Special Education, Theology, Writing, Medical Technology, Public Policy, Computer Science, Computer Engineering, Economics, Broadcasting, Management, Business, Information Science

ATHLETIC PROFILE

Estimated Number of Baseball Scholarships: 4
Conference Affiliation: Chicagoland Collegiate Athletic Conference
Program Profile: A highly-regarded sport at the NAIA level, St. Francis plays its games at Gillespie Field, one of the finest baseball facilities in the Midwest. The field just recently had a facelift. A new infield was installed in 1995. The field is a grass turf & the stadium seats 1,000 people. Among the many features of the program, the Saints take a 2-week trip to Texas to open the season each year.
History: St. Francis began its beseball program in 1972. Gordie Gillespie, who retired from St. Francis after the 1995 season, served as the head coach from 1977 up until that year. In 1993, he became college baseball's all-time winningest coach.
Achievements: 8 NAIA World Series Appearances, National Champs in 1993, 12 Conference Titles including 5 in the past six years, 2 former players currently play on the major league level with 3 others in the minor league. Better than 20 draft picks through the years.
Coaching: Tony Delgado , Head Coach, is entering his fourth season with the program after serving as an assistant to Gordi Gillespie for 14 years and also playing for him for four years. He compiled a record of 90-81 through three years. He was a two-time All-District shortstop and an All-American guard in basketball. John Ernst, Arnie Blaylock and Larry Grant - Assistant Coaches.
Roster for 1998 team/In State: 39 **Out of State:** 1 **Out of Country:** 0
Total Number of Varsity/Jr. Varsity: 32 /18 **Percent of Graduation:** 92%
Number of Seniors on 1998 Team: 11 **Most Recent Record:** 25 - 25 - 0
Freshmen Receiving Fin Aid/Athletic: 5 **Academic:** 1
Number of Fall Games: 24 **Number of Spring Games:** 56
Positions Needed for 1999/2000: Pitchers, Catchers, 1st Base, Shortstop
Baseball Camp Dates: June 7-11, June 14-18
Schedule: Texas-Arlington, St. Joseph, Bellevue, Oklahoma City, Southeastern Oklahoma State, Incarnate Word, St. Mary's, Dallas Baptist, Lewis, St. Xavier
Style of Play: Very aggressive, fundamentally sound and know all situations.

Wabash Valley College

2200 College Drive
Mt. Carmel, IL 62863
Coach: Rob Fournier

NJCAA
Warriors/Red, White
Phone: (618) 262-8641
Fax: (618) 262-8641

ACADEMIC

Type: 2 Yr., Public, Coed
Programs of Study: Contact school for programs of study.

ATHLETIC PROFILE

Estimated Number of Baseball Scholarships: 24
Conference Affiliation: GRAC - Great Rivers Athletic Conference
Achievements: 3rd in nation in 1989 - over 30 players drafted; 2 in 1998.
Coaching: Rob Fournier, Head Coach, is entering his third year with the program. He compiled a record of 77-32 Mark Flatten, Assistant Coach, is entering his third year with the program.
Roster for 1998 team/In State: 2 **Out of State:** 40 **Out of Country:** 0
Total Number of Varsity/Jr. Varsity: 0 **Percent of Graduation:** 95%
Most Recent Record: 40 - 6 - 0 **Number of Sophomores on 1998 Team:** 20
Number of Fall Games: 20 **Number of Spring Games:** 56+
Positions Needed for 1999/2000: Pitcher, Shortstop, 2nd Base, Outfielder
Schedule: Volunteer State, Bellevue, Rend Lake, Spring trip in Panama City-TBA
Style of Play: Aggressive, love to run and put pressure on defense.

Waubonsee Community College

Route 47
Sugar Grove, IL 60554
Coach: Dave Randall
Email: Daver@wcc.gwcc.cc.il.us

NJCAA
Chiefs/Vermillion, Gold
Phone: (630) 466-7900
Fax: (630) 466-9108

ACADEMIC

Founded: 1967 **Type:** 2 Yr., Public, Jr. College, Coed
Student/Faculty Ratio: 18:1 **Male/Female Ratio:** 2:1
Undergraduate Enrollment: 8,000 **Graduate Enrollment:** None
Scholarships/Academic: Yes **Athletic:** No **Fin Aid:** Yes
Total Expenses by: Semester **In State:** $ 1,800 **Out of State:** $ 1,800
Degrees Conferred: Associate Degrees
Programs of Study: Associates for all Bachelor of Art and Science Degrees

ATHLETIC PROFILE

Conference Affiliation: Skyway Conference
Program Profile: We play an 18 game Fall season followed by 56 games in the Spring including a weeks trip to Florida.
History: Our recent history since playing in NJCAA Division III includes 3 second places in Region IV and 1 championship. In 1996, we finished a runner-up at the NJCAA Division III World Seniors.
Achievements: We have been nationally ranked NJCAA Division III for the past seven years. We finished second in NJCAA Division III finals in 1996. We have 2 Region IV, Division III Titles and 3 second place finishes. We were Skyway Conference Champions in 1998.
Coaching: Dave Randall, Head Coach, 21 years at Waubonsee as head coach. Mark Nilles - Assistant Coach.
Roster for 1998 team/In State: 20 **Out of State:** 4 **Out of Country:** 0
Total Number of Varsity/Jr. Varsity: 24 **Percent of Graduation:** 80%
Number of Seniors on 1998 Team: 8 **Number of Sophomores on 1998 Team:** 0
Freshmen Receiving Fin Aid/Athletic: 0 **Academic:** 5
Number of Fall Games: 18 **Number of Spring Games:** 56
Positions Needed for 1999/2000: All **Most Recent Record:** 32 - 20 - 0
Schedule: Joliet Junior, College of DuPage, Harper, Kankee Community, Kishwaukee, South Suburban, Madison Area Tech, Erie Community, College of Lake County, Oakton Community
Style of Play: Aggressive base warning, like to steal, and players must be able to bunt.

Western Illinois University

#204 Western Hall
Macomb, IL 61455
Coach: Kim Johnson

NCAA I
Fighting Leatherneck/Purple, Gold
Phone: (309) 298-1521
Fax: (309) 298-1960

ACADEMIC

Founded: 1902
Religion: Non-Affiliated
Web-site: http://www.wiu.edu
Student/Faculty Ratio: 15:1
Undergraduate Enrollment: 9,644
Scholarships/Academic: Yes **Athletic:** Yes
Total Expenses by: Year **In State:** $ 7,573

Type: 4 Yr., Public, Coed
Campus Housing: Yes
SAT/ACT/GPA: 1010/18
Male/Female Ratio: 47:53
Graduate Enrollment: 2,540
Fin Aid: Yes
Out of State: $ 11,489

Degrees Conferred: BA, BFA, BB, BS, BSED, MS, MA
Programs of Study: Accounting, Agriculture, Art, Biochemistry, Communications, Computer Science, Education, Economics, Foreign Languages, Geography, Geology, Health Education, Physical Education, Industrial, Math, Marketing, Music, Philosophy, Physics, Political Science

ATHLETIC PROFILE

Estimated Number of Baseball Scholarships: 7
Conference Affiliation: Mid - Continent Conference
Program Profile: Vince Grady Field (1,200 capacity, natural grass) is one of the finest diamonds in the midwest, equipped with step-down dugouts, electric scoreboard, chain link fence, restroom facilities, batting cages and 4 practice fields are adjacent to game field. Our campus extends over 1,056 acres and is located in rural midwest 40 miles east of Mississippi River, with picnic and recreational areas nearby. We have a 56 game schedule with a south Spring trip.
History: Our program began in the early 1900's with legendary Ray "Rock" Hanson. Dick Pawlow coached here the past 29 years and retired at the end of the 1998 season.
Achievements: 19 players have played professionally; 1995 - 5 players named to All-Conference. Brian Quinn named first team pitcher and second team 2nd base.
Coaching: Kim Johnson ,Head Coach, is entering his first year with the program. He was named Region 4 Coach of the Year in 1996 and Region 24 Coach of the Year in 1998 in Junior College. He has had many JUCO players sign professional contracts. He compiled a record of 181-147 in 7 years. Most of his teams were nationally ranked. Harry Jorgenson & Deon Dittman - Assistant Coaches.
Roster for 1998 team/In State: 25 **Out of State:** 7 **Out of Country:** 0
Total Number of Varsity/Jr. Varsity: 32 **Percent of Graduation:** 98%
Number of Seniors on 1998 Team: 11 **Number of Sophomores on 1998 Team:** 4
Freshmen Receiving Fin Aid/Athletic: 1 **Number of Fall Games:** 9
Positions Needed for 1999/2000: Catcher, 3rd Base, Pitcher, both sides
Schedule: Oral Roberts, Oklahoma State, University of Nebraska, Brigham Young, University of Illinois, University of Iowa, Southern Illinois University, Troy State, University of Missouri
Style of Play: Aggressive both defensively and offensively.

Wheaton College

501 E College Avenue
Wheaton, IL 60187
Coach: Doug Yager

NCAA III
Crusaders/Royal Blue, Orange
Phone: (630) 752-5743
Fax: (630) 752-7007

ACADEMIC

Founded: 1860
Religion: Interdenominational

Type: 4 Yr., Private, Liberal Arts, Coed
Campus Housing: Yes

Web-site: http://www.wheaton.edu/
SAT/ACT/GPA: 100-1100/23-27
Student/Faculty Ratio: 14.4:1
Male/Female Ratio: 50:50
Undergraduate Enrollment: 2,300
Graduate Enrollment: 350
Scholarships/Academic: Yes **Athletic:** Yes **Fin Aid:** Yes
Total Expenses by: Year **In State:** $ 18,190+ **Out of State:** $ 18,190+
Degrees Conferred: BA, BS, BM, BMEd, MA, PHd
Programs of Study: Ancient Languages, Archeology, Art, Biblical Studies, Biology, Business/Economics, Chemistry, Christian Education, Communications, Computer Science/Mathematics, Economics, Education, Enviromental Science, French, Geological Studies, German, History, History/Social Science, Interdisciplinary Studies, Liberal Arts, Engineering, Liberal Arts, Nursing, Literature, Mathematics, Music (6 majors), Philosophy, Physical Education, Physical

ATHLETIC PROFILE

Conference Affiliation: College Conference of Illinois and Wisconsin
Program Profile: We are in the NCAA Division III. We are the in the midst of building a conference and national contender. The playing season is consit of 36 games in the Spring that include a week trip to Florida for Spring training. We play on a natural grass with our grass field being one of the nicest in our conference in the area.
History: Our pogram began in 1892. The "glory" years were in the 1950's and in the 1960's when former Dodger Minor Leaguer Lee Pfund coached the Crusaders. Coach Pfund is also the father of former LA Laker head coach Randy Pfund. Recent history, Coach Finny Rajchal led the Crusaders to a record year in victories in his rookie season.
Achievements: Conference Title (CCI) in 1951; players were - Jay Miller which is now the GM of the New Orleans Zephyrs (Milwaukee Brewers AAA Club), David Philips CCIW All-Conference in 1992, 1993, 7 1994; played professional ball in 1994 for the Minnearous Millers lindependent), Jonathan Rockless was All-Conference in 1995, 1996, and 1997 he was transferred this year to Illinois State where he will be a starter.

William Rainey Harper College

1200 West Algonquin Road
Palatine, IL 60067
Coach: Norm Garrett

NJCAA
Hawks/Gold, Maroon
Phone: (847) 925-6000
Fax: (847) 925-6038

ACADEMIC

Founded: 1965
Type: 2 Yr., Public, Coed
Student/Faculty Ratio: 15:1
Male/Female Ratio: 41:59
Undergraduate Enrollment: 15,900
Graduate Enrollment: None
Scholarships/Academic: No **Athletic:** No **Fin Aid:** Yes
Total Expenses by: Year **In State:** $ 1,200 **Out of State:** $ 5,800
Degrees Conferred: Associate
Programs of Study: Contact school for programs of study.

INDIANA

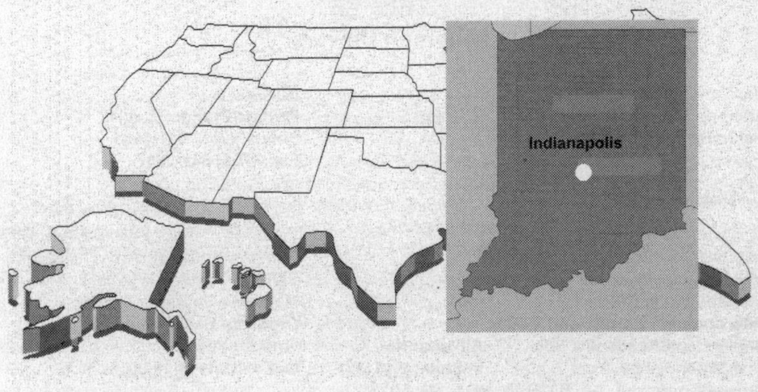

SCHOOL	CITY	AFFILIATION 99	PAGE
Anderson University	Anderson	NCAA III	272
Ball State University	Muncie	NCAA I	272
Bethel College	Mishawaka	NAIA	273
Butler University	Indianapolis	NCAA I	274
De Pauw University	Greencastle	NCAA III	275
Earlham College	Richmond	NCAA III	275
Franklin College	Franklin	NCAA III	276
Goshen College	Goshen	NAIA	276
Grace College	Winona	NAIA	277
Hanover College	Hanover	NCAA III	278
Huntingdon College	Huntington	NAIA	278
Indiana Institute of Technology	Fort Wayne	NAIA	279
Indiana State University	Terre Haute	NCAA I	280
Indiana University	Bloomington	NCAA I	281
Indiana University - Purdue U at FW	Fort Wayne	NCAA II	281
Indiana University - Purdue U-Indianapolis	Indianapolis	NCAA II	282
Indiana University Southeast	New Albany	NAIA	283
Indiana Wesleyan University	Marion	NAIA	283
Manchester College	North	NCAA III	284
Marian College	Indianapolis	NAIA	285
Oakland City College	Oakland City	NCAA II	285
Purdue University	West Lafayette	NCAA I	286
Rose-Hulman Institute of Technology	Terre Haute	NCAA III	286
Saint Francis College	Fort Wayne	NAIA	287
Saint Joseph's College	Rensselaer	NCAA II	288
Taylor University	Upland	NAIA	288
Tri - State University	Angola	NAIA	289
University of Evansville	Evansville	NCAA I	289
University of Indianapolis	Indianapolis	NCAA II	290
University of Notre Dame	Notre Dame	NCAA I	291
University of Southern Indiana	Evansville	NCAA II	292
Valparaiso University	Valparaiso	NCAA I	292
Vincennes University	Vincennes	NJCAA	293
Wabash College	Crawfordsville	NCAA III	294

Anderson University

1100 East 5th Street
Anderson, IN 46012
Coach: Dr. Don Brandon

NCAA III
Ravens/Orange, Black
Phone: (765) 641-4488
Fax: (765) 641-3857

ACADEMIC

Founded: 1917
Type: 4 Yr., Private, Liberal Arts, Coed
Religion: Church of God
Campus Housing: Yes
Web-site: http://www.anderson.edu/
SAT/ACT/GPA: 975+/21+
Student/Faculty Ratio: 15:1
Male/Female Ratio: 42:58
Undergraduate Enrollment: 2,003
Graduate Enrollment: 149
Scholarships/Academic: Yes **Athletic:** No **Fin Aid:** Yes
Total Expenses by: Year **In State:** $ 16,000 **Out of State:** $ 16,00
Degrees Conferred: AA, BA, BSN, MBA, MA, MDIV
Programs of Study: Athletic Training, Business/Marketing, Finance, Management, Accounting, Computer Science, Education, Health Sciences, Psychology, Social Sciences, Philosophy, Theology, Visual and Performing Arts, Music and Communications

ATHLETIC PROFILE

Conference Affiliation: Indiana Collegiate Conference
Program Profile: We are one of the finest collegiate baseball facilities in the MidWest. Our sadium resembles Cincinnati's Riverfront Stadium. It seats 1200 and has a press box, dugouts, an electronic scoreboard, a public address system, a modern backstop, tarps for infield, a home plate and bullpen and 4-80' hitting tunnels. There is a practice field. Indoor facilities include full netted batting cage and several pitching mounds. We are building a new Wellness Center and adding 80,000 sq.ft. for sports and recreation.
History: Our program began in 1941. It moved from NAIA to NCAA III in 1993.
Achievements: ECAC Champs in 1989, 1990, 1992, and 1993; NAIA Area VI Champs in 1984, 1987; NCAA III Mid-East Regional Champs in 1993. NCAA III National 5th place in 1993; NAIA District Champs in 1965; 1978, 1980, 1982, 1984-1992; NCCAA World Series in 199 and 1993. 27 All-Americans; 13 have signed pro contracts; 3 GTE Academic All-Americans since 1992; 68 All-Conference since 1980.
Coaching: Don Brandon, Head Coach, is on his 25th season at AU. He has been Conference Coach of the Year seven times and District Coach of the Year nine times. He was Regional Coach of the Year three times. He has been Director of AU Baseball Camps for 14 years.
Style of Play: Speed, power, solid defense and strong pitching.

Ball State University

HP 120
Muncie, IN 47306-0929
Coach: Rich Maloney
Email: rmaloney@uwp.edu

NCAA I
Cardinals/Cardinal, White
Phone: (765) 285-8242
Fax: (765) 285-8929

ACADEMIC

Founded: 1918
Type: 4 Yr., Public, Coed
Religion: Non-Affiliated
Campus Housing: Yes
Web-site: http://www.bsu.edu/sports
SAT/ACT/GPA: 920/19
Student/Faculty Ratio: 12:1
Male/Female Ratio: 1:1
Undergraduate Enrollment: 18,500
Graduate Enrollment: 2,400
Scholarships/Academic: Yes **Athletic:** Yes **Fin Aid:** Yes
Total Expenses by: Year **In State:** $ 7,934 **Out of State:** $ 13,490
Degrees Conferred: AA, AS, BA, BS, BFA, BGS, BM, MA, MBA, PhD

Programs of Study: Accounting, Actuarial Science, Anthropology, Aquatic Biology, Architecture, Art, Banking/Finance, Botany, Broadcasting, Business, Communications, Mathematics, Philosophy

ATHLETIC PROFILE

Conference Affiliation: Mid-American Conference (MAC)
Program Profile: Ball State plays its home games at Ball Diamond, considered one of the MidWest's finest playing surfaces. The diamond, which features seating for 1,700, measures 330' down each line, 365' to the power alleys and 400' to center field. A full infield tarp, area tarps and brick dust infield enable Cardinals to play when other fields suffer effects of inclement weather. Slots in the outfield fence and the high outside fence provide an excellent batting background. BSU's season gets underway is in March with a trip to Boca Raton.
History: Baseball at Ball State began in 1920 under Orville Sink and grew in 1922 under Paul Williams (coached 35 of next 37 years). Maloney is the seventh coach in 78-year history. Norman Wann coached one year, Ray Louthen had the helm from 1959-1970, Bob Rickel (1971-1982) and Pat Quinn (1983-195) also coached.
Achievements: All American 1st team was Thomas Howard in 1986; All-American 3rd team was Jason Meier in 1997 and Nick Witte in 1996; Honorable Mention was Ed Farris in 1996; drafted players were Darrell Betts in 1995, Dennis Barry in 1972, Dave Rust in 1989, Curt Conley in 1993, Mark Davis in 1987, Don DeWitt in 1980, Greg Dikos in 1979, Ed Farris in 1997, Scott Goss in 1984, Frank Houlk in 1967, Thomas Howard in 1987, Homer Jackson in 1996, Dru Kosko in 1986, Sam McConnell in 1997, Don Presser in 1974, Merv Henmund in 1964, Kenny Reed in 1993, Rick Richmond in 1980, Rob Robins in 1981, Mike Roesler in 1985, Jim Roudebush in 1969, Mike Shebek in 1987, Bruce Stanley in 1996/1997, Clint Wicken Sheimer in 1979, Nick Witte in 1996, Jeff Urban in 1998.
Coaching: Rich Maloney ,Head Coach, is the second coach in the BSU history to record a winning season as a rookie (32-20-1 in 1996). He has a 72-39-1 record, was a third team All-American middle infielder and was drafted by the Atlanta Braves. John Lowery, Assistant Coach, has coached 4 pitchers to the pros in four years.
Roster for 1998 team/In State: 22 **Out of State:** 9 **Out of Country:** 7
Total Number of Varsity/Jr. Varsity: 31 **Percent of Graduation:** 0
Number of Seniors on 1998 Team: 6 **Number of Sophomores on 1998 Team:** 5
Most Recent Record: 39 - 18 - 0 **Number of Spring Games:** 56
Baseball Camp Dates: December 16,17, 26-29
Schedule: Wichita State, North Carolina State, Wake Forest, Michigan, Purdue, Indiana State
Style of Play: AGGRESSIVE!!!

Bethel College

1001 West McKinley Avenue **NAIA**
Mishawaka, IN 46545 **Pilots/Royal, White, Gold**
Coach: Sam Riggleman **Phone: (219) 257-3344**
Email: trulocs@bethel-in.edu **Fax: (219) 257-3385**

ACADEMIC

Founded: 1947 **Type:** 4 Yr., Private, Liberal Arts, Coed
Religion: Missionary Church **Campus Housing:** Yes
Web-site: http://www.bethel-in.edu/ **SAT/ACT/GPA:** 900/20/2.0
Student/Faculty Ratio: 18:1 **Male/Female Ratio:** 40:60
Undergraduate Enrollment: 1,500 **Graduate Enrollment:** 100
Scholarships/Academic: Yes **Athletic:** Yes **Fin Aid:** Yes
Total Expenses by: Year **In State:** $ 16,200 **Out of State:** $ 16,200
Degrees Conferred: AA, AS, AAS, BA, BS, BSN, Masters
Programs of Study: Accounting, American Sign Languages, Art, Biblical Studies, Biology, Business Administration, Business Education, Chemistry, Christian Ministries, Communications, Drama, Elementary Education, Predentistry, Prelaw, Premedicine, Engineering, English, English Education, History, Interior Design, Liberal Arts, Mathematics, Music Education, Nursing, Psychology

ATHLETIC PROFILE

Conference Affiliation: Mid Central Conference
Program Profile: We have two national affiliations, NAIA and NCAA (National Christian College Athletic Association). Our outstanding playing facility has a grass surface with dimensions of RF/LF 335', RC/LC 365' and CF 400. Our Fall program is 6-7 weeks and our weight conditioning program is 50-55 weeks. We have a game schedule in the Spring.
History: The program began in the late 1960's (the exact year is not known).
Achievements: 1997 Conference Champions; 1997 NCCAA National Runner-Up; David Haverstick drafted and signed by Arizona Diamondbacks in 1997; John Urbanski, NAIA 2nd team All-American; John Urbanski, Allen Hodge, Seth Zartham were NCCAA All-American team.
Coaching: Sam Riggleman, Head Coach, compiled a record of 496-380 in 21 seasons. Dave Hicks - Assistant coach. Dick Siler - Assistant. Troy Heckerman - Assistant. Dave Marvin - Assistant.
Roster for 1998 team/In State: 18 **Out of State:** 9 **Out of Country:** 2
Total Number of Varsity/Jr. Varsity: 28 **Percent of Graduation:** 99%
Number of Seniors on 1998 Team: 4 **Number of Sophomores on 1998 Team:** 7
Most Recent Record: 39-15-0
Freshmen Receiving Fin Aid/Athletic: 12/14 **Academic:** 4/12
Number of Fall Games: 7-8 **Number of Spring Games:** 50-55
Positions Needed for 1999/2000: Pitcher, Shortstop
Baseball Camp Dates: June 21-24, June 28-July 1
Schedule: Valparaiso, St. Joseph, St. Xavier, Huntington, Spring Arbor, Mt. Vernon Nazarene
Style of Play: Aggressive, historically solid pitching. Teams play hard.

Butler University

4600 Sunset Avenue
Indianapolis, IN 46208
Coach: Steve Farley

NCAA I
Bulldogs/Blue, White
Phone: (317) 940-9375
Fax: (317) 940-9734

ACADEMIC

Founded: 1855 **Type:** 4 Yr., Private, Liberal Arts, Coed
Religion: Independent **Campus Housing:** Yes
Web-site: http://www.butleruniversity.edu **SAT/ACT/GPA:** 1000
Student/Faculty Ratio: 13:1 **Male/Female Ratio:** 41:59
Undergraduate Enrollment: 3,1000 **Graduate Enrollment:** 1,000
Scholarships/Academic: Yes **Athletic:** Yes **Fin Aid:** Yes
Total Expenses by: Year **In State:** $ 20,000 **Out of State:** $ 20,000
Degrees Conferred: AA, AS, BA, BS, BFA, BM, BSHS, MA, MS, MBA, MM
Programs of Study: Accounting, Art, Biology, Business Administration, Chemistry, Composition, Computer Science, Dance, Economics, Education, Elementary Education, German, Journalism, History, Marketing, Management, Music, Mathematics, Philosophy, Religion, Political Science, Telecommunications, Sociology, Pharmacy, Psychology

ATHLETIC PROFILE

Conference Affiliation: MidWest Collegiate Conference
Program Profile: We have a year-round program,a Division I program and a Southern trip. On the off-season there is a weight program. We have a demanding school. Our natural grass field has big league Ball Park dimensions and an indoor fieldhouse. We have Fall and Spring seasons.
History: We are one of the most rapidly improving Division I program in the MidWest. Our school has been playing baseball for 100 years.
Achievements: 1996 Conference Champs; 1994 and 1996 Coach of the Year. Conference Championships in the 1970's and 1980's. Program has gone from last place to second place in just three years under Coach Farley.
Coaching: Steve Farley - Head Coach. Tony Baldwin - Assistant Coach. Mike Tynca ,Assistant Coach, is a former Orioles pro player. Matt Buczkowski is a former Phillies pro player.
Style of Play: Pitching and defense are the priorities, solid fundamentals, aggressive on defense.

De Pauw University

309 South Locust
Greencastle, IN 46135
Coach: Ed Meyer

NCAA III
Tigers/Gold, Black
Phone: (765) 658-4939
Fax: (765) 658-4964

ACADEMIC

Founded: 1837
Religion: Methodist
Web-site: http://www.depauw.edu
Student/Faculty Ratio: 11:1
Undergraduate Enrollment: 2,100
Scholarships/Academic: Yes **Athletic:** No
Total Expenses by: Year **In State:** $ 21,580

Type: 4 Yr., Public, Liberal Arts, Coed
Campus Housing: Yes
SAT/ACT/GPA: 1150/24
Male/Female Ratio: 45:55
Graduate Enrollment: None
Fin Aid: Yes
Out of State: $ 21,580

Degrees Conferred: BA, BMEd, BMA
Programs of Study: College of Liberal Arts, with a choice of 41 majors including: Biological Sciences, Chemistry, Communications, Education, Economics, Management, International Studies, Political Science, Psychology, Etc. ; Also offers a School of Music with a choice of 5 majors.

ATHLETIC PROFILE

Conference Affiliation: Independent Conference

Earlham College

National Road West
Richmond, IN 47374
Coach: Tom Parkevich

NCAA III
Quakers/Maroon, White
Phone: (765) 983-1414
Fax: (765) 983-1446

ACADEMIC

Founded: 1847
Religion: Society of Friends (Quakers)
Web-site: http://www.earlham.edu/
Student/Faculty Ratio: 11:1
Undergraduate Enrollment: 1,050
Scholarships/Academic: Yes **Athletic:** No
Total Expenses by: Year **In State:** $ 23,546

Type: 4 Yr., Private, Liberal Arts, Coed
Campus Housing: Yes
SAT/ACT/GPA: 1200/25
Male/Female Ratio: 44:56
Graduate Enrollment: None
Fin Aid: Yes
Out of State: $ 23,546

Degrees Conferred: Bachelors
Programs of Study: Business and Management, International Studies, Languages, Letters/Literature, Life Sciences, Natural Sciences, Prelaw, Premed, Psychology, Secondary Education, Social Sciences, Visual and Performing Arts, many Multidisciplinary Studies.

ATHLETIC PROFILE

Conference Affiliation: North Coast Athletic Conference
Program Profile: Earlham was unable to defeat only 2 conference opponents in 1993. Both were ranked in the top 10 in the country. EC plays in one of the nation's finest Div. III facilities. McBride Stadium was formerly a minor league park for the Cincinnati Reds. Seating capacity is 2,000.
History: Earlham is on its way up in the nationally respected NCAC Conference. EC's 5th place finish in the NCAC in 1993 was its highest since joining the conference in 1989. Earlham won the CAC Conference title in its final year in that conference, 1988.

Franklin College

501 E Monroe Street
Franklin, IN 46131
Coach: Lance Marshall
Email: marshall@franklincoll.edu

NCAA III
Grizzlies/Navy, Gold
Phone: (317) 738-8136
Fax: (317) 738-8248

ACADEMIC

Founded: 1834
Religion: Baptist
Web-site: http://www.franklincoll.edu/
Student/Faculty Ratio: 13:1
Undergraduate Enrollment: 900
Scholarships/Academic: Yes **Athletic:** No
Total Expenses by: Year **In State:** $ 16,900
Degrees Conferred: BA, BS

Type: 4 Yr., Private, Liberal Arts, Coed
Campus Housing: Yes
SAT/ACT/GPA: 1000
Male/Female Ratio: 45:55
Graduate Enrollment: None
Fin Aid: Yes
Out of State: $ 16,900

Programs of Study: Accounting, American Studies, Art, Banking and Finance, Biology, Broadcasting, Business and Management, Chemistry, Computer Information Sytems, Computer Sciences, Economics, Education, English, French, History, Information Science, International Business, Journalism, Marketing, Mathematics, Occupational Therapy, Philosophy, Physical Education, Physics, Political Science, Predentistry, Prelaw, Premed, Prevet, Psychology, Recreation and Leisure, Religion, Secondary Education, Spanish, Theatre

ATHLETIC PROFILE

Conference Affiliation: Indiana Collegiate Athletic Conference
Program Profile: Our Fall baseball includes 9 games over six weeks. We have a natural grass facility on campus. Lined with pine trees, it is a gorgeous setting for baseball. It has an outdoor batting cage, 4 bullpens mounds and a portable cage for batting practice. The field's dimension are 325-370 and 395.
History: Our program began in 1942. Franklin finished 34th in Hoosier Collegiate Conference in 1957, finished 2nd in HCC in 1960 and finished tied for 3rd in HCC in 1964.
Coaching: Lance Marshall, Head Coach, is entering his second season with the program. He previously coached at Rockford College and Elmhurst College. He is Associate Scout for the Houston Astros.
Roster for 1998 team/In State: 20 **Out of State:** 1 **Out of Country:** 0
Total Number of Varsity/Jr. Varsity: 0 **Percent of Graduation:** 99%
Number of Seniors on 1998 Team: 2 **Most Recent Record:** 3 - 30 - 0
Freshmen Receiving Fin Aid/Athletic: 0 **Academic:** 12
Number of Fall Games: 9 **Number of Spring Games:** 36
Positions Needed for 1999/2000: Pitcher, Middle Infielder
Baseball Camp Dates: June 15-19; December 28-30
Schedule: Indiana University, Wittenberg, Anderson, DePauw University, Rose Hulman Institute
Style of Play: Based on good fundamental defense and good pitching. Very aggressive offensively.

Goshen College

1700 South Main Street
Goshen, IN 46526
Coach: Todd Bacon

NAIA
Maple/Purple, White
Phone: (219) 535-7493
Fax: (219) 535-7531

ACADEMIC

Founded: 1894
Religion: Mennonite
Web-site: http://www.goshen.edu/
Student/Faculty Ratio: 13:1

Type: 4 Yr., Private, Liberal Arts, Coed
Campus Housing: Yes
SAT/ACT/GPA: Avg. 1120/Ave. 3.3
Male/Female Ratio: 45:55

Undergraduate Enrollment: 1,000
Graduate Enrollment: None
Scholarships/Academic: Yes **Athletic:** Yes **Fin Aid:** Yes
Total Expenses by: Year **In State:** $ 16,810 **Out of State:** $ Varies
Degrees Conferred: BA, BS
Programs of Study: Accounting, Anthropology, Architecture, Art, Art Therapy, Bible and Religion, Biblical Studies, Business, Business Administration, Chemical Engineering, Chemistry, Church Music, Coaching, Communications, Computer Science, Computer Systems, Data Processing, Early Childhood Education, Economics, Education, Elementary Education, English, Environmental Studies, Family Life, French, German, Graphis Design, Health and Safety, History, International Studies, Journalism, Mathematics, Medical Technology, Music, Music Performance, Music Researched, Natural Science, Nursing, Physical Studies, Physics, Political Science, Preengineering, Prelaw, Premed, Prephysical Therapy, Preseminary, Preveterinary, Productions Crafts, Psychology

ATHLETIC PROFILE

Conference Affiliation: Mid - Central Collegiate Conference
Program Profile: We have top notch indoor an outdoor facilities. We play a 10-game Fall schedule, and a 50-game Spring schedule with a Florida trip. We recently spent $25,000 to upgrade the baseball facility and added a new $6.5 million recreation-fitness center.
History: Goshen has played 13 NAIA National Scholar-Athletes in the past ten years.
Achievements: NAIA District Champions in 1994; MCC Conference Champions in 1995; MCC Coach of the Year in 1988 and 1995.

Grace College

200 Seminary Drive
Winona, IN 46590
Coach: Glen Johnson

NAIA
Lancers/Red, White, Black
Phone: (800) 54-GRACE
Fax: (219) 372-5295

ACADEMIC

Founded: 1948
Type: 4 Yr., Private, Liberal Arts, Coed
Religion: Brethren
Campus Housing: Yes
Web-site: http://www.grace.edu/
SAT/ACT/GPA: 920/19/2.0
Student/Faculty Ratio: 16:1
Male/Female Ratio: 42:58
Undergraduate Enrollment: 777
Graduate Enrollment: 124
Scholarships/Academic: Yes **Athletic:** Yes **Fin Aid:** Yes
Total Expenses by: Year **In State:** $ 14,938 **Out of State:** $ 14,938
Degrees Conferred: BA, BS, BM, MS
Programs of Study: Accounting, Art, Art Education, Biblical Studies, Biology, Biology Education, Business Administration, Business Education, Christian Ministries, Communication, Counseling, Criminal Justice, Education (Elementary, Secondary), English, English Education, French, French Education, General Science, German, German Education, Graphic Arts, International Business, Management Information Systems, Mathematics, Mathematics Education, Music Education, Music Management, Physical Education, Sport Broadcasting, Sport Journalism, Sport Management, Sport Medicine, Sport Psychology, Teaching Major, Predentistry, Prelaw, Premed, Prepharmacy, Prephysical Therapy, Psychology, Russian, Science Education, Sociology, Spanish, Spanish Education, Preveterinary Medicine

ATHLETIC PROFILE

Estimated Number of Baseball Scholarships: 4
Conference Affiliation: Mid-Central Conference MCC
Program Profile: We are rebuilding. We have 24 under classmen. Our Fall season is 7 weeks and our Spring season is 17 weeks. We play a total of 56 games and have natural grass , a seating capacity of 200 and new dugouts.
Coaching: Glenn Johnson - Head Coach. Glenn Goldsmith - Assistant Coach.
Total Number of Varsity/Jr. Varsity: 28 **Most Recent Record:** 11 - 39 - 0
Number of Seniors on 1998 Team: 4 **Number of Sophomores on 1998 Team:** 9

Number of Fall Games: 10 **Number of Spring Games:** 55
Positions Needed for 1999/2000: Pitchers, 1st and 3rd base, Outfielders-2
Schedule: Saginaw Valley, Indiana Tech, University of South Carolina-Spartanburg, Grand Valley State, Anderson, Gardner-Webb
Style of Play: Aggressive - hit and run, run, bunt and steal.

Hanover College

P.O. Box 108
Hanover, IN 47243
Coach: Dick Naylor

NCAA III
Panthers/Red, Blue
Phone: (812) 866-7374
Fax: (812) 866-2164

ACADEMIC

Founded: 1827
Type: 4 Yr., Private, Liberal Arts, Coed
Religion: Presbyterian
Campus Housing: Yes
Web-site: http://www.hanover.edu/
SAT/ACT/GPA: 1170/26 Median
Student/Faculty Ratio: 11:1
Male/Female Ratio: 48:52
Undergraduate Enrollment: 1,090
Graduate Enrollment: None
Scholarships/Academic: Yes **Athletic:** No **Fin Aid:** Yes
Total Expenses by: Year **In State:** $ 13,500 **Out of State:** $ 13,500
Degrees Conferred: BA
Programs of Study: Anthropology, Biology, Broadcasting, Business Administration, Chemistry, Communications, Dramatic Arts, Economics, Education, English, Film Arts, French, Geology, German, History, International Relations, Management, Mathematics, Music, Philosophy, Physics, Political Science, Predentistry, Prelaw, Premed, Psychology, Religion, Social Science, Sociology, Spanish, Speech Pathology, Telecommunications, Theatre

ATHLETIC PROFILE

Conference Affiliation: ICAC

Huntingdon College

2303 College Avenue
Huntington, IN 46750
Coach: Mike Frame
Email: mframe@huntingdon.edu

NAIA
Foresters/Red, Forest Green
Phone: (219) 356-4082
Fax: (219) 356-4090

ACADEMIC

Founded: 1897
Type: 4 Yr., Private, Liberal Arts, Coed
Religion: United Brethren
Campus Housing: Yes
Web-site: http://www.huntcol.edu/
SAT/ACT/GPA: 800/18
Student/Faculty Ratio: 12:1
Male/Female Ratio: 49:51
Undergraduate Enrollment: 700
Graduate Enrollment: 50
Scholarships/Academic: Yes **Athletic:** Yes **Fin Aid:** Yes
Total Expenses by: Year **In State:** $ 14,900 **Out of State:** $ 14,900
Degrees Conferred: AA, BA, BS, Masters
Programs of Study: Accounting, Arts, Biblical Studies, Biology, Broadcasting, Business Administration, Chemistry, Communications, Computer Science, Economics, Education, Elementary Education, English, Graphic Art, History, Management, Mathematics, Medical Technology, Ministries, Music, Natural Resources, Philosophy, Physical Education, Physical Fitness/Exercise Science, Predentistry, Preengineering, Prelaw, Premed, Prevet, Psychology, Recreation and Leisure, Religion Science, Secondary Education, Sociology, Special Education, Theatre, Theology

ATHLETIC PROFILE

Estimated Number of Baseball Scholarships: $25,400

Conference Affiliation: Mid-Central Conference
Program Profile: We have an outstanding outdoor facility with lights. There is a great fieldhouse for Winter work. We have won conference 25 out of 38 years. We play a Fall schedule.
History: Our program began in 1897. We have won conference 25 out of 38 years.
Achievements: 8 players drafted since 1974.
Coaching: Mike Frame ,Head Coach, is entering his 13th year with a record of 308-227 . He was MCC Coach of the Year five times. He was NAIA District, Area, and NCCAA Coach of the Year once. He serves as the MCC baseball chairman and is a member of the NAIA National Rating Committee. He serves as an Associate Director of Admission. Bob Boozer, Assistant Coach, is on his second year. His responsibilities include overseeing HC's strength program, working with the outfielders and coaching first base. Dave Goodmiller - Assistant. Russ Lawson - Assistant Coach.
Style of Play: Just try and be fundamentally very solid.

Indiana Institute of Technology

1600 East Washington Blvd
Fort Wayne, IN 46803
Coach: Lance Hershberger
Email: hensberger@indtech.edu

NAIA
Warriors/Black, Orange
Phone: (219) 422-5561
Fax: (219) 422-4584

ACADEMIC

Founded: 1930
Religion: Non-Affiliated
Web-site: http://www.indtech.edu/
Student/Faculty Ratio: 18:1
Undergraduate Enrollment: 1,400
Scholarships/Academic: Yes **Athletic:** Yes
Total Expenses by: Year **In State:** $ 16,430

Type: 4 Yr., Private, Coed, Engineering
Campus Housing: Yes
SAT/ACT/GPA: 860/18/2.0
Male/Female Ratio: 65:35
Graduate Enrollment: None
Fin Aid: Yes
Out of State: $ 16,430

Degrees Conferred: BS, Limited amount of Association Degrees
Programs of Study: Accounting, Computer Engineering, Computer Science, Electrical Engineering and Technology, Engineering and Management, Human Services, Marketing, Mechanical Engineering, Park and Recreations Management, Recreation Therapy, Sport Management, Technical and Business Writing

ATHLETIC PROFILE

Estimated Number of Baseball Scholarships: 12 Full
Conference Affiliation: Wolverine - Hoosier Conference
Program Profile: Our program is entering the 8th year. We play a Fall & Spring baseball (full 65 game schedule) with a 20-25 game junior varsity schedule. We take a Southern trip on Spring break & several weekend trips. We beat at least one ranked opponent on NCAA Div. I, II, III & NAIA level. Last year, we played a great schedule. We have a new indoor facility with 4 batting tunnels, locker room offices, outdoor tunnel & poll way cage. We play in a minor league stadium in Ft. Wayne.
History: The program began in 1991. We went from 11 wins the first year to 34-18 this past year. Our record and schedule have improved every year. We won the NAIA Great Lakes Sectional Tournament in 1996 and participated in the NAIA Great Lakes Regional Tournament in 1996 (The winner of which advanced to the NAIA World Series). We are still a fairly young program and will have our first senior dominated team in 1997.
Achievements: 1996 NAIA Great Lakes Sectional Champs; 1998 Great Lakes Sectional Champs; 1998 NAIA Great Lakes Regional Champs; 1998 NAIA World Series; National Runner-Up players; Troy Bryman was named in 1994 and 1995 Academic All-American; Steve Devine was named 1994 All-District 21 and 1996 All-Sectional; Dameon Smith - was 1996 All-Sectional; Angel Martinez was 1997 All-Sectional; 1998 NAIA Great Lakes All-Sectional; Regional Player of the Year, & many more.
Coaching: Lance Hensberger,Head Coach, is in his 8th year and works with pitchers and catchers. He started the program and is a former successful high school coach at Bishop Divinger in Fort Wayne. He has built Indiana Tech into a formidable program. Steve Devine, Assistant Coach, works with outfielders, heads the junior varsity program and is in change of weight training. He was a great player at Indiana Tech. Kevin Grofino, Assistant Coach, works with catchers and pitchers. He is in his second year and was a former player at Tech. He is also bullpen coach.

Roster for 1998 team/In State: 6 **Out of State:** 19 **Out of Country:** 0
Total Number of Varsity/Jr. Varsity: 25 /14 **Percent of Graduation:** 75%
Number of Seniors on 1998 Team: 8 **Number of Sophomores on 1998 Team:** 0
Freshmen Receiving Fin Aid/Athletic: 6 **Academic:** 2
Number of Fall Games: 5 **Number of Spring Games:** 60
Positions Needed for 1999/2000: Position players
Most Recent Record: 48 - 20 - 0 **Baseball Camp Dates:** December 28-30
Schedule: Notre Dame, Butler University, Michigan State, Western Kentucky University, Cumberland University, St. Joseph, University of Indianapolis, St. Xavier University, Bethel
Style of Play: We are a scrappy team as evidenced by 129 hits by pitches in 1998. We are not a bunch of "pretty boys in oakley sunglasses and fancy warm-up suits". We are "get down dirty" and get after it players". We want "die hands" who love baseball and eat, drink and sleep the game in our program.

Indiana State University

4th and Chestnut Street
Terre Haute, IN 47809
Coach: Bob Warn

NCAA I
Sycamores/Blue, White
Phone: (812) 237-4051
Fax: (812) 237-2913

ACADEMIC

Founded: 1865 **Type:** 4 Yr., Public, Coed
Religion: Non-Affiliated **Campus Housing:** Yes
Web-site: Not Available **SAT/ACT/GPA:** 820/20
Student/Faculty Ratio: 20:1 **Male/Female Ratio:** 49:1
Undergraduate Enrollment: 11,870 **Graduate Enrollment:** 1,500
Scholarships/Academic: Yes **Athletic:** Yes **Fin Aid:** Yes
Total Expenses by: Year **In State:** $ 7,050 **Out of State:** $ 11,346
Degrees Conferred: AA, AS, AAS, BA, BS, BFA, MA, MS, MBA, MFA
Programs of Study: Accounting, Anthropology, Athletic, Banking/Finance, Biology, Business, Chemistry, Communications, Computer, Dietetics, Economics, Education, Engineering, English, Medical, Nursing, Office, Parks/Recreation, Preprofessional Programs, Religion, Safety, Textiles/Clothing, Urban Studies

ATHLETIC PROFILE

Estimated Number of Baseball Scholarships: 4
Conference Affiliation: Missouri Valley Conference
Program Profile: We play on an astro turf infield and a grass outfield. It has a seating capacity of 1,000 and a state of the art lighting system. We are a Top 25 program and our playing season is from February through June. We have a six weeks Fall program.
History: Our program began in1897. The Sycamores placed fifth in the MVC regular season standings. However, we came out of the loser's bracket to annex its seventh trip to the NCAA post-season tournament. The Sycamores were 1-2 at the NCAA MidWest II Regional at Oklahoma City. Indiana State qualified for the College World Series in 1986. Current regime is 850-506.
Achievements: Coach of the Year in 1979, 1983, 1984, and 1986; 86 players in pro ball overall.
Coaching: Bob Warn, Head Coach, started in 1976. Mitch Hannahs, Hitting/Infield, in his third year.
Roster for 1998 team/In State: 17 **Out of State:** 11 **Out of Country:** 0
Total Number of Varsity/Jr. Varsity: 28 **Percent of Graduation:** 70%-80%
Number of Seniors on 1998 Team: 7 **Number of Sophomores on 1998 Team:** 3
Freshmen Receiving Fin Aid/Athletic: 2 **Academic:** 2
Most Recent Record: 37 - 18 - 0 **Number of Spring Games:** 56
Positions Needed for 1999/2000: Pitcher, Catcher
Baseball Camp Dates: All through June
Schedule: Wichita State, SouthWest Missouri State, Illinois, Oral Roberts, Ball State, Louisiana Tech, Creighton, Bradley, McNeese State
Style of Play: Wide - open moving runners all the time.

Indiana University

1001 17th E Street
Bloomington, IN 47408-1590
Coach: Bob Morgan
Email: rgmorgan@indiana.edu

NCAA I
Hosiers/Cream, Crimson
Phone: (812) 855-1680
Fax: (812) 855-9401

ACADEMIC

Founded: 1820
Type: 4 Yr., Public, Coed
Religion: Non-Affiliated
Campus Housing: Yes
Web-site: http://www.indiana.edu/
SAT/ACT/GPA: 800/19
Student/Faculty Ratio: Unknown
Male/Female Ratio: 1:3
Undergraduate Enrollment: 26,000
Graduate Enrollment: 10,000
Scholarships/Academic: Yes **Athletic:** Yes **Fin Aid:** Yes
Total Expenses by: Year **In State:** $ 8,932 **Out of State:** $ 16,798
Degrees Conferred: BA, BS, BFA, MBE, BSGS, AA, MA, MFA, MED, PH.D, OD, JD
Programs of Study: Over 850 degree programs offered including: Business, Sport Marketing and Management, Biology, Sport Communications, Journalism, Criminal Justice, Music, Exercise Science, Political Science, Psychology, Education

ATHLETIC PROFILE

Estimated Number of Baseball Scholarships: 11.7
Conference Affiliation: Big Ten Conference
Program Profile: The Hosiers play at Sembower Field, an all natural stadium that holds 3,500. Its dimensions are L-333, A-370, A 365, and R-333. Playing season is from February through May.
History: Our program began in 1896. Since then, our team is 1,622-1,259-20 entering this season. Since its inception the team has finished 1st four times and won the Big Ten Tournament in 1996.
Achievements: Bob Morgan - 1993 Big Ten Coach of the Year; 1996 MidEast Regional Coach of the Year; major league alumni include Ted Kluszewski, Mikey Morandini, Kevin Orie & John Wehner.
Coaching: Bob Morgan - Head Coach (hitting and infield). Jeff Calcaterna - Pitching Coach and Recruiting Coordinator. Scott Coogins - Catching Coach and Josh Wallace - Outfield Coach.
Roster for 1998 team/In State: 16 **Out of State:** 18 **Out of Country:** 0
Total Number of Varsity/Jr. Varsity: 34 **Percent of Graduation:** 95%
Number of Seniors on 1998 Team: 5 **Number of Sophomores on 1998 Team:** 7
Positions Needed for 1999/2000: 1st Base, 3rd Base, Catcher, All others
Baseball Camp Dates: June 8-12; June 14-19; December 28-30
Style of Play: Very aggressive and disciplined offensively, will make things happen on the bases. Defensively very fundamentally sound; usually a team that will not boast themselves.

Indiana University - Purdue U at Fort Wayne

2101 Coliseum Blvd. E
Fort Wayne, IN 46805-1499
Coach: Tony Vittorio
Email: vitorit@ipfw.edu

NCAA II
Mastadons/Blue, White
Phone: (219) 481-5480
Fax: (219) 481-6002

ACADEMIC

Founded: 1964
Type: 4 Yr., Public, Liberal Arts, Coed
Web-site: http://www.ipfw.indiana.edu/
SAT/ACT/GPA: 700+
Student/Faculty Ratio: 22:1
Male/Female Ratio: 1:1
Undergraduate Enrollment: 11,000
Graduate Enrollment: None
Scholarships/Academic: Yes **Athletic:** Yes **Fin Aid:** Yes
Total Expenses by: Year **In State:** $ 7,000 **Out of State:** $ 11,000
Degrees Conferred: BA, BS, MA, MS

Programs of Study: Accounting, Anthropology, Banking and Finance, Broadcasting, Chemistry, Communications, Computer Science, Criminal Justice, Earth Science, Economics, Education, Electrical Engineering, Engineering, Engineering Technology, English, Fine Arts, French, Geology, German, History, Industrial Engineering, Information Science, Marketing, Mathematics, Mechanical Engineering, Nursing, Personnel Management, Philosophy, Physics, Political Science, Predentistry, Prelaw, Premed, Psychology, Public Administration, Social Science, Spanish, Speech, Speech Pathology, Telecommunications.

ATHLETIC PROFILE

Estimated Number of Baseball Scholarships: 3-In State
Conference Affiliation: Great Lakes Valley Conference
Program Profile: We play a very demanding upbeat intense style of baseball! We have a natural grass field on campus and good indoor facilities. We also play games in Fort Wayne Wizard Park which is right across the street from our campus.
History: Tony Vittorio took over in Fall of 1996. We have spent the last two years putting the foundation down and the wins up.
Achievements: We have broken the school record in wins the last two years. Our record in 1996 was 24-23. We are currently 26-12 with 14 games lefts.
Coaching: Tony Vittorio, Head Coach, compiled a record of 24-23 in 1996. Guy Keller - Pitching Coach. Todd Linklater - Assistant Coach. Dan Ochs - Assistant Coach.
Roster for 1998 team/In State: 25 **Out of State:** 15 **Out of Country:** 0
Total Number of Varsity/Jr. Varsity: 40 **Percent of Graduation:** 100%
Freshmen Receiving Fin Aid/Athletic: 30 **Most Recent Record:** 26 - 12 - 0
Number of Fall Games: 4 **Number of Spring Games:** 52
Positions Needed for 1999/2000: Pitcher
Schedule: Valdosta State, Butler, Indianapolis, St. Joseph, Lewis, University of Missouri - St. Louis, SIU-Edwardsville
Style of Play: Upbeat, intense style of play; pressure on defense play; solid defense.

Indiana University - Purdue University/Indianapolis

901 W New York Street, Ste 105
Indianapolis, IN 46202-5193
Coach: Brian Donohew

NCAA II
Jaguars/Red, Black, Vegas Gold
Phone: (317) 278-2657
Fax: (317) 278-2683

ACADEMIC

Founded: 1969 **Type:** 4 Yr., Public, Liberal Arts, Coed
Religion: Non-Affiliated **Campus Housing:** Yes
Web-site: http://www.iupui.edu/ **SAT/ACT/GPA:** 820/18
Student/Faculty Ratio: 9:1 **Male/Female Ratio:** 40:60
Undergraduate Enrollment: 21,254 **Graduate Enrollment:** 6,742
Scholarships/Academic: Yes **Athletic:** Yes **Fin Aid:** Yes
Total Expenses by: Year **In State:** $ 2,740 **Out of State:** $ 7,812
Degrees Conferred: AA, AS, AAS, BA, BS, BAE, BGS, BSE, BSEE, BSME, BSW, MA, MS, MBA
Programs of Study: Accounting, Anthropology, Art History, Banking and Finance, Biology, Business, Chemistry, City Planning, Communications, Computer Science and Technology, Economics, Education, Engineering, Engineering Technology, Marketing, Mathematics, Nursing, Philosophy, Physics, Political Science, Psychology, Telecommunication, Public Administration

ATHLETIC PROFILE

Estimated Number of Baseball Scholarships: 8
Conference Affiliation: Mid-Continent Conference
Program Profile: We have a brand new facility just built (Indy Sports Complex). It has natural grass turf. Our schedule includes Oral Roberts, Indiana, Notre Dame, Daytona, Purdue, and Butler
History: The program was a club sport in the early 1980's.

Achievements: 15 NAIA All-District Selections; 3 NAIA All-Americans; 1 NAIA District Championship; 1 District Runner-Up.
Coaching: Brian Donohew , Head Coach, is in his third year as a head coach. He began his career at Georgetown College where he was a four-year starter. He played on a team that went 41-11 and finished 5th nationally in NAIA World Series. Assistant Coaches- Mark Flueckiger, Vol Neil Schaffner and Skip Williams
Roster for 1998 team/In State: 27 **Out of State:** 1 **Out of Country:** 0
Number of Seniors on 1998 Team: 7 **Number of Sophomores on 1998 Team:** 6
Freshmen Receiving Fin Aid/Athletic: 7 **Academic:** 0
Most Recent Record: 8 - 38 - 0 **Number of Spring Games:** 56
Positions Needed for 1999/2000: Pitchers Catcher, Mid-Infielder, Outfielder
Baseball Camp Dates: Winter Clinic: 12/27-12/30; Summer/June
Schedule: Oral Roberts, Indiana, Valparaiso, Morehead State, James Madison, Eastern Illionis
Style of Play: Aggressive.

Indiana University SouthEast

4201 Grantline Road
New Albany, IN 47150
Coach: Rick Parr

NAIA
Grenadiers/Red, White, Navy
Phone: (812) 941-2435
Fax: (812) 941-2434

ACADEMIC

Founded: 1941 **Type:** 4 Yr., Public, Coed
Student/Faculty Ratio: 19:1 **Male/Female Ratio:** 39:61
Undergraduate Enrollment: 5,500 **Graduate Enrollment:** 380
Scholarships/Academic: Yes **Athletic:** Yes **Fin Aid:** Yes
Total Expenses by: Year **In State:** $ 2,500+ **Out of State:** $ 7,000+
Degrees Conferred: AA, AS, BA, MS, MA, MBA
Programs of Study: Accounting, Biological, Business, Chemistry, Computer, Communications, Early Childhood Education, Economics, Education, English, Geography, History, Management, Marketing, Math, Music, Nursing, Political Science, Psychology, Secondary Education, Social Science

ATHLETIC PROFILE

Conference Affiliation: Kentucky Athletic Intercollegiate Conference
History: The Grenadiers have had three years straight with 20+ wins in the 1990's. Since 1990, the Grenadiers have not had a losing season.
Achievements: District Champs of 1993; BA Title (National) in 1991.
Coaching: Rick Parr, Head Coach, is entering 12 years as a head coach.

Indiana Wesleyan University

4201 S Washington Street
Marion, IN 46953
Coach: Mark DeMichael
Email: mdemicha@indues.edu

NAIA
Wildcats/Red, Grey
Phone: (765) 677-2318
Fax: (765) 677-2328

ACADEMIC

Founded: 1920 **Type:** 4 Yr., Private, Liberal Arts, Coed
Religion: Wesleyan **Campus Housing:** Yes
Web-site: http://www.indwes.edu/ **SAT/ACT/GPA:** 840/17/2.3
Student/Faculty Ratio: 17:1 **Male/Female Ratio:** 643/1044
Undergraduate Enrollment: 1,563 **Graduate Enrollment:** 124
Scholarships/Academic: Yes **Athletic:** Yes **Fin Aid:** Yes
Total Expenses by: Year **In State:** $ 15,000 **Out of State:** $ 15,000
Degrees Conferred: AA, As, BA, BS, AB, MA, MS, MBA, Med

Programs of Study: Accounting, Art, Art Education, Athletic Training, Biology, Chemistry, Business Administration, Commercial Arts, Criminal Justice, Mathematics, Economics, Education, Physical Education, Social Science, Political Science, Nursing Education, Management, Marketing, Social Studies, Sociology, Psychology

ATHLETIC PROFILE

Estimated Number of Baseball Scholarships: 3
Conference Affiliation: Mid - Central Conference
Program Profile: Our game field and practice field have lights, natural grass, 4 batting tunnels, 6 bullpen mounds, full heated press box, dugouts with bathrooms and a 500 seating capacity. We have a six week Fall season, a 55-65 game Spring season and a Florida trip.
History: The program started in 1969. In 1994, we had a 32 wins in single season record. In 1998, we won 3rd place in NCCAA World Series.
Coaching: Mark DeMichael, Head Coach, is entering his first year with a record of 20-29 and an overall career record of 96-82. He was 1996 and 1997 Commonwealth Coast Conference Coach of the Year. Mike Burchette - Assistant Coach.
Roster for 1998 team/In State: 14 **Out of State:** 11 **Out of Country:** 0
Total Number of Varsity/Jr. Varsity: 25 **Most Recent Record:** 20 - 29 - 0
Number of Seniors on 1998 Team: 4 **Number of Sophomores on 1998 Team:** 0
Freshmen Receiving Fin Aid/Athletic: 6 **Academic:** 5
Number of Fall Games: 8 **Number of Spring Games:** 60
Positions Needed for 1999/2000: Catchers, Shortstop, Centerfield, 1st Base
Schedule: Indiana, Indianapolis, Bethel, Indiana Tech, Mt. Vernon Nazarene, Spring Arbor
Style of Play: Aggressively offesively with sound fundamental defense and solid pitching.

Manchester College

604 College Avenue
North Manchester, IN 46962
Coach: Rick Espeset
Email: rbespeset%staffmc@manchester.edu
NCAA III
Spartans/Black, Gold
Phone: (219) 982-5034
Fax: (219) 982-5032

ACADEMIC

Founded: 1889 **Type:** 4 Yr., Private, Liberal Arts, Coed
Religion: Church of the Brethren **Campus Housing:** Yes
Student/Faculty Ratio: 14:1 **Male/Female Ratio:** 50:50
Undergraduate Enrollment: 1,100 **Graduate Enrollment:** None
Scholarships/Academic: Yes **Athletic:** No **Fin Aid:** Yes
Total Expenses by: Year **In State:** $ 16,500 **Out of State:** $ 16,500
Degrees Conferred: BA, BS, Associate Art, Master, Accounting
Programs of Study: Accounting, Physical Education, Art, Athletic Training, Biology, Business Administration, Chemistry, Coaching, Communications Studies, Computer Science, Criminal Justice, Economics, Elementary Education, Gerontology, Journalism, Mathematics, Medical Technology, Music, Philosophy, Physical Education, Physics, Political Science, Prelaw, Premed, Prenursing

ATHLETIC PROFILE

Conference Affiliation: Indiana Collegiate Athletic Conference
Program Profile: The program is an up and comming Division III program. The program plays a Fall and Spring season on a well kept grass field.
History: The program started in 1911. In the past four years the program has gone from 6-24 to 22-14 last year. In the 1996-1997 season, we set a school record for wins and also brought about a team conference batting title.
Achievements: 3 All-Conference players; 3 All-MidEast selections in '97. Conference titles in 1985.
Coaching: Rick Espeset, Head Coach, is on his fourth year at Manchester (two of these years as a head coach). He compiled a record of 46-24 for two years. He was a 1991 graduate of Gustavus Adolphus College where he also played baseball. Eddie Uschold & Donavan Yarnal-Assistant Coaches.

Roster for 1998 team/In State: 25 **Out of State:** 5 **Out of Country:** 0
Total Number of Varsity/Jr. Varsity: 30 **Percent of Graduation:** 100%
Number of Seniors on 1998 Team: 4 **Number of Sophomores on 1998 Team:** 4
Freshmen Receiving Fin Aid/Athletic: 0 **Academic:** 100%
Number of Fall Games: 9 **Number of Spring Games:** 36
Positions Needed for 1999/2000: 3rd Base, Outfielder, Catcher, Pitchers
Baseball Camp Dates: Sunday in February **Most Recent Record:** 24 - 13 - 0
Schedule: Indiana, Anderson, Rose-Hulman, Wabash College, Emory College, Greenville College
Style of Play: The teams play as hard-nosed and scrappy. The teams has a strong drive to win. We try to do the small things right and let the big things Fall into place.

Marian College

3200 Cold Spring Road
Indianapolis, IN 46222-1997
Coach: Kurt Guldner

NAIA
Knights/Navy, Gold
Phone: (317) 955-6310
Fax: (317) 955-6401

ACADEMIC

Founded: 1936 **Type:** 4 Yr., Private, Liberal Arts, Coed
Religion: Catholic **Campus Housing:** Yes
Web-site: http://www.marian.edu/ **SAT/ACT/GPA:** 860/18/2.0
Student/Faculty Ratio: 13:1 **Male/Female Ratio:** 2:3
Undergraduate Enrollment: 1,400 **Graduate Enrollment:** None
Scholarships/Academic: Yes **Athletic:** Yes **Fin Aid:** Yes
Total Expenses by: Year **In State:** $ 18,350 **Out of State:** $ 18,350
Degrees Conferred: AA, AS, BA, BS, BSN, AN
Programs of Study: Accounting, Art, Art History, Athletic Training, Biology, Business Administration, Chemistry, Coaching Endorsement, Computer Study, Economics, Elementary Education, Finance, Health and Safety, Interior Design, Liberal Arts, Pschology, Nursing, Philosophy, Religion, Sport Management, Sociology, Theater, Theology

ATHLETIC PROFILE

Conference Affiliation: Mid - Central Conference
Program Profile: Marian plays a 60 game schedule each year. The facility is the Summer home of Indianapolis Amauter Baseball Association. It has a seating capacity of 1,000 with lights for night play. Our natural field is one of tops in Indiana. We take a Southern trip each Spring.
History: The program began in 1960. It has had 33 years of straight winning baseball. We play a 60 game schedule which includes a Southern trip.
Achievements: Coach Guldner was Coach of the Year in 1996; the Knights won the MCC in 1993 and 1996; won the MCC Tourney in 1997 to quality for the Great Lakes Regional. In 1996 was the last Honorable Mention All-American; 10 All-Americans and 5 drafted since 1970.
Coaching: Kurt Guldner, Head Coach, was named Coach of the year in 1996. Jeff Custner - Assistant Coach.

Oakland City College

Lucretia Street
Oakland City, IN 47660
Coach: T. Ray Fletcher

NCAA II
Mighty Oaks/Blue, White
Phone: (812) 749-1290
Fax: (812) 749-1291

ACADEMIC

Founded: 1885 **Type:** 4 Yr., Private, Coed
SAT/ACT/GPA: 800/21 **Campus Housing:** Yes
Student/Faculty Ratio: 15:1 **Male/Female Ratio:** 49:51

Undergraduate Enrollment: 742 **Graduate Enrollment:** 10
Scholarships/Academic: Yes **Athletic:** Yes **Fin Aid:** Yes
Total Expenses by: Year **In State:** $ 11,250 **Out of State:** $ 11,250
Degrees Conferred: AA, AS, AAS, BA, BS, M
Programs of Study: Accounting, Biology, Business Administration, Business Education, Elementary Education, English, Humanities, Mathematics, Music, Physical Education, Religion, Science

ATHLETIC PROFILE

Conference Affiliation: AMAC

Purdue University

1790 Mackey Arena
West Lafayette, IN 47907-1790
Coach: Doug Schreiber

NCAA I
Boilermakers/Old Gold, Black
Phone: (765) 494-3189
Fax: (765) 494-0554

ACADEMIC

Founded: 1946 **Type:** 4 Yr., Public, Liberal Arts, Coed
Religion: Non-Affiliated **Campus Housing:** Yes
Web-site: http://www.calumet.purdue.edu/ **SAT/ACT/GPA:** 830+
Student/Faculty Ratio: 30:1 **Male/Female Ratio:** 50:50
Undergraduate Enrollment: 7,500 **Graduate Enrollment:** 800
Scholarships/Academic: Yes **Athletic:** Yes **Fin Aid:** Yes
Total Expenses by: Year **In State:** $ 4,000 **Out of State:** $ 7,000
Degrees Conferred: AA, AS, BA, BS, BSCh, BSE, MA, MS
Programs of Study: Accounting, Banking and Finance, Biology, Biotechnology, Broadcasting, Chemistry, Communications, Computer Science, Computer Technology, Criminal Justice, Economics, Education, Electrical Engineering and Technology, English, French, German, History, Hotel/Restaurant Management, Industrial Engineering, Information Science, International Relations, Marketing, Mathematics, Mechanical Engineering and Technology, Medical Technology, Microbiology, Nursing, Optometry, Philosophy, Physical Therapy, Physics, Political Science

ATHLETIC PROFILE

Conference Affiliation: Big Ten Conference
Program Profile: Named after Purdue legend, Ward 'Piggy' Lambert, the Boilermakers play in an all-grass stadium that holds 1,100 fans. Players have the benefit of using some of the best athletic facilities in the nation. The Purdue baseball team uses the Mollenkopf Athletic Center for off-season conditioning and practice. The 130,000 sq ft center built in 1990 is the largest indoor athletic facility of its kind in the country.
History: 1998 will be the 111th year that Purdue has fielded a team to play collegiate baseball. Boilermaker teams have won 1,392 games since 1888. The university has produced 53 professional players, ten of which made the majors, including Jermaine Allensworth (currently with the Pirates).
Achievements: 16 drafted players in the last 9 years; 2 All-Americans (Mike Billtimier in 1993 and Jermaine Allensworth in 1993); 1997 team boasted a 3.02 team GPA. Back to back 1st round draft picks (Sherard Clinkacales in 1992 and Jermaine Allensworth in 1993).

Rose-Hulman Inst of Technology

5500 Wabash Avenue
Terre Haute, IN 47803
Coach: Jeff Jenkins
Email: jeff.jenkins@rose-hulman.edu

NCAA III
Fightin' Engineers/Black, Scarlet
Phone: (812) 877-8209
Fax: (812) 877-8407

ACADEMIC

Founded: 1874 **Type:** 4 Yr., Private, Coed, Engineering

Religion: Non-Affiliated
Campus Housing: Yes
Web-site: http://www.rose-hulman.edu/
SAT/ACT/GPA: 1200
Student/Faculty Ratio: 14:1
Male/Female Ratio: 14:1
Undergraduate Enrollment: 1,450
Graduate Enrollment: 100
Scholarships/Academic: Yes **Athletic:** No **Fin Aid:** Yes
Total Expenses by: Year **In State:** $ 22,000 **Out of State:** $ 22,000
Degrees Conferred: BS, MS
Programs of Study: Applied Optics, Chemistry, Computer Science, Economics, Engineering (Civil, Chemical, Mechanical, Electrical, Computer), Mathematics, Physical Science, Physics.

ATHLETIC PROFILE

Conference Affiliation: SCAC
Program Profile: Our Top 25 nationally excellent facilities have natural turf and a seating capacity of 1,000. We got a press box, inning by inning scoreboard, full infield tarp, 2 batting cages, and 7 mounds.
History: We began in 1892 . We had a 20 win season prior to 1989, last 8 years 20+ wins and over .500 each season since 1989.
Achievements: Coach of the Year in 1992 and 1996; Academic All-American 8 times in nine years; 2 players signed last two years.
Coaching: Jeff Jenkins, Head Coach, had coached 10 years and graduated from Northern Ohio in 1981. He compiled a record of 206-129 in nine years and 251-194-1 in twelve years of coaching. Jon Prevo, Assistant Coach, is entering his fourth year with the program. Sean Bendel, Assistant Coach, is entering his first year with the program.
Roster for 1998 team/In State: 26 **Out of State:** 16 **Out of Country:** 0
Total Number of Varsity/Jr. Varsity: 42 **Percent of Graduation:** 100%
Number of Seniors on 1998 Team: 3 **Most Recent Record:** 26 - 18 - 0
Freshmen Receiving Fin Aid/Athletic: 0 **Academic:** 40
Number of Fall Games: 9 **Number of Spring Games:** 44
Positions Needed for 1999/2000: Pitchers, Outfielders
Schedule: Manchester, Thomas Moore, Hope, DePauw, Oakland City, Millikin
Style of Play: Aggressive, hit and run, good pitching and defense.

Saint Francis College

2701 Spring Street
NAIA
Fort Wayne, IN 46808
Cougars/Blue, White
Coach: Steve Kovacks
Phone: (219) 434-7414

ACADEMIC

Founded: 1890
Type: 4 Yr., Private, Liberal Arts, Coed
Religion: Catholic
Campus Housing: Yes
Web-site: http://www.stfrancis.sfc.edu/
SAT/ACT/GPA: 890/19
Student/Faculty Ratio: 18:1
Male/Female Ratio: 30:70
Undergraduate Enrollment: 787
Graduate Enrollment: 218
Scholarships/Academic: Yes **Athletic:** Yes **Fin Aid:** Yes
Total Expenses by: Year **In State:** $ 13,800 **Out of State:** $ 13,800
Degrees Conferred: AA, AS, BA, BS, MBA, MSEd, MS
Programs of Study: Accounting, American Studies, Art, Biologoy, Business Administration, Chemistry, Communications, Education, English, Environmental Science, Fine Arts, General Science, Medical Technology, Nursing, Prelaw, Premed, Prevet, Protective Services, Psychology, Religious Studies, Social Work, Special Education.

ATHLETIC PROFILE

Conference Affiliation: Mid - Central Conference

Saint Joseph's College

P.O. Box 875
Rensselaer, IN 47978-
Coach: Mike Moyzis

NCAA II
Pumas/Red, Purple
Phone: (219) 866-6386
Fax: (219) 866-6140

ACADEMIC

Founded: 1891
Type: 4 Yr., Private, Liberal Arts, Coed
Religion: Catholic
Campus Housing: Dorms
SAT/ACT/GPA: 820/18/15 units w/c avg. in core classes/
Web-site: http://www.saintjoe.edu/
Student/Faculty Ratio: 13:1
Male/Female Ratio: 55:45
Undergraduate Enrollment: 1,000
Graduate Enrollment: None
Scholarships/Academic: Yes **Athletic:** Yes **Fin Aid:** Yes
Total Expenses by: Year **In State:** $ 18,380 **Out of State:** $ 18,380
Degrees Conferred: BA, BS, BBA
Programs of Study: Accounting, Biochemistry, Biology, Business Administration, Chemistry, Communications, Computer Information System, Computer Science, Economics, Education, Elementary Education, English, Human Services, Management, Music, Nursing, Philosophy, Physical Education, Social Science, Physics, Political Science, Humanities, Human Services, Geophysics, Psychology, Social Science

ATHLETIC PROFILE

Conference Affiliation: Great Lakes Valley Conference

Taylor University

500 West Reade Avenue
Upland, IN 46989-1001
Coach: Larry Winterholter

NAIA
Trojans/Purple, Gold
Phone: (765) 998-5343
Fax: (765) 998-4920

ACADEMIC

Founded: 1846
Type: 4 Yr., Private, Liberal Arts, Coed
Religion: Interdenominational
Campus Housing: Yes
Web-site: http://www.tayloru.edu/
SAT/ACT/GPA: 1000+
Student/Faculty Ratio: 18:1
Male/Female Ratio: 52:48
Undergraduate Enrollment: 1,800
Graduate Enrollment: None
Scholarships/Academic: Yes **Athletic:** Yes **Fin Aid:** Yes
Total Expenses by: Year **In State:** $ 18,000 **Out of State:** $ 18,000
Degrees Conferred: BA, BS, AA, BMEd
Programs of Study: Accounting, Art, Athletic Training, Biology, Business Administration, Chemistry, Chemistry-Environmental Science, Communication, Computer Graphic Art, Economics, Elementary Education, Mass Communication, Natural Science, Philosophy, Physical Education, Physics

ATHLETIC PROFILE

Conference Affiliation: Mid - Central College Conference
Program Profile: The Trojans play a four week Fall program and a 50 game Spring season with a Spring Break trip to Florida. The home games are played at Taylor Field which has natural grass.
History: The program began in 1934. The Trojans had 30 wins in the 1995 season.
Coaching: Larry Winterholter, Head Coach, coached for 18 years. He was a two-sport letterwinner as a student at Taylor and has also served as a Taylor's Athletic Director (1979-1981). His teams at Taylor have averaged 20 wins per season for the last 16 years.

Tri - State University

1 University Drive
Angola, IN 46703
Coach: Walt Lilley
Email: lilleyw@alena.tristate.edu

NAIA
Thunders/Royal, White, Red
Phone: (219) 665-4174
Fax: (219) 665-4292

ACADEMIC

Founded: 1884
Type: 4 Yr., Private, Coed
Religion: Non-Affiliated
Campus Housing: Yes
Web-site: http://www.tristate.edu/
SAT/ACT/GPA: 800/19
Student/Faculty Ratio: 15:1
Male/Female Ratio: 3:3
Undergraduate Enrollment: 1,200
Graduate Enrollment: None
Scholarships/Academic: Yes **Athletic:** Yes **Fin Aid:** Yes
Total Expenses by: Year **In State:** $ 9,000 **Out of State:** $ 9,000
Degrees Conferred: AA, AS, BA, BS
Programs of Study: Arts and Sciences (Biology, Chemistry, Communications, Computer Science, Corporate English, Criminal Justice, Elementary Education, English, Environmental Science, General Studies, History, Individual Studies, Legal Administration, Mathematics, Physical Education, Physical Science, Premedical, Psychology, Secondary Education, Social Science); Business (Accounting, Applied Management, Business and Arts, Computer Information Systems, General Studies, Management, Marketing, Office Administration); Engineering (Aerospace, Chemical, Civil, Computer, Aided Drafting and Design, Electrical and Computer, Engineering Administration, General Studies, Mechanical)

ATHLETIC PROFILE

Conference Affiliation: Wolverine - Hoosier Athletic Conference
Program Profile: We have a large program for NAIA school and have 48 players that include junior varsity and varsity. Our field is natural surface with dimensions of 335 left lines, 365 gaps and 400. We do a Fall and Spring season and a Spring training trip to Georgia.
History: The program record was not keep prior to 1988 when Coach Lilley took over the program. Since 1988, he has a record of 155 wins and 141 losses. See below for season highlights.
Achievements: 1995 WHAC Post-season Champions; advanced to the NAIA; great Regional - Coach Lilley was named 1995 WHAC Coach of the Year; 3 NAIA Academic All Americans in nine years under Isaac Lucaing; 3 former players in minor league systems.
Coaching: Walt Lilley ,Head Coach, is entering his 10th season as head coach. Dave Wagner, Assistant Coach, entering his first season. Bob Harmon, Assistant Coach, entering his first season.
Style of Play: Aggressive with a priorities and fast runners.

University of Evansville

1800 Lincoln Avenue
Evansville, IN 47722
Coach: Jim Brownlee

NCAA I
Aces/Navy Blue, White
Phone: (812) 479-2059
Fax: (812) 479-2199

ACADEMIC

Founded: 1854
Type: 4 Yr., Private, Liberal Arts, Coed
Religion: Methodist
Campus Housing: Yes
Web-site: http://www.evansville.edu/
SAT/ACT/GPA: 1000/21
Student/Faculty Ratio: 13:1
Male/Female Ratio: 45:55
Undergraduate Enrollment: 2,600
Graduate Enrollment: 100
Scholarships/Academic: Yes **Athletic:** Yes **Fin Aid:** Yes
Total Expenses by: Year **In State:** $ 19,000 **Out of State:** $ 19,000
Degrees Conferred: BS, BA, MA

Programs of Study: Allied Health, Business, Communications, Computer Science, Education, Engineering, Physical Therapy, Premed, Liberal Arts

ATHLETIC PROFILE

Estimated Number of Baseball Scholarships: 4
Conference Affiliation: Missouri Valley Conference
Program Profile: We are in the best conference in the MidWest and averaged 30 wins a season the last ten years. We are building a new facility on campus called Boss Field. It is city owned with a 5,000 seating capacity. We were second in the Missouri Valley Conference Tourney.
History: Evansville has been playing baseball since 1924 and Division I baseball since 1970. Evansville has had winning seasons 9 of the last 10 years averaging 34 wins a year during that time. We are entering fourth year in the Missouri Valley Conference.
Achievements: Won MidWest Region Coach of the Year in 1998; 580 wins in 19 years; Andy Benes number 1 draft pick in 1988; 6 All-Americans; 19 players drafted only 2 drafted out of high school - Sal Fasano 35th round - now in the big leaguers.
Coaching: Jim Brownlee, Head Coach, began coaching in 1979 and compiled a record of 566-508. He was in National Championships in 1969 as a player for Illinois State. He beat Arizona State by 1-0 in 1988 Far West Regional. He won over 40 games 3 times at Evansville. Tim Browlee, Ryan Barett and Ryan Brownlee - Assistant Coaches.
Roster for 1998 team/In State: 18 **Out of State:** 13 **Out of Country:** 0
Total Number of Varsity/Jr. Varsity: 31 **Percent of Graduation:** 100%
Number of Seniors on 1998 Team: 6 **Number of Sophomores on 1998 Team:** 7
Freshmen Receiving Fin Aid/Athletic: 8 **Academic:** 9
Most Recent Record: 29 - 30 - 0 **Number of Spring Games:** 56
Positions Needed for 1999/2000: Pitcher, Outfielder - Power Hitter, Shortstop
Baseball Camp Dates: December 27-30; June 10-15, 17-20
Schedule: Wichita State, Wake Forest, Vanderbilt, SW Missouri, Virginia Tech, Southern Illinois
Style of Play: Very aggressive - lead the nation in 1997 in stolen base 6th in 1997. Very sound fundamental; will be one of the top teams in the Missouri Valley Conference.

University of Indianapolis

1400 East Hanna Avenue
Indianapolis, IN 46227
Coach: Gary Vaught

NCAA II
Greyhounds/Crimson, Grey
Phone: (317) 788-3414
Fax: (317) 788-3472

ACADEMIC

Founded: 1902
Type: 4 Yr., Private, Liberal Arts, Coed
Religion: Methodist
Campus Housing: Yes
Web-site: http://www.uindy.edu/
SAT/ACT/GPA: 800
Student/Faculty Ratio: 13:1
Male/Female Ratio: 45:55
Undergraduate Enrollment: 2,000
Graduate Enrollment: 500
Scholarships/Academic: Yes **Athletic:** Yes **Fin Aid:** Yes
Total Expenses by: Year **In State:** $ 17,500 **Out of State:** $ 17,500
Degrees Conferred: AA, AS, BA, BS, MA, MS, MBA
Programs of Study: Accounting, Biology, Broadcasting, Business Administration, Nursing, Physical Education, Sport Information, Physical Therapy, Journalism, Medical Technology, Electrical Engineering, Mathematics, Prelaw, Premed, Religion

ATHLETIC PROFILE

Conference Affiliation: Great Lakes Valley Conference
Program Profile: Our home field has natural grass and dimensions 335', 365', 405', 375'and 335'. The field has a capacity of 1,000 people. All home games are broadcast on the radio. We have indoor and outdoor hitting cages, a bunting area, an indoor pitching/catching area and a gym.

History: We set school a record for wins in 1997 with 38. In the last three years the program has gone from 19 wins to 38. In 1997, the Greyhounds were ranked nationally as high as #10 and finished ranked #25. In the last three years the Greyhounds have hit .330 as a team and have been ranked in the top 10 defensively in the last three years.
Achievements: Gary Vaught was named MCC Coach of the Year; Jim Carwell was 1995 pitcher for Cincinnati Reds (LHP); John Blackwell was an outfielder drafted by the Arizona Diamondbacks in 1997; Tom Horny was a 1997 2nd team All-American (OF); Pat McDonald was a 1997 2nd team All-American (Relief); Pat McDonald was a 1997 1st team All-American (Relief).
Coaching: Gary Vaught ,Head Coach, previously coached at Kansas State and Oral Roberts University. He was named 1986 MCC Coach of the Year. In 1986-1989, he took the Oral Roberts to the NCAA I Regional. He is a graduate of University of Central (Oklahoma, native of Norman, OK); Scott Norwood, Assistant Coach, is a 1981 graduate from Oral Roberts University and handles infielder and outfielder duties. He was selected as the 1997 AIA Baseball Division I coach and also played in the NJCAA World Series.
Style of Play: We play an exciting " put the pressure on the defense". Hit and run, but score at lEast a run per inning, mentality, bunt runners over. Play exceptional defense which is the key to our success, our roster knows their roles and fulfills them.

University of Notre Dame

Joyce Center, Baseball Office
Notre Dame, IN 46556
Coach: Paul Mainieri

NCAA I
Fighting Irish/Blue, Gold
Phone: (219) 631-6366
Fax: (219) 631-8231

ACADEMIC

Founded: 1842
Religion: Catholic
Web-site: http://www.und.com
Student/Faculty Ratio: 12:1
Undergraduate Enrollment: 7,500
Scholarships/Academic: Yes **Athletic:** Yes
Total Expenses by: Year **In State:** $ 17,500
Type: 4 Yr., Private, Coed, Engineering
Campus Housing: Yes
SAT/ACT/GPA: 1240 average
Male/Female Ratio: 53:47
Graduate Enrollment: 2,400
Fin Aid: Yes
Out of State: $ 17,000
Degrees Conferred: BA, BS, BFA, MA, MS, MBA, MFA, PhD, JD
Programs of Study: Business and Management, Engineering, Letters/Literature, Life Sciences, Multi/Interdisciplinary Studies, Social Sciences

ATHLETIC PROFILE

Estimated Number of Baseball Scholarships: 2
Conference Affiliation: Big East Conference
Program Profile: Facilities include Frank Eck Stadium with 3,000 seats, natural grass and a full size locker room. Notre Dame has the 6th best winning percentage in the 1990's in all of Div. I college baseball. Over the past 25 years, 98% of the student-athletes at Notre Dame have graduated.
History: Our program began in 1892. Seventy former players have played in the major leagues. Notre Dame has 40 or more games for 10 consecutive seasons. NCAA regional in 4 out of the last 7 seasons.
Achievements: 18 players were drafted or signed pro contracts in the last 4 years including 1998 1st round draft choice Brad Lidge (Houston). 1997 season included 2 All-Americans (Brant Ust and Aaron Heilman).
Coaching: Paul Mainieri, Head Coach, played pro ball. He is entering his seventh season with the program. Brian O'Connor, Assistant Coach, played pro ball. Cory Mee, Assistant, played pro ball.
Roster for 1998 team/In State: 2 **Out of State:** 30 **Out of Country:** 0
Total Number of Varsity/Jr. Varsity: 32 **Percent of Graduation:** 100%
Number of Seniors on 1998 Team: 3 **Number of Sophomores on 1998 Team:** 0
Freshmen Receiving Fin Aid/Athletic: 10 **Most Recent Record:** 41 - 17 - 0
Baseball Camp Dates: Early July **Number of Spring Games:** 56
Positions Needed for 1999/2000: 3-Pitchers, Outfielder, Shortstop, Catcher

Schedule: Miami, St. John's, Rutgers, Florida International, Missouri, New Orleans, Michigan, West Virginia, Penn State
Style of Play: Notre Dame will play a very aggressive style of baseball in pitching, base running and offense.

University of Southern Indiana

8600 University Boulevard
Evansville, IN 47712
Coach: Michael Geodde

NCAA II
Screaming Eagles/Blue, Red, White
Phone: (812) 464-1943
Fax: (812) 465-7094

ACADEMIC

Founded: 1965
Religion: Non-Affiliated
Web-site: http://www.usi.edu/
Student/Faculty Ratio: 18:1
Undergraduate Enrollment: 8,230
Scholarships/Academic: Yes **Athletic:** Yes
Total Expenses by: Year **In State:** $ 4,980

Type: 4 Yr., Public, Coed
Campus Housing: Yes
SAT/ACT/GPA: 700+/18+
Male/Female Ratio: 1:2
Graduate Enrollment: None
Fin Aid: Yes
Out of State: $ 8,668

Degrees Conferred: AA, BS, AS, BA, MA, MS, MBA
Programs of Study: Accounting, Business and Management, Science and Technology, Premed, Allied Health, Communications, Education, Psychology, Social Science

ATHLETIC PROFILE

Conference Affiliation: Great Lakes Valley Conference
Program Profile: The USI Baseball Field is located on the USI Campus. It has concession stands, media accommodations and seating for approximately 200 fans. In the outfield, the dimensions measure 355' down the lines, 375' to the power alley and 385' to dead center field. The field has a brick dust infield with grass basepaths. The entire area is maintained by a computerized-underground sprinkler system installed in 1992.
History: The USI baseball program was created in 1971. Over the next 25 years, the squad has won the Great Lakes Valley Conference three times (1983, 1985, 1993) and has been to the NCAA Division II Tournament six times. The team also is 554-502 (.525).
Achievements: 3 GLVC Titles; 6 Appearances in the NCAA Division II Tournament 6 times. 6 players play professional baseball.
Coaching: Mike Geodde, Head Coach, is in his fifth year with the US. He was a former assistant coach for six years at a Division I school and one year as a minor league instructor.
Style of Play: Aggressive, steal, hit and run. Pitching defense oriented.

Valparaiso University

651 SO College Avenue
Valparaiso, IN 46383
Coach: Paul Twenge

NCAA I
Crusaders/Gold, Brown
Phone: (219) 464-5239
Fax: (219) 464-5762

ACADEMIC

Founded: 1859
Religion: Missouri Synod Lutheran
Web-site: http://www.valpo.edu/
Student/Faculty Ratio: 20:1
Undergraduate Enrollment: 3,050
Scholarships/Academic: Yes **Athletic:** Yes
Total Expenses by: Year **In State:** $ 15,960

Type: 4 Yr., Private, Coed, Engineering
Campus Housing: Yes
SAT/ACT/GPA: 900+/20+
Male/Female Ratio: 45:55
Graduate Enrollment: 700
Fin Aid: Yes
Out of State: $ 15,960

Degrees Conferred: AS, BA, BS, MA, MS, Med, JD

Programs of Study: Liberal Arts, Humanities, Sciences, Engineering (Civil, Mechanical, Computer, Electrical), Business Administration, Nursing, Education

ATHLETIC PROFILE

Estimated Number of Baseball Scholarships: 9.5
Conference Affiliation: Mid - Continent Conference
Program Profile: We have a competitive program at Division I level and play from end of February through May. We have natural turf with dimensions of 330, 385, 400, 385 and 330, fences ,500 seating and a press box.
History: We have the winningest program in the athletic conference. In 1998, we finished second in regular season and runner-up in conference tournament.
Achievements: 11th round draft pick in 1997-outfielder Jamie Sykes - was a junior when taken by the Arizona Diamondbacks.
Coaching: Paul Twenge,Head Coach, formerly coached at ARCC from 1982 to 1987. He started coaching at Valparaiso University in 1988. He compiled a record of 333-408-8. John Olson, Assistant Coach, is entering ten years with the program. Tim Holme ,Pitching Coach, is entering eight years with the program. Ryan Trucke,Graduate Assistant Coach, is entering his 5th year.
Roster for 1998 team/In State: 20 **Out of State:** 35 **Out of Country:** 2
Total Number of Varsity/Jr. Varsity: 65 **Percent of Graduation:** 94%
Number of Seniors on 1998 Team: 11 **Number of Sophomores on 1998 Team:** 0
Freshmen Receiving Fin Aid/Athletic: 4 **Academic:** 20
Most Recent Record: 31 - 23 - 1 **Number of Spring Games:** 56
Positions Needed for 1999/2000: Shortstop, Pitcher, Catcher
Schedule: Notre Dame, Indiana, Purdue, Indiana State, Ball State, Tennessee Tech
Style of Play: Hit and run, 12th in the nation for team defense.

Vincennes University

1002 North 1st Street
Vincennes, IN 47591
Coach: Jerry Blemker

NJCAA
Trailblazers/Royal Blue, White
Phone: (812) 888-4237
Fax: (812) 888-4540

ACADEMIC

Founded: 1801 **Type:** 2 Yr., Public, Coed
Student/Faculty Ratio: 16:1 **Male/Female Ratio:** Unknown
Undergraduate Enrollment: 6,500 **Graduate Enrollment:** None
Total Expenses by: Year **In State:** $ 2,486 **Out of State:** $ 6,016
Degrees Conferred: Associate
Programs of Study: Accounting, Actuarial Science, Agricultural Business, Agricultural Technologies, Anthropology, Archaeology, Architectural Technology, Arts/Fine Arts, Biology, Biological Science, Automotive Technology, Aviation Technology

ATHLETIC PROFILE

Conference Affiliation: Independent
Program Profile: We own a field on campus. Playing season consist of 20-games in the Fall and 56 games in the Spring. We play on natural grass.
History: Our program began in 1975.
Achievements: 3 Conference Titles in 1982, 1983 and 1984; Conference Coach of the Year in 1982, 1983 and 1984; 5 All-Americans, 22 Drafted Players.
Coaching: Jerry Blemker - Head Coach. Hank Lopez - Assistant. Derek Parker - Hitting Coach.

Wabash College

P.O. Box 352
Crawfordsville, IN 47933-0352
Coach: Bill Boone
Email: boonew@wabash.edu

NCAA III
Little Giants/Red, White
Phone: (765) 361-6100
Fax: (765) 361-6447

ACADEMIC

Founded: 1832
Religion: Non-Affiliated
Web-site: http://www.wabash.edu/
Student/Faculty Ratio: 1:11
Undergraduate Enrollment: Yes
Scholarships/Academic: Yes **Athletic:** No
Total Expenses by: Year **In State:** $ 22,000
Degrees Conferred: BA, BS

Type: 4 Yr., Private, Lib. Arts, All Male
Campus Housing: Yes
SAT/ACT/GPA: 1100/30
Male/Female Ratio: 100
Graduate Enrollment: None
Fin Aid: Yes
Out of State: $ 22,000

Programs of Study: Biology, Chemistry, Mathematics and Computer Science, Physics, Humanities, Art, Music, Philosophy, Religion, Social Sciences, Economics, History, Political Sciecne, Psychology

ATHLETIC PROFILE

Conference Affiliation: Heartland Collegiate Athletic Conference
Program Profile: We are a competitive Division III program with Fall ball and a Spring Florida Trip. Fall season is in September & Spring season is February through May. We play on natural turf field.
History: We began in 1866. We have been here 113 years excluding a year out for WWI and WW II. Wabash College has won 944 games.
Achievements: Won Conference Championship (Indiana Collegiate Athletic Conference) in 1997. Record of 25-15 in 1996 and 25-9 in 1997.
Coaching: Bill Boone, Head Coach, is entering his first season with the program. Paul Van Wie - Assistant Coach.
Roster for 1998 team/In State: 25 **Out of State:** 10 **Out of Country:** 0
Total Number of Varsity/Jr. Varsity: 23 /12 **Percent of Graduation:** 100%
Number of Seniors on 1998 Team: 2 **Number of Sophomores on 1998 Team:** 8
Freshmen Receiving Fin Aid/Athletic: 0 **Academic:** 35
Number of Fall Games: 8 **Number of Spring Games:** 36
Positions Needed for 1999/2000: Catcher, 3-Pitchers, 2nd Base
Most Recent Record: 25 - 9 - 0
Schedule: Anderson, Illinois Wesleyan, Rose-Hulman, Manchester, DePauw
Style of Play: Aggressive, running style of offense. We like to steal at any time and will take extra base if possible.

IOWA

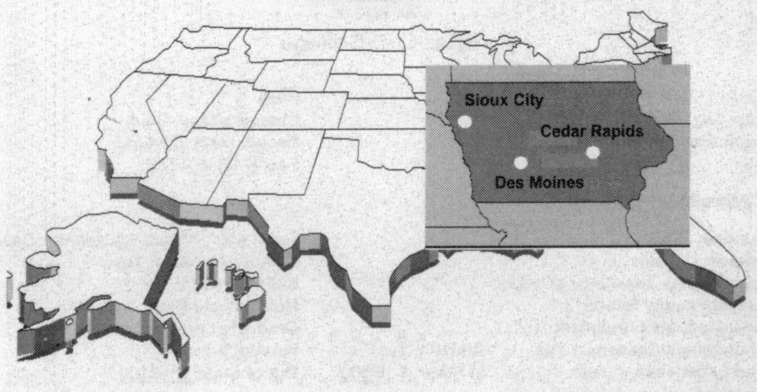

SCHOOL	CITY	AFFILIATION 99	PAGE
Briar Cliff College	Sioux City	NAIA	296
Buena Vista College	Storm Lake	NCAA III	296
Central College	Pella	NCAA III	296
Clarke College	Dubuque	NCAA III\NAIA	297
Coe College	Cedar Rapids	NCAA III	298
Cornell College	Mt. Vernon	NCAA III	298
Des Moines Area Community College	Boone	NJCAA	299
Dort College	Sioux Center	NAIA	299
Ellsworth Community College	Iowa Falls	NJCAA	300
Graceland College	Lamon	NAIA	300
Grand View College	Des Mines	NAIA	301
Grinnell College	Grinnell	NCAA III	301
Indian Hills Community College	Centerville	NJCAA	302
Iowa Central Community College	Ft Dodge	NJCAA	302
Iowa Lakes Community College	Estherville	NJCAA	303
Iowa State University	Ames	NCAA I	304
Iowa Wesleyan College	Mount Pleasant	NAIA	304
Iowa Western Community College	Clarinda	NJCAA	305
Kirkwood Community College	Cedar Rapids	NJCAA	305
Loras College	Dubuque	NCAA III	306
Luther College	Decorah	NCAA III	306
Marshalltown Community College	Marshalltown	NJCAA	307
Morningside College	Sioux City	NCAA II	307
Mount Mercy College	Cedar Rapids	NAIA	308
Mount Saint Clare College	Clinton	NAIA	309
Muscatine Community College	Muscatine	NJCAA I	310
North Iowa Area Community College	Mason City	NJCAA	310
Northwestern College - Iowa	Orange City	NAIA	311
Saint Ambrose University	Davenport	NAIA	311
Simpson College	Indianola	NCAA III	312
Southeastern Community College-North	W Burlington	NJCAA	313
Southwestern Community College	Creston	NJCAA	313
University of Dubuque	Dubuque	NCAA III	314
University of Iowa	Iowa City	NCAA I	314
University of Northern Iowa	Cedar Falls	NCAA I	315
Upper Iowa University	Fayette	NCAA III	316
Waldorf Junior College	Forest City	NJCAA	316
Wartburg College	Waverly	NCAA III	317
William Penn College	Oskaloosa	NCAA III	318

Briar Cliff College

P.O. Box 2100
Sioux City, IA 51102-100
Coach: Boyd Pitkin

NAIA
Chargers/Blue, Gold
Phone: (712) 279-5553
Fax: (712) 279-5592

ACADEMIC

Founded: 1930
Religion: Catholic
Web-site: http://www.briar-cliff.edu/
Student/Faculty Ratio: 13:1
Undergraduate Enrollment: 1,200
Scholarships/Academic: Yes
Total Expenses by: Year
Degrees Conferred: BA, BS

Type: 4 Yr., Private, Liberal Arts, Coed
Campus Housing: Yes
SAT/ACT/GPA: 18
Male/Female Ratio: 1:3
Graduate Enrollment: None
Athletic: Yes
Fin Aid: Yes
In State: $ 16,500
Out of State: $ 16,000

Programs of Study: Majors: Accounting, Art, Biology, Business, Chemistry, Computer Information Systems, Criminal Justice, Elementary Education, English, HPER, History, Human Resource Management, Mass Communications, Photography, Mathematics, Music, Nursing, Psychology, Secondary Education, Social Work, Sociology, Spanish, Theatre, Theology, Writing; Preprofessional Programs: Chiropractic, Church Ministry, Dentistry, Engineering, Law, Medical Technology, Medicine/Physician's Assistant, Occupational Therapy, Optometry, Pharmacy, Physical Therapy, Radiologic Technology, Veterinary Medicine

ATHLETIC PROFILE

Conference Affiliation: Independent Conference

Buena Vista College

610 West 4th Street
Storm Lake, IA 50588
Coach: Larry Anderson

NCAA III
Beavers/Navy, Gold
Phone: (712) 749-2253
Fax: (712) 749-1460

ACADEMIC

Founded: 1891
Undergraduate Enrollment: 1,080
Student/Faculty Ratio: 14:1
Scholarships/Academic: Yes
Total Expenses by: Year
Degrees Conferred: BA, BS

Type: 4 Yr., Private, Coed
SAT/ACT/GPA: 1075/24avg
Male/Female Ratio: 49:51
Athletic: No
Fin Aid: Yes
In State: $ 17,650
Out of State: $ 17,650

Programs of Study: Accounting, Art, Banking/Finance, Biological, Business, Chemistry, Communications, Computer, Criminal Justice, Economics, Education, english, Languages, History, Management, Marketing, Mathematics, Music, Philosophy, Physics, Political Science, Psychology, Religion, Science Education, Social Science, Special Education, Speech, Spanish

ATHLETIC PROFILE

Conference Affiliation: Iowa Conference

Central College

812 University
Pella, IA 50219
Coach: John Edwards

NCAA III
Flying Dutch/Red, White
Phone: (515) 628-5348
Fax: (515) 628-5316

ACADEMIC

Founded: 1853
Type: 4 Yr., Private, Liberal Arts, Coed
Religion: Dutch reformed
Campus Housing: Yes
Web-site: http://www.central.edu/
SAT/ACT/GPA: 1100/23
Student/Faculty Ratio: 18:1
Male/Female Ratio: 50:50
Undergraduate Enrollment: 1,400
Graduate Enrollment: None
Scholarships/Academic: Yes **Athletic:** No **Fin Aid:** Yes
Total Expenses by: Year **In State:** $ 18,000 **Out of State:** $ 18,000
Degrees Conferred: Many
Programs of Study: Accounting, Art, Biology, Business Management, Chemistry, Communications, Computer Information Systems, Computer Science, Economics, Education, English, French, German, Health Science, History, International Business, Journalism, Liberal Arts, Marketing, Mathematics, Medical Techonology, Music, Nursing, Philosophy, Physical Therapy, Political Science, Predentistry, Prelaw, Premed, Prevet, Psychology, Public Relations, Religion, Social Science

ATHLETIC PROFILE

Conference Affiliation: Iowa Intercollegiate Conference
Program Profile: We have a 40 game schedule,a Spring trip South, an excellent indoor practice area and an excellent game facility outdoors.
History: 7 players drafted, 2 All-Americans, 3 Academic All-Americans. Head Coach has been at Central for past 21 years.
Achievements: 7 Academic All-Americans; 6 professional players; 2 Coach of the Year Awards.
Coaching: John Edwards, Head Coach, has been at Central the past 21 years. He has 60 percent wins. He was a former All-American and professional player. Rich Schultz, Assistant Coach, is entering his 4th year and a professional player. Matt Ballou, Assistant Coach, is entering his 7th year.
Roster for 1998 team/In State: 22 **Out of State:** 7 **Out of Country:** 0
Total Number of Varsity/Jr. Varsity: 29 **Percent of Graduation:** 100%
Number of Seniors on 1998 Team: 14 **Number of Sophomores on 1998 Team:** 0
Freshmen Receiving Fin Aid/Athletic: 0 **Academic:** 10
Most Recent Record: 17 - 19 - 0 **Number of Spring Games:** 40
Positions Needed for 1999/2000: LHP, Shortstop
Schedule: Wooster, Upper Iowa, Wartburg, St. Benedict
Style of Play: Aggressive offense running style.

Clarke College

1550 Lake Drive
Dubuque, IA 52001
Coach: Eric Frese
NCAA III\NAIA
Crusaders/Navy Gold
Phone: (319) 588-6657
Fax: (319) 588-6666

ACADEMIC

Founded: 1843
Type: 4 Yr., Private, Liberal Arts, Coed
Religion: Catholic
Campus Housing: Yes
Web-site: http://www.clarke.edu/
SAT/ACT/GPA: 970/20
Student/Faculty Ratio: 12:1
Male/Female Ratio: 36:64
Undergraduate Enrollment: 900
Graduate Enrollment: 102
Scholarships/Academic: Yes **Athletic:** No **Fin Aid:** Yes
Total Expenses by: Year **In State:** $ 15,414 **Out of State:** $ 15,414
Degrees Conferred: AA, BA, BS, BFA, MA, BSN, MED, MS
Programs of Study: Accounting, Art, Biochemistry, Business and Management, Chemistry, Communications, Computer Information Systems, Computer Science, Economics, Education, Music, English, French, German, Journalism, Liberal Arts, Marketing, Mathematics, Medical Technology, Nursing, Philosophy, Physical Theraphy, Political Science, Prelaw, Premed, Prevet, Psychology, Public Relations, Religion, Social Science, Theatre

ATHLETIC PROFILE

Conference Affiliation: Midwest Classic Conference
Program Profile: We have a $4.2 million Sports Complex including a 10,000 sq ft indoor baseball training area, batting cages and dirt pitching mounds. Our complex also has 3 regulation-size basketball courts, which allow plenty of room for indoor workouts. We also have a running track and weight room for off-season conditioning. We play a 36-game varsity schedule.
Achievements: 1 Academic All-American; 2 former players have played professional baseball.

Coe College

1220 - 1st Avenue, NE
Cedar Rapids, IA 52402
Coach: Steve Cook

NCAA III
Kohawks/Red, Gold
Phone: (319) 399-8849
Fax: (319) 399-8721

ACADEMIC

Founded: 1851
Religion: Presbyterian
Web-site: http://www.coe.edu/
Student/Faculty Ratio: 13:1
Undergraduate Enrollment: 1,253
Scholarships/Academic: Yes **Athletic:** No
Total Expenses by: Year **In State:** $ 21,710

Type: 4 Yr., Private, Liberal Arts, Coed
Campus Housing: Yes
SAT/ACT/GPA: 950/20/3.0
Male/Female Ratio: 40:60
Graduate Enrollment: 45
Fin Aid: Yes
Out of State:

Degrees Conferred: BA, BSN, BM, MAT
Programs of Study: Accounting, American Studies, Asian Studies, Biological Sciences, African-American Studies, Business Administration, Education, English, French, German, History, Interdisciplinary Studies, Liberal Arts, Literature, Mathematics, Medical Technology, Physical Sciences, Physics, Political Science, Prelaw, Preveterinary, Psychology, Religious Studies, Sciences, Social Science, Spanish, Theatre

ATHLETIC PROFILE

Conference Affiliation: MCAC

Cornell College

600 First Street W
Mt. Vernon, IA 52314
Coach: Ray Reasland

NCAA III
Rams/Purple, White
Phone: (319) 895-4117
Fax: (319) 895-5895

ACADEMIC

Founded: 1853
Religion: None
Web-site: http://www.cornell-iowa.edu/
Student/Faculty Ratio: 13:1
Scholarships/Academic: Yes **Athletic:** No
Total Expenses by: Year **In State:** $ 21,890

Type: 4 Yr., Private, Liberal Arts, Coed
Campus Housing: Yes
Undergraduate Enrollment: 1,150
Male/Female Ratio: 46:54
Fin Aid: Yes
Out of State: $ 21,890

Degrees Conferred: BA, BSS, BM, BP
Programs of Study: Agriculture and Life Science, Architecture, Art and Planning, Arts and Science, Engineering, Hotel Administration, Human Ecology, Industrial and Labor Relations

ATHLETIC PROFILE

Conference Affiliation: Iowa Conference

Program Profile: Our baseball stadium is on campus adjacent to our indoor training arena. It has natural surface with underground sprinkling system and tarp. The indoor arena holds two full-sized infields with batting cages at each end of the facility.
History: Baseball has been an active part of Cornell athletics since the early 1920's.
Achievements: Jeff Rinak led the nation in triples in 1996 (Junior Athletic Status); Eric Kulba led the nation in stolen bases in 1998.
Coaching: Ray Reasland, Head Coach, Buena Vista Hall of Fame. His rebuilding program in one of the most nationally respected Division III conference in the country. He set records for wins in 1998 and broke ten other team records. Bil Petsch, Assistant Coach, was Wartburg starting shortstop and graduated in 1992.
Roster for 1998 team/In State: 7 **Out of State:** 23 **Out of Country:** 0
Total Number of Varsity/Jr. Varsity: 30 **Percent of Graduation:** 100%
Number of Seniors on 1998 Team: 7 **Number of Sophomores on 1998 Team:** 9
Freshmen Receiving Fin Aid/Athletic: 0 **Academic:** 90%
Most Recent Record: 13 - 23 - 0 **Number of Spring Games:** 36+
Positions Needed for 1999/2000: Catcher, LHP, Power Hitters
Schedule: Upper Iowa University, Wartburg College, Fontbonne, Illinois Wesleyan
Style of Play: Aggressive base running with the ability to manufacture runs when necessary. Solid defense with an emphasis on fundamentals strength training (sports specificity), and discipline.

Des Moines Area Community College

1125 Hancock Drive
Boone, IA 50036
Coach: John Smith

NJCAA
Bears/Blue, White
Phone: (515) 433-5082
Fax: (515) 433-5033

ACADEMIC

Founded: 1966 **Type:** 2 Yr., Jr. College, Coed
Religion: Non-Affiliated **Campus Housing:** No
Total Expenses by: Year **In State:** $ 1,566+ **Out of State:** $ 3,132+
Degrees Conferred: Associate
Programs of Study: Accounting, Agricultural Business, Automotive Technology, Biotechnology, Business amdinistration, Commerce, Management, Commercial Art, Computer Programming, Computer Technologies, Corrections, Criminal Justice

ATHLETIC PROFILE

Conference Affiliation: Iowa Conference - Division I
Program Profile: We have good facilities and practice 6 weeks in the Fall. Practice take place most of the Winter. We play a 56 Spring game schedule.
History: Our program started in 1970. Since 1997, it has had only 1 losing season. Our best record is 41-16.
Achievements: Appeared in National Tourney in 1982; 12 All-Americans; won Iowa Conference in 1982; National Junior College Player of the Year in 1996; 59 players have been drafted or signed in the 24 years; 1 player presently playing in big leagues.
Coaching: John Smith, Head Coach, has 25 years of coaching experience.
Style of Play: Percentage type baseball.

Dort College

498 - 4th Avenue NE
Sioux Center, IA 51250
Coach: Tom Visker

NAIA
Defenders/Black, White, Gold
Phone: (712) 722-6232
Fax: (712) 722-6311

ACADEMIC

Founded: 1955
Religion: Christian Reformed Church
Web-site: http://www.dordt.edu/
Student/Faculty Ratio: 14:1
Undergraduate Enrollment: 1,200
Scholarships/Academic: Yes **Athletic:** Yes
Total Expenses by: Year **In State:** $ 13,100
Type: 4 Yr., Private, Liberal Arts, Coed
Campus Housing: Yes
SAT/ACT/GPA: 19
Male/Female Ratio: 50:50
Graduate Enrollment: None
Fin Aid: Yes
Out of State: $ 13,100
Degrees Conferred: AA, BA, BS (Engineering), BSW (Social Work)
Programs of Study: Agriculture, Business/Office and Marketing/Distribution, Business and Management, Communications, Education, Letters/Literature, Life Sciences, Multi/Interdisciplinary Studies, Psychology, Social Sciences

ATHLETIC PROFILE

Conference Affiliation: South Dakota - Iowa Conference

Ellsworth Community College

1100 College Avenue
Iowa Falls, IA 50126
Coach: Duane Palcic

NJCAA
Panthers/Navy, Gold
Phone: (515) 648-4611
Fax: (515) 648-3128

ACADEMIC

Founded: 1890
Student/Faculty Ratio: Unknown
Undergraduate Enrollment: 835
Scholarships/Academic: No **Athletic:** Yes
Total Expenses by: Year **In State:** $ 5,100
Type: 2 Yr., Jr. College, Coed
Male/Female Ratio: 52:48
Graduate Enrollment: 0
Fin Aid: Yes
Out of State: $ 6,900
Degrees Conferred: Associate
Programs of Study: Accounting, Agricultural Business, Art Education, Arts, Fine Arts, Biology, Biological Scinece, Art Education, Criminal Justice, Child Psychology, Data Processing, Liberal Arts, General Studies, Marketing, Human Services, Interior Design

ATHLETIC PROFILE

Conference Affiliation: JCAC

Graceland College

700 College Avenue
Lamon, IA 50140
Coach: Jeff Douglas

NAIA
Yellow Jackets/Blue, Gold
Phone: (515) 784-5351
Fax: (515) 784-5472

ACADEMIC

Founded: 1895
Religion: LDS
Web-site: http://www.graceland.edu/
Student/Faculty Ratio: 15:1
Undergraduate Enrollment: 1,200
Scholarships/Academic: Yes **Athletic:** Yes
Total Expenses by: Year **In State:** $ 13,600
Type: 4 Yr., Private, Liberal Arts, Coed
Campus Housing: Yes
SAT/ACT/GPA: 21
Male/Female Ratio: 50:50
Graduate Enrollment: None
Fin Aid: Yes
Out of State: $ 13,600
Degrees Conferred: BA, BSN, BS
Programs of Study: Business Administration, Education, Athletic Training, Nursing, Preprofessional Programs, Liberal Studies, Computer Science

ATHLETIC PROFILE

Conference Affiliation: Heart of America Athletic Conference
Program Profile: We play games at Lamoni City Park. Work is currently being done to put a field on Graceland's campus. We have a Spring break tour to Texas and play two double headers in the Metrodome (MN).
History: Graceland had an outstanding program in the early 1980's. We are currently rebuilding the program.
Achievements: Has placed players in the pros.
Coaching: Jeff Douglas - Head Coach.
Style of Play: Try to hit and run a lot. Play hard-nosed old fashioned baseball.

Grand View College

1200 Grand View Avenue
Des Mines, IA 50316
Coach: Lou Yacinich

NAIA
Vikings/Red, White
Phone: (515) 263-2897

ACADEMIC

Founded: 1896
Religion: Evangelical Lutheran
Web-site: http://www.gvc.edu/
Student/Faculty Ratio: 16:1
Undergraduate Enrollment: 1,400
Scholarships/Academic: Yes **Athletic:** Yes
Total Expenses by: Year **In State:** $ 13,600

Type: 4 Yr., Private, Liberal Arts, Coed
Campus Housing: Yes
SAT/ACT/GPA: 1000
Male/Female Ratio: 45:55
Graduate Enrollment: None
Fin Aid: Yes
Out of State: $ 13,600

Degrees Conferred: AA, BA, BS, BSN
Programs of Study: Accounting, Applied Mathematics, Arts, Biology, Broadcasting, Business Administration, Chemistry, Commercial Art, Computer Information System, Computer Science, Criminal Justice, Economics, Education, Elementary Education, English, History, Journalism, Music, Nursing, Philosophy, Physics, Political Science, Prelaw, Premed, Prevet, Psychology, Religion

ATHLETIC PROFILE

Conference Affiliation: Midwest Classic Conference

Grinnell College

P.O. Box 805
Grinnell, IA 50112
Coach: Tim Hollibaugh
Email: hllibaugh@ac.grin.edu

NCAA III
Pioneers/Scarlet, Black
Phone: (515) 269-3822
Fax: (515) 269-3818

ACADEMIC

Founded: 1846
Web-site: http://www.grin.edu/
Student/Faculty Ratio: 9:1
Undergraduate Enrollment: 1,300
Scholarships/Academic: Yes **Athletic:** No
Total Expenses by: Year **In State:** $ 24,000

Type: 4 Yr., Private, Coed
SAT/ACT/GPA: 1250/27/Top 15%
Male/Female Ratio: 45:55
Graduate Enrollment: Unknown
Fin Aid: Yes
Out of State: $ 24,000

Degrees Conferred: BA
Programs of Study: One of the top educational institutions in the country. All majors are available with internship and off campus possibilities.

ATHLETIC PROFILE

Conference Affiliation: Midwest Conference

Program Profile: We have an oustanding natural turf field. It is a power hitter's paradise with a 305 down left field line. It is a great place to play baseball.
History: We are an up and coming team with great history and one of the first teams to play baseball on West of the Mississippi River. Our first game was in 1868.
Achievements: Many All-Conference performers, some All-American players.
Coaching: Tim Hollibaugh ,Head Coach, is entering fourth year as a head coach. He is a graduate of Hanover College in 1990. Steve Larson ,Pitching Coach, is entering his third year and is a graduate of Washington State.
Roster for 1998 team/In State: 3 **Out of State:** 20 **Out of Country:** 1
Total Number of Varsity/Jr. Varsity: 24 **Percent of Graduation:** 100%
Number of Seniors on 1998 Team: 6 **Number of Spring Games:** 34+
Freshmen Receiving Fin Aid/Athletic: 0 **Academic:** 24
Positions Needed for 1999/2000: Pitchers, Shortstops
Baseball Camp Dates: May 11-16; December 14-18
Schedule: McMurry, Howard Payne, Hardin-Simmons, Macalester, Monmouth, Central College
Style of Play: Aggressive offense, fundamental defense and quality pitching has helped build our program into a quality program.

Indian Hills Community College

721 North First Street
Centerville, IA 52544-1223
Coach: Cam Walker

NJCAA
Falcons/Maroon, Gold
Phone: (515) 856-2143
Fax: (515) 856-5527

ACADEMIC

Founded: 1966 **Type:** 2 Yr., Jr. College, Coed
Student/Faculty Ratio: 20:1 **Male/Female Ratio:** 1:1
Undergraduate Enrollment: 3,424 **Graduate Enrollment:** Unknown
Scholarships/Academic: Yes **Athletic:** Yes **Fin Aid:** Yes
Total Expenses by: Year **In State:** $ 3,600 **Out of State:** $ 4,200
Degrees Conferred: AA
Programs of Study: Agricultural Technologies, Automotive Technology, Business Administration, Commerce, Management, Criminal Justice, Drafting/Design, Flight Training, Food Services Technology, Health Services Administration, Laser Technology, Marine and Tool Technology

ATHLETIC PROFILE

Conference Affiliation: Iowa JUCO
Program Profile: Home games are played on Pat Daugherty Field which has new Pro Spec lights. We have an Indoor facility, a multi purpose building, 4 indoor cages and 4 indoor mounds.
History: Indian Hills has made five World Series appearances.
Achievements: 1993 District Coach of the Year, Louisville Slugger Coach of the Year, Diamond Coach of the Year. Over 150 players drafted, 5 big league players, 5 players drafted in 92/93 (4 pitcher in top 20 rounds).
Coaching: Cam Walker, Head Coach, in on his 3rd year and was at IHCC for7 years. Bill Whitaker, Assistant Coach, is on his 8th year. Kevin Benzing, Assistant Coach, is on his 2nd year and coached at Washington University for 4 years.
Style of Play: Aggressive, speed-oriented team, with solid offense. Talented young pitching staff.

Iowa Central Community College

330 Avenue M
Ft Dodge, IA 50501
Coach: Rick Sandquist

NJCAA
Tritons/Navy Blue, White
Phone: (515) 576-0099
Fax: (515) 576-7724

ACADEMIC

Founded: 1966
Type: 2 Yr., Jr. College, Coed
Religion: Non-Affiliated
Campus Housing: Yes
Student/Faculty Ratio:16:1
Male/Female Ratio: 42:58
Undergraduate Enrollment: 2,700
Graduate Enrollment: Unknown
Scholarships/Academic: Yes **Athletic:** Yes **Fin Aid:** Yes
Total Expenses by: Year **In State:** $ 5,100 **Out of State:** $ 6,000
Degrees Conferred: Associate
Programs of Study: Accounting, Automotive Technology, Aviation, Broadcasting, Business, Communications, Community Service, Computer Science, Drafting/Design, Engineering, Journalism, Law, Medical, Occupational Therapy

ATHLETIC PROFILE

Conference Affiliation: NJCAA Region XI Division II
Program Profile: We have a new natural surface facility on campus for Spring of 1998. Our season consists of 56 games in the Spring (Notre Dame trip and Spring trip to Florida). We have a six week Fall season and an off season of weights and plyometrics.
History: Our program began in 1967. We won 2 World Series Appearance in 1996 and 1997.
Achievements: Region Coach of the Year in 1996 and 1997; 2 Regional Titles in 1996 and 1997; 2 World Series Appearances in 1996 and 1997 (National Runner-Up in 1997); 3 All-Americans in 1996-1997; 1 drafted player in 1996.
Coaching: Rick Sandquist - Head Coach. Kevin Ziesman - Assistant Coach. Rick Pederson - Assistant Coach.
Style of Play: We love to run, bunt and play. The game has an in a class way. We are aggressive both offensive and defensively.

Iowa Lakes Community College

300 South 18th Street
Estherville, IA 51334
Coach: John Walz
Email: jwalz@ilcc.cc.ia.us
NJCAA
Lakers/Royal Blue, Gold
Phone: (712) 362-7974
Fax: (712) 362-3969

ACADEMIC

Founded: 1967
Type: 2 Yr., Public, Jr. College, Coed
Religion: Non-Affiliated
Campus Housing: Yes
SAT/ACT/GPA: GED or High School Diploma/
Web-site: http://www.ilcc.cc.ia.us
Student/Faculty Ratio: 60:1
Male/Female Ratio: 50:50
Undergraduate Enrollment: 2,428
Graduate Enrollment: Unknown
Scholarships/Academic: Yes **Athletic:** Yes **Fin Aid:** Yes
Total Expenses by: Year **In State:** $ 8,078 **Out of State:** $ 9,358
Degrees Conferred: AA, AS
Programs of Study: Accounting, Art, Astronomy, Banking/Finance, Botany, Business, Chemistry, Commercial, Computer, Conservation, Criminal, Drafting/Design, Earth Science, Ecology, Economics, Education, Engineering, English, Environmental, Fish/Game, Flight, Geology, Health, History, Jazz, Journalism, Laboratory, Law, Legal, Natural Science, Paralegal

ATHLETIC PROFILE

Conference Affiliation: Iowa-JUCO Conference
Program Profile: We have great facilities. Our season starts in late February and concludes in May. We play on natural grass field.
History: Our program has been running for over twenty years.
Coaching: John Walz, Head Coach, started coaching here in 1996 . He compiled a record of 10-28 in 1996, 17-24 in 1997 and 19-28 in 1998. Curt Petersen - Assistant .
Roster for 1998 team/In State: 13 **Out of State:** 6 **Out of Country:** 5
Total Number of Varsity/Jr. Varsity: 24 **Percent of Graduation:** 0

Number of Seniors on 1998 Team: 0 **Number of Sophomores on 1998 Team:** 12
Freshmen Receiving Fin Aid/Athletic: 8 **Academic:** 2
Schedule: Kirkwood, Iowa Central, Waldorf, College of Lake County, Gulf Coast Community College, SouthEastern Community College, SouthEastern
Style of Play: Aggressive.

Iowa State University

Jacobson Building
Ames, IA 50011
Coach: Lyle Smith

NCAA I
Cyclones/Cardinal, Gold
Phone: (515) 294-4201
Fax: (515) 294-6046

ACADEMIC

Founded: 1858
Type: 4 Yr., Public, Coed
Religion: Non-Affiliated
Campus Housing: Yes
Web-site: http://www.iastate.edu
SAT/ACT/GPA: 3.0
Student/Faculty Ratio: 19:1
Male/Female Ratio: Unknown
Undergraduate Enrollment: 24,726
Graduate Enrollment: None
Scholarships/Academic: Yes **Athletic:** Yes **Fin Aid:** Yes
Total Expenses by: Year **In State:** $ 10,000 **Out of State:** $ 16,280
Degrees Conferred: BA, BS, MS, MA, MFA, Med, PhD
Programs of Study: Accounting, Agriculture, Anthropology, Applied Art, Architecture, Arts, Biochemistry, Biophysics, Botany, Broadcasting, Business and Management, Computer Science, Dietetics, Communications, City/Community/Regional Planning, Linguistic, Meteorology, Microbiology, Russian, Sociology, Religion, Biology, Zoology, Social Work

ATHLETIC PROFILE

Conference Affiliation: Big Twelve Conference
Program Profile: Our stadium,Cap Amon Field, has a seating capacity of 1,400 and natural turf. The team has a 56 game schedule (30 conference games).
History: Our program has existed 104 years. We were College World Series Participants in 1958 and 1970.
Achievements: Runner-Up in the Conference Tourney three times in 1990's; over 70 professionally drafted players; 3 current major league players; five pitchers in the last seven terms drafted in first five rounds of MC draft.
Coaching: Lyle Smith, Head Coach, has coached since 1995/97. He was Pitching/Assistant Coach at ISU for 8 years. He was at Indian Hill Community College for 3 years. He compiled a record of 132-99 in his fourth year of coaching. Tim Murphy, Assistant Coach, is entering his 1st year as an assistant coach. Tony Truman, Assistant Coach, is entering his 1st year as an assistant coach.
Style of Play: Motion/contact style of offense.

Iowa Wesleyan College

601 North Main Street
Mount Pleasant, IA 52641
Coach: Todd Huckabone

NAIA
Tigers/Purple, White
Phone: (319) 385-6349
Fax: (319) 385-6301

ACADEMIC

Founded: 1842
Type: 4 Yr., Private, Liberal Arts, Coed
Religion: United Methodist
Campus Housing: Yes
Web-site: http://www.iwc.edu
SAT/ACT/GPA: 980/19/2.0
Student/Faculty Ratio: 12:1
Male/Female Ratio: 45:55
Undergraduate Enrollment: 828
Graduate Enrollment: None
Scholarships/Academic: Yes **Athletic:** Yes **Fin Aid:** Yes

Total Expenses by: Year **In State:** $ 17,010 **Out of State:** $ 17,010
Degrees Conferred: BA, BME, BSN, BS, BGS
Programs of Study: Accounting, Art, Biology, Business Administration, Business Computer Information Systems, Chemistry, Communications, Computer Science, Criminal Justice, Early Childhood Education, Elementary Education, English, Environmental Health, History, Political Science, International Business, Life Science, Mathematics, Music, Nursing, Physical Education, Psychology, Sociology, Sport Management

ATHLETIC PROFILE

Conference Affiliation: Midwest Classic Conference
Program Profile: Home games are played at Maple Leaf Community Field. Playing season is in March, April, and May.
History: This is my 4th year with the program. Our first year record is 27-19, second year record is 40-19, third year record is 41-17 and fourth year record is 36-16.
Achievements: Conference Champs 1996 and 1997; Player of the Year in Conference 1997; Coach of the Year in Conference 1997.

Iowa Western Community College

923 E Washington
Clarinda, IA 51632
Coach: Therron Brockish

NJCAA
Blue Jays/Lt Blue, Navy, Silver
Phone: (800) 432-5852
Fax: (712) 325-3720

ACADEMIC

Founded: 1945 **Type:** 2 Yr., Jr. College, Coed
Student/Faculty Ratio: 24:1 **Male/Female Ratio:** 1:2
Undergraduate Enrollment: 3,887 **Graduate Enrollment:** Unknown
Scholarships/Academic: Yes **Athletic:** No **Fin Aid:** Yes
Total Expenses by: Year **In State:** $ 5,200 **Out of State:** $ 7,000
Degrees Conferred: AA, AS
Programs of Study: Accounting, Agricultural, Architectural, Automotive Technology, Aviation, business, Computer, Criminal Justice, Deaf Interpreter Training, Drug/Alcohol/Substance Counseling, Engineering, Farm/Ranh, Fashion, Food Services, Graphic Arts, Human Services, Industrial Administration/Design, Journalism, Law, Machine/Tool, Mechanical, Medical, Paralegal

ATHLETIC PROFILE

Conference Affiliation: Iowa JUCO
Program Profile: The Blue Jays play a 14-game Fall season and 50-game Spring season. Home games are played at City Park. IWCC only recruits 24-30 players and does no over recruiting.
History: We started in 1975. The Blue Jays appeared in the JUCO World Series in 1982.
Achievements: 2 All-Americans (Dave Markowsky 1986, Ricardo Calderon 1994), 3 players signed (Ryan Eberly 1988, Ricardo Calderon 1994, Luis Matos 1995).
Total Number of Varsity/Jr. Varsity: 16 **Percent of Graduation:** 64%
Style of Play: Aggressive, fundamentally sound defense.

Kirkwood Community College

6301 Kirkwood Blvd, SW
Cedar Rapids, IA 52404
Coach: John Lewis

NJCAA
Eagles/Royal Blue, White
Phone: (319) 398-4910
Fax: (319) 398-5540

ACADEMIC

Founded: 1966 **Type:** 2 Yr., Jr. College, Coed
Religion: Non-Affiliated **Campus Housing:** No

Student/Faculty Ratio: 22:1 **Male/Female Ratio:** 42:58
Undergraduate Enrollment: 9,665 **Graduate Enrollment:** None
Scholarships/Academic: No **Athletic:** Yes **Fin Aid:** Yes
Total Expenses by: Year **In State:** $ 1,500 **Out of State:** $ 2,800
Degrees Conferred: Associate
Programs of Study: Accounting, Agricultural, Animal, Art, Automotive, Conservation, Corrections, Drafting/Design, Farm/Ranch, Fashion, Fish/Game, Forestry, History, Heating, Refrigerator/Ac, Horticulture, Landscape, Law, Legal Parks/Recreation, Radio/Television, Retail, Robotics, Wildlife Biology

ATHLETIC PROFILE

Conference Affiliation: Iowa Athletic Association
Program Profile: Our baseball field facility is three years old (one of the best in Iowa). Playing season is in March and ends in May. Our field is natural with dimensions of 330-Lines, 360-hole, and 390-center.
History: The program began in 1968. In the last 18 years, we have no losing records (average 30 wins per year). Our overall record is 568-310 in 18 years under Coach Lewis.
Achievements: Coach of the Year in '83, '87, '93 and '95; 4 All-Americans; District Coach of the Year in '93 & '95; Drafted players were 8; Tournament Coach in '95; Conference titles in '93 and '95.
Coaching: John Lewis - Head Coach. Tim Evans - Assist. Coach. Darren Lewis - Assist. Coach.
Style of Play: Bunt - move runners - some hit and run.

Loras College

1450 Alta Vista Street
Dubuque, IA 52001
Coach: Carl Tebon

NCAA III
Duhawks/Purple, Gold
Phone: (319) 588-7732
Fax: (319) 588-7983

ACADEMIC

Founded: 1839 **Type:** 4 Yr., Private, Liberal Arts, Coed
Religion: Catholic **Campus Housing:** Yes
Web-site: http://www.loras.edu/ **SAT/ACT/GPA:** 23/3.2
Student/Faculty Ratio: 13:1 **Male/Female Ratio:** 2:1
Undergraduate Enrollment: 1,500 **Graduate Enrollment:** 300
Scholarships/Academic: Yes **Athletic:** No **Fin Aid:** Yes
Total Expenses by: Year **In State:** $ 11,730 **Out of State:** $ 11,730
Degrees Conferred: Associates, BA, MA
Programs of Study: Accounting, Art Education, Art/Studio, Biology, Business Management, Chemistry, Classical Studies, Computer Science, Early Childhood Education, Engineering, Physics, English, Gerontology, Journalism, Management, Marketing, Mathematics, Computer Science, Music

ATHLETIC PROFILE

Conference Affiliation: Iowa Intercollegiate Athletic Conference
Program Profile: Turf, Patraikis Park, average 45 Fall games a season.
History: In 1906, our record was 638-553-6. We lost to the Chicago White Sox who were led by Shoeless Joe Jackson 8-0. 'Red' Faber was in major league baseball Hall of Fame (White Sox, 1914-33). NBC Sports Commentator Greg Gumbel played basebal at Loras (1964-67).
Achievements: Mike Griebel third team All-American; Al Eggers second team All-Americans.

Luther College

700 College Drive
Decorah, IA 52101
Coach: Paul Solberg

NCAA III
Norse/Blue, White
Phone: (319) 387-1590
Fax: (319) 387-1228

ACADEMIC

Founded: 1861
Type: 4 Yr., Private, Liberal Arts, Coed
Religion: Evangelical Lutheran
Campus Housing: Yes
Web-site: http://www.luther.edu/
Undergraduate Enrollment: 2,400
Student/Faculty Ratio: 14:1
Male/Female Ratio: 40:60
Scholarships/Academic: Yes **Athletic:** No **Fin Aid:** Yes
Total Expenses by: Year **In State:** $ 17,500 **Out of State:** $ 17,500
Degrees Conferred: BA, BS
Programs of Study: Accounting, Anthropology, Art, Biblical Languages, Biology, English, Chemistry, Communications, Computer Science, Economics, Elementary Education, History, Management, Mathematics, Music, Nursing, Philosophy, Physical Education, Physics, Political Science, Psychology, Religion, Social Work, Sociology

ATHLETIC PROFILE

Conference Affiliation: Iowa IAC

Marshalltown Community College

3700 South Center
Marshalltown, IA 50158
Coach: Mike Marquis
NJCAA
Tigers/Navy, Gold
Phone: (515) 752-7106
Fax: (515) 752-8149

ACADEMIC

Founded: 1927
Type: 2 Yr., Jr. College, Coed
Student/Faculty Ratio: 15:1
Male/Female Ratio: 32:68
Undergraduate Enrollment: 1,500
Graduate Enrollment: Unknown
Scholarships/Academic: No **Athletic:** Yes **Fin Aid:** Yes
Total Expenses by: Year **In State:** $ 1,900+ **Out of State:** $ 3,600+
Degrees Conferred: Associate
Programs of Study: Accounting, Business, Community Services, Computer Science, Dental Services, Economics, Electrical/Electronics, Industrial/Heavy Equipment, Machine Tool, Marketing, Nursing, Political Science, Science, Radiological Technology

ATHLETIC PROFILE

Conference Affiliation: Iowa JUCO Region XI
Program Profile: We are an up and coming program . We go to Panama City Beach every Springbreak. We have on campus facilities and our field has been remodeled.
History: Our program started in the 1950's and has been up and down for many years. We are just beginning a sense of importance to our campus.

Morningside College

1501 Morningside College
Sioux City, IA 51106
Coach: Jim Scholten
Email: jls002@alpha.morningside.edu
NCAA II
Mustangs/Maroon, Grey
Phone: (712) 274-5258
Fax: (712) 274-5578

ACADEMIC

Founded: 1894
Type: 4 Yr., Private, Coed
SAT/ACT/GPA: 1000avg/21avg
Campus Housing: Yes
Student/Faculty Ratio: 15:1
Male/Female Ratio: 41:59
Undergraduate Enrollment: 1,175
Graduate Enrollment: 100
Scholarships/Academic: Yes **Athletic:** Yes **Fin Aid:** Yes

Total Expenses by: Year **In State:** $ 14,950 **Out of State:** $ 14,950
Degrees Conferred: BA, BS, M
Programs of Study: Accounting, Art, Biology, Business, Chemistry, Communications, Criminal Justice, Computer, Dramatic Arts, Economics, Education, Engineering, Graphic Arts, History, Humanities, Industrial, Psychology, Math, Music, Natural Science, Nursing, Philosophy, Photography, Preprofessional Programs, Recreation, Religion, Sociology, Special Education

ATHLETIC PROFILE

Estimated Number of Baseball Scholarships: 3
Conference Affiliation: North Central Conference
Program Profile: We play at beautiful Lewis and Clark Stadium which has major league dimensions and seats 4,200. It has a natural surface that is impeccably cared for.
History: Baseball has been the most successful sport at our 105 year old school.
Achievements: Produced 2 All-Americans in the last five years; several drafted players with many more playing in independent professional leagues.
Coaching: Jim Scholten, Head Coach, has over 400 career wins. He is a member of the Iowa Baseball Coaches Hall of Fame. Rich Grife, Assistant Coach, is responsible for the pitchers and has pitched professionally for six years. Jason DeWall, Assistant Coach, is responsible for the hitters and catchers. He was a former All-Conference player at Morningside College.
Roster for 1998 team/In State: 25 **Out of State:** 10 **Out of Country:** 1
Total Number of Varsity/Jr. Varsity: 36 **Percent of Graduation:** 87%
Number of Seniors on 1998 Team: 6 **Most Recent Record:** 30 - 20 - 0
Freshmen Receiving Fin Aid/Athletic: 6 **Academic:** 8
Number of Fall Games: 7 **Number of Spring Games:** 50
Positions Needed for 1999/2000: 3rd Base, Shortstop, Catcher, 3-Pitchers
Baseball Camp Dates: Pitcher-Catcher Camp December 28 and 29
Schedule: Central Missouri, Northern Colorado, All North Central Conference Teams
Style of Play: Aggressive thinking style of play. Players have input on team organization. Bottom line philosophy - have fun playing a great game.

Mount Mercy College

1330 Elmhurst Drive, NE
Cedar Rapids, IA 52402
Coach: Justin Schulte

NAIA
Mustangs/Blue, Gold
Phone: (319) 363-8213
Fax: (319) 363-6341

ACADEMIC

Founded: 1928 **Type:** 4 Yr., Private, Liberal Arts, Coed
Religion: Catholic **Campus Housing:** Yes
Web-site: http://www.mtmercy.edu/ **SAT/ACT/GPA:** 800/18/2.5
Student/Faculty Ratio: 12:1 **Male/Female Ratio:** 35:65
Undergraduate Enrollment: 1,200 **Graduate Enrollment:** None
Scholarships/Academic: Yes **Athletic:** No **Fin Aid:** Yes
Total Expenses by: Year **In State:** $ 15,800 **Out of State:** $ 15,800
Degrees Conferred: BA, BS, BBA
Programs of Study: Art, Biology, Business Administration, (Accounting, Administrative Management, Marketing), Computer Science, Criminal Justice Administration, Education, English, History, Mathematics, Music, Nursing, Political Science, Psychology, Public Relations, Religion, Social Work, Sociology, Preprofessional Studies (Law, Medicine, Physical Therapy)

ATHLETIC PROFILE

Conference Affiliation: Midwest Classics Conference
Program Profile: We have a short Fall season . The Spring season begins in mid-January (indoors) and goes to early May. We play on natural grass.
History: The program began in 1975 and we were Conference Champions in 1996.

Achievements: Conference Coach of the Year in 1996; All-time NAIA stolen base record for individual in 1991 (100).
Coaching: Justin Schulte, Head Coach, is entering his first season with the program. He has been college assistant coach.
Roster for 1998 team/In State: 6 **Out of State:** 23 **Out of Country:**
Total Number of Varsity/Jr. Varsity: 29 **Percent of Graduation:** 90%
Number of Seniors on 1998 Team: 5 **Number of Sophomores on 1998 Team:** 12
Freshmen Receiving Fin Aid/Athletic: 0 **Academic:** 100%
Most Recent Record: 12 - 30 - 0 **Number of Spring Games:** 50
Positions Needed for 1999/2000: Pitcher, Catcher
Schedule: St. Ambrose, Grand View, Mount St. Clare, Upper Iowa, Quincy, Viterbo

Mount Saint Clare College

400 N Bluff Boulevard
Clinton, IA 52732
Coach: Ken Misfeldt

NAIA
Mounties/Purple, Gold
Phone: (319) 242-4153
Fax: (319) 242-8684

ACADEMIC

Founded: 1918 **Type:** 4 Yr., Private, Liberal Arts, Coed
Religion: Franciscan/Catholic **Campus Housing:** Yes
Web-site: None **SAT/ACT/GPA:** 750/18/2.0
Student/Faculty Ratio: 12:1 **Male/Female Ratio:** 3:1
Undergraduate Enrollment: 540 **Graduate Enrollment:** None
Scholarships/Academic: Yes **Athletic:** Yes **Fin Aid:** Yes
Total Expenses by: Year **In State:** $ Varies **Out of State:** Varies
Degrees Conferred: AA, AAS, BA, BGS
Programs of Study: Accounting, Business Administration, Clinical Cytotechnology, Computer Information Systems, Elementary Education, Social Science, Liberal Arts, Fine Arts, Journalism, Music, Science, Social Science, Prelaw, Premed, Precounseling, Arts, Biology, Chemistry, Computer Science, Early Childhood Education, Mathematics, Music, Philosophy, Predentistry, Sociology, Speech Therapy, English as a Second Language

ATHLETIC PROFILE

Estimated Number of Baseball Scholarships: 12
Conference Affiliation: Midwest Classic Conference
Program Profile: We have a year round program with Fall practices and scrimmages. Winter is weight-lifting and conditioning followed by Spring games. We play at Riverview Stadium, which seats 3,000 and has natural grass.
History: The program began in 1993 and is just six years old. Last year we set a school record with 15 wins.
Achievements: 4th last season, highest ever in conference; Chad Jilek (Jr.) and Joe Robbins (Sr.) school's first All-Conference players.
Coaching: Ken Misfeldt, Head Coach, is entering his 1st year as a head coach. He compiled a record of 15-19. He was an assistant at Northern Iowa for four years. He was assistant at Wayne State for two years.
Roster for 1998 team/In State: 22 **Out of State:** 8 **Out of Country:** 2
Total Number of Varsity/Jr. Varsity: 32 **Percent of Graduation:** 76%
Number of Seniors on 1998 Team: 6 **Number of Sophomores on 1998 Team:** 8
Freshmen Receiving Fin Aid/Athletic: 8 **Academic:** 2
Number of Fall Games: 10 **Number of Spring Games:** 50
Positions Needed for 1999/2000: Pitcher, 1st Base, 2nd Base, Catcher
Most Recent Record: 15 - 19 - 0
Schedule: Grand View, Viterbo, St. Ambrose, Missouri Valley
Style of Play: Hustling, "get-after-after" style. We try to think ahead and be entertaining for our teams.

Muscatine Community College

152 Colorado Street
Muscatine, IA 52761
Coach: Nick Zumsande
Email:

NJCAA I
Indians/Royal, Scarlet Red, White
Phone: (319) 288-6066
Fax: (319) 288-6074

ACADEMIC

Founded: 1936
Type: 2 Yr., Jr. College, Coed
Student/Faculty Ratio: 17:1
Male/Female Ratio: Unknown
Undergraduate Enrollment: 1,063
Graduate Enrollment: None
Scholarships/Academic: Yes **Athletic:** Yes **Fin Aid:** Yes
Total Expenses by: Year **In State:** $ 4,000 **Out of State:** $ 5,000
Degrees Conferred: AA, AS
Programs of Study: Accounting, Agricultural Business, Biology, Biological Science, Business Administration, Commerce, Management, Business, Machine Tool Technology, Chemistrt, Child Care, Computer Science, Conservation, Economics, Education, English, Farm/Ranch, Practical Nursing, Psychology

ATHLETIC PROFILE

Conference Affiliation: Iowa JUCO
Program Profile: Abac Field is called Tom Bruner Field and is an old minor league park. In 1997, we spent about $ 250,000.00 for improvements. The surface is anatural grass and there is also an outstanding indoor facility.
History: Our program began in the 1960's.
Achievements: Our Division I program was nationally ranked throughout the 90's. World Series Appearances in 1994; 26 ex-Indians have played professional baseball in 90's; 8 currently;. Many others have played at the major college level.
Coaching: Nick Zumsande, Head Coach, has compiled a record of 317-123. Steve Knocle - Assistant Coach. Angel Matos - Assistant Coach.
Style of Play: Aggressive offensively; believe pitching and defense win games.

North Iowa Area Community College

500 College Drive
Mason City, IA 50401
Coach: Jerry Dunbar

NJCAA
Trojans/Blue, Gold
Phone: (515) 422-4281
Fax: (515) 423-1711

ACADEMIC

Founded: 1918
Type: 2 Yr., Jr. College, Coed
Student/Faculty Ratio: 25:1
Male/Female Ratio: Unknown
Undergraduate Enrollment: 2,728
Graduate Enrollment: None
Total Expenses by: Year **In State:** $ 1,840+ **Out of State:** $ 2,700+
Degrees Conferred: Associate
Programs of Study: Accounting, Agricutural Business, Agricultural Economics, Animal Science, Automtoive Technology, Business Administration, Commerce, Management, Liberal Arts, General studies, Marketing, Retailing, Office Management, Welding Technology

ATHLETIC PROFILE

Conference Affiliation: Iowa Northern Conference

Northwestern College - Iowa

101 College Lane
Orange City, IA 51041
Coach: Mark Bloemendaal
Email: markb@ncwiowa.Edu

NAIA
Red Raiders/Red, Silver
Phone: (712) 737-7136
Fax: (712) 737-7164

ACADEMIC

Founded: 1894
Type: 4 Yr., Private, Liberal Arts, Coed
Religion: Reformed Church of America
Campus Housing: Yes
Web-site: http://www.nwciowa.edu
SAT/ACT/GPA: 18/2.35
Student/Faculty Ratio: 16:1
Male/Female Ratio: 47:57
Undergraduate Enrollment: 1,177
Graduate Enrollment: None
Scholarships/Academic: Yes **Athletic:** Yes **Fin Aid:** Yes
Total Expenses by: Year **In State:** $ 15,174 **Out of State:** $ 15,174
Degrees Conferred: BA
Programs of Study: Art, Biology, Business, Accounting, Education, Music, Sociology, English, Theatre, Spanish, Psychology, Physical Education, Communications, Math, History, Social Work, Environmental Science, Chemistry, Christian Brothers

ATHLETIC PROFILE

Estimated Number of Baseball Scholarships: 4
Conference Affiliation: Nebraska-Iowa Athletic Conference
Program Profile: Our Fall schedule consists of 5 weeks of practice, a 40-50 game in the Spring and a trip to the South. It is a very competitive conference schedule.
History: We had a continuous program since 1967. We generally have a winning season. Our coaches are currently in 7th year and 6th year respectively.
Achievements: 2 players signed in the last four years; 4 Scholar Athletes in the last four years; 2 players named National Player of the Week.
Coaching: Mark Bloemendaal, Head Coach, is entering his 7th season.. He compiled a record of 141-145 and 82-49 in 1997. Dave Nonemacher , Assistant Coach, is entering his 6th year as an assistant coach. He is a former pitcher from Taylor University
Roster for 1998 team/In State: 20 **Out of State:** 12 **Out of Country:** 0
Total Number of Varsity/Jr. Varsity: 0 **Percent of Graduation:** 70%
Number of Seniors on 1998 Team: 8 **Number of Sophomores on 1998 Team:** 32
Freshmen Receiving Fin Aid/Athletic: 8 **Academic:** 6
Number of Fall Games: 8 **Number of Spring Games:** 6
Baseball Camp Dates: Late February **Most Recent Record:** 20 - 21 - 0
Positions Needed for 1999/2000: Pitcher, Infielders, Catcher
Schedule: Biola, Westmont, California Lutheran, Midland Lutheran, Briar Cliff, Morningside
Style of Play: Solid defense; good pitching.

Saint Ambrose University

518 West Locust Street
Davenport, IA 52803
Coach: Jim Callahan

NAIA
Fighting Bees/Blue, White
Phone: (319) 333-6237
Fax: (319) 333-6239

ACADEMIC

Founded: 1882
Type: 4 Yr., Private, Liberal Arts, Coed
Religion: Catholic
Campus Housing: Yes
Web-site: http://www.sau.edu/
SAT/ACT/GPA: 790/20
Student/Faculty Ratio: 15:1
Male/Female Ratio: 49:51
Undergraduate Enrollment: 1,400
Graduate Enrollment: 700-800
Scholarships/Academic: Yes **Athletic:** Yes **Fin Aid:** Yes

Total Expenses by: Year **In State:** $ 16,920 **Out of State:** $ 16,920
Degrees Conferred: BS, BA, MBA, MPT
Programs of Study: Accounting, Art, Business and Management, Communications, Criminal Justice, Education, Engineering, Music, Music Education, Occupational Therapy, Physical Therapy, Protective Service, Public Affairs, Psychology, Sciences, Social Science, Theatre

ATHLETIC PROFILE

Estimated Number of Baseball Scholarships: 7
Conference Affiliation: Midwest Classic Conference
Program Profile: We have a well rounded and very competitive NAIA program. We play a number of Division I NCAA teams with a lot of NAIA ranked teams. We have one of the best indoor and outdoor practice and playing facilities with a natural turf field. We do a 65 game Spring schedule and an 18 game Fall schedule.
History: Our program began in 1893 and became very competitive within the last six years. We won 4 conference titles, 6 post-season tourneys and 1 National Championship Appearance. We produced 5 professional baseball players.
Achievements: Jim Callahan was named Coach of the Year in 1996, 6 Conference Titles, 7 All-Americans, 3 drafted players, 6 free-agent signings; 1996 NAIA Runner-Up at National Championships to Lewis and Clark State; last 6 year ranked in the Top 25.
Coaching: Jim Callahan , Head Coach, is entering his 4th year as a head coach. He has two years of Division I experience. He compiled a record of 91-49 and was named Coach of the Year in 1996. He was NAIA Runner-Up in 1996. Tony Huntley, Assistant Coach, started in 1997.He is a 2-time All-American NJCA and played 3 years of professional ball. He had a four-year conference player team and played on 1996 NAIA Runner-Up team in the World Series.
Roster for 1998 team/In State: 20 **Out of State:** 15 **Out of Country:** 0
Total Number of Varsity/Jr. Varsity: 35 **Percent of Graduation:** 100%
Number of Seniors on 1998 Team: 13 **Most Recent Record:** 19 - 19 - 0
Freshmen Receiving Fin Aid/Athletic: 16 **Academic:** 16
Number of Fall Games: 15 **Number of Spring Games:** 65
Positions Needed for 1999/2000: Pitchers, 1st Base, 3rd Base, Outfielder
Baseball Camp Dates: December?
Schedule: St. Thomas University, Nova SouthEastern, Barry University, Seton Hall, Bradley
Style of Play: Relies on the fundamental baseball. Get a guy on, bunt him over, and drive him in. Great pitching form, staff had 40 complete games this year.

Simpson College

701 North Street
Indianola, IA 50125
Coach: John Sirianni

NCAA III
Storm/Red, Gold
Phone: (515) 961-1620
Fax: (515) 961-1279

ACADEMIC

Founded: 1860 **Type:** 4 Yr, Private, Liberal Arts, Coed
Religion: Methodist **Campus Housing:** Yes
SAT/ACT/GPA: Other factor considered/ **Web-site:** http://www.simpson.edu/
Student/Faculty Ratio: 15:1 **Male/Female Ratio:** 1:1:3
Undergraduate Enrollment: 1,700 **Graduate Enrollment:** None
Scholarships/Academic: Yes **Athletic:** No **Fin Aid:** Yes
Total Expenses by: Year **In State:** $ 17,385 **Out of State:** $ 17,385
Degrees Conferred: BA, Bmus, BS
Programs of Study: Accounting, Advertising, Art Administration, Art Education, Biological Science, Business Administration, Business Education, Chemistry, Communication, Computer Science, Criminal Justice, Economics, Elementary Education, English, Finance, Fine Arts, Health Education, History, Mathematics, Music, Nursing, Philosophy, Political Science, Prelaw, Premed, Religion

ATHLETIC PROFILE

Conference Affiliation: Iowa Intercollegiate Athletic Conference
Achievements: Iowa Conference Title in 1991, 1987, and 1994; Iowa Conference Runner-Up in 1988, 1989, 1990, 1992; Regional Qualifiers in 1990, 1991, 1992, 7 1994; Regional Champons in 1991; NCAA Division III World Series in 1991.
Coaching: John Sirianni, Head Coach, 1985 to the present, .

Southeastern Community College-North Campus

1015 South Gear Avenue
W Burlington, IA 52655
Coach: Lonnie Winston

NJCAA
Blackhawks/Red, Black
Phone: (319) 752-2731
Fax: (319) 752-4957

ACADEMIC

Founded: 1968
Type: 2 Yr., Jr. College, Coed
Student/Faculty Ratio: 24:1
Male/Female Ratio: 38:62
Undergraduate Enrollment: 2,170
Graduate Enrollment: None
Scholarships/Academic: No **Athletic:** Yes **Fin Aid:** Yes
Total Expenses by: Year **In State:** $ 4,000 **Out of State:** $ 5,000
Degrees Conferred: Associate
Programs of Study: Accounting, Agriculture, Agronomy, Automotive, Aviation, Business, Computer Construction, Cosmetology, Criminal Justice, Crop Science, Drafting/Design, Engineering, Medical, English, Law, Liberal Arts, Literature, Machine and Tool Technology, Nursing, Office Management, Practical Nursing, Radiological Technology, Robotics, Welding

Southwestern Community College

1501 Townline Road
Creston, IA 50801
Coach: Bill Krejci
Email: kaejci@swcc.ccia.us

NJCAA
Spartans/Navy, Scarlet, White
Phone: (515) 782-1459
Fax: (515) 782-3312

ACADEMIC

Founded: 1966
Type: 2 Yr., Jr. College, Coed
Student/Faculty Ratio: 20:1
Male/Female Ratio: 2:1
Undergraduate Enrollment: 1,200
Graduate Enrollment: None
Scholarships/Academic: No **Athletic:** Yes **Fin Aid:** Yes
Total Expenses by: Year **In State:** $ 4,500 **Out of State:** $ 5,000
Degrees Conferred: AA, AS, Career Education
Programs of Study: Auto Body, Auto Mechanics, Business, Carpentry, Drafting, Electronics, Liberal Arts, Nursing, Sciences

ATHLETIC PROFILE

Conference Affiliation: Iowa JUCO, Division I
Program Profile: We have excellent indoor and outdoor facilities. Our Fall program is 10 weeks. Yn We have year -round workouts and take a trip in the Spring.
Coaching: Bill Krejci - Head Coach. Matt Thompson - Assistant Coach. Kyle Yamada - Assistant Coach.

Marycrest International University

(Program Discontinued)

University of Dubuque

2000 University Avenue
Dubuque, IA 52001
Coach: Dennis Rima

NCAA III
Spartans/Blue, White
Phone: (319) 589-3229
Fax: (319) 589-3425

ACADEMIC

Founded: 1852
Religion: Presbyterian
Web-site: Not Available
Student/Faculty Ratio: 15:1
Undergraduate Enrollment: 1,000
Scholarships/Academic: Yes **Athletic:** No
Total Expenses by: Year **In State:** $ 20,330
Degrees Conferred: BA, MA, BS

Type: 4 Yr., Private, Liberal Arts, Coed
Campus Housing: Yes
SAT/ACT/GPA: 1000+/19
Male/Female Ratio: 50:50
Graduate Enrollment: 100
Fin Aid: Yes
Out of State: $ 20,330

Programs of Study: Accounting, Aviation, Business, Computer Sicence, English, History, Environmental Science, Education, Physical Education, Biology, Communications, Math, Chemistry, Economics, Music, Political Science, Psychology, Sociology, Religious Studies, Spanish

ATHLETIC PROFILE

Conference Affiliation: Iowa Intercollegiate Athletic Conference
Program Profile: We have a solid and competitive program. In 1996, we got a new natural grass field. We have a nice indoor facility and fitness center. We have 10 practices in the Fall and 36+ games in the Spring (NACC Rule).
History: The program began in early 1900's. We have a great program as anyone who is a decent player is on the team. There is no cutting varsity and junior varsity teams. We are in a very competitive Iowa Conference.
Achievements: Dennis Rima named Coach of the Year in '94; still looking for 1st conference title.
Coaching: Dennis Rima, Head Coach, started in 1989. His overall record is 354-236 (high school and college). His 1st season was 4-29 with no chance to recruit. He won state title in 1985 as a high school coach. He was runner-up in 1984.
Roster for 1998 team/In State: 7 **Out of State:** 13 **Out of Country:** 0
Total Number of Varsity/Jr. Varsity: 40 **Percent of Graduation:** 90%
Number of Seniors on 1998 Team: 2 **Most Recent Record:** 17 - 20 - 0
Freshmen Receiving Fin Aid/Athletic: 0 **Academic:** All
Baseball Camp Dates: December 28-31 **Number of Spring Games:** 37
Positions Needed for 1999/2000: Pitcher, 3rd Base, Outfielder
Schedule: University of Wisconsin-Platteville, Wartburg, Upper Iowa, Simpson, William Penn, Loras
Style of Play: Very aggressive offensively; like to hit and run; steal and move runners along. We build our team on pitching and defense that is what wins championships.

University of Iowa

232 Carver Hawkeye Arena
Iowa City, IA 52242
Coach: Scott Broghamer

NCAA I
Hawkeyes/Black, Gold
Phone: (319) 335-9389
Fax: (319) 335-9417

ACADEMIC

Founded: 1847
SAT/ACT/GPA: 700/17
Student/Faculty Ratio: 15:1
Undergraduate Enrollment: 27,597
Scholarships/Academic: Yes **Athletic:** Yes
Total Expenses by: Year **In State:** $ 6,899

Type: 4 Yr., Public, Coed
Campus Housing: Yes
Male/Female Ratio: 48:52
Graduate Enrollment: 6,436
Fin Aid: Yes
Out of State: $ 13,497

Degrees Conferred: BA, BS, BFA, BLS, BM, BSN, MA, MBA, MFA, MD
Programs of Study: The College of Liberal Arts, The College of Business Administration, The College engineering, The College of Medicine, The College of Nursing, The College of Pharmacy

ATHLETIC PROFILE

Conference Affiliation: Big Ten Conference
Program Profile: The Iowa baseball program traditionally plays a 50-60 game season starting in March and ending in early May. The team holds Fall practice, but does not play any games in the Fall. The program boasts state of the art facilities, including a full size swimming pool for training and rehabilitation, a baseball -exclusive weight romm, an indoor practice facility and a new team clubhouse with every possible amenity. Iowa Field (3,000) features a manicured grass playing surface with an underground irrigation system. Iowa Field has a Daktronics scoreboard with a message center capable of displaying player or team information.
History: The Iowa baseball program began in 1890, and has amassed a 1609-1205-27 record for a winning percentage of .571.
Achievements: Banks has been Conference Coach of the Year, District Coach of the Year, elected to ABCA Hall of Fame, coached 6 All-Americans, 35 First Team All-Conference, 53 players drafted - 3 first round. 5 Hawkeyes earned All-Big 10 honors. Matt Austin, pitcher, earned 2nd Team Academic All-American honors.

University of Northern Iowa

UNI-Dome NW Upper
Cedar Falls, IA 50614-0314
Coach: Dave Schrage

NCAA I
Panthers/Purple, Old Gold
Phone: (319) 273-6323
Fax: (319) 273-3602

ACADEMIC

Founded: 1876
Type: 4 Yr., Public, Liberal Arts, Coed
Religion: Non-Affiliated
Campus Housing: Yes
Web-site: http://www.uni.edu/athletics
SAT/ACT/GPA: 21
Student/Faculty Ratio: 24:1
Male/Female Ratio: 43:57
Undergraduate Enrollment: 12,000
Graduate Enrollment: 1,004
Scholarships/Academic: Yes **Athletic:** Yes **Fin Aid:** Yes
Total Expenses by: Year **In State:** $ 7,222 **Out of State:** $ 11,777
Degrees Conferred: BA, BS, BFA, BLS, BT, BM
Programs of Study: Accounting, Art, American Studies, Anthropology, Asian Studies, Biotechnology, Biology, Chemistry, Communications, Computer, Environment, Earth Science, Finance, General Studies, Geology, Humanities, Management, Natural History, Nutrition/Food, Physics, Science, Religion, Textile/Apparel, Theatre

ATHLETIC PROFILE

Estimated Number of Baseball Scholarships: 8
Conference Affiliation: Missouri Valley Conference
Program Profile: Our home stadium is Waterloo Riverfront Stadium with a seating capacity of 4,277. It has natural grass with the dimensions of 335-360-390-360 and 335. We take annual Spring trips. All the games are in the Spring. We compete in the difficult Missouri Valley Conferece.
History: Our program began in 1893 and 1999 was the 100th year of Northern Iowa baseball. The all-time record is 952-1000-10. We includes such major leaguers as Eddie Watt, Duane Josephson and Steve Dreyer.
Achievements: Dave Schrage was named MVC Coach of the Year in 1995 and 1997; 10 drafted players including 12 in the decade; 2 players drafted in 1998 MLB draft; 1997 team set school record with 32 wins. The team also placed second in Missouri Valley Conference.
Coaching: Dave Schrage, Head Coach, compiled a record of 182-261 in eight years at UNI and an overall record is 239-327 in 11 years as a head coach. He was named 1995 and 1997 Missouri Valley Conference Coach of the Year. He was also All-MVC as a player at Creighton. Todd Rima,

Assistant Coach, owns the school record at UNI for hits, games, bunts, runs, double, amples. Jack and Brian hood - Assistant Coaches.

Roster for 1998 team/In State: 31 **Out of State:** 9 **Out of Country:** 0
Total Number of Varsity/Jr. Varsity: 31 **Percent of Graduation:** 95%
Number of Seniors on 1998 Team: 6 **Most Recent Record:** 26 - 30 - 0
Freshmen Receiving Fin Aid/Athletic: 6 **Academic:** 1
Number of Fall Games: 0 **Number of Spring Games:** 56
Positions Needed for 1999/2000: Corner Outfielders, Middle Infielder, Pitcher
Baseball Camp Dates: TBA Jan-17,31; February 14
Schedule: Wichita State, Fordham, Indiana State, SW Missouri State, Minnesota, SE Missouri State, Iowa, Nebraska, Missouri
Style of Play: Aggressive; good pitching & defense. Top 15 in the nation in fielding percentage in 1997. Looking for hitters who can put the ball in play. Like to keep pressure on other team.

Upper Iowa University

Box 1857
Fayette, IA 52142
Coach: Rick Heller

NCAA III
Peacocks/Col. Blue, White, Navy
Phone: (319) 425-5304
Fax: (319) 425-5334

ACADEMIC

Founded: 1857 **Type:** 4 Yr., Private, Coed
SAT/ACT/GPA: 16 **Campus Housing:** Yes
Student/Faculty Ratio: 15:1 **Male/Female Ratio:** 3:2
Undergraduate Enrollment: 695 **Graduate Enrollment:** 60
Scholarships/Academic: Yes **Athletic:** No **Fin Aid:** Yes
Total Expenses by: Year **In State:** $ 12,500 **Out of State:** $ 12,500
Degrees Conferred: BA, BS, MA, AA
Programs of Study: Accounting, Art, Biological Science, Business,Communication, Computer Conservation/Regulation, Construction Management, Education, English, Fine Arts, Health Care, Human Services, Management, Marketing, Math, Music, Psychology, Public, Recreation, Science

ATHLETIC PROFILE

Conference Affiliation: Iowa Conference
Program Profile: We are a Top level Division III program. We play games in the Metrodome in early March and travel to Florida in late March. We have a tough schedule and play in a beautiful home field. Baseball is a major sport.
History: Our progran began in 1895. We have a long history of successful baseball. The last ten years have been outstanding. We have three Conference Championships, three NCAA Regional Berths, one Regional Championship, one World Series Appearances, and eight straight winning seasons with three season of over 30 wins.
Achievements: 1989 Iowa Conference Coach of the Year; 1993 Iowa Conference Coach of the Year; 1993 Iowa High School Coaches Association; 4-year College Coach of the Year; 1995 Central Region Coach of the Year.
Coaching: Rick Heller - Head Coach. Mark Danker, Pitching Coach, is works full-time and has been with Upper Iowa for eight years. He has coached two conference MVP's, one All-American, and two Pitchers in Pro-Baseball.
Style of Play: Aggressive hustle style. Play short game well. Team this year was pitching and defense oriented. We adopt specific style to the players we have.

Waldorf Junior College

106 S 6th St
Forest City, IA 50436
Coach: Brian Grunzke

NJCAA
Warriors/Purple, Grey
Phone: (515) 582-8263
Fax: (515) 582-8184

ACADEMIC

Founded: 1903
Type: 2 Yr., Jr. College, Coed
Undergraduate Enrollment: 635
SAT/ACT/GPA: 700/15
Student/Faculty Ratio: 11:1
Male/Female Ratio: 1.5:1
Scholarships/Academic: Yes **Athletic:** Yes **Fin Aid:** Yes
Total Expenses by: Year **In State:** $ 12,512 **Out of State:** $ 12,512
Degrees Conferred: Offer 3 years BA Programs
Programs of Study: Accounting, Behavioral Science, Biblical Studies, Biological Science, Business, Chemistry, Community Services, Computer Education, Journalism, Law, Math, Medical, Nursing, Physical Education, Preprofessional Programs, Psychology, Religious, Speech

ATHLETIC PROFILE

Conference Affiliation: Iowa JUCO
Program Profile: We play a Fall schedule with 10-12 games and a Spring schedule with 52-56 games. We have a Winter workout program, and we take a Southern trip.
History: The program began in 1910. Our on campus field was built in 1975.
Achievements: Have had five All-Americans in the last six years.
Style of Play: Aggressive, Hit and Run, running game.

Wartburg College

222 - 9th Street NW
Waverly, IA 50677-0903
Coach: Joel Holst
NCAA III
Knights/orange, Black
Phone: (319) 352-8532
Fax: (319) 352-8528

ACADEMIC

Founded: 1856
Type: 4 Yr., Private, Liberal Arts, Coed
Religion: Lutheran
Campus Housing: Yes
Web-site: http://www.wartburg.edu
SAT/ACT/GPA: 18 minimum
Student/Faculty Ratio: 15:1
Male/Female Ratio: 1:2
Undergraduate Enrollment: 1,450
Graduate Enrollment: None
Scholarships/Academic: Yes **Athletic:** No **Fin Aid:** Yes
Total Expenses by: Year **In State:** $ 17,940 **Out of State:** $ 17,940
Degrees Conferred: BA
Programs of Study: Accounting, Art, Visual Arts Management, Biology, Business Administration, Chemistry, Communications Design, Computer Information Systems, Computer Science, Economics, Educations, Music, Philosophy, Physical Education, Physics, Political Science, Psychology, Religion, Social Work, Sociology, Predentistry, Premed, Prelaw, Preengineering

ATHLETIC PROFILE

Conference Affiliation: Iowa Intercollegiate Athletic Conference
Program Profile: We play at Hertel Field which has natural grass. Lights will be added. We have restroom facilities. The dimensions are 20' down lines and 380' to center. There is an electronic scoreboard. Practice begins in February. A Spring trip is planned annually. We have been to Texas and Florida. Last year we played in the Metrodome in Minneapolis. The season ends early May.
History: The program began in 1935. We have six Iowa Conference titles: 1961, 1962, 1963, 1977, 1978 and 1979. We have four post season appearances in NAIA and in NAIA World Series in 1964. We defeated Joe Niekro and West Liberty State 2-1 in 16 innings, before losing to Grambling and Mayville State.
Coaching: Joel Holst - Head Coach.
Style of Play: Aggressive, hit and run, running game.

William Penn College

201 Trueblood Avenue
Oskaloosa, IA 52577
Coach: Mike Laird

NCAA III
Statesmen/Navy, Gold
Phone: (515) 673-1023
Fax: (515) 673-1373

ACADEMIC

Founded: 1873
Type: 4 Yr., Private, Liberal Arts, Coed
Religion: Quaker
Campus Housing: Yes
Web-site: http://WWW.WmPenn.EDU
SAT/ACT/GPA: 19/2.0
Student/Faculty Ratio: 13:1
Male/Female Ratio: 6:1
Undergraduate Enrollment: 860
Graduate Enrollment: None
Scholarships/Academic: Yes **Athletic:** No **Fin Aid:** Yes
Total Expenses by: Year **In State:** $ 15,800 **Out of State:** $ 15,800
Degrees Conferred: BA, BS
Programs of Study: Accounting, Applied Computer Science, Art, Biology, Biology Education, Business Education, Communication Arts, Computer Information Systems, Elementary Education, Engineering, English, English Education, Health Education, Home Economics, Human Relations, Mathematics, Natural Science, Physical Science, Physical Education, Sociology, Political Science, Sports Administration, Music

ATHLETIC PROFILE

Conference Affiliation: Iowa Intercollegiate Athletic Conference
Program Profile: We got a new natural turf field in 1998, a new large pressbox in 1999, a new large scoreboard in 1996 and new dugouts in 1995. We will likely get a new lighting system (150k) for the 1999 season.
History: The first year of the program was in 1891. We were the dominant program in the IIAC for the last 15 years with: 6 IIAC titles; 7 runner-ups; 10 All-Americans; 12 drafted players; 423 wins; 8 NCAA Appearances; have led NCAA in won/loss, pitching, slugging, double plays.
Achievements: IIAC Coach of the Year four times; 6 IIAC titles; 10 All-Americans; 12 signed players; 2 former pitchers have made it to the big league; ranked top 5 in the NCAA.
Coaching: Mike Laird ,Head Coach, is entering his 16th year with the program. He compiled a record of 423-168-1, 5 IIAC Titles and 8 NCAA Appearances. Jim Overturf ,Assistant Coach, is entering his 2nd year with the program and has 20 years coaching experience. Ken Decook, Assistant Coach, has 20 years coaching experience.
Roster for 1998 team/In State: 15 **Out of State:** 20 **Out of Country:** 0
Total Number of Varsity/Jr. Varsity: 35 **Percent of Graduation:** 0
Number of Seniors on 1998 Team: 35 **Most Recent Record:** 23 - 16 - 0
Baseball Camp Dates: Second week of June **Number of Spring Games:** 50
Positions Needed for 1999/2000: Pitcher, Infielder
Style of Play: Outstanding pitching, aggressive on the bases fundamentally sound, focused, outstanding hitting for serious players only!

KANSAS

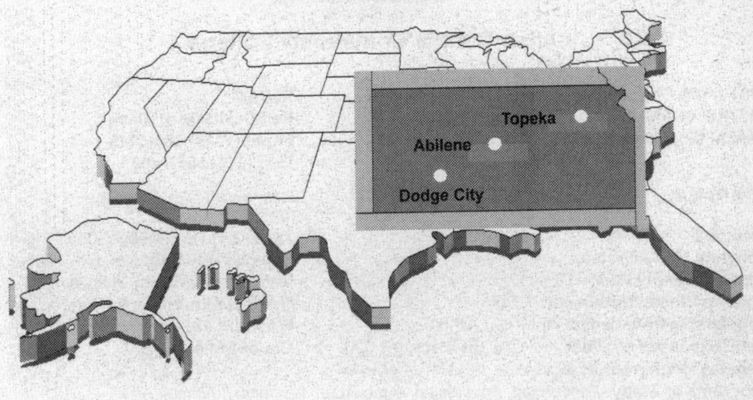

SCHOOL	CITY	AFFILIATION 99	PAGE
Allen County Community College	Iola	NJCAA	320
Baker University	Baldwin City	NAIA	320
Barton County Community College	Great Bend	NJCAA	321
Benedictine College	Atchison	NAIA	321
Bethany College	Lindsborg	NAIA	322
Butler County Community College	El Dorado	NJCAA	323
Central College of Kansas	McPherson	NJCAA	323
Cloud County Community College	Concordia	NJCAA	324
Coffeyville Community College	Coffeyville	NJCAA	324
Colby Community College	Colby	NJCAA	325
Cowley County Community College	Arkansas City	NCAA I	326
Dodge City Community College	Dodge City	NJCAA	326
Emporia State University	Emporia	NCAA II	327
Friends University	Wichita	NAIA	327
Fort Hays State University	Hays	NCAA II	328
Fort Scott Community College	Fort Scott	NJCAA	328
Garden City Community College	Garden City	NJCAA	329
Hesston College	Hesston	NJCAA II	329
Highland Community College	Highland	NJCAA	330
Hutchison Community College	Hutchison	NJCAA	331
Independence Community College	Independence	NJCAA	331
Johnson County Community College	Overland Park	NJCAA	332
Kansas City Kansas Community College	Kansas City	NJCAA	332
Kansas Newman College	Wichita	NAIA	333
Kansas State University	Manhattan	NCAA I	333
Labette Community College	Parsons	NJCAA	334
MidAmerica Nazarene University	Olathe	NAIA	334
Neosho County Community College	Chanute	NJCAA	335
Newman University (Kansas Newman U)	Salina	NAIA	335
Ottawa University	Ottawa	NAIA	336
Pittsburgh State University	Pittsburg	NCAA II	337
Pratt Community College	Pratt	NJCAA	337
Seward County Community College	Liberal	NJCAA	338
Sterling College	Sterling	NAIA	338
Tabor College	Hillsboro	NAIA	339
University of Kansas	Lawrence	NCAA I	339
Washburn University	Topeka	NCAA II	340
Wichita State University	Wichita	NCAA I	340

Allen County Community College

1801 North Cottonwood
Iola, KS 66749
Coach: Dr. Valis McLean

NJCAA
Red Devils/Red, Black
Phone: (316) 365-5116
Fax: (316) 365-7406

ACADEMIC

Founded: 1923
Religion: Non-Affiliated
Student/Faculty Ratio: 12:1
Undergraduate Enrollment: 1,747
Scholarships/Academic: No **Athletic:** Yes
Total Expenses by: Year **In State:** $ 1,020
Type: 2 Yr., Jr. College, Coed
Campus Housing: No
Male/Female Ratio: Unknown
Graduate Enrollment: None
Fin Aid: Yes
Out of State: $ 4,800
Degrees Conferred: Associate
Programs of Study: Accounting, Advertising, Agricultural, Agronomy, Animal, Arts, Banking/Finance, Behavioral, Biological, Communications, Computer, Crop Science, Engineering, Medical Fashion, Library, Machine/Tool Technology, Management, Pharmacy, Printing, Physics, Psychology, Retail Management, Robotics, Science, Social Science, Theatre, Word Processing

ATHLETIC PROFILE

Conference Affiliation: Kansas Jayhawk Conference
Program Profile: Home games are played at Red Devil Field.

Baker University

P.O. Box 65
Baldwin City, KS 66006
Coach: Darrin Loe

NAIA
Wildcats/Black, Orange
Phone: (785) 594-8316
Fax: (785) 594-8377

ACADEMIC

Founded: 1858
Religion: Methodist
Web-site: http://www.bakeru.edu/
Student/Faculty Ratio: 18:1
Undergraduate Enrollment: 850
Scholarships/Academic: Yes **Athletic:** Yes
Total Expenses by: Year **In State:** $ 14,800
Type: 4 Yr., Private, Liberal Arts, Coed
Campus Housing: Yes
SAT/ACT/GPA: 19+
Male/Female Ratio: 1:2
Graduate Enrollment: 1,800
Fin Aid: Yes
Out of State: $ 14,800
Degrees Conferred: BA, BS, BFA, BM, BE, BME, MS, MBA
Programs of Study: Accounting, Banking and Finance, Biology, Business, Chemistry, Communications, Computer Science, Economics, Education, English, Fine Arts, French, German, History, Languages, Life Science, Mathematics, Music, Philosophy, Physics, Political Science, Predentistry, Prelaw, Premed, Psychology, Religion, Sociology, Spanish, Physical Education

ATHLETIC PROFILE

Conference Affiliation: Heart of America Athletic Conference
History: Coach Harris has revived a 'sleeping' baseball program by winning 200 games in the last 8 seasons and winning 3 championships.
Achievements: 1992 District 10 Coach of the Year; 1993 HAAC Conference Coach of the Year; 1993 Conference Champions.
Coaching: Darrin Loe - Head Coach.
Style of Play: We adjust our play to the talent on the team. We emphasize offense as we finished 4th in the nation in team batting and averaged 8.1 runs per game.

Barton County Community College

245 NE 30th Road
Great Bend, KS 67530
Coach: Mike Warren

NJCAA
Cougars/Columbia Blue, Gold
Phone: (316) 792-9373
Fax: (316) 786-1161

ACADEMIC

Founded: 1965
Type: 2 Yr., Jr. College, Coed
Web-site: http://www.barton.cc.ks.us
SAT/ACT/GPA: None
Student/Faculty Ratio: 18:1
Male/Female Ratio: 44:56
Undergraduate Enrollment: 6,800
Graduate Enrollment: None
Scholarships/Academic: Yes **Athletic:** Yes **Fin Aid:** Yes
Total Expenses by: Year **In State:** $ 3,384 **Out of State:** $ 5,745
Degrees Conferred: AA
Programs of Study: Administration of Justice, Agricultural, Anthropology, Cultural, Biological, Cosmetology, Dental, Automtoive, Dietetics, Drafting, Economics, Medical, Occupational Therapy, Preprofessional Programs

ATHLETIC PROFILE

Conference Affiliation: Kansas Jayhawk Community College
Program Profile: Our on campus field is seven years old with on going additions. It features walk-in dugouts with triple A lighting indoor. Our facility has 12,500 square feet of work-out spaces, two indoor batting cages, hitting stations and portable indoor mounds with a weight room facility. There is enough room for a full infield practice.
History: Our program began in 1975 and has an overall record of 591-389. There have only been three head coaches in the history of the program. We won 15 Conference Championships, 6 Sub-Regional Championships and 3 Region III Championships.
Achievements: Won six Conference Championships and 3 Region VI Sub-Regional Championships. Mike Warren was named Coach of the Year Honors three-times.
Coaching: Mike Warren, Head Coach, is in his 15th season at BCCC with a record of 370-226. His teams have won 6 Conference Championships and 3 Region VI Championships. He received Coach of the Year Honors three-times. He was the pitcher for the NJCA All-Star USA team which won the Bronze Medal in the Tournament of the Americans in Merida, Mexico Tournament Weluded Cuban National Team. He compiled a record of 467-335 in 18 seasons. Steve Johnson ,Assistant Coach, played and pitched at Barton Community College and University of Alabama - Birmingham. He spent three years in St. Louis Cardinals Organization reaching triple A level and pitched two seasons in Independent League, Tri-Cobras, Washington.
Roster for 1998 team/In State: 15 **Out of State:** 12 **Out of Country:** 0
Total Number of Varsity/Jr. Varsity: 27 **Number of Fall Games:** 20
Number of Sophomores on 1998 Team: 13 **Number of Spring Games:** 56
Freshmen Receiving Fin Aid/Athletic: 12 **Academic:** 2
Positions Needed for 1999/2000: Pitcher, Outfielders, 1st Base, 3rd Base
Baseball Camp Dates: January 16,23,30; February 6,13,20; June 7-10, 14-17
Schedule: Cowley College, Seminole, Pima, Yavapai, Butler, Seward
Style of Play: Pitching-defense-speed. We are good defensively with a good pitching and we like to put pressure on offense. Will run, hit and run, and bunt any time.

Benedictine College

1020 N 2nd Street
Atchison, KS 66002
Coach: Dan Griggs

NAIA
Ravens/Black, Red, White
Phone: (913) 367-5340
Fax: (913) 367-2564

ACADEMIC

Founded: 1857
Religion: Catholic
Web-site: http://www.benedictine.edu/
Student/Faculty Ratio: 13:1
Undergraduate Enrollment: 1,000
Scholarships/Academic: Yes **Athletic:** Yes
Total Expenses by: Year **In State:** $ 15,500
Degrees Conferred: BA, BS
Type: 4 Yr., Private, Liberal Arts, Coed
Campus Housing: Yes
SAT/ACT/GPA: 18
Male/Female Ratio: 50:50
Graduate Enrollment: None
Fin Aid: Yes
Out of State: $ 15,500
Programs of Study: Accounting, Astronomy, Biochemistry, Biology, Business, Chemistry, Computer Science, Economics, Education, English, French, Journalism, Physics, Natural Science, Sociology, Political Science, Religion, Philosophy, Technical Marketing

ATHLETIC PROFILE

Conference Affiliation: Heart of America Athletic Conference
Program Profile: We are an upscale program (4 Conference Championships in the last 6 years - 2 Regional Appearances in the last 3 yrs.) noted for aggressive hitting (average 6.8 runs per game last 75 game) and strong pitching. Roces Field has had many renovations and improvements. We have new dugouts, new hitting cages, new nets and new bull pens.
History: The program began in 1922 but had no team from 1931-1955. Since 1955, we have had 23 winning seasons and 13 since 1980. We have seven straight winning records. We have had players go on the majors. Two players went last year (1997) to the Texas Independents League.
Achievements: Won Tourney in the HAAC; the Ravens have won titles in 1993, 1992, 1995 and 1997; have All-American pitcher last year (1996).
Coaching: Dan Griggs,Head Coach, is on his his 3rd year as head coach with an overall record of 59-41 which is .590% wherein it is 56-27 .674 % in the NAIA.
Style of Play: Aggressive hitters (.330 average 6.8 runs per game); grow light on bases paths. Good pitching - have had league in staff era in the last two years.

Bethany College

421 North First Street
Lindsborg, KS 67456
Coach: Mike Waldie
NAIA
Swedes/Royal, Gold
Phone: (785) 227-3380x8174
Fax: (785) 227-2021

ACADEMIC

Founded: 1881
Religion: Lutheran
Web-site: http://www.bethany.bethanylb.edu
Student/Faculty Ratio: 13:1
Undergraduate Enrollment: 700
Scholarships/Academic: Yes **Athletic:** Yes
Total Expenses by: Year **In State:** $ 15,500
Degrees Conferred: Bachelors
Type: 4 Yr., Private, Coed, Engineering
Campus Housing: Yes
SAT/ACT/GPA: 910/19/2.5
Male/Female Ratio: 60:40
Graduate Enrollment: None
Fin Aid: Yes
Out of State: $ 15,500
Programs of Study: Art, Communications, English, Music, Religion, Natural Science, Social Science, Biology, Chemistry, Computer Information Systems, Mathematics, Engineering, Economics, Elementary Education, Political Science, Psychology, Recreation, Sociology, Social Work, Physical Education

ATHLETIC PROFILE

Conference Affiliation: Kansas Collegiate Athletic Conference
Program Profile: We have a limited Fall baseball season from Feb 1 to May. We have excellent facilities for a small college, emphasis is on the true Student/Athlete.
History: From 1973 to the present; the Swedes have won 6 conference titles and made 7 trips to District 10 tournament.

Achievements: Conference Titles in 1973, 1974, 1980, 1986, 1989; Coach Dodge named Conference Coach of the Year; 4 All-Conference and 2 All-District players in 1993.
Coaching: Mike Waldie - Head Coach.
Style of Play: Defensively solid; average but adequate on the mound. Offense is built on speed - hit and run, steal, agreesive both at the plate and on the bases. Average power.

Butler County Community College

901 West Haverhill Road
El Dorado, KS 67042
Coach: B.D. Parker

NJCAA
Grizzlies/Purple, Gold
Phone: (316) 322-3201
Fax: (316) 322-3319

ACADEMIC

Founded: 1927
Type: 2 Yr., Jr. College, Coed
Student/Faculty Ratio: 17:1
Male/Female Ratio: 40:60
Undergraduate Enrollment: 7,500
Graduate Enrollment: None
Scholarships/Academic: No **Athletic:** Yes **Fin Aid:** Yes
Total Expenses by: Year **In State:** $ 4,000 **Out of State:** $ 5,500
Degrees Conferred: Associate
Programs of Study: Accounting, Advertising, Agricultural, Art, Automotive, Behavioral, Biological, Business, Chemistry, Commerical, Communications, Computer, Constructions, Criminal Justice, Cytotechnology, Drafting/Design, Education, Education, Engineering, English, Farm/Ranch Management, Fire Science, History, Hotel and Restaurant Management, Markeitng, Mathematics, Music, Nursing, Physics, Political Science, Psychology, Real Estate, Social Science, Theatre

ATHLETIC PROFILE

Conference Affiliation: WPCC-PCAA

Central College of Kansas

1200 S Main Street
McPherson, KS 67460-1403
Coach: Benji Rodriguez
Email: benjir@centralcollege.edu

NJCAA
Tigers/Royal Blue, Gold
Phone: (316) 241-0723
Fax: (316) 241-6032

ACADEMIC

Founded: 1884
Type: 2 Yr., Private, Coed
Religion: Non-Affiliated
Campus Housing: Yes
Undergraduate Enrollment: 320
SAT/ACT/GPA: 660/14
Student/Faculty Ratio: 16:1
Male/Female Ratio: 1:1
Scholarships/Academic: Yes **Athletic:** Yes **Fin Aid:** Yes
Total Expenses by: Year **In State:** $ 12,250 **Out of State:** $ 12,250
Degrees Conferred: AA, AGS, BS
Programs of Study: Accounting, Agricultural, Architectural, Art, Automotive, Aviation, Banking/Finance, Behavioral, Biblical, Computer, Construciton, Criminal, Drafting/Design, Economics, Management, Museum, Nutrition, Religion, Theology

ATHLETIC PROFILE

Conference Affiliation: NJCAA Region VI
Achievements: All-Americans 1996 - Brett Carter (IF), 1995 - Mike Shank (OF), 1995 - Marco Gonzalez (IF); 1996 Region VI Coach of the Year Marty Carver

Cloud County Community College

2221 Campus Dr
Concordia, KS 66901-1002
Coach: Rod Stacken
Email: rodemg.cloudccc.ks.us

NJCAA
Thunderbirds/Black, Gold
Phone: (785) 243-1435
Fax: (785) 243-1043

ACADEMIC

Founded: 1965
Type: 2 Yr., Public, Jr. College, Coed
Religion: Non-Affiliated
Campus Housing: Yes
Web-site: http://www.cloudcc.cc.ks.us
SAT/ACT/GPA: None
Undergraduate Enrollment: 700
Student/Faculty Ratio: 16:1
Scholarships/Academic: Yes **Athletic:** Yes **Fin Aid:** Yes
Total Expenses by: Year **In State:** $ 4,000 **Out of State:** $ 4,700
Degrees Conferred: Associate
Programs of Study: Aviation, Behavioral, Biological, Broadcasting, Criminal, Drafting/Design, Fashion, Farm/Ranch Management, History, Humanities, Nursing, Science, Travel/Tourism

ATHLETIC PROFILE

Estimated Number of Baseball Scholarships: 12
Conference Affiliation: Kansas JayHawk Community College Conference
Program Profile: We play at City of Concordia Sports Complex which is natural grass, and has limited seating with measurements of 330 down lines, 360 center. We will lenghten fence soon.
History: We started in the late 1980's and the early 1990's were the most successfull period of the program. We finished 6th in1996 season & advanced to the semi-finals of the conference tourney.
Coaching: Rod Stacken, Head Coach, is on his 8th year as head coach. Mike Baumann, Assistant Coach, is on his 7th year.
Roster for 1998 team/In State: 17 **Out of State:** 6 **Out of Country:** 0
Total Number of Varsity/Jr. Varsity: 23 **Number of Fall Games:** 20
Number of Seniors on 1998 Team: 14 **Number of Spring Games:** 52
Freshmen Receiving Fin Aid/Athletic: 7 **Academic:** 2
Positions Needed for 1999/2000: Catcher, 1st Base, Shortstop, Pitcher
Schedule: Seward County, Butler County, Hutchison
Style of Play: Play for the big inning - score every opportunity. Stay out of the big inning defensively.

Coffeyville Community College

400 West 11th
Coffeyville, KS 67337
Coach: Dave Teske

NJCAA
Ravens/Red, Black
Phone: (316) 252-7096
Fax: (316) 252-7088

ACADEMIC

Founded: 1923
Type: 2 Yr., Jr. College, Coed
Undergraduate Enrollment: 2,133
Campus Housing: No
Student/Faculty Ratio: 20:1
Male/Female Ratio: 1:1.3
Scholarships/Academic: Yes **Athletic:** Yes **Fin Aid:** Yes
Total Expenses by: Year **In State:** $ Varies **Out of State:** $ Varies
Degrees Conferred: Associate
Programs of Study: Accounting, Agribusiness, Agricultural Economics, Agricultural Education, Agricultural Science, Agricultural Technology, Anumal Science, Applied Science, Automotive Technology, Biology, Biological Science, Plant Science, Broadcasting, Business Administration, Commerce, Management, Business Education, Carpentry, Chemistry, Communications, Computer Programming, Computer Science, Construction Technology, English, History, Home Economics

ATHLETIC PROFILE

Estimated Number of Baseball Scholarships: 30
Conference Affiliation: Kansas Jayhawk Conference Athletic Association
Program Profile: LeClere Park is our home playing field with dimensions of 330' down lines, 340' power alleys and 350' center. The field has a new baseball complex.
History: CCC has evolved from having an Assistant Football and Basketball coaching part-time in the late 1970's to having its own full-time coach and assistant. We were winners of the 1994 sub-regional.
Achievements: 1994 Sub-regional Champions, 1994 Region VI Runner-Up, former players in pro's - Randy Young (Astros). Won 9 out of the last 10 games, 4 All-Conference players.
Coaching: Dave Teske, Head Coach, played with the Mets Organization. Coached Keri Alaska to NBC Championships in 1994. Heath Askew - played with Oklahoma State University and played in College World Series and was drafted by Marlins.
Roster for 1998 team/In State: 24 **Out of State:** 14 **Out of Country:** 0
Total Number of Varsity/Jr. Varsity: 35 **Percent of Graduation:** 98%
Number of Seniors on 1998 Team: 13 **Most Recent Record:** 23 - 30 - 0
Freshmen Receiving Fin Aid/Athletic: 15 **Academic:** 5
Number of Fall Games: 20 **Number of Spring Games:** 35
Positions Needed for 1999/2000: Catcher, Pitcher, Outfielder, Shortstop
Schedule: Connors State, Cowley County Community College, NEO Oklahoma, Seminole Junior
Style of Play: Very aggressive and hard working team.

Colby Community College

1255 S Range
Colby, KS 67701
Coach: Ryan Carter
Email: carter@katie.colby.cc.ks.us

NJCAA
Trojans/Blue, White
Phone: (785) 462-3984
Fax: (785) 462-4688

ACADEMIC

Founded: 1964 **Type:** 2 Yr., Jr. College, Coed
Religion: Non-Affiliated **Campus Housing:** No
Student/Faculty Ratio: 35:1 **Male/Female Ratio:** 48:52
Undergraduate Enrollment: 850 **Graduate Enrollment:** None
Scholarships/Academic: Yes **Athletic:** Yes **Fin Aid:** Yes
Total Expenses by: Year **In State:** $ 4,500 **Out of State:** $ 6,000
Degrees Conferred: AS
Programs of Study: Accounting, Agriculture, Agronomy, Animal, Art, Behavioral, Biological, Broadcasting, Business, Chemistry, Commerical, Computer, criminal Justice, Earth Science, Economics, Education, Engineering, Farm/Ranch Management, Music, Management Science, Wildlife Biology, Zoology

ATHLETIC PROFILE

Estimated Number of Baseball Scholarships: 10
Conference Affiliation: Jayhawks Conference
Program Profile: We were one of the top teams in the conference the last three years. We compete in the biggest conference in the country. The baseball field is on campus, it has natural grass and measurements of 345-left line; 370-left alley; 380-center field; 350-rightfield; & 330-rightfield line. We have a 20 game Fall season & 56 game Spring season. The schedule includes a trip to Arizona.
History: Our program began in 1972. We were one of the top teams in Jayhawks West Conference for the last three years, finishing in top three every year.
Achievements: 1995 Region 6 Champions; 1996 West Region Runner-Up; 1997 Jayhawk West Conference Runner-Up (tied); 1995 Region 6 Coach of the Year.
Roster for 1998 team/In State: 1 **Out of State:** 23 **Out of Country:** 3
Total Number of Varsity/Jr. Varsity: 27 **Percent of Graduation:** 98%
Number of Seniors on 1998 Team: **Number of Sophomores on 1998 Team:** 11
Freshmen Receiving Fin Aid/Athletic: 13 **Academic:** 4

Number of Fall Games: 20
Number of Spring Games: 56
Positions Needed for 1999/2000: All
Most Recent Record: 34 - 22 - 0
Baseball Camp Dates: December
Schedule: Butler, Seward, Yavapai, Pima, Hutchinson, Barton, Cochise CC, Garden City CC, Lamar

Cowley County Community College

125 S Second St., P.O. Box 1147
Arkansas City, KS 67005
Coach: Dave Burroughs

NCAA I
Tigers/Orange, Black
Phone: (316) 441-5225
Fax: (314) 441-5390

ACADEMIC

Founded: 1922
Type: 2 Yr., Jr. College, Coed
Religion: Non-Affiliated
Campus Housing: No
Student/Faculty Ratio: 20:1
Male/Female Ratio: 55:45
Undergraduate Enrollment: 2,900
Graduate Enrollment: None
Scholarships/Academic: Yes **Athletic:** Yes **Fin Aid:** Yes
Total Expenses by: Year **In State:** $ Varies **Out of State:** $ Varies
Degrees Conferred: AA, AS, AGS, AAS
Programs of Study: Accounting, Agriculture, Agronomy, Aircraft/Missile Maintenance, Art, Business, Chemistry, Corrections, Engineering, Management, Law, Journalism, Radiological, Religion

ATHLETIC PROFILE

Conference Affiliation: Jayhawk East Conference
Program Profile: We play in a new City Ball Park stadium which seats 500. We play a Spring season.
History: We won back to back conference championships 1995-1996.
Achievements: 1994-1995 Coach of the Year, Region VI Champions Runner-up; 1995-1996 back to back Conference Champions, Region VI Champions, and went to Central District.
Coaching: Dave Burroughs, Head Coach, has coached eleven years. He was assistant coach for four years and has three years of professional baseball experience. Darren Burroughs, Assistant/Pitching Coach, has coached eight years and has ten years professional experience. He was junior college All-American and played two years pro ball for Royals. Scott Hennessey, Outfield/Base running Coach, has coached two years and has two years of professional experience.
Style of Play: Good pitching and defense. Likes to rely on power hitting and offensive baseball. Likes to play situational baseball and sound fundamental baseball.

Dodge City Community College

2501 North 14th
Dodge City, KS 67801
Coach: Mike Jones

NJCAA
Conquistadors/Black, Purple
Phone: (316) 227-9312
Fax: (316) 225-9334

ACADEMIC

Type: 2 Yr., Jr. College, Coed
Degrees Conferred: Associate
Programs of Study: Accounting, Agriculture, Crop Science, Animal Science, Arts/Fine Arts, Automotive Technology, Biology, Biological Science, Broadcasting, Business Administration, Commerce, Management, Chemistry, Child Care/Child and Family Studies, Communication, Communications Equipment Technology, Computer Information Systems, Computer Programming, Computer Science, Construction Technology, Engineering, English, Fashion, Merchandising, Medical Records Services, Military Science, Mathematics, Journalism, Physical Education, Psychology, Practical Nursing

ATHLETIC PROFILE

Estimated Number of Baseball Scholarships: 24
Conference Affiliation: Kansas Jayhawk Community College Conference
Program Profile: Our games are played at Cavalier Field with a seating capacity of 1,000. We also have a locker room and weight room facility.
Coaching: Michael Jones, Head Coach, is in his 1st year as head coach of the program. He was an assistant coach for several years. Dan La Joie - Assistant Coach.
Roster for 1998 team/In State: 10 **Out of State:** 20 **Out of Country:** 5
Total Number of Varsity/Jr. Varsity: 0 **Percent of Graduation:** 90%
Number of Seniors on 1998 Team: 0 **Number of Sophomores on 1998 Team:** 11
Number of Fall Games: 20 **Number of Spring Games:** 0

Emporia State University

1200 Commercial Street
Emporia, KS 66801
Coach: Brian Embery

NCAA II
Hornets/Black, Gold
Phone: (316) 341-5354
Fax: (316) 341-5603

ACADEMIC

Founded: 1863
Type: 4 Yr., Public, Coed
Religion: Non-Affiliated
Campus Housing: Yes
Web-site: http://www.emporia.edu
SAT/ACT/GPA: 700/18/2.0
Student/Faculty Ratio: 20:1
Male/Female Ratio: 50:50
Undergraduate Enrollment: 4,000
Graduate Enrollment: 2,000
Scholarships/Academic: Yes **Athletic:** Yes **Fin Aid:** Yes
Total Expenses by: Year **In State:** $ 5,942 **Out of State:** $ 10,306
Degrees Conferred: AS, BA, BSEd, BFA, BM, BME, MA, MBA
Programs of Study: Contact school for program of study.

ATHLETIC PROFILE

Conference Affiliation: MIAA

Friends University

2100 University
Wichita, KS 67213
Coach: Mark Carvalho

NAIA
Falcons/Scarlet, Grey
Phone: (316) 295-5700
Fax: (316) 269-3818

ACADEMIC

Founded: 1898
Type: 4 Yr., Private, Liberal Arts, Coed
Religion: Non-Affiliated
Campus Housing: Yes
Web-site: Not-Available
SAT/ACT/GPA: 18
Student/Faculty Ratio: 15:1
Male/Female Ratio: 48:52
Undergraduate Enrollment: 800
Graduate Enrollment: 800
Scholarships/Academic: Yes **Athletic:** Yes **Fin Aid:** Yes
Total Expenses by: Year **In State:** $ 13,000 **Out of State:** $ 13,000
Degrees Conferred: BA, BS, BFA, MA, MS, MBA
Programs of Study: Fine Arts and Business are strong areas of study. Management, Education, Psychology

ATHLETIC PROFILE

Conference Affiliation: KCAC

Program Profile: We play on a brand new natural grass field with state of the art lighting and scoreboards. We also have stadium seating.
History: Coach Dukes has been here since 1994. There is no statistical information prior to 1982. Coach Duke's overall record is 35-37.
Style of Play: We want to play a mixture of running and some power. I believe in strong defense and being aggressive. We will run and be exciting to watch with our speed.

Fort Hays State University

600 Park Street
Hays, KS 67601
Coach: Bob Fornelli

NCAA II
Tigers/Black, Gold
Phone: (785) 628-4357
Fax: (785) 628-4383

ACADEMIC

Founded: 1902
Type: 4 Yr., Public, Liberal Arts, Coed
Web-site: http://ww.fhsu.edu/
SAT/ACT/GPA: None
Student/Faculty Ratio: 18:1
Male/Female Ratio: 46:54
Undergraduate Enrollment: 4,200
Graduate Enrollment: 1,200
Scholarships/Academic: Yes **Athletic:** Yes **Fin Aid:** Yes
Total Expenses by: Year **In State:** $ 5,200 **Out of State:** $ 8,150
Degrees Conferred: AS, BA, BS, BBA, BFA, BGS, BM, BSAF, MA, MS, MBA, MFA
Programs of Study: Accounting, Art, Biological, Business, Chemistry, Communications, Computer, Earth Science, Economics, Education, English, Fine Arts, Languages, History, Management, Marketing, Music, Nursing, Philosophy, Political Science, Psychology, Social Science, Speech Pathology

ATHLETIC PROFILE

Conference Affiliation: RMAC
Program Profile: We are a strong baseball program with 30 plus wins for the last five seasons. We ranked in the NCAA II Top 20 for the last five seasons. Our stadium size is 400 with an artificial turf-infield and grass outfield. We play a Spring season only.
History: The program began in 1966.
Achievements: 1995 RMAC Conference Regular Season Champions; RMAC Post-season Tournament Champions; Coach of the Year in 1995.
Coaching: Bob Fornelli, Head Coach, is in his 3rd year of coaching and was a 1992-1996 assistant coach at Butler Community College. He played for two years at Butler.

Fort Scott Community College

2108 S Horton
Fort Scott, KS 66701
Coach: Dave LaRoche
Email: @fsccax.ftscott.cc.ks.us

NJCAA
Greyhounds/Maroon, Grey
Phone: (316) 223-2700
Fax: (316) 223-4927

ACADEMIC

Type: 2 Yr., Jr. College, Coed
Degrees Conferred: Associate
Programs of Study: Undergraduate Studies, Cosmetology, Nursing

ATHLETIC PROFILE

Estimated Number of Baseball Scholarships: 24

Conference Affiliation: Kansas Jayhawk League
Program Profile: We have been contenders for state title in the past three years. We have three 35+ seasons in the past three years. We have an all-grass infield, an 8-foot wood fence, a 24 ft. 9 inning scoreboard, dugouts, a concession stand, hitting tunnels and a restrooms.
History: We began in 1974 and improved to be contenders in conference and region every year.
Achievements: Runner-Up in the last three years in Jayhawk League - East; 8 players drafted in the last three years; 1 NJCAA All-Americans; 15 All-Conference players.
Coaching: Dave LaRoche - Head Coach. Matt Patrick, Assistant Coach, is in his 5th year with the program.
Roster for 1998 team/In State: 24 **Out of State:** 14 **Out of Country:** 1
Total Number of Varsity/Jr. Varsity: 39 **Percent of Graduation:** 0
Number of Seniors on 1998 Team: **Number of Sophomores on 1998 Team:** 12
Freshmen Receiving Fin Aid/Athletic: 15 **Academic:** 5
Number of Fall Games: 10 **Number of Spring Games:** 56
Positions Needed for 1999/2000: Catcher, Pitcher, Infielder
Most Recent Record: 14 - 42 - 0
Schedule: Cowley, Seminole, Conners State, Crowder, Maplewood, Labette County
Style of Play: Hustle, play hard and have fun.

Garden City Community College

801 Campus Drive
Garden City, KS 67846
Coach: Jeff Curtis

NJCAA
Broncbusters/Brown, Gold
Phone: (316) 276-9599
Fax: (316) 276-9646

ACADEMIC

Founded: 1919
Type: 2 Yr., Jr. College, Coed
Web-site: http://www.gccc.cc.ks.us
SAT/ACT/GPA: None
Student/Faculty Ratio: 20:1
Male/Female Ratio: 55:45
Undergraduate Enrollment: 2,300+
Graduate Enrollment: Unknown
Scholarships/Academic: Yes **Athletic:** Yes **Fin Aid:** Yes
Total Expenses by: Year **In State:** $ 3,600 **Out of State:** $ 4,900
Degrees Conferred: Associate
Programs of Study: Accounting, Agricultural, Athletic, Automotive, Business, Carpentry, Computer Science, Cosmetology, Construction, Criminal Justice, Engineering, Drafting/Design, Law, Nursing, Radiological, Retail, Science, Robotics, Sports Medicine

ATHLETIC PROFILE

Conference Affiliation: Jayhawk League
Program Profile: We are a nationally recognized program with outstanding facilities. William Stadium is a natural surface with a seating capacity of 800, full press box and triple AAA lighting. Buster Academy houses six full length cages, pitching mounds and soft toss station.
History: Our program began in 1973.
Achievements: Numerous drafted players.
Coaching: Jeff Curtis, Head Coach, is in his 2nd year of coaching. He coached five years at Fort Scott Community College. Chris Saldana - Assistant Coach.
Style of Play: Running with a solid defense.

Hesston College

325 S College Dr, Box 3000
Hesston, KS 67062
Coach: Art Mullet

NJCAA II
Larks/Maroon, Gold, Silver
Phone: (316) 327-8278
Fax: (316) 327-8427

ACADEMIC

Founded: 1909
Type: 2 Yr., Private, Coed
Undergraduate Enrollment: 450
Campus Housing: Yes
Student/Faculty Ratio: 13:1
Male/Female Ratio: 50:50
Scholarships/Academic: Yes **Athletic:** No **Fin Aid:** Yes
Total Expenses by: Year **In State:** $ 13,700 **Out of State:** $ 13,700
Programs of Study: Two-year degree in Aviation, Business, Early Childhood, Nursing. Two-year transfer program over 40 different majors including Automotive, Aviation, Electronics, Medical, Business, Biblical, Office

ATHLETIC PROFILE

Conference Affiliation: Great Plains Junior College Conference
Program Profile: We have a five week Fall season and a 40 game Spring schedule. We have a new baseball facility on campus that has natural grass with lights. We are a very competitive program in light of being a non-scholarship program. There are excellent facilities for both inside and outside practice. We are a top quality academic institution.
History: The program began in the early 60's. The quality of the program is stronger now than it has ever been. A new facility has given a huge boast to the program.
Achievements: 5 players received All-Americans honors; numerous players continue on into 4 year programs.
Coaching: Art Mullet, Head Coach, has been coaching baseball for 26 years. He has coached 20 years in colleges and four years of Minor Leagues with the Pittsburgh Pirates. He played, coached and managed four years in Shenandoah Valley League, Harrisonburg, Virginia.
Style of Play: Team averages approximately 5 runs per game, hit average .300. Emphasis on pitching and defense. Works hard to do the "little" things correctly.

Highland Community College

Highway 36 West
Highland, KS 66035
Coach: Rick Eberly
NJCAA
Scotties/Royal Blue, Gold
Phone: (785) 442-6043
Fax: (785) 442-6104

ACADEMIC

Type: 2 Yr., Jr. College, Coed
Degrees Conferred: Associate
Programs of Study: Accounting, Advertising, Agricultural Business, Agricultural Economics, Agronomy, Carpentry, Chemistry, Biology, Biological Science, Education, Emergency Medical Technology, Automotive Technology, Farm and Ranch Management, Cytotechnology, Computer Science, Dairy Science, Data Processing, Construction Technology

ATHLETIC PROFILE

Conference Affiliation: Jayhawk Conference
Program Profile: We play a 20 games Fall schedule and a 56 game Spring schedule. We use the city field which is located on campus (all natural). We have a very nice weight room & indoor facility.
History: We have participated as an Independent in Region III until joining Jayhawk Conference in 1996-1997. We competed on the East half of the conference.
Achievements: 1996 Rodney Eberly drafted 12th by St. Louis currently playing at University of Albama-Birmingham.
Coaching: Rick Eberly,Head Coach, is a graduate of Texas Wesleyan College. He played at Iowa Western, Texas Wesleyan, Clarinda Iowa A's and Toronto Blue Jays. He coached at Tarkio College for 8 years. His teams were heart of America Conference Champs in 1989, 1990, and 1991. His teams were in HCC for 7 years and were in the East Region Playoffs in 1993, 1995 and 1996 (4th Place). He compiled an overall record of 293-296. His HCC Coaching record is 121-158. Pat Tritsch - Assistant Coach.
Style of Play: We like to play a very aggressive style both offensively abd defensively and keep the pressure on the opposing team.

Hutchison Community College

1300 North Plum
Hutchison, KS 67502
Coach: John Burgi

NJCAA
Blue Dragons/Blue, White
Phone: (316) 665-3441
Fax: (316) 665-3394

ACADEMIC

Founded: 1928
Type: 2 Yr., Jr. College, Coed
Web-site: http://www.hutchcc.edu
SAT/ACT/GPA: None
Undergraduate Enrollment: 3,900
Graduate Enrollment: None
Scholarships/Academic: No **Athletic:** No
Fin Aid: Yes
Total Expenses by: Year **In State:** $ 3,600
Out of State: $ 5,000
Degrees Conferred: Associate
Programs of Study: Accounting, Advetising, Agricultural, Baking and Finance, Biological, Broadcasting, Business, Carpentry, Chemistry, Computer, Construction, Corrections, Cytotechnology, Dental, Drafting/Design, Economics, Education, English, Farm and Ranch Management, Fashion Merchadising, Fire Science, Forestry, General Engineering, Geology, History, Insurance, Journalism, Mathematics, Medical Technology, Music, Nursing, Occupational Therapy

ATHLETIC PROFILE

Conference Affiliation: Jayhawk - Western Division Conference
Program Profile: The HCC program has grown during the last four years. We have won 75% of our games and just this past year won the Western Kanasa Subregional. We also play at Hobart - Detter Stadium which is considered the nicest junior college facility in the MidWest.
History: The program began in 1975 and has grown since 1991 when baseball was emphasized. We had a 1997 banner year advancing one game short of the NJCAA World Series.
Achievements: We have had 14 player drafted in the last four years.
Coaching: John Burgi, Head Coach, is in his 19th year here and in his 7th year at HCC. Rick Sabath, Assistant Coach, is in his 2nd year at HCC. He was an assistant coach at Kansas. Darin Vaughan, Assistant Coach, is in his 2nd year at HCC.
Style of Play: We concentrate on sound pitching. We want the pitchers who will challenge hitters and throw it in the zone. Offensively we believe in situational hitter and we like to be balanced throughout the lineup.

Independence Community College

College Avenue and Brookside Drive
Independence, KS 67301
Coach: Paul Marquez

NJCAA
Pirates/Blue, Gold
Phone: (800) 842-6063
Fax: (316) 331-0153

ACADEMIC

Founded: 1925
Type: 2 Yr., Public, Jr. College, Coed
Web-site: http://www.indy.ks.us.com
Campus Housing: Yes
Student/Faculty Ratio: 14:1
Male/Female Ratio: 1:1
Undergraduate Enrollment: 1,200
Graduate Enrollment: None
Scholarships/Academic: Yes **Athletic:** Yes
Fin Aid: Yes
Total Expenses by: Year **In State:** $ 6,400+
Out of State: $ Varies
Degrees Conferred: AA, AS
Programs of Study: Accounting, Biological, Business, Chemistry, Cosmetology, Drafting/Design, Early Childhood, Engineering, English, History, Humanities, Liberal Arts, Mathematics, Music, Physical Education, Physical Science, Preengineering, Spanish

ATHLETIC PROFILE

Estimated Number of Baseball Scholarships: 24

Conference Affiliation: Jayhawk Conference, East Division
Program Profile: ICC plays on all natural grass surface field called Emerson Field. Emerson is 3,200 feet down the line, 365 feet to the alleys and 390 to the center. The fieldhouse is the Pirate's indoor facility. It can hold a full-size infield, a batting cage, and an indoor mound.
History: The program began seven years ago. We have consistently gotten better. Every year our wins have been more. We started from the ground up. This program was built one brick at a time. Pirate baseball was built with desire, dedication and hard work.
Achievements: ICC has had several Academic All-Americans. Pirate who have been drafted: Frankie Garcia, Christy Rosa, Matt Hoffman (twice), and Mike Bishop.
Coaching: Paul Marquez, Head Coach, is in his 6th year at ICC. He built the program from the ground up and is pleased with his progress. Marquez is a graduate of Pittsburgh State University. Dan Davis, Assistant Coach, is a graduate of Southern Illinois University of Carbondale.
Roster for 1998 team/In State: 16 **Out of State:** 12 **Out of Country:** 0
Total Number of Varsity/Jr. Varsity: 35 **Percent of Graduation:** 100%
Number of Seniors on 1998 Team: **Number of Sophomores on 1998 Team:** 2
Freshmen Receiving Fin Aid/Athletic: 24 **Academic:** 9
Number of Fall Games: 40 **Number of Spring Games:** 56
Positions Needed for 1999/2000: Middle Infielder (SS only), OF, Pitcher, Catcher
Schedule: Cowley County, Neosho County, Lafayette County, Kansas City, Butler County, Laredo
Style of Play: Aggressive and fundamental.

Johnson County Community College

12345 College Blvd
Overland Park, KS 66210
Coach: Kent Shelly
Email: kshelly@johnco.cc.ks.us
NJCAA
Cavaliers/Brown, Gold
Phone: (913) 469-8500
Fax: (913) 469-4473

ACADEMIC

Type: 2 Yr., Jr. College, Coed
Degrees Conferred: Associate
Programs of Study: Accounting, Art/Fine Arts, Automotive Technology, Aviation Technology, Business Administration, Commerce, Management, Civil Engineering, Commercial Arts, Computer Science, Computer Technology, Culinary Arts, Data Processing, Deaf Interpreter Training, Dental Services, Drafting/Design, Energy Management Technology, Fashion Merchadising, Interior Design, Electronics, Engineering Technology, Physical Therapy, Nursing

ATHLETIC PROFILE

Conference Affiliation: East Jayhawk Conference
Program Profile: Our field has natural grass and is always in perfect condition. The field was used for the photo of umpire Steve Paleroid on Sports Illustrated. It is the best field in the Jayhawk Conference. We have a regular season.
History: We have only two head coaches in the history of the program (Sonny Maynard from 1973 to 1986 with a record of 504-176); (Kent Shelly from 1987 to the present with a record of 317-161).
Achievements: 7 East Jayhawks Conference Titles; 8 Eastern Sub-Regional Titles; 5 NJCAA Region 6 Titles; 7 All-Americans; 31 Players have signed as a free-agent or drafted players by the Major League Organizations; 3 USA Junior College All-Stars.
Coaching: Kent Shelly, Head Coach, is in his 12th season. He has a tremendous impact on the program, compiling an impressive 292-138 career mark (.677), four Eastern sub-regional championships and two Region VI championships. He was named Coach of the Year. In 1994, he served as a head coach for Team USA. He was selected to a three year term as a president of the NJCAA Baseball Coaches Association. Carl Heinrich, Assistant Head Coach, is in his 6th season. He served as a program coordinator of athletics. He also monitors all facility operations for the athletic department and schedules all events.
Style of Play: Blue Coller work philosophy - fundamentally sound offense and defense posses good overall team speed.

Kansas City Kansas Community College

7250 State Avenue
Kansas City, KS 66112
Coach: Steve Burleson

NJCAA
Blue Devils/Blue, White, Red
Phone: (913) 596-9656
Fax: (913) 596-9676

ACADEMIC

Founded: 1923
Type: 2 Yr., Jr. College, Coed
Student/Faculty Ratio: 19:1
Male/Female Ratio: 40:60
Undergraduate Enrollment: 6,000
Graduate Enrollment: None
Scholarships/Academic: Yes **Athletic:** Yes **Fin Aid:** Yes
Total Expenses by: Year **In State:** $ 6,200 **Out of State:** $ 9,550
Degrees Conferred: AA, AS, AGS, AAS
Programs of Study: Accounting, Education, Engineering, Etc..

ATHLETIC PROFILE

Conference Affiliation: Jayhawk Conference
Program Profile: Home games are played at Mears Brett Field.
Coaching: Steve Burleson - Head Coach. Matt Goldbeck - Assistant Coach.

Kansas Newman College

3100 McCormick Avenue
Wichita, KS 67213
Coach: Paul Sanagorski

NAIA
Jets/Scarlet, Royal
Phone: (316) 942-4291
Fax: (316) 942-4483

ACADEMIC

Founded: 1933
Type: 4 Yr., Private, Liberal Arts, Coed
Religion: Catholic
Campus Housing: Yes
Web-site: http://www.newmanu.edu
SAT/ACT/GPA: None
Student/Faculty Ratio: 10:
Male/Female Ratio: Unknown
Undergraduate Enrollment: 2,000
Graduate Enrollment: None
Scholarships/Academic: Yes **Athletic:** Yes **Fin Aid:** Yes
Total Expenses by: Year **In State:** $ 13,000 **Out of State:** $ 13,000
Degrees Conferred: AS, BA, BS
Programs of Study: Accounting, Biology, Business Administration, Chemistry, Communications, Computer Science, Cytotechnology, Education, English, Fine Arts, Graphic Design, Health Science, History, Management, Marketing, Mathematics, Medical Laboratory Technology, Nursing, Prelaw

ATHLETIC PROFILE

Conference Affiliation: Independent

Kansas State University

1800 College Ave
Manhattan, KS 66502
Coach: Mike Clark

NCAA I
Wildcats/Purple, White
Phone: (913) 532-5723
Fax: (913) 532-6093

ACADEMIC

Founded: 1863
Type: 4 Yr., Public, Coed
Religion: Non-Affiliated
Campus Housing: Yes

Web-site: Not-Available
SAT/ACT/GPA: 21avg
Student/Faculty Ratio: 16:1
Male/Female Ratio: 54:46
Undergraduate Enrollment: 16,990
Graduate Enrollment: 3,675
Scholarships/Academic: Yes **Athletic:** Yes **Fin Aid:** Yes
Total Expenses by: Year **In State:** $ 6,000 **Out of State:** $ 11,700
Degrees Conferred: AA, AS, BA, BS, BFA, MA, MS, MFA
Programs of Study: Contact school for programs of study.

ATHLETIC PROFILE

Conference Affiliation: Big Eight Conference
Program Profile: We play at Frank Myers Field which has natural grass and 5,000 seats. The field is 340 left, 325 right, 411 alleys and 400 to straight away center field.
History: Our program began in 1897.
Achievements: 1995 - placed third in the Big 8. 1990 Big Eight Coach of the Year.
Coaching: Mike Clark - Head Coach. Rocky Ward - Assistant. Mike Hensley - Pitching Coach.

Labette Community College

200 South 14th
Parsons, KS 67357
Coach: Tom Hilton

NJCAA
Cardinals/Red, White
Phone: (316) 421-0911
Fax: (316) 421-5303

ACADEMIC

Founded: 1923
Type: 2 Yr., Jr. College, Coed
Student/Faculty Ratio: 14:1
Male/Female Ratio: 33:67
Undergraduate Enrollment: 2,600
Graduate Enrollment: None
Scholarships/Academic: No **Athletic:** Yes **Fin Aid:** Yes
Total Expenses by: Year **In State:** $ 3,200 **Out of State:** $ 5,000
Degrees Conferred: Associate
Programs of Study: Contact school for programs of study.

MidAmerica Nazarene University

2030 East College Way
Olathe, KS 66062
Coach: Todd Garrett
Email: rhill@mnu.edu

NAIA
Pioneers/Scarlet, White, Royal
Phone: (913) 791-3278
Fax: (913) 791-3456

ACADEMIC

Founded: 1966
Type: 4 Yr., Private, Liberal Arts, Coed
Religion: Nazarene
Campus Housing: Yes
Web-site: http://www.mnu.edu
SAT/ACT/GPA: 700+/18+
Student/Faculty Ratio: 20:1
Male/Female Ratio: 5:7
Undergraduate Enrollment: 1,300
Graduate Enrollment: 150
Scholarships/Academic: Yes **Athletic:** Yes **Fin Aid:** Yes
Total Expenses by: Year **In State:** $ 16,892 **Out of State:** $ 16,892
Degrees Conferred: AA, BA, BSN, MBA, Med
Programs of Study: Accounting, Agribusiness, Biological Science, Business, Chemistry, Christian Education, Church Music, Communications, Computer Science, History, International, Management, Mathematics, Languages, Music, Physics, Psychology, Religion, Secondary Education, Spanish

ATHLETIC PROFILE

Conference Affiliation: Heart of America Athletic Conference

Program Profile: The MNU Baseball program plays in the Heart of America Athletic Conference (HAAC). The season begins in February and ends in May with playoffs. We have a natural grass playing surface boasting the best facilities in the HAAC. We have cages, bullpens and artificial turf.
History: Our program began in 1973. Have competed in the Heart of America Conference since '81.
Achievements: 1984 Coach of the Year (HAAC); NCCAA District 5 Coach of the Year in 1991, 1993, 1996, and 1997; NCCAA District V Champions in 1991, 1993, 1996, and 1997.
Coaching: Todd Garrett, Head Coach, is in his 5th year. He is a two-time NCCAA All-American Catcher. Jason Drummond, Assistant Coach, is in his 3rd year and is a two-time NCCAA All-American Outfielder. Rick McLain, Assistant Coach, is in his 2nd year and is a former semi-pro pitcher from Florida.
Roster for 1998 team/In State: 10 **Out of State:** 15 **Out of Country:** 0
Total Number of Varsity/Jr. Varsity: 25 **Percent of Graduation:** 85%-90%
Number of Seniors on 1998 Team: 2 **Number of Sophomores on 1998 Team:** 0
Freshmen Receiving Fin Aid/Athletic: 7 **Academic:** 4
Number of Fall Games: 0 **Number of Spring Games:** 50
Most Recent Record: 5 - 28 - 0 **Baseball Camp Dates:** June 7-11; June 14-18
Positions Needed for 1999/2000: Infielder, Pitcher
Schedule: Baker, Benedictine, Washburn, Ouachita Baptist University, Henderson, Harding University, Lindenwood University, Culver Stockton
Style of Play: Aggressive hitting and base running demonstrating fundamental baseball on defense.

Neosho County Community College

1000 S Allen
Chanute, KS 66720
Coach: Steve Murry

NJCAA
Panthers/Black, Orange
Phone: (316) 431-2820
Fax: (316) 431-0082

ACADEMIC

Founded: 1936 **Type:** 2 Yr., Jr. College, Coed
Student/Faculty Ratio: 17:1 **Male/Female Ratio:** 50:50
Undergraduate Enrollment: 2,000 **Graduate Enrollment:** None
Scholarships/Academic: Yes **Athletic: Yes** **Fin Aid:** Yes
Total Expenses by: Year **In State:** $ 3,000 **Out of State:** $ 4,000
Degrees Conferred: AA, AS
Programs of Study: Business, Technical, Medical, Technician, Transfer Programs

ATHLETIC PROFILE

Conference Affiliation: Jayhawk East
Program Profile: We have a disciplined program with 56 Spring games and 40 Fall games. Hudson Field is well-manicured and has huge dugouts and a Bermuda grass field.
History: The program began in 1972. The Panthers began winning in 1988 and have not had a losing season since.
Achievements: Conference title in 1994, 11 pro contracts, 50 players continued on to Division I schools.
Coaching: Steve Murry, Head Coach, is in his 10th year, with only one losing season.
Style of Play: Very fast with great hitting.

Newman University

(Former Kansas Newman U)

100 East Claflin
Salina, KS 67401
Coach: Tim Bellew

NAIA
Coyotes/Purple, Gold
Phone: (913) 827-5541
Fax: (913) 827-0927

ACADEMIC

Founded: 1886
Type: 4 Yr., Private, Coed
SAT/ACT/GPA: 22avg
Campus Housing: Yes
Student/Faculty Ratio: 14:1
Male/Female Ratio: 54:46
Undergraduate Enrollment: 500
Graduate Enrollment: None
Scholarships/Academic: Yes **Athletic:** Yes **Fin Aid:** Yes
Total Expenses by: Year **In State:** $ 12,100 **Out of State:** $ 12,100
Degrees Conferred: AA, AAS, BA, BS
Programs of Study: Accounting, Art, Biology, Chemistry, Communications, Computer, Criminal Justice, Dramatic Arts, Economics, History, Mathematics, Music, Physics, Prelaw, Psychology, Religion, Secondary Education, Social Science, Spanish, Special Education, Speech, Studio Art

ATHLETIC PROFILE

Conference Affiliation: KCAC

Ottawa University

1001 South Cedar
Ottawa, KS 66067
Coach: Jarrod Titus
Email: titus@ott.edu
NAIA
Braves/Black, Gold
Phone: (785) 242-5200
Fax: (785) 229-1015

ACADEMIC

Founded: 1863
Type: 4 Yr., Private, Liberal Arts, Coed
Religion: American Baptist
Campus Housing: Yes
Undergraduate Enrollment: 575
SAT/ACT/GPA: 17
Student/Faculty Ratio: 16:1
Male/Female Ratio: 60:40
Scholarships/Academic: Yes **Athletic:** Yes **Fin Aid:** Yes
Total Expenses by: Year **In State:** $ 12,800 **Out of State:** $ 12,800
Degrees Conferred: BA
Programs of Study: Accounting, American Studies, Art, Athletic Training, Biology, Business Administration, Chemistry, Communications,Computer Information Systems, Economics, Education, Health Education, History, Humanities, Human Services, Management, Mathematics, Medical

ATHLETIC PROFILE

Estimated Number of Baseball Scholarships: 40
Conference Affiliation: KCAC
Program Profile: Facilities include an indoor practice facility with weight room cages. We have Fall and Spring seasons. There are 3 fields of which 2 are grass and 1 is dirt . The stadium seats 1,000.
History: We started in 1988.
Achievements: Conference Champs in 1995, 1997 and 1998; 4 All-Americans; 4 All-Regional or 25 All-Conference in the last four years; Jarrod Titus was named Coach of the Year in 1995, 1997, and 1998; 1 player drafted.
Coaching: Jarrod Titus, Head Coach, compiled a record of 80-66 in 1995. He was KCAC Coach of the Year three out of four years. He was a Louisville Slugger Aux for excellence in coaching for three years. He was Big Eight Player of the Week and was once named All-Conference player. Danny Ochs - Assistant.
Roster for 1998 team/In State: 19 **Out of State:** 24 **Out of Country:** 1
Total Number of Varsity/Jr. Varsity: 0 **Percent of Graduation:** 100%
Number of Seniors on 1998 Team: 10 **Number of Sophomores on 1998 Team:** 17
Freshmen Receiving Fin Aid/Athletic: All **Academic:** 15
Number of Fall Games: 12 **Number of Spring Games:** 42
Positions Needed for 1999/2000: Shortstop, Pitcher
Baseball Camp Dates: Summer-Undecided
Schedule: University of Kansas, University of Missouri, Fort Hays State University
Style of Play: Very aggressive offensively; strategic defense.

Pittsburgh State University

1701 South Broadway
Pittsburg, KS 66762
Coach: Steve Bever

NCAA II
Gorillas/Crimson, Gold
Phone: (316) 232-7951
Fax: (316) 232-7951

ACADEMIC

Founded: 1903
SAT/ACT/GPA:20avg
Student/Faculty Ratio: 23:1
Undergraduate Enrollment: 5,825
Scholarships/Academic: Yes **Athletic:** Yes
Total Expenses by: Year **In State:** $ 4,950

Type: 4 Yr., Public, Coed
Campus Housing: Yes
Male/Female Ratio: 59:41
Graduate Enrollment: 1,250
Fin Aid: Yes
Out of State: $ 8,100

Degrees Conferred: BA, BS, BBA, BSED, BFA, BGS, BET, BSN
Programs of Study: Accounting, Art, Banking/Finance, Biological, Broadcasting, Business, Chemistry, Computer, Design, Economics, Education, Engineering, English, Languages, Math, Geography, Medical, Music, Preprofessional Programs, Psychology, Science, Secondary Education, Social Science, Speech

ATHLETIC PROFILE

Conference Affiliation: MIAA-Mid-America Intercollegiate Athletic Association
Program Profile: We play at Ortolani Field on campus which has a new facility. We will be playing our third full season there in 1998. It has natural grass with dimensions of 330 down the lines and 400 to the center. There is a wooden fence from dugout to dugout, 55' dugouts with bathrooms and storage in the dugouts. We play in the Fall and in the Spring plus do off-season conditioning.
History: Our program was reinstated in 1991 after a one year absence. We have built the program from the ground up and have continued to make progress yearly.
Achievements: Coach of the Year in 1997, Conference Regular Season Runner-Up; 38-18 in 1997, made in the NCAA Regional Tournament. Had an MVP of the Conference; MVP position player and pitcher for the region; 1st team All-American utility; 2nd team All-American Pitcher in 1997. Have had 2 pitchers drafted.
Coaching: Steve Bever - Head Coach. Gary Grimaldi - Infield Coach. John Potocnik - Pitching Coach. Brad Buckley - Catcher's Coach. Mike Manderiano - Outfield Coach. Jake Hanson - Assistant Pitching Coach.
Style of Play: Aggressive offensive team. Our team like offensive execution, hit and run, bunt and steal. Work very hard on the team defense.

Pratt Community College

348 NE SR 61
Pratt, KS 67124
Coach: Jeff Brewer

NJCAA
Beavers/Royal Blue, White
Phone: (316) 672-5641
Fax: (316) 672-5288

ACADEMIC

Founded: 1968
Undergraduate Enrollment: 2,000
Student/Faculty Ratio: 3:1
Scholarships/Academic: Yes **Athletic:** Yes
Total Expenses by: Year **In State:** $ 3,056

Type: 2 Yr., Jr. College, Coed
Campus Housing: Yes
Male/Female Ratio: 2:1
Fin Aid: Yes
Out of State: $ 6,460+

Degrees Conferred: Associate
Programs of Study: Accounting, Agriculture, Aircraft/missile Maintenance, Athletic Training, Automotive, Aviation, Broadcasting, Carpentry, Construction, Education, Energy, Farm/Ranch Management, Graphic Arts, Management, Preprofessional Programs, Science, Speech, Sports Medicine, Wildlife

ATHLETIC PROFILE

Conference Affiliation: Jayhawk West Conference
Program Profile: Stanion Field has lights and a seating capacity for 500 fans. Our improvements in the last five years are worth $75,000.
History: The program began in 1968.
Achievements: 3 drafted players, several Division I and II players.

Seward County Community College

PO Box 1137
Liberal, KS 67905-1137
Coach: Galen McSpadden

NJCAA
Saints/Green, White
Phone: (316) 629-2730
Fax: (316) 626-3005

ACADEMIC

Type: 2 Yr., Jr. College, Coed
Religion: Non-Affiliated
Campus Housing: No
Degrees Conferred: Associate
Programs of Study: Accounting, Agribusiness, Art/Fine Arts, Biology, Biological Science, Business Administration, Commerce, Management, Chemistry, Communications, Computer Scinece, Data Processing, Economics, Education, Elementary Education, English, Farm/Ranch Management, Fish/Game, History, Journalism, Literature, Music, Natural Science, Nursing, Physical Education, Psychology, Social Work, Sociology

ATHLETIC PROFILE

Conference Affiliation: Jayhawk Conference

Sterling College

Box 98
Sterling, KS 67579
Coach: Greg Stewart

NAIA
Warriors/Navy, Silver
Phone: (316) 278-4227
Fax: (316) 278-4319

ACADEMIC

Founded: 1887
Religion: Presbyterian
Web-site: http://www.sterling.edu/
Student/Faculty Ratio: 13:1
Undergraduate Enrollment: 500

Type: 4 Yr., Private, Liberal Arts, Coed
Campus Housing: Yes
SAT/ACT/GPA: 900/18/2.0
Male/Female Ratio: 45:55
Graduate Enrollment: N/A

Scholarships/Academic: Yes **Athletic:** Yes **Fin Aid:** Yes
Total Expenses by: Year **In State:** $ 14,150 **Out of State:** $ 14,150
Degrees Conferred: BA, BS, AA, AS
Programs of Study: Accounting, Agronomy, Behavioral Science, Biology, Business Administration, Chemistrty, Computer Science, Education, Elementary Education, English, Fine Arts, History, Mathematics, Music, Nutrition, Philosophy, Political Science, Prelaw, Psychology, Secondary Education, Special Education, Speech

ATHLETIC PROFILE

Conference Affiliation: Kansas Intercollegiate Athletic Conference
Program Profile: Our pogram has excellent facilities with indoor/outdoor hitting tunnels. We play a 42 game season plus do a Spring trip. We have 10 JV games per year. Third place was our loWest finish in the last 7 years. We have a winning program with 4 conference championships.

History: Sterling has had a baseball program almost continually since 1887. The modern program started in 1950's by Coach Clair Gleason.
Achievements: District Play-offs 4 out of the last 7 years; 15 All-KCAC players in the past 5 years.

Tabor College

400 S Jefferson Street
Hillsboro, KS 67063
Coach: Ryan S. Basbin
Email: ryanb@tcnet.tabor.edu

NAIA
Bluejays/Royal Blue, Gold
Phone: (316) 947-3121
Fax: (316) 947-3789

ACADEMIC

Founded: 1908
Type: 4 Yr., Private, Liberal Arts, Coed
Religion: Mennonite Brethren
Campus Housing: Yes
Web-site: http://www.tabor.edu/
SAT/ACT/GPA: None
Student/Faculty Ratio: 13:1
Male/Female Ratio: 1:1
Undergraduate Enrollment: 500
Graduate Enrollment: None
Scholarships/Academic: Yes **Athletic:** Yes **Fin Aid:** Yes
Total Expenses by: Year **In State:** $ Varies **Out of State:** $ Varies
Degrees Conferred: BA, BS
Programs of Study: Accounting, Biology, Botany, Business Law, Business Administration, Chemistry, Communication, Computer Science, Economics, Education, History, Management, Marketing, Mathematics, Medical Technology, Philosophy, Physics, Religion, Psychology

ATHLETIC PROFILE

Conference Affiliation: KCAC
Coaching: Ryan S. Basbin - Head Coach, entering second season with the program. Brett Carter - Assistant Coach.
Roster for 1998 team/In State: 13 **Out of State:** 17 **Out of Country:** 0
Number of Seniors on 1998 Team: 6 **Most Recent Record:** 9 - 25 - 0
Freshmen Receiving Fin Aid/Athletic: 13 **Academic:** 9
Number of Fall Games: 5 **Number of Spring Games:** 42
Positions Needed for 1999/2000: Pitcher, Infielders
Schedule: Ft. Myers, Oklahoma Baptist, Newman, LSU-Shreveport, Southern Nazarene, Ottawa
Style of Play: Aggressive, fundamental baseball.

University of Kansas

220 Allen Field House
Lawrence, KS 66045
Coach: Bobby Randall
Email: mbogby@falcon.cc.ukans.edu

NCAA I
Jayhawks/Crimson, Blue
Phone: (785) 864-7907
Fax: (785) 864-5802

ACADEMIC

Founded: 1866
Type: 4 Yr., Public, Coed
Religion: Non-Affiliated
Campus Housing: Yes
Web-site: http://www.jayhawks.edu
SAT/ACT/GPA: 1000+/20+/3.5
Student/Faculty Ratio: 16:1
Male/Female Ratio: 50:50
Undergraduate Enrollment: 18,000
Graduate Enrollment: 7,000
Scholarships/Academic: Yes **Athletic:** Yes **Fin Aid:** Yes
Total Expenses by: Year **In State:** $ 7,000 **Out of State:** $ 13,600
Degrees Conferred: BA, BGS, MA, MBA, MS
Programs of Study: Aerospace, Anthropology, Architecture, Art, Astronomy, Cellular Biology, Engineering, Broadcasting, Economics, Languages, Design, Cytotechnology, Humanities, Illustration, Linguistics, Magazine, Theatre, Voice, Women's Studies

ATHLETIC PROFILE

Estimated Number of Baseball Scholarships: 11.7
Conference Affiliation: Big 12 Conference
Program Profile: Hoglund Ballpark is currently under renovation and will seat 2,000+. Playing season is February thru June. We have a natural field with dimensions of 350, 375, 378, 375 & 350.
History: Our program began in 1879. It stopped 1933-1936 and 1943 -1945. We attended regional in 1993 and 1994 and College World Series in 1993.
Achievements: Have 73 total drafted (29 in the 1990's); 12 All-Americans.
Coaching: Bobby Randall, Head Coach, compiled a record of 375-377 (74-74 at Kansas). He was an assistant coach at Iowa State for 3 years and head coach at iowa for 11 years. He is in his 3rd season at Kansas and graduated from Kansas State. He played professionally for Dodgers and Twins. Wilson Kelmer and Mike Bard - Assistant Coaches.
Roster for 1998 team/In State: 11 **Out of State:** 16 **Out of Country:** 0
Total Number of Varsity/Jr. Varsity: 27 **Most Recent Record:** 17 - 19 - 0
Number of Seniors on 1998 Team: 6 **Number of Sophomores on 1998 Team:** 6
Freshmen Receiving Fin Aid/Athletic: 4 **Academic:** 0
Positions Needed for 1999/2000: Varies **Number of Spring Games:** 56
Baseball Camp Dates: June 9-10; June 15-18; July 21-24; August 6-9
Schedule: Baylor, Texas Tech, Arkansas, Oklahoma, Missouri, Wichita State, Oklahoma State
Style of Play: Our team is based strongly on pitching and defense. Offensively we play an aggressive style on the basepaths and at the plate.

Washburn University

1700 College Avenue
Topeka, KS 66621
Coach: Steve Anson

NCAA II
Inchabods/Navy, White
Phone: (785) 231-1134
Fax: (785) 231-1091

ACADEMIC

Founded: 1865 **Type:** 4 Yr., Public, Coed
SAT/ACT/GPA: 22avg **Campus Housing:** Yes
Student/Faculty Ratio: 17:1 **Male/Female Ratio:** 40:60
Undergraduate Enrollment: 5,670 **Graduate Enrollment:** 760
Scholarships/Academic: Yes **Athletic:** Yes **Fin Aid:** Yes
Total Expenses by: Year **In State:** $ 6,600 **Out of State:** $ 9,000
Degrees Conferred: AA, AS, AAS, BA, BS, BFA, BM, MA
Programs of Study: Accounting, Anthropology, Art, Banking and Finance, Biological Science, Chemistry, Communications, Computer, Criminal, Dramatic Arts, Early Childhood Education, Economics, Education, English, History, Information Management, Marketing, Math, Medical, Music, Philosophy, Physics, Political Science, Psychology, Public, Secondary Education, Social Science

ATHLETIC PROFILE

Conference Affiliation: (MIAA) Mid-America Intercollegiate Athletics Association
Program Profile: We have an on campus stadium that measures 330, 375 and 400. It has natural grass and it seats 850.
Achievements: MIACC Coach of the Year in 1994; 1988 NAIA Player of the Year-JP Wrihtt; drafted by the Twins-currently AAA Pitcher: Rick DeHart-Expos; a Pitcher Chad Redrieves-Royals; Davey Lopes played, and has a record of 66-69.

Wichita State University

1845 Fairmount
Wichita, KS 67260-0018
Coach: Gene Stephenson

NCAA I
Shockers/Black, Gold
Phone: (316) 978-3636
Fax: (316) 978-3963

ACADEMIC

Founded: 1895
Religion: Non-Affiliated
Web-site: http://www.twsu.edu
Student/Faculty Ratio: 18:1
Undergraduate Enrollment: 11,515
Scholarships/Academic: Yes **Athletic:** Yes
Total Expenses by: Year **In State:** $ 9,153
Type: 4 Yr., Public, Coed
Campus Housing: Yes
SAT/ACT/GPA: 2.0 out of state
Male/Female Ratio: 45:55
Graduate Enrollment: 3.154
Fin Aid: Yes
Out of State: $ 13,725
Degrees Conferred: BA, BS, MA, MS, MBA
Programs of Study: Accounting, Business Administration, Economics, Finance, Real Estate, International Business, Marketing, Entreprenuenership (Secondary Education), Math, German, Spanish, Social Studies, French, History, Biology, Physical Education, Sport Business, K-12, Exercices, Fine Arts, Art Education, Art History, Graphic Design, Music Education, Health Professions, Dental Hygiene, Gerontology, Health Science, Nursing, Public Health, Liberal Arts, Anthropology,. Biochemistry, Advertising, Communications, Etc..

ATHLETIC PROFILE

Conference Affiliation: Missouri Valley Conference
Program Profile: During the last 19 years , we have had the winningest program. We had College World Series appearances. We had 15 NCAA regional appearances. We were 1989 CWS Champions, Missouri Valley Conference Champions and NCAA CWS runner-up three times. Eight of our players were named Academic All-American 13 times. We had two All-American of the Year honorees. Eck Stadium/Tyler Field seats 5,665 and has the largest collegiate baseball scoreboard.
History: We began in 1899 and stopped in 1970. Our program was revived in 1978 when Gene Stephenson took over.
Achievements: Gene Stephenson was NCAA Coach of the Year in 1982, 1989 and 1993. He had 1,000 wins in 1995 (faster than any other collegiate baseball coach). He has coached 3 NCAA Players of the Year, 15 major leaguers and 72 players who have gone to play professional baseball.
Coaching: Gene Stephenson - Head Coach. Brent Kemnitz - Assistant Coach/Pitching, has helped twice to lead the NCAA in team ERA. 31 WSU pitchers have earned All-MVC honors 52 times.

KENTUCKY

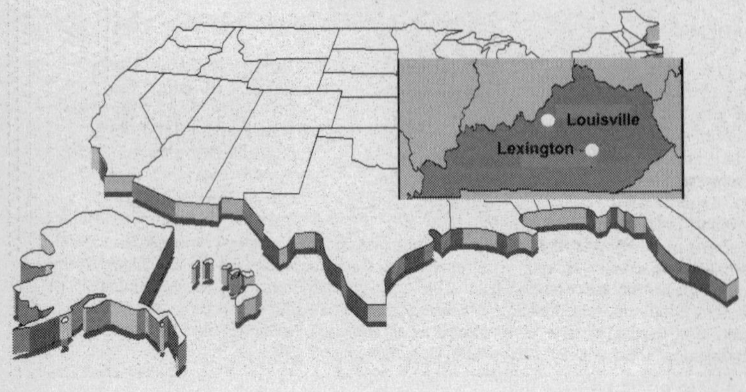

SCHOOL	CITY	AFFILIATION 99	PAGE
Alice Lloyd College	Pippa Passes	NAIA	343
Asbury College	Wilmore	NAIA	343
Bellarmine College	Louisville	NCAA II	344
Berea College	Berea	NAIA	344
Campbellsville College	Campbellsville	NAIA	345
Centre College	Danville	NCAA III	346
Cumberland College	Williamsburg	NAIA	346
Eastern Kentucky University	Richmond	NCAA I	347
Georgetown College	Georgetown	NAIA	347
Kentucky State University	Frankfort	NCAA II	348
Kentucky Wesleyan College	Owensboro	NCAA II	348
Lindsey Wilson College	Columbia	NAIA	349
Morehead State University	Morehead	NCAA I	349
Murray State University	Murray	NCAA I	350
Northern Kentucky University	Highland Heights	NCAA II	350
Pikeville College	Pikeville	NAIA	351
Saint Catharine College	St. Catharine	NJCAA	352
Thomas More College	Crestview Hills	NCAA III	352
Union College	Barbourville	NAIA	353
University of Kentucky	Lexington	NCAA I	354
University of Louisville	Louisville	NCAA I	354
Western Kentucky University	Bowling Green	NCAA I	355

Alice Lloyd College

100 Purpose Road
Pippa Passes, KY 41844
Coach: Scott Cornett

NAIA
Eagles/Royal, White
Phone: (606) 368-2101
Fax: (606) 368-6213

ACADEMIC

Founded: 1923
Type: 4 Yr., Private, Liberal Arts, Coed
SAT/ACT/GPA: 900 avg/18 avg
Campus Housing: No
Student/Faculty Ratio: 3:1
Male/Female Ratio: 49:51
Undergraduate Enrollment: 386
Graduate Enrollment: 102
Scholarships/Academic: Yes **Athletic:** Yes **Fin Aid:** Yes
Total Expenses by: Year **In State:** $ 8,800 **Out of State:** $ 10,000
Degrees Conferred: AA, BA, BS
Programs of Study: Business Administration, Elementary Education, History, Management, Physical Therapy, Predentistry, Prelaw, Premed, Prepharmacy, Secondary Education

ATHLETIC PROFILE

Estimated Number of Baseball Scholarships: 3
Conference Affiliation: Tennessee Virginia Athletic Conference
Program Profile: We play a Fall and Spring season with an outside competition. Outfield is all natural 400 CF, 330 down the lines, and 85 in power alleys. We play on top of a beautiful mountain in Eastern Kentucky.
History: Our program began in 1979 and has grown each year.
Achievements: None - working to have achievements.
Roster for 1998 team/In State: 19 **Out of State:** 6 **Out of Country:** 0
Total Number of Varsity/Jr. Varsity: 25 **Most Recent Record:** 18 - 20 - 0
Number of Seniors on 1998 Team: 2 **Number of Sophomores on 1998 Team:** 10
Number of Fall Games: 10 **Number of Spring Games:** 40
Schedule: Northern, Montreat College, Brewton Parker, Pikeville, Shawnee State, Bluefield, Milligan, Tennessee Wesleyan
Style of Play: Like to play hard, disciplined and aggressive, good pitching.

Asbury College

1 Macklem Drive
Wilmore, KY 40356
Coach: Tom Raven

NAIA
Eagles/Purple, White
Phone: (606) 858-3511
Fax: (606) 858-3921

ACADEMIC

Founded: 1890
Type: 4 Yr., Private, Liberal Arts, Coed
Religion: Non-Denominational
Campus Housing: Yes
Web-site: http://www.asbury.edu/
SAT/ACT/GPA: 830/ 20
Student/Faculty Ratio: 14:1
Male/Female Ratio: 44:56
Undergraduate Enrollment: 1,167
Graduate Enrollment: 4
Scholarships/Academic: Yes **Athletic:** No **Fin Aid:** Yes
Total Expenses by: Year **In State:** $ 13, 547 **Out of State:** $ 13,547
Degrees Conferred: BA, BS, Master of Philosophy in Economics
Programs of Study: Accounting, Applied Mathematics, Art, Biochemistry, Biology, Broadcasting, Business and Management, Chemistry, Computer Science, Education, Psychology, Religious Education, Science Education, Social Science, Nursing, Journalism, Physical Education

ATHLETIC PROFILE

Conference Affiliation: Independent Conference

Program Profile: We play a 50+ game schedule and have excellent indoor/outdoor facilities. The Fall program is 4-weeks and the Spring program is 19-weeks.
History: We have an 11-year history and our 1995 record was 19-14.

Bellarmine College

2001 Newburg Road
Louisville, KY 40205
Coach: Tommy Malone

NCAA II
Knights/Silver, Red
Phone: (502) 452-8380
Fax: (502) 452-8450

ACADEMIC

Founded: 1950
Type: 4 Yr., Private, Liberal Arts, Coed
Religion: Catholic
Campus Housing: Yes
Web-site: http://www.bellarmine.edu/
SAT/ACT/GPA: 950/21/2.5
Student/Faculty Ratio: 14:1
Male/Female Ratio: 41:59
Undergraduate Enrollment: 1,250
Graduate Enrollment: 950
Scholarships/Academic: Yes **Athletic:** Yes **Fin Aid:** Yes
Total Expenses by: Year **In State:** $ 15,050 **Out of State:** $ 15,050
Degrees Conferred: BA, BS, BSN, MA, MEd, MAT, MBA, MLS
Programs of Study: Accounting, Art, Art Administration, Biology, Business Administration, Chemistry, Communication, Computer Engineering, Computer Science, Economics, Education, English, History, Mathematics, Music, Nursing, Philosophy, Political Science, Psychology, Sociology

ATHLETIC PROFILE

Conference Affiliation: Great Lakes Valley Conference
Program Profile: We are in the Top Division II conference in the country. We have outstanding facilities. We play a Fall and Spring schedule. The climate is usually great for baseball. We have a 10-team conference with an automatic bid to NCAA tournaments
History: Our program began in the 1950's when the school began. We have improved since then. Entered conference in late 1970's. We have been to the NCAA tournament 4 times with the most recent in 1989.
Achievements: We won the Conference last in 1989. We have 2 All-Americans. We had number of playerss drafted over the years.
Coaching: Tommy Malone - Head Coach.
Style of Play: Aggressive with a power and a speed.

Berea College

CPO 2344
Berea, KY 40409-999
Coach: Don Richardson
Email: admission@berea.edu

NAIA
Mountaineers/Blue, White
Phone: (606) 986-9341x5430
Fax: (606) 986-7505

ACADEMIC

Founded: 1855
Type: 4 Yr., Private, Liberal Arts, Coed
Religion: Nonsectarian Christian
Campus Housing: No
Web-site: http://www.berea.edu/
SAT/ACT/GPA: 950/ 21
Student/Faculty Ratio: 14:1
Male/Female Ratio: 45:55
Scholarships/Academic: No **Athletic:** No **Fin Aid:** Yes
Total Expenses by: Year **In State:** $ 7,000 **Out of State:** $ 7,000
Degrees Conferred: BA, BS
Programs of Study: Biblical Studies, Guidance, Ministries, Religious Education, Theology

ATHLETIC PROFILE

Conference Affiliation: Kentucky Intercollegiate Athletic Conference

Program Profile: Wyatt Field has natural grass with a measurements of 325-left, 370;left center, 412 -center, 385-right center and 327-right. Our Spring schedule has 26 games maximum.
History: The record is not available.
Achievements: 1993; KIAC District 32 Champions; 1984 Donny Harper Honorable Mention All-American; 1951 and 1964 KIAC Champions.
Coaching: Don Richardson, Head Coach, started with the program in 1996. He coached Madison Central High School for 35 years (1957-1992) and won over 900 games. In 1982, we were undefeated State Champs (40-0) and Coach Richardson was National Coach of the Year.
Roster for 1998 team/In State: 21 **Out of State:** 9 **Out of Country:** 0
Total Number of Varsity/Jr. Varsity: 21 **Most Recent Record:** 9 - 18 - 0
Number of Seniors on 1998 Team: 2 **Number of Sophomores on 1998 Team:** 2
Freshmen Receiving Fin Aid/Athletic: 0 **Academic:** 11
Number of Fall Games: 0 **Number of Spring Games:** 26
Positions Needed for 1999/2000: Pitcher, Catcher, 1st Base, Outfielder
Schedule: Indiana - SouthEast, Lindsey Wilson, Pikeville, Cumberland, Bethel, Brescia College
Style of Play: Fundamentally sound relying; on sound defense with good offense and aggressive base running.

Campbellsville College

1 University Drive
Campbellsville, KY 24718
Coach: Beauford Sander

NAIA
Tigers/Maroon, Grey
Phone: (502) 789-5056
Fax: (502) 789-5059

ACADEMIC

Founded: 1906 **Type:** 4 Yr., Private, Liberal Arts, Coed
Religion: Baptist **Campus Housing:** No
Web-site: http://www.campbellsvil.edu/ **SAT/ACT/GPA:** 890/ 19
Student/Faculty Ratio: 16:1 **Male/Female Ratio:** 1:9
Undergraduate Enrollment: 1,329 **Graduate Enrollment:** 37
Scholarships/Academic: Yes **Athletic:** Yes **Fin Aid:** Yes
Total Expenses by: Year **In State:** $ 9,720 **Out of State:** $ 9,720
Degrees Conferred: AA, AS, BA, BS, BM, BSMT, MA
Programs of Study: Accounting, Art, Athletic Training, Biology, Business Administration, Economics, Office Management, Chemistry, English, History, Journalism, Mathematics, Pre-Professional Courses, Psychology, Social Work, Sociology, Sports Medicine/Exercise Science,

ATHLETIC PROFILE

Conference Affiliation: Mid - South Conference
Program Profile: Campbellsville's home field is Tiger Field located on the college campus. The student support is a plus with the on-campus facility. The field itself is 330' down the lines and 385' to center field and 370' to the gaps. Five years ago, Beauford Sanders was hired as Head Coach and the field has shown gradual improvements each year.
History: In 1963, Campbellsville began playing as a four-year school. The Tigers were 1992 Western Division Champions, District 32 Runner-up and 1993 third place finish. Campbellsville had their best season ever in 1995 when they participated in the NAIA National playoffs and were Tournament and regular season KIAC Champions.
Achievements: 1992 W Division Champions; Runner-Up District Tourney in 1993; Conference Runner-Up in 1994; Conference Runner-Up and District Runner-Up in 1995-1996; Conference Champions Mid-South Regional Runner-Up in 1996; 1995 Coach of the Year; 1995 Mid-South Regional Coach of the Year; KIAC Coach of the Year.
Coaching: Beauford Sander, Head Coach, was named Coach of the Year in the KIAC.
Style of Play: Aggressive - team accomplishments placed over individual. Make something happen.

Centre College

600 West Walnut Street
Danville, KY 40422
Coach: Ed Rall

NCAA III
Colonels/Gold, White
Phone: (606) 238-5488
Fax: (606) 236-6081

ACADEMIC

Founded: 1819
Type: 4 Yr., Private, Liberal Arts, Coed
Religion: Informal Presbyterian
Campus Housing: Yes
Web-site: http://www.centre.edu/
SAT/ACT/GPA: 1130/25/3.4
Student/Faculty Ratio: 10:1
Male/Female Ratio: 50:50
Undergraduate Enrollment: 1,000
Graduate Enrollment: None
Scholarships/Academic: Yes **Athletic:** No **Fin Aid:** Yes
Total Expenses by: Year **In State:** $ 19,500 **Out of State:** $ 19,500
Degrees Conferred: BA, BS
Programs of Study: Art, Biology, Chemistry, Classics, Economics, Elementary Education, English, French, German, Government, History, Math, Music, Philosophy, Physics, Psychobiology, Psychology, Religion, Prelaw, Premed, Secondary Education

ATHLETIC PROFILE

Conference Affiliation: Southern Collegiate Athletic Conference
Program Profile: We play on a natural grass field and our season starts on March 1 and ends on May 9. Facilities include indoor batting cage and mounds. We broke our school record for most wins in season in 1997.
History: Our program began in 1890. Centre lead our conference titles wherein we won seven times. The Conference began in 1963.
Achievements: We won 7 Conference Titles.
Coaching: Ed Rall - Head Coach. Bryan Cross - Assistant Coach.

Cumberland College

7526 College Station Drive
Williamsburg, KY 40769-1386
Coach: Terry Stigall

NAIA
indians/Maroon, White
Phone: (606) 539-4389
Fax: (606) 549-4479

ACADEMIC

Founded: 1889
Type: 4 Yr., Private, Liberal Arts, Coed
Religion: Southern Baptist
Campus Housing: No
Web-site: http://www.cumber.edu/
SAT/ACT/GPA: None
Student/Faculty Ratio: 15:1
Male/Female Ratio: 52:48
Undergraduate Enrollment: 1,500
Graduate Enrollment: None
Scholarships/Academic: Yes **Athletic:** Yes **Fin Aid:** Yes
Total Expenses by: Year **In State:** $ 12,606 **Out of State:** $ Varies
Degrees Conferred: Bachelor - Arts, Science, Music, General Studies, MEd
Programs of Study: Art, Biology, Business Administration, Chemistry, Communications, Computer Information Systems, Elementary Education, English, Health, History, History and Political Science, Mathematics, Medical Technology, Movement and Leisure Studies, Music, Physics, Political Science, Psychology, Religion, Sociology, Special Education, Theatre Arts

ATHLETIC PROFILE

Conference Affiliation: KIAC

Eastern Kentucky University

118 Alumni Coliseum
Richmond, KY 40475
Coach: Jim Ward
Email: athpark@acs.eku.edu

NCAA I
Colonels/Maroon, White
Phone: (606) 622-2120
Fax: (606) 622-5108

ACADEMIC

Founded: 1909
Type: 4 Yr., Public, Coed
Web-site: http://www..eku.edu
Campus Housing: Yes
Student/Faculty Ratio: 16:1
Male/Female Ratio: 1:2
Undergraduate Enrollment: 15,000
Graduate Enrollment: 2,000
Scholarships/Academic: Yes **Athletic:** Yes **Fin Aid:** Yes
Total Expenses by: Year **In State:** $ 6,036 **Out of State:** $ 9,626
Degrees Conferred: AA, BA, BS, BFA, BBA, BM, BSN, MA, MS
Programs of Study: Anthropology, Banking/Finance, Chemistry, Construction, Corrections, Dietetics, Economics, English, Environmental, Fashion, History, Insurance, Interior Design, Industrial, Law, Management, Marketing, Philosophy, Real Estate, Religion, Wildlife

ATHLETIC PROFILE

Estimated Number of Baseball Scholarships: 10
Conference Affiliation: Ohio Valley Conference
Program Profile: We have a very structured, disciplined program. Turkey Hughes Field has Bermuda grass and a seating capacity of 1,200 .
History: Our program began in 1920. Hall of Fame Earl Combs played at EKU (Leadoff hitter for 1927 Yankees). We had 12 Conference Titles since 1950.
Achievements: 4 Conference Titles under Coach Ward; 4 Coach of the Year honors; 3 All-Americans; 28 players drafted.
Coaching: Jim Ward,Head Coach, has an overall career record of 825-601-4. Career record at EKU is 514-416-4. Jason Stein and T.C. Brewer - Assistant Coaches.
Roster for 1998 team/In State: 13 **Out of State:** 12 **Out of Country:** 0
Total Number of Varsity/Jr. Varsity: 25 **Percent of Graduation:** 95%
Number of Seniors on 1998 Team: 7 **Number of Sophomores on 1998 Team:** 1
Freshmen Receiving Fin Aid/Athletic: 3 **Number of Spring Games:** 56
Positions Needed for 1999/2000: Outfielder, Pitcher, Catcher
Most Recent Record: 16 - 20 - 1
Schedule: Georgia Southern, Eastern Illinois, Univ. of Kentucky, Western Kentucky, Furman, Xavier
Style of Play: Very aggressive, steal a lot of bases, and play solid defense. Pitchers should work fast, change speed, and most importantly throw strikes.

Georgetown College

400 E College Street
Georgetown, KY 40324
Coach: Jim Hinerman

NAIA
Tigers/Ornage, Black, Gold
Phone: (502) 863-8207
Fax: (502) 868-8892

ACADEMIC

Founded: 1829
Type: 4 Yr., Private, Liberal Arts, Coed
Religion: Baptist
Campus Housing: Yes
Web-site: http://www.gtc.georgetown.ky.us/
SAT/ACT/GPA: 930/ 20
Student/Faculty Ratio: 10:1
Male/Female Ratio: 50:50
Undergraduate Enrollment: 1,200
Graduate Enrollment: 200
Scholarships/Academic: Yes **Athletic:** Yes **Fin Aid:** Yes
Total Expenses by: Year **In State:** $ 5,432 **Out of State:** $ 5,432
Degrees Conferred: BA, BS, MA

Programs of Study: Accounting, American Studies, Biological Sciences, Business Administration, Chemistry, Economics, Elementary Education, Environmental Science, History, Marketing/Finance, Mathematics, Medical Technology, Philosophy, Physical Education, Physics, Political Science, Pre-Professional Courses, Psychology, Sociology

ATHLETIC PROFILE

Conference Affiliation: KIAC
Program Profile: Robert N. Wilson Field is 2-years old, seats 500 and has a natural grass base.
Achievements: 1988 World Series (5th place); 6 District 32 Titles; 12 KIAC titles; 7 Academic and Athletic All-Americans.
Coaching: Jim Hinerman - Head Coach.
Style of Play: Fundamentally sound.

Kentucky State University

400 East Main Street
Frankfort, KY 40601
Coach: Elwood Johnson

NCAA II
Thorobreds/Green, Gold
Phone: (502) 227-6018
Fax: (502) 227-6466

ACADEMIC

Founded: 1858
Type: 4 Yr., Public, Coed
Web-site: Not Available
SAT/ACT/GPA: 800/19
Student/Faculty Ratio: 14:1
Male/Female Ratio: 50:50
Undergraduate Enrollment: 800
Graduate Enrollment: None
Scholarships/Academic: Yes **Athletic:** Yes **Fin Aid:** Yes
Total Expenses by: Year **In State:** $ 13,250 **Out of State:** $ 13,250
Degrees Conferred: Associate in Nursing, BA, BS
Programs of Study: Business and Management, Communications, Education, Health Science, Life Science, Psychology, Social Science

ATHLETIC PROFILE

Conference Affiliation: Great Lakes Valley Conference

Kentucky Wesleyan College

3000 Frederica Street
Owensboro, KY 42301
Coach: Ron Clark

NCAA II
Panthers/Purple, White
Phone: (502) 926-3111
Fax: (502) 684-5028

ACADEMIC

Founded: 1858
Type: 4 Yr., Private, Liberal Arts, Coed
Religion: United Methodist
Campus Housing: No
Web-site: http://www.kwc.edu/
SAT/ACT/GPA: 800/ 19
Student/Faculty Ratio: 14:1
Male/Female Ratio: 50:50
Undergraduate Enrollment: 800
Graduate Enrollment: N/A
Scholarships/Academic: Yes **Athletic:** Yes **Fin Aid:** Yes
Total Expenses by: Year **In State:** $ 13,250 **Out of State:** $ 13,250
Degrees Conferred: Associate in Nursing, BA, BS
Programs of Study: Business and Management, Communications, Education, Health Sciences, Life Sciences, Psychology, Social Sciences

ATHLETIC PROFILE

Conference Affiliation: Great Lakes Valley Conference

Program Profile: The Panthers play an NCAA 56-game schedule from February to May. We play at Panther Park which was remodeled in the late 1980's to host the Babe Ruth World Series.
History: Our college modern era began in 1961. The Panthers have participated in three NCAA Regionals -1962, 1967 and 1988.
Achievements: 7 professional signees; 12 All-NCAA Regional Players; 24 All-Conference selections; 1993 Conference Player of the Year.
Coaching: Ron Clark, Head Coach, has coached at Division I, II, and Junior College levels. He has 20 years of experience and has both played and coached at the Division II National Championships.
Style of Play: Aggressive running style. We play in a big ball park and speed is essential. Extensive weight training program. the program includes six weeks of Fall practice.

Lindsey Wilson College

210 Lindsey Wilson Street
Columbia, KY 42728
Coach: Mike Talley

NAIA
Raiders/Blue, White
Phone: (502) 384-8070
Fax: (502) 384-8078

ACADEMIC

Founded: 1903
Type: 4 Yr., Private, Liberal Arts, Coed
Religion: Methodist
Campus Housing: Yes
Web-site: Not Available
SAT/ACT/GPA: 860/ 18
Student/Faculty Ratio: 20:1
Male/Female Ratio: 60:40
Undergraduate Enrollment: 1,320
Graduate Enrollment: 50
Scholarships/Academic: Yes **Athletic:** Yes **Fin Aid:** Yes
Total Expenses by: Year **In State:** $ 12,510 **Out of State:** $ 12,510
Degrees Conferred: AA, BA, BS, MA
Programs of Study: All Liberal Art types including: Business and Management, Computer Science, Education, and all Preprofessional Programs

ATHLETIC PROFILE

Estimated Number of Baseball Scholarships: 6
Conference Affiliation: KIAC
Program Profile: We have a varsity and junior varsity program. Our baseball field is on campus and we compete in the nationally ranked Mid-South Region.
History: The program turned into a four-year institution in 1987. We ranked 7th in the nation in team batting average in 1997. We ranked 5th in the nation in team home runs in 1997.
Achievements: 1997 KIAC Conference Titles; 1 first team All-American, 2 Honorable Mention All-Americans; 2 players drafted since 1995.
Coaching: Mike Talley ,Head Coach, started with the program in 1993 and compiled a record of 165-136. Brian Garrett , Assistant Coach, started with the program in 1994.
Roster for 1998 team/In State: 27 **Out of State:** 15 **Out of Country:** 1
Total Number of Varsity/Jr. Varsity: 46 **Percent of Graduation:** 0
Number of Seniors on 1998 Team: 4 **Number of Sophomores on 1998 Team:** 6
Freshmen Receiving Fin Aid/Athletic: 14 **Most Recent Record:** 28 - 20 - 0
Number of Fall Games: 5 **Number of Spring Games:** 60
Schedule: Cumberland University, Union University, Lambuth University, Webber College, Eckerd
Style of Play: We are an exciting team to watch. We like to swing the bat and score runs. 96 home runs in 1997.

Morehead State University

Baseball Office
Morehead, KY 40351-1689
Coach: John Jarnagan

NCAA I
Eagles/Blue, Gold
Phone: (606) 783-2882
Fax: (606) 783-5035

ACADEMIC

Founded: 1887
Religion: Non-Affiliated
SAT/ACT/GPA: Must be greater than 400/
Student/Faculty Ratio: 18:1
Undergraduate Enrollment: 8,300
Scholarships/Academic: Yes **Athletic:** Yes
Total Expenses by: Year **In State:** $ 5,850
Degrees Conferred: AA
Type: 4 Yr., Public, Coed
Campus Housing: No
Web-site: http://www.morehead-st.edu
Male/Female Ratio: 45:55
Graduate Enrollment: 1,500
Fin Aid: Yes
Out of State: $ 9,450
Programs of Study: Has 72 undergraduate programs; 15 associate level degress and 10 preprofessional programs. Has four colleges: Education and Behavioral Sciences, Humanities, Science and Technology - divided into 21 academic departments; 24 graduate programs.

ATHLETIC PROFILE

Conference Affiliation: Ohio Valley Conference
Program Profile: Our campus is set in the foothills of the Appalachian Mountains, providing a picturesque background setting for a baseball field. We have an Indoor hitting and pitching facility next to the field. Home and visitor clubhouses lead into dugouts. Allen Field seats 1,200.
History: The program began in 1924. Steve Hamilton, former Yankees left-handed pitcher, was head coach from 1976-1989. His overall record was 305-275 for 14 years with OVC Championships.
Achievements: Brad Allison - 1993 freshman All-american. Butch Fulks - 1992 3rd team All-American DH. Sean Hogan - 2nd in Division I strikeout./9 innings in 1992. OVC Champs in 1969, 1973, 1983, 1993; 19 players drafted since 1980, including for major leaguers.
Style of Play: Aggressive hitting, hit and run, disciplined and detailed.

Murray State University

15th and Main Streets
Murray, KY 42071
Coach: Mike Thieke
NCAA I
Racers/Blue, Gold
Phone: (502) 762-4892
Fax: (502) 762-6814

ACADEMIC

Founded: 1922
Web-site: http://www.murraystate.edu
Student/Faculty Ratio: 18:1
Undergraduate Enrollment: 6,625
Scholarships/Academic: Yes **Athletic:** Yes
Total Expenses by: Year **In State:** $ 5,500
Type: 4 Yr., Public, Coed
SAT/ACT/GPA: 22avg
Male/Female Ratio: 47:53
Graduate Enrollment: 1,275
Fin Aid: Yes
Out of State: $ 8,900
Degrees Conferred: AA, AS, BA, BS, BFA, BSN, BSA, MA, MS
Programs of Study: Accounting, Art, Biology, Business, Chemistry, Engineering, Construction, Comsumer Affairs, Dietetics, Earth Science, Finance, Manufacturing, Marketing, Music, Medical, Middle School, Occupational, Parks/Recreation Management, Education, Speech, Theatre

ATHLETIC PROFILE

Conference Affiliation: Ohio Valley Conference

Northern Kentucky University

Albright Health Center Nunn Drive
Highland Heights, KY 41099-7500
Coach: Bill Aker
NCAA II
Norse/Gold, Black
Phone: (606) 572-6474
Fax: (606) 572-5427

ACADEMIC

Founded: 1968
Type: 4 Yr., Public, Coed
Student/Faculty Ratio: 16:1
Campus Housing: Yes
Web-site: http://www.nku.edu/
SAT/ACT/GPA: 18
Undergraduate Enrollment: 11,600
Graduate Enrollment: 800
Scholarships/Academic: Yes **Athletic:** Yes **Fin Aid:** Yes
Total Expenses by: Year **In State:** $ 3,110 **Out of State:** $ 4,850
Degrees Conferred: BA, BS, BFA, BMus, BMusEd, BSN, BSW, MA, MBA, JD
Programs of Study: Accounting, Anthropology, Art Education, Biological Science, Business Education, Chemistry, English, Finance, Geology, Geography, Graphic Design, History, Journalism, Justice Studies, Management, Marketing, Mathematics, Philosophy, Physical Education, Physics

ATHLETIC PROFILE

Conference Affiliation: Great Lakes Valley Conference
Program Profile: We participate in probably the toughest conference in the country (GLVC). Our field is ten years old , has natural grass and seats about 500. Our surface is brick-dirt/clay.
History: Our program was developed in 1971. Bill Aker has been the head coach from the start. His record is 742-496. The program has had five losing seasons and 10 winning seasons in a row. Eleven times NKU has won at lEast 30 games. Four times we have won 40 games. The best year was 1997 when our record was 49-7 and we were 7th in the country.
Achievements: Coach of the Year five times; 3 in the Great Lakes Region; 1 in the NAIA Area VI and 1 in the GLVC in 1992; We've had 7 All-Americans, the latest was Brandon Chestnut in 1994. Our latest drafters were Scott Wiggin & Randy Hamilton in 1997 to the Yankees & Mets respectively.
Coaching: Bill Aker,Head Coach, has coached the program from the start to the present. He was coach of the Year five times. Jeff Ketzer , Assistant Coach, is in his 2nd year. His specialty is defense. In 1997, our team was 12th in the country as far as fielding percentage goes. He played and graduated from Northern Kentucky and is currently working on his Master's Degree in Education.
Style of Play: We are not going to hit the ball out of the park. We like to shoot the alleys and turn singles into doubles, doubles into triples. We are very aggressive on the bases. We make other teams make the plays. We are very fundamentally sound and our strength is obviously defense. Our kids work hard and thus we have a great tradition at NKU.

Paducah Community College

(Program Discontinued)

Pikeville College

214 Sycamore Street
Pikeville, KY 41501
Coach: Johnnie LeMaster

NAIA
Bears/Black, Orange
Phone: (606) 432-9312
Fax: (606) 432-9328

ACADEMIC

Founded: 1889
Type: 4 Yr., Private, Coed
Religion: Non-Affiliated
Campus Housing: Yes
Undergraduate Enrollment: 775
SAT/ACT/GPA: 18avg
Student/Faculty Ratio: 14:1
Male/Female Ratio: 31:69
Scholarships/Academic: Yes **Athletic:** Yes **Fin Aid:** Yes
Total Expenses by: Year **In State:** $ 10,000 **Out of State:** $ 10,000
Degrees Conferred: AS, BA, BS, BBA
Programs of Study: Accounting, Biological, Business Administration, Education, Chemistry, Computer Science, Early Childhood Education, Elementary Education, English, History, Management, Mathematics, Nursing, Religion, Science, Secondary Education, Social Science

ATHLETIC PROFILE

Conference Affiliation: KIAC

Saint Catharine College

2735 Bardstown Road
St. Catharine, KY 40061
Coach: Brad Shelton

NJCAA
Patriots/Purple, Gold
Phone: (606) 336-5082
Fax: (606) 336-5031

ACADEMIC

Founded: 1931
Type: 2 Yr., Private, Coed
SAT/ACT/GPA: 12
Campus Housing: Yes
Student/Faculty Ratio: 13:1
Male/Female Ratio: 39:61
Undergraduate Enrollment: 400
Graduate Enrollment: 0
Scholarships/Academic: Yes **Athletic:** Yes **Fin Aid:** Yes
Total Expenses by: Year **In State:** $ 7,650 **Out of State:** $ 7,650
Degrees Conferred: AA, AS
Programs of Study: Accounting, Agricultural, Animal, Art, Biblical, Biological Science, Chemistry, Computer, Criminal Justice, Economics, Education, Farm/Ranch, History, Horticulture, Humanities, Insurance, Journalism, Landscape, Architecture, Landscaping, Land Use Management, Liberal Arts, Mathematics, Music, Physical Education, Range Management Science, Social Science, Spanish

ATHLETIC PROFILE

Estimated Number of Baseball Scholarships: 24
Conference Affiliation: NJCAA Region VII
Program Profile: We are the only junior college program in Kentucky. We have a natural grass playing field, brick dust, 2 cages, 4 indoor mounds and baseball specific weight facilities. We have a 2 month Fall season , play 56 games in the Spring and take a trip in the Spring.
History: Our program began in 1991. Our three seasons under Coach Brad Shelton have been most successful. Our 1996 record was 16-11 and our 1997 record was 27-10. Currently , we have a 1998 season of 23-9 with 18 games remaining.
Achievements: Has two players drafted, several All-Region players; ranked nationally in team batting average in 1998.
Coaching: Brad Shelton, Head Coach, is entering his 3rd year with the program. He is a 1995 graduate of Ausburg College and holds six Ausburg career and season hitting records (66-30) . He was named the school's 1995 Outstanding Student Athlete. In his first season as a head coach, the Patriots were state runner-up and all sophomores received offers from a four year school.
Roster for 1998 team/In State: 25 **Out of State:** 3 **Out of Country:** 0
Total Number of Varsity/Jr. Varsity: 28 **Number of Seniors on 1998 Team:** 15
Freshmen Receiving Fin Aid/Athletic: 10 **Academic:** 5
Number of Fall Games: 12 **Number of Spring Games:** 56
Positions Needed for 1999/2000: 2 Middle Infielders, 2 Catchers, Pitcher
Schedule: Vincinnes, Wabash Valley, Sinclair, Walters State, Roane, Indiana Purdue Fort Wayne
Style of Play: We play hard-nosed, fundamentally sound baseball. We make things happen with our speed and execution. Our program is disciplined on and off the field. Our players are expected to maintain a strong code of conduct.

Sue Bennett College

(School Closed)

Thomas More College

333 Thomas More Parkway
Crestview Hills, KY 41017-3428
Coach: Todd Asalon

NCAA III
Saints/Blue, Silver
Phone: (606) 344-3532
Fax: (606) 344-3632

ACADEMIC

Founded: 1921
Religion: Roman Catholic
Web-site: http://www.thomasmore.edu/
Student/Faculty Ratio: 12:1
Undergraduate Enrollment: 1,500
Scholarships/Academic: Yes **Athletic:** No
Total Expenses by: Year **In State:** $ 13,500
Degrees Conferred: BA, BS, BSN

Type: 4 Yr., Private, Liberal Arts, Coed
Campus Housing: Yes
SAT/ACT/GPA: 18
Male/Female Ratio: 44:56
Graduate Enrollment: None
Fin Aid: Yes
Out of State: $ 13,500

Programs of Study: Accounting, Art, Biology, Business Administration, Chemistry, Computer Science, Computer Information Systems, Criminal Justice, Drama, Economics, Education, English, Fine Arts, Gerontology, Histroy, International Studies, Mathematics, Medical Technology, Microcomputer, Nursing, Philosophy, Physics, Political Science, Prelaw, Premed, Psychology, Sociology, Theology

ATHLETIC PROFILE

Conference Affiliation: Independent
Program Profile: We are in the NCAA Division III which is a non-scholarship program. We have a full Fall schedule. We have a Spring trip to Florida and a 30 man roster in the program. Our baseball field is on campus and has a natural turf surface.
History: Our program began in 1956. In 1994, we had the best season in school history winning 29 out of 38 games. We captured the Conference title and tournament. In 1995 , we tied for first place in regular season conference. In 1995, our record was 29-9 which is the the most wins.
Achievements: Conference Champs in 1994, 1995, and 1996 (AMC); All-American was Ron Ryan in 1996 and 1997; Drafted was David Justice by Cleveland Indians.
Coaching: Todd Asalon,Head Coach, started coaching from 1995 to the present. His overall record is 85-65. Tim McClatchey - Assistant Coach (1997).
Roster for 1998 team/In State: 13 **Out of State:** 20 **Out of Country:** 0
Total Number of Varsity/Jr. Varsity: 33 **Percent of Graduation:** 95%
Freshmen Receiving Fin Aid/Athletic: 0 **Academic:** 33
Number of Fall Games: 9 **Number of Spring Games:** 36
Positions Needed for 1999/2000: Pitcher **Most Recent Record:** 9 - 0 - 0
Baseball Camp Dates: All of July
Schedule: Miami University, Lehigh University, Morehead State University, College of Wooster, Wittenberg University, Ohio Wesleyan University
Style of Play: Aggressive with solid defense and pitching.

Union College

310 College Street
Barbourville, KY 40906
Coach: Darin Wilson

NAIA
Bulldogs/Orange, Black
Phone: (606) 546-1355
Fax: (606) 546-1286

ACADEMIC

Founded: 1879
Religion: Methodist
SAT/ACT/GPA: Varies according to GPA/
Student/Faculty Ratio: 14:1
Undergraduate Enrollment: 700
Scholarships/Academic: Yes **Athletic:** Yes
Total Expenses by: Year **In State:** $ 12,000
Degrees Conferred: Bachelors, Masters

Type: 4 Yr., Private, Liberal Arts, Coed
Campus Housing: Yes
Web-site: http://www.unionky.edu/
Male/Female Ratio: 50:50
Graduate Enrollment: 300
Fin Aid: Yes
Out of State: $ 12,000

Programs of Study: Education, Business, Social Science, Physical Sciences, Sport Management, Athletic Training, Science, Premed, Prelaw

ATHLETIC PROFILE

Conference Affiliation: KIAC

University of Kentucky

Memorial Coliseum
Lexington, KY 40506
Coach: Keith Madison

NCAA I
Wildcats/Royal Blue, White
Phone: (606) 257-4754
Fax: (606) 323-4999

ACADEMIC

Founded: 1865
Religion: Non-Affiliated
Web-site: http://www.uky.edu/
Student/Faculty Ratio: 20:1
Undergraduate Enrollment: 19,000
Scholarships/Academic: Yes **Athletic:** Yes
Total Expenses by: Year **In State:** $ 3,600

Type: 4 Yr., Public, Coed
Campus Housing: Yes
SAT/ACT/GPA: NCAA Minimums
Male/Female Ratio: 47:53
Graduate Enrollment: 6,000
Fin Aid: Yes
Out of State: $ 6,100

Degrees Conferred: BA, BS, BFA, MA, MS, MBA, MFA, MEd, PhD, EdD, JD
Programs of Study: Business/Office and Marketing/Distribution, Business and Management, Communications, Education, Engineering, Health Sciences, Social Sciences

ATHLETIC PROFILE

Conference Affiliation: SouthEastern Conference
Program Profile: We are a program that has been in the Top 25, 9 for the last 13 years. In 20 year s(since 1978), we have had 80 players drafted into the major leagues. Our stadium is a miniature Wrigley Field (bricks) & seats 2,200. We have an outstanding Bermuda grass playing surface.
History: The first game was played 1896. We have been in the SEC since the beginning of the league. Keith Madison has been coaching at UK for 20 years. Hé is third on All-time SEC win list. CM Newton, the UK Athletic Director was an All-Conference baseball player for the Wildcats before signing with the Yankees.
Achievements: Over 80 players drafted during the past 20 years. 15 players have reached major during Madison's tenure; numerous All-American player; most recent were Scott Down in 1997 third round pick by the Cubs, Chad Green in 1996 first round by the Brewers and made the 1996 Olympic team, and Jeff Abott in 1995 3rd round pick by the White Sox and now playing outfielder for Chicago.
Coaching: Keith Madison - Head Coach. Daron Schoenrock - Pitching Coach. Jan Weisberg - Assistant Coach. Jeff Young - Volunteer Coach. Curtis Whitney - Student Assistant Coach.
Style of Play: We are very aggressive offensively trying to put pressure on the defense with the steal and hit and run. During Keith Madison's 20 years at Kentucky we have developed a good reputation for developing pitcher sending more to the major league than any SEC during that time.

University of Louisville

Student Activities Center
Louisville, KY 40292
Coach: Lelo Prado

NCAA I
Cardinal/Red, Black, White
Phone: (502) 852-0103
Fax: (502) 852-4932

ACADEMIC

Type: 4 Yr., Public, Liberal Arts, Coed, Engineering
Religion: Non-Affiliated
Web-site: http://www.louisville.edu/
Student/Faculty Ratio: 12:1
Undergraduate Enrollment: 23,000
Scholarships/Academic: Yes **Athletic:** Yes

Founded: 1798
Campus Housing: Yes
SAT/ACT/GPA: 820/ 17
Male/Female Ratio: 48:52
Graduate Enrollment: 4,000
Fin Aid: Yes

Total Expenses by: Year **In State:** $ 6,570 **Out of State:** $ 11,090
Degrees Conferred: AA, AAS, BA, BS, BFA, MA, MS, MBA, MFA, PhD, JD (170 Degrees)
Programs of Study: Business, Dentistry, Engineering, Medicine, Sports Administration

ATHLETIC PROFILE

Conference Affiliation: Conference USA
Program Profile: Our program is on the rise with Lelo Prado as a head coach. He won 2 NCAA Division II National Championships at the University of Tampa. Our home facility is Cardinal Stadium which has a seating capacity of 22,000.
History: We began in 1909 and Division I play began in 1912. Hall of Fame Coach John Heldman (1937-65) had coached 28 years and has a .500 winning percentage or better. Former Coach Gene Baker had the most wins in his 1st 3 years (87).
Achievements: ABCA Coach of the Year Division I in 1992 and 1993; 3 trips to the World Series; 7 straight Regional Tournaments at Tampa; had 17 All-Americans at Tampa and 8 Spartans were drafted, including New York Yankees 1 Baseman Tino Matinez.
Coaching: Lelo Prado - Head Coach. Brian Mundorf - Assistant Coach. Larry Owens - Assistant Coach. Keith Chester - Assistant Coach.
Style of Play: Aggressive - hard-nosed, get after your opponent when stepping between the lines.

Western Kentucky University

1 Big Red Way
Bowling Green, KY 42101
Coach: Joel Murrie
Email: joel.murrie@wku.edu

NCAA I
Hilltoppers/Red, White
Phone: (502) 745-6023
Fax: (502) 745-3444

ACADEMIC

Founded: 1906
Religion: Non-Affiliated
Web-site: http://www.wku.edu/
Student/Faculty Ratio: 20:1
Undergraduate Enrollment: 12,654
Scholarships/Academic: Yes **Athletic:** Yes
Total Expenses by: Year **In State:** $ 5,480

Type: 4 Yr., Public, Coed
Campus Housing: Yes
SAT/ACT/GPA: 890/ 18
Male/Female Ratio: 40:60
Graduate Enrollment: 2,067
Fin Aid: Yes
Out of State: $ 9,210

Degrees Conferred: AAS, BA, BS, BFA, MS, MA
Programs of Study: Accounting, Advertising, Anthropology, Biochemistry, Biology, Botany, Communications, Computer Science, Creative Writing, Economics, Education, Engineering, Environmental Science, Finance, Fine Arts, Journalism, Mathematics, Liberal Arts, Library Science, Physical Science, Medical Technology, Religion, Social Science

ATHLETIC PROFILE

Conference Affiliation: Sun Belt Conference
Program Profile: Nick Denes Field is the home field of the Hilltoppers and their Spring season runs from February 14 through May 16. The field is natural grass with a seating capacity of 1,050 and has a dimensions of 330 down the lines, 400 in the center and the alleys are 370.
History: The program began in 1910 , has an overall record of 1167-929-10 during those years and has a .555 winning percentage. For the past 18 years, WKU has been guided by the same coach, Joel Murrie. He has compiled a 566-437-5 record including an NCAA Appearance in 1980.
Achievements: Ohio Valley Conference Coach of the Year in 1980; Ohio Valley Conference Coach of the Year North Division in 1981; Sun Belt Conference Coach of the Year in 1985; Ohio Valley Conference Champion in 1980. Players drafted in 1997 were Catcher Erick Kosa, who was drafted in 21st round by the Indians, Josh Patton signed contract with team in Northern Independent League and Dan Grice played with the Independent team in California.
Coaching: Joel Murrie, Head Coach, is entering 20 years as head coach. He was named numerous times Ohio Valley Conference Coach of the Year. He compiled a record of 566-437-5. Dan Mosier - Assistant Coach. Clyde Keller - Assistant Coach.
Style of Play: The team rely on the strong pitching, defense and timely hitting to win the ball games.

LOUISIANA

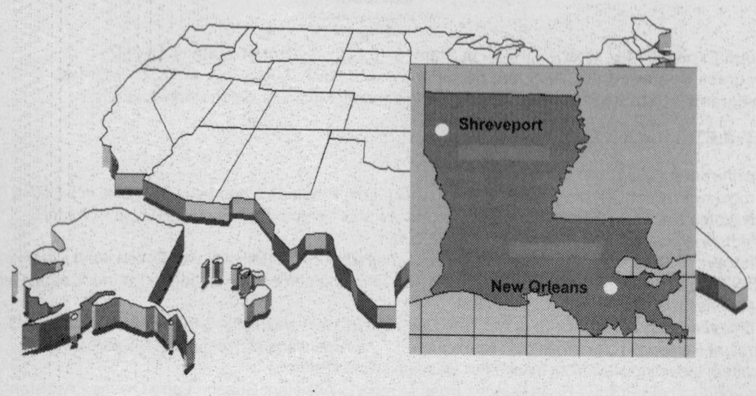

SCHOOL	CITY	AFFILIATION 99	PAGE
Bossier Parish Community College	Bossier City	NJCAA	357
Centenary College	Shreveport	NCAA I	357
Delgado Community College	New Orleans	NJCAA	358
Grambling State University	Grambling	NCAA I	358
Louisiana College	Pineville	NAIA	359
Louisiana State U and A & M C	Baton Rouge	NCAA I	359
Louisiana State University-Shreveport	Shreveport	NAIA	360
Louisiana Tech University	Ruston	NCAA I	361
Loyola University - New Orleans	New Orleans	NAIA	361
McNeese State University	Lake Charles	NCAA I	362
Nicholls State University	Thibodaux	NCAA I	363
Northeast Louisiana University	Monroe	NCAA I	363
Northwestern State University- Louisiana	Natchitoches	NCAA I	364
Southern University	Baton Rouge	NCAA I	365
Southeastern Louisiana University	Hammond	NCAA I	366
Tulane University	New Orleans	NCAA I	366
University of New Orleans	New Orleans	NCAA I	367
University of Southwestern Louisiana	Lafayette	NCAA I	367

Bossier Parish Community College

2719 Airline Drive
Bossier City, LA 71111
Coach: Jay Artigues

NJCAA
Cavaliers/Maroon, Gold
Phone: (318) 746-5233
Fax: (318) 742-8664

ACADEMIC

Type: 2 Yr., Public, Jr. College, Coed
Campus Housing: Yes
Undergraduate Enrollment: 4,400
Student/Faculty Ratio: 35:65
Scholarships/Academic: Yes **Athletic:** Yes **Fin Aid:** Yes
Total Expenses by: Year **In State:** $ 1,200 **Out of State:** $ Varies
Degrees Conferred: Associates
Programs of Study: Contact school for programs of study.

ATHLETIC PROFILE

Estimated Number of Baseball Scholarships: 24
Conference Affiliation: Mississippi-Lou Conference
Program Profile: We play on natural grass surface with measurements of 330 down the lines, 380 in the gaps and 400 to the center.
History: The program is seven years old.
Coaching: Jay Artigues, Head Coach, is entering his 1st year with the program. Brian St. Andre - Assistant Coach.
Roster for 1998 team/In State: 32 **Out of State:** 5 **Out of Country:** 1
Total Number of Varsity/Jr. Varsity: 35 **Percent of Graduation:** 0
Number of Seniors on 1998 Team: **Number of Sophomores on 1998 Team:** 7
Freshmen Receiving Fin Aid/Athletic: 18 **Baseball Camp Dates:** December 28-30
Number of Fall Games: 20 **Number of Spring Games:** 57
Positions Needed for 1999/2000: Pitcher, 1st Base, 3rd Base
Schedule: Meridian, Eastern Oklahoma

Centenary College

2911 Centenary Blvd.
Shreveport, LA 71134-1188
Coach: Ed McCann

NCAA I
Gentlemen/Maroon, White
Phone: (318) 869-5095
Fax: (318) 869-5154

ACADEMIC

Founded: 1825
Type: 4 Yr., Private, Liberal Arts, Coed
Religion: Methodist
Campus Housing: Yes
Web-site: http://www.centenary.edu/
SAT/ACT/GPA: 900/22
Student/Faculty Ratio: 11:1
Male/Female Ratio: 48:52
Undergraduate Enrollment: 755
Graduate Enrollment: 165
Scholarships/Academic: Yes **Athletic:** Yes **Fin Aid:** Yes
Total Expenses by: Year **In State:** $ 16,000 **Out of State:** $ Varies
Degrees Conferred: BA, BS, MA, MS, MBA
Programs of Study: Accounting, Art, Art Administration, Biblical Studies, Biochemistry, Biology, Biophysics, Business Administration, Chemistry, Communications, Computer Science, Dance, Earth Science, Economics, Education, Elementary Education, Engineering and Applied Science, English, French, Geology, Health Education, Health Science, Physical Therapy, Physics, Political Science, Predentistry, Prelaw, Premed, Prevet, Psychology, Religion, Science Education, Secondary Education, Social Science, Spanish, Speech Pathology, Theatre, Voice

ATHLETIC PROFILE

Estimated Number of Baseball Scholarships: 6.5

Conference Affiliation: Trans America Athletic Conference
Program Profile: We are in second tier Division I. New facilities are in the works. Our season runs from February through May. The team plays all their home games at Centenary Park, a natural grass field with a capacity of 1,000. The field measures 325' down the right and left field lines and 355' to dead center. Camps are a real part of the program. We recruite nationwide.
History: The Gents baseball program began in the early 1900's and is still going strong today. In 1990, Centenary won 40 games and we were ranked 40th by Collegiate Baseball. Centenary has won the TAAC Western Division title four times since 1988 and finished 2nd in the TAAC Tournament twice since 1992.
Achievements: Twenty former Gent players have been drafted by the major leagues. We won the TAAC Western Division Title four times since 1988 and finished second at the TAAC Tournament twice since 1992.
Coaching: Ed McCann, Head Coach, is entering his 1st season with the program. Daryl Hondelson, Justin Kern and Scott Leach - Assistant Coaches.
Roster for 1998 team/In State: 9 **Out of State:** 28 **Out of Country:** 1
Total Number of Varsity/Jr. Varsity: 38 **Percent of Graduation:** 85%
Number of Seniors on 1998 Team: 10 **Number of Sophomores on 1998 Team:** 4
Most Recent Record: 21 - 35 - 0 **Number of Spring Games:** 56
Positions Needed for 1999/2000: Center, Middleinfielder, Outfielder, Pitcher
Baseball Camp Dates: December 12-13; 29-31 Summer TBA
Schedule: LSU, Arkansas, TCU, University Central Florida, NorthEast Louisiana, NorthWestern
Style of Play: Play the short game with the occasional long ball. Put runners in motion to make things happen.

Delgado Community College

501 City Park Avenue
New Orleans, LA 70119
Coach: Joseph Scheuermann

NJCAA
Dolphins/Green, Gold
Phone: (504) 483-1959
Fax: (504) 483-4895

ACADEMIC

Founded: 1921 **Type:** 2 Yr., Jr. College, Coed
Student/Faculty Ratio: 18:1 **Male/Female Ratio:** 38:62
Undergraduate Enrollment: 14,950 **Graduate Enrollment:** None
Scholarships/Academic: No **Athletic:** Yes **Fin Aid:** Yes
Total Expenses by: Year **In State:** $ 1,200 **Out of State:** $ 2,700
Degrees Conferred: Associate
Programs of Study: Aircraft/Missile Maintenance, Architectural, Art, Automotive, Business, Commercial Art, Computer, Criminal, Dental, Education, Electrical/Electronics, Engineering, Fire Science, Industrial Design, Interior Design, Liberal Arts, Machine/Tool, Medical, Music, Nursing

ATHLETIC PROFILE

Conference Affiliation: Mississippi-Louis Conference

Grambling State University

Box 868
Grambling, LA 71245
Coach: Wilbert Ellis

NCAA I
Tigers/Black, Gold
Phone: (318) 274-2218
Fax: (318) 274-2761

ACADEMIC

Founded: 1901 **Type:** 4 Yr., Public, Coed
SAT/ACT/GPA: 700avg/17avg **Campus Housing:** Yes
Student/Faculty Ratio: 21:1 **Male/Female Ratio:** 42:58

Undergraduate Enrollment: 8,150 **Graduate Enrollment:** 575
Scholarships/Academic: Yes **Athletic:** Yes **Fin Aid:** Yes
Total Expenses by: Year **In State:** $ 5,600 **Out of State:** $ 7,600
Degrees Conferred: ,AS, BA, BS, MA, MS
Programs of Study: Accounting, Anthropology, Art, Automotive, Biological Science, Business Administration, Computer, Construction, Criminal Justice, Cardiopulmonary, Construction, Cytotechnology, Drafting, Economics, Education, Geography, History, journalism, Mathematics, Medical, Music, political Science, Psychology, Public, Radio/Television, Recreation/Secondary/Special Education, Speech/Languages, Hearing Specialist, Theatre

ATHLETIC PROFILE

Conference Affiliation: SouthWestern Athletic Conference

Louisiana College

Box 566
Pineville, LA 71359
Coach: Randy Dietz

NAIA
Wildcats/Orange, Blue
Phone: (318) 487-7131
Fax: (318) 487-7174

ACADEMIC

Founded: 1906 **Type:** 4 Yr., Private, Coed
SAT/ACT/GPA: 800/20 **Campus Housing:** Yes
Student/Faculty Ratio: 17:1 **Male/Female Ratio:** 37:63
Undergraduate Enrollment: 983 **Graduate Enrollment:** None
Scholarships/Academic: Yes **Athletic:** Yes **Fin Aid:** Yes
Total Expenses by: Year **In State:** $ 10,000 **Out of State:** $ 10,000
Degrees Conferred: AS, BA, BS, BGS, BM, BSN
Programs of Study: Art, Biological, Business, Chemistry, Communications, Criminal Justice, Dramatic Arts, Economics, Elementary Education, Health, History, Management, Math, Medical, Nursing, Philosophy, Preprofessional Programs, Psychology, Public, Religion, Science, Secondary

ATHLETIC PROFILE

Conference Affiliation: Gulf Coast Athletic Conference
Program Profile: Billy Allgood Field has lights, bleachers, natural turf and seats approximately 300. Facilities include a weight room & 5 hitting tunnels. We play a Fall program & a Spring schedule.
History: Our program was revived in 1970. We play an extremely tough schedule. Our most outstanding win was against the defending NCAA champs. In 1995, LSU scored 7-5 in Baton Rouge.
Achievements: We won conference and reprensented conference regional tourney in 1987. Eight former players play professional baseball.

Louisiana State University and A and M C

P.O. Box 25095
Baton Rouge, LA 70894
Coach: Skip Bertman

NCAA I
Tigers/Purple, Gold
Phone: (504) 388-4148
Fax: (504) 388-4066

ACADEMIC

Founded: 1860 **Type:** 4 Yr., Public, Coed
Religion: All Denominations **Campus Housing:** Yes
Web-site: http://sports.lsu.edu/wsoccer.htm **SAT/ACT/GPA:** 910 min/19 min/2.0
Student/Faculty Ratio: 18:1 **Male/Female Ratio:** 2:1
Undergraduate Enrollment: 35,000 **Graduate Enrollment:** ?
Scholarships/Academic: Yes **Athletic:** Yes **Fin Aid:** Yes

Total Expenses by: Year **In State:** $ 6,539 **Out of State:** $ 10,439
Degrees Conferred: Bachelors, Masters, PhD, Professional
Programs of Study: Bachelor of Science, Bachelor of Science and Forestry, Bachelor of Arts, Bachelor of Science, Bachelor of Science in Geology, Bachelor of Architecture, Bachelor Fine Arts, Bachelor of Interior Design, Bachelor of Landscape Architecture, Bachelor of Science in Biological Enginering, Chemical Engineering, Civil Engineering, Construction Management, Electrical Engineering, Bachelor in General Studies, Bachelor of Arts in Mass Communications, and various Masters Degree.

ATHLETIC PROFILE

Conference Affiliation: Southern Conference
Program Profile: We play on a natural grass field. Our stadium has a seating capacity of 7,006. It has a 56-game regular season plus SEC and NCAA Tournaments. LSU has led the nation in attendance in the past two seasons. We drew over 250,000 fans in 1997.
History: Our program began in 1893. LSU has won four College World Series titles in the 1990's. We won six SEC Championships and six 50-win seasons this decade. LSU has the highest all-time win percentage in the NCAA tournament play.
Achievements: Skip Bertman is a five-time National Coach of the Year. LSU has won 12 SEC titles including six in the 1990's. LSU has had 11 first team All-Americans in the last nine seasons. We won 4 National Championships this decade (1991, 1993, 1996, and 1997).
Coaching: Skip Bertman, Head Coach, has been National Coach of the Year five times. Jim Schwankee - Assistant Coach. Dan Canevari - Assistant Coach. Tim Lanier - Volunteer Coach.
Style of Play: Power hitting club set NCAA HR record with 188 homers in 1997; team does not bunt or steal very often, mostly relying on scoring runs in bunches.

Louisiana State University-Shreveport

One University Place
Shreveport, LA 71115-2399
Coach: Kit Laird

NAIA
Pilots/Navy, Gold
Phone: (318) 798-4109
Fax: (318) 798-4179

ACADEMIC

Founded: 1965
Type: 4 Yr., Public, Coed
SAT/ACT/GPA: 1000+/20
Campus Housing: No
Student/Faculty Ratio: 19:1
Male/Female Ratio: 40:60
Undergraduate Enrollment: 3,900
Graduate Enrollment: 575
Scholarships/Academic: Yes **Athletic:** No **Fin Aid:** Yes
Total Expenses by: Year **In State:** $ 2,200 **Out of State:** $ 5,200
Degrees Conferred: BA, BS, MA, MS, MBA, MED
Programs of Study: Accounting, Art, Banking/Finance, Biology, Business, Chemistry, Communications, Computer, Criminal Justice, Economics, Education, English, French, Geography, History, Journalism, Liberal Arts, Management, Marketing, Math, Medical, Physical Education, Physics, Political Scinece, Preprofessional Programs, Psychology, Public, Secondary Education, Social Science, Spanish, Special Education

ATHLETIC PROFILE

Conference Affiliation: Independent Conference
Program Profile: The program is very competitive with other college programs. Our facilities include a natural grass field with dimensions of 335' Left and Right field, 385' in powers allies and 406' Center-Field. We have two batting cages and one indoor batting cage.
History: Our program started in 1990 and we have a 600 winning percentage. In Spring of 1997, we played NCAA Division.
Achievements: Big State Conference Champs in 1997. Made Regional playoffs for the first time in school's history in 1997.

Coaching: Kit Laird, Head Coach, was an assistant at Kansas Newman College in the last five years. Four out of the last five years, our team led the nation in hitting three straight years. Mike Hickok ,Assistant Coach, is on his 1st year and played for the LSUS for the past two years. He led the team in hitting last year with a .430 BA. He also coached for two years at Higland High School in California in 1993-1994.
Style of Play: Very aggressive.

Louisiana Tech University

PO Box 3046
Ruston, LA 71272
Coach: Jeff Richardson

NCAA I
Bulldogs/Red, Blue, White
Phone: (318) 257-4111
Fax: (318) 257-4437

ACADEMIC

Founded: 1894
Type: 2 Yr., Public, Coed
SAT/ACT/GPA: 21avg
Campus Housing: Yes
Student/Faculty Ratio: 26:1
Male/Female Ratio: 54:46
Undergraduate Enrollment: 8,475
Graduate Enrollment: 1,550
Scholarships/Academic: Yes **Athletic:** Yes **Fin Aid:** Yes
Total Expenses by: Year **In State:** $ 5,400 **Out of State:** $ 7,150
Degrees Conferred: AS, BA, BS, BLFA, MA, MS, MBA, MFA
Programs of Study: Accounting, Agricultural, Animal Science, Architecture, Banking and Finance, Botany, Business, Computer, Dietetics, Engineering, Fashion, Forestry, Languages, Geography, Geology, Horticulture, Journalism, Management, Medical, Photography, Physics, Preprofessional Programs, Psychology, Special Education, Speech, Writing, Wildlife, Zoology

ATHLETIC PROFILE

Conference Affiliation: Sun Belt Conference
Program Profile: We are a fully funded Division I. We have a 2,000-seat concrete and brick stadium with a roof, locker rooms and a player's lounge connected to the dugouts. The field is natural grass and has measurements of 320' down the lines, 360' Rt center gap, 370 LT center gap and 395' center field.
History: First year of the program was in 1945. We won 6 NCAA Regional Appearances. Thirteen former Bulldogs have played in the Major Leagues.
Achievements: 8 Conference Championships; 7 All-Americans, 3 Freshman All-Americans, over 30 players drafted.

Loyola University - New Orleans

6363 St Charles Ave
New Orleans, LA 70181
Coach: Don Moreau

NAIA
Wolfpack/Maroon, Gold
Phone: (504) 865-3082
Fax: (504) 865-3081

ACADEMIC

Founded: 1912
Type: 4 Yr., Private, Liberal Arts, Coed
Religion: Catholic
Campus Housing: Yes
Web-site: http://www.loyno.edu
SAT/ACT/GPA: 1040/23/3.53
Student/Faculty Ratio: 10:1
Male/Female Ratio: 60:40
Undergraduate Enrollment: 3,500
Graduate Enrollment: 2,000
Scholarships/Academic: Yes **Athletic:** No **Fin Aid:** Yes
Total Expenses by: Year **In State:** $ 20,060 **Out of State:**
Degrees Conferred: Associate
Programs of Study: Contact school for program of study.

ATHLETIC PROFILE

Conference Affiliation: Gulf Coast Athletic Conference
Program Profile: The nonconference playing season includes NCAA Division I SouthEastern Louisiana, McNeese State, Nicholls State and Southern. We also play NCAA Mississippi College and Millsaps College. Conference action includes Mobile, Springhill College, Belhaven College, Louisiana College and William Carey. Our home Riverview Field is natural grass with 1500 seats.
History: Loyola had a great baseball history under former Head Coach Louis "Rags" Schuerman. The program started in 1924 and ended in 1972 but was reinstated in 1991 under Head Coach Don Moreau. We used to be the best collegiate baseball program in Louisiana until LSU, Tulane and UNO became powers in the 1970s.
Achievements: The Loyola's baseball team has won several championships in the past, including Dixie Conference and Gulf States Conference Championships. Loyola was the 1st Gulf Coast Athletic Conference Championship to go to the NAIA National Tournaments. Zack Boaura, Alan Montreau, John Schroedor and Tom Schwaner have gone to major leagues and over 100 players have played in the minors.
Coaching: Don Moreau, Head Coach,is on his 6th season and was named American Legion 2nd District Eastern Division Coach of the Year twice. Bret Simpson - Assistant Coach.
Style of Play: Conservative on defense, gamble on offense.

McNeese State University

P.O. Box 92724
Lake Charles, LA 70609
Coach: Mike Bianco

NCAA I
Cowboys/Blue, Gold
Phone: (318) 475-5482
Fax: (318) 475-5478

ACADEMIC

Founded: 1939
Type: 4 Yr., Public, Coed
Religion: Non-Affiliated
Campus Housing: Yes
Web-site: http://www.mcneese.edu/
SAT/ACT/GPA: NCAA-req/17
Student/Faculty Ratio: 25:1
Male/Female Ratio: 48:52
Undergraduate Enrollment: 6,000
Graduate Enrollment: 2,000
Scholarships/Academic: Yes **Athletic:** Yes **Fin Aid:** Yes
Total Expenses by: Year **In State:** $ 4,800 **Out of State:** $ 8,342
Degrees Conferred: AA, AS, BA, BS, BM, BMEd, BSN, MS, MA
Programs of Study: Accounting, Agricultural, Animal Science, Architecture, Biological Science, Botany, Broadcasting, Business, Computer, Criminal Justice, Engineering, Ecology, Education, Languages, Forestry, Geology, History, Management, Marketing, Math, Medical, Music, Nursing, Personnel,Management, Petroleum, Physics, Preprofessional Programs, Psychology, Social Science, Speech, Statistics, Wildlife, Zoology

ATHLETIC PROFILE

Estimated Number of Baseball Scholarships: 11.2
Conference Affiliation: Southland Conference
Program Profile: Our stadium has a seating capacity of 2,500 (grandstand), grass field, double wall, indoor batting cages , bull-pens, outside cages and pens, fenced-in complex (wooden) and a 55-ft, digital scoreboard. There is a 1,000 square foot indoor facilitiy that includes an office, a locker room, a meeting room and a lounge.
History: Division I play began in 1954. We joined Southland Conference in 1972. The cowboys have been to three regional tournaments. With state-of-the-art indoor facilities, MSU has been ranked in the top five for pitching and fielding at the end of the season for the last three years.
Achievements: Southland Conference Champs in 1988, Tournament Champs in 1993; Tony Robichaux Coach of the Year in 1988; average 4 players a year to get drafted; 1995 had 9 drafted among the most in the country.

Coaching: Mike Bianco, Head Coach, helped LSU to the College World Series Championship this past season. He was an assistant coach at LSU since 1992. He served as the Tigers third base coach. He graduated from LSU and began his coaching career at NorthWestern State, serving on the staff. Daniel Tomlin, Assistant Coach, played four years at NorthWestern Stateand won 3 conference titles. He was an assistant coach for two years at LSU and won two national championships. Chad Clement and Clint Caruer - Assistant Coaches.
Roster for 1998 team/In State: 10 **Out of State:** 23 **Out of Country:** 0
Total Number of Varsity/Jr. Varsity: 0 **Percent of Graduation:** 70%-80%
Number of Seniors on 1998 Team: 11 **Number of Sophomores on 1998 Team:** 10
Freshmen Receiving Fin Aid/Athletic: 2 **Academic:** 3
Most Recent Record: 30 - 26 - 0 **Number of Spring Games:** 56
Positions Needed for 1999/2000: Pitchers, Catchers, Mid-infielder, Powerful Hitter
Baseball Camp Dates: December 19-23, 4 in June and July
Schedule: LSU, Rice, UCLA, Texas, Baylor, USL
Style of Play: Home runs - hit 73 in 1997 and looking for more 100 in 1998; playing an intense mental game knowing the game better than the other team.

Nicholls State University

PO Box 2032
Thibodaux, LA 70310
Coach: Jim Pizzolatto

NCAA I
Colonels/Red, Grey
Phone: (504) 448-4808
Fax: (504) 448-4814

ACADEMIC

Founded: 1948 **Type:** 4 Yr., Public, Coed
SAT/ACT/GPA: 18avg **Campus Housing:** Yes
Student/Faculty Ratio: 22:1 **Male/Female Ratio:** 41:59
Undergraduate Enrollment: 6,260 **Graduate Enrollment:** 820
Scholarships/Academic: Yes **Athletic:** Yes **Fin Aid:** Yes
Total Expenses by: Year **In State:** $ 5,250 **Out of State:** $ 7,900
Degrees Conferred: AA, AS, BA, BS, MA, MBA
Programs of Study: Allied Health, Business and Management, Business/Office and Marketing/Distribution, Computer Science, Education, Engineering, Home Economics

ATHLETIC PROFILE

Conference Affiliation: Southland Conference
Program Profile: We play a 56-game Spring schedule with a league conference tournament at the end of regular season. Raymond E. Didier Field is an above average facility that features a natural grass surface.
History: The Nicholls State University baseball program has had 29 winning seasons since the program started in 1960. Highlights include being the Division II national runner-up in 1970 and also participating in the D II Regionals four times and D I Regionals twice including 1989 and 1992.
Achievements: The Colonels have also captured four conference championships. Former Colonel players are on major league rosters as of the 1996 season including Darryl Hamilton of Texas, Scott Sanders of San Diego and Mike Moehler of the Oakland A's.
Coaching: Jim Pizzolatto,Head Coach, begins his 1st season at Nicholls State after guiding NAIA power St. Thomas University in Miami (FL) to a 178-67 record in four seasons. Prior to his stint at St. Thomas, Pizzolatto was an assistant at the Univ. of Miami from 1986 to 992 under Ron Fraser.
Style of Play: It will revolve around the team's defense and pitching.

Northeast Louisiana University

Malone Stadium
Monroe, LA 71209
Coach: Ray 'Smoke' Laval
Email: TBA

NCAA I
Indians/Maroon, Gold
Phone: (318) 342-5395
Fax: (318) 342-5367

ACADEMIC

Founded: 1931
Type: 4 Yr., Public, Coed
SAT/ACT/GPA: 20avg
Campus Housing: Yes
Student/Faculty Ratio: 20:1
Male/Female Ratio: 42:58
Undergraduate Enrollment: 10,400
Graduate Enrollment: 1,140
Scholarships/Academic: Yes **Athletic:** Yes **Fin Aid:** Yes
Total Expenses by: Year **In State:** $ 4,600 **Out of State:** $ 6,750
Degrees Conferred: AA, AS, AGS, BA, BS, BFA, BM, BME, MA, MS, MBA
Programs of Study: Accounting, Advertising, Agricultural, Art, Banking and Finance, Biological Science, Broadcasting, Business, Chemistry, Computer, Construction, Criminal Justice, Early Childhood Education, Engineering, Foreign Languages, Geography, Geology, History, Industrial, Information, Insurance, Occupational, Pharmacy, Preprofessioonal Programs, Psychology, Real Estate, Special Education, Speech, Toxicology

ATHLETIC PROFILE

Conference Affiliation: Southland Conference
Program Profile: We have one of the finest facilities in the country. The grand stands seat 2,000. There is an indoor and an outdoor hitting facility, a player's lounge, first class locker rooms with wooden lockers,a picnic area, Etc. Average attendance is 1,200. The field has a natural surface with dimensions of 330-375-330.
History: The program began in 1955 and has won nine conference titles. We appeared in the NCAA Regionals in 1993 and 1995. Coach Laval has turned the program around since his arrival in 1994. He has a record of 129-94 and has won 30 games or more the last three years. He led the team to a 1st conference title in 12 years and an NCAA Appearance in only his 2nd season. In 1996, the team was 41-19 and won the regular season title. It finished 3rd in SLC Tour and was snubbed by the NCAA. We broke 30 school records.
Achievements: 1995 Louisiana Sports writers Coach of the Year; Titles in 1995 and 1996. AA-DJ Loland, Corey Artieta, Corey Taylor and Ben Sheets. Drafted: Shannon Cooley and Denny Bair. Others majors: Chuck Finley and Terry Mathews.
Coaching: Ray Laval, Head Coach, coached 11 years at LSU (6 CWS appearances and 2 national championships. Brad Holland, Assistant Coach, is on his 1st year. He is recruiting coordinator and infield coach and also handles administrative duties. Allen Chance ,Assistant Coach,is on his 5th year and coaches outfielders and first base. He also works with recruiting and has administrative duties. Coach Stacey Wilcox works on field maintenance and assists with the hitters.
Style of Play: Pitch by pitch, high intensity aggressive baseball. Solid fundamentals. Aggressive on the bases.

Northwestern State University - Louisiana

College Avenue, Athletic Fieldhouse
Natchitoches, LA 71497
Coach: John Cohen
NCAA I
Demons/Purple, White
Phone: (318) 357-4139
Fax: (318) 357-4221

ACADEMIC

Founded: 1922
Type: 4 Yr., Public, Coed
Religion: Non-Affiliated
Campus Housing: Yes
Web-site: http://www.nsudemons.com
SAT/ACT/GPA: 17
Student/Faculty Ratio: 17:1
Male/Female Ratio: 45:55
Undergraduate Enrollment: 8,000
Graduate Enrollment: 1,000
Scholarships/Academic: Yes **Athletic:** Yes **Fin Aid:** Yes
Total Expenses by: Year **In State:** $ 5,018 **Out of State:** $ 9,303
Degrees Conferred: AA, AS, BA, BM, BS, MS, MFA

Programs of Study: Accounting, Advertising, Animal Science, Anthropology, Art, Biological Science, Botany, Broadcasting, Business, Dance, Early Childhood Education, Engineering, English, Fine Arts, History, Information, Journalism, Marketing, Management, Math, Medical, Music, Nursing

ATHLETIC PROFILE

Estimated Number of Baseball Scholarships: 3
Conference Affiliation: Southland Conference
Program Profile: Facilities feature an astro-turf infield with a Bermuda outfielder.
History: The Demon baseball program is over 50 years old.
Achievements: 1998 Southland Conference Coach of the Year; 6 out of 8 Regular Season Conference Titles; 1998 four drafted.
Coaching: John Cohen, Head Coach, started his 1st year with the program. He was formerly assistant coach for seven years at Missouri with a record of 40-20 at NSU. Sean McCann, Assistant Coach, started his 2nd year with the program. Bill Wright and Andrew Sawyer ,Assistant Coaches, both started their 1st year with the program.
Roster for 1998 team/In State: 14 **Out of State:** 15 **Out of Country:** 1
Total Number of Varsity/Jr. Varsity: 30 **Percent of Graduation:** 70%
Number of Seniors on 1998 Team: 6 **Number of Sophomores on 1998 Team:** 0
Most Recent Record: 40 - 20 - 0 **Number of Spring Games:** 56
Positions Needed for 1999/2000: Pitcher, Mid-infielders, Outfielder
Baseball Camp Dates: Winter and Summer camp dates
Schedule: Louisiana State University, Rice, UCLA, Alabama, McNeese State, Lamar
Style of Play: Speed and quickness; hit and run, steal, move runners. Solid defense; we have some rebuilding to do. Good combination of pitching and hitting to win games. NorthWestern Louisiana focuses on playing solid defense with an aggressive hitters and fundamentally sound pitching staff.

Southern University

P.O. Box 10850
Baton Rouge, LA 70813
Coach: Roger Cador

NCAA I
Jaguars/Blue, Gold
Phone: (504) 771-3170
Fax: (504) 771-4400

ACADEMIC

Founded: 1880 **Type:** 4 Yr., Public, Coed
SAT/ACT/GPA: 700avg/17avg **Campus Housing:** Yes
Student/Faculty Ratio: 20:1 **Male/Female Ratio:** 1:1
Undergraduate Enrollment: 10,000 **Graduate Enrollment:** 1,200
Scholarships/Academic: Yes **Athletic:** Yes **Fin Aid:** Yes
Total Expenses by: Year **In State:** $ 5,110 **Out of State:** $ 7,600
Degrees Conferred: AA, AS, AAS, BA, BS, BM, BME, MA, MS
Programs of Study: Accounting, Agricultural, Animal Science, Art, Biological Science, Broadcasting, Business, Cardiopulmonary, Chemistry, Cloting/Textiles, Communications, Computer, Cytotechnology, Dietetics, Economics, Education, Health, History, Journalism, Marketing, Math

ATHLETIC PROFILE

Conference Affiliation: SouthWestern Athletic Conference (SWAC)
Program Profile: We play our home games at Lee-Hines Field. The field was opened in the Spring of 1991. Our facilities are on campus. We play on natural grass, the stadium seats 600 and has dimensions of 330-LF, 365-alleys, 400-CF and 320-RF.
History: The program, which began in 1949, has won 67 games in 46 years with 24 conference titles (the most by any of the conferenc members).
Achievements: Coach of the Year Honors in 1987, 1989, 1992, and 1995; 5 Conference Championships in 1987, 1988, 1991, 1993; All-Americans were Kenneth Clark in 1987, Wilson Bennett in 1992; 20 players drafted to the pros.
Style of Play: Fundamentally sound - take what the other team gives you. Stay out of the big inning on defense. Keep the double play in order. At the plate, be aggressive.

Southeastern Louisiana University

PO Box 309, SLU - Mailing Address
Hammond, LA 70402
Coach: Greg Marten

NCAA I
Lions/Green, Gold
Phone: (504) 549-2253
Fax: (504) 549-3495

ACADEMIC

Founded: 1925
Religion: Non-Affiliated
Web-site: http://www.selu.edu/athletics
Student/Faculty Ratio: 32:1
Undergraduate Enrollment: 13,640
Scholarships/Academic: Yes **Athletic:** Yes
Total Expenses by: Year **In State:** $ 4,379

Type: 4 Yr., Public, Coed
Campus Housing: Yes
SAT/ACT/GPA: Open Admission/
Male/Female Ratio: 38:62
Graduate Enrollment: 1,690
Fin Aid: Yes
Out of State: $ 2,615

Degrees Conferred: AA, AS, AAS, BA, BS, BGS, MA, MS
Programs of Study: Biology, Chemistry, Physics, Computer Science, Communications, Theatre, English, Foreign Languages, General Studies, History, Government, Math, Music, Psychology, Sociology, Social Work, Criminal Justice, Visual Arts, Accounting, Economics, Business Education, Teacher Education, Counseling, Family Study, Education Leadership, Kinesiology, Health Studies, Special Education, Nursing

ATHLETIC PROFILE

Conference Affiliation: The Southland Conference
Program Profile: We are a Division I baseball program. Our stadium has seats 3,000 (1,000 chairback & box seats) & the field is natural grass. Our season was February 6 thru May 16 of 1998.
History: The program began in 1935 and we won 18 Conference Championships. In 1975 Division II College World Series, we finished 3rd in the nation. In 1980 , we went to D I and in 1992-1994 we went to Division NCAA Regionals.
Achievements: Our coach was TransAmerica Athletic Conference Coach of the Year in 1992 and 1993. We were TAAC Champions in 1992 and 1994. Since Greg Martin's tenure at SLU, there were 21 players that have played or are still playing pro baseball. Jeff Williams was (LHP) in 1996 and Mizuno was 3rd team All-American.
Coaching: Greg Marten, Head Coach, is a 1975 graduate of SLU and a two-time TAAC Coach of the Year. He started coaching at SLU from 1991 to the present. John Brechtel, Assistant Coach, started in 1991 as a hitting coach. Mark Gosnell ,Assistant Coach, started in 1992 as a defensive coach. Mark Willoughby, Assistant Coach, started in 1996 as a pitching coach.
Style of Play: Aggressive offensively. We hit for power (90 home runs in 1997). We play pretty much by the book.

Tulane University

James W Wilson Ctr for Athletics
New Orleans, LA 70118
Coach: Rick Jones

NCAA I
Green Wave/Olive Green, Sky Blue
Phone: (504) 862-8239
Fax: (504) 865-5512

ACADEMIC

Founded: 1834
Student/Faculty Ratio: 11:1
Web-site: http://www.tulane.edu
Undergraduate Enrollment: 6,400
Scholarships/Academic: Yes **Athletic:** Yes
Total Expenses by: Year **In State:** $ 30,000

Type: 4 Yr., Private, Coed
Campus Housing: Yes
SAT/ACT/GPA: 1289/29/3.6
Graduate Enrollment: 5,000
Fin Aid: Yes
Out of State: $ 30,000

Degrees Conferred: Associate
Programs of Study: Contact school for program of study.

ATHLETIC PROFILE

Conference Affiliation: Conference USA
Program Profile: We do a NCAA 56-game regular season schedule from the 2nd week in February to the 2nd week in May. We play at Turchin Stadium on Tulane campus in New Orleans. Turchin Stadium was renovated in 1997, has a natural grass field and seats 5,000
History: We began in 1893. In 1996, we will be in our 103rd year of Tulane baseball. Green Wave has been to eight NCAA regionals in the past 16 years. Tulane began to play Conference USA in 1996. We have been to the NCAA six of the last 12 years.
Achievements: Rick Jones has 11 Coach of the Year awards; 1996 Conference USA Tournament Champs; 1997 Conference USA Regular Season Champs; Jason Navarro was named All-American.
Coaching: Rick Jones, Head Coach, has a 73-50 (.594) record in two seasons at Tulane. He was NAIA Coach of the Year at Elon College in 1989. Brian Ferrae - Assistant Coach/Recruiting Coordinator. Jim Schlossnagle - Assistant/pitching coach. Ron Cooper - Assistant Coach.

University of New Orleans

Lakefront Arena - Athletic Dept
New Orleans, LA 70148
Coach: Tom Schwaner

NCAA I
Privateers/Royal, Grey
Phone: (504) 280-7021
Fax: (504) 280-7240

ACADEMIC

Founded: 1958
Type: 4 Yr., Public, Coed
Religion: Non-Affiliated
Campus Housing: Yes
Web-site: http://www.uno.edu
SAT/ACT/GPA: 950/20
Student/Faculty Ratio: 16:1
Male/Female Ratio: 43:57
Undergraduate Enrollment: 10,999
Graduate Enrollment: 3,738
Scholarships/Academic: Yes **Athletic:** Yes **Fin Aid:** Yes
Total Expenses by: Year **In State:** $ 8,145 **Out of State:** $ 10,937
Degrees Conferred: BA, BS, BGS, MA, MS, MBA, PhD
Programs of Study: Accounting, Anthropology, Banking/Finance, Biological, Business, Communications, Computer, Dental, Economics, Education

ATHLETIC PROFILE

Conference Affiliation: Sun Belt Conference
Program Profile: We play on a natural turf field that has a seats 5,000. We hosted Milwaukee Brewers AAA affiliate for 4 years ending in the Summer of 1996.
History: In 1973, we were a Division II Regionals. In 1974, we were at Division II World Series. In 1977, 1979, 1980, 1981, 1982, 1984, 1985, 1987, 1988, and 1996 we were at D I Regionals. In 1984, we were Division World Series.
Achievements: We were 1974 Division II South Regular Champs. We were 1978 and 1979 Sun Belt Conference champs. In 198 ,Division I South Regional Champs; 1989 American South Conference Champs through 1996 from 1972; 78 players drafted; 9 getting to the major leagues.
Coaching: Tom Schwaner, Head Coach, was 1989 American South Conference Coach of the Year. He was 21 years at UNO, 12 as head coach. He played professionally. Jeff Twitty ,Pitching Coach, pitched for Royals (1980 AL championship team). Jim Boehne ,Assistant Coach, played professionally. All three coaches have combined 37 years of Division I coaching.
Style of Play: This year which is 1997 is offensive type team.

University of Southwestern Louisiana

201 Reinhardt Drive
Lafayette, LA 70506-4297
Coach: Tony Robichaux

NCAA I
Ragin' Cajuns/Red, White
Phone: (318) 482-6189
Fax: (318) 482-6649

ACADEMIC

Founded: 1898
Type: 4 Yr., Public, Coed
SAT/ACT/GPA: Open Admission
Campus Housing: Yes
Student/Faculty Ratio: 15:1
Male/Female Ratio: 48:52
Undergraduate Enrollment: 14,500
Graduate Enrollment: 2,500
Scholarships/Academic: Yes **Athletic:** Yes **Fin Aid:** Yes
Total Expenses by: Year **In State:** $ 4,536 **Out of State:** $ 8,136
Degrees Conferred: BS, BA
Programs of Study: Accounting, Advertising, Agricultural, Animal Science, Anthropology, Banking/Finance, Broadcasting, Business, Chemistry, Communications, Community Services, Computer, Criminal Justice, Dance, Dietetics, Dramatics Arts, Economics, Education, English, Fashion Design, Fine Arts, French, Geography, Horticulture, Industrial, Journlisn, Land Use, Nursing, Office, Preprofessional Programs, Special Education, Speech, Statistis, Telecommunications, Urban Studies, Wildlife Management

ATHLETIC PROFILE

Conference Affiliation: Sun Belt Conference
Program Profile: Stadium: M.L. 'Tigue' Moore field has seats 5,000 and is natural grass. There are box seats down both lines. It has a state of the art club house behind the 3rd base dugout.
History: We were American South Champs in 1988, 1989, 1990, and 1991. We were Sun Belt Champs in 1997. We were at NCAA Regionals in 1988, 1990, 1991, 1992, and 1997. We were at Regional Finals in 1991.
Achievements: All-Americans: Dado Ramos, Gary Hought, Javi De Jesus, Trey Poland, and Cody Robbins. Players in majors: Ron Guidry, Donne Wall, Xavier Hernandez, and Chris Howard.
Coaching: Tony Robichaux, Head Coach, is the winningest coach in McNeese State history. He was 1997 Sun Belt Coach of the Year and LA-Coach of the Year. Wade Simoneaux was former coach of LA. All-Star Baseball Club Teams were regular qualifiers for Connie UACK World Series. Anthony Babineaux played for the USL during 1991 and 1992 Regional seasons.
Style of Play: "Pitching and defense".

MAINE

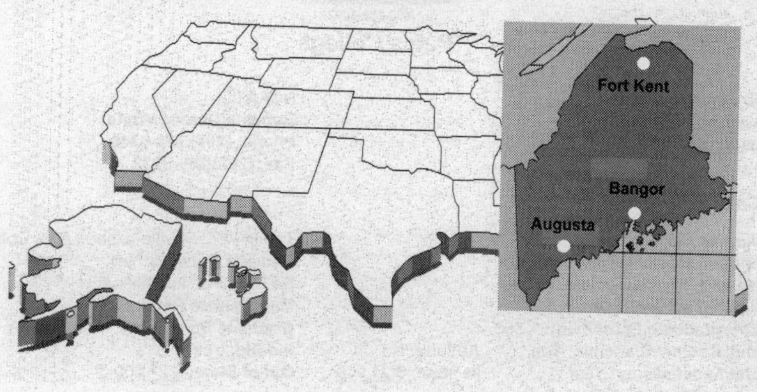

SCHOOL	CITY	AFFILIATION 99	PAGE
Bates College	Lewiston	NCAA III	370
Bowdoin College	Brunswick	NCAA III	370
Colby College	Waterville	NCAA III	370
Husson College	Bangor	NAIA	371
Saint Joseph's College	Windham	NAIA	372
University of Maine	Orono	NCAA I	372
University of Maine - Farmington	Farmington	NCAA III\NAIA	373
University of Maine - Presque Isle	Presque Isle	NAIA	373
University of Southern Maine	Gorham	NCAA III	374

Bates College

130 Central Avenue
Lewiston, ME 04240
Coach: Robert Flynn

NCAA III
Bobcats/Garnet, White
Phone: (207) 786-6348
Fax: (207) 786-8232

ACADEMIC

Founded: 1855
Religion: Non-Affiliated
Web-site: http://www.bates.edu/
Student/Faculty Ratio: 11:1
Undergraduate Enrollment: 1,550
Scholarships/Academic: Yes **Athletic:** No
Total Expenses by: Year **In State:** $ 21,000
Degrees Conferred: Bachelors

Type: 4 Yr., Private, Liberal Arts, Coed
Campus Housing: Yes
SAT/ACT/GPA: Optional
Male/Female Ratio: 50:50
Graduate Enrollment: None
Fin Aid: Yes
Out of State: $ 21,000

Programs of Study: African Studies, American Studies, Anthropology, Art, Biochemistry, Biology, Chemistry, Classics, Economics, English, French, Geology, German, History, Interdisciplinary Studies, Mathematics, Medieval Studies, Music, Philosohy, Physics, Political Science, Psychology, Religion, Russian, Social Science, Spanish, Speech, Theatre, Women's Studies

ATHLETIC PROFILE

Conference Affiliation: ECAC, NIESCAC

Bowdoin College

Morrell Gymnasium
Brunswick, ME 04011
Coach: Michael Connelly

NCAA III
Polar Bears/White
Phone: (207) 725-3751
Fax: (207) 725-3019

ACADEMIC

Founded: 1795
Undergraduate Enrollment: 1,605
SAT/ACT/GPA: No standarized tests required/
Student/Faculty Ratio: 11:1
Scholarships/Academic: No **Athletic:** No
Total Expenses by: Year **In State:** $ 31,950
Degrees Conferred: BA

Type: 4 Yr., Private, Liberal Arts, Coed
Campus Housing: Yes
Web-site: http://www.bowdoin.edu/
Male/Female Ratio: 50:50
Fin Aid: Yes
Out of State: $ 31,950

Programs of Study: Fine Arts, Archeology, Art History, Classics, English, French, German, History, Music, Philosophy, Religion, Romance, Russian, Spanish, Studio Art, Biology, Mathematics, Biochemistry, Chemistry, Physics, Natural Sciences, Geology, Computer Science, Chemical Physics, Physics, Sociology, African Studies, Asian Studies, Environmental Studies, Latin American

ATHLETIC PROFILE

Conference Affiliation: NESCAC, ECAC

Colby College

150 Drive Hill Drive
Waterville, ME 04091
Coach: Tom Dexter

NCAA III
White Mules/Blue, Grey
Phone: (207) 872-3369
Fax: (207) 872-3420

ACADEMIC

Founded: 1813
Religion: Non-Affiliated
Web-site: http://www.colby.edu/
Student/Faculty Ratio: 11:1
Undergraduate Enrollment: 1,750
Scholarships/Academic: No **Athletic:** No
Total Expenses by: Year **In State:** $ 27,900
Degrees Conferred: BA
Type: 4 Yr., Private, Liberal Arts, Coed
Campus Housing: Yes
SAT/ACT/GPA: 640/27
Male/Female Ratio: 50:50
Graduate Enrollment: None
Fin Aid: Yes
Out of State: $ 27,900
Programs of Study: 49 Majors- largest English, Economics, Psychology, Government, Biology

ATHLETIC PROFILE

Conference Affiliation: NESCAC

Husson College

One College Circle
Bangor, ME 04401
Coach: John Kolasinski

NAIA
Braves/Green, Gold
Phone: (207) 941-7700
Fax: (207) 941-7841

ACADEMIC

Founded: 1898
Religion: Non-Affiliated
Web-site: Not Available
Student/Faculty Ratio: 15:1
Undergraduate Enrollment: 1,000
Scholarships/Academic: Yes **Athletic:** No
Total Expenses by: Year **In State:** $ 14,000
Degrees Conferred: AS, BS, MS
Type: 4 Yr., Private, Coed
Campus Housing: Yes
SAT/ACT/GPA: 740+
Male/Female Ratio: 40:60
Graduate Enrollment: 200
Fin Aid: Yes
Out of State: $ 14,000
Programs of Study: Accounting, Banking and Finance, Business Administration, Computer Science, Court Reporting, Education, Management Information Systems, Marketing, Nursing, Physical Therapy, Personnel Management, Professional Studies, Secretarial Studies, Sport Management

ATHLETIC PROFILE

Conference Affiliation: Maine Athletic Conference
Program Profile: We have a Fall schedule, a 40 game Spring schedule and a Florida trip. We play 75% of home games at a million dollar facility built by author Stephen King.
History: Our program began in 1958. We were New England Champions in 1993 and 1995 and Runner-Ups in 1990 and 1991.
Achievements: In the past seven years, 2 New England Champions in 1993 and 1995; Runner-Up 1990 and 1991; District Champions in 1973, 1975, 1993; 1990 New England Coach of the Year; 3 Honorable Mention All-Americans; 14 players All-New England in the past four years; 30 All-England; 3 All-Area.
Coaching: John Kolasinski, Head Coach, started his 9th year at Husson. He was NAIA District Coach of the Year in 1995, 1994, and 1990. He was NAIA Northern Regional Coach of the Year in 1994 and NAIA District 5 Baseball Chairman. He is also National Rater and President of Eastern Maine Amateur Baseball League.
Roster for 1998 team/In State: 18 **Out of State:** 8 **Out of Country:** 1
Total Number of Varsity/Jr. Varsity: 27 **Percent of Graduation:** 73%
Number of Seniors on 1998 Team: 2 **Most Recent Record:** 24 - 19 - 0
Number of Fall Games: 9 **Number of Spring Games:** 40
Positions Needed for 1999/2000: Infielder, Centerfielder
Schedule: Point Loma Nazarene, Biola, Southern California, Wilmington College, Dominican College, Thomas College, Colby College, Bowdoin College, Master's College
Style of Play: Aggressive like to run and hit and run, corner men must hit power.

Saint Joseph's College

278 White Bridge Road
Windham, ME 04084
Coach: Will Sanborn
Email: rplourde@sjcme.edu

NAIA
Monks/Royal Blue, White
Phone: (207) 893-6672
Fax: (207) 893-7860

ACADEMIC

Founded: 1912
Religion: Roman Catholic
Web-site: http://www.sjcme.edu/
Student/Faculty Ratio: 15:1
Scholarships/Academic: Yes **Athletic:** No
Total Expenses by: Year **In State:** $ 17,365
Degrees Conferred: Associate

Type: 4 Yr., Private, Liberal Arts, Coed
Campus Housing: No
Undergraduate Enrollment: 1,310
Male/Female Ratio: Unknown
Fin Aid: Yes
Out of State: $ 17,365

Programs of Study: Education, Business Education, History, Mathematics, Prevet, Premed, Communications, Education, Elementary Education, Life Science, Natural Science, Nursing, Physical Education, Philosophy, Psychology

ATHLETIC PROFILE

Conference Affiliation: Maine Athletic Conference
Program Profile: We have both Fall and Spring baseball. Our 45 game schedule versus Division I, II and III opponents. Our baseball field is lighted and has a wooden fence, an electronic scoreboard, brick dugouts, a press box, a locker room, double batting cages and 8 warm-up pitching mounds.
History: We won 6 NAIA District 5 Baseball Championships since 1986.
Achievements: Will Sanborn won the Al Card Sportmanship Award in 1993 from the Collegiate Baseball Umpires Association.
Coaching: Will Sanborn, Head Coach, is a 1986 graduate of Saint Joseph's College. Ron Plourde, Assistant Coach, graduated from St. Joe's and played on some of the College's best baseball teams. A Lewiston native, he was a three-year starter for the Monks. He was chosen All-New England in his sophomore season.
Roster for 1998 team/In State: 15 **Out of State:** 9 **Out of Country:** 0
Total Number of Varsity/Jr. Varsity: 24 **Percent of Graduation:** 0
Number of Seniors on 1998 Team: 6 **Number of Sophomores on 1998 Team:** 2
Style of Play: Strong pitching and defense combined with explosive offense.

University of Maine

5745 Mahaney Clubhouse
Orono, ME 04469-5745
Coach: Paul Kostacopoulos

NCAA I
Blackbears/Navy, White
Phone: (207) 581-1090
Fax: (207) 581-3987

ACADEMIC

Type: 4 Yr., Public, Liberal Arts, Coed, Engineering
Religion: Non-Affiliated
Web-site: http://www.maine.edu/
Student/Faculty Ratio: 14:1
Undergraduate Enrollment: 7,500
Scholarships/Academic: Yes **Athletic:** Yes
Total Expenses by: Year **In State:** $ 9,681
Degrees Conferred: BA, BS, MA, MS, MBA, Med, PhD, EdD, JD

Founded: 1865
Campus Housing: Yes
SAT/ACT/GPA: Varies
Male/Female Ratio: 50:50
Graduate Enrollment: 2,000
Fin Aid: Yes
Out of State: $ 16,551

Programs of Study: College of Arts and Humanities, College of Business Administration, College of Education, College of Engineering, College of Sciences, College of Social Behavioral Sciences, College of Natural Resources, Forestry and Agriculture

ATHLETIC PROFILE

Conference Affiliation: North Atlantic Conference
Program Profile: Our 4,500-seat stadium has natural grass and lights. We have a multi-million dollar cluhouse, with team locker rooms, training facilities, offices ,lounges, 4 batting screens, 12 mounds, a practice field, full indoor facilities,a sprinkler system and 2 tarps. It is one of the top baseball facilities in the country.
History: We have a 100-year old program, including 13 regional appearances and 7 College World Series Appearances.
Achievements: 10 All-Americans; 70 players drafted over the last 22 years, 7 to the major leagues.
Coaching: Paul Kostacopoulus - Head Coach.
Style of Play: Aggressive hitting and pitching with a solid defense. Fundamentally sound in aspect of the game. Aggressive baser unning with emphasis on a mission style of hitting, getting on, moving the runner or dirving them in.

University of Maine - Farmington

86 Main Street
Farmington, ME 04938
Coach: Richard Meader

NCAA III\NAIA
Beavers/Maroon, Gold, White
Phone: (207) 778-7147
Fax: (207) 778-8177

ACADEMIC

Founded: 1863
Undergraduate Enrollment: 2,000
Web-site: http://www.umf.maine.edu/
Student/Faculty Ratio: 16:1
Scholarships/Academic: Yes
Athletic: No
Total Expenses by: Year
In State: $ 8,500
Degrees Conferred: BA, BS

Type: 4 Yr., Public, Liberal Arts, Coed
Campus Housing: Yes
SAT/ACT/GPA: None
Male/Female Ratio: 30:70
Fin Aid: Yes
Out of State: $ 13,000

Programs of Study: Education, Liberal Arts, Business and Economics, Health and Rehabilitation, Psychology, Social Sciences, Letters/Literature, Multi/Interdisciplinary Studies

ATHLETIC PROFILE

Conference Affiliation: MAC
Program Profile:

University of Maine - Presque Isle

181 Main Street
Presque Isle, ME 04769
Coach: Charles Hamel
Email: hamele@polaris.umdi.maine.edu

NAIA
Owls/Royal Blue, Gold
Phone: (207) 768-9421
Fax: (207) 768-9476

ACADEMIC

Founded: 1903
Religion: Non-Affiliated
Web-site: http://www.umpi.maine.edu/
Student/Faculty Ratio: 12:1
Undergraduate Enrollment: 1,500
Scholarships/Academic: Yes
Athletic: No
Total Expenses by: Year
In State: $ 7,274
Degrees Conferred: AA, AS, BA, BFA, BLS, BSW, Masters

Type: 4 Yr., Public, Liberal Arts, Coed
Campus Housing: Yes
SAT/ACT/GPA: 760
Male/Female Ratio: 1:4
Graduate Enrollment: None
Fin Aid: Yes
Out of State: $ 11,324

Programs of Study: Accounting, Athletic Training, Art, Psychology, Sociology, Biology, Business, Communications, Criminal Justice, Elementary Education, English, Environmental Studies, Fine Arts, Fitness and Wellness, International Studies, Political Science, Liberal Studies, Mathematics, Physical Education, Prelaw, Premed, Recreation and Leisure Services, Social Work

ATHLETIC PROFILE

Conference Affiliation: NorthEast Region Conference
Program Profile: We have a 150 acre campus in Northern Maine. We play Fall ball in September and Spring Fall from April through May. We play on a natural grass field.
History: We began circa 1950's when we were Arcostock State Teacher's College
Roster for 1998 team/In State: 12 **Out of State:** 1 **Out of Country:** 0
Total Number of Varsity/Jr. Varsity: 13 **Percent of Graduation:** 0
Number of Seniors on 1998 Team: 1 **Number of Sophomores on 1998 Team:** 3
Most Recent Record: 3 - 24 - 0 **Number of Spring Games:** 27
Positions Needed for 1999/2000: Pitchers, Middle Infield
Style of Play: Very aggressive.

University of Southern Maine

Hill Gymnasium
Gorham, ME 04036
Coach: Ed Flaherty

NCAA III
Huskies/Crimson, White, Navy
Phone: (207) 780-5474
Fax: (207) 780-5182

ACADEMIC

Founded: 1970
Religion: Non-Affiliated
Web-site: http://www.usm.maine.edu/
Student/Faculty Ratio: 14:1
Undergraduate Enrollment: 3,600
Scholarships/Academic: Yes **Athletic:** No
Total Expenses by: Year **In State:** $ 9,000

Type: 4 Yr., Public, Coed
Campus Housing: Yes
SAT/ACT/GPA: 950/20/2.5
Male/Female Ratio: 40:60
Graduate Enrollment: 1,000
Fin Aid: Yes
Out of State: $ 14,000

Degrees Conferred: AA, AS, BA, BS, MA, Med
Programs of Study: Applied Chemistry, Art, Biology, Premed, Prevet, Predental, Communications, Criminilogy, Economics, English, Environmental Science and Policy, French, Geography-Anthropology, Geology, History, Mathematics, Music, Philosophy, Physics, Political Science, Psychology, Social Work, Social Science, Sociology, Management, Computer Science, Engineering

ATHLETIC PROFILE

Conference Affiliation: Little East Conference
Program Profile: We have made 8 straight NCAA tournament appearances. Our field has natural turf with measurements of 330-390-340. We have a 36-game Spring season, a 9-game Fall schedule and a 12-game Spring trip to Florida.
History: 1991 NCAA Division III Champions; 1989, 1991-92 Division III World Series; 1987-95 NCAA Regional tournament team.
Achievements: 1991 Coach of the Year (Division III); 16 All-Americans since 1986; 1991 NCAA Division III Champion; 8 players drafted by pros; 1987-1995 NCAA Tournament; 1989, 1990-1991 New England Coach of the Year; 1989, 1991-1992 Regional Coach of the Year; 3 College World Series Appearances.
Coaching: Ed Flaherty ,Head Coach, has coached 5 years. He was All-American in 1975. He coached high school 4 years & won 1 State Title. He led USM to post-season play 11 straight years.
Style of Play: Basic fundamentals, big emphasis on hitting, adapt to the talent level of the team.

Westbrook College

(Program Discontinued)

MARYLAND

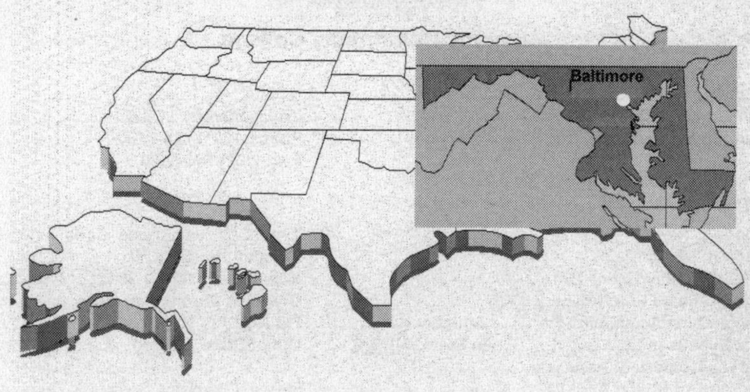

SCHOOL	CITY	AFFILIATION	PAGE
Allegany Community College	Cumberland	NJCAA	376
Anne Arundel Community College	Arnold	NJCAA	376
Baltimore City Community College	Baltimore	NJCAA	376
Bowie State University	Bowie	NCAA II	377
Catonsville Community College	Catonsville	NJCAA	377
Cecil Community College	North East	NJCAA	378
Charles County Community College	LaPlata	NJCAA	379
Chesapeake College	Wye Mills	NJCAA	379
Columbia Union College	Tacoma Park	NCAA II	379
Coppin State College	Baltimore	NCAA I	380
Dundalk Community College	Baltimore	NJCAA	380
Frederick Community College	Frederick	NJCAA	381
Frostburg State University	Frostburg	NCAA III	381
Garrett Community College	McHenry	NJCAA	382
Hagerstown Junior College	Hagerstown	NJCAA	383
Harford Community College	Bel Air	NJCAA II	383
John Hopkins University	Baltimore	NCAA III	384
Montgomery College - Germantown	Germantown	NJCAA	385
Montgomery College-Rockville College	Rockville	NJCAA	385
Mount Saint Mary's College	Emmitsburg	NCAA I	386
Prince George's Community College	Largo	NJCAA	386
St. Mary's College - Maryland	St. Mary's City	NCAA III	387
Salisbury State College	Salisbury	NCAA III	387
Towson State University	Towson	NCAA I	388
US Naval Academy	Annapolis	NCAA I	388
University of Maryland	College Park	NCAA I	389
University of Maryland - Baltimore County	Baltimore	NCAA I	389
University of Maryland - Eastern Shore	Princess Ann	NCAA I	390
Washington College	Chestertown	NCAA III	391
Western Maryland College	Westminster	NCAA III	391

Allegany Community College

Willowbrook Road
Cumberland, MD 21502
Coach: Steve Bazarnic

NJCAA
Trojans/Green, White
Phone: (301) 724-7700
Fax: (301) 784-5650

ACADEMIC

Founded: 1961
Religion: Non-Affiliated
Student/Faculty Ratio: 15:1
Undergraduate Enrollment: 2,960
Scholarships/Academic: No **Athletic:** No
Total Expenses by: Year **In State:** $ 1,900
Type: 2 Yr., Jr. College, Coed
Campus Housing: No
Male/Female Ratio: 35:65
Graduate Enrollment: None
Fin Aid: Yes
Out of State: $ 3,200
Degrees Conferred: Associate
Programs of Study: Accounting, Automotive, Art, Banking/Finance, Chemistry, Computer, Criminal, Dental, Education, Engineering, Management, Therapy, Medical, Liberal Arts, Forestry, Nursing, Technology, Science

ATHLETIC PROFILE

Conference Affiliation: Maryland JUCO

Anne Arundel Community College

101 College Parkway
Arnold, MD 21012
Coach: Clayton Jacobson

NJCAA
Pioneers/Royal, White, Red
Phone: (410) 541-2300
Fax: (410) 541-2233

ACADEMIC

Founded: 1961
Religion: Non-Affiliated
Student/Faculty Ratio: 22:1
Undergraduate Enrollment: 12,400
Scholarships/Academic: No **Athletic:** Yes
Total Expenses by: Year **In State:** $ 1,900
Type: 2 Yr., Jr. College, Coed
Campus Housing: No
Male/Female Ratio: 42:58
Graduate Enrollment: None
Fin Aid: Yes
Out of State: $ 6,400
Degrees Conferred: Associate
Programs of Study: Accounting, American Studies, Applied Art, Architectural, Astronomy, Behavioral Science, Biological, Botany, Broadcasting, Business, Computer, Corrections, Criminal, Education, Engineering, Environmental, Landscape, Law, Marketing, Photography, Real Estate, Retail Science, Telecommunications

ATHLETIC PROFILE

Conference Affiliation: Maryland JUCO

Baltimore City Community College

2901 Liberty Heights Avenue
Baltimore, MD 21215
Coach: Greg Branch

NJCAA
Red Devils/Red, White
Phone: (410) 462-8320
Fax: (410) 462-8329

ACADEMIC

Type: 2 Yr., Jr. College, Coed

Degrees Conferred: Associate
Programs of Study: Accounting, Business Administration, Commerce, Management, Computer Information Systems, Computer Scinece, Corrections, Data Processing, Dental Services, Drafting/Design, Early Childhood Education, Electrical/Electronics Technology, Emergency Medical Technology, Engineering, Fashion and Design Technology, Law Enforcement, Police Science, Medical Records Services, Human Services, Office Management

ATHLETIC PROFILE

Conference Affiliation: Maryland JUCO

Bowie State University

14000 Jericho Park Road
Bowie, MD 20715
Coach: Will Gardner
Email: scott.rouch@bowiestate.edu

NCAA II
Bulldogs/Black, Gold
Phone: (301) 464-6683
Fax: (301) 464-7524

ACADEMIC

Founded: 1865
Religion: Non-Affiliated
Web-site: http://www.bowiestate.edu
Student/Faculty Ratio: 15.5:1
Undergraduate Enrollment: 2,330
Scholarships/Academic: Yes **Athletic:** Yes
Total Expenses by: Year **In State:** $ 3,557+

Type: 4 Yr., Public, Liberal Arts, Coed
Campus Housing: Yes
SAT/ACT/GPA: 950/18/2.2
Male/Female Ratio: 1:2
Graduate Enrollment: 1,629
Fin Aid: Yes
Out of State: $ 5,968+

Degrees Conferred: BA, BS, MA, MS, MED
Programs of Study: Air Traffic Control, Architecture, Automotive, Aviation, Business, Commercial Art, Computer, Corrections, Criminal Justice, Deaf Interpreter Training, Engineering, International, Law, Legal Studies, Manufacturing, Medical, Photography, Real, Estate, Recreation, Science

ATHLETIC PROFILE

Estimated Number of Baseball Scholarships: 6-10
Conference Affiliation: CIAA
Program Profile: Player are involved in practice, conditioning all year long. Emphasis is put on academics - particularly in Fall. Older ball park that is undergoing slow renovation. It has natural turf and will accommodate approximately 400 fans. Season runs mid-February to mid-May.
History: We have come on strong recently - winning CIAA Championships in 1996 and 1997.
Achievements: CIAA Conference Champs in '96 & '97; Mike Gibson-drafted by Chicago Cubs in '93.
Coaching: Will Gardner, Head Coach, started his 1st season in 1998.
Roster for 1998 team/In State: 18 **Out of State:** 6 **Out of Country:** 1
Total Number of Varsity/Jr. Varsity: 30 **Percent of Graduation:** 46%
Number of Seniors on 1998 Team: 2 **Most Recent Record:** 7 - 23 - 0
Freshmen Receiving Fin Aid/Athletic: 0 **Academic:** 6
Number of Fall Games: 6 **Number of Spring Games:** 45
Positions Needed for 1999/2000: All **Baseball Camp Dates:** Undetermined
Schedule: Virginia State University, Shenandoah University, Fairmont State, Binghamton
Style of Play: Gutsy!! We will manufacture a lot of runs using a variety of offensive strategies. Discipline and conditioning will enable us to play as hard in the 9th as we did in the 1st.

Catonsville Community College

800 South Rolling Road
Catonsville, MD 21228
Coach: Patrick Crouse

NJCAA
Cardinals/Red, Black
Phone: (410) 455-4197
Fax: (410) 455-4998

ACADEMIC

Founded: 1957
Type: 2 Yr., Jr. College, Coed
Religion: Non-Affiliated
Campus Housing: No
Student/Faculty Ratio: 21:1
Male/Female Ratio: 46:54
Undergraduate Enrollment: 10,735
Graduate Enrollment: None
Scholarships/Academic: No **Athletic:** Yes **Fin Aid:** Yes
Total Expenses by: Year **In State:** $ 1,500 **Out of State:** $ 4,200
Degrees Conferred: Associate
Programs of Study: Air Traffic Control, Architecture, Automotive, Aviation, Business, Commercial Art, Computer, Corrections, Criminal Justice, Deaf Interpreter Training, Engineering, International, Law, Legal Studies, Manufacturing, Medical, Photography

ATHLETIC PROFILE

Conference Affiliation: Region XX
Program Profile: We play a Fall and Spring schedule for a total of 55 games. We play home games on a natural grass field that seats 1,000.
History: The program began in 1967-1968.

Cecil Community College

1000 North East Road
North East, MD 21901
Coach: Charlie O'Brien
NJCAA
Seahawks/Green, Gold
Phone: (410) 287-6060
Fax: (410) 287-1062

ACADEMIC

Founded: 1968
Type: 2 Yr., Public, Jr. College, Coed
Student/Faculty Ratio: 14:1
Male/Female Ratio: 1:3
Undergraduate Enrollment: 1,100
Graduate Enrollment: None
Scholarships/Academic: Yes **Athletic:** Yes **Fin Aid:** Yes
Total Expenses by: Credit **In State:** $ 60/credit **Out of State:** $ 190/credit
Degrees Conferred: Associates
Programs of Study: Accounting, Business Administration, Computer Graphics, Computer Programming, Computer Technology, Criminal Justice, Education, Electrical/Electronics Technology, Law Enforcement, Liberal Arts, Marketing, Nursing, Photography, Robotics, Water Resources

ATHLETIC PROFILE

Estimated Number of Baseball Scholarships: 4-5
Conference Affiliation: Region 20
Program Profile: Facilities include: dugouts, a fully enclosed field, a score board, a grass field with measurements of 315 down the lines and 365 to the center.
History: We are in the Top one third of the region. Our record in 1997 was 21-13.
Achievements: 8 All-Americans; 10 drafted players.
Coaching: Charlie O'Brien, Head Coach, started his 2nd year with the program and compiled a record of 21-13. He was five years at Keystone Junior College with a record of 96-45. He was two years at West Chester University and five years at ACBC Scranton Wilkes-Barre Twins. Clyde Van Dyke - Assistant Coach.
Roster for 1998 team/In State: 16 **Out of State:** 10 **Out of Country:** 0
Total Number of Varsity/Jr. Varsity: 26 **Number of Fall Games:** 20
Number of Seniors on 1998 Team: 9 **Baseball Camp Dates:** 40
Freshmen Receiving Fin Aid/Athletic: 6 **Academic:** 3
Positions Needed for 1999/2000: 10-12 **Most Recent Record:** 21 - 13 - 0
Schedule: Potomac State University, Del Tech, Dundalk, Gloucester, Charles, Frederick
Style of Play: Aggressive offensively, defensively very sound, and fundamentally sound. Pitching is the question mark.

Charles County Community College

Box 910 Mitchell Rd
LaPlata, MD 20646-0910
Coach: John Ford

NJCAA
Hawks/Green, Gold
Phone: (301) 934-2251
Fax: (301) 934-7697

ACADEMIC

Founded: 1958
Religion: Non-Affiliated
Undergraduate Enrollment: 5,900
Scholarships/Academic: No **Athletic:** No
Total Expenses by: Year **In State:** $ 1,900
Type: 2 Yr., Jr. College, Coed
Campus Housing: No
Graduate Enrollment: None
Fin Aid: Yes
Out of State: $ 5,250
Degrees Conferred: Associate
Programs of Study: Accounting, Biological, Business, Computer, Data Processing, Early Childhood Education, Education, Electrical/Electronics Technology, Human Services, Liberal Arts, Nursing, Paralegal Studies

Chesapeake College

PO Box 8
Wye Mills, MD 21679-0008
Coach: TBA

NJCAA
Skipjacks/Navy, Green
Phone: (410) 822-5400
Fax: (410) 827-9466

ACADEMIC

Type: 2 Yr., Public, Coed
Degrees Conferred: Associate
Programs of Study: Accounting, Agricultural Technology, Art/Fine Arts, Aviation Technology, Business Administration, Commerce, Management, Computer Programming, Computer Scinece, Computer Technology, Corrections, Criminal Justice, Data Processing, Early Childhood Education, Humanities, Liberal Arts, General Studies, General Studeis, Mathematics, Physical Education

ATHLETIC PROFILE

Conference Affiliation: Maryland JUCO

Columbia Union College

7600 Flower Avenue
Tacoma Park, MD 20912
Coach: Brad Durby

NCAA II
Pioneers/Royal Blue, Gold, White
Phone: (301) 891-4195
Fax: (301) 891-4026

ACADEMIC

Founded: 1904
Religion: Seventh Day Adventist
Student/Faculty Ratio: 14:1
Scholarships/Academic: Yes **Athletic:** Yes
Total Expenses by: Year **In State:** $ 13,500
Type: 4 Yr., Private, Liberal Arts, Coed
Undergraduate Enrollment: 950
Male/Female Ratio: 40:60
Fin Aid: Yes
Out of State: $ 13,500
Degrees Conferred: AA, BA, BS
Programs of Study: Accounting, Banking/Finance, Biochemistry, Broadcasting, Business Administration, Chemistry, Communications, Computer Science, Education, English, Health Science, History, Information Science, Journalism, Management, Mathematics, Medical Laboratory Technology, Music, Nursing, Personnel/Management, Physics, Predentistry, Prelaw, Premed, Psychology, Religion

ATHLETIC PROFILE

Conference Affiliation: Independent

Coppin State College

2500 W North Ave
Baltimore, MD 21216-3698
Coach: Paul Blair

NCAA I
Eagles/Royal, Gold
Phone: (410) 383-5686
Fax: (410) 669-6154

ACADEMIC

Founded: 1900
Type: 4 Yr., Public, Coed
Religion: Non-Affiliated
Campus Housing: Yes
Web-site: Not Available
SAT/ACT/GPA: 820/68
Student/Faculty Ratio: 25:1
Male/Female Ratio: 1:3
Undergraduate Enrollment: 2,925
Graduate Enrollment: 350
Scholarships/Academic: Yes **Athletic:** Yes **Fin Aid:** Yes
Total Expenses by: Year **In State:** $ 7,967 **Out of State:** $ 11,972
Degrees Conferred: BA, BS, BN, MA, MS
Programs of Study: Adapted Physical Education, Biology, Chemistry, Computer Science, Criminal Justice, General studies, Engineering, Nursing, Philosophy, Preprofessional Programs, Concentrations, Special Education

ATHLETIC PROFILE

Conference Affiliation: Mid-Eastern Athletic Conference
Program Profile: We are an up and coming program. Home games are played at Joe Cannon Stadium located ten miles off campus (three miles South of BWI Airport). It has Left and Rightfield lines 310', Power Alley, 375' and Centerfield 410'. The stadium has a natural grass field and seats 1,000. The Eagles play 50-56 games in the Spring.
History: The Eagles baseball program began in 1967. Over the years, the team was affiliated with NAIA, NCAA Division II and Now Division I. The School's first post season appearance was in 1979 in the NAIA District tournament.
Achievements: 1995 - MSAC Champs, NCAA Players; 1996 MEAC Northern Division Champs; 2 Players of the Year, 1 Rookie of the Year, NCAA Stolen Base and Batting Champions.
Style of Play: We look for what the opponents offer to determine style of play. We love to force the action and keep the pressure on.

Dundalk Community College

7200 Sollers Point Road
Baltimore, MD 21222
Coach: Elliot Oppenheim

NJCAA
Lions/Red, White
Phone: (410) 285-9741
Fax: (410) 285-9903

ACADEMIC

Founded: 1970
Type: 2 Yr., Jr. College, Coed,
Religion: Non-Affiliated
Campus Housing: No
Undergraduate Enrollment: 3,300
Graduate Enrollment: None
Scholarships/Academic: No **Athletic:** No **Fin Aid:** Yes
Total Expenses by: Year **In State:** $ 1,500 **Out of State:** $ 4,300
Degrees Conferred: Associate
Programs of Study: Accounting, Business, Child Development, Communications, Computer, Electrical/Electronics Technology, Education, Engineering, Guidance, Labor Studies, Liberal Arts, Medical, Mental Health, Office Management, Paralegal, Photography, Physical Fitness/Movement, Real Estate

ATHLETIC PROFILE

Conference Affiliation: Marland Juco, Region XX
Program Profile: We are one of the Top Ten in the NJCAA Division II. Our stadium seats 2,500, has natural turf, dugouts and a field with measurements of 324-LF, 405-CFand 294-RF.
History: We have twenty-six years of baseball. We played ten years of winning baseball. We were the only team to make final "4" in five years in a row. In the last two years we were champions and twice runner-ups.
Achievements: Has 9 Coach of the Year Honors; 2 Regional Championships; 1 State Championship; 8 All-Americans for the last five years; 12 players drafted by Marlins, Mariners.
Coaching: Elliott Oppenheim - Head Coach. Scott Roane - Pitching Coach, pitched for NJCAA Champs, Essex CC. Lance Mauck - Catching Coach, All-District at Davis Elkins. Frank Lotman, ecruiting coach, has been in baseball for 35 years as a coach, a scout recuiter, and a player.
Style of Play: Aggressive - most of the team has green-light to run. We swing in many 3-0 counts.

Essex Community College

(Program Discontinued)

Frederick Community College

7932 Opossumtown Pike
Frederick, MD 21702-2097
Coach: Dan Taylor

NJCAA
Cougars/Green, Gold
Phone: (301) 846-2502
Fax: (301) 846-2498

ACADEMIC

Type: 2 Yr., Jr. College, Coed
Degrees Conferred: Associate
Programs of Study: Accounting, Agricultural Business, Agricultural Scinece, Art/Fine Arts, Aviation Technology, Chemistry, Child Care/Child and Family Studies, Communications, Computer Technology, Construction Management, Criminal Justice, Data Processing, Drafting/Design Technology, Elementary Education, Engineering, Liberal Arts, General Studies, English, Finance/Banking

ATHLETIC PROFILE

Conference Affiliation: Maryland JUCO

Frostburg State University

Physical Education Center
Frostburg, MD 21532
Coach: Phil Caruso

NCAA III
Bobcats/Red, White, Black
Phone: (301) 687-4273
Fax: (301) 687-4780

ACADEMIC

Type: 4 Yr., Public, Liberal Arts, Coed, Engineering
Religion: Non-Affiliated
Web-site: http://www.fsu.umd.edu/
Student/Faculty Ratio: 17:1
Undergraduate Enrollment: 4,543
Scholarships/Academic: Yes **Athletic:** No
Total Expenses by: Year **In State:** $ 9,160
Degrees Conferred: BA, BS, BFA, MS, MA, MBA

Founded: 1898
Campus Housing: Yes
SAT/ACT/GPA: 840/ 20
Male/Female Ratio: 48:52
Graduate Enrollment: 875
Fin Aid: Yes
Out of State: $ 12,700

Programs of Study: 34 Majors, 31 Minors, 14 Distinctive areas of study and 26 Special clusters of courses with disciplines: Preprofessional , Accounting, Actuarial Science, Biology, Business Administration, Chemistry, Computer Science, Education, English, Fine Arts, General Science, Economics, Mass Communications, Math, Music, Philosophy, Physics, Political Science, Psychology

ATHLETIC PROFILE

Conference Affiliation: Independent Conference
Program Profile: Our program is highly instructional, individually and team oriented. It has been a successful one for over 30 years. Our enclosed ball park is in the center of the campus. Our indoor facilities include a baseball room (three cages and mounds), arena and practice gym. Field has natural grass, and large in dimensions.
History: Baseball has existed regularly since 1926. Our current program, under Coach Wells, began in 1965. We were primarily NAIA until 1978 when it became strictly NCAA Division III.
Achievements: NAIA World Series; NAIA Regional Tournaments; NCAA Tournaments in 1984, 1987; ECAC Tournaments in 1989, 190, 1991, 1992, 1993,1994, and 1996; Coach Wells was named Coach of the Year Awards.
Style of Play: Aggressive offense - bunt, run slash as a regular seacourse. Emphasis on fundamentals - do the 'little' things well. Defense loaded with a pickoff plays and aggressive defense against the bunt and running game.

Garrett Community College

PO Box 151
McHenry, MD 21541
Coach: Ed Wildesen

NJCAA
Lakers/Navy Blue, Teal
Phone: (301) 387-3025
Fax: (301) 387-3055

ACADEMIC

Founded: 1971
Type: 2 Yr., Jr. College, Coed
Web-site: Not-Available
SAT/ACT/GPA: Open Door
Student/Faculty Ratio: 12:1
Male/Female Ratio: 50:50
Undergraduate Enrollment: 750
Graduate Enrollment: None
Scholarships/Academic: Yes **Athletic:** Yes **Fin Aid:** Yes
Total Expenses by: Hour **In State:** $ 60/hr **Out of State:** $ 130/hr
Degrees Conferred: AA, AAS
Programs of Study: Our program offers a variety of transfer and career advancement programs leading to associate in Arts or Associate in Applied Science degrees as well as one-year certificate programs.

ATHLETIC PROFILE

Conference Affiliation: MD JUCO
Program Profile: Baseball complex is one of the nicest field in Maryland. Play 56 Spring games and 30-40 Fall games.
History: Program began in 1973-74. We have had only 4 head coaches. Despite having only 350 full students at Garrett, the baseball program continues to compete on the Division I level, making it one of the 10 smallest colleges in Division I. Sixteen years have provided above .500 records and 14 above .600.
Achievements: Has had 22 players drafted and 8 All-Americans. 1997 MD JUCO Conference Champion (Regular Season).
Coaching: Ed Wildesen, Head Coach, started with the program from 1994 to the present. He has 21 years of combined coaching experience. He was four years at Garrett and coached the 1997 team to the MD JUCO Conference Championship. We are first in school history to break the school record winning streak. We had the highest winning percentage since 1978. Cliff Everett, Assistant Coach, is also the head of residence. Jeff Martin - Assistant Coach.
Style of Play: Defense, pitching, desire, and playing with all their heart and class are all stressed. If needed, runs are manufactured through aggressive offensive play.

Hagerstown Junior College

11400 Robinwood Drive
Hagerstown, MD 21742-6590
Coach: Carl Dixon

NJCAA
Hawks/Green, White, Black
Phone: (301) 790-2800
Fax: (301) 733-0097

ACADEMIC

Founded: 1946
Type: 2 Yr., Jr. College, Coed
Student/Faculty Ratio: 35:1
Male/Female Ratio: 1:1
Scholarships/Academic: Yes **Athletic:** Yes **Fin Aid:** Yes
Total Expenses by: Year **In State:** $ 1,096 **Out of State:** $ 3,960
Degrees Conferred: Associate
Programs of Study: Behavioral Sciences and Social Sciences, Business, Criminal Justice, Engineering and Mathematics, Health Science, Humanities, Physical and Health Science, General Studies

ATHLETIC PROFILE

Estimated Number of Baseball Scholarships: 5
Conference Affiliation: Maryland JUCO
Program Profile: Our overall program includes: academic, facilities, baseball, and conference is one of the best in the country. We have a 20-game Fall, a 40-game Spring and a 10 or 11 days game Spring trip to Florida. Our baseball field is natural grass and has measurements of left-field-349, center-395 and right-field-354. Our stadium holds about 2,000.
History: Our program started in 1950. In the last nine years we compiled a record of 194-148. We went to Junior College World Series in 1993, and placed sixth. We have second appearances at the series. This program plays in one of the top Junior College conference in the country.
Achievements: Darryl Powell-Mid-East Coach of the Year in 1993; Louisville Slugger Region Coach of the Year; Diamond D-1 Junior College Coach of the Year; Conference Titles-10; All-Americans-4; drafted players-30.
Coaching: Carl Dixon, Head Coach, started his 1st year with the program. Mike Martin - Assistant.
Roster for 1998 team/In State: 14 **Out of State:** 12 **Out of Country:** 0
Total Number of Varsity/Jr. Varsity: 0 **Percent of Graduation:** 25%
Number of Seniors on 1998 Team: 9 **Most Recent Record:** 19 - 13 - 0
Freshmen Receiving Fin Aid/Athletic: 5 **Academic:** 2
Number of Fall Games: 25 **Number of Spring Games:** 50
Positions Needed for 1999/2000: Shortstop, 3rd Base
Schedule: Indian River Community College, Allegheny College, Essex Community College, Seminole Community College, Daytona Beach Community College
Style of Play: We do a lot of running and sound defense.

Harford Community College

401 Thomas Run Road
Bel Air, MD 21015-4199
Coach: Tim Lindecamp

NJCAA II
Fighting Owls/Blue, Grey
Phone: (410) 836-4000
Fax: (410) 836-4133

ACADEMIC

Type: 2 Yr., Jr. College, Coed
Degrees Conferred: Associate
Programs of Study: Accounting, Art/Fine Arts, Audio Engineering, Automtoive Technology, Behavioral Scinece, Biology, Biological Science, Broadcasting, Business Administration, Commerce, Management, Chemistry, Child Care/Child and Family Studies, Commercial Art, Communications, Computer Information Systems, Computer Science, Criminal justice, Drafting/Design, Early Childhood Education, Electrical/Electronics Technology, Paralegal Studies, Philosophy, Photography

ATHLETIC PROFILE

Conference Affiliation: Maryland Junior College Athletic Conference
Program Profile: The Fighting Owls have a lighted diamond. Games are played at Thomas Run Park on the other college campus. It has an outstanding facility.
History: We have had a baseball program since in 1963.
Coaching: Tim Lindecamp,Head Coach, started his 1st year at Harford Community College. The staff is to be named.
Style of Play: Keep the defense on their toes. Aggressive hit and run, steal, and bunt. Do not wait for the three run homer. Take the Eastern base. Sound defensive and good pitching.

John Hopkins University

Charles and 34th Street
Baltimore, MD 21218
Coach: Robert Babb

NCAA III
Blue Jays/Columbia Blue, Black
Phone: (410) 516-7485
Fax: (410) 516-7482

ACADEMIC

Type: 4 Yr., Private, Liberal Arts, Coed, Engineering
Religion: Non-Affiliated
Web-site: http://www.jhu.edu/
Student/Faculty Ratio: 9:1
Undergraduate Enrollment: 3,400
Scholarships/Academic: Yes **Athletic:** No
Total Expenses by: Year **In State:** $ 32,000
Founded: 1876
Campus Housing: Yes
SAT/ACT/GPA: 1100 avg/2.5
Male/Female Ratio: 60:40
Graduate Enrollment: 1,200
Fin Aid: Yes
Out of State: $ 32,000
Degrees Conferred: BA, BS, MA, MS, PhD, MD
Programs of Study: Arts and Sciences, Engineering (Biomedical, Chemical, Civil, Computer Science, Electrical, Computer, Mechanics, Geography, Environmental, Materials Science, Math, Mechanical), Anthropology, Behavioral Biology, Biology, Biophysics, Chemistry, Classics, Cognitive Science, Comparative American Cultures, Earth and Planetary Science, East Asian Studies, Economics, English, Environmental Earth Sciences, History, Humanistic Studies, Math, Music, Natural Sciences, Neuroscience, Philosophy, Physics and Astronomy, Political Science, Psychology, Public Health, Social and Behavioral Sciences, Sociology, Writing Seminars

ATHLETIC PROFILE

Conference Affiliation: University Athletic Association, Centennial
Program Profile: Our facility includes indoor/outdoor batting cages. We play 20 intersquad Fall and 36 Spring games.
History: Johns Hopkins has had 16 straight winning seasons and 8 straight league titles and NCAA appearances in 1992-1994. We played in Cuba 1986 , Soviet Union 1988 and Czechoslovakia and Russia 1992. We take a 2-week trip to Florida each Spring.
Achievements: 1 1st team All-American; 1 3rd team All-American; 2 1st team Academic All-Americans.
Coaching: Robert Babb, Head Coach, started his 19th year as a head coach of the Blue Jays. During his tenure, the Blue Jays have captured 10 Middle Atlantic Conference SouthEast League Titles. He enters the 1998 season as the winningest coach in school history. Jack Newell - Assistant Coach.
Roster for 1998 team/In State: 2 **Out of State:** 30 **Out of Country:** 0
Total Number of Varsity/Jr. Varsity: 15 **Percent of Graduation:** 100%
Number of Seniors on 1998 Team: 5 **Most Recent Record:** 36 - 4 - 0
Freshmen Receiving Fin Aid/Athletic: 0 **Academic:** 5%
Number of Fall Games: 20 **Number of Spring Games:** 41
Positions Needed for 1999/2000: Pitcher
Schedule: Montclair State, Rowan, Emory, College of New Jersey, Brandies

Montgomery College - Germantown Campus

20200 Observation Drive
Germantown, MD 20876
Coach: Tom Cassera

NJCAA
Gryphons/Dark Green, Silver
Phone: (301) 353-7743
Fax: (301) 353-7728

ACADEMIC

Founded: 1946
Religion: Non-Affiliated
Student/Faculty Ratio: Unknown
Undergraduate Enrollment: 4,000
Scholarships/Academic: No **Athletic:** No
Total Expenses by: Cr-Hr **In State:** $ 131/cr-hr
Degrees Conferred: AA, AS, AAS

Type: 2 Yr., Public, Liberal Arts, Coed
Campus Housing: No
Male/Female Ratio: Unknown
Graduate Enrollment: None
Fin Aid: Yes
Out of State: $ 181/cr-hr

Programs of Study: Accounting, Advertising Art, Architectural and Constructional Technology, Arts and Sciences, Auto Tech, Geography, Business Administration, Computer Application, Engineering Technology, Fire Science, General Studies, Hospitality Management, Interior Design, Landscape Technology, Medical Technology, Health Technology, Paralegal Studies, Photography, Physical Education, Visual Communications, Technical Writing, Television

ATHLETIC PROFILE

Conference Affiliation: Maryland JUCO
Program Profile: We have outdoor and indoor facilities and play on natural grass. We have a 40-60 game season in the Spring.
Achievements: 1998 Region XX Coach of the Year (Division III) in first year as a coach; 1998 Region Champs, District Runner-Ups; 2 All-Americans.
Coaching: Tom Cassera ,Head Coach, started in 1998 and compiled a record of 26-7, Region XX/Division III NJCAA Coach of the Year. He played at Towson State University (Towson Maryland). Adolfo Wittgreen - Assistant Coach.
Roster for 1998 team/In State: 20 **Out of State:** 8 **Out of Country:** 2
Total Number of Varsity/Jr. Varsity: 30 **Percent of Graduation:** 70%
Number of Seniors on 1998 Team: 10 **Most Recent Record:** 26 - 7 - 0
Number of Fall Games: 20 **Number of Spring Games:** 40
Positions Needed for 1999/2000: Left Pitcher, Outfielders, Catcher
Baseball Camp Dates: June 22-August 6; 4-one week sessions
Schedule: Allegheny CC, Gloucester CC, Potomac State CC, Pitt CC, Louisburg College
Style of Play: Aggressive offensively with a solid defense. Sound defense with aggressive offense and a pitching staff that does not quit.

Montgomery College-Rockville College

51 Mannakee Street
Rockville, MD 20850
Coach: Kirk Krikstan

NJCAA
Knights/Burgundy, Gold
Phone: (301) 279-5218
Fax: (301) 251-7586

ACADEMIC

Founded: 1965
Religion: Non-Affiliated
Student/Faculty Ratio: 21:1
Undergraduate Enrollment: 14,300
Scholarships/Academic: No **Athletic:** No
Total Expenses by: Year **In State:** $ 2,000
Degrees Conferred: Associate

Type: 2 Yr., Public, Coed
Campus Housing: No
Male/Female Ratio: 47:53
Graduate Enrollment: None
Fin Aid: Yes
Out of State: $ 5,200

Programs of Study: Accounting, Advertising, Architectural, Art, Automtoive, Biological Science, Business, Cartography, City/Community/Regional Planning, Commercial Art, Computer, Corrections, Construction, Criminal, Data Processing, Dietetics, Education, Geography, Gerontology, Illustration, Law, Math, Photography, Recreation, Theatre

Mount Saint Mary's College

Route 15
Emmitsburg, MD 21727
Coach: Scott Thompson

NCAA I
Mountaineers/Blue, White
Phone: (301) 447-5296
Fax: (301) 447-5300

ACADEMIC

Founded: 1808
Religion: Catholic
Web-site: http://www.msmary.edu/
Student/Faculty Ratio: 16:1
Undergraduate Enrollment: 1,400
Scholarships/Academic: Yes **Athletic:** Yes
Total Expenses by: Year **In State:** $ 21,135
Degrees Conferred: BA, BS

Type: 4 Yr., Private, Liberal Arts, Coed
Campus Housing: Yes
SAT/ACT/GPA: 980-1150
Male/Female Ratio: 47:53
Graduate Enrollment: 400
Fin Aid: Yes
Out of State: $ 21,135

Programs of Study: Accounting, Biochemistry, Dramatic Arts, Economics, English, Fine Arts, History, Human Development, Languages, Literature, Mathematics, Music, Natural Science, Philosophy, Physics, Political Science, Psychology, Public Policy

ATHLETIC PROFILE

Conference Affiliation: NorthEast Conference
Program Profile: Golibart Field has natural grass, seats approximately 100 in bleachers. The traditional season is Spring, with a nontraditional season in Fall.
History: The program began in the 1870's and is the Mount's oldest sport. Babe Ruth was discovered here. Team became Division I in 1989.

Prince George's Community College

301 Largo Road
Largo, MD 20772
Coach: William Vaughan

NJCAA
Owls/Blue, Gold
Phone: (301) 322-0513
Fax: (301) 350-7868

ACADEMIC

Founded: 1958
Religion: Non-Affiliated
Web-site: Not-Available
Student/Faculty Ratio: 22:1
Undergraduate Enrollment: 1,500
Scholarships/Academic: Yes **Athletic:** No
Total Expenses by: Year **In State:** $ 10,405
Degrees Conferred: Associate

Type: 2 Yr., Jr. College, Coed
Campus Housing: No
SAT/ACT/GPA: 1200
Male/Female Ratio: 45:55
Graduate Enrollment: None
Fin Aid: Yes
Out of State: $ 13,705

Programs of Study: Accounting, Engineering, Art, Business, Computer, Constrcutions, Management, Drafting/Design Technology, Education, Electrical/Electronics Technology

St. Mary's College - Maryland

(New Program)

Somerset Field house
St. Mary's City, MD 20686
Coach: Lew Jenkins
Email: jlmason@honors.smcm.edu

NCAA III
Seahawks/Blue, White, Gold
Phone: (301) 862-0320
Fax: (301) 862-0480

ACADEMIC

Founded: 1840
Type: 4 Yr., Public, Liberal Arts, Coed
Religion: Non-Affiliated
Campus Housing: Yes
Web-site: http://www.smcm.edu/
SAT/ACT/GPA: 1290
Student/Faculty Ratio: 13:1
Male/Female Ratio: 45:55
Undergraduate Enrollment: 1,600
Graduate Enrollment: None
Scholarships/Academic: Yes **Athletic:** No **Fin Aid:** Yes
Total Expenses by: Year **In State:** $ 11,500 **Out of State:** $ 14,000
Degrees Conferred: BA
Programs of Study: 19 Majors offered, including strong programs in: Biology, Chemistry, Premed, Economics, Education, History, Theatre Arts, Anthropology, Mathematics, and other general Liberal Arts discipline

ATHLETIC PROFILE

Conference Affiliation: CAC
Program Profile: We offer a top schedule (10 Division II in Fall, 45 in Spring). We play in a premier Capital Athletic Conference. We sent a team to Division III World Series regionals every year of our existence but once. Travel extensively to Columbus, Ohio and Miami, Florida each year. We have a top coaching staff including Maryland Hall of Fame Coach Lew Jenkins and are about to begin an extensive facility renovation that will to be completed in 1999. It will be a multi-million dollar, publicly funded facility on campus with a new field house and new baseball field.
History: We are one of the two "Public Honors" colleges in America, dedicated to offering a top quality academic experience at a public college cost. We are considered one of the best buys in American education (1st in 1996 US News and World Report among liberal arts colleges, offering top experience for a reasonable cost).
Coaching: Lew Jenkins, Head Coach, winningest high school baseball coach in history in state of Maryland at the time of his retirement in 1993 with a 326 wins record. He has coached USA Junior Olympic team four times. He coached 1 dozen major leaguers, 2 dozen 1st draft choices and was at Georgetown University prior to SMC. Jim Mason, Assistant Coach, is responsible for the pitching and he was coordinator at SMC for four years. He was college pitching coach for 6 years. Mike Cavallini and Pestone - Assistant Coaches.
Style of Play: Aggressive - we play hard, push opponents to limits, look for players who can run, hit and throw. We stress good pitching, team defense, and unity purpose.

Salisbury State College

1101 Camden Avenue
Salisbury, MD 21801
Coach: Robb Disbennett

NCAA III
Seagulls/Maroon, Gold
Phone: (410) 543-6345
Fax: (410) 546-2639

ACADEMIC

Founded: 1925
Type: 4 Yr., Public, Liberal Arts, Coed
Religion: Non-Affiliated
Campus Housing: Yes
Web-site: http://www.ssu.umd.edu/
SAT/ACT/GPA: 980-1050
Student/Faculty Ratio: 17:1
Male/Female Ratio: 50:50
Undergraduate Enrollment: 6,000
Graduate Enrollment: None
Scholarships/Academic: Yes **Athletic:** No **Fin Aid:** Yes

Total Expenses by: Year **In State:** $ 8,500 **Out of State:** $ 13,000
Degrees Conferred: BA, BS, BFA, BSN, BSW, MA, MS, MBA, MED
Programs of Study: Accounting, Biology, Broadcasting, Business Administration, Chemistry, Communications, Dramatic Arts, Earth Science, Economics, Education, English, Environmental Science, Fine Arts, French, History, Management, Marine Science, Marketing, Mathematics, Prelaw, Premed, Psychology, Recreation, Social Science, Respiratory Therapy

ATHLETIC PROFILE

Conference Affiliation: ECAC, Capital Conference
Program Profile: We have artificial turf infield, indoor batting and a Nautilus room. We play 35 games and take a 5-game Spring vacation trip. The season is March, April, and 2 weeks in May. There are 20 session Fall workouts.
History: Our scheduling prior to 1964 was non-continuous. It was continuous since 1964.
Achievements: 1977 District NCAA Coach of the Year; 4 NAIA Tourney teams; 5 NCAA Tourney teams; 8 times conference winners; 3 All-Americans; 2 signed contracts.
Coaching: Robb Disbennett - Head Coach.

Towson University

8000 York Road
Towson, MD 21252-0001
Coach: Mike Gottlieb

NCAA I
Tigers/Black, Gold
Phone: (410) 830-3775
Fax: (410) 830-3748

ACADEMIC

Founded: 1866
Religion: Non-Affiliated
Web-site: http://www.towson.edu/
Student/Faculty Ratio: 18:1
Undergraduate Enrollment: 13,000
Scholarships/Academic: Yes **Athletic:** Yes

Type: 4 Yr., Public, Liberal Arts, Coed
Campus Housing: Yes
SAT/ACT/GPA: 1000/3.0
Male/Female Ratio: 45:55
Graduate Enrollment: 2,000
Fin Aid: Yes

Total Expenses by: Year **In State:** $ 10,1000 **Out of State:** $ 15,800
Degrees Conferred: BA, BS, BFA, BM, MA, MS, MAT, MFA, MEd, MM
Programs of Study: Accounting, Art, Art Education, Biology, Business Administration, Chemistry, Communications, Computer Science, Dance Early Childhood Education, Economics, Elementary Education, English, French, General Education, Geography, German, Health Science, Mass Communications, Physical Education, Physics, Political Science, Psychology, Social Science

ATHLETIC PROFILE

Conference Affiliation: America East Conference
History: We are a Div. I program since 1980 and went to NCAA Div. I Tournament in 1988 & 1991.
Coaching: Mike Gottlieb - Head Coach. John Matthews - Assistant Coach. Mike Vota - Assistant.

US Naval Academy

566 Brownson Road
Annapolis, MD 21402
Coach: Bob MCDonald

NCAA I
Midshipmen/Navy, Gold
Phone: (410) 293-2831
Fax: (410) 268-6418

ACADEMIC

Founded: 1845
Religion: Non-Affiliated
Web-site: http://www.nadn.navy.mil/
Student/Faculty Ratio: 1:8
Undergraduate Enrollment: 4,000

Type: 4 Yr., Public, Coed, Engineering
Campus Housing: Yes
SAT/ACT/GPA: 1200
Male/Female Ratio: 90% men
Graduate Enrollment: None

Scholarships/Academic: Yes **Athletic:** No **Fin Aid:** Yes
Total Expenses by: Year **In State:** Free if Appointed **Out of State:** Free if Appoint
Degrees Conferred: BS
Programs of Study: Aerospace Engineering, Chemistry, Computer Science, Economics, Electrical Engineering, English, Engineering, General Studies, History, Humanities, Marine, Mathematics, Mechanical, Naval, Oceanography, Physics, Political Science, Systems Engineering

ATHLETIC PROFILE

Conference Affiliation: Patriot League Conference
Program Profile: Home games are played at Max Bishop Stadium which has a seating capacity of 5,000 and a natural grass field. Playing season is late February to early May.
History: Program began in 1893.
Achievements: Regional Coach of the Year in 1992; PAC 10 North Coach of the Year; 2 PAC 10 North Championships; 42 players drafted; 3 current Major Leaguers.

University of Maryland

P.O. Box 295
College Park, MD 20741
Coach: Tom Bradley

NCAA I
Terrapins/Red, White, Black, Gold
Phone: (301) 314-7122
Fax: (301) 405-0955

ACADEMIC

Founded: 1856
Religion: Non-Affiliated
Web-site: http://www.umd.edu/
Student/Faculty Ratio: 15:1
Undergraduate Enrollment: 25,000

Type: 4 Yr., Public, Liberal Arts, Coed
Campus Housing: Yes
SAT/ACT/GPA: 1200/3.5
Male/Female Ratio: 50:50
Graduate Enrollment: 5,000

Scholarships/Academic: Yes **Athletic:** Yes **Fin Aid:** Yes
Total Expenses by: Year **In State:** $ 10,737 **Out of State:** $ 16,846
Degrees Conferred: BA, BS, BFS, MA, MS, MFA
Programs of Study: Accounting, Anthropology, Banking and Finance, Biology, Fine Arts, Business Administration, Communications, Computer Science, Criminal Justice, Electrical Engineering, History, Mathematics, Journalism, Science

ATHLETIC PROFILE

Conference Affiliation: Atlantic Coast Conference
Program Profile: We do a NCAA 56 game schedule from mid-February to the middle of May. We play at Shipley Field, located in College Park on the University of Maryland campus with lights and a new scoreboard. Shipley Field is a natural grass field , was built in 1956 and seats 2,500 people. The stadium was named for the legendary coach, Burton Shipley.
History: Our program began in 1896. The Terps have been to 5 regionals & have won 3 ACC championships. Program has sent 96 players to professional baseball & 17 to the major leagues.

University of Maryland - Baltimore County

5401 Wilkens Avenue
Baltimore, MD 21228
Coach: John Jancuska

NCAA I
Retrievers/Black, Gold, Red
Phone: (410) 455-2239
Fax: (410) 455-1159

ACADEMIC

Type: 4 Yr., Public, Liberal Arts, Coed, Engineering
Religion: Non-Affiliated
Web-site: http://www.ab.umd.edu/
Student/Faculty Ratio: 17:1

Founded: 1966
Campus Housing: Yes
SAT/ACT/GPA: 1100
Male/Female Ratio: 45:55

Undergraduate Enrollment: 10,600 **Graduate Enrollment:** 2,000
Scholarships/Academic: Yes **Athletic:** Yes **Fin Aid:** Yes
Total Expenses by: Year **In State:** $ 9,200 **Out of State:** $ 13,000
Degrees Conferred: BA, BS, MA, MS, MFA, PhD
Programs of Study: Art, Biochemistry, Biological Science, Chemistry, Computer Science, Economics, Engineering, Geography, Mathematics, Nursing, Philosophy, Physics, Political Science, Psychology, Social Work, Sociology, Theater

ATHLETIC PROFILE

Conference Affiliation: Big South Conference
Program Profile: UMBC Complex houses our 1,000-seat field which has natural grass and lights.
History: The program began in 1966
Coaching: John Jancuska, Head Coach, 22 years.

University of Maryland - Eastern Shore

P.O. Box 1060 UMES
Princess Ann, MD 21853
Coach: Kaye Pinhey
Email: kpinhey@umes.umd.edu
NCAA I
Hawks/Maroon, Grey
Phone: (410) 651-6539
Fax: (410) 651-7600

ACADEMIC

Founded: 1886 **Type:** 4 Yr., Public, Coed
Religion: Non-Affiliated **Campus Housing:** Yes
Web-site: http://www.umes.umd.edu/ **SAT/ACT/GPA:** None
Student/Faculty Ratio: 25:1 **Male/Female Ratio:** 2:1
Undergraduate Enrollment: 2,200 **Graduate Enrollment:** 300
Scholarships/Academic: Yes **Athletic:** Yes **Fin Aid:** Yes
Total Expenses by: Year **In State:** $ 7,570 **Out of State:** $ 12,107
Degrees Conferred: BA, BS, MA, MS, PhD
Programs of Study: Accounting, Agriculture, Air Traffic Control, Biology, Business and Management, Chemistry, Communications, Computer Science, Criminal Science, Ecology, Education, Engineering, Environmental Science, Fashion Merchandise, History, Liberal Arts, Marine Biology, Mathematics, Medical Laboratory Technology, Music, Physical Education, Physical Therapy, Predentistry, Prelaw, Premed, Radiological Technology, Social Sciences

ATHLETIC PROFILE

Estimated Number of Baseball Scholarships: 2
Conference Affiliation: Middle Eastern Athletic Conference
Program Profile: The program at University of Maryland is one of organization and intensity. Players must love the game to be successful. The facilities include field on campus, indoor and outdoor batting cages and a natural surface. Playing season begins February and ends in May. Off-season takes place during the months of September through November.
Coaching: Kaye Pinhey - Head Coach. Brian Hollamon, Assistant Coach, started his 2nd year. He graduated from Salisbury State University with a Bachelors degree in Marketing and Management. He played in four different World Series. He is working on his Masters degree in guidance and counseling. He was ESAC All-Conference player in 1993 as a shortstop.
Roster for 1998 team/In State: 17 **Out of State:** 8 **Out of Country:** 0
Total Number of Varsity/Jr. Varsity: 25 **Percent of Graduation:** 95%
Number of Seniors on 1998 Team: 3 **Number of Sophomores on 1998 Team:** 2
Freshmen Receiving Fin Aid/Athletic: 1 **Baseball Camp Dates:** Future Dates
Number of Fall Games: 0 **Number of Spring Games:** 56
Positions Needed for 1999/2000: All **Most Recent Record:** 11 - 41 - 0
Schedule: University of Maryland-College Park, William and Mary, Naval Academy, Providence College, Georgetown University
Style of Play: We play a very offensive- minded game. Speed is very important to the team's success. Good pitching is also a key to stay within reach of the opponents.

Washington College

300 Washington Avenue
Chestertown, MD 21620
Coach: Al Streelman

NCAA III
Sho'men/Maroon, Black
Phone: (410) 778-7239
Fax: (410) 778-7741

ACADEMIC

Founded: 1782
Religion: Non-Affiliated
Web-site: http://www.washcoll.edu/
Student/Faculty Ratio: 12:1
Undergraduate Enrollment: 1,006
Scholarships/Academic: Yes **Athletic:** No
Total Expenses by: Year **In State:** $ 24,290
Type: 4 Yr., Private, Liberal Arts, Coed
Campus Housing: Yes
SAT/ACT/GPA: 1100
Male/Female Ratio: .8:1
Graduate Enrollment: 70
Fin Aid: Yes
Out of State: $ 24,290
Degrees Conferred: BA, BS, MA
Programs of Study: American Studies, Art, Behavioral Neuroscience, Biology, Business Management, Chemistry, Drama, Economics, English, Environmental Studies, French, German, History, Humanities, Intercultural Studies, Interdisciplinary Studies (Student-designed), Mathematics, Music, Philosophy, Physics, Political Science, Psychology, Sociology, Spanish

ATHLETIC PROFILE

Conference Affiliation: Centennial Conference
Program Profile: Our field is natural, fence enclosed and seats 1,000. Our Fall baseball program is approximately 4 weeks. Winter is a weight program. We take a Florida trip during Spring break. Our schedule has 30-32 games annually. We have an indoor practice facility which is A#1. Our weight and conditioning room is A#1.
History: Our program has been in existence since before the turn of the century. We are a member of a newly formed conference. We finished tied for 2nd in 1994 with a 17-10 record.
Achievements: Ed Athey was selected 1995 College Coach of the Year by the State of Maryland Baseball Association.

Western Maryland College

2 College Hill
Westminster, MD 21157
Coach: David G. Seibert

NCAA III
Green Terror/Green, Gold
Phone: (410) 857-2583
Fax: (410) 857-2586

ACADEMIC

Founded: 1867
Religion: Non-Affiliated
Web-site: Not Available
Student/Faculty Ratio: 14:1
Undergraduate Enrollment: 1,200
Scholarships/Academic: Yes **Athletic:** No
Total Expenses by: Year **In State:** $ 19,500
Type: 4 Yr., Private, Liberal Arts, Coed
Campus Housing: Yes
SAT/ACT/GPA: 950+
Male/Female Ratio: 1:1
Graduate Enrollment: None
Fin Aid: Yes
Out of State: $ 19,500
Degrees Conferred: BA, BS, MA, MS
Programs of Study: Art, Art History, Biology, Business Administration, Chemistry, Communications, Economics, English, Exercise Science, Physical Education, French, German, History, Math, Music, Philosophy, Physics, Political Science, Psychology, Religious Studies, Social Work, Sociology, Spanish, Theatre Arts

ATHLETIC PROFILE

Conference Affiliation: Centennial Conference

Program Profile: The team begins training early with a Fall baseball program. The season includes a trip to Cocoa, Florida during Spring break where we play five junior varsity games.
History: Our program began in 1881. First intercollegiate was offered at WMC.The Green Terror finished the season with an 18-12 overall record and 9-9 in the Centennial Conference. Senior outfielder Rick Estes boasted the team's highest batting average .391,
Achievements: 1984 Middle Atlantic Conference Champions; 1989 SouthWest Conference Champions; 1995 MSABC College Coach of the Year
Coaching: Dave G. Siebert, Head Coach, is a native of Palmyra, PA. started his 18th year as the leader of the Western Maryland College baseball team. He has over 200 wins. The 1978 WMC graduate received his bachelors degree in Physical Education and earned his Masters degree in Educational Administration in 1981. He participated on both football and baseball teams while in college. He coached the 1984 team to the Conference Championship and 1989 they won the SouthWest League Championship. He was Maryland's College Coach of the Year. Brian Van Deusen, Assistant Coach, started his 3rd year with the coaching staff.
Roster for 1998 team/In State: 17 **Out of State:** 13 **Out of Country:** 0
Total Number of Varsity/Jr. Varsity: 30 **Most Recent Record:** 13 - 14 - 0
Number of Fall Games: 3 **Number of Spring Games:** 32
Positions Needed for 1999/2000: All
Style of Play: Emphasized on pitching and defense; aggressive offensively.

MASSACHUSETTS

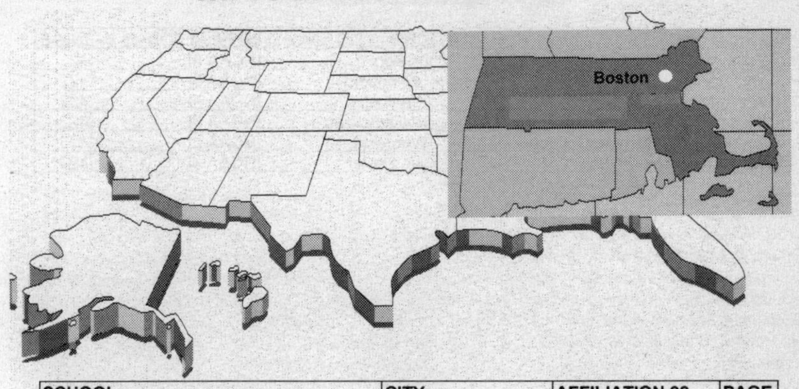

SCHOOL	CITY	AFFILIATION 99	PAGE
American International College	Springfield	NCAA II	395
Amherst College	Amherst	NCAA III	395
Anna Maria College	Paxton	NCAA III	396
Assumption College	Worcester	NCAA II	396
Babson College	Babson Park	NCAA III	397
Becker College - Leicester Campus	Leicester	NCAA III	398
Bentley College	Waltham	NCAA II	398
Boston College	Chestnut Hill	NCAA I	399
Brandies University	Waltham	NCAA III	399
Bridgewater State College	Bridgewater	NCAA III	400
Bunker Hill Community College	Charlestown	NJCAA	400
Clark University	Worcester	NCAA III	401
College of the Holy Cross	Worcester	NCAA I	401
Curry College	Milton	NCAA III	402
Dean College	Franklin	NJCAA	403
Eastern Nazarene College	Quincy	NCAA III	403
Emerson College	Boston	NCAA III	404
Endicott College	Beverly	NCAA III	405
Fitchburg State College	Fitchburg	NCAA III	405
Framingham State College	Framingham	NCAA III	406
Gordon College	Weinham	NCAA III	406
Harvard University	Cambridge	NCAA I	407
Holyoke Community College	Holyoke	NJCAA	407
Massachusetts Maritime Academy	Buzzards Bay	NCAA III	408
Massachusetts Institute of Tech	Cambridge	NCAA III	408
Massasoit Community College	Brockton	NJCAA	409
Merrimack College	North Andover	NCAA II	410
Newbury College	Brookline	NJCAA	411
Nichols College	Dudley	NCAA III	411
Massachusetts College (N Adams State)	North Adams	NCAA III	412
North Shore Community College	Danvers	NJCAA	412
Northeastern University	Boston	NCAA I	412
Northern Essex Community College	Haverhill	NJCAA	413
Quinsigamond Community College	Worcester	NJCAA	414
Roxbury Community College	Roxbury	NJCAA	414
Salem State College	Salem	NCAA III	415
Springfield College	Springfield	NCAA III	415
Springfield Technical Community College	Springfield	NJCAA	416
Stonehill College	North Easton	NCAA II	416
Suffolk University	Boston	NCAA III	417
Tufts University	Medford	NCAA III	418
University of Massachusetts - Amherst	Amherst	NCAA I	419
University of Massachusetts - Boston	Boston	NCAA III	420
University of Massachusetts - Dartmouth	North Dartmouth	NCAA III	420
University of Massachusetts - Lowell	Lowell	NCAA II	421

SCHOOL	CITY	AFFILIATION 99	PAGE
Wentworth Institute of Technology	Boston	NCAA III	421
Western New England College	Springfield	NCAA III	422
Westfield State College	Westfield	NCAA III	422
Williams College	Williamstown	NCAA III	423
Worcester Polytechnic College	Worcester	NCAA III	423
Worcester State College	Worcester	NCAA III	424

American International College

1000 State Street
Springfield, MA 01109
Coach: Chuck Lelas

NCAA II
Yellow Jackets/Black, Gold
Phone: (413) 747-6540
Fax: (413) 731-5710

ACADEMIC

Founded: 1885
Religion: Non-Affiliated
Web-site: http://www.centenary.edu/
Student/Faculty Ratio: 15:1
Undergraduate Enrollment: 1,600
Scholarships/Academic: Yes **Athletic:** Yes
Total Expenses by: Year **In State:** $ 18,000

Type: 4 Yr., Private, Liberal Arts, Coed
Campus Housing: Yes
SAT/ACT/GPA: 800/20
Male/Female Ratio: 55:45
Graduate Enrollment: 400
Fin Aid: Yes
Out of State: $ 18,000

Degrees Conferred: BA, BS, BSN, BSE, MBA
Programs of Study: Business Administration, Criminal Justice, Education, Nursing

ATHLETIC PROFILE

Conference Affiliation: NorthEast 10 Conference
Program Profile: American International College has a year-round program which includes a Fall ball, a Winter training program, a Southern trip to florida and a Spring schedule. The baseball facility is on campus and has natural grass.
History: The team advanced to the 1991 Division II World Series going 3-2 in their first ever tournament Appearance. Baseball began at AIC in 1934 (62 seasons) and carries an overall record of 721-633-14 (.534).
Achievements: At North Adams State - 12 Conference Titles; 7 NCAA Bids; 15 drafted players; Recepient were Jack Butterfield Award-highest honor gives by the New England Coaches Association.

Amherst College

Box 2230
Amherst, MA 01002-5000
Coach: William Thurston

NCAA III
Lord Jeffs/Purple, White, Black
Phone: (413) 542-2284
Fax: (413) 542-2026

ACADEMIC

Founded: 1835
Religion: Non-Affiliated
Web-site: http://www.amherst.edu
Student/Faculty Ratio: 10:1
Undergraduate Enrollment: 1,600
Scholarships/Academic: No **Athletic:** No
Total Expenses by: Year **In State:** $ 30,000

Type: 4 Yr., Private, Liberal Arts, Coed
Campus Housing: Yes
SAT/ACT/GPA: 1200+
Male/Female Ratio: 55:45
Graduate Enrollment: None
Fin Aid: Yes
Out of State: $ 30,000

Degrees Conferred: BA
Programs of Study: American Studies, Anthropology and Sociology, Asian Languages and Civilization, Astronomy, Biology, Black Studies, Chemistry Classics, Economics, English, European Studies, Fine Arts, Geology, German, History, Mathematics and Computer Science, Music Neuro-sciences, Philosophy, Physical Education, Physics, Political Science, Psychology, Religion

ATHLETIC PROFILE

Conference Affiliation: ECAC
Program Profile: We have an indoor baseball cage, video systems, outstanding outdoor facility, batting tunnels, auxillary facilities and a field in the middle of campus.

History: We played and won our first intercollegiate game in 1859 and won 70% of our games in the past 3 years. In the past 33 years, we won 70% of games which is over 550 wins.
Achievements: 4 times New England Coach of the Year; ABCA Coaches Hall of Fame in 1997; USA team Pitching Coach in 1986; Head Coach Australian National Team in 1984 and 1985; won 70% of games in 33 years at Amherst; 19 players drafted; 2 made major leagues; 15 former players in administration of professional baseball; NCAA Regional Selections.
Coaching: Bill Thurston, Head Coach, started his 24th year of his coaching career. Chuck Roys, Assistant Coach, started his 3rd year. He was previously a college coach for 21 years. Joe Sarno, Infield Coach, started his 3rd year. Justin Cronk, Outfield Coach, started his 2nd year.
Roster for 1998 team/In State: 8 **Out of State:** 20 **Out of Country:** 0
Total Number of Varsity/Jr. Varsity: 28 **Percent of Graduation:** 100%
Number of Seniors on 1998 Team: 5 **Number of Sophomores on 1998 Team:** 5
Most Recent Record: 16 - 5 - 0 **Number of Spring Games:** 32
Positions Needed for 1999/2000: Pitches, Outfielders
Baseball Camp Dates: June 11 - July 3
Schedule: Eastern Connecticut State University, Brandies University, St. Thomas University, Aurora University, Allegheny University, University of Massachussetts-Dartmouth, Springfield College
Style of Play: Very aggressive offensive bunt and running game; solid team defense and pitching; stress proper baseball fundamentals.

Anna Maria College

Sunset Lane
Paxton, MA 01612
Coach: Rich Coleman

NCAA III
Amcats/Royal, White
Phone: (508) 849-3447
Fax: (508) 849-3449

ACADEMIC

Founded: 1946 **Type:** 4 Yr., Private, Liberal Arts, Coed
Religion: Roman Catholic **Campus Housing:** Yes
Web-site: http://www.anna-maria.edu **SAT/ACT/GPA:** 1000/2.8
Student/Faculty Ratio: 16:1 **Male/Female Ratio:** 60:40
Undergraduate Enrollment: 500 **Graduate Enrollment:** 1,100
Scholarships/Academic: Yes **Athletic:** No **Fin Aid:** Yes
Total Expenses by: Year **In State:** $ 18,250 **Out of State:** $ 17,000
Degrees Conferred: AA, AS, BA, BFA, BM, BBA, MA, MS, MBA
Programs of Study: Art, Biology, Natural Sciences, Business Administration, CriminalJustice, Education, Music, Music Therapy, Art Therapy, Psychology, Social Work, Paralegal Studies, English

ATHLETIC PROFILE

Conference Affiliation: Commonwealth Coast, ECAC

Assumption College

500 Salisbury Street
Worcester, MA 01615
Coach: Chuck Lane

NCAA II
Greyhounds/Royal Blue, White
Phone: (508) 767-7232
Fax: (508) 798-2568

ACADEMIC

Founded: 1904 **Type:** 4 Yr., Private, Liberal Arts, Coed
Religion: Catholic **Campus Housing:** Yes
Web-site: http://www.assumption.edu/ **SAT/ACT/GPA:** 1000
Student/Faculty Ratio: 12:1 **Male/Female Ratio:** 50:50
Undergraduate Enrollment: 1,900 **Graduate Enrollment:** 700
Scholarships/Academic: Yes **Athletic:** No **Fin Aid:** Yes

Total Expenses by: Year **In State:** $ 20,000 **Out of State:** $ 20,000
Degrees Conferred: BA, BS, MA, CAGS
Programs of Study: Accounting, Biology, Business, Management, Chemistry, Communications, Computer Science, Education English, Languages, Liberal Arts, Medical, Natural Science, Philosophy, Political Science, Rehabilitation Therapy, Religion, Romance Language

ATHLETIC PROFILE

Conference Affiliation: NorthEast 10 Conference
Program Profile: H.L. Rochelesu Field is one of New England's premier playing surfaces. We play a 20-game Fall season and a Southern trip to Ft. Myers.
History: Our program started in 1912 and was the only program in the nation with two Hall of Famer's on staff (Jesse Burkett, Rube Marguard - 1928-1931). We have a team batting average of .338 since 1973 and were 2nd in the nation last year (.361). We had nine 20-win seasons since 1978 and 8 All-Americans.
Achievements: In 1995 has 142 stolen bases, 37 home runs; 8.4 per game.
Style of Play: Aggressive offense - "Get Dirty" defense. Force opponent to make mistakes.

Babson College

Webster Center
Babson Park, MA 02157
Coach: Frank Millerrick

NCAA III
Beavers/Green, White
Phone: (781) 239-4528
Fax: (781) 239-5218

ACADEMIC

Founded: 1919
Type: 4 Yr., Private, Liberal Arts, Coed
Web-site: http://www.babson.edu/
Campus Housing: Yes
Student/Faculty Ratio: 20:1
Male/Female Ratio: 60:40
Undergraduate Enrollment: 1,600
Graduate Enrollment: 300
Scholarships/Academic: Yes **Athletic:** No
Fin Aid: 60%
Total Expenses by: Year **In State:** $ 27,000 **Out of State:** $ 27,000
Degrees Conferred: BS, MBA
Programs of Study: Contact school for program of study.

ATHLETIC PROFILE

Conference Affiliation: NEWMAC
Program Profile: We traditionally ranked in top ten in New England. Beaver Field is called by College Baseball New England "one of the top five places to play in New England". We have a beautifully manicured and enclosed grass field, a press box and also bleacher seating.
History: Baseball has been in existence since 1971 as a varsity sport. We have won 20 or more games 4 of the last 5 years, winning '98 ECAC New England Championships and CAC Titles in 1994, 1995 and 1997.
Achievements: We have produced at least one All-New England selection in three of the past four years. We set school records for runs, hits, home runs, and batting average in the past two years. Head Coach Millerick was named league and New England Coach of the Year in 1996.
Coaching: Frank Millerick , Head Coach, compiled a record of 129-90 in six years. That makes us the schools' leader in wins. Millerick was CAC Coach of the Year in 1994, 1995 and 1996 and New England D III Coach of the Year in 1996. He guided his team to a ECAC New England title in 1998, a first in our program's history.
Roster for 1998 team/In State: 11 **Out of State:** 12 **Out of Country:** 0
Total Number of Varsity/Jr. Varsity: 26 **Percent of Graduation:** 92%
Number of Seniors on 1998 Team: 4 **Most Recent Record:** 23 - 17 - 0
Number of Fall Games: 14 **Number of Spring Games:** 40
Positions Needed for 1999/2000: Pitchers, Infielder
Schedule: Dartmouth, Southern Maine, Bridgewater State, Brandies, Tufts, Bentley
Style of Play: Very aggressive offensively, averaged over seven runs per game in 1998 and hit .320 as a team.

Becker College - Leicester Campus

3 Paxton Street
Leicester, MA 01524
Coach: Herb Whitworth

NCAA III
Hawks/Royal, White, Scarlet
Phone: (508) 791-9241x464
Fax: (508) 892-8131

ACADEMIC

Founded: 1887
Type: 4 Yr., Private, Coed
Undergraduate Enrollment: 1,030
Campus Housing: Yes
Student/Faculty Ratio: 15:1
Male/Female Ratio: 1:4
Scholarships/Academic: Yes **Athletic:** No **Fin Aid:** Yes
Total Expenses by: Year **In State:** $ 14,000 **Out of State:** $ 14,000
Degrees Conferred: BS
Programs of Study: Accounting, Business Administration, Veterinary Science, Early Childhood Education, Elementary Education, Human Resources, Kinesiology, Legal Studies, Marketing, Psychology, Paralegal

ATHLETIC PROFILE

Conference Affiliation: Independent
Program Profile: Becker has two campuses: Worcester and Leicester. The baseball team is housed at the Leicester Campus and we have an on campus field.
Coaching: Herb Whitworth - Head Coach.
Roster for 1998 team/In State: 7 **Out of State:** 8 **Out of Country:** 0
Total Number of Varsity/Jr. Varsity: 15 **Most Recent Record:** 7 - 14 - 0
Number of Seniors on 1998 Team: 1 **Number of Sophomores on 1998 Team:** 0
Number of Fall Games: 10 **Number of Spring Games:** 21
Positions Needed for 1999/2000: Pitchers, Catcher
Schedule: Worcester State, Massachusetts Maritime, Norwich University, Souther Vermont, Teikyo Post, Castleton State

Bentley College

175 Forest Street
Waltham, MA 02154
Coach: Bob Defelice

NCAA II
Falcons/Blue, Gold
Phone: (781) 891-2332
Fax: (781) 891-2648

ACADEMIC

Founded: 1917
Type: 4 Yr., Private, Coed
Religion: Non-Affiliated
Campus Housing: Yes
Web-site: http://www.bentley.edu/
SAT/ACT/GPA: Required
Student/Faculty Ratio: 18:1
Male/Female Ratio: 58:42
Undergraduate Enrollment: 3,116
Graduate Enrollment: 2,007
Scholarships/Academic: Yes **Athletic:** Yes grants **Fin Aid:** Yea
Total Expenses by: Year **In State:** $ 24,000 **Out of State:** $ 24,000
Degrees Conferred: MBA, MS, Certificates, BS, BA, Associates, Five-Year Accelerated
Programs of Study: Accountancy, Business Communications, Business Economics, Computer Information Systems, Economics-Finance, Finance-Bank Management, Marketing, Mathematical Sciences, Paralegal Studies, English, History, International Culture and Economy, Liberal Arts

ATHLETIC PROFILE

Conference Affiliation: NorthEast 10, ECAC, NECAC

Boston College

140 Commonwealth Avenue
Chestnut Hill, MA 02167
Coach: Peter Hughes

NCAA I
Eagles/Maroon, Gold
Phone: (617) 552-3092
Fax: (617) 552-4930

ACADEMIC

Founded: 1863
Religion: Catholic
Web-site: Not Available
Student/Faculty Ratio: 15:1
Undergraduate Enrollment: 8,958
Scholarships/Academic: Yes **Athletic:** Yes
Total Expenses by: Year **In State:** $ 31, 010

Type: 4 Yr., Private, Liberal Arts, Coed
Campus Housing: Yes
SAT/ACT/GPA: 1200/28/3.5
Male/Female Ratio: 48:52
Graduate Enrollment: 5,500
Fin Aid: Yes
Out of State: $ 31,010

Degrees Conferred: BA, BS, MA, MS, PhD
Programs of Study: Arts and Sciences, Management, Nursing, Engineering

ATHLETIC PROFILE

Conference Affiliation: Big East Conference
Program Profile: Our program spans 90 years with 12 coaches. Six of the last nine seasons have resulted in 20+ wins. We have a Spring season only. We play at Commander Shea Field which has a seating capacity of 1,000 and is natural grass.
History: The program was established in 1908. Our 1st no-hitter was thrown by Leo Holleran on May 31, 1914, a 11-0 victory versus Connecticut. Our team has reached the College World Series four times, most recently in 1976. Boston College played Fordham in "Centennial Game" in 1939 at the Baseball Hall of Fame to mark 100 years of baseball.
Achievements: Coach Eddie Pelligrini is a member of the National Collegiate Coaches Hall of Fame and manned the bench for 30 years, including 11 straight winning seasons and three trips to the CWS. Outfielder Kevin Penwell was the only player to win 2 Big East batting titles in 1995 and 1996.
Roster for 1998 team/In State: 19 **Out of State:** 8 **Out of Country:** 0
Total Number of Varsity/Jr. Varsity: 27 **Percent of Graduation:** 100%
Number of Seniors on 1998 Team: 6 **Number of Sophomores on 1998 Team:** 8
Most Recent Record: 14 - 21 - 1 **Number of Spring Games:** 44
Positions Needed for 1999/2000: 3
Schedule: Providence, Notre Dame, West Virginia, Seton Hall, Rutgers, St. John's

Brandies University

415 South Street
Waltham, MA 02254
Coach: Pete Varney

NCAA III
Judges/Blue, White
Phone: (781) 736-3639
Fax: (781) 736-3656

ACADEMIC

Founded: 1948
Student/Faculty Ratio: 9:1
Undergraduate Enrollment: 3,700
Scholarships/Academic: Yes **Athletic:** No
Total Expenses by: Year **In State:** $ 20,000

Type: 4 Yr., Private, Liberal Arts, Coed
Male/Female Ratio: 50:50
Graduate Enrollment: 973
Fin Aid: Yes
Out of State: $ 20,000

Degrees Conferred: BA, MA, MFA, PhD
Programs of Study: Anthropology, Art, Aviation Science, Biology, Business, Chemistry, Professional Chemistry, Communications Arts and Science, Computer Science, Early Childhood Education, Earth Science, Education, Economics, English, French, Geography, History, Management, Science, Mathematics, Music, Philosphy, Physical Education, Physics, Political Science, Psychology, Secondary Science, Social Work, Spanish, Special Education

ATHLETIC PROFILE

Conference Affiliation: University Athletic Association, ECAC, GBL
Achievements: Won in 1988 ECAC Championships; 5 Greater Boston League Titles; University Athletic Association; 9 players have signed professional baseball contracts.
Coaching: Peter Varney, Head Coach, has never had a losing season.
Style of Play: Aggressive on the offense and defense, pitching, power, and a speed.

Bridgewater State College

Park Street
Bridgewater, MA 02325
Coach: Rick Smith

NCAA III
Bears/Red, White
Phone: (508) 697-1352
Fax: (508) 697-1356

ACADEMIC

Founded: 1840
Type: 4 Yr., Public, Liberal Arts, Coed
Religion: Non-Affiliated
Campus Housing: Yes
Web-site: http://www.bridgew.edu/
SAT/ACT/GPA: 850
Student/Faculty Ratio: 17:1
Male/Female Ratio: 33:67
Undergraduate Enrollment: 5,700
Graduate Enrollment: 750
Scholarships/Academic: Yes **Athletic:** No **Fin Aid:** Yes
Total Expenses by: Year **In State:** $ 7,983 **Out of State:** $ 12,077
Degrees Conferred: BA, BB, BSE, MA, MS, MEd (31 degrees)
Programs of Study: Anthropology, Art, Aviation Science, Biology, Business, Chemistry, Professional Chemistry, Communications Art and Science, Early Childhood Education, Earth Science, Economics, Elementary Education, English, French, Geography, History, Management, Science, Mathematics, Music, Philosophy, Physical Education, Physics, Political Science, Psychology, Secondary Education

ATHLETIC PROFILE

Conference Affiliation: MASCAC
Program Profile: We have a 500 seat baseball complex with natural grass and a press box. Field's dimensions to the left/right are 325 and 400 to the center field.
History: Our baseball program began in 1930 and we were a charter member of MASCAC in 1973.
Achievements: MASCAC Titles in 1996, 1997 and 1998; New England Champions in 1996; World Series-3rd place in 1996; Mid-Atlantic Champions in 1997; World Series-7th place in 1997; NCAA New England 4th place. Rick Smith was named Coach of the Year in 1996.
Coaching: Rick Smith ,Head Coach, started as a head coach in 1994 He was named 1996 Coach of the Year, MASCAC Coach of the Year and his record to date is 149-48-1. Doug Vadnais, Assistant Coach, is a former player and graduate of BSC.
Roster for 1998 team/In State: 30 **Out of State:** 10 **Out of Country:** 0
Total Number of Varsity/Jr. Varsity: 40 **Percent of Graduation:** 90%
Number of Seniors on 1998 Team: 5 **Number of Sophomores on 1998 Team:** 10
Number of Fall Games: 9 **Number of Spring Games:** 36
Most Recent Record: 29 - 9 - 0
Schedule: Eastern Connecticut, Southern Maine, Montclair State, William Paterson, Ithaca
Style of Play: Aggressive fundamental baseball with strong emphasis on pitching and defense.

Bunker Hill Community College

New Rutherford Avenue
Charlestown, MA 02129
Coach: Arnold Lindstrom

NJCAA
Bulldogs/Red, White
Phone: (617) 228-2088
Fax: (617) 242-9444

ACADEMIC

Type: 2 Yr., Jr. College, Coed
Degrees Conferred: Associate
Programs of Study: Accounting, Behavioral Science, Business Amdinistration, Commerce, Management, Communications Equipment Technology, Community Services, Computer Programming, Computer Science, Computer Technologies, Criminal Justice, Culinary Arts, Electrical/Electronics Technology, Fire Science, Food Services Management, Hotel/Restaurant Management, Human Services, Law Enforcement, Retail Management

ATHLETIC PROFILE

Conference Affiliation: MCCAC, NSCAA
Program Profile: We have no facility and play on natural grass.
Achievements: NSCAA Small College Coach of the Year.
Style of Play: Depends on the talent.

Clark University

950 Main Street
Worcester, MA 01610
Coach: Mike Reed

NCAA III
Cougars/Scarlet, White, Black
Phone: (508) 793-7164
Fax: (508) 793-8819

ACADEMIC

Founded: 1887
Religion: Non-Affiliated
Web-site: http://www.clarku.edu/
Student/Faculty Ratio: 11:1
Undergraduate Enrollment: 2,100
Scholarships/Academic: Yes **Athletic:** No
Total Expenses by: Year **In State:** $ 20,300

Type: 4 Yr., Private, Liberal Arts, Coed
Campus Housing: Yes
SAT/ACT/GPA: 1150 Avg
Male/Female Ratio: 45:55
Graduate Enrollment: 500
Fin Aid: Yes
Out of State: $ 20,300

Degrees Conferred: BA, MA
Programs of Study: Psychology, Geography, Sciences, Social Science, Art, Biochemistry, Biology, Business and Management, Chemistry, Classic, Computer Science, Earth Science, Film Studies, French, German, Graphic Art, History, Music, Philosophy, Physics, Political Science, Prelaw, Premed

ATHLETIC PROFILE

Conference Affiliation: Constitution Athletic Conference
Program Profile: We have a comprehensive, year-round program which is geared towards teaching the game. Players get a lot of individual attention and will get better in all aspects of the game.
History: Our program began in 1922. We had one winning seasonand are now gaining some respect as a competitive program. This team was 2 wins away from the school record for wins.
Achievements: We raised the team batting average from .222 to .270 in 1997, set numerous school records and raised team win total from 2 to 9 in one year.
Coaching: Mike Reed , Head Coach, is full-time coach and Sports Information Director. He has been a head coach for three years, but his overall coaching experience is 10 years. Dave Wigren ,Part-time Assistant Coach, has 20 years of experience.
Style of Play: Emphasis on the defense, but very aggressive at the plate and on the bases. We take a very simplified approach to the game. We strive to be consistent and execute the fundamentals.

College of the Holy Cross

One College Street
Worcester, MA 01610-2395
Coach: Paul Pearl

NCAA I
Crusaders/White, Purple
Phone: (508) 793-3628
Fax: (508) 793-2229

ACADEMIC

Founded: 1843 **Type:** 4 Yr., Private, Liberal Arts, Coed
Religion: Catholic Jesuit **Campus Housing:** Yes
Web-site: http://www.holycross.edu/ **SAT/ACT/GPA:** 1100+
Student/Faculty Ratio: 15:1 **Male/Female Ratio:** 48:52
Undergraduate Enrollment: 2,700 **Graduate Enrollment:** 0
Scholarships/Academic: No **Athletic:** No **Fin Aid:** Yes
Total Expenses by: Year **In State:** $ 29,280 **Out of State:** $ 29,280
Degrees Conferred: Bachelor of Arts (BA)
Programs of Study: Accounting, Anthropology, Art, Biology, Chemistry, Classics, Computer, Economics, English, Gerontology, History, International, Math, Peach Studies, Preprofessional Programs, Religious, Sociology, Theatre

ATHLETIC PROFILE

Conference Affiliation: Patriot Leage Conference
Program Profile: We play home games at Fitton Field which has a natural surface and has dimensions of 360-421-307. Our playing season is in the Fall and starts from September through October. Spring starts from March through April and consists of 40 games.
History: Our program began in 1876. The first game was at Fitton Field on April, 1905 against Brown. In 1952, we won the College World Series at Omaha.
Achievements: Won College World Series.
Coaching: John Whalen - Head Coach. Paul Praal - Assistant Coach. Tim Whalen - Assistant.
Style of Play: Depends on the talent.

Curry College

1071 Blue Hill Avenue
Milton, MA 02186
Coach: Jack Vallely

NCAA III
Colonels/Purple, White
Phone: (617) 333-2216
Fax: (617) 333-2027

ACADEMIC

Founded: 1879 **Type:** 4 Yr., Private, Liberal Arts, Coed
Religion: Non-Affiliated **Campus Housing:** Yes
Web-site: http://www.curry.edu:8080/ **SAT/ACT/GPA:** 800 - 1000
Student/Faculty Ratio: 15:1 **Male/Female Ratio:** 1:1
Undergraduate Enrollment: 1,500 **Graduate Enrollment:** None
Scholarships/Academic: Yes **Athletic:** No **Fin Aid:** Yes
Total Expenses by: Year **In State:** $ 21,690 **Out of State:** $ 21,690
Degrees Conferred: BA, BS
Programs of Study: Biology, Business Management, Chemistry, Communications, Education, English, Environmental Science, Health Education, Nursing, Philosophy, Physics, Political and History, Psychology, Sociology/Criminal Justice, Visual Arts

ATHLETIC PROFILE

Conference Affiliation: Commonwealth Coastal Conference
Program Profile: Jack Vallely Stadium is on campus and has a grass field with measurements of LF400, CF360 and RF372.
History: Jack Vallely has been head coach since 1948 and just finished his 51st season as head coach. Brian Vallely is the assistant coach & just completed 20 years in this capacity. In 1997, we went to Final Four ECAC Tournament. We won Conference in '97 & CC Tournament in '95 & '97.
Achievements: 1998 collegiate baseball to Tucson, Arizona; Mr. Pavlovich, editor - Jack Vallely named NCAA Division III Coach of the Century; Red Sox honored Vallely at Fenway Park June 29, 1997; 41 players play pro ball.

Coaching: Jack Vallely, Head Coach, started his 50th year of coaching at Curry College. He compiled a record of 716-264-4. He is considered a legend. He is a former major league scouting supervisor for Cincinnati Reds, Oakland Athletics and Cleveland Indians. He has four World Series rings. Brian Vallely, Assistant Coach, graduated from Curry College in 1978.
Roster for 1998 team/In State: 12 **Out of State:** 11 **Out of Country:** 0
Total Number of Varsity/Jr. Varsity: 23 **Percent of Graduation:** 100%
Number of Seniors on 1998 Team: 2 **Number of Sophomores on 1998 Team:** 10
Most Recent Record: 10 - 15 - 1 **Number of Spring Games:** 34
Positions Needed for 1999/2000: Catcher, Pitcher, Outfielders
Schedule: Bates, Worcester State, Franklin Pierce, Colby Sawyer, Roger Williams, Salve Regina
Style of Play: Talent dictates style - some teams run a lot. Recent teams have not had speed. Play for big inning. Club NCAA hitting honors a few times in recent years.

Dean College

99 Main Street
Franklin, MA 02038
Coach: Kevin Burr

NJCAA
Bulldogs/Cardinal, White, Black
Phone: (508) 541-1816
Fax: (508) 541-1817

ACADEMIC

Founded: 1865
Religion: Non-Affiliated
Web-site: Not-Available
Student/Faculty Ratio: 15:1
Scholarships/Academic: Yes **Athletic:** Yes
Total Expenses by: Year **In State:** $ 17,560
Degrees Conferred: AA

Type: 2 Yr., Private, Coed
Campus Housing: No
SAT/ACT/GPA: 600
Male/Female Ratio: 60:40
Fin Aid: Yes
Out of State: $ 17,560

Programs of Study: Accounting, Art, Athletic Training, Broadcasting, Business, Communications, Community Services, Corrections, Drafting/Design, Law, Marketing, Math, Physical Fitness/Exercise Science, Paralegal, Preengineering, Recreation, Retail, Science, Sports Management, Theatre

ATHLETIC PROFILE

Conference Affiliation: Colonial States Athletic Conference, Region 21
Program Profile: We have an excellent field, 24 regular season games and an informal Fall program.
Achievements: Brian Deminico was drafted by A's in 1991.

Eastern Nazarene College

23 E Elm Avenue
Quincy, MA 02170
Coach: Todd Reid
Email: reidt@enc.edu

NCAA III
Crusaders/Red, White
Phone: (617) 745-3648
Fax: (617) 745-3938

ACADEMIC

Founded: 1900
Religion: Christian College, Nazarene
Web-site: http://www.enc.edu
Student/Faculty Ratio: 12:1
Undergraduate Enrollment: 900
Scholarships/Academic: Yes **Athletic:** No
Total Expenses by: Year **In State:** $ 15,600

Type: 4 Yr., Private, Liberal Arts, Coed
Campus Housing: Yes
SAT/ACT/GPA: None
Male/Female Ratio: 45:55
Graduate Enrollment: 600
Fin Aid: Yes
Out of State: $ 15,600

Degrees Conferred: BA, BS, MA, MS
Programs of Study: Liberal Arts, Everything from Physical Education to Physics

ATHLETIC PROFILE

Conference Affiliation: Commonwealth Coast Conference
Program Profile: ENC is a program on the rise. Bradley Field is a natural grass baseball park with unique dimensions: right field is only 300 feet from home plate and a 30 feet high fence makes it a temptation for every left handed hitter.
History: A program with a rich tradition dating back to 1962.
Achievements: Coach of the Year in 1996 & 1997; 2 Scholar Athlete of the Year Awards in 1990's.
Coaching: Todd Reid, Head Coach, started his 2nd year. We have young and enthusiastic players coached into tracks life-lesson and self-motivation.
Roster for 1998 team/In State: 50% **Out of State:** 50% **Out of Country:** 1
Total Number of Varsity/Jr. Varsity: 20 **Percent of Graduation:** 100%
Number of Seniors on 1998 Team: 6 **Number of Sophomores on 1998 Team:** 6
Freshmen Receiving Fin Aid/Athletic: 0 **Academic:** 90%
Number of Fall Games: 8 **Number of Spring Games:** 36
Positions Needed for 1999/2000: Pitchers, Shortstop, Catcher
Most Recent Record: 8 - 22 - 0
Schedule: Suffolk University, Hope, Colby Sawyer, Mt. Vernon Nazarene, Framingham State
Style of Play: We play an aggressive national league style of baseball. We play hard on and off the field. We compete on every pitch like it will be over last.

Emerson College

100 Beacon Street
Boston, MA 02116
Coach: Christian Elias
Email: celias@emerson.edu

NCAA III
Lions/Purple, Black
Phone: (617) 824-8122
Fax: (617) 824-8529

ACADEMIC

Founded: 1880 **Type:** 4 Yr., Private, Liberal Arts, Coed
Religion: Independent **Campus Housing:** Yes
Web-site: http://www.emerson.edu/ **SAT/ACT/GPA:** 1040-1240
Student/Faculty Ratio: 17:1 **Male/Female Ratio:** 45:55
Undergraduate Enrollment: 2,600 **Graduate Enrollment:** 1,000
Scholarships/Academic: Yes **Athletic:** No **Fin Aid:** Yes
Total Expenses by: Year **In State:** $ 27,620 **Out of State:**
Degrees Conferred: BA, BS, BFA, BLI, BM, BSSP, MA, MS, MFA, PhD
Programs of Study: Advertising, Broadcasting, Communication Disorders, Communications, Creative Writing, Dance, Film Arts, Literature, Prelaw, Public Relations, Publishing, Radio and Television, Speech, Speech Pathology, Theatre

ATHLETIC PROFILE

Conference Affiliation: Great NorthEast Athletic Conference
History: Emerson is very excited to be a charter member of the Great NorthEast Athletic Conference, which began play in Spring of 1996.
Coaching: Christian Elias, Head Coach, started his 1st year with the program. His record in 1998 was 7-17 and he led Emerson to its first ever conference playoffs. Skip Lockwood pitched in major league for 12 seasons.
Roster for 1998 team/In State: 8 **Out of State:** 11 **Out of Country:** 0
Total Number of Varsity/Jr. Varsity: 19 **Percent of Graduation:** 100%
Number of Seniors on 1998 Team: 2 **Number of Sophomores on 1998 Team:** 0
Number of Fall Games: 5 **Number of Spring Games:** 24
Positions Needed for 1999/2000: Catcher, Pitchers, 3rd Base
Most Recent Record: 7 - 17 - 0
Schedule: Salem State, Massachussetts Maritime, Worcester, Endicott, Roger Williams, Gordon
Style of Play: Hard and aggressive.

Endicott College

376 Hale Street
Beverly, MA 01915
Coach: Larry Hiser
Email: lhiser@endicott.edu

NCAA III
Gulls/Royal, Kelly, White
Phone: (978) 232-2305
Fax: (978) 232-2600

ACADEMIC

Founded: 1939
Religion: Non-Affiliated
Web-site: http://www.endicott.edu
Student/Faculty Ratio: 11:1
Undergraduate Enrollment: 1,000
Scholarships/Academic: Yes **Athletic:** No
Total Expenses by: Year **In State:** $ 12,970
Type: 4 Yr., Private, Liberal Arts, Coed
Campus Housing: Yes
SAT/ACT/GPA: 800
Male/Female Ratio: 40:60
Graduate Enrollment: None
Fin Aid: Yes
Out of State: $ Varies
Degrees Conferred: BA, BS, BSN
Programs of Study: Advertising-Visual Communications, Athletic, Business, Communications, Criminal, Education, Entrepreneurial, Fashion, Graphic, Interior Design, Liberal Studies, Nursing, Physical Education

ATHLETIC PROFILE

Estimated Number of Baseball Scholarships: Yes
Conference Affiliation: Commonwealth Coast Conference
Program Profile: We are a NCAA Division III, year-round program. We have a well-lighted ball field with a perfect infield surface.
History: This was our first year as varsity. We were Spring 1995 GNAC Runner-Up in 1996 and 1998 and GNAC Champs in 1997. Our historical overall record is 66-52.
Achievements: 1997 Great NorthEast Athletic Conference Champions (10-0); 6 All-GNAC; 1997 Rookie of the Year.
Coaching: Larry Hise, Head Coach, was four years at Ohio Northern University from 1983-1987. He was shortstop, captain as a senior & All-OAC as a junior. He got a Masters in PE from Springfield College in 1991. He started a program at Endicott College. Rick Fisher, Assistant Coach, was a New England College graduate in 1991. He was pitcher /catcher and played varsity hockey.
Roster for 1998 team/In State: 10 **Out of State:** 7 **Out of Country:** 1
Total Number of Varsity/Jr. Varsity: 22 **Percent of Graduation:** 80%
Number of Seniors on 1998 Team: 2 **Most Recent Record:** 17 - 14 - 0
Freshmen Receiving Fin Aid/Athletic: 0 **Academic:** 18
Number of Fall Games: 9 **Number of Spring Games:** 36
Positions Needed for 1999/2000: Middle Infielder, OF, Pitcher
Baseball Camp Dates: Last week of July
Schedule: Virginia Wesleyan, Lynchburg, Guilford, Salem State, Suffolk, Wheaton
Style of Play: Make fundamentals basic to your nature, it removes the surprises from the game.

Fitchburg State College

160 Pearl Street
Fitchburg, MA 01420
Coach: John Sherlock

NCAA III
Falcons/Forest Green, Gold
Phone: (978) 665-4681
Fax: (978) 665-3710

ACADEMIC

Founded: 1894
Web-site: http://www.fsc.edu/
Student/Faculty Ratio: 16:1
Undergraduate Enrollment: 4,300
Scholarships/Academic: Yes **Athletic:** No
Type: 4 Yr., Public, Liberal Arts, Coed
SAT/ACT/GPA: 890
Male/Female Ratio: 45:55
Graduate Enrollment: 900
Fin Aid: Yes

Total Expenses by: Year **In State:** $ 7,200 **Out of State:** $ 11,600
Degrees Conferred: BA, BS, BSEd, MA, MS, MEd
Programs of Study: Accounting, Biology, Business Administration, Chemistry, Communications, Computer Science, Construction Technology, Nursing, Photography, Economics, Education, English, Environmental Science, Film Studies, Geography Art, History, Human Services, Management, Medical Technology, Nursing, Prelaw, Premed, Psychology, Radio and Television, Sociology, Special Education, Technical Writing

ATHLETIC PROFILE

Conference Affiliation: Massachusetts State Athletic Conference
Program Profile: We have a Fall and Spring season and play at Elliot Field which has natural grass.
History: Our program began in 1940. The most wins in a season were 21 in 1980 with a batting average by Doug Haggar of .478 in 1990. Career RBI was Gary Blanchette III in 1985-1988 with a home run career of 21 in 1985-1988. In 1961, P. Jim Herrick led the nation with an 0.19 era.
Achievements: Placed second in the MASCAC in 1993; in 1996 our catcher Steve Balassere was a 1st team All-MASCAC selection and played in collegiate All-Star game at Fenway Park.

Framingham State College

100 State Street
Framingham, MA 01709-101
Coach: Mike Sarno

NCAA III
Rams/Black, Gold
Phone: (508) 626-4614
Fax: (508) 626-4069

ACADEMIC

Founded: 1839
Type: 4 Yr., Public, Liberal Arts, Coed
Web-site: http://www.framingham.edu
SAT/ACT/GPA: 900
Student/Faculty Ratio: 17:1
Male/Female Ratio: 1:3
Undergraduate Enrollment: 3,000
Graduate Enrollment: 600
Scholarships/Academic: Yes **Athletic:** No
Fin Aid: Yes
Total Expenses by: Year **In State:** $ 5,364 **Out of State:** $ 9,412
Degrees Conferred: BA, BS, MA, MS
Programs of Study: Accounting, Art, Biology, Business Administration, Chemistry, Communications, Computer Science, Construction Technology, Economics, Education, English, Environmental Science, Film Studies, Geography, Graphic Art, History, Human Services, Industrial Engineering, Literature, Management, Manufacturing Technology, Marketing, Mathematics, Medical Technology, Nursing, Photography, Prelaw, Premed, Psychology, Sociology, Radio and Television

ATHLETIC PROFILE

Conference Affiliation: Massachusetts State College Athletic Conference
Program Profile: We play at Bowditch Field which has natural grass and is in Framingham, MA.
History: We began in 1969 and have since had six appearances in the ECAC tournament
Achievements: Eric Roepsch 1993 ACBA Division III All-American.

Gordon College

255 Grapevine Road
Weinham, MA 01984
Coach: Scott MacKilligan

NCAA III
Fighting Scots/Blue, Gold, White
Phone: (978) 927-2306x4858
Fax: (978) 524-3000

ACADEMIC

Founded: 1889
Type: 4 Yr., Private, Liberal Arts, Coed
Religion: Non-Denominational
Campus Housing: Yes
Web-site: http://www.gordonc.edu/
SAT/ACT/GPA: SATI preferred
Student/Faculty Ratio: 15:1
Male/Female Ratio: 1:2

Undergraduate Enrollment: 1,224 **Graduate Enrollment:** 38
Scholarships/Academic: Yes **Athletic:** No **Fin Aid:** No
Total Expenses by: Year **In State:** $ 19,990 **Out of State:** $ 19,850
Degrees Conferred: BA, BM, Med
Programs of Study: Accounting, Allied Health, Biology, Business Administration, Chemistry, Communication Arts, Computer Science, Early Childhood Education, Economics, Elementary Education, English, French, International Affairs, Mathematics, Philosophy, Physics, Political Science, Psychology, Sociology, Social Work

ATHLETIC PROFILE

Conference Affiliation: ECAC, CCC

Greenfield Community College

(Program Discontinued)

Harvard University

60 JFK Street
Cambridge, MA 02138
Coach: Joe Walsh

NCAA I
Crimson/Crimson, White, Black
Phone: (617) 495-2629
Fax: (617) 496-9343

ACADEMIC

Founded: 1636 **Type:** 4 Yr., Private, Liberal Arts, Coed
Religion: Non-Affiliated **Campus Housing:** All
Web-site: http://www.harvard.edu/ **SAT/ACT/GPA:** 1200+
Student/Faculty Ratio: 11:1 **Male/Female Ratio:** 55:45
Undergraduate Enrollment: 6,600 **Graduate Enrollment:** 12,800
Scholarships/Academic: Yes **Athletic:** No **Fin Aid:** Yes
Total Expenses by: Year **In State:** $ 27,000 **Out of State:** $ 27,000
Degrees Conferred: All
Programs of Study: Medicine, Law, University Teaching, Business, Arts and Sciences

ATHLETIC PROFILE

Conference Affiliation: Ivy League Conference
Program Profile: In 1997, Collegiate Baseball ranked us #27 in the country. We play at O' Donnell Field which is recognized as the top field in New England.
History: Harvard Baseball began in 1865.
Achievements: 1997 Ivy League Champs; NCAA Play-in Winner versus Army, College Regional (Midwest at Stillwater); went to 2-2 wins over UCLA at Stetson; regular season win over Miami Hurricanes. Coach Joe Walsh named NorthEast Division I Coach of the Year and New England Division I Coach of the Year.
Coaching: Joe Walsh, Head Coach, started his 3rd year as a head coach. He was named NorthEast Division I Coach of the Year & New England Division I Coach of the Year. Gary Donovan, Assistant Coach, started his 3rd year as an assistant coach. Marty Nastasta, Assistant Coach, started his 3rd year as an assistant coach. Ed Gallagher, Assistant Coach, started his 3rd year.
Style of Play: Very aggressive - stolen bases, hit 7 run, bunt hits, intensity, and enthusiastism.

Holyoke Community College

303 Homestead Avenue
Holyoke, MA 01040
Coach: Pat Consedine

NJCAA
Cougars/Dk Green, White, Gold
Phone: (413) 538-7000
Fax: (413) 534-8975

ACADEMIC

Founded: 1946
Type: 2 Yr., Jr. College, Coed
Religion: Non-Affiliated
Campus Housing: No
Student/Faculty Ratio: 17:1
Male/Female Ratio: 40:60
Scholarships/Academic: No **Athletic:** No **Fin Aid:** Yes
Total Expenses by: Year **In State:** $ 2,400 **Out of State:** $ 7,200
Degrees Conferred: Associate
Programs of Study: Accounting, American Studies, Art, Biological, Business, Chemistry, Communications, Hospitality, Law, Liberal Arts, Medical Nursing, Nutrition, Photography, Physics, Radiological, Retail, Theatre, Travel/tourism, Veterinary

ATHLETIC PROFILE

Conference Affiliation: CCAC

Massachusetts Institute of Technology

MIT Box D
Cambridge, MA 02139-4307
Coach: Mac Singleton

NCAA III
Engineers/Cardinal Red, Silver, Grey
Phone: (617) 258-7310
Fax: (617) 258-7343

ACADEMIC

Type: 4 Yr., Private, Liberal Arts, Coed, Engineering
Founded: 1861
Religion: Non-Affiliated
Campus Housing: Yes
Web-site: http://web.mit.edu/
SAT/ACT/GPA: 1400+
Student/Faculty Ratio: 5:1
Male/Female Ratio: 55:45
Undergraduate Enrollment: 4,400
Graduate Enrollment: 5,000
Scholarships/Academic: No **Athletic:** No **Fin Aid:** Yes
Total Expenses by: Semester **In State:** $ 29,000 **Out of State:** $ 29,000
Degrees Conferred: All
Programs of Study: Environment Protection, Marine Engineering, Marine Transportation

ATHLETIC PROFILE

Conference Affiliation: Constitution Athletic Conference
Program Profile: MIT baseball has a Fall and Spring program with an annual training trip to Florida. Our home field has grass, no lights and seats 150.
History: Our program began in 1948.

Massachusetts Maritime Academy

101 Academy Drive
Buzzards Bay, MA 02532
Coach: Bob Corradi
Email: sthompson@mma.mass.edu

NCAA III
Buccaneers/Blue, Gold
Phone: (508) 830-5055
Fax: (508) 830-5056

ACADEMIC

Founded: 1891
Type: 4 Yr., Public, Coed, Engineering
Religion: Non-Affiliated
Campus Housing: Yes
Student/Faculty Ratio: 20:1
Male/Female Ratio: 4:1
Undergraduate Enrollment: 770
Graduate Enrollment: None
Scholarships/Academic: Yes **Athletic:** No **Fin Aid:** Yes
Total Expenses by: Year **In State:** $ 8,445 **Out of State:** $ 14,035
Degrees Conferred: BS
Programs of Study: Environment Protection, Marine Engineering, Marine Transportation

ATHLETIC PROFILE

Conference Affiliation: ECAC, Massachusetts State College Athletic Conference
Program Profile: We are a Division II program. We are in the Massachusetts State College Athletic Conference. We play at Hendy Field on campus. It is completely enclosed, has walk-in dugouts , an excellent natural field surface, a cover for inclement weather, a press box, and an indoor batting cage. Our 32 game schedule starts the last week in March and goes through the first week in April. Our Spring training trip to Florida is in late February .
History: Our program began in 1973 as NCAA Division III. Bob Corradi has been our only head coach for 25 years. Coach Corradi has 361 college victories.
Achievements: 1982 ECAC NorthEast Champs - Massachusetts State College Conference Co-Champions; 1979, 1980, 1982, 1984, 1985 ECAC Tournament Appearance; 4 All-Americans; numerous All NorthEast and All-Conference players; Bob Corradi - MA, BB Coaches Award in 1990; 2 players in the Baseball League; one CCAL All-Star; 361 Career victories.
Coaching: Bob Corradi, Head Coach, got the Coaches Award in 1990 and has a 361record. Greg Perry, Assistant Coach, is a graduate of Westfield State College. Charlie Horran, Assistant Coach, is a graduate of University of Connecticut.
Style of Play: Aggressive with an offensive and defensive discipline. Fundamentally solid teams.

Massasoit Community College

One Massasoit Blvd
Brockton, MA 02402
Coach: Tom Frizzell

NJCAA
Warriors/Green, White
Phone: (508) 588-9100
Fax: (508) 427-1250

ACADEMIC

Founded: 1966
Type: 2 Yr., Public, Coed
Web-site: http://www.hcc.mass.edu/home.html
SAT/ACT/GPA: Open Admission/
Student/Faculty Ratio: 20:1
Male/Female Ratio: 40:60
Undergraduate Enrollment: 6,000
Graduate Enrollment: None
Scholarships/Academic: No **Athletic:** No **Fin Aid:** Yes
Total Expenses by: Year **In State:** $ 2,900 **Out of State:** $ Varies
Degrees Conferred: AA, AS
Programs of Study: Liberal Arts, Business, Law Enforcement, Nursing, Radiological Technology, Respiratory Care, Child Care, Culinary Arts, Physical Therapist Assistant, Art and Graphic Design, Fire Science, Travel and Tourism

ATHLETIC PROFILE

Conference Affiliation: Colonial States Athletic Conference
Program Profile: We have a 15 game Fall scrimmage schedule and a 14 game Florida Spring trip. We do a 32 game regional schedule. Our stadium has an indoor facilities, two batting cages, two indoor mounds, jugs pitching machines and rador guns.
History: Our program started in 1967. We were NJCAA Division II National Champions in 1993, Region XXI Tournament Champions in 1993, 1995, and 1997 Colorado State Conference Champions in 1991, 1992, 1994, 1995 and 1996.
Achievements: National Division II Baseball Coach of the Year in 1993; NJCAA District H Coach of the Year in 1993 and 1995; Region XXI Coach of the Year in 1993, 1995 and 1997; Louisville Slugger Award in 1993, 1995 and 1997; Diamond Sports Coach of the Year in 1993 and 1995.
Coaching: Tom Frizzell ,Head Coach, started in 1991. He was assistant coach at Massasoit CC for three years and National Baseball Division I Coach of the Year 1993. He got NJCAA Region XXI Coach of the Year 1993, 1995 and 1997. He was1993 and 1995 District Coach of the Year. He compiled a record of 233-62-0. Bob Flynn - Assistant Coach.
Roster for 1998 team/In State: 19 **Out of State:** 0 **Out of Country:** 0
Total Number of Varsity/Jr. Varsity: 19 **Percent of Graduation:** 0
Most Recent Record: 31 - 4 - 0 **Number of Sophomores on 1998 Team:** 8
Freshmen Receiving Fin Aid/Athletic: 5 **Academic:** 0
Number of Fall Games: 15 **Number of Spring Games:** 45

Positions Needed for 1999/2000: Shortstop, Catcher, Outfield, Pitcher
Schedule: CC of Rhode Island, University of Connecticut at Avery Point, Quinsigamond Community, Dean Junior, Mitchell Junior, Harvard Junior, Eastern Connecticut State, Bridgewater State
Style of Play: The Massassoit Community College Warriors play an exciting brand of baseball. We stress pitching and defense complimented by an aggressive offense.

Merrimack College

315 Turnpike Street
North Andover, MA 01845
Coach: Barry Rosen
Email: admission@merrimack.edu

NCAA II
Warriors/Navy, Gold
Phone: (978) 837-5000x4214
Fax: (978) 837-5032

ACADEMIC

Type: 4 Yr., Private, Liberal Arts, Coed, Engineering
Founded: 1947
Religion: Catholic
Campus Housing: Yes
Web-site: Not Available
SAT/ACT/GPA: 1000
Student/Faculty Ratio: 14:1
Male/Female Ratio: 50:50
Undergraduate Enrollment: 2,000
Graduate Enrollment: None
Scholarships/Academic: Yes **Athletic:** Yes **Fin Aid:** Yes
Total Expenses by: Year **In State:** $ 21,180 **Out of State:** $ Varies
Degrees Conferred: BA, BS
Programs of Study: Science and Engineering (Biology, Chemistry, Civil Engineering, Computer Science, Math, Physics, Sports Medicine); Liberarl Arts (Political Science, Social, Psychology, Etc.); Business Administration

ATHLETIC PROFILE

Conference Affiliation: NorthEast 10 Conference
Program Profile: We have a highly competitive New England program. Warrior Field has natural grass with measurements of 330 lines, 375 alleys and 390 CF. We have Fall and Spring programs.
History: Our program began in 1978. In the last six years there have been 4 regular season championships, 2 playoff championships, 5 league playoff appearances, 1 regional bid, 2 ECAC Bids with one championship.
Achievements: In the last six years program won New England Coach of the Year in 1996; Conference Regular Season Champs in 1994, 1995, 1996 and 1997; playoff Champs in 1995 and 1996; 3 All-Americans, 3 drafted players; 5 professional signees.
Coaching: Barry Rosen ,Head Coach, started in 1993. He has 21 years coaching experience in high school and was a two-time Boston College Coach of the Year. He won one State Championship and compiled a record of 133-92-2. He won New England Coach of the Year in 1996. He was president of New England Intercollegiate Baseball Association in 1998-1999 and a member of Massachusetts High School Coaches Hall of Fame. Robert Caswell,Assistant Coach, holds the hitting and infield positions and was 3-time New Hampshire Coach of the Year.
Roster for 1998 team/In State: 20 **Out of State:** 6 **Out of Country:** 0
Total Number of Varsity/Jr. Varsity: 25 **Percent of Graduation:** 98%
Number of Seniors on 1998 Team: 2 **Most Recent Record:** 15 - 20 - 0
Freshmen Receiving Fin Aid/Athletic: 0 **Academic:** 12
Number of Fall Games: 15 **Number of Spring Games:** 40
Positions Needed for 1999/2000: Pitcher, Catcher, Middle Infielder
Schedule: University of Tampa, Florida Southern College, University of New Haven, University of Massachusetts - Lowell, US Military Academy at West Point, College of St. Rose
Style of Play: Disciplined and aggressive; we have been known as a power hitting team, with solid defense and pitching with no gimmicks.

Newbury College

129 Fisher Avenue
Brookline, MA 02146
Coach: Stephen Gruenberg

NJCAA
Knights/Green, Gold
Phone: (617) 730-7091
Fax: (617) 730-7146

ACADEMIC

Founded: 1962
Religion: Non-Affiliated
Web-site: http://www.newbury.edu
Student/Faculty Ratio: 13:1
Undergraduate Enrollment: 1,050
Scholarships/Academic: Yes **Athletic:** No
Total Expenses by: Year **In State:** $ 18,736
Type: 2 Yr., Private, Jr. College, Coed
Campus Housing: Yes
SAT/ACT/GPA: None
Male/Female Ratio: 45:55
Graduate Enrollment:
Fin Aid: Yes
Out of State: $ 18,736
Degrees Conferred: Associate
Programs of Study: Accounting, Business Administration, Commerce, Management, Communications, Computer Information Systems, Computer Programming, Criminal Justice, Fashion Design, Graphic Arts, Interior Design, Marketing, Physical Therapy, Tourism

ATHLETIC PROFILE

Conference Affiliation: Independant
History: The Knights' baseball program began in 1991.
Coaching: Stephen Gruenberg, Head Coach, is in his 3rd year. The assistant coaching staff has not been established (To be announced).

Nichols College

Dudley Hill Road
Dudley, MA 01571
Coach: Kevin O'Connell

NCAA III
Bisons/Green, Black, White
Phone: (508) 213-2369
Fax: (508) 943-8250

ACADEMIC

Founded: 1815
Religion: Non-Affiliated
Web-site: http://www.nichols.edu/
Student/Faculty Ratio: 15:1
Undergraduate Enrollment: 800
Scholarships/Academic: Merit **Athletic:** No
Total Expenses by: Year **In State:** $ Varies
Type: 4 Yr., Private, Liberal Arts, Coed
Campus Housing: Yes
SAT/ACT/GPA: 800
Male/Female Ratio: 50:50
Graduate Enrollment: 400
Fin Aid: Need Based
Out of State: $ Varies
Degrees Conferred: BS, BA (BS in Business or Public Administration)
Programs of Study: Accounting, Economics, Finance, General Business, Management, Marketing, Management Information Systems, Sports Management, Liberal Arts

ATHLETIC PROFILE

Conference Affiliation: Commonwealth Coast Conference
Program Profile: Our grass field is located on campus with close proximity to our fieldhouse and residence halls.
Achievements: In 1996, junior John Anderson was selected to the First team All-Conference and to the second team All-New England squads. He finished the season with a .482 batting average that was sixth in the country.
Style of Play: Aggressive, fundamental baseball.

Massachusetts College
(Former North Adams State)

Church Street
North Adams, MA 01247
Coach: Tom Lo Ricco

NCAA III
Mohawks/Blue, Gold
Phone: (413) 662-5403
Fax: (413) 662-5357

ACADEMIC

Founded: 1894
Type: 4 Yr., Public, Liberal Arts, Coed
Web-site: http://www.nasc.mass.edu/
SAT/ACT/GPA: 950
Student/Faculty Ratio: 12:1
Male/Female Ratio: 50:50
Undergraduate Enrollment: 1,400
Graduate Enrollment: 300
Scholarships/Academic: Yes **Athletic:** No **Fin Aid:** Yes
Total Expenses by: Year **In State:** $ 8,800 **Out of State:** $ 13,000
Degrees Conferred: BA, BS, Med
Programs of Study: Liberal Arts, Biology, Chemistry, Engineering, Sociology, Psychology, Education, Business, Computer Science, Business Administration, Health Sciences, Philosophy, Mathematics, Interdisciplinary Studies, History, English, Fine and Performing Arts

ATHLETIC PROFILE

Conference Affiliation: Massachusetts State College Athletic Conference
Program Profile: Home games are played at NASC Athletic Complex. We have a Fall program, a Winter training program, a Spring trip and a Spring schedule.
History: We began in 1955. We have made 10 NCAA appearances and 11 ECAC appearances.
Achievements: Ken Hill plays for Texas Rangers; 4 players playing minor league baseball; 7 drafted in the professional baseball.
Coaching: Tom Lo Ricco, Head Coach, is in his 3rd year as a head coach.

North Shore Community College

1 Ferncroft Road
Danvers, MA 01923
Coach: Michael Muchmore

NJCAA
Sea Hawks/Blue, Grey
Phone: (781) 477-2123
Fax: (781) 477-2111

ACADEMIC

Founded: 1965
Type: 2 Yr., Jr. College, Coed
Undergraduate Enrollment: 3,300
Male/Female Ratio: 41:59
Scholarships/Academic: No **Athletic:** No **Fin Aid:** Yes
Total Expenses by: Year **In State:** $ 1,900 **Out of State:** $ 5,400
Degrees Conferred: Associate
Programs of Study: Accounting, Air Traffic Control, Aviation, Banking/Finance, Business, Criminal, Drug/Alcohol/Substance Abuse, Education, Engineering, Flight Training, Gerontology, Nursing, Occupational, Paralegal, Physical Therapy, Preengineering, Radiological, Real Estate, Respiratory

ATHLETIC PROFILE

Conference Affiliation: MCCAC

Northeastern University

360 Huntington Avenue
Boston, MA 02115
Coach: Neil McPhee

NCAA I
Huskies/Black, Red
Phone: (617) 373-3657
Fax: (617) 373-8988

ACADEMIC

Founded: 1898
Religion: Non-Affiliated
Web-site: http://www.NorthEastern.edu/
Student/Faculty Ratio: 13:1
Undergraduate Enrollment: 24,000
Scholarships/Academic: Yes **Athletic:** Yes
Total Expenses by: Year **In State:** $ 25,334
Type: 4 Yr., Private, Liberal Arts, Coed
Campus Housing: Yes
SAT/ACT/GPA: 1060/24
Male/Female Ratio: 7:4
Graduate Enrollment: 7,000
Fin Aid: Yes
Out of State: $ 25,334
Degrees Conferred: BA, BS, MS, MA, PhD, Associate
Programs of Study: Accounting, Anthropology, Art, Banking/Finance, Computer Technology, Biology, Broadcasting, Business, Chemistry, Communications, Computer Science, Criminal Justice, Economics, Education, Engineering, History, Human Services, Journalism, Marketing, Mathematics, Philosophy, Political Science, Public Administration, Physical Therapy

ATHLETIC PROFILE

Conference Affiliation: North Atlantic Conference
Program Profile: We have a very successful program consistently ranked in the Top 5 in New England. Our home Field is Friedman Diamond. We have an indoor facility. Cabot Cage is one of the best in the country with a fully netted, artifical surface infield and 3 batting cages.
History: Our baseball program began in the 1940's & we have been to a College World Series twice.
Achievements: 8 drafted players in the last 8 years, Coach McPhee named New England Coach of the Year in 1991, 1987; Conference Champs in 1994, participated in NCAA Division I Regional Playoffs in 1994; player drafted in 1994
Coaching: Neil McPhee, Head Coach, started at NU in 1968. He was with the Twins 3 years and 20 years at Newton South High School.
Style of Play: Aggressive base running, combination of power and average. Pitching staff ERA 3.62 Second in the nation in team defense with a .974 in 1993.

Northern Essex Community College

Elliot Way
Haverhill, MA 01830
Coach: Pete Michell
NJCAA
Knights/Blue, Gold
Phone: (978) 556-3820
Fax: (978) 556-3115

ACADEMIC

Founded: 1960
Religion: Non-Affiliated
Student/Faculty Ratio: 17:1
Undergraduate Enrollment: 7,059
Scholarships/Academic: No **Athletic:** No **Aid:** Yes
Total Expenses by: Year **In State:** $ 3,000
Type: 2 Yr., Jr. College, Coed
Campus Housing: No
Male/Female Ratio: 36:64
Graduate Enrollment: None
Out ofFin State: $ 6,600
Degrees Conferred: Associate
Programs of Study: Accounting, Banking/Finance, Business, Commercial, Computer, Criminal Justice, Deaf Interpreter Training, Education, Electrical/Electronics Technology, Engineering, Hotel/Restaurant Management, Information, International, Journalism, Liberal Arts, Machine/Tool Technology, Marketing, Material Science, Nursing

ATHLETIC PROFILE

Conference Affiliation: MCCAC
Program Profile: We play 25 games with a Spring and a Fall program. We have two fields (skin practice field and game field), indoor hitting tunnels, one pitching mounds, CYBEX and free weight fitness room next to team locker and indoor practice areas. Our Spring trip is to Clearwater, Florida.
History: Our is program is ten years old & has a history of state & regional tournament appearances.
Achievements: All-Americans - Larry Rodgers in 1993, John Cail in 1989; Conference Titles in 1986; Finalist in 1988, 1992, and 1994.

Quinsigamond Community College

670 W Boylston Street
Worcester, MA 01606
Coach: Barry Glinski

NJCAA
Chiefs/Blue, White
Phone: (508) 854-4266
Fax: (508) 852-6943

ACADEMIC

Founded: 1963
Type: 2 Yr., Jr. College, Coed
Student/Faculty Ratio: 21:1
Male/Female Ratio: 39:61
Undergraduate Enrollment: 2,900
Graduate Enrollment: None
Scholarships/Academic: Yes **Athletic:** No **Fin Aid:** Yes
Total Expenses by: Year **In State:** $ 1,200 **Out of State:** $ 1,200
Degrees Conferred: Associate
Programs of Study: Accounting, Art, Automotive Technology, Business, Computer, Criminal Justice, Dental, Electrical/Electronics Technology, Fire Science, Hotel/Restaurant Management, Human Services, Liberal Arts, Nursing, Occupational Therapy, Office Management, Preengineering, Radiological, Respiratory, Retail, Travel/Tourism

ATHLETIC PROFILE

Conference Affiliation: NJCAA - Region XXI - MCCAC
Program Profile: We play a 25 game Fall season and a 35 game Spring season. We take a ten day Spring trip to Savannah, Georgia.
History: The program began in 1967 and we have been to JC World Series four-times.
Achievements: Current players in the Major League Baseball are Tanyon Sturtze-Pitcher - Texas Ranger; Rick Betti-Pitcher - Boston Red Sox; Rich Barker - Pitcher - Chicago Cubs.
Coaching: Barry Glinski, Head Coach, compiled an overall record of 549-270-2. Tony Bibik-Assistant Coach. Jim Vail - Assistant Coach.
Style of Play: Extremely basic - fundamentals.

Roxbury Community College

1234 Columbus Avenue
Roxbury, MA 02120-3400
Coach: TBA

NJCAA
Tigers/Orange, Black, White
Phone: (617) 541-2475
Fax: (617) 541-2476

ACADEMIC

Founded: 1973
Type: 2 Yr., Public, Jr. College, Coed
Religion: Non-Affiliated
Campus Housing: No
Undergraduate Enrollment: 2,500
Graduate Enrollment: None
Scholarships/Academic: No **Athletic:** No **Fin Aid:** Yes
Total Expenses by: Credit **In State:** $ 76 Credit **Out of State:** $ 76 Credit
Degrees Conferred: Associates plus Certifications
Programs of Study: Liberal Arts, Arts and Sciences, Business Administration, Nursing, Math

ATHLETIC PROFILE

Conference Affiliation: MCCAC
Program Profile: We started as a club team. Spring of 1998, we became a regular team. We have a state of the art weight room, locker rooms and a track facility. Our natural grass field is 350 ft. down lines, 380 ft CF and 400 right center.
History: Our program began in 1993 and our coach was George Scott until 1997. We were a 1996 State Finalist.
Roster for 1998 team/In State: 13 **Out of State:** 2 **Out of Country:** 0

Total Number of Varsity/Jr. Varsity: 20
Percent of Graduation: 85%
Most Recent Record: 1 - 14 - 0
Number of Sophomores on 1998 Team: 10
Freshmen Receiving Fin Aid/Athletic: Yes **Academic:** Yes
Number of Fall Games: 11
Number of Spring Games: 25
Schedule: Norwak Community College, Massassoit Community College, University of Connecticut - Avery, Quinsigamond, Dean Junior College, Northern Essex Community College
Style of Play: Aggressive on defensive and offense. Strong running team; George Scott is still a consultant.

Salem State College

352 Lafayette Street
Salem, MA 01970
Coach: Ken Perrone

NCAA III
Vikings/Orange, Blue
Phone: (978) 542-6570
Fax: (508) 741-2926

ACADEMIC

Founded: 1854
Type: 4 Yr., Public, Liberal Arts, Coed
SAT/ACT/GPA: 860/2.61
Campus Housing: Yes
Student/Faculty Ratio: 16:1
Male/Female Ratio: 1:1
Undergraduate Enrollment: 4,000
Graduate Enrollment: 900
Scholarships/Academic: No **Athletic:** No **Fin Aid:** Yes
Total Expenses by: Year **In State:** $ 7,198 **Out of State:** $ 9,240
Degrees Conferred: BA, BS, BFA, MS, MBA, MEd
Programs of Study: Art, Aviation Science, Biology, Business Administration, Business Technology and Education, Cartography, Chemistry, Education, Communications, Computer and information Studies, Criminal Justice, Economics, Educational Studies, English, Fire Science, General Studies, Geography, Geological Science, History, Mathematics, Music, Nursing, Office Management, Political Science, Preengineering, Psychology, Social Work, Sociology, Sport/Fitness/Leisure Studies

ATHLETIC PROFILE

Conference Affiliation: Massachusetts State College Athletic Conference
Program Profile: We are a member of the NCAA Division III. We play a 36-game Spring schedule with a trip to Florida during March Break to begin regular season schedule.
History: Since 1983, the Vikings have posted 13 winning seasons and over 300 wins. The Vikings have been selected to post season play 11 times since 1983 including 2 NCAA tournament appearances.
Achievements: NCAA Tournament in 1983 and 1994; MASCAC Champions in 1973, 1990 and 1994; ECAC Tournament in 1984-198; 1989-1993; ECAC New England Champions in 1987.
Coaching: Ken Perrone, Head Coach, is in his 15th season as a head coach.
Style of Play: Hustling, aggressive attitude.

Springfield College

263 Alden Street
Springfield, MA 01109
Coach: Mark Simeone

NCAA III
Chiefs/Maroon, White
Phone: (413) 748-3274
Fax: (413) 748-3537

ACADEMIC

Founded: 1885
Type: 4 Yr., Private, Liberal Arts, Coed
Religion: Non-Affiliated
Campus Housing: Yes
Web-site: http://www.spfid.col.edu
SAT/ACT/GPA: None
Student/Faculty Ratio: 12:1
Male/Female Ratio: 48:52
Undergraduate Enrollment: 2,600
Graduate Enrollment: 930
Scholarships/Academic: Yes **Athletic:** No **Fin Aid:** Yes

Total Expenses by: Year **In State:** $ 19,845 **Out of State:** $ 18,500
Degrees Conferred: BA, BS
Programs of Study: Art, Art Therapy, Training, Biology, Business, Chemistry, Computer Systems Management, Early Childhood Education, English, Environmental Studies, Gerontology, Health Service Administration, History, Human Services, Laboratory Science, Management, Mathematics, Medical Technology, Physical Education, Physical Therapy, Political Science, Psychology, Sociology

ATHLETIC PROFILE

Conference Affiliation: ECAC, NorthEast 10 Conference

Springfield Technical Community College

1 Armory Square
Springfield, MA 01105
Coach: TBA

NJCAA
Rams/Maroon, Gold
Phone: (413) 781-7822
Fax: (413) 781-5805

ACADEMIC

Founded: 1885
Type: 2 Yr., Jr. College, Coed
Religion: Non-Affiliated
Campus Housing: Yes
Student/Faculty Ratio: 19:1
Male/Female Ratio: 51:49
Undergraduate Enrollment: 2,100
Graduate Enrollment: None
Scholarships/Academic: Yes **Athletic: No** **Fin Aid: Yes**
Total Expenses by: Year **In State:** $ 18,500 **Out of State:** $ 18,500
Degrees Conferred: Associate
Programs of Study: Accounting, Architectural, Art, Automotive, Banking/Finance, Business, Computer, Cosmetology, Criminal Justice, Dental, Drafting/Design, Electronics/Electrical Technology, Energy, Engineering, Environmental, Fire Science, Health, Graphic, Landscape, Law

ATHLETIC PROFILE

Conference Affiliation: MACCAC

Stonehill College

320 Washington Street
North Easton, MA 02356
Coach: Patrick Boen
Email: pboen@stonehill.edu

NCAA II
Chieftains/Purple, White
Phone: (508) 565-1351
Fax: (508) 565-1460

ACADEMIC

Founded: 1948
Type: 4 Yr., Private, Liberal Arts, Coed
Religion: Non-Affiliated
Campus Housing: Yes
Web-site: http://www.stonehill.edu/
SAT/ACT/GPA: None
Student/Faculty Ratio: 16:1
Male/Female Ratio: 42:58
Undergraduate Enrollment: 2,000
Graduate Enrollment: None
Scholarships/Academic: Yes **Athletic:** No **Fin Aid:** Yes
Total Expenses by: Year **In State:** $ 24,000 **Out of State:** $ 24,000
Degrees Conferred: BA, BS, BSBA
Programs of Study: American Studies, Communications, Criminal Justice, Economics, Education, Health Care Administration, History, International Studies, English, Mathematics, Philosophy, Political Science, Psychology, Public Administration, Religious, Sociology, Philosophy, Chemistry, Computer Science, Math-Computer, Medical Technology, Business Administration, Accounting

ATHLETIC PROFILE

Conference Affiliation: NorthEast 10 Conference

Program Profile: Stonehill College is located in a beautiful 365 acre campus located 20 miles South of Boston. The facilities include on campus baseball field, natural grass, an 8' fence with tarp, dugouts, 4 bullpen mounds,a batting cage,a pitching machine and a locker room. Indoor facilities include a batting cage, pitching mounds, a full infield area and aweight room. We have a state of the art fitness and recreation center. We play a 10 game Fall schedule which includes 2 tournaments and a 12 week mandatory off season weight training program. We do a Spring trip to Fort Myers, Florida with ten games against the top 20 teams and return North for a 35 game schedule.
History: Our program is 50 years old. We struggled in the past until last last year. In 1998, we broke the school record for most team wins, 25. With a new full-time coaching staff, the program is striving to become one of the top Division teams in New England.
Achievements: In 1998 (25-16), we got school the record for most wins in a season. We ranked 3rd in New England Division II Poll and have 5 Conference All-Stars. We led the league in batting average, ERA fielding %, ranked 15th in the nation in team batting average .360. Sophomore Outfielder Mike Close set school a record for home runs and RBI's in a season and career. P. Tom Malvesti, set a school record for saves in season with 7.
Coaching: Patrick Boen, Head Coach, is in his 2nd year and is also assistant Athletic Director. His overall record is 25-16 in his 1st season. He is a 1989 graduate of Stonehill College where he played baseball and basketball. John Flander ,Asssistant Coach, is a pitching coach and a recruiting coordinator. He is a graduate of Salem State in 1993-1995. He had a number of pitching articles published in coaching magazines and is of the top pitching coaches in New England area.
Roster for 1998 team/In State: 19 **Out of State:** 9 **Out of Country:** 0
Total Number of Varsity/Jr. Varsity: 28 **Percent of Graduation:** 100%
Number of Seniors on 1998 Team: 3 **Number of Sophomores on 1998 Team:** 3
Freshmen Receiving Fin Aid/Athletic: 0 **Academic:** 8
Number of Fall Games: 10 **Number of Spring Games:** 46
Positions Needed for 1999/2000: Shortstop, 2nd Base, 1st Base, Outfielder
Most Recent Record: 25 - 16 - 0 **Baseball Camp Dates:** August
Schedule: Boston College, University of Massachusetts-Lowell, University of New Haven, SIU-Edwardsville, Slippery Rock, Bryant
Style of Play: Pitching - defense along with aggressive base running. We will put pressure on defense, disciplined.

Suffolk University

41 Temple Street
Boston, MA 02114
Coach: Cary McConnell
Email: cmccone@betty.suffolk.edu

NCAA III
Rams/Navy, Grey
Phone: (617) 573-8379
Fax: (617) 227-4935

ACADEMIC

Type: 4 Yr., Private, Liberal Arts, Coed, Engineering **Founded:** 1906
Religion: Non-Affiliated **Campus Housing:** Yes
Web-site: http://www.suffolk.edu **SAT/ACT/GPA:** 820+
Student/Faculty Ratio: 12:1 **Male/Female Ratio:** 45:55
Undergraduate Enrollment: 3,126 **Graduate Enrollment:** 3,000
Scholarships/Academic: Yes **Athletic:** No **Fin Aid:** Yes
Total Expenses by: Year **In State:** $ 23,000 **Out of State:** $ 23,000
Degrees Conferred: AA, AS, BA, BS, MS, MBA, MEd
Programs of Study: Art and Design, Biology, Chemistry, Communications, Journalism, Computer Science, Economics, Education, Engineering, English, Government, History, Math, Medical Science, Modern Languages, Philosophy, Physics, Psychology, Sociology, Theatre, Accounting, Predental, Business Administration, Finance, Management, Marketing, Prevet, Prelaw

ATHLETIC PROFILE

Conference Affiliation: ECAC

Program Profile: We have a beautiful urban downtown Boston campus. On campus facilities include a full state of the art weight room and a gymnasium with an indoor mounds. Off-campus facilities include natural grass field with tunnels. Our program is a full year with Fall workouts and games consisting of strength and conditioning with a weight test. Spring includes five weeks of indoor workouts, a 10-12 Florida trip and then 30+ games up North.
History: We have a 50 year baseball program and a terrific winning tradition. The program has averaged 18+ wins for a number of years.
Achievements: All-Americans were Darwin Hernandez in 1994-1995; Tim Murray, Joe Rizzo, Mike Ramano, and Chris Slatery. Drafted and Signed players were: Mike Ramano - C-Red - AA Top, Darwin Hernandez Massachusetts - Maddogs.
Coaching: Cary McConnell, Head Coach, started his 8th year at the college level. He was two year assistant at College of Wooster, NCAA Division III Runner-Up to the National title. He was head coach for three years at University of Rochelle where the team averaged 20+ wins. He was 3 years at Suffolk University with a record of 31-28. David Masters - Assistant. Dennis Luti - Assistant. Josh Powell - Assistant.
Style of Play: Huge emphasis on pitching and defense, 1995-1996 team 14th in the country in fielding %. The team has hit for power and average a very aggressive. Mistake free style of play.

Tufts University

College Avenue
Medford, MA 02155
Coach: John Casey
Email: jcasey@infonet,tufts.edu

NCAA III
Jumbos/Columbia Blue, Brown
Phone: (617) 627-3232
Fax: (617) 627-3614

ACADEMIC

Type: 4 Yr., Private, Liberal Arts, Coed, Engineering
Religion: Non-Affiliated
Web-site: http://www.tufts.edu/
Student/Faculty Ratio: 14:1
Undergraduate Enrollment: 4,504
Scholarships/Academic: No **Athletic:** No
Total Expenses by: Year **In State:** $ 28,360

Founded: 1852
Campus Housing: Yes
SAT/ACT/GPA: Yes
Male/Female Ratio: 48:52
Graduate Enrollment: 1,534
Fin Aid: Yes
Out of State: $ 28,360

Degrees Conferred: BA, BS, MA, MS
Programs of Study: Biological and Physical Sciences, Education, Engineering, International Relations, Languages, Letters/Literature, Mathematics, Nutritions, Prelaw, Premed, Psychology, Social Sciences, Visual and Performing Arts

ATHLETIC PROFILE

Estimated Number of Baseball Scholarships: 3
Conference Affiliation: NESCAC
Program Profile: Tufts baseball has been among the region's top 10 in each of the last five seasons. We have a regulation-size indoor infield and several batting cages, perfect for Winter practice before the team's Spring trip South. Huskins Field is recognized as one of the finest in the NorthEast.
History: Our record for the last five seasons is 99-59-1.Our program began in 1870 and we were College World Series in 1950. We had post-seasons 9 out of the last 11 seasons. Our overall record since 1900 is 823-671-12.
Achievements: We were ECAC Champions in 1989, 1994, 1996 and 1997. We were NCAA Regional 1995. Dan Mosse was named All-American in 1998. Jeff Taglenti , was named All-American in 1996 and 1997. He was drafted on the 7th round by Boston Red Sox.
Coaching: John Casey ,Head Coach, started his 18th year with the program. Bob Clarke, Assistant Coach, is a former standout at Curry College (Outfielder). Bill Samko, Assistant Coach, is a former head baseball coach at Tufts (1979-1982) and current head football coach (catcher). Matt Lyman, Graduated Assistant, started here in 1996 and is a former 4-year varsity player who works with the infielder and junior program.
Roster for 1998 team/In State: 15 **Out of State:** 15 **Out of Country:** 0

Total Number of Varsity/Jr. Varsity: 30
Percent of Graduation: 100%
Number of Seniors on 1998 Team: 8
Number of Sophomores on 1998 Team: 9
Freshmen Receiving Fin Aid/Athletic: 0
Academic: 20
Number of Fall Games: 0
Number of Spring Games: 33
Baseball Camp Dates: December 28-31
Most Recent Record: 19 - 14 - 0
Positions Needed for 1999/2000: Pitchers, Outfielders
Schedule: Eastern Connecticut, Southern Maine, Brandies, Dartmouth, University of Massachusetts
Style of Play: Excellent on the field and in the classroom.

University of Massachusetts - Amherst

Baseball Office, Boyden Gym 248
Amherst, MA 01003
Coach: Mike Stone

NCAA I
Minutemen/Cardinal, White
Phone: (413) 545-3120
Fax: (413) 545-1752

ACADEMIC

Founded: 1863
Type: 4 Yr., Public, Coed, Engineering
Religion: Non-Affiliated
Campus Housing: Yes
Web-site: http://www.umass.edu/
SAT/ACT/GPA: 950+
Student/Faculty Ratio: 18:1
Male/Female Ratio: 1:1
Undergraduate Enrollment: 18,000
Graduate Enrollment: 6,000
Scholarships/Academic: Yes **Athletic:** Yes **Fin Aid:** Yes
Total Expenses by: Year **In State:** $ 10,170+ **Out of State:** $ 16,570+
Degrees Conferred: AS, BA, BS, BFA, MA, MS, MBA, MFA, MEd, PhD, EdD
Programs of Study: Astronomy, Biochemistry and Molecular Biology, Chemistry, Computer Science, Geography, Geology, Mathematics, Art, Art History, Classics, Comparative Litrature, Dance, English, German, French, Anthropology, College of Science and Behavioral Sciences, Psychology, Engineering, Sport Management, Resource Economics

ATHLETIC PROFILE

Estimated Number of Baseball Scholarships: 3.2
Conference Affiliation: Atlantic 10 Conference
Program Profile: Our field has a suitable grass surface and the stadium seats 1,500. We play 8 games in the Fall and 48 in the Spring.
History: Our program began in 1877. Earl Lorden was considered the father of University of Massachusetts Baseball. He roamed the dugouts at the university for nearly two decades. Dick Bergquist is another of our coaches. He was honored when Lorden Field was officially dedicated in his name.
Achievements: We have 7 All-Americans, current ones are Muchie Dagliere and Doug Clark in 1998. Academic All-Americans were Travis Veracka in 1998 and 3 others. Bill Cooke and Muchie Dagliere were named All-NorthEast Region in 1998 and several more. We had 33 All-Atlantic 10 players, and many more.
Coaching: Mike Stone, Head Coach, started his 11th year as a head coach. He was 5 years at University of Vermont before coming to University of Massachusetts. Scott Weaney, Assistant Coach, started his 3rd year. He was a player at University of Massachusetts and played as a captain. He was named 1991 and 1992 Atlantic 10 All-Academic Team. Raphael Cerrato, Assistant Coach, begins his 2nd season. He spent one year and a half as an assistant coach at the University of Rhode Island, where his responsibilities included defensive alignments, outfield instruction, and strength and conditioning. Ryan Thistle, Assistant Coach, begins his first season as a volunteer coach. He joined the staff after 4 years as a player for the Massachusetts from 1994-1997.
Roster for 1998 team/In State: 20 **Out of State:** 16 **Out of Country:** 0
Total Number of Varsity/Jr. Varsity: 37
Percent of Graduation: 100%
Number of Seniors on 1998 Team: 5
Number of Sophomores on 1998 Team: 7
Freshmen Receiving Fin Aid/Athletic: 9
Academic: 5
Number of Fall Games: 8
Number of Spring Games: 46
Positions Needed for 1999/2000: 2-Pitchers, 1-Catcher, 1-Infielder

Most Recent Record: 27 - 12 - 0
Schedule: W.C. State, South Florida, Virginia Tech, Xavier, Fordham, Harvard
Style of Play: Solid consistent from defense and pitching; aggressive fundamental offense!!

University of Massachusetts - Boston

100 Morrissey Boulevard
Boston, MA 02125
Coach: Mark Bettencourt

NCAA III
Beacons/Blue, White
Phone: (617) 287-7801
Fax: (617) 287-7840

ACADEMIC

Founded: 1964
Religion: Non-Affiliated
Web-site: http://www.umb.edu/
Student/Faculty Ratio: 17:1
Undergraduate Enrollment: 9,451
Scholarships/Academic: Yes **Athletic:** No
Total Expenses by: Year **In State:** $ 5,800

Type: 4 Yr., Public, Coed
Campus Housing: Yes
SAT/ACT/GPA: 910
Male/Female Ratio: 27:32
Graduate Enrollment: 1,155
Fin Aid: Yes
Out of State: $ 11,800

Degrees Conferred: BA, BS, MA, MS, MBA
Programs of Study: Anthroplogy, Biology, Chemistry, Classics, Community Services, Computer Science, Criminal Justice, Dramatic Arts, Economics, Engineering, Physics, English, Fine Arts, French, Geography, German, Gerontology, Human Services, Law, Management, Mathematics, Music, Nursing, Philosophy, Physical Education, Political Science, Psychology, Social Science

ATHLETIC PROFILE

Conference Affiliation: ECAC, Little East Conference

University of Massachusetts - Dartmouth

Old Westport Road
North Dartmouth, MA 02747
Coach: Bruce Wheeler
Email: bwheller@umassd.edu

NCAA III
Corsairs/Blue, Gold, White
Phone: (508) 999-8721
Fax: (508) 999-8867

ACADEMIC

Founded: 1891
Religion: Non-Affiliated
Web-site: http://www.umassd.edu/
Student/Faculty Ratio: 15:1
Undergraduate Enrollment: 4,900
Scholarships/Academic: Yes **Athletic:** No
Total Expenses by: Year **In State:** $ 8,844

Type: 4 Yr., Public, Coed
Campus Housing: Yes
SAT/ACT/GPA: 525v, 525m
Male/Female Ratio: 1:1
Graduate Enrollment: 600
Fin Aid: Yes
Out of State: $ 15,340

Degrees Conferred: BA, BS, BSN, BM, BFA, MFA, MAE, MS, MBA, PhD
Programs of Study: College of Art and Sciences: Biology, Chemistry, Computer Science, Economics, Education, English, French, German, History, Humanities and Social Sciences, Mathematics, Medical Laboratory, Psychology, Sociology, Political Science, Spanish, Accounting, Business Information, Engineering, Computer Engineering, Art History, Music, Painting

ATHLETIC PROFILE

Conference Affiliation: ECAC, NECAC, Little East Conference

University of Massachusetts - Lowell

1 University Avenue
Lowell, MA 01854
Coach: Jim Stone

NCAA II
River Hawks/Red, White, Blue
Phone: (978) 934-2344
Fax: (978) 934-2313

ACADEMIC

Founded: 1896
Religion: Non-Affiliated
Web-site: http://www.uml.edu/
Student/Faculty Ratio: 16:1
Undergraduate Enrollment: 6,400
Scholarships/Academic: Yes **Athletic:** Yes
Total Expenses by: Year **In State:** $ 9,000

Type: 4 Yr., Public, Liberal Arts, Coed
Campus Housing: Yes
SAT/ACT/GPA: 800
Male/Female Ratio: 1.2/1
Graduate Enrollment: 3,000
Fin Aid: Yes
Out of State: $ 14,500

Degrees Conferred: BA, BS, MS, MA, Med
Programs of Study: Health Professions, Engineering, Management, Fine Arts, Arts and Sciences, Business, Communications, Computer Sciences, Education (graduate level only), Letters/Literature, Liberal Arts, Parks/Recreation, Psychology, Protective Services, Public Affairs, Social Sciences

ATHLETIC PROFILE

Conference Affiliation: NECC, ECAC
Achievements: 40 players sign professional baseball contracts.
Coaching: Jim Stone , Head Coach, is in his 32nd season as a head coach. He is graduated from Springfield College in 1960.
Style of Play: Like to run, hit and run, good defense, timely hitting, throw strikes.

Wentworth Institute of Technology

550 Huntington Avenue
Boston, MA 02115
Coach: Mark Woodworth

NCAA III
Leopards/Black, Gold
Phone: (617) 989-4598
Fax: (617) 989-4655

ACADEMIC

Type: 4 Yr., Private, Coed, Engineering
Religion: Non-Affiliated
Web-site: http://www.wit.edu/
Student/Faculty Ratio: 19:1
Undergraduate Enrollment: 2,800
Scholarships/Academic: Yes **Athletic:** No
Total Expenses by: Year **In State:** $ 16,000

Founded: 1925
Campus Housing: Yes
SAT/ACT/GPA: 820
Male/Female Ratio: 3:1
Graduate Enrollment: None
Fin Aid: Yes
Out of State: $ 16,000

Degrees Conferred: AAS, BS, BArch
Programs of Study: Airway Science, Architecture, Building Construction Technology, Engineering, Computer Science, Construction Management, Interior Design, Mechanical Engineering, Technical Management

ATHLETIC PROFILE

Conference Affiliation: Commonwealth Coast Conference
Program Profile: We play a full 36 game Spring schedule including a Spring trip to Miami every year. We are a growing program with no seniors, and the largest squad (21) ever in the team's history. Coach Woodworth is in his 1st season as a head coach.
History: The program restarted in 1983 after 30 years of hiatus.
Achievements: 1996 CC Title; 1995 ECAC Tournament Semi-finalist; 1995 Matt Bruchard - 1st team All-New England (NEICA), 1st team All-ECAC.

Coaching: Mark Woodworth, Head Coach, graduated from Wesleyan University in 1994. He started his 1st year as a head coach and was assistant coach at Falmouth-Cape Cod League in 1995. He was an assistant coach at Albertus Magnus College in 1994. Jason Pethie, Assistant Coach, graduated from Hamilton College in 1994. Mike McClary, Assistant, graduated from Wesleyan University in 1993.
Roster for 1998 team/In State: 10 **Out of State:** 10 **Out of Country:** 0
Total Number of Varsity/Jr. Varsity: 24 **Percent of Graduation:** 100%
Number of Seniors on 1998 Team: 4 **Number of Sophomores on 1998 Team:** 0
Freshmen Receiving Fin Aid/Athletic: 0 **Academic:** 15
Number of Fall Games: 10 **Number of Spring Games:** 36
Positions Needed for 1999/2000: Shortstop, Pitcher
Schedule: Wesleyan, Bridgewater State, Brandies, Salem State
Style of Play: "Smart - we may be beat on talent, but not on brains".

Western New England College

1215 Wilbraham Road
Springfield, MA 01119
Coach: Tony Williams

NCAA III
Golden Bears/Royal, Gold
Phone: (413) 782-1792
Fax: (413) 796-2121

ACADEMIC

Founded: 1919 **Type:** 4 Yr., Private, Liberal Arts, Coed
Web-site: http://www.wnec.edu/ **SAT/ACT/GPA:** 760+
Student/Faculty Ratio: 17:1 **Male/Female Ratio:** 60:40
Undergraduate Enrollment: 2,000 **Graduate Enrollment:** 800
Scholarships/Academic: Yes **Athletic:** No **Fin Aid:** Yes
Total Expenses by: Year **In State:** $16,000 **Out of State:** $ 16,000
Degrees Conferred: AA,BA, BS, MS, MBA, JD
Programs of Study: Business and Management, Engineering, Interdisciplinary Studies, Parks/Recreation, Protective Services, Psychology, Public Affairs, Social Sciences

ATHLETIC PROFILE

Conference Affiliation: Constitution Athletic Conference
Program Profile: We carry 26 players and play Fall baseball. We take a Southern trip for 8 games and play 25 games in Spring season. Facilities include an indoor batting cage,a full diamond on synthetic surface, Nautilus & free weight rooms, 2 outdoor batting cages, a scoreboard and a portable fence.
Achievements: We were 1995 Conference Champs and CAC Coach of the Year in 1995.
Coaching: Tony Williams, Head Coach, played in the Orioles Organization. He was All-New England at University of Massachusetts and coached 8 years in the Cape Cod League. He scouted for the Orioles and the KC Angels.

Westfield State College

Western Avenue
Westfield, MA 01086
Coach: John Griffin

NCAA III
Owls/Blue, White
Phone: (413) 572-5477
Fax: (413) 572-5726

ACADEMIC

Founded: 1838 **Type:** 4 Yr., Public, Liberal Arts, Coed
Web-site: http://www.wsc.mass.edu/ **SAT/ACT/GPA:** 800
Student/Faculty Ratio: 20:1 **Male/Female Ratio:** 1:1
Undergraduate Enrollment: 4,250 **Graduate Enrollment:** 775
Scholarships/Academic: Yes **Athletic:** No **Fin Aid:** Yes

Total Expenses by: Year **In State:** $ 7,000 **Out of State:** $ 11,000
Degrees Conferred: BA, BS, BSE, MA, MS, MEd
Programs of Study: Biology, Business Administration, Chemistry, Communications, Computer Science, Criminal Justice, Economics, Education, English, Fine Arts, French, Geology, Geography, History, Information Science, Management, Mathematics, Music, Political Science, Psychology, Social Science, Spanish, Special Education, Urban Studies

ATHLETIC PROFILE

Conference Affiliation: ECAC, MASCAC
Achievements: 2-time NCAA New England Region Runner-Up; 5 NCAA Tournaments; 2 ECAC Tournament; 8 All-District; 6 All-Americans; 34 All-New England over 21 years.

Williams College

P.O. Box 457
Williamstown, MA 01267
Coach: David Barnard

NCAA III
Ephs/Purple, Gold
Phone: (413) 597-2344
Fax: (413) 597-4272

ACADEMIC

Founded: 1793
Religion: Non-Affiliated
Web-site: http://www.williams.edu/
Student/Faculty Ratio: 11:1
Undergraduate Enrollment: 2,000
Scholarships/Academic: No **Athletic:** No
Total Expenses by: Year **In State:** $ 23,700

Type: 4 Yr., Private, Liberal Arts, Coed
Campus Housing: Yes
SAT/ACT/GPA: 1100
Male/Female Ratio: 50:50
Graduate Enrollment: 42
Fin Aid: Yes
Out of State: $ 23,700

Degrees Conferred: BA, MA
Programs of Study: American Studies, Anthropology, Art, Asian Studies, Astronomy, Astrophyhsics, Biology, Chemistry, Classics, Computer Science, Economics, English, French, Geology, German, Greek, History, Latin, Liberal Arts, Mathematics, Music, Philosophy, Physics, Political Science, Psychology, Religion, Russian, Sociology, Spanish, Theatre

ATHLETIC PROFILE

Conference Affiliation: NECAC, ECAC

Worcester Polytechnic College

100 Institute Road
Worcester, MA 01609
Coach: Ross Eberhart

NCAA III
Engineers/Red, Grey
Phone: (508) 831-5624
Fax: (508) 831-5775

ACADEMIC

Founded: 1874
Religion: Non-Affiliated
Web-site: http://www.wpi.edu/
Student/Faculty Ratio: 18:1
Undergraduate Enrollment: 4,800
Scholarships/Academic: Yes **Athletic:** No
Total Expenses by: Year **In State:** $ 7,255

Type: 4 Yr., Private, Liberal Arts, Coed
Campus Housing: Yes
SAT/ACT/GPA: 890/2.7
Male/Female Ratio: 40:60
Graduate Enrollment: 800
Fin Aid: Yes
Out of State: $ 11,935

Degrees Conferred: BS, BA, BS in Education
Programs of Study: Liberal Arts Major in Economics, English, History, Humanities/Science or Technology, Phiolosophy, Social Science/Technology, Management Engineering, Management Information Systems, Engineering, Biomedical Sciences, Biotechnology, Chemical Engineering

Worcester State College

486 Chandler Street
Worcester, MA 01602
Coach: Dirk Baker

NCAA III
Lancers/Royal Blue, Gold
Phone: (508) 929-8852
Fax: (508) 793-8184

ACADEMIC

Founded: 1874
Type: 4 Yr., Public, Liberal Arts, Coed
Religion: Non-Affiliated
Campus Housing: Yes
Student/Faculty Ratio: 18:1
Male/Female Ratio: 39:61
Undergraduate Enrollment: 5,300
Graduate Enrollment: 1,700
Scholarships/Academic: Yes **Athletic:** No **Fin Aid:** Yes
Total Expenses by: Year **In State:** $ 7,253 **Out of State:** $ 11,641
Degrees Conferred: Master of Science, Master of Education
Programs of Study: Biology, Biotechnology, Business Administration, Chemistry, Communications, Communications Disorders, Computer Science, Economics, Early Childhood Education, Elementary Education, English, Engineering Transfer Program, French, Geography, Health Studies, History, Mathematics, Nursing, Natural Science, Occupational Therapy, Physics, Psychology, Sociology

ATHLETIC PROFILE

Conference Affiliation: MASCAC
Program Profile: We have 36 games in the Spring and 9 games in the Fall. We play games at Tiun Field which is fenced in and is located at City Park.
History: The program started in 1954 and we have played baseball 46 years.
Achievements: We were NESCAC Champs in 1964-1965, MASCAC Champs in 1978-1983. We had 4 players drafted. In 1996, Jason Alcana was #1 hitter NCAA .514.
Coaching: Dirk Baker, Head Coach, was at BU in 1991 and 1993. He was All-New England in 1991. Mike O'Brien, Assistant Coach, was at New Haven in 1996 and CWS in 1995. Jim Kelliher, Assistant, was at Holy Cross in 1966.
Style of Play: Aggressive on the bases and line drive hitters. The pitching staff who throws strikes.

MICHIGAN

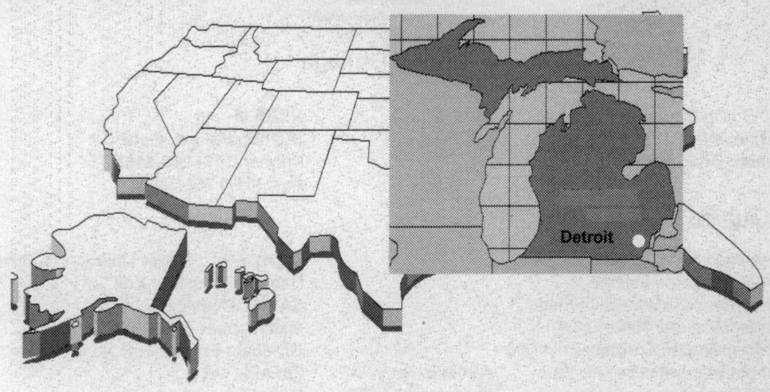

SCHOOL	CITY	AFFILIATION 99	PAGE
Adrian College	Adrian	NCAA III	426
Albion College	Albion	NCAA III	426
Alma College	Alma	NCAA III	427
Aquinas College	Grand Rapids	NAIA	427
Calvin College	Grand Rapids	NCAA III	428
Central Michigan University	Mt Pleasant	NCAA I	428
Concordia College - Ann Arbor	Ann Arbor	NAIA	429
Eastern Michigan University	Ypsilanti	NCAA I	430
Glen Oaks Community College	Centreville	NJCAA	430
Grand Rapids Community College	Grand Rapids	NJCAA	431
Grand Valley State University	Allendale	NCAA II	432
Henry Ford Community College	Dearborn	NJCAA	432
Hillsdale College	Hillsdale	NCAA II/NAIA	433
Hope College	Holland	NCAA III	433
Kalamazoo College	Kalamazoo	NCAA III	434
Kalamazoo Valley Community College	Kalamazoo	NJCAA	434
Kellogg Community College	Battle Creek	NJCAA	435
Lake Michigan College	Benton Harbor	NJCAA	435
Macomb Community College	Warren	NJCAA	436
Madonna University	Livonia	NAIA	436
Michigan State University	East Lansing	NCAA I	437
Mott Community College	Flint	NJCAA	437
Muskegon Community College	Muskegon	NJCAA	438
Northwood University	Midland	NCAA II	438
Oakland University	Rochester	NCAA II	439
Olivet College	Olivet	NCAA III	440
Saginaw Valley State University	University Center	NCAA II	440
Saint Clair County Community College	Port Huron	NJCAA	441
Siena Heights College	Adrian	NAIA	441
Spring Arbor College	Spring Arbor	NAIA	442
University of Detroit Mercy	Detroit	NCAA I	443
University of Michigan - Ann Arbor	Ann Arbor	NCAA I	443
Wayne State University	Detroit	NCAA II	444
Western Michigan University	Kalamazoo	NCAA I	445

Adrian College

110 South Madison Street
Adrian, MI 49221
Coach: Craig Rainey

NCAA III
Bulldogs/Black, Gold
Phone: (517) 265-5161
Fax: (517) 264-3802

ACADEMIC

Founded: 1859
Type: 4 Yr., Private, Liberal Arts, Coed
Religion: United Methodist
Campus Housing: Yes
Web-site: http://www.adrian.edu
SAT/ACT/GPA: Required
Student/Faculty Ratio: 13:1
Male/Female Ratio: 50:50
Undergraduate Enrollment: 1,000
Graduate Enrollment: None
Scholarships/Academic: Yes **Athletic:** No **Fin Aid:** Yes
Total Expenses by: Year **In State:** $ 17,970 **Out of State:** $ 17,970
Degrees Conferred: AA, BS, BA, BFA, Bmus, BMEd, BB
Programs of Study: Accounting, Art, Biology, Business Administration, Chemistry, Criminal Justice, Communication Arts, Earth Science, Economics, English, French, German, Health/Physical Education, International Business, Math, Music, Philosophy, Religion, Sociology, Teacher Education, Medical Technology, Political Science, Prelaw, Premed, Predentistry

ATHLETIC PROFILE

Program Profile: We are a Division III program & have an indoor work-out facility. We play at newly renovated Riverside Park. Our Florida trip is for 10 days & we have two other trips for tournaments.
History: Our program began in 1900. Our last championship was in1993. In 1995, we finished 2nd and had over 100 wins for the past five years.
Achievements: 1993 Conference Champions; 1996 2 All-Region players; last signed player was in 1994.
Coaching: Craig Rainey, Head Coach, started his 6th year as head coach. He compiled a record of 101-99. Mike Duffy, Assistant Coach, is entering his 9th year. He is responsible for hitting & outfielding. Phil Lawrence, Assistant, is entering his 3rd year with the program and is responsible for the infield.
Roster for 1998 team/In State: 20 **Out of State:** 10 **Out of Country:** 0
Total Number of Varsity/Jr. Varsity: 32 **Percent of Graduation:** 100%
Number of Seniors on 1998 Team: 4 **Most Recent Record:** 22 - 16 - 0
Freshmen Receiving Fin Aid/Athletic: 0 **Academic:** 12
Number of Fall Games: 0 **Number of Spring Games:** 45
Positions Needed for 1999/2000: Pitcher, Shortstop
Schedule: Anderson, Toledo, Tri-State University, Hope, Albion
Style of Play: Speed game, defense and pitching.

Albion College

The DOW Center
Albion, MI 49224
Coach: Jim Conway

NCAA III
Britons/Purple, Gold
Phone: (517) 629-0500
Fax: (517) 629-0509

ACADEMIC

Founded: 1835
Type: 4 Yr., Private, Liberal Arts, Coed
Religion: United Methodist
Campus Housing: Yes
SAT/ACT/GPA: V-540-640, Math-530-640/22-28/3.0
Web-site: http://www.albion.edu/
Student/Faculty Ratio: 19:1
Male/Female Ratio: 1:1
Undergraduate Enrollment: 1,800
Graduate Enrollment: None
Scholarships/Academic: Yes **Athletic:** No **Fin Aid:** Yes
Total Expenses by: Year **In State:** $ 21,620 **Out of State:** $ 21,620

Degrees Conferred: BA, BFA
Programs of Study: Accounting, Anthropology, Art, Biology, Business and Management, Chemistry, Communications, Economics, Education, English, Geology, History, Letters/Literature, Life Sciences, Mathematics, Music, Philosophy, Physical Education, Physics, Political Science, Psychology

ATHLETIC PROFILE

Conference Affiliation: MIAA

Alma College

614 West Superior Street
Alma, MI 48801
Coach: John Leister

NCAA III
Scots/Maroon, Cream
Phone: (517) 463-7265
Fax: (517) 463-7018

ACADEMIC

Founded: 1886
Religion: Presbyterian (USA)
Web-site: http://www.alma.edu/
Student/Faculty Ratio: 14:1
Undergraduate Enrollment: 1,350
Scholarships/Academic: Yes **Athletic:** No
Total Expenses by: Year **In State:** $ 19,000

Type: 4 Yr., Private, Liberal Arts, Coed
Campus Housing: Yes
SAT/ACT/GPA: 25 Avg
Male/Female Ratio: 48:52
Graduate Enrollment: None
Fin Aid: Yes
Out of State: $ 19,000

Degrees Conferred: BA, BS
Programs of Study: Accounting, Art, Biochemistry, Business and Management, Chemistry, Computer Information System, Ecology, Health Science, Humanities, Journalism, Liberal Arts, Literature, Mathematics, Modern Languages, Philosophy, Physics, Political Science, Sport Medicine

ATHLETIC PROFILE

Conference Affiliation: MIAA

Aquinas College

1607 Robinson Road, SE
Grand Rapids, MI 49506
Coach: Terry Bocian
Email: bociater@aquinas.edu

NAIA
Saints/Red, White
Phone: (616) 459-8281
Fax: (616) 732-4548

ACADEMIC

Founded: 1922
Religion: Catholic
Web-site: http://www.aquinas.edu/
Student/Faculty Ratio: 15:1
Undergraduate Enrollment: 2,500
Scholarships/Academic: Yes **Athletic:** Yes
Total Expenses by: Year **In State:** $ 18,500

Type: 4 Yr., Private, Liberal Arts, Coed
Campus Housing: Yes
SAT/ACT/GPA: None
Male/Female Ratio: 1:3
Graduate Enrollment: None
Fin Aid: Yes
Out of State: $ 18,500

Degrees Conferred: AA, AS, BA, BS, BFA, M
Programs of Study: Accounting, Art, Art History, Athletic Training, Biology, Business, Chemistry, Commercial Art, Communications, Computer Information Systems, Ecology, Economics, Educations, English, Environmental Science, French, Geography, German, Gerontology, Graphic Art, History, Interior Design, International Business, Liberal Arts, Mathematics, Medical Laboratory Technology, Music, Nuclear Medical Technology, Philosophy, Science, Predentistry, Preengineering, Prelaw

ATHLETIC PROFILE

Estimated Number of Baseball Scholarships: $500-$1,000 per player

Conference Affiliation: WHAC
Program Profile: Our home games are played at Kimble Field.
Achievements: WHAC All-Conference were Chad Addicott, Gary Cook, Jason Switzer, Adam Vanden Toorn, and Chris Waligora. 3 Academic All-Conference players; 3 WHAC All-Conference Honorable Mention, 2 Dennis Molnar Award.
Coaching: Terry Bocian, Head Coach, started his 26th year as head coach at Aquinas College. He also serves as the Athletic Director. He compiled a record of 888-392. He was named the NAIA's State Coach of the Year 8 times and was selected as the NAIA Midwest Region's Coach of the Year. Doug Greenslate, Associate Coach, is responsible for the pitching. He started his 12th season with the program. Edd Mikkelsen - Assistant Coach.
Style of Play: Aggressive offensive; fundamental; very basic defense specialize in defensive fundamentals.

Calvin College

3201 Burton SE
Grand Rapids, MI 49546
Coach: Jeff Pettinga

NCAA III
Knights/Maroon, Gold
Phone: (616) 957-6021
Fax: (616) 957-6060

ACADEMIC

Founded: 1876
Religion: Christian Reformed Churh
Web-site: http://www.calvin.edu/
Student/Faculty Ratio: 16:1
Undergraduate Enrollment: 4,000
Scholarships/Academic: Yes **Athletic:** No
Total Expenses by: Year **In State:** $ 15,865

Type: 4 Yr., Private, Liberal Arts, Coed
Campus Housing: Yes
SAT/ACT/GPA: 940/ 18
Male/Female Ratio: 55:45
Graduate Enrollment: 125
Fin Aid: Yes
Out of State: $ 15,865

Degrees Conferred: BA, BS, BSA, BFA, BSN, BSE, BSW, BSR
Programs of Study: Accounting, Biology, Business Administration (Communications, Mathematics, Social Science), Biochemistry, Film Studies, French, Geography, Geology, German, Music, Nursing, Natural Science, Medical Technology, History, Criminal Justice, Computer Science, Economics, Education, Sociology, Social Science, Telecommunications, Christian Ministry

ATHLETIC PROFILE

Conference Affiliation: Michigan Intercollegiates Athletic Association
Program Profile: We have an outstanding outdoor facility, batting cages and an excellent weight room. We take a quality Spring trip and have a 36 game schedule (NCAA limit).
History: Our program began in 1921 and has been a perennial conference contender.
Coaching: Jeff Pettinga, Head Coach, has 32 years of coaching experience.
Style of Play: Good pitching is emphasized, hiting line-up, emphasiz good defense. Requirements - good speed in the outfield, good hands in the infield, strong arm catching.

Central Michigan University

112 Rose Center
Mt Pleasant, MI 48859
Coach: Judd Folske

NCAA I
Chippewas/Maroon, Gold
Phone: (517) 774-6670
Fax: (517) 774-5391

ACADEMIC

Founded: 1892
Religion: Non-Affiliated
Web-site: Not Available
Student/Faculty Ratio: 20:1
Undergraduate Enrollment: 14,400

Type: 4 Yr., Public, Coed
Campus Housing: Yes
SAT/ACT/GPA: 820avg
Male/Female Ratio: 45:55
Graduate Enrollment: 1,800

Scholarships/Academic: Yes **Athletic:** Yes **Fin Aid:** Yes
Total Expenses by: Year **In State:** $ 7,400 **Out of State:** $ 12,000
Degrees Conferred: BA, BS, BFA, BAA, BSBA, MA, MS
Programs of Study: Numerous Majors offered in each of these areas: Business Administration, Communications, Health-Related Programs, Human Services, Liberal Arts, Fine Arts, Preprofessional Programs, Science and Technology, Elementary Education, Secondary Education

ATHLETIC PROFILE

Conference Affiliation: Mid-American Conference
Program Profile: CMU's Theunissen Stadium, considered one of the finest facilities in the Midwest , seats more than 4,100. The well-groomed playing field is surrounded by a spacious pressbox, large dugouts and a huge electric scoreboard. Outside of the left field fence is another well-maintained field. Over the right field is an infield that is a great practice tool for many individual and team drills. Along the right field line are 3 batting cages for hitting drills. Our baseball complex is 2nd to none.
History: "Chippewa Pride" is the Central Michigan University motto and in baseball it is very evident. CMU has been playing baseball since 1896 and has compiled an all-time record of 1502-836-16 for a winning percentage of .645.
We have been to NCAA play 13 times since 1971. Central reached the NCAA playoffs seven times in the 1980's and three times in the 1990's. CMU has won the Mid-American Conference Championship in 1977, 1980, 1981, 1984, 1986, 1987,1988, 1990, 1994 and 1995. Since becoming division I in 1970, our overall record of 970 wins and 464 losses is the best win-loss percentage (.676) of the 33 major universities in the MidEast region.
Achievements: CMU has 15 All-Americans since 1971 and the Chippewa currently have one player in the major leagues. An additional 8 players are in the minor leagues hoping to reach the majors.

Concordia College - Ann Arbor

4090 Geddes Road
Ann Arbor, MI 48105
Coach: Phil Trapp
Email: trapp@ccdd.edu

NAIA
Cardinals/Red, White
Phone: (734) 995-7342
Fax: (734) 995-4883

ACADEMIC

Founded: 1963
Religion: Lutheran
Web-site: http://www.ccaa.edu/
Student/Faculty Ratio: 12:1
Undergraduate Enrollment: 550

Type: 4 Yr., Private, Liberal Arts, Coed
Campus Housing: Yes
SAT/ACT/GPA: 20/2.5
Male/Female Ratio: 40:60
Graduate Enrollment: N/A

Scholarships/Academic: Yes **Athletic:** Yes **Fin Aid:** Yes
Total Expenses by: Year **In State:** $ 17,450 **Out of State:** $ 17,450
Degrees Conferred: BA
Programs of Study: Art, Biblical Languages, Biology, Business Administration, Communications, Elementary Education, English, General Science, History, Political Science, Mathematics, Music, Church Music, Physical Education, Psychology, Religious Studies, Social Studies, Sociology, Sports Management

ATHLETIC PROFILE

Estimated Number of Baseball Scholarships: 2 Full
Conference Affiliation: Wolverine - Hoosier Athletic Conference
Program Profile: We do 4-6 weeks of Fall practice with 5-6 games. We have a flexible off-season of conditioning and weights (Oct 16 - Dec). We take a 7-10 days Spring trip South (Tennessee, Florida, or other) and play a 40-50 games season.
Coaching: Phil Trapp - Head Coach. Rob Hamuda - Assistant Coach.
Roster for 1998 team/In State: 16 **Out of State:** 5 **Out of Country:** 0
Total Number of Varsity/Jr. Varsity: 25+ **Percent of Graduation:** 18%
Number of Seniors on 1998 Team: 3 **Number of Sophomores on 1998 Team:** 0
Number of Fall Games: 5 **Number of Spring Games:** 50

Baseball Camp Dates: Second week of June **Most Recent Record:** 10 - 30 - 0
Style of Play: Emphasize defensive execution, fundamental soundness, baseball knowledge. Offensive aggressive running, hit and run, bunting, and base-hit baseball team chemistry and individual player development.

Cornerstone College

(Program Discontinued)

Eastern Michigan University

12 Bowen Fieldhouse
Ypsilanti, MI 48197
Coach: Roger Coryell
Email: rogercoryell@emich.edu

NCAA I
Eagles/Green, White
Phone: (734) 487-0315
Fax: (734) 487-6898

ACADEMIC

Founded: 1849
Type: 4 Yr., Public, Coed
Religion: Non-Affiliated
Campus Housing: Yes
Web-site: http://www.emich.edu/
SAT/ACT/GPA: None
Student/Faculty Ratio: 20:1
Male/Female Ratio: 1:4
Undergraduate Enrollment: 25,000
Graduate Enrollment: 10,000
Scholarships/Academic: Yes **Athletic:** Yes **Fin Aid:** Yes
Total Expenses by: Year **In State:** $ 8,112.40 **Out of State:** $ 12,649
Degrees Conferred: BA, BS, BFA, BAE, BBA, BBE, BMP, MA, MS, MBA, MFA
Programs of Study: Accounting, Advertising, Anthropology, Aviation, Banking/Finance, Biochemistry, Biology, Chemistry, Broadcasting, Communications, Computer Science, Criminal Justice, Design, Dramatic Arts, Earth Science, Economics, Education, English, Geography, Geology, Management, Marketing, Microbiology, Music, Nursing, Physics, Political Science, Psychology

ATHLETIC PROFILE

Estimated Number of Baseball Scholarships: 11.7
Conference Affiliation: Mid - American Conference
Program Profile: We play in a highly competitive West Division of the Mid-American Conference. We play at the new Oestrike Stadium that seats 2,500 fans and has a natural playing surface.
History: Our program began in 1949 and our career record is 1,108-942-9.
Achievements: NAIA World Series in 1967, 1968, and 1970; NAIA National Champions in 1970; NCAA College World Series in 1975 (5th place), 1976 (2nd place); MAC Champions in 1975, 1976, 1978 and 1982.
Coaching: Roger Coryell, Head Coach (EMU 1971), was an assistant to Head Coach Ron Oestrike for 16 seasons before taking over the program. Our team has been above .500 for 5 of his 8 seasons as a head coach. Jake Boss - Assistant Coach.
Roster for 1998 team/In State: 25 **Out of State:** 3 **Out of Country:** 2
Total Number of Varsity/Jr. Varsity: 25 **Percent of Graduation:** 90%
Number of Fall Games: 2 **Number of Spring Games:** 54
Positions Needed for 1999/2000: Outfielder, Infielder, Pitcher, Catcher
Most Recent Record: 27 - 27 - 0
Baseball Camp Dates: June 15-18; June 22-25; July 6-9
Style of Play: Very aggressive offensively.

Glen Oaks Community College

62249 Shimmel Road
Centreville, MI 49032
Coach: Joel Mishler

NJCAA
Vikings/Forest Green, Gold
Phone: (616) 467-9945
Fax: (616) 467-9646

ACADEMIC

Founded: 1967
Type: 2 Yr., Public, Jr. College, Coed
Web-site: http://www.glenoaks.cc.mi.us
SAT/ACT/GPA: None
Student/Faculty Ratio: 14:1
Male/Female Ratio: Unknown
Undergraduate Enrollment: 1,300
Graduate Enrollment: None
Scholarships/Academic: Yes **Athletic:** Yes **Fin Aid:** Yes
Total Expenses by: Year **In State:** $ 5,300 **Out of State:** $ 5,900
Degrees Conferred: AA, AAS
Programs of Study: Business, Nursing, Science, Technology, Engineering, Liberal Arts, General Studies

ATHLETIC PROFILE

Estimated Number of Baseball Scholarships: 12
Conference Affiliation: Michigan Community College Athletic Assoc.
Program Profile: We have a small grand stand that seats 360 down the lines. There is an underground sprinkler system and a brick dust in the infield . In a beautiful setting, there is an indoor practice facility right next to the field. We play Fall ball September to October and have a 56 game Spring schedule that includes a the trip to Arizona.
History: Our program began in 1969 and has produced 2 Big Leaguers and numerous pro's. We have competed for Regional XII Championships consistently over the past five years.
Achievements: We are were2nd in the region 4 out of 5 years. Twice we lost to eventual National Champions and once to Runner-Up National Champs. We play in a Strong Region and had 3 All-Americans in the past five years. We had 4 draft choices in the past five years (10th , 11th , 20th , 45th round); 8 professional players in the past five years - some are Independent Leaguers.
Coaching: Joel Mishler, Head Coach,has coached here since 1993 with an overall record of 178-137. J. Osborne, Assistant Coach, stared his 1st first year with the program and coached several seasons at Western Oklahoma CC and Oklahoma State University.
Roster for 1998 team/In State: 19 **Out of State:** 14 **Out of Country:** 0
Total Number of Varsity/Jr. Varsity: 33 **Percent of Graduation:** 80%
Number of Seniors on 1998 Team: **Number of Sophomores on 1998 Team:** 12
Freshmen Receiving Fin Aid/Athletic: 7 **Academic:** 2
Number of Fall Games: 16 **Number of Spring Games:** 56
Positions Needed for 1999/2000: Pitcher, Catcher, Middle Infielder, Outfielder
Baseball Camp Dates: December 21-23; December 28-30
Schedule: Arizona Central, Glendale CC, Mesa CC, Rend Lake, Grand Rapids, Lake Michigan
Style of Play: Fundamentally sound - take pride in our daily approach and work ethic. Play hard and with class - pitchers throw strikes and have a "pitch at a time: mentality. Hitters must be able to bunt, hit and run, and take and honest cut at positive count fastballs.

Grand Rapids Community College

143 Bostwick Avenue, NE
Grand Rapids, MI 49503
Coach: Doug Wabeke
NJCAA
Raiders/Blue, Gold
Phone: (234) 771-3990
Fax: (234) 771-4262

ACADEMIC

Founded: 1914
Type: 2 Yr., Public, Jr. College, Coed
Student/Faculty Ratio: 26:1
Male/Female Ratio: 50:50
Undergraduate Enrollment: 13,700
Graduate Enrollment: None
Scholarships/Academic: No **Athletic:** Yes **Fin Aid:** Yes
Total Expenses by: Year **In State:** $ 1,600 **Out of State:** $ 2,800
Degrees Conferred: Associate
Programs of Study: Accounting, Architecture, Automotive, Business, Communications Computer, Corrections, Criminal, Dental, Drafting/Design, Electrical/Electronics, Engineering, Environmental, Health, Fire, Food, Forestry, Geology, Gerontology, Law, Manufacturing, Nursing, Plastics, Preengineering, Quality Control, Science

ATHLETIC PROFILE

Conference Affiliation: MCCAA

Grand Valley State University

1 Campus Drive
Allendale, MI 49401
Coach: Steve Lyon

NCAA II
Lakers/Blue, Black, White
Phone: (616) 895-3584
Fax: (616) 895-3232

ACADEMIC

Founded: 1963
Type: 4 Yr., Public, Coed
Religion: Non-Affiliated
Campus Housing: Yes
Web-site: Not Available
SAT/ACT/GPA: 19/2.8
Student/Faculty Ratio: 15:1
Male/Female Ratio: Unknown
Undergraduate Enrollment: 12,000
Graduate Enrollment: 3,000
Scholarships/Academic: Yes **Athletic:** Yes **Fin Aid:** Yes
Total Expenses by: Year **In State:** $ 8,362 **Out of State:** $ 12,346
Degrees Conferred: BA, BS, MED, MBA
Programs of Study: Contact school for program of study.

ATHLETIC PROFILE

Conference Affiliation: GLIAC

Henry Ford Community College

5101 Evergreen
Dearborn, MI 48128
Coach: Stu Rose

NJCAA
Hawks/Blue, White
Phone: (313) 845-9647
Fax: (313) 845-6334

ACADEMIC

Founded: 1938
Type: 2 Yr., Jr. College, Coed
Student/Faculty Ratio: 20:1
Male/Female Ratio: 49:51
Undergraduate Enrollment: 15,300
Graduate Enrollment: None
Scholarships/Academic: No **Athletic:** Yes **Fin Aid:** Yes
Total Expenses by: Year **In State:** $ 1,500 **Out of State:** $ 2,500
Degrees Conferred: Associate
Programs of Study: Art, Automotive, Business, Commercial Art, Communications, Constructions, Electrical/Electronics, Graphic Arts, Hospitality, Marketing, Robotics, Theatre, Transportation, Real Estate

ATHLETIC PROFILE

Conference Affiliation: Eastern Collegiate Conference
Achievements: National Runner-up 1994.

Highland Park Community College

(Program Discontinued)

Hillsdale College

201 Oak Street
Hillsdale, MI 49242
Coach: Paul Noce

NCAA II/NAIA
Chargers/Blue, White
Phone: (517) 437-7364
Fax: (517) 437-0014

ACADEMIC

Founded: 1844
Type: 4 Yr., Private, Liberal Arts, Coed
Web-site: Not Available
SAT/ACT/GPA: 1100/20
Student/Faculty Ratio: 13:1
Male/Female Ratio: 50:50
Undergraduate Enrollment: 1,150
Graduate Enrollment: None
Scholarships/Academic: Yes **Athletic:** Yes **Fin Aid:** Yes
Total Expenses by: Year **In State:** $ 17,000 **Out of State:** $ 17,000
Degrees Conferred: BA, BS
Programs of Study: Business and Management, Education, International Studies, Languages, Letter/Literature, Life Sciences, Political Economy, Premed, Prelaw, Social Science

ATHLETIC PROFILE

Conference Affiliation: Great Lakes Intercollegiate Athletic Conference (GLIAC)
Program Profile: Former Major Leaguer Paul Noce is in his 3rd season as Head Coach and is building a solid program. The Chargers play on a beautiful field that is well-maintained. Hillsdale also has a well-equipped sports complex for Winter training. Our team plays a highly competitive schedule.
Achievements: 1990 graduate Troy Salvior was taken in the 25th round by the St. Louis Cardinals.
Coaching: Paul Noce, Head Coach, has 13 years professional baseball experience including two years in the majors (Cubs, Reds). His coaching experience covers both the USA and Korea.
Total Number of Varsity/Jr. Varsity: 32 **Percent of Graduation:** 100%
Style of Play: Aggressive, fundamental baseball

Hope College

P.O. Box 9000
Holland, MI 49422-9000
Coach: Stu Fritz

NCAA III
Flying Dutchmen/Blue, Orange
Phone: (616) 395-7692
Fax: (616) 395-7175

ACADEMIC

Founded: 1866
Type: 4 Yr., Private, Liberal Arts, Coed
Religion: Christian
Campus Housing: Yes
Web-site: http://www.hope.edu/
SAT/ACT/GPA: None
Student/Faculty Ratio: 13:1
Male/Female Ratio: 45:55
Undergraduate Enrollment: 2,900
Graduate Enrollment: None
Scholarships/Academic: Yes **Athletic:** No **Fin Aid:** Yes
Total Expenses by: Year **In State:** $ 19,874 **Out of State:** $ 19,874
Degrees Conferred: BA, BS
Programs of Study: Liberal Arts with concentrated study in 39 academic ares including Business and Management, Letters/Literature, Life Sciences, Physical Sciences, Psychology, Social Sciences

ATHLETIC PROFILE

Conference Affiliation: Michigan Intercollegiate Athletic Association
Program Profile: Hope College has won the Michigan Intercollegiate Athletic Association baseball championship 4 of the last 6 years and 6 times since 1985. The season begins with an 11-game Southern trip. The Ekdal J. Buys Athletic Complex on the campus of Hope College features a baseball field with enclosed dugouts and pressbox.

History: Hope College has sponsored baseball since 1872. It appears the 1st game was played on June 8, 1872, when Hope lost to Grand Haven 30-12 in a game that took 2 hours, 45 minutes.
Achievements: Hope College senior Mark Kuiper (Class of 1995) was voted 1st team GTE Academic All-american for a 2nd consecutive year. He was the 1st Hope player to bat better than .400 in 2 seasons. He is now attending the Wayne State Medical School.
Coaching: Stu Fritz, Head Coah, will begin his 5th season at the helm of the Flying Dutchman in 1997. He is a member of the Kinesiology Faculty and is also an assistant football coach.
Style of Play: We use an aggressive style of play and work hard on defense.

Kalamazoo College

1200 Academy Street
Kalamazoo, MI 49006
Coach: Randy Jones

NCAA III
Hornets/Orange, Black
Phone: (616) 383-7392
Fax: (616) 337-7401

ACADEMIC

Founded: 1833
Type: 4 Yr., Private, Liberal Arts, Coed
Religion: American Baptist
Campus Housing: Yes
Web-site: http://www.kzoo.edu/
SAT/ACT/GPA: 1100/24/3.0
Student/Faculty Ratio: 15:1
Male/Female Ratio: 1:1
Undergraduate Enrollment: 1,250
Graduate Enrollment: None
Scholarships/Academic: Yes **Athletic:** No **Fin Aid:** Yes
Total Expenses by: Year **In State:** $ 24,249 **Out of State:** $ 21,975
Degrees Conferred: BA
Programs of Study: 24 Majors, 30 concentrations and special programs including Anthropology, Biology, Business Administration, Chemistry, Computer Science, Dramatic Arts, Economics, English, Fine Arts, French, German, Health Science, History, Management, Mathematics, Music, Philosophy, Physics, Political Science, Predental, Prelaw, Premed, Psychlogy, Religion, Secondary Education

ATHLETIC PROFILE

Conference Affiliation: Michigan Intercollegiate Conference

Kalamazoo Valley Community College

P.O. Box 4070
Kalamazoo, MI 49003
Coach: Greg Cowles

NJCAA
Cougars/Royal, White
Phone: (616) 372-5421
Fax: (616) 372-5172

ACADEMIC

Founded: 1966
Type: 2 Yr., Jr. College, Coed
Web-site: Not-Available
SAT/ACT/GPA: Non-competitive
Student/Faculty Ratio: Unknown
Male/Female Ratio: 45:55
Undergraduate Enrollment: 9,300
Graduate Enrollment: None
Scholarships/Academic: Yes **Athletic:** Yes **Fin Aid:** Yes
Total Expenses by: Credit **In State:** $ 38/cr **Out of State:** $ 74/cr
Degrees Conferred: Associate
Programs of Study: Accounting, Automotive, Business, Computer, Dental, Medical, Law, Marketing, Engineering, Nursing, Plastics, Respiratory, Science, Secretarial

ATHLETIC PROFILE

Conference Affiliation: MCCAA

Kellogg Community College

450 North Avenue
Battle Creek, MI 49017
Coach: Russ Bortell

NJCAA
Bruins/Royal Blue, Silver
Phone: (616) 965-3931
Fax: (616) 962-2215

ACADEMIC

Founded: 1956
Type: 2 Yr., Jr. College, Coed
Student/Faculty Ratio: 20:1
Male/Female Ratio: 45:55
Undergraduate Enrollment: 7,000
Graduate Enrollment: None
Scholarships/Academic: No **Athletic:** Yes **Fin Aid:** Yes
Total Expenses by: Year **In State:** $ 4,000 **Out of State:** $ 5,500
Degrees Conferred: Associate
Programs of Study: Accounting, Anthropology, Art, Administration, Automotive, Banking/Finance, Biological, Broadcasting, Business, Chemistry, Communications, Corrections, Criminal, Dental, Drafting/Design Technology, Education, Engineering, Fire Science, Food Services, Gerontology, History, Legal, Machine/Tool Technology, Office Management, Paralegal, Pharmacy, Philosophy, Retail, Robotics, Science, Speech, Technical Writing, Theatre

ATHLETIC PROFILE

Estimated Number of Baseball Scholarships: 11
Conference Affiliation: Michigan Community College Athletic Association
Program Profile: We play at a city facility, Bailey Park, which seats 6,000. It is one of the best facilities in the Midwest. Our Spring season is approximately 50 games. We do a 6-8 week Fall program. We do conditioning in the Winter.
History: Our program began in 1976 - 1977.
Achievements: 16 players have been drafted.
Coaching: Russ Bortell, Head Coach, started coaching the program in 1987-1988. His record is 173-167-6. Jim Miller and Mot Boumon - Assistant Coaches.
Roster for 1998 team/In State: 26 **Out of State:** 3 **Out of Country:** 0
Total Number of Varsity/Jr. Varsity: 0 **Percent of Graduation:** 70%
Baseball Camp Dates: Winter **Number of Sophomores on 1998 Team:** 15
Freshmen Receiving Fin Aid/Athletic: 7 **Academic:** 2
Most Recent Record: 16 - 20 - 0 **Number of Spring Games:** 54
Positions Needed for 1999/2000: 14
Schedule: Volunteer State, Columbia State, Grand Rapids
Style of Play: Aggressive.

Lake Michigan College

2755 East Napier
Benton Harbor, MI 49022-1899
Coach: Tom Ackerman

NJCAA
Indians/Red, Grey
Phone: (616) 927-3571
Fax: (616) 927-8176

ACADEMIC

Type: 2 Yr., Public, Coed
Campus Housing: No
Degrees Conferred: Associate
Programs of Study: Accounting, Art/Fine Arts, Biology, Biological Science, Business Administration, Commerce, Management, Chemistry, Computer Programming, Computer Science, Corrections, Criminal justice, Data Processing, Dental Services, Dietetics, Drafting/Design Technology, Economics, Education, Electrical/Electronics Technology, Food Services Management, Geography

Macomb Community College

14500 E Twelve Mile Road
Warren, MI 48093
Coach: Riechl Mayne

NJCAA
Monarchs/Blue, White
Phone: (810) 445-7476
Fax: (810) 445-7491

ACADEMIC

Founded: 1954
Type: 2 Yr., Jr. College, Coed
Religion: Non-Affiliated
Campus Housing: No
Web-site: http://www.macomb.cc.mi.us
SAT/ACT/GPA: None
Undergraduate Enrollment: 28,000+
Graduate Enrollment: None
Total Expenses by: Year **In State:** $ 2,300 **Out of State:** $ 3,000
Degrees Conferred: Associate
Programs of Study: Accounting, Architectural Technology, Automotive Technology, Aviation Technology, Behavioral Science, Business Administration, Commerce, Management, Computer Technology, Paralegal Studies, Office Management, Physical Therapy, Surveying Technology, Nursing, Criminal Justice, Physical Therapy, Plastics

ATHLETIC PROFILE

Conference Affiliation: Michigan Community College Athletic Association
Program Profile: The baseball program makes its outdoor home on Monarch Field with a seating capacity of 1,000. Indoor practice facilities include a complete synthetic infield, two batting cages, pitching machines, sliding pits, a running track and a weight room.
History: The program began in 1970 and the team finished 20-20 that season, but has since had great success winning MCCAA Division titles in 1971, 1977, 1979, 1983, 1984, 1985, 1986, 1989, 1994 and 1995. We were Regional champs in 1983 and 1995.
Achievements: Macomb has had several players drafted by major league teams. Led by former Boston and Toronto Catcher Ernie Whitt, Tops All-American 1971. In all, Macomb has had seven players drafted into the pro-ranks.

Madonna University

36600 Schoolcraft Road
Livonia, MI 48150
Coach: Greg Haeger

NAIA
Crusaders/Blue, Gold, White
Phone: (313) 432-5609
Fax: (313) 432-5611

ACADEMIC

Founded: 1947
Type: 4 Yr., Private, Liberal Arts, Coed
Religion: Catholic
Campus Housing: Yes
Web-site: http://www.munet.edu/
SAT/ACT/GPA: 18
Student/Faculty Ratio: 18:1
Male/Female Ratio: 1:3
Undergraduate Enrollment: 4,000
Graduate Enrollment: 560
Scholarships/Academic: Yes **Athletic:** Yes **Fin Aid:** Yes
Total Expenses by: Year **In State:** $ 11,593 **Out of State:** $11,593
Degrees Conferred: Bachelor, Master
Programs of Study: 50 Under Graduate Majors

ATHLETIC PROFILE

Conference Affiliation: Independent Conference
Program Profile: Our indoor facility has two cages, four mounds and a pitching machine. Fall season is six weeks and we have an off-season weight lifting and conditioning program. We play a 65-game regular season with a 13-day Southern trip and an 8-day trip to San Diego. Home games are played on a natural turf field at Madonna University Park.
History: Our program is entering its eighth year and has compiled a record of 222-146 (.603).

Achievements: 1993 District 23 Regular season Champions; 1995 NAIA Great Lakes Sectional Champions.
Style of Play: Fundamental baseball. Aggressive offense, and baserunnning. Solid pitching and defense.

Michigan State University

304 Jenison Fieldhouse
East Lansing, MI 48824
Coach: Ted Mahan

NCAA I
Spartnas/Green, White
Phone: (517) 355-4486
Fax: (517) 9636

ACADEMIC

Founded: 1855
Religion: Non-Affiliated
Web-site: http://www.msu.edu/
Student/Faculty Ratio: 25:1
Undergraduate Enrollment: 31,000
Scholarships/Academic: Yes **Athletic:** Yes
Total Expenses by: Year **In State:** $ 17,320

Type: 4 Yr., Public, Coed
Campus Housing: Yes
SAT/ACT/GPA: 1120/ 24
Male/Female Ratio: 48:52
Graduate Enrollment: 9,000
Fin Aid: Yes
Out of State: $31,450

Degrees Conferred: AA, BA, BS, MS, PhD, AAS
Programs of Study: Agriculture and Natural Resources, Arts and Letters, Business, Communication, Arts and Science, Education, Engineering, Human Ecology/Medicine, Natural Science, Nursing, Osteophathe Medicine, Social Science, Veterinary Medicine

ATHLETIC PROFILE

Conference Affiliation: Big 10 Conference
Program Profile: MSU plays 50+ games in a regular season. We play at Kobs Field which seats 4,000 and has natural grass. Oldsmobile Park seats 6,006 and has natural grass. It is a Class A ballpark for Royals Affiliate--Lansing Lugnuts). Kobs Field recently upgraded with a new electronic scoreboard. Ted Mahan assumed head coaching duties in 1995-1996 for Tom Smith, who retired after being associated with the MSU Baseball program for 28 years. MSU played two Fall games in September 1996 at Oldsmobile Park.
History: MSU baseball began in 1884 and we were Big Ten Champions in 1979, 1971, 1954. MSU players who went on to the major league include Kirk Gibson, Mel Behney, Rob Ellis, Dean Look, Steve Carvey, Dick Billings, Tim Birtsas, Ed Hobaugh, Dann Howith, Jack Kralick, John Leister, Al Luplow, Rick Miller, Ron Perranoski, Ron Pruitt, Dick Radatz, Robin Roberts, Tom Yewcic, Hobie Landrith, Mike Marshall and Mike Wallace. Current players in the major league include Tim Crabtree, Dave Reinfelder, Dan Masteller.
Achievements: NCAA District IV Title in 1954 and placed 3rd in the College World Series; has produced 5 Big Ten Batting Champions and 6 Big Ten winningest pitchers, along with 8 1st team, 10 2nd team and 93rd team All-Americans; 55 1st team All-Big Ten Selections; several drafted players.
Coaching: Ted Mahan,Head Coach, is in his 4th year and was MSU assistant coach for 4 years. He assisted at Michigan for 3 years and played 4 years of baseball at Michigan as a catcher.
Style of Play: Aggressive, fundamental baseball.

Mott Community College

1401 East Court Street
Flint, MI 48503
Coach: Dan Shelton
Email: athletics@mcc.edu

NJCAA
Bears/Black, Gold
Phone: (810) 232-2161
Fax: (810) 762-0562

ACADEMIC

Founded: 1923
Student/Faculty Ratio: 23:1

Type: 2 Yr., Public, Jr. College, Coed
Male/Female Ratio: 39:61

Undergraduate Enrollment: 10,900 **Graduate Enrollment:** None
Scholarships/Academic: No **Athletic:** Yes **Fin Aid:** Yes
Total Expenses by: Year **In State:** $ 1, 800 **Out of State:** $ 3,100
Degrees Conferred: Associate
Programs of Study: Architecture, Automotive, Business, Chemistry, Computer Information Systems, Construction, Corrections, Deaf Interpreter, Dental Services, Engineering, Gerontology, Law, Paralegal Studies, Photography, Quality Control

ATHLETIC PROFILE

Estimated Number of Baseball Scholarships: 24
Conference Affiliation: MCCAA
Program Profile: Our program is on an up swing. We play in the Fall and in the Spring on a natural grass field. The stadium size seats about 1,500.
History: Mott has been to the National Tournament several times.
Achievements: We were Conference Co-Champions in 1997.
Coaching: Dan Shelton, Head Coach, is in his 4th year and has coached 18 years. His high school record is 362-169. Charlie Sumpter - Assistant Coach.
Roster for 1998 team/In State: 24 **Out of State:** 0 **Out of Country:** 0
Total Number of Varsity/Jr. Varsity: 24 **Percent of Graduation:** 0
Number of Seniors on 1998 Team: 12 **Number of Sophomores on 1998 Team:**
Freshmen Receiving Fin Aid/Athletic: 10 **Most Recent Record:** 24 - 20 - 0
Number of Fall Games: 0 **Number of Spring Games:** 56
Positions Needed for 1999/2000: Shortstop, Pitcher, Catcher
Style of Play: Aggressive offense, conservative defense.

Muskegon Community College

221 South Quarterline Road
Muskegon, MI 49442
Coach: Cap Pohlman

NJCAA
Jayhawks/Royal, Gold
Phone: (616) 777-0381
Fax: (616) 777-0255

ACADEMIC

Founded: 1926 **Type:** 2 Yr., Jr. College, Coed
Student/Faculty Ratio: 35:1 **Male/Female Ratio:** 48:52
Undergraduate Enrollment: 5,170 **Graduate Enrollment:** None
Scholarships/Academic: No **Athletic:** Yes **Fin Aid:** Yes
Total Expenses by: Year **In State** Associate: $ 1,200 **Out of State:** $ 2,200
Degrees Conferred: Associate
Programs of Study: Accounting, Advertising, Anthropology, Art, Automtoive, Banking/Finance, Business, Engineering, Computer, Criminal Justice, Drafting/Design Technology, Economics

ATHLETIC PROFILE

Conference Affiliation: MCCAA

Northwood University

3225 Cook Road
Midland, MI 48640
Coach: Stephen Jacksa

NCAA II
Timberwolves/Col Blue, White, Navy
Phone: (517) 837-4200
Fax: (517) 837-4484

ACADEMIC

Founded: 1960 **Type:** 4 Yr., Private, Coed
Web-site: Not Available **SAT/ACT/GPA:** 900/19-20

Student/Faculty Ratio: 9:1
Male/Female Ratio: 55:45
Undergraduate Enrollment: 1,400
Graduate Enrollment: None
Scholarships/Academic: Yes **Athletic:** Yes **Fin Aid:** Yes
Total Expenses by: Year **In State:** $ 15,300 **Out of State:** $ 15,300
Degrees Conferred: AA, BBA
Programs of Study: Accounting, Advertising, Business, Marketing

ATHLETIC PROFILE

Conference Affiliation: Great Lakes Intercollegiate Athletic Conference (GLIAC)
Program Profile: Our new stadium is under construction and will be in operation for the Fall of 1998. It will have natural grass but seating capacity has not yet been determined.
History: The baseball program began in 1963.
Achievements: Stephen Jacksa is in his 1st year . We do not know the details yet.
Coaching: Stephen Jacksa - Head Coach. Art Felton - Assistant Coach. Wolly Brzenk - Assistant.
Style of Play: Like to run - aggressive and solid defense.

Oakland University

2200 Squirrel Road
Rochester, MI 48309
Coach: Greg Porter

NCAA II
Pioneers/Gold, Black
Phone: (248) 370-4059
Fax: (248) 370-4056

ACADEMIC

Type: 4 Yr., Public, Liberal Arts, Coed, Engineering
Founded: 1955
Religion: Non-Affiliated
Campus Housing: Yes
Web-site: http://www.acs.oakland.edu/
SAT/ACT/GPA: Only used as a guide
Student/Faculty Ratio: 19:1
Male/Female Ratio: 40:60
Undergraduate Enrollment: 14,000
Graduate Enrollment: None
Scholarships/Academic: Yes **Athletic:** Yes **Fin Aid:** Yes
Total Expenses by: Year **In State:** $ 8,000 **Out of State:** $ 14,000
Degrees Conferred: Bachelor, Master, Doctorate
Programs of Study: Accounting, Anatomy, Anthropology, Art, History, Biochemistry, Biology, Business, Chemistry, Communications, Computer Science, Cytotechnology, Economics, Education, Engineering, Environmental Science, Finance, French, German, Journalism, Math, Marketing, Medical Laboratory, Music, Nursing, Philosophy, Physical Therapy, Physics, Political Science, Psychology, Toxicology, Prelaw, Premed, Predentistry

ATHLETIC PROFILE

Estimated Number of Baseball Scholarships: 7.5
Conference Affiliation: Mid-Continent Conference
Program Profile: Our field has natural turf, an enclosed park, ample seating, a public address,a press box, an indoor Winter facility and a bubble (football size).
History: We started in 1970 as an Independent Div. II member of GLIAC Conference in 1974-1997.
Achievements: GLIAC Tournament Champions in 1994; Matt Byrd was drafted by Atlanta Bravez Organization in 1994-1996; Matt McClellan was drafted by Blue Jays Organization in 1997-1998; Bill Masching was drafted by Detroit Tigers Organization in 1996-1997.
Coaching: Greg Porter,Head Coach, started his 1st year with the program. Jay Alexander and Frank Divito - Assistant Coaches.
Roster for 1998 team/In State: 26 **Out of State:** 0 **Out of Country:** 0
Total Number of Varsity/Jr. Varsity: 26 **Percent of Graduation:** 100%
Number of Seniors on 1998 Team: 2 **Number of Sophomores on 1998 Team:** 4
Freshmen Receiving Fin Aid/Athletic: 9 **Academic:** 4
Most Recent Record: 14 - 16 - 0 **Number of Spring Games:** 30
Positions Needed for 1999/2000: Pitching, Middle Infielder
Schedule: Notre Dame, Michigan, MSU, Oral Roberts, Central Michigan, Eastern Michigan
Style of Play: Aggressive, stealing, bunting, hit and run.

Olivet College

300 South Main Street
Olivet, MI 49076
Coach: Eddie Uschold

NCAA III
Fighting Comets/Red, White, Black
Phone: (616) 749-6654
Fax: (616) 749-7229

ACADEMIC

Founded: 1844
Type: 4 Yr., Private, Coed
Religion: Non-Affiliated
Campus Housing: Yes
Web-site: Not-Available
SAT/ACT/GPA: 18
Student/Faculty Ratio: 14:1
Male/Female Ratio: 2:1
Undergraduate Enrollment: 780
Graduate Enrollment: None
Scholarships/Academic: Yes **Athletic:** No **Fin Aid:** Yes
Total Expenses by: Year **In State:** $ 16,000 **Out of State:** $ 16,000
Degrees Conferred: BA
Programs of Study: Education, Insurance and Business Administration are the most popular. Typical Liberal Arts Institution curriculum offering general academic program including Business and Management, Communications, Education, Liberal Art Education, Psychology and Sociology

ATHLETIC PROFILE

Conference Affiliation: Michigan Intercollegiate Athletic Association
Program Profile: Olivet College is located in beautiful South Central Michigan, twenty miles of East Battle Creek and 35 minutes west of Michigan State.
History: Our program began in 1905. We are a founding and original member of the nation's oldest athletic conference (MIAA) in the country. Last league title was 1981. We went from 11-21, 17-17 to 25-13 during the last three years. In 1995 we had a school record for wins (25 wins), It was the first winning season in school history.
Achievements: Vern Ruhle, major league pitcher was an Olivet baseball alumni.
Coaching: Eddie Uschold, Head Coach, started his 1st year with the program and has 7 years experience at the collegiate level. He was an assistant coach at Kent State, Tylor Junior College and Manchester College. He was a head coach of Tyler Texans and Athletes in Action. Twenty-three players he has coached have signed pro contracts.
Roster for 1998 team/In State: 28 **Out of State:** 6 **Out of Country:** 3
Freshmen Receiving Fin Aid/Athletic: 0 **Academic:** All
Most Recent Record: 17 - 17 - 0 **Number of Spring Games:** 44
Positions Needed for 1999/2000: All open
Schedule: Hope, Manchester College, Grand Valley, Adrian, Albion
Style of Play: Sound aggressive, fundamental baseball.

Saginaw Valley State University

7400 Bay Road
University Center, MI 48710
Coach: Walt Head

NCAA II
Cardinals/Navy, Red, White
Phone: (517) 791-7334
Fax: (517) 790-0545

ACADEMIC

Type: 4 Yr., Public, Liberal Arts, Coed, Engineering
Founded: 1963
Religion: Non-Affiliated
Campus Housing: Yes
Web-site: Not-Available
SAT/ACT/GPA: 17/2.0
Student/Faculty Ratio: Unknown
Male/Female Ratio: 46:54
Undergraduate Enrollment: 8,500
Graduate Enrollment: 1,050
Scholarships/Academic: Yes **Athletic:** Yes **Fin Aid:** Yes
Total Expenses by: Year **In State:** $ 7,600 **Out of State:** $ Varies
Degrees Conferred: Bachelors

Programs of Study: Accounting, Art, Banking/Finance, Biological, Business, Chemistry, Communications, Computer, Criminal Justice, Design, Dramatic Arts, Economics, Political Science, Preprofessional Programs, Psychology, Secondary Education

ATHLETIC PROFILE

Conference Affiliation: GLIAC
Program Profile: The SVSU baseball field may have some of the best facilities in the GLIAC. The season begins in the Fall. The field is natural grass and the stadium seats 1,500 people.
History: We began in 1979 & won a conference champs in 1995. We were affiliated with the NAIA from 1979-1989 & have played in NCAA Div. II since 1990. We were NAIA Regional in 1986-1987.
Achievements: Won 1995 Conference Titles; Walt Head named NAIA Distrist 1985 and 1986 Coach of the Year; 1995 league champions. Roger Mason (RHP) in the major league 9 years with the Tigers, Giants, and pitched for the Phillies in the World Series. Mike Villino (RHP) drafted in 1995 by the Giants. Jeff Paluk (RHP) drafted in 1995 by the Dodgers.
Coaching: Walt Head, Head Coach, was 1985 and 1986 Coach of the Year. He compiled a record of 432-323-4 in 17 years of coaching. He was GLIAC Coach of the Year in 1996. Jeff Paluk and Mickey Kimel - Assistant Coaches.
Roster for 1998 team/In State: 30 **Out of State:** 1 **Out of Country:** 6
Total Number of Varsity/Jr. Varsity: 42 **Percent of Graduation:** 96%
Number of Seniors on 1998 Team: 10 **Number of Sophomores on 1998 Team:** 6
Freshmen Receiving Fin Aid/Athletic: 0 **Academic:** 5
Most Recent Record: 32 - 20 - 0 **Number of Spring Games:** 56
Positions Needed for 1999/2000: Catcher, Centerfielder, 3-Pitchers
Schedule: Boston College, Dayton, Central Michigan, Missouri - St. Louis, Ashland, Mercyhurst
Style of Play: Power team - broke school record for home runs and doubles, batting average, RBI, eight starter back for 1999 season.

Saint Clair County Community College

323 Erie St
Port Huron, MI 48060
Coach: Rick Smith

NJCAA
Skippers/Maize, Blue
Phone: (810) 989-5671
Fax: (810) 984-4730

ACADEMIC

Founded: 1923 **Type:** 2 Yr., Jr. College, Coed
Student/Faculty Ratio: 18:1 **Male/Female Ratio:** 40:60
Scholarships/Academic: No **Athletic:** Yes **Fin Aid:** Yes
Total Expenses by: Year **In State:** $ 1,600 Associate **Out of State:** $ 3,200
Degrees Conferred: Associate
Programs of Study: Accounting, Advertising, Agriculture, Architectural, Art, Broadcasting, Business, Commercial, Communications, Computer, Corrections, Criminal, Drafting/Design, Journalism, Liberal Arts, Machine/Tool Manufacturing, Marketing, Mental Health, Nursing, Plastics, Quality control, Robotics, Science, Welding

ATHLETIC PROFILE

Conference Affiliation: MCCAA

Siena Heights University

1247 East Siena Heights Drive
Adrian, MI 49221
Coach: Gordie Theisen

NAIA
Saints/Navy, Gold
Phone: (517) 264-7870
Fax: (517) 264-7737

ACADEMIC

Founded: 1919
Religion: Dominican
Web-site: http://www.sienahts.com
Student/Faculty Ratio: 13:1
Undergraduate Enrollment: 1,000
Scholarships/Academic: Yes **Athletic:** Yes
Total Expenses by: Year **In State:** $ 15,500
Type: 4 Yr., Private, Liberal Arts, Coed
Campus Housing: Yes
SAT/ACT/GPA: 22
Male/Female Ratio: 45:55
Graduate Enrollment: 300
Fin Aid: Yes
Out of State: $ 15,500
Degrees Conferred: AA, BA, AFA, BFA, BS, BAS, AS
Programs of Study: Accounting, American Studies, Art, Biology, Business Administration, Management, Marketing, Chemistry, Child Development, Computer Information Systems, Human Services, Criminal Justice, Gerontology, Psychology, Public Administration, Music, Prelaw

ATHLETIC PROFILE

Estimated Number of Baseball Scholarships: $25,000
Conference Affiliation: Wolverine - Hoosier Athletic Conference
Program Profile: Our playing field is on campus. We have a 60 game varsity and a 20 game junior varsity schedule. We have an outstanding indoor practice facility and one of the most competitive and challenging schedules in the Midwest.
History: Our program started in 1973 and we were NAIA District Champs in 1989 and 1994. We were a NAIA World Series participant in 1994. We are consistently #1 or #2 in conference.
Achievements: NAIA District Championships in 1989 and 1994; Regional Champs and World Series Berth in 1994; 3 drafted players in the 1990's; 2 All-Americans; 3 more players signed as undrafted free-agents.
Coaching: Gordie Theisen, Head Coach, arrived in the Summer of 1987. His team has won 310 games since then. Mike Kaczmarek, Assistant Coach, is in his 5th year with the program. Vince Socco, Assistant Coach, started his 2nd year with the program.
Roster for 1998 team/In State: 33 **Out of State:** 6 **Out of Country:** 1
Total Number of Varsity/Jr. Varsity: 40 **Percent of Graduation:** 96%
Number of Seniors on 1998 Team: 9 **Most Recent Record:** 24 - 28 - 0
Freshmen Receiving Fin Aid/Athletic: 7 **Academic:** 7
Number of Fall Games: 6 **Number of Spring Games:** 60
Positions Needed for 1999/2000: Pitcher, Middle Infielder, Outfielder
Schedule: Auburn, Birmingham Southern, Cumberland, Indiana Tech, Ohio Dominican, Michigan
Style of Play: Aggressive offensive philosophy, deep pitching staff; we use about 12 pitcher and 18 position players on a regular basis.

Southwestern Michigan College

(Program Discontinued)

Spring Arbor College

Main Street
Spring Arbor, MI 49283
Coach: Hank Burbridge

NAIA
Cougars/Navy, Gold
Phone: (517) 750-6503
Fax: (517) 750-2745

ACADEMIC

Founded: 1873
Religion: Free Methodist
Web-site: http://www.admin.arbor.edu
Student/Faculty Ratio: 25:1
Undergraduate Enrollment: 1,900
Scholarships/Academic: Yes **Athletic:** Yes
Total Expenses by: Year **In State:** $ 15,310
Type: 4 Yr., Private, Liberal Arts, Coed
Campus Housing: Yes
SAT/ACT/GPA: 20
Male/Female Ratio: 1:3
Graduate Enrollment: 800
Fin Aid: Yes
Out of State: $ 15,310
Degrees Conferred: Bachelors, Associate

Programs of Study: Exercise Sports, Premed, Communications, Education, Christian Ministries, Psychology, Biology, Music, Arts, Chemistry, English, Biochemistry, French, Spanish, Geography, History, Greek, Math, Philosophy, Political Science, Religion, Social Work, Sociology, Speech, Urban Studies, Accounting, Business

ATHLETIC PROFILE

Conference Affiliation: Wolverine - Hoosier Athletic Conference
Program Profile: Our facilities include indoor/outdoor batting cages and a 500 seat stadium. We play Fall and Spring seasons.
History: Our program began in 1964. We won NCCAA (National Christian College Athletic Association) National Championships in 1992 and 1993.
Achievements: NAIA Coach of the Year, NAIA Area Coach of the Year for the past three years; District NCCAA Coach of the Year for four years; NCCAA National Coach of the Year in 1991 and 1992; NAIA and NCCAA Hall of Fame; 3 NAIA District and 2 NAIA Area Championships.
Coaching: Hank Burbridge, Head Coach, has been here 33 years. He ranked 7th nationally in the NAIA and serves on USA Baseball Board. He was a head coach of the National 1996 team Olympic Trials. He was head coach of USA Team in President Cup in Seoul, Korea.
Style of Play: Aggressive, fundamental baseball. Good mental toughness, constantly hustling.

University of Detroit Mercy

4001 W McNichols Rd
Detroit, MI 48219-0900
Coach: Bob Miller

NCAA I
Titans/Red, White, Blue
Phone: (313) 993-1725
Fax: (313) 993-1765

ACADEMIC

Founded: 1877
Religion: Jesuit
Web-site: Not Available
Student/Faculty Ratio: 18:1
Undergraduate Enrollment: 7,000
Scholarships/Academic: Yes **Athletic:** Yes
Total Expenses by: Year **In State:** $ 15,000

Type: 4 Yr., Private, Liberal Arts, Coed
Campus Housing: No
SAT/ACT/GPA: 870+/20+
Male/Female Ratio: 44:56
Graduate Enrollment: None
Fin Aid: Yes
Out of State: $ 15,000

Degrees Conferred: ASBA, BS, BCE, BEE, BFA, MA, MS, DMD
Programs of Study: School of Architecture, College of Business and Adnimistration, School of Education, College of Engineering and Science, Health and Human Services, College of Liberal Arts, School of Nursing, Professional schools of Law and Dentistry

ATHLETIC PROFILE

Conference Affiliation: Midwestern Collegiate Conference
Program Profile: The Titans play a 56-game schedule against MCC, MAC and Big 10 schools. We play at our beautiful ball park, similar to Wrigley Field. It has natural turf and seats 1,500.
History: The Detroit baseball program began in 1941 and has had only four coaches during that span. Current Head Coach, Bob Miller, is entering his 32nd year as head man at Detroit.
Achievements: Made the NCAA Tournaments five times in their 55 year history. Head Coach Bob Miller has been the head coach of the Titans since the 1965 campaign.
Coaching: Bob Miller, Head Coach, started his 35th year as a head coach.
Style of Play: Sound defense and pitching.

University of Michigan - Ann Arbor

1000 S State St
Ann Arbor, MI 48104
Coach: Geoff Zahn

NCAA I
Wolverines/Maize, Blue
Phone: (734) 647-4550
Fax: (734) 647-4589

ACADEMIC

Type: 4 Yr., Public, Liberal Arts, Coed, Engineering
Founded: 1817
Religion: Non-Affiliated
Campus Housing: Yes
Web-site: http://www.umich.edu/˜mgoblue/
SAT/ACT/GPA: 1030+
Student/Faculty Ratio: 15:1
Male/Female Ratio: 52:48
Undergraduate Enrollment: 22,000
Graduate Enrollment: 14,000
Scholarships/Academic: Yes **Athletic:** Yes **Fin Aid:** Yes
Total Expenses by: Year **In State:** $ 9,559 **Out of State:** $ 19,881
Degrees Conferred: AB, BS, BFA, BBA, Bmus, BSN, MA, MS, MBA, MFA, PhD, MD, JD
Programs of Study: Accounting, Anthropology, Art, Architecture, Astronomy, Atmospheric/Oceanic Studies, Biblical, Biology, Botany, Business, Chemistry, Computer, Dentistry, Design, Economics, Education, Engineering, Geology, History, Literature, Management, Math, Medieval, Movement, Music, Natural Resources, Nursing, Oceanography, Pharmacy, Philosophy, Etc..

ATHLETIC PROFILE

Estimated Number of Baseball Scholarships: 11
Conference Affiliation: Big 10 Conference
Program Profile: Baseball at the University of Michigan has been played on the current site of Ray Fisher Stadium since 1923. It was built in 1948 and had renovations in 1973 and in 1983. Moby Benedict installed the fence with the dimensions including 330 down the lines, 375 in the gaps and 400 to dead center. It has a message scoreboard, concession stand, Etc..
History: The 1996 baseball season was a learning experience for 1st year head coach Geoff Zahn. Coach Zahn earned Big Ten Coach of the Year in 1997 leading the Wolverines to their first Big Ten title since 1987.
Achievements: 15 All-Americans; numerous GTE-COSIDA Academic All-Americans; Jim Abbott was named Big Ten Athlete of the Year; 7 Big Ten Players of the Year; 4 Most Valuable Player; numerous All-Tournament.
Coaching: Geoff Zahn, Head Coach, started in the 1995/96 season. He is a former big league pitcher and former pitching coach at Pepperdine in 1994.
Roster for 1998 team/In State: 25 **Out of State:** 15 **Out of Country:** 0
Total Number of Varsity/Jr. Varsity: 40
Baseball Camp Dates: 7/12-16; 7/26-29
Number of Seniors on 1998 Team: 13
Number of Sophomores on 1998 Team: 6
Number of Fall Games: 0
Number of Spring Games: 53

Wayne State University

5101 John C Lodge Drive
Detroit, MI 48202
Coach: Rod George
NCAA II
Tartars/Green, Gold
Phone: (313) 577-7540
Fax: (313) 577-5997

ACADEMIC

Founded: 1868
Type: 4 Yr., Public, Liberal Arts, Coed
Web-site: Not Available
SAT/ACT/GPA: 20 avg
Student/Faculty Ratio: 9:1
Male/Female Ratio: 43:57
Undergraduate Enrollment: 20,230
Graduate Enrollment: 14,000+
Scholarships/Academic: Yes **Athletic:** Yes **Fin Aid:** Yes
Total Expenses by: Year **In State:** $ 3,800 **Out of State:** $ 7,900
Degrees Conferred: BA, BS, BFA, BGS, BM, BPA, BSMS, BSW, MA, MS, MBA, MFA, PhD
Programs of Study: Accounting, Ancient Civilization, Anthropology, Art, Banking/Finance, Biological, Broadcasting, Chemistry, Classics, Communications, Computer, Criminal, Dance, Design, Dietetics, Geography, Geology, History, Humanities, International, Journalism, Linguistics, Etc..

ATHLETIC PROFILE

Conference Affiliation: GLIAC

Western Michigan University

Athletic Department
Kalamazoo, MI 49008
Coach: Fred Decker

NCAA I
Broncos/Brown, Gold
Phone: (616) 387-8149
Fax: (616) 387-8604

ACADEMIC

Founded: 1903
Religion: Non-Affiliated
Web-site: http://www.wmich.edu/
Student/Faculty Ratio: 17:1
Undergraduate Enrollment: 19,803
Scholarships/Academic: Yes **Athletic:** No
Total Expenses by: Year **In State:** $ 8,000
Type: 4 Yr., Public, Coed
Campus Housing: Yes
SAT/ACT/GPA: None
Male/Female Ratio: 45:55
Graduate Enrollment: 5,896
Fin Aid: Yes
Out of State: $ 12,000
Degrees Conferred: BA, BS, BFA, MA, MS, MFA, PhD
Programs of Study: Business and Management, Business/Office and Marketing/Distribution, Communications, Education, Engineering, Parks/Recreation, Protective Services, Public Affairs, Fine Arts, Health and Human Services

ATHLETIC PROFILE

Conference Affiliation: Mid - American Conference
Program Profile: Hyames Field seats 4,000. Its main feature is a bank extending down right field line. It was the site of the first two College World Series engagements (1947-48). Former President George Bush played First base for Yale in the 1948 title game.
History: Our program started in 1911. Coaches Judson Hyames and Charlie Maher are in the Collegiate Baseball Coaches Hall of Fame. Currently, Coach Fred Decker has 601 career wins, tops in WMU history for any sport.
Achievements: School has approved 15 NCAA Tournaments - top finishes were 2nd place at 1995 World Series and tied for 3rd in 1952.
Coaching: Fred Decker, Head Coach, was 2nd team All-american outfielder in 1963 and 1964 at WMU. He is a member of the school's athletic Hall of Fame and tops in WMU for any sport.
Style of Play: We have good team speed and will try to take advantage of it.

MINNESOTA

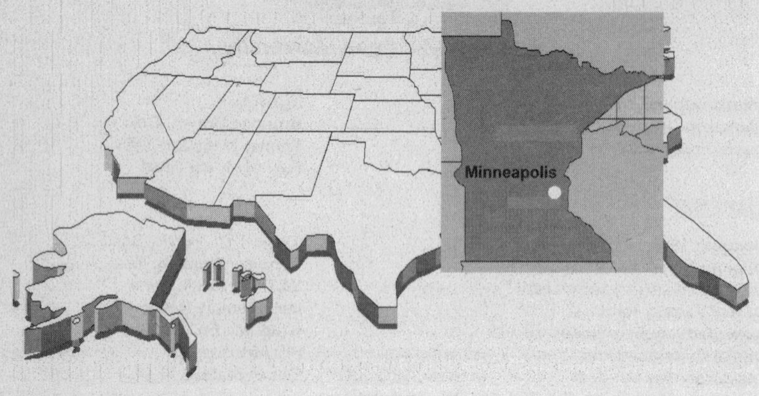

SCHOOL	CITY	AFFILIATION 99	PAGE
Anoka - Ramsey Community College	Coon Rapids	NJCAA	447
Augsburg College	Minneapolis	NCAA III	447
Bemidji State University	Bemidji	NCAA II	447
Bethany Lutheran College	Mankato	NJCAA	448
Bethel College	St. Paul	NCAA III	449
Brainerd Community College	Brainerd	NJCAA	449
Carleton College	Northfield	NCAA III	450
College of Saint Scholastica	Duluth	NCAA III/NAIA	450
Concordia College - Moorhead	Moorhead	NCAA III	451
Concordia College - St. Paul	St. Paul	NAIA	451
Fergus Falls Community College	Fergus Falls	NJCAA	452
Gustavus Adolphos College	St. Peter	NCAA III	453
Hamline University	St. Paul	NCAA III	453
Hibbing Community College	Hibbing	NJCAA	454
Itasca Community College	Grand Rapids	NJCAA	455
Macalester College	St. Paul	NCAA III	455
Mankato State University	Mankato	NCAA II	456
Mesabi Range Community College	Virginia	NJCAA	457
North Hennepin Community College	Brooklyn Park	NJCAA	457
Northland Community College	Thief River Falls	NJCAA	458
Riverland Community College	Austin	NJCAA III	458
Rochester Community College	Rochester	NJCAA	458
Saint Cloud State University	St. Cloud	NCAA II	459
Saint John's University	Collegeville	NCAA III	460
Saint Mary's University - Minnesota	Winona	NCAA III	460
Saint Olaf College	Northfield	NCAA III	461
Southwest State University	Marshall	NCAA II	462
University of Minnesota	Minneapolis	NCAA I	462
University of Minnesota - Duluth	Duluth	NCAA II	463
University of Minnesota - Morris	Morris	NCAA II	463
University of Saint Thomas	St. Paul	NCAA III	464
Vermilion Community College	Ely	NJCAA	465
Willmar Community College	Willmar	NJCAA	465
Winona State University	Winona	NCAA II	466

Anoka - Ramsey Community College

11200 Mississippi Blvd, NW
Coon Rapids, MN 55433
Coach: Tom Yelle

NJCAA
Rams/Black, Gold
Phone: (612) 422-3521
Fax: (612) 422-3341

ACADEMIC

Founded: 1965
Type: 2 Yr., Jr. College, Coed
Undergraduate Enrollment: 6,378
SAT/ACT/GPA: Recommended
Scholarships/Academic: No **Athletic:** No **Fin Aid:** Yes
Total Expenses by: Year **In State:** $ 1,935 **Out of State:** $ 3,770
Degrees Conferred: Associate
Programs of Study: Accounting, Air Traffic Control, Business, Data Processing, Film, Health, Law, Liberal Arts, Marketing, Medical, Nursing, Occupational Therapy, Office Management, Optical Technology, Physical Therapy, Preengineering Science

ATHLETIC PROFILE

Conference Affiliation: MCCC

Augsburg College

2211 Riverside Avenue
Minneapolis, MN 55454
Coach: Mark Strandemo

NCAA III
Auggies/Maroon, Grey
Phone: (612) 330-1249
Fax: (612) 330-1372

ACADEMIC

Founded: 1869
Type: 4 Yr., Private, Liberal Arts, Coed
Religion: Lutheran
Campus Housing: Yes
Web-site: http://www.augsburg.edu/
SAT/ACT/GPA: 850/22
Student/Faculty Ratio: 1:18
Male/Female Ratio: 1:1.5
Undergraduate Enrollment: 2,900
Graduate Enrollment: 150
Scholarships/Academic: Yes **Athletic:** No **Fin Aid:** Yes
Total Expenses by: Year **In State:** $ 18,000 **Out of State:** $ 18,000
Degrees Conferred: BA, BS, MA, MSW, PA
Programs of Study: Natural Science, Social Science, Fine Arts, Excellent Internship Program, Business and MIS

ATHLETIC PROFILE

Conference Affiliation: MIAC
Program Profile: We have an indoor artificial turf facility on campus for practice.
History: Conference Championship 1987.

Bemidji State University

1500 Birchmont Drive, NE
Bemidji, MN 56601
Coach: Jim Grimm

NCAA II
Beavers/Green, White
Phone: (218) 755-2958
Fax: (218) 755-3898

ACADEMIC

Founded: 1919
Type: 4 Yr., Public, Liberal Arts, Coed
Web-site: Not Available
SAT/ACT/GPA: 700/17

Student/Faculty Ratio: 11:1 **Male/Female Ratio:** 1:2
Undergraduate Enrollment: 4,900 **Graduate Enrollment:** 550
Scholarships/Academic: Yes **Athletic:** Yes **Fin Aid:** Yes
Total Expenses by: Year **In State:** $ 5,200 **Out of State:** $ 7,600
Degrees Conferred: AA, AS, BA, BS, BFA, MA, MS
Programs of Study: Accounting, Anthropology, Art, Biological, Broadcasting, Business, Chemistry, Communications, Community Services, Computer, Criminal Justice, Early Childhood, Earth Science, Economics, Education, English, Languages, Geography, Geology, Health, Journalism, Management, Medical, Preprofessional Programs, Etc..

ATHLETIC PROFILE

Conference Affiliation: Northern Sun Intercollegiate
Program Profile: We have a year round program beginning with a 4 week Fall practice. There is an off -season conditioning program and then Winter practice in our indoor facilities. We do 7-10 game Spring trip to Florida and a 40-50 game schedule.
History: The history of BSU baseball dates back to the Spring of 1952. Since that time, BSU baseball has been rich in tradition and pride. Since the transitions over the years, Bemidji has been to a college world series (1992) and is in the midst of having 4 winning seasons in the last 6 years.
Achievements: Coach Smith was twice named NAIA District 15 Coach of the Year at Loras College (Iowa) 1979, 1980. He has the best winning percentage at BSU with Conference titles 1982, 1988, Runner-up in 1992. Three of his players were drafted into pros - Bryan Asp, Kerry Taylor, Tim Veith.
Coaching: Jim Grimm - Head Coach.
Total Number of Varsity/Jr. Varsity: 15 /12 **Percent of Graduation:** 83%
Style of Play: A team that plays to win every game. We are in a hitters conference, so we like to score runs and bank the ball around the park. We play with grit, heart and determination. Our players get along well and we have a lot of fun.

Bethany Lutheran College

734 Marsh Street
Mankato, MN 56001
Coach: Art Westphal
Email: aWest@blc.edu
NJCAA
Vikings/Red, White
Phone: (507) 386-5375
Fax: (507) 386-5355

ACADEMIC

Founded: 1927 **Type:** 2 Yr., Private, Coed
SAT/ACT/GPA: Consideration **Campus Housing:** Yes
Student/Faculty Ratio: 15:1 **Male/Female Ratio:** 45:55
Undergraduate Enrollment: 375 **Graduate Enrollment:** None
Scholarships/Academic: Yes **Athletic:** Yes **Fin Aid:** Yes
Total Expenses by: Year **In State:** $ 12,200 **Out of State:** $ 12,200
Degrees Conferred: AA, AS
Programs of Study: Liberal Arts, General Studies

ATHLETIC PROFILE

Conference Affiliation: Minnesota Community College Conference
Program Profile: We are entering the fourteenth year of our program. We average 22 wins per year. Our season runs from early March through uthe end of May. We have a natural grass field with a seating capacity of 500. The dimensions of our field are: 320 down lines, 365 in the alleys, and 385 to the center.
History: In 1985 , after a 10-year hiatus, the administration of Bethany decided it was time to again have baseball on its campus. Coach Art Westphal was selected as a coach to revive the program. Since then, his teams have posted an impressive 282-146 record. Since 1990, the Vikings have won 6 Division Championships, 2 State Championships and 3 Region XIII Championships.
Achievements: Won 6 Division Titles; 3 Region WIII Championships; 5 All-americans; 3 Professional Players (Minor League); Region XIII Coach of the Year in 1994, 1995, and 1996.

Coaching: Art Wesphal, Head Coach, 24 years experience at high school and collegiate levels and serves as recommending scout for Atlanta Braves. He was NJCAA Region XIII Coach of the Year in 1994, 1995 and 1996. Derek Woodley, Assistant Coach, started his 7th season.
Style of Play: As always, the Vikings will rely on the team's speed and aggressiveness. The Vikings like to bunt, hit and run, and steal as much as possible. Over the years, the trade mark of the Vikings has been the pitchers' ability to throw strikes.

Bethel College

3900 Bethel Drive
St. Paul, MN 55112-6999
Coach: Ken Neuhaus

NCAA III
Royals/Blue, Gold
Phone: (612) 638-6143
Fax: (612) 638-6001

ACADEMIC

Founded: 1871
Religion: Baptist
Web-site: Not-Available
Student/Faculty Ratio: 15:1
Undergraduate Enrollment: 1,900
Scholarships/Academic: Yes **Athletic:** No
Total Expenses by: Year **In State:** $ 17,990
Degrees Conferred: BA, BS, BAEd, Med

Type: 4 Yr., Private, Liberal Arts, Coed
Campus Housing: Yes
SAT/ACT/GPA: 22
Male/Female Ratio: 45:55
Graduate Enrollment: 220
Fin Aid: Yes
Out of State: $ 17,990

Programs of Study: Accounting, Art, History, Biblical Studies, Bilogy, Business and Management, Chemistry, Communications, Computer Science, Creative Writing, Education, Music, Physical Science, English, Family Studies, Finance, History, International Studies, Leberal Arts, Leterature, Management Information Systems, Mathematrics, Ministries, Molecular Biology, Nursing, Philosophy

ATHLETIC PROFILE

Conference Affiliation: Minnesota (MIAC)
Program Profile: We have a 22-man roster and a 39-game schedule. We play in the Metrodome, a minor league stadium. We do a Spring trip to Ft Myers, Florida .Our experienced baseball team looks to improve because 14 from the 1995 team that won 19 games are returning. The Royals have averaged 20 wins per season over the past 4 years.
Achievements: Bethel teams have set the school record for wins 4 of the 7 years Coach Neuhaus has been a head coach.
Coaching: Ken Neuhaus, Head Coach, is in 16th year in college coaching and his 9th year at Bethel College. He assisted at Iowa and Southern Illinois. His MS is from Southern Illinois and his BA is from Wisconsin - Eau Claire.

Brainerd Community College

501 West College Drive
Brainerd, MN 56401
Coach: Jim Russell

NJCAA
Raiders/Red, White
Phone: (218) 828-2525
Fax: (218) 828-2710

ACADEMIC

Founded: 1938
Student/Faculty Ratio: 21:1
Undergraduate Enrollment: 2,025
Scholarships/Academic: No **Athletic:** No
Total Expenses by: Year **In State:** $ 2,000
Degrees Conferred: Associate

Type: 2 Yr., Jr. College, Coed
Male/Female Ratio: 40:60
Graduate Enrollment: None
Fin Aid: Yes
Out of State: $ 3,900

Programs of Study: Acocunting, Business Administration, Horticulture, Liberal Arts, Marketing, Nursing

Carleton College

One North College Street
Northfield, MN 55057
Coach: Bill Nelson

NCAA III
Knights/Maize, Blue
Phone: (507) 646-4051
Fax: (507) 646-5550

ACADEMIC

Founded: 1866
Religion: Non-Affiliated
SAT/ACT/GPA: ACT above 25 and top 10% of class/
Student/Faculty Ratio: 10:1
Undergraduate Enrollment: 1,800
Scholarships/Academic: No **Athletic:** No
Total Expenses by: Year **In State:** $ 26,000
Degrees Conferred: BA

Type: 4 Yr., Private, Liberal Arts, Coed
Campus Housing: Yes
Web-site: http://www.carleton.edu
Male/Female Ratio: 1:1
Graduate Enrollment: None
Fin Aid: Yes
Out of State: $ 23,950

Programs of Study: 33 Majors including: Area and Ethnic Studies, Art, Biology, Chemistry, Economics, History, International Relations, Languages, Letter/Literature, Life Sciences, Mathematics, Music, Philosophy, Physics, Psychology, Religion, Social Science, Theology, Visual and Performing Arts

ATHLETIC PROFILE

Conference Affiliation: Minnesota Intercollegiate Athletic Conference
Program Profile: Practice begins indoors on Feb 1 and is held 5-6 days a week to the end of Winter term. The outdoor portion of the regular season begins with a Spring break trip during the final 2 weeks of March and ends with last conference game in early May. Our school has 2 swimming pools, 2 gyms, 7000-seat football stadium, 400 m all-weather track, 220 yard indoor track, 12 outdoor tennis courts, 20 miles of skiing and running and biking trails.
History: Carleton's financial aid philosophy is to make every effort to meet the full demonstrated financial need of each student offered admission to the college & to continue meeting that need. Policy applies to all need-based grants from the college, as well as loans & work-study contracts.
Achievements: MIAC Champions in 1990 and 1991; 1 All-American in 1989 and 1990. John Nielson, Marvin Stoloz named MIAC Co-MVP's in 1991.
Coaching: Bill Nelson ,Head Coach, is in his 6th year and was assistant coach for two years. He is the manager of Dundas Dukes, a local amateur ball club which won two Minnesota Championships in 1982 and 1988.
Style of Play: All-out, base-stealing, hit and run, Etc. Smart players, smart baseball.

College of Saint Scholastica

1200 Kenwood Avenue
Duluth, MN 55811
Coach: John Baggs
Email: jbaggs@css.edu

NCAA III/NAIA
Saints/Black, Royal Blue
Phone: (218) 723-6298
Fax: (218) 723-5958

ACADEMIC

Founded: 1912
Religion: Roman Catholic
Web-site: http://www.css.edu/
Student/Faculty Ratio: 13:1
Undergraduate Enrollment: 1,800
Scholarships/Academic: Yes **Athletic:** No
Total Expenses by: Year **In State:** $ 19,000
Degrees Conferred: BA, BS, BSN, MSN, MA, MS

Type: 4 Yr., Private, Liberal Arts, Coed
Campus Housing: Yes
SAT/ACT/GPA: None
Male/Female Ratio: 30:70
Graduate Enrollment: None
Fin Aid: Yes
Out of State: $ 19,000

Programs of Study: Accounting, Biology, Broadcasting, Business Administration, Chemistry, Communications, Computer Science, Economics, Education, English, History, Hotel/Restaurant Management, International Business, Journalism, Management, Marketing, Mathematics, Medical Laboratory Technology, Music, Nursing, Pharmacy, Photography, Physical Therapy, Predentistry, Prelaw, Premed, Psychology, Religion, Social Science

ATHLETIC PROFILE

Conference Affiliation: Upper MidWest Athletic Conference
Program Profile: Our Fall season is in September and consists of 9 games. Our Spring season goes from February through May. We play at Wade Stadium with a seating capacity of 4,200.
History: Our program is 13 years old. We played Regional Playoffs in 1995, 1996 and 1997.
Achievements: We won 3 Conference Championships including tournament and 3 playoffs appearances over the last four years. We were nationally ranked top 20 in 1997 and 1998.
Coaching: John Baggs, Head Coach, started his 7th year with a record of 165-109. He graduated from Iowa State in 1989. Tim Anderson, Assistant Coach, graduated from St. Scholastica in 1992.
Roster for 1998 team/In State: 15 **Out of State:** 14 **Out of Country:** 0
Total Number of Varsity/Jr. Varsity: 29 /12 **Percent of Graduation:** 100%
Number of Seniors on 1998 Team: 2 **Number of Sophomores on 1998 Team:** 6
Freshmen Receiving Fin Aid/Athletic: 0 **Academic:** All
Number of Fall Games: 9 **Number of Spring Games:** 36
Positions Needed for 1999/2000: All **Most Recent Record:** 33 - 13 - 0
Baseball Camp Dates: November 27-29, August
Schedule: Kansas, Purdue, Minnesota, University of Wisconsin-Oshkosh, Carthage, St. Cloud
Style of Play: Aggressive, fundamentally solid baseball. Top 10 in the country in stolen bases and fielding percentage.

Concordia College - Moorhead

901 South 8th Street
Moorhead, MN 56562
Coach: Don Burgau

NCAA III
Cobbers/Maroon, Gold
Phone: (218) 299-4434
Fax: (218) 299-4189

ACADEMIC

Founded: 1891 **Type:** 4 Yr., Private, Liberal Arts, Coed
Religion: Lutheran **Campus Housing:** Yes
Web-site: http://www.cord.edu/ **SAT/ACT/GPA:** 900+/21+
Student/Faculty Ratio: 15:1 **Male/Female Ratio:** 40:60
Undergraduate Enrollment: 3,000 **Graduate Enrollment:** None
Scholarships/Academic: Yes **Athletic:** No **Fin Aid:** Yes
Total Expenses by: Year **In State:** $ 13,500 **Out of State:** $ 13,500
Degrees Conferred: BA, BS
Programs of Study: Accounitng, Advertising, Art, Biology, Broadcasting, Business and Management, Chemistry, Classic, Comunications, Computer Science, Creative Writing, Criminal Justice, Music, History, Humanities, Physical Education, Mathematics, Nursing, Political Science, Philosophy, Political Science, Religion, Social Work, Sociology

ATHLETIC PROFILE

Conference Affiliation: MIAC

Concordia College - St. Paul

275 North Syndicate
St. Paul, MN 55104
Coach: Mike Streitz

NAIA
Comets/Royal, Gold
Phone: (651) 641-8854
Fax: (651) 641-8787

ACADEMIC

Founded: 1893
Religion: Lutheran
Web-site: http://www.csp.edu/
Student/Faculty Ratio: 17:1
Undergraduate Enrollment: 1,200
Scholarships/Academic: Yes **Athletic:** No
Total Expenses by: Year **In State:** $ 13,700
Degrees Conferred: AA, BA, MA

Type: 4 Yr., Private, Liberal Arts, Coed
Campus Housing: No
SAT/ACT/GPA: 17+
Male/Female Ratio: 45:55
Graduate Enrollment: 4
Fin Aid: Yes
Out of State: $ 13,700

Programs of Study: Accounting, Banking and Finance, Biblical Languages, Biology, Business Administration, Economics, Education, English, Environmental Science, Fine Arts, History, Languages, Literature, Management, Marketing, Mathematics, Music, Natural Science, Physical Science, Prelaw, Premed, Psychology, Relgious Education, Social Science, Speech Science

ATHLETIC PROFILE

Conference Affiliation: UMAC

Fergus Falls Community College

1414 College Way
Fergus Falls, MN 56537
Coach: Kent Bothwell

NJCAA
Spartans/Blue, Gold
Phone: (218) 739-7541
Fax: (218) 739-7475

ACADEMIC

Founded: 1962
Undergraduate Enrollment: 1,100
Student/Faculty Ratio: 20:1
Scholarships/Academic: Yes **Athletic:** No
Total Expenses by: Year **In State:** $ Varies
Degrees Conferred: Associate

Type: 2 Yr., Jr. College, Coed
Campus Housing: Yes
Male/Female Ratio: 40:60
Fin Aid: Yes
Out of State: $ Varies

Programs of Study: Contact school for programs of study.

ATHLETIC PROFILE

Conference Affiliation: Minnesota Community College Conference
Program Profile: We play on a natural grass field. We have above average playing surface and above average facilities for our area. We love baseball, work hard at it and play a hard aggressive game. We place 5 to 6 athletes a year at Division I, II or III.
History: Our baseball program started in 1960. The program is well respected in the area. Our school is known for its solid baseball program and one that college coaches and pro scouts check each year. It is a baseball program where an athlete can improve his skills.
Achievements: 16 players drafted by the Pro's; Coach of the Year Honors in 1986, 1991, 1992 and 1995; 6 All-Americans.
Coaching: Kent Bothwell ,Head Coach, has 16 years experience, and is in his 2nd year at Fergus Falls CC. He was State and Regional Qualifier in 1996. Todd Johnson, Assistant Coach, has Division II coaching experience. He is in his 31st year as an assistant at FFCC. He is excellent on techniques and mental toughness and a graduate and former assistant at South Dakota State. He also works with outfielders and catchers.
Roster for 1998 team/In State: 18 **Out of State:** 2 **Out of Country:** 0
Total Number of Varsity/Jr. Varsity: 20 **Percent of Graduation:** 95%
Most Recent Record: 22 - 8 - 0 **Number of Sophomores on 1998 Team:** 10
Baseball Camp Dates: February **Number of Spring Games:** 40
Positions Needed for 1999/2000: Pitcher, 3rd Base, 1st Base, OF
Style of Play: We normally have solid pitching and defense. We are very aggressive offensively and make things happen. We really like speed, stealing bases, bunting (drag sac squeeze push) hit and run. We will also hit with some power and consistently hit the ball hard.

Gustavus Adolphos College

800 College Avenue
St. Peter, MN 56082
Coach: Mike Carroll

NCAA III
Gusties/Black, Gold
Phone: (507) 933-7617
Fax: (507) 933-8412

ACADEMIC

Founded: 1862
Type: 4 Yr., Private, Liberal Arts, Coed
Religion: ELCA (Lutheran)
Campus Housing: Yes
Web-site: http://www.gac.edu/
SAT/ACT/GPA: 1100/25
Student/Faculty Ratio: 17:1
Male/Female Ratio: 45:55
Undergraduate Enrollment: 2,300
Graduate Enrollment: None
Scholarships/Academic: Yes **Athletic:** No **Fin Aid:** Yes
Total Expenses by: Year **In State:** $ 19,500 **Out of State:** $ Varies
Degrees Conferred: BA
Programs of Study: Sciences, Health and Fitness, Communications, Accounting, Art, Athletic Training, Biology, Chemistry, Classics, Computer Science, Criminal Justice, Economics, Education, English, Environmental Studies, General Sciences, Geography, Geology, History, International Management, Management, Math, Music, Nursing, Philosophy, Physical Education and Health, Physics, Physical Science, Political Science, Psychology, Religion, Sociology/Anthropology, Speech, Theatre, Preprofessional Programs: Actuarial Science, Architecture, Arts Administration, Church Vocations, Dentistry, Engineering, Law, Medicine, Ministry, Occupational Therapy, Optometry

ATHLETIC PROFILE

Conference Affiliation: Minnesota Intercollegiate Athletic Conference
Program Profile: The Gustavus baseball team has struggled in recent years. However, the return of Barry Bowles, who led the Gusties to 3 straight conference titles in the late 1970's should help turn things around. Facilities are outstanding. The playing field is natural grass.
History: The program began in 1903. The Gusties have won 13 conference titles which is the 3rd highest total in the conference. Gustavus dominated conference play in the 1920's and 1930's and again in the 1970's. Due to a large turnover of head coaches in the 1980's, results were mixed. It appears the program is stable again with the return of head coach Barry Bowles.
Achievements: NAIA District 13 Coach of the Year in 1980; directed the Gusties to 3 straight conference titles in 1978, 1979 and 1980. During the 1978-1980 period, the team compiled an overall record of 66-23-1 and MIAC 46-6.
Style of Play: We have strong emphasis on speed and base running. Offensively and defensively, the team will be built up the middle of the field with a concentration on starting pitching.

Hamline University

1536 Hewitt Avenue
St. Paul, MN 55104
Coach: Barry Boevers
Email: bsboever@piper.hamline.edu

NCAA III
Pipers/Red, Grey, Black
Phone: (612) 523-2035
Fax: (612) 523-2390

ACADEMIC

Founded: 1854
Type: 4 Yr., Private, Liberal Arts, Coed
Religion: Methodist
Campus Housing: Yes
Web-site: http://www.hamlin.edu/
SAT/ACT/GPA: 20/3.0
Student/Faculty Ratio: 12:1
Male/Female Ratio: 3:5
Undergraduate Enrollment: 1,550
Graduate Enrollment: 300
Scholarships/Academic: Yes **Athletic:** No **Fin Aid:** Yes
Total Expenses by: Year **In State:** $ 20,500 **Out of State:** $ 20,500
Degrees Conferred: BA, MA

Programs of Study: Art, Anthropology, Economics, Psychology, Math, Management, Physical Education, English, Physics, Political Science, Sociology, Spanish, Philosophy, Legal Studies, History, Exercise and Sports Science, Environmental Studies, Chemistry, Biology, Etc.. 8 Preprofessional Programs

ATHLETIC PROFILE

Conference Affiliation: Minnesota Intercollegiate Athletic Conference (MIAC)
Program Profile: Our home games are played at Midway Stadium just a half mile from campus. Midway is also the home park of the St. Paul Saints minor league team. By Fall of 1998, all practice facilities will be new or renovated. We will have the new $ 8 million Walker Fieldhouse. Early March games are played in the Metro Dome.
History: Hamline has a great tradition of teaching of baseball. Many past players have gone to be highly successful teachers and coaches. Jim Senske (1962 graduate) is the all-time winningest coach in Minnesota High School baseball with 564 career wins.
Achievements: Hamline's finest season was in 1996. They set school records for total wins and conference wins. Sophomore Kevin Truax was named Conference MVP and All-Region. Hamlin ranked 11th nationally in stolen bases that year.
Coaching: Barry Boevers, Head Coach, entered his 5th season with the program and compiled a record of 53-87. Dan Headline, Assistant Coach, entered his 10th year with the program and is a 1986 Hamline alumni. Ron Woodbury, Assistant, entered his 9th year with the program and is a 1973 Hamline alumni.
Roster for 1998 team/In State: 27 **Out of State:** 1 **Out of Country:** 0
Total Number of Varsity/Jr. Varsity: 28 **Percent of Graduation:** 100%
Number of Seniors on 1998 Team: 4 **Number of Sophomores on 1998 Team:** 4
Freshmen Receiving Fin Aid/Athletic: 0 **Academic:** 8
Number of Fall Games: 0 **Number of Spring Games:** 39
Positions Needed for 1999/2000: Pitchers, Outfielder, Shortstop, 2nd Base
Schedule: St.Thomas, Concordia, Washington University, St. Olaf, St. John's, Bethel, Macalester, Carleton, St. Marys, Gustavus Adolphus
Style of Play: We emphasize pitching defense and team speed. We stress being fundamentally sound, well organized and working hard.

Hibbing Community College

1515 E 25th Street
Hibbing, MN 55746
Coach: Mike Turnbull

NJCAA
Cardinals/Red, Black, White
Phone: (218) 262-6748
Fax: (218) 262-6717

ACADEMIC

Founded: 1917 **Type:** 2 Yr., Jr. College, Coed
Student/Faculty Ratio: 1,100 **Male/Female Ratio:** 50:50
Undergraduate Enrollment: 22:1 **Graduate Enrollment:** None
Scholarships/Academic: Yes **Athletic:** No **Fin Aid:** Yes
Total Expenses by: Year **In State:** $ Varies **Out of State:** $ Varies
Degrees Conferred: Associate
Programs of Study: Accounting, Business, Drafting/Design, Fire Science, History, Law, Media, Occupational Therapy, Physical Therapy, Radiological Technology

ATHLETIC PROFILE

Conference Affiliation: Minnesota Conference
Program Profile: We have indoor and outdoor cages, fly to Florida during Spring Break and play in a very nice park that hosted the Minnesota State American Legion tournament in 1995.
History: Started in the Spring of 1973 as a club team. Our first official year as a varsity sport was 1974. Head Coach Schmitz was a Captain on that first team. We had three players in the Top 10 in the nation for home runs in 1994.

Achievements: Doug Schmitz has been president of the Coaches Association 2 different times. Our team has qualified for the state playoffs 7 out of the last 9 years.
Style of Play: Aggressive, hard-working baseball.

Itasca Community College

1851 East Highway 169
Grand Rapids, MN 55744
Coach: Justin Lamppa

NJCAA
Vikings/White, Blue
Phone: (218) 327-4226
Fax: (218) 327-4350

ACADEMIC

Type: 2 Yr., Public, Jr. College, Coed, Engineering
Founded: 1922
Religion: Non-Affiliated
Campus Housing: Yes
Web-site: http://www.it.cc.mn.us
SAT/ACT/GPA: None
Student/Faculty Ratio: 24:1
Male/Female Ratio: 58:42
Undergraduate Enrollment: 1,120
Graduate Enrollment: None
Scholarships/Academic: Yes **Athletic:** No **Fin Aid:** Yes
Total Expenses by: Year **In State:** $ Varies **Out of State:** $ Varies
Degrees Conferred: AA, AS, AAS
Programs of Study: Associated in Arts, Natural Resources/Forestry, Word Processing, Practical Nursing, Business Management, Legal Assistant, Business and Office Technology, Human Services, Associated in Science

ATHLETIC PROFILE

Conference Affiliation: Minnesota Community College Conference
Program Profile: The program is very organized and very successful. Legion Field seats 850 people. Playing season begins on March 1st and ends on May 28th.
History: The program began in 1977. We were 1998 State Champions of Minnesota Community College and got 4 Consecutive Northern Division Champships.
Achievements: 1998 achievements: Scott Marquett was named All-American and 6 of 9 starters received a baseball scholarship to a four-year school.
Coaching: Justin Lamppa , Head Coach, started his 3rd year. He graduated from University of Wisconsin. He ws Superior in 1997. He has a Corporate and Community Health Degree and a minor in coaching. He compiled a record of 53-18 in three years.
Roster for 1998 team/In State: 22 **Out of State:** 3 **Out of Country:** 0
Total Number of Varsity/Jr. Varsity: 25 **Percent of Graduation:** 92%
Positions Needed for 1999/2000: All **Number of Sophomores on 1998 Team:** 11
Freshmen Receiving Fin Aid/Athletic: 0 **Academic:** 25
Most Recent Record: 30 - 6 - 0 **Number of Spring Games:** 28
Schedule: Madison Technology, Riverland, Willimar, North Hennipen, Anoka
Style of Play: We are very aggressive and put a lot of pressure on the opposing defense.

Macalester College

1600 Grand Avenue
St. Paul, MN 55105
Coach: Steve Hauser
Email: hauser@macalester.edu

NCAA III
Scots/Blue, Orange
Phone: (651) 696-6774
Fax: (651) 696-6328

ACADEMIC

Founded: 1874
Type: 4 Yr., Private, Liberal Arts, Coed
Religion: Presbyterian
Campus Housing: Yes
Web-site: http://www.macalester.edu/
SAT/ACT/GPA: 1200+/27+
Student/Faculty Ratio: 1:10
Male/Female Ratio: 50:50
Undergraduate Enrollment: 1,750
Graduate Enrollment: None

Scholarships/Academic: Yes **Athletic:** No **Fin Aid:** Yes
Total Expenses by: Year **In State:** $ 20,000 **Out of State:** $ 20,000
Degrees Conferred: BA
Programs of Study: Anthropology, Art, Biology, Chemistry, Classics, Communication Studies, Computer Science, Dance, Dramatic Arts, East Asian Studies, Economics, Education, English, Environmental Studies, French, Geography, Geology, German, History, Humanities, Individually Designed Major, International Studies, Japan Studies, Latin American Studies, Legal Studies, Linguistics, Mathematics, Music, Neuroscience, Philosophy, Physics, Political Science, Psychology, Religious Studies, Russian, Russian/Central and Eastern European Studies, Sociology, Spanish

ATHLETIC PROFILE

Conference Affiliation: Minnesota Intercollegiate Athletic Conference
Program Profile: Facilities include a state of the art artificial turf infield, a grass outfield, a newly constructed batting tunnel & a 30,000 sq. ft. indoor training facility with 3 major league batting cages.
History: The program has been down in the past. We have a new emphasis on athletics with a new full-time coach and a $6 million outdoor athletic facilities in the past 4 years!
Achievements: Steve Hauser was named Coach of the Year in 1995.
Coaching: Steve Hauser ,Head Coach, started in 1994. He was a former Division I pitcher and an assistant coach at Division II level for four years. Our building program is a commitment at Macalester. He was named Coach of the Year in 1995 and compiled a record of 81-115. Matt Parrington - Assistant Coach.
Roster for 1998 team/In State: 9 **Out of State:** 18 **Out of Country:** 1
Total Number of Varsity/Jr. Varsity: 28 **Percent of Graduation:** 100%
Number of Seniors on 1998 Team: 4 **Most Recent Record:** 22 - 21 - 1
Schedule: St. Thomas, St. Johns **Number of Spring Games:** 44
Positions Needed for 1999/2000: Pitcher **Baseball Camp Dates:** February, March
Style of Play: We have an aggressive style of play and stress the fundamentals of the game.

Mankato State University

Paul Allan SID MSU 28 PO Box 8400
Mankato, MN 56002-8400
Coach: Dean Bowyer

NCAA II
Mavericks/Purple, Gold
Phone: (507) 389-2689
Fax: (507) 389-2904

ACADEMIC

Founded: 1868 **Type:** 4 Yr., Public, Liberal Arts, Coed
Religion: Non-Affiliated **Campus Housing:** Yes
Web-site: http://www.makato.msus.edu/ **SAT/ACT/GPA:** 960/23
Student/Faculty Ratio: 25:1 **Male/Female Ratio:** 49:51
Undergraduate Enrollment: 11,000 **Graduate Enrollment:** 2,500
Scholarships/Academic: Yes **Athletic:** Yes **Fin Aid:** Yes
Total Expenses by: Year **In State:** $ 6,848 **Out of State:** $ 10,035
Degrees Conferred: BA, BS, MA, MS, MBA
Programs of Study: Accounting, Anthropology, Art, Athletic, Banking/Finance, Biological Science, Business, Chemistry, Computer, Dietetics, Earth Science, Economics, Education, Engineering, English, Geography, History, International, Journalism, Management, Marketing, Math, Music, Medical, Nursing, Parks/Recreation, Physical, Psychology, Public Health, Theatre

ATHLETIC PROFILE

Conference Affiliation: North Central Conference
Program Profile: We are one of the top NCAA Division II baseball programs in the country. Mankato State has had 27 players sign professional contracts since 1977. MSU has a renovated field with a sprinkler system installed in 1994. There is a practice infield adjacent to the main complex. MSU also has a 70 x 35 double batting tunnel that is turf.
History: Our program began in 1964. Dean Bowyer has been with the Mavericks for 23 years.

Achievements: 10 NCC division titles, 9 NCC Championships, 12 NCAA post-season appearances, 3 NCAA Div II College World Series appearances, 1986 4th at Series, 2 All-American selections, several All-Region and All-Conference picks, some 26 players have signed pro contracts (2 all the way to the majors), NCC Coach of the Year several times during career (All past achievements under the direction of Bowyer).
Coaching: Dean Bowyer, Head Coach, entered his 25th year with the Mavericks. He has a 634-259-6 lifetime record and led MSU to nine North Central Conference titles, 12 trips to NCAA post-season play and three NCAA Division II College World Series berths.
Style of Play: The Mavericks have always been a team that has relied upon good defense, good pitching and timely hitting. While our teams of the early 1980's were oriented towards the big offensive inning, we rely more on speed and hitting for average.

Mesabi Range Community College

1001 Chestnut St, West
Virginia, MN 55792-3448
Coach: Tom Stackpool

NJCAA
Norse/Green, Gold
Phone: (218) 749-7756
Fax: (218) 749-7782

ACADEMIC

Type: 2 Yr., Jr. College, Coed
Degrees Conferred: Associate
Programs of Study: Accounting, Alcohol/Drug/Substance Abuse Counseling, Preengineering Sequence, Human Services, instrumentation Technology, Liberal Arts, General Studies, Marketing, Retailing, Merchandising, Paralegal Studies, Secretarial

ATHLETIC PROFILE

Conference Affiliation: Minnesota Community College Conference
Program Profile: Our program is 3 years old with seasons from March to June. We play at Huck Field in Virginia which is natural grass field. We play a 28 game schedule.
History: Our program began in 1995 and we have increased our wins each year.
Style of Play: We have aggressive base-running and work to create runs. Our goal is to score as many as we have hits.

Normandale Community College

(Program Discontinued)

North Hennepin Community College

7411 - 85th Avenue North
Brooklyn Park, MN 55445
Coach: Doug Schidgen

NJCAA
Norsemen/Blue, Silver
Phone: (612) 424-0796
Fax: (612) 493-0560

ACADEMIC

Type: 2 Yr., Jr. College, Coed
Degrees Conferred: Associate
Programs of Study: Accounting, Automotive Technology, Business Administration, Commerce, Management, Commercial Art, Construction Management, Electronic Engineering Technology, Fire Science, Graphic Arts, Law Enforcement, Police Science, Liberal Arts, General Studies, Manufacturing Technology, Marketing, Retailing/Merchandising, Material Science, Nursing, Paralegal Studies, Retail Management

ATHLETIC PROFILE

Conference Affiliation: MCCC

Northland Community College

Highway 1 East
Thief River Falls, MN 56701
Coach: John Ott

NJCAA
Pioneers/Blue, Red
Phone: (218) 681-0729
Fax: (218) 681-0878

ACADEMIC

Founded: 1965
Type: 2 Yr., Jr. College, Coed
Student/Faculty Ratio: 13:1
Male/Female Ratio: 1:1
Undergraduate Enrollment: 1,000
Graduate Enrollment: None
Scholarships/Academic: Yes **Athletic:** No **Fin Aid:** Yes
Total Expenses by: Year **In State:** $ 4,700 **Out of State:** $ 6,900
Degrees Conferred: Associate
Programs of Study: Accounting, Aerospace, Architectural, Athletic, Aviation, Broadcasting, Business Administration, Communications, Computer, Criminal Justice, Drafting/Design

ATHLETIC PROFILE

Conference Affiliation: Minnesota Community College Conference
Program Profile: We play 28 games on a campus baseball field. We take a Spring trip to Omaha, Nebraska. Our playing season begins March 1st and ends June 1st.
Achievements: 1994 Regional Semifinal, 1994 State Tournament. 1993 All-American Mitch Bernstein, 1991 pro ball Shawn Ohman; 2 professional players, 2 All-Americans.

Riverland Community College

(Former Austin CC)

1900 - 8th Avenue, NW
Austin, MN 55912-1470
Coach: Herb Hoffer
Email: hhoffer@river.cc.mn.us

NJCAA III
Blue Devils/Blue, White
Phone: (507) 433-0373
Fax: (507) 433-0515

ACADEMIC

Founded: 1940
Type: 2 Yr., Jr. College, Coed
Undergraduate Enrollment: 1,400
SAT/ACT/GPA: Recommended
Scholarships/Academic: No **Athletic:** No **Fin Aid:** Yes
Total Expenses by: Year **In State:** $ 2,100 **Out of State:** $ 4,000
Degrees Conferred: Associate
Programs of Study: Business, Child Care, Human Services, Law, Liberal Arts, Literature, Nursing, Occupational Therapy, Physical Therapy

ATHLETIC PROFILE

Conference Affiliation: MCCC - Southern Division
Program Profile: We play at two fields. We have a college facility and also play at beautiful well-lit Marcussen Park in downtown Park.
Achievements: We have had 7 players get scholarship money. Previous to that, none signed with four-year schools.

Rochester Community College

851 - 30th Avenue, SE
Rochester, MN 55904
Coach: Brian Laplante

NJCAA
Yellow Jackets/Royal Blue, Yellow
Phone: (507) 285-7106
Fax: (507) 285-7496

ACADEMIC

Founded: 1915
Type: 2 Yr., Jr. College, Coed
Student/Faculty Ratio: 18:1
Male/Female Ratio: 36:64
Undergraduate Enrollment: 3,950
Graduate Enrollment: None
Scholarships/Academic: No **Athletic:** No **Fin Aid:** Yes
Total Expenses by: Year **In State:** $ 2,000 **Out of State:** $ 4,000
Degrees Conferred: Associate
Programs of Study: Broadcasting, Business, Computer, Dental Services, Engineering, Human Services, Journalism, Law, Liberal Arts, Marketing, Medical, Nursing, Office Management, Pharmacy, Physical Therapy, Preengineering, Radiological

ATHLETIC PROFILE

Conference Affiliation: MCCC Minnesota Community College Conference
Program Profile: We play 32 games. The Yellow Jackets play on a natural grass.
Achievements: Past achievements were: All-State Kelly Fitzgerald in 1974 - Outfielder; Steve Curry 1980 Pitcher, Joe Warren 1981 Catcher, Mike Malde 1983 Infielder, Andy Devine 1989 and 1990 Infielder, Matt Teal 1993 Infielder, Craig Koehler 1997 Infielder. Past All-Americans were Joe Warren in 1981 as a Catcher and Andy Devine in 1990 as an Infielder.
Coaching: Brian Laplante ,Head Coach, stared his 3rd year and graduated in 1995 from Winona State University. He was an assistant baseball coach at Winona State from 1994 to 1995. Chadfield Minnesota American Legion Coach from 1991-1995.
Style of Play: Hit and run, basic pitching and defense, fundamentally sound.

Saint Cloud State University

720 - 4th Avenue South
St Cloud, MN 56301-4498
Coach: Denny Lorsung

NCAA II
Huskies/Cardinal, Black
Phone: (320) 255-3208
Fax: (320) 255-2099

ACADEMIC

Founded: 1869
Type: 4 Yr., Public, Liberal Arts, Coed
Web-site: Not Available
SAT/ACT/GPA: 1000/25
Student/Faculty Ratio: 21:1
Male/Female Ratio: 48:52
Undergraduate Enrollment: 12,849
Graduate Enrollment: 1,259
Scholarships/Academic: Yes **Athletic:** Yes **Fin Aid:** Yes
Total Expenses by: Year **In State:** $ 5,581 **Out of State:** $ 7,793
Degrees Conferred: BA, BS
Programs of Study: Accounting, Advertising, Anthropology, Arts, Banking/Finance, Biological Science, Broadcasting, Business Administration, Chemistry, Earth Science, Elective Studies, Geography, International Business and Relations, Journalism, Preprofessional Programs, Psychology, *** contact school for more information.

ATHLETIC PROFILE

Conference Affiliation: Northern Division of the North Central Conference (NCAA II)
Program Profile: Our Division II program has excellent indoor practice facilities. Games are played at Dick Putz Stadium, a stadium that was recognized as the finest field in the country by the U.S. High School Coaches Association.
Achievements: We won the NCC Title in 1991.
Coaching: Denny Lorsung, Head Coach, started his 19th year at St. Cloud. Andy Bulson, Assistant Coach, started his 2nd year and is a former SCSU pitcher.
Style of Play: The style of play is dependent on the skill of the players.

Saint John's University

#1 Champion Drive
Collegeville, MN 56321-7277
Coach: Jerry Haugen
Email: jthaugen@csbsju.edu

NCAA III
Johnies/Blue, Red
Phone: (320) 363-2756
Fax: (320) 363-3130

ACADEMIC

Type: 4 Yr., Private, Liberal Arts, All Male
Founded: 1858
Religion: Roman Catholic
Campus Housing: Yes
Web-site: Not-Available
SAT/ACT/GPA: 10/2.8
Student/Faculty Ratio: 12:1
Male/Female Ratio: 100:0
Undergraduate Enrollment: 1,750
Graduate Enrollment: Unknown
Scholarships/Academic: Yes **Athletic:** No **Fin Aid:** Yes
Total Expenses by: Year **In State:** $ 20,000 **Out of State:** $ 20,000
Degrees Conferred: BA, BS
Programs of Study: Accounting, Art, Biology, Chemistry, Classics, Communications, Computer Science, Economics, Elementary Education, English, French, German, Government, History, Humanities, Liberal Studies, Management, Mathematics, Medical Technology, Medieval Studies, Music, Natural Science, Nursing, Nutrition, Peace Studies, Philosophy, Physics, Psychology, Social Science, Social Work, Sociology, Spanish, Theatre, Theology, Preprofessional Programs

ATHLETIC PROFILE

Conference Affiliation: Minnesota Intercollegiate Athletic Conference
Program Profile: We have a Top Division III program with excellent indoor facilities and a natural turf field used only for baseball.
History: We have a long history of baseball at SJU. Our 1st game was played in 1889. In 1993, Avitas Humisl signed with Cleveland and spent many years as an executive with the Cubs. Ernie Sowada pitched a 1942 undefeated season. We have been Conference Champions in every decade since the 1930's.
Achievements: Coach of the Year in 1994; Conference Title in 1994; 1993 and 1994 National Batting Champion NCAA Division III: Jon Pold .562 and Ryan Roder was .540; Last All-American first team was in 1997; 4 1st team Academic All-Americans; last drafted player was in 1993.
Coaching: Jerry Haugen, Head Coach, is on his 22nd year. He got top 30 in wins for active Division III coaches. He was ABCA Research Committee Chair, ABCA Clinic Committee Co-Chair and MIAC Coaches' Chair. Mike Carr, Assistant Coach, entered his 10th year. Mike Trewick, Assistant, entered his 3rd year.
Total Number of Varsity/Jr. Varsity: 41 **Most Recent Record:** 24 - 13 - 0
Number of Seniors on 1998 Team: 6 **Number of Sophomores on 1998 Team:** 0
Number of Fall Games: 0 **Number of Spring Games:** 40-45
Positions Needed for 1999/2000: Outfielder, Shortstop
Baseball Camp Dates: 1st Sunday of February for six consecutive sundays
Schedule: University of Minnesota, St. Cloud State
Style of Play: We have exceptional defense and solid pitching. We are a hitting team with a decent power. We will run more this year.

Saint Mary's University - Minnesota

700 Terrace Heights
Winona, MN 55987
Coach: Nick Whaley
Email: dnaddali@smumn.edu

NCAA III
Cardinals/Red, White, Navy
Phone: (507) 457-1577
Fax: (507) 457-6440

ACADEMIC

Founded: 1919
Type: 4 Yr., Private, Liberal Arts, Coed
Religion: Non-Affiliated
Campus Housing: Yes

Web-site: http://www.smumn.edu/ **SAT/ACT/GPA:** 20
Student/Faculty Ratio: 15:1 **Male/Female Ratio:** 50:50
Undergraduate Enrollment: 1,300 **Graduate Enrollment:** 7,000
Scholarships/Academic: Yes **Athletic:** No **Fin Aid:** Yes
Total Expenses by: Year **In State:** $ 15,000 **Out of State:** $ 15,000
Degrees Conferred: BA, BS
Programs of Study: Accounting, Art:Graphic Design, Art:Art Studio, Biology, Chemistry, Computer Science, Criminal Justice, Electronic Publishing, Elementary Education, English Education, French, History, Life Science, Marketing, Mathematics, Mathematics Education, Music Merchandising, Philosophy, Physics, Political Science, Social Science, Sociology, Theatre, Theatre Education

ATHLETIC PROFILE

Conference Affiliation: Minnesota Intercollegiate Athletic conference
Program Profile: We have a competitive program with an excellent field on campus and a new fieldhouse. We have a great baseball setting.
History: We were 12 MIAC Conference Champions.
Achievements: We have won 12 MIAC Conference Champs, more than anyone else in the MIAC.
Coaching: Nick Whaley, Head Coach, entered his 2nd year with the program. He compiled a record of 34-34. Steve Lahti - Assistant Coach.
Roster for 1998 team/In State: 14 **Out of State:** 11 **Out of Country:** 0
Total Number of Varsity/Jr. Varsity: 25 **Percent of Graduation:** 90%
Number of Seniors on 1998 Team: 11 **Number of Sophomores on 1998 Team:** 9
Freshmen Receiving Fin Aid/Athletic: 0 **Academic:** 10
Most Recent Record: 17 - 17 - 0 **Number of Spring Games:** 40
Positions Needed for 1999/2000: Pitcher, Infielder
Schedule: St. Thomas, St. John's, Fontbonne, St. Scholastica, Winona State, St. Olaf
Style of Play: We are disciplined, hardworking and enthusiastic.

Saint Olaf College

1520 St. Olaf Avenue **NCAA III**
Northfield, MN 55057 **Oles/Black, Gold**
Coach: Matt McDonald **Phone: (507) 646-3250**
Fax: (507) 646-3572

ACADEMIC

Founded: 1874 **Type:** 4 Yr., Private, Coed
Religion: Lutheran **Campus Housing:** Yes
Web-site: http://www.stolaf.edu/ **SAT/ACT/GPA:** 25
Student/Faculty Ratio: 11:1 **Male/Female Ratio:** 2.4:3
Undergraduate Enrollment: 2,888 **Graduate Enrollment:** None
Scholarships/Academic: Yes **Athletic:** no **Fin Aid:** Yes
Total Expenses by: Year **In State:** $ 15,000 **Out of State:** $ 15,000
Degrees Conferred: BA, BS, BM
Programs of Study: Art, Art History, Asian Studies, Biology, Chemistry, Classic, Dance, Economics, English, Fine Arts, French, Mathematics, Music, Nursing, Physical Education, Physics, Political Science, Philosophy, Prelaw, Premed, Predentistry, Psychology, Social Studies, Social Work

ATHLETIC PROFILE

Conference Affiliation: Minnesota Intercollegiate Athletic Conference
Program Profile: We have an excellent completely enclosed field on campus. Our fieldhouse includes 2 batting cages, 4 mounds and a complete infield.
History: One of the best in NCAA III, 14 MIAC titles and 13 NCAA Tournament appearances in the last quarter century.
Style of Play: We play aggressive base running and solid defense.

Southwest State University

1501 State Street
Marshall, MN 56258
Coach: Paul Blanchard
Email: blanchard@ssu.SouthWest.msus.edu

NCAA II
Mustangs/Brown, Gold
Phone: (507) 537-7268
Fax: (507) 537-6578

ACADEMIC

Founded: 1967
Religion: Non-Affiliated
Web-site: http://www.SouthWest.com
Undergraduate Enrollment: 3,300
Scholarships/Academic: Yes **Athletic:** Yes
Total Expenses by: Year **In State:** $ 6,047

Type: 4 Yr., Public, Liberal Arts, Coed
Campus Housing: Yes
SAT/ACT/GPA: 20/2.5
Student/Faculty Ratio: 14:1
Fin Aid: Yes
Out of State: $ 9,268

Degrees Conferred: AA, BS, BA, MS, MA
Programs of Study: Agronomy, Athletic Training, Business, Preprofessional Programs, Education, Health, Psychology, Management, Chemistry, Political Science, Marketing, Sports Management, Business Administration, Sociology, Speech, Music, Literature, Computer Science, Art, Accounting, Philosophy, Women's Studies, Theatre Arts, History, Math

ATHLETIC PROFILE

Estimated Number of Baseball Scholarships: 2
Conference Affiliation: Northern Sun Intercollegiate Conference
Program Profile: We have a campus grass surface field and use a city municipal field also. We have two batting cages outdoor and indoor.
History: Our program began in 1970. We won 3 conference titles & 2 conference tournament titles in 1996 & 1997. We got a 31-13 record in 1997 which is the school record for victories & fewest loses.
Achievements: 1997 NSIC Tournament Champions.
Coaching: Paul Blanchard, Head Coach, entered his 2nd year as head coach at SouthWest State University. He compiled a record of 64-29 in two years of coaching. Chris Hmielewski, Assistant Coach, entered his 2nd year as a pitching coach.
Roster for 1998 team/In State: 28 **Out of State:** 9 **Out of Country:** 0
Total Number of Varsity/Jr. Varsity: 38 **Percent of Graduation:** 100%
Number of Seniors on 1998 Team: 4 **Baseball Camp Dates:** Summer
Freshmen Receiving Fin Aid/Athletic: 6 **Academic:** 5
Most Recent Record: 33 - 16 - 0 **Number of Spring Games:** 54
Schedule: Winona, North Dakota, Mankato State, South Dakota State, Wayne State, Augustana
Style of Play: We put athletes in the best possible position to be successful.

University of Minnesota

516 15th Avenue, SE
Minneapolis, MN 55455
Coach: John Anderson
Email: ebacheolo@gold.tc.umn.edu

NCAA I
Golden Gophers/Maroon, Gold
Phone: (612) 625-4057
Fax: (612) 625-0359

ACADEMIC

Founded: 1851
Religion: Non-Affiliated
Student/Faculty Ratio: 25:1
Undergraduate Enrollment: 24,000
Scholarships/Academic: Yes **Athletic:** Yes
Total Expenses by: Year **In State:** $ 7,500

Type: 4 Yr., Public, Coed
Campus Housing: Yes
Male/Female Ratio: 53:47
Graduate Enrollment: 14,000
Fin Aid: Yes
Out of State: $ 13,563

Degrees Conferred: BA, BS, MA, MS, MBA, DMD, JD
Programs of Study: Contact school for programs of study.

ATHLETIC PROFILE

Conference Affiliation: Big 10 Conference
Program Profile: Minnesota baseball plays a 50-60 games per year starting in the early February. The team travels to warm climate parts of the USA until the start of March, when the team plays 15-20 games at the Metrodome. The team plays the other half of its games at Siebert Field, a symmetrical ballpark with an awesome homefield atmosphere.
History: The University of Minnesota begins its 122nd year. The University of Minnesota has posted 83 winning seasons, 35 consecutive winning seasons, 17 Big Ten Championships, 21 NCAA Appearances, five College World Series appearances, and three NCAA Titles. Prominant alumni include future Hall of Fame-Paul Molitor, and Dave Winfield. Current pro's include: Denny Neagle, Brent Gates, and Dan Wilson.
Achievements: 26 All-Americans; 17 Conference Titles; Dick Siebert-All-time winningest coach (754-360-8, 295-151-3 in the Big Ten); current Coach John Anderson compiled a record of 560-369-3, and 233-133 in the Big Ten; 4 Conference Titles; named Big Ten Coach of the Year in 1982. Over 100 drafted players and currently eight are in the major leagues.
Coaching: John Anderson, Head Coach, is in his 18th season (Minnesota '77) and has a career record of 560-369-3 for 16 years at Minnesota. Rob Fornasiere, Assistant Coach, is in his 15th year (La Crose '78). Mike Dee, Assistant Coach, is in his 12th year. Herb Isalsson - Volunteer Coach.
Style of Play: We play an aggressive style of sound fundamental baseball. We hit the ball extremely well and play a sound defense. Each year we have at least two starting pitchers who give us a chance to beat every team in the country.

University of Minnesota - Duluth

10 University Drive
Duluth, MN 55812
Coach: Scott Hanna

NCAA II
Bulldogs/Maroon, Gold
Phone: (218) 726-7967
Fax: (218) 726-6529

ACADEMIC

Founded: 1947
Type: 4 Yr., Public, Liberal Arts, Coed
Web-site: Not Available
SAT/ACT/GPA: 22 avg
Student/Faculty Ratio: 17:1
Male/Female Ratio: 53:47
Undergraduate Enrollment: 7,015
Graduate Enrollment: 350
Scholarships/Academic: Yes **Athletic:** Yes **Fin Aid:** Yes
Total Expenses by: Year **In State:** $ 7,600 **Out of State:** $ 13,500
Degrees Conferred: AA, AS, BA, BS, BAA, BAS, BM, Ma, MS, MBA
Programs of Study: American Studies, Anthropology, Biological Science, Chemistry, Communications, Computer, Criminology, Dramatic Arts, Early Childhood Education, Earth Science, Economics, Education, English, Geography, Geology, History, Industrial, Interdisciplinary, International, Math, Music, Philosophy, Physics, Political Science, Psychology, Speech

ATHLETIC PROFILE

Conference Affiliation: WCHA, Northern Sun Conference

University of Minnesota - Morris

E. 2nd Street
Morris, MN 56267
Coach: Mark Fohl

NCAA II
Cougars/Maroon, Gold
Phone: (320) 589-6421
Fax: (320) 589-6428

ACADEMIC

Founded: 1959
Type: 4 Yr., Public, Liberal Arts, Coed
Web-site: Not Available
SAT/ACT/GPA: 820/17 min

Student/Faculty Ratio: 15:1
Male/Female Ratio: 45:55
Undergraduate Enrollment: 1,933
Graduate Enrollment: None
Scholarships/Academic: Yes **Athletic:** No **Fin Aid:** Yes
Total Expenses by: Year **In State:** $ 8,000 **Out of State:** $ 15,000
Degrees Conferred: BA
Programs of Study: Contact school for program of study.

ATHLETIC PROFILE

Conference Affiliation: Northern Sun Conference

University of Saint Thomas

2115 Summit Avenue
St. Paul, MN 55105
Coach: Dennis Denning
NCAA III
Tommies/Purple, White, Grey
Phone: (651) 962-5924
Fax: (651) 962-5910

ACADEMIC

Founded: 1885
Type: 4 Yr., Private, Liberal Arts, Coed
Religion: Catholic
Campus Housing: No
Web-site: http://www.stthomas.edu/
SAT/ACT/GPA: 800/20
Student/Faculty Ratio: 17:1
Male/Female Ratio: 50:50
Undergraduate Enrollment: 5,000
Graduate Enrollment: 5,000
Scholarships/Academic: Yes **Athletic:** No **Fin Aid:** Yes
Total Expenses by: Year **In State:** $ 16,800 **Out of State:** $ 16,800
Degrees Conferred: BA, MA, MS, MBA, EdD, Mdiv
Programs of Study: Accounting, Advertising, Art History, Asian Studies, Banking and Finance, Biology, Broadcasting, Business Administration, Chemistry, Communications, Computer Science, Criminal Justice, Dramatic, Arts, Education, English, French, Geography, Geology, German, History, International Business, Journalism, Latin, Literature, Management, Marketing, Mathematics, Music, Philosophy, Psychology, Public Relations, Public Administration, Russian, Social Science, Spanish, Speech, Telecommunications, Theology, Urban Studies

ATHLETIC PROFILE

Conference Affiliation: MIAC
Program Profile: Has an excellent facilities-fieldhouse, inside/outside batting cages, and grass field.
History: The program began in the 1950's. UST has won 13 Conference Titles and recently we have won 3 conference titles in a row and have been nationally ranked the past three years.
Achievements: We have had 4 All-Americans the past four years and have had 3 players sign professional contracts.
Coaching: Dennis Denning, Head Coach, stared in 1995. While the Toms have always been competitive in baseball, he compiled a 138-38 record. In Denning's first season at UST, the 1995 Toms placed second in the MIAC and reached the NCAA Tournaments for the first time since 1986 in a 28-13 finished 36-3 in regular season and forge a school-record 14-game streak. Don Roney - Assistant Coach.
Roster for 1998 team/In State: 30 **Out of State:** 6 **Out of Country:** 0
Total Number of Varsity/Jr. Varsity: 40 **Percent of Graduation:** 100%
Number of Seniors on 1998 Team: 7 **Most Recent Record:** 37 - 11 - 0
Freshmen Receiving Fin Aid/Athletic: 0 **Academic:** 100%
Number of Fall Games: 0 **Number of Spring Games:** 48
Positions Needed for 1999/2000: Pitchers, Shorstop
Schedule: University of Minnesota, Augustana, St. John's, Southern Maine, Amherst, North Union
Style of Play: Our goals are to never be out-hustled, never be surprised or out-smarted, always control, do not lose it and to always have a positive team personality.

Vermilion Community College

1900 E Camp St
Ely, MN 55731
Coach: Ray Podominick
Email: r.podominick@mail.vcc.mnscu.edu

NJCAA
Ironmen/Royal Blue, Gold
Phone: (218) 365-7200
Fax: (218) 365-7207

ACADEMIC

Founded: 1922
Religion: Non-Affiliated
Web-site: http://www.vcc.mnscu.edu
Student/Faculty Ratio: 14:1
Undergraduate Enrollment: 700
Scholarships/Academic: No **Athletic:** No
Total Expenses by: Year **In State:** $ 6,400
Degrees Conferred: AA, AS, AAS

Type: 2 Yr., Public, Jr. college, Coed
Campus Housing: Yes
SAT/ACT/GPA: Open Admission/
Male/Female Ratio: 2:1
Graduate Enrollment: None
Fin Aid: Yes
Out of State: $ 8,650

Programs of Study: Natural Resources, Forestry, Wildlife, Aviation, Parks and Recreation, Law Enforcement, Water Resources, Wilderness Management; Transfer Programs: AA, AS

ATHLETIC PROFILE

Conference Affiliation: Minnesota Community College Conference
Program Profile: We have a beautiful natural grass field that has hosted the American Legion World Series. We play at the site of the American Legion World Series.
History: Our program began in 1991.
Achievements: We participated in the Region 13 Tournament in 1997.
Coaching: Ray Podominick, Head Coach, is coaching his 1st year at college level. He was a pitcher at Bemidji State University in 1984 - 1986. He did previous coaching at VFW and Legion Levels.
Roster for 1998 team/In State: 15 **Out of State:** 10 **Out of Country:** 0
Total Number of Varsity/Jr. Varsity: 23 **Percent of Graduation:** 0
Number of Seniors on 1998 Team: 10 **Most Recent Record:** 16 - 12 - 0
Number of Fall Games: 0 **Number of Spring Games:** 32
Positions Needed for 1999/2000: Probably start all sophomores
Style of Play: Our personal philosophy is strong in the areas of pitching and defense. We provide players with opportunitys to transfer to a four-year school if they choose to.

Willmar Community College

PO Box 797
Willmar, MN 56201
Coach: Dwight Kotila

NJCAA
Warriors/Red, Silver
Phone: (320) 231-5130

ACADEMIC

Founded: 1961
Student/Faculty Ratio: 35:1
Undergraduate Enrollment: 1,150
Scholarships/Academic: No **Athletic:** No
Total Expenses by: Year **In State:** $ 2,000
Degrees Conferred: Associate

Type: 2 Yr., Jr. College, Coed
Male/Female Ratio: 40:60
Graduate Enrollment: None
Fin Aid: Yes
Out of State: $ 4,000

Programs of Study: Accounting, Agriculture, Art, Broadcasting, Business, Communications, Community Service, Computer, Criminal Justice, Drafting/Design, Engineering, Gerontology, Humanities, Interdisciplinary, Journalism, Law, Liberal Arts, Management, Math, Mental Health

ATHLETIC PROFILE

Conference Affiliation: Minnesota Community College Conference (Southern Division)
Program Profile: We have an 18 player roster. We play a 28-game schedule and our home field is Baker Park which seats 2,000.

Winona State University

PO Box 5838
Winona, MN 55987-5838
Coach: Gary Grob

NCAA II
Warriors/Purple, White
Phone: (507) 457-5206
Fax: (507) 457-5606

ACADEMIC

Founded: 1858
Type: 4 Yr., Public, Liberal Arts, Coed
Web-site: Not Available
SAT/ACT/GPA: 700/17 min
Student/Faculty Ratio: 20:1
Male/Female Ratio: 40:60
Undergraduate Enrollment: 7,000
Graduate Enrollment: 500
Scholarships/Academic: Yes **Athletic:** Yes **Fin Aid:** Yes
Total Expenses by: Year **In State:** $ 7,500 **Out of State:** $ 9,500
Degrees Conferred: AA, AS, BA, BS, MA, MS, MBA, Phd, JD
Programs of Study: Accounting, Advertising, Banking/Finance, Biological, Broadcasting, Business, Chemistry, Communications, Community Services, Computer, Criminal, Dramatic Arts, Earth Science, Economics, Education, English, Geography, Geology, History, International, Journalism, Management, Marketing, Medical, Praks/Recreation, Preprofessional Programs, Speech

ATHLETIC PROFILE

Conference Affiliation: Northern Sun Intercollegiate Conference
Program Profile: We have a highly successful Spring program that plays at an on-campus natural surface site. We have had outstanding success in the post-season under NAIA affiliation, but now we have switched affiliation to NCAA II. Our coach is the winningest collegiate coach in the history of Minnesota.
History: Our program began in 1919 and since then over 1,100 games have been played with Winona State University winning .630 percent of the games.
Achievements: Numerous conference, district, and area Coach of the Year awards; many conference championships; a great number of All-Conference, All-District, All-Area, and All-American selections; several players have gone on to sign professional contracts.
Coaching: Gary Grob, Head Coach, was an NAIA Baseball Hall of Fame selection and has more wins in Minnesota collegiate history than any other collegiate coach in Minnesota.
Style of Play: We will use big-inning strategy, but also like to run and gun (bunt, fake bunt, and slash). We will depend on good defense and pitching depth.

MISSISSIPPI

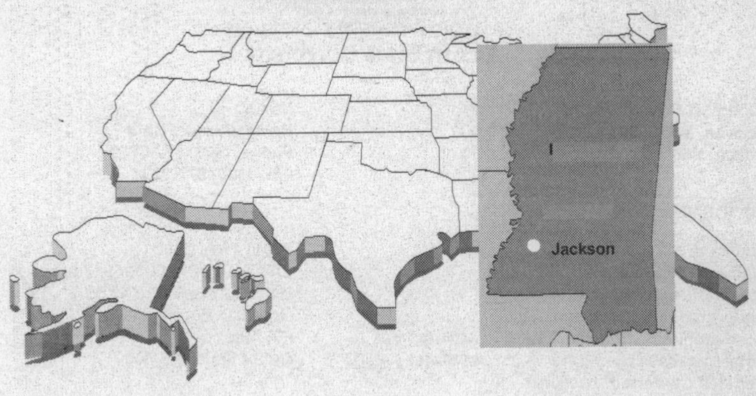

SCHOOL	CITY	AFFILIATION 99	PAGE
Alcorn State University	Lorman	NCAA I	468
Belhaven College	Jackson	NAIA	468
Coahoma Community College	Clarksdale	NJCAA	469
Copiah - Lincoln Community College	Wesson	NJCAA	469
Delta State University	Cleveland	NCAA II	470
East Central Community College	Decatur	NJCAA	470
East Mississippi Community College	Scooba	NJCAA	471
Hinds Community College	Raymond	NJCAA	471
Holmes Community College	Goodman	NJCAA	472
Itawamba Community College	Fulton	NJCAA	472
Jackson State University	Jackson	NCAA I	473
Jones County Junior College	Ellisville	NJCAA	473
Meridian Community College	Meridian	NJCAA	474
Millsaps College	Jackson	NCAA III	474
Mississippi College	Clinton	NCAA II	475
Mississippi Delta Community College	Moorhead	NJCAA	476
Mississippi Gulf Coast Community College	Perkinston	NJCAA	476
Mississippi State University	Mississippi State	NCAA I	477
Mississippi Valley State University	Itta Bena	NCAA I	477
Northeast Mississippi Community College	Booneville	NJCAA	478
Northwest Mississippi Community College	Senatobia	NJCAA	478
Pearl River Community College	Poplarville	NJCAA	479
Rust College	Holly Springs	NCAA III	479
Southwest Mississippi Community College	Summit	NJCAA	480
University of Mississippi (Ole Mississippi)	University	NCAA I	481
University of Southern Mississippi	Hattiesburg	NCAA I	481
William Carey College	Hattiesburg	NAIA	482

Alcorn State University

1000 ASU Drive #510
Lorman, MS 39096
Coach: Willie McGowan

NCAA I
Braves/Purple, Gold
Phone: (601) 877-3750
Fax: (601) 877-3821

ACADEMIC

Founded: 1871
Type: 4 Yr., Coed
Web-site: Not Available
SAT/ACT/GPA: 700avg/17avg
Student/Faculty Ratio: 20:1
Male/Female Ratio: 45:55
Undergraduate Enrollment: 3,040
Graduate Enrollment: 210
Scholarships/Academic: Yes **Athletic:** Yes **Fin Aid:** Yes
Total Expenses by: Year **In State:** $ 4,500 **Out of State:** $ 5,500
Degrees Conferred: Associate
Programs of Study: General Studies

ATHLETIC PROFILE

Conference Affiliation: SouthWestern Athletic Conference
Program Profile: The Alcorn State University baseball team plays on the beautiful Braves Field that is natural grass. The stadium accommodates 1,100 spectators during the baseball season.
Achievements: Willie McGowan was named SouthWestern Athletic Conference Coach of the Year in 1981, 1978 and 1976. We were SWAC Eastern Division Champions in 1997.
Coaching: Willie McGowan, Head Coach, has been at Alcorn for 26 years and has compiled over 400 wins. Ron Krause - Assistant. Matthew Parish and Tyrone Marshall-graduate assistants.
Style of Play: We are a hit and run team that pushes the runner; defense oriented.

Belhaven College

1500 Peachtree Street
Jackson, MS 39202-1789
Coach: Mike Hutcheon

NAIA
Blazers/Gold, Green
Phone: (601) 968-5984
Fax: (601) 968-9998

ACADEMIC

Founded: 1883
Type: 4 Yr., Private, Liberal Arts, Coed
Religion: Presbyterian
Campus Housing: Yes
Web-site: http://www.belhaven.edu
SAT/ACT/GPA: 960/20/2.0
Student/Faculty Ratio: 18:1
Male/Female Ratio: 1:2.5
Undergraduate Enrollment: 1,300
Graduate Enrollment: 100
Scholarships/Academic: Yes **Athletic:** Yes **Fin Aid:** Yes
Total Expenses by: Year **In State:** $ 7,025 **Out of State:** $ 7,025
Degrees Conferred: BA, BS, BM
Programs of Study: Accounting, Art, Biblical Studies, Biology, Business Administration, Chemistry, Combined Science, Computer Information Systems, Computer Science, Dance, Elementary Education, English, History, Humanities, Mathematics, Music, Philosophy, Sports Administration, Sports Medicine, Sports Ministry, Prelaw, Premed, Psychology

ATHLETIC PROFILE

Conference Affiliation: Gulf Coast Athletic Conference
Program Profile: We have a 56 game Spring schedule. February 7 through mid May vs. NAIA, NCAA Division I and II opponents. Home games are at McLeod Field adjacent to campus. The stadium has 500 seats and is near downtown Jackson. It has a grass playing surface and wood outfield fence.
History: We were founded in 1962 and have won 6 District championships in NAIA competition.

Achievements: We won first NAIA District 30 Title in 1994and appeared in the South Regional for the first time in the program's history. We missed the 1995 GCAC playoffs on extra-innings loss. 5 All-americans since 1989; 3 GCAC Players of the Year since 1989; two GCAC Coach of the Year awards, 3 MLB signees.
Coaching: Mike Hutcheon ,Head Coach, (B.Ed at Wayne State University in 1984) is in his 2nd year as head coach. He assisted at Manatee CC in 1991-1993 and assisted at Hasting College in 1990. He was a graduate assistant at Mississippi State in 1988-1989 and got a Master of Athletic Administration from Mississippi State in 1989.

Coahoma Community College

3240 Friars Point Road
Clarksdale, MS 38614
Coach: Johnny Noah

NJCAA
Tigers/Maroon, White
Phone: (601) 627-2571

ACADEMIC

Type: 2 Yr., Jr. College, Coed
Campus Housing: No
Degrees Conferred: Associate
Programs of Study: Accounting, Agricultural Technologies, Art/Fine Arts, Biology, Biological Science, Business Administration, Commerce, Management, Economics, Chemistry, Computer Programming, Computer Science, Criminal Justice, Drafting/Design, Early Childhood Education, Education, Electronics Engineering Technology, Elementary Education, English, Graphic Arts, Health Education, Liberal Arts, General Studies, Medical Technology, Radio & Television Studies

ATHLETIC PROFILE

Conference Affiliation: MJCA

Copiah - Lincoln Community College

PO Box 649
Wesson, MS 39191
Coach: Keith Case

NJCAA
Wolfpack/Royal, White
Phone: (601) 643-8412
Fax: (601) 643-8225

ACADEMIC

Type: 2 Yr., Jr. College, Coed
Campus Housing: No
Degrees Conferred: Associate
Programs of Study: Accounting, Art Education, Biology, Biological Science, Business Administration, Commerce, Management, Chemistry, Child Care/Child and Family Studies, Civil Engineering Technology, Computer Programming, Cosmetology, Data Processing, Drafting/Design Technology, Economics, Elementary Education, Electrical and Electronics Technology, Health Education, Liberal Arts, General Studies, Nursing

ATHLETIC PROFILE

Conference Affiliation: Mississippi Association of Community and Junior College
Program Profile: We play on natural grass (tifton 419) that is overseeded with perennial rye grass during playing season. Pollie Sullivan Stadium currently seats 600.
Achievements: Had 2 players drafted since 1992; 10 All-Region players since 1992.
Coaching: Keith Case, Head Coach, has 15 years of coaching experience. Six were at a junior college. He was a graduate of Mississippi State University. Chad Caillet, Assistant Coach, is a Copiah Lincoln alumni. Rusty Miller, Assistant Coach, is a SouthEast Louisiana University alumni.
Style of Play: We have strong pitching and defense and athletic players that are aggressive. Offensively , the team works very hard to be able to use the entire field.

Delta State University

Box 3161
Cleveland, MS 38733
Coach: Mike Kinnison

NCAA II
Statesmen/Forest Green, White
Phone: (601) 846-4291
Fax: (601) 846-4297

ACADEMIC

Founded: 1924
Type: 4 Yr., Public, Liberal Arts, Coed
Religion: Non-Affiliated
Campus Housing: Yes
Web-site: Not Available
SAT/ACT/GPA: 17/2.0
Student/Faculty Ratio: 24:1
Male/Female Ratio: 40:60
Undergraduate Enrollment: 3,900
Graduate Enrollment: 200
Scholarships/Academic: Yes **Athletic:** Yes **Fin Aid:** Yes
Total Expenses by: Year **In State:** $ 2,798 **Out of State:** $ 4,273
Degrees Conferred: BA, BBA, BCA, BFA, BSCJ, BSE, BSGS, MBA, EDS, MCA, MSNS
Programs of Study: Education, Business, Aviation, Nursing, Premed, Accounting, Criminal Justice, Sports Management, Sports Medicine, Physical Therapy, Occupational Therapy, Physical Education, Environmental Science, Chemistry

ATHLETIC PROFILE

Estimated Number of Baseball Scholarships: 9.0
Conference Affiliation: Gulf South Conference
Program Profile: Our program is a member of NCAA Division II. We play on a lighted natural grass called Ferris Field with a seating capacity of 1,500 . Our season runs from February through May.
History: Our program began in 1959.
Achievements: 1997 GSC Coach of the Year; 8 Conference Championships since 1978, 16 Regional, 6 World Series Appearances, 3rd place finish in 1994 and 1996 World Series; 40 professional signees.
Coaching: Mike Kinnison, Head Coach, became the school's first-ever full-time assistant in 1994. He was 1997 GSC Coach of the Year. He compiled a record of 74-32 in two years and is a former All-American at Delta State Unviersity.
Roster for 1998 team/In State: 29 **Out of State:** 11 **Out of Country:** 0
Total Number of Varsity/Jr. Varsity: 40 **Percent of Graduation:** 85%
Number of Seniors on 1998 Team: 15 **Number of Sophomores on 1998 Team:** 10
Freshmen Receiving Fin Aid/Athletic: 7 **Academic:** 1
Baseball Camp Dates: June, July **Number of Spring Games:** 56
Positions Needed for 1999/2000: Pitcher, Outfielder, Middle Infielder
Most Recent Record: 39 - 12 - 0
Schedule: University of Mississippi, University of Tampa, Florida Southern University, University of West Florida, University of North Alabama, Cumberland University
Style of Play: We emphasize on defense fundamentals and sound pitching staff. We have an aggressive and competitive team emphasis.

East Central Community College

PO Box 129
Decatur, MS 39327
Coach: Jamie Clark
Email: jclark@eccc.cc.ms.us

NJCAA
Warriors/Black, Gold
Phone: (601) 635-2111
Fax: (601) 635-4099

ACADEMIC

Founded: 1928
Type: 2 Yr., Jr. College, Coed
Website: http://www.eccc.cc.ms.us
Campus Housing: No
Undergraduate Enrollment: 1,500
Graduate Enrollment: None

Scholarships/Academic: No **Athletic:** No **Fin Aid:** Yes
Total Expenses by: Year **In State:** $ 4,000 **Out of State:** $ 5,100
Degrees Conferred: Associate
Programs of Study: Accounting, Art Educaion, Art/Fine Arts, Behavioral Science, Biology, Biological Science, Business Administration, Commerce, Management, Carpentry, Chemistry, Computer Science, Cosmetology, Data Processing, Draftng/Design Technology, Early Childhood Education, Preengineering, Electrical and Electronics Technology, English

ATHLETIC PROFILE

Conference Affiliation: Mississippi JCAA

East Mississippi Community College

PO Box 158
Scooba, MS 39358
Coach: William Baldner

NJCAA
Lions/Black, Red
Phone: (601) 476-8442
Fax: (601) 476-5039

ACADEMIC

Founded: 1927
Type: 2 Yr., Jr. College, Coed
Religion: Non-Affiliated
Campus Housing: Yes
Student/Faculty Ratio: 20:1
Male/Female Ratio: 2:1
Undergraduate Enrollment: 400
Graduate Enrollment: None
Scholarships/Academic: Yes **Athletic:** Yes **Fin Aid:** Yes
Total Expenses by: Year **In State:** $ 820+ **Out of State:** $ 870+
Degrees Conferred: AA
Programs of Study: Accounting, Agronomy, Soil and Crop Science, Art/Fine Arts, Automotive Technology, Aviation Technology, Biology, Biological Science, Business Administration, Commerce, Management, Chemistry, Computer Science, Computer Technology, Cosmetology, Criminal Justice, Drafting/Design, Economics, Education, Electrical/Electronics Technology, Law Enforcement

ATHLETIC PROFILE

Conference Affiliation: Mississippi Community College Conference
Program Profile: The home game field has natural grass. Poole Field seats 500 and is surrounded by fine trees. There is a Bermuda infield and a St. Augustine outfield.
History: Our program began in 1930. Several players have gone to Division I schools and many others have contributed to society in coaching, law, education and medical fields.
Achievements: Rodney Batts, Delta State, was drafted by the Phillies. Jason Page , Delta State, played in Division II World Series. Tony Montgomery ,Delta State, played in Division II World Series.
Coaching: William Baldner ,Head Coach, is a 1978 graduate from Ohio University and coached five years high school baseball in Ohio. He worked under Ron Polk at Mississippi State for two years as a Georgia, Infielder and Pitcher. Ashley Robinson, Assistan Coach, is a fomer player EMCC and works with catchers, outfielders.
Style of Play: We believe in combustion of defense and aggressive base running.

Hinds Community College

PO Box 1286 HCC
Raymond, MS 39154
Coach: Rick Clarke

NJCAA
Eagles/Maroon, White
Phone: (601) 857-3362
Fax: (601) 857-3645

ACADEMIC

Founded: 1917
Type: 2 Yr., Jr. college, Coed
Undergraduate Enrollment: 9,100
Graduate Enrollment: None
Scholarships/Academic: No **Athletic:** No **Fin Aid:** Yes

Total Expenses by: Year **In State:** $ 3,000 **Out of State:** $ 5,100
Degrees Conferred: Associate
Programs of Study: Accounting, Agriculture, Art/Fine Arts, Business Administration, Child Development, Child Psychology, Civil Engineering Technology, Biology, Biological Science, Commercial Arts, Communications, Graphics, Computer

ATHLETIC PROFILE

Conference Affiliation: Region XXIII Conference

Holmes Community College

PO Box 399
Goodman, MS 39079
Coach: Quinby Morgan

NJCAA
Bulldogs/Maroon, White
Phone: (601) 472-2312
Fax: (601) 472-9157

ACADEMIC

Founded: 1928
Type: 2 Yr., Jr. College, Coed
Web-site: Not-Available
SAT/ACT/GPA: Required
Undergraduate Enrollment: 2,400
Graduate Enrollment: None
Scholarships/Academic: No **Athletic:** Yes **Fin Aid:** Yes
Total Expenses by: Year **In State:** $ 2,500 **Out of State:** $ 3,500
Degrees Conferred: Associate
Programs of Study: Agricultural Science, Biology, Biological Science, Business Administration, Commerce, Management, Business Education, Child Care/Child and Family Studies, Elementary Education, Engineering, Finance/Banking, Data Processing, Drafting/Design Technology, Medical Records Services, Medical Technology, Music Education, Nursing, Pharmacy, Physical Therapy

ATHLETIC PROFILE

Conference Affiliation: MJCAA

Itawamba Community College

602 W Hill St
Fulton, MS 38843
Coach: Chuck Box

NJCAA
Indians/Red, Blue
Phone: (601) 862-8000
Fax: (601) 862-9540

ACADEMIC

Founded: 1947
Type: 2 Yr., Jr. College, Coed
Student/Faculty Ratio: 20:1
Male/Female Ratio: 1:1.3
Undergraduate Enrollment: 2,400
Graduate Enrollment: None
Scholarships/Academic: Yes **Athletic:** Yes **Fin Aid:** Yes
Total Expenses by: Year **In State:** $ 2,645 **Out of State:** $ 3,445
Degrees Conferred: Associate
Programs of Study: Accounting, Agricultural Business, Art Education, Art/Fine Arts, Biology, Biological Science, Business Administration, Commerce, Management, Chemistry, Child Care/Child and Family Studies, Child Psychology, Child Development, Computer Science, Computer Technologies, Data Processing

ATHLETIC PROFILE

Conference Affiliation: Mississippi Junior College Association
Program Profile: The Indians play a NJCAA 50-game schedule plus eight Fall games. The home games are played on campus at John S. Crubaugh Field.

Achievements: 1993 Coach of the Year, 1987 and 1983 All Star Coach. In 13 seasons 81 players have signed with 4-year schools, and 8 have signed pro contracts.
Style of Play: We play fundamentally sound.

Jackson State University

1325 West Lynch Street
Jackson, MS 39217
Coach: Robert Braddy

NCAA I
Tigers/Blue, White
Phone: (601) 968-2291
Fax: (601) 968-7008

ACADEMIC

Founded: 1877
Type: 4 Yr., Public, Coed
Religion: Non-Affiliated
Campus Housing: Yes
Web-site: Not-Available
SAT/ACT/GPA: 700avg/17avg
Student/Faculty Ratio: 17:1
Male/Female Ratio: 43:57
Undergraduate Enrollment: 5,455
Graduate Enrollment: 890
Scholarships/Academic: Yes **Athletic:** Yes **Fin Aid:** Yes
Total Expenses by: Year **In State:** $ 5,400 **Out of State:** $ 7,600
Degrees Conferred: BA, BS, BBA, BM, BME, BSE, BSW, MA, MS, MBA
Programs of Study: Accounting, Art/Fine Arts, Biology, Biological Science, Business Administration, Commerce, Management, Business Economics, Business Education, Chemistry, Child Care/Child and Family Studies, Communications, Computer Science, Criminal Justice, Predentistry, Journalism, Economics, Electrical and Electronics Technology, Fire Science, Health Education, Law Enforcement, Police Science, Political Science

ATHLETIC PROFILE

Conference Affiliation: SWAC

Jones County Junior College

900 S Court Street
Ellisville, MS 39437
Coach: Bobby Glaze

NJCAA
Bobcats/Cardinal, Gold
Phone: (601) 477-4087
Fax: (601) 477-4017

ACADEMIC

Type: 2 Yr., Public, Liberal Arts, Coed
Founded: 1911
Religion: Non-Affiliated
Campus Housing: Yes
SAT/ACT/GPA: Act must have been taken/
Undergraduate Enrollment: 4,500
Scholarships/Academic: Yes **Athletic:** Yes **Fin Aid:** Yes
Total Expenses by: Year **In State:** $ 1,454 **Out of State:** $ 2,029
Degrees Conferred: AA
Programs of Study: Accounting, Agriculture, Art, Biological Science, Business, Chemistry, Data Processing, Drafting/Design Technology, Economics, Education, Electrical/Electronics Technology, Medical, Engineering, Forest, Horticulture, Law, Math, Music

ATHLETIC PROFILE

Estimated Number of Baseball Scholarships: 10
Conference Affiliation: Mississippi Junior College Conference
Program Profile: We have a 50 game Spring schedule. Our natural turf field is upgraded yearly.
History: We played in the1950's and shut down at some point. We started again in 1969.
Achievements: Ryan Kennedy was drafted by the Colorado Rockies in 1996.

Coaching: Bobby Glaze, Head Coach, started his 8th year at Jones. He was 10 years at Laurel High School winning a state championship in 1989. Jay Reeves, Assistant Coach, started his 1st year with the program. He is responsible for the pitchers and was drafted by the Atlanta Braves in 1982.
Roster for 1998 team/In State: 23 **Out of State:** 6 **Out of Country:** 0
Total Number of Varsity/Jr. Varsity: 0 **Percent of Graduation:** 75%
Positions Needed for 1999/2000: Pitchers **Number of Sophomores on 1998 Team:** 18
Freshmen Receiving Fin Aid/Athletic: 10 **Academic:** 4
Number of Fall Games: 6 **Number of Spring Games:** 50
Schedule: Mississippi Gulf Coast, Hinds, Pearl River, Okaloosa Walton, Chipola
Style of Play: We are big inning oriented offensively and have good team speed.

Mary Holmes College

(Program Discontinued)

Meridian Community College

910 Highway 19 North
Meridian, MS 39307
Coach: Scott Berry

NJCAA
Eagles/Green, White
Phone: (601) 484-8680
Fax: (601) 484-8635

ACADEMIC

Founded: 1937 **Type:** 2 Yr., Jr. College, Coed
Web-site: http://www.mcc.cc.ms.us **SAT/ACT/GPA:** None
Student/Faculty Ratio: 16:1 **Male/Female Ratio:** 31:69
Undergraduate Enrollment: 2,850 **Graduate Enrollment:** None
Scholarships/Academic: No **Athletic:** Yes **Fin Aid:** Yes
Total Expenses by: Year **In State:** $ 950 **Out of State:** $ 2,000
Degrees Conferred: Associate
Programs of Study: Broadcasting, Computer Graphics, Computer Technologies, Dental Services, Drafting/Design Technology, Electrical and Electronics Technology, Emergency Medical Technology, Medical Record Services, Fire Science, Horticulture, Hotel/Restaurant Management, Machine/Tool Technology, Physical Therapy, Respiratory Therapy

ATHLETIC PROFILE

Conference Affiliation: Mississippi Conference
Program Profile: Our team ranked 1st in the NJCAA Division I for the entire 1997 season. We participated in JUCO World Series 3 out of the last 5 years and finished 2nd in 1996. We play 20 games in the Fall from August through October . In the Spring ,we play 56 games from February through May. We have a natural playing surface and our stadim seats 3000.
Achievements: Region XXXIII Champions in 1992 - 1994, 1996 - 1997; Mississippi Conference champions in 1992, 1994-1997; Eastern District Champions in 1993, 1994 and 1996.
Coaching: Scott Berry - Head Coach.

Millsaps College

1701 N State Street
Jackson, MS 39210
Coach: Jim Page

NCAA III
Majors/Purple, White
Phone: (601) 974-1196
Fax: (601) 974-1209

ACADEMIC

Founded: 1890 **Type:** 4 Yr., Private, Liberal Arts, Coed
Religion: United Methodist **Campus Housing:** Yes
Web-site: http://www.millsaps.edu/ **SAT/ACT/GPA:** 960/ 21

Student/Faculty Ratio: 13:1 **Male/Female Ratio:** 47:53
Undergraduate Enrollment: 1,209 **Graduate Enrollment:** 200
Scholarships/Academic: Yes **Athletic:** No **Fin Aid:** Yes
Total Expenses by: Year **In State:** $ 18,788 **Out of State:** $ 18,788
Degrees Conferred: BA, BS, BBA, BMus, MBA, MA, MLS, BLS
Programs of Study: Accounting, Biology, Business Administration, Chemistry, Classics, Computer Science, Dramatic Arts, Economics, Elementary Education, English, Fine Arts, French, Geology, History, Management, Mathematics, Music, Philosophy, Physics, Political Science, Psychology, Religion, Science Education, Social Science, Spanish

ATHLETIC PROFILE

Conference Affiliation: Southern Collegiate Athletic Conference
Program Profile: We play highly successfully in SCAC play and won 5 consecutive SCAC championships between 1990-94. We had our first appearance in the NCAA Division III championships in 1995. We finished the season ranked 21st in the country.
History: Baseball has been played on and off throughout Millsaps' history.
Achievements: Jim Page is four-time SCAC Coach of the Year and our program won a record 5 straight SCAC Titles.
Coaching: Jim Page, Head Coach, is a 1985 graduate of Millsaps. He was a standout third baseman/pitcher at Millsaps and Conference Coach of the Year. He is a former member of the South Region Selection Committee.
Style of Play: We play everything aggressively. We want to keep the pressure on the opposition by running, swinging the bat aggressively and going at them on the mound.

Mississippi College

PO Box 4245 **NCAA II**
Clinton, MS 39058 **Choctaws/Navy, Old Gold**
Coach: Tom Gladney **Phone: (601) 925-3346**
Email: gladney@mc.edu **Fax: (601) 924-6517**

ACADEMIC

Founded: 1826 **Type:** 4 Yr., Private, Liberal Arts, Coed
Religion: Southern Baptist **Campus Housing:** No
Web-site: Not Available **SAT/ACT/GPA:** 22 avg/3.0
Student/Faculty Ratio: 18:1 **Male/Female Ratio:** 39:61
Undergraduate Enrollment: 2,600 **Graduate Enrollment:** 800
Scholarships/Academic: Yes **Athletic:** No **Fin Aid:** Yes
Total Expenses by: Year **In State:** $ 13,000 **Out of State:** $ 13,000
Degrees Conferred: BA, BS, MBA, Med, JD
Programs of Study: Accounting, Business and Management, Communications, Computer Science, Education, Home Economics, Religion, Psychology, Social Science

ATHLETIC PROFILE

Conference Affiliation: Gulf South Conference
Program Profile: We play at Frierson Field which has grass and seats 1,500. Our playing/practice season consists of 22 total weeks with 5-6 games in the Fall and 16-17 games in the Spring.
History: Mississippi College became a member of the Gulf South Conference in 1972.
Achievements: 1993 - 3 All-Conference 2nd Team, 2 NCAA Division II All-South Central Region, 3 All-Academic GSC, 1 GTE Academic All-District (VI), 1 GTE Academic All-American.
Coaching: Tom Gladney, Head Coach since 1984, got a BS/ED in 1978 and a MA/ED from MC in 1979. He was Academic All-GSC player and chairman of National Div. II Baseball All-American/COY Selection Committee. Doug Shanks, Grad Asst, in his 3rd year as pitching coach. He got his BBS from Liberty. Michael Young, Grad Asst, played for MC and was MVP in 1993. He was in the 1992-93 MS Sports All-College Team and graduated from MC in 1993. Mike McNeer, Student Assistant, was All-Conference and All-South Central Region.
Roster for 1998 team/In State: 30 **Out of State:** 9 **Out of Country:** 0

Total Number of Varsity/Jr. Varsity: 39
Most Recent Record: 17-21-0
Number of Seniors on 1998 Team: 5
Most Recent Record: 36 - 19 - 0
Freshmen Receiving Fin Aid/Athletic: 0
Academic: 22
Number of Fall Games: 9
Number of Spring Games: 40
Positions Needed for 1999/2000: Catcher, RHP, LHP, Shortstop
Schedule: Howard Payne University, Mary Hardin Baylor University, Huntington College, Belhaven College, University of the Ozarks

Mississippi Delta Community College

PO Box 668
Moorhead, MS 38761
Coach: Terry Thompson

NJCAA
Trojans/Red, Black
Phone: (601) 246-6311
Fax: (601) 246-8627

ACADEMIC

Founded: 1926
Type: 2 Yr., Jr. College, Coed
Student/Faculty Ratio: 20:1
Male/Female Ratio: 46:54
Undergraduate Enrollment: 2,500
Graduate Enrollment: None
Scholarships/Academic: No **Athletic:** Yes **Fin Aid:** Yes
Total Expenses by: Year **In State:** $ 2,500 **Out of State:** $ 3,500
Degrees Conferred: Associate
Programs of Study: Accounting, Advertising, Agricultural Business, Agricultural Economics, American Studies, Applied Art, Art Education, Behavioral Science, Biology, Biological Science, Business Administration, Commerce, Management, Business Machine Technology, Child Psychology, Child Development, Civil Engineering Technology, Commercial Arts, Computer Technologies, Criminal Justice, Data Processing, Elementary Education, English, Farm/Ranch Management, Electrical/Electronics Technology, Medical Record Services, Music, Music Education

ATHLETIC PROFILE

Conference Affiliation: MSCA

Mississippi Gulf Coast Community College

Box 47
Perkinston, MS 39573
Coach: Cooper Farris

NJCAA
Bulldogs/Royal Blue, Gold
Phone: (601) 928-6348
Fax: (601) 928-6359

ACADEMIC

Founded: 1923
Type: 2 Yr., Public, Coed
Religion: Non-Affiliated
Campus Housing: Yes
Student/Faculty Ratio: 20:1
Male/Female Ratio: 50:50
Undergraduate Enrollment: 12,000
Graduate Enrollment: None
Scholarships/Academic: Yes **Athletic:** Yes **Fin Aid:** Yes
Total Expenses by: Semester **In State:** $ 1,300 **Out of State:** $ 2,000
Degrees Conferred: Associate, Technical
Programs of Study: Accounting, Advertising, Business, Art, Education, Etc..

ATHLETIC PROFILE

Estimated Number of Baseball Scholarships: 10
Conference Affiliation: Mississippi Association of Community and Junior College
Program Profile: Ken 'Curly' Farris Field has a seating capacity of 1,000, a natural grass and has dimensions 370-LCF, 400-CF and 360-RCF. Playing season starts February through May which consists of a 50 game schedule. Fall season starts from September and goes through October.

History: We started in 1964. We have 16 State Championships and 12 Runner-Ups. We have been in state regional playoffs in the last nine years and went to JUCO World Series in 1991.
Achievements: Coach Farris started in 1990 and has had 9 All-Americans, 19 players drafted and 82 went on to play senior college ball South Division Championships 8 times.
Coaching: Cooper Farris, Head Coach, graduated from Delta State University in 1977. He was 9 years at the Gulf Coast and 12 years in high school in Mississippi and Texas. He has an overall 653-272 record. Michael Cudd, Assistant Coach, graduated from Delta State University 1992 and was at the Gulf Coast for three years.
Roster for 1998 team/In State: 24 **Out of State:** 6 **Out of Country:** 0
Total Number of Varsity/Jr. Varsity: 30 **Percent of Graduation:** 95%
Number of Seniors on 1998 Team: 15 **Most Recent Record:** 36 - 19 - 0
Freshmen Receiving Fin Aid/Athletic: 12 **Academic:** 6
Number of Fall Games: 8 **Number of Spring Games:** 50
Positions Needed for 1999/2000: Pitchers, Outfielders, Catchers
Style of Play: We believe in pressure, hit and run and defense.

Mississippi State University

PO Drawer 5327
Mississippi State, MS 39762
Coach: Pat McMahon
Email: canderson@athletics.msstate.edu

NCAA I
Bulldogs/Maroon, White
Phone: (601) 325-3597
Fax: (601) 325-3600

ACADEMIC

Founded: 1878
Type: 4 Yr., Public, Liberal Arts, Coed
Religion: Non-Affiliated
Campus Housing: Yes
Web-site: http://www.msstate.edu/
SAT/ACT/GPA: 17
Student/Faculty Ratio: 19:1
Male/Female Ratio: 50:50
Undergraduate Enrollment: 13,500
Graduate Enrollment: 3,000
Scholarships/Academic: Yes **Athletic:** Yes **Fin Aid:** Yes
Total Expenses by: Year **In State:** $ 8,271 **Out of State:** $ 11,091
Degrees Conferred: BA, BBA, BFA, BGS, BS, BLA, BPA, MA, MS, MAM, MBA
Programs of Study: Accounting, Agriculture, Anthropology, Biology, Business and Management, Chemistry, Communications, Computer, Education, Engineering, English, Finance, Management

ATHLETIC PROFILE

Estimated Number of Baseball Scholarships: 11.7
Conference Affiliation: SouthEastern Conference (SEC)
Program Profile: Our stadium is Dudy Noble Field & has natural grass, a capacity of 14,750 & includes 8,000 in the outfield terrace. We have the largest on-campus college baseball facility in the country.
History: Our program began in 1885 and we were NCAA regional participants 21 times. We had College World Series Appearances in 1979, 1981, 1985, 1990 and 1997.
Achievements: 30 All-Americans since 1949; SEC Champions 10 times (1948, 1949, 1965, 1966, 1970, 1971, 1979, 1985, 1987 and 1989. We had 28 former Bulldogs players in the major leagues including 6 All-Stars.
Coaching: Pat McMahon, Head Coach, is in his 2nd year; after serving as an associate head coach. Jim Case, Assistant, is in his 2nd year. Tommy Raffo, Assistant Coach, is in his 2nd year.
Schedule: LSU, Alabama, Florida, Auburn, South Carolina, Arkansas

Mississippi Valley State University

PO Box 743 MVSU
Itta Bena, MS 38941
Coach: Cleotha Wilson

NCAA I
Delta Devils/Green, White
Phone: (601) 254-3398
Fax: (601) 254-6641

ACADEMIC

Founded: 1950
Type: 4 Yr., Public, Coed
SAT/ACT/GPA: 700avg/17avg
Campus Housing: Yes
Undergraduate Enrollment: 2,170
Graduate Enrollment: 15
Scholarships/Academic: Yes **Athletic:** Yes **Fin Aid:** Yes
Total Expenses by: Year **In State:** $ 5,200 **Out of State:** $ 7,350
Degrees Conferred: BA, BS, BME, BSW, MA, MS
Programs of Study: Accounting, Art/Fine Arts, Administration, Commerce, Management, Chemistry, Communications, Computer Science, Criminal Justice, Education, Elementary Education, Engineering, Physical Education, Political Science, Public Administration, Secondary Education, Office Management, Social Work

ATHLETIC PROFILE

Conference Affiliation: SouthWestern Conference

Northeast Mississippi Community College

101 Cunningham Blvd
Booneville, MS 38829
Coach: Ray Scott

NJCAA
Tigers/Black, Gold
Phone: (601) 720-7309
Fax: (601) 728-1165

ACADEMIC

Founded: 1948
Type: 2 Yr., Jr. College, Coed
Student/Faculty Ratio: Unknown
Male/Female Ratio: 48:52
Undergraduate Enrollment: 2,775
Graduate Enrollment: None
Scholarships/Academic: No **Athletic:** Yes **Fin Aid:** Yes
Total Expenses by: Year **In State:** $ 2,800 **Out of State:** $ 3,600
Degrees Conferred: Associate
Programs of Study: Accounting, Agriculture, Art Education, Art/Fine Arts, Biblical Studies, Biology, Biological Studies, Business Administration, Commerce, Management, Business Economics, Business Education, Carpentry, Chemistry, Child Care/Child and Family Studies, Child Psychology, Civil Engineering Technology, Commercial Art, Communications, Computer Information Systems, Computer Management, Computer Science, Crimnal Justice, Computer Management, Drafting/Design, Electrical/Electronics Technology, Fashion Merchandising, Food, Marketing, Foresty, Forest Technology, Home Economics Education, Interior Design

ATHLETIC PROFILE

Conference Affiliation: MACJC

Northwest Mississippi Community College

510 North Panole
Senatobia, MS 38668
Coach: Donny Castle

NJCAA
Rangers/Navy, Cardinal Red, Grey
Phone: (601) 562-3419
Fax: (601) 562-3423

ACADEMIC

Founded: 1927
Type: 2 Yr., Jr. College, Coed
Religion: Non-Affiliated
Campus Housing: No
Web-site: http://www.nwcc.cc.ms.us
SAT/ACT/GPA: None
Undergraduate Enrollment: 4,200
Graduate Enrollment: None
Scholarships/Academic: No **Athletic:** No **Fin Aid:** Yes
Total Expenses by: Year **In State:** $ 2,400 **Out of State:** $ 3,400
Degrees Conferred: Associate

Programs of Study: Accounting, Agricultural Economics, Agricultural Science, Aircraft and Missile Maintenance, Applied Art, Art/Fine Arts, Automotive Technology, Broadcasting, Business Administration, Management, Commerce, Carpentry, Child Care/Child and Family Studies, Civil Engineering Technology, Commercial Arts, Computer Science, Computer Technology, Cosmetology, Preengineering, Data Processing, Dental Services, Drafting/Design Technology, Education, Electronics Engineering Technology, Funeral Services, Home Economics

ATHLETIC PROFILE

Conference Affiliation: Mississippi Association of Jr. and Community Colleges
Program Profile: We have a rich tradition program that has claimed numerous championships on the state, region and national level. Our team has made two consecutive trips to the Division II College World Series in Millington in the last two years. Our stadium has a grass field with a capacity of 500. It has a four room press box that was recently built..
History: Our program began in 1927. Jim Miles was head coach for 22 years and recently stepped down. Donny Castle, his assistant of 19 years, took over the helm a month ago.

Pearl River Community College

Hwy 11 N Station
Poplarville, MS 39470
Coach: Jim Nightengale

NJCAA
Wildcats/Maroon, Gold
Phone: (601) 795-1326
Fax: (601) 795-1176

ACADEMIC

Founded: 1909
Type: 2 Yr., Jr. College, Coed
Student/Faculty Ratio: 18:1
Male/Female Ratio: 34:66
Undergraduate Enrollment: 2,780
Graduate Enrollment: None
Scholarships/Academic: No **Athletic:** Yes **Fin Aid:** Yes
Total Expenses by: Year **In State:** $ 2,600 **Out of State:** $ 3,600
Degrees Conferred: Associate
Programs of Study: Business Administration, Commerce, Management, Drafting/Design, Electrical/Electronics Technology, Liberal Arts, General Studies, Marketing, Retailing Merchandising, Medical Secretarial Studies, Nursing, Respiratory Therapy, Secretarial Studies, Office Management

ATHLETIC PROFILE

Conference Affiliation: MACJC

Rust College

150 Rust Avenue
Holly Springs, MS 38635
Coach: Avery Mason

NCAA III
Bearcats/Blue, White
Phone: (601) 252-8101
Fax: (601) 252-6107

ACADEMIC

Founded: 1866
Type: 4 Yr., Private, Coed
SAT/ACT/GPA: 17avg
Campus Housing: Yes
Student/Faculty Ratio: 18:1
Male/Female Ratio: 36:64
Undergraduate Enrollment: 1,130
Graduate Enrollment: None
Scholarships/Academic: Yes **Athletic:** No **Fin Aid:** Yes
Total Expenses by: Year **In State:** $ 8,300 **Out of State:** $ 8,300
Degrees Conferred: AS, BA, BS
Programs of Study: Accounting, Biology, Biological Science, Business Administration, Commerce, Management, Chemistry, Communications, Computer Science, Early Childhood Education, Economics, Education, Elementary Education, English, History, Physics, Political Science, Science, Education, Social Work, Sociology

ATHLETIC PROFILE

Conference Affiliation: Independent
Program Profile: Rust College Baseball program is rebuilding for the 1997-1998 season. At the present, we are building Bearcat Field It is a natural grass field and seats 250 fans. It can also accommodate many standers.
History: Rust College baseball program beagn in the early 1900's. It has always been a Christian school (private institution) so scholarships for baseball has been probihited. In 1986 , our Rust College baseball program had a remarkable 32-9 season under the direction of Bo Sellers the coach untill 1996-1997 season. In 1998, Coach Avery Mason took over.
Achievements: 1969 Gulf Coast Athletic Conference Champions, 1984 SIAC Division III, 3rd Place; players drafted were Anthony Berry (Texas Rangers) 1989 Outfielder, Otis Edwards (Cleveland Indians) 91-93 Outfielder, and Jerome Williams (Chicago Cubs) 1989 Outfielder.
Coaching: Avery Mason, Head Coach. At this present time Rust College has a 1st year coach. He was a graduate Assistant Coach at Alcorn State University. Before Alcorn State, he coached the high school level in Lancanster California at Antelope Valley High School. An assistant coach is being recruited.
Style of Play: Coach Mason is bringing in a new free style offense and a web tight defense. The key to winning in baseball is to have a good +pitching and a better than average defense making all routine plays.

Southwest Mississippi Community College

College Drive
Summit, MS 39666
Coach: Larry Holmes

NJCAA
Bears/Royal Blue, Cardinal Red
Phone: (601) 276-2000
Fax: (601) 276-3888

ACADEMIC

Type: 2 Yr., Jr. College, Coed
Campus Housing: No
Degrees Conferred: Associated
Programs of Study: Accounting, Advertising, Automotive Technology, Biology, Biological Science, Business Administration, Commerce, Management, Business Education, Carpentry, Chemistry, Computer Science, Construction Technology, Cosmetology, Education, Electrical and Electronics Technology, Marketing, Retailing Merchandising, Music, Music Education, Physical Sciences

ATHLETIC PROFILE

Conference Affiliation: Mississipi Conference
Program Profile: We have a 2 year JUCO program with a limit of 24 scholarship players per year. Eighteen of the players must come from a recruiting district inside Mississipi. Six players are allowed from outside of the state. Our baseball field is 6 years old,has natural turf Bermuda and dimensions of 325 foul lines, 370 alleys and 390 center field. The Fall season starts after Labor Day (six weeks), The Spring season starts middle of February and is 50 games.
History: Mississippi started offering scholarships nine years ago. SMCC has had 3 winning seasons in those nine years. Twenty five players have moved on to senior college programs or pro-ball and 15 of those players signed Division 1. Seven have played pro-ball.
Achievements: Seven former SMCC players have gone to play pro-ball, three of those players signed straight out of SMCC.
Coaching: Larry Holmes, Head Coach, started his 6th year and has a record of 78-132. He is a graduate of William Carey College-Hattiesburg, MS. He pitched for three years at WCC. Butch Holme, Assistant Coach, is a former head coach of SMCC (10 years). He graduated from Mississippi State University, was a four year Letterman Baseball and led SEC in Earned Run Average.
Style of Play: We are aggressive on offense, routine on defense. We have a better chance of winning in low scoring games.

University of Mississippi (Ole Mississippi)

PO Box 217
University, MS 38677
Coach: Pat Harrison
Email: TBA

NCAA I
Rebels/Cardinal Red, Navy Blue
Phone: (601) 232-7538
Fax: (601) 232-7006

ACADEMIC

Founded: 1848
Type: 4 Yr., Public, Coed
Religion: Non-Affiliated
Campus Housing: No
Web-site: http://www.olemiss.edu/
SAT/ACT/GPA: 720
Student/Faculty Ratio: 18:1
Male/Female Ratio: 49:51
Undergraduate Enrollment: 10,369
Graduate Enrollment: 2,173
Scholarships/Academic: Yes **Athletic:** Yes **Fin Aid:** Yes
Total Expenses by: Semester **In State:** $ 3,568 **Out of State:** $ 3,980
Degrees Conferred: BA, BS, BFA, BAc, BAE, BALM, BBA, BE, BM, BPA, BSCE, BSChE, BSCS, BSE, BSES, BSEE, BSG, BSHE, BSME, BSPharm, BSW, MA, MS, MBA, MFA, MEd, PhD, EdD, JD
Programs of Study: Accounting, Advertising, Anthropology, Art, Art Education, Art History, Banking/Finance, Biological Science, Biomedical Science, Broadcasting, Business Administration, Chemical Engineering, Chemistry, Civil Engineering, Computer Science, Court Reporting Design, Dramatic Arts, Early Childhood, Economics, Electrical Engineering, Elemenatry Education, Engineering, English, French, Geological Engineering, Geology, German, History, Insurance, Journalism, Leisure Management, Management, Management Information Systems, Marketing, Mathematics, Mechanical Engineering, Medical Laboratory Technology, Music, Music Education, Personnel Management, Pharmacy, Philosophy, Physics, Political Science, Psychology, Public Administration, Real Estate, Social Science, Spanish, Special Education, Speech Pathology, Telecommunications, Theatre

ATHLETIC PROFILE

Conference Affiliation: SouthEastern Conference (West Division)
Program Profile: Our home field is Oxford University Stadium/Swayze Field which seats 3,000. The field is natural grass and the stadium was voted 7th -best in the country in 1992 by Baseball America Magazine. It includes a spacious locker room, a coaches' locker room and office, a players' lounge, batting tunnels, a training room, Etc.
History: The program has made four NCAA College World Series appearances. The Rebels have won the SEC Championship six times and have won the SEC West Division Title nine times. The last NCAA Regional appearance the Rebel made was in 1995 when the Rebels participated in the NCAA Atlantic I Regional.
Achievements: The Rebels have won six SEC titles and have had 10 student/athletes to receive All-American honors. Ole Miss has had 86 players play professional baseball and has had 20 who played in the Major League.
Coaching: Pat Harrison ,Head Coach, completed his 2nd season as skipper of the Rebels. His overall record now is 156-148-2 after one season at Ole Miss. He was head coach for 2 seasons at Pepperdine & another at The Master's College. The coaching staff is a young one. Keith Kessinger, who is also finishing his first year at Ole Miss, coaches infielders & hitters. First-year coach Darby Carmichael works with the pitchers & catchers. Harrison works with the pitcher & hitters.
Style of Play: Our program plays hit-and-run in certain situations. The team will lay down on occasional bunt to keep the defense off-balance.

University of Southern Mississippi

Box 5017
Hattiesburg, MS 39401
Coach: Corky Palmer

NCAA I
Golden Eagles/Black, Gold
Phone: (601) 266-5017
Fax: (601) 266-6595

ACADEMIC

Founded: 1910
Type: 4 Yr., Public, Liberal Arts, Coed
Web-site: http://www.usm.edu
SAT/ACT/GPA: 21avg
Student/Faculty Ratio: 17:1
Male/Female Ratio: 44:56
Undergraduate Enrollment: 10,939
Graduate Enrollment: 2,718
Scholarships/Academic: Yes **Athletic:** Yes **Fin Aid:** Yes
Total Expenses by: Year **In State:** $ 5,580 **Out of State:** $ 8,475
Degrees Conferred: Bachelors, Masters, Doctoral
Programs of Study: Accounting, American Studies, Advertising, Anthropology, Architecture, Art, Fine Arts, Biology, Biological Science, Business Administration, Commerce, Management, Chemistry, Commmunity Services, Computer Engineering, Computer Science, Economics, Computer Technologies, Film Studies, Science Education, Science Education, Real Estate, Pathology, Speech, Nursing, Music, Music Education, Physical Education

ATHLETIC PROFILE

Conference Affiliation: Conference USA
Program Profile: The Golden Eagles play their home games at modern Pete Taylor Park, which holds 3,500 people and was first opened in 1985. The field is a natural grass surface and the distances are 340' down the lines and 400' to center. USM traditionally plays around 35 home games per season against some of the nation's top teams. Southern Miss is also among the nation's attendance leaders each year.
History: Baseball became a full-time sport at USM in 1947, however records go back as far as 1913. Under head coach Hill Denson, USM has posted 11 consecutive winning seasons. Denson is one of just three head baseball coaches at USM since 1950 and is the school's most successful head coach. Under Denson, the Eagles have made two NCAA tournament appearances. We are a regular contender for the conference championship.
Achievements: During Denson's tenure as head coach USM has produced eight All-Americans, 32 All-Conference selections and has sent 28 players into professional baseball. In 1994, Tommy Davis was a first team All-America selection and in 1995 Derek Reams was a first team Academic All-American. Denson was named Metro Conference Coach of the Year in 1989 and 1990. Four USM players were named to the Conference USA All-Freshman team in 1996.
Coaching: Carlton "Corky" Palmer - Head Coach. Dan Wagner - Assistant. Scott Dwyer - Assistant.
Style of Play: We are fundamentally sound, aggressive and disciplined.

William Carey College

498 Tuscan Avenue
Hattiesburg, MS 39401
Coach: Bobby Halford

NAIA
Crusaders/Red, White, Black
Phone: (601) 582-6111
Fax: (601) 582-6454

ACADEMIC

Founded: 1906
Type: 4 Yr., Private, Liberal Arts, Coed
Religion: Baptist
Campus Housing: Yes
Web-site: Not Available
SAT/ACT/GPA: 18+
Student/Faculty Ratio: 13:1
Male/Female Ratio: 1:1
Undergraduate Enrollment: 2,200
Graduate Enrollment: 200
Scholarships/Academic: Yes **Athletic:** Yes **Fin Aid:** Yes
Total Expenses by: Year **In State:** $ 7,500 **Out of State:** $ 7,500
Degrees Conferred: BS, BA, BFA, BSN, BM, MBA, M Ed
Programs of Study: Business, Education, Art, Nursing, English, History, Math, Psychology, Biology

ATHLETIC PROFILE

Conference Affiliation: Gulf Coast Athletic Association

MISSOURI

SCHOOL	CITY	AFFILIATION 99	PAGE
Avila College	Kansas City	NAIA	484
Central Methodist College	Fayette	NAIA	484
Central Missouri State University	Warrensburg	NCAA II	485
College of the Ozarks	Point Lookout	NAIA	485
Crowder College	Neosho	NJCAA	486
Culver - Stockton College	Canton	NAIA	487
East Central College	Union	NJCAA	488
Evangel College	Springfield	NAIA	488
Fontbonne College	Clayton	NCAA III	489
Hannibal - LaGrange College	Hannibal	NAIA	489
Harris - Stowe State College	St. Louis	NAIA	490
Jefferson College	Hillsboro	NJCAA	491
Kemper Military College	Boonville	NJCAA	491
Lincoln University	Jefferson City	NCAA II	491
Lindenwood College	St. Charles	NAIA	492
Longview Community College	Lees Summit	NJCAA	493
Maple Woods Community College	Kansas City	NJCAA	493
Maryville University - Saint Louis	St. Louis	NCAA III	494
Mineral Area College	Park Hills	NJCAA	494
Missouri Baptist College	St. Louis	NAIA	495
Missouri Southern State College	Joplin	NCAA II	495
Missouri Valley College	Marshall	NAIA	496
Missouri Western State College	St. Joseph	NCAA II	496
North Central Missouri College	Trenton	NJCAA	497
Northwest Missouri State University	Maryville	NCAA II	497
Rockhurst College	Kansas City	NCAA II	498
Saint Louis Community College - Florissant	St. Louis	NJCAA	499
Saint Louis Community College - Forest Park	St. Louis	NJCAA	499
Saint Louis Community College - Meramec	Kirkwood	NJCAA	500
Saint Louis University	St. Louis	NCAA I	500
Southeast Missouri State University	Cape Girardeau	NCAA I	501
Southwest Baptist University	Bolivar	NCAA II	501
Southwest Missouri State University	Springfield	NCAA I	502
Three Rivers Community College	Poplar Bluff	NJCAA	502
Truman State University	Kirksville	NCAA II	503
University of Missouri - Columbia	Columbia	NCAA I	504
University of Missouri - Rolla	Rolla	NCAA II	504
University of Missouri - Saint Louis	St. Louis	NCAA II	505
Washington University - Saint Louis	St. Louis	NCAA III	506
Webster University	Webster Grove	NCAA III	506
Westminster College	Fulton	NCAA III	507
William Jewell College	Liberty		507

Avila College

11901 Wornall Road
Kansas City, MO 64145-1698
Coach: Jim Huber

NAIA
Eagles/Purple, Gold
Phone: (816) 942-8400
Fax: (816) 942-3362

ACADEMIC

Founded: 1916
Religion: Catholic
Web-site: http://www.avila.edu/
Student/Faculty Ratio: 13:1
Undergraduate Enrollment: 1,200
Type: 4 Yr., Private, Liberal Arts, Coed
Campus Housing: Yes
SAT/ACT/GPA: 22/3.2
Male/Female Ratio: 40:60
Graduate Enrollment: 200
Scholarships/Academic: Yes **Athletic:** Yes **Fin Aid:** Yes
Total Expenses by: Year **In State:** $ 16,010 **Out of State:** $ 16,010
Degrees Conferred: BA, BS, BSBA, BSN, BSMT, BSW, BFA, MS, MBA
Programs of Study: Art, Communication, English, General Studies, History, Mathematics, Music, Natural Sciences, Political Sciences, Psychology, Sociology, Theater, Theology, Etc.

ATHLETIC PROFILE

Conference Affiliation: Midland Collegiate Athletic Conference
Program Profile: Stadium-Zarda Family Athletic Complex seats 800 & has a natural grass surface.
History: The program began in 1989 with Head Coach Dave Klein who coached both as assistant and head, until 1990. Then Coach Toeben took over for the seasons of 1991-1992. Jim Huber came along in 1992 and is still the current head coach who in 1992 sent his team to the playoffs .In 1994, with a forty-five win season, he led his team to the regional finals. This past season his team won forty-one games.
Achievements: Coach of the Year; District 16 - Jim Huber in 1994; Gary Haarman and Joe Simone - Honorable Mention All-Americans.
Coaching: Jim Huber, Head Coach, started in 1993. He began as an assistant coach at Avila in 1992 and has 23 years of baseball experience. With 135 wins, he is the winningest basebal coach in Avila's history.
Style of Play: Huber's style of play involves aggressive, strong defense with aggressive base running. He believes the key to success will be team unity for the completion of a specific goal. Huber wants a confident attitude and sets goal to accomplish a winning season.

Central Methodist College

411 Central Methodist Square
Fayette, MO 65248
Coach: Jim Dapkus

NAIA
Eagles/Green, Black
Phone: (660) 248-6352
Fax: (660) 248-1632

ACADEMIC

Founded: 1852
Religion: Methodist
Web-site: http://www.cmc.edu/
Student/Faculty Ratio: 14:1
Type: 4 Yr., Private, Libera Arts, Coed
Campus Housing: Yes
SAT/ACT/GPA: 1840/18
Male/Female Ratio: 50:50
Scholarships/Academic: Yes **Athletic:** Yes **Fin Aid:** Yes
Total Expenses by: Year **In State:** $ 14,500 **Out of State:** $ 14,500
Degrees Conferred: AA, AS, BA, BS, BSEd, BSN, BM, BMEd, Med
Programs of Study: Accounting, Athletic Training, Biology, Business Administration, Chemistry, communications, Community Services, Computer Science, Criminal Justice, Dramatic Arts, Economics, Education, English, French, German, History, Languages, Management, Mathematics, Music, Music History, Nursing, Philosophy, Physical Science, Political Science, Prelaw, Psychology, Religion, Social Science

ATHLETIC PROFILE

Conference Affiliation: HAAC

Central Missouri State University

206 MPB
Warrensburg, MO 64093
Coach: Brad Hill

NCAA II
Mules/Red, Black
Phone: (660) 543-4800
Fax: (660) 543-8034

ACADEMIC

Founded: 1871
Type: 4 Yr., Public, Liberal Arts, Coed
Religion: Non-Affiliated
Campus Housing: Yes
Web-site: Not Available
SAT/ACT/GPA: 17 avg
Student/Faculty Ratio: 17:1
Male/Female Ratio: 48:52
Undergraduate Enrollment: 11,200
Graduate Enrollment: 1,500
Scholarships/Academic: Yes **Athletic:** Yes **Fin Aid:** Yes
Total Expenses by: Year **In State:** $ 5,084 **Out of State:** $ 7,268
Degrees Conferred: AS, AA, BA, BS, BFA, BM, BME, BSBA, MA, MS, MBA, Med
Programs of Study: Accounting, Actuarial Science, Agriculture, Banking/Finance, Biological, Broadcasting, Earth Science, Business, Chemistry, Communications, Computer, Conservation and Regulation, Criminal, Design, Dietetics, Drafting/Design, Earth Sceince, Economics, Engineering, Fashion, Film, Geography, History, Medical, Education, Speech

ATHLETIC PROFILE

Estimated Number of Baseball Scholarships: 2
Conference Affiliation: MIAA
Program Profile: We have a new $1.2 million James R. Crone Stadium including lights, clubhouse, and coaches' office. The stadium seats 800 and has a natural grass surface.
Achievements: 5 straight Conference Championships, 4 Division II Championships Appearances in the last five years; 3 1st team All-Americans in 1998; 24 drafted players, 37 All-Americans; 10 Academic All-Americans.
Coaching: Brad Hill, Head Coach, compiled a record of 167-43 in a four year period. He was previously assistant coach and recruiting coordinator at University of Kansas. Rob Davis and Bill Dwight - Assistant Coaches.
Roster for 1998 team/In State: 22 **Out of State:** 6 **Out of Country:** 0
Total Number of Varsity/Jr. Varsity: 28 **Percent of Graduation:** 80%
Number of Seniors on 1998 Team: 5 **Most Recent Record:** 39 - 8 - 0
Freshmen Receiving Fin Aid/Athletic: 9 **Academic:** 2
Number of Fall Games: 4 **Number of Spring Games:** 50
Positions Needed for 1999/2000: 3rd Base, Catcher, Infielder
Schedule: Central Oklahoma, Central Arkansas, University of Missouri, Mankato State
Style of Play: We play an aggressive, stressed team defense. We are defense minded and led Division II in 5 offensive categories in 1998.

College of the Ozarks

College Avenue
Point Lookout, MO 65726
Coach: Dr. Bob Smith
Email: blsmith@cofo.edu

NAIA
Bobcats/Maroon, White
Phone: (417) 334-6411
Fax: (417) 335-2618

ACADEMIC

Founded: 1906
Type: 4 Yr., Private, Liberal Arts, Coed
Religion: Non-Affiliated
Campus Housing: Yes

Web-site: http://www.cofo.edu
SAT/ACT/GPA: 18
Student/Faculty Ratio: 13:1
Male/Female Ratio: 50:50
Undergraduate Enrollment: 1,500
Graduate Enrollment: None
Scholarships/Academic: Yes **Athletic:** Yes **Fin Aid:** Yes
Total Expenses by: Year **In State:** $ 2,350 **Out of State:** $ 2,350
Degrees Conferred: BA, BS
Programs of Study: Aviation, Biological Science, Business, Chemistry, Computer, Criminal Justice, Education, English, History, Management, Media, Mathematics, Music, Nursing, Philosophy, Political Science, Psychology, Social Science

ATHLETIC PROFILE

Conference Affiliation: West Collegeiate Athletic Association
Program Profile: We have a top schedule of which half of the opponents are Division II. Fall practice is 8 weeks. We play on a natural turf field and have a 5 or 6 game season.
History: We started in 1967 on a limited basis. We were OCC Champs from 1978 to 1987, National Batting Champs in 1982 & ICAA Champs from 1988 to 1991. We were in the NAIA Playoffs from 1978 to 1997, District 16 Champs in 1984, Runner-Up in 1983/1988 & Sectional Runner-Up in 1997.
Achievements: Dr. Bob Smith has a 583-445 recordand was Coach of the Year for each conference title. He was 1984 District 16 NAIA Coach of the Year and voted College of the Ozarks Hall of Fame.
Coaching: Dr. Bob Smith, Head Coach, started the baseball program in 1967. Coached all but in 1973, 1974 and 1975 with a record of 603-457. He graduated from Arkansas 1968.
Roster for 1998 team/In State: 15 **Out of State:** 8 **Out of Country:** 3
Total Number of Varsity/Jr. Varsity: 26 **Percent of Graduation:** 48%
Number of Seniors on 1998 Team: 7 **Most Recent Record:** 24 - 19 - 0
Freshmen Receiving Fin Aid/Athletic: 8 **Academic:** 0
Number of Fall Games: 0 **Number of Spring Games:** 54
Positions Needed for 1999/2000: Pitcher, Shortstop, Outfielder, 3rd Base
Schedule: Bellevue, Kansas Newman, Arkansas Tech, Central Arkansas, Henderson, Avila
Style of Play: We are aggressive, put the ball in play, hit and run, steal and have good defense.

Crowder College

601 Laclede
Neosho, MO 64850
Coach: Andy Summers
NJCAA
Roughriders/Royal, White
Phone: (417) 451-5530
Fax: (417) 451-4280

ACADEMIC

Founded: 1964
Type: 2 Yr., Public, Coed
Religion: Non-Affiliated
Campus Housing: No
Undergraduate Enrollment: 1,700
Graduate Enrollment: None
Scholarships/Academic: Yes **Athletic:** Yes **Fin Aid:** Yes
Total Expenses by: Year **In State:** $ 7,465 **Out of State:** $ 5,455
Degrees Conferred: AA, AS
Programs of Study: Varied

ATHLETIC PROFILE

Conference Affiliation: Mid American Conference
Achievements: We had 33 players drafted in the past 14 seasons and our team ranked annually in the National NJCAA. We have 700 lifetime JUCO wins.
Total Number of Varsity/Jr. Varsity: 33 **Percent of Graduation:** 90%

Culver - Stockton College

One College Hill
Canton, MO 63435-1299
Coach: Doug Bletcher
Email: dbletcher@culver.edu

NAIA
Wildcats/Royal Blue, White
Phone: (217) 231-6374
Fax: (217) 231-6442

ACADEMIC

Founded: 1853
Type: 4 Yr., Private, Liberal Arts, Coed
Religion: Non-Affiliated
Campus Housing: Yes
Web-site: http://www.culver.edu
SAT/ACT/GPA: 18/2.0
Student/Faculty Ratio: 15:1
Male/Female Ratio: 1:2
Undergraduate Enrollment: 1,100
Graduate Enrollment: None
Scholarships/Academic: Yes **Athletic:** Yes **Fin Aid:** Yes
Total Expenses by: Year **In State:** $ 14,100 **Out of State:** $ 14,100
Degrees Conferred: BA, BS, BFA, BME, BSN
Programs of Study: Accounting, Art, Art Management, Biology, Business and Management, Chemistry, Computer Science, Criminal Justice, Education, Foreign Languages, Health Science, History, Marketing, Mathematics, Music, Nursing, Philosophy, Political Science, Engineering, Preprofessional Programs, Psychology, Religion, Psychology, Religion, Social Science

ATHLETIC PROFILE

Conference Affiliation: Heart of America Athletic Conference
Program Profile: Play a 65 game schedule which includes an annual ten day Spring trip. Regular season includes multiple overnight trips. Our full Fall workout schedule includes 35 Fall scrimmages. Fall workout season begins on the second day of classes and concludes normally on or about second weeek in November. Our on -campus facility has natural turf with dimensions of Left-field 301', Left-Center 355', Center-Field 428', Right-Center 370', and Right-Field 340'. Indoor facilities include, batting tunnels, multiple independent hitting stations, pitching mounds and tartan surface infield. Our new baseball complex will be completed by 1999 season. Our new facility will include: stadium seating, walk-in dugouts, home and visiting club-houses, offices, training facilities, weight room, laundry room, equipment room, outdoor and indoor batting tunnels, indoor pitching mounds, umpire dressing rooms, and a full service - working media press box. Recruiting is accomplished on a nation -wide basis. Our current staff utilizes historical contacts with professional scouts, junior college coaches, high school coaches and Summer leage coaches. Wildcat Baseball offers the opportunity to experience baseball the professional way. All players are encouraged to " chase your dreams, and enjoy the trip".
History: We were playoff qualifiers six of the ten years. Our program began in 1890 and we had back-to-back Conference Championships including a 1998 World Series.
Achievements: 1994 All-American Shortstop, 1996 All-American Outfielder, 1997 All-American Outfielder, 1995, 1996, 1997 Conference Player of the Year, 1997 Conference Coach of the Year, 1997 NAIA West Region Coach of the Year, 1997 Conference Championship (First in school's history), nine players received All-Conference selections in 1997, school received its first national ranking ever in 1997.
Coaching: Doug Bletcher, Head Coach, started his 1st year with the program. He was a former associate head coach for two years at Culver Stockton and six years at Pomona-Pitzer. He has 23 years of coaching experience. Paul Fregeau and Greg Pentony are responsible for the pitchers and the catchers. John Ulibarri and Scott Daly are strength and conditioning coaches.
Roster for 1998 team/In State: 10 **Out of State:** 25 **Out of Country:** 0
Total Number of Varsity/Jr. Varsity: 15 **Percent of Graduation:** 90%
Number of Fall Games: 0 **Number of Spring Games:** 60
Positions Needed for 1999/2000: Pitcher, Middle Infielder
Most Recent Record: 39-17-0
Style of Play: We play aggressive, attacking, execution style ball. Well employ a tactical style to generate scoring opportunity. We do location pitching, strike, and produce positive defensive results. We challenge hitters intelligently with tempo. We respect the game

East Central College

PO Box 529
Union, MO 63084
Coach: TBA

NJCAA
Rebels/Col Blue, White
Phone: (314) 583-5195
Fax: (314) 583-6637

ACADEMIC

Founded: 1968
Type: 2 Yr., Public, Coed
Student/Faculty Ratio: 20:1
Male/Female Ratio: 39:61
Undergraduate Enrollment: 3,000
Graduate Enrollment:
Scholarships/Academic: No **Athletic:** Yes **Fin Aid:** Yes
Total Expenses by: Year **In State:** $ 1,100 **Out of State:** $ 2,300
Degrees Conferred: Associate
Programs of Study: Accounting, Agronomy, Anthropology, Automotive, Biological Science, Botany, Communications, Computer, Constructions, Criminal Justice, Drafting/Design Technology, Education, Electrical/Electronics Technology, Medical, Forestry, Horticulture, Humanities, Law, Liberal Arts, Marketing, Nursing, Philosophy, Physics, Sciences

ATHLETIC PROFILE

Conference Affiliation: MCCAC

Evangel College

1111 N Glenstone
Springfield, MO 65802
Coach: Kevin Roepke

NAIA
Crusaders/Maroon, White
Phone: (417) 865-2815
Fax: (417) 865-9599

ACADEMIC

Founded: 1955
Type: 4 Yr., Private, Liberal Arts, Coed
Religion: Assemblies of God
Campus Housing: No
Web-site: Not Available
SAT/ACT/GPA: 750/18
Student/Faculty Ratio: 18:1
Male/Female Ratio: 46:54
Undergraduate Enrollment: 1,500
Graduate Enrollment: None
Scholarships/Academic: Yes **Athletic:** Yes **Fin Aid:** Yes
Total Expenses by: Year **In State:** $ 10,540 **Out of State:** $ 10,540
Degrees Conferred: AA, BA, BS
Programs of Study: 35 Fields of Study including: Allied Health, Business and Management, Business/Office and Marketing/Distribution, Communications, Education, Letters/Literature, Social Sciences

ATHLETIC PROFILE

Conference Affiliation: Heart of America Athletic Conference
Program Profile: The team is a NAIA member. We have 1,500 students and Christian and Liberal Arts college. We have a 50-55 game schedule. We play on a natural grass field and the team consists of 30-36 players. Springfield has a population of about 140,000 people.
History: Our program began in 1965.
Achievements: 1996 HAAC Conference Champs (15-3); 1996 HAAC Conference Coach of the Year; 1995 All-American - Russ Burns; 2 players drafted in the past ten years.
Coaching: Kevin Roepke, Head Coach; started in 1995 and the team posted a 23-21 record. This was the most wins in a season since 1982. He compiled an overall record of 71-58-1 in only three seasons of coaching.
Style of Play: We are aggressive at the plate. Like speed. Will run bases hard and cover lots of ground in the outfielder. We believe that pitching is the most important position.

Fontbonne College

6800 Wydown Blvd
Clayton, MO 63105
Coach: Darin Hendrickson
Email: dheadric@fontbonne

NCAA III
Griffins/Purple, Gold
Phone: (314) 889-1466
Fax: (314) 889-4507

ACADEMIC

Founded: 1917
Type: 4 Yr., Private, Liberal Arts, Coed
Religion: Non-Affiliated
Campus Housing: Yes
Web-site: http://www.fontbonne.edu/
SAT/ACT/GPA: 900/19
Student/Faculty Ratio: 15:1
Male/Female Ratio: 1:3
Undergraduate Enrollment: 2,000
Graduate Enrollment: None
Scholarships/Academic: Yes **Athletic:** No **Fin Aid:** Yes
Total Expenses by: Year **In State:** $ 10,000 **Out of State:** $ 15,000
Degrees Conferred: BA, BBA, BFA, BS, MAA, MBA, MFA, MSCD, MSCE, MST
Programs of Study: Applied Mathematics, Art, Biology, Broadcasting, Business, Communication Disorders, Computer Science, Deaf Education, Dietetics, Drawing, English, Fashion, Painting, Sculpture, Special Education, Studio Major, Mathematics, Human Services

ATHLETIC PROFILE

Conference Affiliation: St. Louis Intercollegiate Athletic Conference
Program Profile: Our 42 game schedule includes a 9 game trip to Ft. Myers, Florida. We host a three weekend 4 team tournaments at home! We play at Shaw Park at Clayton, Missouri. It is a new field with lights and a natural surface.
History: The program began in 1995 under Darin Hendrickson. The Griffins have a 91-42 mark, including 1998 Tourn. Appearances in the Central Region & an average of 30 wins in 3 seasons.
Achievements: 1998 Coach of the Year; Ryan Bouer, was drafted by San Diego in the 25th round in 1998. We were Top 10 in all offensive categories as a team in 1998, second most wins (41). beat Division I St. Louis University (27-7) and 21st team All-Region players.
Coaching: Darin Hendrickson, Head Coach, began our program in 1995. He compiled a record of 91-42. He is a former SLUE pitcher and current record holder in several categories. He got a College World Series victory in 1991. Bobby Hill, Assistant Coach, played at Memphis University, Fontbonne in 1997.
Roster for 1998 team/In State: 10 **Out of State:** 18 **Out of Country:** 0
Total Number of Varsity/Jr. Varsity: 27 **Percent of Graduation:** 95%
Number of Seniors on 1998 Team: 8 **Baseball Camp Dates:** June 12-16
Freshmen Receiving Fin Aid/Athletic: 0 **Academic:** All
Number of Fall Games: 9 **Number of Spring Games:** 44
Positions Needed for 1999/2000: Catcher, Pitcher, Infielder
Most Recent Record: 41 - 7 - 0
Schedule: Carthage, Wartburg, St. Scholastica, MacMurray, Benedictine, Washington University
Style of Play: We combine speed and power, have a much-improved defense, 3 extremely powerful hitters in the middle of the line-up and combined 42 home runs during the 1998 season. We have scrappy pitchers who throw strikes and a very competitive staff.

Hannibal - LaGrange College

2800 Palmyra Road
Hannibal, MO 63401
Coach: Scott Ashton
Email: sashton@hlg.edu

NAIA
Trojans/Red, Blue
Phone: (573) 221-0411
Fax: (573) 221-9424

ACADEMIC

Founded: 1858
Type: 4 Yr., Private, Liberal Arts, Coed
Religion: Southern Baptist
Campus Housing: No

Web-site: http://www.hlg.edu
SAT/ACT/GPA: 18
Student/Faculty Ratio: 14:1
Male/Female Ratio: 37:63
Undergraduate Enrollment: 900
Graduate Enrollment: None
Scholarships/Academic: Yes
Athletic: Yes
Fin Aid: Yes
Total Expenses by: Year
In State: $ 9,400
Out of State: $ 9,400
Degrees Conferred: AA, AS, AAS, BA, BS, BCE, BRS, BSEd, BSN
Programs of Study: Accounting, Banking/Finance, Biological, Business, Christian Studies, Communications, Computer, Criminal, Early Childhood Education, Education, English, Fine Arts, Humanities, Management, Marketing, Mathematics, Music, Nursing and Allied Health, Personnel Management, Sciences, Secondary Education

ATHLETIC PROFILE

Conference Affiliation: American West Association

Harris - Stowe State College

3026 Laclede
St. Louis, MO 63103
Coach: Tony Dattoli
NAIA
Hornets/Black, Gold
Phone: (314) 340-3500
Fax: (314) 340-5762

ACADEMIC

Founded: 1857
Type: 4 Yr., Public , Coed
Undergraduate Enrollment: 1,700
Campus Housing: Yes
Web-site: http://www.hssc.edu
SAT/ACT/GPA: 950/20
Student/Faculty Ratio: 15:1
Male/Female Ratio: 1:4
Scholarships/Academic: Yes
Athletic: Yes
Fin Aid: Yes
Total Expenses by: Year
In State: $ 2,000
Out of State: $ 4,000
Degrees Conferred: BS, BA, CJ, Urban Education
Programs of Study: Business Administration, Criminal Justice, Early Chidhood, Elementary Education, Secondary Education, Urban Education

ATHLETIC PROFILE

Estimated Number of Baseball Scholarships: 4
Conference Affiliation: American West Conference
Program Profile: We have new training facilities coming in 1999-2000. Our current playing field is natural surface with updated and new equipment.
Achievements: Tony Dattoli was named All-Americans; Conference Titles in 1994.
Coaching: Tony Dattoli, Head Coach, started his 1st year. He was our previous assistant coach for 4 years. As a player for Harris-Stowe, he was named All-American during the 1993 season. Bob Farrell - Assistant Coach.
Roster for 1998 team/In State: 29
Out of State: 0
Out of Country: 1
Total Number of Varsity/Jr. Varsity: 30
Percent of Graduation: 55%
Number of Seniors on 1998 Team: 5
Number of Sophomores on 1998 Team: 4
Freshmen Receiving Fin Aid/Athletic: 13
Academic: 7
Number of Fall Games: 4
Number of Spring Games: 56
Positions Needed for 1999/2000: Pitchers
Most Recent Record: 18 - 23 - 0
Baseball Camp Dates: Undecided on dates
Schedule: Central Missouri State University, Southern Illinois University - Edwardsville, Freed-Hardeman University, University of Missouri - St. Leo, Mayville State, Missouri Baptist College
Style of Play: We are offensively aggressive and defensively minded.

Jefferson College

1000 Viking Dr, PO Box 1000
Hillsboro, MO 63050
Coach: Dave Oster

NJCAA
Vikings/Red, White, Blue
Phone: (314) 789-3951
Fax: (314) 789-4012

ACADEMIC

Founded: 1963
Type: 4 Yr., Public, Coed
Undergraduate Enrollment: 4,220
Campus Housing: Yes
Student/Faculty Ratio: 23:1
Male/Female Ratio: 45:55
Scholarships/Academic: No **Athletic:** Yes **Fin Aid:** Yes
Total Expenses by: Year **In State:** $ 1,100 **Out of State:** $ 1,900
Degrees Conferred: Associate
Programs of Study: Accounting, Architectural, Art, Automotive, Business, Computer, Criminal Justice, Data Processing, Drafting/Design Technology, Education, Electronics/Electrical Technology, Medical Laboratory, History, Law, Laser, Liberal Arts, Machine/Tool Technology, Marketing, Math, Mechanical, Nursing, Psychology, Public, Retail, Robotics, Science, Spanish, Speech

ATHLETIC PROFILE

Conference Affiliation: MCCAC

Kemper Military College

701 Third Street
Boonville, MO 65233-1699
Coach: Jason Campbell

NJCAA
Yellowjackets/Black, Gold
Phone: (660) 882-5623
Fax: (660) 882-3332

ACADEMIC

Type: 2 Yr., Public, Coed,
Campus Housing: No
Degrees Conferred: Associate
Programs of Study: Contact school for programs of study.

ATHLETIC PROFILE

Conference Affiliation: Independent

Lincoln University

820 Chestnut Street
Jefferson City, MO 65102-0029
Coach: Sergio Espinal

NCAA II
Tigers/Blue, White
Phone: (573) 681-5334
Fax: (314) 681-5998

ACADEMIC

Founded: 1866
Type: 4 Yr., Public, Coed
Web-site: Not Available
SAT/ACT/GPA: 820/18
Student/Faculty Ratio: 18:1
Male/Female Ratio: 40:60
Undergraduate Enrollment: 3,300
Graduate Enrollment: 323
Scholarships/Academic: Yes **Athletic:** Yes **Fin Aid:** Yes
Total Expenses by: Year **In State:** $ 5,000 **Out of State:** $ 8,000
Degrees Conferred: AA, AAS, BA, BS, MA, MBA, Med

Programs of Study: Accounting, Agriculture, Art, Bilogy, Business, Chemistry, Computer Information Systems, Computer Science, Criminal Justice, Economics, Electrical/Electronic Technology, Marketing, Mathematics, Mechanical Design Technology, Music Education, Nursing, Philosophy, Physical Education, Physics, Political Science, Psychology, Public Adminstration, Social Science, Sociology, Special Education

ATHLETIC PROFILE

Conference Affiliation: Mid - Americ Conference
Program Profile: Our new playing surface has been completed. The bleachers and dug-outs were built in May 1994.
Coaching: Sergio Espinal, Head Coach, started his 5th year as a head coach. He is a former standout at Oklahoma State and a former professional player.
Style of Play: We believe in hustling, running, good defense, bunting, pitching & we never give-up.

Lindenwood College

209 South Kingshighway
St. Charles, MO 63301
Coach: Shane Boywer
Email: tbroyles@lc.lindenwood.edu

NAIA
Lions/Gold, Black
Phone: (314) 949-4808
Fax: (314) 949-4910

ACADEMIC

Founded: 1827
Religion: Presbyterian
Web-site: Not Available
Student/Faculty Ratio: 16:1
Undergraduate Enrollment: 6,800
Scholarships/Academic: Yes **Athletic:** No
Total Expenses by: Year **In State:** $ 16,000

Type: 4 Yr., Private, Liberal Arts, Coed
Campus Housing: Yes
SAT/ACT/GPA: 860/18
Male/Female Ratio: 50:50
Graduate Enrollment: 6,800
Fin Aid: Yes
Out of State: $ 16,000

Degrees Conferred: BA, BS, MA, MS, MBA, MPA
Programs of Study: Accounting, Art, Art History, Biology, Business, Chemistry, Computer Science, Corporate Communications, Criminal Justice, Early Childhood Education, Elementary Education, Fashion Marketing, French, History, Human Resources, Management, Marketing, Mass Communications, Mathematics, Physical Education, Political Science, Psychology, Public Administration, Secondary Education, Sociology, Special Education, Theatre, Prelaw, Premed

ATHLETIC PROFILE

Conference Affiliation: Heart of America Conference
Program Profile: Our new facilities include a 1/2 acre weightroom, new sod, grandstands, dug-outs, a warning track and a multi-purpose building. Seating is approximately 750.
History: The program is relatively new with all facilities being new or upgraded. Lindenwood has been to regional tourney twice ,one game away from series. We are getting better recruits with new coach and new facilities.
Achievements: Conference Champs twice in old conference. Took 4th last year in the Heart of America Conference. We are in the Top 4 and go to tourney. Three players have signed professional contracts: Joe Hoster by Cardinals AA, Tim Nihard by Twins and Jon Stephens by Evansville Otters.
Coaching: Shane Boyer, Head Coach, started his 5th year at Lindenwood. He was head coach at Marycrest International. He was assistant for two seasons under his father Dean Bowyer at Mankato State University. He was graduate assistant at Indiana State for one year. Tom Broyles, Assistant Coach, started his 3rd year with the program as a pitching coach.
Style of Play: This year we will run, run, run, with a little power. We are very aggressive.

Longview Community College

500 SW Longview Road
Lee's Summit, MO 64081
Coach: Mark Lyford

NJCAA
Lakers/Royal Blue, White
Phone: (816) 672-2441
Fax: (816) 672-2420

ACADEMIC

Founded: 1969
Type: 2 Yr., Jr. College, Coed
Student/Faculty Ratio: 22:1
Male/Female Ratio: 40:60
Undergraduate Enrollment: 8,950
Graduate Enrollment: None
Scholarships/Academic: No **Athletic:** Yes **Fin Aid:** Yes
Total Expenses by: Year **In State:** $ 1,250 **Out of State:** $ 2,900
Degrees Conferred: Associate
Programs of Study: Accounting, Agricultural, Automotive, Biologial, Business, Chemistry, Computer, Corrections, Criminal Justice, Drafting/Design Technology, General Studies, Liberal Arts, Quality Control Technology, Etc..

ATHLETIC PROFILE

Estimated Number of Baseball Scholarships: 10
Conference Affiliation: Independent
Program Profile: Longview Community College is located in a beautiful Lee's Summit, Missouri. We are in a suburb of South Kansas City. Longview is only minutes from the Truman Sports Complex (Royal and Chiefs) and Longview Lake. Longview plays home games at Lakers Field located on campus with our baseball field is next to our recreation center. We take pride in our home field advantage.
History: Since the beginning of the program in 1980, Longview has enjoyed great success, including three trips to the NJCAA World Series, seven District Championships and three Runner-Up finishes.
Achievements: Longview enjoyed its most successful seasons in 1993 and 1994, earning trips to the NJCAA World Series where finished 5th both years. In its 18 years of existence, Longview has had 7 All-Americans and 2 drafted players.
Coaching: Mark Lyford, Head Coach, begins his 2nd year as a head coach of the Lakers. In his initial season, he guided the Lakers to their best record in four seasons, missing a trip to the NJCAA World Series. Ryan Rana - Assistant Coach.
Total Number of Varsity/Jr. Varsity: 31 **Most Recent Record:** 22 - 27 - 0
Number of Seniors on 1998 Team: 8 **Number of Sophomores on 1998 Team:** 0
Number of Fall Games: 20 **Number of Spring Games:** 56
Positions Needed for 1999/2000: Pitcher, 3rd Base, Outfielder
Style of Play: Our goal is to limit our opponent to less than seven runs per game defensively. Offensively, we strive to score each inning. This formula spells success.

Maple Woods Community College

2601 NE Barry Road
Kansas City, MO 64156
Coach: TBA

NJCAA
Centaurs/Green, White, Black
Phone: (816) 437-3132
Fax: (816) 437-3049

ACADEMIC

Founded: 1969
Type: 2 Yr., Jr. College, Coed
Student/Faculty Ratio: 27:1
Male/Female Ratio: 43:57
Undergraduate Enrollment: 5,100
Graduate Enrollment: None
Scholarships/Academic: No **Athletic:** Yes **Fin Aid:** Yes
Total Expenses by: Year **In State:** $ 1,200 **Out of State:** $ 3,000
Degrees Conferred: Associate

Programs of Study: Accounting, Aviation, Biological, Chemistry, Computer, Criminal, Data Processing, Electrical/Electronics Technology, Engineering, Heating/Refrigeration/Air Conditioning, Law Enforcement, Liberal Arts, Machine/Tool Technology, Marketing, Preengineering, Science, Travel/Tourism, Veterinary Technology

ATHLETIC PROFILE

Conference Affiliation: MACC

Maryville University - Saint Louis

13550 Conway Road
St. Louis, MO 63141
Coach: Joe Berchelmann

NCAA III
Saints/Red, White
Phone: (314) 529-9313
Fax: (314) 529-9947

ACADEMIC

Founded: 1872
Type: 4 Yr., Private, Coed
Religion: Non-Affiliated
Campus Housing: Yes
Web-site: http://www.maryvillestl.edu/
SAT/ACT/GPA: 950/20
Student/Faculty Ratio: 17:1
Male/Female Ratio: 1:3
Undergraduate Enrollment: 1,300
Graduate Enrollment: 400
Scholarships/Academic: Yes **Athletic:** No **Fin Aid:** Yes
Total Expenses by: Year **In State:** $ 16,300 **Out of State:** $ 16,300
Degrees Conferred: BA, BS, BFA
Programs of Study: Art (Studio and International Design), Business, Communications, Education, History, English, Nursing, Physical Therapy, Occ. Therapy, Music, Psychology, Accounting, Management, Business Administration, Biology, Chemistry, Science

ATHLETIC PROFILE

Conference Affiliation: SLIAC

Mineral Area College

PO Box 1000, Hwy 67 and 32
Park Hills, MO 63601-1000
Coach: Jim Komar

NJCAA
Cardinals/Red, White
Phone: (573) 431-4593
Fax: (573) 431-2166

ACADEMIC

Founded: 1922
Type: 2 Yr., Public, Coed
Undergraduate Enrollment: 3,100
Graduate Enrollment: None
Scholarships/Academic: No **Athletic:** No **Fin Aid:** Yes
Total Expenses by: Hour **In State:** $ 35cr/hr **Out of State:** $ 50cr/hr
Degrees Conferred: Associate
Programs of Study: Business, Computer, Construction, Criminal Justice, Drafting/Design, Education, Electrical/Electronics, Fashion, Fine Arts, History, Law, Liberal Arts, Manufacturing, Marketing, Mathematics, Music, Nursing, Office Management, Physical Education, Prengineering, Radiological, Science, Social Science

ATHLETIC PROFILE

Conference Affiliation: West MCCAC

Missouri Baptist College

One College Park Drive
St. Louis, MO 63141-8698
Coach: Andrew V. Carter
Email: athletics@mobap.edu

NAIA
Spartans/Royal Blue, White
Phone: (314) 434-1115
Fax: (314) 434-7596

ACADEMIC

Founded: 1950
Type: 4 Yr., Private, Liberal Arts, Coed
Religion: Southern Baptist
Campus Housing: Yes
Web-site: http://www.mobap.edu
SAT/ACT/GPA: 840/18/2.0
Student/Faculty Ratio: 18:1
Male/Female Ratio: 3:2
Undergraduate Enrollment: 871
Graduate Enrollment: None
Scholarships/Academic: Yes **Athletic:** Yes **Fin Aid:** Yes
Total Expenses by: Year **In State:** $ 12,990 **Out of State:** $ 12,990
Degrees Conferred: AA, AS, BA, BS, BSEd, BSN
Programs of Study: Accounting, Behavioral Science, Biblical Studies, Biology, Business Administration, Chemistry, Communications, Computer Information Systems, Computer Science, Management, Mathematics, Military Science, Music, Natural Science, Nursing, Philosophy, Physical Education, Predental, Prelaw, Premed, Prevet, Psychology, Religion, Secondary Education, Social Science, Theology

ATHLETIC PROFILE

Estimated Number of Baseball Scholarships: 12
Conference Affiliation: American West Conference
Program Profile: We have a top NAIA program and play both Fall and Spring schedule consisting of a total of 67 contests. We play on campus in the newly renovated baseball field which is natural grass surface.
History: The past ten years the program has averaged 30 wins a season.
Achievements: 6 consecutive AMC Championships; 4 consecutive Coach of the Year Awards; 4 consecutive Sear's Coach of the Year Awards, 15 players signed professionally in the past 10 years.
Coaching: Andrew V. Carter ,Head Coach, started his 7th year with the program. He played two years at MBC. He was an assistant coach for five years. Mike Reid - Assistant Coach.
Roster for 1998 team/In State: 13 **Out of State:** 15 **Out of Country:** 0
Total Number of Varsity/Jr. Varsity: 28 **Percent of Graduation:** 92%
Number of Seniors on 1998 Team: 6 **Number of Sophomores on 1998 Team:** 3
Freshmen Receiving Fin Aid/Athletic: 3 **Academic:** 3
Number of Fall Games: 7 **Number of Spring Games:** 60
Positions Needed for 1999/2000: Pitcher **Most Recent Record:** 33 - 15 - 0
Schedule: SouthWest Missouri State, University of Missouri, SouthEast Missouri State, Southern Illinois-Edwardsville, Arkansas Tech
Style of Play: We are very aggressive, very fundamental.

Missouri Southern State College

3950 East Newman Road
Joplin, MO 64801
Coach: Warren Turner

NCAA II
Lions/Green, Gold
Phone: (417) 625-9312
Fax: (417) 625-9397

ACADEMIC

Founded: 1937
Type: 4 Yr., Public, Coed
Religion: Non-Affiliated
Campus Housing: Yes
Web-site: http://www.mssc.ecu/
SAT/ACT/GPA: 17/
Student/Faculty Ratio: 25:1
Male/Female Ratio: 4:5
Undergraduate Enrollment: 5,600
Graduate Enrollment: None
Scholarships/Academic: Yes **Athletic:** Yes **Fin Aid:** Yes

Total Expenses by: Year **In State:** $ 2,128 **Out of State:** $ 4,256
Degrees Conferred: AA, AS, Aas, BA, BS, BSBA, BSE, BGS
Programs of Study: Accounting, Biology, Broadcasting, Business Administration, Chemistry, Computer Science, Criminal Justice, Dramatic Arts, Economics, Education, Fine Arts, History, Management, Mathematics, Music, Nursing, Physics, Predentistry, Premed, Social Science

ATHLETIC PROFILE

Conference Affiliation: MIAA

Missouri Valley College

500 East College
Marshall, MO 65340
Coach: Tim Linhart

NAIA
Vikings/Purple, Orange
Phone: (816) 831-4195
Fax: (816) 831-4038

ACADEMIC

Founded: 1889
Type: 4 Yr., Private, Liberal Arts, Coed
Religion: Presbyterian
Campus Housing: Yes
Web-site: http://www.murlin.com/~webfx/mvc/
SAT/ACT/GPA: None
Student/Faculty Ratio: 10:1
Male/Female Ratio: 50:50
Undergraduate Enrollment: 1,100
Graduate Enrollment: None
Scholarships/Academic: Yes **Athletic:** Yes **Fin Aid:** Yes
Total Expenses by: Year **In State:** $ 9,500 **Out of State:** $ 9,500
Degrees Conferred: AA, BA, BS, Preprofessional
Programs of Study: Accounting, Acturial Science, Biology, Business Administration, Computer Science, Criminal Justice, Economics, Elementary Education, English, Finance, Human Services, Management, Marketing, Mass Communications, Mathematics, Philosophy, Religion

ATHLETIC PROFILE

Conference Affiliation: Heart of America Athletics
Program Profile: We have a rebuilt program that is very solid. Two coaches that are ex-professional players so it is great way to learn. We have great indoor and outdoor facilities. Our field is in the city park and which has nice grass fields. The strong point of our program is a consistant motivation to get better.
Achievements: 1994 was second in HAAC; 1995 was 4th place in the HAAC. Had many players picked on the All-Conference; 2 players that were picked up in an Independent League.

Missouri Western State College

4525 Downs Drive
St Joseph, MO 64507
Coach: Doug Minnis

NCAA II
Griffons/Black, Gold
Phone: (816) 271-4484
Fax: (816) 271-4544

ACADEMIC

Founded: 1915
Type: 4 Yr., Public, Liberal Arts, Coed
Web-site: Not Available
SAT/ACT/GPA: 18 avg
Student/Faculty Ratio: 18:1
Male/Female Ratio: 40:60
Undergraduate Enrollment: 5,121
Graduate Enrollment: None
Scholarships/Academic: Yes **Athletic:** Yes **Fin Aid:** Yes
Total Expenses by: Year **In State:** $ 5,350 **Out of State:** $ 7,100
Degrees Conferred: AS, BA, BSBA, BSE, BSN, BSW
Programs of Study: Accounting, Agriculture, Art, Biology, Chemistry, Communications, Computer, Criminal, Early Childhood, Economics, Education, Engineering, English, Languages, History, Management, Math, Medical, Natural Resources, Parks/Recreation, Etc.

ATHLETIC PROFILE

Conference Affiliation: MIAA

North Central Missouri College

1301 Main Street
Trenton, MO 64683
Coach: Tom Jemnwain

NJCAA
Pirates/Red, White
Phone: (660) 359-3948
Fax: (660) 359-2899

ACADEMIC

Founded: 1925
Type: 2 Yr., Public, Coed
Undergraduate Enrollment: 782
Campus Housing: Yes
Student/Faculty Ratio: Unknown
Male/Female Ratio: 35:65
Scholarships/Academic: Yes **Athletic:** Yes **Fin Aid:** Yes
Total Expenses by: Year **In State:** $ 4,277 **Out of State:** $ 4,637
Degrees Conferred: AA, AAS, AES
Programs of Study: Academic Transfer, Agriculture, Computer Science, Construction Technology, Criminal Justice, Nursing

ATHLETIC PROFILE

Estimated Number of Baseball Scholarships: 15-20
Program Profile: Games are played at Busleigh Grimes Field in Eastside Park, owned by the city of Trenton. The field is natural grass with a grass infield.
History: The program was reinstated in 1989 after a lapse of several years. We usually have 20-25 players on the team, mostly from North mission. We play in the NJCAA Division II (Region XXVI).
Achievements: We have several of our players go on to play at the four-year level, mainly in Division II.

NorthWest Missouri State University

800 University Avenue
Maryville, MO 64468-6001
Coach: Jim Johnson
Email: desserr@acad.nwmissouri.edu

NCAA II
Bearcats/Green, White
Phone: (660) 562-1212
Fax: (660) 562-1900

ACADEMIC

Founded: 1905
Type: 4 Yr., Public, Coed
Religion: Non-Affiliated
Campus Housing: Yes
Web-site: http://www.nwmissouri.edu
SAT/ACT/GPA: 860/21/2.0
Student/Faculty Ratio: 26:1
Male/Female Ratio: 47:53
Undergraduate Enrollment: 6,200
Graduate Enrollment: 500
Scholarships/Academic: Yes **Athletic:** Yes **Fin Aid:** Yes
Total Expenses by: Year **In State:** $ 6,405 **Out of State:** $ 8,295
Programs of Study: Accounting, Agricultural, Banking/Finance, Botany, Broadcasting, Early Childhood, Earth Science, Economics, History, Horticulture, Humanities, Journalism, Philosophy, Preprofessional Programs, Science, Special Education, Speech, Zoology

ATHLETIC PROFILE

Conference Affiliation: MIAA
Program Profile: Bearcat Field has natural turf and is in a beautiful setting in the heart of the NorthWest campus. It has permanent seating for 500, a 56 game season and dimensions of 400-CF, 330-RF and LF. Our indoor facility includes: bull pens, 3 cages, a practice arena, a team meeting program,a baseball locker room training room, an athletic strength room and a video room.

History: The NorthWest baseball program began in 1968. We had MIAA Championships in 1973, 1975, 1978, 1980, 1982 and 1983 (2nd most titles in 11 teams conference). Sixteen of our players signed in 19 seasons. We had 50 All-Americans since 1971.
Achievements: Jim Johnson was named Coach of the Year twice in 15 seasons. We were MIAA Champions 6 times.
Coaching: Jim Johnson, Head Coach, compiled a record of 333-291-3. Dale Kisker, Pitching Coach, started with the program in 1996. Bobby Elder, Assistant Coach, played at Oral Roberts U.
Roster for 1998 team/In State: 17 **Out of State:** 17 **Out of Country:** 1
Total Number of Varsity/Jr. Varsity: 37 **Most Recent Record:** 21 - 18 - 0
Number of Seniors on 1998 Team: 9 **Number of Sophomores on 1998 Team:**
Freshmen Receiving Fin Aid/Athletic: 2 **Academic:** 0
Number of Fall Games: 10 **Number of Spring Games:** 40
Positions Needed for 1999/2000: Outfielder, Pitcher
Baseball Camp Dates: January dates available
Schedule: Central Missouri State, Iowa State, North Dakota State, Nebraska - Omaha
Style of Play: We play aggressive offense, put the ball on the ground and move runners up. We do not wait for the big inning, we create and manufacture runs.

Rockhurst College

1100 Rockhurst Road
Kansas City, MO 64110-2561
Coach: Gary Burns

NCAA II
Hawks/Royal Blue, White
Phone: (816) 501-4130
Fax: (816) 501-4119

ACADEMIC

Founded: 1910 **Type:** 4 Yr., Private, Liberal Arts, Coed
Religion: Catholic/Jesuit **Campus Housing:** Yes
Web-site: http://vax1.rockhurst.edu/ **SAT/ACT/GPA:** 700/24/2.5
Student/Faculty Ratio: 14:1 **Male/Female Ratio:** 40:60
Undergraduate Enrollment: 1,500 **Graduate Enrollment:** 1,500
Scholarships/Academic: Yes **Athletic:** Yes **Fin Aid:** Yes
Total Expenses by: Year **In State:** $ 17,000 **Out of State:** $ 17,000
Degrees Conferred: BA, BS, BA Elem Ed, BSBA, BSN, MS, MBA
Programs of Study: Accounting, Banking and Finance, Biology, Business Administration, Chemistry, Communications, Community Services, Computer Engineering, Computer Science, Economics, Education, English, French, Geography, History, Information Science, International Relations, Management, Marketing, Nursing, Occupational Therapy, Personnel Management, Philosophy, Physical Therapy, Political Science, Predentistry, Prelaw, Premed, Psychology, Religion, Social Science, Spanish, Theology

ATHLETIC PROFILE

Estimated Number of Baseball Scholarships: 9
Conference Affiliation: Independent
Program Profile: We play at Hidden Valley Park which is lighted, has natural grass & is in Blue Springs.
History: The Rockhurst program began in 1994 after a 20 year absence. In the first 2 seasons, Rockhurst was 28-24 in 1994 and 44-25 in 1995. In 1995 , Rockhurst ended the season ranked 19th. nationally by the NAIA.
Achievements: We have been in the Top 25 in the nation for 4 years. Some players signed pro.
Coaching: Gary Burns,Head Coach, graduated Vanderbilt in 1982. He has 14 years of coaching experience at Vanderbilt, Indiana State, Clemson and Rockhurst. He compiled a record of 173-104.
Roster for 1998 team/In State: 85% **Out of State:** 15% **Out of Country:** 0
Total Number of Varsity/Jr. Varsity: 35 **Percent of Graduation:** 100%
Number of Seniors on 1998 Team: 7 **Baseball Camp Dates:** June, July
Freshmen Receiving Fin Aid/Athletic: 70% **Academic:** 40%
Number of Fall Games: 20 **Number of Spring Games:** 56

Positions Needed for 1999/2000: Pitcher, Catcher, Shortstop
Most Recent Record: 34 - 17 - 0
Schedule: Kansas, Wichita State, Vanderbilt, Iowa State, SouthWest Missouri, Central Missouri
Style of Play: We play aggressive offense - steal bases, hit and run. We throw strikes, and get ahead in the court. We are team oriented.

Saint Louis Community College - Florissant

3400 Pershall Road
St Louis, MO 63135
Coach: Donne Hillerman

NJCAA
Norsemen/Col Blue, Navy
Phone: (314) 595-4278
Fax: (314) 595-2232

ACADEMIC

Type: 2 Yr., Jr. College, Coed
Campus Housing: No
Degrees Conferred: Associate
Programs of Study: Accounting, Art/Fine Arts, Broadcasting, Business Administration, Commerce, Management, Chemical Engineering Technology, Child Care/Child and Family Studies, Civil Engineering Technology, Commercial Art, Communications, Computer Science, Computer Programming, Computer Technology, Criminal Justice, Data Processing, Elementary Education, Emergency Medical Technology, Law Enforcement, Legal Studies, Liberal Arts, General Studies, Music, Nursing, Photography, Radio/Television, Journalism, Mathematics, Real Estate

ATHLETIC PROFILE

Conference Affiliation: West Conference

Saint Louis Community College - Forest Park

5600 Oakland Avenue
St. Louis, MO 63110
Coach: Mike Wallis
Email: wallismo.aol.com

NJCAA
Highlanders/Red, White
Phone: (314) 644-9724
Fax: (314) 644-9959

ACADEMIC

Type: 2 Yr., Jr. College, Coed
Campus Housing: No
Degrees Conferred: Associate
Programs of Study: Accounting, Art/Fine Arts, Automtoive Technology, Biology, Biological Science, Biomedical Technology, Black-American Studies, Business Administration, Commerce, Management, Child Care/Child and Family Studies, Child Psychology, Commercial Art, Communications, Computer Science, Criminal Justice, Culinary Arts, Data Processing, Electronics Engineering Technology, Hotel and Restaurant Management, Engineering, Sciences, Funeral Services, Mathematics

ATHLETIC PROFILE

Program Profile: Michael Wallis is in his 2nd year at Forest Park . In the past the basebal program was a little down. In his 1st year we ended ranked 10th in the country and we had a very good recruiting class. We fly to Houston, Texas and play San Jacinto on February 13 - 16.
History: We will go on March 7th to Millington Tennessee at USA baseball complex and then proceed down to Delgado in New Orleans. From there, we go to Pennsicola and to Panama City. We end at Okaloosa Walton and then come back home to St. Louis.
Achievements: Conference Coach of the Year; 1 3rd team All-American and 2 All-Region players which are all returning.
Coaching: Michael Wallis - Head Coach. Gale Wallis - Assistant Coach.
Style of Play: We play strong pitching with strong defense and speed.

Saint Louis Community College - Meramec

11333 Big Bend
Kirkwood, MO 63122
Coach: Joe Swiderski

NJCAA
Warriors/Green, Gold
Phone: (314) 984-7396
Fax: (314) 984-7273

ACADEMIC

Founded: 1965
Type: 2 Yr., Jr. College, Coed
Student/Faculty Ratio: 20:1
Male/Female Ratio: 40:60
Undergraduate Enrollment: 15,000
Graduate Enrollment: None
Scholarships/Academic: Yes **Athletic:** Yes **Fin Aid:** Yes
Total Expenses by: Year **In State:** $ 4,072+ **Out of State:** $ 4,472+
Degrees Conferred: Associate
Programs of Study: Accounting, Advertising, Architecture, Art, Banking/Finance, Broadcasting, Business, Computer, Corrections, Creative Writing, Medical, Law, Literature, Materials, Music, Nursing, Paralegal, Photography, Real Estate, Science

ATHLETIC PROFILE

Conference Affiliation: MCCAC (West Community College Athletic Conference)
Program Profile: We are one of the three schools under the St. Louis Community College system with 30,000+ students. We are a true community college that does not have on campus housing. We have a modest all grass playing field. Our Fall season starts in late August and runs through mid-October.
History: We are entering into our 31st season. Our overall school record is 1071-370. There have only been two coaches to ever lead the Warriors: Ric Lessman and Todd Whaley. Our main goal is to move players on to the next level. The level is different for each student athlete.
Achievements: Meramec has won 18 Conference Championships and played in 11 World Series (Most in country tied with Seminole). We have had 27 NJCAA All-Americans and won National Champions in 1974. Fifty-six players have played professional baseball, nine in the major leagues. We have had over 250 players continue on to four-year universities and colleges.

Saint Louis University

221 North Grand
St. Louis, MO 63103
Coach: Bob Hughes

NCAA I
Billikens/Blue, White
Phone: (314) 977-3172
Fax: (314) 977-3178

ACADEMIC

Founded: 1818
Type: 4 Yr., Private, Coed
Religion: Jesuit
Campus Housing: Yes
Web-site: http://www.slu.edu/
SAT/ACT/GPA: 1150/24
Student/Faculty Ratio: 10:1
Male/Female Ratio: 48:52
Undergraduate Enrollment: 11,243
Graduate Enrollment: None
Scholarships/Academic: Yes **Athletic:** Yes **Fin Aid:** Yes
Total Expenses by: Year **In State:** $ 13,900 **Out of State:** $ 13,900
Degrees Conferred: BA, BS, MA, MS, MBA, PhdEd, JD
Programs of Study: Arts and Sciences, Business Administration, Allied Health, Nursing, Social Services, Medicine, Law, Public Health, Philosophy and Letters, Physical Therapy, Engineering

ATHLETIC PROFILE

Conference Affiliation: West Conference

Southeast Missouri State University

One University Plaza
Cape Girardeau, MO 63701
Coach: Mark Hogan

NCAA I
Indians/Red, Black
Phone: (573) 651-2645
Fax: (573) 651-2810

ACADEMIC

Founded: 1873
Type: 4 Yr., Public, Coed
Web-site: Not Available
SAT/ACT/GPA: 990/21
Student/Faculty Ratio: 17:1
Male/Female Ratio: 44:56
Undergraduate Enrollment: 6,409
Graduate Enrollment: 721
Scholarships/Academic: Yes **Athletic:** Yes **Fin Aid:** Yes
Total Expenses by: Year **In State:** $ 4,704+ **Out of State:** $ 6,552
Degrees Conferred: AA, AAS, BA, BS, BGS, BSBA, BSED, BSM, MA, MS
Programs of Study: Accounting, Advertising, Animal, Art, Banking/Finance, Biological, Business, Chemistry, Computer, Dietetics, Earth Science, Engineering, Nursing, Parks/Recreation, Etc..

ATHLETIC PROFILE

Conference Affiliation: Ohio Valley Conference
Program Profile: The SouthEast Missouri State Indians are members of the nine-team Ohio Valley Conference with the winner advancing to the NCAA tournament. In 1996, the Indians played teams from the SouthEastern, Missouri Valley, Sun Belt, Conference USA, and Big Eight Conference. Home field is Capana Park which seats 500, has natural grass and is lighted for night games.
History: We began in 1959 and have a record of 669-512-10 (.562) in 38 years of play. We were very successful at Division II level winning seven MIAA Conference titles. We will begin a 6th at Division I level in 1997 with prior finishes at 2nd, 3rd, 4th, 5th, and 6th place.
Achievements: Former player Rex Crosnoe was 1995 OVC Player of the Year. David Michel was 1995 Pitcher of the Year. There were 7 pro-signees and 2 All-Americans since 1989.
Coaching: Mark Hogan, Head Coach, has a record of 57-44-1. In two years at SouthEast, his record was 434-300-3. He coached at high schools, junior colleges and four-year colleges totaling 15 years experience. He was named Alabama JUCO Coach of the Year in 1988 and Gulf-South Conference Coach of the Year 1992.
Style of Play: We are very aggressive and put much emphasis on defense.

Southwest Baptist University

1600 University
Bolivar, MO 65613
Coach: John Katrosh
Email: jkatrosh@sbuniv.edu

NCAA II
Bearcats/Purple, White
Phone: (417) 328-1746
Fax: (417) 328-1745

ACADEMIC

Founded: 1878
Type: 4 Yr., Private, Liberal Arts, Coed
Religion: Southern Baptist
Campus Housing: Yes
Web-site: http://www.bearcat.sbuniv.edu/
SAT/ACT/GPA: 820/18/2.0
Student/Faculty Ratio: 17:1
Male/Female Ratio: 45:55
Undergraduate Enrollment: 3,200
Graduate Enrollment: 997
Scholarships/Academic: Yes **Athletic:** Yes **Fin Aid:** Yes
Total Expenses by: Year **In State:** $ 11,048 **Out of State:** $ 11,048
Degrees Conferred: BA, BBA, BS, MED, MBA, MS
Programs of Study: College of Education and Social Sciences, College of Science and Mathematics, College of Business, College of Music, Arts and Letters, College of Christian Studies

ATHLETIC PROFILE

Estimated Number of Baseball Scholarships: 5.5

Conference Affiliation: Mid American Athletic Association
Program Profile: We have a year-round program with an excellent natural turf field. Our natural grass infield has dimensions of 330 down lines and 410 in the center. Our facility is located on a 17 acre campus with two full batting cages, soft toss screen and four practice mounds. There are locker rooms, a concession stand and an adjacent field called Dodge Field that seats 200.
History: The progran began in the 1960's as a small NAIA Division II and has grown into a highly competitive NCAA Division II program. We made conference tournament in 1993-1995 and finished 25-21 in 1997.
Achievements: Pitcher Bruce Long played for Phillies Organization in 1983. Jack Funderburic was pre-season All-American in 1996 and 1997. We finished 2nd in Division and made playoffs 3 of 8 years in the conference.
Coaching: John Katrosh, Head Coach, started his 9th year in the program. He got his BA from Trenton State College and was NI drafted 17th Minnesota-Twins in 1971. He is beginning his 28th year in coaching/MED at University of Arkansas in 1989. Greg Yudevich, Assistant Coach, got his BA from Sterling College, Kansas. He has been Pitching Coach at SBU for the past 2 years.Tom House Disciple. Jack Funderburk, Graduate Assistant, started his 1st year.
Roster for 1998 team/In State: 24 **Out of State:** 12 **Out of Country:** 0
Total Number of Varsity/Jr. Varsity: 39 **Percent of Graduation:** 50%
Number of Seniors on 1998 Team: 7 **Most Recent Record:** 24 - 31 - 0
Freshmen Receiving Fin Aid/Athletic: 4 **Academic:** 8
Number of Fall Games: 8 **Number of Spring Games:** 48
Positions Needed for 1999/2000: Pitchers, Catcher, Middle Infielder
Schedule: University of Missouri-Columbia, SouthWest Missouri State University, Central Missouri State University, Pittsburg State University
Style of Play: Our disciplined program stresses the fundamentals taught in a Christian atmosphere.

Southwest Missouri State University

901 South National
Springfield, MO 65804
Coach: Keith Guttin

NCAA I
Bears/Maroon, White
Phone: (417) 836-5343
Fax: (417) 836-8475

ACADEMIC

Founded: 1905
Type: 4 Yr., Public, Coed
Religion: Non-Affiliated
Campus Housing: Yes
Web-site: http://www.smsu.edu/
SAT/ACT/GPA: 19+
Student/Faculty Ratio: 19:1
Male/Female Ratio: 47:53
Undergraduate Enrollment: 17,500
Graduate Enrollment: 1,600
Scholarships/Academic: Yes **Athletic:** Yes **Fin Aid:** Yes
Total Expenses by: Year **In State:** $ 7,476 **Out of State:** $ 10,266
Degrees Conferred: BA, BS, BFA, BSEd, BSN, BSW, Macc, MA, MS, MBA, MsEd
Programs of Study: Accounting, Administrative Office Systems, Agriculture, Agronomy, Animal Science, Biology, Business Education, Cartography, Communications, Computer Science, Construction Technology, Elementary Education, Economics,Geography, Geology, Education, Management, Marketing, Mathematics, Music, Nursing, Philosophy, Physical Education, Physics

ATHLETIC PROFILE

Conference Affiliation: Missouri Valley Conference

Three Rivers Community College

2080 Three Rivers Blvd
Poplar Bluff, MO 63901
Coach: Stacey Burkey

NJCAA
Raiders/Black, Gold
Phone: (573) 840-9613
Fax: (573) 840-9604

ACADEMIC

Founded: 1966
Type: 2 Yr., Jr. College, Coed
Web-site: http://www.trcc.cc.mo.us
SAT/ACT/GPA: Open
Undergraduate Enrollment: 3,000
Graduate Enrollment: None
Scholarships/Academic: Yes **Athletic:** Yes **Fin Aid:** Yes
Total Expenses by: Year **In State:** $ 2,300 **Out of State:** $ 2,700
Degrees Conferred: AA, AS
Programs of Study: Agricultural, Art, Biology, Business, Education, Engineering, English, Languages, Forestry, History, Journalism, Library, Mathematics, Medical, Ministry, Music, Optometry, Pharmacy, Physical Education, Psychology, Social Work

ATHLETIC PROFILE

Conference Affiliation: West Community College Athletic
Program Profile: Home games are played on campus at Raider Field with dimentions of: LF-330, LC-375, CF-400, RC-375 and RF-330. It is a grass field. We have a 56-game regular season schedule in the Spring.
Achievements: Thirteen former players are currently playing professionally. In 1994, we got 1st team All-American Alan Mahaffey. We were Region 16 champions in 1990 and 1992.
Coaching: Stacey Burkey - Head Coach.

Truman State University

100 East Normal
Kirksville, MO 63501
Coach: B. J. Pumroy
Email: bjpumroy@truman.edu
NCAA II
Bulldogs/Purple, Black, White
Phone: (660) 785-4261
Fax: (660) 785-4189

ACADEMIC

Founded: 1867
Type: 4 Yr., Public, Liberal Arts, Coed,
Web-site: http://www.truman.edu/
SAT/ACT/GPA: None
Student/Faculty Ratio: 16:1
Male/Female Ratio: 45:55
Undergraduate Enrollment: 5,800
Graduate Enrollment: 250
Scholarships/Academic: Yes **Athletic:** Yes **Fin Aid:** Yes
Total Expenses by: Year **In State:** $ 6,800 **Out of State:** $ 9,300
Degrees Conferred: BA, BS, BFA, MAE, MA, MS, MBA
Programs of Study: Accounting, Business, Chemistry, Biology, English, Political Science, Communication, Education, Health and Exercise Science

ATHLETIC PROFILE

Conference Affiliation: Mid America Intercollegiate Athletic Association
Program Profile: We are a very demanding academic institution where school comes before baseball. We adhere to the 132 days of practice rule using seven weeks in the Fall and 15 in the Spring. Our field is located on campus and, after recent improvements, is considered one of the best in the conference.
History: The program began in 1966. Since then, we have had three pitchers in the major league and five others signed contracts.
Achievements: In the past five years, we have had 18 Academic All-Conference selections, 2 Academic All-Region selections and an Academic All-American. We have also had our first draft pick since 1980 and he has made the All-Star team twice in A ball and once in AA.
Coaching: B.J. Pumroy - Head Coach. Kyle Plackemeier - Assistant Coach.
Style of Play: We are an emerging program who plays to a high level while not losing site of sportsmanship and doing things with class. We are honest with ourselves teammates and coaches and we recognize that academics are the focus of the collegiate experience.

University of Missouri - Columbia

P.O. Box 677
Columbia, MO 65202
Coach: Tim Jamieson

NCAA I
Tigers/Black, Old Gold
Phone: (573) 882-0731
Fax: (573) 882-4720

ACADEMIC

Type: 4 Yr., Public, Liberal Arts, Coed, Engineering
Founded: 1839
Religion: Non-Affiliated
Campus Housing: Yes
Web-site: http://www.missori.edu/
SAT/ACT/GPA: 700 Min/17 Min/
Student/Faculty Ratio: 19:1
Male/Female Ratio: 50:50
Undergraduate Enrollment: 17,165
Graduate Enrollment: 4,191
Scholarships/Academic: Yes **Athletic:** Yes **Fin Aid:** Yes
Total Expenses by: Year **In State:** $ 8,200 **Out of State:** $ 14,000
Degrees Conferred: BA, BS, BFA, AB, BSEd, BGS, BSN, BJ, BM, MA, MS, MFA, BSW, MBA, BES
Programs of Study: Over 200 Majors including: Accounting, Advertising, Agriculture, Animal Science, Anthropology, Archaelogy, Art History, Atmospheric Sciences, Banking/Finance, Biological Science, Broadcasting, Business, Chemistry, Classics, Communication, Computer Sceince, Design, Dietetics, Dramatic Arts, Economics, Education, Engineering (Chemical, Civil, Computer, Electrical, Industrial, Mechanical), English, Film/Fine Arts, Food, Geography, Geology, History, Hotel/Restaurant, Insurance, Journalism, Linguistics, Management, Marketing, Math, Medical, Meteorology, Music, Nursing, Parks/Recreation, Philosophy, Physics, Political Science, Psychology

ATHLETIC PROFILE

Conference Affiliation: Big 12 Conference
Program Profile: Missouri plays its home games at Simmons Field, which seats 2,500. It has a natural grass surface and lights.
History: Since its inception in 1891, the Missouri Baseball program has played 103 seasons of baseball. Its record stands at 1,613 (W), 1,028 (L), 18 (T).
Achievements: Jamieson earned Big Eight coach of the Year award in 1996. MU won its first and last Big 8 Title. We have 8 active players in professional and minor league ranks. A total of 100 players have signed professional contracts.
Coaching: Tim Jamieson, Head Coach, started his 5th year at MU as a head coach. He was an assistant coach at MU for 6 years. He was an assistant coach at the University of New Orleans for 6 years.
Style of Play: We have a big-inning oriented offense supported by a sound defense and solid pitching.

University of Missouri - Rolla

P.O. Box 249
Rolla, MO 65401
Coach: Travis Boulware

NCAA II
Miners/Gold, Silver
Phone: (573) 341-4191
Fax: (573) 341-4880

ACADEMIC

Founded: 1871
Type: 4 Yr., Public, Coed, Engineering
Religion: Non-Affiliated
Campus Housing: Yes
Web-site: http://www.umr.edu/
SAT/ACT/GPA: 820/18
Student/Faculty Ratio: 17:1
Male/Female Ratio: 2:1
Undergraduate Enrollment: 3,300
Graduate Enrollment: 1,500
Scholarships/Academic: Yes **Athletic:** Yes **Fin Aid:** Yes
Total Expenses by: Year **In State:** $ 4,500 **Out of State:** $ 10,500
Degrees Conferred: BA, BS, MS, PhD

Programs of Study: Engineering, Science, Some Liberal Arts, Premed, Computer Science, Aeronautical Engineering, Applied Mathematics, Ceramic Engineering, Chemical Engineering, Chemistry, Civil Engineering, Computer Science, Economics, Electrical Engineering, English, Geological Engineering, Geology, Geophysics, History, Life Science, Management, Mathematics, Mechanical Engineering, Metallurgical Engineering, Mining and Mineral Engineering, Nuclear Engineering, Petroleum and Natural Gas Engineering, Philosophy, Physics, Psychology

ATHLETIC PROFILE

Conference Affiliation: MIAA

University of Missouri - Saint Louis

8001 Natural Bridge Road
St. Louis, MO 63121
Coach: Jim Brady
Email: athdefo@jinx.umsl.edu
NCAA II
Rivermen/Cardinal Red, Gold
Phone: (314) 516-5647
Fax: (314) 516-5503

ACADEMIC

Founded: 1963
Type: 4 Yr., Public, Coed
Religion: Non-Affiliated
Campus Housing: Yes
Web-site: http://www.umsl.edu/
SAT/ACT/GPA: 24
Student/Faculty Ratio: 14:1
Male/Female Ratio: 50:50
Undergraduate Enrollment: 12,844
Graduate Enrollment: 2,732
Scholarships/Academic: Yes **Athletic:** Yes **Fin Aid:** Yes
Total Expenses by: Year **In State:** $ 7,545 **Out of State:** $ 13,500
Degrees Conferred: BA, NS, MA, MS, Med, MBA, PhD, BFA, BGS, BM, BSBA, BSEd, BSN, BSPA
Programs of Study: Anthropology, Art History, Biology, Business Administration, Chemistry, Communication, Computer Science, Criminal Justice, Economics, Education, English, French, German, History, Management, Mathematics, Music, Nursing, Philosophy, Physics, Political Science, Psychology, Public Administration, Social Science, Spanish, Special Education

ATHLETIC PROFILE

Estimated Number of Baseball Scholarships: 2.5
Conference Affiliation: Great Lakes Valley Conference
Program Profile: Perennially, we are in the Top 20 NCAA II. We made collegiate baseball poll, a Regional Appearance and finished 17th in the nation in 1998. Our last World Series Appearance was in 1996. We have a Fall and Spring schedule. Our playing surface is natural grass.
History: We began in 1971 and had NCAA Regional Tournaments in 1972, 1973, 1975, 1976, 1977, 1978, 1979, 1984, 1992, 1993, 1996 and 1998. We were in NCAA II World Series in 1972, 1973, 1977, 1993 and 1996.
Achievements: Jim Brady was named Region Coach of the Year in 1993 and 1996. All-Americans were 24, including 10 since 1992. Drafted players were 23 , including 9 since 1992.
Coaching: Jim Brady, Head Coach, started in 1986. He compiled a record of 370-212. He was named Region Coach of the Year in 1993 and 1996. He played at Meramec CC, Missouri and SouthWest Missouri State and ever had a losing season. Deron Spink, Assistant Coach, is a former standout player at Sacramento City CC, California and Armstrong State, Georgia.
Roster for 1998 team/In State: 12 **Out of State:** 13 **Out of Country:** 0
Total Number of Varsity/Jr. Varsity: 25 **Percent of Graduation:** 72%
Number of Seniors on 1998 Team: 10 **Number of Sophomores on 1998 Team:** 3
Freshmen Receiving Fin Aid/Athletic: 1 **Academic:** 1
Number of Fall Games: 4 **Number of Spring Games:** 52
Positions Needed for 1999/2000: 8-Pitchers, Catcher, 3rd Base, Mid-infielder, OF
Most Recent Record: 34 - 14 - 0 **Baseball Camp Dates:** June 7-11
Schedule: Missouri, SouthEast Missouri, SIU-Edwardsville, Lewis, St. Joe, Indianapolis

Style of Play: We are aggressive with a combination of both speed and power. We put a heavy emphasis on a player's ability to play sound defense. We emphasize on pitchers that are able to consistently throw strikes, hit their spots, field their position and keep it in the yard.

Washington University - Saint Louis

Campus Box 1067
St. Louis, MO 63130-4899
Coach: Ric Lessman

NCAA III
Bears/Red, Green
Phone: (314) 935-5945
Fax: (314) 935-5545

ACADEMIC

Founded: 1853
Type: 4 Yr., Private, Coed
Web-site: http://www.wustl.edu/
SAT/ACT/GPA: None
Student/Faculty Ratio: 15:1
Male/Female Ratio: 1:1
Undergraduate Enrollment: 5,000
Graduate Enrollment: 5,000
Scholarships/Academic: Yes **Athletic:** No **Fin Aid:** Yes
Total Expenses by: Year **In State:** $ 27,110 **Out of State:** $ 27,110
Degrees Conferred: BA, BS, MA, MS
Programs of Study: Arts and Sciences, Allied Health, Architecture and Applied Sciences, Business and Management, Computer, Engineering, Letters/Literature

ATHLETIC PROFILE

Conference Affiliation: University Athletic Association
Program Profile: Playing season is in the Fall and consists of 6 weeks and 9 scrimmages. We also do 15 weeks - 36 games plus of tournaments (estimated 45 games total).
History: Our program began in 1946. In 52 years, our overall record is 810-708 which is .53 percent.
Achievements: University Athletic Association Champions in 1995.
Coaching: Ric Lessman, Head Coach, served as a head coach at Meramec Community College in St. Louis and compiled a record 963-318 for a winning percentage of .752. During his 27-year tenure, he never experienced a losing season. He guided Meramec to the National Junior College World Series 9 times. He signed with the New York Yankees as a pitcher in 1955. He was District Coach of the Year 9 times. Dan Fanter, Assistant Coach, is in his 1st year of collegiate coaching.
Style of Play: Pitching is first, defense is second and we figure out someway to score.

Webster University

470 East Lockwood Avenue
Webster Grove, MO 63119
Coach: Marty Hunsucker

NCAA III
Gorloks/Navy, Gold
Phone: (314) 968-6984
Fax: (314) 963-6092

ACADEMIC

Founded: 1915
Type: 4 Yr., Private, Liberal Arts, Coed
Religion: Non-Affiliated
Campus Housing: Yes
Web-site: http://www.websteruniv.edu/
SAT/ACT/GPA: 20/2.4
Student/Faculty Ratio: 13:1
Male/Female Ratio: 49:51
Undergraduate Enrollment: 2,800
Graduate Enrollment: 2,200
Scholarships/Academic: Yes **Athletic:** No **Fin Aid:** Yes
Total Expenses by: Year **In State:** $ 17,460 **Out of State:** $ 17,460
Degrees Conferred: BA, BS, BM, MA, MM, MBA
Programs of Study: Behavioral Science, Business and Management, Communications, Computer Science, Education, Health Sciences, Social Sciences, Visual and Performing Arts

ATHLETIC PROFILE

Conference Affiliation: SLIAC
Program Profile: Our facilities include: indoor/outdoor batting cages, a natural grass field and a seating capacity of 1,000. We have a Fall and Spring schedule which consists of 45-50 games.
History: The program is 13 years old.
Coaching: Marty Hunsucker, Head Coach, started in 1996. He has a BA from Grinnell College and played baseball for 4 years and football for 4 years. His MS is from University of Iowa. Adam Llewellyn - Assistant Coach.
Roster for 1998 team/In State: 22 **Out of State:** 6 **Out of Country:** 0
Total Number of Varsity/Jr. Varsity: 28 **Percent of Graduation:** 98%
Number of Seniors on 1998 Team: 4 **Number of Sophomores on 1998 Team:** 7
Number of Fall Games: 10 **Number of Spring Games:** 45
Positions Needed for 1999/2000: Pitchers, C, SS, CF, 3rd Base, Designated-Hitter
Most Recent Record: 8 - 31 - 0
Schedule: McMurray, Fontbonne College, Central College, Westminster College, Washington
Style of Play: We play very aggressive with straight steal and hit and run. We are based on fundamentals of solid offensive execution! Our ball park is suited for power hitters: short down lines, begins center, no foul territory and power alleys accessable often.

Westminster College

501 Westminster Avenue
Fulton, MO 65251
Coach: Ehren Earleywine

NCAA III
Blue Jays/Royal Blue, White
Phone: (573) 592-5335
Fax: (573) 592-5366

ACADEMIC

Founded: 1851
Type: 4 Yr., Private, Liberal Arts, Coed
Religion: Historically Presbyterian
Campus Housing: Yes
Web-site: http://www.Westminster-mo.edu/
SAT/ACT/GPA: Yes
Student/Faculty Ratio: 12:1
Male/Female Ratio: 6:4
Undergraduate Enrollment: 650
Graduate Enrollment: 0
Scholarships/Academic: Yes **Athletic:** No **Fin Aid:** Yes
Total Expenses by: Year **In State:** $ 17,190 **Out of State:** $ 17,190
Degrees Conferred: BS, BA
Programs of Study: Accounting, Advertising, Art, Biology, Business Administration, Business Communications, Chemistry, Classic, Economics, Education, English, French, History, Mathematics, Philosophy, Physical Education, Physics, Political Science, Prelaw, Premed, Psychology, Religion

ATHLETIC PROFILE

Estimated Number of Baseball Scholarships: 0
Conference Affiliation: SLIAC
Program Profile: Small school with new facilities that include a locker room, a weight room and a training room.
Achievements: Coach Ehren Earleywine spent three years assisting professional All-Star Phil Bradley. Bradley coached the Blue Jays to a 54-45 record and two conference tournament titles in three years.
Coaching: Ehren Earleywine, Head Coach, played for Westminster & earned NAIA All-District 16 & St. Louis Intercollegiate Athletic All-Conference honors during his career. Adam Metz-Assist. Coach.

William Jewell College

500 College Hill
Liberty, MO 64068
Coach: Fred Flook

NAIA
Cardinals/Red, Black
Phone: (816) 781-7700
Fax: (816) 781-3164

ACADEMIC

Founded: 1849
Type: 4 Yr., Private, Liberal Arts, Coed
Religion: Baptist
Campus Housing: Yes
Web-site: http://www.jewell.edu/
SAT/ACT/GPA: 18+
Student/Faculty Ratio: 13:1
Male/Female Ratio: 1:3
Undergraduate Enrollment: 1,200
Graduate Enrollment: None
Scholarships/Academic: Yes **Athletic:** Yes **Fin Aid:** Yes
Total Expenses by: Year **In State:** $ 16,560 **Out of State:** $ 16,560
Degrees Conferred: BA, BS
Programs of Study: Art, Biology, British Studies, Business Administration and Economics, Accounting, Chemistry, Communications, Speech/Theatre, Education, English, History, Languages, Mathematics, Computer Science, Music, Nursing, Oxbridge Honors Program, Philosophy, Physics, Political Science, Psychology, Religion, Sociology

ATHLETIC PROFILE

Conference Affiliation: Heart of America

NEBRASKA

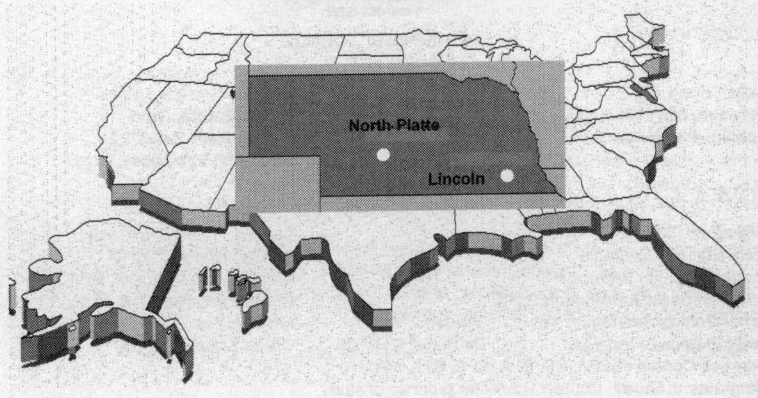

SCHOOL	CITY	AFFILIATION 99	PAGE
Bellevue College	Bellevue	NAIA	510
Creighton University	Omaha	NCAA I	510
Concordia College - Nebraska	Seward	NAIA	511
Dana College	Blair	NAIA	511
Doane College	Crete	NAIA	512
Hastings College	Hastings	NAIA	512
Midland Lutheran College	Fremont	NAIA	513
Nebraska Wesleyan University	Lincoln	NCAA III	513
Peru State College	Peru	NAIA	514
University of Nebraska	Lincoln	NCAA I	515
University of Nebraska - Kearney	Kearney	NCAA II	515
University of Nebraska - Omaha	Omaha	NCAA II	516
Wayne State College	Wayne	NCAA II	517
York College - Nebraska	York	NAIA	517

Bellevue College

Galvin Road
Bellevue, NE 68005
Coach: Mike Evans

NAIA
Bruins/Purple, Gold
Phone: (402) 293-3782
Fax: (402) 293-2020

ACADEMIC

Founded: 1966
Type: 4 Yr., Private, Coed
Web-site: Not Available
SAT/ACT/GPA: 700/18
Student/Faculty Ratio: 27:1
Male/Female Ratio: 46:54
Undergraduate Enrollment: 2,200
Graduate Enrollment: 115
Scholarships/Academic: Yes **Athletic:** Yes **Fin Aid:** Yes
Total Expenses by: Year **In State:** $ 5,000 **Out of State:** $ 5,000
Degrees Conferred: BA, BS, BFA, BPS, BTS, MA
Programs of Study: Contact school for program of study.

ATHLETIC PROFILE

Conference Affiliation: Central Conference
Program Profile: We play in a 1,500 seat stadium that has a natural turf playing field.
History: We began in 1979. We have won 6 straight state titles and ranked 7th in 1994.
Achievements: Nebraska College Coach of the Year 6-times; 1981 Regional Coach of the Year .
Coaching: Mike Evans - Head Coach. Darren Ladd and Mark Mancuso - Assistants. Bill McGuire was a 1st round draft for Seattle. Mark Moncuso was All-Conference UNO. Ron Weis was All-American 2nd Team player.
Total Number of Varsity/Jr. Varsity: 20 /10 **Percent of Graduation:** 90%
Style of Play: We hit and run, run and bunt and steal; aggressive defense; power type of pitching, although we will use the breaking pitch.

Creighton University

2500 Plaza
Omaha, NE 66178
Coach: Jack Dahm

NCAA I
Blue Jays/Blue, White
Phone: (402) 280-5545
Fax: (402) 280-5596

ACADEMIC

Founded: 1878
Type: 4 Yr., Private, Liberal Arts, Coed
Religion: Jesuit
Campus Housing: Yes
Web-site: http://www.creighton.edu/
SAT/ACT/GPA: Sliding Scale
Student/Faculty Ratio: 13:1
Male/Female Ratio: 41:59
Undergraduate Enrollment: 4,000
Graduate Enrollment: 2,000
Scholarships/Academic: Yes **Athletic:** Yes **Fin Aid:** Yes
Total Expenses by: Year **In State:** $ 18,208 **Out of State:** $ 18,208
Degrees Conferred: AA, AS, BA, BS, BFA, MA, MS, MBA, PhD, DMD, MD
Programs of Study: American Studies, Art, Economics, History, Journalism, Medical Physics, Ministry, Music, Communications, Philosophy, Anthropology, Political Science, Theater, Theology, Computer Science, Education, Physics, Advertising,

ATHLETIC PROFILE

Conference Affiliation: Missouri Valley Conference
Program Profile: The Blue Jays play in the largest astro turf multi-purpose complex in the Midwest. The stadium seats 2,500.
History: Creighton has been in the regionals 3 of the 6 six years and finished 3rd in the country in 1991 in a College World Series Appearance. There have been four consecutive 1st t round draft picks (1990, 1991, 1992 and 1993).

Achievements: 1991 Coach of the Year, NCAA World Series (finished 3rd nationally), 4 first-round picks in consecutive years drafted, 3 in 1994; 1995 finished 2nd in the Missouri Valley Conference regular season.
Coaching: Jack Dahm, Head Coach, was formerly an assistant coach at Creighton.
Style of Play: Aggressive, scrappy, pitching and defense.

Concordia College - Nebraska

800 N Columbia Avenue
Seward, NE 68434
Coach: Jeremy Geidel

NAIA
Bulldogs/Navy, White
Phone: (402) 643-7334
Fax: (402) 643-3966

ACADEMIC

Founded: 1894
Religion: Lutheran Church - Missouri Synod
Web-site: http://www.ccsn.edu/
Student/Faculty Ratio: 14:1
Undergraduate Enrollment: 1,100
Scholarships/Academic: Yes **Athletic:** Yes
Total Expenses by: Year **In State:** $13,560
Type: 4 Yr., Private, Liberal Arts, Coed
Campus Housing: Yes
SAT/ACT/GPA: 840/ 18
Male/Female Ratio: 1:3
Graduate Enrollment: 150
Fin Aid: Yes
Out of State: $ 13,560
Degrees Conferred: BA, BSEd, MAEd
Programs of Study: Education, Preprofessional, Commercial Art, Art, Business-Administration/Management, Accounting, Liberal Arts, Sport Management, Sociology, Exercise

ATHLETIC PROFILE

Conference Affiliation: NIAC
Program Profile: Our program is being built. Our city-owned facility includes an excellent game field, a practice field of good quality grass and a rebuilt infield.
History: Our program has been at Concordia for years. Recently, new equipment and practice equipment has been added.
Achievements: Many of our graduates go on to to coach at the high school level located through out the US. We have had two-All-American Scholar Athletes in the last eight years.

Dana College

2848 College Drive
Blair, NE 68008
Coach: Paul Davis

NAIA
Vikings/Red, White
Phone: (402) 426-7374
Fax: (402) 426-7299

ACADEMIC

Founded: 1884
Religion: Evangelical
Web-site: Not Available
Student/Faculty Ratio: 13:1
Undergraduate Enrollment: 650
Scholarships/Academic: Yes **Athletic:** Yes
Total Expenses by: Year **In State:** $ 13,400
Type: 4 Yr., Private, Liberal Arts, Coed
Campus Housing: No
SAT/ACT/GPA: 21 avg
Male/Female Ratio: 46:54
Graduate Enrollment: None
Fin Aid: Yes
Out of State: $ 13,400
Degrees Conferred: BA, BS
Programs of Study: Contact school for program of study.

ATHLETIC PROFILE

Conference Affiliation: Nebraska - Iowa Athletic Conference

Program Profile: Our schedule has around 50 games (25 double headers) and we play 24 conference games. Our Spring Break trip is in March (6-7 days - Oklahoma). Our season is mid-March through early May. Our field is natural, beautiful turf (325', 400', 325'). We have a scoreboard, huge walk-in dugouts, no lights and 4 bullpen mounds.
History: In our first year, we were unknown but we have developed a highly regarded program since the 1960's. We won 5 Conference Championships in the 1970's and 5 more in the 1980's.
Achievements: 5 Conference championships in 1970's' 5 in 1980's; District Champions in 1980; All-American Catcher 1982 (Dale DeBuhr), 2 2nd team All-Americans in the 1980's (John Schnaible-LF, Scott Simms-P), numerous Honorable Mentions; Scott Simms was one of the 9 Academic All-Americans in 1981.
Style of Play: We run offensively, are tight defensively and have decent pitching.

Doane College

1140 Boswell Avenue
Crete, NE 68333
Coach: Jack Hudkins

NAIA
Tigers/Orange, Black
Phone: (402) 826-2161
Fax: (402) 826-8647

ACADEMIC

Founded: 1872
Type: 4 Yr., Private, Liberal Arts, Coed
Religion: Church of Christ
SAT/ACT/GPA: 22 avg
Student/Faculty Ratio: 13:1
Male/Female Ratio: 48:52
Undergraduate Enrollment:
Graduate Enrollment: 0
Scholarships/Academic: Yes **Athletic:** Yes **Fin Aid:** Yes
Total Expenses by: Year **In State:** $ 13,300 **Out of State:** $ 13,300
Degrees Conferred: BA, BS, M
Programs of Study: Accounting, Biological Science, Business Administration, Chemistry, Communications, Computer Science, Elementary Education, English, Environmental Science, German, Human Services, International Studies, Management, Philosophy, Physical Science, Political Science, Psychology, Public Administration, Science, Social Science, Special Education

ATHLETIC PROFILE

Conference Affiliation: NIAC

Hastings College

800 N Tuner
Hastings, NE 68901
Coach: Jim Boeve

NAIA
Broncos/Crimson, White
Phone: (402) 461-7322
Fax: (402) 461-7480

ACADEMIC

Founded: 1882
Type: 4 Yr., Private, Liberal Arts, Coed
Religion: Presbyterian
Campus Housing: No
Web-site: www.hasting.com
SAT/ACT/GPA: 900/23 avg
Student/Faculty Ratio: 13:1
Male/Female Ratio: 1:1
Undergraduate Enrollment: 1,000
Graduate Enrollment: 20
Scholarships/Academic: Yes **Athletic:** Yes **Fin Aid:** Yes
Total Expenses by: Year **In State:** $ 13,600 **Out of State:** $ 13,600
Degrees Conferred: BA, MA, BM, MAT
Programs of Study: Contact school for program of study.

ATHLETIC PROFILE

Conference Affiliation: Nebraska-Iowa Athletic Conference

Program Profile: Hastings College plays a 6-week Fall & 18-week Spring season. The team plays 50 - 60 games each Spring. Home games are played in Duncan Field (dimensions: 370', 408', 367').
History: Our program was resurrected in 1990 after a 15 year absence. The Broncos have won four league straight league titles and have made five consecutive post-season appearances.
Achievements: 1992-1995 Conference Champions. NIAC Players of the Year - Chris Olsen 1993, Jeff Chmelka '94, & Dereck Splitt '95. In 1993, Chris Olsen signed as a free agent with the Phillies.
Coaching: Jim Boeve, Head Coach, was Chairman of NIAC baseball coaches, Chairman on NAIA Great Plains Region Baseball Committee and a member of the NAIA Ratings Committee
Total Number of Varsity/Jr. Varsity: 24 /20 **Percent of Graduation:** 50%
Style of Play: Deep pitching staff with control; strong catching; disciplined hitting; excellent walk to strikeout ratio.

Midland Lutheran College

900 N Clarkson
Fremont, NE 68025
Coach: Jef Field

NAIA
Warriors/Black, Orange
Phone: (402) 721-5480
Fax: (402) 721-9406

ACADEMIC

Founded: 1883
Religion: Lutheran
Web-site: Not Available
Student/Faculty Ratio: 18:1
Undergraduate Enrollment: 1,025
Scholarships/Academic: Yes
Athletic: Yes
Total Expenses by: Year
In State: $ 14,000
Degrees Conferred: AA, BA, BS, BBA, BSN
Programs of Study: Contact school for program of study.

Type: 4 Yr., Private, Liberal Arts, Coed
Campus Housing: No
SAT/ACT/GPA: Top half
Male/Female Ratio: 2:3
Graduate Enrollment: None
Fin Aid: Yes
Out of State: $ 14,000

ATHLETIC PROFILE

Conference Affiliation: Nebraska/Iowa Athletic Conference
Program Profile: Our disciplined program is geared toward the student/athlete. We have had very progressive results for the past three seasons. We have a very nice playing field with natural grass and turf borders.
History: Our program was reinstated 10 years ago. We are now in a top 25 cabaler situation..
Achievements: 1997 NIAC Co-Coach of the Year; 1997 NIAC Tournament Champions; In 1997, we placed 3rd in Great Plains Region. We had several Academic All-Americans.
Coaching: Jef Field, Head Coach, started his 4th season as head coach. Has coached at every level of baseball. Steve Gossett, Pitching Coach, played at Oral Roberts and has some professional playing experience, several as an assistant at UC-Riverside.
Style of Play: We are very aggressive. Our kids play the game the way it was meant to be played. We are very fundamentally sound and seldom beat ourselves.

Nebraska Wesleyan University

500 St. Paul Avenue
Lincoln, NE 68504-2796
Coach: Rich Russo

NCAA III
Plainsmen/Yellow, Brown
Phone: (402) 465-2171
Fax: (402) 465-2126

ACADEMIC

Founded: 1887
Religion: United Methodist
Web-site: http://www.nebwesleyan.edu/
Student/Faculty Ratio: 13:1

Type: 4 Yr., Private, Liberal Arts, Coed
Campus Housing: Yes
SAT/ACT/GPA: None
Male/Female Ratio: 1:1

Undergraduate Enrollment: 1,600 **Graduate Enrollment:** None
Scholarships/Academic: Yes **Athletic:** No **Fin Aid:** Yes
Total Expenses by: Year **In State:** $ 13,300 **Out of State:** $ 13,300
Degrees Conferred: BA, BS
Programs of Study: Full Liberal Arts and Preprofessional Curriculum; Applied Music, Art, Biology, Biochemistry, Business Administration, Business Psychology, Business, Sociology, Chemistry, Communications, Computer Science, Economics, Elementary Education, English, French, German, Health/Physical Science, History, International Business, Mathematics, Music, Physics, Political Science, Psychology, Physical Education, Philosophy, Sport Management

ATHLETIC PROFILE

Conference Affiliation: Nebraska - Iowa Athletics Conference
Program Profile: Our on-campus facility is Osborne-Nickerson Field. It has indoor cages and a natural field. We play 36 games total, have a Fall practice and do a traditional season.
History: Our program went from 1908-1917 and from 1950 to the present.
Achievements: Russon was named Nebraska-Iowa Athletic Conference Coach of the Year for the 1996 season. Two players were named to the NCAA Division III. We were second team All-MidWest Region and 3 players were named 1st team All-NIAC.
Coaching: Rich Russo,Head Coach, finished his 3rd season as a head head coach in 1997. He has 27 years of high school and college coaching experience, including a four-year stint (83-87) as an assistant coach at Nebraska-Omaha. He got his Master's at Kearney State College in 1978.
Style of Play: Nebraska Wesleyan plays a fast-paced, aggressive baseball. We try to run and take advantage of our opportunities while focusing on speed and defense.

Peru State College

Box 10
Peru, NE 68421
Coach: Mark Bayliss

NAIA
Bobcats/Blue, White
Phone: (402) 872-2443
Fax: (402) 872-2302

ACADEMIC

Founded: 1867 **Type:** 4 Yr., Public, Coed
Web-site: Not Available **SAT/ACT/GPA:** 18
Student/Faculty Ratio: 18:1 **Male/Female Ratio:** 47:53
Undergraduate Enrollment: 1,600 **Graduate Enrollment:** 200
Scholarships/Academic: Yes **Athletic:** Yes **Fin Aid:** Yes
Total Expenses by: Year **In State:** $ 4,950 **Out of State:** $ 6,600
Degrees Conferred: AA, BA, BS, BT
Programs of Study: Business and Management, Computer Science, Education, Mathematics, Psychology, Social Science, Trade and Industry

ATHLETIC PROFILE

Conference Affiliation: NAIA MidWest Region, Independent
Program Profile: Varsity program plays a full schedule of 65 games in part located on campus and takes a Spring trip every year. The Fall program lasts seven to eight weeks with games played against top teams in NCAA Division II. Peru State's baseball is a solid program -- among the top in the Midwest.
History: Our program began in 1940's. PSC has progressed from 'just a program offered' to a highly visible program.
Achievements: Pro players -- Scott Kobout, Dan Lajoie, Chris Michaels. All-American -- Shawn Semler.

University of Nebraska

1101 Avery Avenue
Lincoln, NE 68588
Coach: Dave Van Horn
Email: dvanhorn@huskers.unl.edu

NCAA I
Huskers/Scarlet, Cream
Phone: (402) 472-2269
Fax: (402) 472-9641

ACADEMIC

Type: 4 Yr., Public, Liberal Arts, Coed, Engineering
Religion: Non-Affiliated
Web-site: http://www.huskerwebcast.com
Student/Faculty Ratio: 17:1
Undergraduate Enrollment: 25,000
Scholarships/Academic: Yes **Athletic:** Yes
Total Expenses by: Year **In State:** $ 6,812
Founded: 1869
Campus Housing: Yes
SAT/ACT/GPA: 850/20
Male/Female Ratio: 54:46
Graduate Enrollment: 5,100
Fin Aid: Yes
Out of State: $ 10,585
Degrees Conferred: AS, BA, BFA, BS, BBA, BJ, BSAE, BSBSE, MBA
Programs of Study: Contact school for program of study.

ATHLETIC PROFILE

Estimated Number of Baseball Scholarships: 11.7
Conference Affiliation: Big Twelve Conference
Program Profile: A new stadium is to be built in two years. Our current field has artificial infield, natural outfield and a stadium capacity is 1,500. Our budget ranks in the top five in the nation for baseball programs. There are two indoor practice facilities.
History: Husker baseball program began in 1889 & has an overall record of 1441-1162-12. We have 16 winning seasons since 1980 & 3 coaches in 52 years. There were 18 coaches in school history. The most wins in a year is 49 in 1979 & 1980. We have had eight 40 wins seasons in our school history.
Achievements: Conference Titles in 1948 and 1950; NCAA Regional Appearances in 1979, 1980 and 1985; 8 1st team were named All-Americans; 3 in the 1990's; 4 1st round draft picks including 1st Darim Erstad in 1995, 106 professional players since 1950.
Coaching: Dave Van Horn, Head Coach, started his 1st season with the program. He recorded a 24-20 at NU and a 393-168 overall record for 10 years. He was an assistant coach at Arkansas for 2 years and did College World Series Appearances. Rob Childress, Assistant, is in his 2nd year with the program. Mike Anderson, Assistant, is in his 5th year with the program, and coached 1995 1st draft pick Darin Erstad.
Roster for 1998 team/In State: 14 **Out of State:** 17 **Out of Country:** 4
Total Number of Varsity/Jr. Varsity: 35 **Percent of Graduation:** 80%
Number of Seniors on 1998 Team: 7 **Number of Sophomores on 1998 Team:** 4
Freshmen Receiving Fin Aid/Athletic: 9 **Academic:** 2
Most Recent Record: 24 - 20 - 0 **Number of Spring Games:** 56
Positions Needed for 1999/2000: Outfielders, Pitchers, Catchers
Baseball Camp Dates: Winter and Summer
Schedule: Oklahoma, Texas A &M, Texas Tech, Oklahoma State, Texas, Baylor
Style of Play: Our team has power and speed and depth to compete with anyone on our schedule. Our pitching needs to develop, we have a lot of young experienced arms. The guys have potential.

University of Nebraska - Kearney

15th Avenue and 9th HSC #26
Kearney, NE 68849
Coach: Guy Murray

NCAA II
Lopers/Royal Blue, Old Gold
Phone: (308) 865-8022
Fax: (308) 865-8832

ACADEMIC

Founded: 1903
Type: 4 Yr., Public, Liberal Arts, Coed

Web-site: Not Available
SAT/ACT/GPA: 20 avg
Student/Faculty Ratio: 21:1
Male/Female Ratio: 45:55
Undergraduate Enrollment: 6,450
Graduate Enrollment: 1,130
Scholarships/Academic: Yes **Athletic:** Yes **Fin Aid:** Yes
Total Expenses by: Year **In State:** $ 4,500 **Out of State:** $ 5,950
Degrees Conferred: BA, BS, BFA, MA, MS, Med, SPED
Programs of Study: Contact school for program of study.

ATHLETIC PROFILE

Conference Affiliation: Rocky Mountain Athletic Conference
Program Profile: We have 10 of 16 (1972-1989) NAIA District Championships. Our outdoor stadium has cement with a seating capacity of 2,000. We have a natural field with over 12 tons of surface of dirt. There are new lights, a press box, a concession and rest room, 2 locker rooms and 2 indoor cages for hitting(at the field). The indoor has rubberized surfaces size of 85 yards football field and 30' ceiling. Games are from late February through the middle of May.
History: Our program began in 1962. We have about a.500 win loss percentage but have paled many Big 8 and Old SouthWest Conference opponents. We played in Hawaii on 4 different years.
Achievements: Guy Murray was named NAIA District II Coach of the Year 11 times. We got only a couple of conference titles but most years were Independet . We have several All-Americans and drafted players. We currently have 2 players in the minor league.
Coaching: Guy Murray, Head Coach, was Coach of the Year 11 times. He started his 26th year as a head coach. John Arnold , Pitching Coach, started his 4th four year. Tony Murray, Assistant Coach, started his 3rd year. Jamie Dunn, Assistant Coach, started his 1st year.
Style of Play: We have good defense, good hitting, decent pitching and decent base running. We are aggressive on both offense and defense. We expect to pay for conference titles. We were 3rd last year (1996) with only 3 seniors. We were one of the top 2 teams selected to 3 team Regional in California.

University of Nebraska - Omaha

60th and Dodge E Street
Omaha, NE 68182
Coach: Bob Gates
NCAA II
Mavericks/Crimson, Black
Phone: (402) 554-2305
Fax: (402) 554-3694

ACADEMIC

Founded: 1908
Type: 4 Yr., Public, Coed
Web-site: Not Available
SAT/ACT/GPA: 21 avg
Student/Faculty Ratio: 30:1
Male/Female Ratio: 48:52
Undergraduate Enrollment: 13,300
Graduate Enrollment: 2,588
Scholarships/Academic: Yes **Athletic:** Yes **Fin Aid:** Yes
Total Expenses by: Year **In State:** $ 2,500 **Out of State:** $ 5,500
Degrees Conferred: AS, BA, BS, BFA, BBA, BGS
Programs of Study: Contact school for program of study.

ATHLETIC PROFILE

Conference Affiliation: North Central Conference
Program Profile: We have a good baseball program and a good palying field of natural turf.
History: Our program began in 1947. We won North Central Conference in 1977 and 1981.
Achievements: North Central Conference in 1977 and 1981.
Coaching: Bob Gates - Head Coach. Bob Nowaczyk and Raywood - Assistant Coaches.
Style of Play: We promote fundamentals of all phases of the game.

Wayne State College

200 East 10th Street
Wayne, NE 68787
Coach: John Manganaro

NCAA II
Wildcats/Black, Gold
Phone: (402) 375-7313
Fax: (402) 375-7520

ACADEMIC

Founded: 1910
Religion: Non-Affiliated
Web-site: Not-Available
Student/Faculty Ratio: 30:1
Undergraduate Enrollment: 13,300
Scholarships/Academic: Yes **Athletic:** Yes
Total Expenses by: Year **In State:** $ 4,900

Type: 4 Yr., Public, Coed
Campus Housing: Yes
SAT/ACT/GPA: 21avg
Male/Female Ratio: 48:52
Graduate Enrollment: 2,588
Fin Aid: Yes
Out of State: $ 6,100

Degrees Conferred: BA, BS, BFA, MA, MS, MBA
Programs of Study: Accounting, Advertising, Agriculture, Applied Mathematics, Art/Fine Arts, Arts, Biological Science, Business Administration, Commerce, Management, Business Economics, Chemistry, Communications, Computer Information Systems, Computer Science, Creative Writing

ATHLETIC PROFILE

Conference Affiliation: Independent
Program Profile: We are fundamentally oriented with team concept. We have a Spring and Fall season. We have excellent facilities and a safe Midwest setting.
History: Program has developed a winning tradition.
Style of Play: We play fundamentally sound and aggressive.

York College - Nebraska

912 Kiplinger
York, NE 68467-2699
Coach: James King
Email: jking@yc.nc.edu

NAIA
Panthers/Royal Blue, White
Phone: (402) 363-5736
Fax: (402) 363-5738

ACADEMIC

Founded: 1890
Religion: Church of Christ
Web-site: Not Available
Student/Faculty Ratio: 13:1
Undergraduate Enrollment: 423
Scholarships/Academic: Yes **Athletic:** Yes
Total Expenses by: Year **In State:** $ 9,865

Type: 4 Yr., Private, Liberal Arts, Coed
Campus Housing: Yes
SAT/ACT/GPA: 820/ 17
Male/Female Ratio: 1.0-1.5
Graduate Enrollment: None
Fin Aid: Yes
Out of State: $ 9,865

Degrees Conferred: AA, AS, BA, BS
Programs of Study: Bible, Business, Accounting, Business Administration, Finance, Management, Communications, Education, Elementary Education, English, History, Human Resources Management, Liberal Arts, Mathematics, Psychology, Religious Education

ATHLETIC PROFILE

Estimated Number of Baseball Scholarships: 6-7
Conference Affiliation: Midland Collegiate Athletic Conference
Program Profile: We are a new program this year (4 year) after being a junior college which was successful in baseball. We are building a new baseball stadium and facility. We play at city park right now. Play a Fall ball through October and have off-season conditioning. We have a Spring season. We have natural grass turf and our stadium seats 800. The new stadium will seat over 1,000 and have a covered roof.

History: York College began playing baseball as a Jr. College in 1993. The school went to a four-year system and began competing in the NAIA. Our program has been working towards being competitive.

Achievements: 1985-1991 in Junior College Regionals and 1988 were Runner-Up in National Small College Championship and two years went to the NCAA (National Christian College Athletic Association) National Tournament. Coach of the Year Honors; 1 Conference Title and 1 Conference Tournament Championship.

Coaching: James King, Head Coach, entered his 2nd year as a head coach. He was Coach of the Year 4 times at another school. He has 5 Conference or District Titles, 2 Conference Tournament Championships and 8 District (sectional) or Regional Playoff Appearances. He compiled a record of 317-146. He played 3 years of professional baseball and was an associate Scout for New York Yankees for 4 years. John Beck, Assistant Coach, works with the pitchers. He is also a senior player coach. Bobby Dehart - Assistant Coach.

Roster for 1998 team/In State: 5 **Out of State:** 21 **Out of Country:** 1

Total Number of Varsity/Jr. Varsity: 27 **Percent of Graduation:** 80%

Freshmen Receiving Fin Aid/Athletic: 14 **Academic:** 11

Number of Fall Games: 9 **Number of Spring Games:** 58

Positions Needed for 1999/2000: Pitcher, Catcher, Infielder

Most Recent Record: 18 - 24 - 0

Baseball Camp Dates: December 12-19; May 31 - June and July 19-22

Schedule: Kansas State University, Metro State University, Abilene Christian University, Lubbock Christian University, Bellevue University, University of Nebraska-Kearney

Style of Play: We are aggressive, hard-nosed and very scrappy.

NEVADA

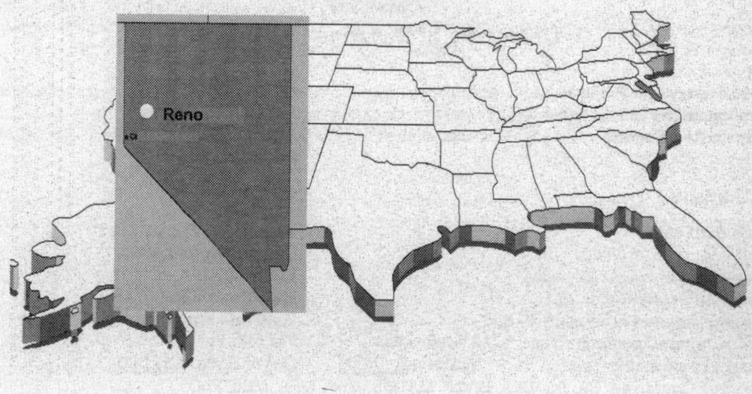

SCHOOL	CITY	AFFILIATION 99	PAGE
University of Nevada - Las Vegas	Las Vegas	NCAA I	520
University of Nevada - Reno	Reno	NCAA I	520

University of Nevada - Las Vegas

4505 S Maryland Parkway
Las Vegas, NV 89154-0004
Coach: Rod Soesbe

NCAA I
Rebels/Scarlet, Grey
Phone: (702) 895-3499
Fax: (702) 895-0989

ACADEMIC

Founded: 1957
Type: 4 Yr., Public, Coed
Religion: Non-Affiliated
Campus Housing: No
Web-site: http://www.unly.edu/
SAT/ACT/GPA: 820/ 18
Student/Faculty Ratio: 25;1
Male/Female Ratio: 46:54
Undergraduate Enrollment: 14,350
Graduate Enrollment: 5,350
Scholarships/Academic: Yes **Athletic:** Yes **Fin Aid:** Yes
Total Expenses by: Year **In State:** $ 7,000 **Out of State:** $ 12,000
Degrees Conferred: BA, BS, BFA, BArch, MA, MS, MBA, MFA, MEd, PhD
Programs of Study: Accounting, Anthroplogy, Applied Mathematics, Architecture, Art, Biochemsitry, Biology, Botany, Management, Comparative Literature, Geography, Geology, Industrial, Insurance, Linguistics, Recreation, Romance Languages, Travel, Zoology

ATHLETIC PROFILE

Conference Affiliation: Western Athletic Conference
Program Profile: UNLV baseball has one of the top 15 facilities in the country!! Our $1.2 million Earl E. Wilson Stadium at Roger Barnson Field is a beautiful natural grass playing surface. Our park's dimensions are 335-400-375-335 and there is a 12-foot high outfield fence.
History: Baseball officially began in 1976 and we a posted 8-40 or more WIV season, including a season high 53 victories in 1980. UNLV had 30 or more games in 19 out of the last 22 years. We have won 30 or more 17 straight season in 1976-1992 & UNLV appeared in the NCAA Tournament 7 times. UNLV captured the 1996 Big West Championship with an overall record of 43-17.
Achievements: 12 All-Americans including 3 straight freshmen All-Americans Selections; 1996 Big West Tournaments Champions; UNLV has had over 100 players play in the professional ranks; top players include Matt Williams (Cleveland Indians), Todd Stattleyer (St. Louis Cardinals), Joe Boever (Pittsburgh Pirates), Tj Matthews (Oakland A's), Erick Ludwick (Oakland A's).
Coaching: Rod Soesbe, Head Coach, started in 1997. He has a record of 24-31 for one year and has 14 seasons overall at URV. Jim Pace, Assistant Coach, played at UNLV in 1982-1985. He works with the pitchers. Mel Stottlemyer, Jr, Assistant Coach, played at UNLV in 1983-1984 and also played with the Kansas City Royals.
Style of Play: We have good offensive punch. We are good defesively up the middle and our pitching should be much more improved!

University of Nevada - Reno

Baseball Office - Lawlor Annex-232
Reno, NV 89557
Coach: Gary Powers

NCAA I
Wolf Pack/Navy Blue, Silver
Phone: (702) 784-4180
Fax: (702) 784-4497

ACADEMIC

Founded: 1874
Type: 4 Yr., Public, Coed
Religion: Non-Affiliated
Campus Housing: Yes
Web-site: http://www.wolfpack.edu
SAT/ACT/GPA: None
Student/Faculty Ratio: Unknown
Male/Female Ratio: 50:50
Scholarships/Academic: Yes **Athletic:** Yes **Fin Aid:** Yes
Total Expenses by: Year **In State:** $ 7,470 **Out of State:** $ 13,240
Degrees Conferred: BA, BS, Masters, PhD

Programs of Study: Engineering, Education, Mining, Agricultural, Journalism, Home Economics, Business, Nursing, School of Medicine, Arts and Science, Community and Health Sciences

ATHLETIC PROFILE

Estimated Number of Baseball Scholarships: 11
Conference Affiliation: Big West Conference
Program Profile: Our home stadium is William Peccole Park and has a natural grass playing surface with seating capacity of 1,300. Included are concessions areas, restrooms, a press box, a ticket office, a home team clubhouse, 3 batting tunnels and bullpen areas. We have a 56 game Spring schedule.
History: We began Division I status in 1970. Prior to 1970 , we were a college Division II program. Our present stadium was built in 1986.
Achievements: 1994 Coach of the Year; 1994 Big West Champions; 1997 and 1998 Big West Division Champions; 1994 and 1997 NCAA Regionals; 3 All-Americans.
Coaching: Gary Powers,Head Coach, started in 1983 and compiled a record of 484-364-4. Stan Stolte ,Assistant Coach, started in 1997. Gary McNamac, Assistant Coach, started in 1998.
Roster for 1998 team/In State: 10 **Out of State:** 20 **Out of Country:** 0
Total Number of Varsity/Jr. Varsity: 30 **Percent of Graduation:** 80%
Number of Seniors on 1998 Team: 6 **Number of Sophomores on 1998 Team:** 4
Freshmen Receiving Fin Aid/Athletic: 7 **Most Recent Record:** 31 - 22 - 0
Number of Fall Games: 0 **Number of Spring Games:** 56
Baseball Camp Dates: June 10-13; June 17-19
Schedule: Stanford, Wichita, Long Beach State, California State-Fullerton, Clemson, Washington
Style of Play: We have a blend of power and speed. We have solid pitching with a sound defense. We are aggressive but disciplined.

NEW HAMPSHIRE

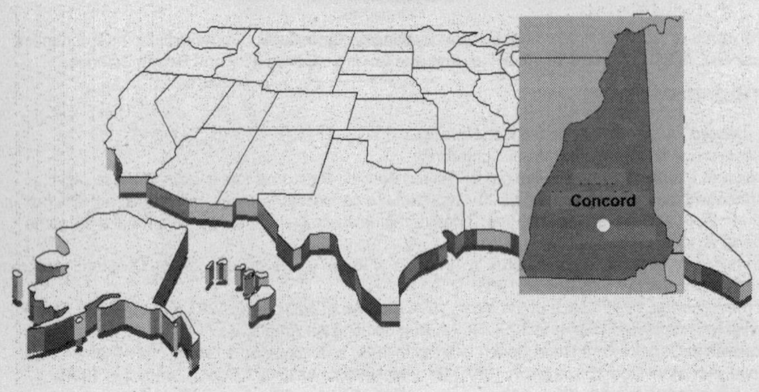

SCHOOL	CITY	AFFILIATION 99	PAGE
Colby - Sawyer College	New London	NCAA III	523
Daniel Webster College	Nashua	NCAA III	523
Dartmouth College	Hanover	NCAA I	524
Franklin Pierce College	Rindge	NCAA II	525
Keene State College	Keene	NCAA II	525
New England College	Henniker	NCAA III	526
New Hampshire College	Manchester	NCAA II	526
Plymouth State College	Plymouth	NCAA III	527
Saint Anselm College	Manchester	NCAA II	528

Colby - Sawyer College

100 Main Street
New London, NH 03257
Coach: Jim Broughton

NCAA III
Chargers/Royal Blue, White, Black
Phone: (603) 526-3607
Fax: (603) 526-2135

ACADEMIC

Founded: 1838
Religion: Non-Affiliated
Web-site: http://www.colby-sawyer.edu/
Student/Faculty Ratio: 12:1
Undergraduate Enrollment: 750
Scholarships/Academic: Yes **Athletic:** No
Total Expenses by: Year **In State:** $ 22,808
Degrees Conferred: AA, BA, BS, BFA

Type: 4 Yr., Private, Liberal Arts, Coed
Campus Housing: No
SAT/ACT/GPA: 870/19
Male/Female Ratio: 1:2
Graduate Enrollment: None
Fin Aid: Yes
Out of State:

Programs of Study: Art, Athletic Training, Biology, Broadcasting, Business, Communications, Education, English, Graphic Art, Liberal Art, Management, Nursing, Psychology, Prelaw, Premed, Secondary Education, Sport Administration, Sports Medicine

ATHLETIC PROFILE

Conference Affiliation: Commonwealth Coast Conference
Program Profile: We have a new program and the 1st class of recruited freshmen will graduate Spring of 1999. The school will open a new field in Spring of 1999. We play Fall and Spring seasons and have large indoor facilities.
History: The program began in 1995. We are in the 4th year of our program . On our 2nd year, we won conference championships. Our overall record is 19-16.
Achievements: 1998 Co-Coach of the Year; Tyler Blout was named 1998 Conference Player of the Year, 1st team All-New England; 2nd team ECAC; Chris Cabe 2nd team ECAC.
Coaching: Jim Broughton , Head Coach, began in 1995 with a record of 44-62. He was named Co-Coach of the Year in 1998. He is a 1992 graduate of University of Southern Maine. We were 1991 NCAA Division III Champs, 1991 & 1992 All-American & 1992 captain. Rick Miller - Assistant Coach.
Roster for 1998 team/In State: 11 **Out of State:** 14 **Out of Country:** 0
Total Number of Varsity/Jr. Varsity: 25 **Most Recent Record:** 19 - 16 - 0
Number of Seniors on 1998 Team: 5 **Number of Sophomores on 1998 Team:** 6
Freshmen Receiving Fin Aid/Athletic: 0 **Academic:** 18
Number of Fall Games: 10 **Number of Spring Games:** 35
Positions Needed for 1999/2000: Pitchers, Centerfield, Shortstop, 3rd Base
Schedule: University of Southern Maine, Plymouth State, Tufts, Keene State, Massachusetts
Style of Play: We pressure the other team, steal bases and hit and run.

Daniel Webster College

20 University Drive
Nashua, NH 03063-1300
Coach: Charles Crawford

NCAA III
Eagles/Blue, White
Phone: (603) 577-6498
Fax: (603) 577-6001

ACADEMIC

Founded: 1965
Web-site: http://www.dwc.edu/
Student/Faculty Ratio: 14:1
Undergraduate Enrollment: 500
Scholarships/Academic: Yes **Athletic:** No
Total Expenses by: Year **In State:** $ 18,500
Degrees Conferred: BS

Type: 4 Yr., Private, Coed
SAT/ACT/GPA: 800+
Male/Female Ratio: 5:1
Graduate Enrollment: None
Fin Aid: Yes
Out of State: $ 18,500

Programs of Study: Air Traffic Control, Aviation Management, Aviation Flight Operations, Business and Management, Computer Science, Computer Systems, Engineering, Engineering Science, Flight Operations, Sports Management

ATHLETIC PROFILE

Conference Affiliation: Great Northeast Athletic Conference
Program Profile: We are a growing Division III program and achieved the best record in school history in 1995. We play at Holman Stadium, the home of a minor league baseball team. DWC plays a very competitive schedule, consisting of 22 games against Division II & III teams from New England.
Achievements: Won the Great Northeast Athletic Conference Championships in 1996.
Style of Play: We are a good pitching team that forces defense to make thorough plays. Our pitching and defense relies on avoiding the "beginning" from opposition.

Dartmouth College

6083 Alumni Gym
Hanover, NH 03755
Coach: Bob Whalen
Email: robert.dwahalen@darmouth.edu

NCAA I
Big Green/Green, White
Phone: (603) 646-2477
Fax: (603) 646-3348

ACADEMIC

Founded: 1769
Type: 4 Yr., Private, Liberal Arts, Coed
Religion: Non-Affiliated
Campus Housing: Yes
Web-site: http://www.dartmouth.edu/
SAT/ACT/GPA: 1100+
Student/Faculty Ratio: 10:1
Male/Female Ratio: 50:50
Undergraduate Enrollment: 4,200
Graduate Enrollment: 1,500
Scholarships/Academic: No **Athletic:** No **Fin Aid:** Yes
Total Expenses by: Year **In State:** $ 28,000 **Out of State:** $ 28,000
Degrees Conferred: BA, MA, MS, MBA, PhD, MD
Programs of Study: Anthropology, Art, Asian, Biochemsitry and Molecular Biology, Biophysical, Classical Archaeology, Classics, Cognititive, Comparative, Drama, English, Earth Science, Environmental, Genetics, Geography, History, Women's Studies

ATHLETIC PROFILE

Conference Affiliation: Ivy League Conference
Program Profile: We have an excellent facility in the middle of the campus that has natural grass with dimensions of LF-316, CF-407 and RF-345.
History: The program began in 1866 and is the oldest program in the school.
Achievements: In 1997, the team finished 19th in the country in team batting average. For the second time, we are in the top 20 in the last 4 years. Dartmouth had 3 players in the major leagues in 1996 : Mike Remlinger (LHP) by the Red, Brad Ausmus (C) by the Astros and Mark Johnson (1Base) by the Pirates.
Coaching: Bob Whalen, Head Coach, works with the outfielders and hitters. He compiled a record of 143-170 since 1990. He was an assistant coach with USA Baseball in 1997. Mike Aoki ,Assistant Coach, works with the recruiting, infielders and hitters. Chris Detolo, Assistant Coach, works with the outfielders and catchers.
Total Number of Varsity/Jr. Varsity: 27
Percent of Graduation: 100%
Number of Seniors on 1998 Team: 5
Number of Sophomores on 1998 Team: 0
Number of Fall Games: 4
Number of Spring Games: 40
Positions Needed for 1999/2000: 4-Pitchers, 2-OF, 2-Infielders, Catcher
Style of Play: We are a very aggressive offensive team that plays solid defense.

Franklin Pierce College

P.O. Box 60
Rindge, NH 03461
Coach: Jayson King

NCAA II
Ravens/Crimson, Grey, Black
Phone: (603) 899-4084
Fax: (603) 899-4328

ACADEMIC

Founded: 1962
Type: 4 Yr., Private, Liberal Arts, Coed
Religion: Non-Affiliated
Campus Housing: Yes
SAT/ACT/GPA: 700+/17+ (both required)
Web-site: http://www.fpc.edu/ ?????
Student/Faculty Ratio: 15:1
Male/Female Ratio: 51:49
Undergraduate Enrollment: 1,300
Graduate Enrollment: 50
Scholarships/Academic: Yes **Athletic:** Yes **Fin Aid:** Yes
Total Expenses by: Year **In State:** $ 20,770 **Out of State:** $ 20,770
Degrees Conferred: BA, BS, MBA
Programs of Study: Accounting, Advertising, American Studies, Anthropology, Archaelogy, Art, Biology, Business Management, Communications, Computer Science, Creative Writing, Criminal Justice, Dance, Drama, Early Childhood Education, Economic Theory, Elementary Education, English, Environmental Science, Fine Arts, Financial Management, Graphic Communications, History, Mass Communications, Mathematics, Music, Political Science, Prelaw, Premed, Prevet, International Business, Journalism, Marketing, Social Work and Counseling, Psychology, Radio And Television Productions, Secondary Education, Sociology, Sports and Leisure Management

ATHLETIC PROFILE

Estimated Number of Baseball Scholarships: 1 3/4
Conference Affiliation: New England Collegiate Conference
Program Profile: We have a six week Fall program, a Southern trip and a Spring season. We have turf, batting cages and mounds.
Coaching: Jayson King, Head Coach, started his 1st season with the program.
Roster for 1998 team/In State: 5 **Out of State:** 23 **Out of Country:** 0
Total Number of Varsity/Jr. Varsity: 28 **Most Recent Record:** 8 - 21 - 0
Number of Seniors on 1998 Team: 2 **Baseball Camp Dates:** January 16-18
Freshmen Receiving Fin Aid/Athletic: 4 **Academic:** 7
Number of Fall Games: 10 **Number of Spring Games:** 29
Positions Needed for 1999/2000: Outfielder, 3rd Base
Schedule: University of Massachusetts - Lowell, Armstrong State, New Haven, Stony Brook
Style of Play: We are aggressive, steal bases, hit and run with good defense and pitching.

Keene State College

229 Main Street
Keene, NH 03431
Coach: Ken Howe

NCAA II
Owls/Red, White
Phone: (603) 358-2809
Fax: (603) 358-2888

ACADEMIC

Founded: 1909
Type: 4 Yr., Public, Liberal Arts, Coed
Religion: Non-Affiliated
Campus Housing: Yes
Web-site: http://www.keene.edu/
SAT/ACT/GPA: None
Student/Faculty Ratio: 20:1
Male/Female Ratio: 42:58
Undergraduate Enrollment: 3,900
Graduate Enrollment: 1,000
Scholarships/Academic: Yes **Athletic:** No **Fin Aid:** Yes
Total Expenses by: Year **In State:** $ 9,188 **Out of State:** $ 14,848
Degrees Conferred: AA, AS, BA, BS, BM, MA

Programs of Study: American Studies, Cytology, Chemistry, Computer Science, Dietetics, Dramatic Arts, Education, English, Environmental Science, Fine Arts, Geography, History, Industrial Technology, Journalism, Mathematics, Music, Music Performance, Political Science, Psychology, Safety Management, Social Science, Spanish, Special Education, Sports Management

ATHLETIC PROFILE

Conference Affiliation: ECAC, NECC

New England College

29 Western Avenue
Henniker, NH 03242-3309
Coach: Jason Hunter

NCAA III
The Pilgrims/Scarlet Red, Royal
Phone: (603) 428-2263
Fax: (603) 428-6023

ACADEMIC

Founded: 1946
Religion: Non-Affiliated
Web-site: http://www.nec.edu/
Student/Faculty Ratio: 16:1
Undergraduate Enrollment: 700
Scholarships/Academic: Yes **Athletic:** No
Total Expenses by: Year **In State:** $ 20,706

Type: 4 Yr., Private, Liberal Arts, Coed
Campus Housing: Yes
SAT/ACT/GPA: Optional
Male/Female Ratio: 53:47
Graduate Enrollment: None
Fin Aid: Yes
Out of State: $ 20,076

Degrees Conferred: AA, BA, BS, MA, MS
Programs of Study: Art, Biology, Business Administration, Communications, Education, Environmental Science Kinesiology, Philosophy, Political Science, Psychology, Sociology, Theatre

ATHLETIC PROFILE

Estimated Number of Baseball Scholarships: 0
Conference Affiliation: Commonwealth Coast Conference
Program Profile: We have a traditional playing season Spring only. We play home games on a campus field with natural turf.

New Hampshire College

2500 North River Road
Manchester, NH 03106-1045
Coach: Bruce A. Joyce
Email: joycebr@nhc.edu

NCAA II
Penmen/Navy Blue, Gold
Phone: (603) 645-9637
Fax: (603) 645-9686

ACADEMIC

Founded: 1932
Religion: Non-Affiliated
Web-site: http://www.nhc.edu
Student/Faculty Ratio: 15:1
Undergraduate Enrollment: 1,200
Scholarships/Academic: Yes **Athletic:** Yes
Total Expenses by: Year **In State:** $ 12,000

Type: 4 Yr., Private, Liberal Arts, Coed
Campus Housing: Yes
SAT/ACT/GPA: 760+
Male/Female Ratio: 50:50
Graduate Enrollment: 1,090
Fin Aid: Yes
Out of State: $ 12,000

Degrees Conferred: AS, AAS, BS, MS, MBA
Programs of Study: Accounting, Business Administration, Business Studies, Communications, Computer Science, Economics, English, Finance, Hotel/Restaurant Management, Liberal Arts, Marketing, Prelaw, Psychology, Social Science, Sports Management, System Analysis

ATHLETIC PROFILE

Conference Affiliation: New England Collegiate (NECC), ECAC

Program Profile: We are in Division II and play approximately 40 games. We do a Southern trip to Fort Myers, Florida. Our Fall schedule consists of 7-8 week s with 12 scheduled games. We also play approximately 20 intrasquad games. Our field is on campus. We have an indoor facility with pitching mounds and a batting cage available year-round.
History: We were a member of New England Intercollegiate Baseball Association until early 1980's. We won many NEIBA Championships and joined NECC in the early 1980's. We consistently ranked among the top teams in New England and the Northeast Region.
Achievements: Bruce Joyce is a two-time NECC Coach of the Year in 1993 and 1997. In 1997 we were NECC and ECAC Champions. Sophomore RHP Marc Perec was 2nd team All-American in 1997. He was also a 1997 NECC Pitcher of the Year and a 1997 Northeast Region Pitcher of the Year. Four players have signed to play Pro Ball.
Coaching: Bruce Joyce, Head Coach, was 11 years at NHC. He was an Alumni winningest coach in the history of NHC. Jay Hoyt, Assistant Coach, was a pitching coach for 10 years at NHC where he also an alumni. Jim Triantafellow, Bench Coach, coached for 15 years at NHC. He has 35 years of coaching experience.
Roster for 1998 team/In State: 10 **Out of State:** 17 **Out of Country:** 0
Total Number of Varsity/Jr. Varsity: 24 **Percent of Graduation:** 100%
Number of Seniors on 1998 Team: 7 **Most Recent Record:** 17 - 17 - 0
Freshmen Receiving Fin Aid/Athletic: 0 **Academic:** 3
Number of Fall Games: 12 **Number of Spring Games:** 34
Positions Needed for 1999/2000: Pitcher, Middle Infielder
Schedule: University of Massachusetts - Lowell; University of New Haven, Dartmouth College, College St. Rose, Merrimack College, Stone Hill College, Mansfield
Style of Play: We play aggressive and are very steady on defense. We are a "scrappy" type of team and have good team speed.

Plymouth State College

Physical Education Center #32
Plymouth, NH 03264
Coach: Dennis McManus
Email: dennism@psc.edu
NCAA III
Panthers/Green, White
Phone: (603) 535-2756
Fax: (603) 535-2758

ACADEMIC

Founded: 1871 **Type:** 4 Yr., Public, Liberal Arts, Coed
SAT/ACT/GPA: 900-1200/2.5 **Campus Housing:** 2300 on campus
Student/Faculty Ratio: 19:1 **Male/Female Ratio:** 50:50
Undergraduate Enrollment: 3,500 **Graduate Enrollment:** 500
Scholarships/Academic: No **Athletic:** No **Fin Aid:** Yes
Total Expenses by: Year **In State:** $ 9,500 **Out of State:** $ 14,500
Degrees Conferred: AA, BA, BFS, BS, BSE, as well as many other minors and master programs
Programs of Study: Actuarial Science, Athletic Training, Business and Management, Computer Science, Education, Health and Physical Education, Liberal Arts, Meteorology, Parks/Recreations, Protective Sciences, Psychology, Public Affairs, Social Sciences, Visual and Performing Arts

ATHLETIC PROFILE

Conference Affiliation: Little East Conference
Program Profile: We are one of the state Division III programs in the region. We have excellent indoor and outdoor facilities and a very solid and stable coaching staff. We play a six weeks Fall schedule and a full Spring schedule . We also go on a Florida trip.
History: The baseball program began in 1948. We have a strong tradition of winning and produce quality people. Dennis McManus is now the coach.
Achievements: Many All-Tourneys; All-Conference and drafted players.
Coaching: Dennis McManus, Head Coach, started his 16th year as head coach. Has become synonomous with Panther baseball. He is a 1973 PSC graduate. After a stint as an assistant baseball coach, he has now been a head coach since 1985. He led the Panthers to 8 post-season berth in 13 seasons and is PSC's all-time winningest baseball coach with a 227-213-1 record (.516).
Roster for 1998 team/In State: 11 **Out of State:** 12 **Out of Country:** 0

Total Number of Varsity/Jr. Varsity: 23
Percent of Graduation: 90%
Number of Seniors on 1998 Team: 8
Number of Sophomores on 1998 Team: 6
Freshmen Receiving Fin Aid/Athletic: 0
Academic: 2
Number of Fall Games: 13
Number of Spring Games: 36
Positions Needed for 1999/2000: Pitcher, Shortstop, Catcher
Most Recent Record: 20 - 19 - 0
Schedule: Eastern Connecticut, University Southern Maine, University Massachusetts-Darmouth, Darmouth College, Bridgewater State, Trinity College
Style of Play: We are very aggressive and run a lot. We have hit over 300 in the last 14 years.

Saint Anselm College

100 St. Anselm Drive
Manchester, NH 03102
Coach: Bob Kerrigan

NCAA II
Hawks/Royal, White
Phone: (603) 641-7800
Fax: (603) 641-7172

ACADEMIC

Founded: 1889
Type: 4 Yr., Private, Liberal Arts, Coed
Religion: Order of Saint Benedict
Campus Housing: Yes
Web-site: http://www.anselm.edu/
SAT/ACT/GPA: 1090/24
Student/Faculty Ratio: 17:1
Male/Female Ratio: 46:54
Undergraduate Enrollment: 1,950
Graduate Enrollment: None
Scholarships/Academic: Yes
Athletic: Yes
Fin Aid: Yes
Total Expenses by: Year
In State: $ 22,010
Out of State: $ 22,010
Degrees Conferred: BA, BSN
Programs of Study: Biology, Business and Management, Chemistry, Computers, Criminal Justice, Economics, Education, Engineering, English, Health Sciences, History, Languages, Liberal Arts, Life Sciences, Mathematics, Nursing, Parks/Recreation, Political Science, Protective Services, Psychology, Public Affairs, Social Sciences and many others.

ATHLETIC PROFILE

Conference Affiliation: Northeast 10, ECAC
Coaching: Bob Kerrigan, Head Coach, started his 4th season as a skipper of the Hawk's program in the Spring of 1999. He came to St. Anselm more than qualified for the position, having spent almost his entire career coaching the sport. Prior to coming to the Hilltop, Kerrigan established himself as a New Hampshire High School coaching legend. He coached in the high school ranks for 28 years including the last 26 at Manchester West High School. During that tenure, he became one of the winningest coaches in New Hampshire state champions.

University of New Hampshire

(Program Discontinued)

NEW JERSEY

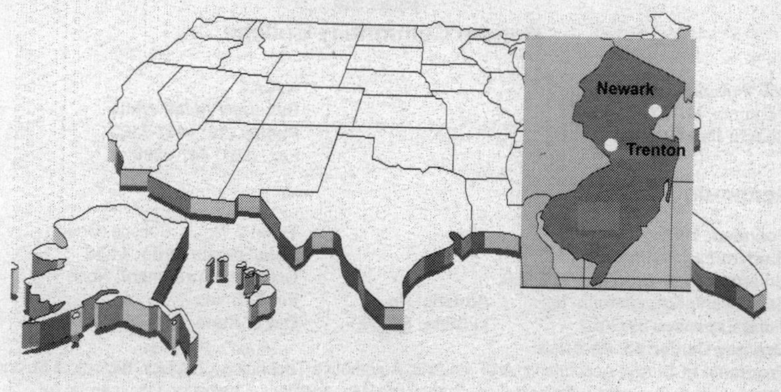

SCHOOL	CITY	AFFILIATION 99	PAGE
Bergen Community College	Paramus	NJCAA	530
Bloomfield College	Bloomfield	NAIA	530
Brookdale Community College	Lincroft	NJCAA	530
Burlington County College	Pemberton	NJCAA	531
Caldwell College	Caldwell	NAIA	531
Camden County College	Blackwood	NJCAA	532
County College of Morris	Randolph	NJCAA	532
Drew University	Madison	NCAA III	532
Fairleigh Dickinson University - Madison	Madison	NCAA III	533
Fairleigh Dickinson University - Teaneck	Teaneck	NCAA I	533
Gloucester County College	Sewell	NJCAA III	534
Jersey City State College	Jersey City	NCAA III	535
Kean College - New Jersey	Union	NCAA III	535
Mercer County Community College	Trenton	NJCAA	536
Middlesex County College	Edison	NJCAA	536
Monmouth University	West Long Branch	NCAA I	537
Montclair State College	Upper Montclair	NCAA III	538
NJ Institute of Technology	Newark	NCAA II	538
Ocean County College	Toms River	NJCAA III	539
Princeton University	Princeton	NCAA I	539
Ramapo College of New Jersey	Mahwah	NCAA III	540
Raritan Valley Community College	Somerville	NJCAA	541
Richard Stockton College	Pomona	NCAA III	541
Rider University	Lawrenceville	NCAA I	542
Rowan University	Glassboro	NCAA III	543
Rutgers University - U of New Jersey	New Brunswick	NCAA I	543
Rutgers University - Camden	Camden	NCAA III	544
Rutgers University - Newark	Newark	NCAA III	544
Saint Peter's College	Jersey City	NCAA I	545
Salem Community College	Carneys Point	NJCAA	546
Seton Hall University	South Orange	NCAA I	546
Stevens Institute of Technology	Hoboken	NCAA III	547
Sussex County Community College	Newton	NJCAA	547
College of New Jersey (Trenton State)	Ewing	NCAA III	548
Union County College	Cranford	NJCAA	548
William Paterson College	Wayne	NCAA III	549

Bergen Community College

400 Paramus Road
Paramus, NJ 07652-1595
Coach: Ray Gressler

NJCAA
Bulldogs/Violet, White
Phone: (201) 447-7183
Fax: (201) 447-0298

ACADEMIC

Founded: 1965
Type: 2 Yr., Jr. College, Coed
Student/Faculty Ratio: 14:1
Male/Female Ratio: 44:56
Undergraduate Enrollment: 8,650
Graduate Enrollment: None
Scholarships/Academic: No **Athletic:** No **Fin Aid:** Yes
Total Expenses by: Year **In State:** $ 1,500 **Out of State:** $ 5,500
Degrees Conferred: Associate
Programs of Study: Accounting, Art/Fine Arts, Automotive Technology, Biology, Biological Science, Broadcasting, Business Administration, Commerce, Management, Chemistry, Commercial Art, Communications, Computer Science, Computer Programming, Computer Technology, Criminal Justice, Drafting/Design, Early Childhood Education, Engineering Science, Electrical/Electronic Technology, Hotel/Restaurant Management, Legal Management, Legal Secretarial Studies, Finance/Banking, Mathematics, Medical, Philosophy, Photography, Physical Fitness/Exercise

ATHLETIC PROFILE

Conference Affiliation: Garden State Athletic Conference

Bloomfield College

467 Franklin Street
Bloomfield, NJ 07003
Coach: Jay Blackwell

NAIA
Deacons/Maroon, Gold
Phone: (973) 748-9000
Fax: (973) 743-3998

ACADEMIC

Founded: 1868
Type: 4 Yr., Private, Coed
Religion: Presbyterian
Campus Housing: Yes
Web-site: http://www.bloomfield.edu
SAT/ACT/GPA: 860/18/2.0
Student/Faculty Ratio: 17:1
Male/Female Ratio: 35:65
Undergraduate Enrollment: 1,900
Graduate Enrollment: None
Scholarships/Academic: Yes **Athletic:** Yes **Fin Aid:** Yes
Total Expenses by: Year **In State:** $ 15,500 **Out of State:** $ 15,500
Degrees Conferred: BA, BS
Programs of Study: Accounting, Biology, Business Administration, Chemistry, Communications, Computer Information Systems, Creative Arts and Technology, Criminal Justice, Economics, English, History, Humanities, Philosophy, Political Science, Psychology, Religion, Sociology

ATHLETIC PROFILE

Conference Affiliation: CCAC

Brookdale Community College

765 Newman Springs Rd
Lincroft, NJ 07738
Coach: Paul MacLaughlin

NJCAA
Jersey Blues/Navy, Red, White
Phone: (773) 224-2379
Fax: (732) 224-2155

ACADEMIC

Type: 2 Yr., Jr. College, Coed
Campus Housing: No
Degrees Conferred: Associate
Programs of Study: Accounting, Applied Art, Art/Fine Arts, Automotive Technology, Business Administration, Commerce, Management, Chemistry, Communications, Computer Programming, Computer Science, Criminal Justice, Drafting/Design, Early Childhood Education, Education, Electronics/Electrical Technology, English, Fashion, Merchandising, Food Services, Management, Insurance, Liberal Arts, General Studies, Library Science, Marketing, Retailing, Merchandising, Music, Nursing, Science, Social Science, Sociology

Burlington County College

Pemberton-Browns Mills Rd
Pemberton, NJ 08068
Coach: Jamie Galioto

NJCAA
Barons/Red, Grey, White
Phone: (609) 894-9311
Fax: (609) 894-4973

ACADEMIC

Founded: 1966
Type: 2 Yr., Public, Coed
Web-site: http://www.bcc.edu/
SAT/ACT/GPA: None
Student/Faculty Ratio: 23:1
Male/Female Ratio: 39:61
Undergraduate Enrollment: 7,150
Graduate Enrollment: None
Scholarships/Academic: Yes **Athletic:** Yes **Fin Aid:** Yes
Total Expenses by: Year **In State:** $ 1,400 Tuition **Out of State:** $ 3,800 Tuition
Degrees Conferred: Associate
Programs of Study: Accounting, Applied Art, Archetectural Technology, Art/Fine Arts, Art Therapy, Automotive Technology, Biology, Biological Science, Business Administration, Commerce, Management, Chemical Engineering, Technology, Chemistry, Civil Engineering, Communication Equipment Technology, Law Enforcement, Liberal Arts, General Studies, Music, Nursing, Philosophy, Physics, Political Science, Psychology, Radiological Technology, Science

ATHLETIC PROFILE

Conference Affiliation: Garden State

Caldwell College

8 Ryerson Avenue
Caldwell, NJ 07006-6195
Coach: Charles Honeker

NAIA
Cougars/Scarlet, White, Gold
Phone: (973) 228-4424
Fax: (973) 403-0334

ACADEMIC

Founded: 1956
Type: 4 Yr., Private, Liberal Arts, Coed
Religion: Catholic
Campus Housing: Yes
Web-site: http://www.caldwell.edu/
SAT/ACT/GPA: 860+/18/2.0
Student/Faculty Ratio: 12:1
Male/Female Ratio: 45:55
Undergraduate Enrollment: 2,000
Graduate Enrollment: 300
Scholarships/Academic: Yes **Athletic:** Yes **Fin Aid:** Yes
Total Expenses by: Year **In State:** $ 17,000 **Out of State:** $ 17,000
Degrees Conferred: BA, BS, Master of Arts
Programs of Study: Art, Biology, Business Administration, Communication Arts, Education, English, Foreign Languages, History and Political Science, Mathematics and Computer Science, Music, Natural and Physical Sciences, Psychology, Religious Studies and Philosophy, Sociology

ATHLETIC PROFILE

Conference Affiliation: CACC

Camden County College

PO Box 200
Blackwood, NJ 08012
Coach: Bob Arra

NJCAA
Cougars/Blue, White
Phone: (609) 227-7200
Fax: (609) 374-4890

ACADEMIC

Founded: 1967
Type: 2 Yr., Jr. College, Coed
Student/Faculty Ratio: 25:1
Male/Female Ratio: 41:59
Undergraduate Enrollment: 15,585
Graduate Enrollment: None
Scholarships/Academic: No **Athletic:** No **Fin Aid:** Yes
Total Expenses by: Year **In State:** $ 1,500 **Out of State:** $ 1,700
Degrees Conferred: Associate
Programs of Study: Accounting, Animal Science, Applied Art, Art/Fine Arts, Automotive Technology, Business Administration, Commerce, Management, Communications, Computer Programming, Computer Technology, Criminal Justice, Data Processing, Dental Services, Dietetics, Early Childhood Education, Education, Food Services Management, Fire Science, Liberal Arts

ATHLETIC PROFILE

Conference Affiliation: GSAC

County College of Morris

214 Center Grove Rd
Randolph, NJ 07869
Coach: TBA

NJCAA
Titans/Red, Gold
Phone: (973) 328-5251
Fax: (973) 328-5330

ACADEMIC

Founded: 1969
Type: 2 Yr., Jr. College, Coed
Student/Faculty Ratio: 19:1
Male/Female Ratio: 47:53
Undergraduate Enrollment: 10,000
Graduate Enrollment: None
Scholarships/Academic: Yes **Athletic:** Yes **Fin Aid:** Yes
Total Expenses by: Year **In State:** $ 2,000 **Out of State:** $ 6,000
Degrees Conferred: Associate
Programs of Study: Accounting, Advertising, Agriculture, Art/Fine Arts, Aviation Administration, Commerce, Management, Music, Nursing, Photography, Medical Laboratory Technology

ATHLETIC PROFILE

Conference Affiliation: Garden State Athletic Conference
Achievements: 3-time Region XIX Coach of the Year, 1 Mideast Coach of the Year, 7 Region XIX Championships in 15 years, 8 All-Americans, 38 drafted.
Coaching: 3 coaches; pitching instructor, hitting instructor and 1 part time coach.

Drew University

36 Madison Avenue
Madison, NJ 07940
Coach: Vincent Masco

NCAA III
Rangers/Oxford Blue, Lincoln Green
Phone: (973) 408-3443
Fax: (973) 408-3014

ACADEMIC

Founded: 1867
Religion: United Methodist
Web-site: http://www.drew.edu/
Student/Faculty Ratio: 10:1
Undergraduate Enrollment: 1,318
Scholarships/Academic: Yes **Athletic:** No
Total Expenses by: Year **In State:** $ 19,128
Type: 4 Yr., Private, Liberal Arts, Coed
Campus Housing: Yes
SAT/ACT/GPA: 1100
Male/Female Ratio: 40:60
Graduate Enrollment: 1,336
Fin Aid: Yes
Out of State: $ 19,128
Degrees Conferred: BA, BS, MA, PhD
Programs of Study: American Studies, Anthropology, Art, Behavioral Sciences, Biology, Chemistry, Computer Science, Economics, English, French, German, Mathematics, Music, Philosophy, Physics, Political Science, Psychology, Religion, Sociology

ATHLETIC PROFILE

Conference Affiliation: Middle Atlantic - Freedom League
Program Profile: Drew's baseball program has its own stadium with NCAA dimensions. It has a natural field and bleachers with the capacity of 500. There is a non-traditional Fall season and a Spring trip followed by the traditional Spring season consisting of 38 games. Our games count toward total number of games allowed , record does not count.
History: The program began in 1931 and has accumulated an overall record of 436-492-7.
Achievements: 1995 Co-Coach of the Year; ECAC Semi-finals; Coach Masco recently was selected as Jersey Nine Coach of the Year in 1991 and MAC Northeast Coach of the Year in 1992.
Coaching: Vincent Masco, Head Coach, was 1995 Conference Co-Coach of the Year. He was 1991 Jersey Nine Coach of the Year and MAC Northeast Coach of the Year.
Style of Play: We do aggressive base running , use the stolen bases, hit & run and bunt and steal.

Fairleigh Dickinson University - Madison

285 Madison Avenue
Madison, NJ 07940
Coach: Jack Sullivan

NCAA III
Jersey Devils/Columbia, Navy, White
Phone: (973) 443-8826
Fax: (973) 443-8796

ACADEMIC

Founded: 1958
Web-site: http://www.fdu.edu
Student/Faculty Ratio: 15:1
Undergraduate Enrollment: 2,203
Scholarships/Academic: Yes **Athletic:** No
Total Expenses by: Year **In State:** $ 20,416
Type: 4 Yr., Private, Liberal Arts, Coed
SAT/ACT/GPA: 950
Male/Female Ratio: 50:50
Graduate Enrollment: 1,545
Fin Aid: Yes
Out of State: $ 20,416
Degrees Conferred: BA, BS, MA, MAT, MBA, MS, MPA, DMD
Programs of Study: Accounting, Biology, Business Management, Chemistry, Clinical Laboratory Science, Computer Science, Economics, Electronic Filmmaking and Digital Video Design, English Languages and Literature, Finance, Fine Arts, French Languages and Literature, History, Hotel/Restaurant Management, Humanities, Marine Biology, Marketing, Mathematics

ATHLETIC PROFILE

Conference Affiliation: ECAC, MAACAC

Fairleigh Dickinson University - Teaneck

1000 River Road
Teaneck, NJ 07666
Coach: Dennis Sasso

NCAA I
Knights/Black, FDU Blue, White
Phone: (201) 692-2245
Fax: (201) 692-9361

ACADEMIC

Founded: 1942
Type: 4 Yr., Private, Liberal Arts, Coed
Religion: Non-Affiliated
Campus Housing: Yes
Web-site: http://www.fdu.edu/
SAT/ACT/GPA: 900+
Student/Faculty Ratio: 15:1
Male/Female Ratio: 50:50
Undergraduate Enrollment: 4,000
Graduate Enrollment: None
Scholarships/Academic: Yes **Athletic:** Yes **Fin Aid:** Yes
Total Expenses by: Year **In State:** $ 19,858 **Out of State:** $ 19,858
Degrees Conferred: BS, BA
Programs of Study: Accounting, Arts, Biology, Business Management, Chemistry, Economics, English Language and Literature, Finance, History, International Studies, Marine Biology, Marketing, Mathematics, Philosophy, Psychology, Science, Sociology, Preprofessional Courses

ATHLETIC PROFILE

Conference Affiliation: Northeast, ECAC
Program Profile: We are NCAA Division I and our game schedule is from the 1st week of March until the middle of May. We play at Knights Stadium on campus which has natural grass, seats 1,000 and has dimensions of LF-323', LC-374', CF-351',RC-357,RF-325'.
History: Our program began in 1950 and has compiled an overall record of 648-634-7 (.505). We have 7 years in post season play, 10 regular season conference championships, 32 players signed major league contracts and 6 players still playing professional baseball in minor leagues. One of our players reached the major leagues--Mike Laga (class of 1980) and played with the Detroit Tigers and St. Louis Cardinals.
Achievements: Dennis Sasso Northeast Conference Coach of the Year 1987, 1988 and 1993; Northeast Conference Regular Season Champions in 1986, 1987, 1988, 1993 and 1994; 1 Academic All-American; 7 All-Northeast Region Americans; 13 players signed pro contracts; 14 players drafted under Sasso, including 2 in 1997.
Coaching: Dennis Sasso, Head Coach, started his 13th year.
Style of Play: We play aggressive and fundamentals are emphasized.

Gloucester County College

1400 Tanyard Rd
Sewell, NJ 08080-9518
Coach: Barry Davis

NJCAA III
Roadrunners/Blue, Gold
Phone: (609) 468-5000
Fax: (609) 468-0280

ACADEMIC

Founded: 1968
Type: 2 Yr., Jr. College, Coed
Student/Faculty Ratio: 21:1
Male/Female Ratio: 1:2
Undergraduate Enrollment: 5,500
Graduate Enrollment: None
Scholarships/Academic: Yes **Athletic:** No **Fin Aid:** Yes
Total Expenses by: Year **In State:** $ 1,573 **Out of State:** $ 1,573
Degrees Conferred: Associate
Programs of Study: Arts and Sciences, Communications, Options, Education, Health/Physical Education and Recreation, Biology, Business, Accounting, Automotive, Computer, Engineering, Banking/Finance, Certificate Programs

ATHLETIC PROFILE

Conference Affiliation: Garden State Athletic Conference
Program Profile: We do an annual Spring trip to Jacksonville, Florida. We have an enclosed natural grass field with enclosed dugouts. We were the only program to qualify for all 4 NJCAA Division III national tournaments. We play a 50-game Spring season and a 17-game Fall season.

History: Our program started in 1971 (team was 2-16). We won 1st NJCAA Region 19 title in 1978 (19-6). We had the best success in the last 6 years under Barry Davis : 2 national titles, 4 NJCAA Region 19 crowns and 4 Garden State Athletic Conference titles, 211-53-1 in last 6 years and 166-35-1 in last 4 years.
Achievements: Under Barry Davis we were: NJCAA Division III national championships in 1992-93; won ABCA JC Coach of the Year honors 1992-93; 211-53-1 in 6 years; only team to qualify for all 4 NJCAA Division national tournaments (1992-95); won Garden State Athletic Conference and NJCAA Region 19 crowns 1992-95; 5 players currently in pro ball; 9 have been drafted; 8 All-Americans.
Coaching: Barry Davis, Head Coach, is in his 6th year. He is the former assistant to George Mason and Frostburg State. He also coached in the Shenandoah League. He is a 2-time All-Conference SS at Bridgewater College (BS 1987), Frostburg (MS 1989)and became GCC coach in 1990 (age 24). Steve Lindner, Assistant Coach, former Div. I player at Virginia, played 2 years independent ball in the pros. Mike Stankiewicz, Assistant Coach, was Div. I player Temple. He coached 5 years at Chestnut Hill Academy.
Style of Play: We play aggressive and fundamentally sound.

New Jersey City University
(Jersey City State College)

2039 Kennedy Boulevard
Jersey City, NJ 07305
Coach: Ken Heaton

NCAA III
Gothic Knights/Green, Gold
Phone: (201) 200-3079
Fax: (201) 200-2365

ACADEMIC

Founded: 1929
Type: 4 Yr., Public, Coed
Religion: Non-Affiliated
Campus Housing: Yes
Web-site: Not Available
SAT/ACT/GPA: 950
Student/Faculty Ratio: 15:1
Male/Female Ratio: 1:3
Undergraduate Enrollment: 8,000
Graduate Enrollment: ?
Scholarships/Academic: Yes **Athletic:** No **Fin Aid:** Yes
Total Expenses by: Year **In State:** $ 8,527 **Out of State:** $ 9,997
Degrees Conferred: BA, BS, BFA, BSN, MA, MS
Programs of Study: Accounting, Banking/Finance, Biology, Broadcasting, Business Administration, Communications, Computer Science, Criminal Justice, Economics, Education, English, Fine Arts, Geography, Geology, Health Science, History, Management, Marketing, Mathematics, Medical Technology, Music, Nursing, Philosophy, Political Science, Prelaw, Premed, Psychology

ATHLETIC PROFILE

Conference Affiliation: ECAC

Kean College - New Jersey

1000 Morris Avenue
Union, NJ 07083
Coach: Neil Ioviero

NCAA III
Cougars/Royal, White, Silver
Phone: (908) 527-2002
Fax: (908) 527-2002

ACADEMIC

Founded: 1855
Type: 4 Yr., Public, Liberal Arts, Coed
Web-site: http://www.kean.edu/
SAT/ACT/GPA: 950+/2.0
Student/Faculty Ratio: 18:1
Male/Female Ratio: 1:4
Undergraduate Enrollment: 4,000
Graduate Enrollment: 5,000
Scholarships/Academic: Yes **Athletic:** No **Fin Aid:** Yes
Total Expenses by: Year **In State:** $ 10,908 **Out of State:** $ 12,090
Degrees Conferred: BA, BS, BFA, BSN, BSW, MA, MS

Programs of Study: School of Business, Government and Technology, School of Liberal Arts, School of Natural Science, Nursing and Mathematics, School of Education

ATHLETIC PROFILE

Conference Affiliation: New Jersey Athletic Conference
Program Profile: We play a 36 game schedule on natural grass in every competitive conference. Kean plays in the best Division III conference in the country. The team travels to Daytona, FL for a 10 day Spring trip. In 1994, the college spent $50,000 to install a new infield and enclosed fencing. In Summer of 1995, we added dugouts and a scoreboard to complete the field renovation. It is the best field in the conference.
History: We have a new head coach. His 1996 record was 22-18 before 24-12.
Achievements: He had I player drafted on 15th round by the Beavers-Ton Ciravolo. 3 All-Americans.
Coaching: Neil Ioviero, Head Coach, compiled a record of 25-7 in 1997. He was NJ All-State player at Rutgers University. Jorge Perez - Assistant Coach.
Roster for 1998 team/In State: 38 **Out of State:** 0 **Out of Country:** 0
Total Number of Varsity/Jr. Varsity: 38 **Baseball Camp Dates:** TBA
Number of Seniors on 1998 Team: 12 **Most Recent Record:** 25 - 7 - 0
Number of Fall Games: 7 **Number of Spring Games:** 36
Schedule: St. Thomas, Northwood, Montclair State, John Hopkins
Style of Play: Our team has speed, power defense and pitching.

Mercer County Community College

1200 Old Trenton Road
Trenton, NJ 08690
Coach: Rick Freeman

NJCAA
Vikings/Kelly Green, Gold
Phone: (609) 586-4800
Fax: (609) 588-5148

ACADEMIC

Founded: 1966 **Type:** 2 Yr., Jr. College, Coed
Student/Faculty Ratio: 25:1 **Male/Female Ratio:** 45:55
Undergraduate Enrollment: 8,800 **Graduate Enrollment:** None
Scholarships/Academic: Yes **Athletic:** Yes **Fin Aid:** Yes
Total Expenses by: Year **In State:** $ 1,700 **Out of State:** $ 5,100
Degrees Conferred: Associate
Programs of Study: Accounting, Architectural, Art, Automotive, Aviation, Banking/Finance, Botany, Business, Computer Criminal Education, Engineering, Math Technology, Sciences

ATHLETIC PROFILE

Conference Affiliation: Garden State Athletic Conference
Program Profile: We play on a natural turf field which has a seating capacity of 1,000. We won the 1996 Division II World Series and were 1997 Region 19 Runner-Up.
History: We began in 1965 and won World Series in 1981 and 1996.
Achievements: Region 19 Coach of the Year in 1996; 4 All-Conference Player in 1997; 3 drafted Players for the past two years.
Coaching: Rick Freeman - Head Coach. Assistant Coaches - Ange Capuano, Frank Taylor, Steve Wilfing, Tore Carr.
Style of Play: We have sound fundamentals and play aggressively. We hope to have a team with an idea!

Middlesex County College

155 Mill Road
Edison, NJ 08818-3050
Coach: Michael Lepore

NJCAA
Colts/Navy Blue, White
Phone: (732) 906-4675
Fax: (732) 906-4179

ACADEMIC

Founded: 1964 **Type:** 2 Yr., Jr. College, Coed
Web-site: http://www.middlesex.cc.nj.us **SAT/ACT/GPA:** None
Student/Faculty Ratio: 44:1 **Male/Female Ratio:** 50:50
Undergraduate Enrollment: 12,500 **Graduate Enrollment:** None
Scholarships/Academic: No **Athletic:** Yes **Fin Aid:** Yes
Total Expenses by: Year **In State:** $ 1,500 **Out of State:** $ 2,900
Degrees Conferred: Associate
Programs of Study: Accounting, Advertising, Applied Art, Art/Fine Arts, Automotive Technology, Biology, Biological Science, Biotechnology, Business Administration, Commerce, Management, ChemistryChild Care/Child and Family Studies, Civil Engineering Technology, Commercial Art, Computer, Graphics, Computer Information Systems, Computer Programming, Computer Science, Computer Technology, Construction Technology, Fashion Design and Technology

ATHLETIC PROFILE

Conference Affiliation: Garden State Athletic Conference
Program Profile: Our Fall season is in September. Spring season includes a practicet in January and games from March until May. We have a 2 year old beautiful baseball stadium with natural grass measurements of 350 down the lines and to the center.
History: Michael Lepore has been the pitching coach for the past 10 years and was appointed head coach for the 1997-1998 season. We have been one of the top teams in our conference and region for my tenure at Middlessex.
Achievements: We have come in 2nd place in our Region Tournament several times. We have had 5 All-Americans in the past 10 years.
Coaching: Michael Lepore, Head Coach, started his 1st. He was high school coach for 24 years and got several conference and state championships. He was assistant for 10 years at Middlesex County College. Robert Cleffi, Assistant Coach, was a high school coach 15 years where he won several conference and state championships.
Roster for 1998 team/In State: 35 **Out of State:** 0 **Out of Country:** 2
Most Recent Record: 23 - 7 - 0 **Percent of Graduation:** 75%
Number of Fall Games: 14 **Number of Spring Games:** 37
Schedule: Brookdale CC, Gloucester CC, Raritan Valley, Lackwanna JC, Nassau
Style of Play: We play good defense with full use of speed.

Monmouth University

Cedar Avenue **NCAA I**
West Long Branch, NJ 07764 **Hawks/Royal, White**
Coach: Dean Ehehalt **Phone: (732) 263-5186**
Email: dehehalt@monmouth.edu **Fax: (732) 571-3535**

ACADEMIC

Founded: 1955 **Type:** 4 Yr., Private, Coed
Religion: Non-Affiliated **Campus Housing:** Yes
Web-site: http://www.monmouth.edu/ **SAT/ACT/GPA:** 960
Student/Faculty Ratio: 12:1 **Male/Female Ratio:** 44:56
Undergraduate Enrollment: 4,500 **Graduate Enrollment:** 2,000
Scholarships/Academic: Yes **Athletic:** Yes **Fin Aid:** Yes
Total Expenses by: Year **In State:** $ 13,000 **Out of State:** $ 18,800
Degrees Conferred: AA, BA, BS, MA, MS, MBA, Med, Liberal Arts
Programs of Study: Business and Management, Computer Science, Communications, Education, Health Science, Multi/Interdisciplinary Studies, Psychology, Social Sciences

ATHLETIC PROFILE

Estimated Number of Baseball Scholarships: 2-3 available
Conference Affiliation: Northeast Conference

Program Profile: We are members of the NCAA Division I were NCAA Regional participants in 1998. We have an on campus facility. The team plays on a natural grass field with dimensions of 320 - 390 - 320.
History: We started in 1958 and 1983 was the first year of Division I. In 1996, Monmouth had a record for wins in a season: 25. In 1996-1997, we became a Division I team that has had a back to back 20 win season. Our school record for wins in 1998 is 30 (NCAA Tournament).
Achievements: 1996 Northeast Conference - 1st place. In 1998, Joe McCrought was 2nd team All-American (ABCA/rankings).
Coaching: Dean Ehehalt, Head Coach, entered his 6th year with the program. He compiled a record of 110-124 for 5 years at Monmouth. Our overall coaching career is 7 years. Joe Litterio and Jeff Bertanlinardo - Assistant Coaches.
Roster for 1998 team/In State: 26 **Out of State:** 24 **Out of Country:**
Total Number of Varsity/Jr. Varsity: 30 **Percent of Graduation:** 100%
Number of Seniors on 1998 Team: 7 **Baseball Camp Dates:** July 1999
Freshmen Receiving Fin Aid/Athletic: 6 **Academic:** 6
Number of Fall Games: 5 **Number of Spring Games:** 50
Positions Needed for 1999/2000: Catcher, Pitcher, Centerfielder
Schedule: Seton Hall, Maine, Florida Atlantic, Rutges, Illinois State
Style of Play: We play aggressive strong pitching and defensive.

Montclair State College

Normal Avenue
Upper Montclair, NJ 07043
Coach: Norm Shoenig

NCAA III
Red Hawks/Scarlet, White
Phone: (973) 655-5281
Fax: (973) 655-5390

ACADEMIC

Founded: 1908 **Type:** 4 Yr., Public, Coed
Web-site: http://www.montclair.edu/ **SAT/ACT/GPA:** 900
Student/Faculty Ratio: 30:1 **Male/Female Ratio:** 10:1
Undergraduate Enrollment: 9,500 **Graduate Enrollment:** 3,500
Scholarships/Academic: Yes **Athletic:** No **Fin Aid:** Yes
Total Expenses by: Year **In State:** $ 9,228 **Out of State:** $ 10,540
Degrees Conferred: School of Business, School of Arts, College of Humanities, Social Sciences
Programs of Study: School of Business, School of Arts, College of Education and Human Services and Special Programs

ATHLETIC PROFILE

Conference Affiliation: New Jersey Athletic Conference
Program Profile: Pittser Field has natural grass and a 600 capacity. We do 21 weeks for NCAA practice and games. We play 36 Spring games including a Virginia trip and a 10-day trip to either California, North Carolina or Florida with outstanding competition. We play 9 Fall games versus Division I teams including a 2-day, 4-team tournament. Our indoor facilities include a 70' batting cage, 40' short cage and 3 astroturf regulation mounds. We have an outside batting cage on astroturf practice area, 4 cages, 5 soft toss nets, and 4 mounds.
History: Montclair's baseball started with a 6-game season in 1929 and then picked back up again in 1933. The overall record is 1049-527-20 (.664). We won the program's 2nd Division III National Championship in 1993.

New Jersey Institute of Technology

323 University Heights
Newark, NJ 07102
Coach: Dave Sawicki

NCAA II
Highlanders/Red, White, Blue
Phone: (973) 596-5827
Fax: (973) 596-8440

ACADEMIC

Founded: 1881
Type: 4 Yr., Public, Coed, Engineering
Religion: Non-Affiliated
Campus Housing: Yes
Web-site: http://www.njit.edu/
SAT/ACT/GPA: Required
Student/Faculty Ratio: 14;1
Male/Female Ratio: 82:18
Undergraduate Enrollment: 3,400
Graduate Enrollment: 2,500
Scholarships/Academic: Yes **Athletic:** No **Fin Aid:** Yes
Total Expenses by: Year **In State:** $ 11,200 **Out of State:** $ 15,800
Degrees Conferred: BA, BS, BArch, BSCE, BSChemE, BSEE, BSET, BSME, MA, MArch, MS, PhD
Programs of Study: Actuarial Sciences, Architecture, Chemical Engineering, Chemistry, Civil Engineering, Computer Science, Mathematics, Physics, Science, Technology and Society, Statistics

ATHLETIC PROFILE

Conference Affiliation: New York Collegiate Athletic Conference, NYCAC
Program Profile: This is our 1st year of the program at Division I level. Our campus field is 2 years old an has indoor and outdoor batting cages. Our school is making commitment to athletics. NJIT is one of the top academic institutions as per Money Magazine in 1997.
History: In 1997, we made a big jump from low level D III to a very strong D II conference.
Achievements: Our coach is in his 1st year at our school. He built FDU Madison into a Region tournament team and Perennial MAC. We are Middle Atlantic Conference playoffs contenders.

Ocean County College

College Drive
Toms River, NJ 08754
Coach: Bernie Lega

NJCAA III
Vikings/Kelly, Stone
Phone: (732) 255-0345
Fax: (732) 255-0408

ACADEMIC

Type: 2 Yr., Jr. College, Coed
Degrees Conferred: Associate
Programs of Study: Accounting, Broadcasting, Business Administration, Commerce, Management, Civil Engineering Technology, Community Services, Computer Science, Construction Technology, Criminal Justice, Electrical Engineering Technology, Elementary Education, Fire Science, Gerontology, Nursing, Paralegal, Manufacturing Technology, Real Estate, Retail Management

ATHLETIC PROFILE

Conference Affiliation: Garden State Athletic Conference
Program Profile: We play on a natural grass field with measurements of 320 left, 352 leftcenter, 400 left, 362 rightcenter and 320 right.
Roster for 1998 team/In State: 22 **Out of State:** 0 **Out of Country:** 0
Total Number of Varsity/Jr. Varsity: 22 **Percent of Graduation:** 0
Number of Seniors on 1998 Team: 16 **Most Recent Record:** 18 - 12 - 0
Freshmen Receiving Fin Aid/Athletic: 0 **Academic:** 2
Number of Fall Games: 10 **Number of Spring Games:** 36
Positions Needed for 1999/2000: All position and pitcher
Schedule: Brookdale, Gloucester, Camden, Middle State
Style of Play: We play aggressive solid defense and good pitching.

Princeton University

P.O. Box 71
Princeton, NJ 08544
Coach: Scott Bradley

NCAA I
Tigers/Black, Orange
Phone: (609) 258-5059
Fax: (609) 258-4477

ACADEMIC

Type: 4 Yr., Private, Liberal Arts, Coed, Engineering
Founded: 1746
Religion: Non-Affiliated
Campus Housing: Yes
Web-site: http://www.princeton.edu/
SAT/ACT/GPA: 1260+/ 27+
Student/Faculty Ratio: 5:1
Male/Female Ratio: 57:43
Undergraduate Enrollment: 4,500
Graduate Enrollment: 1,700
Scholarships/Academic: No **Athletic:** No **Fin Aid:** Yes
Total Expenses by: Year **In State:** $ 30,690 **Out of State:** $ 30,690
Degrees Conferred: BA, BS, MA, PhD
Programs of Study: Aeronautical Engineering, Anthropology, Archeology, Architectural Engineering, Computer Engineering, Asian Studies, Astrophysics, Biology, Chemistry, Computer Science, Economics, Fine Arts, Geology, History, International Relations, Math, Music, Philosophy, Physics, Political Science, Psychology, Religion, Social Science

ATHLETIC PROFILE

Conference Affiliation: Ivy League Conference
Program Profile: We have an outstanding program with outstanding facilities. Our baseball stadium seats 2,000 and JV field is the same size. We have outdoor cages and the best indoor facility in the Northeast. There is an indoor field, cages, warm-up areas, Etc.
History: Founded in 1864, baseball was the first collegiate sport at Princeton. The first televised game was May 17, 1969. We have made 4 NCAA appearances: 1951, 1965, 1985 and 1991. Our record overall is 1788-1403-46.
Achievements: Set NCAA records; most runs scored (17) in 2nd inning; most batted in (16) in any inning; 1985 District NCAA Coach of the Year; 1985 and 1991 EIBL Champs and were in NCAA's both years. 14 players have ebeen drafted.
Style of Play: We play good, sound fundamental baseball, relying on a combination of good hitting, sound defense and reliable pitching.

Ramapo College of New Jersey

505 Ramopo Valley Road
Mahwah, NJ 07430
Coach: Dan Palumbo
NCAA III
Roadrunners/Scarlet, Gold, White
Phone: (201) 529-7066
Fax: (201) 684-7958

ACADEMIC

Founded: 1969
Type: 4 Yr., Public, Liberal Arts, Coed
Religion: Non-Affiliated
Campus Housing: Yes
Web-site: http://www.ramapo.edu
Undergraduate Enrollment: 4,800
Student/Faculty Ratio: 15:1
Male/Female Ratio: 49:51
Scholarships/Academic: Yes **Athletic:** No **Fin Aid:** Yes
Total Expenses by: Year **In State:** $ 5,578+ **Out of State:** $ 6,763+
Degrees Conferred: BA, BS
Programs of Study: Accounting, American Studies, Biology, Business Administration, Management, Marketing, Chemistry, Clinical Laboratory Science, Communications, Arts, Graphic Design, Journalism, Public Communications, Radio/Television, Writing, Computer Science, Contemporary Arts, Economics, Environmental Science, Environmental Studies, History, Fine Arts, Information Systems, Literature, Law and Society, Mathematics, Metropolitan Studies, Nursing, Physics, Political Science, Social Work, Sociology, Anthropology, Philosophy, Psychology, Elementary Education, Women's Studies, Sociology

ATHLETIC PROFILE

Conference Affiliation: New Jersey Athletic Conference
Program Profile: We take an annual Florida trip. We were 1984 National Championships. We have a newly renovated field and a ball park with dimensions of 330, 380, 400, 380 and 325. The field has natural turf and tournament qualified field specifications.

History: Our college opened its doors in 1970. In 1976, we joined conference and in 1978 we netted a 20-win season. We have had two 20-win seasons and five 30-win seasons.
Achievements: NCAA Division III National Champions in 1984; NCAA Regional Champions in 1984; NJAC Champions in 1984; NJAC Champions in 1980, 1983 and 1984; 7 NCAA Tournament Bid's; 7 All-Americans; 3 NJAC Rookie of the Year, 1 NJAC Athlete of the Year; 1 ECAC Tournament Bid; 8 - 20+ win seasons; 5 - 30+ win seasons.
Style of Play: Aggressive.

Raritan Valley Community College

PO Box 3300
Somerville, NJ 08876
Coach: Gary Cowan
Email: oormosi.raritanval.edu

NJCAA
Golden Lions/Green, Gold
Phone: (908) 218-8868
Fax: (908) 231-8814

ACADEMIC

Founded: 1965 **Type:** 2 Yr., Jr. College, Coed
Undergraduate Enrollment: 4,500 **Graduate Enrollment:** None
Scholarships/Academic: No **Athletic:** No **Fin Aid:** Yes
Total Expenses by: Year **In State:** $ 1,600 **Out of State:** $ 5,700
Degrees Conferred: Associate
Programs of Study: Accounting, Arts, Automotive Technology, Biology, Biological Science, Commercial Arts, Computer Information Systems, Computer Programming, Computer Science, Construction Technology, Criminal Justice, Data Processing, Drafting/Design, Early Childhood Education, Education

ATHLETIC PROFILE

Conference Affiliation: Garden State Athletic Conference
Program Profile: We have a natural grass field, indoor and outdoor pitching moundsan indoor batting cage, a gym, weights, a swimming pool, a trainer/stretching coach and a tarped field.
History: Raritan Valley Community College struggled in baseball until the arrival of Head Coach Gary Cowan. Since 1991, the Golden Lions have appeard in the Region XIX tournament yearly. From 1994 to the present, we have been ranked in the Top 10 nationally among Division III junior colleges.
Achievements: Conference Titles in 1995; Coach of the Year in 1995; drafted player was Carlton McKenzie in 1997 by Pittsburgh Pirates; Tim Dockey - Independent League, Greg Belson 1998, Mike Cavallo in 1996, Bill Maier in 1991 1st team All-Americans.
Coaching: Gary Cowan, Head Coach, compiled a record of 213-154. He played with Houston Astros. John Kroger, Assistant Coach, played with the New York Yankees, the Chicago White Sox and the St. Louis Cardinals.
Roster for 1998 team/In State: 15 **Out of State:** 6 **Out of Country:** 0
Total Number of Varsity/Jr. Varsity: 21 **Most Recent Record:** 33 - 10 - 0
Number of Seniors on 1998 Team: 5 **Positions Needed for 1999/2000:** Undecided
Freshmen Receiving Fin Aid/Athletic: 0 **Academic:** 15
Number of Fall Games: 15 **Number of Spring Games:** 50
Baseball Camp Dates: Available upon request
Schedule: Gloucester CC, Middlesex CC, Brookdale CC, Morris CC, SouthEastern CC, Lenoir CC
Style of Play: We are aggressive, offensively and defensively. We emphasize pitchers, catchers and aggressive base running.

Richard Stockton College

Jimmy Leeds Road
Pomona, NJ 08240
Coach: John Gurzo

NCAA III
Osprey/Black, White
Phone: (609) 652-4217
Fax: (609) 748-5510

ACADEMIC

Founded: 1969
Type: 4 Yr., Public, Liberal Arts, Coed
Religion: Non-Affiliated
Campus Housing: Yes
Web-site: http://www.stockton.edu/
SAT/ACT/GPA: 1150
Student/Faculty Ratio: 16:1
Male/Female Ratio: 1:1.2
Undergraduate Enrollment: 5,600
Graduate Enrollment: 250
Scholarships/Academic: Yes **Athletic:** No **Fin Aid:** Yes
Total Expenses by: Year **In State:** $ 8,000 **Out of State:** $ 8,500
Degrees Conferred: BA, BS
Programs of Study: Actuarial Sciences, Allied Health, Business, Computer Science, Engineering, English, Environmental Science, Journalism, Life Sciences, Marine Biology, Prelaw, Premed, Professional Studies, Social Science, Visual and Performing Arts

ATHLETIC PROFILE

Conference Affiliation: New Jersey Athletic Conference
Program Profile: We play a 36-game Spring schedule and take a Southern trip on Spring break. We do a 9-game Fall schedule. We are in the top-rated NCAA Div. III baseball conference in the nation.
History: We have a 6 year old varsity program.
Achievements: Ranked 12th all-time NCAA Division III, stolen bases in a single season; 1994 stolen bases NCAA All-Division Champion, Gary Gottlob 40-40. The team has an average of over 90 stolen bases/year over the last six seasons.
Coaching: John Gurzo, Head Coach, compiled a 103-69 for six seasons. He is a former pro Senior Professional Baseball League Player.
Style of Play: We do an aggressive offense, an aggressive base running, a consistent pitching and defense, defense, defese.

Rider University

2083 Lawrenceville Road
Lawrenceville, NJ 08648
Coach: Sonny Pittaro

NCAA I
Broncs/Cranberry, White
Phone: (609) 896-5000
Fax: (609) 896-0341

ACADEMIC

Founded: 1865
Type: 4 Yr., Private, Liberal Arts, Coed
Religion: Non-Affiliated
Campus Housing: Yes
Web-site: http://www.rider.edu/
SAT/ACT/GPA: 1055
Student/Faculty Ratio: 13:1
Male/Female Ratio: 48:52
Undergraduate Enrollment: 2,800
Graduate Enrollment: 1,200
Scholarships/Academic: Yes **Athletic:** Yes **Fin Aid:** Yes
Total Expenses by: Year **In State:** $ 15,880 **Out of State:** $ 15,880
Degrees Conferred: AA, AS, BA, BS, MA, MBA
Programs of Study: Business (11 majors), Communications, Computer Sciences, Liberal Arts, Prelaw, Premed, Psychology, Sociology, Teacher Education

ATHLETIC PROFILE

Conference Affiliation: MAAC
Program Profile: We were voted top 100 Division I programs of the decade by Baseball America. We have a grass field that is fully enclosed and seats 1,000 spectators.
History: The program began in 1929 and we have had 56 seasons. We went to College World Series in 1967 and ranked 5th in the nation.
Achievements: 8 NCAA Regional since 1984, East Regional Final Round (final 16 in nation) in 1987; 9 Conference Titles; 34 pros in the last 28 years.
Coaching: Sonny Pittaro, Head Coach, compiled a record of 612 wins since 1971. He was second Vice-President of the American Baseball Coaches Association.
Roster for 1998 team/In State: 19 **Out of State:** 9 **Out of Country:** 0

Total Number of Varsity/Jr. Varsity: 27
Percent of Graduation: 100%
Number of Seniors on 1998 Team: 3
Number of Sophomores on 1998 Team: 6
Number of Fall Games: 3
Number of Spring Games: 50
Most Recent Record: 25 - 25 - 0
Schedule: Delaware, Le Moyne, St. John's, Seton Hall, Rutgers, Villanova
Style of Play: Aggressive and fundamentally strong.

Rowan University

201 Mullica Hill road
Glassboro, NJ 08028
Coach: John Colege

NCAA III
Profs/Brown, Gold
Phone: (609) 256-4687
Fax: (609) 256-4916

ACADEMIC

Founded: 1923
Type: 4 Yr., Public, Liberal Arts, Coed
Religion: Non-Affiliated
Campus Housing: Yes
Web-site: http://www.rowan.edu/
SAT/ACT/GPA: 1040-1190
Student/Faculty Ratio: 17:1
Male/Female Ratio: 4:5
Undergraduate Enrollment: 8,941
Graduate Enrollment: None
Scholarships/Academic: Yes **Athletic:** No **Fin Aid:** Yes
Total Expenses by: Year **In State:** $ 9,040 **Out of State:** $ 12,170
Degrees Conferred: BA, BS, MA, MS, MBA
Programs of Study: Art, Biological Science, Chemistry, Communications, Computer Science, Economics, Elementary Education, English, Engineering, Geography, Health and Physical Education, History, Law/Justice, Liberal Studies, Mathematics, Music, Physical Science, Physics, Political Science, Psychology, School Nursing, Sociology, Spanish, Theatre

ATHLETIC PROFILE

Conference Affiliation: New Jersey Athletic Conference
Program Profile: We play on a natural grass field with dimensions of 320', 360' and 320'.
History: Play began in 1941 and was stopped in 1947 because of World War II. In 15 seasons, the Profs have an all-time record of 797-490-16 for a .618 winning percentage.
Achievements: NCAA Division III National Champs in 1978 and 1979; 9 NCAA Division III Regional Tournaments Appearances in 1976, 1977, 1978, 1979, 1980, 1984, 1986, 1993 and 1996.

Rutgers University - University of New Jersey

P.O. Box 5061
New Brunswick, NJ 08903
Coach: Fred Hill

NCAA I
Scarlet Knights/Scarlet
Phone: (732) 445-3553
Fax: (732) 445-4623

ACADEMIC

Type: 4 Yr., Public, Liberal Arts, Coed, Engineering
Founded: 1766
Religion: Diverse
Campus Housing: Yes
Web-site: http://www.rutgers.edu/athletics
SAT/ACT/GPA: 1100
Student/Faculty Ratio: 22:1
Male/Female Ratio: 49:51
Undergraduate Enrollment: 22,470
Graduate Enrollment: 9,500
Scholarships/Academic: Yes **Athletic:** Yes **Fin Aid:** Yes
Total Expenses by: Year **In State:** $ 10,239 **Out of State:** $ 13,334
Degrees Conferred: BA, BS, MA, PhD
Programs of Study: Arts, Business and Management, Communications, Engineering, Environmental Studies, Languages, Life Sciences, Nursing, Physical Education, Premed, Psychology, Social Sciences, Political Science, English

ATHLETIC PROFILE

Conference Affiliation: Atlantic 10 Conference

Rutgers University - Camden

3rd and Linden Street
Camden, NJ 08102
Coach: Keith Williams

NCAA III
Scarlet Raptors/Scarlet, Black
Phone: (609) 225-6198
Fax: (609) 225-6024

ACADEMIC

Founded: 1927
Religion: Non-Affiliated
Web-site: http://www.camden-www.rutgers.edu/
Student/Faculty Ratio: 15:1
Undergraduate Enrollment: 3,455
Scholarships/Academic: Yes **Athletic:** No
Total Expenses by: Year **In State:** $ 6,105
Type: 4 Yr., Public, Liberal Arts, Coed
Campus Housing: Yes
SAT/ACT/GPA: 1030
Male/Female Ratio: 1:1
Graduate Enrollment: 1,587
Fin Aid: Yes
Out of State: $ 10,986
Degrees Conferred: BA, BS, MA, MS, MSW
Programs of Study: Bachelor of Arts: Afro-American Studies, Art, Biology, Chemistry, Computer Science, Criminal Justice, Economics, English, French, German, History, Student-Proposed Major, Mathematics, Music, Philosophy, Political Science, Psychology, General Studies, Social Work, Sociology, Spanish, Theatre Arts, Urban Studies; Bachelor of Science: Biomedical Technology

ATHLETIC PROFILE

Conference Affiliation: New Jersey Athletic Conference
Program Profile: Rutgers Camden plays its home games at the newly refurbished Memorial Park in Cinnaminson, New Jersey. The team will eventually play in a new 7,000-seat stadium to be built 2 blocks from campus. The new stadium will be the home of an independent minor league team.
History: Rutgers Camden has fielded a baseball team since 1951. From 1956 to 1981, Rutgers Camden was a member of the New Jersey Athletic Conference (NJAC).
Achievements: 1996 Coach of the Year; Won Delaware Valley Conference Championships in 1957, 1958, 1960, 1961, 1966, 1967, 1968 and 1970.
Coaching: Keith Williams, Head Coach, entered his 1st year with the program. He was coach and hitting instructor for various club teams in Australia in 1991-1994. Michael Tomasetti and John Wink - Assistant Coaches.
Roster for 1998 team/In State: 19 **Out of State:** 0 **Out of Country:** 0
Total Number of Varsity/Jr. Varsity: 0 **Percent of Graduation:** 100%
Number of Fall Games: 0 **Number of Spring Games:** 25
Positions Needed for 1999/2000: Pitcher **Baseball Camp Dates:** TBA
Most Recent Record: 6 - 19 - 0
Schedule: William Paterson, Montclair State University, College of New Jersey, Allentown, Rowan
Style of Play: We play scrappy with a no quit attitude.

Rutgers University - Newark

42 Warren Street
Newark, NJ 07102
Coach: Hyman Stanford

NCAA III
Scarlet Raiders/Red, White, Black
Phone: (973) 353-5474
Fax: (973) 353-1431

ACADEMIC

Type: 4 Yr., Public, Liberal Arts, Coed, Engineering
Religion: Non-Affiliated
Web-site: http://www.rutger.edu/newark/
Founded: 1766
Campus Housing: Yes
SAT/ACT/GPA: None

Student/Faculty Ratio: 12:1 **Male/Female Ratio:** 46:54
Undergraduate Enrollment: 6,000 **Graduate Enrollment:** 3,500
Scholarships/Academic: Yes **Athletic:** No **Fin Aid:** Yes
Total Expenses by: Year **In State:** $ 7,500 **Out of State:** $ 11,000
Degrees Conferred: BA, BS
Programs of Study: Business, Marketing, Management, Computer Science, Literature, Education, Criminal Justice, Mathematics, Prelaw, Engineering, Psychology, Premed, Social Sciences

ATHLETIC PROFILE

Conference Affiliation: New Jersey Athletic Conference
Program Profile: The Scarlet Raiders play in the tough New Jersey Athletic Conference where four teams out of ten have won the World Series. We have a great ball park, sort of like Fenway in downtown Newark. It has natural grass and has a seating capacity of 450.
History: The baseball program began around 1930 but we have only been recognized as a legitimate program since 1990 when we went 26-11.
Achievements: Tom Kaechele was a New Jersey Coach of the Year in 1992 and 1994. Since 1990, our program has been to the NCAA Regionals 4 times. He had 8 All-Americans, 8 players drafted and 2 signed as a free-agent at the try-outs.

Saint Peter's College

2461 Kennedy Boulevard
Jersey City, NJ 07306
Coach: Dan O'Lear

NCAA I
Peacocks/Peacock Blue, White
Phone: (201) 915-9459
Fax: (201) 915-9102

ACADEMIC

Founded: 1872 **Type:** 4 Yr., Private, Liberal Arts, Coed
Religion: Roman Catholic (Jesuit) **Campus Housing:** Yes
Web-site: http://www.spc.edu/ **SAT/ACT/GPA:** 750+
Student/Faculty Ratio: 14:1 **Male/Female Ratio:** 45:55
Undergraduate Enrollment: 3,000 **Graduate Enrollment:** 800
Scholarships/Academic: Yes **Athletic:** Yes **Fin Aid:** Yes
Total Expenses by: Year **In State:** $ 18,218 **Out of State:** $ 18,218
Degrees Conferred: AA, AAS, BA, BS, MA, MBA, Med
Programs of Study: Accounting, American Studies, Art History, Biological Chemistry, Biology, Business Management, Chemistry, Clinical Laboratory, Medical Technology, Toxilogy, Computer Science, Economics, Mathematics, Elementary Education, English, History, Marketing, Management, Political Science, Philosophy, Physics, Psychology, Sociology, Theology

ATHLETIC PROFILE

Conference Affiliation: Metro Atlantic Athletic Conference
Program Profile: We play a NCAA Division I schedule that goes from early March to middle May. We play at Joseph J. Jaroschak Field which opened in 1989 in Lincoln Park in Jersey City. The dimensions are: LF 330, LC 370, CF 404, RC 370 and RF 330. The field opened for the1990 season. The Rev.Victor R.Yanitelli, S.J. Recreational Life Center opened in 1975. It is a multi-purpose facility with a huge air-supported rooftop bubble that covers 5 tennis courts and a running track. It also serves as an open training area for baseball, softball, soccer and football.
History: The program began in 1935. We were MAAC Champs in 1994 (last play in to W.VA) and qualified for MAAC Tournament 1996.
Achievements: 1992 and 1995 MAAC South Coach of the Year; 1994 and 1990 NJ Division I Coach of the Year; 1990-1994 NJ Division I Coach of the Year; 1994 MAAC Champs; member of USA Baseball's Ambassador Committeee; 1994-1995 USA Baseball's Laison to Cuba's National Team; 6 players in pros.
Style of Play: We play scrappy, hit and run, steal bases, bunt and do situationnal hitting.

Salem Community College

460 Hollywood Avenue
Carneys Point, NJ 08069-2799
Coach: Greg DeCastro
Email: uena@prodigy.com

NJCAA
Oaks/Green, White
Phone: (609) 351-2693
Fax: (609) 351-2690

ACADEMIC

Founded: 1972
Type: 2 Yr., Public, Liberal Arts, Coed
Web-site: http://www.salem.cc.nj.us
SAT/ACT/GPA: None
Undergraduate Enrollment: 1,100
Graduate Enrollment: None
Scholarships/Academic: Yes **Athletic:** Yes **Fin Aid:** Yes
Total Expenses by: Year **In State:** $ 3,000 **Out of State:** $ 3,000
Degrees Conferred: AA, AS
Programs of Study: Accounting, Agricultural Technology, Biology, Biological Science, Business Administration, Commerce, Management, Chemistry, Communications, Community Services, Computer Information Services, Computer Technology, Criminal Justice, Drafting and Design, Journalism, Legal, Health Education, Nursing, Physical Education, Political Science, Office Management, Social Science, Sociology

ATHLETIC PROFILE

Conference Affiliation: NJCAA Region XIX
Program Profile: We play Division II and do tuition scholarships only. We have a natural field with a rural setting. Our season goes from March through May. Our scrimmage season is in the Fall. We have no dormitories but there are privately operated apartments across the street from the campus.
History: Since 1972, we have advanced to the semi-finals of the Regional Tournament in 1996.
Achievements: We were at semi-finals in the Regional Tournament in 1996. We have had 9 All-Region players in the last 6 years.
Coaching: Greg DeCastro, Head Coach, did his 1st year in 1997-1998. John Ditzler - Assistant Coach.
Style of Play: We play aggressive, fundamental, "throw strikes and play good defense".

Seton Hall University

400 S Orange Avenue
South Orange, NJ 07079
Coach: Mike Sheppard

NCAA I
Pirates/Blue, White
Phone: (973) 761-9557
Fax: (973) 761-9061

ACADEMIC

Founded: 1856
Type: 4 Yr., Private, Liberal Arts, Coed
Religion: Catholic
Campus Housing: Yes
Web-site: http://www.shu.edu/
SAT/ACT/GPA: 960-1150
Student/Faculty Ratio: 16:1
Male/Female Ratio: 1:1
Undergraduate Enrollment: 4,600
Graduate Enrollment: 4,500
Scholarships/Academic: Yes **Athletic:** Yes **Fin Aid:** Yes
Total Expenses by: Year **In State:** $ 21,000 **Out of State:** $ 21,000
Degrees Conferred: BA, BS, MS, MA, PhD, EdD
Programs of Study: 40 majors at the undergraduate level, as well as many minors, certificates and special programs that include: Business, Arts, Sciences, Nursing, Education, Theology, Law

ATHLETIC PROFILE

Conference Affiliation: Big East Conference
Program Profile: The Seton Hall baseball program is one of the Northeast's & nation's most successful programs. The Pirates play on a natural field located on campus & is named after one of the Seton Hall's most successful coaches, Owen T. Carroll. Seton Hall's baseball field seats 1,500.

History: Seton Hall's baseball program began in 1863. It sports an all-time mark of 1,516-830-20 in 2,367 games played. Seton Hall has participated in the NCAA Tournament 11 times including two College World Series Appearances in 1974 and 1975. Since joining the Big East, the Pirates have won and league crown (1987) and appeared in the Big East Tournament a record of 11 times.
Achievements: Current Pirate Head Coach Mike Sheppard has been honored as the Big East Coach of the Year three times (1985, 1987 and 1989). We were 1987 Big East Champions. The Pirate program has produced 9 All-Americans. Under Sheppard, the program has had 70 players sign professional contracts including six from the 1997 squad.
Coaching: Mike Sheppard, Head Coach, has been at Seton Hall for 27 years. He ranks among the top 20 active coaches in winning percentage. He compiled a record of 819-405-9. Robert Sheppard and Ed Lyons, Assistant Coaches, are responsible for the pitching. Fred Honke,Volunteer Assistant, is responsible for the hitting.
Style of Play: We are aggressive and hustle.

Stevens Institute of Technology

Castle Point Terrace
Hoboken, NJ 07030
Coach: Mike Lippencott

NCAA III
Ducks/Red, Grey
Phone: (201) 216-8038
Fax: (201) 216-8244

ACADEMIC

Type: 4 Yr., Private, Some, Coed, Engineering
Founded: 1870
Religion: Non-Affiliated
Campus Housing: Yes
Web-site: http://www.stevens-tech.ecu/
SAT/ACT/GPA: 1100 at lEast/3.5
Student/Faculty Ratio: 9:1
Male/Female Ratio: 4:1
Undergraduate Enrollment: 1,400
Graduate Enrollment: None
Scholarships/Academic: Yes **Athletic:** No
Fin Aid: Yes
Total Expenses by: Year **In State:** $ 26,000
Out of State: $ 26,000
Degrees Conferred: BE, BA, BS, ME, MS, PhD
Programs of Study: Applied Mathematics, Biochemistry, Biology, Chemistry, Computer Information Systems, Computer Science, Engineering, English, History, Humanities, Liberal Arts, Management Information System, Material Science, Mathematics, Optics, Philosophy, Physics, Polymer Science, Predentistry, Prelaw, Premed, Science, Statistic, Telecommunications, Water Resources

ATHLETIC PROFILE

Conference Affiliation: ECAC, IAC
Achievements: IAC Coach of the Year in 1994; Conference Champions in IAC in 1994; Youth camp dates ran well in 1996. We have limited numbers but we are growing.
Coaching: Mike Lippencott - Head Coach.

Sussex County Community College

One College Hill
Newton, NJ 07860
Coach: Todd Poltersdorf

NJCAA
Skylanders/Royal Blue, Kelly Green
Phone: (973) 300-2230
Fax: (973) 300-2254

ACADEMIC

Type: 2 Yr., Jr. College, Coed
Campus Housing: No
Degrees Conferred: Associate
Programs of Study: Accounting, Art/Fine Arts, Biology, Biological Science, Broadcasting, Business Administration, Commerce, Management, Chemistry, Computer Information Systems, Criminal Justice, Graphic Arts, Human Services, Mathematics

ATHLETIC PROFILE

Conference Affiliation: Garden State Athletic Conference
Program Profile: We are a Division III Junior College and play all our home games at Skylands Park, Home of the New York, Penn League and New Jersey Cardinals. The stadium has a seating capacity is 4,800 and natural grass.
History: It is my 4th year here, 3rd as Head Coach. We have increased our wins by 7 for the last 2 years. This season is the most wins in school's history (17).
Achievements: 2 players made to the Conference and to the Region.
Coaching: Todd Poltersdorf - Head Coach. Berine Nousky - Assistant. Jeff Sponder - Assistant.
Style of Play: We play very aggressive, like to run and take pride in defense.

College of New Jersey
(Former Trenton State)

P.O. Box 7718
Ewing, NJ 08628
Coach: Rick Dell
Email: mchugh@vm.tenj.edu

NCAA III
Lions/Navy, Gold
Phone: (609) 771-2230
Fax: (609) 637-5133

ACADEMIC

Founded: 1855
Type: 4 Yr., Public, Liberal Arts, Coed
Religion: Non-Affiliated
Campus Housing: Yes
Web-site: http://www.trenton.edu/
SAT/ACT/GPA: 1100+
Student/Faculty Ratio: 15:1
Male/Female Ratio: Unknown
Undergraduate Enrollment: 5,167
Graduate Enrollment: 944
Scholarships/Academic: Yes **Athletic:** No **Fin Aid:** Yes
Total Expenses by: Year **In State:** $ 10,123 **Out of State:** $ 12,398
Degrees Conferred: BA, BS, BFA, BSN, MA, MD
Programs of Study: Childhood Education, Economics, Education, Engineering Science, Health and Physical Education, Music, Nursing, Philosophy, Physics, Political Science, Psychology, Secondary Education, Sociology, Special Education for the Developmentally Handicapped

ATHLETIC PROFILE

Conference Affiliation: New Jersey Athletic Conference
History: This year is 75th anniversary of our baseball program. We had NCAA bids in 1979, 1981, 1985, 1986,1987, 1990, 1991, 1992, 1993, 1994 and 1998. In 1991we were a finalist in College World Series.
Achievements: 20 All-American players since 1979; 15 players signed pro contracts since 1979.
Coaching: Rick Dell, Head Coach, started with the program in 1982 and compiled a record of 429-233-8. He was named Coach of the Year in 1991 and 1994. Brian Carter - Assistant.
Roster for 1998 team/In State: 90 **Out of State:** 10 **Out of Country:** 0
Total Number of Varsity/Jr. Varsity: 42 **Baseball Camp Dates:** July
Number of Fall Games: 9 **Number of Spring Games:** 36
Schedule: Columbia, Wilmington, Montclair, William Paterson, John Hopkins, Kean

Union County College

1033 Springfield Avenue
Cranford, NJ 07016
Coach: Vinnie Retino

NJCAA
Owls/Red, White, Black
Phone: (908) 709-7093
Fax: (908) 709-8092

ACADEMIC

Founded: 1933
Type: 2 Yr., Jr. College, Coed
Student/Faculty Ratio: 25:1
Male/Female Ratio: 36:64

Undergraduate Enrollment: 10,900 **Graduate Enrollment:** None
Scholarships/Academic: No **Athletic:** Yes **Fin Aid:** Yes
Total Expenses by: Year **In State:** $ 1,600 **Out of State:** $ 5,600
Degrees Conferred: Associate
Programs of Study: Accounting, American Studies, Architecture, Art/Fine Arts, Biology, Biological Science, Business Administration, Commerce, Management, Chemistry, Civil Engineering, Communications, Computer Science, Computer Information

ATHLETIC PROFILE

Conference Affiliation: Garden State Conference

William Paterson College

300 Pompton Road
Wayne, NJ 07470
Coach: Jeff Albies

NCAA III
Pioneers/Orange, Black
Phone: (973) 720-2210
Fax: (973) 720-3017

ACADEMIC

Founded: 1855 **Type:** 4 Yr., Public, Liberal Arts, Coed
Religion: Non-Affiliated **Campus Housing:** Yes
Web-site: http://www.wilpaterson.edu/ **SAT/ACT/GPA:** 1000+/ 21
Student/Faculty Ratio: 19:1 **Male/Female Ratio:** 45:55
Undergraduate Enrollment: 10,500 **Graduate Enrollment:** 2,300
Scholarships/Academic: Yes **Athletic:** No **Fin Aid:** Yes
Total Expenses by: Year **In State:** $ 8,250 **Out of State:** $ 10,300
Degrees Conferred: BA, BS, BFA, MA, MS, MBA, Med
Programs of Study: Business and Management, Communications, Health Sciences, Psychology, Social Sciences, Teacher Education, Visual and Performing Arts

ATHLETIC PROFILE

Conference Affiliation: New Jersey Athletic Conference
Program Profile: We are a nationally recognized Division III program. We won 2 NCAA Division II National Championships in 1992 and 1996. We won Regional Championships and 11 Conference Championships in the last 15 years.
History: William Paterson is among the nation's elite in college baseball. Since 1975, the baseball program has a 639-235 win-loss record.
Achievements: 25 All-American baseball players; 19 players drafted in the 20 years; 11 Conference Championships in the past 16 years; Dan Pasqua - New York Yankees - Chicago White Sox - 10 years in the Big League.
Coaching: Jeff Albies, Head Coach, is entering his 23rd year of coaching. Bob Lautherhahn , Assistant Coach, entered his 16th year as a part- time coach. Tom Kraljic,Assistant Coach, entered 10th year as a part-time coach. Sean Rooney, Assistant Coach, entered his 4th year.
Style of Play: We are aggressive and like to run.

NEW MEXICO

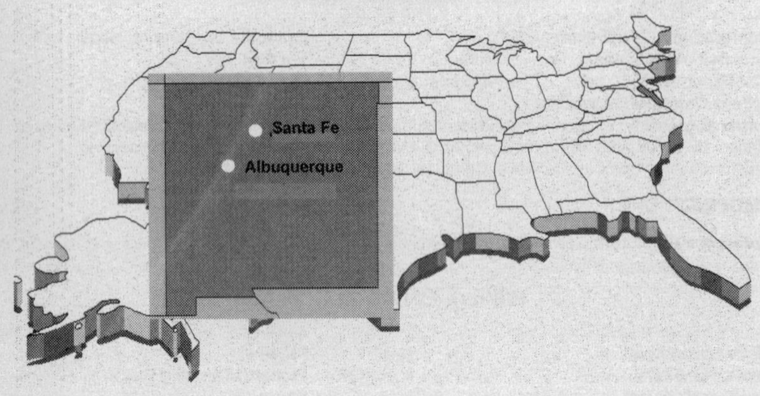

SCHOOL	CITY	AFFILIATION 99	PAGE
College of the Southwest	Hobbs	NAIA	551
Eastern New Mexico University	Portales	NCAA II	551
New Mexico Highlands University	Las Vegas	NCAA II	552
New Mexico Junior College	Hobbs	NJCAA	552
New Mexico Military Institute	Roswell	NJCAA	553
New Mexico State University	Las Cruces	NCAA I	554
University of New Mexico	Albuquerque	NCAA I	554

College of the SouthWest

6610 Lovingston Highway
Hobbs, NM 88240
Coach: Jim Marshall

NAIA
Mustangs/Red, Blue, White
Phone: (505) 392-6561
Fax: (505) 392-6006

ACADEMIC

Founded: 1962
Type: 4 Yr., Private, Liberal Arts, Coed
Religion: Non-Denominational
Campus Housing: Yes
Web-site: http://www.csw.edu
SAT/ACT/GPA: None
Student/Faculty Ratio: 14:1
Male/Female Ratio: 25:75
Undergraduate Enrollment: 682
Graduate Enrollment: None
Scholarships/Academic: Yes **Athletic:** Yes **Fin Aid:** Yes
Total Expenses by: Year **In State:** $ 8,790 **Out of State:** $ 8,790
Degrees Conferred: BA, BS, BAS, BBA
Programs of Study: Accounting, Biology, Business Administration, Chemistry, Elementary Education, English, Fine Arts, Geology, History, Management, Marketing, Mathematics, Psychology, Secondary Education, Social Science, Special Education

ATHLETIC PROFILE

Conference Affiliation: Independent Conference

Eastern New Mexico University

Station 17
Portales, NM 88130
Coach: Phil Clabaugh

NCAA II
Greyhounds/Green, Silver, White
Phone: (505) 562-2889
Fax: (505) 562-2822

ACADEMIC

Founded: 1934
Type: 4 Yr., Public, Liberal Arts, Coed
Religion: Non-Affiliated
Campus Housing: Yes
Web-site: http://www.enmu.edu
SAT/ACT/GPA: 700/17 min
Student/Faculty Ratio: 22:1
Male/Female Ratio: 40:60
Undergraduate Enrollment: 4,000
Graduate Enrollment: 500
Scholarships/Academic: Yes **Athletic:** Yes **Fin Aid:** Yes
Total Expenses by: Year **In State:** $ 4,840 **Out of State:** $ 9,106
Degrees Conferred: AA, AS, BS, BFA, BAE, BBA, BM, BSE, MA, MS, MBA
Programs of Study: Accounting, Agricultural, Business Management, Anthropology, Biological Science, Business Administration, Chemistry, Communications, Computer Science, Economics, Education, French, Geology, History, Information Science, Journalism, Marketing, Mathematics, Personnel Management, Physics, Political Science, Psychology, Social Science, Statistics

ATHLETIC PROFILE

Estimated Number of Baseball Scholarships: 6.5
Conference Affiliation: Lone Star Conference
Program Profile: Greyhound Field has natural & dimensions of 406' to the center, 372' to the left & 362' down right field line. It has a seating for 2,000 with plenty of observation space in the outfield.
History: Our program was resurrected in 1992. We had continual improvement over the six years. We finished as high as 2nd in the conference. Coach Phil Clabaugh started the program up in 1991.
Achievements: ABCA NCAA Division II South Central Region players: Andy Gray (1994), Shane Shallenger (1995), Steve Montaya (1996), Mike Dunston (1997), Bryan Silva (1997). Draftees were John Arnold (C, by Atlanta Braves in 1996) and Chris Price (P/OF by Colorado Rockies in 1997).
Coaching: Phil Clabaugh, Head Coach, started his 6th year at Eastern. He was 4 years at Western New Mexico. In his first season there, they won the Rocky Mountain Athletic Conference

Championship by winning the post-season tournament. He received his BA and MA from Northwest Oklahoma.
Roster for 1998 team/In State: 10 **Out of State:** 14 **Out of Country:** 0
Total Number of Varsity/Jr. Varsity: 24 **Percent of Graduation:** 40%
Number of Seniors on 1998 Team: 6 **Number of Sophomores on 1998 Team:** 0
Freshmen Receiving Fin Aid/Athletic: 2 **Number of Spring Games:** 60
Positions Needed for 1999/2000: Catcher, Outfielder (center-right), Pitchers
Schedule: Texas Tech, University of New Mexico, New Mexico State, St. Mary's, Texas A&M-Kingsville, Abilene Christian
Style of Play: We are tough, hard-nosed, hard working and fundamentally sound.

New Mexico Highlands University

Baseball Office
Las Vegas, NM 87701
Coach: Steve Jones

NCAA II
Cowboys/Purple, White
Phone: (505) 454-3587
Fax: (505) 454-3001

ACADEMIC

Founded: 1893 **Type:** 4 Yr., Public, Liberal Arts, Coed
Web-site: Not Available **SAT/ACT/GPA:** NCAA Minimum
Student/Faculty Ratio: 17:1 **Male/Female Ratio:** 42:58
Undergraduate Enrollment: 2,250 **Graduate Enrollment:** 821
Scholarships/Academic: Yes **Athletic:** Yes **Fin Aid:** Yes
Total Expenses by: Year **In State:** $ 4,776 **Out of State:** $ 9,474
Degrees Conferred: BA, BS, MA, MS, MBA, Med, MSW
Programs of Study: Accounting, Biological Sciences, Business Administration, Computer Technology, Environmental Sciences, History, Journalism, Management Information Systems, Marketing, Mathematics, Physical Fitness and Movements, Political Science, Preprofessional Programs, Psychology, Radio and Television Technology, Recreation and Leisure Service, Social Science, Technical Education, Travel and Tourism

ATHLETIC PROFILE

Conference Affiliation: Mile High Intercollegiate Baseball League, RMAC
Program Profile: We are rebuilding the program. We have good playing facilities :elevation 7,000 ft, 56 games per season and cold climate until mid-March. In case of cold weathe, we have an indoor facility. We take a Spring break trip.
History: Our program began 1956,;1967 NAIA National Champions;1968 NAIA National Runner-Up.
Achievements: NAIA District VII Coach of the Year 1992, 2 players drafted.
Total Number of Varsity/Jr. Varsity: 26 **Percent of Graduation:** 60%
Style of Play: We keep the game simple, play for big inning if possible. We play very aggressive base running.

New Mexico Junior College

5317 Lovington Highway
Hobbs, NM 88240
Coach: Ray Birmingham

NJCAA
Thunderbirds/Gold, Scarlet
Phone: (505) 392-5503
Fax: (505) 392-5871

ACADEMIC

Founded: 1966 **Type:** 2 Yr., Public, Coed
Religion: Non-Affiliated **Campus Housing:** Yes
Student/Faculty Ratio: 15:1 **Male/Female Ratio:** 1:4
Undergraduate Enrollment: 2,700 **Graduate Enrollment:** None
Scholarships/Academic: Yes **Athletic:** Yes **Fin Aid:** Yes

Total Expenses by: Semester **In State:** $ 1,800 **Out of State:** $ 1,800
Degrees Conferred: Associate
Programs of Study: Accounting, Agricultural, Automotive Technology, Business/Finance, Biological Science, Chemistry, Computer, Construction, Cosmetology, Drafting/Design, Education, Medical, Petroleum, Nursing, Recreation, Sports Medicine, Science, Theatre, Welding

ATHLETIC PROFILE

Estimated Number of Baseball Scholarships: 12
Conference Affiliation: Western Junior College Athletic Conference
Program Profile: We have a 60 game semester, 56 regular season games,a big league park & annual temperatures of 75°F. We have an outstanding facility & one of the top programs in the country.
History: The program began in 1990 and has a record of 403-145. We have been nationally ranked 6 out of 9 years. We got two conference titles, two regional runner-ups and 52 drafted players.
Achievements: 6 All-Americans; 52 drafted players.
Coaching: Ray Birmingham, Head Coach, is in his 6th year at NMJC. He won the 1981 NM Class AAAA State Championship. Has 19 years of coaching experience. Kevin Lallmann, Assistant Coach, is in his 6th season at NMJC.
Style of Play: We have good pitching and a strong offensive team.

New Mexico Military Institute

101 West College Blvd
Roswell, NM 88201
Coach: Dale Smith

NJCAA
Broncos/Scarlet, Black
Phone: (505) 624-8282
Fax: (505) 624-8287

ACADEMIC

Founded: 1891
Type: 2 Yr., Public, Coed
Religion: Non-Affiliated
Campus Housing: Yes
Web-site: Not-Available
SAT/ACT/GPA: 700/17
Student/Faculty Ratio: 18:1
Male/Female Ratio: 74:26
Undergraduate Enrollment: 435
Graduate Enrollment: None
Scholarships/Academic: Yes **Athletic:** Yes **Fin Aid:** Yes
Total Expenses by: Year **In State:** $ 5,480 **Out of State:** $ 7,175
Degrees Conferred: AA, High School Diploma
Programs of Study: Accounting, Art, Banking/Finance, Biology, Business, Chemistry, Computer, Criminal, Economics, English, History, Humanities, Law, Liberal Arts, Mathematics, Military Science, Physics, Preengineering, Prelaw, Premed, Prevet, Science, Social Science, Sports Administration

ATHLETIC PROFILE

Conference Affiliation: Independent (RegionV)
Program Profile: We play in our recently completed $700,000.00 baseball field. It is the only sport facility on campus. It has natural grass, permanent bleachers, brick walls, a press area and a concession area.
History: We are currently in 7th year.
Achievements: We won Frontier Conference Championship and the WJCAC Championship. Gene Hardman was the only athlete to win 2 consecutive All-America honors in baseball for his work as catcher. He was a member of the Bronco team which also included Dallas Cowboy great Roger Staubach, who played center and was a relief pitcher.
Coaching: Dale Smith, Head Coach, has been sole mentor of the Bronco baseball program since 1991. He graduated from NMMI in 1974 where he was a member of the Bronco football team. He attended Panhandle OK State, until a career-ending injury occurred. He played baseball 13 years as catcher which saw him advance to the semi-pros.
Style of Play: We play aggressive, make things happen, use starting runners and do not go by the book.

New Mexico State University

Box 30001, Dept 3145
Las Cruces, NM 88003
Coach: Rocky Ward
Email: nmsu32@prodigy.net

NCAA I
Aggies/Crimson, White
Phone: (505) 646-5813
Fax: (505) 646-2741

ACADEMIC

Founded: 1888
Type: 4 Yr., Public, Coed, Engineering
Religion: Non-Affiliated
Campus Housing: Yes
Web-site: http://www.nmsu.edu
SAT/ACT/GPA: 1000/20/2.5
Student/Faculty Ratio: 18.2:1
Male/Female Ratio: 50:50
Undergraduate Enrollment: 15,000
Graduate Enrollment: None
Scholarships/Academic: Yes **Athletic:** Yes **Fin Aid:** Yes
Total Expenses by: Year **In State:** $ 7,288 **Out of State:** $ 12,592
Degrees Conferred: AA, AS, AAS, BA, BS, BFA, BSA, BSN, BM, BSPE, BSW, MA, MS, MBA, MFA
Programs of Study: Agricultural Business Management, Agricultural Engineering, Agriculture, Banking/Finance, Biochemistry, City/Community/Regional Planning, Civil Engineering, Communications, Computer Science, Fisheries, Geological Science, Engineering, Geology, Horticulture, Latin American Studies, Mexican-American Studies, Microbiology, Range Management

ATHLETIC PROFILE

Estimated Number of Baseball Scholarships: 4.5
Conference Affiliation: Big West Conference
Program Profile: We are a young growing program. In 1997, we got new lights. In 1998, we got new dugouts,a locker office, locker rooms, seating, an oufield fence, a 1999 scoreboard, a concession stand, public restrooms, additional seating, a press box, a grass field, perfect weather (no rain-warm weather) and a 2,000 occupancy.
History: NMSU started baseball in 1962. The Aggies have a career record of 712-838 overall and are still making progress.
Achievements: Our 1997 team ranked 5th in scoring; 1998 team 3rd in scoring (10-15), 4th batting average (351); 5 All-Conference players; 1 Freshman All-American.
Coaching: Rocky Ward, Head Coach, he is in his 3rd year with the program. He compiled a record of 44-61 for two years. He is responsible for the hitters. Tim Touma, Assistant Coach, is in his 3rd year with the program and is responsible for pitchers. Brad Meador, Assistant Coach, is in his 2nd year with the program and is responsible for the defense.
Roster for 1998 team/In State: 16 **Out of State:** 27 **Out of Country:** 1
Total Number of Varsity/Jr. Varsity: 44 **Most Recent Record:** 23 - 28 - 0
Number of Seniors on 1998 Team: 11 **Number of Sophomores on 1998 Team:** 0
Freshmen Receiving Fin Aid/Athletic: 6 **Academic:** 7
Baseball Camp Dates: Weekends in Spring **Number of Spring Games:** 56
Positions Needed for 1999/2000: Pitchers, Catcher, 3rd Base 1st Base
Schedule: Long Beach, Washington State, Utah, Fullerton, Nebraska, Nevada
Style of Play: We play solid defense and pitch with a powerful offense.

University of New Mexico

1414 University SE
Albuquerque, NM 87131
Coach: Rich Alday

NCAA I
Lobos/Cherry, Silver
Phone: (505) 925-5720
Fax: (505) 925-5509

ACADEMIC

Type: 4 Yr., Public, Liberal Arts, Coed, Engineering
Founded: 1887
Religion: Non-Affiliated
Campus Housing: Yes
Web-site: http://www.unm.edu/
SAT/ACT/GPA: 850/2.25

Student/Faculty Ratio: 19:1 **Male/Female Ratio:** 45:55
Undergraduate Enrollment: 25,000 **Graduate Enrollment:** 3,500
Scholarships/Academic: Yes **Athletic:** Yes **Fin Aid:** Yes
Total Expenses by: Year **In State:** $ 6,683.80 **Out of State:** $ 12,693.40
Degrees Conferred: BS, MS, MS, PhD
Programs of Study: Over 170 accredited disciplines; Accounting, Anthropology, Architecture, Art, Art Education, Art History, Biochemistry, Biology, Business Computer Systems, Business Education, Engineering, Communications, Computer Science, Creative Writing, Criminology, Dance, Earth Science, Elementary Education, Economics, Music, Nursing, Pharmacy, Philosophy, Physical Education, Physical Therapy, Sociology

ATHLETIC PROFILE

Conference Affiliation: Western Athletic Conference
Achievements: 1995 Mark Wulfert was drafted by the San Diego Padres in the 11th round.

NEW YORK

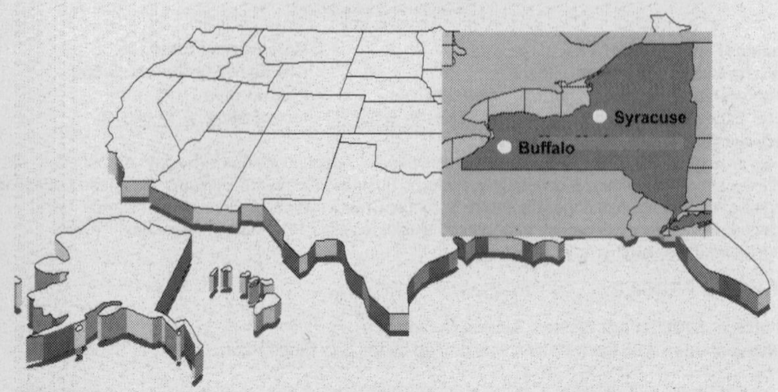

SCHOOL	CITY	AFFILIATION 99	PAGE
Adelphi University	Garden City	NCAA II	558
Alfred State College	Alfred	NJCAA I	558
Baruch College	New York City	NCAA III	559
Broome Community College	Binghamton	NJCAA	560
Canisius College	Bufallo	NCAA I	560
CUNY - Bronx Community College	Bronx	NJCAA	561
CUNY - John Jay College of Criminal Justice	New York	NCAA III	561
CUNY - Lehman College	Bronx	NCAA III	562
CUNY - Manhattan Community College	New York	NJCAA	562
CUNY - Queens College	Flushing	NCAA II	563
CUNY - Queensborough Community College	Bayside	NJCAA	563
Clarkson University	Potsdam	NCAA III	564
Clinton Community College	Plattsburgh	NJCAA	564
College of Saint Rose	Albany	NCAA II	565
College of Staten Island	Staten Island	NCAA III	565
Columbia - Greene Community College	Hudson	NJCAA	566
Columbia University	New York	NCAA I	566
Concordia College - New York	Bronxville	NCAA II	567
Cornell University	Ithaca	NCAA I	568
Corning Community College	Corning	NJCAA	568
Dominican College	Orangeburg	NCAA II/NAIA	569
Dowling College	Oakdale	NCAA II	570
Dutchess Community College	Poughkeepsie	NJCAA	570
Erie Community College	Buffalo	NCAA III	571
Finger Lakes Community College	Canandaigua	NJCAA	572
Fordham University	Bronx	NCAA I	572
Fulton - Montgomery Community College	Johnstown	NJCAA	573
Genesee Community College	Batavia	NJCAA	574
Hamilton College	Clinton	NCAA III	574
Hartwick College	Oneonta	NCAA III	575
Herkimer County Community College	Herkimer	NJCAA	575
Hilbert College	Hamburg	NCAA III	576
Hofstra University	Hempstead	NCAA I	576
Hudson Valley Community College	Troy	NJCAA	577
Iona College	New Rochelle	NCAA III	577
Ithaca College	Ithaca	NCAA III	578
Jamestown Community College	Jamestown	NJCAA	579
Jefferson Community College	Watertown	NJCAA	579
Kingsborough Community College	Brooklyn	NJCAA	580
Le Moyne College	Syracuse	NCAA I	581
Long Island University - Brooklyn Campus	Brooklyn	NCAA I	581
Long Island University - C.W. Post Campus	Brookville	NCAA I	582
Manhattan College	Riverdale	NCAA I	582
Manhattanville College	Purchase	NCAA III	583
Marist College	Poughkeepsie	NCAA I	583

SCHOOL	CITY	AFFILIATION 99	PAGE
Mercy College	Dobbs Ferry	NCAA II	584
Mohawk Valley Community College	Utica	NJCAA	584
Molloy College	Rockville	NCAA II	585
Monroe Community College	Rochester	NJCAA I	585
Mount Saint Mary College	Newburgh	NCAA III	586
Nassau Community College	Garden City	NJCAA	587
New York Institute of Technology	Old Westbury	NCAA I	587
Niagara County Community College	Sanborn	NJCAA	588
Niagara University	Niagara University	NCAA I	588
Nyack College	Nyack	NAIA	589
Orange County Community College	Middletown	NCAA III	590
Pace University	Pleasantville	NCAA	590
Polytechnic University	Brooklyn	NCAA III	591
Rensselaer Poly Institute	Troy	NCAA III	592
Rochester Institute of Technology	Rochester	NCAA III	592
Rockland Community College	Suffern	NJCAA	593
Saint Bonaventura University	St. Bonaventura	NCAA I	593
Saint Francis College - New York	Brooklyn Heights	NCAA I	594
Saint John Fisher College	Rochester	NCAA III	594
Saint John's University - New York	Jamaica	NCAA I	594
Saint Joseph's College - New York	Patchogue	NCAA III	595
Saint Lawrence University	Canton	NCAA III	596
Saint Thomas Aquinas College	Sparkill	NAIA	596
Schenectady County Community College	Schenectady	NJCAA	597
Siena College	Londonville	NCAA I	597
Skidmore College	Saratoga Springs	NCAA III	598
State University of New York - Binghamton	Binghamton	NCAA III	598
State University of New York - Brockport	Brockport	NCAA III	599
State University of New York - Cobleskill	Cobleskill	NJCAA	600
State University of New York - Cortland	Cortland	NCAA III	600
State University of New York - Farmingdale	Farmingdale	NJCAA	601
State University of New York - Fredonia	Fredonia	NCAA III	602
State University of New York - New Paltz	New Paltz	NCAA III	602
State University of New York - Old Westbury	Old Westbury	NCAA III	603
State University of New York - Oneonta	Oneonta	NCAA III	604
State University of New York - Oswego	Oswego	NCAA III	604
State University of New York - Stony Brook	Stony Brook	NCAA II	605
State University of New York - Maritime	Bronx	NCAA III	605
Suffolk County Community College	Selden	NJCAA	606
Suffolk-West Community College	Brentwood	NJCAA	607
Ulster County Community College	Stone Ridge	NJCAA	607
University of Albany	Albany	NCAA II	608
University of Rochester	Rochester	NCAA III	608
Union College	Schenectady	NCAA III	609
Utica College - Syracuse University	Utica	NCAA III	609
US Merchant Marine Academy	Kings Point	NCAA III	610
US Military Academy	West Point	NCAA I	610
Vassar College	Poughkeepsie	NCAA III	611
Wagner College	Staten Island	NCAA I	612
Westchester Community College	Valhala	NJCAA	612

Adelphi University

South Avenue
Garden City, NY 11530
Coach: Ron Davies

NCAA II
Panthers/Black, Gold
Phone: (516) 877-4240
Fax: (516) 877-4237

ACADEMIC

Founded: 1896
Religion: Non-Affiliated
Web-site: http://www.adelphi.edu/
Student/Faculty Ratio: 12:1
Undergraduate Enrollment: 4,100
Scholarships/Academic: Yes **Athletic:** Yes
Total Expenses by: Year **In State:** $ 19,200
Degrees Conferred: Varied

Type: 4 Yr., Private, Liberal Arts, Coed
Campus Housing: Yes
SAT/ACT/GPA: 900
Male/Female Ratio: 1:1.3
Graduate Enrollment: 2,000
Fin Aid: Yes
Out of State: $ 19,200

Programs of Study: Business and Management, Communications, Education, Health Sciences, Life Sciences, Multi/Interdisciplinary Studies, Nursing, Physical Education, Psychology, Social Sciences

ATHLETIC PROFILE

Estimated Number of Baseball Scholarships: 7
Conference Affiliation: New York Collegiate Athletic Conference
Program Profile: Our Division II campus field was built in 1993 ,seats 500 and is on campus. We were 1994 Division II College World Series Finalists. We did 1993, 1996 NCAA Division II National Championship Tournament Appearances.
History: Our program began at Adelphi in 1947. A standout player in the late fifties took over the coaching reigns in 1964, that player is Ron Davies, currently in his 35th year at the helm of the team with over 700 victories.
Achievements: Adelphi has reached the Division II College World Series in three of the last 5 years, finishing 3rd twice. The Panthers have won 17 conference titles and have qualified for the NCAA tournament 10 times. Adelphi has had 9 All-Americans selections, including the "National Player of the Year in 1993"; numerous Panthers have gone on to professional baseball careers, including 6 in the last 10 years. Former major league Joe Sambito attended Adelphi.
Coaching: Ron Davies, Head Coach, has coached 35 years and has 740 victories. Tom Sowinski, Assistant Coach, was named All-American pitcher at St. John's in 1968 and has been with the staff for 12 years. John David, Assistant Coach, was a former head coach at Dowling for 13 years. He is in his 2nd year with Adelphi.
Roster for 1998 team/In State: 25 **Out of State:** 4 **Out of Country:** 0
Total Number of Varsity/Jr. Varsity: 29 **Percent of Graduation:** 90%
Number of Seniors on 1998 Team: 6 **Most Recent Record:** 23 - 12 - 0
Number of Fall Games: 8 **Number of Spring Games:** 40
Positions Needed for 1999/2000: Shortstop, 1st Base, Pitcher
Schedule: New Haven, Armstrong State, William Paterson, Montclair State, St. Rose, Dowling
Style of Play: Adelphi is a strong hitting team that is very fundamentally sound. Versatile players are valued and the team is close-knit with a drive to succeed.

Alfred State College

Department of Athletics
Alfred, NY 14802
Coach: Tom Kenney

NJCAA I
Pioneers/Clue, Gold
Phone: (607) 587-4360
Fax: (607) 587-4331

ACADEMIC

Founded: 1896
Student/Faculty Ratio: 20:1

Type: 4 Yr., Coed
Male/Female Ratio: 30:70

Undergraduate Enrollment: 3,500 **Graduate Enrollment:** 4,000
Scholarships/Academic: Yes **Athletic:** Yes **Fin Aid:** Yes
Total Expenses by: Year **In State:** $ 13,000 **Out of State:** $ 13,000
Degrees Conferred: AS, AAS, BFA, MA
Programs of Study: Contact school for program of study.

ATHLETIC PROFILE

Conference Affiliation: WNYAC - Western New York Athletic Conference
Program Profile: The program is in its 4th season with a 96-64 overall record. We are a Division I Junior College SUNY College of Technology. We play on natural grass and conference season is in the Fall which consist of 20 games and a 45 games schedule in the Spring. Some scholarship funds are available.
History: The program beagn in 1994-1995 with an overall record is 96-94. We won Region III Championship last year 1996-1997 with a record of 46-17. We won the WNYAC title Fall of 1997.
Achievements: Regional title in 1996-1997; Conference Title in 1997; 1997 draft was Geronimo Cruz Catcher by the Texas Rangers in the 17th round; 1997 Academic All-American was Chad Donovan Outfielder.
Coaching: Tom Kenney, Head Coach, is a graduate of Brockport State. He entered his 4th year as a head coach. He compiled a record of 96-64. He is G.M in NCAA sanctioned and Wooden Bat Summer Collegiate League. He was in the NCBL Northeastern Collegiate Baseball League and Hornell Doggers. Skip Herman, Pitching Coach, entered his 3rd year as an assistant coach. He was at Ashland University, Ohio.
Style of Play: Sound fundamentally, run, pitching and defense.

Baruch College

17 Lexington Avenue
New York City, NY 10010-
Coach: Buddy Hefferman

NCAA III
Statesmen/Blue, White
Phone: (718) 714-4855
Fax: (212) 387-1277

ACADEMIC

Founded: 1968 **Type:** 4 Yr., Public, Coed
Religion: Non-Affiliated **Campus Housing:** Yes
Web-site: Not-Available **SAT/ACT/GPA:** 990+/23+
Student/Faculty Ratio: 30:1 **Male/Female Ratio:** 43:57
Undergraduate Enrollment: 12,300 **Graduate Enrollment:** 2,450
Scholarships/Academic: Yes **Athletic:** No **Fin Aid:** Yes
Total Expenses by: Year **In State:** $ 5,152 **Out of State:** $ 7,752
Degrees Conferred: BA, BS, MBA, BBA
Programs of Study: Accounting, Actuarial Science, Advertising, Communications, Computer Science, Comsumer Research, Economics, Education, English, Finance, Hebrew, History, Industrial, Psychology, Journalism, Management, Marketing, Mathematics, Office Administration, Operation Research, Personnel Management

ATHLETIC PROFILE

Conference Affiliation: Knickerbocker, CUNY
Program Profile: Our facilities include gym, armory & batting cages. We play on a natural grass field.
Achievements: 3 Conference All-Stars.
Coaching: Buddy Hefferman - Head Coach. Bob Greenburg - Assistant Coach. Frank Dursi - Pitching Coach. Scott Losch - Assistant Coach.
Style of Play: Running game and defense.

Broome Community College

PO Box 1017
Binghamton, NY 13902-
Coach: Jason Cronin

NJCAA
Hornets/Black, Gold
Phone: (607) 778-5003
Fax: (607) 778-5370

ACADEMIC

Founded: 1946
Type: 2 Yr., Jr. College, Coed
Student/Faculty Ratio: 20:1
Male/Female Ratio: 1:1
Undergraduate Enrollment: 6,100
Graduate Enrollment: None
Scholarships/Academic: Yes **Athletic:** No **Fin Aid:** Yes
Total Expenses by: Year **In State:** $ 2,030 **Out of State:** $ 2,030
Degrees Conferred: Associate
Programs of Study: Business and Office Technologies, Computing, Engineering, Health, Liberal Arts and Related Fields, Technology

ATHLETIC PROFILE

Conference Affiliation: Region III
Program Profile: Our program competes in a very competitive group of up-state New York. We play a 40-game schedule, which includes a trip South. Our home field is natural grass with major league dimensions. We have a winning tradition.
History: The baseball program began in 1952, and since then we have had only 5 losing seasons. We have produced numerous All-Americans, All-Region and some players that were drafted.
Achievements: In the last 11 years: 2 1st team All-American, 1 Academic All-American, 5 players drafted, 15 1st team All-Region and numerous transfers to 4-year colleges.

Canisius College

2001 Main Street
BuFallo, NY 14208-
Coach: Don Colpoys

NCAA I
Golden Griffins/Blue, Gold
Phone: (716) 888-2970
Fax: (716) 888-3174

ACADEMIC

Founded: 1870
Type: 4 Yr., Private, Liberal Arts, Coed
Religion: Jesuit
Campus Housing: Yes
Web-site: http://www.canisius.edu/
SAT/ACT/GPA: 1050
Student/Faculty Ratio: 17:1
Male/Female Ratio: 51:49
Undergraduate Enrollment: 3,300
Graduate Enrollment: 1,500
Scholarships/Academic: Yes **Athletic:** Yes **Fin Aid:** Yes
Total Expenses by: Year **In State:** $ 13,000 **Out of State:** $ 13,000
Degrees Conferred: BS, BA, MBA, PA, MPA, MS, MSEd
Programs of Study: Accounting, Anthropology, Art, Athletic, Banking/Finance, Biology, Business, Chemistry, Economics, International, Languages, Management, Marketing, Medical, Religion, Social Science, Urban, Women's Studies

ATHLETIC PROFILE

Conference Affiliation: Metro Atlantic Athletic Conference
Program Profile: We do a NCAA 56 game schedule. We do a five week season in the Fall (12-14 games) and 42-44 games in the Spring from mid-March to early May. We play at the astro turf covered Demske Sports Complex which has lights and is on campus. We have a competitive Junior Varsity program that plays 20 games per year.
History: Baseball has been played every year at Canisius since the late 1940's, however a Griffs team was fielded as early as 1903, making baseball the oldest sport at Canisius.

Achievements: Conference Titles in 1985 and 1994; 62 victories over the past 3 seasons. Joe Mamott (1994) was 6th round draft choice of the Boston Red Sox.
Coaching: Don Colpoys, Head Coach, started in 1977 and was 1994 MAAC Coach of the Year. He has professional experience in the St.Louis Cardinal Organization as a catcher.
Style of Play: 1997 team was offensive oriented with plenty of speed and power.

CUNY - Bronx Community College

181 University Avenue
Bronx, NY 10453-
Coach: Adolpho De Jesus

NJCAA
Broncos/Green, Gold
Phone: (718) 289-5265
Fax: (718) 295-5038

ACADEMIC

Type: 2 Yr., Jr. College, Coed
Campus Housing: No
Degrees Conferred: Associate
Programs of Study: Accounting, Art/Fine Arts, Biology, Biological Science, Black/African - American Studies, Business Administration, Commerce, Management, Business Education, Chemistry, Child Care/Child and Family Education, Data Processing, Electrical Engineering Technology, History, Human Services, International Studies, Liberal Arts, General Studies, Marketing, Retailing, Merchandising, Mathematics, Medical Laboratory Technology, Music, Nuclear Medical Technology

CUNY - John Jay College of Criminal Justice

899 Tenth Avenue
New York, NY 10019-
Coach: Lou DeMartino
Email: tfreaney@faculty.jjay.cuny.edu

NCAA III
Bloodhounds/Blue, Gold
Phone: (212) 237-8396
Fax: (212) 237-8474

ACADEMIC

Founded: 1964
Type: 4 Yr., Private, Liberal Arts, Coed
Web-site: Not Available
SAT/ACT/GPA: None
Student/Faculty Ratio: 20:1
Male/Female Ratio: Even
Undergraduate Enrollment: 10,500
Graduate Enrollment: 2,000
Scholarships/Academic: Yes **Athletic:** No **Fin Aid:** Yes
Total Expenses by: Year **In State:** $ 1,700 **Out of State:** $ 5,000
Degrees Conferred: BA, BS, AA
Programs of Study: Behavioral Science, Computer Information Systems, Corrections, Criminal Justice, Criminology, Fire Science, Forensic Studies, Law Enforcement, Prelaw, Psychology, Public Administration, Safety and Security Technology, Toxicology

ATHLETIC PROFILE

Conference Affiliation: Knickerbocker and CUNY
Program Profile: Our indoor facilities are one of the best in the New York City area with three batting cages, pitching mounds, pool, cardiovascular fitness center, Etc..
History: In 25 years we have won over 19 Conference League and Tournaments and one ECAC Championship/NCAA in 1996.
Achievements: Coach of the Year 12 times; 24 All-Americans; 7 pro contracts.
Coaching: Lou DeMartino, Head Coach, is in his 25th year as a head coach. He has a record of 405-324 and coaches the Austrian National Junior and Cadet National Teams during the Summer. Vito Francavilla - Assistant Coach.
Roster for 1998 team/In State: 24 **Out of State:** 1 **Out of Country:** 0
Total Number of Varsity/Jr. Varsity: 0 **Percent of Graduation:** 70%-80%
Number of Seniors on 1998 Team: 8 **Most Recent Record:** 15 - 14 - 0
Number of Fall Games: 9 **Number of Spring Games:** 36

Positions Needed for 1999/2000: Catcher, Pitcher
Schedule: RPI, Mt. St. Mary, Old Westbury, Cortland, Oswego
Style of Play: In 1997 and 1998 we led NCAA III in stoeln bases. This year's team will be running again.

CUNY - Lehman College

250 Bedford Park Blvd. West
Bronx, NY 10475-
Coach: Robert Gordian

NCAA III
Lightning/Royal Blue, Kelly Green
Phone: (718) 960-7746
Fax: (718) 960-1132

ACADEMIC

Founded: 1968
Religion: Non-Affiliated
Student/Faculty Ratio: 18:1
Undergraduate Enrollment: 8,300
Scholarships/Academic: Yes **Athletic:** No
Total Expenses by: **In State:** $ 5,200

Type: 4 Yr., Public, Coed
SAT/ACT/GPA: 900+/20+
Male/Female Ratio: 4:9
Graduate Enrollment: 1,553
Fin Aid: Yes
Out of State: $ 1,553

Degrees Conferred: AA, AS, BA, BS, MBA
Programs of Study: Accounting, Afro-American Studies, American Studies, Ancient Civilization, Anthropology, Biology, Business, Chemistry, Communications, Computer Science, Criminal Justice, Dance, Dietetics, Economics, Education, English, Family/Consumer Studies, Fine Arts, French, Geography, Geology, German, Greek, Health Care, Hebrew, History, International Relations, Italian, Languages, Latin American Studies, Management, Mathematics, Music, Nursing, Philosophy

ATHLETIC PROFILE

Conference Affiliation: ECAC, CUNY, Knickerbocker
Program Profile: We play on a natural grass field. The Apex has excellent gymnasium facilities . We have a 34 regular season and a 2.0 GPA is required to play.
Achievements: CUNY Finals Appearance in 8 of the last 10 years; last CUNY Title in 1995; 1996 ECAC Metro NY/NJ Champs; 1995 Led the nation in team batting average. Coach Reyes currently plays for Waterbury Spirit; last player drafted in 1996 was Robert Riggio (Brewers).
Coaching: Robert Gordian - Head Coach. David Lois - Assistant Coach. Juan "Kiko" Reyes - Assistant Coach. Victor Ayala, Jr. - Assistant Coach.
Style of Play: Aggressive, one hundred percent effort wanted at all times on offense and defense. Players should have good work ethics and winning attitudes.

CUNY - Manhattan Community College

199 Chambers Street
New York, NY 10007-
Coach: Demitri Segalic

NJCAA
Panthers/Blue, Orange
Phone: (212) 346-8268
Fax: (212) 346-8275

ACADEMIC

Founded: 1963
Student/Faculty Ratio: 17:1
Undergraduate Enrollment: 16,850
Scholarships/Academic: No **Athletic:** No
Total Expenses by: Year **In State:** $ 1,440

Type: 2 Yr., Jr. College, Coed
Male/Female Ratio: 33:67
Graduate Enrollment: None
Fin Aid: Yes
Out of State: $ 1,800

Degrees Conferred: Associate
Programs of Study: Accounting, Bank/Finance, Business Administration, Communications, Computer Programming, Education, Emergency Medical Technology, Engineering Science, Human Services, Liberal Arts, Marketing, Physical Education, Public Administration, Real Estate, Recreation/Leisure Services, Respiratory Therapy

ATHLETIC PROFILE

Conference Affiliation: MCCAC

CUNY - Queens College

65 - 30 Kissena Blvd
Flushing, NY 11367-
Coach: Yuki Yamada

NCAA II
Knights/Blue, Silver
Phone: (718) 997-2780
Fax: (718) 997-2799

ACADEMIC

Founded: 1937
Type: 2 Yr., Public, Liberal Arts, Coed
Web-site: Not Available
SAT/ACT/GPA: 900 avg
Student/Faculty Ratio: 18:1
Male/Female Ratio: 40:60
Undergraduate Enrollment: 14,460
Graduate Enrollment: 3,290
Scholarships/Academic: Yes **Athletic:** Yes **Fin Aid:** Yes
Total Expenses by: Year **In State:** $ 3,150 **Out of State:** $ 5, 750
Degrees Conferred: AA, AS, BA, BS, MA, MS, MBA, PhD, JD
Programs of Study: Business and Management, Communications, Computer Science, Education, Letters/Literature, Psychology, Social Science, Visual and Performing Arts

ATHLETIC PROFILE

Conference Affiliation: NYCAC
Program Profile: Our well-groomed field is on campus and has natural grass. There are 6 indoor batting cages.
Achievements: 1950 Bob Mueller, White Sox. 1958 Mel Seiden, White Sox. 1959 Louis BeBole, Phillies. 1963 Jeff Maloney, Twins. 1974 Mark Goodman, Yankees. 1976 Billy Hiss, Indians. 1990 Keith Baaske, Royals.

CUNY - Queensborough Community College

222-05 56th Avenue
Bayside, NY 11364-1497
Coach: TBA

NJCAA
Tigers/Blue, Red, White
Phone: (718) 631-6322
Fax: (718) 631-6333

ACADEMIC

Founded: 1957
Type: 2 Yr., Jr. College, Coed
Student/Faculty Ratio: 22:1
Male/Female Ratio: 43:57
Undergraduate Enrollment: 8,000
Graduate Enrollment: None
Scholarships/Academic: No **Athletic:** No **Fin Aid:** Yes
Total Expenses by: Year **In State:** $ 2,100 **Out of State:** $ 8,200
Degrees Conferred: Associate
Programs of Study: Accounting, Art, Business Administration, Computer Programming, Computer Technology, Drafting/Design, Electrical Engineering Science Technology, Medical Laboratory Technology, Nursing, Office Management

ATHLETIC PROFILE

Conference Affiliation: Region XV, NJCAA - CUNY
Program Profile: We have a new field, 15 minutes from the college. It is grass and has 325-400-330 dimensions. There are indoor hitting stations, 2 gyms and a weight room. We travel every year to the South. We went to Dominican Republic in 93.
History: Program began in 1980; 2 Region Championships; 7 consecutive city championships (CUNY); 1994 Coach of the Year; All-Americans: Mike Soto LHP (Sophomore), Al Acosta 1B (graduated). Ferguson George (OF) drafted 40th round by Royals in 1994.

Achievements: 1989 Region Champs; 1994 Region Champs; 1995 City Champs; 1996 City Champs; 1997 City Champs. All-American in 1997 was Rob Dito; Drafted in 1996 was Jose Lopez; Drafted in 1997 was Chris Silva; Drafted in 1997 was James McGowen.

Clarkson University

Box 5830 - Athletic Office
Potsdam, NY 13699-5830
Coach: Mike Nicholson

NCAA III
Golden Knights/Green, Gold
Phone: (315) 268-3759
Fax: (315) 268-7613

ACADEMIC

Type: 4 Yr., Private, Liberal Arts, Coed, Engineering
Founded: 1896
Religion: Non-Affiliated
Campus Housing: Yes
Web-site: http://www.clarkson.edu/
SAT/ACT/GPA: None
Student/Faculty Ratio: 15:1
Male/Female Ratio: 3:1
Undergraduate Enrollment: 2,425
Graduate Enrollment: 320
Scholarships/Academic: Yes **Athletic:** No **Fin Aid:** Yes
Total Expenses by: Year **In State:** $ 25,079 **Out of State:** $ Varies
Degrees Conferred: Bachelors, Masters, Doctorates
Programs of Study: Engineering, Business, Science, Liberal Arts

ATHLETIC PROFILE

Conference Affiliation: Upstate Collegiate Athletic Association
Program Profile: Our Spring season is 35-40 games. We play on Snell Field (natural grass) that has a seating capacity of 2,000. There is a batting cage indoor practice facility.
History: Our program officially started in 1929. Our best seasons were in 1940's, 1950's and 1960's. Jack Phillips and Emerson Roser played major league ball with NY Yankees and Phillips played on 1984 World Champions as well as Pittsburgh and Detroit.
Achievements: Several players from 1940's and 1950's; played professional ball - most notably Jack Phillips; 1947 World Series New York Yankees; Emerson Roser - New York Yankees.
Coaching: Mike Nicholson - Head Coach. Todd Kirkey - Assistant Coach.
Roster for 1998 team/In State: 18 **Out of State:** 8 **Out of Country:** 0
Total Number of Varsity/Jr. Varsity: 26 **Percent of Graduation:** 99%
Number of Seniors on 1998 Team: 3 **Most Recent Record:** 7 - 24 - 0
Freshmen Receiving Fin Aid/Athletic: 0 **Academic:** 90%
Number of Fall Games: 0 **Number of Spring Games:** 35
Positions Needed for 1999/2000: Everywhere
Schedule: Ithaca, Rensselaer, St. Lawrence

Clinton Community College

Lakeshore Dr, Rt 9 S
Plattsburgh, NY 12901-
Coach: Tom Neale

NJCAA
Cougars/Navy, Orange
Phone: (518) 562-4220
Fax: (518) 562-4222

ACADEMIC

Founded: 1969
Type: 2 Yr., Jr. College, Coed
Student/Faculty Ratio: 25:1
Male/Female Ratio: 46:54
Undergraduate Enrollment: 2,175
Graduate Enrollment: None
Scholarships/Academic: No **Athletic:** No **Fin Aid:** Yes
Total Expenses by: Year **In State:** $ 1,900 **Out of State:** $ 3,600
Degrees Conferred: Associate

Programs of Study: Accounting, Business Administration, Criminal Justice, Humanities, Law Enforcement, Liberal Arts, Medical Laboratory Technology, Nursing, Physical Education, Retail Management, Science, Social Science

ATHLETIC PROFILE

Conference Affiliation: Iowa JUCO

College of Saint Rose

432 Western Avenue
Albany, NY 12203-
Coach: Bob Bellizzi

NCAA II
Golden Knights/Black, Gold, White
Phone: (518) 454-2041
Fax: (518) 458-5457

ACADEMIC

Founded: 1920
Type: 4 Yr., Private, Liberal Arts, Coed
Religion: Independent
Campus Housing: Yes
Web-site: http://www.strose.edu/
SAT/ACT/GPA: 920+
Student/Faculty Ratio: 17:1
Male/Female Ratio: 27:73
Undergraduate Enrollment: 1,886
Graduate Enrollment: None
Scholarships/Academic: Yes **Athletic:** Yes **Fin Aid:** Yes
Total Expenses by: Year **In State:** $ 10,610 **Out of State:** $ 10,610
Degrees Conferred: Numerous undergraduate and graduate
Programs of Study: Accounting, American Studies, Art Education, Biochemistry, Biology, Business Administration, Chemistry, Communications Disorders, Communications, Computer Information Systems, Elementary Education, English, Graphic Design, History, Political Science, Religious Studies, Mathematics, Medical Technology, Music, Music Education, Psychology, Religious Studies

ATHLETIC PROFILE

Estimated Number of Baseball Scholarships: 9 Full
Conference Affiliation: New York Collegiate Athletic Conference
Program Profile: Our program has over 30 wins in its 7 years of competing exclusively Division II level. Bleeker Stadium seats 2,000 natural grass and lights.
History: The program began in 1979 and has been to 3 NCAA Tournaments in the past five years.
Achievements: Have had 2 All-Americans in the last three years who were both drafted. Have won one conference title and have not finished lower than 2nd in 6 of the 7 years in the NYCAC.
Coaching: Bob Bellizzi, Head Coach, is the founder of the program which is widely considered to be among the most respected and fastest growing in the East. He was named 1994 NYCAC Coach of the Year and 1994 American Baseball Coaches Association Northeast Coach of the Year. He is among the top five active winningest coaches by wins, took 1990 team to NAIA World Series. He compiled a record of 550-247-1 over 20 years. Ken Hodge - Assistant Coach.
Roster for 1998 team/In State: 24 **Out of State:** 2 **Out of Country:** 2
Total Number of Varsity/Jr. Varsity: 28 /25 **Percent of Graduation:** 90%
Number of Seniors on 1998 Team: 4 **Most Recent Record:** 23 - 22 - 0
Number of Fall Games: 20 **Number of Spring Games:** 55
Positions Needed for 1999/2000: 3rd Base, Shortstop, 2nd Base, 1st Base, OF, Pitch
Schedule: Queens, Massachussetts-Lowell, Adelphi, New Haven, Mercyhurst, Rensselaer
Style of Play: Saint Rose is renowned for excellent pitching and defense; team likes to be aggressive on offense - especially on the base paths.

College of Staten Island

2800 Victory Boulevard
Staten Island, NY 10214-
Coach: Bill Cali

NCAA III
Dolphins/Maroon, Blue
Phone: (718) 982-3160
Fax: (718) 982-3138

ACADEMIC

Founded: 1976 | **Type:** 4 Yr., Public, Coed
Web-site: http://www.csi.cuny.eud/ | **SAT/ACT/GPA:** 1020 up/80 and better
Student/Faculty Ratio: 19:1 | **Male/Female Ratio:** 1:1.5
Undergraduate Enrollment: 10,674 | **Graduate Enrollment:** 1,522
Scholarships/Academic: Yes | **Athletic:** No | **Fin Aid:** Yes
Total Expenses by: Year | **In State:** $ Varies | **Out of State:** $ Varies
Degrees Conferred: Associates, Bachelors in Arts and Science, Masters
Programs of Study: Accounting, American Studies, Anthropology, Biochemistry, Biology, Business Administration, Chemistry, Communications, Computer Science, Dramatic Arts, Economics, Education, Engineering, English, Film Arts, Fine Arts, History, International Studies, Languages, Political Science, Psychology, Social Science, Spanish, Women's Studies

ATHLETIC PROFILE

Conference Affiliation: CUNY, Skyline Conference

Columbia - Greene Community College

PO Box 1000
Hudson, NY 12534-
Coach: Bob Godlewski
Email: MERRITT@VAXA.SUNYCGCC.EDU

NJCAA
Twins/Grey, Navy
Phone: (518) 828-4181x3212
Fax: (518) 828-8543

ACADEMIC

Founded: 1969 | **Type:** 2 Yr., Public, Jr. College, Coed
Web-site: http://www.sunycgcc.edu | **SAT/ACT/GPA:** Not Required
Student/Faculty Ratio: 16:1 | **Male/Female Ratio:** 45:55
Undergraduate Enrollment: 1,500 | **Graduate Enrollment:** None
Scholarships/Academic: Yes | **Athletic:** No | **Fin Aid:** Yes
Total Expenses by: Year | **In State:** $ 5,000 | **Out of State:** $ 10,000
Degrees Conferred: AA, AS, AA, AOS, Cert.
Programs of Study: Business Administration, Computer Science, Accounting, Nursing, Automotive Technology, Liberal Arts, Fine Arts

ATHLETIC PROFILE

Conference Affiliation: Mountain Valley Conference
History: We began in 1965 with establishment of institution. We are a Region 3, Division 3 athletic program. We were National World Series Contenders in 1996 and 1997, Regional Champs in 1996 and 1997 and Mt. Valley Conference Participants.
Achievements: Robert Godlewski in 1996 and 1997 was named Coach of the Year; All-Americans were DeShawn Ziths in 1997 by Baltimore Orioels, James Shook in 1997and Mickey Brantley in 1998 by Seattle.
Coaching: Bob Godlewski, Head Coach, has a career record of 71-41-1. John Isabella - Assistant.
Roster for 1998 team/In State: 17 | **Out of State:** 0 | **Out of Country:** 3
Total Number of Varsity/Jr. Varsity: 20 | **Most Recent Record:** 17 - 6 - 0
Baseball Camp Dates: June 29 - July 3 | **Number of Spring Games:** 29
Positions Needed for 1999/2000: Catcher, Pitcher
Schedule: Erie, Finger Lakes, Corning, Herkimer, Fulton-Montgomery, Hudson Valley

Columbia University

Dodge Physical Fitness Center
New York, NY 10027-
Coach: Mikio Aoki

NCAA I
Lions/Blue, White
Phone: (212) 854-2543
Fax: (212) 854-6200

ACADEMIC

Type: 4 Yr., Private, Liberal Arts, Coed, Engineering
Founded: 1754
Religion: Non-Affiliated
Campus Housing: No
Web-site: http://www.columbia.edu/
SAT/ACT/GPA: 1100+/25+
Student/Faculty Ratio: 7:1
Male/Female Ratio: 48:52
Undergraduate Enrollment: 4,000
Graduate Enrollment: 13,000
Scholarships/Academic: No **Athletic:** No **Fin Aid:** Yes
Total Expenses by: Year **In State:** $ 27,000 **Out of State:** $ 27,000
Degrees Conferred: BA, BS
Programs of Study: Over 60 majors including Computer Sciences, Letters/Literature, Life Sciences, Multi/Interdisciplinary Studies, Physical Sciences, Psychology, Social Sciences, Engineering

ATHLETIC PROFILE

Conference Affiliation: Ivy League Conference
Program Profile: Facilities include grass field, indoor cages and a turf practice facility.
History: The first year of the program was in 1884.
Achievements: Eddie Collins and Lou Gehring were named Hall of Fame. Gene Larkin and Frank Seminala most recent Big Leaguers.
Coaching: Mikio Aoki, Head Coach, entered his 1st year with the program.
Roster for 1998 team/In State: **Out of State:** **Out of Country:** 0
Total Number of Varsity/Jr. Varsity: 26 **Percent of Graduation:** 100%
Number of Seniors on 1998 Team: 5 **Baseball Camp Dates:** TBA
Number of Fall Games: 4 **Number of Spring Games:** 45
Positions Needed for 1999/2000: Pitcher, Infielder, Outfielder
Schedule: Rutgers, St. John's, Indiana, Harvard, Purdue, Dartmouth
Style of Play: Aggressive.

Concordia College - New York

171 White Plains Road
Bronxville, NY 10708-
Coach: Bob Greiner

NCAA II
Clippers/Blue, Gold
Phone: (914) 337-9300
Fax: (914) 395-4500

ACADEMIC

Founded: 1881
Type: 4 Yr., Private, Liberal Arts, Coed
Religion: Lutheran
Campus Housing: Yes
Web-site: Not Available
SAT/ACT/GPA: No minimum
Student/Faculty Ratio: 10:1
Male/Female Ratio: 41:58
Undergraduate Enrollment: 600
Graduate Enrollment: None
Scholarships/Academic: Yes **Athletic:** Yes **Fin Aid:** Yes
Total Expenses by: Year **In State:** $ 18,340 **Out of State:** $ 18,340
Degrees Conferred: BA, BS, B.Mus
Programs of Study: Behavioral Science, Biology, Business Administration, Church Music, Education, English, Environmetal Science, History, Interdisciplinary Studies, Mathematics, Music Education, Social Work

ATHLETIC PROFILE

Conference Affiliation: NYCAC
Program Profile: Concordia plays Division II baseball. Its conference consists of 8 teams, two of which (Adelphi and St. Rose) are nationally ranked. Concordia plays between 30-35 games in the Spring. Included in the schedule are Division II powers New Haven, Sacred Heart and Quinipiac.
History: Concordia has been an NCAA Division II program since the mid 1980's. Prior to that, they were a nationally ranked NAIA school. In the last 15 years, Concordia's overall record is 282-211. Concordia has 3 active major leaguers: John Doherty, Scott Lewis, and Willie Fraser.

Achievements: Concordia's past coaches have received 3 Coach of the Year honor as well as 2 Conference Titles. Concordia has had 12 players play professional baseball.
Coaching: Bob Greiner, Head Coach, was previously coach at Manhattanville College and Pace U.
Style of Play: We will strive to play excellent defense, and surround that with effective pitching and an aggressive style of offensive baseball..

Cornell University

Teagle Hall, Campus Rd.
Ithaca, NY 14853-
Coach: Tom Ford

NCAA I
Big Red/Red, White
Phone: (607) 255-6604
Fax: (607) 255-2969

ACADEMIC

Founded: 1865
Religion: Non-Affiliated
Web-site: http://www.cornell.edu/
Student/Faculty Ratio: 20:1
Undergraduate Enrollment: 13,000
Scholarships/Academic: No **Athletic:** No
Total Expenses by: Year **In State:** $ 18,409
Type: 4 Yr., Private, Liberal Arts, Coed
Campus Housing: Yes
SAT/ACT/GPA: 1200
Male/Female Ratio: 52:48
Graduate Enrollment: 5,000
Fin Aid: Yes
Out of State: $ 32,074
Degrees Conferred: BA, BS, BFA, Barch, MA, MS, MFA
Programs of Study: Colleges of Agriculture and Life Science, Architecture, Art and Planning, Arts and Science, Engineering, Hotel Administration, Human Ecology, Industrial and Labor Relations

ATHLETIC PROFILE

Conference Affiliation: Ivy League Conference
Program Profile: Facilities include and artificial indoor facility and a natural turf game field which is called Hoy Field.
History: The program's inception, amid in the 1800's.
Achievements: 1995 has 3 All-Ivy League players; League Rookie of the Year-Doug Pritts 2nd team.
Coaching: Tom Ford, Head Coach, played at Ithaca College and graduated in 1979. He assisted at Ithaca for 11 years.
Style of Play: We want an ideal balance between academics and athletics.

Corning Community College

1 Academic Drive
Corning, NY 14830
Coach: Jeff Manwaring

NJCAA
Barons/Red, Black, White
Phone: (607) 962-9396
Fax: (607) 962-9401

ACADEMIC

Founded: 1956
Student/Faculty Ratio: 21:1
Undergraduate Enrollment: 3,426
Scholarships/Academic: No **Athletic:** No
Total Expenses by: Year **In State:** $ 2,400
Type: 2 Yr., Jr. College, Coed
Male/Female Ratio: 46:54
Graduate Enrollment: None
Fin Aid: Yes
Out of State: $ 4,800
Degrees Conferred: Associate
Programs of Study: Accounting, Automotive, Business, Computer Information Systems, Criminal Justice, Electrical/Electronics Technology, Engineering, Fire Science, Humanities, Human Services, Liberal Arts, Math, Nursing, Travel and Tourism

ATHLETIC PROFILE

Conference Affiliation: Mid-State Athletic Conference

Program Profile: Corning Community College is completing construction of a new baseball complex off campus. Play will begin at the natural grass facility for the 1997 season. The new park will be hitter friendly, 320' down lines, 380' center fieldand small foul territory. The field will be fully enclosed.
History: The baseball program was rejuvenated after a ten year hiatus in 1993 by head coach Jeff Manwaring (brother of Houston Astros catcher Kirt Manwaring).
Coaching: Jeff Manwaring, Head Coach, played his college ball at the University of Richmond as a catcher. He received his degree in Physical Education in 1978. He coached high school ball for ten years before restarting the Corning program.

Dominican College

470 Western Highway
Orangeburg, NY 10962
Coach: Rick Giannetti

NCAA II/NAIA
Chargers/Red, Black, White
Phone: (914) 398-3008
Fax: (914) 398-3042

ACADEMIC

Founded: 1952
Type: 4 Yr., Private, Liberal Arts, Coed
Religion: Catholic
Campus Housing: No
Web-site: Not Available
SAT/ACT/GPA: 820+
Student/Faculty Ratio: 12:1
Male/Female Ratio: 1:3
Undergraduate Enrollment: 2,000
Graduate Enrollment: 1,000
Scholarships/Academic: Yes **Athletic:** Yes **Fin Aid:** Yes
Total Expenses by: Semester **In State:** $ 8,000 **Out of State:** $ 8,000
Degrees Conferred: AA, BA, BS, BSN, BSW
Programs of Study: Business/Management, Education, Health Sciences, Liberal Arts, Interdisciplinary Studies, Nursing, Occupational Therapy, Psychology, Social Science, Special Education

ATHLETIC PROFILE

Estimated Number of Baseball Scholarships: 5
Conference Affiliation: Central Atlantic Collegiate Conference (CACC)
Program Profile: We play a 65 games season which includes a Fall and Spring season. In the Spring we take trips to Florida and Delaware.
History: Our program began in the early 1980'; have not had a losing season since before 1985.
Achievements: Rick Giannetti won the Conference Coach of the Year for the past six seasons and have been named Northeast Region Coach of the Year in 1996 and 1997. We have had 40 All-Americans since 1986 and 16 players sign pro contracts. Coach Giannetti record at DC is 228-120 for eight years while overall record is 273-153 in ten years.
Coaching: Rick Giannetti, Head Coach, won Conference Coach of the Year for the past six seasons. Started coaching at DC in 1990. He has over 300 wins as a coach and has been to 2 College World Series as a coach. Anthony Magnelle and Sean Moran - Assistant Coaches.
Roster for 1998 team/In State: 24 **Out of State:** 16 **Out of Country:** 0
Total Number of Varsity/Jr. Varsity: 35 **Percent of Graduation:** 90%
Number of Seniors on 1998 Team: 6 **Baseball Camp Dates:** July
Freshmen Receiving Fin Aid/Athletic: 15 **Academic:** 5
Number of Fall Games: 15+ **Number of Spring Games:** 50+
Positions Needed for 1999/2000: Pitchers, Centerfielder, Middle Infielder
Most Recent Record: 30 - 20 - 0
Schedule: FDU, Iona, Wilmington, Nova SouthEastern University, Palm Beach Atlantic, Adelphi
Style of Play: Aggressive, a lot of hitting and running.

Dowling College

Idle Hour Boulevard
Oakdale, NY 11769
Coach: Chris McKnight

NCAA II
Golden Lions/Blue, Gold
Phone: (516) 244-3019
Fax: (516) 244-3317

ACADEMIC

Founded: 1955
Type: 4 Yr., Private, Liberal Arts, Coed
Religion: Non-Affiliated
Campus Housing: Yes
SAT/ACT/GPA: NCAA Div II Requirements/
Web-site: http://www.dowling.edu
Student/Faculty Ratio: 23:1
Male/Female Ratio: 1:4
Undergraduate Enrollment: 5,940
Graduate Enrollment: 1,000
Scholarships/Academic: Yes **Athletic:** Yes **Fin Aid:** Yes
Total Expenses by: Semester **In State:** $ 2,501/sem **Out of State:** $ 2,501/sem
Degrees Conferred: BA, BS, MBA, MS
Programs of Study: Accounting, Aero, Airway Science, Arts, Biology, Computer Information Systems, Computer Science, Economics, Education, Elementary Education, English, Finance, History, Humanities, Management, Marketing, Math, Music, Natural Science, Political Science, Psychology, Romance, Languages, Social Science, Special Education, Speech, Drama Arts, Travel and Tourism, Visual Arts

ATHLETIC PROFILE

Conference Affiliation: NYCAC
Program Profile: The Golden Lions play a 10 game Fall season anda 45 game Spring season with trips down South and on the East coast. Our field has a natural playing surface and overlooks the Great South Bay.
History: The program began in 1974 and first year of NCAA was in 1983.
Achievements: 4 players in the 90's have signed pro contracts; 1998 ECAC Champions; finished 2 in NYCAC; 19 players All-Conference and All-Star in the last three years.
Coaching: Chris McKnight, Head Coach, enteried his 4th season as a head coach. He is the former head coach at SUNY Old Westbury. He is in his 12th year as a college coach. Gary Puccio, Assistant Coach is the former head coach at Manhattan College.
Style of Play: We are very aggressive on the base paths. We do the little things right. We play for a run on inning.

Dutchess Community College

53 Pendell Road
Poughkeepsie, NY 12601
Coach: Joe Derosa

NJCAA
Falcons/Blue, Gold
Phone: (914) 431-8000
Fax: (914) 431-8990

ACADEMIC

Founded: 1957
Type: 2 Yr., Public, Jr. College, Coed
Web-site: Not Available
SAT/ACT/GPA: None
Student/Faculty Ratio: 25:1
Male/Female Ratio: 50:50
Scholarships/Academic: No **Athletic:** No **Fin Aid:** Yes
Total Expenses by: Year **In State:** $ 2,300+ **Out of State:** $ 4,600+
Degrees Conferred: Associate Degrees
Programs of Study: Advertising, Architecture, Biological Science, Business, Communications, Computer Science, Dietetics, Electromechanical Engineering, Food Services, General Studies, Humanities, Math, Mechanical, Medical, Recreation, Retail Estate

ATHLETIC PROFILE

Conference Affiliation: Region XV, Mid-Hudson Conference

Program Profile: Fall baseball consists of 7 weeks with 15-20 scrimmage. We do off-season conditioning for seven weeks. Spring season consists of 20 weeks with a 45-50 game schedule and a pre-season Southern trip. Our indoor facility includes two batting cages, soft-toss, t-stations, pitcher's mounds and infield . We have an aerobics room and weight training. Our outdoor facility is a 40 ft dugout with dimensions lf/335, cf/390, rf/330. It has natural grass with grass baselines.
History: We are very competitive within the Region XV and an extended schedule throughout Northeast into Maryland area. We are 1990 Eastern District Champions and participated in the NJCAA College World Series and a grant JCT-Colorado. Our record for the past 4 years was 103-57. We were 1996 Eastern District Finalis and 1997 and 1998 Mid-Hudson Conference Champions.
Achievements: 1990 participated in NJCAA College World Series; 1996 Region XV Division I Champions; Eastern District Finalist; 1997-1998 Mid-Hudson Conference Champions; 1996 Region XV Coach of the Year - Division I; All-Americans were: 1st team Les Funk in 1990, 2nd team Greg Goodemote in 1992 and 3rd team Justin Taber in 1997. Players entering professional baseball are Frank Cimorelli, Jeff Pierce and Tim Tyrell.
Coaching: Joe Derosa, Head Coach, is in his 8th year at DCC. He was high school varsity coach for 15 years . Scott DeGeorge, Assistant Coach, is in his 3rd year at DCC and is 25 years old. Keith Stohr - Assistant Coach.
Roster for 1998 team/In State: 17 **Out of State:** 0 **Out of Country:** 1
Total Number of Varsity/Jr. Varsity: 18 **Percent of Graduation:** 95%
Number of Seniors on 1998 Team: **Number of Sophomores on 1998 Team:** 4
Freshmen Receiving Fin Aid/Athletic: 0 **Academic:** 1
Number of Fall Games: 20 **Number of Spring Games:** 50
Positions Needed for 1999/2000: Pitchers, Catcher, Shortstop
Baseball Camp Dates: June 29 - July 17
Schedule: Queensborough, Suffolk West, Suffolk, Brookdale, Briar Cliff, Rockland, Montgomey, Pitt
Style of Play: We maximize attention to offensive and defensive misuse that contribute to winning and losing games. We focus on discipline and give attention to details.

Erie Community College

6205 Main Street
Buffalo, NY 14221
Coach: Joe Bauth

NCAA III
Kats/Black, Red, Grey
Phone: (716) 851-1290
Fax: (716) 634-6397

ACADEMIC

Founded: 1946 **Type:** 2 Yr., Jr. College, Coed
Student/Faculty Ratio: 18:1 **Male/Female Ratio:** 50:50
Undergraduate Enrollment: 6,870 **Graduate Enrollment:** None
Scholarships/Academic: No **Athletic:** No **Fin Aid:** Yes
Total Expenses by: Year **In State:** $ 2,100+ **Out of State:** $ 4,100+
Degrees Conferred: Associate
Programs of Study: Contact school for program of study.

ATHLETIC PROFILE

Conference Affiliation: Western New York Conference
Program Profile: The Kats play on Erie North Field which has dugouts, infield tarp and a batting tunnel (inside and out).
History: A new tradition began in July 1991 when Joe Bauth was hired . Kats went 0-21 but in a year of a new tradition went 11-12. Bauth has won over 60% and has qualified for Regional Playoffs 5 years in a row. Numerous players sent on to a four-year school to continue careers.
Achievements: 2 All-Americans - Seitt Davis in 1997 & Robb Vogth in 1995; Academic All-American in 1996 D.J. Odombina; former player-Joe Mamott drafted round 6th Red Sox via Canisius College.
Coaching: Joe Bauth, Head Coach, has coached 5 seasons. The Erie CC record is 91-95 with All-Region. Joe Mamott, Pitching Coach, graduated from Erie CC 1991 and Canisius College. He played for the Red Sox for 3 years. Scott Jusink, Outfielder Coach,is a 1995 Erie CC graduate and played at Bruch University.
Style of Play: We are aggressive -- fundamental, pressure orientated.

Finger Lakes Community College

4355 Lakeshore Drive
Canandaigua, NY 14424
Coach: Bob Lowden

NJCAA
Lakers/Navy, Gold
Phone: (716) 394-3500
Fax: (716) 394-5005

ACADEMIC

Founded: 1965
Type: 2 Yr., Jr. College, Coed
Student/Faculty Ratio:
Male/Female Ratio: Unknown
Undergraduate Enrollment: 3,000
Graduate Enrollment: None
Scholarships/Academic: Yes **Athletic:** No **Fin Aid:** Yes
Total Expenses by: Year **In State:** $ 5,000 **Out of State:** $ 7,500
Degrees Conferred: Associate
Programs of Study: Business, Conservation, Criminal Justice

ATHLETIC PROFILE

Conference Affiliation: Mid-State Athletic Conference
Program Profile: We play 40 games in the Spring and 20 in the Fall. We play in a natural turf field with full infield tarp, outdoor hitting tunnel and 200 seats. The dimensions are 305' down the lines and 410' in the center. We have an indoor hitting tunnel and pitching mounds.
History: Our program started in 1974 and has steadily grown. The Lakers 4th in the country in 1992 and 7th in 1994.
Achievements: NJCAA District Coach of the Year 1992, 1994. Region III Coach of the Year 1992, 1994. Region III Champions 1992, 1994.
Coaching: Bob Lowden, Head Coach, previously assisted at Ball State University. He was 1994 Head Coach of East team in US Olympic Festival, 1991-1993 Guest Coach for the Italian Baseball Federation and played at Miami University and Monroe.
Style of Play: We emphasize speed and aggressive base running. We put emphasis on pitching and defense. We stole home 8 out of 11 attempts in 1995.

Fordham University

441 E Fordham Road
Bronx, NY 10458
Coach: Dan Gallagher

NCAA I
Rams/Cardinal, White
Phone: (718) 817-4290
Fax: (718) 817-4278

ACADEMIC

Founded: 1841
Type: 4 Yr., Private, Liberal Arts, Coed
Religion: Jesuit
Campus Housing: Yes
Web-site: http://www.fordham.edu/
SAT/ACT/GPA: 900-1200/3.0
Student/Faculty Ratio: 27:1
Male/Female Ratio: 45:55
Undergraduate Enrollment: 9,000
Graduate Enrollment: 5,000
Scholarships/Academic: Yes **Athletic:** Yes **Fin Aid:** Yes
Total Expenses by: Year **In State:** $ 26,000 **Out of State:** $ 26,000
Degrees Conferred: Bachelor, Masters, Doctoral, Professional
Programs of Study: American Studies, Anthropology, Art, Biology, Broadcasting, Business, Chemistry, Economics, Journalism, Medieval, Peace, Public, Theology, Urban, Women's Studies

ATHLETIC PROFILE

Estimated Number of Baseball Scholarships: 5-8
Conference Affiliation: Atlantic 10 Conference

Program Profile: Games are played from mid-March to early May. Home games are played in 7,500 seat Jack Coffey Field (natural grass, located on campus). The field is named for Jack Coffey, the winningest coach in the program's history. The current Coach Dan Gallagher, ranks second. We have an indoor training facility which includes four batting cages and six mounds.
History: Our program began in 1859 and the oldest program in the US.
Achievements: 6 Conference Titles in the last 11 years; 4 ECAC Championships and 4 NCAA Appearances. Fordham is the school of current New York Met Pitcher Pete Harnisch. 15 players drafted in the last 10 years and was named 1991 Patriot League Coach of the Year. In 1996 Tom Stein was a Freshman All-American.
Coaching: Dan Gallagher, Head Coach, compiled a record of approximately more than 346-293, making him the second winningest coach in the program's history.
Roster for 1998 team/In State: 20 **Out of State:** 8 **Out of Country:** 0
Total Number of Varsity/Jr. Varsity: 28 **Percent of Graduation:** 99%
Number of Seniors on 1998 Team: 5 **Number of Sophomores on 1998 Team:** 6
Freshmen Receiving Fin Aid/Athletic: 7 **Academic:** 7
Number of Fall Games: 3 **Number of Spring Games:** 53
Schedule: South Alabama, Univ. of Florida, Stetson, Vermont, University of Massachusetts, Xavier
Style of Play: We are aggressive, disciplined and fundamental.

Fulton - Montgomery Community College

2805 State Hwy 67
Johnstown, NY 12095
Coach: Mike Mulligan
NJCAA
Raiders/Royal Blue, White
Phone: (518) 762-4651
Fax: (518) 762-4334

ACADEMIC

Founded: 1964 **Type:** 2 Yr., Jr,. College, Coed
Student/Faculty Ratio: 21:1 **Male/Female Ratio:** 40:60
Undergraduate Enrollment: 2,000 **Graduate Enrollment:** None
Scholarships/Academic: No **Athletic:** No **Fin Aid:** Yes
Total Expenses by: Year **In State:** $ 2,100 **Out of State:** $ 4,100
Degrees Conferred: Associate
Programs of Study: Accounting, Automotive Technology, Banking and Finance, Behavioral Science, Biological Science, Business Administration, Carpentry, Communications, Constructions Technology, Conservation, Electrical/Electronics Technology, Flight Training, Forestry, History

ATHLETIC PROFILE

Conference Affiliation: Mountain Valley Conference
Program Profile: We have an on campus playing field. We have Fall and Spring seasons and indoor practice facilities.
History: The program began in 1988. We took 7 trips to post-season.
Achievements: 1 Conference Title; 7 trip to post-season; 4 All-Americans; numerous All-Region players.
Coaching: Mike Mulligan - Head Coach. Dwight Doepel - Assistant Coach.
Roster for 1998 team/In State: 15 **Out of State:** 0 **Out of Country:** 0
Total Number of Varsity/Jr. Varsity: 15 **Percent of Graduation:** 80%
Number of Seniors on 1998 Team: **Number of Sophomores on 1998 Team:** 2
Freshmen Receiving Fin Aid/Athletic: 0 **Academic:** 12
Number of Fall Games: 20 **Number of Spring Games:** 37
Positions Needed for 1999/2000: Pitcher, Catcher, Infielder, Outfielder
Most Recent Record: 10 - 7 - 0
Schedule: Monroe, Fingerlakes, Erie, Mohawk Valley, Hudson Valley, Schenectady, Columbia

Genesee Community College

College Road
Batavia, NY 14020
Coach: Barry Garigen

NJCAA
Cougars/Navy, Gold, White
Phone: (716) 343-0055
Fax: (716) 343-1869

ACADEMIC

Founded: 1966
Type: 2 Yr., Public, Jr. College, Coed
SAT/ACT/GPA: Placement purposes only
Campus Housing: Yes
Student/Faculty Ratio: 17:1
Male/Female Ratio: 40:60
Undergraduate Enrollment: 2,500
Graduate Enrollment: 0
Scholarships/Academic: Yes **Athletic:** Yes **Fin Aid:** Yes
Total Expenses by: Year **In State:** $ 7,000 **Out of State:** $ 7,250
Degrees Conferred: AS, AAS
Programs of Study: General Studies, OTA, PTA, Nursing, Business

ATHLETIC PROFILE

Conference Affiliation: Western New York Athletic Conference
Program Profile: Our outside on site facility has: a batting cage and a field with dimensions of 325' down lines, 365 alley and 400' center. There is a new $ 3.0 million facility for some Spring games. Indoors we have a gym,a pool and a fitness center. Fall season consists of a 20-25 game and Spring season 35-45 game.
History: Our program began in 1978, we were 2nd place in Region III in 1980 and at Regional competition for playoffs most every year.
Achievements: 1 player drafted - played with Piller thru triple A (Mickey Hyde).

Hamilton College

198 College Hill Road
Clinton, NY 13323
Coach: Mike Davis

NCAA III
Continentals/White, Blue
Phone: (315) 859-4755
Fax: (315) 859-4117

ACADEMIC

Founded: 1812
Type: 4 Yr., Private, Liberal Arts, Coed
Web-site: http://www.hamilton.edu/
SAT/ACT/GPA: 1050+
Student/Faculty Ratio: 11:1
Male/Female Ratio: 53:47
Undergraduate Enrollment:
Graduate Enrollment: None
Scholarships/Academic: No **Athletic:** No **Fin Aid:** Yes
Total Expenses by: Year **In State:** $ 26,000 **Out of State:** $ 26,000
Degrees Conferred: BA
Programs of Study: Anthropology, Arts, Biochemistry, Biology, Chemistry, Classics, Comparative Literature, Computer Science, Creative Writing, Economics, English, French, Geology, German, Greek, History, International Studies, Latin, Linguistic, Literature, Mathematics, Modern Languages, Molecular Biology, Music, Philosophy, Physics, Political Science, Psychology, Public Affairs

ATHLETIC PROFILE

Conference Affiliation: NESCAC
Program Profile: We only have a Spring season! We play a 20-game Northern schedule, a 10-12 game schedule and take a Southern trip Cocoa Expo, Cocoa FL.
History: Hamilton's baseball program is over 100 years old.
Achievements: Matt Klump was named NCAA 2nd team All-Star in 1996 as a sophomore. Brian Guastella was named All-ECAC for his freshman year of 1995.

Coaching: Mike Davis, Head Coach, enters his 5th year as a head coach at Hamilton College. He started in both football and baseball at Idaho State garnering All-Big Sky honors in both sports. He coached at Rome Catholic High for nine years winning three Section III Titles.
Style of Play: We have a defensive approach to winning. Good pitching and good defense will win many games! Offensively, we want to be smart and do the basics - fundamentaly sound.

Hartwick College

West Street
Oneonta, NY 13820
Coach: Dan Pepicelli

NCAA III
Hawks/Blue, White
Phone: (607) 431-4706
Fax: (607) 431-4018

ACADEMIC

Founded: 1797
Type: 4 Yr., Private, Liberal Arts, Coed
Religion: Non-Affiliated
Campus Housing: Yes
Web-site: http://www.hartwick.edu/
SAT/ACT/GPA: Optional
Student/Faculty Ratio: 13:1
Male/Female Ratio: 47:53
Undergraduate Enrollment: 1,500
Graduate Enrollment: None
Scholarships/Academic: Yes **Athletic:** No **Fin Aid:** Yes
Total Expenses by: Year **In State:** $ 26,375 **Out of State:** $ 26,375
Degrees Conferred: BA, BS
Programs of Study: Accounting, Anthropology, Arts, Biochemistry, Biology, Business Administration, Chemistry, Computer Science, Economics, English, French, Geology, German, History, Information Science, Management, Mathematics, Medical Technology, Music, Nursing, Philosophy, Physics, Political Science, Prelaw, Premed, Prevet, Psychology, Religion, Sociology

ATHLETIC PROFILE

Conference Affiliation: ECAC, Upstate New York
Program Profile: We play and practice at a minor league facility called Damaschke Field, a home of the Class A Oneonta Yankees. It has a seating capacity of 3,500, indoor batting cages, outdoor astro-turf and a Fall practice facility.
History: The program began around 1900 and our winning tradition started in 1992. Our 1992 record was 19-13, 1993 record was 20-13, 1994 record was 25-13, 1995 record was 19-15 and 1996 record 17-16-1.
Achievements: 1992, 1994 and 1996 ECAC Upstate New York Champions; 1994 NCAA Tournament Bid.
Coaching: Dan Pepicelli, Head Coach, is taking over the reigns of the Hartwick baseball after the Hawks posted a 10-22-campaign last year. He served as an assistant coach for the 3 years, serving as a hitting coach and outfield instructor. The Hawks set school records for batting average under Pepicelli in 1996 and 1997.

Herkimer County Community College

Reservoir Road
Herkimer, NY 13350
Coach: Henry Testa

NJCAA
Generals/Green, Gold
Phone: (315) 866-0300
Fax: (315) 866-7253

ACADEMIC

Founded: 1966
Type: 2 Yr., Jr. College, Coed
Student/Faculty Ratio: 23:1
Male/Female Ratio: 40:60
Undergraduate Enrollment: 2,300
Graduate Enrollment: None
Scholarships/Academic: Yes **Athletic:** No **Fin Aid:** Yes
Total Expenses by: Year **In State:** $ 2,200 **Out of State:** $ 3,500
Degrees Conferred: Associate

Programs of Study: Accounting, Broacasting, Business, Computer, Conservation, Cosntruction, Corrections, Court Reporting, Criminal Justice, Drafting/Design, Fine Arts, Health, History, Humanities, Paralegal, Physical, Radio/Television, Sports/Recreation, Science, Travel/Tourism

ATHLETIC PROFILE

Conference Affiliation: Mountain Valley Conference
Program Profile: Play a Fall and a Spring season which consists of 45 games. We have an enclosed field in the campus. Facilities include a brand new field, dugouts and uniforms.
History: We are slowly gaining respect & made regional playoffs this year with several returning starters.
Coaching: Henry Testa, Head Coach, is a full time professor of accounting. He is in his 3rd year. His current Fall record is 7-1. Ken Ashe - Assistant Coach.
Style of Play: We play aggressive, running style and emphasize defense.

Hilbert College

8200 S Park Avenue
Hamburg, NY 14075
Coach: Jeremy Ross

NCAA III
Hawks/Blue, Silver, White
Phone: (716) 649-7900x243
Fax: (716) 649-6429

ACADEMIC

Founded: 1957
Type: 4 Yr., Private, Coed
Web-site: Not Available
SAT/ACT/GPA: 900+/20+
Student/Faculty Ratio: 14:1
Male/Female Ratio: 35:65
Undergraduate Enrollment: 950
Graduate Enrollment: None
Scholarships/Academic: Yes **Athletic:** No **Fin Aid:** Yes
Total Expenses by: Year **In State:** $ 13,500 **Out of State:** $ 13,500
Degrees Conferred: AA, AS, AAS, Bachelors, Baccalaureate, Associate
Programs of Study: Criminal Justice, Legal Assistant, Psychology, English Business Administration, Human Services, Accounting, Management Information System

ATHLETIC PROFILE

Conference Affiliation: Independent, ECAC
Program Profile: The 1995/96 Hilbert College baseball season will mark the 4th season as a Division III varsity sport and the beginning of a great deal of success for the program.
History: Our Div. III status began in the 92/93 season after much success at the junior college level.
Coaching: Fred Falkowski, Head Coach, is the former assistant coach at Rochester and head coach at the University of Buffalo.
Style of Play: We play fundamentally sound, enthusiastic and disciplined baseball.

Hobart and Williams Smith College

(Program Discontinued)

Hofstra University

100 Hampstead Turnpike
Hempstead, NY 11550
Coach: Reginald C. Jackson

NCAA I
Flying Dutchmen/Blue, Gold
Phone: (516) 463-5065
Fax: (516) 463-7514

ACADEMIC

Founded: 1935
Type: 4 Yr., Private, Liberal Arts, Coed
Religion: Non-Affiliated
Campus Housing: Yes
Web-site: http://www.hofstra.edu/
SAT/ACT/GPA: None

Student/Faculty Ratio: 16:1 **Male/Female Ratio:** 47:53
Undergraduate Enrollment: 8,716 **Graduate Enrollment:** 3,875
Scholarships/Academic: Yes **Athletic:** Yes **Fin Aid:** Yes
Total Expenses by: Year **In State:** $ 12,790 **Out of State:** $ 12,790
Degrees Conferred: AAS, BA, BS, BFA, BBA, BE, BSE, PhD, JD, MS, MA, MBA
Programs of Study: Humanities, Comparative Literature and Languages, Drama and Dance, English, Fine Arts, Art History and Humanities, French, Music, Mathematics, Engineering and Computer Science, Biology, Chemistry, Computer Science, Geology, Mathematics, Physics, Economics, History, Philosophy, Political Science, Psychlogy, Sociology, Anthropology, American

ATHLETIC PROFILE

Estimated Number of Baseball Scholarships: 10
Conference Affiliation: America East Conference
Program Profile: Our Fall program begins at the start of the school year. We play 10-15 games with some travel for 30 days only. We have a two weeks weight team program that goes until the Spring training. The Spring season starts with a trip to Florida. We play a regular season of 48 games. Our home field is natural grass infield/outfield.
Achievements: Playoffs in 1998.
Coaching: Reginald C. Jackson - Head Coach. Kevin Delaney and Larry Minor - Assistant Coaches.

Hudson Valley Community College

80 Vandenburgh Avenue **NJCAA**
Troy, NY 12180 **Vikings/Dartmouth Green, White**
Coach: Tom Reinisch **Phone: (518) 270-7328**
Email: reinitho@hucc.edu **Fax: (518) 270-4855**

ACADEMIC

Type: 2 Yr., Jr. College, Coed
Web-site: http://www.hvcc.edu
Degrees Conferred: Associate
Programs of Study: Contact school for program of study.

ATHLETIC PROFILE

Conference Affiliation: Mountain Valley Conference
Program Profile: Program has a playing season in the Fall & in the Spring. It is consists of 60 game.
History: Has three trips to World Series in Grand Junction.
Achievements: Travis Smith a shortstop was second team All-American in 1997; David Sunkens pitcher was named All-Mountain Valley Conference.
Coaching: Tom Reinisch - Head Coach. Jeffrey Di Nuzzo - Assistant Coach.
Roster for 1998 team/In State: 22 **Out of State:** 0 **Out of Country:** 0
Number of Fall Games: 18 **Number of Spring Games:** 42
Positions Needed for 1999/2000: Pitcher, Shortstop, Centerfield
Schedule: Columbia Green, Ocean County College, Onondaga Community College

Iona College

715 North Avenue **NCAA III**
New Rochelle, NY 10801 **Gaels/Maroon, Gold**
Coach: Al Zoccolillo **Phone: (914) 633-2305**
Fax: (607) 633-2662

ACADEMIC

Founded: 1940 **Type:** 4 Yr., Private, Liberal Arts, Coed
Religion: Catholic **Campus Housing:** Yes

Web-site: http://www.iona.edu/
SAT/ACT/GPA: 820
Student/Faculty Ratio: 12:1
Male/Female Ratio: 1:1
Undergraduate Enrollment: 5,200
Graduate Enrollment: 1,000
Scholarships/Academic: Yes **Athletic:** Yes **Fin Aid:** Yes
Total Expenses by: Year **In State:** $ 17,000 **Out of State:** $ 17,000
Degrees Conferred: AA, AAS, BA, BS, MA, MS, MBA, Med
Programs of Study: Accounting, Biochemistry, Biology, Chemistry, Computer and Information Science, Business, Education, Prephysical Therapy, Communications, Psychology, Teacher Education, Computer Science, Law, Math, Health Science

ATHLETIC PROFILE

Conference Affiliation: Metro Atlantic Athletic Conference
Program Profile: Our ball park was built in 1989 and the field measures 300' and 320' on lines, 370' gaps, 401' centerfield. We play both a Fall and Spring season.
History: Our program began in 1940.
Achievements: Conference Coach of the Year in 1983, 1984, and 1992; 2nd Place in the Conference in 1993; ECAC Finalist in 1992; received at large bid in 1993; over 50 players drafted; 3 major leaguers; 1994 MAAC finalist; 1 player drafted in 1994.
Coaching: Al Zoccolillo - Head Coach.
Style of Play: Power, hit and run.

Ithaca College

108 Ceracche Athletic-Danby Road
Ithaca, NY 14850
Coach: George Valensente

NCAA III
Bombers/Navy, White
Phone: (607) 274-3749
Fax: (607) 274-1667

ACADEMIC

Founded: 1892
Type: 4 Yr., Private, Liberal Arts, Coed
Religion: Non-Affiliated
Campus Housing: Yes
Web-site: http://www.ithaca.edu/
SAT/ACT/GPA: None
Student/Faculty Ratio: 12:1
Male/Female Ratio: 47:53
Undergraduate Enrollment: 5,600
Graduate Enrollment: 200
Scholarships/Academic: Yes **Athletic:** No **Fin Aid:** Yes
Total Expenses by: Year **In State:** $ 19,849 **Out of State:** $ 19,849
Degrees Conferred: BA, BS, BFA, BM, MS, MM
Programs of Study: Accounting, Finance, Human Resources Management, International Business, Management, and Marketing, Corporate Communications, Film, Photography, Arts, Journalism, Media Studies, Telecommunications, Health Services, Athletic Training, Exercise Science, Clinical Science, Physical Therapy, Community Health Education, Health and Physical Education, Health Information Management, Physical Education Teacher, Recreation, Anthropology, Applied Psychology, Musical Theatre, Computer Science, Sociology, Spanish, Music, Religion

ATHLETIC PROFILE

Conference Affiliation: Non-Conference
Program Profile: Ithaca plays its home games on award-winning Freeman Field, 1 of the most attractive grass fields in the country. It is equipped with permanent dugouts, a pressbox and 2 bullpens. The Bombers have 1 of the most successful small college programs with 20 consecutive appearances in the Div. III playoffs, NCAA champs in 1980 & 1988 & 57 straight winning years.
History: Ithaca 1st competed on collegiate level in 1930/31. A season later, legendary Coach James 'Bucky' Freeman took the helm for 31 seasons, forging a 281-82-2 record. His 1962 club beat Missouri in the College World Series before elimination by a 1-run decision to Florida State and Texas. Carlton 'Carp' Wood followed Freeman, guiding the Bombers to a 233-75-2 (.755) over the next 13 years. Wood was succeeded by Freeman protege George Valesente in 1978/79.
Achievements: 30 All-Americans; numerous players play pro baseball.

Coaching: George Valesente - Head Coach. Frank Fazio - Hitting Coach. Fritz Hamburg - Catchers (defense) and infield (3rd base). Brian Angeluchlo - Outfield (1st base).
Roster for 1998 team/In State: 24 **Out of State:** 9 **Out of Country:** 0
Total Number of Varsity/Jr. Varsity: 25/20 **Percent of Graduation:** 95%
Number of Seniors on 1998 Team: 6 **Number of Sophomores on 1998 Team:** 7
Freshmen Receiving Fin Aid/Athletic: 0 **Academic:** 85%
Number of Fall Games: 13 **Number of Spring Games:** 39
Positions Needed for 1999/2000: Pitcher, Middle Infielder, Catcher
Most Recent Record: 27 - 15 - 0
Schedule: Rollins, Florida Tech, LeMoyne, Mansfield State University, St. Leo, Shippensburg
Style of Play: Aggressive attack offensively. Good pitching and solid defense.

Jamestown Community College

525 Falconer Street
Jamestown, NY 14701
Coach: Kerry Kellogg

NJCAA
Jayhawks/Kelly Green, Gold
Phone: (716) 665-5220x321
Fax: (716) 665-6632

ACADEMIC

Founded: 1950 **Type:** 2 Yr., Public, Jr. College, Coed
Student/Faculty Ratio: 12:1 **Male/Female Ratio:** 1:1
Undergraduate Enrollment: 4,300 **Graduate Enrollment:** None
Scholarships/Academic: Yes **Athletic:** No **Fin Aid:** Yes
Total Expenses by: Year **In State:** $ 2,400 **Out of State:** $ 4,800
Degrees Conferred: Associates
Programs of Study: Accounting, Business, Communications, Computer, Criminal Justice, Engineering, Humanities, Law Enforcement, Liberal Arts, Nursing

ATHLETIC PROFILE

Conference Affiliation: Western New York Athletic Conference
Program Profile: We do a split season - approximately 20-25 games in the Fall and 25-30 games in the Spring. stadium has a seating capacity of 4,000, on campus; Minor League Field.
History: Greatest playing facility in WNY. Minor league ball park with lights - promotes a full Fall schedule of 25 games. Split season with 35 games in Spring.
Achievements: Not yet.
Coaching: Kerry Kellogg - Head Coach, fourth year with the program. BS degree at St. Petersburg JC, University of Florida. Montreal Expos (minors); pitched several years, strong baseball background. Past two years .500 percentage in Division III.
Roster for 1998 team/In State: 16 **Out of State:** 3 **Out of Country:** 0
Total Number of Varsity/Jr. Varsity: /19 **Percent of Graduation:** 80+%
Number of Seniors on 1998 Team: **Number of Sophomores on 1998 Team:** 6
Freshmen Receiving Fin Aid/Athletic: 0 **Academic:** 15
Number of Fall Games: 25 **Number of Spring Games:** 35
Positions Needed for 1999/2000: Pitcher, Retool every year!!
Most Recent Record: 14 - 16 - 0
Schedule: Erie Community College, Monroe Community College, CCFL
Style of Play: Let your bats, arms and gloves speak and not your mouth. Play hard and work hard. Proper practice prevents poor performance.

Jefferson Community College

Outer Coffeen Street
Watertown, NY 13601
Coach: Paul Alteri

NJCAA
Cannoneers/Cranberry, White
Phone: (315) 786-2497
Fax: (315) 786-2459

ACADEMIC

Founded: 1961
Type: 2 Yr., Public, Jr. College, Coed
SAT/ACT/GPA: Recommended but not required/
Web-site: http://www.sunyjefferson.edu
Student/Faculty Ratio: 17:1
Male/Female Ratio: 45:55
Undergraduate Enrollment: 3,500
Graduate Enrollment: 0
Scholarships/Academic: Yes **Athletic:** No **Fin Aid:** Yes
Total Expenses by: Year **In State:** $ 3,142 **Out of State:** $ 5,384
Degrees Conferred: AAS, AS, AA
Programs of Study: Accounting, Business, Computer Information Systems, Computer Science, Criminal Justice, Early Childhood, Early Childhood, Engineering Science, Hospitality Tourism, Human Services, Liberal Arts, Math, Office Technology, Paralegal, Registered Nursing, Retail Business Management, Science Laboratory Technology

ATHLETIC PROFILE

Conference Affiliation: Mid-State Athletic Conference
Program Profile: Our home games are played at the Watertown Fairgrounds Duffy Stadium, home of the Cleveland Indians single "A" farm club. The all-natural stadium seats 3,000 to 4,000 people.
History: Our program was dropped in 1996 (Spring). Paul Alteri took the team over in the Summer of 1996 and started from scratch. Now play both Fall and Spring season and go South for week during Spring break. The excitement is here at JCC; interest and individuality of our program is at an all time high!
Achievements: In our first season 1997 Rich Rhodes was selected 2nd team All-Region at 1st base.
Coaching: Paul A. Alteri, Head Coach, started in 1996. He compiled a record of 14 wins & 27 losses. He was a graduate of Le Moyne College, Syracuse, New York in 1996. Mark Alteri - Assistant Coach.
Roster for 1998 team/In State: 18 **Out of State:** 0 **Out of Country:** 1
Total Number of Varsity/Jr. Varsity: 21 **Percent of Graduation:** 100%
Number of Seniors on 1998 Team: 13 **Most Recent Record:** 10 - 15 - 0
Freshmen Receiving Fin Aid/Athletic: 0 **Academic:** All
Number of Fall Games: 12 **Number of Spring Games:** 30
Positions Needed for 1999/2000: Pitcher, Catcher, Middle Infielder
Schedule: Erie, Finger Lakes, Schenectady, Fulton-Montgomey, Broome, Onondaga, Mohawk
Style of Play: Discipline with the bats, aggressive on the bases!

Kingsborough Community College

2001 Oriental Blvd
Brooklyn, NY 11235
Coach: Bob Tertsas
NJCAA
The Wave/Blue, Orange
Phone: (718) 368-5737
Fax: (718) 368-4634

ACADEMIC

Type: 2 Yr., Jr. College, Coed
Campus Housing: No
Degrees Conferred: Associate
Programs of Study: Accounting, Art/Fine Arts, Biology, Biological Science, Broadcasting, Business Administration, Commerce, Management, Chemistry, Computer Programming, Computer Science, Data Processing, Early Childhood Education

ATHLETIC PROFILE

Conference Affiliation: CUNY

Le Moyne College

Springfield Road
Syracuse, NY 13214
Coach: John King

NCAA I
Dolphins/Green, Gold
Phone: (315) 445-4411
Fax: (315) 445-4678

ACADEMIC

Founded: 1946
Type: 4 Yr., Private, Liberal Arts, Coed
Religion: Jesuit
Campus Housing: Yes
Web-site: http://www.lemoyne.edu/
SAT/ACT/GPA: 1000+
Student/Faculty Ratio: 13:1
Male/Female Ratio: 47:53
Undergraduate Enrollment: 1,800
Graduate Enrollment: None
Scholarships/Academic: Yes **Athletic:** Yes **Fin Aid:** Yes
Total Expenses by: Year **In State:** $ 11,700 **Out of State:** $ 11,700
Degrees Conferred: BA, BS, MBA
Programs of Study: Business and Management, Education, Letters/Literature, Life Science, Psychology, Social Science, Accounting, Biology, Chemistry, Computer Science, Economics, History, Industrial Relations, Mathematics, Physics, Philosophy, Political Science, Psychology

ATHLETIC PROFILE

Conference Affiliation: Metro Atlantic Athletic Conference
Program Profile: NCAA Division I, Rockfield has a seating capacity of 1,000 and has a measurements of 320-380-320.
History: Since going to Division I in 1988; 7 Conference Champions including 1998 Regular Season and Tournament Championships.
Achievements: 1998 MAAC Coach of the Year; 4 All-Americans; 37 Professional players; 4 went to the major league.
Coaching: John King, Head Coach, entered his 2nd year with the program. He compiled a record of 44-38. Bob Nandin ,Assistant Coach, was a professional player for 10 years with the Toronto and Detroit. It is his 2nd year of professional coaching. Peter Huy Assistant Coach, is responsible for the pitchers and played with the Red Sox Organization, major league in 1992.
Roster for 1998 team/In State: 24 **Out of State:** 7 **Out of Country:** 1
Total Number of Varsity/Jr. Varsity: 32 **Percent of Graduation:** 99%
Number of Seniors on 1998 Team: 6 **Baseball Camp Dates:** July 5-9, 1999
Freshmen Receiving Fin Aid/Athletic: 6 **Academic:** Several
Number of Fall Games: 12 **Number of Spring Games:** 44
Positions Needed for 1999/2000: Pitcher, Infielder
Most Recent Record: 26 - 15 - 0
Style of Play: Low key, even keeled, self-disciplined.

Long Island University - Brooklyn Campus

1 University Plaza
Brooklyn, NY 11201
Coach: Frank Giannone

NCAA I
Blackbirds/Blue, White
Phone: (718) 488-1030
Fax: (718) 488-1669

ACADEMIC

Founded: 1926
Type: 4 Yr., Private, Liberal Arts, Coed
Religion: Non-Sectarian
Campus Housing: No
Web-site: http://www.brooklyn.liunet.edu/
SAT/ACT/GPA: 820/17
Student/Faculty Ratio: 12.5:1
Male/Female Ratio: 33:67
Undergraduate Enrollment: 6,253
Graduate Enrollment: 1,736
Scholarships/Academic: Yes **Athletic:** Yes **Fin Aid:** Yes
Total Expenses by: Year **In State:** $ 13,390 **Out of State:** $ 13,390

Degrees Conferred: BA, BS, AA, MBA, PhD
Programs of Study: Accounting, Anthropology, Banking/Finance, Biology, Broadcasting, Business, Chemistry, Communications, Computer, Economics, English, Fine Arts, History, Information Science, Languages, Library Science, Pharmacy, Political, Social Science

ATHLETIC PROFILE

Conference Affiliation: Northeast Conference

Long Island University - C.W. Post Campus

Northern Boulevard
Brookville, NY 11548
Coach: Richard Vining

NCAA I
Pioneers/Green, Gold
Phone: (516) 299-2939
Fax: (516) 626-0150

ACADEMIC

Founded: 1954
Type: 4 Yr., Private, Liberal Arts, Coed
Religion: Non-Affiliated
Campus Housing: Yes
Web-site: http://www.cwpost.liunet.edu/cwis/cwp/post.html
SAT/ACT/GPA: 840
Student/Faculty Ratio: 16:1
Male/Female Ratio: 38:62
Undergraduate Enrollment: 4,500
Graduate Enrollment: 3,600
Scholarships/Academic: Yes **Athletic:** Yes **Fin Aid:** Yes
Total Expenses by: Year **In State:** $ 21,000 **Out of State:** $ 21,000
Degrees Conferred: AA, BA, BS, BFA, MA, MS, MBA, MFA, D
Programs of Study: Acting, Art, Biology, Broadcasting, Business, Chemistry, English, Environmental, Interdisciplinary, International, Math, Molecular Biology, Preprofessional Programs, Public, Radiologic, Teachers of Special Education/Speech/Hearing Handicapped

ATHLETIC PROFILE

Conference Affiliation: Metropolitan Conference
History: The program began in 1958.

Manhattan College

Manhattan College Parkway
Riverdale, NY 10471
Coach: Steve Trimper

NCAA I
Jaspers/White, Green
Phone: (718) 862-7486
Fax: (718) 862-8020

ACADEMIC

Type: 4 Yr., Private, Liberal Arts, Coed, Engineering
Founded: 1851
Religion: Roman Catholic
Campus Housing: Yes
Web-site: http://www.mancol.edu/
SAT/ACT/GPA: 1000
Student/Faculty Ratio: 15:1
Male/Female Ratio: 50:50
Undergraduate Enrollment: 3,500
Graduate Enrollment: None
Scholarships/Academic: Yes **Athletic:** Yes **Fin Aid:** Yes
Total Expenses by: Year **In State:** $ 23,000 **Out of State:** $ 23,000
Degrees Conferred: BA, BS, MA, MBA, PhD
Programs of Study: Athletic Training, Biotechnology, Chemistry, Engineering, Health, History, Humanities, Human Services, International, Literature, Math, Mechanical, Languages, Physics, Religious, Science, Special Education

ATHLETIC PROFILE

Conference Affiliation: Metro Atlantic Athletic Conference

Program Profile: Has a four straight years of more win than before. Won 4 All-MAAC in 1997; MAAC Player of the Year in 1997.
History: Our program began in 1903 and we are famous for inventing the 7th inning stretch. We the Division III longest program.
Achievements: 1996 Coach of the Year; 1997 Player of the Year.

Manhattanville College

2900 Purchase Street
Purchase, NY 10577
Coach: Michael McCarthy

NCAA III
the Valiants/Valiant Red, White
Phone: (914) 323-5280
Fax: (914) 323-5130

ACADEMIC

Founded: 1841
Religion: Sacred Heart
Web-site: http://www.mville.edu/
Student/Faculty Ratio: 10:1
Undergraduate Enrollment: 900
Scholarships/Academic: Yes **Athletic:** No
Total Expenses by: Year **In State:** $ 23,000

Type: 4 Yr., Private, Liberal Arts, Coed
Campus Housing: Yes
SAT/ACT/GPA: 1000
Male/Female Ratio: 1:2
Graduate Enrollment: 700
Fin Aid: Yes
Out of State: $ 23,000

Degrees Conferred: BA, BS, MA, MAT, MFA
Programs of Study: Art, Art History, Biochemistry, Biology, Business Management, Chemistry, Computer Science, Design, Dramatic Arts, Economics, Education, English, Environmental Science, Finance, Philosophy, Photography, Physics, Political Science, Predentistry, Prelaw, Premed

ATHLETIC PROFILE

Conference Affiliation: Skyline Conference
Achievements: Several All-Conference Palyers.
Style of Play: Aggressive.

Marist College

290 North Road
Poughkeepsie, NY 12601
Coach: John Szefc

NCAA I
Red Foxes/Red, White, Black
Phone: (914) 575-3000
Fax: (914) 471-0466

ACADEMIC

Founded: 1946
Religion: Catholic
Web-site: http://www.marist.edu/
Student/Faculty Ratio: 15:1
Undergraduate Enrollment: 3,200
Scholarships/Academic: Yes **Athletic:** Yes
Total Expenses by: Year **In State:** $ 19,000

Type: 4 Yr., Private, Liberal Arts, Coed
Campus Housing: Yes
SAT/ACT/GPA: 1000+/23/85%
Male/Female Ratio: 55:45
Graduate Enrollment: 500
Fin Aid: Yes
Out of State: $ 19,000

Degrees Conferred: BA, BS, MA, MS, MFA, MBA
Programs of Study: Accounting, American Studies, Biochemistry, Biology, Business Administration, Chemistry, Communications, Computer Science, Criminal Justice, Economics, Education, Fashion Design, Film Arts, History, Journalism, Management, Mathematics, Medical Laboratory Technology, Political Science, Psychology, Social Science

ATHLETIC PROFILE

Conference Affiliation: Metro Atlantic Conference
History: The inception of the program was six years ago.

Mercy College

555 Broadway
Dobbs Ferry, NY 10522
Coach: Bill Sullivan

NCAA II
Flyers/Navy, Carolina Blue, White
Phone: (914) 674-7566
Fax: (914) 674-7281

ACADEMIC

Founded: 1950
Type: 4 Yr., Private, Liberal Arts, Coed
Web-site: Not Available
SAT/ACT/GPA: 700+
Student/Faculty Ratio: 15:1
Male/Female Ratio: 3:1
Undergraduate Enrollment: 6,500
Graduate Enrollment: 1,000
Scholarships/Academic: Yes **Athletic:** Yes **Fin Aid:** Yes
Total Expenses by: Year **In State:** $ 10,000 **Out of State:** $ 10,000
Degrees Conferred: BA, BS, MS
Programs of Study: Accounting, Actuarial Sciences, Animal Science, Banking and Finance, Behavioral Science, Biology, Broadcasting, Business Administration, Chiropractic, Communications, Computer Science, Criminal Justice, Education, English, French, Graphic Design, History, Italian, Journalism, Management, Marketing, Mathematics, Medical Laboratory Technology, Music, Nursing, Political Science, Predentistry, Prelaw, Premed, Prepharmacy, Psychology, Social Science, Spanish

ATHLETIC PROFILE

Conference Affiliation: New York Collegiate Athletic Conference
Program Profile: We have an on campus playing facility with a natural grass surfac and are not a stadium layout. We have a 50 Spring games schedule and a 6-10 games schedule in the Fall.
History: Our programs started in 1950. Mercy competes in one of the most competitive conference in Division II.
Achievements: Last conference titles was in 1990; All-American in 1990 was Chris Walpole; Brian Sweeneyn - Lancaster Jethawks Single A Seattle Mariners Organization.
Coaching: Bill Sullivan, Head Coach, is entering his fourth season. He graduated from La Salle University in 1991and was seventh overall at Mercy. Ray Alonso, Assistant Coach, started his 3rd season and graduated from Mercy College in 1995. Bill Rosenweiz , Assistant Coach, started his 1st season and is a graduate from Albany State University in 1995.
Style of Play: Offensively our best weapon is our speed. Like to run and run often. Team's goal will be 130 stolen bases. Showed good gap power in the Fall of 1997. To win we will need a solid pitching and defense.

Mohawk Valley Community College

1101 Sherman Drive
Utica, NY 13501-5394
Coach: Joe Milazzo

NJCAA
Hawks/Green, White
Phone: (315) 792-5571
Fax: (315) 792-5695

ACADEMIC

Founded: 1946
Type: 2 Yr., Jr. College, Coed
Web-site: http://www.mvcc.edu
SAT/ACT/GPA: None
Student/Faculty Ratio: 11:1
Male/Female Ratio: 20:80
Undergraduate Enrollment: 1,950
Graduate Enrollment: 300
Scholarships/Academic: Yes **Athletic:** Yes **Fin Aid:** Yes
Total Expenses by: Year **In State:** $ 10,000 **Out of State:** $ 10,000
Degrees Conferred: Associate
Programs of Study: Accounting, Advertising, Aircraft/Missile Maintenance, Biology, Business, Chemistry, Communications Equipment Technology, Computer Programming, Data Processing, Electrical/Electronics Technology, Engineering and Applied Science

ATHLETIC PROFILE

Conference Affiliation: Mountain Valley Conference

Molloy College

1000 Hempstead Avenue
Rockville, NY 11571-5002
Coach: Bernie Havern

NCAA II
Lions/Maroon, Grey
Phone: (516) 678-5000
Fax: (516) 256-2231

ACADEMIC

Founded: 1955
Type: 4 Yr., Private, Liberal Arts, Coed
Religion: Catholic
Campus Housing: Yes
Web-site: http://www.molloy.edu/
SAT/ACT/GPA: 100
Student/Faculty Ratio: 11:1
Male/Female Ratio: 20:80
Undergraduate Enrollment: 1,950
Graduate Enrollment: 300
Scholarships/Academic: Yes **Athletic:** Yes **Fin Aid:** Yes
Total Expenses by: Year **In State:** $ 10,000 **Out of State:** $ 10,000
Degrees Conferred: AA, BA, MS, MA
Programs of Study: Accounting, Art, Biology, Business Management, Cardio-Respiratory Sciences, Communications, Computer Science, English, French, Gerontology, History, Interdisciplinary Studies, International Peace and Justice, Mathematics, Music, Nursing, Philosophy, Political Science, Psychology, Social Work, Sociology, Theology, Preparation for Teaching Certification in Secondary, Elementary and Special Education

ATHLETIC PROFILE

Conference Affiliation: New York Collegiate Athletic Conference
Program Profile: Newly renovated field.
History: Our program began in 1993 as NCAA team. Our 1st year record was 15-18. Our team has traveled to Dominican Republic and Puerto Rico to play ball.
Achievements: Two All-Region Players.
Coaching: Bernie Havern - Head Coach.
Style of Play: Fundamental game.

Monroe Community College

1000 E Henrietta Rd
Rochester, NY 14623
Coach: Dudley 'Skip' Bailey

NJCAA I
Tribunes/Black, Gold
Phone: (716) 292-2833
Fax: (716) 292-3845

ACADEMIC

Type: 2 Yr., Public, Liberal Arts, Coed, Engineering
Founded: 1960
Religion: Non-Affiliated
Campus Housing: No
Undergraduate Enrollment: 8,000
Graduate Enrollment: None
Total Expenses by: Year **In State:** $ 3,000 **Out of State:** $ Varies
Degrees Conferred: Associates
Programs of Study: Accounting, Humanities, Mathematics, Social Science, Natural Science, Business Administration, Biological Technological, Chemical Technology, Civil Technology, Communications and Media Arts, Computer Information Systems, Computer Science, Computer Technology, Construction Technology, Criminal Justice, Dental Assisting, Electrical Engineering

ATHLETIC PROFILE

Estimated Number of Baseball Scholarships: 10
Conference Affiliation: Western New York Conference

Program Profile: Monroe Community College is one of the most successful programs in the country having won the Penn-York Conference Championships 16 times in the past 18 years. We have an on campus baseball facility of natural grass. Fall season has 20 games & Spring season has 45 games.
History: 1966 was MCC's first season. Dave Chamberlain was a head coach for 32 season with a record of 735-232; Reional Championships; 4 Junior College World Series Division I.
Achievements: 27 All-Americans and 22 drafted players.
Coaching: Dudley Skip Bailey, Head Coach, is in his 3rd year as head coach. It his 19th year with the program and he works with the hitting and infield. Pete Dawes, Assistant Coach, is in his 13th season and works with the pitchers and catchers. Mike Chamberlain, Asistant Coach, is in his 6th season and works with outfielders, base running and coaches 3rd base.
Roster for 1998 team/In State: 18 **Out of State:** 6 **Out of Country:** 0
Total Number of Varsity/Jr. Varsity: 24 **Percent of Graduation:** 75%
Baseball Camp Dates: March **Number of Sophomores on 1998 Team:** 12
Freshmen Receiving Fin Aid/Athletic: 5 **Academic:** 2
Number of Fall Games: 20 **Number of Spring Games:** 45
Positions Needed for 1999/2000: All **Most Recent Record:** 43 - 14 - 0
Schedule: Brevard CC, Rockland CC, Briar Cliff CC, Alfred State College, Onondaga CC, Erie CC
Style of Play: Aggressive offense (built around team speed), defense (solid up the middle), utilize all players. Allow pitchers who are qualified to hit and play positions.

Mount Saint Mary College

330 Powell Avenue
Newburgh, NY 12550
Coach: Tom McTamaney

NCAA III
Blue Knights/Royal Blue, Gold
Phone: (914) 569-3594
Fax: (914) 562-6762

ACADEMIC

Founded: 1960 **Type:** 4 Yr., Private, Liberal Arts, Coed
Religion: Catholic **Campus Housing:** Yes
Web-site: http://www.msmc.edu/ **SAT/ACT/GPA:** 950/18
Student/Faculty Ratio: 16:1 **Male/Female Ratio:** 1:2.5
Undergraduate Enrollment: 1,900 **Graduate Enrollment:** 400
Scholarships/Academic: Yes **Athletic:** No **Fin Aid:** Yes
Total Expenses by: Year **In State:** $ 14,730 **Out of State:** $ 14,730
Degrees Conferred: BA, BS, BSN, MBA, MSEd, MSM
Programs of Study: Accounting, Biology, Business Management/Administration, Chemistry, Communications, Computer Science, Elementary Education, English, Political Science, International Studies, Mathematics, Medical Technology, Nursing, Predentistry, Social Science, Sociology, Theatre

ATHLETIC PROFILE

Conference Affiliation: Knickerbocker, Skyline Conference
Program Profile: The team played at Cronomer Park with a seating capacity of 1,500 which has a natural grass field and an indoor hitting facility for the Winter. The program has both a Fall and a Spring season.
History: We started NCAA affiliation season of 1989 in Division III. We won Knickerbocker Conference in our first year as members (1991) and again in 1994. We received a ECAC bid in 1992 and 1994.
Achievements: Over 50 players drafted since 1989. Skyline Conference Champions in 1995-1998; ECAC Metro Champ; Runner-Up ECAC; NCAA Regional Berth 2-times; NCAA Tournament in 1998.
Coaching: Tom McTamaney, Head Coach, entered his 6th season with the program and compiled a record of 107-61. Lou Arrotta - Assistant Coach.
Roster for 1998 team/In State: 26 **Out of State:** 0 **Out of Country:** 0
Total Number of Varsity/Jr. Varsity: 26 **Percent of Graduation:** 88%-99%
Number of Seniors on 1998 Team: 10 **Number of Sophomores on 1998 Team:** 6

Number of Fall Games: 10 **Number of Spring Games:** 32
Positions Needed for 1999/2000: Infielder, Pitcher, Catcher
Most Recent Record: 25 - 9 - 0
Schedule: Western Connecticut, SUNY-Oneonta, SUNY-Old Westbury, Staten Island, Dowling
Style of Play: Aggressive players.

Nassau Community College

1 Education Drive
Garden City, NY 11530
Coach: Larry Minor
NJCAA
Lions/Orange, Blue
Phone: (516) 572-7522
Fax: (516) 228-3531

ACADEMIC

Founded: 1959
Type: 2 Yr., Jr. College, Coed
Student/Faculty Ratio: 8:1
Male/Female Ratio: 71:29
Undergraduate Enrollment: 7,623
Graduate Enrollment: None
Scholarships/Academic: Yes **Athletic:** Yes **Fin Aid:** Yes
Total Expenses by: Year **In State:** $ 1,950 **Out of State:** $ 3,800
Degrees Conferred: Associate
Programs of Study: Accounting, Applied Arts, Banking/Finance, Business, Civil Engineering Technology, Engineering Science, Humanities, Law Enforcement, Liberal Arts, Marketing, Mathematics, Operating Room Technology, Paralegal Studies, Contact school admission office for more information on academic and admission.

ATHLETIC PROFILE

Conference Affiliation: Region XV

New York Institute of Technology

P.O. Box 8000
Old Westbury, NY 11568
Coach: Bob Hirschfield
NCAA I
Bears/Royal, Gold
Phone: (516) 686-7513
Fax: (516) 626-0750

ACADEMIC

Type: 4 Yr., Private, Liberal Arts, Coed, Engineering
Founded: 1955
Web-site: http://www.nyit.edu/
SAT/ACT/GPA: NCAA Requirements
Student/Faculty Ratio: 18:1
Male/Female Ratio: 6:4
Undergraduate Enrollment: 6,000
Graduate Enrollment: 4,000
Scholarships/Academic: Yes **Athletic:** Yes **Fin Aid:** Yes
Total Expenses by: Year **In State:** $ 16,000 **Out of State:** $ 16,000
Degrees Conferred: AAS, BA, BS, BFA, BArch, MA, MS, MFA, DO
Programs of Study: Accounting, Advertising, Architectural Technology, Architecture, Art, Biology, Business and Management, Chemistry, Communications, Computer Information Systems, Computer Science, Economics, Education, Electrical Engineering/Technology, Mathematics, Political Science

ATHLETIC PROFILE

Conference Affiliation: Independent
Program Profile: We have an excellent natural turf facility in a secluded North shore (Lorry Island), environment . Our facility has :1,000 seats , a press box and an electronic scoreboard. The team has a locker room, laundry facilities & 4 outdoor batting cages. OurFall season consists of 5 weeks.
History: We were Division I in 1981. We have an overall record in Division I with of 408-325, and an overall playoff record of 24-16. We participated in NCAA playoffs 3 times (twice as Division II member and once as a Division I member). We have been nationally ranked at various times in the late 1980's.

Achievements: Has 8 conference titles since 1981; 3 Coach of the Year Honors; 3 All-Americans (last one in 1991) Al Watson, Anaheim Angels-1st round pick; 42 players drafted or signed by professional organization since 1981.
Coaching: Bob Hirschfield, Head Coach, was at New York Tech since 1978 . He was pitching coach since 1978-1981 and head coach since 1982. Bill Asermely, Scott Hatten and Bill Timmes - Assistant Coaches.
Roster for 1998 team/In State: 27 **Out of State:** 1 **Out of Country:** 0
Total Number of Varsity/Jr. Varsity: 28 **Percent of Graduation:** 95%
Number of Seniors on 1998 Team: 2 **Most Recent Record:** 14 - 28 - 0
Freshmen Receiving Fin Aid/Athletic: 7 **Academic:** 3
Number of Fall Games: 4 **Number of Spring Games:** 52
Positions Needed for 1999/2000: Pitcher, Centerfield, Catcher
Baseball Camp Dates: August 16-20/(516) 922-7133
Schedule: University of Miami, Georgia Southern Unviersity, West Virginia, St. John's University, Seton Hall University, George Mason University
Style of Play: Sound defense and quality pitching - most of the drafted players have been pitchers.

Niagara County Community College

3111 Saunders Settlement Road
Sanborn, NY 14132
Coach: Dave Nemi

NJCAA
Trailblazers/Royal, Gold
Phone: (716) 731-3271
Fax: (716) 731-2116

ACADEMIC

Founded: 1962 **Type:** 2 Yr., Jr. College, Coed
Student/Faculty Ratio: 15:1 **Male/Female Ratio:** 43:57
Undergraduate Enrollment: 5,663 **Graduate Enrollment:** None
Scholarships/Academic: No **Athletic:** No **Fin Aid:** Yes
Total Expenses by: Year **In State:** $ 2,100 **Out of State:** $ 4,000
Degrees Conferred: Associate
Programs of Study: Accounting, Animal Science, Biological Science, Business Administration, Communications, Criminal Justice, Data Processing, Drafting/Design, Horticulture, International Business, Labor Relations, Mathematics, Operating Room Technology, Radiological Technology

ATHLETIC PROFILE

Conference Affiliation: Western New York Athletic Conference
Program Profile: We have a Fall and a Spring program. The team plays 25 games in the Fall and 45 games in the Spring. Ourfacilities are located on campus campus.
History: Our program has been in existence for 30 years. For the past 8 years,we finished in the top ten in NYS.
Achievements: Won 1994 Western New York Athletic Conference Champs, 1995 seeded 1 in NYS, All-American in 1995 - Steve Strack. NYS Player of the Year.
Coaching: David Nemi ,Head Coach, is on his 14th season. Tony Nemi ,Associate Coach, is on his 14th season. Charlie Webb,Assistant Coach, is on his 5th season. Aaron Goloa ,Pitching Coach, is on his 3rd season.
Style of Play: Fundamentally sound and aggressive play.

Niagara University

Lewiston Road
Niagara University, NY 14109-2039
Coach: Jim Mauro
Email: jfm@niagara.edu

NCAA I
Purple Eagles/Purple, White
Phone: (716) 286-8602
Fax: (716) 286-8609

ACADEMIC

Founded: 1856
Religion: Vincentian
Web-site: http://www.niagara.edu/
Student/Faculty Ratio: 17:1
Undergraduate Enrollment: 2,225
Type: 4 Yr., Private, Liberal Arts, Coed
Campus Housing: Yes
SAT/ACT/GPA: 1000
Male/Female Ratio: 2:1
Graduate Enrollment: 650
Scholarships/Academic: Yes **Athletic:** Yes **Fin Aid:** Yes
Total Expenses by: Year **In State:** $ 18,500 **Out of State:** $ 18,500
Degrees Conferred: BA, BS, MBA, MED
Programs of Study: Business and Management, Communications, Health Sciences, Multi/Interdisciplinary Studies, Physical Sciences, Social Sciences, Prelaw, Biology, Education, Nursing, Hotel Management, Criminal Justice

ATHLETIC PROFILE

Conference Affiliation: Metro Atlantic Athletic Conference
Program Profile: Home games are played on John P. Bobo field (natural grass, seats 300). The program has a stable coaching staff, and we play both a Fall (10 games) and Spring (40-46 games) season in a competitive conference. We have a recently renovated infield.
History: The records at the university do not go back very far, but the program was conducted in 1940's.
Achievements: Won the 1997 MAAC North Division Regular Season Title; Jim Mauro - 1997 MAAC North Coach of the Year; Aaron Mindel - 1997 MAAC North Player of the Year, Carm Penaro drafted by Arizona Diamondbacks in 1996.
Coaching: Jim Mauro - Head Coach. Bob Kowalski - Assistant Coach. John Goodfellow - Assistant.
Style of Play: Strong defense team. Pitching has some players coming back from injuries, if healthy, will be a strength. Fairly balanced line-up with some power. Like to move runners and be aggressive on basepaths.

Nyack College

1 South Boulevard
Nyack, NY 10960
Coach: Jason Beck
NAIA
Figthing Parsons/Purple, Gold
Phone: (914) 358-1710
Fax: (914) 353-2147

ACADEMIC

Founded: 1882
Religion: Christian and Missionary Alliance
Web-site: Not Available
Type: 4 Yr., Private, Liberal Arts, Coed
Campus Housing: Yes
SAT/ACT/GPA: 860
Scholarships/Academic: Yes **Athletic:** Yes **Fin Aid:** Yes
Total Expenses by: Year **In State:** $ 13,500 **Out of State:** $ 13,500
Degrees Conferred: BA, BS, Bmus, MA, MS
Programs of Study: Biblical Studies, Business and Economics, Christian Studies, Communication, Education, English, History, Humanities, Management, Ministries, Missions, Music, Music Theory and Composition, Natural Science, Performing Arts, Philosophy, Psychology, Religion, Religious Education, Religious Music, Secondary Education, Social Science, Voice

ATHLETIC PROFILE

Conference Affiliation: NAIA, NCCAA, Central Atlantic Collegiate Conference
Program Profile: We are in NAIA Division I. Nyack baseball includes a Fall program, a Florida Spring training and a Spring season of 30+ games. We play on a natural grass field.
History: Our program began in 1963. We are NCCAA District champs/NCCAA District runner-up '94.
Achievements: NCCAA Conference Champs in 1982; Kurt Huber was 1994 Honorable Mention in the NCCAA.

Orange County Community College

115 South Street
Middletown, NY 10940
Coach: Tony Mancuso

NCAA III
Colts/Navy Blue, Orange
Phone: (914) 341-4211
Fax: (914) 341-4216

ACADEMIC

Founded: 1950
Type: 2 Yr., Jr. College, Coed
Religion: Non-Affiliated
Campus Housing: No
Undergraduate Enrollment: 2,000+
Graduate Enrollment: None
Total Expenses by: Year **In State:** $ Varies **Out of State:** $ Varies
Degrees Conferred: Associate
Programs of Study: Accounting, Architectural Technology, Biology, Biological Science, Business Administration, Commerce, Management, Computer Information Systems, Computer

ATHLETIC PROFILE

Conference Affiliation: Mid-Hudson Conference, NJCAA Region XV
Program Profile: At OCCC we are the other alternative for high school athletes in Orange County. We recruit primarily in our county giving the athlete an opportunity to work, go to class, and play ball. We have a Fall and Spring season and work hard to get our graduates into four year colleges.
History: The baseball program at OCCC started in the late 1950's or early 1960's. During the 1970's the school enjoyed moderate success, but fell on hard times in the 1980's. Beginning in 1994 with a new coaching staff OCCC has been successful by recruiting good ball players and is slowly becoming a program of note in Region XV.
Achievements: OCCC has made the Region XV tournament 3 out of the last 4 years and had 1 ball player, Tim Spindler, drafted by the New York Yankees.
Coaching: Tony Mancuso, Head Coach, has been here four years and has a 37-55 record. Tom Gioradano, Assistant Coach/Pitching Coach, has coached four years. Mike Scott, Assistant Coach/Catching Coach, has coached one year.
Style of Play: We play hardnose, fundamentally solid baseball. We never quit even though we had a poor 1996 season the school we played knew that we would not lose quietly.

Pace University

861 Bedford Road
Pleasantville, NY 10570
Coach: Fred Calaicone
Email: fcalaicone@fsmail.pace.edu

NCAA
Setters/Blue, Grey, Gold
Phone: (914) 773-3413
Fax: (914) 773-3491

ACADEMIC

Founded: 1963
Type: 4 Yr., Private, Coed
Religion: Non-Affiliated
Campus Housing: Yes
Web-site: http://www.pace.edu
SAT/ACT/GPA: 900
Student/Faculty Ratio: 21:1
Male/Female Ratio: 1:2
Undergraduate Enrollment: 3,500
Graduate Enrollment: None
Scholarships/Academic: Yes **Athletic:** Yes **Fin Aid:** Yes
Total Expenses by: Year **In State:** $ 21,000 **Out of State:** $ 21,000
Degrees Conferred: AA, AS, AAS, BA, BS, BBA, BFA, LLM, MBA, MSN
Programs of Study: Business and Management, Equestrian Science, Communications, Bioengineering and Biomedical, Engineering, International Studies, Psychology, Social Sciences

ATHLETIC PROFILE

Estimated Number of Baseball Scholarships: 10
Conference Affiliation: Independent

Program Profile: We are a Division I top level for East. Our stadium has a seating capacity of 1,000 and is a natural grass field which has a dimensions of 330, 390, 330, gaps is 370. We play 50 games in the Spring and 6 in the Fall. We have 5 step down dugouts, double cages and a large working area for large bull pens on both sides.
History: We began in 1949 and were Division I for ten years. We take a trip to Arizona, Miami, North Carolina. Chapel Hill, Virginia, New Mexico and a few places in Florida.
Achievements: 3 Conference Titles; 6 All-Americans; 31 drafted in 12 years.
Coaching: Fred Calaicone - Head Coach. Tim Kelly - Assistant Coach.
Roster for 1998 team/In State: 12 **Out of State:** 7 **Out of Country:** 1
Total Number of Varsity/Jr. Varsity: 30 **Percent of Graduation:** 100%
Number of Seniors on 1998 Team: 5 **Number of Sophomores on 1998 Team:** 6
Freshmen Receiving Fin Aid/Athletic: 14 **Academic:** 16
Number of Fall Games: 6 **Number of Spring Games:** 50
Positions Needed for 1999/2000: Catcher, 2 OF, 2nd Base, 3 Pitchers
Most Recent Record: 17 - 24 - 0
Schedule: Florida Atlantic, Maine, Richmond, West Virginia, Michigan State, Purdue, Seton Hall
Style of Play: Like to run - must hit and make DP's.

Polytechnic University

6 Metrotech Center
Brooklyn, NY 11201
Coach: Darrel Tiebout
Email: athletic@poly.edu
NCAA III
Blue Jays/Blue, Grey
Phone: (718) 637-5900
Fax: (718) 637-5959

ACADEMIC

Type: 4 Yr., Private, Coed, Engineering **Founded:** 1854
Religion: All **Campus Housing:** Yes
Web-site: http://www.poly.edu/ **SAT/ACT/GPA:** None
Student/Faculty Ratio: 18:1 **Male/Female Ratio:** 7:1
Undergraduate Enrollment: 1,200 **Graduate Enrollment:** 1,000
Scholarships/Academic: Yes **Athletic:** No **Fin Aid:** Yes
Total Expenses by: Year **In State:** $ 18,000 **Out of State:** $ 18,000
Degrees Conferred: BS, Masters, PhD
Programs of Study: Mechanical Engineering, Electrical Engineering, Civil Engineering, Computer Science, Computer Engineering, Technical Writing, Chemical Engineering, Pure Science, Humanities

ATHLETIC PROFILE

Conference Affiliation: Independent Conference
Program Profile: We play a Spring season. Our facility is a field in Farmingdale, New York and has natural turf. The Spring season is from March to May.
History: Our program began in 1971 and we became an NCAA team in 1973.
Achievements: Won the Independent Athletic Conference Champions 1980; lasr 2 seasons winning team.
Coaching: Darrel Tiebout, Head Coach, coached baseball for 26 years. He coached 1 year high school baseball. He coached four players who are in the Major League. Linton Dyer, Assistant Coach, played six years of baseball at W. Kansas City Royals, and Sandlot Ball for six years.
Total Number of Varsity/Jr. Varsity: 12 **Percent of Graduation:** 100%
Number of Seniors on 1998 Team: 2 **Most Recent Record:** 3 - 6 - 0
Positions Needed for 1999/2000: All **Number of Spring Games:** 15
Schedule: Stevens Tech, SUMC, St. Joseph's, NYU, Nyack, Baruch
Style of Play: Our goal is to have solid defense with a good pitcher to enhance player's skills. Aggressive offensively and playing fundamental defense.

Rensselaer Poly Institute

110 - 8th Street
Troy, NY 12180
Coach: Karl Steffen

NCAA III
Engineers/Red, White
Phone: (518) 276-6185
Fax: (518) 276-2717

ACADEMIC

Type: 4 Yr., Private, Liberal Arts, Coed, Engineering
Founded: 1824
Religion: Non-Affiliated
Campus Housing: Yes
Web-site: http://www.rpi.edu/
SAT/ACT/GPA: 1090+28
Student/Faculty Ratio: 11:1
Male/Female Ratio: 80:20
Undergraduate Enrollment: 5,000
Graduate Enrollment: 2,400
Scholarships/Academic: Yes **Athletic:** Yes **Fin Aid:** Yes
Total Expenses by: Year **In State:** $ 28,000 **Out of State:** $ 28,000
Degrees Conferred: BS, Barch, Ms, MBA, MFA, PhD
Programs of Study: Aeronautical Engineering, Architecture, Biology, Biomedical Engineering, Chemical Engineering, Chemistry, Engineering, Computer Science, Economics, Geology, Interdisciplinary Studies, Management, Mathematics, Philosophy, Physics, Predentistry, Prelaw, Premed, Psychology, Science Technology

ATHLETIC PROFILE

Conference Affiliation: ECAC, EAA, NYSWCAA
Achievements: Rensselaer has qualified for the NCAA Tournament five straight years and six of the last seven years. In 1996, the team advanced to the World Series for the first time ever, won the NCAA Division III team ERA Title, and fielder three All-Americans. In recent years, has won numerous conference titles and several of its players have earned All-Conference, All-Leagues, and All-Americans honors.
Coaching: Karl Steffen, Head Coach, has coached 11 years and guided the program to 6 NCAA Tournaments, the only 6 in the program's history. He has compiled a .643 winning percentage.

Rochester Institute of Technology

51 Lomb Memorial Drive
Rochester, NY 14623
Coach: Rob Grow

NCAA III
Tigers/Orange, White
Phone: (716) 475-2614
Fax: (716) 475-5675

ACADEMIC

Type: 4 Yr., Private, Liberal Arts, Coed, Engineering
Founded: 1829
Religion: Non-Affiliated
Campus Housing: Yes
Web-site: http://www.rir.edu/
SAT/ACT/GPA: 950+/24
Student/Faculty Ratio: 13:1
Male/Female Ratio: 65:35
Undergraduate Enrollment: 10,600
Graduate Enrollment: 2,000
Scholarships/Academic: Yes **Athletic:** No **Fin Aid:** Yes
Total Expenses by: Year **In State:** $ 20,835 **Out of State:** $ 20, 835
Degrees Conferred: AAS, AS, BS, BA, BFA, MS, MA, MGA, MST, PhD
Programs of Study: Accounting, Aeronautical Engineering, Banking/Finance, Biology, Business, Chemistry, Communications, Computer Science, Criminal Justice, Economics, Film and Fine Arts, Management, Marketing, Photography, Physics, Polymer Science, Social Science

ATHLETIC PROFILE

Conference Affiliation: EAA, ECAC

Rockland Community College

145 College Road
Suffern, NY 10901
Coach: Dan Keeley

NJCAA
Hawks/Green, Orange
Phone: (914) 574-4452
Fax: (914) 574-4430

ACADEMIC

Founded: 1959
Type: 2 Yr., Jr. College, Coed
Undergraduate Enrollment: 8,000
Graduate Enrollment: None
Scholarships/Academic: No **Athletic:** Yes **Fin Aid:** Yes
Total Expenses by: Year **In State:** $ 2,600 **Out of State:** $ 5,200
Degrees Conferred: Associate
Programs of Study: Accounting, Advertising, Automotive Technology, Banking/finance, Business, Communications, Criminal Justice, Data Processing, Drafting/Design, Electrical Design, Electrical Engineering, Electro Mechanical Technology, Environmental Science, Fire Science, Forestry

ATHLETIC PROFILE

Conference Affiliation: Mid-Hudson, NJCAA Region XV

Saint Bonaventura University

Athletic Department
St. Bonaventura, NY 14778
Coach: Larry Sudbrook

NCAA I
Bonnies/Brown, White
Phone: (716) 375-2641
Fax: (716) 375-2280

ACADEMIC

Founded: 1858
Type: 4 Yr., Private, Liberal Arts, Coed
Religion: Catholic
Campus Housing: Yes
Web-site: http://www.cs.sbu.edu/
SAT/ACT/GPA: 1000
Student/Faculty Ratio: 18:1
Male/Female Ratio: 60:40
Undergraduate Enrollment: 2,050
Graduate Enrollment: 650
Scholarships/Academic: Yes **Athletic:** Yes **Fin Aid:** Yes
Total Expenses by: Year **In State:** $ 19,600 **Out of State:** $ 19,600
Degrees Conferred: BA, BS, MA, MS, MBA
Programs of Study: Accounting, Biology, Business and Management, Chemistry, Computer Science, Physics, Political Science, Prelaw, Premed, Physical Education, Predentistry, History, Modern Language, Social Science, German, Greek, Finance, Marketing, Journalism

ATHLETIC PROFILE

Conference Affiliation: Atlantic Ten Conference
Program Profile: Indoor facilities consist of two gyms and a new state of the art weight lifting facility. Team plays a full 56 game Division I schedule on a natural turf at McGraw-Jennings Field.
History: Hall of Fame members ,John McGraw and Hugh Jennings started and played in early 1900's. Our program went Division I in 1985. We had Atlantic Ten Tourney Appearances (top 4 out of 12) in 1994 and 1995.
Achievements: 9 players drafted in the 1990's.
Coaching: Larry Sudbrook - Head Coach. Chris Goyette - Assistant Coach.
Style of Play: Program stresses pitching, defense, and speed.

Saint Francis College - New York

180 Remsen Street
Brooklyn Heights, NY 11201
Coach: Frank Delgeorge

NCAA I
Terries/Red, Blue
Phone: (718) 522-2300
Fax: (718) 522-1274

ACADEMIC

Founded: 1884
Type: 4 Yr., Private, Liberal Arts, Coed
Religion: Franciscan Brothers
Campus Housing: No
Web-site: Not Available
SAT/ACT/GPA: 820/18
Student/Faculty Ratio: 24:1
Male/Female Ratio: 45:55
Undergraduate Enrollment: 2,300
Graduate Enrollment: None
Scholarships/Academic: Yes **Athletic:** Yes **Fin Aid:** Yes
Total Expenses by: Year **In State:** $ 8,000 **Out of State:** $ 8,000
Degrees Conferred: AS, AAS, BA, BS
Programs of Study: Accounting, Aviation Management, Biology, Biomedical Science, Broadcasting, Business Administration, Communications, Computer Information Systems, Computer Science, Criminal Justice, Economics, Elementary Education, English, Film Studies, Finance, Health Services, History, Interdisciplinary Studies, Liberal Arts, Management, Marketing, Mathematics, Medical Technology Physical Education, Political Science, Predentistry, Prelaw, Premed, Psychology, Secondary Education, Social Science, Special Education

ATHLETIC PROFILE

Conference Affiliation: Northeast, ECAC

Saint John Fisher College

3690 East Avenue
Rochester, NY 14618
Coach: Robert Simms

NCAA III
Cardinals/Cardinal Red, Gold
Phone: (716) 385-8309
Fax: (716) 385-7308

ACADEMIC

Founded: 1948
Type: 4 Yr., Private, Liberal Arts, Coed
Religion: Roman Catholic
Campus Housing: Yes
Web-site: Not Available
SAT/ACT/GPA: 950/21
Student/Faculty Ratio: 14:1
Male/Female Ratio: 50:50
Undergraduate Enrollment: 1,500
Graduate Enrollment: 1,000
Scholarships/Academic: Yes **Athletic:** No **Fin Aid:** Yes
Total Expenses by: Year **In State:** $ 19,000 **Out of State:** $ 19,000
Degrees Conferred: BA, BS
Programs of Study: Business and Management, Communications, Letters/Literature, Psychology, Social Sciences

ATHLETIC PROFILE

Conference Affiliation: ECAC

Saint John's University - New York

800 Utopia Parkway
Jamaica, NY 11439
Coach: Ed Blankmeyer
Email: blankme@st.johns.edu

NCAA I
Red Storm/Red, White, Navy
Phone: (718) 990-6148
Fax: (718) 990-1988

ACADEMIC

Founded: 1870
Type: 4 Yr., Private, Liberal Arts, Coed
Religion: Vincentian
Campus Housing: Yes
Web-site: http://www.stjohns.edu/
SAT/ACT/GPA: 820/70
Student/Faculty Ratio: 15:1
Male/Female Ratio: 1:1
Undergraduate Enrollment: 15,000
Graduate Enrollment: 3,000
Scholarships/Academic: Yes **Athletic:** Yes **Fin Aid:** Yes
Total Expenses by: Year **In State:** $ 17,000 **Out of State:** $ 17,000
Degrees Conferred: BA, BS, BFA, MA, MBA, MS
Programs of Study: Accounting, American Studies, Anthropology, Banking and Finance, Biology, Broadcasting, Business, Chemistry, Communications, Computer Science, Criminal Justice, Economics, Education, English, Environmental Science, Fine Arts, Journalism, Management, Marketing, Mathematics, Nursing, Pharmacy, Philosophy, Physical Education Physics, Political Science, Psychology, Religion, Social Science, Toxilogy

ATHLETIC PROFILE

Conference Affiliation: Big East Conference
Program Profile: We are considered a top program in the Northeast. The McCallen Field is the best stadium in the Metropolitan area. A new stadium will be constructed in the near future. Indoor and weight training facilities are of high quality. We are very conducive for indoor-Winter training.
History: Our program began in 1906. St. John's has appeared in six College World Series with their last appearance in 1980. The Red Storm has appeared in the Final AP Poll 16 times since 1959 and has won four conference titles.
Achievements: 1996 Big East Coach of the Year; 1997 Big East Champions; last year three junior pitchers drafted; 6 all-time winningest program in the country; 26 NCAA Appearances; most Big East Conference Championships.
Coaching: Ed Blankmeyer, Head Coach, coached 16 years and was Association Academic Coach at Seton Hall. He compiled an overall record of 89-52. Kevin McMullan, Assistant Coach, was years head coach at Indiana University for 4 years, prior to arriving at St. John's (3 years at SJU). Mike Maesten - Pitching Coach, (4 years at SJU).
Roster for 1998 team/In State: 20 **Out of State:** 14 **Out of Country:** 0
Total Number of Varsity/Jr. Varsity: 34 **Percent of Graduation:** 90%
Number of Seniors on 1998 Team: 4 **Number of Sophomores on 1998 Team:** 8
Freshmen Receiving Fin Aid/Athletic: 10 **Academic:** 6
Number of Fall Games: 4 **Number of Spring Games:** 52
Positions Needed for 1999/2000: LHP, Catcher, Shortstop
Schedule: VCU, North Carolina State, Florida International, Notre Dame, Central Florida
Style of Play: Team built on pitching and defense and speed.

Saint Joseph's College - New York

155 W Roe Boulevard
Patchogue, NY 11772-2603
Coach: Tim Mundell

NCAA III
Golden Eagles/Navy, Gold, White
Phone: (516) 447-3290
Fax: (516) 447-3347

ACADEMIC

Founded: 1925
Type: 4 Yr., Private, Liberal Arts, Coed,
Student/Faculty Ratio: 15:1
Male/Female Ratio: 4:6
Undergraduate Enrollment: 2,500
Graduate Enrollment: 150
Scholarships/Academic: Yes **Athletic:** No **Fin Aid:** Yes
Total Expenses by: Year **In State:** $ 8,350 **Out of State:** $ 8,548
Degrees Conferred: BA, BS, MA, Therapeutic Ed.
Programs of Study: Accounting, Biology, Business Administration, Child Study, Classics, Computer Science, Education, English, Fine Arts, History, Human Relations, Mathematics, Modern Languages, Philosophy, Physical Education, Physical Sciences, Recreation, Religious Studies, Social Science, Psychology, Religious Studies, Social Science, Speech Communications, Interdisciplinary Courses

ATHLETIC PROFILE

Conference Affiliation: Independent Athletic Conference and Knickerbocker (ECAC)

Saint Lawrence University

Augsburg Center, Park and Leigh Sts
Canton, NY 13617
Coach: Tom Fay

NCAA III
Saints/Scarlet, Brown
Phone: (315) 379-5882
Fax: (315) 379-5589

ACADEMIC

Founded: 1856
Type: 4 Yr., Private, Liberal Arts, Coed
Religion: Non-Affiliated
Campus Housing: Yes
Web-site: http://www.stlawu.edu/
SAT/ACT/GPA: None
Student/Faculty Ratio: 12:1
Male/Female Ratio: 1:1
Undergraduate Enrollment: 1,950
Graduate Enrollment: 100
Scholarships/Academic: Yes **Athletic:** No **Fin Aid:** Yes
Total Expenses by: Year **In State:** $ 28,815 **Out of State:** $ 28,815
Degrees Conferred: BA, BS, MA, MS, Med
Programs of Study: Anthropology, Art, Asian Studies, Biology, Biophysics, Chemistry, Computer Science, Creative Writing, Ecology, Economics, Engineering, English, Environmental Science, French, Geology, Geophysics, German, History, Literature, Mathematics, Modern Languages, Music, Philosophy, Physical Education, Physics, Political Science, Psychology, Recreation and Leisure, Religion, Romance Languages, Social Sciences, Spanish, Theatre

ATHLETIC PROFILE

Conference Affiliation: Upstate Collegiate Athletic Association
Program Profile: We have indoor facilities: Leithead Field House. It has a full-sized tartan turf infield, 2 batting cages and a 4-mound bull pen.

Saint Thomas Aquinas College

125 Route 340
Sparkill, NY 10976
Coach: James Romeo

NAIA
Spartans/Maroon, Gold
Phone: (914) 398-4058
Fax: (914) 359-8136

ACADEMIC

Founded: 1952
Type: 4 Yr., Private, Coed
Web-site: Not Available
SAT/ACT/GPA: 830+
Student/Faculty Ratio: 18;1
Male/Female Ratio: 50;50
Undergraduate Enrollment: 1,400
Graduate Enrollment: 40
Scholarships/Academic: Yes **Athletic:** Yes **Fin Aid:** Yes
Total Expenses by: Year **In State:** $ 15,000 **Out of State:** $ 15,000
Degrees Conferred: BA, BS, Med
Programs of Study: Accounting, Applied Art, Applied Mathematics, Business Administration, Communications, Computer Information Systems, Criminal Justice, Education, Engineering, English, Finance, Fine Arts, History, Humanities, Journalism, Mathematics, Medical Laboratory Technology, Modern Languages, Natural Science, Premed, Psychology, Recreation and Leisure, Religion Romance, Social Science, Spanish, Speech Education

ATHLETIC PROFILE

Conference Affiliation: CACC

Schenectady County Community College

78 Washington Avenue
Schenectady, NY 12305
Coach: Tim Andi
Email: gonzaldm@gw.sunnyscc.edu

NJCAA
Royals/Royal Blue, Gold
Phone: (518) 381-1356
Fax: (518) 346-0379

ACADEMIC

Founded: 1969
Type: 2 Yr., Public, Jr. College, Coed
Web-site: http://www.crisny.org.edu/
SAT/ACT/GPA: Not Required
Student/Faculty Ratio: 18:1
Male/Female Ratio: 1:1
Undergraduate Enrollment: 1,800
Graduate Enrollment: None
Scholarships/Academic: Yes **Athletic:** No **Fin Aid:** Yes
Total Expenses by: Year **In State:** $ 2,440 **Out of State:** $ 5,500
Degrees Conferred: Associate Degrees
Programs of Study: Aviation Science, Business Administration, Computer Science, Drama, Human Services, Mathematics, Music, Sciences, Telecommunications, Accounting, Administrative Assistant, Criminal Justice, Culinary Arts, Early Childhood Education

ATHLETIC PROFILE

Conference Affiliation: Mountain Valley Conference
Program Profile: We practice in an indoor facility starting in February each year, play Fall and Spring schedule. We have a natural grass field and go to Florida for Spring training each March before starting the regular season.
History: The program started in 1970. We have made regional playoffs ten straight years. We have won over 20 games for eight straight years. We had over ten players drafted over that time and a number of players transfer to Division I, II, and III baseball programs.
Achievements: Coach Tim Andi was named Region III Coach of the Year this past year as well as Mountain Valley Conference Coach of the Year; we have 3 All-Region players this year; 4 All-Conference and have had 2 All-Americans in the past.
Coaching: Tim Andi, Head Coach, started in 1980 and compiled a record of 160-68 overall. We played at Le Moyne College, Division II in Syracuse, New York and played briefly in minor leagues. Jeff Brown ,Assistant Coach, played Division I at St. John's University. Some drafted by Tigers.
Roster for 1998 team/In State: 22 **Out of State:** 2 **Out of Country:** 1
Total Number of Varsity/Jr. Varsity: 25 **Percent of Graduation:** 100%
Number of Seniors on 1998 Team: 12 **Number of Sophomores on 1998 Team:** 0
Number of Fall Games: 20 **Number of Spring Games:** 40
Positions Needed for 1999/2000: Pitchers, Catchers
Schedule: Monroe CC, Columbia Green, Hudson Valley, Fulton Motgomery, Finger Lakes, Erie C
Style of Play: Good pitching and fielding, like to steal in right situattion. Play smart baseball and do not beat themselves.

Siena College

515 London Road
Londonville, NY 12211-1462
Coach: Tony Rossi
Email: rossi@siena.edu

NCAA I
Saints/Green, Gold
Phone: (518) 786-5044
Fax: (518) 783-2992

ACADEMIC

Founded: 1939
Type: 4 Yr., Private, Liberal Arts, Coed
Religion: Roman Catholic
Campus Housing: Yes
Web-site: http://www.siena.edu/
SAT/ACT/GPA: 1000/80
Student/Faculty Ratio: 16:1
Male/Female Ratio: 1:1
Undergraduate Enrollment: 2,700
Graduate Enrollment: 400
Scholarships/Academic: Yes **Athletic:** Yes **Fin Aid:** Yes

Total Expenses by: Year **In State:** $ 19,595 **Out of State:** $ 19,595
Degrees Conferred: BA, BS
Programs of Study: Business (Accounting, Finance, Marketing and Management), Education, English, History, Letters/Literature, Life Sciences, Political Science, Psychology, Social Science

ATHLETIC PROFILE

Estimated Number of Baseball Scholarships: 3
Conference Affiliation: Metro Atlantic Athletic Conference
Program Profile: We are a small Division I and top NAIAC indoor facility. Our field has a natural surface and we have a 56 game schedule, a Southern trip and Fall and Spring seasons.
History: Our program began in 1941 and has 2 major league. Billy Marshall was named American League Rockie of the Year in 1954 with Cleveland Indians; over 35 pro-players; Division II until going Division I in 1978.
Achievements: Coach of the Year in 1991, 1995 and 1996; Conference Champs in 1995, 1996 and 1997; 3 drafted players in 1996 and 2 in 1997; All-American in 1996.
Coaching: Tony Rossi, Head Coach, started his 32nd year of coaching. He was named Coach of the Year in 1997, 1996 and 1995. Paul Thompson, Assistant Coach, started his 8th year. Tony Curd, Assistant Coach, started his 4th year.
Roster for 1998 team/In State: 17 **Out of State:** 13 **Out of Country:** 1
Total Number of Varsity/Jr. Varsity: 31 **Percent of Graduation:** 98%
Number of Seniors on 1998 Team: 8 **Baseball Camp Dates:** July 27-31
Freshmen Receiving Fin Aid/Athletic: 5 **Academic:** 6
Number of Fall Games: 2 **Number of Spring Games:** 54
Positions Needed for 1999/2000: 1st Base, 2-OF, 3rd Base, Pitcher
Most Recent Record: 15 - 32 - 0
Schedule: Seton Hall, University of Massachusetts, Stetson, University of Central Florida
Style of Play: Speed, pitching, and defense.

Skidmore College

815 North Broadway
Saratoga Springs, NY 12866
Coach: Ron Plurde

NCAA III
Thoroughbreds/White, Gold, Green
Phone: (518) 580-5000
Fax: (518) 584-5396

ACADEMIC

Founded: 1911 **Type:** 4 Yr., Private, Liberal Arts, Coed,
Religion: Presbyterian **Campus Housing:** Yes
Web-site: http://www.skidmore.edu/ **SAT/ACT/GPA:** 1100/24
Student/Faculty Ratio: 10:1 **Male/Female Ratio:** 40:60
Undergraduate Enrollment: **Graduate Enrollment:** None
Scholarships/Academic: No **Athletic:** No **Fin Aid:** Yes
Total Expenses by: Year **In State:** $ 15,250 **Out of State:** $ 15,250
Degrees Conferred: BA, BS, MA
Programs of Study: Anthropology, Art, Biology, Biochemistry, Business, Economics, Chemistry, Physical Education, Computer Science, Philosophy, Elementary Education, Economics-Sociology

ATHLETIC PROFILE

Conference Affiliation: ECAC

State University of New York - Binghamton

P.O. Box 6000
Binghamton, NY 13902-6000
Coach: Tim Sinicki

NCAA III
Colonials/Dark Green, White
Phone: (607) 777-2525
Fax: (607) 777-4597

ACADEMIC

Founded: 1946
Type: 4 Yr., Public, Coed
Religion: Non-Affiliated
Campus Housing: Yes
Web-site: http://www.binghamton.edu
SAT/ACT/GPA: 1150
Student/Faculty Ratio: 13:1
Male/Female Ratio: 1:1.2
Undergraduate Enrollment: 9,349
Graduate Enrollment: 2,627
Scholarships/Academic: Yes **Athletic:** Yes **Fin Aid:** Yes
Total Expenses by: Year **In State:** $ 8,433 **Out of State:** $ 13,333
Degrees Conferred: BA, BS, BFA, MA, MS, MFA, MEd, PhD
Programs of Study: Accounting, American Studies, Athropology, Art, Art History, Biochemistry, Biology, Business and Management, Chemistry, Classics, Comparative Literature, Computer Science, Creative Writing, Ecology, Economics, Engineering, English, Environmental Studies, Film Studies, French, Geography, Geology, Geophysics, German, History, Liberal Arts, Life Sciences, Literature, Mathematics, Nursing, Philosophy, Physical Education, Political Science, Predentistry, Prelaw, Premed, Prevet, Psychology, Social Science, Theatre

ATHLETIC PROFILE

Conference Affiliation: State University of New York Atheltic Conference
Program Profile: We have a 45-game schedule (9 Fall/36 Spring). We play games on campus at Varsity Field. Our team takes an annual Southern trip. We have a natural grass playing surface. Our indoor facilities include 2 year-round batting cages and indoor pitching mounds.
History: Our program began in 1948 and has enjoyed its most success in the past 2 seasons with back-to-back 17- and 20-win seasons ncluding postseason invite in 1995. Six of our players have signed pro contracts.
Achievements: 1995 has 3 All-Conference players; 1 Regional All-American; 7 players named to the Academic All-Conference team; 1996 has 1 All-Conference Selection; 8 Academic All-Conference Selections; 4 players in the past 12 years have been drafted to play pro ball.
Coaching: Tim Sinicki, Head Coach, is a Division I pitcher at Western Carolina and was drafted by the Pirates in 1986 as a pitcher. He coached at Broome CC for 3 years and was 5th Spring at Binghamton.
Style of Play: Fundamentals stressed, aggressive style on offense (hit and run, stealing, taking extra bases).

State University of New York - Brockport

350 New Campus Drive
Brockport, NY 14420
Coach: Mark Rowland
NCAA III
Golden Eagles/Green, Gold
Phone: (716) 395-5329
Fax: (716) 395-2160

ACADEMIC

Founded: 1867
Type: 4 Yr., Public, Coed
Religion: Non-Affiliated
Campus Housing: Yes
Web-site: http://www.brockport.edu/
SAT/ACT/GPA: Required
Student/Faculty Ratio: Unknown
Male/Female Ratio: 46:54
Undergraduate Enrollment: 7,000
Graduate Enrollment: 2,000
Scholarships/Academic: No **Athletic:** No **Fin Aid:** Yes
Total Expenses by: Year **In State:** $ 8,265 **Out of State:** $ 11,581
Degrees Conferred: All
Programs of Study: Accounting, American Studies, Anthropology, Art History, Art Studio, Biological Science, Business Administration, Chemistry, Communications, Computer Science, Criminal Justice, Dance, Earth Science, Economics, English, French, Geology, Health Science, History, International Business and Economics, International Studies, Liberal Studies, Mathematics, Nursing, Philosophy

ATHLETIC PROFILE

Conference Affiliation: SUNYAC West

Program Profile: Our facilities include a natural, newly renovated playing surface with dugouts, seating for 500, an athletic weight room, an indoor batting cage with a a juggs machine. The Physical Education facilities, are among the finest in NY state. They include: hundreds of acres of playinfields, two swimming pools, indoor hockey rink, scores of tennis courts and several gymnasiums. The Golden Eagles play both a Fall and Spring season.
History: Our program began in 1947 and was dropped in 1950 and reinstated in the mid 1950's until it was dropped again in the late 1970's. We were reinstated again in 1984 and have enjoyed a fine tradition since then. There have been 9 head coaches between 1969 and 1989.
Achievements: Won SUNYAC West Title in 1991, 1992 and 1994; ECAC Upstate NY Runner-Up in 1994 and 1995. In the Summer of 1996 two former players participated in professional baseball.
Coaching: Mark Rowland, Head Coach, was elected to the position in May of 1996 after serving as an assistant coach under former head coach Jim DeBell, who retired.
Style of Play: Aggressive style of play is emphasized - taking extra bases when possible, stealing, hit and rug and bunting. Fundamentals are stressed most. The strength of the squad is usually hitting attack, but a strong core of pitchers returns to bolster the staff.

State University of New York - Cobleskill

Route 7
Cobleskill, NY 12043
Coach: John Price

NJCAA
Tigers/Orange, Black
Phone: (518) 255-5127
Fax: (518) 234-5333

ACADEMIC

Type: 4 Yr.,Coed
Religion: Non-Affiliated
Web-site: http://www.cobleskill.edu/
Degrees Conferred: Bachelors
Programs of Study: Contact school for program of study.

State University of New York - Cortland

P.O. Box 2000
Cortland, NY 13045
Coach: Steve Owens

NCAA III
Red Dragons/Red, White
Phone: (607) 753-4950
Fax: (607) 753-4929

ACADEMIC

Founded: 1868
Religion: Non-Affiliated
Web-site: http://www.cortland.edu/
Student/Faculty Ratio: 20:1
Undergraduate Enrollment: 5,000
Scholarships/Academic: Yes **Athletic:** No
Total Expenses by: Year **In State:** $ 10,000

Type: 4 Yr., Public, Liberal Arts, Coed
Campus Housing: Yes
SAT/ACT/GPA: 1000
Male/Female Ratio: 40:60
Graduate Enrollment: 1,400
Fin Aid: Yes
Out of State: $ 15,000

Degrees Conferred: BS, BA, BSE, MA, MS
Programs of Study: African American Studies, Anthropology, Art, Biology, Chemistry, Cinema Study, Communications, Early Secondary and Elementary Education, Economics, Economics Management, English, Environmental Studies, French, Geography, Geology, Health Education, History, Mathematics, Philosophy, Physical Education, Physics, Political Science, Psychology, Social Studies, Spanish, Speed and Heavy

ATHLETIC PROFILE

Conference Affiliation: SUNYAC

Program Profile: We play at Wallace Field with a press box, dugouts, wind screen, outdoor cages and a seating capacity of 500. Lusk Fieldhouse is 100 yards long is netted and has cages.
History: The program began in 1992 & we have a 5-30 win season in a row. We had 9-20 win seasons in a row & 1-40 win season in a row . We have the 6th winningest program in the country in 1990's.
Achievements: 1992-1998 achievements: 8 NCAA All-Americans; 2 Academic All-Americans; 4 pro players.
Coaching: Steve Owens, Head Coach, has coached from 1992-1998. He has a career record of 209-72, 6 NCAA, 3 World Series and back to back 3rd place finishes in the country. John Brown and Mike Urtz - Assistant Coach.
Roster for 1998 team/In State: 25 **Out of State:** 5 **Out of Country:** 0
Total Number of Varsity/Jr. Varsity: 31 **Most Recent Record:** 40 - 5 - 0
Number of Seniors on 1998 Team: 6 **Baseball Camp Dates:** July 13-17
Positions Needed for 1999/2000: Pitchers
Schedule: Florida Tech, Mansfield, Anderson, Lehigh, Ithaca
Style of Play: Aggressive at plate and on bases.

State University of New York - Farmingdale

Nold Hall, Melville Road
Farmingdale, NY 11735
Coach: Ken Rocco

NJCAA
Rams/Green, Grey, Gold
Phone: (516) 420-2123
Fax: (516) 420-3624

ACADEMIC

Founded: 1912 **Type:** 2 Yr., Public, Coed
Student/Faculty Ratio: 17:1 **Male/Female Ratio:** 53:47
Undergraduate Enrollment: 7,700 **Graduate Enrollment:** None
Scholarships/Academic: No **Athletic:** No **Fin Aid:** Yes
Total Expenses by: Year **In State:** $ 8,500 **Out of State:** $ 12,500
Degrees Conferred: Associates
Programs of Study: Aerospace Science, Architectural Technology, Aviation Administration and Technology, Biological Science, Biomedical Technology, Construction Technology, Criminal Justice, Flight Training, General Engineering, Horticulture, Industrial Administration, Landscape Architecture, Manufacturing Technology

ATHLETIC PROFILE

Program Profile: Our playing field has natural grass with measurements of 320 down the lines and 380 to the center. It has a seating capacity of 4,000 and an indoor batting cage. Playing season starts March 10 and goes through May 10 . We then have the playoffs.
History: Since 1971, we have been in region 15 tournaments all but 3 years. We have a win and loss record career or 441-305.
Achievements: All-Americans were Wayne Schwing, Mike Pepio, Frank Hornig, Ball Decollibus, Matt Gervasio, Tom Tuttle, Lou Oroligio, Todd Kerpa & Mike Murray. We have 6 Sportmanship Awards.
Coaching: Ken Rocco - Head Coach.
Roster for 1998 team/In State: 20 **Out of State:** 0 **Out of Country:** 0
Total Number of Varsity/Jr. Varsity: 0 **Percent of Graduation:** 92%
Most Recent Record: 15 - 16 - 0 **Number of Sophomores on 1998 Team:** 3
Number of Fall Games: 12 **Number of Spring Games:** 42
Positions Needed for 1999/2000: Pitcher, Middle Infielder
Schedule: Queensboro, Navy, Annapolis, Dutchess, Nassau, Suffolk

State University of New York - Fredonia

Dods Hall
Fredonia, NY 14063
Coach: Dale Till

NCAA III
Bvlue Devils/Blue, White
Phone: (716) 673-3334
Fax: (716) 673-3624

ACADEMIC

Founded: 1826
Type: 4 Yr., Public, Liberal Arts, Coed
Religion: Non-Affiliated
Campus Housing: Yes
Web-site: http://www.cs.fredonia.edu/
SAT/ACT/GPA: 1000
Student/Faculty Ratio: 16:1
Male/Female Ratio: 2:3
Undergraduate Enrollment: 4,500
Graduate Enrollment: 200
Scholarships/Academic: Yes **Athletic:** No **Fin Aid:** Yes
Total Expenses by: Year **In State:** $ 3,400 **Out of State:** $ 8,300
Degrees Conferred: Bachelors, Masters
Programs of Study: Accounting, Art, Biology, Business Administration, Chemistry, Communications, Computer Information Science, Cooperative Agriculture, Cooperative Engineering, Earth Science, Economics, Elementary Education, English, Geology, Health Service Administration, History, Mathematics, Medical technology, Music, Philosophy, Physics, Political Science, Psychology

ATHLETIC PROFILE

Conference Affiliation: SUNYAC, ECAC
Program Profile: The Fredonia State Blue Devils play a Fall and Spring program, competing in approximately 50 games during the season. The team has won 332 games in the past 15 years, averaging 23 victories per season. The Western division champs of their conference (SUNYAC) in both 1990 and 1991, the squad captured the conference crown in 1990 and won the ECAC Upstate NY Division III championship in 1982.
History: Our program began in 1963. Our current Head Coach Dale Till is only the third head coach in the history of the program and is currently mid-way through his 16th season as head coach. Assistant Coach Dave Criscione has also been with the program since 1980.
Achievements: Co-Coach of the Year (SUNYAC) 1989-1990; SUNYAC Champions in 1989-1990; ECAC Upstate NY Division III Champions in 1982; 3 players drated by pros; Coach Till member of Fredonia State Sports Hall of Fame and Western New York Softball Hall of Fame.
Coaching: Dale Till, Head Coach, graduated from Fredonia State. He played varsity ball for four years and set several hitting records.

State University of New York - New Paltz

75 South mznheim
New Paltz, NY 12561
Coach: Michael Juhl

NCAA III
Hawks/Orange, Blue
Phone: (914) 257-3915
Fax: (914) 257-3920

ACADEMIC

Type: 4 Yr., Public, Liberal Arts, Coed, Engineering
Founded: 1828
Religion: Non-Affiliated
Campus Housing: Yes
Web-site: http://www.newpaltz.edu/
SAT/ACT/GPA: None
Student/Faculty Ratio: 25:1
Male/Female Ratio: 40:60
Undergraduate Enrollment: 5,000
Graduate Enrollment: 500
Scholarships/Academic: Yes **Athletic:** No **Fin Aid:** Yes
Total Expenses by: Year **In State:** $ 9,500 **Out of State:** $ 13,500
Degrees Conferred: BA, BS, BFA, MA, MAT, MA, MFA
Programs of Study: Education, Engineering, Liberal Arts and Science, Business Administration, Fine Arts, Performing Arts

ATHLETIC PROFILE

Conference Affiliation: SUNYAC
Program Profile: Our Division II program is looking to improve. Loren Gambell Field is a natural grass with a seating capacity of 200 people which has a dimensions of 318 down the lines, 384 to the center. We have excellent indoor facilities including a 300'x125' bubble (air structure) to set up full infield, 2 batting tunnels and indoor mounds.
History: Our program has been on the downward slide in the last six years.
Coaching: Mike Juhl, Head Coach, was hired in August 1 to replace the previous coach with a 20-106 record over the past 6 seasons. Coach Juhl is a former Philadelphia Phillies pitcher who made his triple A debut in 1995. An Honorable Mention Junion College All-American from FCCT, he should be able to pass his baseball knowledge to his players. Look for good things to happen at SUNY, starting with his first recruting class in 1998-1999. Jim Ferraro - Assistant Coach.
Style of Play: Little baseball hit-run. Play defense and throw strikes. We have a small ball park and no power. Loaded with pitching but need to play defense.

State University of New York - Old Westbury

Clark Center Building
Old Westbury, NY 11568-0210
Coach: John Lonardo

NCAA III
Panthers/Forest Green, White
Phone: (516) 876-3241
Fax: (516) 876-3209

ACADEMIC

Founded: 1968
Type: 4 Yr., Pubblic, Coed
Web-site: http://www.oldWestbury.edu/
SAT/ACT/GPA: 800
Student/Faculty Ratio: 25:1
Male/Female Ratio: 45:55
Undergraduate Enrollment: 3,800
Graduate Enrollment: 800
Scholarships/Academic: No **Athletic:** No **Fin Aid:** Yes
Total Expenses by: Year **In State:** $ 7,600 **Out of State:** $ 11,900
Degrees Conferred: BA, BS
Programs of Study: Business, Accounting, Economics, Management, Education, Arts and Sciences, American Studies, Anthropology, Applied Physics, Art History, Art Studio, Biochemistry, Biology, Biophysics, Chemistry, Communications, Comparative Literature, Computer

ATHLETIC PROFILE

Conference Affiliation: Knickerbocker
Program Profile: We play major college baseball in a small school atmosphere. We have a brand new stadium . The Jackie Robinson Sports facility is to be built in 1999-2000 and will seat 1,500. It will include a press box, changing room, dug-outs, a scoreboard, & a state of the art training facility.
History: The program began in 1989.
Achievements: John Lonardo was named Coach of the Year in 1994 and 1995; Conference Champions in 1993, 1994 and 1995; Tournament champions in 1995, 1997 and 1998; NCAA Regional in 1997; 5 All-Region players; team leaders stolen bases in 1994, 1995 and 1998.
Coaching: John Lonardo ,Head Coach, started in 1994 . He compiled a record of 113-60 (.653). He was named Coach of the Year in 1994 and 1995. Hector Aristy - Assistant Coach.
Roster for 1998 team/In State: 27 **Out of State:** 0 **Out of Country:** 0
Total Number of Varsity/Jr. Varsity: 35 **Percent of Graduation:** 85%
Number of Seniors on 1998 Team: 5 **Number of Sophomores on 1998 Team:** 6
Number of Fall Games: 9 **Number of Spring Games:** 36
Most Recent Record: 26 - 14 - 0
Schedule: Eastern Connecticut, North Carolina Wesleyan, William Paterson, Adelphi
Style of Play: Highly aggressive offense and defense. Strong pitching and defense.

State University of New York - Oneonta

Athletic Department
Oneonta, NY 13820
Coach: Rick Ferchen
Email: szlosett@snyoneva.cc.oneonta.edu

NCAA III
Red Dragons/Red, White
Phone: (607) 436-3594
Fax: (607) 436-3088

ACADEMIC

Founded: 1889
Religion: Non-Affiliated
Web-site: http://www.oneonta.edu
Student/Faculty Ratio: 21:1
Undergraduate Enrollment: 5,500
Scholarships/Academic: Yes **Athletic:** No
Total Expenses by: Year **In State:** $ 9,600

Type: 4 Yr., Public, Liberal Arts, Coed
Campus Housing: Yes
SAT/ACT/GPA: 1000/21/85
Male/Female Ratio: 2:3
Graduate Enrollment: 250
Fin Aid: Yes
Out of State: $ 14,500

Degrees Conferred: BA, BS, MA, MS
Programs of Study: Accounting, Anthropology, Art History, Art Studio, Biology, Business Economics, Chemistry, Computer Science, Earth Science, Economics, Elementary Education, Environmental Sciences, Geography, Geology, History, Home Economics, Mathematics, Meteorology, Psychology, Philosophy, Sociology

ATHLETIC PROFILE

Conference Affiliation: SUNYAC
Program Profile: We are a highly competitive top 30 program with an outstanding playing field. It has natural grass with a seating capacity of 1,000. Our indoor facility is a $15 million dollar field house with 2 batting cages. We have Fall and Spring seasons with a Florida trips and tournaments.
History: We have always been a solid program. In recent years (5 years), the program has become a nationally known program and top five in the New York region.
Achievements: Has 4 Coach of the Year Award at Division I and III; 6 Conference Titles; numerous All-Americans and drafted players.
Coaching: Rick Ferchen, Head Coach, started his 17th year as a head coach. He compiled a record of 387-302, coached 3 years at Oneonta State and compiled a record of 64-44. Bill Gru and Tom Marks - Assistant Coaches.
Roster for 1998 team/In State: 24 **Out of State:** 0 **Out of Country:** 0
Most Recent Record: 24 - 15 - 0 **Percent of Graduation:** 100%
Number of Fall Games: 9 **Number of Spring Games:** 36
Positions Needed for 1999/2000: Catcher, 1st Base, Pitcher, 2nd Base
Baseball Camp Dates: December, 17-29; February
Schedule: Cortland State, RPI, Ithaca, Brandies, Mt. St. Mary, John Hopkins
Style of Play: Aggressive base running, good defense and pitching. Fundamental and non-phoney play; have fun playing the game.

State University of New York - Oswego

Route 104
Oswego, NY 13126
Coach: Frank Paino

NCAA III
Lakers/Forest Green, Black
Phone: (315) 341-2405
Fax: (315) 341-2766

ACADEMIC

Founded: 1861
Religion: Non-Affiliated
Web-site: http://www.oswego.edu/
Student/Faculty Ratio: 19:1
Undergraduate Enrollment: 7,621
Scholarships/Academic: Yes **Athletic:** No

Type: 4 Yr., Public, Liberal Arts, Coed
Campus Housing: Yes
SAT/ACT/GPA: 900+
Male/Female Ratio: 48:52
Graduate Enrollment: 1,129
Fin Aid: Yes

Total Expenses by: Year **In State:** $ 9,500 **Out of State:** $ 11,500
Degrees Conferred: BA, BS, BFA, MA, MS, MFA
Programs of Study: Accounting, American Studies, Anthropology, Applied Mathematics, Art, Biology, Elementary Education, Broadcasting, Business Administration, Chemistry, Geochemistry, Geology, German, History, Human Development, English, French, Management, Marketing, Mathematics, Meteorology, Music, Philosophy, Physics, Political Science, Psychology, Secondary Education, Sociology, Spanish, Theatre, Zoology

ATHLETIC PROFILE

Conference Affiliation: SUNYAC, ECAC
Program Profile: We are a top 5 New York State Division III. We have off season workouts in our astro-turf, fully netted fieldhouse. There are 2 athletic weight rooms, a full major league tarp, a digital scoreboard and cement dugouts.
History: We have won 7 conference championships in the last decade.
Achievements: 1988 Coach of the Year, 3 ECAC Tournament bids.
Coaching: Frank Paino, Head Coach, is in his 10th year with the program. He is a Coastal Carolina graduate and made 4 Regional Appearances and 2 World Series trips. He was also the strength coordinator at Oswego State University and got 2 NCAA records double plays.
Style of Play: Very aggressive, power baseball; weight lifting is very evident.

State University of New York - Stony Brook

USB Sport Complex
Stony Brook, NY 11794-3500
Coach: Matt Senk

NCAA II
Seawolves/Scarlet, Grey
Phone: (516) 632-9226
Fax: (516) 632-7122

ACADEMIC

Founded: 1957
Type: 4 Yr., Public, Liberal Arts, Coed
Religion: Non-Affiliated
Campus Housing: Yes
Web-site: http://www.sunysb.edu/
SAT/ACT/GPA: 1100/25
Student/Faculty Ratio: 22:1
Male/Female Ratio: 1:1
Undergraduate Enrollment: 11,000
Graduate Enrollment: 5,000
Scholarships/Academic: Yes **Athletic:** Yes
Fin Aid: Yes
Total Expenses by: Year **In State:** $ 6,700 **Out of State:** $ 14,500
Degrees Conferred: BA, BS, BE, MA, MAT, MFA
Programs of Study: Biological Science, Communications and the Arts, Computer and Physical Science, Education, Engineering and Environmental Design, Exercise Science, Health Profession, Physical Therapy, Social Science

ATHLETIC PROFILE

Conference Affiliation: New England Collegiate (NECC), ECAC
Program Profile: The Seawolves play at University Field located on USB campus with state-of-the-art scoreboard. The facilities also include indoor and outdoor hitting tunnels.
History: USB Baseball began in 1966. 1996 will mark the 31st season of USB baseball. Division II play began in 1996. The Seawolves made their first NCAA Division III Regional appearance in 1995. ECAC Co-Champion 1992, ECAC Runner-up 1994.

State University of New York - Maritime

FT Schuyler
Bronx, NY 10465
Coach: James Kenny

NCAA III
Privateers/Red, White, Blue
Phone: (718) 409-7331
Fax: (718) 409-7331

ACADEMIC

Founded: 1874
Type: 4 Yr., Public, Coed, Engineering
SAT/ACT/GPA: 990+
Campus Housing: No
Student/Faculty Ratio: 15:1
Male/Female Ratio: 90:10
Undergraduate Enrollment: 725
Graduate Enrollment: 190
Scholarships/Academic: Yes **Athletic:** No **Fin Aid:** Yes
Total Expenses by: Year **In State:** $ 11,000 **Out of State:** $ 11,000
Degrees Conferred: BS, MS
Programs of Study: Afro-American Studies, Anthropology, Architecture, Asian Studies, Biochemistry, Biology, Business Administration, Chemical Engineering, Chemistry, Civil Engineering, Classics, Communications, Computer Science, Creative Writing, Dance, Earth Science, Economics, Education, Electrical Engineering, English, French, Geography, Geology, German, Managemenr, Marine Science, Mathematics, Music, Nursing, Philosophy, Physics, Political Science, Predentistry, Prelaw, Premed, Psychology, Social Science, Spanish, Speech, Speech Pathology

ATHLETIC PROFILE

Conference Affiliation: ECAC

Suffolk County Community College

533 College Road
Selden, NY 11784
Coach: Eric Brown

NJCAA
Clippers/Blue, White
Phone: (516) 451-4136
Fax: (516) 451-4609

ACADEMIC

Founded: 1959
Type: 2 Yr., Jr. college, Coed
Student/Faculty Ratio: 27:1
Male/Female Ratio: 50:50
Undergraduate Enrollment: 12,000
Graduate Enrollment: None
Scholarships/Academic: Yes **Athletic:** No **Fin Aid:** Yes
Total Expenses by: Year **In State:** $ 1,850 **Out of State:** $ 1,850
Degrees Conferred: Associate
Programs of Study: 62 areas of study. Strongest in Liberal Arts, Business and Accounting, Criminal Justice, Nursing

ATHLETIC PROFILE

Conference Affiliation: Region XV
Program Profile: We have a Fall program that starts from February through October. We play a 20 game Fall season and Spring season is about 35 games with a Southern trip. Suffolk field has ameasurements of 330 down the lines and fences. It has a sod infield and a scoreboard.
History: Our program began in 1960.
Achievements: Umpires Award in the last two years; three All-Americans in 11 years of coaching (Eric Brown); 1998 Region XV Champs; 1998 World Series.
Coaching: Eric Brown ,Head Coach, has coached 11 years. He was PAS Summer head coach. Joe Kosina and Ron Albaum - Assistant Coaches.
Roster for 1998 team/In State: 21 **Out of State:** 0 **Out of Country:** 0
Total Number of Varsity/Jr. Varsity: 21 **Most Recent Record:** 23 - 9 - 0
Number of Seniors on 1998 Team: **Number of Sophomores on 1998 Team:** 0
Freshmen Receiving Fin Aid/Athletic: 12 **Academic:** 0
Number of Fall Games: 21 **Number of Spring Games:** 35
Positions Needed for 1999/2000: Catcher, Outfielders, Pitchers
Schedule: Rockland CC, Briar Cliff College, Bronx Community College, Suffolk West, Dutchess CC
Style of Play: Fundamental principles of baseball.

Suffolk-West Community College

Crooked Hill Road
Brentwood, NY 11717
Coach: Randy Cadin

NJCAA
Longhorns/Red, White, Black
Phone: (516) 273-6475
Fax: (516) 273-6475

ACADEMIC

Founded: 1974
Type: 2 Yr., Jr. College, Coed
Student/Faculty Ratio: 18:1
Male/Female Ratio: 34:66
Undergraduate Enrollment: 6,100
Graduate Enrollment: None
Scholarships/Academic: No **Athletic:** No **Fin Aid:** Yes
Total Expenses by: Year **In State:** $ 2,100 **Out of State:** $ 4,100
Degrees Conferred: Associate
Programs of Study: Accounting, Banking/Finance, Business Administration, Criminal Justice, Drug/Alcohol/Substance Abuse Counseling, Electrical/Electronic Technology, Liberal Arts, Marketing, Medical Technology, Nursing, Office Management, Real Estate, Retail Management

ATHLETIC PROFILE

Conference Affiliation: Region XV Conference
Program Profile: Our field features are: a batting tunnel, a hitting area, bullpens and a natural grass field (325 LF-355 PA-400 CF-305 RF). We got 12-6 Region XV 2nd place. We travel to 4-year schools in the Fall and play junior colleges in the Spring. We have no fence.Our season starts on March 6 and goes through May 13.
History: Our program began in 1974. 1997 was my first year my best season ever. We were 26-14-1, Conference Champions, Regional XV Champions and Participated in the NJCAA Division III College World Series and ranked 8th in the nation.
Achievements: Region XV and District F Coach of the Year; 2 All-Americans in 1997; 1 second team; 1 third team; 5 All-Region players in 1997.
Coaching: Randy Caden -Head Coach. Mike McCabe - Assistant Coach
Style of Play: We run and have a lot of power. Last season (1997) 194 SB's - 225 SBA's in 46 games.

Ulster County Community College

Cottekill Rd
Stone Ridge, NY 12484
Coach: Bill Schiller

NJCAA
Senators/Blue, White, Red
Phone: (914) 687-5277
Fax: (914) 687-5254

ACADEMIC

Founded: 1961
Type: 2 Yr., Jr. College, Coed
Student/Faculty Ratio: Unknown
Male/Female Ratio: 55:45
Undergraduate Enrollment: 1,450
Graduate Enrollment: None
Scholarships/Academic: Yes **Athletic:** No **Fin Aid:** Yes
Total Expenses by: Year **In State:** $ 3,850 **Out of State:** $ 7,700
Degrees Conferred: AS, AAS, AOS
Programs of Study: Variety of transfer and career programs.

ATHLETIC PROFILE

Conference Affiliation: Mid-Hudson Conference
Program Profile: We have a natural grass field in a 2,000 seat stadium with lights. We ranked nationally 2 years in a row Division III Jr. college (3rd and 5th). We play full a Fall season and 45 games in the Spring.
Achievements: 2-time Coach of the Year, 1 All-American, 2 players drafted by Major League Baseball.

University of Albany

1400 Washington Avenue
Albany, NY 12222
Coach: Doug O'Brey

NCAA II
Great Danes/Purple, Gold
Phone: (518) 442-3014
Fax: (518) 442-3076

ACADEMIC

Founded: 1896
Type: 4 Yr., Public, Liberal Arts, Coed
Religion: Non-Affiliated
Campus Housing: Yes
Web-site: Not Available
SAT/ACT/GPA: 1000/90
Student/Faculty Ratio: 17:1
Male/Female Ratio: 52:48
Undergraduate Enrollment: 11,400
Graduate Enrollment: None
Scholarships/Academic: Yes **Athletic:** Yes **Fin Aid:** Yes
Total Expenses by: Year **In State:** $ 9,685 **Out of State:** $ 14,585
Degrees Conferred: BA, BS, MA, MS, Med, PhD
Programs of Study: Accounting, Afro-American Studies, Ancient Civilization, Anthropology, Archaeology, Biochemistry, Biology, Business Administration, Caribbean Studies, Chemistry, Chinese, Communications, Computer Science, Criminal Justice, Economics, Education, English, Fine Arts, French, Geography, Geology, German, Greek, History, Human Biology, Music, Philosophy, Physics, Political Science, Predentistry, Prelaw, Premed, Psychology, Religion, Russian

ATHLETIC PROFILE

Conference Affiliation: ECAC

University of Rochester

River Campus Sport Complex
Rochester, NY 14627
Coach: Bob Hartz

NCAA III
Yellow Jackets/Navy, Gold
Phone: (716) 275-6027
Fax: (716) 461-5081

ACADEMIC

Type: 4 Yr., Private, Liberal Arts, Coed, Engineering
Founded: 1850
Religion: Non-Affiliated
Campus Housing: Yes
Web-site: http://www.rochester.edu/
SAT/ACT/GPA: 1190
Student/Faculty Ratio: 9:1
Male/Female Ratio: 50:50
Undergraduate Enrollment: 3,000
Graduate Enrollment: 3,000
Scholarships/Academic: Yes **Athletic:** No **Fin Aid:** Yes
Total Expenses by: Year **In State:** $ 30,000 **Out of State:** $ 30,000
Degrees Conferred: BA, BS, MA, MS, PhD, EdD
Programs of Study: Anthropolgy, Applied Mathematics, Art, Astronomy, Biochemistry, Biology, Chemistry, Classic, Computer Science, Earth Science, Economics, Engineering, English, Environemntal Science, French, Geology, German, Health Science, History, Mathematics, Music, Natural Science, Nursing, Philosophy, Physics, Political Science, Psychology, Religion, Science

ATHLETIC PROFILE

Conference Affiliation: University Athletic Association, Upstate Collegiate Athletic
Program Profile: We have a full 6-week Fall program featuring 9 contests and an out-of-season weight program. Our Spring season is : 42 games and a 12-day Florida trip. We have a full indoor cage and artificial turf infield and can play games indoors. Towers Baseball Field is our outdoor facility. It has hitting tunnels and an outdoor artificial turf practice area.
History: We had a 20+ winning season 5 out of last 7 years. Our tradition is offensive baseball. In 1991, we led the nation in hitting with .376 team average.

Achievements: 1990 ECAC Champions; 1993 UAA 3rd place; 1989 Tom Havens 1st team All-American signed athletics; 1993 has 3 All-Region; 1992-1993 Academic All-american Ben Lanning; 1992-1993 Academic All-american; 1992 All-American Jim Ritzel.
Style of Play: Very aggressive both offensively and defensively, put preesure on defense by having physically strong hitters. Pitchers will be in 8-85 range and be true pitchers, changing speed and going right after the hitters.

Union College

Union Avenue
Schenectady, NY 12308
Coach: Gary Reynolds

NCAA III
Dutchmen/Garnet, White
Phone: (518) 388-6548
Fax: (518) 388-6695

ACADEMIC

Type: 4 Yr., Private, Liberal Arts, Coed, Engineering
Founded: 1795
SAT/ACT/GPA: 13000/27/Top 15% rank
Web-site: http://www.union.edu/
Student/Faculty Ratio: 12:!
Male/Female Ratio: 50:50
Undergraduate Enrollment: 2,000
Graduate Enrollment: 110
Scholarships/Academic: No **Athletic:** No
Fin Aid: Yes
Total Expenses by: Year **In State:**
Out of State: $ 29,990
Degrees Conferred: BS, MBA, MS, MD, JD
Programs of Study: Africana Studies, American Studies, Anthropology, Art History, Biological Sciences, Business Administration, Chemistry, Chinese, Civil Engineering, Classics, Computer Science, Computer Systems Engineering, Music, Philosophy, Political Science, Psychology

ATHLETIC PROFILE

Conference Affiliation: Upstate Collegiate Athletic Association UCCA
Program Profile: We have a Fall and Spring program. We play 14 games in the Fall and 25 games in the Spring with 8-10 games additional in Florida. Buck Eggins Field is natural grass with a measurements of 345 left/right, 400 center. We have strong indoor facilities.
History: We started in the late 1800's and were NCAA in 1965. We got small College Championships in 1973, 1979, 1986, 1987 and 1996. We were ECAC Championship Participants and Champions in 1973 and 1986.
Achievements: 1986 ECAC Championship; 1987 ECAC Runner-Up; 1996 ECAC Participant; 1986-1987 tied school win record; 1996 set school win record; 2 players have signed Minor League Contract during Coach Reynold's tenure.
Coaching: Gary Reynolds -Head Coach. Dave Degostino, Assistant Coach, is a 1995 Union College graduate and a career 347 hitter. He has a school record of a 30 game hit streak and signed a contract with the Northeast League. He was a 3-time WYS D I All-Star and MVP in 1995 of all Division , Regional NY State All-Star game.
Roster for 1998 team/In State: 10 **Out of State:** 14 **Out of Country:** 0
Total Number of Varsity/Jr. Varsity: 24 **Percent of Graduation:** 100%
Number of Seniors on 1998 Team: 5 **Most Recent Record:** 17 - 15 - 0
Freshmen Receiving Fin Aid/Athletic: 0 **Academic:** 75%
Number of Fall Games: 14 **Number of Spring Games:** 35
Positions Needed for 1999/2000: Pitcher, 3rd Base, 1st Base
Schedule: RPI, St. Lawrence, University at Albany, Hartwick, University of Rochester, Williams
Style of Play: Aggressive - running game offensively, solid fundamentally on defense.

Utica College - Syracuse University

1600 Burrstone Road
Utica, NY 13502
Coach: Don Guido

NCAA III
Pioneers/Blue, Orange
Phone: (315) 792-3378
Fax: (315) 792-3211

ACADEMIC

Founded: 1947
Type: 4 Yr., Private, Liberal Arts, Coed
Religion: Non-Affiliated
Campus Housing: Yes
Web-site: Not Available
SAT/ACT/GPA: Not required
Student/Faculty Ratio: 10:1
Male/Female Ratio: 40:60
Undergraduate Enrollment: 1,600
Graduate Enrollment: None
Scholarships/Academic: No **Athletic:** Yes **Fin Aid:** Yes
Total Expenses by: Year **In State:** $ 21,262 **Out of State:** $ 21,262
Degrees Conferred: BA, BS
Programs of Study: Allied Health, Biology, Business and Management, Communications, Criminal Justice, Elementary Education, Humanities, Journalism, Natural Sciences and Mathematics, Nursing, Occupational/Physical Therapy, Parks/Recreation, Philosophy, Political Science, Protective Services, Psychology, Public Relations, Social Sciences

ATHLETIC PROFILE

Conference Affiliation: Eastern College Athletic Conference (ECAC)
Program Profile: We are a very competitive Division III program playing many of the Division 3 teams in New York State. The field is located on campus which is a natural grass. We play both a Fall and a Spring season.
Coaching: Donald Guido - Head Coach, Le Moyne graduate in 1971. James Murner - Assistant Coach, Utica College graduate in 1995.
Roster for 1998 team/In State: 20 **Out of State:** 1 **Out of Country:** 0
Total Number of Varsity/Jr. Varsity: 21 **Percent of Graduation:** 95%
Number of Seniors on 1998 Team: 3 **Most Recent Record:** 10 - 15 - 0
Number of Fall Games: 10 **Number of Spring Games:** 35
Schedule: Ithaca, RPI, Oneonta State, University of Rochester, St. Lawrence, RIT
Style of Play: Very aggressive team play. We love to hit and run and will steal according to our personnel. The bunting game is important to us also.

US Merchant Marine Academy

Steamboat Road
Kings Point, NY 11024
Coach: Tim McNulty

NCAA III
Mariners/Blue, Grey
Phone: (516) 773-5474
Fax: (516) 773-5469

ACADEMIC

Founded: 1943
Type: 4 Yr., Public, Coed
Web-site: http://www.usmma.edu/
SAT/ACT/GPA: 1050
Student/Faculty Ratio: 12:1
Male/Female Ratio: 8:1
Undergraduate Enrollment: 950
Graduate Enrollment: None
Degrees Conferred: BS
Programs of Study: Service Academy- Charge no tuition and offers Engineering and Business.

ATHLETIC PROFILE

Conference Affiliation: ECAC, Skyline Conference

US Military Academy

Odia - Building 639
West Point, NY 10996
Coach: Dan Roberts

NCAA I
Black Knights/Black, Gold, Grey
Phone: (914) 938-3712
Fax: (914) 938-2210

ACADEMIC

Type: 4 Yr., Public, Liberal Arts, Coed, Engineering
Founded: 1802
Religion: Non-Affiliated
Campus Housing: Yes
Web-site: http://www.usma.edu/
SAT/ACT/GPA: No cut-offs listed
Student/Faculty Ratio: 15:1
Male/Female Ratio: 8:1
Undergraduate Enrollment: 4,000
Graduate Enrollment: None
Scholarships/Academic: No **Athletic:** No
Fin Aid: Free education
Total Expenses by: Year **In State:** $ Varies **Out of State:** $ Varies
Degrees Conferred: BS
Programs of Study: Behavioral Science, Engineering, Foreign Languages, General Management, Letter/Literature, Life Sciences, Mathematical Science, Military Science, Physical Science, Social Science

ATHLETIC PROFILE

Conference Affiliation: Patriot League Conference
Achievements: Dan Roberts was named 1994 Patriot League Coach of the Year. 2 All-Americans; Patriot League Northern Division Champions in 1994.
Coaching: Dan Roberts, Head Coach, has been at the controls of Army baseball for the past 12 years. His teams have been below the .500 mark only 3 times and 6 times have surpassed the 20-victory mark on the season. His 1994 team set the school record for most victories in a season when they finished 25-17 mark.
Style of Play: Basic, fundamental baseball; hit, throw, catch.

Vassar College

Raymond Avenue, Box 259
Poughkeepsie, NY 12603
Coach: Andy Barlow
Email: anbarlow@vassar.edu
NCAA III
Brewers/Burgunday, Grey, White
Phone: (914) 437-5344
Fax: (914) 437-7033

ACADEMIC

Founded: 1861
Type: 4 Yr., Private, Liberal Arts, Coed
Religion: Non-Affiliated
Campus Housing: Yes
Web-site: http://www.vassar.edu/
SAT/ACT/GPA: 1200+
Student/Faculty Ratio: 11:1
Male/Female Ratio: 40:60
Undergraduate Enrollment: 2,250
Graduate Enrollment: None
Scholarships/Academic: Yes **Athletic:** No
Fin Aid: Yes
Total Expenses by: Year **In State:** $ 27,000 **Out of State:** $ 27,000
Degrees Conferred: BA
Programs of Study: African Studies, American Studies, Anthropology, Art Education, Asian Studies, Biochemistry, Biology, Chemistry, Computer Science, Dramatic Arts, Economics, Elementary Education, Engineering, English, Film Arts, Fine Arts, Foreign Language, Geography, Geology, International Studies, Math, Music, Philosophy, Physics, Political Science, Prelaw, Premed

ATHLETIC PROFILE

Conference Affiliation: Independent
Program Profile: We are a Division III program with excellent indoor facilities including batting cages, a fieldhouse and a weight room called Nautillos Room. We have gym space for full infield and outfield and a drills training room. Our outdoor facility (Prentcoss Field) includes: excellent playing surface, two home and two away bullpen mounds and dugouts. We have an 8 game Fall season and a 30 game Spring season that includes a Southern trip over Spring break.
History: The program began in 1991. In eight years, we are at the point where the team can play with any Division III opponent in the region.
Coaching: Andy Barlow, Head Coach, started in 1995. He graduated from University of Vermont in 1985. He graduated from Maryland in Sports Management. Pete Egbert - Assistant Coach.
Roster for 1998 team/In State: 4 **Out of State:** 13 **Out of Country:** 0

Most Recent Record: 8 - 18 - 0
Percent of Graduation: 100%
Number of Seniors on 1998 Team: 3
Number of Sophomores on 1998 Team: 17
Freshmen Receiving Fin Aid/Athletic: 0
Academic: 2
Number of Fall Games: 8
Number of Spring Games: 30
Positions Needed for 1999/2000: Pitchers, Catcher, Middle Infielder, Outfielder
Schedule: Skidmore, Union, Oneonta, Drew, Utica-Tech, University of Massachusetts, John Jay
Style of Play: Lots of running and execution.

Wagner College

631 Howard Avenue
Staten Island, NY 10301
Coach: Rich Vitaliano

NCAA I
Seahawks/Green, White
Phone: (718) 390-3154
Fax: (718) 390-3347

ACADEMIC

Founded: 1883
Type: 4 Yr., Private, Liberal Arts, Coed
Religion: Lutheran
Campus Housing: No
Web-site: Not Available
SAT/ACT/GPA: 820/18
Student/Faculty Ratio: 35:1
Male/Female Ratio: 45:55
Undergraduate Enrollment: 1,800
Graduate Enrollment: 340
Scholarships/Academic: Yes **Athletic:** Yes **Fin Aid:** Yes
Total Expenses by: Year **In State:** $ 20,000 **Out of State:** $ 20,000
Degrees Conferred: BA, BS, MS, MA
Programs of Study: Accounting, Anthropology, Arts Administration, Banking/Finance, Biology, Business Administration, Chemistry, Computer Science, Criminal Justice, English

ATHLETIC PROFILE

Conference Affiliation: Northeast Conference
Program Profile: Our home field is natural grass and seats 2,000. The Seahawks play a 30 game schedule.
Coaching: Rich Vitaliano, Head Coach, started his 8th season at the helm of the Seahawks baseball program. Head Coach Rich Vitaliano has compiled a record of 99-183-3 after leading the Seahawks to the Northeast Conference Tournament two years ago. He had a successful stint at Grymes Hill. In just his first season, he led Wagner to a three-way tie for the top spot in the Northeast conference and was rewarded with Coach of the Year honors in the conference.

Westchester Community College

75 Grasslands Road
Valhalla, NY 10595
Coach: Mike Geradi

NJCAA
Vikings/Blue, Orange
Phone: (914) 785-6950
Fax: (914) 785-6989

ACADEMIC

Founded: 1946
Type: 2 Yr., Coed
Student/Faculty Ratio: 30:1
Male/Female Ratio: 43:57
Undergraduate Enrollment: 17,600
Graduate Enrollment: None
Scholarships/Academic: No **Athletic:** No **Fin Aid:** Yes
Total Expenses by: Year **In State:** $ 2,385 **Out of State:** $ 5,608
Degrees Conferred: Associate
Programs of Study: Accounting, Automotive Technology, Banking/Finance, Biomedical Technology, Business Administration, Communications, Computer Information Systems, Engineering Science, Engineering Technology, Humanities, International Business, Law Enforcement, Liberal Arts, Pharmacy, Radiological Technology

ATHLETIC PROFILE

Program Profile: We play a Fall season with 25 games from August 25 to October 6. Spring pitching starts January 15. Spring season is 45 games from March 18 to May 20. The home playing field has natural grass and is day only. Thirty players have signed pro contracts in the 4 years.
Achievements: 1993 Region XV Champs; Victor Davila and John Qual - currently in the minor leagues.
Style of Play: Aggressive

NORTH CAROLINA

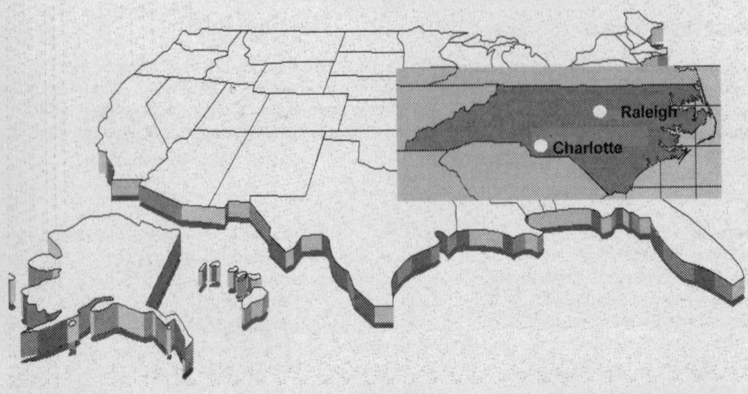

SCHOOL	CITY	AFFILIATION 99	PAGE
Appalachian State University	Booone	NCAA I	615
Barton College	Wilson	NCAA II	615
Belmont Abbey College	Belmont	NCAA II	616
Brevard College	Brevard	NJCAA	616
Campbell University	Buies Creek	NCAA I	617
Catawba College	Salisbury	NCAA II	618
Chowan College	Murfreesboro	NCAA III	618
Davidson College	Davidson	NCAA I	619
Duke University	Durham	NCAA I	620
East Carolina University	Greenville	NCAA I	620
Elizabeth City State University	Elizabeth City	NCAA II	621
Elon College	Elon College	NCAA I	621
Gardner - Webb University	Boiling Springs	NCAA II	622
Greensboro College	Greensboro	NCAA III	623
Guilford College	Greensboro	NCAA III	623
High Point University	High Point	NCAA II	624
Lenoir Community College	Kinston	NJCAA	625
Lenoire - Rhyne College	Hickory	NCAA II	625
Louisburg College	Louisburg	NJCAA	626
Mars Hill College	Mars Hill	NCAA II	626
Methodist College	Fayetteville	NCAA III	627
Montreat College	Montreat	NAIA	627
Mount Olive College	Mount Olive	NCAA II	628
North Carolina A & T State University	Greensboro	NCAA I	628
North Carolina State University	Raleigh	NCAA I	629
North Carolina Wesleyan College	Rocky Mount	NCAA III	630
Pfeiffer University	Misenheimer	NCAA II	631
Saint Andrews College	Laurinburg	NCAA II	632
Saint Augustine's College	Raleigh	NCAA II	632
Shaw University	Raleigh	NCAA II	633
Southeastern Community College	Whiteville	NJCAA	633
Surry Community College	Dobson	NJCAA	634
University of North Carolina - Asheville	Asheville	NCAA I	634
University of North Carolina - Chapel Hill	Capel Hill	NCAA I	635
University of North Carolina - Charlotte	Charlotte	NCAA I	636
University of North Carolina - Greensboro	Greensboro	NCAA I	637
University of North Carolina - Pembroke	Pembroke	NCAA II	637
University of North Carolina - Wilmington	Wilmington	NCAA I	638
Wake Forest University	Winston - Salem	NCAA I	639
Western Carolina University	Cullowhee	NCAA I	640
Wingate University	Wingate	NCAA II	640

Appalachian State University

309 Broome - Kirk Gym
Booone, NC 28608
Coach: Troy Heustess

NCAA I
Mountaineers/Black, Gold
Phone: (828) 262-6097
Fax: (828) 262-6106

ACADEMIC

Founded: 1899
Type: 4 Yr., Public, Liberal Arts, Coed
Religion: Non-Affiliated
Campus Housing: Yes
Web-site: http://www.appstate.edu/
SAT/ACT/GPA: 1076
Student/Faculty Ratio: 16:1
Male/Female Ratio: 52:48
Undergraduate Enrollment: 13,000
Graduate Enrollment: None
Scholarships/Academic: Yes **Athletic:** Yes **Fin Aid:** Yes
Total Expenses by: Year **In State:** $ 4,848 **Out of State:** $ 11,600
Degrees Conferred: BA, BS, BFA, BM, BSBA, BSCJ, BSW< BT, MA, MS, MBA, MFA, Med, EdD
Programs of Study: Over 170 majors to choose from in all areas of study including Arts and Science, Business and Management, Education, Fine and Applied Arts, Music, Natural Sciences, Parks/Recreation, Protective Services, Public Affairs, Psychology, Social Sciences, and over 300 majors

ATHLETIC PROFILE

Conference Affiliation: Southern Conference
Program Profile: We are a NCAA Division I program. We play a 56-game schedule with Fall and Spring seasons. We have an on-campus baseball stadium with natural grass and 1,500 seating capacity. There is an astroturf practice facility. We have do a 6-week Fall season. We moved to a new on-campus, lighted stadium in 1996.
History: Our program dates back to the 1930's and is a very successful program in regards to win-loss records (won 65% of games over past 20 years).
Achievements: Since 1974: 41 players signed or draft; 5 All-americans; 3 Conference Titles; 5 Regular season titles, Coach of the Year honors, and 3 former player played in the major league.

Barton College

P.O. Box 5328
Wilson, NC 27893
Coach: Roger May

NCAA II
Bulldogs/Royal, White
Phone: (252) 399-6518
Fax: (252) 399-6516

ACADEMIC

Founded: 1902
Type: 4 Yr., Private, Liberal Arts, Coed
Religion: Disciples of Christ
Campus Housing: Yes
Web-site: http://www.barton.com
SAT/ACT/GPA: 820+/17
Student/Faculty Ratio: 14:1
Male/Female Ratio: 1:2
Undergraduate Enrollment: 1,400
Graduate Enrollment: None
Scholarships/Academic: Yes **Athletic:** Yes **Fin Aid:** Yes
Total Expenses by: Year **In State:** $ 5,900 **Out of State:** $ 6,525
Degrees Conferred: BA, BS, BFA, BLS
Programs of Study: Biological/Physical Sciences (Biology, Cell Biology, Chemistry, Environmental Science, General Science, Medical Technology), Business Programs (Accounting, Business Administration, Economics, Finance, Management, Management of Human Resources, Marketing), Communications, Perfoming/Visual Arts (Art Education, Communications, Drama, Music, Studio Art), Education (Elementary K-6, Middle School 6-9, Deaf and the Hard of Hearing K-12), English/Modern Languages (English, French, Hispanic Studies, Writing), History, Social Sciences/Social Work (American Studies, Geography, History, International Studies, Political Science, Social Studies, Social Work, Sociology), Mathematics, Nursing, Physical Education/Sports Studies

ATHLETIC PROFILE

Conference Affiliation: Carolinas - Virginia Athletic Conference
Program Profile: We are one of the top NAIA programs in the country. Our outstanding facility has been rated 2nd twice in the Beam Clay Ballpark of the Year contest. A fieldhouse with baseball locker rooms was added in 1993. We play 56 games per year.
Achievements: 2-time CIAC Coach of the Year; 1993 District 26 Coach of the Year; 1993 CIAC Champions; 1 former player currently in professional baseball.
Coaching: Roger May - Head Coach.
Style of Play: Pitchers with control. Sound defense - prefer aggressive offense, hit and run. Hitters with power potential work hard and play hard each day.

Belmont Abbey College

100 Belmont
Belmont, NC 28012
Coach: Pat Dolan

NCAA II
Crusaders/Red, Black
Phone: (704) 825-6804
Fax: (704) 825-6570

ACADEMIC

Founded: 1876
Religion: Catholic
Web-site: http://www.bac.edu/
Student/Faculty Ratio: 15:1
Undergraduate Enrollment: 1,000
Type: 4 Yr., Private, Liberal Arts, Coed
Campus Housing: Yes
SAT/ACT/GPA: Varies
Male/Female Ratio: 1:5
Graduate Enrollment: None
Scholarships/Academic: Yes **Athletic:** Yes **Fin Aid:** Yes
Total Expenses by: Year **In State:** $ 16,160 **Out of State:** $ 17,600
Degrees Conferred: BA, BS
Programs of Study: Accounting, Biological Sciences, Business Administration, Chemistry, Computer Information Systems, Economics, Education, Elementary Education, English, History, Management, Mathematics, Medical Technology, Philosophy, Political Science, Predentistry, Prelaw, Premed, Psychology, Recreation and Leisure, Recreation Therapy, Secondary Education, Social Science, Sports Administration, Theology

ATHLETIC PROFILE

Conference Affiliation: Carolinas Intercollegiate Athletic Conference
Program Profile: We play both a traditional and nontraditional season with a maximum of 56 games between the two. Our game field is on campus and has : natural turf, a 300-seat capacity, 2 cages beside field,an infield tarp and a small hill around outfield that serves as a warning track. A Junior Varsity Program was started in 1996-1997.
History: Our program was restarted in '90 after a 17 year absence. The best record to date is 17-28.
Style of Play: Believe in pitching, defense, putting pressure on other team while on offense.

Brevard College

400 N Broad Street
Brevard, NC 28712
Coach: Gill Payne
Email: gpayne@brevard.edu

NJCAA
Tornadoes/Blue, White
Phone: (828) 884-8.00
Fax: (828) 884-3790

ACADEMIC

Founded: 1853
Religion: Methodist
Web-site: http://www.brevard.edu
Student/Faculty Ratio: 15:1
Undergraduate Enrollment: 700
Type: 2 Yr., Private , Coed
Campus Housing: Yes
SAT/ACT/GPA: None
Male/Female Ratio: 60:40
Graduate Enrollment: None

Scholarships/Academic: Yes **Athletic:** Yes **Fin Aid:** Yes
Total Expenses by: Year **In State:** $ 15,300 **Out of State:** $ 15,300
Degrees Conferred: AA, AS, BA, BS, Jr. College Diploma
Programs of Study: Accounting, Agriculture, Anatomy, Art, Behavioral Science, Biblical, Botany, Broadcasting, Communications, Computer, Creative Writing, Forestry, Graphic Arts, Guidance, History, Philosophy, Physical, Recreation, Sports Medicine, Religion

ATHLETIC PROFILE

Estimated Number of Baseball Scholarships: 12
Conference Affiliation: TVAC
Program Profile: We finished 3rd in the nation at JUCO World Series in Grand junction, Colorado in 1998. We have a mid-February through mid-May playing season, use an auxiliary gym with indoor cage, pool and weight room. Our natural field has 600 seats available and an excellent facility.
History: Our program started in 1992. We were at JUCO World Series in 1994 and 1998. We will be 1999-2000 first year NAIA Participant.
Achievements: 1998 Region X Coach of the Yeat, Eastern District Coach of the Year, ABCA Regional Coach, Louisville Slugger Coaches Award; Region X champs and Eastern District Champs in 1998; 12 All-American and 17 drafted players since 1992.
Coaching: Gill Payne, Head Coach, started with the program in 1998. He was a former head coach at Bristol University in Tennessee, and won two NAIA Small College National Championship. He also coaches the Front Royal Cardinals in the Summer Valley League.
Roster for 1998 team/In State: 10 **Out of State:** 20 **Out of Country:** 0
Total Number of Varsity/Jr. Varsity: 30/20 **Percent of Graduation:** 90%
Number of Seniors on 1998 Team: **Number of Sophomores on 1998 Team:** 14
Freshmen Receiving Fin Aid/Athletic: 24 **Academic:** 11
Number of Fall Games: 9 **Number of Spring Games:** 56
Most Recent Record: 45-17 - 0 **Baseball Camp Dates:** July 12-16
Positions Needed for 1999/2000: Pitcher, Catcher (possible Shortstop)
Schedule: Spartanburg Methodist College, Pitt Community College, Louisburg College, Pensacola Junior College, St. Louis/Meramec Community College, Black Hawk College
Style of Play: We are aggressive and love to hit. We are building a reputation for pitching to go with a hitting reputation.

Campbell University

P.O. Box 10
Buies Creek, NC 27506
Coach: Chip Smith
Email: smith@mailcenter.campbell.edu
NCAA I
Fightin Camels/Black, Orange, White
Phone: (910) 893-1325
Fax: (901) 893-1330

ACADEMIC

Founded: 1887
Type: 4 Yr., Private, Liberal Arts, Coed
Religion: Baptist
Campus Housing: Yes
Web-site: http://www.campbell.edu/
SAT/ACT/GPA: 800
Student/Faculty Ratio: 20:1
Male/Female Ratio: 1:2
Undergraduate Enrollment: 2,100
Graduate Enrollment: 2,500
Scholarships/Academic: Yes **Athletic:** Yes **Fin Aid:** Yes
Total Expenses by: Year **In State:** $ 13,500 **Out of State:** $ 13,500
Degrees Conferred: BA, BS, MA, MED, MBA, Pharm. Doc, JD
Programs of Study: Accounting, Applied Science, Art, Biology, Business Administration, Chemistry, Economics, Elementary Education, Mass Communications, Mathematics, Journalism, Music, Psychology, Religion, Philosophy, Physical Education, Social Science, Sport Management, Prelaw, Premedicine, Computer Information System, Drama, English

ATHLETIC PROFILE

Estimated Number of Baseball Scholarships: 9.9
Conference Affiliation: Trans American Athletic Conference

Program Profile: We are a top Division I program in a great conference with one of the top playing surface & indoor facilities in the South. Our playing season is year-round. We have a natural grass field of tiffway 419 Bermuda/oversized with rye called Taylor Field & has a seating capacity of 2,000.
History: We have a long history of major leaguers including Cal Koone, Gaylord and Jim Perry.
Achievements: Past conference title were in Big South Conference; drafted players each year.
Coaching: Chip Smith - Head Coach. Randy Hood, Assistant Coach, is responsible for recruiting and is also coordinator. Jeff Bock - Pitching Coach.
Roster for 1998 team/In State: 12 **Out of State:** 13 **Out of Country:** 1
Total Number of Varsity/Jr. Varsity: 26 **Percent of Graduation:** 85%-100%
Number of Seniors on 1998 Team: 2 **Number of Sophomores on 1998 Team:** 5
Freshmen Receiving Fin Aid/Athletic: 11 **Academic:** 1
Most Recent Record: 28 - 30 - 0 **Number of Spring Games:** 56
Positions Needed for 1999/2000: Pitcher, Mid-infielder, Shortstop, Outfielder
Baseball Camp Dates: December 21-22, December 28-29
Schedule: Stetson, Florida Atlantic, Central Florida, North Carolina, Troy State, Jacksonville
Style of Play: We have aggressive, hard-nosed, fundamentally sound student athletes.

Catawba College

2300 West Innes Street
Salisbury, NC 28144-2488
Coach: Jim Gantt

NCAA II
Indians/Blue, White
Phone: (704) 637-4469
Fax: (704) 637-5705

ACADEMIC

Founded: 1851
Religion: United Church of Christ
Web-site: http://www.catawba.edu/
Student/Faculty Ratio: 15:1
Undergraduate Enrollment: 1,100
Type: 4 Yr., Private, Liberal Arts, Coed
Campus Housing: Yes
SAT/ACT/GPA: 700 Min
Male/Female Ratio: 50:50
Graduate Enrollment: 100
Scholarships/Academic: Yes **Athletic:** Yes **Fin Aid:** Yes
Total Expenses by: Year **In State:** $ 15, 852 **Out of State:** $ 15, 852
Degrees Conferred: BA, Med
Programs of Study: Accounting, Biology, Business and Management, Chemistry, Communications, Computer Science, Education, English, French, History, Law, Mathematics, Medical Technology, Philosophy, Political Science, Preprofessional, Psychology, Religion, Social Sciences, Sport Medicine

ATHLETIC PROFILE

Conference Affiliation: South Atlantic Conference
Achievements: Catawba has won 12 Conference Titles, nearly one every six years. The most recent were back titles in 1992 and 1993. Catawba most recent pro player is Heath Bust, who was drafted by the Colorado Rockies in the 18th round of the 1995 draft.
Coaching: Jim Gantt - Head Coach.

Chowan College

P.O. Box 1848
Murfreesboro, NC 27855
Coach: Steve Flack
Email: flacks@micah.chowan.edu

NCAA III
Braves/Columbia Blue, Navy
Phone: (919) 398-6228
Fax: (919) 398-1390

ACADEMIC

Founded: 1848
Religion: Baptist
Web-site: Not Available
Type: 4 Yr., Private, Liberal Arts, Coed
Campus Housing: Yes
SAT/ACT/GPA: 820

Student/Faculty Ratio: 15:1 **Male/Female Ratio:** 40:60
Undergraduate Enrollment: 850 **Graduate Enrollment:** None
Scholarships/Academic: Yes **Athletic:** No **Fin Aid:** Yes
Total Expenses by: Year **In State:** $ 13,400 **Out of State:** $ 13,400
Degrees Conferred: Associate Degrees, BS
Programs of Study: Bachelors Degrees: Art (Graphic Design, Studio), Biology (Allied Health/Laboratory), Business Administration (Accounting, Information Systems, Small Business Management, Marketing), Elementary Education, English, English Education, History, Liberal Studies, Mathematics, Mathematics Education, Music, Printing Production and Imaging Technology, Religion, Physical Education (Teacher Licensure, Athletic Training, Sport Management, Sport Science), Physical Science (Chemistry or Physics), Psychology, Prelaw, Premed, Predental, Preveterinary Medicine, Prepharmacy, Prephysical Therapy, Preoptometry

ATHLETIC PROFILE

Conference Affiliation: Independent Conference
Program Profile: The 1998 will be the first year Chowan College will be eligible for the Division III playoffs after a transition from a junior college into a four-year school. Varsity and Junior Varsity program involves 45 players.
History: The baseball program is in its 40th year as a four-year Division III program school. We become an official Division program on September 1, 1997.
Achievements: The college record in the past four seasons as a provisional member of the Division III has been 90-46 (.662%).
Coaching: Steve Flack, Head Coach, started his 5th year with the program. He has 17 years high school experience, 5 years college experience and volleyball league for four years.
Roster for 1998 team/In State: 8 **Out of State:** 39 **Out of Country:**
Total Number of Varsity/Jr. Varsity: 47 **Percent of Graduation:** 100%
Number of Seniors on 1998 Team: 7 **Number of Spring Games:** 40
Freshmen Receiving Fin Aid/Athletic: 0 **Academic:** 21
Positions Needed for 1999/2000: Pitchers, Shortstop, 1st Base
Schedule: North Carolina Wesleyan, Methodist College, Ferrum College, University of New Haven, St. Xavier University, Frostburg State University, Salisbury State University, Barton College
Style of Play: We are aggressive and have team power.

Davidson College

P.O. Box 1750
Davidson, NC 28038
Coach: Dick Cooke

NCAA I
Wildcats/Red, Black
Phone: (704) 892-2368
Fax: (704) 892-2556

ACADEMIC

Founded: 1837 **Type:** 4 Yr., Private, Liberal Arts, Coed
Religion: Presbyterian **Campus Housing:** Yes
Web-site: http://www.davidson.edu/ **SAT/ACT/GPA:** 1240-1410/27-30
Student/Faculty Ratio: 8:1 **Male/Female Ratio:** 52:48
Undergraduate Enrollment: 1,550 **Graduate Enrollment:** None
Scholarships/Academic: Yes **Athletic:** Yes **Fin Aid:** Yes
Total Expenses by: Year **In State:** $ 26,013 **Out of State:** $ 26,013
Degrees Conferred: AB, BS
Programs of Study: Anthropology, Sociology, Art, Biology, Chemistry, Classical Studies, Economics, English, French, German, Russian, Japanese, History, Mathematics, Music, Philosophy, Physics, Political Science, Psychology, Religion, Spanish, Theatre, Interdisciplinary

ATHLETIC PROFILE

Conference Affiliation: Southern Conference
Program Profile: We are a competitive Division I program. We play home games at Wildcat Park which seats 800 and is located 20 miles from Charlotte.

Achievements: 1995 - Rhett Engerick drafted by the Marlins in the 47th round but will be returning for his senior year; placed 4th in the conference; Big South Conference Coach of the Year; 8 players drafted to pros.
Coaching: Dick Cooke, Head Coach, is a graduate of Richmond and was a Boston Red Sox in 1979-1982.He coached at Richmond and Belmont Abbey from 1989-1990.
Style of Play: We are conservative offensively and look for hitters who can drive the ball.

Duke University

P.O. Box 90555
Durham, NC 27708
Coach: Steve Traylor

NCAA I
Blue Devils/Royal Blue, White
Phone: (919) 684-2358
Fax: (919) 681-7866

ACADEMIC

Founded: 1838
Type: 4 Yr., Private, Liberal Arts, Coed
Religion: United Methodist
Campus Housing: Yes
Web-site: http://www.duke.edu/
SAT/ACT/GPA: 12,00/3.75
Student/Faculty Ratio: 12:1
Male/Female Ratio: 55:45
Undergraduate Enrollment: 6,000
Graduate Enrollment: 4,000
Scholarships/Academic: Yes **Athletic:** Yes **Fin Aid:** Yes
Total Expenses by: Year **In State:** $ 32,000 **Out of State:** $ 32,000
Degrees Conferred: BA, BS, MA, MS, MBA, D, MD, JD, Mdiv
Programs of Study: Engineering, Letters/Literature, Life Sciences, Psychology, Social Science

ATHLETIC PROFILE

Estimated Number of Baseball Scholarships: 9
Conference Affiliation: Atlantic Coast Conference
Coaching: Steve Traylor - Head Coach.
Roster for 1998 team/In State: 2 **Out of State:** 22 **Out of Country:**
Total Number of Varsity/Jr. Varsity: 24 **Percent of Graduation:** 94%
Number of Seniors on 1998 Team: 4 **Number of Sophomores on 1998 Team:** 0
Freshmen Receiving Fin Aid/Athletic: 3 **Academic:** 0
Most Recent Record: 38 - 20 - 0 **Number of Spring Games:** 56
Positions Needed for 1999/2000: Undecided
Baseball Camp Dates: 1st week in August
Schedule: Florida State, Clemson, Georgia Tech, South Carolina, Rice, South Alabama

East Carolina University

Scales Fieldhouse
Greenville, NC 27858
Coach: Keith LeClair

NCAA I
Pirates/Purple, Gold
Phone: (252) 328-4604
Fax: (252) 328-4647

ACADEMIC

Founded: 1907
Type: 4 Yr., Public, Coed
Religion: Non-Affiliated
Campus Housing: Yes
Web-site: http://www.ecu.edul
SAT/ACT/GPA: 820/18 mim
Student/Faculty Ratio: 25:1
Male/Female Ratio: 1:3
Undergraduate Enrollment: 14,300
Graduate Enrollment: 3,400
Scholarships/Academic: Yes **Athletic:** Yes **Fin Aid:** Yes
Total Expenses by: Year **In State:** $ 900 **Out of State:** $ 7,600
Degrees Conferred: BA, BS, BFA, BM, BSA, BSBA, BSBE, MA, MS, MBA, MFA, Med, PhD

Programs of Study: Offers 106 undergraduate and 92 graduate majors in the Schools of Allied Health Sciences, Art, Arts/Sciences, Business, Education, Health and Human Performance, Human Environmental Sciences, Industry/Technology, Music, Nursing, Social Work

ATHLETIC PROFILE

Conference Affiliation: Colonial Athletic Association
Program Profile: ECU baseball is played at Harrington Field, located on the Southeast corner of campus adjacent to ECU's other athletic facilities. It features a natural grass playing surface with a seating capacity of 2,500. Harrington's dimensions are 320' down the lines, 390' to the power alleys, and 410' to dead center.
History: The baseball program began play in 1951. The Pirates have made 14 appearances in NCAA tournaments; won the NAIA championship in 1961; won 14 conference championships.
Achievements: 1974 George Williams Southern Conference Coach of the Year; 1993 Gary Overton was East Region Coach of the Year; 1990 CAA Coach of the Year; 1961 NAIA Champions; 1966, 1968, 1970, 1974 - Southern Conference Champions; 1982 - wins inaugural ECAC Southern Conference Champions; 1984-ECAc South Conference Champions; 1993 - CAA Champions.
Coaching: Keith Laclair - Head Coach.
Style of Play: We play a balanced attack and stress on defense.

Elizabeth City State University

Campus Box 900
Elizabeth City, NC 27909
Coach: Chuck Cullens

NCAA II
Vikings/Royal, White
Phone: (252) 335-3392
Fax: (252) 335-3675

ACADEMIC

Founded: 1891
Type: 4 Yr., Public, Liberal Arts, Coed
Web-site: Not Available
SAT/ACT/GPA: 750 avg
Student/Faculty Ratio: 13:1
Male/Female Ratio: 39:61
Undergraduate Enrollment: 2,130
Graduate Enrollment: None
Scholarships/Academic: Yes **Athletic:** Yes **Fin Aid:** Yes
Total Expenses by: Year **In State:** $ 5,150 **Out of State:** $ 10,500
Degrees Conferred: BA, BS, BSEd
Programs of Study: Contact school for program of study.

ATHLETIC PROFILE

Conference Affiliation: CIAA

Elon College

2500 Campus Box
Elon College, NC 27244
Coach: Mike Kennedy

NCAA I
Fightin' Christian/Cardinal, Grey
Phone: (336) 584-2420
Fax: (336) 538-2686

ACADEMIC

Founded: 1889
Type: 4 Yr., Private, Liberal Arts, Coed
Religion: United Church of Christ
Campus Housing: Yes
Web-site: http://www.elon.edu/
SAT/ACT/GPA: None
Student/Faculty Ratio: 17:1
Male/Female Ratio: 40:60
Scholarships/Academic: Yes **Athletic:** Yes **Fin Aid:** Yes
Total Expenses by: Year **In State:** $ 16,200 **Out of State:** $ Varies
Degrees Conferred: BA, BS, Med, MBA, MPT
Programs of Study: 41 majors, including Business Administration, Computer Science, Education, Physics, Sociology

ATHLETIC PROFILE

Estimated Number of Baseball Scholarships: 6-7
Conference Affiliation: Big South Conference
Program Profile: In 1998 we were a first year Division I program. In 1997, we were in NCAA Division III South Central Region Championship Game. Our final ranking was 14. Collegiate baseball ranked Elon 24th in a decade among Division II schools. We have outstanding surface Bermuda/Rye grass with dimensions of 317 down the lines, 380 center and 327 right. We play 56 game season.
History: The program began in 1899. Elon has had just six losing season since 1925.
Achievements: Has 10 Coach of the Year Honors; 19 Conference Championships; 4 National Tournament Appearances; 10 District, Division, or Regional Post-Season Appearances.
Coaching: Mike Kennedy, Head Coach, started his 2nd season with the program. He was 55-33 NCAA Division II South Central Regional in 1997. He was South Atlantic Conference Coach of the Year in 1997. He was a former Oakland A's Minor League player and a two-time Honorable Mention NAIA All-American Catcher as a player at Elon. Mike Rickard - Assistant Coach. Snapper Lawson - Assistant Coach.
Roster for 1998 team/In State: 15 **Out of State:** 17 **Out of Country:** 0
Total Number of Varsity/Jr. Varsity: 32 **Percent of Graduation:** 90%
Number of Seniors on 1998 Team: 8 **Number of Sophomores on 1998 Team:**
Freshmen Receiving Fin Aid/Athletic: 9 **Academic:** 4
Most Recent Record: 23 - 19 - 0 **Number of Spring Games:** 56
Positions Needed for 1999/2000: 3rd Base, Outfielder, Catcher
Baseball Camp Dates: Last two weeks of July
Schedule: Miami, Tulane, South Carolina, NC State, Duke University, University of North Carolina, Winthrop University, Coastal Carolina, Charleston Southern
Style of Play: We are aggressive ,hit and run and to steal bases.

Gardner - Webb University

Main Street
Boiling Springs, NC 28017
Coach: Clyde Miller

NCAA II
Running Bulldogs/Red, Black
Phone: (704) 434-4343
Fax: (704) 434-4739

ACADEMIC

Founded: 1905
Type: 4 Yr., Private, Liberal Arts, Coed
Religion: Southern Baptist
Campus Housing: Yes
Web-site: http://www.fardner-webb.edu/
SAT/ACT/GPA: 820
Student/Faculty Ratio: 17:1
Male/Female Ratio: 40:60
Undergraduate Enrollment: 2,000
Graduate Enrollment: 500
Scholarships/Academic: Yes **Athletic:** Yes **Fin Aid:** Yes
Total Expenses by: Year **In State:** $ 14,000 **Out of State:** $ 14,000
Degrees Conferred: MA, BA, BS
Programs of Study: Accounting, Biology, Business Administration, Chemistry, Communications, Computer Science, Elementary Education, English, French, Health Education, Management Information Systems, Mathematics, Medical Technology, Social Science, Pschology, Physical Education

ATHLETIC PROFILE

Conference Affiliation: South Atlantic Conference
Program Profile: We are a member of the NCAA Division II program. We compete in the South Atlantic conference. Our field is a natural grass which is not lighted but has a permanent batting tunnel and a seating capacity of 350. The field's dimensions are 350', 340', 390', 380' and 327'.
History: We began as a senior college in 1972. We made transfer from Junior College status at that time. We are members of the Carolina's Conference untill Fall of 1989 as a SAC became a comprehensive sports conference.
Achievements: Terry Wright was a 1994 3rd team NCAA Division II All-American. In 1994,we led Divisioin II in triples (12) Mickey Munn was a 1991 NAIA All-American Honorable Mention.

Coaching: Clyde Miller, Head Coach, started his 9th season at GWU. 1998 will mark 32nd year with as a head coach in collegiate ranks. Andy Collins,Assistant Coach, started his 2nd year as a full-time assistant coach. He is a former two sport (football and baseball) letterman at GWU. Landy Cox, Student Assistant Coach, played at GWU in 1995 and 1996.
Style of Play: We are aggressive on offense and defense. We like to hit and run and run and hit. We stress base running and game type situations in practices. Pitching could be a strong point for the 1998 season.

Greensboro College

815 W Market Street
Greensboro, NC 27358
Coach: Scott Rash
Email: baseball@gborocollege.edu

NCAA III
The Pride/Green, White, Grey
Phone: (336) 272-7102
Fax: (336) 230-9686

ACADEMIC

Founded: 1838
Religion: Methodist
Web-site: http://www.gborocollege.edu/
Student/Faculty Ratio: 14:1
Scholarships/Academic: Yes **Athletic:** No
Total Expenses by: Year **In State:** $ 16,000
Degrees Conferred: BA, BS

Type: 4 Yr., Private, Liberal Arts, Coed
Campus Housing: Yes
SAT/ACT/GPA: 900/2.0
Male/Female Ratio: 50:50
Fin Aid: Yes
Out of State: $ 16,000

Programs of Study: Accounting, Biological Science, Business Administration, Chemistry, Elementary Education, English, French, History, Interdisciplinary Studies, Liberal Arts, Management, Mathematics, Medical Laboratory Technology, Music, Physical Education, Political Science, Predentistry, Prelaw, Premed, Prevet, Psychology, Radiological Technology, Religion, Secondary Education, Spanish, Special Education, Sports Medicine, Theatre

ATHLETIC PROFILE

Conference Affiliation: Dixie Intercollegiate Athletic Conference
Program Profile: We play at War Memorial Stadium, oldest active minor league ball park in the country.
History: Our program began in 1993, averaged twenty wins/season with Dixie Championships and NCAA Tournament Berth in 1998.
Achievements: Scott Rash has earned 2 DIAC Coach of the Year awards since starting the program in 1993. In six seasons Coach Rash has had 17 All-Conference selections; 13 All-Region selections and 1 player sign professional contract.
Coaching: Scott Rash, Head Coach, was named DIAC Coach of the Year. He compiled a record of 121-109-1. Dan Albert and Ryan Waelchli - Assistant Coaches.
Roster for 1998 team/In State: 12 **Out of State:** 13 **Out of Country:** 0
Total Number of Varsity/Jr. Varsity: 30 **Percent of Graduation:** 90%
Number of Seniors on 1998 Team: 3 **Positions Needed for 1999/2000:** Pitchers
Freshmen Receiving Fin Aid/Athletic: 0 **Academic:** All
Number of Fall Games: 9 **Number of Spring Games:** 40
Most Recent Record: 27 - 15 - 0
Style of Play: We are aggressive offensively and defensively.

Guilford College

5800 W Friendly Avenue
Greensboro, NC 27410
Coach: Gene Baker
Email: bakergo@rascal.guilford.edu

NCAA III
Quakers/Crimson, Silver
Phone: (336) 316-2161
Fax: (336) 316-2953

ACADEMIC

Founded: 1837
Religion: Society of Friends (Quakers)
Web-site: http://www.guilford.edu/
Student/Faculty Ratio: 14:1
Undergraduate Enrollment: 1,300
Scholarships/Academic: Yes **Athletic:** No
Total Expenses by: Year **In State:** $ 1,900
Type: 4 Yr., Private, Liberal Arts, Coed
Campus Housing: Yes
SAT/ACT/GPA: 900/20
Male/Female Ratio: 1:1
Graduate Enrollment: None
Fin Aid: Yes
Out of State: $ Varies
Degrees Conferred: AB, BS, BFA
Programs of Study: Biology, Business and Management, Chemistry, Criminal Justice, Dentistry, Education, History, Justice and Policy, Law, Letters/Literature, Liberal Arts, Management, Medicine, Parks/Recreation, Philosophy, Physical Education, Physics, Psychology, Public Affairs, Sport Management, Sport Medicine, Social Sciences

ATHLETIC PROFILE

Conference Affiliation: Old Dominion Athletic Conference
Program Profile: We are a competitive Division III baseball program playing on campus at McBone Field with a seating capacity of 750 in Greensboro, North Carolina. Our schedule includes full allotment of games Fall and Spring with championships season beginning in mid-February.
History: Baseball has been sponsored at Guilford since 1913. A member of the NAIA in the 1970's and 1980's. Guilford made two trips to the NAIA World Series. Since joining the NCAA III ODAC in 1992 Guilford has played in three of seven conference tournament finals.
Achievements: ODAC Champs in 1992 and 1993; 1998 has 2 All-Conference; 2 All-Tournaments; 1All-South Region; 1 Academic All-Region; Tony Womack - drafted by the Pittsburgh Pirates.
Coaching: Gene Baker, Head Coach, started his 1st year with the program and compiled a record of 21-23. He has 11 years of coaching experience with an overall record of 220-379. He was named Academic All-American in 1981 at Austin Peay.
Roster for 1998 team/In State: 20 **Out of State:** 10 **Out of Country:** 0
Total Number of Varsity/Jr. Varsity: 30 **Percent of Graduation:** 100%
Number of Seniors on 1998 Team: 8 **Number of Sophomores on 1998 Team:** 4
Freshmen Receiving Fin Aid/Athletic: 0 **Academic:** 30
Number of Fall Games: 9 **Number of Spring Games:** 40
Most Recent Record: 21 - 23 - 0 **Baseball Camp Dates:** 8/10-14
Positions Needed for 1999/2000: Shortstop, Outfielder, Pitcher, Catcher
Schedule: Navy, Duke, Methodist, North Carolina Wesleyan, Virginia Wesleyan, Ferrum
Style of Play: We have an aggressive offensive philosophy utilizing many players in situational strategies offensively, defensively and on the mound.

High Point University

(New Program)

University Station
High Point, NC 27262
Coach: Jim Speight

NCAA II
Panthers/Purple, White
Phone: (336) 841-9276
Fax: (336) 841-9182

ACADEMIC

Founded: 1924
Religion: United Methodist
Web-site: http://www.highpoint.edu
Student/Faculty Ratio: 20:1
Undergraduate Enrollment: 2,500
Scholarships/Academic: Yes **Athletic:** Yes
Total Expenses by: Year **In State:** $ 15,500
Type: 4 Yr., Private, Liberal Arts, Coed
Campus Housing: Yes
SAT/ACT/GPA: Sliding Scale
Male/Female Ratio: 45:55
Graduate Enrollment: 300
Fin Aid: Yes
Out of State: $ 15,500
Degrees Conferred: BA, BS, MBA

Programs of Study: Business and Management, Communications, Computer Science, Education, Prelaw, Premed, Psychology, Social Science, Sports Management, Sport Medicine

Lenoire - Rhyne College

P.O. Box 7356
Hickory, NC 28603
Coach: Frank Pait

NCAA II
Panthers/Purple, White
Phone: (828) 328-7136
Fax: (828) 328-7399

ACADEMIC

Founded: 1891
Religion: Lutheran
Web-site: http://www.lrc.edu/
Student/Faculty Ratio: 11:1
Undergraduate Enrollment: 1,400
Scholarships/Academic: Yes **Athletic:** Yes
Total Expenses by: Year **In State:** $ 15,740

Type: 4 Yr., Private, Liberal Arts, Coed
Campus Housing: yes
SAT/ACT/GPA: 900/18
Male/Female Ratio: 60:40
Graduate Enrollment: None
Fin Aid: Yes
Out of State: $ 15,740

Degrees Conferred: BA, BS, BME, MA, Education and Couseling
Programs of Study: Accounting, Anthropology, Art, Astronomy, Biology, Business, Chemistry, Classics, Computer Science, Dance, Drama, Earth Science, Education, Environmental Studies, Geography, Sport Studies, Mathematics, Military Science, Nursing, Office Science, Sociology, Social Science

ATHLETIC PROFILE

Conference Affiliation: Carolinas Conference

Lenoir Community College

231 Highway 58 South
Kinston, NC 28502
Coach: Lind Hartsell

NJCAA
Lancers/Col Blue, White
Phone: (252) 527-6223
Fax: (252) 527-1199

ACADEMIC

Founded: 1960
Student/Faculty Ratio: 15:1
Undergraduate Enrollment: 2,070
Scholarships/Academic: No **Athletic:** Yes
Total Expenses by: Year **In State:** $ 590

Type: 2 Yr., Jr. College, Coed
Male/Female Ratio: 43:57
Graduate Enrollment: None
Fin Aid: Yes
Out of State: $ 4,600

Degrees Conferred: Associate
Programs of Study: Accounting, Agriculture, Art/Fine Arts, Aviation Technology, Aviation Management, Business Administration, Commerce, Management, Computer Programming, Cosmetology, Court Reporting, Criminal Justice, Drafting/Design Technology, Elementary Education, Electronic Engineering Technology, Finance/Banking, Insurance, Industrial and Heavy Equipment Technology, Liberal Arts, General Studies, Law Enforcement, Library Science, Marketing, Retailing, Merchandising, Mental Health, Nursing, Postal Management, Reatil Management

ATHLETIC PROFILE

Conference Affiliation: Independent Conference
Program Profile: We have a solid program located and are in a Minor league town (40,000 pop). We have a cold climate and indoor facilities.
Coaching: Lind Hartsell, Head Coach, started his 4th year.

Louisburg College

North Main
Louisburg, NC 27549
Coach: Russ Frazier

NJCAA
Hurricanes/Navy, White
Phone: (919) 496-2521
Fax: (919) 496-7330

ACADEMIC

Founded: 1787
Type: 2 Yr., Private, Liberal Arts, Coed
Religion: Methodist
Campus Housing: Yes
Student/Faculty Ratio: 20:1
Male/Female Ratio: 60:40
Undergraduate Enrollment: 500
Graduate Enrollment: None
Scholarships/Academic: Yes **Athletic:** Yes **Fin Aid:** Yes
Total Expenses by: Year **In State:** $ 13,000 **Out of State:** $ 13,000
Degrees Conferred: AA
Programs of Study: Accounting, Agricultural, Animal, Art, Biblical, Biological Science, Chemistry, Computer, Criminal Justice, Economics, Education, Farm/Ranch Management, History, Horticulture, Humanities, Insurance, Journalism, Landscape, Liberal Arts, Mathematics, Music, Physical Education, Range Management Science, Social Science, Spanish

ATHLETIC PROFILE

Conference Affiliation: Region 10 Conference - NJCAA
Program Profile: We play on Frazier Field which has natural turf and has a seating capacity of 2,000. We have a .736 percentage in 38 years.
Achievements: 10 Major Leaguers - Otis Nixon (Dodgers) and Chad Fonville (White Sox) current; NJCAA Hall of Fame.
Coaching: Russ Frazier - Head Coach. Sam White - Assistant Coach.
Style of Play: We use the style that fits the personnel.

Mars Hill College

P.O. Box 370
Mars Hill, NC 28754
Coach: Ed Hodge

NCAA II
Lions/Royal, Gold
Phone: (828) 689-1173
Fax: (828) 689-1501

ACADEMIC

Founded: 1856
Type: 4 Yr., Private, Liberal Arts, Coed
Religion: Baptist
Campus Housing: Yes
Web-site: http://www.mhc.edu/
SAT/ACT/GPA: 820
Student/Faculty Ratio: 13:1
Male/Female Ratio: 52:48
Undergraduate Enrollment: 1,200
Graduate Enrollment: None
Scholarships/Academic: Yes **Athletic:** Yes **Fin Aid:** Yes
Total Expenses by: Year **In State:** $ 12,700 **Out of State:** $ 12,700
Degrees Conferred: BA, BS, BM, BSM, BFA
Programs of Study: Business Administration and Economics, Business/Office and Marketing/Distribution, Education, Fine Arts, Health, Humanities, Life Science, Natural Science and Mathematics, Physical Education and Recreation, Social Behavioral Sciences, Sport Medicine

ATHLETIC PROFILE

Conference Affiliation: SAC - 8 Conference

Methodist College

5400 Ramsey Street
Fayetteville, NC 28311
Coach: Tom Austin

NCAA III
Monarchs/Green, Gold
Phone: (910) 630-7176
Fax: (910) 630-1300

ACADEMIC

Founded: 1954
Religion: United Methodist
Web-site: http://www.methodist.com
Student/Faculty Ratio: 17:1
Undergraduate Enrollment: 1,500
Scholarships/Academic: Yes **Athletic:** No
Total Expenses by: Year **In State:** $ 15,650
Degrees Conferred: BS, BA
Programs of Study: Business and Management, Education, Social Sciences

Type: 4 Yr., Private, Liberal Arts, Coed
Campus Housing: Yes
SAT/ACT/GPA: 710
Male/Female Ratio: 55:45
Graduate Enrollment: None
Fin Aid: Yes
Out of State: $ 15,650

ATHLETIC PROFILE

Conference Affiliation: Dixie Intercollegiate Athletic Conference

Montreat College

P.O. Box 1267
Montreat, NC 28757
Coach: Darin Chaplain
Email: dchaplain@montreat.edu

NAIA
Cavaliers/Blue, Gold
Phone: (828) 669-8011
Fax: (828) 669-8014

ACADEMIC

Founded: 1916
Religion: Presbyterian
Web-site: http://www.montreat.edu/
Student/Faculty Ratio: 12:1
Undergraduate Enrollment: 500
Scholarships/Academic: Yes **Athletic:** Yes
Total Expenses by: Year **In State:** $ 14,542
Degrees Conferred: BA, BS
Programs of Study: Accounting, Bible Studies, Business and Management, Ecology, Economics, English, Environmental Studies, History, Human Services, Liberal Arts, Mathematics, Missionary Studies, Religion, Secondary Education, Social Sciences

Type: 4 Yr., Private, Liberal Arts, Coed
Campus Housing: Yes
SAT/ACT/GPA: 860/18/2.2
Male/Female Ratio: 50:50
Graduate Enrollment:
Fin Aid: Yes
Out of State:

ATHLETIC PROFILE

Estimated Number of Baseball Scholarships: 4.2
Conference Affiliation: Tennessee - Virginia Athletic Conference
Program Profile: Our new program has moved to the top of the TVAC conference. The Cavaliers have indoor facilities and a top notch playing surface. Montreat plays both in the Fall and in the Spring with about 65 games total.
History: Montreat went four year in 1993 and has become a big success. Montreat has claimed two of the last 3 conference titles and will continue to be at the top. Montreat was formerly called Montreat-Anderson and has had many players drafted and signed to professional contracts.
Achievements: Conference Titles in 1996 and 1998; Conference Coach of the Year in 1996; Regional Coach of the Year in 1996; Joe Snyder was named All-American
Coaching: Darin Chaplain, Head Coach, was Conference Coach of the Year in 1996 and Regional Coach of the Year. He started coaching in 1993-to the present with an overall record of 160-141. Billy Conley, Jamie Jessee, and Kent Cox - Assistant Coaches.

Roster for 1998 team/In State: 20 **Out of State:** 15 **Out of Country:** 1
Total Number of Varsity/Jr. Varsity: 38 **Percent of Graduation:** 95%
Number of Seniors on 1998 Team: 6 **Most Recent Record:** 35 - 19 - 0
Freshmen Receiving Fin Aid/Athletic: 29 **Academic:** 20
Number of Fall Games: 10 **Number of Spring Games:** 55
Positions Needed for 1999/2000: LHP, 3rd Base, Outfielder, Shortstop
Schedule: Birmingham Southern, Lincoln Memorial University, Lenoir Rhyne College, Limestone College, Bluefield College, Tennessee Wesleyan
Style of Play: We are very disciplined and fundamentally sound. Montreat is very aggressive and will play very hard each and every game. We are very sound defensively; will always be prepared and intense.

Mount Olive College

634 Henderson Street
Mount Olive, NC 28365
Coach: Carl Lancaster

NCAA II
Trojans/Green, White
Phone: (919) 658-5056
Fax: (919) 658-1753

ACADEMIC

Founded: 1951
Type: 4 Yr., Private, Liberal Arts, Coed
Religion: Non-Affiliated
Campus Housing: Yes
Web-site: http://www.horizon.moc.edu/
SAT/ACT/GPA: 820/18/2.0
Student/Faculty Ratio: 17:1
Male/Female Ratio: 50:50
Undergraduate Enrollment: 1,600
Graduate Enrollment: None
Scholarships/Academic: Yes **Athletic:** Yes **Fin Aid:** Yes
Total Expenses by: Year **In State:** $ 12,460 **Out of State:** $ 12,460
Degrees Conferred: BA, BS, BAS
Programs of Study: Accounting, Art, Biology, English, English Composition, Fine Arts, History, General Studies, Music, Psychology, Recreation, Leisure Studies, Business Administration, Management and Organization Development, Church Ministries, Criminal Justice, Human Resources Development, Business Management, Visual Communications

ATHLETIC PROFILE

Conference Affiliation: Carolinas Conference
Program Profile: We have a first class playing facility, a press box and a dressing room. We play on natural grass. The average yearly temperature is 72 degrees.
History: MOC was a junior college until 1986 and was a member of NAIA from 1987 to 1995 and from 1995 to 1997 a member of NCAA Division I.
Achievements: CVAC Coach of the Year in 1991, 1992, 1995, 1996 and 1997; Conference Titles in 1992; Area III Champion in 1992; NAIA World Series in 1992; NCAA Regionals in 1996 and 1997.
Coaching: Carl Lancaster - Head Coach. Anthony Cobb - Assistant Coach.
Style of Play: We are very aggressive; we like to get players moving, hit and run.

North Carolina A & T State University

1601 East Market Street
Greensboro, NC 27411
Coach: Keith Shumate

NCAA I
Aggies/Navy, Old Gold
Phone: (336) 334-7371
Fax: (336) 334-7272

ACADEMIC

Type: 4 Yr., Public, Liberal Arts, Coed, Engineering
Founded: 1890
Religion: Non-Affiliated
Campus Housing: Yes
Web-site: Not Available
SAT/ACT/GPA: 920

Student/Faculty Ratio: 16:1 **Male/Female Ratio:** 50:50
Undergraduate Enrollment: 7,050 **Graduate Enrollment:** 1,000
Scholarships/Academic: Yes **Athletic:** Yes **Fin Aid:** Yes
Total Expenses by: Year **In State:** $ 5,540 **Out of State:** $ 13,000
Degrees Conferred: BA, BS, BFA, BSN, BSW, MA, MS, PhD
Programs of Study: Accounting, Marketing, Finance, Electrical, Industrial, Architectural, Mechanical Engineering, Computer Science, Animal Science, Elementary Education, Physical Education, Nursing, Technology, Transportation

ATHLETIC PROFILE

Estimated Number of Baseball Scholarships: 7
Conference Affiliation: Mid-Eastern Athletic Conference (MEAC)
Program Profile: We have a growing program. We play 56 games and a tournament. We play on natural grass in Memorial Stadium. Single A home of New York Yankees. Greensboro affiliate seats 12,000.
History: We are historically a black university. Our program has produced some quality athletes. Most notably was Al Holland Sr., a former major league relief pitcher. We are a "Diamond in the Royal " type program wherein opportunities abound.
Achievements: Former major leaguer - Al Holland pitched at A & T. He later pitched in the World Series with Phillies. Recent best draft was Cory Lima - RHP 25th round '97 draft with Florida Marlin.
Coaching: Keith Shumate, Head Coach, started with the program in 1996-1997. He inherited a 4-45 team with no recruits. He had 8 wins on his first year; 16 wins on his second year and an overall record of 24-64 with only five recruits. Our greatest recruiting class was in 1998.
Roster for 1998 team/In State: 24 **Out of State:** 5 **Out of Country:** 0
Total Number of Varsity/Jr. Varsity: 29 **Percent of Graduation:** 100%
Number of Seniors on 1998 Team: 5 **Baseball Camp Dates:** TBA
Freshmen Receiving Fin Aid/Athletic: 8 **Academic:** 4
Most Recent Record: 16 - 34 - 0 **Number of Spring Games:** 0
Positions Needed for 1999/2000: Pitcher
Schedule: UNC-Charlotte, Duke University, Western Carolina, UNC-Greensboro, Liberty University
Style of Play: We play an aggressive, running game on offense, scrappy, play overall. We are a young team (18 new players) in coach's first big recruiting class. We can not be afraid to make mistakes. We should have a great middle defense in 1999.

North Carolina State University

Box 8501
Raleigh, NC 27695-8501
Coach: Elliot Avent

NCAA I
Wolfpack/Red, White
Phone: (919) 515-3612
Fax: (919) 515-5443

ACADEMIC

Founded: 1887 **Type:** 4 Yr., Public, Coed, Engineering
Religion: Non-Affiliated **Campus Housing:** Yes
Web-site: http://www.ncsu.edu/ **SAT/ACT/GPA:** None
Student/Faculty Ratio: 14:1 **Male/Female Ratio:** 58:42
Undergraduate Enrollment: 18,000 **Graduate Enrollment:** 9,000
Scholarships/Academic: Yes **Athletic:** Yes **Fin Aid:** Yes
Total Expenses by: Year **In State:** $ 6,500 **Out of State:** $ 15,082
Degrees Conferred: Contact school.
Programs of Study: College of Agricultural and Life Sciences, College of Education and Psychology, College of Engineering, College of Forest Resources, College of Humanities and Social Sciences, College of Management, College of Physical and Mathematical Sciences, College of Textiles, College of Veterinary Medicine

ATHLETIC PROFILE

Conference Affiliation: Atlantic Coast Conference

Program Profile: Our facilities include: a $100,000 scoreboard, lights, natural turf with dimensions: 340-380-410-380-340, indoor cages and mounds. NC State baseball has become synonymous with success. We have averaged 45+ wins per season over past 6 years. NC State is looking for players who strive for success in the classroom and on the field. We have an Academic Support Program for our athletes. Doak Field has a capacity of 2,500. 1996 attendance was 26,513 for 29 dates.
History: Our program dates back to 1903. The recruiting classes have been ranked in the top 25 nationally the last four years, with the 1993 class being ranked 7th in the nation. The 1993 team set a new school record for wins with 49. We have been to the NCAA regionals 9 times in the last 11 years. Our season runs from early February through May.
Achievements: Ranked 2nd nationally; 1st seed in NCAA Regional Tournament in 1993; 12 NCAA Tournament Appearance75 first team All-Conference, 19 All-Americans, 72 players went to pros (22 since 1988); 3 players on 1993 US National team.
Coaching: Elliot Avent - Head Coach. Billy Best - Assistant Coach.
Style of Play: We have a defense style of play.

North Carolina Wesleyan College

3400 N Wesleyan Boulevard
Rocky Mount, NC 27804
Coach: Charlie Long
Email: clong@ncwc.edu

NCAA III
Battling Bishops/Royal Blue, Gold
Phone: (252) 985-5219
Fax: (252) 985-5252

ACADEMIC

Founded: 1956
Religion: Methodist
Web-site: http://www.ncwc.edu/
Student/Faculty Ratio: 13:1
Undergraduate Enrollment: 1,200
Scholarships/Academic: Yes **Athletic:** No
Total Expenses by: Year **In State:** $ 12,000
Degrees Conferred: BA, BS

Type: 4 Yr., Private, Liberal Arts, Coed
Campus Housing: Yes
SAT/ACT/GPA: 800
Male/Female Ratio: 50:50
Graduate Enrollment: None
Fin Aid: Yes
Out of State: $ Varies

Programs of Study: Accounting, Biology, Business Administration, Chemistry, Computer Information Systems, Elementary Education, English, Environmental Science, Food Services and Hotel Management, History, Justice Studies, Mathematics, Middle Grades Education, Philosophy-Religious Studies, Physical Education, Political Science, Psychology, Religious Studies, Secondary Education Certification, Sociology-Anthropology, Theater

ATHLETIC PROFILE

Conference Affiliation: Dixie Intercollegiate Athletic Conference
Program Profile: Home games are played at a beautiful Bauer Field, rated one of the finest small college facilities in the nation. It is fully enclosed with a 7 foot fence and windscreen and equipped with 3 fully astro turf batting cages, 50 foot dugouts complete with water coolers, flooring and padded seats. We haveindividual personlized lockers, bathrooms, a concession stand, a press box, and four bullpens. We have a 500 seat newly renovated bleacher section, an automatic sprinkler system, a new 36x9 foot 9-inning scoreboard and a beautiful tifton grass.
History: For the past 17 seasons, we have averaged 37 wins per season while capturing 13 Dixie Intercollegiate Athletic Conferences. We also have made 16 trips to the NCAA tournament. We have been ranked in the NCAA Division III. We participated in 9 College World Series. Each year we play a competitive schedule. Many players have been recognized for their individual accomplishments.
Achievements: We won the NCAA Division III National championship in 1989, went to 9 College World Series and won the NCAA South Regional Championship.

Pfeiffer University

P.O. Box 960
Misenheimer, NC 28109
Coach: Marty Reed

NCAA II
Falcons/Black, Old Gold
Phone: (704) 463-1360x2426
Fax: (704) 463-5051

ACADEMIC

Founded: 1885
Type: 4 Yr., Private, Liberal Arts, Coed
Religion: Methodist
Campus Housing: Yes
Web-site: http://www.pfeiffer.edu
SAT/ACT/GPA: 800/17
Student/Faculty Ratio: 15:1
Male/Female Ratio: 50:50
Undergraduate Enrollment: 1,000
Graduate Enrollment: 400
Scholarships/Academic: Yes **Athletic:** Yes **Fin Aid:** Yes
Total Expenses by: Year **In State:** $ 13,260 **Out of State:** $ 13,260
Degrees Conferred: BA, BS, MBA, Master of Organizational Management, Christian, Education
Programs of Study: Accounting, Arts Administration, Biology, Business Administration, Chemistry, Economics, Elementary Education, Law, Journalism, Engineering, Sociology, Sport Management, Sport Medicine, Psychology, Physical Education History, Mathematics

ATHLETIC PROFILE

Estimated Number of Baseball Scholarships: 3.5
Conference Affiliation: Carolinas - Virginia Athletic Conference
Program Profile: The Pfeiffer's baseball program is based on integrity, honesty and hardwork. For the past two years the baseball program has maintained a 3.0 team GPA and has had more scholar athletes than any other program at Pfeiffer. Falcons play on Joe Ferebee Field, named in honor of ABCA Hall of Fame coach. We have a natural grass facility with huge dimensions and plenty of foul-ground make it an excellent pitcher's park. There are top full batting cages. An indoor, an outdoor, and three indoor pitching mounds allow players to work and get better year-round.
History: Under Coach Joe Ferebee, the Falcons enjoyed much success, including a 2nd place national ranking in 1968. Even after Coach Ferebee's retirement in 1987, the Falcons have maintained a very competitive program.
Achievements: Coach Joe Refebee lead the Falcons to 667 wins (North Carolina record) and 10 Conference Championships; Coach Refebee was named NAIA District Coach of the Year 5 times and is also a member of the NAIA and ABCA Hall of Fames; 46 players have signed professional baseball contracts and 8 of those players were All-Americans; in 1996 pitcher Vinny Maddalone was named to the All-South Atlantic Reion team and in 1998 pitcher Adam Davidson earned CVAC Player of the Year honors by posting 10 and 2 record with a 1.5% ERA.
Coaching: Marty Reed, Head Coach, entered his 4th season. He compiled a record of 72-21. He began his coaching career in 1990 as the top assistant at the University of Tampa winning National Championships in 1992 and 1993. He has coached 12 All-Americans; 3 Region Players of the Year and Division II Player of the Year in 1990. Prior to coaching Reed pitched in the California Angels Organization from 1984 and 1989 compiling a career of 50-26. David Lee - Assistant Coach.
Roster for 1998 team/In State: 23 **Out of State:** 10 **Out of Country:** 0
Total Number of Varsity/Jr. Varsity: 33 **Percent of Graduation:** 87%
Number of Seniors on 1998 Team: 2 **Number of Sophomores on 1998 Team:** 9
Freshmen Receiving Fin Aid/Athletic: 2 **Academic:** 5
Number of Fall Games: 14 **Number of Spring Games:** 48
Positions Needed for 1999/2000: Catchers, Outfuelder, Starting Pitcher
Most Recent Record: 24 - 24 - 0
Baseball Camp Dates: June 8-12; June 14-19; June 22-26; June 29-July 1
Schedule: Mt. Olive College, Coker, Longwood College, St. Andrews, Catawba, Duke, Eckerd
Style of Play: The Falcons play an extremely aggressive style of baseball. Every player in the line-up will steal, hit and run, bunt, anything to put pressure on the opposing defense. Defensively, pitchers must throw strikes and keep runners close on the bases while position players must emphasize throwing, catching and taking care of the baseball.

Saint Andrews College

1700 Dogwood Mile
Laurinburg, NC 28352
Coach: Joe Critcher

NCAA II
Knights/White, Blue
Phone: (910) 277-5276
Fax: (910) 277-5272

ACADEMIC

Founded: 1958
Type: 4 Yr., Private, Liberal Arts, Coed
Religion: Presbyterian
Campus Housing: Yes
Web-site: http://www.sapc.edu/
SAT/ACT/GPA: 820/17/2.0
Student/Faculty Ratio: 12:1
Male/Female Ratio: 1:1
Undergraduate Enrollment: 600
Graduate Enrollment: None
Scholarships/Academic: Yes **Athletic:** Yes **Fin Aid:** Yes
Total Expenses by: Year **In State:** $ 18,300 **Out of State:** $ 18,300
Degrees Conferred: BA, BS
Programs of Study: Allied Health Biochemistry, Biology, Business Administration, Chemistry, Communications, Dramatic Arts, Economics, Elementary Education, English, Fine Arts, French, History, Languages, Literature, Management, Mathematics, Music, Philosophy, Physical Education, Physics, Political Science, Psychology, Religion, Sports Medicine

ATHLETIC PROFILE

Conference Affiliation: Carolinas - Virginia
Program Profile: We play a 52-game schedule. This is our 1st season as an NCAA D II school. The Knights play home games at Clark Field (on natural grass), which seats 5,000. We have a 42-player roster.
History: 2 Carolinas Conference titles, 1 NAIA District title, ranked in top 10 NAIA for 5 straight years, won 29 straight games. Gary Swanson's 8-year record at St. Andrews is 287-143. Became NAIA in 1989.
Achievements: Coach Swanson was 1994 Carolinas Conference Coach of the Year; 18 players drafted into pro baseball; 6 NAIA All-Americans; 22 All-Region; 37 All-Conference.
Style of Play: We play aggressive, base stealing, good pitching and power hitting.

Saint Augustine's College

1315 Oakwood Avenue
Raleigh, NC 27610
Coach: Dr. Henry E. White
Email: hwhite@es.st.aug.edu

NCAA II
Falcons/Blue, White
Phone: (919) 516-4174
Fax: (919) 804-9731

ACADEMIC

Founded: 1867
Type: 4 Yr., Private, Liberal Arts, Coed
Religion: Non-Affiliated
Campus Housing: Yes
SAT/ACT/GPA: NCAA Requirements for athletes/
Web-site: http://www.st.aug
Student/Faculty Ratio: 18:1
Male/Female Ratio: 1:4
Undergraduate Enrollment: 1,700
Graduate Enrollment: None
Scholarships/Academic: Yes **Athletic:** Yes **Fin Aid:** Yes
Total Expenses by: Year **In State:** $ 12,000 **Out of State:** $ 12,000
Degrees Conferred: BA, BS
Programs of Study: Accounting, Biological, Business, Chemistry, Communications, Computers, Criminal Justice, Early Childhood Education, Economics, Engineering, Education, English, Fine Arts, History, Industrial, Medical, Math, Music, Office, Physical Education/Therapy, Physics, Political Science, Prelaw, Premed, Psychology, Social Science, Spanish, Urban Studies

ATHLETIC PROFILE

Conference Affiliation: Central Intercollegiate Athletic Association

Program Profile: Our playing season is in the Spring. Our facilities are on campus with a natural playing surface.
History: St. Augustine's baseball program has existed for over 75 years. It is one of the best baseball programs in this conference. Henry White have been a head coach for so long at St. Augustine College wherein he saw the program grow to become one of the best competitive programs in the State of North Carolina.
Achievements: Coach of the Year in 1985-1987, 1990-1991; Conference Champions 1984, 1985-87; Tournament Champion 1984.
Coaching: Henry E. White, Head Coach got his PhD, MS & BS in Physical Education. He became the head coach in 1982. Since that time , we have grown as one of the top programs in the HDCU's.
Style of Play: We are a running team; we concentrate on putting pressure on the defense.

Shaw University

118 East South Street
Raleigh, NC 27601
Coach: Bobby Sanders

NCAA II
Bears/Maroon, White
Phone: (919) 546-8281
Fax: (919) 546-8299

ACADEMIC

Founded: 1865
Type: 4 Yr., Private, Liberal Arts, Coed
Religion: Baptist
Campus Housing: No
Web-site: Not Available
SAT/ACT/GPA: 17 avg
Student/Faculty Ratio: 13:1
Male/Female Ratio: 42:58
Undergraduate Enrollment: 4,245
Graduate Enrollment: None
Scholarships/Academic: Yes **Athletic:** Yes **Fin Aid:** Yes
Total Expenses by: Year **In State:** $ 9,600 **Out of State:** $ 9,600
Degrees Conferred: AA, BA, BS
Programs of Study: Accounting, Behavioral Science. Biology, Biological Science, Business, Management, Commercial, Chemistry, Communications, Computer Information Systems, Elementary Education, International Studies, Physical Education, Music, Social Science, Recreation Therapy, Speech Pathology

Southeastern Community College

PO Box 151
Whiteville, NC 28472
Coach: Chuck Baldwin

NJCAA
Rams/Orange, Royal, White
Phone: (910) 642-7141
Fax: (910) 642-5658

ACADEMIC

Founded: 1963
Type: 2 Yr., Jr. College, Coed
Religion: Non-Affiliated
Campus Housing: No
Student/Faculty Ratio: 20:1
Male/Female Ratio: 5:2
Undergraduate Enrollment: 1,800
Graduate Enrollment: None
Scholarships/Academic: No **Athletic:** Yes **Fin Aid:** Yes
Total Expenses by: Year **In State:** $ 3,500 **Out of State:** $ 5,500
Degrees Conferred: Associate
Programs of Study: Transfer, Technology and Vocational areas of study offered.

ATHLETIC PROFILE

Conference Affiliation: NJCAA Region X
Program Profile: We have a natural bermuda grass playing field with a200-seat capacity. Fall practice is from September to mid-October. Spring season is March to May. We have great weather and only 4 games were lost due to rain in the last 3 years. The temperature in January/February is 50-70 degrees and in March/April it is 60-80 degrees..

History: Our program began in 1968 and was dropped in 1972. It was reinstated in 1974 and dropped again in 1983. It was reinstated in 1987.
Achievements: 2 drafted during the 1974-1983 period. 4 drafted in 1987-1994 period with 3 in the last 2 years.
Style of Play: We play aggressive - good defense.

Surry Community College

P.O. Box 304
Dobson, NC 27017
Coach: Mark Tucker
Email: tuckerm@surry.cc.nc.us
NJCAA
Knights/Royal Blue, White
Phone: (336) 386-8121
Fax: (336) 386-8951

ACADEMIC

Founded: 1964
Type: 2 Yr., Public, Jr. College, Coed
Religion: Non-Affiliated
Campus Housing: No
Web-site: http://www.surry.cc.nc.us
SAT/ACT/GPA: High School Diploma
Student/Faculty Ratio: 20:1
Male/Female Ratio: 1:2
Undergraduate Enrollment: 3,000
Graduate Enrollment: None
Scholarships/Academic: Yes **Athletic:** No **Fin Aid:** Yes
Total Expenses by: Year **In State:** $ 831 **Out of State:** $ 2,582
Degrees Conferred: Associate Degrees
Programs of Study: College Transfer: Accounting, Automotive, Business Administration, Computer Engineering, Criminal Justice, Electrical, Electronics, Agriculture, Information Systems, Mechanical

ATHLETIC PROFILE

Conference Affiliation: Region X
Program Profile: We have 20-25 Fall games and 45-50 Spring games. We play on natural grass field that measures 330-left, 385-center and 305 right.
History: Our program started in 1995-1996. Eighteen of our players continued playing careers at four-year schools. We won 27 games in 1997 (27-20) and 28 games with a record of 28-15 in 1998.
Achievements: Finished 5th at 1998 NJCAA World Series; 3 All-Americans in the past three years; 1 player drafted in 1997 in the 14th round.
Coaching: Mark Tucker, Head Coach, was Region X Coach of the Year in 1997 and compiled a record of 68-56 in three years. He was 1998 District/Region Coach of the Year. Roy Vernon, Assistant Coach, entered his 3rd year and was also Associate Scout with Cincinnati Reds.
Roster for 1998 team/In State: 25 **Out of State:** 1 **Out of Country:** 0
Total Number of Varsity/Jr. Varsity: 26 **Percent of Graduation:** 89%
Number of Seniors on 1998 Team: 10 **Most Recent Record:** 28 - 15 - 0
Freshmen Receiving Fin Aid/Athletic: 0 **Academic:** 6
Number of Fall Games: 24 **Number of Spring Games:** 50
Positions Needed for 1999/2000: LHP, Shortstop, Catcher
Schedule: Spartanburgh - Methodist, Brevard, Norwalk C Tech, Louisburg, Cuyahoga CC
Style of Play: We play an aggressive, hustling style of play.

University of North Carolina - Asheville

One University Heights
Asheville, NC 28804-3299
Coach: Bill Hillier
Email: mgore@unca.edu
NCAA I
Bulldogs/Royal Blue, White
Phone: (828) 251-6920
Fax: (828) 251-6903

ACADEMIC

Founded: 1927
Type: 4 Yr., Public, Liberal Arts, Coed
Religion: Non-Affiliated
Campus Housing: Yes

Web-site: http://www.cs.unca.edu/ **SAT/ACT/GPA:** 1180/3.0
Student/Faculty Ratio: 19:1 **Male/Female Ratio:** 47:53
Undergraduate Enrollment: 3,400 **Graduate Enrollment:** 300
Scholarships/Academic: Yes **Athletic:** Yes **Fin Aid:** Yes
Total Expenses by: Year **In State:** $ 6,137 **Out of State:** $ 12,557
Degrees Conferred: BA, BS, BFA, M
Programs of Study: Accounting, Actuarial Science, Applied Mathematics, Art, Atmospheric Science, Biology, Business and Management, Chemistry, Classics, Communications, Computer Information Systems, Computer Science, Economics, Education, English, Environmental Science, Finance, French, German, Greek, Health Services, History, Latin, Literature, Marketing, Mathematics, Music, Philosophy, Physics, Political Science, Psychology, Social Science, Spanish, Theatre

ATHLETIC PROFILE

Estimated Number of Baseball Scholarships: 5.5
Conference Affiliation: Big South Conference
Program Profile: We play a NCAA maximum 56 game schedule. We have a stadium and Greenwood field is natural grass. We have a brand new $ 6 miilion dollar health and fitness center, weight room and indoor track.
History: The first year of the progam was in 1986. Since Hilliers first year; we reached our best year last year. We had our most wins and our best conference finish: 3rd place..
Achievements: Three rising seniors were drafted and signed this Summer; Shortstop Wiggins 17th ; RHP Simon Nerris 19th; OF Ludwigsen 28th round.
Coaching: Bill Hillier, Head Coach, started coaching in 1995. He is the winningest head coach in the history of the program. He was an associate head coach at Duke for 7 seasons before coming to Asheville. Has put over 25 players in Major League baseball. Has improved the record at UNCA each of his 3 seasons. He compiled a record of 18-34 in 1996, 20-33 in 1997; and 27-33 in 1998. Eric Filipek ,Assistant Coach, is a UNCA graduate and two-time All-Big South Conference , OH; 1994 UNCA Athlete of the Year. He is in his 2nd year as an assistant coach and in his 1st year as a head assistant coach.
Roster for 1998 team/In State: 7 **Out of State:** 16 **Out of Country:** 1
Total Number of Varsity/Jr. Varsity: 24 **Percent of Graduation:** 100%
Number of Seniors on 1998 Team: 5 **Number of Sophomores on 1998 Team:** 0
Freshmen Receiving Fin Aid/Athletic: 7 **Academic:** 0
Most Recent Record: 27 - 32 - 0 **Number of Spring Games:** 56
Positions Needed for 1999/2000: Pitcher, Hitting
Baseball Camp Dates: October, December 18-26
Schedule: Florida State, Auburn, Georgia, Maryland, East Carolina, Ohio University
Style of Play: We are hard hitting and aggressive offensively; defensively solid; pitching challenge hitters.

University of North Carolina - Chapel Hill

P.O. Box 2126
Capel Hill, NC 27514
Coach: Mike Fox
NCAA I
Tar Heels/Carolina Blue, White
Phone: (919) 962-2351
Fax: (919) 962-3865

ACADEMIC

Founded: 1793 **Type:** 4 Yr., Public, Liberal Arts, Coed
Religion: Non-Affiliated **Campus Housing:** Yes
Web-site: http://www.ga.unc.edu/ **SAT/ACT/GPA:** None
Student/Faculty Ratio: 10:1 **Male/Female Ratio:** 1/1.4
Undergraduate Enrollment: 15,363 **Graduate Enrollment:** 8,778
Scholarships/Academic: Yes **Athletic:** Yes **Fin Aid:** Yes
Total Expenses by: Year **In State:** $ 8,361 **Out of State:** $ 17,493
Degrees Conferred: Bachelors, Masters, Doctoral, Professional Degree

Programs of Study: African Studies, American Studies, Art, Astronomy, History, Biostatistics, Biology, Dental, Economics, Engineering, Geology, Geography, Health, Math, Recreation, Political, Physical, Physics, Sociology, Religious

ATHLETIC PROFILE

Conference Affiliation: Atlantic Coast Conference
Program Profile: Home games are played at Boshamer Stadium. It has natural grass and was voted the number 1 facility in Collegiate Baseball in 1987. It is lighted with a seating capacity of 2,500. It has new turf for the infield and a padded, ply-wood-backed outfield wall like those used in major league parks were added in the last two years. Possible future renovations include: replacing bench seating with individual seats for spectators, adding a new outfield turf and erected permanent concession stands and a ticket booth.
History: The program began in 1867. The 1998 Tar Heels are young but experienced squad with excellent speed, improved offense.
Achievements: There were 11 players named All-ACC; 3 went to the major leagues, 6 went to pro ball; BJ Surhoff was named All-American, National Player of the Year, and ACC Athlete of the Year.
Coaching: Mike Fox, Head Coach, entered his 1st year with the program. He coached 16 years at North Carolina Wesleyan, and was 2nd winning % among Division III coaches. Roger Williams, Assistant Coach, entered his 5th year with the program and still holds ACC single game strike-out record. Chad Holbrook, Assistant Coach, entered his 5th year with the program.
Roster for 1998 team/In State: 18 **Out of State:** 11 **Out of Country:** 0
Total Number of Varsity/Jr. Varsity: 29 **Percent of Graduation:** 90+%
Number of Seniors on 1998 Team: 5 **Number of Sophomores on 1998 Team:** 0
Freshmen Receiving Fin Aid/Athletic: 3 **Baseball Camp Dates:** TBA
Most Recent Record: 42 - 23 - 0 **Number of Spring Games:** 56+
Positions Needed for 1999/2000: Pitchers, Outfielder, Shortstop
Schedule: Florida State, Clemson, Wake Forest, Georgia Tech, Fresno State, NC State
Style of Play: We hustle, play hard, aggressive offensively.

University of North Carolina - Charlotte

9201 University City Boulevard
Charlotte, NC 28223
Coach: Loren Hibbs

NCAA I
49ers/Green, White
Phone: (704) 547-3935
Fax: (704) 547-4918

ACADEMIC

Founded: 1946 **Type:** 4 Yr., Public , Coed, Engineering
Web-site: http://www.uncc.edu/ **SAT/ACT/GPA:** Varies
Student/Faculty Ratio: 16:1 **Male/Female Ratio:** 49:51
Undergraduate Enrollment: 13,770 **Graduate Enrollment:** 2,670
Scholarships/Academic: Yes **Athletic:** Yes **Fin Aid:** Yes
Total Expenses by: Year **In State:** $ 3,050 **Out of State:** $ 6,800
Degrees Conferred: AS, AA, Barch, BSBA, BSEE, BET, BSME, BSN, BSW
Programs of Study: Accounting, African Studies, Anthropology, Architecture, Biological Science, Business Administration, Chemistry, Civil Engineering, Computer Science, Criminal Justice, Dance, Dramatic Arts, Economics, Electrical Engineering, Elementary Education, Engineering Technology, English, Fine Arts, French, Geograpjy, German, History, Human Services, Management, Mathematics, Mechanical Engineering, Music, Nursing, Political Science, Philosophy, Physics

ATHLETIC PROFILE

Conference Affiliation: Conference USA
Program Profile: The 49ers compete on Tom and Lib Phillips Field, a natural grass surface, with seating capacity of up to 2,000 people. The 49ers locker facility is right next to the field in the 1.2 million dollar Wachovia Fieldhouse. The fieldhouse holds the coaches offices and has over 30 individual lockers. The program competes in Conference USA and regularly plays the top teams in the Southeast.

History: The program began in 1979 and in that time the 49ers have moved from the Sun Belt Conference to the Metro and now in Conference USA. The 49ers have won two regular season conference championships and one tournament title. The 49ers made their lone NCAA appearance in 1993 after winning the 1993 Metro tournament.
Achievements: 1993 Metro Tournament Champions; 1993 NCAA MidEast Regional; 1994 and 1995 Metro Season Champions; 1984 Gary Robinson, Sun Belt Coach of the Year; 1994 Loren Hibbs - Metro Coach of the Year; 3 Freshman All-Americans; 35 have gone to professional baseball.
Coaching: Loren Hibbs, Head Coach, played collegiately at Wichita State and has brought that winning tradition to UNCC. Hibbs was the 1994 Metro Coach of the Year and has the highest winning percentage for all 49er baseball coaches. Has guided the 49ers to two regular season titles and I tournament title in just four years. He holds the NCAA record for runs scored in season with 125.
Style of Play: The 49ers are a team that like to play aggressive baseball. Speed has been an essential element over the past couple of years. The 1996's team stole 137 bases, ranking 5th nationally. As a whole, anything may go when the 49ers have runners on the base

University of North Carolina - Greensboro

1000 Spring Garden Street
Greensboro, NC 27412
Coach: Mike Gaski
Email: mewils502@homans.uncg.edu

NCAA I
Spartans/Gold, Blue
Phone: (336) 334-3247
Fax: (336) 334-4063

ACADEMIC

Founded: 1891
Type: 4 Yr., Public, Liberal Arts, Coed
Web-site: http://www.uncg.edu/
SAT/ACT/GPA: Floating scale
Student/Faculty Ratio: 14:1
Male/Female Ratio: 35:65
Undergraduate Enrollment: 12,000
Graduate Enrollment: 2,500
Scholarships/Academic: Yes **Athletic:** Yes **Fin Aid:** Yes
Total Expenses by: Year **In State:** $ 6,000 **Out of State:** $ 14,500
Degrees Conferred: BA, BS, BFA, MA, MS, MFA, Med, PhD, EdD
Programs of Study: UNCG is organized into the Graduate School, The College of Arts and Sciences and six Professional Schools: The Joseph M. Bryan School of Business and Economics, School of Education, School of Health and Human Performance, School of Human Environmental Sciences, School of Music, School of Nursing

ATHLETIC PROFILE

Conference Affiliation: Southern Conference
Program Profile: In 1999 UNCG will open a new $4.5 million baseball stadium with approximately 1,000 permanent seating and hillside blanket seating for an additional 2,000 fans. This natural grass field will be located in the heart of campus and have state of the art lighting and support facilities.
History: UNCG began intercollegiate baseball in 1991 and gained Division I status in 1992. In only their 2nd year of Division I play the Spartans established a winning season. The Spartans completed their 3rd season of Division I play with a record of 39-18 and trip to the NCAA South Regionals in Baton Rouge, LA, where they finished 3rd place.
Achievements: Mike Gaski was named two-time Coach of the Year in conference; 2 Conference Championships; 2 All-Americans; 5 Freshmen All-Americans; 1 Academic All-American; numerous players have gone on to professional ranks.
Coaching: Michael Gaski, Head Coach, began the baseball program in 1991 and in 6 years of Division I play has a 191-126 record and 2 conference championships and 2 NCAA Tournament Appearances. Neil Avent - Assistant Coach.

University of North Carolina - Pembroke

Box 1510
Pembroke, NC 28372-1510
Coach: Danny Davis
Email: davisd@sassette.uncp.edu

NCAA II
Braves/Black, Gold
Phone: (910) 521-6498
Fax: (910) 521-6540

ACADEMIC

Founded: 1887
Religion: Non-Affiliated
Web-site: http://www.uncp.edu
Student/Faculty Ratio: 16:1
Undergraduate Enrollment: 3,000
Scholarships/Academic: Yes **Athletic:** Yes
Total Expenses by: Year **In State:** $ 2,446
Degrees Conferred: BA, BS, MA, MS, MBA
Programs of Study: Has 53 major and 40 minor programs.

Type: 4 Yr., Public, Liberal Arts, Coed
Campus Housing: Yes
SAT/ACT/GPA: NCAA Requirements
Male/Female Ratio: 40:60
Graduate Enrollment: 300
Fin Aid: Yes
Out of State: $ 6,081

ATHLETIC PROFILE

Conference Affiliation: Peach Belt Athletic Conference
Program Profile: The program has excellent facilities: lights, natural grass field and a well-maintained playing field. We have great weather so we have outside practice year-round. We have Top Division II conference competition.
Coaching: Danny Davis - Head Coach. Trae McKee - Assistant Coach.
Number of Fall Games: 0 **Number of Spring Games:** 56
Most Recent Record: 24 - 25 - 0 **Baseball Camp Dates:** June 22-25
Positions Needed for 1999/2000: Mainly Pitchers
Schedule: Kennesaw State, North Florida, Armstrong Atlantic State, Columbus State, Mt. Olive
Style of Play: We have hustling, aggressive execution of fundamentals and like hard working young men.

University of North Carolina - Wilmington

601 S College Road
Wilmington, NC 28403
Coach: Mark Scalf
Email: scalfm@uncwil.edu

NCAA I
Seahawks/Teal, Gold, Navy
Phone: (910) 962-3570
Fax: (910) 962-3686

ACADEMIC

Founded: 1947
Religion: Non-Affiliated
Web-site: http://www.uncwil.edu/
Student/Faculty Ratio: 16:1
Undergraduate Enrollment: 8,700
Scholarships/Academic: Yes **Athletic:** Yes
Total Expenses by: Year **In State:** $ 8,000
Degrees Conferred: BA, BS, BSW, MBS, MSA, Med, MS in Accountancy, MS, MA, MA in Teaching.
Programs of Study: Bachelor of Arts, Bachelor of Science, Preprofessional Programs

Type: 4 Yr., Public, Liberal Arts, Coed
Campus Housing: Yes
SAT/ACT/GPA: 970
Male/Female Ratio: 41:59
Graduate Enrollment: 250
Fin Aid: Yes
Out of State: $ 15,000

ATHLETIC PROFILE

Estimated Number of Baseball Scholarships: 7
Conference Affiliation: Colonial Athletic Association
Program Profile: UNC Wilmington competes in the highly regarded Colonial Athletic Association in one of the most desirable locations in the country. The Seahawks also have a tough non-conference schedule that features many ACC opponents as well as nationally ranked foes. Brooks Field is one of the top collegiate facilities in the country, and new dressing facilities are in the planning stage.
History: The program was very successful during its infancy as a junior college program and has continued that trend into the NCAA Division I ranks. The Seahawks have won the regular season title in the CAA, featured two-Coach of the Year selections and three Player of the Year choices. In addition, many players have been drafted and signed with professional teams through the years.
Achievements: CAA Coach of the Year: Bobby Guthrie in 1989, Mark Scalf in 1995; CAA Player of the Year: Trent Mongero in 1989, Battle Holley in 1994 and Bryant Britt in 1996.

Coaching: Mark Scalf, Head Coach, compiled a record of 165-179 in six years with the program after serving as as assistant coach with the program for eight seasons. Todd Wilkenson - Assistant.
Roster for 1998 team/In State: 19 **Out of State:** 10 **Out of Country:** 0
Total Number of Varsity/Jr. Varsity: 30 **Percent of Graduation:** 0
Number of Seniors on 1998 Team: 7 **Number of Sophomores on 1998 Team:** 10
Freshmen Receiving Fin Aid/Athletic: 6 **Number of Spring Games:** 56
Positions Needed for 1999/2000: Pitcher, Catcher, Outfielder
Schedule: North Carolina State, UNC-Chapel Hill, Wake Forest, VCU, Old Dominion, Ball State
Style of Play: The Seahawks emphasize fundamentals with an aggressive approach to the game.

Wake Forest University

1834 Wake Forest Rd.
Winston - Salem, NC 27109
Coach: George Greer
Email: greer@wfu.edu

NCAA I
Demon Deacons/Old Gold, Black
Phone: (336) 758-5255
Fax: (336) 758-4565

ACADEMIC

Founded: 1834 **Type:** 4 Yr., Private, Liberal Arts, Coed
Religion: Non-Affiliated **Campus Housing:** Yes
Web-site: http://www.wfu.edu/ **SAT/ACT/GPA:** 1270/29
Student/Faculty Ratio: 11.4:1 **Male/Female Ratio:** 1:1
Undergraduate Enrollment: 3,841 **Graduate Enrollment:** 2,226
Scholarships/Academic: Yes **Athletic:** Yes **Fin Aid:** Yes
Total Expenses by: Year **In State:** $ 26,700 **Out of State:** $ 26,700
Degrees Conferred: BA, BS, MA, MS, MBA, Med, PhD, MD, JD.
Programs of Study: Anthropology, Art History, Studio Art, Chemistry, Classical Studies, Communications, Economics, English, French, German, Greek, History, Latin, Music, Philosophy, Physics, Politics, Psychology, Religion, Russians, Sociology, Spanish, Theatre, Biology, Computer Science, Health and Exercise Science, Mathematical Economics, Mathematics, Elementary Education, Education, Dentistry, Engineering, Forestry, Environmental Studies, Medieval Technology, Physician's Assistant, Business, Analytical Finance, Professional Accountancy

ATHLETIC PROFILE

Estimated Number of Baseball Scholarships: 11.7
Conference Affiliation: Atlantic Coast Conference
Program Profile: We are a competitive baseball program in one of the nation's top conferences, the ACC. Gene Hooks Stadium that has a seating capacity of 2,500 in permanent brick grandstand. It has a natural grass field. Our season generally runs from early mid-February through June.
History: The program began in the late 1800's. Wake Forest owns the ACC's only College World Series Championships (1955). Most recently, the team captured the 1998 ACC title and advanced to the NCAA South Regionals.
Achievements: 16 players have earned All-American honors; 32 players have signed pro contracts in the last 11 years; 28 players have reached the Major League (most recently Mike Buddie, 1998 New York Yankees); 4 ACC championships.
Coaching: George Greer, Head Coach, came to Wake Forest in 1988. His record at Wake Forest University is 383-258-2. His 17 years coaching record is 589-380-6. Bobby Moranda - Assistant.
Roster for 1998 team/In State: 4 **Out of State:** 27 **Out of Country:** 0
Total Number of Varsity/Jr. Varsity: 31 **Percent of Graduation:** 79%
Number of Seniors on 1998 Team: 6 **Number of Sophomores on 1998 Team:** 10
Freshmen Receiving Fin Aid/Athletic: 4 **Baseball Camp Dates:** June 1999
Most Recent Record: 43 - 23 - 0 **Number of Spring Games:** 56
Positions Needed for 1999/2000: Outfielder, Catcher, Pitcher, 2nd Base, Shortstop
Schedule: Florida State, Georgia Tech, Clemson, Auburn, Georgia, North Carolina
Style of Play: We play solid, fundamental baseball based on quality pitching and good defense.

Western Carolina University

WCU Athletics Baseball, Ramsey Center
Cullowhee, NC 28723
Coach: Rodney Hennon

NCAA I
Catamounts/Purple, Gold
Phone: (828) 227-2021
Fax: (828) 227-7688

ACADEMIC

Founded: 1889
Type: 4 Yr., Public, Coed
SAT/ACT/GPA: 850avg
Campus Housing: Yes
Student/Faculty Ratio: 17:1
Male/Female Ratio: 49:51
Undergraduate Enrollment: 5,685
Graduate Enrollment: 866
Scholarships/Academic: Yes **Athletic:** Yes **Fin Aid:** Yes
Total Expenses by: Year **In State:** $ 4,250 **Out of State:** $ 10,700
Degrees Conferred: BA, BFA, BS, BSBA, BSN, MBA, MA, MS
Programs of Study: 90 programs leading to bachelors degree and 70+ programs leading to Masters degree.

ATHLETIC PROFILE

Conference Affiliation: Southern Conference
Program Profile: We have a high profile program in the Southern Conference with an outstanding 1,500 seat stadium with a chairback seating and alumni bleacher seats and includes modern restroom and concession facilities and covered twin batting cages in a beautiful setting. Playing surface is a natural with underground irrigation system. Our team plays a full 56-game Spring schedule that goes from early February until mid-May. Our Fall practice runs from early September to mid-October.
History: Our program began in 1938 and has run continously for 59 seasons with a 1180-821-6 record. The school joined the Southern Conference in 1977 and has produced 9 regular season conference championships, 8 tournament championships and made 9 trips to the NCAA post-season play. Team have been nationally ranked (top 25) in the Fall polls 3 times in the last 10 seasons.
Achievements: Our program has produced 8 All-American selcetions, 6 Academic All-Americans, 10 Southern Conference Players of the Year, 7 Conference Coaches of the Year, 44 Major League Baseball signees, and 5 top five round draft selections since 1990. Three products have played Major League Baseball and one is a major League Baseball pitching coach.
Coaching: Rodney Hennon, Head Coach, is in his 2nd season. He served as a assistant coach for 3 seasons before being named a head coach. He is a two-time All-Southern Conference, All-NCAA South Region and two-time Academic All-American selection as a player at Western Carolina. Mike Tidick, Assistant Coach, is in his 1st season and was a Southern Conference Player of the Year in 1994. He played in the Chicago White Sox Organization. Dan Kyslinger, Assistant Coach, is in his 1st season and played at Georgia Tech and Western Carolina. He was 5th round draft choice of Milwaukee Brewers in 1992.
Style of Play: We like to be aggressive, hitting and running the bases. WCU also emphasizes a solid fundamental defense to compliment quality pitching.

Wingate University

Campus Box 3054
Wingate, NC 28174
Coach: Bill Nash
Email: bilnash@wingate.edu

NCAA II
Bulldogs/Blue, Gold
Phone: (704) 233-8242
Fax: (704) 233-8169

ACADEMIC

Founded: 1895
Type: 4 Yr., Private, Liberal Arts, Coed
Religion: Baptist
Campus Housing: Yes
Web-site: http://www.wingate.edu/
SAT/ACT/GPA: 850+
Student/Faculty Ratio: 15:1
Male/Female Ratio: 1:3
Undergraduate Enrollment: 1,400
Graduate Enrollment: 150

Scholarships/Academic: Yes **Athletic:** Yes **Fin Aid:** Yes
Total Expenses by: Year **In State:** $ 16,000 **Out of State:** $ 16,000
Degrees Conferred: AA, AS, BA, BS, MBA
Programs of Study: Accounting, Biology, Business and Management, Chemistry, Communications, Computer Information Systems, Economics, Education, English, Fine Arts, Journalism, Liberal Arts, Mathematics, Music, Parks Management, Preengineering, Prelaw, Premed, Prevet, Religion, Social Science, Speech, Sports Medicine, Telecommunications

ATHLETIC PROFILE

Estimated Number of Baseball Scholarships: 5
Conference Affiliation: South Atlantic Conference
Program Profile: The Bulldogs play at the Ron Christopher Stadium constructed in 1994 with dimensions of 330-35-400-365-330. It has an indoor cage and mounds. Our Fall season is five weeks with 3-4 scrimmages off-season work-outs programs and a 50+ game schedule. We were nationally ranked in 1998.
Achievements: 1994, 1995, 1996 and 1998 South Atlantic Conference Tournament Champions1994, 1995 and 1996 NCAA Regional Tournament. Bill Nash was 1995 Baseball Coaches Association College Coach of the Year.
Coaching: Bill Nash, Head Coach, is a graduate of Wake Forest University. He has a Masters Degree from UNCC. Paul Knight ,Assistant Coach, is a graduate of Methodist College. He has a Masters from the University of Richmond.
Roster for 1998 team/In State: 15 **Out of State:** 10 **Out of Country:** 0
Total Number of Varsity/Jr. Varsity: 28 **Most Recent Record:** 30 - 20 - 0
Number of Seniors on 1998 Team: **Number of Sophomores on 1998 Team:** 0
Freshmen Receiving Fin Aid/Athletic: 5 **Academic:** 6
Number of Fall Games: 3 **Number of Spring Games:** 53
Schedule: Kennesaw State, Savannah State, Presbyterian, Carson Newman, Mt. Olive

NORTH DAKOTA

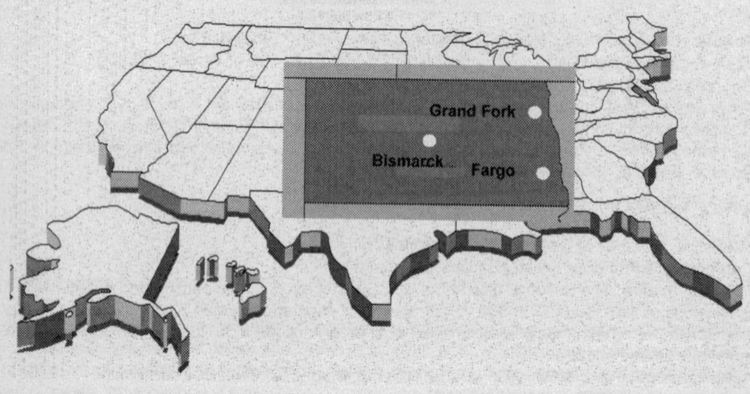

SCHOOL	CITY	AFFILIATION 99	PAGE
Bismarck State College	Bismarck	NJCAA III	643
Dickinson State University	Dickinson	NAIA	643
Jamestown College	Jamestown	NAIA	644
Mayville State University	Mayville	NAIA	644
Minot State University	Minot	NAIA	645
North Dakota State University	Fargo	NCAA II	646
North Dakota State University - Bottineau	Bottineau	NJCAA	646
University of Mary	Bismark	NAIA	647
University of North Dakota	Grand Forks	NCAA II	647
University of North Dakota - Williston	Williston	NJCAA	648
Valley City State University	Valley City	NAIA	649

Bismarck State College

1500 Edwards Avenue
Bismarck, ND 58501
Coach: Buster Gillis

NJCAA III
Mystics/Kelly, Gold, White
Phone: (701) 224-5480
Fax: (701) 224-5555

ACADEMIC

Type: 2 Yr., Public, Coed
Campus Housing: No
Web-site: http://www.bsc.nodak.edu
Degrees Conferred: Associate
Programs of Study: Agriculture, Automotive Technology, Business Administration, Commerce, Management, Biology, Biological, Carpentry, Chemical Engineering Technology, Chemistry, Commercial Art, Computer Science, Criminal Justice, Education, Electrical/Electonics Technology, Elementary Education, Energy Management, English, Farm/Ranch Management, Health Education, Journalism, Management, Public Administration, Physical education, Political Science, Psychology, Retail Management, Welding Technology

ATHLETIC PROFILE

Conference Affiliation: Mon - Dak NDJC
Program Profile: The Mystics play at Municipal Ball Park which is a natural grass with a seating capacity of 3,000. We play a Spring baseball which consists of approximately 20 games.
History: We belong to the NDJC Conference and ,as of this year, the Mon Dak Conference is becoming the shortage of Junior College teams in our area. We play a lot of the NAIA school in North Dakota. As a result, the win-loss record is not so good. We have made 1 trip to the National Tourney and that was in 1992.
Achievements: Scott Nustad became involved in the program here in the Spring of 1992. That was the first year in our program that we were going to NJCAA Division III. We qualified for the National Tournament and had only our second All-american ever. Buster Gillis was Region XIII and District C and Diamond Sports/ABCA Region Coach of the Year.

Dickinson State University

291 Campus Drive
Dickinson, ND 58601-4896
Coach: Hank Biesiot

NAIA
Blue Hawks/Blue, Grey
Phone: (701) 483-2735
Fax: (701) 227-2006

ACADEMIC

Founded: 1918
Religion: Non-Affiliated
Web-site: Not Available
Student/Faculty Ratio: 18:1
Undergraduate Enrollment: 1,585
Scholarships/Academic: Yes **Athletic:** Yes
Total Expenses by: Year **In State:** $ 4,650

Type: 4 Yr., Public, Liberal Arts, Coed
Campus Housing: No
SAT/ACT/GPA: 19 avg
Male/Female Ratio: 43:57
Graduate Enrollment: None
Fin Aid: Yes
Out of State: $ 7,500

Degrees Conferred: AA, AS, AAS, BA, BS
Programs of Study: Accounting, Agricultural, Art, Biology, Business, Chemistry, Communications, Computer, Early Childhood Education, Earth Science, Education, English, Fine Arts, Geography, History, Journalism, Management, Mathematics, Music, Nursing, Political Science, Secondary Education, Social Science, Spanish, Speech

ATHLETIC PROFILE

Conference Affiliation: NDCAC

Jamestown College

407 - 15th Avenue NE, #10
Jamestown, ND 58401-3401
Coach: Steve Olson

NAIA
Jimmies/Black, Orange
Phone: (701) 252-3467
Fax: (701) 253-4318

ACADEMIC

Founded: 1883
Religion: Presbyterian
Web-site: Not Available
Student/Faculty Ratio: 18:1
Undergraduate Enrollment: 1,085
Scholarships/Academic: Yes **Athletic:** Yes
Total Expenses by: Year **In State:** $ 11,600
Degrees Conferred: BA

Type: 4 Yr., Private, Liberal Arts, Coed
Campus Housing: No
SAT/ACT/GPA: 950/22 avg
Male/Female Ratio: 47:53
Graduate Enrollment: None
Fin Aid: Yes
Out of State: $ 11,600

Programs of Study: Business and Management, Health Sciences, Life Science, Mathematics, Psychology, Social Sciences, Teacher Education

ATHLETIC PROFILE

Conference Affiliation: NDCAC
Program Profile: Home games are played at Jack Brown Stadium.

Mayville State University

330 3rd St NE
Mayville, ND 58257
Coach: Scott Berry

NAIA
Comets/Royal Blue, White
Phone: (701) 786-4771
Fax: (701) 786-4748

ACADEMIC

Founded: 1889
Religion: Non-Affiliated
Web-site: http://www.masu.nodak.edu
Student/Faculty Ratio: 18:1
Undergraduate Enrollment: 750
Scholarships/Academic: Yes **Athletic:** Yes
Total Expenses by: Year **In State:** $ 5,868
Degrees Conferred: AA, BA, BS, BGS

Type: 4 Yr., Public, Coed
Campus Housing: Yes
SAT/ACT/GPA: Open enrollment/2.0
Male/Female Ratio: 50:50
Graduate Enrollment: None
Fin Aid: Yes
Out of State: $ 8,928

Programs of Study: Business and Management, Business/Office and Marketing/Distribution, Computer Studies, Sciences, Social Science, Teacher Education, Child Development, Professional Programs

ATHLETIC PROFILE

Conference Affiliation: North Dakota College Athletic Conference
Program Profile: We are a tradition-rich program with 12 conference championships in a row. We participated in the national playoffs 9 of the last 10 years. We have excellent indoor and outdoor facilities. Presently holds one of the best winning percentages in the NAIA baseball.
History: Our program began in the 1940's. Conference affiliation began in 1957. We have won 32 conference championships in 41 years and are acknowledged as the most successful baseball program in the state. Our longstanding tradition has attracted top quality student-athletes into the program. Twelve of our players have signed professional contracts since 1988.
Achievements: Coach of the Year 11 times, 14 conference titles in 16 years (12 in a row), 13 NAIA All-Americans (3 of them 1st or 2nd team). 10 NAIA Scholar-Athletes. 13 players have signed professional contracts.

Coaching: Scott Berry, Head Coach, has coached 16 years with a 419-252 record. He coaches pitchers and hitters. Curt Greive, Assistant, coaches outfielders and 3rd base. Aaron Funders, Assistant, coaches infielders.
Style of Play: We are fundamentally sound and aggressive. Our ritching staff is acknowledged for their consistency and competitiveness. MSU believes in an offensive offense and offensive defense. Applying constant pressure on the opponent is a priority. The offensive game plan is very diverse with an attacking style is a priority in the philosophy.

Minot State University

500 University Ave W
Minot, ND 58707
Coach: Bob Holte

NAIA
Beavers/Green, Grey, Black
Phone: (800) 777-0750
Fax: (701) 858-3631

ACADEMIC

Founded: 1906
Type: 2 Yr., Public, Coed
Religion: Non-Affiliated
Campus Housing: Yes
Web-site: http://www.165.234.172.78/homepage.htm
SAT/ACT/GPA: None
Student/Faculty Ratio: 19:1
Male/Female Ratio: 2:1
Undergraduate Enrollment: 450
Graduate Enrollment: None
Scholarships/Academic: Yes **Athletic:** Yes **Fin Aid:** Yes
Total Expenses by: Year **In State:** $ 5,066 **Out of State:** $ 5,842
Programs of Study: We offer 22 vocational-technical programs or options, Flowershop and Greenhouse Technology, Horticulture-Floral Design, Greenhouse Technology, Landscape Design, Turf Management, Information Processing, Marketing and Management, Office Education, Parks and Recreation, Urban Forestry, Wildlife and Fisheries Technology, Water Quality Technology

ATHLETIC PROFILE

Estimated Number of Baseball Scholarships: 10
Conference Affiliation: North Dakota Athletic Conference
Program Profile: The program is only in its 4th year of varsity. Our practice facility includes MSU Dome which has a seating capacity of 8,000. Our playing season includes a Southern trip in the Spring . We start conference April 1. Our field is natural grass with a seating capacity of 2,500. It was a minor league ball park.
History: We are in our 4th year of playing. We have placed 3rd and 2nd in conference tourney.
Achievements: In 1997 had 4 players in the top 10 (#32, #9, #5); runs per game (#6, #2), hit, game (#4, #2), (double #4, #1, #5); RBI's per game (#12, #8), HR per game (#1); total home run (#13), overall team is second #2 highest BA in nation; 3All-Conference in 1996, 4 in 1997 and 2 1998.
Coaching: Bob Holte - Head Coach. lance Schoenwall - Assistant Coach.
Roster for 1998 team/In State: 12 **Out of State:** 10 **Out of Country:** 12
Total Number of Varsity/Jr. Varsity: 45 **Most Recent Record:** 14 - 19 - 0
Number of Seniors on 1998 Team: 8 **Number of Sophomores on 1998 Team:** 5
Freshmen Receiving Fin Aid/Athletic: 4 **Academic:** 10
Number of Fall Games: 0 **Number of Spring Games:** 40
Positions Needed for 1999/2000: Shortstop, Pitchers-3
Style of Play: We practice hard and play hard. We like to run a lot with team speed.

North Dakota State University

University Drive
Fargo, ND 58105
Coach: Mitch McLeod

NCAA II
Bison/Green, Gold
Phone: (701) 231-8853
Fax: (701) 231-8872

ACADEMIC

Founded: 1890
Type: 4 Yr., Public, Liberal Arts, Coed
Religion: Non-Affiliated
Campus Housing: No
Web-site: Not Available
SAT/ACT/GPA: 21 avg
Student/Faculty Ratio: 20:1
Male/Female Ratio: 60:40
Undergraduate Enrollment: 9,784
Graduate Enrollment: 9,784
Scholarships/Academic: Yes **Athletic:** Yes **Fin Aid:** Yes
Total Expenses by: Year **In State:** $ 5,700 **Out of State:** $ 9,250
Degrees Conferred: Masters, Bachelors
Programs of Study: 79 Bachelors degree programs, 50 Master' degree programs, 21 Doctoral and Professional Programs. In nine academic colleges - Agriculture, Engineering, Architecture, Human Development and Education, Humanities and Social Sciences, Pharmacy, Science and Math

ATHLETIC PROFILE

Conference Affiliation: North Central Conference
Program Profile: We have a $5.6 million dollars stadium. We play on natural turf with a full locker facility, weight room and hitting tunnels under the stadium. It has a seating capacity of 4,700 including 12 skybores. We play Fall baseball with a tearing ball beginning inside a large sport area.
History: We had seven players in five years move on to play pro ball.
Coaching: Mitch McLeod - Head Coach. Blair Tweet - Assistant Coach.
Style of Play: Play hard!!

North Dakota State University - Bottineau

105 Simrall Boulevard
Bottineau, ND 58318
Coach: Craig Irwin
Email: irwin@warplo.cs.misu.nodak.edu
NJCAA
Lumberjacks/Green, Black
Phone: (701) 228-5452
Fax: (701) 228-5468

ACADEMIC

Type: 2 Yr., Public, Coed
Campus Housing: No
Degrees Conferred: Associate
Programs of Study: Contact school for program of study.

ATHLETIC PROFILE

Conference Affiliation: Montana-Dakota Conference
Program Profile: We do Fall workouts with instruction using indoor batting cages and pitching mounds. Spring ball usually is preceded by indoor workouts. Our playing field is in the process of being built. Our current field is a skin infield.
Coaching: Craig Irwin, Head Coach, is in his 1st year as head coach. He was head legion baseball coach for 13 years. He compiled a record of 596-149 which is equivalent to 80%. He helped the team win 3 state titles. Took 8 trips in 13 years. In four years, he compiled a record of 79-45. He was an assistant coach for six years and won 1 high school state championship. Mike Getzlaff - Assistant Coach.
Roster for 1998 team/In State: 8 **Out of State:** 1 **Out of Country:** 7
Total Number of Varsity/Jr. Varsity: 18 **Percent of Graduation:** 0
Number of Seniors on 1998 Team: 8 **Number of Spring Games:** 25-30
Freshmen Receiving Fin Aid/Athletic: 0 **Academic:** 8
Positions Needed for 1999/2000: Pitchers, Catchers, Middle Infielder
Schedule: Minot State University, Dawson Community College, Bismark State College, UND-Williston, Jamestown College, Valley City State
Style of Play: We believe in building a program with pitching and defense. We have an aggressive style of offense with the ability to manufacture runs by way of the bunt or hit and run. Power in the line-up is nice but emphasis on the fundamentals of hitting are stressed.

University of Mary
(New Program)

7500 University Drive
Bismark, ND 58504-9652
Coach: Steve LeGrand
Email: Morander@umary.edu

NAIA
Marauders/Royal, Orange, White
Phone: (701) 255-7500
Fax: (701) 255-7687

ACADEMIC

Founded: 1955
Religion: Catholic
Web-site: Not Available
Student/Faculty Ratio: 18:1
Undergraduate Enrollment: 2,200
Scholarships/Academic: Yes **Athletic:** Yes
Total Expenses by: Year **In State:** $ 11,255

Type: 4 Yr., Private, Coed
Campus Housing: No
SAT/ACT/GPA: None
Male/Female Ratio: 39:61
Graduate Enrollment: 157
Fin Aid: Yes
Out of State: $ 11,255

Degrees Conferred: AA, BA, BS, M
Programs of Study: Accounting, Addiction Counseling, Athletic Training, Biology, Business Administration, Business Communications, Clinical Laboratory Science, Communications, Computer Information Systems, Early Childhood Education, English, Mathematics, Math, Science, Music, Nursing, Occupational Therapy, Pastoral Ministry, Physical Education, Psychology, Radiologic Technology, Respiratory Care, Social and Behavioral Science, Social Work, Special Education

ATHLETIC PROFILE

Estimated Number of Baseball Scholarships: 4
Conference Affiliation: North Dakota Collegiate Athletic Conference
Program Profile: We have two fields both grass. One is on campus and the other is in a city park in Bismark where most of the varsity games are played. Other practice areas are the gymnasium and a golf range that is roofed with a turf surface inside.
History: The program began in 1996 (went 10-10). Coach LeGrand arrived in 1997. The team went 29-7 and tied for regular season title and finished 2nd in NDCAC tournament. In 1998 ,with a vastly improved schedule , the team went 25-24 and once again finished 2nd in the NDCAC.
Achievements: We finished 2nd in NDCAC.
Coaching: Steve LeGrand, Head Coach, has a six years overall coaching career. He was head college coach for 3 years in the NAIA and 3 in Minnesota Junior College. He compiled a record of 130-72 with 4 conference championships and 1 runner-up finish. He was named Coach of the Year in Minnesota Community College Northern Division in 1981 and 1982. Gerald Urland and Steve Ambuhe - Assistant Coaches.
Roster for 1998 team/In State: 18 **Out of State:** 27 **Out of Country:** 0
Total Number of Varsity/Jr. Varsity: 48 **Most Recent Record:** 25 - 24 - 0
Number of Seniors on 1998 Team: 13 **Number of Sophomores on 1998 Team:** 10
Freshmen Receiving Fin Aid/Athletic: 5 **Academic:** 12
Number of Fall Games: 0 **Number of Spring Games:** 40
Positions Needed for 1999/2000: Pitcher, 3rd Base, 1st Base, Outfielder
Style of Play: Aggressive.

University of North Dakota

PO Box 9013
Grand Forks, ND 58202-9013
Coach: Kelvin Ziegler
Email: keziegle@badlens.nodak.edu

NCAA II
Fighting Sioux/Kelly Green, White
Phone: (701) 777-2980
Fax: (701) 777-4352

ACADEMIC

Founded: 1883
Religion: Non-Affiliated

Type: 4 Yr., Public, Coed
Campus Housing: Yes

Web-site: http://www.nodak.edu
SAT/ACT/GPA: 2.0 grade-point
Student/Faculty Ratio: 15:1
Male/Female Ratio: 50:50
Undergraduate Enrollment: 9,500
Graduate Enrollment: 1,500
Scholarships/Academic: Yes **Athletic:** Yes **Fin Aid:** Yes
Total Expenses by: Year **In State:** $ 6,160 **Out of State:** $ 10,000
Degrees Conferred: BA, BS, BFA, MA, MS, MFA, MD
Programs of Study: There are over 165 different fields of study so here are the 11 academic divisions: Arts and Sciences, Aerospace Sciences, Business and Public Administration, Engineering and Mines, Fine, Fine Arts and Communications, Nursing, Education and Human Development, Medicine and Health Sciences, Law; graduate School and Continuing Education

ATHLETIC PROFILE

Estimated Number of Baseball Scholarships: 3.5
Conference Affiliation: North Central Conference
Program Profile: UND plays at Kraft Field, a grass, 1,500-seat facility. The program has been one of the most successful in the region, reaching the NCAA II College World Series in 1993 and winning over 100 games last five seasons (1997 season was shortened after 18 games due to flood).
History: The program was restarted in 1956 after a 36-year absence. UND has won 200+ games in the 1990's.
Achievements: Mike Rerick, 1998 draft choice choice (22nd round) by St. Louis Cardinals; Tavis Johnson was a 1995 draft choice by Minnesota Twins; Mark Varriano was a 1995 draft choice by Boston Red Sox; Carter Rogalla and Mike Rerick was a 1996 All-Central Region first team picked.
Coaching: Kelvin Ziegler, Head Coach, in his 3rd year was a assistant for 3 years. His current record is 116-67-1 in five seasons. He got 20 wins season each year and was All-Conference infielder at Minot State. Ryan Kragh, John Somrock and Kyle Yamada - Assistant Coaches.
Roster for 1998 team/In State: 40 **Out of State:** 60 **Out of Country:** 0
Total Number of Varsity/Jr. Varsity: 32 **Percent of Graduation:** 100%
Number of Seniors on 1998 Team: 4 **Number of Sophomores on 1998 Team:** 0
Freshmen Receiving Fin Aid/Athletic: 6 **Most Recent Record:** 37 - 15 - 0
Number of Fall Games: 0 **Number of Spring Games:** 52
Positions Needed for 1999/2000: Pitcher, Middle Infielder, 3rd Base
Schedule: South Dakota State, North Dakota State Nebraska-Omaha, Nebraska-Kearney
Style of Play: Aggressive - Ziegler's teams are known for hitting and pitching. Our team also plays solid defense and runs aggressively.

University of North Dakota - Williston

1426 University Avenue
Williston, ND 58802
Coach: Len Stanley

NJCAA
Tetons/Green, White
Phone: (701) 774-4200
Fax: (701) 774-4275

ACADEMIC

Founded: 1957
Type: 2 Yr., Public, Coed
Religion: Non-Affiliated
Campus Housing: No
Student/Faculty Ratio: 18:1
Male/Female Ratio: 41:59
Undergraduate Enrollment: 850
Graduate Enrollment: 0
Scholarships/Academic: No **Athletic:** Yes **Fin Aid:** Yes
Total Expenses by: Year **In State:** $ 3,500 **Out of State:** $ 6,000
Degrees Conferred: Associate
Programs of Study: Contact school for program of study.

ATHLETIC PROFILE

Conference Affiliation: Montana-Dakota Conference

Valley City State University

101 College Street SW
Valley City, ND 58072
Coach: Cory Anderson
Email: cory-anderson@mail.vcsu.nodak.edu

NAIA
Vikings/Cardinal, Royal Blue
Phone: (701) 845-7413
Fax: (701) 845-7245

ACADEMIC

Founded: 1890
Religion: Non-Affiliated
Web-site: Not Available
Student/Faculty Ratio: 15:1
Undergraduate Enrollment: 1,118
Scholarships/Academic: Yes **Athletic:** Yes
Total Expenses by: Year **In State:** $ 5,853

Type: 4 Yr., Public, Liberal Arts, Coed
Campus Housing: No
SAT/ACT/GPA: 850/18/2.0
Male/Female Ratio: 47:53
Graduate Enrollment: None
Fin Aid: Yes
Out of State: $ 8,659

Degrees Conferred: BA, BS, BSEd
Programs of Study: Business and Management, Business/Office and Management/Distribution, Humanities, Preprofessional Programs, Sciences, Teacher Education

ATHLETIC PROFILE

Conference Affiliation: North Dakota College Athletic Conference
Program Profile: Our practice started in January, February and part of March. We have a fieldhouse and a cage facility. We go on a Southern trip the 2nd week in March. Our home field is natural grass.
History: Our school was chartered in 1889. Our program began in the early 1900's and we won 5 conference titles and one District title in the past 13 years..
Achievements: 5 Conference Titles, 2 players drafted, 1 NAIA Regional appearances.
Coaching: Cory Anderson is our 6th year Head Coach and is a 1988 graduate of VCSU with Bachelor of Science Degree. He was assistant coach 1989-1991.
Style of Play: We like to stress fundamentals, rely on hitting and speed more than power (big park). The best athletes who can hit and run play for us.

OHIO

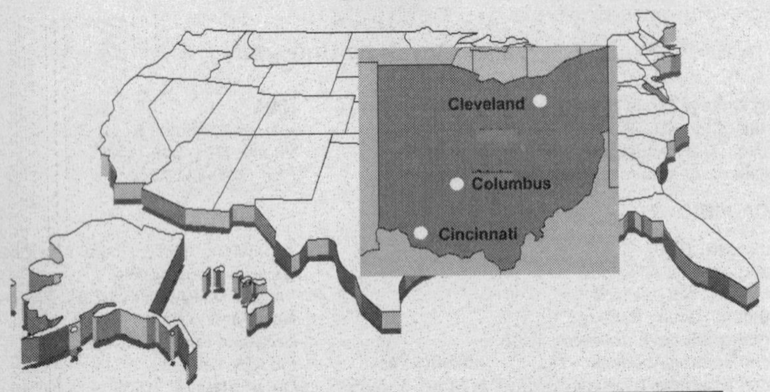

SCHOOL	CITY	AFFILIATION 99	PAGE
Ashland University	Ashland	NCAA II	652
Baldwin - Wallace College	Berea	NCAA III	652
Bluffton College	Bluffton	NCAA III	653
Bowling Green State University	Bowling Green	NCAA I	654
Capital University	Columbus	NCAA III	654
Case Western Reserve University	Cleveland	NCAA III	655
Cedarville College	Cedarville	NAIA	655
Cleveland State University	Cleveland	NCAA I	656
College of Mount Saint Joseph	Cincinnati	NCAA III	657
College of Wooster	Wooster	NCAA III	658
Columbus State Community College	Columbus	NJCAA	658
Cuyahoga Community College	Parma	NJCAA	659
Defiance College	Defiance	NCAA III	659
Denison University	Granville	NCAA III	660
Heidelberg College	Tiffin	NCAA III	660
Hiram College	Hiram	NCAA III	661
John Carroll University	University Heights	NCAA III	662
Kent State University	Kent	NCAA	663
Kenyon College	Gambier	NCAA III	663
Lakeland Community College	Kirtland	NJCAA	664
Malone College	Canton	NAIA	664
Marietta College	Marietta	NCAA III	665
Miami University - Ohio	Oxford	NCAA I	666
Mount Union College	Alliance	NCAA III	667
Mount Vernon Nazarene College	Mount Vernon	NAIA	667
Muskingum College	New Concord	NCAA III	668
Oberlin College	Oberlin	NCAA III	669
Ohio Dominican College	Columbus	NCAA III	669
Ohio Northern University	Ada	NCAA III	670
Ohio State University	Columbus	NCAA I	671
Ohio University	Athens	NCAA I	672
Ohio Wesleyan University	Delaware	NCAA III	672
Otterbein College	Westerville	NCAA III	673
Owens Community College	Toledo	NJCAA	673
Shawnee State University	Portsmounth	NAIA	674
Sinclair Community College	Dayton	NJCAA	675
Tiffin University	Tiffin	NAIA	675
University of Akron	Akron	NCAA I	676
University of Cincinnati	Cincinnati	NCAA I	676
University of Dayton	Dayton	NCAA I	677
University of Findlay	Findlay	NAIA	677
University of Rio Grande	Rio Grande	NAIA	678
University of Toledo	Toledo	NCAA I	678
Urbana University	Urbana	NAIA	679
Walsh University	North Canton	NAIA	679

SCHOOL	CITY	AFFILIATION 99	PAGE
Wilmington College	Wilmington	NCAA III	680
Wittenberg University	Springfield	NCAA III	680
Wright State University	Dayton	NCAA I	681
Xavier University	Cincinnati	NCAA I	682
Youngstown State University	Youngstown	NCAA I	682

Ashland University

Kates Gymnasium
Ashland, OH 44805
Coach: John Schaly

NCAA II
Eagles/Purple, White
Phone: (419) 289-5444
Fax: (419) 289-5468

ACADEMIC

Founded: 1878
Type: 4 Yr., Private, Liberal Arts, Coed
Religion: Brethren Church
Campus Housing: Yes
Web-site: http://www.ashland.edu/
SAT/ACT/GPA: Open Enrollment/
Student/Faculty Ratio: 13:1
Male/Female Ratio: 50:50
Undergraduate Enrollment: 1,800
Graduate Enrollment: 300
Scholarships/Academic: Yes **Athletic:** Yes **Fin Aid:** No
Total Expenses by: Year **In State:** $ 17,950 **Out of State:** $ 17,950
Degrees Conferred: BA, BS, MEd, MBA
Programs of Study: Accounting, Biology, Broadcasting, Business Administration, Chemistry, Communications, Computer Science, Criminal Justice, Economics, Education, English, Geology, History, Hotel/Restaurant Management, Journalism, Management, Marketing, Math, Medical Laboratory Technology, Music, Nursing, Philosophy, Physics, Political Science, Predentistry, Prelaw, Premed, Psychology, Public Administration, Social Science, Speech

ATHLETIC PROFILE

Conference Affiliation: Great Lakes Intercollegiate Athletic Conference
Program Profile: We have great facilities: natural grass, 300 seats & locker rooms . Conard Fieldhouse has Tarton surface for indoor practice. We play at Donges Field.
History: The team played in 1995 Division II World Series. Our program began in 1920 and has built a great tradition. There have been only 4 head coaches in the program's history, and it plays in one of the toughest Division II conferences in the nation. The school record for wins was in 1994 with 31. Last year, Ashland went 37-21 overall and 18-5 in the conference.
Coaching: John Schaly - Head Coach. Mark Johnson - Assistant Coach.

Baldwin - Wallace College

275 Eastland Road
Berea, OH 44017
Coach: Bob Fisher

NCAA III
Yellow Jackets/Brown, Gold
Phone: (440) 826-2182
Fax: (440) 826-2192

ACADEMIC

Founded: 1845
Type: 4 Yr., Private, Liberal Arts, Coed
Religion: Methodist
Campus Housing: Yes
Web-site: http://www.balwinw.edu/
SAT/ACT/GPA: 1050/ 21
Student/Faculty Ratio: 14:1
Male/Female Ratio: 40:60
Undergraduate Enrollment: 4,200
Graduate Enrollment: 600
Scholarships/Academic: Yes **Athletic:** No **Fin Aid:** Yes
Total Expenses by: Year **In State:** $ 17,500 **Out of State:** $ 17,500
Degrees Conferred: BA, BS, BM, BME, MBA, MAEd
Programs of Study: Accounting, Banking/Finance, Biology, Business Administration, Chemistry, Communications, Computer Science, Dance, Earth Science, Education, Geology, Engineering, Health, Marketing, Mathematics, Medical Laboratory, Physical Education, Prepsychology, Prepathology

ATHLETIC PROFILE

Conference Affiliation: Ohio Athletic Conference (OAC)

Program Profile: We have a Fall camp that includes weekend scrimmages, off-season and physical training. Winter practice is mid-January through Florida trip. Facilities include spacious indoor fieldhouse and astro-turf football field to practice outdoors year-round.
History: Our program began in 1895. Coach Fisher's era started in 1968. BW was 81-47 in OAC during the 1970's' 103-36 in the conference during the 1980's; 82-58 thru far in the 1990's.
Achievements: 15 players signed pro contract since 1970; OAC Champions in 1985; OAC regular season champs in 1986 and 1988; NCAA Regional Bid in 1985, 1986, 1988 and 1991.
Coaching: Bob Fisher, Head Coach, was Coach of the Year four times. He started coaching at BW in 1968. He compiled a record of 458-428-11.. James Timmer - Infield Coach .
Roster for 1998 team/In State: 18 **Out of State:** 8 **Out of Country:** 0
Total Number of Varsity/Jr. Varsity: 44 **Percent of Graduation:** 96%
Number of Seniors on 1998 Team: 7 **Most Recent Record:** 12 - 12 - 0
Freshmen Receiving Fin Aid/Athletic: 0 **Academic:** 17
Number of Fall Games: 0 **Number of Spring Games:** 36
Positions Needed for 1999/2000: Pitchers, Catchers, Middle Infielders
Schedule: Marietta, Wooster, Wittenberg, Allegheny, Ohio Northern
Style of Play: Short game using bunting skill, hit and run attack; aggressive defense.

Bluffton College

280 W College Avenue
Bluffton, OH 45817-1196
Coach: Greg Brooks

NCAA III
Beavers/NorthWestern Purple, White
Phone: (419) 358-3225
Fax: (419) 358-3232

ACADEMIC

Founded: 1899 **Type:** 4 Yr., Private, Liberal Arts, Coed
Religion: Mennonite **Campus Housing:** Yes
Web-site: http://www.bluffton.edu/ **SAT/ACT/GPA:** 20
Student/Faculty Ratio: 15:1 **Male/Female Ratio:** 1:2
Undergraduate Enrollment: 725 **Graduate Enrollment:** 251
Scholarships/Academic: Yes **Athletic:** No **Fin Aid:** Yes
Total Expenses by: Year **In State:** $ 15,197 **Out of State:** $ 15,197
Degrees Conferred: BA, BS, BM, MA
Programs of Study: 35 Different areas of study with a Business and Education as the two largest: Art, Biology, Chemistry, Communications, Computer Science, Criminal Justice, Economics/Business and Accounting, Education, English, Family and Consumer Sciences, General Education, German, Greek, Health/Physical Education, English, Humanities, Liberal Arts and Sciences, Mathematics, Music, Peace and Conflict Studies, Philosophy, Physics, Political Science, Psychology, Recreation Management, Religion, Special Education, Sociology, Social Sciences, Social Work

ATHLETIC PROFILE

Conference Affiliation: Independent Conference
Program Profile: We play on campus at Sears Athletic Complex (natural grass).Our 40+ games schedule includes NAIA and MCAA Division III teams and a week long trip to Florida over Spring Break. We play in conference tournament every season.
History: Our program began in 1951. We had only nine coaches in 44 years of program. Only 12 losing seasons out of 44 years. Our college has been a playing club ball since the 1920's.
Achievements: Seven players received major league playoffs.
Coaching: Greg Brooks, Head Coach, has the longest tenure of any BC baseball coach with 18 years. He has a BA and MA in secondary education.
Style of Play: We play conservative, fundamental baseball.

Bowling Green State University

Intercollegiate Athletics
Bowling Green, OH 43043
Coach: Danny Schmitz

NCAA I
Falcons/Brown, Orange
Phone: (419) 372-7065
Fax: (419) 372-6015

ACADEMIC

Founded: 1910
Type: 4 Yr., Public, Coed
Religion: Non-Affiliated
Campus Housing: Yes
Web-site: http://www.bgsu.edu/
SAT/ACT/GPA: 22.2avg/3.10
Student/Faculty Ratio: 18:1
Male/Female Ratio: 44:56
Undergraduate Enrollment: 14,800
Graduate Enrollment: 2,400
Scholarships/Academic: Yes **Athletic:** Yes **Fin Aid:** Yes
Total Expenses by: Year **In State:** $ 7,576 **Out of State:** $ 12,134
Degrees Conferred: A, BA, BS, BFA, MA, MS, MBA, MFA, MEd, PhD
Programs of Study: American Culture, Apparel Design/History, Art, Asian, Biological, Classical, Computer Creative Writing, English, Environmental, Ethnic, Fashion, Preprofessional Programs

ATHLETIC PROFILE

Conference Affiliation: Mid - American Conference
Program Profile: Bowling Green plays its outdoor season beginning in March. Its home park, Warren E. Steller Field (cap. 2,500/natural grass), is considered one of the finest facilities in the Midwest. During the Winter months, the Falcons train at the $8.7 million fieldhouse where they use two spacious batting cages and the 90-yard indoor turf room.
History: Baseball has been played at BGSU since 1915, though the first varsity season was not until 1918. The all time record stands at 1,091-925-25 over 77 seasons spanning 79 years. Over that time, BG has won 9 conference titles, including the MAC championship in 1972 and 1995.
Achievements: We sent many players to the major league, narrowly missing a trip to the College World Series; 4 Falcons have earned All-Americans over the years.
Coaching: Danny Schmitz, Head Coach, is a former minor league player and coach. He served 3 seasons as an assistant coach at Eastern Michigan, where he earned his undergraduate degree in Physical Education in 1979.
Style of Play: BG plays an aggressive style of baseball, stressing good fundamentals and defense. Program goes by the theory that hard work and practice will pay dividends.

Capital University

2199 E Main Street
Columbus, OH 43209-2394
Coach: Brian Arnold

NCAA III
Crusaders/Purple, White
Phone: (614) 236-6203
Fax: (614) 236-6178

ACADEMIC

Founded: 1830
Type: 4 Yr., Private, Liberal Arts, Coed
Religion: Lutheran
Campus Housing: Yes
Web-site: http://www.capital.edu/
SAT/ACT/GPA: 870/ 17
Undergraduate Enrollment: 1,900
Graduate Enrollment: 1,900
Scholarships/Academic: Yes **Athletic:** No **Fin Aid:** Yes
Total Expenses by: Year **In State:** $ 18,500 **Out of State:** $ 18,500
Degrees Conferred: BA, BFA, General Studies, Social Work, Music, Nursing
Programs of Study: Accounting, Art, Art Education, Art Therapy, Biology, Business, Chemistry, Communications, Computer Science, Criminilogy, Economics, Education, Elementary Education, English, Finance, French, Health Education, Liberal Arts, Management, Marketing, Math, Music, Nursing, Philosophy, Physical Education, Political Science, Predentistry, Prelaw, Premed, Psychology, Public Administration, Social Science

ATHLETIC PROFILE

Conference Affiliation: Ohio Athletic Conference
Program Profile: Spring program, natural grass.
History: Program began in 1900.
Achievements: 1995 Tri - Coach of the Year - Jeff Bricker; Jim Mayer was 1st team All-American in 1994, 1994 and 1995 (OF).
Coaching: Brian Arnold, Head Coach, entered his 2nd year as a head coach and was former assistant coach at Capital University for six years.
Style of Play: Aggressive.

Case Western Reserve University

10900 Euclid Avenue
Cleveland, OH 44106
Coach: Jerry Seimon

NCAA III
Spartans/Royal, White
Phone: (216) 368-5379
Fax: (216) 368-5475

ACADEMIC

Founded: 1880
Religion: Non-Affiliated
Web-site: http://www.cwru.edu/
Student/Faculty Ratio: 8:1
Undergraduate Enrollment: 3,200
Scholarships/Academic: Yes **Athletic:** No
Total Expenses by: Year **In State:** $ 23,000
Degrees Conferred: BS, BA, MS

Type: 4 Yr., Private, Liberal Arts, Coed
Campus Housing: Yes
SAT/ACT/GPA: 1100/ 25
Male/Female Ratio: 65:35
Graduate Enrollment: 4,000
Fin Aid: Yes
Out of State: $ 23,000

Programs of Study: Accounting, Aerospace Engineering, Anthropology, Applied Mathematics, Art, Astronomy, Biochemistry, Communications, Comparative Literature, Computer Engineering, Computer Science, Dentistry, Earth Science, Economics, Electrical Engineering, English, Environmental Science, Finance, Geology, Gerontology, Law, Management, Math, Mechanical Engineering, Medical Technology, Medicine, Music, Natural Science, Nursing, Philosophy, Physics, Political Science, Religion, Psychology

ATHLETIC PROFILE

Conference Affiliation: North Coast Athletic, University Athletic Association
Program Profile: We compete in 2 conferences and play in round-robin tournament in Cocoa Beach Florida. Outdoor Spring schedule runs from mid March - first of May. We have an Ivy League caliber education.
History: The Cleveland State baseball program began in 1966, but was preceeded by the Fenn College baseball program that began in 1932. CSU has had 8 coaches and several winning seasons. The best player could be Matt Carpenter who was drafted by the Colorado Rockies in the expansion draft.

Cedarville College

P.O. Box 601
Cedarville, OH 45314-0601
Coach: Norris Smith

NAIA
Yellow Jackets/Blue, Yellow
Phone: (937) 766-7645
Fax: (937) 766-5556

ACADEMIC

Founded: 1887
Religion: Baptist
Web-site: http://www.cedarville.edu/
Student/Faculty Ratio: 18:1

Type: 4 Yr., Private, Liberal Arts, Coed
Campus Housing: Yes
SAT/ACT/GPA: 1020/ 22
Male/Female Ratio: 43:57

Undergraduate Enrollment: 2,450 **Graduate Enrollment:** N/A
Scholarships/Academic: Yes **Athletic:** Yes **Fin Aid:** Yes
Total Expenses by: Year **In State:** $ 13,164 **Out of State:** $13,164
Degrees Conferred: BA, BME, BSEE, BSME, BSN, AA
Programs of Study: Accounting, American Studies, Applied Psychology, Athletic Training, Bible, Biology, Broadcasting, Business, Communication Technology, Business Education, Chemistry, Communication Arts, Computer Information Sytems, Criminal Justice, Electrical Engineering, Elementary Education, English, Finance, History, History-Political Science, International Studies, Management, Marketing, Mathematics, Music, Music Education, Nursing, Physical Education, Political Science, Predentistry, Prelaw, Premed, Prevet, Psychology, Public Administration, Science, Social Science, Social Work, Sociology, Spanish, Spanish Education, Speech Education

ATHLETIC PROFILE

Conference Affiliation: Mi-Ohio Conference

Central State University

(Program Discontinued)

Cleveland State University

2451 Euclid Avenue
Cleveland, OH 44115
Coach: Jay Murphy

NCAA I
Vikings/Gold, Green, White
Phone: (216) 687-4822
Fax: (216) 687-9242

ACADEMIC

Type: 4 Yr., Public, Liberal Arts, Coed, Engineering **Founded:** 1964
Religion: Non-Affiliated **Campus Housing:** Yes
SAT/ACT/GPA: Open Enrollment for OH Residents/ **Web-site:** http://www.csuohio.edu/
Student/Faculty Ratio: 27:1 **Male/Female Ratio:** 52:48
Undergraduate Enrollment: 15,656 **Graduate Enrollment:** 4,500
Scholarships/Academic: Yes **Athletic:** Yes **Fin Aid:** Yes
Total Expenses by: Year **In State:** $ 8,590 **Out of State:** $ 12,046
Degrees Conferred: BA, BS
Programs of Study: College of Arts and Sciences, College of Business Administration, College of Education, College of Engineering, Graduate Degrees, College of Law

ATHLETIC PROFILE

Estimated Number of Baseball Scholarships: 8
Conference Affiliation: Midwestern Collegiate Conference
Program Profile: Cleveland State Baseball field is located in the near - by grass diamond with lights, tarp, press box, and seating for 1,500. Dimensions are 320 down the line, 360 in the gaps and 359 to center. CSU plays an ambitious 56 game Division I schedule.
History: 1932 as Fenn College and 1966 as Cleveland State. Jay Murphy is the 5th head coach at CSU which sent 20 players on to play professionally. Most notable is Jerry Dylzenski with the Indians, White Sox, and Pirates. Al Mohorcic was drafted by Texas Rangers and the Yankess. Ken Robinson was drafted by the Toronto Blue Jays.
Achievements: 1992 Jay Murphy's George Washington Team won the Atlantic Ten West Division and Tournament Championship which earned GW berth in the NCAA Tournament. Under Murphy's tutelage, the young Vikings are expected to make a strong bid for the conference & tournament titles.
Coaching: Jay Murphy, Head Coach, compiled a record of 22-28 in 1997. He was named Co-Coach of the Year in 1982-1984 at Skidmore College in Saratoga, New York. He was an assistant coach at Kent State in 1985-1987. He was an assistant coach at George Washington in 1987-1991 and head coach at George Washington from 1992-1996. Dave Sprochi & Dennis Healy - Assistant Coaches.
Roster for 1998 team/In State: 32 **Out of State:** 6 **Out of Country:** 0
Total Number of Varsity/Jr. Varsity: 28+ **Percent of Graduation:** 95%

Number of Seniors on 1998 Team: 5 **Number of Sophomores on 1998 Team:** 12
Most Recent Record: 11 - 19 - 0 **Number of Spring Games:** 56
Positions Needed for 1999/2000: Pitcher, 3rd Base, Infielder
Baseball Camp Dates: June 22-26; July 6-10
Schedule: UNC-Charlotte, North Carolina, Old Dominion, Notre Dame, Ohio State
Style of Play: CSU is a high powered offense that averages 9 runs a game. In 1997, a team record 57 runs were hit and the 1998 team is on a pace to shatter that record.

College of Mount Saint Joseph

5701 Delhi Road
Cincinnati, OH 45233-1670
Coach: Chuck Murray

NCAA III
Lions/Blue, Gold
Phone: (513) 244-4402
Fax: (513) 244-4928

ACADEMIC

Founded: 1920 **Type:** 4 Yr., Private, Liberal Arts, Coed
Religion: Catholic **Campus Housing:** No
Web-site: Not Available **SAT/ACT/GPA:** 400/19
Student/Faculty Ratio: 15:1 **Male/Female Ratio:** 32:68
Undergraduate Enrollment: 2,500 **Graduate Enrollment:** 200
Scholarships/Academic: Yes **Athletic:** No **Fin Aid:** Yes
Total Expenses by: Year **In State:** $ 15,130 **Out of State:** $ 15,130
Degrees Conferred: BA, BS, MA, AA, AS
Programs of Study: Art, Behavioral Science, Biology, Business, Chemistry, Education, humanities, Liberal Arts, Mathmatics, Music, Nursing, Physical Therapy, Religious and Pastoral Studies, Preprofessional Programs

ATHLETIC PROFILE

Conference Affiliation: ICAC
Program Profile: We are in our 6th year of baseball in 1999. We play at beautiful Midland Field home of Connie Mack champion at Midland Redskin. It has 2 indoor mounds and batting cages. Grass surface seating is 750-1,000 people.
History: In 1994, we had 9 wins and 18 losses playing in NAIA - Mid-Ohio. 1995 NAIA Independent had 20 wins and 29 losses; qualified for sectional play. 1996 had 19 wins and 10 losses dual membership NCAA 3 and NAIA. AMC regular season post-season champions. Qualify NAIA Sectional. 1997 has 25 wins and 16 losses - NAIA Sectional Qualifier; 1998 - last year as dual NAIA-NCAA membership; 1999 Full fledged NCAA III; 1998 has 24 wins and 14 losses.
Achievements: In 1996, Joe Regruth was named AMC Coach of the Year. He got 1996 AMC Regular Season Post-season titles; In 1996 and 1997, Kyle Hensley was named Academic All-American; 1996 Mike Ayers signed as a free-agent by Pittsburgh Pirates; 1995 - 1998 Qualified for NAIA Sectional Play.
Coaching: Chuck Murray, Head Coach, was an assistant coach in 1994-1996. He became a head coach in 1997. Our record in 1997 was 25-16 and in 1998 24-14. Mark Hopkins, Assistant Coach, started coaching in 1994 to the present. Joe Nichols, Assistant, started in 1997 to the present.
Roster for 1998 team/In State: 24 **Out of State:** 1 **Out of Country:** 1
Total Number of Varsity/Jr. Varsity: 26 **Most Recent Record:** 24 - 14 - 0
Number of Seniors on 1998 Team: 4 **Number of Sophomores on 1998 Team:** 6
Number of Fall Games: 0 **Number of Spring Games:** 42
Schedule: Anderson, DePauw, Manchester, Cincinnati, Thomas Moore, Wabash, Otterbein
Style of Play: We are fundamentally sound and do not beat ourselves. We hustle and give 100% at all times.

College of Wooster

Beall Avenue
Wooster, OH 44691
Coach: Tim Pettorini

NCAA III
Fighting Scots/Black, Old Gold
Phone: (330) 263-2180
Fax: (330) 263-2537

ACADEMIC

Founded: 1866
Religion: Presbyterian
Web-site: http://www.wooster.edu/
Student/Faculty Ratio: 12:1
Scholarships/Academic: Yes **Athletic:** No
Total Expenses by: Year **In State:** $ 24,500
Type: 4 Yr., Private, Liberal Arts, Coed
Campus Housing: Yes
SAT/ACT/GPA: 1160
Male/Female Ratio: 50:50
Fin Aid: Yes
Out of State: $ 24,500
Degrees Conferred: BA, Bmus, Bed
Programs of Study: Extensive Listing and Self - Designed Major. 37 Majors, 7 Special Programs, 10 Preprofessional Programs including: Afro-American Studies, Art, Biology, Business Economics, Chemistry, Classical Studies, Communications, Computer Science, Dramatic Arts, Economics, Education, English, French, Geology, German, History, Mathematics, Music, Philosophy, Physics

ATHLETIC PROFILE

Conference Affiliation: North Coast Athletic Conference
Program Profile: Wooster's home field is Art Murray Field -- natural grass, permanent outfield fence, warning track, two dugouts, electronic scoreboard, enclosed press box and concession stand.
Achievements: NCAA Division III 1994 MidEast Regional Champions; 7 1st team All-Americans; 3 2nd team; 4 3rd team; 3 Academic All-Americans; 2 NCAC Pitcher of the Year; 4 NCAC Players of the Year; 2 World Series Appearances in 1989 and 1995; 10 players signed or drafted by professional team since 1970.
Coaching: Tim Pettorini, Head Coach, has coached 16 years. He was NCAC Coach of the Year in 1987-1988, 1990 and 1995.
Style of Play: Offesively, we are very aggressive and run whenever possible. Defensively, we are fundamentally sound with a good pitching.

Columbus State Community College

550 East Spring Street
Columbus, OH 43216-1609
Coach: Greg Weyrich

NJCAA
Cougars/Blue, White
Phone: (614) 287-5348
Fax: (614) 227-5395

ACADEMIC

Founded: 1963
Religion: Non-Affiliated
Student/Faculty Ratio: 21:1
Undergraduate Enrollment: 17,050
Scholarships/Academic: No **Athletic:** No
Total Expenses by: Year **In State:** $ 1,900
Type: 2 Yr., Jr. College, Coed
Campus Housing: No
Male/Female Ratio: 42:58
Graduate Enrollment: None
Fin Aid: Yes
Out of State: $ 4,200
Degrees Conferred: Associate
Programs of Study: Accounting, Banking, Finance, Business Administration, Corrections, Education, Liberal Arts, Marketing, Real Estate, Social Science, Sports Administration***Contact school admission for more information on academic and admission.

ATHLETIC PROFILE

Conference Affiliation: OCCAC (Ohio Community College Athletic Conference)

Program Profile: The team plays at McCoy Park in Columbus, Ohio with natural field and dimensions of 340-400-340. We are a Division III Junior College member of the Ohio Community College Athletic Conference.
History: Our program began in 1988.
Achievements: Coach of the Year Division III in 1992 - Harry Caruso; Division III World Series in 1992; Conference champs in 1992; 5 All-American players: 1991 had 1, 1992 had 2, 1993 had 1 and 1997 had 1; 4 drafted pro players.
Coaching: Greg Weyrich - Head Coach. Tom Venditelli - Assistant Coach. Bill Schultz - Assistant.
Style of Play: We are aggressive with a speed, hit and run and single and double. We have less power but a strong defense is preferred.

Cuyahoga Community College

11000 Pleasant Valley Rd
Parma, OH 44130
Coach: Tim Dowdell

NJCAA
Challengers/Red, White, Blue
Phone: (216) 987-5458
Fax: (216) 987-3622

ACADEMIC

Founded: 1966
Type: 2 Yr., Jr. College, Coed
Religion: Non-Affiliated
Campus Housing: No
Undergraduate Enrollment: 13,200
Graduate Enrollment: 0
Scholarships/Academic: No **Athletic:** Yes
Fin Aid: Yes
Total Expenses by: Year **In State:** $ 2,000
Out of State: $ 4,500
Degrees Conferred: Associate
Programs of Study: Automotive, Aviation, Business, Commercial Art, Computer, Court Reporting, Medical, Graphic Arts, Labor, Law, Manufacturing Technology, Real Estate, Science

ATHLETIC PROFILE

Conference Affiliation: Ohio Community College Athletic Conference
Program Profile: We have been highly successful over the past 10 years. We had 8 regional appearances, including a Regional Champs in 1989. Mottl Field is a top notch facility including lights, dugouts and a pressbox.
History: Our program began in 1972. The team has had over 30 former players that were drafted or signed to a professional contract. The school had Regional Championships in 1976 and 1989. Coach Dowdell is in his 11th year with an overall record of 255-178.
Achievements: Coach Dowdell was Region XII NJCAA Coach of the Year in 1989. Third baseman Dave Kane was first team All-American in 1995; 4 conference titles in the 8 years of the conference; 32 players drafted or signed.
Coaching: Tim Dowdell has been Head Coach for 10 years and has a 255-178 record. Ken Nedoma was 4 years at CCC. Jay Arndt, Hitting Coach, was 2 years at CCC with a .347 team. He got a BA in 1995.
Style of Play: We are very aggressive with a premium placed on team speed, pitching and defense.

Defiance College

701 North Clinton Street
Defiance, OH 43512
Coach: Craig Rutter

NCAA III
Yellow Jackets/Purple, Gold
Phone: (419) 783-2341
Fax: (419) 783-2369

ACADEMIC

Founded: 1850
Type: 4 Yr., Private, Liberal Arts, Coed
Religion: United Church of Christ
Campus Housing: Yes
Web-site: http://www.defiance.edu/
SAT/ACT/GPA: 820+/ 18
Student/Faculty Ratio: 14:1
Male/Female Ratio: 1:1

Undergraduate Enrollment: 900 **Graduate Enrollment:** 50
Scholarships/Academic: Yes **Athletic:** No **Fin Aid:** Yes
Total Expenses by: Year **In State:** $ 17,000 **Out of State:** $ 17,000
Degrees Conferred: BS, BA, MA
Programs of Study: Accounting, Art, Biology, Business Administration, Chemistry, Communication, Education, Finance, History, Management, Mathematics, Physical Education, Social Work, Sport Management

ATHLETIC PROFILE

Conference Affiliation: Michigan Intercollegiate Athletic Association
Program Profile: Facilities are new with the possibility of a press box. Playing season is in Spring only. Our field is natural grass.
History: We have been around a long time and do not know when it started. Craig Rutter came in 1983, can not find much information before that.
Achievements: HBCC Coach of the Year in 1985; AMC Coach of the Year in 1995; Association of Mideast Colleges Titles in 1995.
Coaching: Craig Rutter, Head Coach, compiled a record of 243-292-5.
Roster for 1998 team/In State: 20 **Out of State:** 1 **Out of Country:** 0
Total Number of Varsity/Jr. Varsity: 21 **Percent of Graduation:** 96%
Number of Seniors on 1998 Team: 5 **Number of Sophomores on 1998 Team:** 6
Freshmen Receiving Fin Aid/Athletic: 0 **Academic:** 8
Most Recent Record: 13 - 11 - 0 **Baseball Camp Dates:** June 16-18
Positions Needed for 1999/2000: I'll look at anyone
Schedule: Indiana University, BGSU, University of Toledo, MIACC Schedule
Style of Play: Aggressive! Take nothing for granted. Score first, throw strikes, work fast, close the deal. Play hard or go home. Sprint everywhere!

Denison University

P.O. Box M
Granville, OH 43023
Coach: Dan Briggs

NCAA III
Big Red/Red, White
Phone: (740) 587-6714
Fax: (740) 587-6362

ACADEMIC

Founded: 1825 **Type:** 4 Yr., Private, Liberal Arts, Coed
Religion: Non-Affiliated **Campus Housing:** Yes
Web-site: http://louie.cc.denison.edu/ **SAT/ACT/GPA:** 1050+/ 27
Student/Faculty Ratio: 11:1 **Male/Female Ratio:** 50:50
Undergraduate Enrollment: 2,000 **Graduate Enrollment:** None
Scholarships/Academic: Yes **Athletic:** No **Fin Aid:** Yes
Total Expenses by: Year **In State:** $ 23,730 **Out of State:** $ 23,730
Degrees Conferred: BS, BA
Programs of Study: Art, Biology, Black Studies, Chemistry, Cinema, Classical Studies, Communications, Computer Science, Dance, International Studies, Latin American, Mathematics, Music, Philosophy, Physical Education, Physics, Political Science, Psychology, Religion, Sociology

ATHLETIC PROFILE

Conference Affiliation: North Coast Athletic Conference

Heidelberg College

310 E Market Street
Tiffin, OH 44883
Coach: Chris Keshock
Email: cheshock@mail.heidelberg.edu

NCAA III
Student Princes/Black, Red, Orange
Phone: (419) 448-2009
Fax: (419) 448-2025

ACADEMIC

Founded: 1874
Type: 4 Yr., Private, Liberal Arts, Coed
Religion: United Church of Christ
Campus Housing: Yes
Web-site: http://www.heidelburg.edu/
SAT/ACT/GPA: 900/ 17 Flexible
Student/Faculty Ratio: 14:1
Male/Female Ratio: 51:49
Undergraduate Enrollment: 1,100
Graduate Enrollment: 100
Scholarships/Academic: Yes **Athletic:** No **Fin Aid:** Yes
Total Expenses by: Year **In State:** $ 19,800 **Out of State:** $ 19,800
Degrees Conferred: BA, BS, MA, Med, MBA
Programs of Study: 35 majors in all fields including: Accounting, Allied Health, Anthropology, Business and Management, Biology, Chemistry, Communications, Computer Science, Education, English, French, Health Science, Philosophy, Physical Science, Premed, Psychology, Social Science, Sport Medicine, Zoology

ATHLETIC PROFILE

Conference Affiliation: Ohio Athletic Conference, NCAA III
Program Profile: We have been rebuilding for the past few years and still looking for newcomers to play the right way. Indoor facilities: regulation size gym and auxillary gym with cages for batting. Outdoor: school owned property; grass, new outfield fence, bull pens, outdoor cage. We are building a new pressbox with a locker room at the field. We play in the Fall and in the Spring.
History: The last time we went to a conference tournament was in 1987. We have in rebuilding stages in the last 3 years under Head Coach Chris Keshock who started in 1994 (program began in the 1940's).
Achievements: 1997 player signed a free agent professional baseball contract.
Coaching: Chris Keshock - Head Coach. Marc Adkins - Graduate Assistant Coach. Jim Dillard - Volunteer Coach. Tony Mattia - Volunteer Assistant Coach. Part time assistant position is open.
Style of Play: Changes according to player's talent level.

Hiram College

State Rt. 700
Hiram, OH 44234
Coach: Howard Jenter
NCAA III
Terriers/Navy, Red
Phone: (330) 569-5348
Fax: (330) 569-5392

ACADEMIC

Founded: 1850
Type: 4 Yr., Private, Liberal Arts, Coed
Religion: Disciples of Christ Church
Campus Housing: Yes
Web-site: http://www.hiram.edu/
SAT/ACT/GPA: Selective
Student/Faculty Ratio: 13:1
Male/Female Ratio: 1:1
Undergraduate Enrollment: 1,000
Graduate Enrollment: N/A
Scholarships/Academic: Yes **Athletic:** No **Fin Aid:** Yes
Total Expenses by: Year **In State:** $ 22,000 **Out of State:** $ 22,000
Degrees Conferred: BA
Programs of Study: Art, Art History, Biology, Chemistry, Classical Studies, Communications, Comparative Studies, Computer Science, Economics, Elementary Education, English, Environmental Studies, French, German, History, International Economics and Management, Management, Mathematics, Music, Philosophy, Physics, Political Science, Psychology, Religion Studies, Sociology, Spanish, Theatre Arts, Exercise and Sport Science, Photography, Health Care

ATHLETIC PROFILE

Conference Affiliation: Ohio Athletic Conference
Program Profile: We provide both varsity and junior varsity. We have a natural grass surface and a fieldhouse for Winter workouts. We have Spring training and go to Florida every year.
Achievements: 5 Conference Champions; 2 Regional All-Americans in the last 2 seasons.
Coaching: Howard Jenter - Head Coach. Ron Aulet - Assistant Coach.

Roster for 1998 team/In State: 32 **Out of State:** 4 **Out of Country:**
Total Number of Varsity/Jr. Varsity: 36 **Percent of Graduation:** 95%
Number of Seniors on 1998 Team: 5 **Baseball Camp Dates:** June 1999
Freshmen Receiving Fin Aid/Athletic: 0 **Academic:** 8
Most Recent Record: 17 - 23 - 0 **Number of Spring Games:** 40
Positions Needed for 1999/2000: Pitchers, Catcher, Middle Infielder
Schedule: Wooster, Marietta, Allegheny, Ohio Wesleyan
Style of Play: We have an aggressive offense and like to "make things happen".

John Carroll University

20700 North Park Boulevard
University Heights, OH 44118
Coach: Brian Brewer
Email: Bbrewer@jcuaxa.jcu.edu
NCAA III
Blue Streaks/Blue, Gold
Phone: (216) 397-4660
Fax: (216) 397-3043

ACADEMIC

Founded: 1886
Type: 4 Yr., Private, Liberal Arts, Coed
Religion: Catholic and Jesuit
Campus Housing: Yes
Web-site: http://www.jcu.edu
SAT/ACT/GPA: 1030/21/2.85
Student/Faculty Ratio: 16:1
Male/Female Ratio: 51:49
Undergraduate Enrollment: 3,253
Graduate Enrollment: 800
Scholarships/Academic: Yes **Athletic:** No **Fin Aid:** Yes
Total Expenses by: Year **In State:** $ 19,745 **Out of State:** $ 19,745
Degrees Conferred: BA, BS, MBA, MS, MA
Programs of Study: Liberal Arts, Business Administration, (6 Majors), Communications, Preprofessional Programs, Teacher Training, Science, Mathematics, Physical Education, Education, Humanities, Fine Arts

ATHLETIC PROFILE

Conference Affiliation: Ohio Athletic Conference
Program Profile: We have a nice and improving grass ball park with measurements of 345 down the lines, 368 alleys and 398 centerfield. We got a new playing field that has: an in-ground pop-up sprinkling system, dugouts, a pressbox, wrap-around bleachers, a dugout to dugout, a 6-8 ft. outfield chainlink fence, a totally wind screened and 2 outdoor cages.
History: Our program began in 1973. We got 9 conference championships in Presidents Athletic Conference, 8 in 10 years (1980-1990); joined OAC in 1990. Member of PAC Conference for a while and then moved to OAC in 1989. Started last three years 6th - 4th - 2nd place finishes.
Achievements: Conference Coach of the Year in 1992 and 1998; Jon Widokis was named 1998 All-American 3rd team and 1st team GTE Academic.
Coaching: Brian Brewer, Head Coach, graduated from Marietta in 1993. He was named 1992 All-American. He guided the Blue Streaks to a 62-61 record the past three years back to back Conference Tournament with a 3 year 31-23 conference record. Marc Thibeault - Assistant Coach.
Roster for 1998 team/In State: 20 **Out of State:** 15 **Out of Country:** 0
Total Number of Varsity/Jr. Varsity: 36 **Percent of Graduation:** 100%
Number of Seniors on 1998 Team: 5 **Number of Sophomores on 1998 Team:** 12
Freshmen Receiving Fin Aid/Athletic: 0 **Academic:** 100%
Most Recent Record: 25 - 18 - 0 **Number of Spring Games:** 45
Positions Needed for 1999/2000: Pitcher, Shortstop
Schedule: Marietta College, Wooster, Ohio Wesleyan, Wittenberg University, Newburry, Wartburg
Style of Play: Aggressive - fundamentally sound!!

Kent State University

238 MAC Center
Kent, OH 44242
Coach: Rick Rembielak

NCAA
Golden Flashes/Navy, Gold
Phone: (330) 672-3696
Fax: (330) 672-2112

ACADEMIC

Founded: 1910
Religion: Non-Affiliated
Web-site: http://www.kent.edu
Student/Faculty Ratio: 18:1
Undergraduate Enrollment: 17,000
Scholarships/Academic: Yes **Athletic:** Yes
Total Expenses by: Year **In State:** $ 9,374

Type: 4 Yr., Public, Coed
Campus Housing: Yes
SAT/ACT/GPA: 700/17
Male/Female Ratio: 1:4
Graduate Enrollment: 4,500
Fin Aid: Yes
Out of State: $ 14,034

Degrees Conferred: BA, BS, BBA, MA, MS, BFA, BM, MFA
Programs of Study: College of Arts and Sciences, College of Business Administration, College of Education, College of Fine and Professional Arts, School of Nursing, School of Technology

ATHLETIC PROFILE

Estimated Number of Baseball Scholarships: 11.7
Conference Affiliation: Mid-American Conference
Program Profile: Gene Michael Field has a capacity of 2,500-seat and natural grass. Kent Field House is a 100 yards turf indoor facility for early season training. We regularly take 3-4 trips to South, including Spring break week. We compete in 12-team Mid-American Conference . Tournament winner received automatic bid to NCAA Regional play.
History: Our program started in 1915 and recorded its 1000th win in school's history during the 1997 season. We have won conference titles in four of the last six years (1992, 1993, 1994 and 1997); notable Kent baseball alumni: Thurman Munson, Gene Michael, Steve Stone, Dustin Hermanson and Travis Miller.
Achievements: 7 All-Americans, including 4 in the 1990's; 6 MAC Pitchers of the Year in the last eight years; 17 All-District and 59 All-MAC selections this decade.
Coaching: Rick Rembielak, Head Coach, (Akron '88), has a record of 160-112-1 and five years as a head coach.He was an assistant coach for six years prior (Kent is 340-200-1 in that time). Greg Beals - Assistant Coach, (Kent '95). Mike Birkbeck - Pitching Coach, (Akron '85). Dan Masteller - Volunteer Coach, (Michigan State '91).
Roster for 1998 team/In State: 32 **Out of State:** 3 **Out of Country:** 1
Total Number of Varsity/Jr. Varsity: 35 **Percent of Graduation:** 70%
Number of Seniors on 1998 Team: 7 **Number of Sophomores on 1998 Team:** 9
Freshmen Receiving Fin Aid/Athletic: 8 **Most Recent Record:** 28 - 29 - 0
Number of Fall Games: 20 **Number of Spring Games:** 56
Positions Needed for 1999/2000: Pitcher, Shortstop, 2nd Base, Catcher
Baseball Camp Dates: 5 weekends in November-February
Schedule: Georgia Tech, Coastal Carolina, UNC-Charlotte, Florida Atlantic, Louisville, Purdue
Style of Play: Pitching and defense oriented. Stress fundamentals and player's development.

Kenyon College

Duff Street
Gambier, OH 43022
Coach: Matthew Burdette
Email: burdette@kenyon.edu

NCAA III
Lords/Purple, White
Phone: (614) 427-5810
Fax: (614) 427-5402

ACADEMIC

Founded: 1824
Religion: Non-Denominational

Type: 4 Yr., Private, Liberal Arts, Coed
Campus Housing: Yes

Web-site: http://www.kenyon.edu/
Student/Faculty Ratio: 10:1
Undergraduate Enrollment: 1,550
Scholarships/Academic: Yes **Athletic:** No
Total Expenses by: Year **In State:** $ 25,600
SAT/ACT/GPA: 1150
Male/Female Ratio: 46:54
Graduate Enrollment: None
Fin Aid: Yes
Out of State: $ 25,830
Degrees Conferred: BA, BS
Programs of Study: Life Sciences, Psychology, Social Sciences, Letters/Literature, Philosophy, Religion, Theology, Visual and Performing Arts

ATHLETIC PROFILE

Conference Affiliation: NCAC
Program Profile: Our team usually plays before capacity or near capacity at Mavel Field which is natural turf.
History: The program started in 1947. We have a record of 317-220-15 in 49 years; 31 seasons at .500 or better; has a trip to NCAA Division III Tournament.
Achievements: Kenyon had Conference Palyer of the Year in 1989, 1991, 1992 and 1993; 10 All-Americans.

Lakeland Community College

770 Clocktower Drive
Kirtland, OH 44094-5198
Coach: Kevin Rhomberg
NJCAA
Lakers/Blue, Silver
Phone: (440) 953-4826
Fax: (440) 953-7269

ACADEMIC

Type: 2 Yr., Jr. College, Coed
Campus Housing: No
Degrees Conferred: Associate
Programs of Study: Accounting, Business Administration, Commerce, Management, Civil Engineering Technology, Computer Information Systems, Corrections, Criminal Justice, Data Processing, Dental Services, Early Childhood Education, Electrical/Electronics Technology, Medical Technology, Fire Science, Graphic Arts, Law Enforcement, Human Services, Engineering Technology, Nursing, Paralegal Studies, Tourism/Travel

ATHLETIC PROFILE

Conference Affiliation: OCCAC

Malone College

515 - 25th Street, NW
Canton, OH 44709
Coach: Jay Martin
NAIA
Pioneers/Red, White
Phone: (330) 471-8286
Fax: (330) 471-8296

ACADEMIC

Founded: 1892
Religion: Friends
Web-site: http://www.malone.edu/
Student/Faculty Ratio: 14:1
Undergraduate Enrollment: 1,725
Scholarships/Academic: Yes **Athletic:** Yes
Total Expenses by: Year **In State:** $ 15,900
Type: 4 Yr., Private, Liberal Arts, Coed
Campus Housing: Yes
SAT/ACT/GPA: 870/ 18Min/2.5
Male/Female Ratio: 36:64
Graduate Enrollment: 310
Fin Aid: Yes
Out of State: $ 15,900
Degrees Conferred: BA, BS, MA

Programs of Study: Accounting, Art, Art Education, Bible, Biology, Business Administration, Chemistry, Commercial , Communication Arts, Computer Science, Education, Sports, Elementary Education, Psychology, Social Science, Internal Affairs, Law and Society, Liberal Arts, Management, Mathematics, Music, Nursing, Physical Education, Sport Medicine, Social Studies, Sport Science, Theology, Premed, Prepharmacy, Prephysical Therapy

ATHLETIC PROFILE

Conference Affiliation: Mid - Ohio Conference
Estimated Number of Baseball Scholarships: 6.5
Program Profile: We have a solid program of 35 years with numerous conference championships and a first class facility with a natural grass field. We have a Spring season but also compete in a few Fall tournaments.
History: The program began in 1963 and has achieved 11 conference titles and one College world Series (NAIA) Appearance in 1973.
Achievements: Malone has had eight players drafted into the major leagues, numerous conference titles, three NAIA All-Americans, numerous Conference Coach of the Year honors.
Coaching: Jay Martin, Head Coach, started in 1996 (2 complete seasons). He compiled a record of 30-52 at Malone college. He played shortstop at NCAA Division III at Wheaton College with numerous All-Conference honors. Tom Crank - Assistant Coach.
Roster for 1998 team/In State: 25 **Out of State:** 5 **Out of Country:** 0
Total Number of Varsity/Jr. Varsity: 30 **Percent of Graduation:** 90%
Number of Seniors on 1998 Team: 5 **Number of Sophomores on 1998 Team:** 7
Most Recent Record: 14 - 27 - 0 **Number of Spring Games:** 49
Positions Neede for 1999/2000: Pitcher primarily, but all areas
Schedule: Ohio Dominican College, Mt. Vernon Nazarene College, Mount Union College, Baldwin Wallace College, College of Wooster, Wals University
Style of Play: Aggressive style but also emphasis on fundamental aspects of play.

Marietta College

215 Fifth Street
Marietta, OH 45750-3031
Coach: Don Schaly
Email: webert@mcnet.marietta.edu

NCAA III
Pioneers/Navy Blue, White
Phone: (740) 376-4673
Fax: (740) 376-4674

ACADEMIC

Founded: 1835 **Type:** 4 Yr., Private, Liberal Arts, Coed
Web-site: http://www.marietta.edu/ **SAT/ACT/GPA:** 1000/20/2.5
Student/Faculty Ratio: 12:1 **Male/Female Ratio:** 50:50
Undergraduate Enrollment: 1,200 **Graduate Enrollment:** 100
Scholarships/Academic: Yes **Athletic:** No **Fin Aid:** Yes
Total Expenses by: Year **In State:** $ 20,000 **Out of State:** $ 20,000
Degrees Conferred: BA, BS, MA
Programs of Study: Computer Science, Engineering, Business, Sport Medicine, Accounting, Advertising, Athletic Training, Biology, Chemistry, Communications, Education, Marketing

ATHLETIC PROFILE

Conference Affiliation: Ohio Athletic Conference
Program Profile: We are a highly competitive Division III program and play NCAA 36-game schedule + 2-tournament rule to get 47 games. Pioneer Park is the premier Division III playing facility in the country. It has a state-of-the-art lighting system and a 3-story press facility was added recently. Our natural grass facility hosted the Division III World Series for 12 years.
History: Our program began in 1874. MC record in 104 years is 1,283-561 (.696 winning percentage); has won 3 national championships (1981, 1983, 1986) and 21 conference titles (including 8 of last 10); 14 Midwest regional titles; also have 5 national runners-up finishes. Marietta led Division III schools in 1995 season attendance and average with 18,150 total and 789 average fans per game.

Achievements: Coach Schaly was OAC Coach of the Year in 1997; Joe Thomas was 1st team All-American and Division III National Player of the Year; Bob Davies was 2nd team All-American; Joe was drafted by the Red Sox in the 21st round and Bob was drafted by Minnesota Twins in 4th round; Conference Champs in 1997. Joe was the OAC's MVP; Bob the OAC's Pitcher of the Year Award.
Coaching: Don Schaly, Head Coach, started in 1964. He was OAC Coach of the Year in 1997. He compiled a record of 1,224-297. Tom Weber, Associate Coach, started in 1994. Ken Nedoma, Pitching Coach, started in 1997. Joe Kornokovich, Student Assistant Coach, started in 1997.
Roster for 1998 team/In State: 23 **Out of State:** 13 **Out of Country:** 0
Total Number of Varsity/Jr. Varsity: 36 **Percent of Graduation:** 90+%
Number of Seniors on 1998 Team: 3 **Number of Sophomores on 1998 Team:** 10
Number of Fall Games: 0 **Number of Spring Games:** 37
Baseball Camp Dates: June 12-14; June 15-16; July 14-16; 7/26-30; 9/2-6
Style of Play: " Aggressive in all phases" - Coach Don Schaly.

Miami University - Ohio

110 Withrow Court
Oxford, OH 45056
Coach: Tracy Smith

NCAA I
Redhawks/Red, White
Phone: (513) 529-1809
Fax: (513) 529-6729

ACADEMIC

Founded: 1809
Type: 4 Yr., Pulic, Liberla Arts, Coed
Religion: Non-Affiliated
Campus Housing: Yes
Web-site: http://www.muohio.edu/
SAT/ACT/GPA: 1200/26/3.0
Student/Faculty Ratio: 22:1
Male/Female Ratio: 45:55
Undergraduate Enrollment: 16,000
Graduate Enrollment: 1,800
Scholarships/Academic: Yes **Athletic:** Yes **Fin Aid:** Yes
Total Expenses by: Year **In State:** $ 11,790 **Out of State:** $ 17,546
Degrees Conferred: BA, BS, MA, MS, PhD
Programs of Study: Accounting, American Studies, Anthropology, Architecture, Art, Athletic Training, Botany, Broadcasting, Business, Chemistry, Classics, Communications, Computer Science, Creative Writing, Criminal Justice, Earth Science, Economics, Education, Elementary Education, Engineering, English, Environmental Design, Finance, French, Geography, Geology, German, Greek, History, Journalism, Management, Marketing, Mathematics, Music, Nursing, Philosophy, Physical Education, Physics, Political Science, Premed, Psychology, Public Administration, Public Relations, Sociology, Pathology, Sports Administration

ATHLETIC PROFILE

Estimated Number of Baseball Scholarships: 11.7
Conference Affiliation: Mid - American Conference
Program Profile: Miami University's Stanley G. Mackie Field is centrally located on campus and is a picturesque college ballpark. The Redhawks begin their home schedule on February 22 on the natural grass field with 1,5000 seats stadium capacity. The home of Miami baseball since 1915, will maintain renovations following the 1999 season.
History: The program began in 1915 to the present. Miami University baseball has had its share top-notch players. Known as the "Cradle of Coaches", 45 Miamians have gone in the Major League Baseball draft. Such notable Miami alumni include: Baseball Hall of Famer Walt "Smokey" Alston, Charlie Liebrant, Tim Naehring, Bill Earley and Bill Doran.
Achievements: Gary Cooper in 1972, Dennis Smith in 1973, Mark Nackriing in 1977, and Bill Doran in 1979 were All-Americans; over 40 drafted players; 1997 Big League Roster Players: Tim Naehrin - Boston Red Sox and Dave Swarthbaugh - Cubs.
Coaching: Tracy Smith, Head Coach, entered his 3rd year with the program. He is a Miami 1988 graduate. He started in 1997 with a record of 60-54 (.526). He took the team to MAC Tournament in 1997 for the first time in 15 years had repeat trip losing in MAC Champis in 1998. He was a four-year starter at Miami drafted by Chicago Cubs and played 2-plus seasons in the minors. Tim Kinkelaar and Matt Jackson-Assistant Coaches.
Roster for 1998 team/In State: 21 **Out of State:** 11 **Out of Country:** 0

Total Number of Varsity/Jr. Varsity: 32 **Percent of Graduation:** 100%
Number of Seniors on 1998 Team: 5 **Number of Sophomores on 1998 Team:** 3
Most Recent Record: 33 - 26 - 0 **Number of Spring Games:** 59
Schedule: Wichita State, Purdue, Indiana, Ball State, Kentucky, Bowling

Mount Union College

1972 Clark Avenue
Alliance, OH 44601
Coach: Paul Hesse
Email: sportsinfo.demattm@muc.edy

NCAA III
Purple Raiders/Purple, White, Blue
Phone: (330) 823-4878
Fax: (330) 821-0425

ACADEMIC

Founded: 1846 **Type:** 4 Yr., Private, Liberal Arts, Coed
Religion: Methodist **Campus Housing:** Yes
Web-site: http://www.muc.edu/ **SAT/ACT/GPA:** 950/ 20
Student/Faculty Ratio: 15:1 **Male/Female Ratio:** 1:1
Undergraduate Enrollment: 1,700 **Graduate Enrollment:** None
Scholarships/Academic: No **Athletic:** No **Fin Aid:** Yes
Total Expenses by: Year **In State:** $ 18,000 **Out of State:** $ 18,000
Degrees Conferred: BA, BS
Programs of Study: Accounting, American Studies, Art, Biology, Business Administration, Chemistry, Communications, Computer Science, Cytotechnology, Economics, Education, Geology, Mathematics, Medical Technology, Philosophy, Physical Education, Physics and Astronomy, Sport Management, Sport Medicine

ATHLETIC PROFILE

Conference Affiliation: Ohio Athletic Conference
Program Profile: Facilities include a fieldhouse and cages. We have a 36 game season , a 10 game Florida trip, and play on natural grass. The playing surface has measurements of 330-365-380-365-350. The center has a double height fence, two bull-pens, four mounds, two batting cages and an electronic scoreboard.
Achievements: 6 All-Conference in 1998; last conference title was in 1961.
Coaching: Paul Hesse, Head Coach, has a BS from Kent State in 1982 and a MA in 1986. He compiled a record of 41-32 (21-14 league). Tim Lake, Assistant Coach, graduated from Wooster in 1996. Jay Bartos graduated from Akron University in 1998. Dave Herbert, Assistant Coach, graduated Baldwin - Wallace in 1973. Derek Common, Assistant Coach, got a Bowling Green BS in 1993 and a MA in 1995.
Roster for 1998 team/In State: 60 **Out of State:** 7 **Out of Country:** 0
Total Number of Varsity/Jr. Varsity: 32 /35 **Percent of Graduation:** 100%
Number of Seniors on 1998 Team: 4 **Number of Sophomores on 1998 Team:** 0
Freshmen Receiving Fin Aid/Athletic: 0 **Academic:** 36
Most Recent Record: 19 - 17 - 0 **Number of Spring Games:** 36
Positions Needed for 1999/2000: Pitcher, Outfielder, 1st Base, 3rd Base
Schedule: Wooster, Marietta, Baldwin - Wallace, Ohio Wesleyan, Allegheny, Point Park
Style of Play: Aggressive power baseball, solid fundamental defense, pitching aggressive with strike zone.

Mount Vernon Nazarene College

800 Martinsburg
Mount Vernon, OH 43050
Coach: Keith Veale

NAIA
Cougars/Blue, Green
Phone: (740) 397-6862
Fax: (740) 392-5079

ACADEMIC

Founded: 1964
Type: 4 Yr., Private, Liberal Arts, Coed
Religion: Nazarene
Campus Housing: No
Web-site: http://www.mvnc.edu/
SAT/ACT/GPA: 18/2.0
Student/Faculty Ratio: 19:1
Male/Female Ratio: 45:55
Undergraduate Enrollment: 1,200
Graduate Enrollment: 20
Scholarships/Academic: Yes **Athletic:** Yes **Fin Aid:** Yes
Total Expenses by: Year **In State:** $ 12,300 **Out of State:** $ 12,300
Degrees Conferred: AA, AAS, BA, BS, M
Programs of Study: Accounting, Applied Art, Art, Biblical Studies, Biochemistry, Biology, Broadcasting, Business, Chemistry, Communications, Computer Science and Technology, Criminal Justice, Early Childhood Education, Education, Elementary Education, English, Health Science, History, Human Services, Liberal Arts, Literature, Management, Marketing, Mathematics, Medical Technology, Modern Languages, Music, Nursing, Philosophy, Physical Education, Predentistry, Prelaw, Premed, Prevet, Psychology, Religion, Science, Secondary Education, Social Sciences, Spanish, Special Education, Sports Administration, Sports Medicine, Theatre, Theology

ATHLETIC PROFILE

Conference Affiliation: America MidEast Conference
Program Profile: We have a beautiful natural grass facility with sprinkler system and a press box. We have an indoor hitting facility, one of the best facilities we play on. Play begins mid-March through mid-to-late May.
History: The program began in 1969; record in 1998 is 37-12 mid-Ohio Conference Champs; 1997 record was 47-8 MOC Champs; Great Lakes Regional Champs, World Series Berth; 1996 record was 43-3 MOC Champs; NCCA National Champs in 1995, 1996 & 1997.
Achievements: 13 players drafted or signed since 1983. Tim Belcher #1 pick in the country in 1973; 4 conference titles in a row, Conference Coach of the Year in 1995 and 1998.
Coaching: Keith Veale, Head Coach, began coaching in 1990. He was softball coach 3 years. NAIA District Titles in 1988, 1991 and 1994; NCCAA National Championships in 1995 and 1996. Compiled a record of 296-134 at Mt. Vernon Nazarene; compiled a record of 204-50 over the past five years.
Roster for 1998 team/In State: 21 **Out of State:** 5 **Out of Country:** 0
Total Number of Varsity/Jr. Varsity: 26 **Most Recent Record:** 37 - 12 - 0
Number of Seniors on 1998 Team: 4 **Number of Sophomores on 1998 Team:** 7
Number of Fall Games: 3 **Number of Spring Games:** 0
Positions Needed for 1999/2000: Catcher, Pitcher, Middle Infielder
Schedule: Ohio Dominican, Ohio Wesleyan, Wooster, Point Park, Tiffin, Shawnee State
Style of Play: Dictated by personnel.

Muskingum College

163 Stormont Street
New Concord, OH 43762
Coach: Gregg Thompson
NCAA III
Fighting Huskies/Black, Magenta
Phone: (740) 826-8318
Fax: (740) 826-8300

ACADEMIC

Founded: 1837
Type: 4 Yr., Private, Liberal Arts, Coed
Religion: Presbyterian Church, USA
Campus Housing: Yes
Web-site: http://www.muskingum.edu/
SAT/ACT/GPA: None
Student/Faculty Ratio: 15:1
Male/Female Ratio: 1:1
Undergraduate Enrollment: 1,200
Graduate Enrollment: 100
Scholarships/Academic: Yes **Athletic:** No **Fin Aid:** Yes
Total Expenses by: Year **In State:** $ 15,385 **Out of State:** $ 15,385
Degrees Conferred: BA, BS

Programs of Study: Accounting, American Studies, Art, Biology, Business, Chemistry, Christian Education, Computer Science, Earth Science, Economics, Elementary Education, English, Environmental Science, French, Geology, German, History, Humanities, International Affairs, Journalism, Math, Music, Philosophy, Physical Education, Physics, Political Science, Predentistry

ATHLETIC PROFILE

Conference Affiliation: Ohio Athletic Conference
Program Profile: We do a 40-game schedule that includes a7-day Florida trip. We playe at Mose Morehead Field (seats 200). Our solid indoor facilities provide quality practice during Winter months.
History: Our team was organized in 1905. We affiliated with NCAA Division III since its inception. We will mark the 101st year of Muskingum baseball in 1996.

Oberlin College
(New Program)

200 Woodland Avenue
Oberlin, OH 44074
Coach: Eric Lahertta

NCAA III
Yeomen/Crimson, Gold
Phone: (440) 775-8502
Fax: (440) 775-8957

ACADEMIC

Founded: 1833
Undergraduate Enrollment: 2,500
Web-site: http://www.oberlin.edu
Student/Faculty Ratio: 15:1
Scholarships/Academic: Yes **Athletic:** No
Total Expenses by: Year **In State:** $ 25,000
Type: 4 Yr., Private, Liberal Arts, Coed
Campus Housing: Yes
SAT/ACT/GPA: 1100/26
Male/Female Ratio: 50:50
Fin Aid: Yes
Out of State: $ 25,000
Degrees Conferred: BA, Bmus, MA
Programs of Study: Anthropology, Archaelogy, Astronomy, Biology, Chemistry, Computer Science, Creative Writing, Arts, Economics, Fine Arts, Geology, Law, Literature, Mathematics, Music, Education, Philosophy, Physics, Political Science, Psychology, Social Science,

ATHLETIC PROFILE

Conference Affiliation: North Coast Athletic Conference

Ohio Dominican College

1216 Sunbury Road
Columbus, OH 43219
Coach: Paul Page
Email: page@odc.edu

NCAA III
Panthers/Black, Gold
Phone: (614) 251-4535
Fax: (214) 251-2556

ACADEMIC

Founded: 1911
Religion: Roman Catholic
Web-site: http://www.odc.edu/
Student/Faculty Ratio: 16:1
Undergraduate Enrollment: 1,977
Scholarships/Academic: Yes **Athletic:** Yes
Total Expenses by: Year **In State:** $ 14,070
Type: 4 Yr., Private, Liberal Arts, Coed
Campus Housing: Yes
SAT/ACT/GPA: 800/ 22/2.5
Male/Female Ratio: 40:60
Graduate Enrollment: N/A
Fin Aid: Yes
Out of State: $ Varies
Degrees Conferred: BS, BA
Programs of Study: Accounting, Art, Biology, Business Administration, Business Administration with Fashion Merchandising Concentration, Chemistry, Communication Arts, Computer Science, Criminal Justice, Economics, Elementary Education, International Business, Mathematics, Philosophy, Political Science, Political Science with Environmental Issues Concentration, Psychology

ATHLETIC PROFILE

Estimated Number of Baseball Scholarships: 3.5
Conference Affiliation: American MidEast Conference
Program Profile: We are the 5th winningest team in the NAIA over the past 10 years.We consistently play 55 varsity games and 12-15 junior varsity games. The Panthers play home games at the on-campus facility called Panther Valley, which is a natural surface and easily one of the finest in Ohio.
History: Ohio Dominican began its fine baseball tradition in 1970. They joined the Mid-Ohio Conference 2 years later, and in 24 years of conference affiliation have won 8 conference championships and advanced to regional play 7 times. The Panthers have been in post-season play for 13 consecutive years.
Achievements: Coach Paul Page was named MOC Coach of the Year in 1992 and District 22 Coach of the Year in 1992 and 1993; program boast 19 All-Americans and 6 Academic All-Americans, as well as 8 MOC Titles. At least 11 former players have played or are playing in the professional ranks.
Coaching: Paul Page, Head Coach, is former assistant coach to Ron Polk and Don Schley, with whom he won two NCAA Division III National Titles. He is now one of the top winningest active NAIA coaches. His overall record career is 419-181. Duane Theiss, Scott Mardale, and Ron Casserly - Assistant Coaches.
Roster for 1998 team/In State: 25 **Out of State:** 12 **Out of Country:**
Total Number of Varsity/Jr. Varsity: 38 **Percent of Graduation:** 90%
Number of Seniors on 1998 Team: 7 **Most Recent Record:** 39 - 16 - 0
Freshmen Receiving Fin Aid/Athletic: 3 **Academic:** 0
Number of Fall Games: 5 **Number of Spring Games:** 58
Positions Needed for 1999/2000: Catchers, Pitchers
Schedule: Cumberland, Wright State, Mt. Vernon Nazarene, Ohio Wesleyan, Wooster
Style of Play: An aggressive, running game with an emphasis on pitching and defense.

Ohio Northern University

King Horn Center
Ada, OH 45810
Coach: Herb Strayer
Email: h-strayer@onu.edu
NCAA III
Polar Bears/Black, Burnt Orange
Phone: (419) 772-2442
Fax: (419) 772-2470

ACADEMIC

Founded: 1871 **Type:** 4 Yr., Private, Coed
Religion: Methodist **Campus Housing:** Yes
Web-site: http://www.onu./edu/ **SAT/ACT/GPA:** 21+
Student/Faculty Ratio: 13:1 **Male/Female Ratio:** 54:46
Undergraduate Enrollment: 2,400 **Graduate Enrollment:** 400
Scholarships/Academic: Yes **Athletic:** No **Fin Aid:** Yes
Total Expenses by: Year **In State:** $ 18,600 **Out of State:** $ 18,600
Degrees Conferred: BS, BA, BFA
Programs of Study: Arts and Science, Business, Education, Engineering, Health Science, Law, Pharmacy

ATHLETIC PROFILE

Conference Affiliation: Ohio Athletic Conference
Program Profile: We have a natural field with dimensions of 330-375-400. There are :10 warning trap, a dug-out, a pitching mound inside field ,grassed 1st and t 3rd baselines, a press box and a fill 165-165 tarp.
History: Winning program in 1903 -1998 with a record of .580; OAC Champions in 1923, 1949, 1974, 1976, 1982 and 1983; NCAA Mideast in 1974, 1976, 1980, 1981, 1982, 1983, 1985 and 1995; 1974 World Series NCAA Top Ten; 3rd in 1974; 9th in 1980; 7th in 1982.
Achievements: 5 times Coach of the Year; ONC; 4 ONC titles; 3 All-Americans; 6 drafted players.
Coaching: Herb Strayer- Head Coach. Greg Roberts, assistant hitting instructor, entered his 12th year.

Roster for 1998 team/In State: 25 **Out of State:** 3 **Out of Country:** 0
Total Number of Varsity/Jr. Varsity: 23 **Percent of Graduation:** 99%
Number of Seniors on 1998 Team: 4 **Number of Sophomores on 1998 Team:** 6
Freshmen Receiving Fin Aid/Athletic: 0 **Academic:** 15
Most Recent Record: 16 - 15 - 0 **Number of Spring Games:** 36
Positions Needed for 1999/2000: Pitcher
Schedule: Marietta, John Carroll, Rose Hulman, Augustana, Baldwin Wallace, Ohio Wesleyan
Style of Play: We stress defense and pitching. We want smart players who view academic as a number one with baseball as a bonus

Ohio State University

410 Woody Hayes Drive
Columbus, OH 43210
Coach: Bob Todd

NCAA I
Buckeyes/Scarlet, Grey
Phone: (614) 292-1075
Fax: (614) 292-2351

ACADEMIC

Type: 4 Yr., Public, Liberal Arts, Coed, Engineering **Founded:** 1878
Religion: Non-Affiliated **Campus Housing:** Yes
Web-site: http://www.acs.ohio-state.edu/ **SAT/ACT/GPA:** 1000/23
Student/Faculty Ratio: 14:1 **Male/Female Ratio:** 50:50
Undergraduate Enrollment: 42,000 **Graduate Enrollment:** 7,000
Scholarships/Academic: Yes **Athletic:** Yes **Fin Aid:** Yes
Total Expenses by: Year **In State:** $ 9,385 **Out of State:** $ 16,252
Degrees Conferred: BA, BS, MS, MA, PhD
Programs of Study: 11,000 Courses, 129 graduate fields, 121 programs leading to Master Degree, 99 leading to Doctorate Degree: Allied Health, Business and Management, Communications, Education, Engineering, Home Economics, Social Sciences

ATHLETIC PROFILE

Conference Affiliation: Big Ten Conference
Program Profile: Bill Davis Stadium has a seating capacity of 3,000 and has dimensions of 330-370-400-370-330. The field is natural grass. The season goes from February through June.
History: Our program began in 1881. OSU has made 12 NCAA tournament appearances and 4 College World Series Appearances. OSU won the CWS in 1996 and was runner-up in 1965. OSU has won 12 Big Ten Championships and 4 Big Ten Tournament Championships.
Achievements: Bob Todd was named Big Ten Coach of the Year in 1991 and 1994; assistant for USA Baseball at the 1994 World Games, OSU has had 35 All-Americans and 74 first All-Big Ten selections; Bob Todd has had 34 professional baseball signess.
Coaching: Bob Todd, Head Coach, entered his 12th season as a head coach. He compiled a record of 563-306-1 since 1984. He averaged 41 wins per season. Greg Cypret and Pat Bangtson - Assistant Coach.
Roster for 1998 team/In State: 30 **Out of State:** 4 **Out of Country:** 1
Total Number of Varsity/Jr. Varsity: 40 **Percent of Graduation:** 0
Number of Seniors on 1998 Team: 7 **Number of Sophomores on 1998 Team:** 0
Most Recent Record: 37 - 16 - 0 **Number of Spring Games:** 53
Schedule: USC, Miami, Houston, Illinois, Penn State, Indiana
Style of Play: Fundamentally sound, low on errors; No mental mistakes ;usually a power hitting club; Always a solid-hitting club through the entire lineup; An aggressive pitching unit.;Always a confident team - four Big Ten Titles in the 1990's, will attest to the fact. Our team is never out of a game because players are so confident in their own abilities and those of the coaching staff.

Ohio University

108 Convocation Ctr
Athens, OH 45701
Coach: Joe Carbone

NCAA I
Bobcats/Green, White
Phone: (614) 593-1180
Fax: (614) 593-2420

ACADEMIC

Founded: 1804
Religion: Non-Affiliated
Web-site: http://www.ohiou.edu
Student/Faculty Ratio: 21:1
Undergraduate Enrollment: 16,000
Scholarships/Academic: Yes **Athletic:** Yes
Total Expenses by: Year **In State:** $ 10,614

Type: 4 Yr., Public, Liberal Arts, Coed
Campus Housing: Yes
SAT/ACT/GPA: Very Selective
Male/Female Ratio: 20:1
Graduate Enrollment: 3,000
Fin Aid: Yes
Out of State: $ 15,570

Degrees Conferred: AA, AS, BA, BS, BSC, MA, MS, MBA, MFA
Programs of Study: Accounting, Advertising, Airway Sciences, Anthropology, Broadcasting, Chemical Engineering, Civil Engineering, Communications, Criminal Justice, Economics, Engineering, Food Science, Geography, Languages, Marketing, Mathematics, Microbiology

ATHLETIC PROFILE

Conference Affiliation: Mid America Conference
Program Profile: We do a MAC schedule and competitive Southern trips. Spring season starts February 27 and ends in May 11.We have a new 3,000 seats stadium. The grass stadium is a part of a new athletic mall. We have excellent pitching and hitting facilities. There is a solid weight and conditioning program. We have an excellent academic reputation.
History: We began in 1892. We are in our 106th season which has 76 winning seasons (464-160) We have the winningest coach in the history. We were in 11 NCAA playoffs and finished 4th in the 1970 College World Series . Joe Carbone took over the program in 1989. To the present; he has 2 MAC Championships and two-time MAC Coach of the Year.He was 1997 Mid-East Region Coach of the Year and has a 1459-957-7 (.604) all-time record.
Achievements: Has 6 first team All-Americans; 7 2nd team; 3 3rd team; 2 Academic All-Americans; 115 players drafted; 17 major league players. Mike Schmidt, Steve Swisher and Bob Brenly.
Coaching: Joe Carbone, Head Coach, played for Bobcats 1968-70 and played for Kansas City Royals after graduating. He won one MAC championship. Bill Toadvine - Assistant Coach.
Style of Play: Aggressive, fundamentally sound, good pitching, stress good defense.

Ohio Wesleyan University

116 Edwards Gymnasium
Delaware, OH 43015
Coach: Roger Ingles

NCAA III
Battling Bishops/Red, Black
Phone: (740) 368-3738
Fax: (740) 368-3751

ACADEMIC

Founded: 1842
Religion: Methodist
Web-site: http://www.owu.edu/
Student/Faculty Ratio: 13:1
Undergraduate Enrollment: 1,700
Scholarships/Academic: Yes **Athletic:** No
Total Expenses by: Year **In State:** $ 18,228

Type: 4 Yr., Private, Liberal Arts, Coed
Campus Housing: Yes
SAT/ACT/GPA: None
Male/Female Ratio: 50:50
Graduate Enrollment: None
Fin Aid: Yes
Out of State: $ 18,228

Degrees Conferred: BA, BFA, BM
Programs of Study: Accounting, Astronomy, Biochemistry, Earth Science, Economics, Education, International Business, Journalism, Prelaw, Psychology, Religion, Anthropology, Psychology

ATHLETIC PROFILE

Conference Affiliation: North Coast Athletic Conference
Program Profile: OWV is among the top 5 Division III programs in the country. We have been to 7 straight NCAA National playoffs; regularly in the Top 10 nationally. We have outstanding indoor and outdoor facilities. We have averaged over 32 wins/year since 1990 (1994 35-8, 1995 36-6).
History: Our program began in 1889. Branch Rickey was player and coach. The all-time overall record is 1007-868-17. We have won over 20 for 10 straight seasons and been nationally ranked every year since 1986; have had 9 players sign professionally.
Achievements: Since 1984, Coach Ingles has received National, Regional and League Coach of the Year honors. OWU has had 18 All-Americans; 5 All-Region; 115 All-Conference and 6 players drafted, also won 7 NCAC Titles; 10 NCAA bids; 2 Regional Runner-Up.
Coaching: Roger Ingles, Head Coach, is in his 14th season. He is all-time winningest coach at OWU.
Style of Play: Our style is dependent on our talent We like to run, hit and run, play aggressive. We are an outstanding defensive club with a great pitching. We are a very aggrewssive offensive and defensive team. OWU is recognized for a great pitching, defense and team's hitting. Our club executes well and is well conditioned.

Otterbein College

West College Avenue and Grove Street
Westerville, OH 43081
Coach: Dick Fishbaugh

NCAA III
Cardinals/Red, Tan
Phone: (614) 823-3521
Fax: (614) 823-1966

ACADEMIC

Founded: 1847
Type: 4 Yr., Private, Liberal Arts, Coed
Religion: Methodist
Campus Housing: Yes
Web-site: http://www.otterbein.edu/
SAT/ACT/GPA: 820+/ 20+
Student/Faculty Ratio: 13:1
Male/Female Ratio: 43:57
Undergraduate Enrollment: 2,397
Graduate Enrollment: 93
Scholarships/Academic: Yes **Athletic:** No **Fin Aid:** Yes
Total Expenses by: Year **In State:** $ 19,053 **Out of State:** $ 19,053
Degrees Conferred: BA, BS, BFA, MEd
Programs of Study: Accounting, Art, Business Administration, Broadcasting, Chemistry, Communications, Education, Computer Science, Dance, Economics, Engineering, English, French, Health Education, History, Individualized Degree, International Studies, Journalism, Life Science, Mathematics, Music, Nursing, Philosophy, Pyhysical Education, Physics/Astronomy, political Science, Predentistry, Prelaw, Premed, Prephysical Therapy, Prevet, psychology, Public Relations, Religion, Sociology, Spanish, Sports Medicine, Theatre, Visual Arts

ATHLETIC PROFILE

Conference Affiliation: Ohio Athletic Conference

Owens Community College

PO Box 10,000
Toledo, OH 43699-1947
Coach: Rich Pivoriunas

NJCAA
Express/Red, White
Phone: (419) 661-7409
Fax: (419) 661-7095

ACADEMIC

Founded: 1938
Type: 2 Yr., Jr. College, Coed
Religion: Non-Affiliated
Campus Housing: No
Student/Faculty Ratio: 17:1
Male/Female Ratio: 53:47

Undergraduate Enrollment: 1,437 **Graduate Enrollment:** None
Scholarships/Academic: No **Athletic:** No **Fin Aid:** Yes
Total Expenses by: Year **In State:** $ 1,800 **Out of State:** $ 3,400
Degrees Conferred: Associate
Programs of Study: Biomedical Technology, Computer Programming, Drafting/Design Technology, Education, Electrical Engineering Technology, Law Enforcement, Marketing, Mechanical Engineering Technology, Office Management, Quality Control Technology, Robotics

ATHLETIC PROFILE

Conference Affiliation: OCCAC

Shawnee State University

James A Rhodes Athletic Center
Portsmounth, OH 45662
Coach: Pat Rigsby
Email: prigsby@shawnee.edu
NAIA
Bears/Blue, Grey
Phone: (740) 355-2537
Fax: (740) 355-2381

ACADEMIC

Founded: 1986 **Type:** 4 Yr., Public, Coed, Engineering
Religion: Non-Affiliated **Campus Housing:** Yes
Web-site: http://www.shawnee.edu/ **SAT/ACT/GPA:** Open enrollment
Student/Faculty Ratio: 15:1 **Male/Female Ratio:** 1:2
Undergraduate Enrollment: 3,500 **Graduate Enrollment:** 0
Scholarships/Academic: Yes **Athletic:** No **Fin Aid:** Yes
Total Expenses by: Year **In State:** $ 8,190 **Out of State:** $ 10,443
Degrees Conferred: BA, BS, BFA
Programs of Study: Accounting, Applied Mathematics, Arts, Biology, Business Administration, Computer Science, Computer Technology, Dentistry, Education, Elementary Education, English, Finance, Fine Arts, Humanities, Liberal Arts, Management, Mathematics, Medical Laboratory Technology, Natural Science, Nursing, Occupational Therapy, Physical Education, Physical Science, Physical Therapy, Plastic Technology, Prelaw, Premed, Prevet, Radiological Technology, Real Estate, Respiratory, Therapy, Science, Social Science

ATHLETIC PROFILE

Conference Affiliation: AMC
Program Profile: Our 1998 record was 35-11. We do a 45-50 game schedule including trips to North Carolina, Tennessee and Florida. We have a rigorous off-season strength and conditioning program. Our home field is Bruch Rickey Park. It has lights and a with a brick wall . The park was recently renovated to include a new infield and warning track.
History: The Bears program began in 1992 under the direction of major league All-Star Al Oliver. The first winning season was in 1995, followed by a 1997 record of 27-16 & a 1998 record of 35-11.
Achievements: 5 All-Conference performers in 1998, including a National Player of the Week and a Conference Player of the Year; 1 player drafted and 2 other signed with independent profession team in 1998; Shawnee State was 2nd in hitting in the NAIA and 6th in pitching.
Coaching: Pat Rigsby ,Head Coach, is the winningest coach. He compiled a record of 77-40 equal to .658 in percentage. He is associate scout with the Cleveland Indians. He is a former professional player and assistant with independent professional teams. Tom Benjamin ,Pitching Coach, has four year professional experience and played at University of Nebraska.
Roster for 1998 team/In State: 26 **Out of State:** 4 **Out of Country:** 0
Total Number of Varsity/Jr. Varsity: 30 **Percent of Graduation:** 100%
Number of Seniors on 1998 Team: 8 **Most Recent Record:** 35 - 11 - 0
Freshmen Receiving Fin Aid/Athletic: 0 **Academic:** 5
Number of Fall Games: 0 **Number of Spring Games:** 45
Positions Needed for 1999/2000: Pitcher, Catcher, Shortstop, Centerfield
Schedule: Lambuth, Mt. Vernon Nazarene, West Virginia, Ohio Dominican
Style of Play: Aggressive style of play with an emphasis on power and speed offensively.

Sinclair Community College

444 West Third Street
Dayton, OH 45402
Coach: Jim Harrison

NJCAA
Tartans/Scarlet, Grey
Phone: (937) 226-3039
Fax: (937) 512-3056

ACADEMIC

Founded: 1887
Type: 2 Yr., Jr. College, Coed
Religion: Non-Affiliated
Campus Housing: No
Student/Faculty Ratio: 23:1
Male/Female Ratio: 37:63
Undergraduate Enrollment: 20,950
Graduate Enrollment: None
Scholarships/Academic: No **Athletic:** Yes **Fin Aid:** Yes
Total Expenses by: Year **In State:** $ 1,400 **Out of State:** $ 3,500
Degrees Conferred: Associate
Programs of Study: Accounting, Applied Art, Banking/Finance, Communications, Drafting/Design, Education, Law Enforcement, Liberal Arts, Physical Education, Physical Therapy, Public Administration, Real Estate, Retail Management, Transportation Technology, Travel/Tourism

ATHLETIC PROFILE

Conference Affiliation: OCCAC
Program Profile: We play on a natural field. Playing season is in March 8 through May 26.
History: Our program began in 1973.
Achievements: Won 10 Conference Titles; drafted players - Chris Spurling, Eric Starchler
Coaching: Jim Harrison - Head Coach. Tony De Saro - Assistant. Dave McMenamin - Assistant.
Style of Play: Run and hit, hit and run.

Tiffin University

155 Miami Street
Tiffin, OH 44883
Coach: Lonny Allen
Email: lallen@tiffin.edu

NAIA
Dragons/Green, Gold
Phone: (419) 448-3359
Fax: (419) 443-5007

ACADEMIC

Founded: 1888
Type: 4 Yr., Private, Liberal Arts, Coed
Religion: Non-Affiliated
Campus Housing: Yes
Web-site: http://www.tiffin.edu
SAT/ACT/GPA: 860/ 18/2.0
Student/Faculty Ratio: 19:1
Male/Female Ratio: 57:43
Undergraduate Enrollment: 9,210
Graduate Enrollment: 4,400
Scholarships/Academic: Yes **Athletic:** Yes **Fin Aid:** Yes
Total Expenses by: Year **In State:** $ 10,450 **Out of State:** $ 10,450
Degrees Conferred: BA, BBA, BCJ, ABA
Programs of Study: BBA in Liberal Studies in Humanities and Social Studies. BBA in Accounting, Administrative Management, Finance, Hospitality Management, Information Systems, International Studies, Management, Marketing. BCJ in Corrections, Forensic Psychology, Law Enforcement

ATHLETIC PROFILE

Estimated Number of Baseball Scholarships: 4
Conference Affiliation: American MidEast Conference
Program Profile: Tiffin University team plays at new TU Athletic Complex, a natural field stadium with large 9 inning scoreborad.
History: We started intercollegiate play in 1972 and have challenged for conference titles over the last three seasons.
Achievements: 1992 Matt Miga NAIA All-American, only a few draftees players most recently Greg Prenzlin with the Canton Crocodiles.
Coaching: Lonny Allen, Head Coach, coached since 1992 and compiled a record of 133-144-1. Chad Trias and Jim Easson - Assistant Coaches.

Roster for 1998 team/In State: 40 **Out of State:** 6 **Out of Country:** 3
Total Number of Varsity/Jr. Varsity: 27 /22 **Percent of Graduation:** 100%
Number of Seniors on 1998 Team: 5 **Number of Sophomores on 1998 Team:** 12
Freshmen Receiving Fin Aid/Athletic: 17 **Academic:** 12
Number of Fall Games: 15 **Number of Spring Games:** 57
Most Recent Record: 14 - 22 - 0 **Baseball Camp Dates:** Early June
Positions Needed for 1999/2000: 1st Base, 3rd Base, Pitcher
Schedule: Embry-Riddle, Mt. Vernon, Indiana Tech, Wooster, Ohio Dominican
Style of Play: Offense aggressive, defense fundamental.

University of Akron

302 Buchtel Common
Akron, OH 44325
Coach: Dave Fross

NCAA I
Zips/Blue, Gold
Phone: (330) 972-7277
Fax: (330) 972-5473

ACADEMIC

Founded: 1870 **Type:** 4 Yr., Public, Coed
Web-site: http://www.uakron.edu/athletics **Campus Housing:** Yes
SAT/ACT/GPA: Taken test and completion of college prep curriculum/
Student/Faculty Ratio: 20:1 **Male/Female Ratio:** 47:53
Undergraduate Enrollment: 20,037 **Graduate Enrollment:** 3,568
Scholarships/Academic: Yes **Athletic:** Yes **Fin Aid:** Yes
Total Expenses by: Year **In State:** $ 3,625 **Out of State:** $ 7,951.40
Degrees Conferred: AA, AS, BA, BS, BFA, MA, MS, MBA
Programs of Study: Accounting, Art, Advertising, Biology, Business Administration, Chemistry, Classics, Communications, Communicative Disorder, Computer Science, Construction Technology, Cytotechnology, Dance, Economics, Elementary Education, Engineering, English, Finance, Geography, Geology, History, Humanities, Management, Marketing, Mathematics, Medical Science, Psychology, Music, Nursing, Philosophy, Political Science, Physical Education, Physics, Social Science, Social Work, Sociology, Special Education.

ATHLETIC PROFILE

Conference Affiliation: Mid - American Conference

University of Cincinnati

Mail Location 0021
Cincinnati, OH 45221
Coach: Brian Cleary

NCAA I
Beatcats/Black, Red
Phone: (513) 556-0566
Fax: (513) 556-5059

ACADEMIC

Founded: 1819 **Type:** 4 Yr., Public, Liberal Arts, Coed
Religion: Non-Affiliated **Campus Housing:** Yes
Web-site: http://www.uc.edu/ **SAT/ACT/GPA:** 860+
Student/Faculty Ratio: 17:1 **Male/Female Ratio:** 48:52
Undergraduate Enrollment: 15,000 **Graduate Enrollment:** 20,000
Scholarships/Academic: Yes **Athletic:** Yes **Fin Aid:** Yes
Total Expenses by: Year **In State:** $ 9,500 **Out of State:** $ 15,500
Degrees Conferred: BS, BA, Master and Doctoral Degrees
Programs of Study: Accounting, Anthropology, Architecture, Arts, Biochemistry, Biology, Broadcasting, Business and Management, Chemistry, Communications, Computer Information Systems, Computer Science, Pharmacy, Criminal Justice, Physical Education, Natural Science

ATHLETIC PROFILE

Conference Affiliation: Conference USA
Program Profile: In 1993, we got new facilities with lights.
History: Our program is over 100 years old. The captain of our 1900 team was Miller Huggins who later managed the Great Yankee teams of the 1920's.
Achievements: Brian Cleary - Head Coach.

University of Dayton

300 College Park
Dayton, OH 45469
Coach: Chris Sorrell

NCAA I
Flyers/Red, Blue
Phone: (937) 229-4456
Fax: (937) 229-4461

ACADEMIC

Founded: 1850
Religion: Catholic (Marianist)
Web-site: http://www.udayton.edu/
Student/Faculty Ratio: 14:1
Undergraduate Enrollment: 6,000
Scholarships/Academic: Yes **Athletic:** Yes
Total Expenses by: Year **In State:** $ 19,900

Type: 4 Yr., Private, Liberal Arts, Coed
Campus Housing: Yes
SAT/ACT/GPA: 1093/25
Male/Female Ratio: 1:1
Graduate Enrollment: 3,000
Fin Aid: Yes
Out of State: $ 19,900

Degrees Conferred: BA, BS, BFA, BGS, BM, MA, MBA
Programs of Study: Biological Sciences, Business, Communications and the Arts, Computer and Physical Sciences, Education, Engineering and Environmental Design, Health Professions, Social Sciences

ATHLETIC PROFILE

Conference Affiliation: Atlantic Ten Conference

University of Findlay

1000 N Maint Street
Findlay, OH 45840
Coach: Doug Coate

NAIA
Oilers/Orange, Black
Phone: (419) 424-4541
Fax: (419) 424-4618

ACADEMIC

Founded: 1882
Religion: Church of God
Web-site: http://www.findlay.edu/
Student/Faculty Ratio: 17:1
Undergraduate Enrollment: 3,200
Scholarships/Academic: Yes **Athletic:** Yes
Total Expenses by: Year **In State:** $ 19,238

Type: 4 Yr., Private, Liberal Arts, Coed
Campus Housing: Yes
SAT/ACT/GPA: 740/18
Male/Female Ratio: 1:1
Graduate Enrollment: 400
Fin Aid: Yes
Out of State: $ 19,238

Degrees Conferred: AA, BA, BS, MBA
Programs of Study: Agriculture, Bilingual Education, Business and Management, Enviromental and Hazardous Material Management, Equestrine Studies, Education, Health Science, Premed, Prevet, Social Sciences

ATHLETIC PROFILE

Conference Affiliation: Mid - Ohio Conference
Program Profile: The Oiler program strives and emphasizes hard work, dedication, discipline and pride both in the classroom and on the field. Our field is 2 years old and has an all grass infield that measures 327 down lines, 400 center and 367 alleys. Oiler Field is at Swale Park.

History: Baseball began in 1908. There were no teams in 1909-10, 1919, 1924, 1927, 1935, 1944-45. In 78 years of hardball, the Oilers have totaled a 559-598-17 record. In the last 10 years, the Oilers have had only 2 losing seasons. In 1994, the Oilers broke or tied 11 season team records and had 10 players named to the Dean's list.

University of Rio Grande

College Avenue
Rio Grande, OH 45674
Coach: Brent Clark

NAIA
Redmen/Red, White
Phone: (740) 245-5353
Fax: (740)245-7555

ACADEMIC

Founded: 1876
Religion: Non-Affiliated
Web-site: Not Available
Student/Faculty Ratio: 20:1
Undergraduate Enrollment: 2,000
Scholarships/Academic: Yes **Athletic:** Yes
Total Expenses by: Year **In State:** $ 10,100

Type: 4 Yr., Private, Liberal Arts, Coed
Campus Housing: No
SAT/ACT/GPA: 820/ 18
Male/Female Ratio: 50:50
Graduate Enrollment: 150
Fin Aid: Yes
Out of State: $ 10,500

Degrees Conferred: AA, AS, AAS, BS, MEd
Programs of Study: Accounting, Art, Biochemistry, Biology, Business and Management, Chemistry, Communications, Computer Science, Economics, Education, English, Finance, Health Sciences, Communications, Computer Science, Economics, Education, International Business, Liberal Arts, Mathematics, Music, Nursing, Physical Fitness/Exercise Science, Physical Science, Physics, Premed, Psychology, Social Science, Special Education, Theatre

ATHLETIC PROFILE

Conference Affiliation: Mid - Ohio Conference

University of Toledo

2801 West Bancroft Street
Toledo, OH 43606
Coach: Joe Kruzel
Email: sokane@pop3.utoledo.edu

NCAA I
Rockets/Midnight Blue, Gold
Phone: (419) 530-2526
Fax: (419) 530-4428

ACADEMIC

Founded: 1872
Religion: Non-Affiliated
Web-site: http://www.utoledo.edu
Student/Faculty Ratio: 19:1
Undergraduate Enrollment: 17,500
Scholarships/Academic: Yes **Athletic:** Yes
Total Expenses by: Year **In State:** $ 7,316

Type: 4 Yr., Public, Liberal Arts, Coed
Campus Housing: Yes
SAT/ACT/GPA: 900/18
Male/Female Ratio: 50:50
Graduate Enrollment: 2,000
Fin Aid: Yes
Out of State: $ 12,064

Degrees Conferred: BA, BS, MA, MS, MBA, MBA
Programs of Study: Allied Health, Business and Management, Business/Office and Marketing/Distribution, Communications, Education, Engineering, Parks/Recreation, Protective Services, Public Affairs, Social Science

ATHLETIC PROFILE

Conference Affiliation: Mid American Conference
Program Profile: Our games are played at our baseball complex at Scott Park. It is natural field and seats 1,500.
Achievements: Denny S tark - 4th round, Seattle in 1996; Bryan Braswell - 4th round, Houston in 1996; Bill Bronikowski - 20th round , NY Yankees in 1997.

Coaching: Joe Kruzel, Head Coach, is in his 6th year. He graduated from Toledo in 1989. Steve Parrell ,Assistant Coach, is in his 5th year. He is a 1988 graduate of Ohio State. Mike Kendall, Pitching Coach, is in his 1st year. He graduated from San Diego State in 1995.
Style of Play: Aggressive running style.

Urbana University

579 College Way
Urbana, OH 43078
Coach: Al Fulk

NAIA
Blue Knights/Blue, Grey
Phone: (937) 484-1325
Fax: (937) 484-1389

ACADEMIC

Founded: 1850
Type: 4 Yr., Private, Liberal Arts, Coed
Religion: Swedenborgian
Campus Housing: No
Web-site: Not Available
SAT/ACT/GPA: 19 avg
Student/Faculty Ratio: 16:1
Male/Female Ratio: 51:49
Undergraduate Enrollment: 1,000
Graduate Enrollment: None
Scholarships/Academic: Yes **Athletic:** Yes **Fin Aid:** Yes
Total Expenses by: Year **In State:** $ 14,500 **Out of State:** $ 14,500
Degrees Conferred: AA, BA, BS
Programs of Study: Contact school for program of study.

ATHLETIC PROFILE

Conference Affiliation: Mid-Ohio Conference
Program Profile: Our field is natural grass with a brick dust infield. Playing season is from March 1 through May 15.
History: Our program began in 1965.
Achievements: Coach of the Year 1991 and 1992.
Coaching: Al Fulk , Head Coach, has coached for 15 years. Jason Cordiar is in his 2nd year.
Style of Play: Power.

Walsh University

2020 Easton NW
North Canton, OH 44720
Coach: Tim Mead

NAIA
Cavaliers/Maroon, Gold
Phone: (800) 362-9846
Fax: (330) 490-7038

ACADEMIC

Founded: 1959
Type: 4 Yr., Private, Liberal Arts, Coed
Religion: Catholic
Campus Housing: Yes
Web-site: http://www.walsh.edu/
SAT/ACT/GPA: 860/18
Student/Faculty Ratio: 20:1
Male/Female Ratio: 1:1
Undergraduate Enrollment: 1,400
Graduate Enrollment: 300
Scholarships/Academic: Yes **Athletic:** Yes **Fin Aid:** Yes
Total Expenses by: Year **In State:** $ 15,400 **Out of State:** $ 15,400
Degrees Conferred: Ass., BA, BS, MA
Programs of Study: General Liberal Arts, Business, Nursing, Education, Predental, Premed, Preoptical, Prevet, Prelaw, Physical Therapy, Prenatural Resources, International Studies, Communications, Computer Science, English, History, Mathematics, Sociology, Psychology, Philosophy, Theology

ATHLETIC PROFILE

Conference Affiliation: Mid-Ohio Conference

Wilmington College

Box 1246, 251 Luduvic Street
Wilmington, OH 45177
Coach: Greg Hughes

NCAA III
Quakers/Green, White
Phone: (937) 382-6661
Fax: (937) 382-8566

ACADEMIC

Founded: 1870
Religion: Quaker
Web-site: http://www.wilmington.edu/
Student/Faculty Ratio: 17:1
Undergraduate Enrollment: 1,100
Scholarships/Academic: Yes **Athletic:** No
Total Expenses by: Year **In State:** $ 17,090
Degrees Conferred: BA, BS
Programs of Study: Business, Education, Athletic Training, Social Work, Biology, Chemistry, Psychology, Criminal Justice

Type: 4 Yr., Private, Liberal Arts, Coed
Campus Housing: Yes
SAT/ACT/GPA: 19
Male/Female Ratio: 50:50
Graduate Enrollment: None
Fin Aid: Yes
Out of State: $ 17,090

ATHLETIC PROFILE

Conference Affiliation: ICAC
Program Profile: We are a rebuilding program with much tradition. Hughes is the first recruiting class that was 22 deep. There are 10 Quakers returning which should result in a bright future for WC. We have a nice grass surface which is very well maintained. We play from late February to early May. We have a good Auxillary facility.
History: The program began in 1920. Our first record kept was in 1921 and was 3-3. We became a strong program in the 1980's. We had 3 players drafted in the decade. Greg Hughes is in his second season as a coach. Notable former coaches include Jim Schmidtz who is now a head coach at Earten Illinois and Brooks Lawrence ,former pitcher,is with the Cincinnati Reds.
Achievements: Several players drafted in 1980's.
Coaching: Greg Hughes, Head Coach, entered his 2nd season as a head coach. He was an assistant coach at Eastern Kentucky University before coming to Wilmington College in August of 1996. Also coached 12 years at Indiana Tech where he played before heading to EKU. We are looking for big things at Wilmington College with a first recruiting class.
Style of Play: Class program that does things the right way. Swing the bat, steal bases, and offensively throw strikes. Change speed, work on fast pitching.

Wittenberg University

P.O. Box 720
Springfield, OH 45501
Coach: Jay Lewis
Email: jlewis@wittenberg.edu

NCAA III
Tigers/Red, White
Phone: (937) 327-6494
Fax: (513) 327-6340

ACADEMIC

Founded: 1844
Religion: Lutheran
Web-site: http://www.wittenberg.edu/
Student/Faculty Ratio: 15:1
Undergraduate Enrollment: 2,100
Scholarships/Academic: Yes **Athletic:** No
Total Expenses by: Year **In State:** $ 18,500
Degrees Conferred: BA

Type: 4 Yr., Private, Liberal Arts, Coed
Campus Housing: Yes
SAT/ACT/GPA: 1000/2.75
Male/Female Ratio: 1:1
Graduate Enrollment: None
Fin Aid: Yes
Out of State: $ 18,500

Programs of Study: American Studies, Art, Biology, Chemistry, Computer Science, East Asian Studies, Economics, Education, English, French, Geography, Geology, German, History, Management, Mathematics, Music, Philosophy, Physics, Political Science, Psychology, Religion, Russian Area Studies, Sociology, Spanish, Theatre-Dance

ATHLETIC PROFILE

Conference Affiliation: North Coast Athletic Conference
Program Profile: We have a strong Division III program that competes in one of the best conference in the region. Our stadium is an old minor league field built in 1942 with a seating capacity of 1,500.
History: Our records go back to 1950. Recently , we averaged 26 wins a season for the past 13 years.
Achievements: 9 All-Americans; 9 All-Region players in the 1990's; 4 professional players in the 1990's, regular season titles in 1991 and 1996.
Coaching: Jay Lewis, Head Coach, entered his 3rd season with a record of 50-30. For two years he was assistant coach at St. Parish Graham high School where he helped lead the Falcons to a Division II State Runner-Up finish in 1995. In addition, he helped coach perennial power Piqua in the American Legion League. He is a native of St. Paris, Ohio and a graduate of Graham.
Roster for 1998 team/In State: 40 **Out of State:** 3 **Out of Country:** 0
Total Number of Varsity/Jr. Varsity: 40 **Percent of Graduation:** 100%
Number of Seniors on 1998 Team: 10 **Most Recent Record:** 24 - 11 - 2
Freshmen Receiving Fin Aid/Athletic: 0 **Academic:** 100%
Number of Fall Games: 9 **Number of Spring Games:** 40
Positions Needed for 1999/2000: Outfielders, Pitchers
Schedule: Wooster, Ohio Wesleyan, Marietta, Allegheny, Thomas More, John Carrol
Style of Play: Aggressive style of offense and very disciplined strong style of defense.

Wright State University

3640 Colonel Glenn Hwy
Dayton, OH 45435-0001
Coach: Ron Nischwitzs

NCAA I
Raiders/Green, Gold
Phone: (937) 775-2771
Fax: (937) 775-2368

ACADEMIC

Type: 4 Yr., Public, Liberal Arts, Coed, Engineering **Founded:** 1967
Religion: Non-Affiliated **Campus Housing:** Yes
Web-site: http://www.wright.edu/ **SAT/ACT/GPA:** General
Student/Faculty Ratio: 17:1 **Male/Female Ratio:** 47:53
Undergraduate Enrollment: 15,732 **Graduate Enrollment:** 7,500
Scholarships/Academic: Yes **Athletic:** Yes **Fin Aid:** Yes
Total Expenses by: Year **In State:** $ 9,063 **Out of State:** $ 12,771
Degrees Conferred: BA, BS, BBA, MA, MD, MS
Programs of Study: Accounting, Biology, Business Administration, Communications, Computer Science, Education, Engineering, Health Science, History, Mathematics, Philosophy, Physical Education, Physical Sciences, Social Sciences

ATHLETIC PROFILE

Conference Affiliation: Midwestern Collegiate Conference
Program Profile: We have a fine facility. We just added $15 million in dugouts, seats, scoreboard, restroom and lights. We have natural turf and fences measuring 320-400-320. The season is from mid-February to mid-May. We compete in the Midwestern Collegiate Conference. We have won conference 4 of the last 5 years.
History: Our program began Division I competition in 1988 after finishing second in the country in Division II in 1987. The last five years we have averaged 40 wins per season. We are moving into a new baseball facility which will be lighted, fully irrigated and hold 4,000 seat stadium. 1993 record: 39-15-0. 1994 record: 39-21. 1995 record: 33-28.

Achievements: 25 players to the professional baseball. Most recent is Brian Anderson with the Cleveland Indians.
Coaching: Ron Nischwitz, Head Coach, has been at WSU for 23 years with over 700 wins. Bo Billinski - Associate Coach. Dan Bassler - Assistant Coach.
Style of Play: Aggressive and strong defense.

Xavier University

3800 Victor Parkway
Cincinnati, OH 45207-6114
Coach: John Morrey

NCAA I
Musketeers/Blue, White
Phone: (513) 745-2890
Fax: (513) 745-4390

ACADEMIC

Founded: 1831
Religion: Jesuit
Web-site: http://www.xu.edu
Student/Faculty Ratio: 16:1
Undergraduate Enrollment: 3,500
Scholarships/Academic: Yes **Athletic:** Yes
Total Expenses by: Year **In State:** $ 18,500

Type: 4 Yr., Private, Liberal Arts, Coed
Campus Housing: Yes
SAT/ACT/GPA: 900+/20+
Male/Female Ratio: 46:54
Graduate Enrollment: 2,000
Fin Aid: Yes
Out of State: $ 18,500

Degrees Conferred: BA, BS, AA, BFA, BSBA, BSN
Programs of Study: Over 50 majors including: Allied Health, Business and Management, Communications, Education, Health Sciences, Letters/Literature, Psychology, Social Sciences

ATHLETIC PROFILE

Conference Affiliation: Atlantic 10 Conference
Program Profile: Hayden Field has a natural grass surface and seats 500.

Youngstown State University

One University Plaza
Youngstown, OH 44555
Coach: Mike Florak

NCAA I
Penguins/Red, White, Black
Phone: (330) 742-3485
Fax: (330) 742-2733

ACADEMIC

Founded: 1908
Religion: Non-Affiliated
Web-site: Not Available
Student/Faculty Ratio: 25:1
Undergraduate Enrollment: 12,000
Scholarships/Academic: Yes **Athletic:** Yes
Total Expenses by: Year **In State:** $ 7,666

Type: 4 Yr., Public, Liberal Arts, Coed
Campus Housing: Yes
SAT/ACT/GPA: 820/17
Male/Female Ratio: 49:51
Graduate Enrollment: 1,140
Fin Aid: Yes
Out of State: $ 11,302

Degrees Conferred: AA, AAB, AAS, BA, BE, BM, BFA, MS, MBA, MBA
Programs of Study: Composed of eight schools and colleges which are further divided into various major departments: Applied Science and Technology, Arts and Sciences, Business Administration, Engineering, Fine and Performing Arts, Education, Graduate School, Northeastern Ohio Universities College of Medicine.

ATHLETIC PROFILE

Estimated Number of Baseball Scholarships: 3
Conference Affiliation: Mid-Continent Conference
Program Profile: We have a new facility. Our multi-million dollar stadium is also used by Cleveland Indians AA Niles Palisades. Our playing field is natural grass.

History: Youngstown State has been playing baseball for 42 years. Dave Dravecky graduated from here. We had most wins in 1995 with a record of 37. We have had a winning season 3 of the last 4 years.
Achievements: Coach of the Year in 1995; East Division Champs in 1995; Playoffs in 1995.
Coaching: Mike Florak, Head Coach, entered his 1st year with the program. He was President's Athletic Conference Coach of the Year. He was previously at Waynesburg College. He was a 4-year starter at Ohio University and was drafted by the Seattle Mariners in 1985. An assistant coach is to be named later.
Roster for 1998 team/In State: 30 **Out of State:** 5 **Out of Country:** 0
Total Number of Varsity/Jr. Varsity: 35 **Percent of Graduation:** 90%
Number of Seniors on 1998 Team: 6 **Baseball Camp Dates:** TBA
Freshmen Receiving Fin Aid/Athletic: 5 **Academic:** 1
Positions Needed for 1999/2000: All **Most Recent Record:** 17 - 31 - 0
Schedule: Oral Roberts, Ohio University, Ohio State, Kent State, East Carolina, Valparaiso
Style of Play: Aggressive; first class program that excels academically and athletically.

OKLAHOMA

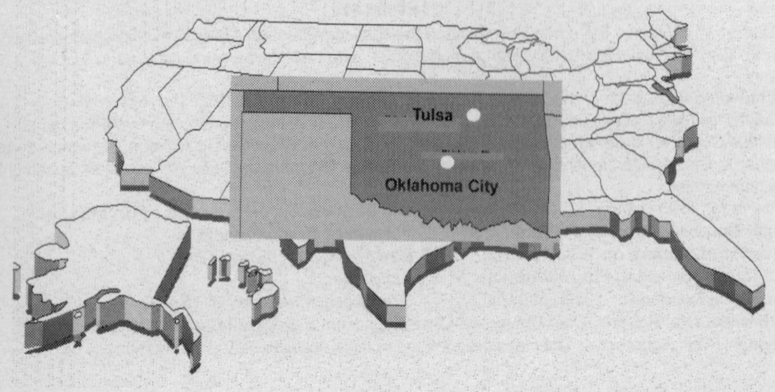

SCHOOL	CITY	AFFILIATION 99	PAGE
Bacone College	Muskogee	NJCAA I	685
Cameron University	Lawton	NCAA II	685
Carl Albert State College	Poteau	NJCAA	686
Connors State College	Warner	NJCAA	686
East Central University	Ada	NCAA II	687
Eastern Oklahoma State College	Wilburton	NJCAA	688
Murray State College	Tishomingo	NJCAA	688
Northeastern OK A & M JC	Miami	NJCAA	688
Northeastern State University	Tahlequah	NCAA II/NAIA	689
Northwestern Oklahoma State University	Alva	NCAA III	689
Oklahoma Baptist University	Shawnee	NAIA	690
OK Christian U of Science & Arts	Oklahoma City	NAIA	690
Oklahoma City University	Pklahoma City	NAIA	691
Oklahoma State University	Stillwater	NCAA I	691
Oral Roberts University	Tulsa	NCAA I	692
Redlands Community College	El Reno	NJCAA II	693
Rose State College	Midwest City	NJCAA	693
Seminole State College	Seminole	NJCAA	694
Southern Nazarene University	Bethany	NAIA	694
Southeastern Oklahoma State University	Durant	NCAA II	695
Southwestern Oklahoma State University	Weatherford	NCAA II	695
University of Central Oklahoma	Edmond	NCAA II	696
University of Oklahoma	Norman	NCAA I	697
University of Science & Arts of OK	Chickasha	NAIA	697
Western Oklahoma State College	Altus	NJCAA	698

Bacone College

99 Old Bacone Road
Muskogee, OK 74403
Coach: Wayne Kenmemer

NJCAA I
Warriors/Red, White
Phone: (918) 683-4581
Fax: (918) 687-5913

ACADEMIC

Type: 2 Yr., Private, Coed
Campus Housing: No
Degrees Conferred: Associate
Programs of Study: Arts/fine Arts, Business Administration, Commerce, Management, Business Education, Computer Science, Home Economics, Horticulture, Journalism, Liberal Arts, General Studies, Native American Studies, Natural Resources Management, Nursing, Radiological Technology, Secretarial Studies, Office Management

ATHLETIC PROFILE

Conference Affiliation: Bi - State Region II Conference
Program Profile: Our schedule covers all top 20 teams in the area. We play a Fall and Spring schedule of maximum allowable games. We have an indoor and outdoor practice facility. We do extensive weight and speed training. Our field has a natural playing surface.
History: We are the only JC program in OK to win a national title(1965). Our winning tradition failed off in the early 1990's but now it is being restored. Andy Summers has 12 years as head coach & his program has gone from last in the conference to 3rd behind Seminole JC & Conners State College.

Cameron University

2800 Gore
Lawton, OK 73505
Coach: Ron Ihler

NCAA II
Aggies/Gold, Black
Phone: (580) 581-2479
Fax: (580) 581-5537

ACADEMIC

Founded: 1908
Religion: Non-Affiliated
Web-site: Not Available
Student/Faculty Ratio: 28:1
Undergraduate Enrollment: 5,225
Scholarships/Academic: Yes **Athletic:** Yes
Total Expenses by: Year **In State:** $ 4,200

Type: 4 Yr., Public, Liberal Arts, Coed
Campus Housing: No
SAT/ACT/GPA: 700/17
Male/Female Ratio: 45:55
Graduate Enrollment: 420
Fin Aid: Yes
Out of State: $ 6,200

Degrees Conferred: AAS, AS, BA, BFA, MS
Programs of Study: Accounting, Agricultural Sciences, Art Education, Art/Fine Arts, Biology, Business Administration, Computer Science, Criminal Justice, Data Processing, Drafting/Design, Elementary Education, English, Music Education, Physics, Political Science, Psychology

ATHLETIC PROFILE

Conference Affiliation: Lone Star Conference
Program Profile: We play on a natural grass with a dimensions of 330 LF, 365 LC, 400 CF, 365 RC, 330 RF. The seating capacity is approximately 1,000.
History: We were a Junior College program until 1968 and NAIA until 1980. We were NCAA Division II since then.
Achievements: 1992 Lone Star Conference Champions; 1992 Coach of the Year in Lone Star; Ron Cain 1989 NAIA All-American; Tyler Williams 1992 NCAA All-American; professionals Jason Younker signed 1990, current Pittsburg Pirate pitcher Jason Christiansen signed 1991, Dennis Milius drafted in 1992.

Coaching: Ron Ihler, Head Coach, entered his 15th year as head coach at Cameron. He was named Conference Coach of the Year. Kent Holland, Assistant Coach, is an ex-Cameron University player and entered his first season as an assistant coach.
Style of Play: As Earl Weaves said " There's nothing better than the three run homers ".

Carl Albert State College

1507 South McKenna
Poteau, OK 74953-5208
Coach: Mark Pollard
Email: tdavis@casc.cc.ok.us

NJCAA
Vikings/Royal, White, Red
Phone: (918) 647-1280
Fax: (918) 647-1369

ACADEMIC

Type: 2 Yr., Private, Coed
Campus Housing: No
Degrees Conferred: Associates
Programs of Study: Accounting, Agricultural Business, Art Education, Biology, Biological Science, Business Administration, Commerce, Management, Business Education, Early Childhood Education, Elementary Education, Journalism, Mathematics, Psychology, Physical Science, Office Management

ATHLETIC PROFILE

Conference Affiliation: Twin State Conference
Program Profile: We have an on campus facility. It has a simple layout, outstanding playing surface between the lines, natural grass and a seating capacity of 5.000. We have a Fall scrimmage season that goes from August 15 through November 1. We have 56 games in the Spring season that goes from March 1 through May 15.
History: 1969 program began as a Division I - Bi-State Conference; declared Division II in 1992-1993; Regional Champs;Central District Champions; NJCAA Division II College World Series in 1992-1993, 1993-1994, 1994-1995; Regional Runner-Up in 1995-1996 and 1996-1997.
Achievements: Division II District Coach of the Year in 1993; Division II District A Coach of the Year in 1994; Division II District A Coach of the Year in 1995; Conference Champions in 1993, 1994, 1995, and 1997; All-Americans were Kendall Dillon in 1993, Mark Johnson in 1993, Ronnie Sockey in 1994, Justin Crase in 1995, Shane Wooter and Brian Stout in 1996, Aaron Thompson in 1997; Academic All-Americans were Steve Kendruck in 1994, Jeff Nolan in 1996,and Wes McGouen in 1997. Drafted players were Jeff Frye by Boston Red Sox in 1986, Buckly Groom by Oakland "A" in 1984, Jeff Sexton by Cleveland Indians in 1992, Jason Shuck by New York Mets in 1997.
Coaching: Mark Pollsrd, Head Coach, entered 15 years of coaching. He compiled a record of 461-375. John Ward, Assistant Coach, entered four years as an assistant coach.
Style of Play: Aggressive, fundamental baseball attemp to play game the right way!! Solid 2-year program.

Connors State College

Rt 1 Box 1000
Warner, OK 74469
Coach: Perry Keith

NJCAA
Cowboys/Black, Orange
Phone: (918) 463-2931
Fax: (918) 463-2233

ACADEMIC

Type: 2 Yr., Public, Coed
Web-site: http://www.connors.cc.ok.us
Degrees Conferred: Associate
Programs of Study: Accounting, Agricultural Education, Agricultural Technology, Animal Science, Art Education, Biology, Biological Science, Business Administration, Commerce, Management, Chemistry, Computer Science, Criminal Justice, Child Psychology, Data Processing, Drafting/Design Education, Law Enforcement, English, Liberal Arts, Physical Education, Postal Management, Psychology, Zoology

ATHLETIC PROFILE

Conference Affiliation: Region II Conference
Program Profile: BIF Thompson field is located on campus just 200 yards from Russel Hall. The playing field is graced by an 8 foot outfield wall. Our dugout is built on the side of a 2,500 sq. ft. indoor workout facility that houses 2 pitching mounds, 2 batting cages, and a soft toss area. This is truly one of the best indoor facilities in junior college baseball. Our natural field measures LF-326, LCF-369, CF-397, RCF-370, RF-327.
History: Perry Keith (took over in 1985) has put together a baseball program that baseball people know from coast to coast. Connors State is known yearly as one of the best JUCO's in the country. Year after year ,Connor's State has turned out players to major universities and professional baseball averaging over 50 wins per year.
Achievements: Ranked Top 10 of NJCAA National Poll from 1985 to 1997. JUCO World Series 1985, Region II Champions 1985, 1986, and 1996, Region II Runner-Up from 1987 to 1997, 50 players drafted, 12 All-Americans, 10 Academic All-Americans.
Coaching: Perry Keith, Head Coach, has coached 13 seasons at Connors State. The Cowboys have had over 50 players under Keith's regime.They have been ranked in Top 10 in NJCAA National Poll in all 13 years. Keith has won more games than any coach in Connors State baseball history with a phenominal record of 684-177. Ryan McCoe,Assistant Coach, spent his 2nd season after a stellar playing career at Southwest Mission State and Connors State College.
Style of Play: Aggressive; we play and play. Spend a lot of time on the field getting better. Our kids love to fly around and play, but we love to play.

East Central University

East 14th Street
Ada, OK 74820
Coach: Ron Hill
Email: rhuckeby@mailclerk.ecok.edu

NCAA II
Tigers/Black, Orange
Phone: (580) 436-4940
Fax: (580) 436-8361

ACADEMIC

Founded: 1909
Religion: Non-Affiliated
Web-site: Not Available
Student/Faculty Ratio: 25:1
Undergraduate Enrollment: 3,950
Scholarships/Academic: Yes **Athletic:** Yes
Total Expenses by: Year **In State:** $ 4,200
Degrees Conferred: BA, BS, BM, MS

Type: 4 Yr., Public, Liberal Arts, Coed
Campus Housing: No
SAT/ACT/GPA: 19 avg
Male/Female Ratio: 42:58
Graduate Enrollment: 500
Fin Aid: Yes
Out of State: $ 6,250

Programs of Study: Accounting, Art Education, Biological, Biology, Business Economics, Criminal Justice, Ecology, Education, Electrical Engineering, Law Enforcement, Ealry Childhood Education, Physics, Political Scinece, Social Work, Psychology, Music, Music Education, English

ATHLETIC PROFILE

Conference Affiliation: Lone Star Conference (North Division)
Program Profile: ECU has been a long standing OIC member until 1997, when we entered the Lone Star Conference. Tiger Field is a natural surface with 340' each line and 390' center field. Our indoor facility has two cages and a weight room. There are five outdoor cages.
Achievements: Brian Williams was Academic All-American in 1995; Brandon Bowers - All-American in 1997 Honorable Mention; Ron Hill Coach of the Year (Conference OIC) in 1993.
Coaching: Ron Hill, Head Coach, entered his 8th year. He was Conference Coach of the Year in 1993. He compiled a record of 138-215 in his 8th year coaching career. He played 2nd team All-Conference. Steve Womack - Assistant Coach.
Style of Play: Pitching staff will throw a lot of ground balls. Offensive - gap hitting team. This team will be able to bunt and hit and run. Average team speed.

Eastern Oklahoma State College

1301 West Main
Wilburton, OK 74578
Coach: Todd Shelton

NJCAA
Mountaineers/Blue, Gold
Phone: (918) 465-2361
Fax: (918) 465-4495

ACADEMIC

Founded: 1907
Type: 2 Yr., Public, Coed
Undergraduate Enrollment: 2,475
Campus Housing: No
Student/Faculty Ratio: 45:1
Male/Female Ratio: 37:63
Scholarships/Academic: No **Athletic:** Yes **Fin Aid:** Yes
Total Expenses by: Year **In State:** $ 3,500 **Out of State:** $ 5,200
Degrees Conferred: Associate
Programs of Study: Accounting, Agricultural Business, Agricultural Economics and Education, Soil and Crop Science, Animal Science, Animal Science, Art Education, Art/Fine Arts, Biology, Biological Science, Business Administration, Commerce, Management, Chemistry, Computer Science, Computer Technology, Corrections, Criminal Justice, Economics, Education, Electrical Engineering Technology, History, Horticulture, Mathematics, Medical Assistant, Political Science, Psychology, Farm/Ranch Management, Veterinary Science, Wildlife Management

ATHLETIC PROFILE

Conference Affiliation: Bi - State Conference
Program Profile: Play on a natural grass which is sitting in the valley.
History: Has a new coaching staff.
Coaching: Todd Shelton, Head Coach, played at McLennan Community College, Oklahoma. He coached at Cumberland University, Northeast and entered his 1st year at Eastern Oklahoma State. Jon Aven ,Assistant Coach, Director/Coordinator , was at MidAmerica All-Star baseball camps with former head coach Gary Ward . His specialty is hitting and outfield. Kelly Dickinson, Assistant Coach, played at McLennan Community College and Delta State . His specialty is pitching and he is a recruiting assistant.
Style of Play: We will put up big numbers of offensive with a solid defense.

Murray State College

1100 Byrd Street
Tishomingo, OK 73460
Coach: Mike McBrarer

NJCAA
Aggies/Blue, Red
Phone: (580) 371-2371
Fax: (580) 371-9844

ACADEMIC

Founded: 1908
Type: 2 Yr., Public, , Coed,
Religion: Non-Affiliated
Campus Housing: No
Undergraduate Enrollment: 1,706
Student/Faculty Ratio: 20:1
Total Expenses by: Year **In State:** $ 1,354+ **Out of State:** $ 3,274+
Degrees Conferred: Associate
Programs of Study: Agricultural Education, Agricultural Science, Animal Science, Art/Fine Arts, Business Administration, Commerce, Management, Business Education, Chemistry, Child Care, Child and Family Studies, Computer Information Systems, Computer Science, Conservation

Northeastern Oklahoma A and M JC

200 I NE Street
Miami, OK 74354-0001
Coach: Roger Ward

NJCAA
Golden Norsemen/Blue, Gold
Phone: (918) 542-8441
Fax: (918) 542-2680

ACADEMIC

Founded: 1919
Type: 2 Yr., Public, Coed
Religion: Non-Affiliated
Campus Housing: Yes
Undergraduate Enrollment: 2,600
SAT/ACT/GPA: Required
Scholarships/Academic: No **Athletic:** No **Fin Aid:** Yes
Total Expenses by: Year **In State:** $ 3,100 **Out of State:** $ 5,000
Degrees Conferred: Associate
Programs of Study: Contact school for program of study.

ATHLETIC PROFILE

Conference Affiliation: Bi-State East Conference

Northeastern State University

600 North Grand
Tahlequah, OK 74464
Coach: Kevin Riggs
NCAA II/NAIA
Redmen/Green, White
Phone: (918) 456-5511
Fax: (918) 458-2339

ACADEMIC

Founded: 1851
Type: 4 Yr., Public, Coed
Religion: Non-Affiliated
Campus Housing: Yes
Web-site: http://www.nsuok.edu/
SAT/ACT/GPA: 19+
Student/Faculty Ratio: 20:1
Male/Female Ratio: 40:60
Undergraduate Enrollment: 7,500
Graduate Enrollment: 1,800
Scholarships/Academic: Yes **Athletic:** Yes **Fin Aid:** Yes
Total Expenses by: Year **In State:** $ 53.50/hr **Out of State:** $ 127/hr
Degrees Conferred: BS, BA, BFA, MA, MS, MBA, OD
Programs of Study: Mathematics, Science, Nursing, Biology, Chemistry, Computer Science, Medical Technology, Nursing, Physics, Geography, History, Native American Studies, Political Science, Psychology, Sociology, Allied Health Administration, Criminal Justice, Social Work, Accounting, Business Administrarion, Business Education, Marketing, Finance, Mangement, Art

ATHLETIC PROFILE

Conference Affiliation: Lone Star Conference
Program Profile: The program has 30 wins per years for 11 years. We have excellent indoor facilities. The team plays on a natural grass field.
Achievements: Coach of the Year in 1989, 1991 and 1996; 3 Conference Titles; 3 All-Americans; 15 Players signed pro contracts.
Coaching: Kevin Riggs - Head Coach. Jay Franklin, Pitching Coach.
Style of Play: Fundamentally strong - manufacture runs.

Northwestern Oklahoma State University

709 Oklahoma Blvd
Alva, OK 73717
Coach: Joe Phillips
NCAA III
Rangers/Red, Black
Phone: (580) 327-1700
Fax: (580) 327-1881

ACADEMIC

Founded: 1895
Type: 4 Yr., Public, Coed
SAT/ACT/GPA: 20avg
Campus Housing: Yes
Student/Faculty Ratio: 21:1
Male/Female Ratio: 46:54
Undergraduate Enrollment: 1,600
Graduate Enrollment: 250
Scholarships/Academic: Yes **Athletic:** Yes **Fin Aid:** Yes

Total Expenses by: Year **In State:** $ 6,000 **Out of State:** $ 8,000
Degrees Conferred: BA, BS, MS
Programs of Study: Accounting, Agricultural Business, Biology, Biological Science, Business Administration, Commerce, Management, Business Education, Chemistry, Communications, Computer Information Systems, Computer Science, Early Childhood Education, Journalism, Law Enforcement, Mathematics, Medical Laboratory Technology, Physical Education, Nursing, Music, Music Education

ATHLETIC PROFILE

Conference Affiliation: OK Intercollegiate

Oklahoma Baptist University

500 West University
Shawnee, OK 74801
Coach: Bobby Cox

NAIA
Bison/Green, Gold
Phone: (405) 878-2136
Fax: (405) 878-2069

ACADEMIC

Founded: 1910
Religion: Southern Baptist
Web-site: Not Available
Student/Faculty Ratio: 14:1
Undergraduate Enrollment: 2,400
Scholarships/Academic: Yes **Athletic:** Yes
Total Expenses by: Year **In State:** $ 10,380

Type: 4 Yr., Pricate, Liberal Arts, Coed
Campus Housing: No
SAT/ACT/GPA: 800/17
Male/Female Ratio: 48:52
Graduate Enrollment: 30
Fin Aid: Yes
Out of State: $ 10,380

Degrees Conferred: AA, BA, BS, BFA, BM, BMA, M
Programs of Study: Accounting, Banking/Finance, Biological Science, Broadcasting, Business Administration, Communications, Computer Science, Dramatic Arts, Education, English, Fine Arts, French, German, History, Information Scinece, Journalism, Marketing, Mathematics, Music, Nursing, Personnel Management, Physics, Poltical Science, Preprofessional Programs, Psychology, Religion, Social Science, Spanish, Speech, Telecommunications

ATHLETIC PROFILE

Conference Affiliation: Sooner Athletic Conference
Achievements: The team has gone to the NAIA World Series twice in 1989 and 1996. The team won District 9 Title and the Sooner Athletic Conference in 1996.
Coaching: Bobby Cox, Head Coach, has been head coach for 13 years. He was leader of OBU coaches and District Coach of the Year 3 times. He was Conference Coach of the 2 times, Area Coach of the Year and Region Coach of the Year.
Style of Play: Aggressive blend of speed and consistent hitting. Pitching - rich squad in 1996.

Oklahoma Christian University of Science and Arts

Box 11000
Oklahoma City, OK 73136
Coach: Johnny Inman

NAIA
Eagles/Maroon, Green
Phone: (405) 425-5354
Fax: (405) 425-5351

ACADEMIC

Founded: 1950
Religion: Church of Christ
Web-site: http://www.oc.edu/
Student/Faculty Ratio: 18:1
Undergraduate Enrollment: 1,500

Type: 4 Yr., Private, Liberal Arts, Coed
Campus Housing: Yes
SAT/ACT/GPA: None
Male/Female Ratio: 52:48
Graduate Enrollment: 50

Scholarships/Academic: Yes **Athletic:** Yes **Fin Aid:** Yes
Total Expenses by: Year **In State:** $ 12,000 **Out of State:** $ 12,000
Degrees Conferred: BA, BS, BBA, BFA, BME, BSE
Programs of Study: Art and Design, Behavioral and Social Science, Biblical Studies, Business, Communications, Education, Language and Literature, Music, Science and Engineering

ATHLETIC PROFILE

Conference Affiliation: Sooner Conference

Oklahoma City University

2501 North Blackwelder
Pklahoma City, OK 73106
Coach: Denney Crabaugh

NAIA
Chiefs/Blue, White
Phone: (405) 521-5156
Fax: (405) 521-5816

ACADEMIC

Founded: 1902
Type: 4 Yr., Private, Liberal Arts, Coed
Religion: Methodist
Campus Housing: Yes
Web-site: http://www.okcu.edu
SAT/ACT/GPA: 19
Student/Faculty Ratio: 18:1
Male/Female Ratio: 1:4
Undergraduate Enrollment: 3,200
Graduate Enrollment: 1,600
Scholarships/Academic: Yes **Athletic:** Yes **Fin Aid:** Yes
Total Expenses by: Year **In State:** $ 5,200 **Out of State:** $ 5,200
Degrees Conferred: BA, BS
Programs of Study: Accounting, Advertising Asian Studies, Banking and Finance, Biology, Broadcasting, Business Administration, Chemistry, Communications, Computer Science, Criminal Justice, Dance, Dramatic Arts, Economics, Education, Fine Arts, Journalism, Law Enforcement, Management, Marketing, Mathematics, Nursing, Political Science, Social Science

ATHLETIC PROFILE

Conference Affiliation: Sooner Athletic Conference
Program Profile: We have been NAIA nationally ranked every year since 1986. We have a natural grass field, a 335-380-400 fence, building with offices, a locker room and 2 carpeted indoor tunnels located on field site.
History: Our program began in 1976. We played in NCAA Division I until 1986. We have been to the NAIA World Series 3 times since 1986 and finished 4th twice 3rd in 1992.
Achievements: District 9 Champs in 1986, 1988 and 1992; 16 All-Americans including the 1994 National Player of the Year; 35 professional players since 1989.
Coaching: Denney Crabaugh - Head Coach.
Style of Play: Up-tempo - try to put a lot of pressure on the defense. Pitching has been a major strength over the years. We are proud that 20 of the 35 professional players have been pitchers. Only three were drafted before they played at OCU.

Oklahoma State University

100 Reynolds Stadium
Stillwater, OK 74078
Coach: Tom Holiday

NCAA I
Cowboys/Orange, Black
Phone: (405) 744-5849
Fax: (405) 744-8941

ACADEMIC

Founded: 1890
Type: 4 Yr., Public, Coed
Religion: Non-Affiliated
Campus Housing: Yes
Web-site: http://www.okstate.com
SAT/ACT/GPA: 1030/22/3.0
Student/Faculty Ratio: 26:1
Male/Female Ratio: 54:46

Undergraduate Enrollment: 14,500 **Graduate Enrollment:** 3,496
Scholarships/Academic: Yes **Athletic:** Yes **Fin Aid:** Yes
Total Expenses by: Year **In State:** $ 6,992 **Out of State:** $ 10,750
Degrees Conferred: BA, BS, MA, MS, MBA, DO, DVM
Programs of Study: Accounting, Advertising, Architecture, Banking/Finance, Education, Film, Fire, Geography, Geology, Industrial, Manufacturing, Marketing, Mining and Petroleum, Preprofessional Programs, Religion, Speech, Zoology

ATHLETIC PROFILE

Conference Affiliation: Big Twelve Conference
Program Profile: Oklahoma State has won 15 consecutive league titles and traveled to the College World Series a record 7 consecutive seasons in the 1980's. The stadium, which holds an estimated 4,000 fans, is a shrine to Cowboy's Baseball, including Hall of Fame banners. The turf is natural grass , a hitter's ball park and state of the art.
History: Oklahoma State began baseball in 1909 and has played 84 years since. The Cowboys have won 25 Big 8 titles, which include 15 straight NCAA appearances. OSU holds 10 NCAA records. Coach Gary Ward is the 3rd winningest, active Division I coach.
Achievements: Oklahoma State won the NCAA championship in 1959 and has finished 5 times as runner-up. The program has won 15 consecutive Big 8 titles and made 15 consecutive trips to the NCAA regionals in those years. 17 players have been named All-American, and 127 were drafted by proffessional baseball; 30 additional players have signed free agent contracts.
Coaching: Tom Holiday, Head Coach, entered his 2nd season with the program. In his first season at the helm of the Oklahoma State Baseball team, he guided the Cowboys to their 30th NCAA Regional Appearances, a 46 win season and a 2nd place finish in the Big 12 Conference. He was drafted by the Pittsburgh in Niagara Falls. John Farrell, Assistant Coach, entered his 2nd season with the program. He brought 13 years of experience in professional baseball to Oklahoma State. He was hired as a pitching coach in the Fall of 1996. He was drafted in 1984 by the Cleveland Indians in the 2nd round of the amateur draft. Robbie Wine ,Assistant Coach, begins his 2nd season as the hitting coach. He spent 9 years in professional baseball as a player and 5 years as a coach.
Schedule: Texas A and M, Texas Tech, North Carolina State, Oklahoma, Baylor, San Diego State
Style of Play: Pitching - defense; aggressive offense; speed - power combination ten runs per game average.

Oral Roberts University

7777 South Lewis Avenue
Tulsa, OK 74133
Coach: Sunny Gollaway

NCAA I
Golden Eagles/Blue, Gold
Phone: (918) 495-7130
Fax: (918) 495-7123

ACADEMIC

Founded: 1963 **Type:** 4 Yr., Private, Liberal Arts, Coed
Religion: **Campus Housing:** Yes
Web-site: http://www.orusports.com **SAT/ACT/GPA:** 1050/23
Student/Faculty Ratio: 15:1 **Male/Female Ratio:** 44:56
Undergraduate Enrollment: 4,716 **Graduate Enrollment:**
Scholarships/Academic: Yes **Athletic:** Yes **Fin Aid:** Yes
Degrees Conferred: BA, BS, BSE, MA
Programs of Study: Education, Nursing, Business, Theology, Arts and Sciences, School of Life Long Education, Art, Accounting, Biological Science, Computer Science, Dramatic Arts, Broadcasting, Ministries, Music, Physics, Political Science

ATHLETIC PROFILE

Estimated Number of Baseball Scholarships: TBA
Conference Affiliation: Mid-Continent Conference

Program Profile: Our home field is called T.L. Johnson. The stadium has a seating capacity of 2,500 and is natural grass. There are indoor cages, a locker room, coaches' offices, a player's lounge and a training room.
History: The first year of the program was in 1966. We had a .639 winning percentage in our 33 year history. We had 10 NCAA Regional Appearances including a 1998 College World Series Appearances in 1978. We have 8 first team All-Americans. 40 wins 8 times and 50 wins twice.
Achievements: 10 NCAA Regional Appearances; 1998 College World Series 8 All-Americans.
Coaching: Sunny Gollaway, Head Coach, entered 3 years with the program with a record of 103-74 and was named Mid-Continent Coach of the Year. Bob Miller - Assistant Coach.
Roster for 1998 team/In State: 18 **Out of State:** 17 **Out of Country:** 0
Total Number of Varsity/Jr. Varsity: 35 **Baseball Camp Dates:** TBA
Number of Seniors on 1998 Team: 6 **Number of Sophomores on 1998 Team:** 8
Freshmen Receiving Fin Aid/Athletic: 4 **Academic:** 4
Positions Needed for 1999/2000: TBA **Number of Spring Games:** 56
Most Recent Record: 45 - 20 - 0
Schedule: Oklahoma, Oklahoma Ste, Arkansas, Texas, TCO, Kansas
Style of Play: Very aggressive but balanced between speed and power offensively. High emphasis is placed on pitching and defense.

Redlands Community College

1300 Country Club Road
El Reno, OK 73036
Coach: Don Brown

NJCAA II
Cougars/Gold, Burgundy
Phone: (405) 262-2552
Fax: (405) 422-1200

ACADEMIC

Founded: 1938 **Type:** 2 Yr., Jr. College, Coed
Religion: Non-Affiliated **Campus Housing:** No
Student/Faculty Ratio: 18:1 **Male/Female Ratio:** 40:60
Undergraduate Enrollment: 2,000 **Graduate Enrollment:** None
Scholarships/Academic: Yes **Athletic:** Yes **Fin Aid:** Yes
Total Expenses by: Year **In State:** $ 1,790+ **Out of State:** $ 3,600+
Degrees Conferred: Associate
Programs of Study: Accounting, Agricultural, Animal, Art, Banking/Finance, Behavioral, Biological Science, Botany, Business, Computer, Criminal Justice, Drafting/Design, Electrical/Electronics Technology, Medical, Farm/Ranch Management, Health, History, Journalism, Law, Liberal Arts, Literature, Math, Music, Natural Science, Office Management, Physics, Psychology, Political Science, Science, Speech, Zoology

ATHLETIC PROFILE

Conference Affiliation: Bi-State Conference
Program Profile: The home playing field has natural grass, batting cages and seats approximately 300. We play a Fall and Spring season.
History: 1996 appearance in the NJCAA Division II World Series - placed 5th in the Nation.
Achievements: District Coach of the Year (1995-1996); NJCAA Division II Regional District Champions 1995-1996; All-Americans 7 in the last 4 years; Drafted players - 2 in the last 8 years.
Coaching: Don Brown - Head Coach.
Style of Play: Traditional Baseball.

Rose State College

6420 SE 15th St
MidWest City, OK 73110
Coach: Lloyd Cummings
Email: lcummings@ms.rose.cc.ok.us

NJCAA
Raiders/Navy, Gold
Phone: (405) 733-7421
Fax: (405) 736-0359

ACADEMIC

Type: 4 Yr., Coed
Campus Housing: No
Degrees Conferred: Associate
Programs of Study: Accounting, Art/Fine Arts, Aviation Technology, Biology, Biological Science, Business Administration, Commerce, Management, Chemistry, Child Care/Child and Family Studies, Child Psychology, Computer Information Systems, Court Reporting, Chemistry, Drafting/Design, English, Environmental, Finance/Banking, History, Home Economics, Human Ecology, Library Science, Mathematics, Medical, Psychology, Physical Education, Sociology, Speech

ATHLETIC PROFILE

Conference Affiliation: Bi-State Conference
Program Profile: We are in the process of improving our facilities with restrooms, covered seating , a pressbox, a storage facility and a concession stand. We play on a natural turf field.
History: We had a strong program in the late 1970's and early 1980's but just average lately.
Coaching: Lloyd Cummings - Head Coach.
Style of Play: Fundametal baseball, move runners, play good defense.

Seminole State College

P.O. Box 351
Seminole, OK 74818-0351
Coach: Lloyd Simmons

NJCAA
Trojans/Blue, Red, White
Phone: (405) 382-9950
Fax: (405) 382-3122

ACADEMIC

Founded: 1931
Religion: Non-Affiliated
Student/Faculty Ratio: 20:1
Undergraduate Enrollment: 1,650
Scholarships/Academic: Yes **Athletic:** Yes
Total Expenses by: Year **In State:** $ 4,866

Type: 2 Yr., Jr. College, Coed
SAT/ACT/GPA: Open
Male/Female Ratio: 9:1
Graduate Enrollment: None
Fin Aid: Yes
Out of State: $ 4,866

Degrees Conferred: Associate
Programs of Study: Accounting, Art/Fine Arts, Behavioral Science, Biology, Biological Science, Business Administration, Commerce, Management, Computer Science, Elementary Education, Law Enforcement, Liberal Arts, General Studies, Medical Laboratory Technology, Nursing, Physical

ATHLETIC PROFILE

Conference Affiliation: Bi-State Conference
Coaching: Lloyd Simmons, Head Coach, started his 24th year as a head coach.
Style of Play: Too early to know, but we should have good depth.

Southern Nazarene University

6729 NW 39th Expressway
Bethany, OK 73008
Coach: Scott Selby
Email: sselby@snu.edu

NAIA
Crimson Storm/Crimson
Phone: (405) 491-6630
Fax: (405) 491-6387

ACADEMIC

Founded: 1899
Religion: Nazarene
Web-site: http://www.snu.edu/
Student/Faculty Ratio: 17:1
Undergraduate Enrollment: 1,800+

Type: 4 Yr., Private, Liberal Arts, Coed
Campus Housing: Yes
SAT/ACT/GPA: 19
Male/Female Ratio: 2:1
Graduate Enrollment: 200

Scholarships/Academic: Yes **Athletic:** Yes **Fin Aid:** Yes
Total Expenses by: Year **In State:** $ 11,000 **Out of State:** $ 11,000
Degrees Conferred: Bachelor of Science and Art, Masters of Education and Business
Programs of Study: 3 Colleges, 21 Courses of Study including: Accounting, Art Education, Chemistry, Communication, Computer Science, Education, English, Music, Nursing, Prelaw, Premed

ATHLETIC PROFILE

Conference Affiliation: Sooner Athletic Conference
Program Profile: We are building a new facilities with a natural field, a press box, dressing rooms, a concession, a track and a seating facility for 2,000.
History: 1997 record was 8-42 and 1998 record was 20-31.
Achievements: 1 player drafted in 1997 catcher - Mike Wade by Baltimore.
Coaching: Scott Selby, Head Coach, was a former assistant coach in high school. He played in college and was named All-Conference. He was All-District for 3 years. He compiled a record of 21-30 as a head coach. Sean Karn - Assistant Coach.
Roster for 1998 team/In State: 27 **Out of State:** 11 **Out of Country:** 1
Total Number of Varsity/Jr. Varsity: 40 **Percent of Graduation:** 95%
Number of Seniors on 1998 Team: 5 **Number of Sophomores on 1998 Team:** 11
Freshmen Receiving Fin Aid/Athletic: 6 **Academic:** 5
Number of Fall Games: 13 **Number of Spring Games:** 62
Positions Needed for 1999/2000: Pitcher, Outfielder
Most Recent Record: 21 - 30 - 0
Baseball Camp Dates: 2nd week in June
Schedule: Kansas State, UCO, SouthEastern, St. Mary, Incarnate Word, OCU
Style of Play: Fundamentally sound with team power and solid defense.

Southeastern Oklahoma State University

Station A
Durant, OK 74701-0609
Coach: Mike Metheny

NCAA II
Savages/Blue, Gold
Phone: (580) 924-0121
Fax: (580) 924-7313

ACADEMIC

Founded: 1909
Religion: Non-Affiliated
Web-site: Not Available
Student/Faculty Ratio: 20:1
Undergraduate Enrollment: 3,650

Type: 4 Yr., Public, Liberal Arts, Coed
Campus Housing: No
SAT/ACT/GPA: 19 avg
Male/Female Ratio: 45:55
Graduate Enrollment: 450

Scholarships/Academic: Yes **Athletic:** Yes **Fin Aid:** Yes
Total Expenses by: Year **In State:** $ 4,400 **Out of State:** $ 6,650
Degrees Conferred: BA, BS, BAED, BM, MA, MS, MED
Programs of Study: Accounting, Aerospace Engineering, Art Education, Art/Fine Arts, Automotive Technology, Computer Science, Business Education, Ecology, Economics, Medical Technology, Music, Music Education, Cell Biology, Criminal Justice, Business Administration, Retail Management, Social Science, Sociology

ATHLETIC PROFILE

Conference Affiliation: OIC

Southwestern Oklahoma State University

100 Campus Drive
Weatherford, OK 73096
Coach: Charles Teasley

NCAA II
Bulldogs/Navy, White
Phone: (580) 774-3263
Fax: (580) 774-7059

ACADEMIC

Founded: 1901
Religion: Non-Affiliated
Web-site: Not Available
Student/Faculty Ratio: 18:1
Undergraduate Enrollment: 4,600
Scholarships/Academic: Yes **Athletic:** Yes
Total Expenses by: Year **In State:** $ 4,100

Type: 4 Yr., Public, Liberal Arts, Coed,
Campus Housing: No
SAT/ACT/GPA: 19+
Male/Female Ratio:
Graduate Enrollment: 500
Fin Aid: Yes
Out of State: $ 6,300

Degrees Conferred: Bachelors, Masters
Programs of Study: Southwestern is composed of 5 schools which are further divided into various departments. The schools include: Arts and Science, Business, Education, Health Science and Graduate School

ATHLETIC PROFILE

Conference Affiliation: NAIA Division I District 9, Oklahoma Intercollegiate Conf.
Program Profile: Southwestern Oklahoma plays on a natural grass field (Rankin Williams Field) on the Swosu Campus. The Bulldogs start their schedule in February and conclude the season in May.

University of Central Oklahoma

100 North University Drive
Edmond, OK 73034
Coach: Wendell D. Simmons

NCAA II
Bronchos/Bronze, Blue
Phone: (405) 974-2980
Fax: (405) 974-3820

ACADEMIC

Founded: 1890
Religion: Non-Affiliated
Web-site: http://www.ucok.edu
Student/Faculty Ratio: 23:1
Undergraduate Enrollment: 12,048
Scholarships/Academic: Yes **Athletic:** Yes
Total Expenses by: Year **In State:** $ 3,800

Type: 4 Yr., Public, Liberal Arts, Coed
Campus Housing: Yes
SAT/ACT/GPA: 910/19/2.7
Male/Female Ratio: 2:1
Graduate Enrollment: 3,286
Fin Aid: Yes
Out of State: $ 3,800

Degrees Conferred: BA, BS, MA, MS, MBA, MED
Programs of Study: Accounting, Actuarial Science, Advertising, Applied Mathematics, Art, Art Education, Economics, Business Economics, Criminal Justice, Contruction Technology, Design, Journalism, Reading Education, Nutrition, Philosophy, Photography, Graphic Arts, Food Service

ATHLETIC PROFILE

Estimated Number of Baseball Scholarships: 7
Conference Affiliation: Lone Star Conference
Program Profile: Our field is natural grass.
History: We have been in existence for 7 years.Our record is 210 wins and 154 loses. We were National Runner-Up in Division II in 1997, Lone Star Conference Champions in 1994 and 1997, and NCAA South Central Region Champs in 1997. We nationally ranked in the top twenty in 1994, 1995, 1996, 1997 and 1998.
Achievements: Lone Star Conference Coach of the Year in 1994 and 1997, NCAA Division II South Central Region Coach of the Year in 1997; College Coach of the Year in Oklahoma in 1997; 3 All-American in 1997; 3 drafted in 1997.
Coaching: Wendell D. Simmons - Head Coach. Todd Kelley - Assistant Coach.
Roster for 1998 team/In State: 26 **Out of State:** 4 **Out of Country:** 3
Total Number of Varsity/Jr. Varsity: 16 **Percent of Graduation:** 90%
Number of Seniors on 1998 Team: 5 **Number of Sophomores on 1998 Team:** 5
Freshmen Receiving Fin Aid/Athletic: 2 **Academic:** 3
Number of Fall Games: 4 **Number of Spring Games:** 52
Positions Needed for 1999/2000: 6 **Most Recent Record:** 38 - 14 - 0

Baseball Camp Dates: May 28 - June 16
Schedule: Central Missouri State, SouthEastern Oklahoma State University
Style of Play: Very aggressive mix of power and speed.

University of Oklahoma

401 W Imhoff
Norman, OK 73019-0650
Coach: Larry Cochell

NCAA I
Sooners/Crimson, Cream
Phone: (405) 325-8354
Fax: (405) 325-8374

ACADEMIC

Type: 4 Yr., Public, Liberal Arts, Coed, Engineering
Founded: 1890
Religion: Non-Affiliated
Campus Housing: Yes
Web-site: http://www.ou.edu
SAT/ACT/GPA: 1030/23/3.0
Student/Faculty Ratio: 30:1
Male/Female Ratio: 50:50
Undergraduate Enrollment: 15,000
Graduate Enrollment: 5,000
Scholarships/Academic: Yes **Athletic:** Yes **Fin Aid:** Yes
Total Expenses by: Year **In State:** $ 7,163 **Out of State:** $ 11,203
Degrees Conferred: 200 Masters and Doctoral
Programs of Study: Business, Meteorology, Education, Engineering, Fine Arts, Geosciences, Architecture, Psychology, Marketing, Music, Political Science, Science Education, Journalism, Linguistics, Drama, Dance, Botany, Zoology, Economics, Physics, Sociology, Social Work

ATHLETIC PROFILE

Conference Affiliation: Big Twelve Conference
Program Profile: We have a 56 game season starting in early February. We play on natural field. Our stadium size is 2,700. We are beginning renovations to add concession, restroom & seats. We were (Field of the Year) Bean Clay Diamond of the Year in 1994. Kesut Stadium was built in 1981.
History: Our program began in 1898. We won College World Series Champions in 1951 and 1994. We were members of the 1922-1928 Old Missouri Valley Conference, the 1929-1948 Big Six Conference, the 1949-1960 Big Seven Conference, the 1961-1996 Big 8 Conference and the Big 12 in 1997.
Achievements: 1997 Big Twelve Conference Tournament Champion; NCAA Regional Champions in 1994-1995; 1994 National Coach of the Year. Over 130 drafted players; 30 All-Americans.
Coaching: Larry Cochell, Head Coach, is the only coach in the history to take 3 different schools to College World Series. He sent more than 100 players to the pros. Jackson Todd, Pitching Coach, is was a former OU player in 1971-1973. He has been playing professional ball for 13 seasons. Bill Mostello, Assistant Coach, works with infielders and hitters and was Alaska League Manager of the Year in 1990-1991.
Style of Play: Put pressure on defense with a sound running game and quality pitching and defense.

University of Science and Arts of Oklahoma

PO Box 82345
Chickasha, OK 73018-0001
Coach: L. J. Powell

NAIA
Dovers/Dark Green, Old Gold
Phone: (405) 224-3140
Fax: (405) 522-3176

ACADEMIC

Founded: 1908
Type: 4 Yr., Public, Coed
Religion: Non-Affiliated
Campus Housing: No
Web-site: Not Available
SAT/ACT/GPA: 18+
Student/Faculty Ratio: 19:1
Male/Female Ratio: 35:65
Undergraduate Enrollment: 1,740
Graduate Enrollment: None
Scholarships/Academic: Yes **Athletic:** Yes **Fin Aid:** Yes

Total Expenses by: Year **In State:** $ 4,968 **Out of State:** $ 7,128
Degrees Conferred: Associate
Programs of Study: Accounting, Art Education, Fine Arts, Biology, Biological Science, Business Economics, Business Education, Music, Music Education, Data Processing, Political Science, English, History, Psychology, Theatre

ATHLETIC PROFILE

Conference Affiliation: Oklahoma Intercollegiate Conference
History: The program began in 1994-1995 school year and displayed steady growth.
Coaching: L. J. Powell - Head Coach. Jan Moore - Assistant Coach.

Western Oklahoma State College

2801 North Main
Altus, OK 73521
Coach: Jim Luetjan

NJCAA
Pioneers/Green, Gold
Phone: (580) 477-2000
Fax: (580) 477-7777

ACADEMIC

Founded: 1926
Religion: Non-Affiliated
Student/Faculty Ratio: 22:1
Undergraduate Enrollment: 1,740
Scholarships/Academic: No **Athletic:** Yes
Total Expenses by: Year **In State:** $ 1,000

Type: 4 Yr., Coed
Campus Housing: No
Male/Female Ratio: 46:54
Graduate Enrollment: None
Fin Aid: Yes
Out of State: $ 2,800

Degrees Conferred: Associate
Programs of Study: Agriculture, Aviation Administration, Aviation Technology

OREGON

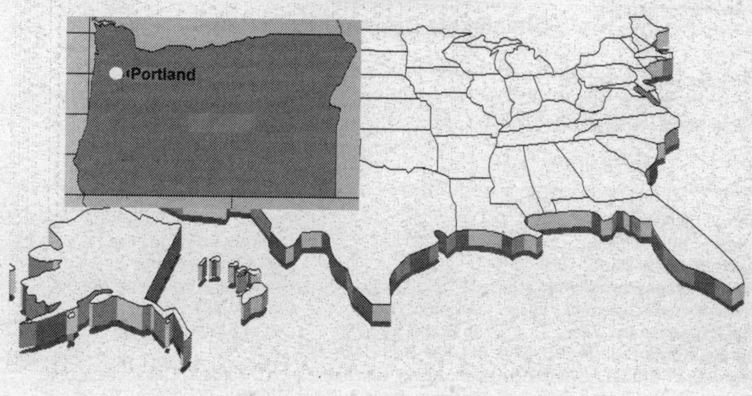

SCHOOL	CITY	AFFILIATION 99	PAGE
Chemeketa Community College	Salem	NWAACC	700
Clackamas Community College	Oregon City	NWAAC	700
Concordia College - Portland	Portland	NAIA	701
Eastern Oregon State College	La Grande	NCAA III	701
George Fox University	Newberg	NCAA III\NAIA	702
Lewis and Clark College	Portland	NAIA III	703
Linfield College	McMinnville	NCAA III\NAIA	703
Oregon State University	Corvallis	NCAA I	704
Pacific University	Forest Grove	NCAA III\NAIA	705
Treasure Valley Community College	Ontario	NJCAA	706
University of Portland	Portland	NCAA I	706
Western Baptist College	Salem	NAIA	707
Western Oregon University	Monmouth	NCAA II/NAIA	707
Willamette University	Salem	NCAA III	708

Chemeketa Community College

4000 Lancaster Drive, NE
Salem, OR 97309-7070
Coach: Steve Hendrickson

NWAACC
Storm/Kelly Green, Black
Phone: (503) 399-5081
Fax: (503) 390-5496

ACADEMIC

Founded: 1880
Type: 2 Yr., Private, Jr. College, Coed
Religion: Non-Affiliated
Campus Housing: Yes
Student/Faculty Ratio: 16:1
Male/Female Ratio: 7:1
Undergraduate Enrollment: 2,200
Graduate Enrollment: None
Scholarships/Academic: Yes **Athletic:** No **Fin Aid:** Yes
Total Expenses by: Year **In State:** $ 23,786 **Out of State:** $ 23,786
Degrees Conferred: BA, BS, BFA, BLI, BM, BSSP, MA, MS, MFA
Programs of Study: Advertising, Broadcasting, Communication Disorders, Communications, Creative Writing, Dance, Film Arts, Literature, Prelaw, Public Relation, Publishing, Radio and Television, Speech, Speech Pathology, Theatre

ATHLETIC PROFILE

Estimated Number of Baseball Scholarships: 9 Full
Conference Affiliation: Southern Division
Program Profile: We have an on-campus facilities with natural turf which is fully lighted and has stadium 1,200 seats. Indoor and outdoor hitting facilities are available. Fall season runs September 25 to November 10 which will include approximately 20 games. Spring schedule runs March 10 to May 30 and includes 40 games.
History: We sarted in 1969 in the old OCCAA Conference and entered the NWAACC in 1989. We were NWAACC Champions in 1994.
Achievements: 1994 NWAACC Coach of the Year; 16 drafted with 9 still active; 1990 NWAACC Player of the Year - Ricky Warl; 1996 NWAACC Player of the Year - Cody Barney.
Coaching: Steve Hendrickson, Head Coach, has coached 18 years at Jr. College level. He compiled a record of 311-246. He was 1994 Coach of the Year & 1994 NWAACC Coach of the Year.
Roster for 1998 team/In State: 20 **Out of State:** 4 **Out of Country:** 0
Total Number of Varsity/Jr. Varsity: 24 **Percent of Graduation:** 75%
Number of Seniors on 1998 Team: 605 **Number of Sophomores on 1998 Team:** 0
Freshmen Receiving Fin Aid/Athletic: 11 **Academic:** 4
Number of Fall Games: 20 **Number of Spring Games:** 40
Most Recent Record: 21 - 19 - 0 **Baseball Camp Dates:** June 10-15
Positions Needed for 1999/2000: Catcher, Outfielder, Middle Infielder
Schedule: Yavapai, Mt. Hood CC, Lower Columbia, Lane, Glendale, Edmonds, South Mountain JC
Style of Play: Solid defense, aggressive pitching & offensive style to fit make up of the current team.

Clackamas Community College

19600 South Molalla Avenue
Oregon City, OR 97045
Coach: Robin Robinson

NWAAC
Cougars/Navy, Scarlet
Phone: (503) 657-8400
Fax: (503) 655-5153

ACADEMIC

Founded: 1966
Type: 2 Yr., Public, Jr. College, Coed
Religion: Non-Affiliated
Campus Housing: No
Undergraduate Enrollment: 4,700
Graduate Enrollment: None
Scholarships/Academic: Yes **Athletic:** Yes **Fin Aid:** Yes
Total Expenses by: Year **In State:** $ 1,100 **Out of State:** $ 3,800
Degrees Conferred: Associate

Programs of Study: Accounting, Anthropology, Automotive Technology, Biological Science, Business, Computer, Criminal Justice, Dental Service, Drafting/Design, Economics, Education, English, Fine Arts, Forestry, Gerontology, Horticulture, Hotel/Restaurant Management, Journalism, Law, Liberal Arts, Manufacturing, Marketing, Mechanical, Nursing, Occupational therapy, Office, Philosophy, Real Estate, Theatre, Water Resources

ATHLETIC PROFILE

Conference Affiliation: Northwest Athletic Association of Community Colleges
Program Profile: We went to the playoffs in 1994 for the first time since 1977. We play Fall ball September 25 to November 15. Spring season is February 1-May 31 and we play 36 games. We have excellent natural grass facilities, a large baseball area and a small seating capacity.
History: We began in 1969 and affiliated with NJCAA .About 10 years ago, we went to the NWAACC because of cash. Our program has had 5 coaches. We always have a large turnout. We had 2 earlier good playoff seasons and then stayed in the middle until now; we are back at the top.
Achievements: 3 players drafted in 5 years.
Coaching: Robin Robinson, Head Coach, has been 6 years at Clackamas. He graduated from willamette in 1979 and received his Masters from Lewis and Clark. He spent 10 years as high school coach when he was named 1988 High School Coach of the Year.
Style of Play: We run; top 5 in NWAACC in SB's last 3 seasons and we hit and run..."'we like to make things happen!" We have been in the top of the NWAACC in pitching stats also. 'We pitch smart (not high velocity), to get fly ball, ground ball outs!" 'We teach baseball, not just practice skills."

Concordia College - Portland

2811 NE Holman
Portland, OR 97211
Coach: Brian Mullan

NAIA
Cavaliers/Navy, White
Phone: (503) 280-8691
Fax: (503) 280-8591

ACADEMIC

Founded: 1905
Type: 4 Yr., Private, Liberal Arts, Coed
Religion: Non-Affiliated
Campus Housing: Yes
Web-site: http://www.cu-portland.edu/
SAT/ACT/GPA: 950
Student/Faculty Ratio: 17:1
Male/Female Ratio: 1:1
Undergraduate Enrollment: 1,150
Graduate Enrollment: None
Scholarships/Academic: Yes **Athletic:** Yes **Fin Aid:** Yes
Total Expenses by: Year **In State:** $ 14,500 **Out of State:** $ 14,500
Degrees Conferred: BA, BS, Med
Programs of Study: Accounting, Art, Biology, Business, Chemistry, Economics, Elementary Education, English, Environmental Science, Health Care, Humanities, Human Resources Management, International Business, Management, Mathematics, Marketing, Science, Physical

ATHLETIC PROFILE

Conference Affiliation: NCCAA

Eastern Oregon State College

1410 L Avenue
La Grande, OR 97850-2899
Coach: West McCallister

NCAA III
Mountaineers/Royal, Gold
Phone: (541) 962-3364
Fax: (541) 962-3577

ACADEMIC

Founded: 1929
Type: 4 Yr., Public, Liberal Arts, Coed
Religion: Non-Affiliated
Campus Housing: No

Student/Faculty Ratio: 13:1 **Male/Female Ratio:** Unknown
Undergraduate Enrollment: 1,800 **Graduate Enrollment:** None
Scholarships/Academic: Yes **Athletic:** No **Fin Aid:** Yes
Total Expenses by: Year **In State:** $ 8,500 **Out of State:** $ 8,500
Degrees Conferred: BA, BS, MA, MS, AA, AS
Programs of Study: The School of Arts and Sciences, the School of Education and Business Programs, Agriculture - Cooperative Program with Oregon State University, Nursing - Cooperative Program with Oregon Health Sciences University

ATHLETIC PROFILE

Conference Affiliation: Cascade Conference
Program Profile: Spring season includes a 45-game regular schedule.We do a Fall term intrasquad 'league' . We play at Snowflake Field which is natural grass and has a capacity of 250. It opened in 1974, is on campus and has no lights.
History: Our first team was in Spring of 1930. We did not field a team for 10 years (off-and-on). Our program has had only 3 head coaches (including current head coach). We were 7 times Conference Champions or Co-Champs, 3 times won Division title and one as District champion.
Achievements: Conference Coach of the Year in 1990, currently have a former player in the Braves Organization.

George Fox University

414 N Meridian Street **NCAA III\NAIA**
Newberg, OR 97132 **Bruins/Navy, White, Grey**
Coach: Patrick Bailey **Phone: (503) 554-2914**
Email: pbailey@georgefox.edu **Fax: (503) 544-3864**

ACADEMIC

Founded: 1891 **Type:** 4 Yr., Private, Liberal Arts, Coed
Religion: Quaker (Friends) **Campus Housing:** Yes
Web-site: http://www.gfc.edu/ **SAT/ACT/GPA:** Formula
Student/Faculty Ratio: 16:1 **Male/Female Ratio:** 60:40
Undergraduate Enrollment: 1,350 **Graduate Enrollment:** 565
Scholarships/Academic: Yes **Athletic:** No **Fin Aid:** Yes
Total Expenses by: Year **In State:** $ 20,390 **Out of State:** $ 20,390
Degrees Conferred: BA, BS, Masters, PhD
Programs of Study: 30 majors including: Biblical Studies, Biology, Business and Management, Chemistry, Christian Ministry Communication Arts, Communications/Video Productions, Letters/Literature, Life Science, Math, Music, Psychology, Economics, Education, Religion, Sociology/Social Sciences, Teacher Education

ATHLETIC PROFILE

Conference Affiliation: Northwest Conference of Independent Colleges
Program Profile: We have a manicured all grass field with artificial turf bull pens and other areas. There are dug-outs , 4 outdoor and 3 indoor batting cages. The indoor facility includes room for full infield practice along with four indoor pitching mounds.
History: The program began in 1864, and we joined NAIA in 1965. We joined Northwest Conference in 1995 and NCAA Division III in 1998. We were Conference Champions 7 of the last 10 years.
Achievements: Coach of the Year in 1997 for the Northwest Conference of Independent Colleges. Was named Conference Coach of the Year 4 of the last 6 years in high school.
Coaching: Patrick Bailey, Head Coach, entered his 4th year with the program. He college record is 79-39 while his high school record was 607-311. He coached high school and college for 16 years. Geoff Loomis, Assistant Coach, was Pacific 10 North Player of the Year in 1992. He was drafted in 1992 and played 3 years in the Oakland Organization. Jim Reicherbach - Assistant Coach.
Roster for 1998 team/In State: 14 **Out of State:** 24 **Out of Country:** 0
Total Number of Varsity/Jr. Varsity: 36 **Percent of Graduation:** 100%
Number of Seniors on 1998 Team: 10 **Number of Sophomores on 1998 Team:** 8

Most Recent Record: 25 - 13 - 0
Number of Spring Games: 41
Positions Needed for 1999/2000: 7
Baseball Camp Dates: December, June
Schedule: Lewis and Clark State College, Albertson's College, University of Portland, California Lutheran University, Linfield College, Willamette University
Style of Play: Offensive: steal, hit and run; run production hitting skills; drag bunting, push bunting, aggressive style. Defensive: most valuable possession defensively - 27 outs; defense based on minimizing big inning allowed and getting outs.

Lewis and Clark College

0615 SW Palatine Hill Rd.
Portland, OR 97219
Coach: Jerry Gatto
Email: gatto@clark.edu

NAIA III
Pioneers/Orange, Black
Phone: (503) 768-7062
Fax: (503) 768-7058

ACADEMIC

Founded: 1867
Type: 4 Yr., Private, Liberal Arts, Coed
Religion: Non-Affiliated
Campus Housing: No
Web-site: Not Available
SAT/ACT/GPA: None
Student/Faculty Ratio: 16:1
Male/Female Ratio: 4:5
Undergraduate Enrollment: 1,800
Graduate Enrollment: None
Scholarships/Academic: Yes **Athletic:** No **Fin Aid:** Yes
Total Expenses by: Year **In State:** $ Varies **Out of State:** $ Varies
Degrees Conferred: BA, BS, MA, MS, JD
Programs of Study: Anthropology, Art, Biology, Business, Chemistry, Communications, Economics, Education, English, History, Interdisciplinary, International, Management, Math, Music, Philosophy, Physics, Political Psychology, Religion, Social Science, Spanish

ATHLETIC PROFILE

Conference Affiliation: NCIC
Program Profile: Our baseball complex has a seating capacity of 350. BOK is 125. It has cages and a natural turf field. Playing season goes from February 25 to May 13-15 including playoffs.
History: 50 years of baseball; 1947-1997. Playoffs 14 of 18 years; six District II Championship (NAIA) one Area I (West Coast) Championship; World Series Appearance in 1990.
Achievements: Coach of the Year five times; District II NAIA; Area I Coach of the Year in 1990; District II Hall of Fame three Conference Titles; 12 dozen drafted players over 18-20 year period.
Coaching: Jerry Gatto, Head Coach, started his 17th season. He was Coach of the 5 times District II NAIA and Area Coach of the Year in 1990. Mick Ellet - Assistant Coach. Mike Meyer - Assistant.
Style of Play: Aggressive - offensive. Pressure oriented, hopefully. Sound fundamentally defensively.

Linfield College

900 SE Baker Street
McMinnville, OR 97128
Coach: Scott Carnahan
Email: scarnahan@linfield.edu

NCAA III\NAIA
Wildcats/Scarlet, Navy, White
Phone: (503) 434-2229
Fax: (503) 434-2453

ACADEMIC

Founded: 1849
Type: 4 Yr., Private, Liberal Arts, Coed
Religion: Baptist
Campus Housing: Yes
Web-site: http://www.linfield.edu/
SAT/ACT/GPA: 900/2.8
Student/Faculty Ratio: 17:1
Male/Female Ratio: 45:55
Undergraduate Enrollment: 1,600
Graduate Enrollment: None

Scholarships/Academic: Yes **Athletic:** No **Fin Aid:** Yes
Total Expenses by: Year **In State:** $ 26,000 **Out of State:** $ 26,00
Degrees Conferred: BA, BS, MEd
Programs of Study: Accounting, Anthropology, Art, Biology, Botany, Business, Chemistry, Communications, Computer Science, Creative Writing, Earth Science, Ecology, Economics, Education, English, Finance, French, German, Health Education, History, Humanities, Information Science, International Business, Japanese, Journalism, Liberal Arts, Management, Mathematics, Medical Technology, Modern Languages, Music, Natural Science, Nursing, Philosophy, Physical Education, Physics, Political Science, Predentistry, Prelaw, Premed, Prevet, Psychology, Public Relations, Radio and Televions, Religion Science, Sociology, Spanish, Theatre

ATHLETIC PROFILE

Conference Affiliation: Northwest Conference of Independent Colleges
Program Profile: We are a Top 25 program with great facilities. Linfield is a long time NAIA member that became NCAA III in 1998-1999. We play a 36 game regular season schedule with the varsity and a 24 game schedule with our junior varsity. We play on Helser Field which is natural grass. We have great facilities including Wright Stadium and Rutschaman Fieldhouse. They are Division I facilities!!
History: Our program started in 1926. Since 1950 , Linfield has won or shared 28 NCIC Conference Championships. The program has been very competitive with all schools nationally at the NAIA level and we have won 2 national championships. We have a very good tradition and the support from alumni and community.
Achievements: Coach Carnahan has been the NCIC Coach of the Year 8 times in 14 years. He also coached the USA team in 1993, 1995 and 1996. He was the team leader for the USA during the Atlanta Summer Olympics. Currently we have four players playing professionally with the most noticeable being with the Brosous of the Oakland A's. Our right fielder signed with the Toronto Tufts this past Summer - was in 18th round pick.
Coaching: Scott Carnahan, Head Coach, was Coach of the Year 8 times. He is in his 15th year as a baseball head coach. He is recognized as one of the top baseball clinicians in the Northwest. He was a featured speaker at the 1994 American Baseball Coaches National Clinic held in Chicago and has been a featured speaker at various coaching clinics held in the Pacific Northwest. He was the team leader for the USA Baseball delegation for the Olympics Games held in Atlanta during the Summer of 1996. Jim Ray, Assistant Coach, is in his 20th year as an assistant coach for the Wildcats. His primary responsibility is supervising the outfielders. Bryan Tebeau, Assistant Coach, is in his 3rd year as assistant coach. He graduated from Linfield in 1988. He pitched two seasons for Coach Carnahan. Clyde Powell ,Assistant Coach, begins his 1st season. He will supersvise the junior varsity team this Spring. Mike Lord - Assistant Coach. Casey Powell - Assistant Coach.
Total Number of Varsity/Jr. Varsity: 44 **Percent of Graduation:** 98%
Positions Needed for 1999/2000: Pitchers **Number of Spring Games:** 36
Most Recent Record: 25 - 13 - 0 **Schedule:** LC State
Style of Play: Aggressive - like to run; team hit .369 this year; .385 in conference.

Oregon State University

Gill Coliseum 127
Corvallis, OR 97331
Coach: Pat Casey
NCAA I
Beavers/Orange, Black
Phone: (541) 737-2825
Fax: (541) 737-4002

ACADEMIC

Founded: 1868 **Type:** 4 Yr., Public, Coed
Religion: Non-Affiliated **Campus Housing:** Yes
Web-site: http://www.orst.edu/ **SAT/ACT/GPA:** 970/23
Student/Faculty Ratio: 16:1 **Male/Female Ratio:** 57:43
Undergraduate Enrollment: 11,280 **Graduate Enrollment:** 2,881
Scholarships/Academic: Yes **Athletic:** Yes **Fin Aid:** Yes
Total Expenses by: Year **In State:** $ 3,500 **Out of State:** $ 10,116
Degrees Conferred: BA, BS, BFA, MA, MS, MAIS, MAT, PhD

Programs of Study: Agriculture, Business, Engineering, Forestry, Health and Human Performance, Home Economics and Education, Liberal Arts, Pharmacy, Science, Anthropology, American Studies, History, Geology, Computer Science, Geography, Microbiology, Mathematics, Music, Natural Resources, Physics, Philosophy, Political Science, Poultry Science, Psychology, Sociology

ATHLETIC PROFILE

Conference Affiliation: Pacific 10 Conference
Program Profile: Oregon State offers a major-league program in every sense of the term. Home games and practices are at Coleman Field, which seats over 2,300. In 1999, Goss Stadium at Coleman Field will open. It will provide an enlarged press box and improved seating. Coleman Field is grass, indoor practice on McAlexander Fieldhouse is artificial turf. Season runs early February thru Mid-May.
History: OSU began playing varsity baseball in 1907 and has fielded a team ever since, with breaks only for World War I and World War II. Only two coaches most of the time - Ralph Coleman (1923-1931 and 1938-1966) and Jack Riley (1973-1994). They captured the Pacific Coast Conference and Pacific 10 Northern Division since 1926.
Achievements: 14 Major Leaguers, including Mike Thurman of Montreat Expos in 1997; 49 players drafted, including 3 in 1st round; numerous others signed with a pro teams as a free-agent. Alumni include Ken Forsch and Steve Lyons; 20 League Championships; 1952 College World Series Appearance; 11 All-Americans; 6 league Coach of the Year Honors; 3 Academic All-Americans.
Coaching: Pat Casey, Head Coach, started his 4th year as a head coach and compiled a record of 95-52-3. The 10th year overall record is 266-165-4. He came to OSU after 6 highly successful seasons at nearby George Fox College. Dan Spencer, Assistant Coach, entered his 2nd year and was 135-79 head coach at Green River Community College. Ron Northcutt, Assistant Coach, came to OSU from George Fox with Casey.
Style of Play: Aggressive and offense.

Pacific University

2043 College Way
Forest Grove, OR 97116
Coach: Greg Bradley

NCAA III\NAIA
Boxers/Red, Black
Phone: (503) 359-2142
Fax: (503) 359-2209

ACADEMIC

Founded: 1849
Type: 4 Yr., Private, Liberal Arts, Coed
Religion: Non-Affiliated
Campus Housing: Yes
Web-site: http://www.pacifcu.edu/
SAT/ACT/GPA: None
Student/Faculty Ratio: 14:1
Male/Female Ratio: 42:58
Undergraduate Enrollment: 1,050
Graduate Enrollment: 750
Scholarships/Academic: Yes **Athletic:** Yes **Fin Aid:** Yes
Total Expenses by: Year **In State:** $ 19,000 **Out of State:** $ 19,000
Degrees Conferred: BA, BS, MA, MS, D, OD
Programs of Study: Accounting, Banking and Finance, Biology, Biology, Business Administration, Chemistry, Computer Science Creative Writing, Dramatic Arts, Economics, Elementary Education, Exercise Science, French, German, History, Humanities, Japanese, Literature, Management, Marketing, Mathematics, Music, Philosophy, Physical Education, Physics, Political Science, Psychology, Science, Social Science, Sociology, Spanish

ATHLETIC PROFILE

Conference Affiliation: NCIC

Portland State University

(Program Discontinued)

Treasure Valley Community College

650 College Blvd
Ontario, OR 97914
Coach: Gary Van Tol
Email: gary_van_tol@tucc.cc.or.u

NJCAA
Chukars/Orange, Navy Blue
Phone: (541) 889-6493
Fax: (541) 881-2732

ACADEMIC

Founded: 1962
Type: 2 Yr., Public, Jr. College, Coed
Religion: Non-Affiliated
Campus Housing: Yes
SAT/ACT/GPA: We have our own placement test
Web-site: http://www.tucc.or.us
Student/Faculty Ratio: 20:1
Male/Female Ratio: 48:52
Undergraduate Enrollment: 2,000
Scholarships/Academic: Yes **Athletic:** Yes **Fin Aid:** Yes
Total Expenses by: Year **In State:** $ 6,195 **Out of State:** $ 6,915
Degrees Conferred: AA, AS
Programs of Study: Agricultural, Agronomy, Biological Science, Business, Chemistry, Commerical Art, Computer, Criminal Justice, Crop Science, Drafting/Design, Economics, Education, English, Forestry, History, Humanities, Law, Liberal Arts, Math, Music, Natural Resources, Range, Science, Theatre, Welding, Wildlife

ATHLETIC PROFILE

Estimated Number of Baseball Scholarships: 12
Conference Affiliation: Scenic West Athletic Conference
Program Profile: Our program prides itself on hard work and preparing our student-athletes for the future. Facilities include an indoor artificial turf workout area, a weight room, a training room, a sauna,a whirl pool, indoor batting cages, outdoor batting cages, a natural grass baseball field, lights and a seating capacity for 500-700 people. We have dry climate, and great weather. Spring season starts early February. Home games open March 1st.
History: The program began in 1962. Rick Baumann is the winningest coach at Treasure Valley. Gary Van Tol took over the program in 1995-1996.
Achievements: College World Series in 1990 (5th) and 1976; Region 18 Champions in 1990 and 1992; Former Major Leagues: Wayne Nordhagen, Lenn Sakata, and Jeff Lahii, Current players: Reck Bauer (5th Rd.) Orioles - 'A' Ball, (1996) John Margaria (21st Rd.) Angels - 'A' Ball; 18 All-Americans, 6 Academic All-Americans.
Coaching: Gary Van Tol, Head Coach, entered his 3rd year with the program. He graduated from Gonzaga University in 1990 and has an overall record of 30-59. Reck Baumann ,Pitching Coach, is in his 16th year and graduated from Idaho State University in 1973). Eric Smith, Assistant Coach, is in his 5th year and graduated from Treasure Valley CC in 1991 and Boise State University in 1995. Tracy Bratcher - Assistant Coach.
Roster for 1998 team/In State: 2 **Out of State:** 26 **Out of Country:** 5
Total Number of Varsity/Jr. Varsity: 25 **Percent of Graduation:** 95%
Number of Seniors on 1998 Team: 10 **Baseball Camp Dates:** June
Freshmen Receiving Fin Aid/Athletic: 7 **Academic:** 5
Number of Fall Games: 20 **Number of Spring Games:** 56
Positions Needed for 1999/2000: Pitcher, Shortstop, Catcher, 1st Base, Centerfield
Most Recent Record: 24 - 33 - 0
Schedule: Saddleback, Cypress, Riverside, Southern Idaho, Dixie, Utah Valley
Style of Play: Scrappy and aggressive; emphasis placed on pitching, team defense and offensive execution.

University of Portland

5000 N Willamette Blvd
Portland, OR 97203
Coach: Chris Sperry

NCAA I
Pilots/Navy, Red
Phone: (503) 283-7707
Fax: (503) 283-7242

ACADEMIC

Type: 4 Yr., Private, Coed, Engineering
Founded: 1901
Religion: Roman Catholic
Campus Housing: Yes
Web-site: http://www.uofport.edu/
SAT/ACT/GPA: 1000+
Student/Faculty Ratio: 17:1
Male/Female Ratio: 46:54
Scholarships/Academic: Yes **Athletic:** Yes **Fin Aid:** Yes
Total Expenses by: Year **In State:** $ 21,000 **Out of State:** $ 21,000
Programs of Study: Business and Management, Communications, Education, Engineering, Health Science, Life Science, Social Science

ATHLETIC PROFILE

Conference Affiliation: West Coast Conference
Program Profile: We play on a 1,500 seats stadium on campus. We have full inside facilities with appropriate hitting tunnels for training in inclement weather.
History: Our program started in 1908. The program since its inception has been a regionally strong program, playing a mixture of NCAA Division I program and NAIA program in the Northwest. Since 1992 , the program has upgraded its schedule to predominately NCAA Division I and joined the West Coast Conference in 1996.
Achievements: Coach Terry Pollreisz was the NCAA 1989 District VIII Coach of the Year. PAC Ten North Tournament Champions 1989 and 1991. Rick Falkner and Jason Geis are recent 2nd and 3rd Team All-Americans, Geoff Loomis was named 1992 PAC Ten North Player of the Year.

Western Baptist College

500 Deer Park Drive, SE
Salem, OR 97301
Coach: Paul Gale
NAIA
Warriors/Royal, Gold
Phone: (503) 375-7021
Fax: (503) 315-2947

ACADEMIC

Founded: 1939
Type: 4 Yr., Private, Liberal Arts, Coed
Religion: Independent Baptist
Campus Housing: Yes
Web-site: http://www.wbc.edu
SAT/ACT/GPA: 800
Student/Faculty Ratio: 17:1
Male/Female Ratio: 1:2
Undergraduate Enrollment: 5,720
Graduate Enrollment: None
Scholarships/Academic: Yes **Athletic:** Yes **Fin Aid:** Yes
Total Expenses by: Year **In State:** $ 17,570 **Out of State:** $ 17,000
Degrees Conferred: AA, BA, BS
Programs of Study: Accounting, Bible Studies, Community Services, Education, Elementary Education, English, Family Studies, Finance, Humanities, Human Performances, Interdisciplinary Studies, Liberal Arts, Management and Communications, Mathematics, Minitries, Music, Prelaw

ATHLETIC PROFILE

Conference Affiliation: Cascade Collegiate Conference

Western Oregon University

NPE Building
Monmouth, OR 97361
Coach: Terry Baumgartner
Email: baumgartner@fsa.wou.edu
NCAA II/NAIA
Wolves/Red, Grey
Phone: (503) 838-8448
Fax: (503) 838-8370

ACADEMIC

Founded: 1856
Type: 4 Yr., Public, Liberal Arts, Coed
Religion: Non-Affiliated
Campus Housing: No

Web-site: Not Available
SAT/ACT/GPA: 750
Student/Faculty Ratio: 20:1
Male/Female Ratio: 40:60
Undergraduate Enrollment: 3,800
Graduate Enrollment: 200
Scholarships/Academic: No **Athletic:** No **Fin Aid:** Yes
Total Expenses by: Year **In State:** $ 7,200 **Out of State:** $ 12,150
Degrees Conferred: AA, BA, BS, MA, MS, MED
Programs of Study: Biological, Business, Chemistry, Computer, Corrections, Economics, Education, English, Fine Arts, Fire Services, Geography, History, Humanities, Interdisciplinary Studies, International Business, Languages, Law, Mathematics, Music, Natural Science, Physical Science, Physical Education, Political Scinece, Psychology, Public Affairs, Science, Social Science

ATHLETIC PROFILE

Estimated Number of Baseball Scholarships: 2
Conference Affiliation: Cascade Conference
Program Profile: Our field is natural grass with a seating capacity of 500. We have two outdoor and indoor batting cages. We do 5 weeks practice in the Fall and 56 games in the Spring. We start playing in February and end in May. Our program is very competitive.
History: Our program began in 1924. It has a great history of winning and is one of the strongest programs in Pacific Northwest and West Coast. We have had 6 straight winning seasons and 6 straight post-season berths.
Achievements: Won Conference Titles in 1995, finished Runner-Up in 1996-1998; Coach of the Year in 1995; 26 players have gone on the pro's; 13 in the 1990's.
Coaching: Terry Baumgartner, Head Coach, started with the program in 1995 with an overall record of 115-74. He was named All-District performer as a pitcher in 1989, 1991 and 1992 at Western Oregon. He was Coach of the Year. Brooke Knight and Garrett Alford - Assistant Coaches.
Roster for 1998 team/In State: 26 **Out of State:** 1 **Out of Country:** 1
Total Number of Varsity/Jr. Varsity: 0 **Percent of Graduation:** 98%
Positions Needed for 1999/2000: Pitcher, Catcher, 3rd Base, 1st Base, Outfielder
Most Recent Record: 32-19-0
Schedule: Lewis and Clark State, Albertson, Oregon State University, Chico State, Willamette
Style of Play: Sound defense, aggressive on the bases, aggressive on the mound. Play hard and get dirty.

Willamette University

900 State Street
Salem, OR 97301
Coach: David Wong
Email: dwong@willamette.edu
NCAA III
Bearcats/Cardinal, Old Gold
Phone: (503) 370-6011
Fax: (503) 370-6379

ACADEMIC

Founded: 1842
Type: 4 Yr., Private, Liberal Arts, Coed
Religion: Methodist
Campus Housing: Yes
Web-site: http://www.willamette.edu/
SAT/ACT/GPA: 1250/27/3.8
Student/Faculty Ratio: 13:1
Male/Female Ratio: 40:60
Undergraduate Enrollment: 1,700
Graduate Enrollment: 700
Scholarships/Academic: Yes **Athletic:** No **Fin Aid:** Yes
Total Expenses by: Year **In State:** $ 28,000 **Out of State:** $ 28,000
Degrees Conferred: BA, BS, BM
Programs of Study: American Studies, Art, Biology, Business Administration, Economics, Chemistry, Comparative Literature, Computer Science, English, Environmental Science, French, German, History, Humanities, International Studies, Japanese Studies, Math, Music, Philosophy, Physics, Psychology, Religion Studies, Media Studies, Spanish, Theatre

ATHLETIC PROFILE

Conference Affiliation: Northwest Conference

Program Profile: We have great facilities. The stadium has a seating capacity 1,200. There are covered dug-outs and two batting cages. The season runs March 1 to May 14. Turf is natural grass and the field includes a tarp. We are rarely rained out at home.

History: Our program officially began in 1925 with a formation of Northwest Conference. WU has won 10 Conference Titles and several Bearcats have made it in professionall baseball, the latest being Tony Barron of the Phillies.

Achievements: 3 players have signed pro contracts in 1990's; 10 Conference Titles.

Coaching: David Wong, Head Coach, compiled a record 175-132-3 late in his 8th season. He was an All-American football player at Willamette before playing 5 seasons of minor league baseball. His first season was in 1991. Tom Bush, John Horner and Jeff Sigado - Assistant Coaches.

Roster for 1998 team/In State: 18 **Out of State:** 10 **Out of Country:** 0

Total Number of Varsity/Jr. Varsity: 28 **Percent of Graduation:** 1005

Number of Seniors on 1998 Team: 5 **Number of Sophomores on 1998 Team:**

Freshmen Receiving Fin Aid/Athletic: 0 **Academic:** 8

Most Recent Record: 27 - 7 - 0 **Number of Spring Games:** 41

Positions Needed for 1999/2000: Pitchers

Schedule: Portland, Oregon State, Lewis-Clark State, Chico State, Linfield, George Fox

Style of Play: Solid pitching, solid defense, ability to execute offensively in situations like hit and run and moving runners over.

PENNSYLVANIA

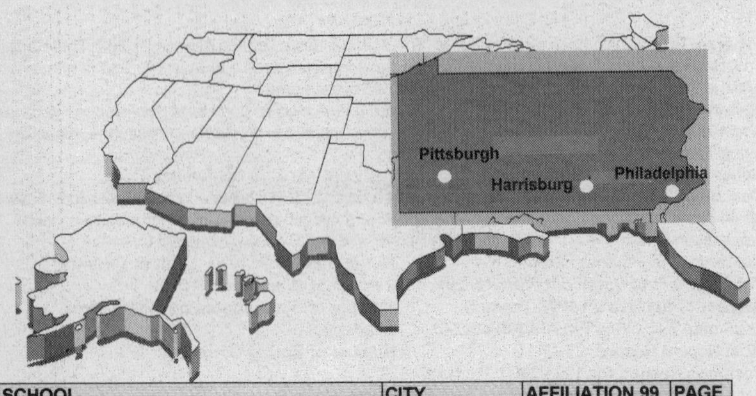

SCHOOL	CITY	AFFILIATION 99	PAGE
Albright College	Reading	NCAA III	712
Alleghany College	Meadville	NCAA III	712
Allentown College St. Francis De Sales	Center Valley	NCAA III	713
Alvernia College	Reading	NCAA III	714
Beaver College	Glenside	NCAA III	715
Bloomsburg University	Bloomsburg	NCAA II	715
Bucknell University	Lewisburg	NCAA I	716
Bucks County Community College	Newton	NJCAA	716
Butler County Community College	Butler	NJCAA	717
California University - Pennsylvania	California	NCAA II	717
Clarion University	Clarion	NCAA II	718
College Misericordia	Dallas	NCAA III	718
Community College of Allegheny C - Allegheny	Pittsburgh	NJCAA	719
Community College of Allegheny C - South	West Mifflin	NJCAA	719
Delaware County Community College	Media	NJCAA	720
Delaware Valley College	Doylestown	NCAA III	720
Dickinson College	Carlisle	NCAA III	721
Drexel University	Philadelphia	NCAA I	721
Duquesne University	Pittsburgh	NCAA I	722
East Stroudsburg University	East	NCAA II	723
Eastern College	St. David	NCAA III	723
Edinboro University	Edinboro	NCAA II	724
Elizabethtown College	Elizabethtown	NCAA III	724
Franklin and Marshall College	Lancaster	NCAA III	725
Gannon University	Erie	NCAA II	725
Geneva College	Beaver Falls	NAIA	726
Gettysburg College	Gettysburg	NCAA III	726
Grove City College	Grove City	NCAA III	727
Haverford College	Haverford	NCAA III	728
Indiana University - Pennsylvania	Indiana	NCAA II	728
Juniata College	Huntingdon	NCAA III	729
Keystone College	LaPlume	NJCAA	729
King's College - Pennsylvania	Wilkes-Barre	NCAA III	730
Kutztown University	Kutztown	NCAA II	731
La Roche College	Pittsburgh	NCAA III	731
La Salle University	Philadelphia	NCAA I	732
Lackawanna Junior College	Scranton	NJCAA	732
Lafayette College	Easton	NCAA I	733
Lebanon Valley College	Annville	NCAA III	734
Lehigh University	Bethlehem	NCAA I	734
Lincoln University - Pennsylvania	Lincoln	NCAA III	735
Lock Haven University	Lock Haven	NCAA II	735
Luzerne County Community College	Nanticoke	NJCAA	736
Mansfield University	Mansfield	NCAA II	737
Marywood College	Scranton	NCAA III	737

SCHOOL	CITY	AFFILIATION 99	PAGE
Mercyhurst College	Erie	NCAA II	738
Messiah College	Gratham	NCAA III	738
Millersville University - Pennsylvania	Millersville	NCAA II	739
Moravian College	Bethlehem	NCAA III	740
Muhlenberg College	Allentown	NCAA III	740
Neumann College	Aston	NCAA III	741
Pennsylvania State University	University Park	NCAA I	742
PA State University - Beaver Campus	Monaca	NJCAA	742
Pennsylvania State University - Behrend	Erie	NCAA III	743
Phila College of Pharmacy & Science	Philadelphia	NAIA	743
Phila College Textiles/Science	Philadelphia	NCAA II	744
Point Park College	Pittsburgh	NAIA	744
Saint Joseph's University	Phila	NCAA I	745
Saint Vincent College	Latrobe	NAIA	746
Shippensburg University	Shippensburg	NCAA II	746
Slippery Rock University	Slippery Rock	NCAA II	747
Susquehanna University	Sellinsgrove	NCAA III	747
Swarthmore College	Swarthmore	NCAA III	748
Temple University	Philadelphia	NCAA I	748
Thiel College	Greenville	NCAA III	749
University of Pennsylvania	Philadelphia	NCAA I	749
University of Pittsburgh	Pittsburgh	NCAA I	750
University of Pittsburg, The - Johnstown	Johnstown	NCAA II	751
University of Scranton	Scranton	NCAA III	751
Ursinus College	Collegeville	NCAA III	752
Villanova University	Villanova	NCAA I	752
Washington and Jefferson College	Washington	NCAA III	753
Waynesburg College	Waynesburg	NCAA III	753
West Chester University	West Chester	NCAA II	754
Westminster College	New Wilmington	NCAA II	755
Westmoreland County Community College	Youngwood	NJCAA	755
Widener University	Chester	NCAA III	755
Wilkes University	Wilkes - Barre	NCAA III	756
York College- Pennsylvania	York	NCAA III	757

Albright College

13th and Bern Streets
Reading, PA 19612
Coach: Jeff Feiler

NCAA III
Lions/Cardinal, White
Phone: (610) 921-7828
Fax: (610) 921-7566

ACADEMIC

Founded: 1856
Type: 4 Yr., Private, Liberal Arts, Coed
Religion: Methodist
Campus Housing: Yes
Web-site: http://www.albright.edu
SAT/ACT/GPA: None
Student/Faculty Ratio: 12:1
Male/Female Ratio: 48:52
Undergraduate Enrollment: 1,100
Graduate Enrollment: None
Scholarships/Academic: Yes **Athletic:** No **Fin Aid:** Yes
Total Expenses by: Year **In State:** $ 24,502 **Out of State:** $ 20,000
Degrees Conferred: BA, BS
Programs of Study: Accounting, Biology, Business, Chemistry, Computers, Economics, Education, Education, English, Environmental, Family Studies, Fine Arts, French, German, History, Management, Marketing, Math, Medical, Nutrition, Philosophy, Physics, Political Science

ATHLETIC PROFILE

Conference Affiliation: Middle Atlantic Conference
Program Profile: Games are played on campus at Kelchner Field , a natural grass field. We play from February through May and have a 5 or 6 Fall program. We have excellent indoor facilities available in the school life sports center.
History: We began in 1895. The 1897 team went unbeaten (7-0). The 1913 team won 12 in a row (18-3). The 1927 team went 10-0. The 1959, 1967 and 1996 teams won MAC league titles. Under fourth-year Head Coach Stan Hyman, the 1994 team set 27 school records. In 1995 ,we won a ECAC Southern Championship. The 1996 team captured its first MAC Commonwealth League title in nearly 30 years. Hyman was named Coach of the Year in 1996.
Achievements: MAC Commonwealth League Champions in 1996 and 1998. Ranked as high as 10th in the Division III Poll in 1994, 19th in 1996. Last season (1996) tied defending national champions William Paterson 16-16 prior to Pioneer's winning 23 straight en route to the title. In Hyman's tenure, Lions have posted a 70-38-1 record, including three consecutive 20-wins seasons and two straight post-season titles. Pitching staff has ranked in the Top 10 three times in the last four years. The 1995 staff finished fifth overall in ERA. All-MAC centerfield Mark Hilyard signed pro contract after the 1996 season.
Coaching: Jeff Feiler, Head Coach, entered his 1st year with the program. He graduated from Wake Forest in 1992 where he ws a 3 -time letter winner. Kurt Krebs, Assistant Coach, entered his 1st year with the program. He graduated from Albright College in 1998 where he was a four-time letter winner.
Roster for 1998 team/In State: 23 **Out of State:** 12 **Out of Country:** 0
Total Number of Varsity/Jr. Varsity: 35 **Percent of Graduation:** 90%
Number of Seniors on 1998 Team: 3 **Most Recent Record:** 27 - 13 - 0
Freshmen Receiving Fin Aid/Athletic: 0 **Academic:** 4
Number of Fall Games: 9 **Number of Spring Games:** 36
Positions Needed for 1999/2000: Pitcher, 3rd Base, Shorstop
Schedule: Montclair State, College of New Jersey, Delaware Valley, Rowan, Kean, Kutztown
Style of Play: Emphasis on pitching and defense with an aggressive approval to both hitting base running.

Alleghany College

P.O. Box 34
Meadville, PA 16335
Coach: Mike Ferris

NCAA III
Gators/Navy, Gold
Phone: (814) 332-2830
Fax: (814) 337-1217

ACADEMIC

Founded: 1815
Religion: Methodist
Web-site: http://www.alleg.edu/
Student/Faculty Ratio: 12:1
Undergraduate Enrollment: 1,800
Scholarships/Academic: Yes **Athletic:** No
Total Expenses by: Year **In State:** $ 24,080
Degrees Conferred: BS, BA
Type: 4 Yr., Private, Liberal Arts, Coed
Campus Housing: Yes
SAT/ACT/GPA: 540-640/22-27
Male/Female Ratio: 50:50
Graduate Enrollment: None
Fin Aid: Yes
Out of State: $ 24,080
Programs of Study: Art, Biology, Chemistry, Computer Science, Classics, Communication Arts, Economics, English, Environmental Science, Geology, History, International Studies, Mathematics, Modern Languages, Music, Philosophy, Physics, Political Science, Psychology, Religious Studies, Sociology/Anthropology, Women's Studies

ATHLETIC PROFILE

Conference Affiliation: North Coast Athletic Conference
Program Profile: We are one of the top outdoor facilities in Pennsylvania. It has natural grass, an enclosed playing area, an artificial turf batting tunnel and bullpen catching areas. There is a full infield tarp, a digital scoreboard, a press box and an infield underground watering system. We have a Fall program, a Spring trip to Fort Myers, Florida and an off-season weightlifting program. We have a JV program.
Achievements: 1996 Championhip game of NCAA Regional participants; 2 players named to the All-Americans; Pitcher Matt Perry drafted in 26th round by the Chicago Cubs; 7 players signed pro contracts in the last 10 years.
Coaching: Mike Ferris, Head Coach, was the former assistant coach for three years.

Allentown College St. Francis De Sales

2755 Station Avenue
Center Valley, PA 18034
Coach: Tim Neiman
NCAA III
Centaurs/Navy Blue, Scarlet
Phone: (610) 282-1100
Fax: (610) 282-2279

ACADEMIC

Founded: 1964
Religion: Catholic
Web-site: http://www.allencol.edu/
Student/Faculty Ratio: 15:1
Undergraduate Enrollment: 1,100
Scholarships/Academic: Yes **Athletic:** No
Total Expenses by: Year **In State:** $ 17,720
Degrees Conferred: BA, BS, Master's
Type: 4 Yr., Private, Liberal Arts, Coed
Campus Housing: Yes
SAT/ACT/GPA: 1080
Male/Female Ratio: 50:50
Graduate Enrollment: 1,200
Fin Aid: Yes
Out of State: $ 17,720
Programs of Study: Biology, Communications, Chemistry, Criminal Justice, Dance, English, Environmental Studies, History, Liberal Studies, History, Management, Politics, Philosophy, Social Work, Spanish, Television and Film, Theatre, Theology, Accounting, Computer Science, Finance, Marketing, Mathematics, Nursing, Physician Assistant, Psychology, Sport Management

ATHLETIC PROFILE

Conference Affiliation: Middle Atlantic States Collegiate Athletic Conference
Program Profile: Allentown College offers a highly competitive, nationally ranked Division III baseball program. The Centaurs' home field, located on campus, consists of a field with major league dimensions, two outdoor batting cages and a multi-million dollar year-round practice facility.
History: The Allentown College baseball program began in 1969 and has grown into a regional power house. The Centaurs became 1998 MAC Champions in their 1st year in the conference and made their first NCAA Tournament Appearance in 1997 after winning the ECAC South Region Championship.

Achievements: In 1998, Coach Neiman became our all-time winningest coach as he notched his 200th victory and earned Coach of the Year honors in the MAC Freedom League. The Centaurs won two straight PAC Titles in 1996 and 1997. Five players have gone on to play professionally, including All-American Brian Manning.
Coaching: Tim Neiman, Head Coach, took over the Centaur program in 1990 and has a 210-100-1 record.. Sean Irey, Assistant Coach, was a four-year varsity letter winner at University of Connecticut where he was selected to the All-Big East Conference Team as a sophomore.
Roster for 1998 team/In State: 20 **Out of State:** 6 **Out of Country:** 0
Total Number of Varsity/Jr. Varsity: 40 **Percent of Graduation:** 100%
Number of Seniors on 1998 Team: 5 **Most Recent Record:** 26 - 9 - 1
Freshmen Receiving Fin Aid/Athletic: 0 **Academic:** 10
Number of Fall Games: 9 **Number of Spring Games:** 36
Positions Needed for 1999/2000: Pitcher, Outfielder, Shortstop
Baseball Camp Dates: 6/22-26; 6/29-7/3
Schedule: Montclair State University, Rowan University, University of Massachusetts-Darmouth, Chapman College, Wisconsin-Lacrosse, York College
Style of Play: The Centaurs' style of play consists of aggressive base running, solid defense and good pitching.

Alvernia College

400 St. Bernadine Street
Reading, PA 19607
Coach: Yogi Lutz

NCAA III
Crusaders/Maroon, Gold
Phone: (610) 796-8315
Fax: (610) 796-8349

ACADEMIC

Founded: 1958 **Type:** 4 Yr., Private, Coed
Religion: Catholic **Campus Housing:** Yes
Web-site: http://www.alvernia.edu **SAT/ACT/GPA:** None
Student/Faculty Ratio: 11:1 **Male/Female Ratio:** 30:70
Undergraduate Enrollment: 800 **Graduate Enrollment:** 0
Scholarships/Academic: Yes **Athletic:** No **Fin Aid:** Yes
Total Expenses by: Year **In State:** $ 15,500 **Out of State:** $ 15,500
Degrees Conferred: BA, BS, BSN, Associate in Science
Programs of Study: Accounting, Addictions Studies, Banking/Finance, Biological, Business, Chemistry, Communications, Computer, Criminal Justice, Education, English, Health, History, Math, Medical, Nursing, Optometry, Philosophy, Political Science, Preprofessional Programs, Psychology, Religion, Science, Secondary Education, Social Science, Spanish, Theology

ATHLETIC PROFILE

Conference Affiliation: Pennsylvania Athletic, Eastern College Athletic Conference
Program Profile: We do a NCAA 45-game schedule (36 Spring, 9 Fall) which runs from the 1st week of March to the middle of May. Included in the Spring schedule is a 9-day, 10-game Florida trip. Home games are played on campus at Crusader Field. Our field surface is natural grass.
History: NCAA Division III play began in 1994. 1996 will mark the 14th year of Crusader baseball. Our 1995 team qualified as the 4th seed in the Division III regional tournament.
Achievements: 1993-1995 PAC Champions; finished 6th in 1995 Regional Tournament; Paul Yoder was named Palyer of the Year in the ECAC; Paul Yoder was drafted and signed by the New York Mets in the 26th round.
Coaching: Yogi Lutz, Head Coach, was a two-time PAC Coach of the Year in 1993 and 1995. He won his 200th game in 1995.
Style of Play: Fundamental, power baseball.

Beaver College

450 South Easton Road
Glenside, PA 19038
Coach: Stan Exeter

NCAA III
Knights/Scarlet, Grey
Phone: (215) 572-2194
Fax: (215) 572-2159

ACADEMIC

Founded: 1853
Type: 4 Yr., Private, Liberal Arts, Coed
Religion: Presbyterian
Campus Housing: Yes
Web-site: http://www.beaver.ed/
SAT/ACT/GPA: None
Student/Faculty Ratio: 13:1
Male/Female Ratio: 30:70
Undergraduate Enrollment: 1,200
Graduate Enrollment: 1,090
Scholarships/Academic: Yes **Athletic:** No **Fin Aid:** Yes
Total Expenses by: Year **In State:** $ 20,990 **Out of State:** $ 20,990
Degrees Conferred: BA, BS, BFA
Programs of Study: Accounting, Art, Art Education, Fine Arts, Biology, Busines Administration, Management, Marketing, Chemistry, Communications, Computer Science, Education, Mathematics, Engineering, Optometry, Philosophy, Physical Therapy, Political Science

ATHLETIC PROFILE

Conference Affiliation: Keystone, PAC

Bloomsburg University

Nelson Fieldhouse
Bloomsburg, PA 17815
Coach: Matt Haney

NCAA II
Huskies/Maroon, Gold
Phone: (570) 389-4375
Fax: (570) 389-2099

ACADEMIC

Founded: 1839
Type: 4 Yr., Public, Coed
Religion: Non-Affiliated
Campus Housing: Yes
Web-site: http://www.bloomu.edu/
SAT/ACT/GPA: 900
Student/Faculty Ratio: 18:1
Male/Female Ratio: 1:4
Undergraduate Enrollment: 6,300
Graduate Enrollment: 1,500
Scholarships/Academic: Yes **Athletic:** Yes **Fin Aid:** Yes
Total Expenses by: Year **In State:** $ 3,790 **Out of State:** $ 6,380
Degrees Conferred: BA, BS, BSEd, BSN, BSOA, MA, MS, MBA
Programs of Study: Accounting, Adult Health, Anthropology, Applied Music, Art History, Art Studio, Biology, Business Administration, Business Economics, Chemistry, Computer Information System, Computer Science, Early Childhood Education, Earth Science, Economics, Elementary Education, Engineering and Liberal Arts, English, Finance, Geology, German, History, Humanities, Management, Marketing, Mathematics, Nursing, Political Science, Social Science, Sociology

ATHLETIC PROFILE

Conference Affiliation: Pennsylavania State Athletic Conference
Program Profile: We have a natural grass field with grass base paths and measurements of LF line 330, LC 364, Center 375, RC 353 and RF line 340. Season: Our Fall season goes from September to the 2nd week of October & Spring season goes from the end of February to the 2nd week of May..
History: Our program dates back to 1934 . No records were kept prior to 1934. A 586-504-5 overall record was recorded. We made a first World Series appearance in 1995 in Div. II (Montgomery). We were 9th in the final poll in 1995 with a 37-21 overall record.

Bucknell University

Baseball Office
Lewisburg, PA 17837
Coach: Gene Depew
Email: depew@bucknell.edu

NCAA I
Bisons/Navy, Orange
Phone: (717) 524-1232
Fax: (717) 524-1660

ACADEMIC

Type: 4 Yr., Private, Liberal Arts, Coed, Engineering
Religion: Non-Affiliated
Web-site: http://www.bucknell.edu/
Student/Faculty Ratio: 23:1
Undergraduate Enrollment: 3,300
Scholarships/Academic: No **Athletic:** No
Total Expenses by: Year **In State:** $ 26,000

Founded: 1846
Campus Housing: Guaranted
SAT/ACT/GPA: 3300
Male/Female Ratio: 51:49
Graduate Enrollment: None
Fin Aid: Yes
Out of State: $ 26,000

Degrees Conferred: BA, BS, MA, MS
Programs of Study: Accounting, Animal, Anthropology, Art, Biochemistry, Biology, Business and Management, Computer, Environmental, Engineering, Religion, Social Sciences, Statitics, Theatre, Women's Studies

ATHLETIC PROFILE

Conference Affiliation: Patriot League Conference
Program Profile: The Fall program consists of six weeks while the Spring program consists of 16 weeks. We take a trip to Florida. We have excellent indoor facilities and a 1st class natural grass playing field.
History: Our baseball program started in the late 1800's. Christy Mathewson played here.
Achievements: League Champions in 1996; East Regional/NCAA Tournament in 1996; Patriot League Coach of the Year in 1993 and 1996; Andy Nezelek drafted in the 5th round in 1989 by the Atlanta Braves.
Coaching: Gene Depew, Head Coach, begins his 17th season as the Bison's head coach and is just the 4th coach since World War II. He is a 1971 Bucknell graduate and won his first Patriot League "Coach of the Year" honor in 1992. Brian Hoyt, Assistant Coach, begins his 6th season as a member of the Bison's coaching staff. He is a 1987 graduate of Bucknelll and spent 4 years on the Bison's squad playing outfield for Coach Depew. Brian Rieddell, Assistant Coach, enters his 1st season. He worked with the Bucknell University pitchers in 1998. He is a 1995 graduate of Shippensburg with a degree in Math.
Roster for 1998 team/In State: 15 **Out of State:** 15 **Out of Country:** 0
Total Number of Varsity/Jr. Varsity: 30 **Percent of Graduation:** 100%
Number of Seniors on 1998 Team: 8 **Number of Sophomores on 1998 Team:** 0
Freshmen Receiving Fin Aid/Athletic: 1 **Academic:** 6
Number of Fall Games: 6 **Number of Spring Games:** 50

Bucks County Community College

Swamp Road
Newton, PA 18940
Coach: Geroge Armstrong

NJCAA
Centurions/Navy, Col. Blue, White
Phone: (215) 968-8450
Fax: (215) 968-8452

ACADEMIC

Founded: 1965
Religion: Non-Affiliated
Student/Faculty Ratio: 17:1
Undergraduate Enrollment: 10,000
Scholarships/Academic: Yes **Athletic:** No
Total Expenses by: Year **In State:** $ 1,600

Type: 2 Yr., Public, Jr. College, Coed
Campus Housing: No
Male/Female Ratio: 1:2
Graduate Enrollment: 0
Fin Aid: Yes
Out of State: $ 2,400

Degrees Conferred: Associate
Programs of Study: Accounting, American Studies, Art/Fine Arts, Biology, Biological Science, Biotechnology, Broadcasting, Business Administration, Commerce, Management, Chemical Engineering Technology, Chemistry, Child Care/Child and Family Studies

ATHLETIC PROFILE

Conference Affiliation: Independent

Butler County Community College

PO Box 1203
Butler, PA 16003
Coach: Tom Roper

NJCAA
Pioneers/Blue, White, Orange
Phone: (724) 287-8711
Fax: (724) 285-6047

ACADEMIC

Founded: 1965
Religion: Non-Affiliated
Student/Faculty Ratio: 24:1
Undergraduate Enrollment: 3,225
Scholarships/Academic: No **Athletic:** No
Total Expenses by: Year **In State:** $ 1,200

Type: 2 Yr., Public, Jr. College, Coed
Campus Housing: No
Male/Female Ratio: 38:62
Graduate Enrollment: 0
Fin Aid: Yes
Out of State: $ 3,500

Degrees Conferred: Associate
Programs of Study: Accounting, Architectural Technology, Biology, Biological Science, Business Administration, Commerce, Management, Civil Engineering Technology, Communications, Computer Information Systems, Computer Programming, Computer Technology, Criminology, Drafting/Design, Meteorology, Nursing, Parks/Recreation, Quality Control Technology, Retail Management

ATHLETIC PROFILE

Conference Affiliation: PCAA

California University - Pennsylvania

250 University Avenue, Box 34
California, PA 15419
Coach: Mike Conte

NCAA II
Vulcans/Scarlet, Black
Phone: (724) 938-5837
Fax: (724) 938-5849

ACADEMIC

Founded: 1847
Religion: Non-Affiliated
Web-site: http://www.cup.edu
Student/Faculty Ratio: 20:1
Undergraduate Enrollment: 5,000
Scholarships/Academic: Yes **Athletic:** Yes
Total Expenses by: Year **In State:** $ 4,450

Type: 4 Yr., Public, Liberal Arts, Coed
Campus Housing: Yes
SAT/ACT/GPA: 910/20/2.5
Male/Female Ratio: 50:50
Graduate Enrollment: 1,000
Fin Aid: Yes
Out of State: $ 7,750

Degrees Conferred: BA, BS, MA, Med
Programs of Study: Liberal Arts, Education, Science and Technology, Human Services

ATHLETIC PROFILE

Conference Affiliation: PSAC
Program Profile: We have Fall evaluation and off-season conditioning. Our 56-game Spring schedule includes a Florida Spring trip. Our field is enclosed by a cyclone fence and its dimensions are: left - 320, Center-410 and Right - 330.

History: We have an excellent baseball tradition and are in the largest Division II conference in the country. We won numerous conference championships and participated in NCAA Regionals twice in the last 10 years.
Achievements: PSAC West Champs in 1977, 1979, 1981, 1983 and 1985; PSAC Runner-Up in 1977, 1981, 1983 and 1990; PSAC State Champs in 1979; NCAA Regional in 1979 and 1983; 9 All-Americans, 26 players drafted into pros.
Coaching: Mike Conte - Head Coach.
Style of Play: Aggressive style of play that is geared to personnel from year to year. Daring brash style.

Clarion University

112 Tippin Gym
Clarion, PA 16214
Coach: Rich Herman

NCAA II
Golden Eagles/Blue, Gold
Phone: (814) 226-1997
Fax: (814) 226-2082

ACADEMIC

Founded: 1867
Type: 4 Yr., Public, Coed
Religion: Non-Affiliated
Campus Housing: Yes
Web-site: http://www.clarion.edu
SAT/ACT/GPA: 850/2.0
Student/Faculty Ratio: 17:1
Male/Female Ratio:
Undergraduate Enrollment: 6,000
Graduate Enrollment: None
Scholarships/Academic: Yes **Athletic:** Yes **Fin Aid:** Yes
Total Expenses by: Year **In State:** $ 7,789 **Out of State:** $ 13,145
Degrees Conferred: Bachelors, Masters
Programs of Study: Computer Science, Rehab Sciences, Accounting, Biology, Education, Marketing, Economics, Political Science, Chemistry, Math, French, Philosophy, Art, Theatre, General Studies, Music, Communications, History, Physics, Real Estate, Psychology

ATHLETIC PROFILE

Conference Affiliation: PSAC

College Misericordia

301 Lake Street
Dallas, PA 18612
Coach: Charles Edkens
Email: cedkins@miseri.edu

NCAA III
Cougars/Blue, White, Gold
Phone: (717) 674-6397
Fax: (717) 674-5785

ACADEMIC

Founded: 1924
Type: 4 Yr., Private, Liberal Arts, Coed
Religion: Catholic
Campus Housing: Yes
Web-site: http://www.miseri.edu/
SAT/ACT/GPA: Varies
Student/Faculty Ratio: 14:1
Male/Female Ratio: 35:65
Undergraduate Enrollment: 1,200
Graduate Enrollment: None
Scholarships/Academic: Yes **Athletic:** No **Fin Aid:** Yes
Total Expenses by: Year **In State:** $ 19,480 **Out of State:** $ 19,480
Degrees Conferred: BS, BA, MS
Programs of Study: Accounting, Biology, Business Administration, Computer Science, Early Childhood, Elementary Education, English, History, Humanities, Management, Marketing, Mathematics, Medical Laboratory Technology, Natural Science, Nursing, Physical Therapy, Predentistry, Prelaw, Premed, Social Science

ATHLETIC PROFILE

Conference Affiliation: Pennsylvania Athletic Conference

Program Profile: Diamond Tex Infield is an excellent indoor facility . We are a small competitive Division III school with a strong schedule. We play a Fall as well as Spring season.
History: We are a former NAIA program that has been in Division III for 7 years. We were in one conference finals in 1997 and 1998. Our Southern trip takes us to Cocoa, Florida.
Achievements: 1997 outfielder Jeff Campist All-MIA Atlantic Region and All-ECAC South Region; 1997 Chuck Edkins received Coach of the Year honors in conference.
Coaching: Charles Edkens, Head Coach, has been a full-time head coach for 8 years . He was named Conference Coach of the Year.
Roster for 1998 team/In State: 20 **Out of State:** 8 **Out of Country:** 0
Total Number of Varsity/Jr. Varsity: 29 **Percent of Graduation:** 100%
Number of Seniors on 1998 Team: 5 **Most Recent Record:** 14 - 15 - 0
Freshmen Receiving Fin Aid/Athletic: 0 **Academic:** 8
Number of Fall Games: 10 **Number of Spring Games:** 36
Positions Needed for 1999/2000: Pitcher, Catcher
Schedule: Allentown, Wilkes, Susquehanna, Alvernia, Drew, Wesley
Style of Play: Controlled aggression - put pressure on defense whenever possible.

Community College of Allegheny C - Allegheny

808 Ridge Avenue
Pittsburgh, PA 15212-6097
Coach: Bob Janada

NJCAA
Cougars/Columbia, Black, White
Phone: (412) 237-2563
Fax: (412) 237-4522

ACADEMIC

Type: 2 Yr., Public, Jr. College, Coed
Campus Housing: No
SAT/ACT/GPA: Open
Student/Faculty Ratio: 25:1 **Male/Female Ratio:** 1:1.6
Undergraduate Enrollment: 4,337 **Graduate Enrollment:** None
Scholarships/Academic: Yes **Athletic:** No **Fin Aid:** Yes
Total Expenses by: Year **In State:** $ 1,920 **Out of State:** $ 2,880
Degrees Conferred: AA, AS, AAS
Programs of Study: Accounting, Art, Aviation Administration/Technology, Behavioral Science, Biological Science, Computer, Medical, Humanities, Human, History, Pscyhology, Public, Purchasing/Inventory, Retail, Social Science, Theatre

ATHLETIC PROFILE

Conference Affiliation: Western PA Collegiate, PA Collegiate Athletic Association
Program Profile: We play both Fall and Spring seasons and our facilities are off campus.
History: We began NJCAA regional play in 1983. We have won numerous conference titles and competed at the Division III World Series in 1993.
Achievements: Our athletes achieve all-conference and all-state honors consistently. We have had as many as 3 All-Americans in 1 season! Individual awards include top finishers in hitting averages as well as team hitting averages.

Community College of Allegheny C - South

1750 Clairton Road
West Mifflin, PA 15122
Coach: Kerry Hetrick

NJCAA
Tigers/Black, Gold
Phone: (412) 469-6319
Fax: (412) 469-6371

ACADEMIC

Type: 2 Yr., Public, Jr. College, Coed
Campus Housing: No

Degrees Conferred: Associate
Programs of Study: Contact school for program of study.

Community College of Beaver County
(Program Discontinued)

Delaware County Community College

901 S Media Line Road
Media, PA 19063-1094
Coach: Paul Motta

NJCAA
Phantoms/Blue, Gold
Phone: (610) 359-5047
Fax: (610) 359-5002

ACADEMIC

Founded: 1896
Type: 2 Yr., Private, Jr. College, Coed
Religion: Non-Affiliated
Campus Housing: Yes
Web-site: Not-Available
SAT/ACT/GPA: 770+
Student/Faculty Ratio: 16:1
Male/Female Ratio: 50:50
Undergraduate Enrollment: 1,375
Graduate Enrollment: None
Scholarships/Academic: Yes **Athletic:** No **Fin Aid:** Yes
Total Expenses by: Year **In State:** $ 18,000 **Out of State:** $ 18,000
Degrees Conferred: BA, BS, AS
Programs of Study: Agribusiness, Agriculture, Agronomy and Environmental Science, Animal Science, Biology, Business Administration, Chemistry, Computer Information Systems, Criminal Justice, Horticulture, Life Science, Mathematics, Ornamental, Horticulture

ATHLETIC PROFILE

Conference Affiliation: PCAA

Delaware Valley College

Route 202
Doylestown, PA 18901
Coach: Frank Wolfgang

NCAA III
Aggies/Green, Gold
Phone: (215) 345-1500
Fax: (215) 340-1609

ACADEMIC

Founded: 1896
Type: 4 Yr., Private, Coed
Religion: Non-Affiliated
Campus Housing: Yes
Web-site: http://www.devalcol.edu
SAT/ACT/GPA: 770+
Student/Faculty Ratio: 16:1
Male/Female Ratio: 50:50
Undergraduate Enrollment: 1,375
Graduate Enrollment: None
Scholarships/Academic: Yes **Athletic:** No **Fin Aid:** Yes
Total Expenses by: Year **In State:** $ 18,000 **Out of State:** $ 18,000
Degrees Conferred: BA, BS, AS
Programs of Study: Agribusiness, Agriculture, Agronomy and Environmental Science, Animal Science, Biology, Business Administration, Chemistry, Computer Information Systems, Criminal Justice, Horticulture, Life Science, Mathematics, Ornamental Horticulture

ATHLETIC PROFILE

Conference Affiliation: MAC, ECAC

Dickinson College

Kline Center
Carlisle, PA 17013
Coach: Brad Shover

NCAA III
Red Devils/Red, White
Phone: (717) 245-1652
Fax: (717) 245-1441

ACADEMIC

Founded: 1773
Religion: United Methodist
Web-site: http://www.dickinson.edu/
Student/Faculty Ratio: 10:1
Undergraduate Enrollment: 1,950
Scholarships/Academic: Yes **Athletic:** No
Total Expenses by: Year **In State:** $ 26,260
Degrees Conferred: BA, BS

Type: 4 Yr., Private, Liberal Arts, Coed
Campus Housing: Yes
SAT/ACT/GPA: Not Required
Male/Female Ratio: Unknown
Graduate Enrollment: None
Fin Aid: Yes
Out of State: $ 26,260

Programs of Study: 31 majors including American Studies, Anthropology, Asian Studies, Biology, Chemistry, Computer Science, Dramatic Arts, Economics, English, Fine Arts, Foreign Languages, French, Geology, German, Greek, History, Humanities, International Studies, Latin, Mathematics, Music, Natural Sciences, Philosophy, Physics, Political Science, Psychology, Religion, Russian, Russian and Soviet Area Studies, Social Sciences, Spanish

ATHLETIC PROFILE

Conference Affiliation: MAC, ECAC
Coaching: Brad Shover, Head Coach, is a former minor league franchise owner.
Style of Play: We like to play an aggressive game. We are not a power-hittng team. We play for one run at a time. We need to play a good defense to be successful.

Drexel University

314 Chestnut Sts.
Philadelphia, PA 19104
Coach: Don Maines
Email: maines@post.drexel.edu

NCAA I
Dragons/Navy Blue, Gold
Phone: (215) 895-1782
Fax: (215) 895-2037

ACADEMIC

Founded: 1891
Religion: Non-Affiliated
Web-site: http://www.drexel.edu/
Student/Faculty Ratio: 13:1
Undergraduate Enrollment: 5,300
Scholarships/Academic: Yes **Athletic:** Yes
Total Expenses by: Year **In State:** $ 25,000
Degrees Conferred: Bachelors, Masters, Doctoral

Type: 4 Yr., Private, Coed
Campus Housing: None
SAT/ACT/GPA: Varies
Male/Female Ratio: 65:35
Graduate Enrollment: 2,900
Fin Aid: Yes
Out of State: $ 25,000

Programs of Study: Accounting, Architecture, Atmospheric Sciences, Biology, Business and Management, Chemistry, Communications, Computer Information Systems, Computer Science, Construction Management, Economics, Education, Engineering, Environmental Science, Graphic Art, Humanities, Interior Design, International Business, Literature, Management Information System, Marketing, Mathematics, Music, Natural Science, Nutrition, Operation Research, Philosophy, Photography, Physical Science, Physics, Political Science, Prevet, Psychology, Science, Science Education, Social Science, Sociology, Technical Writing

ATHLETIC PROFILE

Estimated Number of Baseball Scholarships: 5.5
Conference Affiliation: America East Conference

Program Profile: Drexel Field has measurements of 340 to right, 390 to right center field, 408-center field, 375 left center field & 330 to the left. It has a natural grass surface with a capacity of 1,000.
History: Began Division I in 1974; Liberty Bell Classics Champion in 1993.
Achievements: 1995 Freshmen All-American 2nd base Dennis Helrowski, 1996 Freshman All-American catcher Lou Marchetti, 1998 Freshman All-American left handed pitcher Bruce Boehm.
Coaching: Don Maines, Head Coach, began coaching the program in 1990. He graduated from East Stroudsburg in 1982. He compiled a record of 186-229-3. Darren Maines - Assistant Coach. Chris Caknan - Assistant Coach.
Roster for 1998 team/In State: 8 **Out of State:** 18 **Out of Country:** 1
Total Number of Varsity/Jr. Varsity: 27 **Percent of Graduation:** 90%
Number of Seniors on 1998 Team: 3 **Number of Sophomores on 1998 Team:** 10
Freshmen Receiving Fin Aid/Athletic: 22 **Academic:** 15
Most Recent Record: 17 - 32 - 1 **Number of Spring Games:** 56
Positions Needed for 1999/2000: Catcher, Pitcher
Baseball Camp Dates: December 28th - 31
Schedule: Oklahoma, Delaware, Virginia Commonwealth, Marist, Villanova, Florida International
Style of Play: Aggressive style, hard-nosed play.

Duquesne University

600 Forbes Avenue
Pittsburgh, PA 15282-1010
Coach: Mike Wilson
Email: duathletics@dug.edu

NCAA I
Dukes/Red, White, Royal Blue
Phone: (412) 396-6565
Fax: (412) 396-4746

ACADEMIC

Founded: 1878 **Type:** 4 Yr., Private, Coed
Religion: Catholic **Campus Housing:** Yes
Web-site: http://www.duq.edu/ **SAT/ACT/GPA:** 1091/24/3.47
Student/Faculty Ratio: 16:1 **Male/Female Ratio:** 49:51
Undergraduate Enrollment: 5,572 **Graduate Enrollment:** 3,928
Scholarships/Academic: Yes **Athletic:** Yes **Fin Aid:** Yes
Total Expenses by: Year **In State:** $ 22,275 **Out of State:** $ 22,275
Degrees Conferred: BA, BS, MA, MS, MPT, MSLP, PhD
Programs of Study: There are nine schools with over 65 areas of study included are Liberal Arts, Natural and Environmental Science, Law, Business and Administration, Pharmacy, Music, Education

ATHLETIC PROFILE

Conference Affiliation: Atlantic 10 Conference
Program Profile: The Dukes enjoy an all natural 2 year old playing facility. It has 2 astro turf practice fields and an indoor 65x65 yard astro turf practice facility. Our schedule includes 56 games and we take a Southern trip from first week in March to the third week. We play in the Atlantic 10. The Dukes played MEAC for the rights to go to the NCAA Regionals.
History: The Duquesne program started in 1957 under "Doc" Skender. Mike Wilson is the 3rd head coach for the Dukes. Mike has moved the Dukes up to the 149 spot in the NCAA RPI rankings. The Dukes have quickly moved to the top conference schedule that includes teams from the SEC, Big East, MAC and TAAC.
Achievements: Past achievements include: 1st team All-Conference players Jeff Rojik in 1997; BJ Barns in 1997 and Jeff Rojik in 1994, Louisville Slugger Freshmen All-American; BJ Barns in 1997 and Easton reflex Defense Award Runner-Up; Bryan Cornell in 1997.
Coaching: Mike Wilson, Head Coach, entered his 6th year as a head coach. He was an assistant coach at Pitt for one year. He compiled a record of 66-132 since 1994. His conference record is 30-44. He was first team NAIA shortstop at Chadron State. He is a graduate of Umpire Development School. He was Major League Umpire for Gulf Coast and Citrus Leagues. Norm Frey and Jerry Unitas - Assistant Coaches. He is a Western Pennsylvania Sports Hall of Fame member. Joe Hill, Assistant Coach, was former coach for Hays Larks in Kansas Jayhawks League. Jay Stoner - Assistant Coach, former head coach for the Sandusky Bay Stars in the NCAA Sanctioned Great Lakes League.

Roster for 1998 team/In State: 33 **Out of State:** 2 **Out of Country:** 0
Number of Seniors on 1998 Team: 4 **Number of Sophomores on 1998 Team:** 0
Positions Needed for 1999/2000: Pitcher
Schedule: Pittsburgh Pirates, Seton Hall, Northern Iowa, Illinois State, Xavier, Virginia Tech, Kent State, Ohio University, Akron, Penn State
Style of Play: Depends on the abilities of the players we have. We use what we are best at. We do play relentless high percentage baseball with an emotion at all times.

East Stroudsburg University

Baseball Office
East Stroudsburg, PA 18301
Coach: Roger Barren

NCAA II
Warriors/Red, Black
Phone: (717) 422-3263
Fax: (717) 422-3306

ACADEMIC

Founded: 1893
Type: 4 Yr., Public, Liberal Arts, Coed
Religion: Non-Affiliated
Campus Housing: Yes
Web-site: http://www.esu.edu/
SAT/ACT/GPA: 1000
Student/Faculty Ratio: 21:1
Male/Female Ratio: 3:5
Undergraduate Enrollment: 4,800
Graduate Enrollment: 600
Scholarships/Academic: Yes **Athletic:** No **Fin Aid:** Yes
Total Expenses by: Year **In State:** $ 3,900 **Out of State:** $ 5,600
Degrees Conferred: AS, BA, BS, BFA, MA, MS, Med
Programs of Study: Business, Education, Letters/Literature, Life Science, Social Science

ATHLETIC PROFILE

Conference Affiliation: PSAC
Program Profile: We do a 6-week Fall program that includes 8-10 games plus scrimmages. We do 10-day Spring trip to Florida. We play 46-48 Spring games. We have excellent indoor facilities that include a permanent batting cage plus 4 pitching mounds.
Achievements: 4 players signed professionally in recent years, including Joel Bennett in 1991 who is pitching in Red Sox Organization, led all minors in strikeouts in 1993 (221).
Coaching: Roger Barren, Head Coach, is in his 5th year after assisting.He has 15 years coaching experience overall and holds Bachelors and Masters.

Eastern College

10 Fairview Drive
St. David, PA 19087
Coach: Don Hare

NCAA III
Golden Eagles/Maroon, Gold, White
Phone: (610) 341-1735
Fax: (610) 341-1317

ACADEMIC

Founded: 1952
Type: 4 Yr., Private, Liberal Arts, Coed
Religion: Baptist, Christian
Campus Housing: Yes
Web-site: http://www.Eastern.edu
SAT/ACT/GPA: 1050
Student/Faculty Ratio: 12:1
Male/Female Ratio: 36:64
Undergraduate Enrollment: 1,000
Graduate Enrollment: 600
Scholarships/Academic: Yes **Athletic:** No **Fin Aid:** Yes
Total Expenses by: Year **In State:** $ 8,500 **Out of State:** $ 8,500
Degrees Conferred: BA, BS, MA
Programs of Study: Art History, Astronomy, Biblical Studies, Biology, Business Administration, Chemistry, Communications, Elementary Education, Health and Physical Education, History, Mathematics, Medical Technology, Music, Nursing, Philosophy, Political Science, Psychology, Social Work, Sociology

ATHLETIC PROFILE

Conference Affiliation: Pennsylvania Athletic Conference
Program Profile: We a solid NCAA Division III baseball program. We play on one of the finest natural grass fields in the Delaware Valley. We do a competitive schedule with Winter training in Florida.
History: Eastern is celebrating 30 years of quality baseball under the guidance of Skip Hare.
Style of Play: Aggressive offense, stingy defense. Great teaching/experience program.

Edinboro University

McComb Fieldhouse
Edinboro, PA 16444
Coach: John Radovich

NCAA II
Fighting Scots/Red, White
Phone: (814) 732-2776
Fax: (814) 732-2596

ACADEMIC

Founded: 1857
Type: 4 Yr., Public, Liberal Arts, Coed
Web-site: Not Available
SAT/ACT/GPA: 700/17
Student/Faculty Ratio: 19:1
Male/Female Ratio: 43:57
Undergraduate Enrollment: 6,850
Graduate Enrollment: 640
Scholarships/Academic: Yes **Athletic:** Yes **Fin Aid:** Yes
Total Expenses by: Year **In State:** $ 5,900 **Out of State:** $ 10,250
Degrees Conferred: AA, AS, BA, BS, BFA, Ma, MS, MFA, MED
Programs of Study: Accounting, Anthropology, Art, Biology, Business, Chemistry, Communications, Computer, Criminal, Earth Science, Economics, Education, English, Geography, Geology, History, Humanities, Math, Medical, Natural Science, Preprofessional Programs, Psychology, Russian, Special Education, Speech, Social Science

ATHLETIC PROFILE

Conference Affiliation: Pennsylvania State Athletic Conference
Program Profile: We have a tremendous facility for baseball that was completely renovated 4 years ago. We play Fall and Spring schedules with a maximum of 56 games.
History: Our program began in 1966 with a complete turn-around over the last 5 years with the school emphasizing baseball more.
Achievements: Since 1991, numerous All-Conference, All-Region players. 2 players drafted in the last 4 years.
Coaching: John Radovich, Head Coach, has coached for 11 years at the college level. His first 4 were at JC in Pittsburgh. Our staff also includes volunteer assistants.
Style of Play: Very hard, aggressive, running style.

Elizabethtown College

One Alpha Drive
Elizabethtown, PA 17022
Coach: Gary Pritchard

NCAA III
Blue Jays/Blue, Grey
Phone: (717) 361-1137
Fax: (717) 361-1488

ACADEMIC

Founded: 1899
Type: 4 Yr., Private, Liberal Arts, Coed
Religion: Church of Brethren
Campus Housing: Yes
Web-site: http://www.etown.edu/
SAT/ACT/GPA: 1000 +
Student/Faculty Ratio: 14:1
Male/Female Ratio: 1:2
Undergraduate Enrollment: 1,529
Graduate Enrollment: None
Scholarships/Academic: Yes **Athletic:** No **Fin Aid:** Yes
Total Expenses by: Year **In State:** $ 21,580 **Out of State:** $ 21,580

Degrees Conferred: BA, BS
Programs of Study: Accounting, Biochemistry, Biology, Business Administration, Chemical Physics, Chemistry, Chemistry Management, Communications, Computer Engineering, Computer Science, Early Childhood Education, Economics, Education, Engineering, English, Environmental Science, History, Industrial Engineering, International Business, Mathematics, Medical Technology, Modern Languages, Music, Music Education, Music Therapy, Philosophy, Physics, Political Philosophy, Political Science, Mathematics, Social Studies, Social Work, Sociology, Anthropology

ATHLETIC PROFILE

Conference Affiliation: MAC

Franklin and Marshall College

P.O. Box 3003
Lancaster, PA 17604-3003
Coach: Mark Cole

NCAA III
Diplomats/Blue, White
Phone: (717) 339-4530
Fax: (717) 399-4440

ACADEMIC

Founded: 1787
Religion: Non-Affiliated
Web-site: http://www.fandm.edu/
Student/Faculty Ratio: 11:1
Undergraduate Enrollment: 1,800
Scholarships/Academic: Yes **Athletic:** No
Total Expenses by: Year **In State:** $ 27,000
Type: 4 Yr., Private, Liberal Arts, Coed
Campus Housing: Yes
SAT/ACT/GPA: 1200
Male/Female Ratio: 55:45
Graduate Enrollment: None
Fin Aid: Yes
Out of State: $ 27,000
Degrees Conferred: BA, BS
Programs of Study: African Studies, American Studies, Anthropology, Art, Art History, Asian Studies, Astronomy, Biology, Business Administration, Classics Chemistry, Computer Science, Economics, English, Environmental Science, French, Geoscience, German, Government, Music, Hebrew, History, Mathematics, Philosophy, Psychology, Religion, Russian, Sociology, Spanish

ATHLETIC PROFILE

Conference Affiliation: Centennial Conference
Program Profile: We have a competitive program and play Division I, Division II and nationally recognized Division III teams. We have a Fall competition in Columbus, Ohio. We do 2 Southern trips to North Carolina and Florida. Our indoor facility is a 55,000 sq. ft. fieldhouse. Our baseball field has measurements of 320 down the lines with 410 center field.
History: Our team began in 1873. We got MAC affiliation in the 1994 season when the Centennial Conference was instituted. The last 3 years, we were 1st, 2nd and 3rd in the Centennial Conference. In 1996, we ranked as high as 18th in the Division Polls.
Coaching: Mark Cole - Head Coach. Troy Steffy - Assistant Coach. Mark Hrcumman - Assistant Coach. Jon Robbins - Assistant Coach.
Style of Play: Aggressive style of play that includes creating opportunities and making the most of the opponents. Fundamentals are stressed, taught and expected.

Gannon University

University Square
Erie, PA 16541
Coach: Chris Jones

NCAA II
Knights/Maroon, Gold
Phone: (814) 871-7416
Fax: (814) 871-7794

ACADEMIC

Founded: 1925
Religion: Roman Catholic
Type: 4 Yr., Private, Liberal Arts, Coed
Campus Housing: Yes

Web-site: http://www.gannon.edu/
SAT/ACT/GPA: 900+
Student/Faculty Ratio: 15:1
Male/Female Ratio: 49:51
Undergraduate Enrollment: 4,000
Graduate Enrollment: 500
Scholarships/Academic: Yes **Athletic:** Yes **Fin Aid:** Yes
Total Expenses by: Year **In State:** $ 17,000 **Out of State:** $ 17,000
Degrees Conferred: Associates, BS, Masters, Preprofessional
Programs of Study: Offers 62 Bachelors degrees, 10 Preprofessional Programs, 11 Associates degrees, 16 Masters degrees through five academic areas: Business Administration, Education, Health Sciences, Humanities and Science, Engineering. The programs include: Accounting, Business, Economics, Finance, Industrial Distribution, International Business, Management, Marketing, Anthropology, Arts and Humanities, Communications, Criminal Justice, English, Languages, History, Human Services, Liberal Arts, Mental Health, Premed, Predentistry, Prepharmacy, Preoptometry, Prevet Medicine, Science, Early Childhood, Elementary/Second Education, Nursing, Medical, Dietetics, Special Education, Mortuary Science, Paralegal, Philosophy

ATHLETIC PROFILE

Conference Affiliation: ECAC

Geneva College

3200 College Avenue
Beaver Falls, PA 15010
Coach: Alan Sumner
NAIA
Tornadoes/White, Gold
Phone: (724) 847-6650
Fax: (724) 847-5001

ACADEMIC

Founded: 1848
Type: 4 Yr., Private, Coed
Religion: Christian
Campus Housing: Yes
Web-site: http://www.geneva.edu/
SAT/ACT/GPA: 21
Student/Faculty Ratio: 18:1
Male/Female Ratio: 45:55
Undergraduate Enrollment: 1,500
Graduate Enrollment: 70
Scholarships/Academic: Yes **Athletic:** Yes **Fin Aid:** Yes
Total Expenses by: Year **In State:** $ 16,284 **Out of State:** $ 16,284
Degrees Conferred: AS, BA, BS, MA
Programs of Study: Accounting, Applied Mathematics, Bible Studies, Biology, Broadcasting, Business Administration, Computer Science, Education, Electrical Engineering, Elementary Education, English, Guidance, History, Human Resources, Industrial Engineering, Medical Technology, Ministries, Music, Philosophy, Physics, Political Science, Premed, Psychology, Radio and Television, Science, Secondary Education, Spanish, Speech, Speech Pathology

ATHLETIC PROFILE

Conference Affiliation: Mid-State Conference

Gettysburg College

300 N Washington Street
Gettysburg, PA 17325
Coach: John Campo
NCAA III
Bullets/Orange, Blue
Phone: (717) 337-6413
Fax: (717) 337-6528

ACADEMIC

Founded: 1832
Type: 4 Yr., Private, Liberal Arts, Coed
Religion: Lutheran
Campus Housing: No
Web-site: http://www.gettysburg.edu/
SAT/ACT/GPA: 1000 (500/500)
Student/Faculty Ratio: 12:1
Male/Female Ratio: 1:1
Undergraduate Enrollment: 2,210
Graduate Enrollment: None
Scholarships/Academic: Yes **Athletic:** No **Fin Aid:** Yes

Total Expenses by: Year **In State:** $ 25,450 **Out of State:** $ 25,450
Degrees Conferred: BA, BS
Programs of Study: Anthropology, Sociology, Art, Art History, Biochemistry, Biology, Chemistry, Classical Studies, Computer Science, Economics, English, French, German, Greek, Health and Exercise Sciences, Latin, History, Management, Mathematics, Music, Music Education, Philosophy, Physics, Political Science, Psychology, Sociology, Spanish, Theatre Arts, Women's Studies

ATHLETIC PROFILE

Conference Affiliation: Centennial Conference
Program Profile: Gettysburg's playing field is one of the best in Division III. It has a seating capacity of 100, an enclosed fence, a warning track around the fence and all natural turf. The measurements are: distance to L/RF is 300 feet, to dead center is 420 feet, a 35 foot distance between home plate and the backstop. There is a press row with all electrical and telecommunications wiring behind the backstop. We have an electric scoreboard in RF and a complete sound system used through all home games.
History: Our rich history of baseball can be traced to the Civil War days when Abner Doubleday was in Gettysburg as a commanding officer. Gettysburg began playing in 1863, but officially started in 1880. At the turn of the century, Gettysburg produced Hall of Famer Eddie Plank, one of the greatest LHers of all time. Since then, it has produced a large number of minor league players, but only one reaching the majors for a short 2-week period at the end of regular season.
Achievements: Conference or Division Champs in 1987-1989, 1991; Brian Golden was strikeout leader in 1988, pitcher Marc Favieri was All-American in 1990; pitcher James Sauve was All-SEC in 1993. Large number of players named All-Conference since 1987.
Coaching: John Campo, Head Coach, is in his 3rd year as a head coach. He guided the Gettysburg to the Conference Title and in 1988 took the Bullets to the NACC Division III playoffs. In 1991, he was named Conference Coach of the Year.
Style of Play: We are aggressive on the basepaths and on defense, focus on consistent hitting over long ball hitting and constantly take advantage of opponent's mental mistakes.

Grove City College

100 Camous Drive
Grove City, PA 16127
Coach: Rob Skaricich

NCAA III
Wolverines/Red, White
Phone: (724) 458-3836
Fax: (724) 458-3855

ACADEMIC

Type: 4 Yr., Private, Liberal Arts, Coed, Engineering
Religion: Presbyterian
Web-site: http://www.gcc.edu/
Student/Faculty Ratio: 15:1
Undergraduate Enrollment: 2,300
Scholarships/Academic: Yes **Athletic:** No
Total Expenses by: Sem **In State:** $ 5,326 **Out of State:** $ 5,326

Founded: 1876
Campus Housing: Yes
SAT/ACT/GPA: 1250/27avg
Male/Female Ratio: 1:1
Graduate Enrollment: 30
Fin Aid: Yes

Degrees Conferred: BA, BS, BMUS, BSME, BSEE
Programs of Study: Engineering, Education, Accounting, Economics, Business, Financial Management, International Business, Prelaw, Premed, Prevet, Predental, Political Science, Psychology, Music, Spanish, French, History, English, Philosophy, Math, Computers, Biology, Chemistry, Christian Thought, Christian Ministries, Molecular Biology, Applied Physics, Biochemistry

ATHLETIC PROFILE

Conference Affiliation: President's Athletic Conference
Program Profile: We play on a grass field. We do approximately 22 games and a conference tournament to decide the champion. The 2-day event is held at a neutral site.
History: Our program began in 1959 and we have posted a winning record in each of the past 5 seasons.
Achievements: 2 Academic All-Americans; 1 All-Mideast Honorable Mention (NCAA III).

Haverford College

370 Lancaster Avenue
Haverford, PA 19041-1392
Coach: Ed Molush

NCAA III
Black Squirrels/Scarlet, Black
Phone: (610) 896-1117
Fax: (610) 896-4995

ACADEMIC

Founded: 1833
Type: 4 Yr., Private, Liberal Arts, Coed
Religion: Non-Affiliated
Campus Housing: Yes
Web-site: http://www.haverford.edu/
SAT/ACT/GPA: 1200+
Student/Faculty Ratio: 11:1
Male/Female Ratio: 50:50
Undergraduate Enrollment: 1,200
Graduate Enrollment: 0
Scholarships/Academic: No **Athletic:** No **Fin Aid:** Yes
Total Expenses by: Year **In State:** $ 29,520 **Out of State:** $ 29,520
Degrees Conferred: BA, BS
Programs of Study: Archaeology, Astronomy, Biology, Chemistry, Classics, Comparative Literature, East Asian Studies, Economics, English, Fine Arts, French, Geology, German, History, History of Art, Mathematics, Music, Philosophy, Physics, Political Science, Psychology, Religion, Russian

ATHLETIC PROFILE

Conference Affiliation: Centennial Conference
Program Profile: We are a top Division III program. We play Fall and Spring and take an annual trip to Florida, Texas or California. We have a superb natural grass field and a 60,000 sq. ft. indoor artificial turf facility. There are indoor and outdoor batting cages.
History: We began in 1916. We are a strong contender in the Middle Atlantic Conference and ,since 1994, in the Centennial Conference. We produced 3 pro players in US and several in Italy and Australia. We often compete against Division I programs.
Achievements: Chaon Garland 3rd round draft choice by the Oakland A's.
Coaching: Ed Molush, Head Coach, went to the Temple All-College World series in 1971. He reached Triple A in the Phillies system. He coached at LaSalle High School. He is a top pitching clinician.
Style of Play: Emphasis on bat control and speed; sound fundamentals; versality, and strong defense.

Indiana University - Pennsylvania

107 Memorial Fieldhouse
Indiana, PA 15705
Coach: Tom Kennedy

NCAA II
Indians/Crimson, Grey
Phone: (724) 357-7830
Fax: (724) 357-7804

ACADEMIC

Founded: 1875
Type: 4 Yr., Public, Coed
Religion: Non-Affiliated
Campus Housing: No
Web-site: Not Available
SAT/ACT/GPA: 900+
Student/Faculty Ratio: 19:1
Male/Female Ratio: 45:55
Undergraduate Enrollment: 12,500
Graduate Enrollment: 1,500
Scholarships/Academic: Yes **Athletic:** Yes **Fin Aid:** Yes
Total Expenses by: Year **In State:** $ 7,926 **Out of State:** $ 13,124
Degrees Conferred: AA, BA, BS, BFA, MA, MS, MBA, MFA, Med, PhD, EdD
Programs of Study: Accounting, Anthropology, Art, Biology, Business, Chemistry, Computer Science, Criminology, Dietetics, Economics, English, Finance, Fine Arts, Geography, Geology, German, Health and Physical Education, History, Hotel and Restaurant Management, Journalism, Mathematics, Music, Natural Science, Philospohy, Physical Education, Political Science, Education, Safety Science

ATHLETIC PROFILE

Conference Affiliation: Pennsylvania State Athletic Conference
Program Profile: Owen J. Dougherty Field has natural grass and dimensions of L-345, C-405 and R-350. We do a 48 game schedule in the Spring. We will have a Spring training trip to Ft. Myers, Florida.
History: The program began in 1909; 1960 won NAIA District 30 And Area 8; 1964 won District 30; 1971 3rd place finish NAIA World Series; 1988 PSAC Champion; 1009 PSAC Champion.
Achievements: Professional players: Bruce Yards (LA Dodgers), Kevin McMullan (NY Yankees), Ed Hartman (Pgh Pirates), and Garry Warn (Pgh Pirates).
Coaching: Tom Kennedy, Head Coach, entered his 3rd year as a head coach. He was an assistant coach for 17 years. Bruce Yard, Assistant Coach, was named All-PSAC shortstop. He played 5 years with the Dodgers
Style of Play: Aggressive, emphasis on speed defense and pitching.

Juniata College

Kennedy Sports Center
Huntingdon, PA 16652
Coach: Bill Berrier

NCAA III
Eagles/Blue, Gold
Phone: (814) 641-3515
Fax: (814) 641-3508

ACADEMIC

Founded: 1876
Type: 4 Yr., Private, Liberal Arts, Coed
Religion: Church of the Brethren
Campus Housing: Yes
Web-site: http://www.juniata.edu/
SAT/ACT/GPA: 900
Student/Faculty Ratio: 14:1
Male/Female Ratio: 50:50
Undergraduate Enrollment: 1,200
Graduate Enrollment: N/A
Scholarships/Academic: Yes **Athletic:** No **Fin Aid:** Yes
Total Expenses by: Year **In State:** $ 22,000 **Out of State:** $ 22,000
Degrees Conferred: BA, BS
Programs of Study: Juanica does not offer majors, but instead develops personalized program of emphasis.

ATHLETIC PROFILE

Conference Affiliation: MAC
Program Profile: Baseball is the oldest sport at Juniata. Langdon Field is all natural grass and is located right on the campus.
Coaching: Bill Berrier - Head Coach.
Roster for 1998 team/In State: 20 **Out of State:** 4 **Out of Country:** 0
Total Number of Varsity/Jr. Varsity: 24 **Percent of Graduation:** 100%
Freshmen Receiving Fin Aid/Athletic: 0 **Academic:** All
Number of Fall Games: 6 **Number of Spring Games:** 35
Positions Needed for 1999/2000: OF, Pitchers
Most Recent Record: 21 - 17 - 0
Style of Play: "Two guarantees for baseball players at Juniata: first, you will receive a good education; second, you will learn sound, fundamental baseball with the opportunity to play an outstanding schedule". William Berrier.

Keystone College

College Avenue
LaPlume, PA 18440
Coach: Michael Collins

NJCAA
Giants/Orange, Navy
Phone: (717) 945-5141
Fax: (717) 945-7916

ACADEMIC

Founded: 1868
Type: 2 Yr., Private, Jr. College, Coed
Undergraduate Enrollment: 1,000
Graduate Enrollment: None
Scholarships/Academic: No **Athletic:** No **Fin Aid:** Yes
Total Expenses by: Year **In State:** $ 14,200 **Out of State:** $ 14,200
Degrees Conferred: Associate
Programs of Study: Accounting, Fine Arts, Biology, Biological Science, Business Administration, Commerce, Management, Chemistry, Child Care/Child and Family Studies, Communications, Computer Information Systems, Criminal Justice, Culinary Arts, Cytotechnology, Early Childhood Education, Environmental Engineering Technology, Hotel and Restaurant Management, Liberal Arts, General Studies, Medical Technology, Nursing, Occupational Therapy, Manufacturing Technology, Medical Technology, Tourism and Travel, Water Resources, Wood Sciences

ATHLETIC PROFILE

Conference Affiliation: NJCAA Region XIX Conference
Program Profile: Keystone has an on campus playing field. We offer an outdoor cage and an indoor cage. Keystone plays 15-20 Fall games and 35-40 Spring games . The Giants travel to Florida for a week during Spring break.
History: The program began in 1886. Our most famous alumni was Christy Mathewson who graduated in 1889. Our field is named after the Hall of Famer known as the " Christian Gentlemen". In recent years Keystone has sent over 60 players on to Division I and II schools to play baseball.
Achievements: We have had over 40 Junior College All-Americans.
Coaching: Michael Collins, Head Coach, is in his 2nd year as head coach. He was an assistant coach for the Scranton Wilkes Barde Twins of the ACBL. He played Division I baseball at St. Joseph's University in Philadelphia. Jamei Sheuchik , Assistant Coach, was a head coach of the Troop Dukes Amateur Baseball Tyeam. He is a Keystone graduate. He also played college baseball at East Stroudsburg University.
Style of Play: We play aggressive and intelligent baseball. I (Michael Collins) like to use my whole arsenal, therefore there is no one term to categorize our style of play. We bunt a lot, steal bases, but we also expect our big hitters to drive in the runs.

King's College - Pennsylvania

133 North River Street
Wilkes-Barre, PA 18711
Coach: Al Brogna

NCAA III
Monarchs/Red, Gold
Phone: (570) 208-5855
Fax: (570) 208-5937

ACADEMIC

Founded: 1946
Type: 4 Yr., Private, Coed
Religion: Roman Catholic
Campus Housing: Yes
Web-site: http://www.kings.edu/
SAT/ACT/GPA: Average 1050
Student/Faculty Ratio: 17:1
Male/Female Ratio: 1:1
Undergraduate Enrollment: 1,700
Graduate Enrollment: 500
Scholarships/Academic: Yes **Athletic:** No **Fin Aid:** Yes
Total Expenses by: Year **In State:** $ 20,000 **Out of State:** $ Varies
Degrees Conferred: BA, BS, MA
Programs of Study: Accounting, Biology, Business Adminstration, Chemistry, Communications, Computer Science, Computer and Information Systems, Criminal Justice, Early Childhood Education, Economics, Elementary Education, English, Finance, French, General Science, Gerontology, Health Information systems, Marketing, Mathematics, Medical Technology, Philosophy, Physician Assistant, Physics, Political Science, Predentistry, Prelaw, Premed, Preoptometry, Prepharmacy, Prevet, Psychology, Secondary Education, Sociology, Special Education, Theatre, Theology

ATHLETIC PROFILE

Conference Affiliation: MAC, ECAC

Kutztown University

P.O. Box 730
Kutztown, PA 19530
Coach: Matt Royer

NCAA II
Bears/Gold, Maroon
Phone: (610) 683-4063
Fax: (610) 683-1379

ACADEMIC

Founded: 1866
Type: 4 Yr., Public, Liberal Arts, Coed
Religion: Non-Affiliated
Campus Housing: Yes
Web-site: http://www.kutztown.edu/
SAT/ACT/GPA: 1050 Avg
Student/Faculty Ratio: 8:1
Male/Female Ratio: 1/1.5
Undergraduate Enrollment: 6,000
Graduate Enrollment: None
Scholarships/Academic: Yes **Athletic:** Yes **Fin Aid:** Yes
Total Expenses by: Year **In State:** $ 8,000 **Out of State:** $ 13,000
Degrees Conferred: BA, BFA, BS, BSBA, Education, Engineering
Programs of Study: Anthropology, Economics, English, Geography, Mathematics, Music, Philosophy, Political Science, Psychology, Sociology, Communications, Biology, Chemistry, Computer and Information Science, Criminal Justice, Environmental Science, Geology, Mathematics, Nursing, Physics, Accounting, Economics, Management, Marketing, Education

ATHLETIC PROFILE

Conference Affiliation: PSAC, ECAC

La Roche College

9000 Babcoack Boulevard
Pittsburgh, PA 15237
Coach: Vince Mezza

NCAA III
Red Hawkins/Red, White
Phone: (472) 536-1046
Fax: (412) 635-1012

ACADEMIC

Founded: 1863
Type: 4 Yr., Private, Liberal Arts, Coed
Religion: Catholic
Campus Housing: Yes
Web-site: http://www.La Roche.edu
SAT/ACT/GPA: Varies
Student/Faculty Ratio: 20:1
Male/Female Ratio: 40:60
Undergraduate Enrollment: 1,500
Graduate Enrollment: 350
Scholarships/Academic: Yes **Athletic:** No **Fin Aid:** Yes
Total Expenses by: Year **In State:** $ 15,000 **Out of State:** $ 15,000
Degrees Conferred: BA, BS, MS
Programs of Study: Accounting, Applied Art, Art, Applied Mathematics, Astronomy, Biology, Business Administration, Chemistry, Commercial Art, Communications, Computer Information Systems, Creative Writing, Earth Science, Education, English, Environmental Science, Finance, Graphic Art, History, human Services, Interior Design, International Business, Journalism, Literature, Management, Mathematics, Medical Technology, Natural Science, Nursing, Predentistry, Prelaw, Premed, Prevet, Psychology, Public Relations, Radiological Technology, Religion, Respiratory Therapy, Secondary Education, Social Work, Sociology, Technical Writing

ATHLETIC PROFILE

Conference Affiliation: Allegheny Mountain Conference
Program Profile: We have a small college program with Fall and Spring seasons. We have an on-campus field. We take a Spring trip to Florida each year.
History: Our program began in 1983/1984. We qualified for post-season playoffs in 1990, 1991, 1993. We made District Runner-up in 1990, 1991.
Achievements: 1991 Coach of the Year; NAIA District 18 - Jim Tinkey Conference Runner-Up in 1990-1991.

La Salle University

1900 West Olney
Philadelphia, PA 19141-1199
Coach: Larry Conti

NCAA I
Explorers/Blue, Gold
Phone: (215) 951-1637
Fax: (215) 951-1694

ACADEMIC

Founded: 1863
Religion: Roman Catholic
Web-site: http://www.lasalle.edu/
Student/Faculty Ratio: 15:1
Undergraduate Enrollment: 2,900
Scholarships/Academic: Yes **Athletic:** Yes
Total Expenses by: Year **In State:** $ Varies

Type: 4 Yr., Private, Liberal Arts, Coed
Campus Housing: Yes
SAT/ACT/GPA: 1000 +/Required
Male/Female Ratio: 40:60
Graduate Enrollment: 1,400
Fin Aid: Yes
Out of State: $ Varies

Degrees Conferred: AA, AS, BA, BS, MBA, MSN
Programs of Study: Accounting, Banking/Finance, Biochemistry, Biology, Business, Chemistry, Communications, Economics, Education, Management, Marketing, Preprofessional Programs, Quantitative Methods, Religion, Statistics

ATHLETIC PROFILE

Conference Affiliation: Atlantic 10 Conference
Program Profile: We play very good baseball Division I. We do five weeks in the Fall and 17 weeks in the Spring . We do a 54 games schedule. We take a March Florida trip and play 7 games. The home game field is natural grass, seats approximately 300, and is known as one of the best fields in the East. High school playoffs and championship games are played on it. We have American Legion games and tryout camps.
History: The program dates back to 1948, possibly earlier. No records were kept.
Achievements: Tom Filer pitched for Yankees, Red Sox and Mets; Steve O'Donnell was named All-American in 1988.

Lackawanna Junior College

501 Vine St.
Scranton, PA 18509
Coach: Tony DiMattia

NJCAA
Falcons/Blue, White
Phone: (717) 961-7814
Fax: (717) 961-7858

ACADEMIC

Founded: 1894
Religion: Non-Affiliated
Student/Faculty Ratio: 20:1
Undergraduate Enrollment: 1,200
Scholarships/Academic: Yes **Athletic:** No
Total Expenses by: Year **In State:** $ 8,200

Type: 2 Yr., Private, Jr. college, Coed
Campus Housing: No
Male/Female Ratio: 50:50
Graduate Enrollment: None
Fin Aid: Yes
Out of State: $ 8,500

Degrees Conferred: Associate Degree
Programs of Study: Accounting, Business, Computer Information Systems, Criminal Justice, Education, Human Services, Liberal Arts, Marketing, Medical Secretarial Studies, Office Management

ATHLETIC PROFILE

Estimated Number of Baseball Scholarships: $23,000
Conference Affiliation: NJCAA Region 19 Division II
Program Profile: The Falcons play in one of the top junior college conferences in the country. Several home games are played in the beautiful 10,000 seat Lackwanna County multi-purpose stadium.

History: Baseball was brought back in 1991. Since then, Lackawanna has had a number of players move on to four year schools Four members of the the Falcons have been drafted into pro-ball since Coach Bartoletti arrived in 1994.
Achievements: Harry Zoziarski drafted in 1994 NY Mets; Ron Chiavacci drafted in 1996 Texas; Dan Nelson drafted in 1996 NY Meys; Ron Chiavacci re-drafted by 1997 Cal-Angels.
Roster for 1998 team/In State: 21 **Out of State:** 1 **Out of Country:** 0
Total Number of Varsity/Jr. Varsity: 0 **Percent of Graduation:** 85%
Number of Seniors on 1998 Team: 8 **Number of Sophomores on 1998 Team:** 0
Freshmen Receiving Fin Aid/Athletic: 10 **Academic:** 2
Positions Needed for 1999/2000: All positions
Schedule: Brookdale, Potomac State, Gloucester, Mercer, Delaware Tech

Lafayette College

Kirby Fieldhouse
Easton, PA 18042
Coach: Lloyd Brewere

NCAA I
Leopards/Maroon, White
Phone: (610) 330-5476
Fax: (610) 330-5702

ACADEMIC

Founded: 1826 **Type:** 4 Yr., Private, Liberal Arts, Coed
Religion: Non-Affiliated **Campus Housing:** Yes
Web-site: http://www.lafayette.edu/ **SAT/ACT/GPA:** Optional
Student/Faculty Ratio: 11:1 **Male/Female Ratio:** 40:60
Undergraduate Enrollment: 2,000 **Graduate Enrollment:** None
Scholarships/Academic: Yes **Athletic:** No **Fin Aid:** Yes
Total Expenses by: Year **In State:** $ 29,000 **Out of State:**
Degrees Conferred: MBA, MBS
Programs of Study: American Studies, Anthropology and Sociology, Art, Biochemistry, Computer, Economics and Business, Engineering, English, Geology, Government and Law, History, Religion, Ethical, Health, Women's Studies

ATHLETIC PROFILE

Conference Affiliation: Patriot League Conference
Program Profile: We have a year-round program. We do five to six weeks in the Fall (in season). We do 2 1/2 months of conditioning and strength training (out of season). We do a 46 game Spring schedule that includes 1 week in Fort Meyers. We have natural turf with measurements of 330 lines, and 400 center. The seating capacity is 1,000. We have an excellent indoor facility . We have scrimmage capability with outfielders and a 3,500 sq. feet strength center.
History: The program began in 1865. Our record is 1,521-1,248-32 which is .549 winning percentage. We were in the College World Series in 1953, 1954 and 1958 We went to the ECAC Tournament in 1992 and the South II Regionals in 1990.
Achievements: Won the MAC Western Section Championship in 1971 and 1972; Crowned the 1990 ECC Champions; several drafted players; 16 All-Patriot League since 1991.
Coaching: Lloyd Brewer, Head Coach, was a former player at Carolina and finished 3rd in 1978 CWS . He was named 1st teal All-ACC in 1980.
Roster for 1998 team/In State: 8 **Out of State:** 17 **Out of Country:** 0
Total Number of Varsity/Jr. Varsity: 25 **Percent of Graduation:** 100%
Number of Seniors on 1998 Team: 2 **Number of Sophomores on 1998 Team:** 10
Freshmen Receiving Fin Aid/Athletic: 0 **Academic:** 50%
Number of Fall Games: 6 **Number of Spring Games:** 46
Positions Needed for 1999/2000: Pitchers, 2- OF, Catcher, 1st Base, Midd-Infielder
Most Recent Record: 10 - 26 - 0
Schedule: Rutgers, Seton Hall, Monmouth, Navy, Army, Marist
Style of Play: Aggressive and fundamentally sound.

Lebanon Valley College

101 North College Avenue
Annville, PA 17003
Coach: John Gergle Jr.

NCAA III
Dutchman/Blue, White
Phone: (717) 867-6271
Fax: (717) 867-6019

ACADEMIC

Founded: 1866
Type: 4 Yr., Private, Liberal Arts, Coed
Web-site: Not Available
SAT/ACT/GPA: Required
Student/Faculty Ratio: 15:1
Male/Female Ratio: 50:50
Undergraduate Enrollment: 1,670
Graduate Enrollment: $ 214
Scholarships/Academic: Yes **Athletic:** No **Fin Aid:** Yes
Total Expenses by: Year **In State:** $ 20,750 **Out of State:** $ 20,750
Degrees Conferred: AA, AS, BA, BS, BM, MBA
Programs of Study: Contact school for program of study.

ATHLETIC PROFILE

Conference Affiliation: Middle Atlantic Conference (MAC)
Program Profile: We built a new field stadium in 1998. The field is natural and has dimensions of 325' lines, 370' Left-Center and Right-Center and 415' Center. We have a seating capacity of 5,000. There is an inside practice sport center.
History: Our program began approximately in 1866.
Achievements: 1993 NCAA Division Title; ICAC Title.
Coaching: John Gergle - Head Coach. Keith Evans, Assistant Coach, handles 3rd base. John Gabriel - Hitting Instruction. Joseph Yacklovich - 1st base coach.
Style of Play: We do defense and pitching and also hit and run. We play for one run at a time.

Lehigh University

641 Taylor Street
Bethlehem, PA 18015
Coach: Sean Leary
Email: spl3@lehigh.edu

NCAA I
Engineers/Brown, White
Phone: (610) 758-4315
Fax: (610) 758-6629

ACADEMIC

Founded: 1865
Type: 4 Yr., Private, Coed
Religion: Non-Affiliated
Campus Housing: Yes
SAT/ACT/GPA: (avg) 460-570 V, 570-680 M/
Web-site: http://www.lehigh.edu/
Student/Faculty Ratio: 11:1
Male/Female Ratio: 60:40
Undergraduate Enrollment: 4,400
Graduate Enrollment: 2,000
Scholarships/Academic: Varies **Athletic:** Yes **Fin Aid:** Yes
Total Expenses by: Year **In State:** $ 15,000 **Out of State:** $ 15,000
Degrees Conferred: BA, BS, MS, MBA, MEd, PhD, EdD
Programs of Study: Accounting, American Studies, Anthropology, Architecture, Art, Biology, Chemistry, Classics, Computer Science, Economics, East Asian Studies, English, French, Geology, International Careers, International Relations, Journalism, Science Writing, Predental, Premed, Mathematics, Music, Natural Science, Philosophy, Physics, Russian Studies, Geophysics, Molecular Biology, Business and Economics, Engineering and Applied Science, Electrical Engineering

ATHLETIC PROFILE

Conference Affiliation: Patriot League Conference
Program Profile: We are a NCAA Division I program with indoor and outdoor practice facilities. The Engineers play home games at Murray H. Goodman Field. It has a full length professional scoreboard and a natural grass surface. The 8 games Fall season is used primarily as a preparation for the 46 games Spring season.

History: The program began in 1885. We have 110 years of baseball. From 1967-1994, Lehigh Baseball history was molded by Stan Schultz, the Engineer's coach for an unprecedented 28 years before stepping down after 1997 season. They completed 4 straight winning seasons from '81-'84.
Achievements: Ben Talbot was drafted in 32nd round by Angels in 1997. 1984 East Coach Conference Title; Paul Hartzel went to major league with Angels, Orioles and Twins. Greg Fitz received minor league contract with White Sox in 1990. Dave Norwood was drafted by Indians, but decided to remain in school; 2 Lehigh catchers were drafted in the early 1970's; Joe Carroll was drafted by Texas Ranger in 1976.
Coaching: Sean Leary, Head Coach, begins his 2nd season as a head coach. He was an assistant coach for 2 seasons. He compiled a record of 49-70-2 in 1996 and was a two-year starter shortstop that boasted a .296 in seven years.
Roster for 1998 team/In State: 10 **Out of State:** 20 **Out of Country:** 0
Total Number of Varsity/Jr. Varsity: 30 **Percent of Graduation:** 88%
Number of Seniors on 1998 Team: 5 **Most Recent Record:** 13 - 26 - 0
Number of Fall Games: 8 **Number of Spring Games:** 46
Positions Needed for 1999/2000: Pitcher, Shortstop
Schedule: Central Florida, University of Penn, Long Island, CW Post, Navy, Army, Georgetown
Style of Play: Fundamental, disciplined and aggressive.

Lincoln University - Pennsylvania

P.O. Box 179
Lincoln University, PA 19352
Coach: Robert Bryars

NCAA III
Lions/Orange, Blue
Phone: (601) 932-8300
Fax: (601) 932-0815

ACADEMIC

Founded: 1854
Type: 4 Yr., Public, Liberal Arts, Coed
Religion: Non-Affiliated
Campus Housing: Yes
Web-site: http://www.lincoln.edu/
SAT/ACT/GPA: 800
Student/Faculty Ratio: 12:1
Male/Female Ratio: 40:60
Undergraduate Enrollment: 1,270
Graduate Enrollment: 200
Scholarships/Academic: Yes **Athletic:** No **Fin Aid:** Yes
Total Expenses by: Year **In State:** $ 7,000 **Out of State:** $ 9,000
Degrees Conferred: BA, BS, M
Programs of Study: Accounting, Actuarial Science, Anthropology, Banking and finance, Biology, Business Administration, Chemistry, Computer Science, Criminal Justice, Economics, Education, English, French, History, Human Services, International Relations, Journalism, Management, Mathematics, Medical Technology, Music, Nursing, Philosophy, Physical Education, Physics, Political Science, Predental, Preengineering, Prelaw, Premed, Prevet, Psychology, Public Affairs, Recreation and Leisure, Recreation Therapy, Religion, Russian Work, Sociology, Spanish

ATHLETIC PROFILE

Conference Affiliation: EPAC, ECAC

Lock Haven University

Thomas Fieldhouse
Lock Haven, PA 17745
Coach: Smokey Stover

NCAA II
Bald Eagles/Cardinal, White
Phone: (717) 893-2102
Fax: (800) 233-8978

ACADEMIC

Founded: 1870
Type: 4 Yr., Public, Liberal Arts, Coed
Religion: Non-Affiliated
Campus Housing: Yes
Web-site: http://www.lhup.edu/
SAT/ACT/GPA: 900+

Student/Faculty Ratio: 18:1
Male/Female Ratio: 45:55
Undergraduate Enrollment: 3,400
Graduate Enrollment: 200
Scholarships/Academic: Yes **Athletic:** Yes **Fin Aid:** Yes
Total Expenses by: Year **In State:** $ 7,700 **Out of State:** $ 12,900
Degrees Conferred: BA, BS, BFA, MA
Programs of Study: Aeronautical/Astronautical/Space Engineering, Arts and Science, Business and Management, Communications, Computer Science, Education/Human Services, Engineering, Health Science and Recreation, Psychology, Protective Service, Social Sciences

ATHLETIC PROFILE

Conference Affiliation: PSAC, ECAC
Program Profile: Our Division II program is in a very competitive conference. Our new baseball field was built in 1994. We do a Fall season and a 46 game Spring season on a natural grass field.
Achievements: Paul Smokey - Head Coach.

Luzerne County Community College

1333 S Prospect St
Nanticoke, PA 18634-3899
Coach: Al Cihocki

NJCAA
Minutemen/Red, Blue, White
Phone: (570) 740-0429
Fax: (570) 740-0377

ACADEMIC

Founded: 1812
Type: 2 Yr, Private, Liberal Arts, Coed
Religion: United Methodist
Campus Housing: Yes
Web-site: http://www.lycoming.edu/
SAT/ACT/GPA: 1070/21
Student/Faculty Ratio: 13:1
Male/Female Ratio: 1:1
Undergraduate Enrollment: 1,500
Graduate Enrollment:
Scholarships/Academic: Yes **Athletic:** No **Fin Aid:** LFAA, FAFSA
Total Expenses by: Year **In State:** $ 19,900 **Out of State:** $ 19,900
Degrees Conferred: BA, BS, BFA
Programs of Study: One Year - Certificate of Specialization: General Studies, Liberal Arts/Sciences Program. Two Year - Associate in Applied Science - General Studies, Automated Manufacturing, Computer Aided Drafting, Computer Systems, Electronics Engineering

ATHLETIC PROFILE

Conference Affiliation: EPCC, PCAA
Program Profile: We have a natural field on campus that has a pavilion behind the bleachers. It is used by fans for cook-outs.
History: LCCC had a baseball team since 1968. The team has played at many sites until it had its own facilities. Our college campus moved from Wilkes-Barre to Nanticoke in 1974.
Achievements: Eastern PA Collegiate Conference Champions. PA Collegiate Athletic Association State Champions.
Coaching: Al Cihocki, Head Coach, was a professional player for Cleveland and Baltimore. He is in the International League Hall of Fame. He managed teams in Dominican Republic and Puerto Rico.
Style of Play: We like to play aggressively -- hit and run, etc.-- but this style of play depends on the talent at hand.

Mansfield University

Baseball Office I
Mansfield, PA 16933
Coach: Harry Hillson

NCAA II
Mountaineers/Scarlet, Black
Phone: (717) 662-4457
Fax: (717) 662-4116

ACADEMIC

Founded: 1857
Type: 4 Yr., Public, Liberal Arts, Coed
Web-site: Not Available
SAT/ACT/GPA: 950/21+
Student/Faculty Ratio: 15:1
Male/Female Ratio: 6:4
Undergraduate Enrollment: 2,847
Graduate Enrollment: 224
Scholarships/Academic: Yes **Athletic:** Yes **Fin Aid:** Yes
Total Expenses by: Year **In State:** $ 7,400 **Out of State:** $ 13,000
Degrees Conferred: AA, AS, BA, BS, MA, MS
Programs of Study: Over 60 different majors: Allied Health, Business and Management, Communications, Education, Home Economics, Life Science, Psychology, Social Sciences

ATHLETIC PROFILE

Conference Affiliation: Pennsylvania State Athletic Conference
Program Profile: We are an outstanding top 10 program with a top-notch facility. We have a full infield tarp, 3 turf batting cages and restrooms.
History: Our program dates back to 1865 and has produced over 100 professional players.
Achievements: Division champs 1960, 1970, 1972, 1980, 1984, 1987, 1990, 1992. PSAC state champs 1960, 1970, 1976, 1992-93. Regional Champs 1975-76, 1979-80, 1992-93. 3rd at Division III World Series 1979. College World Series 1992-93. Runner-up at Division II Championship, 2nd national ranking 1992. 1992-93 North Atlantic Regional Coach of the Year. 26 players drafted in 17 years. 1997 PSA State Champions (5 out of the last six years).
Coaching: Harry Hillson, Head Coach, became head coach in 1987, attended Cortland State where he was All-SUNYAC Conference team 3 years. He played 1 season of minor league baseball and became assistant at Mansfield in 1983. He is a member of the ABCA Coaching and Teaching Committee. None of his teams have finished with less than a .324 batting average. Three of his teams were ranked among the top 5 in Division II.
Style of Play: Hustling, hard-hitting club.

Marywood College

2300 Adams Avenue
Scranton, PA 18509
Coach: Joe Ross
NCAA III
Pacers/Green, White
Phone: (717) 961-4724
Fax: (717) 961-4730

ACADEMIC

Founded: 1915
Type: 4 Yr., Private, Coed
Religion: Catholic
Campus Housing: No
Web-site: Not Available
SAT/ACT/GPA: 780+
Student/Faculty Ratio: 11:1
Male/Female Ratio: 25:75
Undergraduate Enrollment: 1,948
Graduate Enrollment: 979
Scholarships/Academic: Yes **Athletic:** No **Fin Aid:** Yes
Total Expenses by: Year **In State:** $ 14,750 **Out of State:** $ 14,750
Degrees Conferred: AA, BA, BFA, MA, MS, MBA, MFA
Programs of Study: Visual and Performing arts, Health Sciences, Business and Management, Communications, Computer and Information Sciences, Law, Nursing, Prelaw, Social Sciences, Teacher Education

ATHLETIC PROFILE

Conference Affiliation: Pennsylvania Athletic Conference
Program Profile: Marywood has made a genuine commitment to the baseball program as is evident by the construction of the new field. The field will be grass. We play a 36-game schedule, including a limited Fall campaign and a Spring break trip to the South.
History: This program began in 1995. After posting a 1-20 record during their initial season, the pacers logged a 7-23 mark in 1996 despite not haveing a senior on the roster.

Coaching: Joe Ross, Head Coach,is a former Middle Atlantic Conference (3-time) and Mid-Atlantic Regional (twice). He was All-State at the University of Scranton. He was the JV Coach at Bishop O'Hara H.S., and Varsity Coach at Lakeland H.S.
Style of Play: Right now, because we are just establishing our program, we play a very fundamental style. We are aggressive and look to move runners offensively. Defensively, we still want to be aggressive and consistent. We are more of a bunt and run team than we are a power squad.

Mercyhurst College

501 E 38th Street
Erie, PA 16546
Coach: Scot Worwood

NCAA II
Lakers/Blue, Kelly, White
Phone: (814) 824-2441
Fax: (814) 824-2204

ACADEMIC

Founded: 1926
Type: 4 Yr., Private, Liberal Arts, Coed
Religion: Catholic
Campus Housing: Yes
Web-site: http://www.utopia.mercy.edu/
SAT/ACT/GPA: 950/18/2.5
Student/Faculty Ratio: 16:1
Male/Female Ratio: 54:46
Undergraduate Enrollment: 3,000
Graduate Enrollment: 110
Scholarships/Academic: Yes **Athletic:** Yes **Fin Aid:** Yes
Total Expenses by: Year **In State:** $ 17,500 **Out of State:** $ Varies
Degrees Conferred: BA, BS, Med
Programs of Study: Accounting, Anthropology, Archaeology, Art Administration, Art Therapy, Banking/Finance, Biology, Broadcasting, Businesss Administration, Chemistry, Communications, Criminal Justice, Dance, Earth Science, Education, English, Environmental Science, Geology, Graphic Design, History, Interior Design, Journalism, Management, Marketing, Mathematics, Medical Laboratory, Prelaw, Premed, Predentistry, Psychology, Religion, Social Science, Studio Art

ATHLETIC PROFILE

Estimated Number of Baseball Scholarships: 9
Conference Affiliation: Great Lakes Intercollegiate Athletic Conference
Program Profile: We have the top baseball field in the area. It has natural grass .We play one-fourth to one-half of our home games in Jerry Hunt Park. It is one of the top minor parks in USA..
History: We began in 1972-1973 . Our team reached national stature in the last 10 years. We had South Regional Division II Appearances in the last 10 years. We consistently ranked in the top 20 of Division II.
Achievements: 5 players drafted in the past 4 years; 4 All-Americans; 2 Players of the Year GLIAC.
Coaching: Scot Worwood, Head Coach, was a an assistant coach at Indianapolis for 4 years. He built our team to a national powerhouse in just 4 years. Our team won 39 games. For 2 straight years, we ranked 4th . Joe Spano, Assistant Coach, entered his 2nd year with the program. He was a former All-American and All-Regional at Lewis University.
Total Number of Varsity/Jr. Varsity: 25 **Percent of Graduation:** 95%
Freshmen Receiving Fin Aid/Athletic: 100% **Academic:** 100%
Baseball Camp Dates: December 20th **Number of Spring Games:** 56
Positions Needed for 1999/2000: Numerous
Most Recent Record: 19 - 23 - 0
Schedule: Tampa, Slippery Rock, Millersville, Boston, Ashland, Saginaw Valley, Grand Valley
Style of Play: Aggressive, fundamental baseball.

Messiah College

No Street Address
Gratham, PA 17027
Coach: Frank Montgomery

NCAA III
Falcons/Blue, White
Phone: (717) 691-6018
Fax: (717) 691-6044

ACADEMIC

Founded: 1909
Type: 4 Yr., Private, Liberal Arts, Coed
Religion: Non-Affiliated
Campus Housing: Yes
Web-site: http://www.messiah.edu/
SAT/ACT/GPA: 900 + / 21
Student/Faculty Ratio: 15:1
Male/Female Ratio: 42:58
Undergraduate Enrollment: 2,375
Graduate Enrollment: N/A
Scholarships/Academic: Yes **Athletic:** No **Fin Aid:** Yes
Total Expenses by: Year **In State:** $ 16,300 **Out of State:** $ 16,300
Degrees Conferred: BA, BS
Programs of Study: Accounting, Art History, Behavioral Science, Biblical, Biochemistry, Biology, Business Administration, Chemistry, Civil Engineering, Communications, Computer Science, Economics, Education, Eletrical Engineering, English, Family and Consumer Studies, Fine Arts, French, German, History, Home Economics, Humanities, international Business, Journalism, Management, Marketing, Mathematics, Mechanical Engineering, Medical Laboratory Technology, Ministries, Music, Natural Science, Nursing, Personnel Management, Physics, Political Science, Predental, Prelaw, Premed, Prevet, Psychology, Religion, Religious Education, Social Science, Spanish, Sorts Medicine

ATHLETIC PROFILE

Conference Affiliation: Middle Atlantic Conference

Millersville University - Pennsylvania

P.O. Box 1002
Millersville, PA 17551-0302
Coach: Glen Gallagher
NCAA II
Marauders/Black, Gold
Phone: (717) 872-3361
Fax: (717) 871-2125

ACADEMIC

Founded: 1855
Type: 4 Yr., Public, Liberal Arts, Coed
Religion: Non-Affiliated
Campus Housing: Yes
Web-site: http://www.marauder.millersv.edu/
SAT/ACT/GPA: 1030
Student/Faculty Ratio: 18:1
Male/Female Ratio: 4:6
Undergraduate Enrollment: 5,500
Graduate Enrollment: 2,000
Scholarships/Academic: Yes **Athletic:** 'Partial' **Fin Aid:** Yes
Total Expenses by: Year **In State:** $ 9,000 **Out of State:** $ 13,000
Degrees Conferred: BA, BS, BSEd, BFA, BSN, MA, MS, Med
Programs of Study: Anthropology, Art, Business, Biology, History, International Studies, Mathematics, Economics, Oceanography, Meteorology, Earth Science, Political, Occupational Safety and Hygiene Management

ATHLETIC PROFILE

Conference Affiliation: PSAC, Eastern Division
Program Profile: Biemesderfer Field (500-seat capacity), no lights, season March - May, natural grass field.
History: Our Intercollegiate Program began in 1889. We are the 1st sport in MU athletics history with a record of 437-379-9 since 1970. Our team won PSAC titles in 1968, 1974-75. We got PSAC Eastern Division crowns in 1974-75 and 1982. Our 1988 Marauder diamondmen won the ECAC Division II South tournament championship. Under former head coach Dr. Joe Abromaitis, MU posted seven 20-win seasons between 1982 and 1992.
Achievements: 1 player in the major league-Jim Todd who pitched for the Oakland A's Oraganization.
Coaching: Glen Gallagher, Head Coach, entered his 3rd year as ahead coach.

Moravian College

1200 Main Street
Bethlehem, PA 18018
Coach: Ed Little
Email: admissions@moravian.edu

NCAA III
Greyhounds/Blue, Grey
Phone: (610) 861-1534
Fax: (610) 861-3940

ACADEMIC

Founded: 1742
Type: 4 Yr., Private, Liberal Arts, Coed
Religion: Non-Affiliated
Campus Housing: Yes
Web-site: http://www.moravian.edu
SAT/ACT/GPA: 1000-1100
Student/Faculty Ratio: 15:1
Male/Female Ratio: 50:50
Undergraduate Enrollment: 1,250
Graduate Enrollment: MBA only
Scholarships/Academic: Yes **Athletic:** No **Fin Aid:** Yes
Total Expenses by: Year **In State:** $ 22,000 **Out of State:** $ 22,000
Degrees Conferred: BA, BS, Bmus
Programs of Study: Art History, Biology, Business and Management, Chemistry, Criminal Justice, Economics, Education, Journalism, Letters/Literature, Life Science, Psychology, Religion, Social Sciences

ATHLETIC PROFILE

Conference Affiliation: Middle Atlantic Conference, Commonwealth League
Program Profile: Our playing facility is called Gillespie Field. Our playing season is 6 weeks in the Fall. The Spring season is from late January through the last weekend in April. Our playing field is natural grass. Our stadium has dimensions of LF-343, RF-338 and CF-432.
History: The program has 53 winning seasons in 62 years of varsity competition.
Achievements: Conference Champions in 1985, 1990, 1992; Coach of the Year in 1985; 1997 Freshman pitcher Mark Slavin (Stroudsburgh, PA) lead the country in ERA 0.50. ERA was the 3rd lowest in Division III history, and the best ever posted by a freshman.
Coaching: Ed Little, Head Coach, compiled a record of 230-204-1. Frank Matla, Assistant Coach, has been pitching coach for 11 years. Bob Zerfass, Assistant Coach, has been hitting coach 5 years.
Roster for 1998 team/In State: 24 **Out of State:** 14 **Out of Country:** 0
Total Number of Varsity/Jr. Varsity: 24 /14 **Percent of Graduation:** 100%
Number of Seniors on 1998 Team: 3 **Number of Sophomores on 1998 Team:** 8
Freshmen Receiving Fin Aid/Athletic: 0 **Academic:** 16
Number of Fall Games: 8 **Number of Spring Games:** 36
Positions Needed for 1999/2000: Pitcher, 1st Base, Middle Infielder
Schedule: Allentown, Massachusetts - Dartmouth, Kutztown, Lehigh, East Stroudsburg, Ursinus
Style of Play: Solid pitching and good defense mixed with a speed.

Muhlenberg College

2400 Chew Street
Allentown, PA 18104
Coach: Bob Macaluso

NCAA III
Mules/Cardinal Grey
Phone: (610) 821-3320
Fax: (610) 821-3537

ACADEMIC

Founded: 1848
Type: 4 Yr., Private, Liberal Arts, Coed
Religion: Lutheran
Campus Housing: Yes
Web-site: http://www.muhlberg.edu/
SAT/ACT/GPA: 1150+
Student/Faculty Ratio: 25:1
Male/Female Ratio: 50:50
Undergraduate Enrollment: 1,800
Graduate Enrollment: N/A
Scholarships/Academic: Yes **Athletic:** No **Fin Aid:** Yes
Total Expenses by: Year **In State:** $ 24,000 **Out of State:** $ 24,000
Degrees Conferred: BA, BS

Programs of Study: Accounting, American Studies, Art, Biochemistry, Biology, Business Administration, Chemistry, Classiscs, Communication Studies, Computer Science, Economics, English, Environmental Science, French, German, Greek, History, Human Resources Administration, Informations Science, International Studies, Latin, Mathematics, Music, Natural Science, Philosophy, Philosophy/Political Thought, Physical Science, Physics, Political Science, Political Economy, Prelaw, Premed, Preministry, Psychology, Religion, Russian Studies, Social Science, Social Work, Sociology, Spanish, Theatre Arts

ATHLETIC PROFILE

Conference Affiliation: Centennial Conference
Program Profile: Our team plays a 30-game schedule. We do a Spring trip in March to North Carolina and Virginia and play top opponents. Our Fall season is organized with practices and scrimmages with local colleges. Our home field is a legion field used to host state tournaments.
History: Baseball started at Muhlenberg in 1922. The team won Middle Atlantic Conference South titles in 1971, 1980. We are now in the new Centennial Conference.
Style of Play: Our team is aggressive on the basepaths and forces other teams to make good plays. Our fundamentals will be solid and our team will always be prepared for all situations. Our pitchers will go after hitters. We emphasize on control and staying ahead. Our players will have fun playing but will go out to win every time.

Neumann College

One Neumann Drive
Aston, PA 19014-1298
Coach: Len Schuler

NCAA III
Knights/Blue, White
Phone: (610) 558-5627
Fax: (610) 558-5657

ACADEMIC

Founded: 1965
Type: 4 Yr., Private, Liberal Arts, Coed
Religion: Catholic
Campus Housing: No
Web-site: Not Available
SAT/ACT/GPA: 900 avg
Student/Faculty Ratio: 12:1
Male/Female Ratio: 3:1
Undergraduate Enrollment: 1,300+
Graduate Enrollment: 100+
Scholarships/Academic: Yes **Athletic:** No **Fin Aid:** Yes
Total Expenses by: Year **In State:** $ 12,890 **Out of State:** $ 12,890
Degrees Conferred: AA, BA, BS, MS
Programs of Study: Accounting, Biological Science, Business Administration, Communications, Computer Science, Early Childhood Education, Elementary Education, English, Information, Science, Medical Laboratory Technology, Nursing, Political Science, Prelaw, Psychology, Religion

ATHLETIC PROFILE

Conference Affiliation: Pennsylvania Athletic Conference
Program Profile: Bruder Athletic Field has natural grass . It is fully enclosed with 330 down right and left field, 370 right left center gaps and 400 dead center. There is seating for 150 people. It has an indoor batting cage with indoor mounds for pitching. We take a Spring trip to Florida. We play an average of 30-35 games during Spring schedule.
History: Our program began in 1990. The 1997 has a record of 11 wins-most in the program's history. During the first 8 years, Neumann was all commuter students. In 1997-1998, on campus housing was made available. This should open our recruiting area.
Achievements: 1992 - 2 players named NAIA District 19 Honorable Mention All-District. 1993 - 2 players named NAIA District 1st Team All-District, 2 players named NAIA 2nd Team All-District. 1994-2 players named 1st team All-PAC; 1 named 2nd team. 1995-freshman outdoor named All-PAC 1st team. 1996-Freshman infielder named All-PAC 1st team.
Coaching: Len Schuler, Head Coach, is in his 7th year and also serves as Women's Baseball Coach and Director of Athletics.

Style of Play: We previously relied on hit and run, stolen base and fundamentals. We want solid pitching have a need to manufactors runs. We are looking to improve infield defense and add power to the line-up. We are also looking for extra help with a pitching staff.

Pennsylvania State University

112 Bryce Jordan Center
University Park, PA 16801
Coach: Joe Hindelang
Email: jpd8@psu.edu

NCAA I
Nittany Lions/Blue, White
Phone: (814) 863-0239
Fax: (814) 865-2594

ACADEMIC

Founded: 1855
Religion: Non-Affiliated
Web-site: http://www.psu.edu/
Student/Faculty Ratio: 16:1
Undergraduate Enrollment: 36,000
Scholarships/Academic: Yes **Athletic:** Yes
Total Expenses by: Year **In State:** $ 10,374

Type: 4 Yr., Public, Coed
Campus Housing: Yes
SAT/ACT/GPA: 1200
Male/Female Ratio: 55:45
Graduate Enrollment: 4,000
Fin Aid: Yes
Out of State: $ 16,714

Degrees Conferred: Baccalaurate, Masters, Doctoral, Post-Docs
Programs of Study: Over 180 Major fields including: Agriculture, Architecture, Business and Management, Communications, Education, Engineering, Health Sciences, Liberal Arts, Social Sciences

ATHLETIC PROFILE

Estimated Number of Baseball Scholarships: 4
Conference Affiliation: Big Ten Conference
Program Profile: Play on grass field with a seating capacity of 2,000.
Achievements: 1996 Big Ten Champs; 1996 Coach of the Year; 1998 1st round draft; Nate Bump RHP was 3rd team All-American.
Coaching: Joe Hindelang, Head Coach, entered his 8th season with the program. Jeff Ditch, Asssitant, is in his 5th year with the program. Randy Ford, Asssitant, entered his 10th year with the program.
Roster for 1998 team/In State: 22 **Out of State:** 10 **Out of Country:** 0
Total Number of Varsity/Jr. Varsity: 32 **Percent of Graduation:** 72%
Number of Seniors on 1998 Team: 9 **Number of Sophomores on 1998 Team:** 8
Freshmen Receiving Fin Aid/Athletic: 6 **Academic:** 2
Most Recent Record: 28 - 24 - 0 **Number of Spring Games:** 56
Positions Needed for 1999/2000: Pitcher
Schedule: Virginia, Duke, Notre Dame, Illinois Minnesota, George Mason
Style of Play: In the first place is dominating pitching, in the second place is hitting through the lineup and in the third place is defensively playing consistent. We attempt to place as much offensive pressure on the opposition, while limiting our opponents to three outs an inning.

Pennsylvania State University - Beaver Campus

Brodhead Road
Monaca, PA 15061
Coach: Jim Karwoski

NJCAA
Blue Devils/Blue, Red
Phone: (724) 773-3880
Fax: (724) 773-3853

ACADEMIC

Founded: 1964
Male/Female Ratio: 62:38
Undergraduate Enrollment: 750+
Scholarships/Academic: No **Athletic:** No

Type: 2 Yr., Public, Coed
SAT/ACT/GPA: Test Required/
Graduate Enrollment: None
Fin Aid: Yes

Total Expenses by: Year **In State:** $ 8,650 **Out of State:** $ 14,200
Degrees Conferred: Associate
Programs of Study: Agricultural Business, Biology, Biological Science, Biomedical Technology, Electrical Engineering Technology, Hotel and Restaurant Management, Liberal Arts, General Studies, Manufacturing Technology, Mechanical Engineering Technology, mechanical Engineering Technology, Physical Science

ATHLETIC PROFILE

Conference Affiliation: CCAC

Pennsylvania State University - Behrend College

5091 Station Road
Erie, PA 16563-0400
Coach: Paul Benim
Email: prb3@psu.edu

NCAA III
Lions/Blue, White, Red
Phone: (814) 898-6322
Fax: (814) 898-6013

ACADEMIC

Type: 4 Yr., Public, Liberal Arts, Coed, Engineering
Founded: 1947
Religion: Non-Affiliated
Campus Housing: Yes
Web-site: Not Available
SAT/ACT/GPA: 1100
Student/Faculty Ratio: 18:1
Male/Female Ratio: 1:1
Undergraduate Enrollment: 3,200
Graduate Enrollment: None
Scholarships/Academic: Yes **Athletic:** No **Fin Aid:** No
Total Expenses by: Year **In State:** $ 10,500 **Out of State:** $ 15,100
Degrees Conferred: BA, BS
Programs of Study: 25 baccalaureate. Programs Including Business (Economics, Management, Accounting, Management Information System), Biology, Chemistry, Communications, Engineering, Mathematics, Political Science, Psychology, Sciences, Social Science

ATHLETIC PROFILE

Conference Affiliation: Allegheny Mountain Collegiate Conference
History: We were 1981 District 18 Champions. We have been in existence 34 years. Tom Lawless was 8 years in the majors.
Achievements: 1981 was the most victories with a 20-11 record.
Coaching: Paul Benim, Head Coach, has an MS in Counseling from Edinboro and a BA in Business and Behavioral Science from PSC. He spent 3 years as a softball coach at Behrend. His team got the 1993 ECAC Championship. He compiled a record of 126-90 in six years.
Roster for 1998 team/In State: 09 **Out of State:** 1 **Out of Country:** 0
Total Number of Varsity/Jr. Varsity: 20 **Most Recent Record:** 15 - 8 - 0
Number of Seniors on 1998 Team: 1 **Number of Sophomores on 1998 Team:** 10
Number of Fall Games: 10 **Number of Spring Games:** 40
Positions Needed for 1999/2000: Catcher, 1st Base, RHP, LHP
Baseball Camp Dates: TBA
Schedule: Allegheny College, Frostburgh State University, Delaware Valley, Maryville College
Style of Play: Aggressive with everything, will run (1997 and 1998). Top twenty Division III in stolen bases per game; throw first pitch strikes - get ahead.

Phila College of Pharmacy and Science

600 South 43rd Street
Philadelphia, PA 19104
Coach: TBA

NAIA
Blue Devils/Royal, White
Phone: (215) 596-8817
Fax: (215) 895-1100

ACADEMIC

Founded: 1821
Religion: Non-Affiliated
Web-site: Not Available
Student/Faculty Ratio: 14:1
Undergraduate Enrollment: 1,600
Scholarships/Academic: Yes **Athletic:** Yes
Total Expenses by: Year **In State:** $ 19,800

Type: 4 Yr., Private, Coed
Campus Housing: No
SAT/ACT/GPA: 900/18
Male/Female Ratio: 2:3
Graduate Enrollment: 200
Fin Aid: Yes
Out of State: $ 19,800

Degrees Conferred: BS, MS, PhD, PharmD
Programs of Study: Biological Science, Biochemistry, Chemistry, Health Science, Medical Laboratory Technology, Microbiology, Pharmacy, Science, Toxicology, Occupational Therapy, Physician's Assistant

ATHLETIC PROFILE

Conference Affiliation: Independent
Program Profile: We are highly academic-oriented. The schedule consists of three to four games per week.
History: The Blue Devils have always been successful versus a similar size program.
Achievements: The Blue Devils have been a consistent playoff participant.

Phila College of Textiles and Science

School House Lane
Philadelphia, PA 19144
Coach: Don Flynn

NCAA II
Rams/Maroon, White
Phone: (215) 951-2630
Fax: (215) 951-2859

ACADEMIC

Founded: 1884
Web-site: http://www.philacol.edu/
Student/Faculty Ratio: 18:1
Undergraduate Enrollment: 1,700
Scholarships/Academic: Yes **Athletic:** Yes
Total Expenses by: Year **In State:** $ 19,000

Type: 4 Yr., Private, Coed
SAT/ACT/GPA: 700 Min / 17 Min
Male/Female Ratio: 37:63
Graduate Enrollment: 580
Fin Aid: Yes
Out of State: $ 19,000

Degrees Conferred: AS, BS, MS, MBA
Programs of Study: Accounting, Banking/Finance, Biochemistry, Chemistry, Computer Science, Fashion Merchandising, Information Science, Interior Design, International Business, Management, Marketing, Polymer Science, Psychology, Retailing, Textiles

ATHLETIC PROFILE

Conference Affiliation: New york Collegiate Athletic Conference
Program Profile: Alumni Field has natural grass. The Rams play a Spring season only. Spring Break is spent in Florida playing 7-10 games.

Point Park College

201 Wood Street
Pittsburgh, PA 15222
Coach: Mark Jackson

NAIA
Pioneers/Green, Black
Phone: (412) 392-3845
Fax: (412) 391-1980

ACADEMIC

Type: 4 Yr., Private, Liberal Arts, Coed, Engineering
Religion: Non-Affiliated
Web-site: Not Available

Founded: 1960
Campus Housing: No
SAT/ACT/GPA: 825+

Student/Faculty Ratio: 18:1 **Male/Female Ratio:** 5:7
Undergraduate Enrollment: 1,100 **Graduate Enrollment:** 120
Scholarships/Academic: Yes **Athletic:** Yes **Fin Aid:** Yes
Total Expenses by: Year **In State:** $ 15,500 **Out of State:** $ 15,500
Degrees Conferred: AA, AS, BA, BFA, MA, MBA
Programs of Study: Accounting, Art Administration, Biology, Business Administration, Civil Engineering, Communications, Computer Science, Dance, Design, Early Childhood Education, Electrical Engineering, Elementary Education, English, Environmental Science, Fashion, Merchandising, Film Production, History, Hotel/Restaurant Mangement, Human Resources, Journalism, Legal Studies, Management, Mathematics, Mechanical Engineering, Performing Arts, Photography, Political Science, Psychology, Secondary Education, Theatre, Visual Arts

ATHLETIC PROFILE

Conference Affiliation: Keystone Empire Collegiate Conference
Program Profile: Home field is Pullman Park. We play a 65-game schedule which includes a trip to Florida. We competed in the NAIA World Series 5 of the last 10 years.
History: Our program began in 1968. We were 17-time District Champions, 9-time NAIA Champions and World Series participants. We got a national record for a winning streak of 41 games in 1990.
Achievements: Point Park captured the District 18 Title 16 times, including 8 consecutive years from 1985-1992; had many All-americnas, and several players go on to professional baseball.

Saint Joseph's University

5600 City Avenue
Phila, PA 19131
Coach: Jim Ertel
Email: wemaster@sjvhawks.com

NCAA I
Hawks/Crimson, Grey
Phone: (610) 660-1718
Fax: (610) 660-1724

ACADEMIC

Founded: 1851 **Type:** 4 Yr., Private, Liberal Arts, Coed
Religion: Catholic (Jesuit) **Campus Housing:** Yes
Web-site: http://www.sju.edu/ **SAT/ACT/GPA:** Varies
Student/Faculty Ratio: 20:1 **Male/Female Ratio:** 49:51
Undergraduate Enrollment: 3,000 **Graduate Enrollment:**
Scholarships/Academic: Yes **Athletic:** Yes **Fin Aid:** Yes
Total Expenses by: Year **In State:** $ 24,725 **Out of State:** $ 24,725
Degrees Conferred: BS, BA, MS, MA, MBA
Programs of Study: Accounting, Banking and Finance, Biology, Business Administration, Chemistry, Computer Science, Criminal Justice, Economics, Elementary Education, English, Fine Arts, Food Marketing, French, German, Health Care, History, Humanities, Human Services, Psychology, Information Science, International Relations, Labor Studies, Management, Marketing, Mathematics, Philosophy, Physics, Political Science, Psychology, Public Administration, Religion, Secondary Education, Social Science, Spanish

ATHLETIC PROFILE

Conference Affiliation: Atlantic 10 Conference
Program Profile: We play a full 56-games in NCAA Division I ranked Atlantic 10. Our regular season goes from late February to early May. We have a large indoor facility for Winter workouts. We do a Fall program and off -season conditioning/skills work. Our ballpark has a setting with a 110-foot light standard.
History: We are on of the oldest sport institutions, dating back to 1894. Our varsity program began in 1910.
Achievements: 2 NCAA Tourney Appearances in 1971 and 1974; numerous draftees including current MLB Pitcher Jamie Moyer; produced 3 All-Americans and 5 Academic All-Americans.
Coaching: Jim Ertel, Head Coach, graduated fromTemple in 1971. He was an assistant for 10 years. Ken Krsolovic, Assistant Coach, graduated from Toledo in 1993. Jack Stanczak, Assistant Coach, graduated from Villanova in 1993.

Roster for 1998 team/In State: 20 **Out of State:** 8 **Out of Country:** 2
Total Number of Varsity/Jr. Varsity: 30 **Number of Fall Games:** 56
Number of Seniors on 1998 Team: 5 **Number of Sophomores on 1998 Team:** 5
Schedule: Florida, Florida State, West Virginia, Massachusetts, Delaware, Villanova, Virginia Commonwealth, Akron, Fordham
Style of Play: We emphasize defense and the hit and run.

Saint Vincent College

300 Fraser Purchase Road
Latrobe, PA 15650
Coach: Randy Morgan

NAIA
Bearcats/Green, Gold
Phone: (724) 539-9761
Fax: (724) 532-5050

ACADEMIC

Founded: 1846
Type: 4 Yr., Private, Liberal Arts, Coed
Religion: Roman Catholic
Campus Housing: Yes
Web-site: http://www.stvincent.edu/
SAT/ACT/GPA: 840+
Student/Faculty Ratio: 12:1
Male/Female Ratio: 50:50
Undergraduate Enrollment: 1,200
Graduate Enrollment: None
Scholarships/Academic: Yes **Athletic:** Yes **Fin Aid:** Yes
Total Expenses by: Year **In State:** $ 18,000 **Out of State:** $ 18,000
Degrees Conferred: AA, AS, BA, BS, BFA, Mdiv, D
Programs of Study: Accounting, Banking/Finance, Biochemistry, Biology, Business Administration, Chemistry, Communications, Computer Science, Design, Management, Marketing, Math, Medical Laboratory Technology, Music, Philosophy, Photography, Physics, Political Science, Prelaw, Premed, Psychology, Religion, Social Science, Studio Art

ATHLETIC PROFILE

Conference Affiliation: Pennsylvania State Athletic Conference

Shippensburg University

1871 Old Main Drive
Shippensburg, PA 17257
Coach: Bruce D. Peddie

NCAA II
Red Raiders/Red, Blue, White
Phone: (717) 532-1508
Fax: (717) 532-4045

ACADEMIC

Founded: 1871
Type: 4 Yr., Public, Liberal Arts, Coed
Religion: Non-Affiliated
Campus Housing: Yes
SAT/ACT/GPA: 1000 class rank, upper 2/5/
Web-site: http://www.ship.edu/
Student/Faculty Ratio: 20:1
Male/Female Ratio: 4:5
Undergraduate Enrollment: 5,500
Graduate Enrollment: 1,000
Scholarships/Academic: Yes **Athletic:** Yes **Fin Aid:** Yes
Total Expenses by: Year **In State:** $ 3,969 **Out of State:** $ 6,568
Degrees Conferred: BA, BS, BSBA, Minors and Preprofessional Options
Programs of Study: Art, Biology, Medical Technology, Chemistry, Communications/Journalism, English, French, Geography, Earth and Space Science, Public Administration, History, Mathematics, Mathematics/Computer Science, Physics, Applied Physics, Psychology, Sociology, Speech Communication, Accounting, Business Education, Office Administration, Management, Marketing, Criminal Justice, Social Work, Elementary Education, Prelaw, Premed, Predentistry, Prepharmacy

ATHLETIC PROFILE

Estimated Number of Baseball Scholarships: 6
Conference Affiliation: Pennsylvania State Athletic Conference

Program Profile: We have as enclosed park with grass and a seating capacity of 1,500. It has a hitting area, cages, infield and a large indoor facility.
History: The baseball team was founded in 1874, making it the oldest intercollegiate team on campus. Tom Crist became coach in 1950 and took conference titles in 1954 and 1958. The program has had winning seasons from 1969-1988, 21 years in a row.
Achievements: 1996 Conference Regional Coach of the Year; Conference Champs in 1977, 1981, 1984, 1986, 1987, 1989 and 1996; Regional Champs in 1977, 1991 and 1996; 13 All-Americans, 23 drafted player 3 in 1998.
Coaching: Bruce D. Peddie - Head Coach, compiled a record of 76-66. Doug Senott - Assistant.
Roster for 1998 team/In State: 24 **Out of State:** 5 **Out of Country:** 1
Total Number of Varsity/Jr. Varsity: 30 **Percent of Graduation:** 98%
Number of Seniors on 1998 Team: 5 **Number of Sophomores on 1998 Team:** 9
Freshmen Receiving Fin Aid/Athletic: 7 **Most Recent Record:** 28 - 20 - 0
Number of Fall Games: 0 **Number of Spring Games:** 56
Positions Needed for 1999/2000: Catcher, Pitcher
Schedule: Tampa, Florida Southern, St. Leo, Mansfield, Slippery Rock, Millersville
Style of Play: Piching - defense, hard-nosed.

Slippery Rock University

Athletic Department
Slippery Rock, PA 16057
Coach: Jeff Messer

NCAA II
Rockets/Green, White
Phone: (412) 738-2813
Fax: (412) 738-2626

ACADEMIC

Founded: 1889 **Type:** 4 Yr., Public, Liberal Arts, Coed
Religion: Non-Affiliated **Campus Housing:** Yes
Web-site: http://www.sru.edu/ **SAT/ACT/GPA:** 800+
Student/Faculty Ratio: 25:1 **Male/Female Ratio:** 40:60
Undergraduate Enrollment: 7,500 **Graduate Enrollment:** 750
Scholarships/Academic: Yes **Athletic:** Yes **Fin Aid:** Yes
Total Expenses by: Year **In State:** $ 7,800 **Out of State:** $ 13,000
Degrees Conferred: BA, BS, BE, BN, BBA
Programs of Study: Accounting, Anthropology, Art, Biology, Business Administration, Chemistry, Communications, Computer Science, Economics, Elementary Education, Finance, Geography, Geology, Health Education, Management, Marketing, Mathematics, Philosophy, Physical Education

ATHLETIC PROFILE

Conference Affiliation: PSAC

Susquehanna University

Houts Gym
Sellinsgrove, PA 17870
Coach: Tim Briggs

NCAA III
Crusaders/Maroon, Orange
Phone: (717) 372-4417
Fax: (717) 372-4048

ACADEMIC

Founded: 1858 **Type:** 4 Yr., Private, Liberal Arts, Coed
Religion: Evangelical Lutheran Church **Campus Housing:** Yes
Web-site: http://www.susqu.edu/ **SAT/ACT/GPA:** 25/75% 960 - 1170
Student/Faculty Ratio: 14:1 **Male/Female Ratio:** 1:1
Undergraduate Enrollment: 1,500 **Graduate Enrollment:** N/A
Scholarships/Academic: Yes **Athletic:** No **Fin Aid:** Yes
Total Expenses by: Year **In State:** $ 22,770 **Out of State:** $ 22,770

Degrees Conferred: Associates, Bachelors
Programs of Study: The School of Art and Science offers Biochemistry, Biology, Chemistry, Classics, Computer Science, Economics, Elementary Education, English, Environmental Science, French, Geoscience, German, Greek, History, Information Systems, International Studies, Latin, Mathematics, Philosophy, Physics, Political Science, Pyschology, Religion, Sociology and Spanish. The School of Fine Arts offers Art, Art History, Communications and Theatre Arts, Music, Church Music, Music Education and Music Performance. The Sigmund Wels School of Business offers Accounting, Business Administration and Economics.

ATHLETIC PROFILE

Conference Affiliation: Middle Atlantic Conference
Program Profile: We have a limited Fall program. We do a highly competitive Spring schedule, 36 games and an annual Spring trip to Florida. We were a NCAA Division III national play-off participant in 1992 and 1995.
History: We had 4 consecutive winning seasons since Coach Christodulu took over the program. We were 1992 League Champions, 1995 MAC Overall Champions, 5 Regional All-Americans and had 2 Academic All-Americans.
Achievements: Coach Greg Christodulu was named Coach of the Year. He has been to the National Playoffs and won his first MAC Title in 1995. Seven players in 1995 attained All-League status and 3 received All-American honors. We have had 7 Regional All-Americans and two players in professional baseball over the past two seasons.

Swarthmore College

500 College Avenue
Swarthmore, PA 19081
Coach: Frank Agovino

NCAA III
Garnets/Garnet, White
Phone: (610) 328-8218
Fax: (610) 328-7798

ACADEMIC

Founded: 1864
Type: 4 Yr., Private, Liberal Arts, Coed
Religion: Quaker
Campus Housing: Yes
Web-site: http://www.swarthmore.edu/
SAT/ACT/GPA: 1250 / 21
Student/Faculty Ratio: 10:1
Male/Female Ratio: 1:1
Undergraduate Enrollment: 1,350
Graduate Enrollment: N/A
Scholarships/Academic: Yes **Athletic:** No **Fin Aid:** Yes
Total Expenses by: Year **In State:** $ 25,900 **Out of State:** $ 25,900
Degrees Conferred: BA, BS
Programs of Study: Art, Art History, Asian Studies, Astronomy, Astrophysics, Biology, Black Ctudies, Chemistry, Classics, Computer Science, Economics, Education, Engineering, English, Literature, History, International Relations, Mathematics, Medieval Studies, Modern Languages and Literature, Music and Dance, Philosophy, Physics, Political Science, Psychology, Public Policy, Religion, Sociology and Anthropology, Special Major, Theatre Studies, Women's Studies

ATHLETIC PROFILE

Conference Affiliation: Centennial Conference

Temple University

P.O. box 2842
Philadelphia, PA 19122
Coach: James Wilson

NCAA I
Owls/Red, White
Phone: (215) 204-7447
Fax: (215) 204-7770

ACADEMIC

Founded: 1884
Type: 4 Yr., Public, Coed, Engineering
Religion: Non-Affiliated
Campus Housing: Yes
Web-site: http://www.temple.edu/
SAT/ACT/GPA: 950/2.75
Student/Faculty Ratio: 12:1
Male/Female Ratio: 48:52
Undergraduate Enrollment: 18,000
Graduate Enrollment: 11,000
Scholarships/Academic: Yes **Athletic:** Yes **Fin Aid:** Yes
Total Expenses by: Year **In State:** $ 5,500 **Out of State:** $ 8,000
Degrees Conferred: AAS, BA, BS, BBA, BFA, BArch, BSN, BSEE, MA, MS, MBA, PhD, JD
Programs of Study: Accounting, Actuarial Science, Anthropology, Architectural Engineering, Banking/Finance, Biochemistry, Biology, Biomedical Engineering, Broadcasting, Business Law, Business Administration, Chemistry, Chinese, Civil Engineering, Communications, Community Service, Computer Science, Criminal Justice, Dance, Economics, Education, Electrical Engineering, English, Environmental Science, Foreign Languages, Geography, Geology, History, Horticulture, International Business, International Relations, Journalism, Management, Marketing, Mathematics, Mechanical Engineering, Music, Nursing, Occupational Therapy, Parks and Recreation, Personnel Management, Pharmacy, Philosophy, Physical Therapy, Physics, Political Science, Preprofessionals, Psychology, Religion, Social Science, Speech, Telecommunications, Visual Arts

ATHLETIC PROFILE

Conference Affiliation: ECAC, Atlantic 10 Conference

Thiel College

75 College Avenue
Greenville, PA 16125
Coach: Mark Vennis

NCAA III
Tomcats/Blue, Gold
Phone: (724) 589-2165
Fax: (724) 589-2880

ACADEMIC

Founded: 1866
Type: 4 Yr., Private, Liberal Arts, Coed
Religion: Lutheran
Campus Housing: Yes
Web-site: Not Available
SAT/ACT/GPA: 950/21/2.5
Student/Faculty Ratio: 11:1
Male/Female Ratio: 50:50
Undergraduate Enrollment: 1,020
Graduate Enrollment: None
Scholarships/Academic: Yes **Athletic:** No **Fin Aid:** Yes
Total Expenses by: Year **In State:** $ 19,250 **Out of State:**
Degrees Conferred: BA, BS, AA
Programs of Study: Accounting, Actuarial Science, Art, Biology, Business Administration, Business Communications, Chemistry, Cytotechnology, Communications, Computer Science, Education, English, Environmental Science, History, International Business, Languages, Mathematics, Medical Technology, MIS, Nursing, Philosophy, Physics, Political Science, Engineering, Psychology, Religion, Sociology, Philosophy, Physics, Preprofessional Programs in Dentistry, Medicine, Optometry, Osteopathic Medicine, Pharmacy, Podiatry, Veterinary Medicine Law and Physical Therapy

ATHLETIC PROFILE

Conference Affiliation: Presidents Athletic Conference

University of Pennsylvania

33rd Street Weightman Hall
Philadelphia, PA 19104
Coach: Bob Seddon

NCAA I
Quakers/Red, Blue
Phone: (215) 898-6282
Fax: (215) 573-2599

ACADEMIC

Type: 4 Yr., Private, Liberal Arts, Coed, Engineering
Founded: 1740
Religion: Non-Affiliated
Campus Housing: Yes
Web-site: http://www.upenn.edu/
SAT/ACT/GPA: 1200+
Student/Faculty Ratio: 30:1
Male/Female Ratio: 47:53
Undergraduate Enrollment: 8,000
Graduate Enrollment: 3,000
Scholarships/Academic: Yes **Athletic:** No **Fin Aid:** Yes
Total Expenses by: Year **In State:** $ 25,000 **Out of State:** $ 25,000
Degrees Conferred: AA, BA, BS, BFA, MA, MS, MBA, MFA, MED, PhD, JD
Programs of Study: Various areas of study including Architecture, Business and Management, Communications, Engineering, Letters/Literature, Liberal Arts, Nursing, Premed, Psychology, Social Science

ATHLETIC PROFILE

Conference Affiliation: Ivy League Conference
Program Profile: We take a Southern trip and have a 45-game schedule with national competition. We have 1/2 million dollar facilities with: a locker room, a pressbox and a natural grass field with dimensions of 330-410-330. Our dirt field was built in 1980 and a has seating capacity. We are a strong Division I program. We had 5 regional tourneys in the last 7 years and were 1995 Ivy Champions.
History: Our program began in the 1900's. We are one of the oldest teams in the USA. We finished 2nd or 3rd in the Ivy League for the last 8 years. We got Oklahoma Regional in 1995.
Achievements: 6 Ivy Conference Titles; 14 drafted players; Doug Clanville drafted by the Chicago Cubs and is active; Mark De Roja drafted by Atlanta Brave-Double A is an active player; 14 All-Americans
Coaching: Bob Seddon - Head Coach, has 519 wins record. Bill Wagner - Assistant Coach.
Roster for 1998 team/In State: 0 **Out of State:** 80% **Out of Country:** 0
Total Number of Varsity/Jr. Varsity: 28
Percent of Graduation: 100%
Number of Seniors on 1998 Team: 2
Most Recent Record: 15 - 21 - 1
Freshmen Receiving Fin Aid/Athletic: 0
Academic: 80%
Number of Fall Games: 2
Number of Spring Games: 45
Positions Needed for 1999/2000: Pitcher, Outfielder
Schedule: Fresno State, New Mexico, North Carolina, Harvard, Navy, Seton Hall
Style of Play: We like to run, hit and run. We do not have a lot of power but we do have good defense!!!

University of Pittsburgh

P.O. Box 7436
Pittsburgh, PA 15213
Coach: Joe Gordano

NCAA I
Panthers/Blue, Gold
Phone: (412) 648-8208
Fax: (412) 648-9177

ACADEMIC

Type: 4 Yr., Public, Liberal Arts, Coed, Engineering
Founded: 1887
Religion: Non-Affiliated
Campus Housing: Yes
Web-site: http://www.pitt.edu/
SAT/ACT/GPA: 1230/24
Student/Faculty Ratio: 15:1
Male/Female Ratio: 48:52
Undergraduate Enrollment: 12,933
Graduate Enrollment: 17,000
Scholarships/Academic: Yes **Athletic:** Yes **Fin Aid:** Yes
Total Expenses by: Year **In State:** $ 11,344 **Out of State:** $ 17,704
Degrees Conferred: BA, BS, BSE, MA, MS, MBA, Med, MENG, PhD, EdP, PsyD
Programs of Study: Biological Science, Business, Communications and the Arts, Computer and Physical Science, Education, Engineering and Environmental Design, Health Profession, Social Science. Over 90 majors offered.

ATHLETIC PROFILE

Conference Affiliation: Big East Conference
Program Profile: We have a history of recruiting and developing student-athletes into the best baseball players and students they can be. Our coaching staff is dedicated to the goal of having each player reach his potential.
History: Baseball is the oldest sport at Pittsburgh dating back to 1869, the same year Major League Baseball had its start in this country. Pitt has sent 3 players to the Major Leagues in recent years. Pitt plays in the prestigious Big East Conference that has produced Craig Biggio, John Franco, Charles Nagy, Mo Vaughn and Frank Viola.
Achievements: 1994 Big East Conference Regular Season Champions; numerous individual player honors over the past 3 years. We were 1995 Big East Tournament Champs and a 1995 NCAA Mideast Regular.

University of Pittsburg - Johnstown

450 School House Road
Johnstown, PA 15904
Coach: Stan Williams

NCAA II
Mountain Cats/Blue, Gold
Phone: (814) 269-7170
Fax: (814) 269-2026

ACADEMIC

Type: 4 Yr., Public, Liberal Arts, Coed, Engineering
Founded: 1927
Undergraduate Enrollment: 3,000
Campus Housing: Yes
Web-site: http://www.pitt.edu/~upjweb
SAT/ACT/GPA: 900
Student/Faculty Ratio: 20:1
Male/Female Ratio: 1:1
Scholarships/Academic: Yes **Athletic:** Yes **Fin Aid:** Yes
Total Expenses by: Year **In State:** $ 9,300 **Out of State:** $ 15,000
Degrees Conferred: BA, BS, MEd
Programs of Study: Accounting, Biology, Business and Management, Chemistry, Communications, Computer Science, Creative Writing, Ecology, Economics, Education, Engineering, English, Finance, Geography, Geology, History, Humanities, Journalism, Literature, Mathematics, Medical Laboratory

ATHLETIC PROFILE

Conference Affiliation: Independent Conference

University of Scranton

800 Linden Street
Scranton, PA 18510
Coach: Bill Howerton

NCAA III
Royals/Purple, White
Phone: (570) 941-7440
Fax: (570) 941-4223

ACADEMIC

Founded: 1888
Type: 4 Yr., Private, Coed
Religion: Jesuit
Campus Housing: Yes
Web-site: http://www.uofs.edu/
SAT/ACT/GPA: None
Student/Faculty Ratio: 17:1
Male/Female Ratio: 45:55
Undergraduate Enrollment: 3,200
Graduate Enrollment: 250
Scholarships/Academic: Yes **Athletic:** No **Fin Aid:** Yes
Total Expenses by: Year **In State:** $ 23,000 **Out of State:** $ 23,000
Degrees Conferred: AA, AS, BA, BS, MA, MS, MBA
Programs of Study: Accounting, Advertising, Biochemistry, Biology, Biophysics, Broadcasting, Business, Chemistry, Classics, Communications, Computer Information System, Computer Science, Criminal Justice, Economics, Education, Engineering, English, Finance, French, German,Gerontology, History, Journalism, Marketing, Mathematics, Political Science, Prelaw, Premed, Prevet, Psychology, Religion, Social Science, Theology

.THLETIC PROFILE

Conference Affiliation: MAC

Ursinus College

P.O. Box 1000, Main Street
Collegeville, PA 19426
Coach: Brian D. Thomas

NCAA III
Bears/Black, Old Gold, Red
Phone: (610) 409-3000
Fax: (610) 409-3200

ACADEMIC

Founded: 1869
Type: 4 Yr., Private, Liberal Arts, Coed
Religion: United Church of Christ
Campus Housing: Yes
Web-site: http://www.ursinus.edu/
SAT/ACT/GPA: 1200
Student/Faculty Ratio: 12:1
Male/Female Ratio: 50:50
Undergraduate Enrollment: 1,200
Graduate Enrollment: N/A
Scholarships/Academic: Yes **Athletic:** No **Fin Aid:** Yes
Total Expenses by: Year **In State:** $ 24,400 **Out of State:** $ 24,400
Degrees Conferred: BA, BS
Programs of Study: Biology, Chemistry, Economics and Business, Exercise and Sports Science, English, History, Politics, International Relations, Psychology, French, German, Spanish, Japanese, Philosophy, Religion, Computer Science, Mathematics, Physics, Premed, Prelaw, Education, Preengineering

ATHLETIC PROFILE

Conference Affiliation: Centennial Conference
Program Profile: We have a 6 week Fall program. We play a full 36 game schedule in the Spring. We do a Florida Spring break trip with 10-11 games. Our field is natural grass and is one of the best playing surface in the conference. It has a 328 left and right field fence with a 385 center.
History: The Coach Thomas era is from 1990 to the present. We had 3 post-season bids, one Centennial Conference Championship, one ECAC Championship and one ECAC Runner-Up.
Achievements: 1996 Centennial Conference Championships; 1996 ECAC South Championships; 4 of the last 5 years in post-season; ECAC Tournament; 2nd winningest coach in the Centennial Conference with a record of 57-33.
Coaching: Brian D. Thomas, Head Coach, has 28 years of coaching experience. He has over 500 wins in the region, high school and college combined. Mike Svanson ,Assistant Coach, started from 1990 to the present. He was All-Big Catcher in 1989 and graduated from Villanova University.
Roster for 1998 team/In State: 16 **Out of State:** 8-1 **Out of Country:** 0
Total Number of Varsity/Jr. Varsity: 24-26 **Percent of Graduation:** 100%
Number of Fall Games: 10 **Number of Spring Games:** 36
Positions Needed for 1999/2000: Pitcher **Most Recent Record:** 23 - 12 - 0
Schedule: Rowan University, College of New Jersey, John Hopkins University, Bridgewater State
Style of Play: Sound defense - 1st defensive team in the conference in 1998. We use all weapons on off-run-hit and run, bunt, etc. We strive for a fundamentally sound team with sharp execution.

Villanova University

800 E Lancaster Avenue
Villanova, PA 19085
Coach: George Bennett

NCAA I
Wildcats/Blue, White
Phone: (610) 519-4130
Fax: (610) 519-7987

ACADEMIC

Type: 4 Yr., Private, Coed, Engineering
Founded: 1843
Religion: Order of St. Augustine
Campus Housing: Yes

Web-site: http://www.vill.edu/
SAT/ACT/GPA: 1180/3.6
Student/Faculty Ratio: 13:1
Male/Female Ratio: 1:1
Undergraduate Enrollment: 6,512
Graduate Enrollment: 2,795
Scholarships/Academic: Yes **Athletic:** Yes **Fin Aid:** Yes
Total Expenses by: Year **In State:** $ 26,970 **Out of State:** $ 26,970
Degrees Conferred: AA, AS, BA, BS, MA, MS, MBA, PhD, JD
Programs of Study: Aerospace Studies, African Studies, Arab Studies, Accounting, Art, Astronomy, Astrophysics, Biochemistry, Biology, Business, Classics, Communications, Computer Science, Crimincal Justice, Economics, Education, Engineering, English, Finance, French, Geography, German, History, Humanities, Human Services, Interdisciplinary Studies, International Business, Liberal Arts, Marketing, Meteorology, Military Science, Natural Science, Naval Science, Nursing, Philosophy, Physics, Political Science, Predental, Prelaw, Premed, Prevet, Religion, Social Science, Special Education

ATHLETIC PROFILE

Conference Affiliation: Big East Conference

Washington and Jefferson College

45 South Lincoln Street
Washington, PA 15301
Coach: John Banaszak

NCAA III
Presidents/Red, Black
Phone: (724) 223-6054
Fax: (724) 223-5271

ACADEMIC

Founded: 1781
Type: 4 Yr., Private, Liberal Arts, Coed
Religion: Non-Affiliated
Campus Housing: Yes
Web-site: http://www.washjeff.edu/
SAT/ACT/GPA: 1000/20
Student/Faculty Ratio: 12:1
Male/Female Ratio: 54:46
Undergraduate Enrollment: 1,200
Graduate Enrollment: None
Scholarships/Academic: Yes **Athletic:** No **Fin Aid:** Yes
Total Expenses by: Year **In State:** $ 21,600 **Out of State:** $ 21,600
Degrees Conferred: BA, Liberal Arts College
Programs of Study: Accounting, Art, Biology, Business Administration, Chemistry, Economics, English, French, German, History, Physics, Philosophy, Political Science, Psychology, Sociology, Prelaw, Premed, Predentistry, Education, Human Resources Management

ATHLETIC PROFILE

Conference Affiliation: PAC

Waynesburg College

51 West College Avenue
Waynesburg, PA 15370
Coach: Duane Lanzy

NCAA III
Yellow Jackets/Orange, Black, White
Phone: (724) 852-3230
Fax: (724) 852-4122

ACADEMIC

Founded: 1849
Type: 4 Yr., Private, Liberal Arts, Coed
Religion: Presbyerian
Campus Housing: No
Web-site: http://waynesburg.edu/
SAT/ACT/GPA: None
Student/Faculty Ratio: 16:1
Male/Female Ratio: 47:53
Undergraduate Enrollment: 1,267
Graduate Enrollment: 25
Scholarships/Academic: Yes **Athletic:** No **Fin Aid:** Yes
Total Expenses by: Year **In State:** $ 14,690 **Out of State:** $ 14,690

Degrees Conferred: AA, AS, BA, BSN, BSBA
Programs of Study: Accounting, Biology, Business Administration, Chemistry, Commercial Art, computer Science, Criminal Justice, Economics, Electronic Media, Elementary Education, English, Finance, Health Care, History, Literature, Management, Marketing, Mathematics, Medical Laboratory Technology, Nursing, Political Science, Predental, Prelaw, Premed, Professional Writing, Psychology, Public Administration, Secodary Education, Social Science, Sport Broadcasting and Information, Sport Medicine, Visual Communications

ATHLETIC PROFILE

Conference Affiliation: President's Athletic Conference
Program Profile: We play on a Madison Field which has dimensions of 325 to the left, 375 to the center and 325 to the right. We have two large indoor facilities. We play a traditional 36 game in the Spring, beginning with a trip to Ft. Myers, Florida. Our field is natural grass.
History: The school program began as an NCAA Division III competition in late 1980's. We are affiliated with the President's Athletic Conference whose members includes Bethany, Alfred, Grove City, Thiel, Washintong and Jefferson. Previously, we were an NAIA member.
Achievements: PAC Titles in 1993, 1994 and 1995; In 1997, we were 1st in the country in team batting average for Division III schools, 7th in stolen bases and 8th in slugging percentage.

West Chester University

South Campus
West Chester, PA 19383
Coach: Jack Hopkins

NCAA II
Golden Rams/Purple, Gold
Phone: (610) 436-2152
Fax: (610) 436-1020

ACADEMIC

Founded: 1871
Type: 4 Yr., Public, Coed
Web-site: http://www.wcupa.edu/
SAT/ACT/GPA: 840+
Student/Faculty Ratio: 19:1
Male/Female Ratio: 39:61
Undergraduate Enrollment: 9,400
Graduate Enrollment: 1,900
Scholarships/Academic: Yes **Athletic:** Yes **Fin Aid:** Yes
Total Expenses by: Year **In State:** $ 8,000 **Out of State:** $ 11,900
Degrees Conferred: AA, AS, BA, BS, BFA, MS, MBA, MEd
Programs of Study: Accounting, Biology, Astronomy, Anthropology, Athletic Training, Biochemistry, Biological Science, Business, Cell Biology, Chemistry, Communications, Computer Science, Computer Information Systems, Creative Writing, Criminal Justice, Ecology, Earth Science, Education, English,Fine Arts, Forensic Studies, Geochemistry, International Studies, Liberal Arts, Marketing, Mathematics, Microbiology, Music, Natural Science, Nursing, Philosophy, Physical Education, Physics, Political Science, Predental, Prelaw, Premed, Prevet, Psychology, Public Health, Religion, Science, Social Science, Space Science, Spanish, Special Education, Speech, Speech Pathology, Speech Therapy, Sports Medicine, Theatre

ATHLETIC PROFILE

Conference Affiliation: Diamond Conference, ECAC
Program Profile: Our program has an indoor facility with a batting cage. Serpico Stadium is an on-campus field . It has a tarp and grandstand seating for 1,200. We do a Fall baseball tryout program. Spring schedule includes a Southern trip plus a 50-game schedule.
History: Our program began in 1889. We are the only Division I Men's program in the university and in the entire PA State system.
Achievements: 2-time PSAC Champions; 1-time ECC Champ; over 50 players have played professional baseball.
Style of Play: The foundation of the team is solid defensive play complimented by an aggressive offense.

Westminster College

S Market Street
New Wilmington, PA 16172
Coach: Scot Renninger
Email: rennids@Westminster.edu

NCAA II
Titans/Blue, White
Phone: (724) 946-7311
Fax: (724) 946-7021

ACADEMIC

Founded: 1852
Religion: Presbyterian
Web-site: http://www.Westminster.edu/
Student/Faculty Ratio: 16:1
Undergraduate Enrollment: 1,450
Scholarships/Academic: Yes **Athletic:** Yes
Total Expenses by: Year **In State:** $ 20,000
Degrees Conferred: BA, BS, Bmus

Type: 4 Yr., Private, Liberal Arts, Coed
Campus Housing: Yes
SAT/ACT/GPA: 540m/24
Male/Female Ratio: 42:58
Graduate Enrollment: None
Fin Aid: Yes
Out of State: $ 20,000

Programs of Study: Accounting, Art, Biology, Broadcasting, Communication, Business Administration, Chemistry, Computer Information System, Computer Science, Economics, Elementary Education, Environmental Science, Management, Political Science, Religion, Philosophy, Physics, Prelaw, Premed, Psychology

ATHLETIC PROFILE

Conference Affiliation: Keystone - Empire Collegiate Conference
Program Profile: The team plays a Spring season on a natural surface field.
Achievements: Coach Renniger was named Coach of the Year in 1982.
Coaching: Scott Renniger, Head Coach, coached at Heidelberg College in 1975. He coached at Westminster College in 1978.
Total Number of Varsity/Jr. Varsity: 18 **Percent of Graduation:** 995
Number of Seniors on 1998 Team: 2 **Number of Sophomores on 1998 Team:** 5
Most Recent Record: 3 - 10 - 0

Westmoreland County Community College

Armbrust Road
Youngwood, PA 15697
Coach: Mike Draghi

NJCAA
Wolfpack/Green, White, Gold
Phone: (724) 925-4129
Fax: (724) 925-1150

ACADEMIC

Founded: 1970
Student/Faculty Ratio: 17:1
Undergraduate Enrollment: 6,900
Scholarships/Academic: No **Athletic:** No
Total Expenses by: Year **In State:** $ 1,250
Degrees Conferred: Associate

Type: 2 Yr., Public, Jr. College, Coed
Male/Female Ratio: 38:62
Graduate Enrollment: None
Fin Aid: Yes
Out of State: $ 3,700

Programs of Study: Accounting, Architectural Technology, Business Administration, Commerce, Management, Child Care, Commercial Art, Computer Graphics, Computer Information Systems, Computer Science, Criminal Justice, Culinary Arts, Electronics, Engineering tEchnology, Fashion

Widener University

One University Place
Chester, PA 19013
Coach: Sean Matkowski

NCAA III
Pioneers/Blue, Gold
Phone: (610) 499-4446
Fax: (610) 499-4481

ACADEMIC

Founded: 1821
Type: 4 Yr., Private, Liberal Arts, Coed
Religion: Non-Affiliated
Campus Housing: Yes
Web-site: http://www.widener.edu/
SAT/ACT/GPA: 800/18
Student/Faculty Ratio: 12:1
Male/Female Ratio: 1:1.2
Undergraduate Enrollment: 2,400
Graduate Enrollment: 2,100
Scholarships/Academic: Yes **Athletic:** No **Fin Aid:** Yes
Total Expenses by: Year **In State:** $ 21,800 **Out of State:** $ 21,800
Degrees Conferred: AAS, BA, BS, MA, MS, MBA, MED, EdD, JD
Programs of Study: Business Administration, Engineering, Hospitality Management, Nursing, Human Services, Arts and Science, School of Law, Criminal Justice, Communications Studies, Physical Therapy, Physics, Psychology, Biology, Chemistry, Computer Science, Mathematics, Education, Economics

ATHLETIC PROFILE

Conference Affiliation: Commonwealth League of the MAC
Program Profile: We have a successful Division III program with indoor and outdoor diamonds. We do 30+ games per season including Spring training games at Cocoa Expo, Florida. We have outdoor practice games in the Fall. We do indoor scrimmages with Division I teams from January to February. Our school is located in a suburban Philadelphia area.
History: Baseball has been played at Widener for 120 years, the earliest known season is 1876. There have been many major league draftees and NCAA tournament appearances during the last 20 years. NCAA Division III 's all-time career strikout leader, Phil DiAngelo, attended Widener.
Achievements: MAC Regular Season Champions in 9 out of 11 years; 4 NCAA Division III Regional Tournament Appearances, back-to-back 20-wins season in 1990 and 1991; 11 ABCA All-Americans since 1974; ECAC Player of the Year in 1989 and 1991.
Coaching: Sean Matkowski - Head Coach.
Style of Play: Aggressive - stealing, hit and run, etc.. Emphasis on power pitching average 1 K per inning in 1993.

Wilkes University

P.O. Box 111
Wilkes - Barre, PA 18766
Coach: Joe Folek

NCAA III
Colonels/Blue, Gold
Phone: 800-wilkes u
Fax: (570) 408-9470

ACADEMIC

Type: 4 Yr., Private, Liberal Arts, Coed, Engineering
Founded: 1933
Religion: Non-Affiliated
Campus Housing: Yes
Web-site: http://www.wilkes.edu/
SAT/ACT/GPA: 950
Student/Faculty Ratio: 13:1
Male/Female Ratio: 1:1
Undergraduate Enrollment: 1,780
Graduate Enrollment: None
Scholarships/Academic: Yes **Athletic:** No **Fin Aid:** Yes
Total Expenses by: Year **In State:** $ 19,000 **Out of State:** $ 19,000
Degrees Conferred: BA, BS, MS, MA, PhD
Programs of Study: Business and Management, Communication, Engineering, Health Sciences, Life Sciences, Psychology, Social Sciences

ATHLETIC PROFILE

Conference Affiliation: Mid - Atlantic Conference, Freedon Division
Program Profile: We are a Division III program located in Northeastern, Pennsylvania. Our home field is called Artillery Park. It is a beautiful, old-fashioned style park that was the original home of the Wilkes-Barre Barens. Such greats as Babe Ruth, Whitey Ford, Bob Lemen, just to name a few, have played there. Artillery Park was the first groundkeeping job held by George Toma.
History: Wilkes baseball started in 1946. The Colonels celebrated our 50th anniversary in 1996.

Achievements: The colonels have been MAC Champions 4 times (1994 most recent) and have made two appearances in the Eastern Regional and College World Series. Since the late 1980's we have had 7 players drafted or signed. Our highest and latest pick was in 1995 (6th round, Seatlle); Pitcher Kevin Gryboski -currently pitching Winter ball in Hawaii. Project to start in 1998 in AA-Orlando (still with the Seattle).
Coaching: Joe Folek - Head Coach. Jerry Bauitz - Assistant Coach. Mark Youngblood - Assistant Coach. Rob Klineteb - Assistant Coach.
Style of Play: Aggressive, hard-nosed, old-fashioned baseball.

York College- Pennsylvania

Wolf Gym
York, PA 17405
Coach: Paul Saikia

NCAA III
Spartans/Green, White
Phone: (717) 846-7788
Fax: (717) 849-1626

ACADEMIC

Type: 4 Yr., Private, Liberal Arts, Coed, Engineering
Founded: 1941
Religion: Non-Affiliated
Campus Housing: Yes
Web-site: http://www.ycp.edu/
SAT/ACT/GPA: 970/21
Student/Faculty Ratio: 18:1
Male/Female Ratio: 40:60
Undergraduate Enrollment: 3,300
Graduate Enrollment: None
Scholarships/Academic: Yes **Athletic:** No
Fin Aid: Yes
Total Expenses by: Year **In State:** $ 9,980 **Out of State:** $ 9,980
Degrees Conferred: BA, BS
Programs of Study: Contact school for program of study.

ATHLETIC PROFILE

Conference Affiliation: Capital Athletic Conference
Program Profile: We built a very competitive, regional tourney qualifier, new stadium in 1999. It has a natural grass surface with a seating for 1,000+. We have a Fall and Spring season.
History: The program began in 1969 and qualified for regionals 6 times in the past 10 years. He was 1st or 2nd in conference in the last 6 years.
Achievements: Coach of the Year in 1992 and 1996; Conference Titles in 1992 and 1996; 2 All-Americans; 2 drafted players (Keith Wentz and Ed Fuller).
Coaching: Paul Saikia, Head Coach, began coaching for the program in 1986 . He compiled a record of 198-158 and was named Coach of the Year twice. He played for Southern Illinois University in 1984 and played two years in Alaskan League. Brad Chambers - Assistant Coach.
Roster for 1998 team/In State: 15 **Out of State:** 18 **Out of Country:** 0
Total Number of Varsity/Jr. Varsity: 33
Percent of Graduation: 1005
Number of Seniors on 1998 Team: 5
Most Recent Record: 16 - 18 - 0
Number of Fall Games: 9
Number of Spring Games: 36
Positions Needed for 1999/2000: 3
Schedule: Mary Washington, Montclair State, Rowan, St. Bonaventura, Emory-Riddle, Emory
Style of Play: Aggressive, double hitters, steal, take extra base, and good defense.

RHODE ISLAND

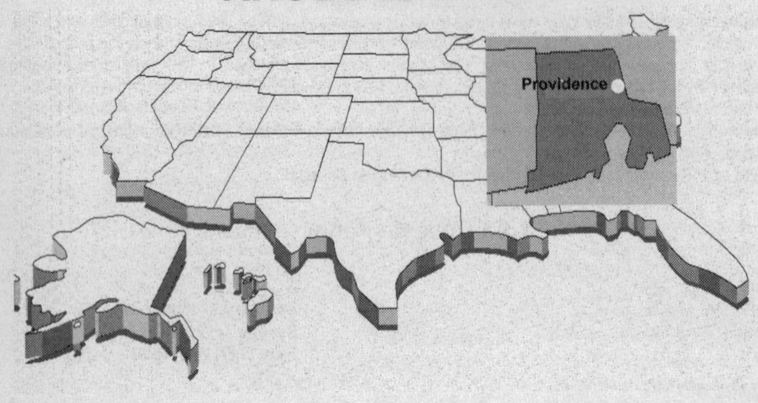

SCHOLL	CITY	AFFILIATION 99	PAGE
Brown University	Providence	NCAA I	759
Bryant College	Smithfield	NCAA II	759
Community College of Rhode Island	Lincoln	NJCAA	760
Johnson & Wales University	Providence	NCAA III	760
Providence College	Providence	NCAA I	761
Rhode Island College	Providence	NCAA III	762
Roger Williams University	Bristol	NCAA III	762
Salve Regina University	Newport	NCAA III	763
University of Rhode Island	Kingston	NCAA I	763

Brown University

285 Hope Street
Providence, RI 02912
Coach: Marek Drabinski
Email: Brett_Boretti@Brown.edu

NCAA I
Bears/Red, Seal Brown, White
Phone: (401) 863-3090
Fax: (401) 863-1463

ACADEMIC

Type: 4 Yr., Private, Liberal Arts, Coed, Engineering
Religion: Non-Affiliated
Web-site: http://www.brown.edu/
Student/Faculty Ratio: 8:1
Undergraduate Enrollment: 5,500
Scholarships/Academic: Ye
Athletic: No
Total Expenses by: Year
In State: $ 32,000
Founded: 1764
Campus Housing: Yes
SAT/ACT/GPA: 580-680v, 640-750m
Male/Female Ratio: 1:1
Graduate Enrollment: 1,600
Fin Aid: Yes
Out of State: $ 32,000
Degrees Conferred: BS, BA, MA, MS
Programs of Study: Art, Behavioral Science, Biology, Biomedical Sciences, Biophysics, Chemistry, Cognitive Science, Comparative Literature, Creative Writing, Electrical, Materials, Computer, Geology, Geophysics, Neurosciences, Religion, Theatre, Women's Studies

ATHLETIC PROFILE

Conference Affiliation: Ivy League Conference
Program Profile: The home field is Edward B. Aldrich Baseball Field with a seating capacity of 1,000. It has natural grass and the dimensions are 340' LF, 405' CF and 325' RF.
History: We are Ivy League and began full competition in 1993 .Our teams have competed in the Eastern Intercollegiate Baseball League for 64 years.
Achievements: Freshman All-American (Louisville Slugger) was Jeff Lawler. Junior RHP-Graeme Brown was drafted out of high school - 12th round. Bill Almon was College Baseball Player of the Year in 1974, drafted by the San Diego Padres, also played for Montreat Expos, Chicago White Sox, Etc. Todd Carey was drafted by the Boston Red Sox.
Coaching: Marek Drabinski, Head Coach, started with the program in 1996-1997. Brett Boretti - Assistant Coach. J.J. koning, Assistant Coach, entered his 2nd year with the program.
Roster for 1998 team/In State: 1
Out of State: 25
Out of Country: 0
Total Number of Varsity/Jr. Varsity: 26
Percent of Graduation: 99%
Number of Seniors on 1998 Team: 1
Number of Sophomores on 1998 Team: 8
Number of Fall Games: 4-6
Number of Spring Games: 48
Most Recent Record: 12-34 - 0
Baseball Camp Dates: June 20-24
Positions Needed for 1999/2000: Outfielder, Pitcher
Schedule: Providence, Boston College, Georgetown, Coastal Carolina, George Mason, Harvard
Style of Play: Aggressive - put pressure on the opponents.

Bryant College

1150 Douglas Pike
Smithfield, RI 02917
Coach: Jonathan Sjogren

NCAA II
Bulldogs/Black, Gold
Phone: (401) 232-6397
Fax: (401) 232-6361

ACADEMIC

Founded: 1863
Religion: Non-Affiliated
Web-site: http://www.bryant.edu/
Student/Faculty Ratio: 20:1
Undergraduate Enrollment: 2,300
Scholarships/Academic: Yes
Athletic: Yes
Total Expenses by: Year
In State: $ 18,500
Type: 4 Yr., Private, Liberal Arts, Coed
Campus Housing: Yes
SAT/ACT/GPA: 820
Male/Female Ratio: 1:1
Graduate Enrollment: 700
Fin Aid: Yes
Out of State: $ 18,500

Degrees Conferred: AS, BA, BS, MS, MBA
Programs of Study: Accounting, Actuarial Science, Business Administration, Communications, Computer Information System, Economics, English, Finance, History, Information Science, International Studies, Management, Marketing

ATHLETIC PROFILE

Conference Affiliation: Northeast 10 Conference
Program Profile: We play home games on a grass field. We take a Florida trip in the Spring.
Achievements: Jon Sjogren - won two-time Northeast 10 Coach of the Year; Darin Dagle was a 1996 1st team All-American; NCAA Tournament in 1986 and 1987.
Coaching: Jonathan Sjogren, Head Coach, was a three-time All-Northeast 10 and two-time All-Northeast. He was an assistant for two years at University of Rhode Island.

Community College of Rhode Island

1762 Louisquisset Pike
Lincoln, RI 02865
Coach: Jay Grenier

NJCAA
Knights/Green, White
Phone: (401) 825-2106
Fax: (401) 825-1062

ACADEMIC

Founded: 1964
Type: 2 Yr., Public, Jr. College, Coed
Religion: Non-Affiliated
Campus Housing: No
Student/Faculty Ratio: 18:1
Male/Female Ratio: 38:62
Undergraduate Enrollment: 11,730
Graduate Enrollment: None
Scholarships/Academic: No **Athletic:** No **Fin Aid:** Yes
Total Expenses by: Year **In State:** $ 1,600 **Out of State:** $ 4,400
Degrees Conferred: Associate
Programs of Study: Accounting, Art, Business, Computer, Corrections, Dental, Drug/Alcohol/Substance Abuse Counseling, Education, Engineering, Electrical/Electronics Technology, Fire, Gerontology, Human, Labor Relations, Law, Liberal Arts, Machine/Tool, Marketing, Mechanical, Medical, Music, Physics, Radiological, Real Estate, Respiratory, Retail, Science, Social Science, Urban Studies

ATHLETIC PROFILE

Conference Affiliation: Colonial States Conference
Program Profile: CCRI has 2 campuses, Warwick and Lincoln. Baseball program takes students from both.

Johnson and Wales University

8 Abbott Park Place
Providence, RI 02903
Coach: Dave Morris

NCAA III
Griffins/Royal Blue, Scarlet, White
Phone: (401) 598-1600x1425
Fax: (401) 598-1601

ACADEMIC

Founded: 1914
Type: 4 Yr., Private, Coed
Religion: Non-Affiliated
Campus Housing: Yes
Web-site: http://www.jwu.edu/
SAT/ACT/GPA: None
Student/Faculty Ratio: 1:25,
Male/Female Ratio: 1:1.25
Undergraduate Enrollment: 7,000
Graduate Enrollment: 1,097
Scholarships/Academic: Yes **Athletic:** No **Fin Aid:** Yes
Total Expenses by: Year **In State:** $ 18,000 **Out of State:** $ 18,000
Degrees Conferred: Associate, Bachelors, Doctorate

Programs of Study: Culinary Arts, Business, Criminal Justice, Hospitality, Marketing/Accounting Technology, Recreation/Leisure Management, Hotel/Restaurant Management, Travel and Tourism

ATHLETIC PROFILE

Conference Affiliation: Great Northeast Athletic Conference
Program Profile: We play a 24-game Spring schedule and 12 games in the Fall. We play with Division III opponents. We have an annual Fall tournament with Rhode Island's eight other programs. Our home field is Pierce Stadium in East Providence. It has natural grass. An indoor practice facility for Winter is available.
History: Our club program elevated to NCAA Division III in 1995-1996. We are one of the founding members of Great Northeast Athletic Conference.
Achievements: GNAC Regular Season Champs in 1996; Dave Morris named Conference Coach of the Year in 1996.
Coaching: Dave Morris, Head Coach, came to JWU after 4 seasons as an assistant and 4 seasons as a head coach at University of Rhode Island (Divison I, Atlantic 10). His team got the Coach District Championship at Clarkson, GA High School and at North Kingstown, RI High School.
Style of Play: Emphasis on fundamentals. The fewer the mistakes, the better the chances of winning. A team that will keep things simple and execute.

Providence College

River Avenue
Providence, RI 02918
Coach: Charlie Hickey

NCAA I
Friars/Black, White
Phone: (401) 865-2273
Fax: (401) 865-1231

ACADEMIC

Founded: 1917
Type: 4 Yr., Private, Liberal Arts, Coed
Religion: Catholic (Dominican)
Campus Housing: Yes (96%)
Web-site: http://www.providence.edu/
SAT/ACT/GPA: 1050/
Student/Faculty Ratio: 13:1
Male/Female Ratio: 4:5
Undergraduate Enrollment: 3,500
Graduate Enrollment: None
Scholarships/Academic: Yes **Athletic:** Yes **Fin Aid:** Yes
Total Expenses by: Year **In State:** $ Varies **Out of State:** $ 20,000
Degrees Conferred: BA, BS, MBA, MA, MS
Programs of Study: Accountancy, African Studies, American Studies, Anthropology, Art, Asian Studies, Biology, Chemistry, Computer Science, Economics, Education, Engineering, English, Finance, Health Services, History, Humanities, Latin American Studies, Management, Marketing, Mathematics, Modern Languages, Music, Philosophy, Political Science, Psychology, Social Science, Social Work, Sociology, Theatre Arts, Theology

ATHLETIC PROFILE

Estimated Number of Baseball Scholarships: 2
Conference Affiliation: Big East Conference
Program Profile: Hendriclhan Field is on campus and has natural grass. It has a full year program.
History: Baseball is the oldest sport at Providence College, beginning in 1921. The Friars play on one of New England's best fields, Hendricken Field which is on campus. PC won the Big East regular season title in 1995 and the tournament championship in 1992. We were co-champions of our division this season.
Achievements: 1992-1995 NCAA Regionals; Big East Regular Season Champs in 1995 and 1996; Big East Tournament in 1992.
Coaching: Charlie Hickey, Head Coach, compiled a record of 58-44 in two years. Sean O'Connor - Assistant Coach.
Roster for 1998 team/In State: 1 **Out of State:** 28 **Out of Country:** 0
Total Number of Varsity/Jr. Varsity: 29 **Percent of Graduation:** 100%
Number of Seniors on 1998 Team: 6 **Number of Sophomores on 1998 Team:** 8
Freshmen Receiving Fin Aid/Athletic: 6 **Academic:** 0

Number of Fall Games: 3 **Number of Spring Games:** 54
Positions Needed for 1999/2000: 8 **Most Recent Record:** 31 - 22 - 0
Schedule: Rutgers, St. John's, Notre Dame, Tulane, Harvard, Alabama
Style of Play: We try to play fundamentally sound baseball with a good pitching and a strong defense. We try no to beat ourselves. We will be younger than in the past few years, so we will have to be patient with a player's development.

Rhode Island College

600 Mount Pleasant Avenue
Providence, RI 02908
Coach: Scott Perry

NCAA III
Anchors/Gold, Burgundy, White
Phone: (401) 456-8007
Fax: (401) 456-8514

ACADEMIC

Founded: 1854
Type: 4 Yr., Public, Liberal Arts, Coed
Religion: Non-Affiliated
Campus Housing: Yes
Web-site: http://www.rhodeislandcollege.edu
SAT/ACT/GPA: 750+
Student/Faculty Ratio: 25:1
Male/Female Ratio: 1:2
Undergraduate Enrollment: 5,000
Graduate Enrollment: 4,000
Scholarships/Academic: Yes **Athletic:** No **Fin Aid:** Yes
Total Expenses by: Year **In State:** $ 8,563 **Out of State:** $ 13,219
Degrees Conferred: BA, BS, BFA, BM, BSN, BSW, MA, MS, Med
Programs of Study: Accounting, Anthropology, Art, Art Education, Art History, Biology, Communications, Chemistry, Public Relations, Computer Science, Dance, Economics, Elementary Education, Telecommunications, Gerontology, Health Education, History, Computer Information Systems, Film Studies, French, Geography, Graphic Arts Technology, Latin American Studies, Management, Marketing, Math, Medieval and Renaissance Studies, Music, Music Education, Nursing, Philosophy, Physical Education, Physics, Political Science, Political Science, Public Administration

ATHLETIC PROFILE

Conference Affiliation: Little East Conference

Roger Williams University

1 Old Ferry Road
Bristol, RI 02809
Coach: Val Innocente

NCAA III
Hawks/Blue, White, Gold'
Phone: (401) 254-3050
Fax: (401) 254-3535

ACADEMIC

Type: 4 Yr., Private, Liberal Arts, Coed, Engineering
Founded: 1956
Religion: Non-Affiliated
Campus Housing: Yes
Web-site: http://www.rwu.edu/
SAT/ACT/GPA: 1050
Student/Faculty Ratio: 20:1
Male/Female Ratio: 56:44
Undergraduate Enrollment: 2,100
Graduate Enrollment: 465
Scholarships/Academic: Yes **Athletic:** No **Fin Aid:** Yes
Total Expenses by: Year **In State:** $ 22,000 **Out of State:** $ 22,000
Degrees Conferred: BA, BS, BFA, B-Arch, Juris Doctor
Programs of Study: Art and Science, Architecture, Business, Engineering, Law

ATHLETIC PROFILE

Conference Affiliation: Commonwealth Coast Conference
Program Profile: The playing season is during the Fall and Spring. Roger Williams University has a lighted, natural grass baseball field.

History: The program began in the 1970's. The team has done consistently well in the past twenty years, around the .500 mark.

Salve Regina University

100 Ochre Point Avenue
Newport, RI 02840
Coach: George Andrade

NCAA III
The Newporters/Navy, White, Kelly
Phone: (401) 847-6650
Fax: (401) 847-0372

ACADEMIC

Founded: 1947
Type: 4 Yr., Private, Liberal Arts, Coed
Religion: Catholic
Campus Housing: Yes
SAT/ACT/GPA: Varies in ratio to academical performance/
Web-site: http://www.salve.edu/
Student/Faculty Ratio: 16:1
Male/Female Ratio: 1:2
Undergraduate Enrollment: 1,377
Graduate Enrollment: 515
Scholarships/Academic: Yes **Athletic:** No **Fin Aid:** Yes
Total Expenses by: Year **In State:** $ 21,900 **Out of State:** $ Varies
Degrees Conferred: Associates, Bachelors, Masters
Programs of Study: Accounting, Administration of Justice, American Studies, Art, Biology and Biomedical Sciences, Business Administration, Chemistry, Cytotechnology, Early Childhood Education, Economics, Elementary Education, English, French, History, Mathematical Science, Medical Technology, Nursing, Philosophy, Politics, Prelaw, Premed, Psychology, Religious Studies, Secondary Education, Social Work, Sociology

ATHLETIC PROFILE

Conference Affiliation: ECAC, Commonwealth Coast Conference

University of Rhode Island

3 Keaney Rd., Suite 1
Kingston, RI 02881
Coach: Frank Leoni

NCAA I
Rams/Lt. Blue, Navy, White
Phone: (401) 874-4550
Fax: (401) 874-5354

ACADEMIC

Type: 4 Yr., Public, Lberal Arts, Coed, Engineering
Founded: 1896
Religion: Non-Affiliated
Campus Housing: Yes
Web-site: http://www.uri.edu/
SAT/ACT/GPA: 960/23 Avg
Student/Faculty Ratio: 16:1
Male/Female Ratio: 1:1
Undergraduate Enrollment: 10,000
Graduate Enrollment: 2,000
Scholarships/Academic: Yes **Athletic:** Yes **Fin Aid:** Yes
Total Expenses by: Year **In State:** $ 11,000 **Out of State:** $ 19,200
Degrees Conferred: 25 Different Majors
Programs of Study: Arts and Science, Business Administration, Engineering, Human Science and Services, Nursing, Pharmacy, Resource Development, Finance, Accounting, Chemistry, Economics, Computer, History, Mechanical, Music, Electrical, Political Science

ATHLETIC PROFILE

Estimated Number of Baseball Scholarships: 2
Conference Affiliation: Atlantic 10 Conference
Program Profile: URI is a well organized program with a great outdoor facility located on campus. The dimensions of the stadium are 315' LF, 400' C, 315' RF and gaps 370.It has natural grass. We do 51 Spring games that start practice in January and end the 3rd week of May. The Fall season consists of 5 weeks and goes from mid-September through the end of October.
History: The program began in 1898.

Achievements: 1998 - Jay Krytoloski was named Atlantic 10 Pitcher of the Year; 2nd team All-Northeast Region (ABC) free agent signee by New York Mets; 1997 Rob Farrell - 2nd team All-Northeast Region (ABCA) free agent signee (Springfield Capitals).
Coaching: Frank Leoni, Head Coach, entered his 6th year with the program. His has a record of 74-172-2. He was a four-year starter as shortstop for URI in 1988-1991. His team recorded the 2nd most wins in school history in 1998. He was at La Roche for three years.
Roster for 1998 team/In State: 14 **Out of State:** 25 **Out of Country:** 0
Total Number of Varsity/Jr. Varsity: 0 **Percent of Graduation:** 100%
Number of Seniors on 1998 Team: 4 **Number of Sophomores on 1998 Team:** 9
Freshmen Receiving Fin Aid/Athletic: 4 **Academic:** 3
Number of Fall Games: 5 **Number of Spring Games:** 51
Positions Needed for 1999/2000: LHP, Catcher, Shortstop, RHP
Most Recent Record: 19 - 24 - 0
Baseball Camp Dates: July 20-24; August 10-14
Schedule: University of Virginia, University of Massachusetts, Xavier, Providence, Harvard, Rutgers
Style of Play: Execute fundamental defense limiting unforced extra base opportunities. Offensively - aggressive on the bases while again executing a simple, fundamental style of hitting attack focusing on the specific situation.

SOUTH CAROLINA

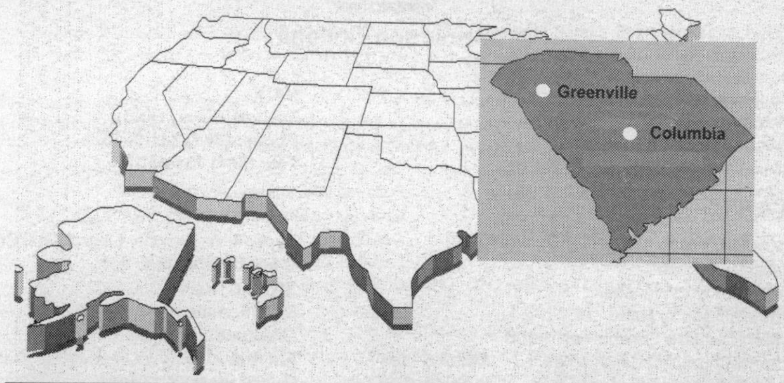

SCHOOL	CITY	AFFILIATION 99	PAGE
Anderson College	Anderson	NAIA	766
Benedict College	Columbia	NAIA	766
Charleston Southern University	Charleston	NCAA I	767
Citadel	Charleston	NCAA I	767
Clemson University	Clemson	NCAA I	768
Coastal Carolina University	Conway	NCAA I	768
Coker College	Hartsville	NCAA II	769
College of Charleston	Charleston	NCAA I	770
Erskine College	Due West	NCAA II	770
Francis Marion College	Florence	NCAA II	771
Furman University	Greenville	NCAA I	772
Lander University	Greenwood	NCAA II	773
Limestone College	Gaffney	NCAA II/NAIA	773
Morris College	Sumter	NAIA	774
Newberry College	Newberry	NCAA II	774
North Greenville College	Tigerville	NAIA	775
Presbyterian College	Clinton	NCAA II	776
Southern Wesleyan University	Central	NAIA	776
Spartanburg Methodist College	Spartanburg	NJCAA	777
University of South Carolina - Aiken	Aiken	NCAA II	778
University of South Carolina - Columbia	Columbia	NCAA I	778
University of South Carolina - Salkehatchie	Allendale	NJCAA	779
University of South Carolina - Spartanburg	Spartanburg	NCAA II	779
Voorhees College	Denmark	NAIA	780
Winthrop University	Rock Hill	NCAA I	780
Wofford College	Spartanburg	NCAA I	781

Anderson College

316 Boulevard
Anderson, SC 29621
Coach: Joe Miller

NAIA
Trojans/Black, Gold
Phone: (864) 231-2013
Fax: (864) 231-5601

ACADEMIC

Founded: 1911
Religion: Baptist
Web-site: Not Available
Student/Faculty Ratio: 13:1
Undergraduate Enrollment: 1,100
Scholarships/Academic: Yes **Athletic:** Yes
Total Expenses by: Year **In State:** $ 13,561

Type: 4 Yr., Private, Liberal Arts, Coed
Campus Housing: Yes
SAT/ACT/GPA: 900/18/2.5
Male/Female Ratio: 40:60
Graduate Enrollment: None
Fin Aid: Yes
Out of State: $ 13,561

Degrees Conferred: AA, BA, BS
Programs of Study: Art, Biological, Business, Communications, Education, English, Fashion, Graphic Art, History, Interior Design, Journalism, Liberal Studies, Literature, Management, Marketing, Music, Psychology, Religion, Speech, Theatre

ATHLETIC PROFILE

Conference Affiliation: NAIA, Independent Conference
Program Profile: We play 53 games in Anderson Memorial Stadium. It seats 5,000 and has natural grass. There are lights, three batting cages and a clubhouse. Our field size is 337, 414, 346 and 397 with 402 gaps. The Atlanta Braves once had a Class A club here.
History: Our program began in 1984. The Trojans have won two junior college conference titles. Since becoming a four-year school, we have finished 2nd two times and have won a national championship in the NCCAA.
Achievements: 1994 NCCAA National Champions; 1995 Runner-Up; 1 player drafted by the Florida Mariners; 4 Conference Championships.
Coaching: Joe Miller - Head Coach.
Style of Play: Speed - hit and run - solid defense.

Benedict College

1600 Harden Street
Columbia, SC 29204
Coach: Yancy King

NAIA
Tigers/Purple, Gold
Phone: (803) 253-5405
Fax: (803) 253-1789

ACADEMIC

Founded: 1870
Religion: Baptist
Web-site: Not Available
Student/Faculty Ratio: 17:1
Undergraduate Enrollment: 1,265
Scholarships/Academic: Yes **Athletic:** Yes
Total Expenses by: Year **In State:** $ 8,500

Type: 4 Yr., Private, Liberal Arts, Coed
Campus Housing: No
SAT/ACT/GPA: 17+
Male/Female Ratio: 33:67
Graduate Enrollment: None
Fin Aid: Yes
Out of State: $ 8,500

Degrees Conferred: BA, BS, BSW
Programs of Study: Accounting, Biological Science, Business Administration, Chemistry, Computer Science, Criminal Justice, Early Childhood Education, Elementary Education, English, Environmental Health, Journalism, Mathematics, Philosophy, Music, Physics, Religion, Social Science

ATHLETIC PROFILE

Conference Affiliation: EIAC

Charleston Southern University

P.O. Box 118087
Charleston, SC 29423-8087
Coach: Gary Murphy

NCAA I
Buccaneers/Navy, Gold
Phone: (843) 863-7591
Fax: (843) 863-7695

ACADEMIC

Founded: 1964
Type: 4 Yr., Private, Liberal Arts, Coed
Religion: Southern Baptist
Campus Housing: Yes
Web-site: http://www.csuniv.edu
SAT/ACT/GPA: 850/20
Student/Faculty Ratio: 15:1
Male/Female Ratio: 1:2
Undergraduate Enrollment: 2,500
Graduate Enrollment: 500
Scholarships/Academic: Yes **Athletic:** Yes **Fin Aid:** Yes
Total Expenses by: Year **In State:** $ 13,310 **Out of State:** $ 13,310
Degrees Conferred: BA, BS, MBA
Programs of Study: Accounting, Biology, Botany, Business, Chemistry, Communications, Criminal Justice, Fine Arts, Economics, Education, English, Geology, History, Liberal Arts, Management, Mathematics, Microbiology, Music, Nursing, Political Science, Psychology, Religion

ATHLETIC PROFILE

Conference Affiliation: Big South Conference
Program Profile: We began Division I play in 1964. We have reconstructed the athletic offces, the weight room , the locker rooms, etc.. We do a NCAA 56-game schedule from the 1st week of February to the middle of May. The 1995-96 season will mark the 31st season of the Buccaneers.
History: Our program began in the former Baptist College. Six years ago ,we went Division I and changed name to Charleston Southern University.
Achievements: Quincy Boyo was drafted by Dodgers from 1993-1994 team; Runner-Up Big South Coach of the Year.
Style of Play: Very aggressive style of play. Look to score runs through a speed oriented offense. Defense will be fundamentally sound through all positions.

Citadel

171 Moultrie Street
Charleston, SC 29409
Coach: Fred Jordan

NCAA I
Bulldogs, Cadets/Col. Blue, White,
Phone: (843) 953-5030
Fax: (843) 953-5058

ACADEMIC

Founded: 1842
Type: 4 Yr., Public, Liberal Arts, Coed
Religion: Non-Affiliated
Campus Housing: Yes
Student/Faculty Ratio: 13:1
SAT/ACT/GPA: 920/19
Undergraduate Enrollment: 2,000
Graduate Enrollment: None
Scholarships/Academic: Yes **Athletic:** Yes **Fin Aid:** Yes
Total Expenses by: Year **In State:** $ 8,410 **Out of State:** $ 12,632
Degrees Conferred: BA, BS
Programs of Study: Biology, Business Administration, Chemistry, Civil Engineering, Computer Science, Education, Eletrical Engineering, English, French, German, Health and PE, History, Mathematics, Physics, Political Science, Psychology, Spanish

ATHLETIC PROFILE

Conference Affiliation: Southern Conference
Program Profile: Our facilities include two 5,000 seats stadiums. We went to the College World Series in 1990 and to the Regionals in 1994.

Clemson University

P.O. Box 31
Clemson, SC 29633
Coach: Jack Leggett

NCAA I
Tigers/Purple, Orange
Phone: (864) 656-1947
Fax: (864) 656-7324

ACADEMIC

Founded: 1889
Type: 4 Yr., Public, Liberal Arts, Coed
Religion: Non-Affiliated
Campus Housing: Yes
Web-site: http://www.clemson.edu/
SAT/ACT/GPA: None
Student/Faculty Ratio: 18:1
Male/Female Ratio: 56:44
Undergraduate Enrollment: 12,000
Graduate Enrollment: 4,500
Scholarships/Academic: Yes **Athletic:** Yes **Fin Aid:** Yes
Total Expenses by: Year **In State:** $ 10,471 **Out of State:** $ 15,785
Degrees Conferred: BS, BA, Masters, PhD
Programs of Study: 73 Undergraduate Programs; 9 Colleges: Agricultural Sciences, Architecture and Environmental Design, Business and Management, Education, Engineering, Forest and Recreation Resources, Liberal Arts, Nursing, Sciences

ATHLETIC PROFILE

Conference Affiliation: Atlantic Coast Conference
Program Profile: Clemson plays its home games at Tiger Field built in 1970. Tiger Field has 3,800 permanent seats and seats up to 5,000 with a hill down the third base line. The playing surface is all grass with a slope towards the outfield fence that serves as a warning tracks.
History: Clemson began playing baseball in 1896. Clemson has appeared in the NCAA tournament 25 times and has been invited to 12 straight NCAA Regionals. Clemson has been to the College World Series eight times with the most recent coming in 1996.
Achievements: Clemson has won the ACC Regular Season title 20 times since 1954. The Tigers have claimed ACC Tournament Championships including three in the 1990's. Current Head Coach Jack Leggett was named the ACC Coach of the Year in 1994 and 1995, his first two season as the Tiger Skipper. In 1996, Clemson Kris Benson was the first player selected in the major league draft. Benson was selected by the Pittsburgh Pirates and was one of the two Tiger pitchers among the top four picks. Team-mates Billy Kock was the 4th overall pick by the Toronto Blue Jays.
Coaching: Jack Leggett, Head Coach, started his 1st season as head coach in 1995. His record at Clemson is 246-88 (.737) in five seasons. He has guided Clemson to two CWS Appearance in 1995 and 1996. The Tigers have been to the NCAA Tournament and won at least 40 games in his 5 years.
Roster for 1998 team/In State: 13 **Out of State:** 25 **Out of Country:** 0
Total Number of Varsity/Jr. Varsity: 38 **Percent of Graduation:** 100%
Number of Seniors on 1998 Team: 4 **Number of Sophomores on 1998 Team:** 0
Freshmen Receiving Fin Aid/Athletic: 6 **Academic:** 1
Most Recent Record: 43 - 16 - 0 **Number of Spring Games:** 56
Positions Needed for 1999/2000: Pitchers, Catcher
Baseball Camp Dates: December 5-6; 3 weeks in June-2 weeks in July
Schedule: Florida State, Georgia Tech, UNLV, North Carolina, North Carolina State, Wake Forest
Style of Play: We play a very aggressive game offensively and defensively. We like to take action to the opposition and force them into mistakes. We like to hit and run; bunt, squeeze and steal bases and be aggressive on the basepaths.

Coastal Carolina University

P.O. Box 261954
Conway, SC 29528
Coach: Gary Gilmore
Email: dhogue@coastal.edu

NCAA I
Chanticleers/Coastal Green, Bronze
Phone: (843) 349-2820
Fax: (843) 349-2893

ACADEMIC

Founded: 1954
Type: 4 Yr., Public, Liberal Arts, Coed
Religion: Non-Affiliated
Campus Housing: Yes
Web-site: http://www.coastal.edu/
SAT/ACT/GPA: 820 Min
Student/Faculty Ratio: 18:1
Male/Female Ratio: 50:50
Undergraduate Enrollment: 4,800
Graduate Enrollment: 2,000+
Scholarships/Academic: Yes **Athletic:** Yes **Fin Aid:** No
Total Expenses by: Year **In State:** $ 2,910 **Out of State:** $ 7,840
Degrees Conferred: BA, BS, MED, MBA
Programs of Study: Accounting, Art, Biology, Business and Management, Computer, Education, English, Finance, History, Interdisciplinary, Marine, Marketing, Math, Political, Psychology, Sociology, Cooperative Golf Management

ATHLETIC PROFILE

Estimated Number of Baseball Scholarships: 11.7
Conference Affiliation: Big South Conference
Program Profile: We have a natural grass playing surface in a modern ,fully -serviced stadium. We have a seating capacity of 1,000, press box facilities, batting cages, a practice infield and a weight room. We had 22 winning seasons out of 25 years at the four-year level. We have gone to most Big South Championships.
History: Our program began in 1974, moved from NAIA to Division II and moved to Division I in 1986. We have won four Big South Tournament Titles. We won 6 straight regular season titles from 1988-1993. We reached NCAA Tourney in 1991.
Achievements: Most notable stars include Kirt Manwaring of the Colorado Rockies and Mickey Brantley who played in the majors with the Seattle Mariners and is now the hitting instructor with the New York Mets. Had two draft picks in 1998 draft. Damien Hart (13th round to Cincinnati), Dorian Cameron (44th round RDSF).
Coaching: Gary Gilmore, Head Coach, entered his 4th year at Coastal. His overall record is 78-89 at Coastal. His overall record is 335-187 for 9 seasons including 5 at USC-Aiken. He played at Coastal from 1978-1980 and holds the school record for stolen bases in season.
Roster for 1998 team/In State: 3 **Out of State:** 21 **Out of Country:** 1
Total Number of Varsity/Jr. Varsity: 30 **Number of Spring Games:** 56
Number of Seniors on 1998 Team: 7 **Number of Sophomores on 1998 Team:** 0
Positions Needed for 1999/2000: Catcher, Infielder
Most Recent Record: 31 - 29 - 0
Schedule: Clemson, North Carolina, Western Carolina, Delaware, Ohio, Kent
Style of Play: Very aggressive style, runners in motion. Built around speed and pitching.

Coker College

300 East College Avenue
Hartsville, SC 29550
Coach: Dave Schmotzer
NCAA II
Cobras/Navy, Gold
Phone: (843) 383-8073
Fax: (843) 383-8167

ACADEMIC

Founded: 1908
Type: 4 Yr., Private, Liberal Arts, Coed
Religion: Non-Affiliated
Campus Housing: Yes
Web-site: http://www.coker.edu/
SAT/ACT/GPA: Varies
Student/Faculty Ratio: 10:1
Male/Female Ratio: 1:1
Undergraduate Enrollment: 906
Graduate Enrollment: None
Scholarships/Academic: Yes **Athletic:** Yes **Fin Aid:** Yes
Total Expenses by: Year **In State:** $ 16,908 **Out of State:** $ 16,908
Degrees Conferred: BA, BS, BME
Programs of Study: Art, Biology, Chemistry, Communication, Dance, Drama, Elementary Education, English, History, Political Science, Physical Education

ATHLETIC PROFILE

Conference Affiliation: Carolinas Conference

College of Charleston

66 George Street
Charleston, SC 29456
Coach: Ralph Ciabattari

NCAA I
Cougars/Maroon, Gold
Phone: (843) 953-5916
Fax: (843) 953-8296

ACADEMIC

Type: 4 Yr., Public, Liberal Arts, Coed, Engineering
Religion: Non-Affiliated
Web-site: http://www.cofc.edu/
Student/Faculty Ratio: 19:1
Undergraduate Enrollment: 10,500
Scholarships/Academic: Yes **Athletic:** Yes
Total Expenses by: Year **In State:** $ 6,500

Founded: 1770
Campus Housing: Yes
SAT/ACT/GPA: 1050/19
Male/Female Ratio: 3:1
Graduate Enrollment: 1,500
Fin Aid: Yes
Out of State: $ 10,700

Degrees Conferred: BA, BS, MA, MS, MED
Programs of Study: Accounting, Anthropology, Art, Biochemistry, Biology, Business and Management, Chemistry, Classics, Communications, Computer Information Systems, Computer Science, Economics, Education, Elementary Education, English, French, Geology, German, Greek, History, Marine Biology, Mathematics, Music, Philosophy, Physical Education, Physics

ATHLETIC PROFILE

Conference Affiliation: TAAC
Program Profile: The home playing field has natural grass and the seating capacity is 1,500. Our playing season runs in accordance with NCAA guidelines. We play a NCAA Division I schedule which usually begins in early February and ends on May 15.
History: The program began in 1990. Our program became part of TAAC Conference in 1992. We will be moving to the Southern Conference in 1999.
Achievements: Sam Moone - Florida Marlins, Robbie Thomas - Dodgers, Thad Rowland - Boston Red Sox.
Coaching: Ralph Ciabattari, Head Coach, has 12 years of coaching experience.
Style of Play: We are a very intense group. We will use speed to create a run production. Pitching will be a strong part of our success. Hitting will be a strong suit of our club.

Erskine College

2 Washington Street
Due West, SC 29639
Coach: Dan Massarelle

NCAA II
Flying Fleet/Maroon, Gold
Phone: (864) 379-8777
Fax: (864) 379-2197

ACADEMIC

Founded: 1839
Web-site: http;//www.erskine.edu
Student/Faculty Ratio: 13:1
Scholarships/Academic: Yes **Athletic:** Yes
Total Expenses by: Year **In State:** $ 19,762

Type: 4 Yr., Private, Liberal Arts, Coed
SAT/ACT/GPA: Required
Male/Female Ratio: 1:3
Fin Aid: Yes
Out of State: $ Varies

Degrees Conferred: BA, BS
Programs of Study: Accounting, Athletic Training, Behavioral Science, Biblical Studies, Biology, Business and Management, Chemistry, Early Childhood Education, Elementary Education, English, French, History, Mathematics, Music, Music Education, Natural Science, Physical Education, Physics, Psychology, Religion, Spanish, Special Education, Sports Administration

ATHLETIC PROFILE

Estimated Number of Baseball Scholarships: 2.9
Conference Affiliation: Carolinas - Virginia Athletic Conference
Program Profile: Erskine's home field is called Grier Field. It seats approximately 800 people It has Bermuda turf and measures 395 to center, 330 lines, and 365 to the power alleys.
History: The first season was in 1905. We won State Championships in 1907, 1909 & 1910 . Under Coach Billy Laval and W.L. Pressly, Erskine went to a State Championship in 1916. Jackie Todd then coached from 1926-1941 with Erskine claiming another state title in 1936. When Harry Stille coached from 1959-1988, Erskine was a consistent powerhouse. They won the Region 3-times & beat USC, 4 consecutive times, Ohio University who was third in nation, UVA who were ACC Champs, Wake Forest, Furman, University of Massachusetts and Yale. UCS Bob O'Hoppe followed Stille and set a school record for number of wins in season with 29. Dan Massarelli, current coach, stopped in 1996.
Achievements: We have no Conference title yet. We have only been a part of a Conference for 4 years, this year being the 3rd year. We had 4 drafted players: Gare Moody, Jim Randall, Erskine Thomas in 1970; Jim Farey in 1991; school record for wins with 29 on Harry Stille (59 in 1988; Coach of the Year for South Carolina in 1984 and 1985; District 6 NAIA in 1964, 1970, 1984, 1985; Coach Bob O'Hoppe in 1991-1995; Coach of the Year District 6 in 1991. In 1993, Erskine was 4th in the nation in fielding and 9th in pitching.
Coaching: Dan Massarelle, Head Coach, entered his 3rd season. He compiled a record of 14-2-1 on his 1st season. He is a 1994 graduate and played at Erskine. Dorn Thorley - Assistant Coach.
Style of Play: We are a team that thrives on putting pressure on the defense. We like to steal, hit/run, bunt/run at any given time. We are an aggressive team which works on fundamentals. We pride ourselves in our offense and hitting.

Francis Marion College

P.O. Box 100547
Florence, SC 29501-0547
Coach: Gerald Griffin

NCAA II
Patriots/Red, White, Blue
Phone: (843) 661-1241
Fax: (843) 661-4645

ACADEMIC

Founded: 1970
Type: 4 Yr., Public], Liberal Arts, Coed
Web-site: http://www.fmarion.edu/
SAT/ACT/GPA: 820
Student/Faculty Ratio: 18:1
Male/Female Ratio: 45:55
Undergraduate Enrollment: 3,600
Graduate Enrollment: 200
Scholarships/Academic: Yes **Athletic:** Yes **Fin Aid:** Yes
Total Expenses by: Year **In State:** $ 6,278 **Out of State:** $ 9,278
Degrees Conferred: BA, BS, BBA, BGS, MBA, ME, MAT
Programs of Study: Accounting, Art, Art Education, Biology, Business Administration, Business Economics, Chemistry, Computer Information Systems, Computer Science, Economics

ATHLETIC PROFILE

Conference Affiliation: Peach Belt Athletic Conference, NCAA Division II
Program Profile: Our program includes a Fall practice and a 40-game (approximation) playing season from late February through the first of May. We were founded in 1973. The Francis Marion baseball program has suffered through only one losing season and has enjoyed 18 20-win seasons. Gerald Griffin began the program and is still head coach. FMU plays at the 1,000-seat natural grass, on-campus Cormell Field.
History: Gerald Griffin began the program in 1973 with only one losing season. Francis Marion won the NAIA District 6 championship in 1974, 1976 and 1988. FMU was selected to the NCAA Division II National playoffs in 1993 and finished 2nd in the South AtlanticRegional.
Achievements: NAIA District 6 Champions; Selected to the NCAA Division II playoffs in 1993; Gerald Griffin was named NAIA District 6 Coach of the Year and Co-Coach of the Year in 1990; Named SC Baseball Coach of the Year in 1979 and 1988; named Palmetto State Conference Coach of the Year in 1990, 1991 and Co-Coach of the Year in 1992. Griffin was elected to NAIA Hall of Fame in 1993.

Coaching: Gerald Griffin, Head Coach, graduated from North Carolina. He is a 2-time All-ACC selection. He played 4 years in the Philadelphia Phillies Organization and coached baseball for 6 years at St. Andrews Presbyterian College before coming to Francis Marion.

Furman University

3300 Poinsett Highway
Greenville, SC 29613
Coach: Ron Smith
Email: kylie.inman@furman.edu

NCAA I
Paladins/Purple, White
Phone: (864) 294-2034
Fax: (864) 294-3127

ACADEMIC

Founded: 1826
Type: 4 Yr., Private, Liberal Arts, Coed
Religion: Non-Affiliated
Campus Housing: Yes
Web-site: http://www.furman.edu/
SAT/ACT/GPA: 100 Appr.
Student/Faculty Ratio: 12:1
Male/Female Ratio: 50:50
Undergraduate Enrollment: 2,500
Graduate Enrollment: None
Scholarships/Academic: Yes **Athletic:** Yes **Fin Aid:** Yes
Total Expenses by: Year **In State:** $ 21,000 **Out of State:** $ 21,000
Degrees Conferred: BA, BM, BGS, BS, MAEd, MSChem
Programs of Study: Accounting, Art, Biology, Business, Chemistry, Computer Science, Economics, Education, English, Foreign, Mathematics, Music, Philosophy, Physics, Political Science, Psychology, Religion, Theatre

ATHLETIC PROFILE

Estimated Number of Baseball Scholarships: 6
Conference Affiliation: Southern Conference
Program Profile: Our baseball program is on the rise under Coach Ron Smith. We have a beautiful 1,000 seat stadium with a state of the art scoreboard. Our playing surface is rye grass with a clay infield.
History: The first year of the program was in 1939 .We went 4 times to NCAA Regional . Our last trip was in 1991. Our last season opponent was Missouri with a record of 8-4 loss. Our overall record is 715-931-11.
Achievements: 15 players in history drafted by major league baseball, Southern Conference Champions in 1965, 1969, 1976 and 1991 (Tournament Only); NCAA Regional in 1965, 1969, 1976, and 1991; David Noyce Freshman All-American LHP; GTE Academic All-American were John Campbell (1971), and Rob Goecker (1992), Southern Conference Player of the Year.
Coaching: Ron Smith, Head Coach, began coaching with the program in 1994 . He compiled a record of 101-146-2. He played baseball and basketball at Furman from 1975-1978. He was shortstop at the 1976 Southern Conference Championships. He played and managed in the Phillies Organization from 1977-1982. Greg McVey, Jeff Massey and Rocky Pitman - Assistant Coaches.
Roster for 1998 team/In State: 7 **Out of State:** 25 **Out of Country:** 0
Total Number of Varsity/Jr. Varsity: 32 **Percent of Graduation:** 85%
Number of Seniors on 1998 Team: 6 **Number of Sophomores on 1998 Team:** 10
Freshmen Receiving Fin Aid/Athletic: 13 **Academic:** 2
Most Recent Record: 21 - 27 - 1 **Number of Spring Games:** 56
Positions Needed for 1999/2000: RHP, LHP, Left-handed hitting corner
Baseball Camp Dates: 2 weeks in June, 2 weeks in July
Schedule: Clemson, South Carolina, Citadel, UNC-Greensboro, Western Carolina, Georgia
Style of Play: Aggressive, hard-nosed play. Emphasis on running game. Pitching and defense are emphasized as the keys to winning.

Lander University

(New Program)

Stanley Avenue
Greenwood, SC 29649
Coach: Rusty Stroupe

NCAA II
Senators/Royal Blue, Gold Trim
Phone: (864) 388-8011
Fax: (864) 388-8889

ACADEMIC

Founded: 1872
Type: 4 Yr., Public, Coed
Religion: Non-Affiliated
Campus Housing: Yes
Web-site: http://www.lander.edu
SAT/ACT/GPA: 850
Student/Faculty Ratio: 1:16
Male/Female Ratio: 2:5
Undergraduate Enrollment: 3,000
Graduate Enrollment: 300
Scholarships/Academic: Yes **Athletic:** Yes **Fin Aid:** Yes
Total Expenses by: Year **In State:** $ 7,300 **Out of State:** $ 8,925
Degrees Conferred: BA, BS, MEd, MBA
Programs of Study: Biology, Business Administration, Chemistry, Computer Science, Elementary Education, Engineering, English, Health Care, Management, History, Mass Communications and Theatre, Mathematics, Allied Health, Music, Nursing, Physical Education, Political Science, Psychology, Sociology, Criminal Justice, Prelaw, Premed, Prepharmacy, Preoptometry

ATHLETIC PROFILE

Estimated Number of Baseball Scholarships: 6
Conference Affiliation: Peach Belt Conference
Program Profile: We play a 56 game schedule. Our stadium seats 2,500 and has Bermuda grass. Our facility includes locker rooms.
History: The program began in 1998. It achieved national ranking in Division II in its 1st season and ranked as high as 20th.
Achievements: We finished 4th of 11 teams in the Peach Belt in the 1st season. The only senior on the team went on to play pro ball.
Coaching: Rusty Stroupe, Head Coach, has been college head coach since 1990. He has a record of 249-147. He was 1994 North Carolina College Baseball Coach of the Year. Chris Rodriguez and Mike Pitts - Assistant Coaches.
Roster for 1998 team/In State: 19 **Out of State:** 8 **Out of Country:** 1
Total Number of Varsity/Jr. Varsity: 28 /14 **Baseball Camp Dates:** Mid-July
Number of Seniors on 1998 Team: 5 **Number of Sophomores on 1998 Team:** 9
Freshmen Receiving Fin Aid/Athletic: 3 **Academic:** 1
Most Recent Record: 24 - 28 - 0 **Number of Spring Games:** 52
Positions Needed for 1999/2000: Pitchers
Schedule: Kennesaw State, North Florida, Georgia, Armstrong State, Presbyterian, Columbus State
Style of Play: Aggressive offensively with emphasis on speed and putting pressure on opponent's defense.

Limestone College

1115 College Drive
Gaffney, SC 29340
Coach: Larry Epperly

NCAA II/NAIA
Saints/Blue, Gold
Phone: (864) 488-4568
Fax: (864) 488-8360

ACADEMIC

Founded: 1845
Type: 4 Yr., Private, Liberal Arts, Coed
Religion: Non-Affiliated
Campus Housing: Yes
Web-site: Not Available
SAT/ACT/GPA: 800/18
Student/Faculty Ratio: 11:1
Male/Female Ratio: 55:45

Undergraduate Enrollment: 500 | **Graduate Enrollment:** None
Scholarships/Academic: Yes | **Athletic:** Yes | **Fin Aid:** Yes
Total Expenses by: Year | **In State:** $ 12,500 | **Out of State:** $ 12,500
Degrees Conferred: BA, BS
Programs of Study: Applied Art, Art, Biology, Business Administration, Computer Science, Early Childhood Education, Education, Elementary Education, English, Guidance, History, Humanities, Liberal Arts, Management, Math, Music, Physical Education, Predentistry, Prelaw, Premed, Psychology, Science, Social Work

ATHLETIC PROFILE

Conference Affiliation: PSAC

Morris College

100 West College Street
Sumter, SC 29150
Coach: Clarence Houck

NAIA
Hornets/Blue, Gold
Phone: (803) 775-9371
Fax: (803) 773-3687

ACADEMIC

Founded: 1908
Type: 4 Yr., Private, Liberal Arts, Coed
Religion: Southern Baptist
Campus Housing: No
Student/Faculty Ratio: 16:1
Male/Female Ratio: 36:64
Undergraduate Enrollment: 890
Graduate Enrollment: None
Scholarships/Academic: Yes | **Athletic:** Yes | **Fin Aid:** Yes
Total Expenses by: Year | **In State:** $ 8,000 | **Out of State:** $ 8,000
Degrees Conferred: BA, BS, BFA
Programs of Study: Contact school for program of study.

ATHLETIC PROFILE

Conference Affiliation: EIAC

Newberry College

2100 College Street
Newberry, SC 29108
Coach: Tim Medlin

NCAA II
Indians/Scarlet, Grey
Phone: (803) 321-5155
Fax: (803) 321-5169

ACADEMIC

Founded: 1856
Type: 4 Yr., Private, Liberal Arts, Coed
Religion: Evangelical Lutheran
Campus Housing: Yes
Web-site: http://www.newberry.edu/
SAT/ACT/GPA: 850/20/2.5
Student/Faculty Ratio: 12:1
Male/Female Ratio: 52:48
Undergraduate Enrollment: 744
Graduate Enrollment: None
Scholarships/Academic: Yes | **Athletic:** Yes | **Fin Aid:** Yes
Total Expenses by: Year | **In State:** $ 17,962 | **Out of State:** $ 17,962
Degrees Conferred: BA, BM, BME, BS
Programs of Study: Art, Biology, Chemistry, Veterinary Technology, Accounting, Economics, Business Administration, Business Administration and Computer Science, Communications, Elementary Education, Special Education, Learning Disabilities, English, French, German, Spanish

ATHLETIC PROFILE

Estimated Number of Baseball Scholarships: 4

Conference Affiliation: South Atlantic Conference
Program Profile: We play on natural turf. Our season begins February 3rd and finishes April 28th.
History: Our program began in 1899. It is in its 100th year of existence.
Achievements: Tim Medlin was named Coach of the Year in 1989 and 1992; District VI Champs in 1975, 1977, 1989 and 1992; Regionals in 1977, 1989 and 1992; World Series in 1977.
Coaching: Tim Medlin, Head Coach, started with the program in 1988. He has a record of 222-222. He was a Newberry graduate. Tom Eachus, Assistant Coach, started in 1991. He is a Newberry graduate. P.K. Fuller, Assistant Coach, started from 1989 to 1991 and from 1995 to the present. He is a Newberry graduate.
Roster for 1998 team/In State: 24 **Out of State:** 6 **Out of Country:** 0
Total Number of Varsity/Jr. Varsity: 30 **Percent of Graduation:** 98%
Number of Seniors on 1998 Team: 3 **Number of Sophomores on 1998 Team:** 11
Freshmen Receiving Fin Aid/Athletic: 6 **Academic:** 0
Most Recent Record: 21 - 32 - 0 **Number of Spring Games:** 55
Positions Needed for 1999/2000: 2-Outfielders, 2-Pitchers, Catcher
Schedule: Mt. Olive, Armstrong Atlantic University, Wingate University, Coker College

North Greenville College

Hwy 414
Tigerville, SC 29688
Coach: Kim Nihert
NAIA
Mounties/Red, Black
Phone: (864) 977-7150
Fax: (864) 977-7152

ACADEMIC

Founded: 1892 **Type:** 4 Yr., Private, Coed
Religion: Southern Baptist **Campus Housing:** Yes
Web-site: Not Available **SAT/ACT/GPA:** 860/18/2.0
Student/Faculty Ratio: 15:1 **Male/Female Ratio:** 1.2:1
Undergraduate Enrollment: 1,100 **Graduate Enrollment:** None
Scholarships/Academic: Yes **Athletic:** Yes **Fin Aid:** Yes
Total Expenses by: Year **In State:** $ 11,680 **Out of State:** $ 11,680
Degrees Conferred: BA
Programs of Study: Art, Biological Science, Business Administration, Communication, Computer Science, General Engineering, Health Science, Liberal Arts, Music, Psychology, Religious Education, Social Science

ATHLETIC PROFILE

Estimated Number of Baseball Scholarships: 3.2
Conference Affiliation: Mid South Conference
Program Profile: We believe in pitching defense. Most of our money is spent in our pitching staff. We have led our conference in ERA the last 2 years. We have a natural surface, large field that is definitely a pitcher's park.
History: 1995 was the last year NGC was a junior college; 1996 marked the 1st season as a 4-year institution.
Achievements: 1995 Region X (NJCAA) Slugger Coach of the Year; 1995 Region X Champs; 4th round (Reds); 1994 DeCombe Connor Outfielder 7th round draft by Reds; 1995 Herb Goodman outfielder.
Roster for 1998 team/In State: 25 **Out of State:** 10 **Out of Country:** 2
Most Recent Record: 31 - 14 - 0 **Percent of Graduation:** 85%
Number of Seniors on 1998 Team: 5 **Baseball Camp Dates:** June 15-29
Freshmen Receiving Fin Aid/Athletic: 10 **Academic:** 5
Number of Fall Games: 20 **Number of Spring Games:** 50
Positions Needed for 1999/2000: Middle Infielders, Pitchers
Schedule: Cumberland, Coker, Lander, Lambuth, Union

Presbyterian College

105 Ashland Avenue, Dept. of Athletics
Clinton, SC 29325
Coach: Doug Kovash

NCAA II
Blue Hose/Blue, Garnet
Phone: (864) 833-8236
Fax: (864) 833-8323

ACADEMIC

Founded: 1880
Type: 4 Yr., Private, Liberal Arts, Coed
Religion: Presbyterian Church, USA
Campus Housing: Yes
Web-site: http://www.presby.edu/
SAT/ACT/GPA: 1000/3.0
Student/Faculty Ratio: 12:1
Male/Female Ratio: 50:50
Undergraduate Enrollment: 1,200
Graduate Enrollment:
Scholarships/Academic: Yes **Athletic:** Yes **Fin Aid:** Yes
Total Expenses by: Year **In State:** $ 19,405 **Out of State:** $ 19,405
Degrees Conferred: BS, BA
Programs of Study: Accounting, Biology, Business Administration, Chemistry, Economics, Elementary Education, English, Fine Arts, History, Mathematics, Music, Physics, Political Science, Psychology, Religion, Philosophy, Social Science, Sociology, Theater Arts, Visual Arts, Engineering, Predentisry, Prelaw, Premed, Prepharmacy

ATHLETIC PROFILE

Estimated Number of Baseball Scholarships: 2.5
Conference Affiliation: South Atlantic Conference
Program Profile: We have a NCAA Division II program with a 56-game schedule plus a conference tournament. Home games are played at PC Baseball Complex. It has natural Bermuda tiftway 419 seed, outstanding playing surface with concrete and astro-turf batting cages. We have a practice field beyond rigth field.
History: In 1988, the program was revived after a 20-year layoff. We have a rich history dating from the early teens to 1968 with players like Chick Galloway (Philidelphia Athletics), Clavor Crocker (Brooklyn Dodgers) & Bob McBee (minor league player and manager). We had Coach of the Year in1988.
Achievements: Coach Doug Kovash was named 1998 SAC Coach of the Year; 1998 SAC Champions; 7 players gradauted to pros in 10 years of the program; 1998 2nd team All-American - Gere Gobbel; 1998 40 wins best in the school history; 1998 1st NCAA Regional Bid.
Coaching: Doug Kovash, Head Coach, was named 1998 SAC Coach of the Year. He is responsible for the hitters, catchers and the pitchers. Shane Spears ,Assistant Coach,is responsible for the hitters, outfielders and the basemen.
Roster for 1998 team/In State: 17 **Out of State:** 13 **Out of Country:** 0
Total Number of Varsity/Jr. Varsity: 35 **Percent of Graduation:** 90%
Number of Seniors on 1998 Team: 7 **Number of Sophomores on 1998 Team:** 10
Most Recent Record: 40 - 20 - 0 **Number of Spring Games:** 56
Style of Play: Fast, aggressive, hit and run ball. All of first middle infielders are base-stealing threats!

Southern Wesleyan University

(Former Central Wesleyan College)

1 Wesleyan Drive, P.O. Box 1020
Central, SC 29630
Coach: Mike Gillespie
Email: swu23@aol.com

NAIA
Warriors/Royal Blue, Gold
Phone: (864) 639-2469
Fax: (864) 639-0826

ACADEMIC

Founded: 1906
Type: 4 Yr., Private, Liberal Arts, Coed
Religion: Wesleyan
Campus Housing: Yes

Web-site: http://www.swu.edu/
SAT/ACT/GPA: 840/18/2.0
Student/Faculty Ratio: 14:1
Male/Female Ratio: 1:2
Undergraduate Enrollment: 420
Graduate Enrollment: None
Scholarships/Academic: Yes **Athletic:** Yes **Fin Aid:** Yes
Total Expenses by: Year **In State:** $ 14,500 **Out of State:** $ 14,500
Degrees Conferred: AS, BA, BS, MA
Programs of Study: Accounting, Biblical Studies, Biology, Business Administration, Chemistry, Education, Elementary Education, English, History, Liberal Arts, Mathematics, Medical Technology, Minitries, Music, Music Education, Nursing, Physical Education, Psychology, Religion, Social Science, Special Education, Theology

ATHLETIC PROFILE

Estimated Number of Baseball Scholarships: 4
Conference Affiliation: Georgia Athletic Conference
Program Profile: Our NAIA program is in a strong GAC. We play a 48 game schedule in the Spring with a Fall season as well. We work hard on fundamentals. Our team drills with a strong conditioning program in the Fall. We are working toward establishing a strong baseball program built with hardwork, dedication, pride, team speed and fundamentally sound student-athletes.
History: Our program started in 1986. We are working toward rebuilding and establishing a quality program.
Achievements: Won National College World Series in 1989 and 1995.
Coaching: Mike Gillespie, Head Coach, entered his 2nd year with the program. He is committed to building a quality program with quality student-athletes. Scott Atkins - Assistant Coach.
Roster for 1998 team/In State: 11 **Out of State:** 8 **Out of Country:** 0
Total Number of Varsity/Jr. Varsity: 24 **Percent of Graduation:** 100%
Number of Seniors on 1998 Team: **Number of Sophomores on 1998 Team:**
Freshmen Receiving Fin Aid/Athletic: 10 **Academic:** 5
Number of Fall Games: 0 **Number of Spring Games:** 48
Positions Needed for 1999/2000: Pitcher, OF, Shorstop
Schedule: Brewton-Parker College, Presbyterian College, Gardnerd-Webb University, Anderson College, Berry College, Montreat College, Southern Polytechnic
Style of Play: Working toward a strong defensive team with great speed - like to move runners with aggressive style of play.

Spartanburg Methodist College

1200 Textile Road
Spartanburg, SC 29301-0009
Coach: Tim Wallace

NJCAA
Pioneers/Royal, White
Phone: (864) 587-4244
Fax: (864) 587-4265

ACADEMIC

Founded: 1919
Type: 2 Yr., Private, Jr. College, Coed
Religion: Methodist
Campus Housing: Yes
Web-site: http://www.smcsc.edu/
SAT/ACT/GPA: 760/15
Student/Faculty Ratio: 16:1
Male/Female Ratio: 50:50
Undergraduate Enrollment: 1,000
Graduate Enrollment: 0
Scholarships/Academic: Yes **Athletic:** Yes **Fin Aid:** Yes
Total Expenses by: Year **In State:** $ 11,720 **Out of State:** $ 11,720
Degrees Conferred: AS, AA, ACJ
Programs of Study: Business, Education, Criminal Justice, Law Enforcement, Liberal Arts, Office Management, Social Science, Science

ATHLETIC PROFILE

Conference Affiliation: NJCAA Region X

University of South Carolina - Aiken

171 University Parkway
Aiken, SC 29801
Coach: Tony Casas

NCAA II
Pacers/Cardinal, White
Phone: (803) 641-3410
Fax: (803) 641-3441

ACADEMIC

Founded: 1961
Religion: Non-Affiliated
Web-site: http://www.usca.sc.edu/
Student/Faculty Ratio: 12:1
Undergraduate Enrollment: 3,300
Scholarships/Academic: Yes **Athletic:** Yes
Total Expenses by: Year **In State:** $ 6,000

Type: 4 Yr., Public, Coed
Campus Housing: Yes
SAT/ACT/GPA: 820
Male/Female Ratio: 35:65
Graduate Enrollment: 500
Fin Aid: Yes
Out of State: $ 10,000

Degrees Conferred: 4 years Baccalaureate Degrees
Programs of Study: Accounting, Banking/Finance, Biology, Business, Chemistry, Computer Science, Criminal Justice, Education, English, History, Marketing, Mathematics, Nursing, Physical Education, Political Science, Psychology, Social Science

ATHLETIC PROFILE

Conference Affiliation: Peach Belt Athletic Conference
Program Profile: Our facilities include a 1,000 capacity stadium. We have a 17,700 sq. ft. clubhouse, a game field, a practice infield and two turfed cages. Playing season starts on February 1st and goes through June. We practice year round.
History: Pacers have been ranked in the Top 10 in NAIA and NCAA Division II for the last 8 years & have been to the World Series 3 times in the past 6 years; 1st in 1993 going into the World Series.
Achievements: Since 1986, 36 players have been drafted/signed into professional baseball. Pacers have been to the College World Series in 1991 and 1993. We also finished Runner-Up in the Regional in 1992. The Pacers have won Peach Belt Conference Titles in 1992 and 1993. We won the regular season title in 1994.
Coaching: Tony Casas, Head Coach, entered his 2nd year as a head coach.
Style of Play: Very aggressive style of play.

University of South Carolina - Columbia

1300 Rosewood Drive
Columbia, SC 29208
Coach: Ray Tanner

NCAA I
Gamecocks/Garnet, Black
Phone: (803) 777-7921
Fax: (803) 777-8226

ACADEMIC

Founded: 1801
Religion: Non-Affiliated
Web-site: http://www.uscsports.com
Student/Faculty Ratio: 17:1
Undergraduate Enrollment: 9,349
Scholarships/Academic: Yes **Athletic:** Yes
Total Expenses by: Year **In State:** $ 7,500

Type: 4 Yr., Public, Coed
Campus Housing: Yes
SAT/ACT/GPA: 1000
Male/Female Ratio: 41:59
Graduate Enrollment: None
Fin Aid: Yes
Out of State: $ 11,000

Degrees Conferred: BA, BS, BFA, MA, MS, MBA, MFA, MED, PhD, EdD, JD
Programs of Study: Accounting, Anthropology, Advertising, Art, Biology, Broadcasting, Business, Chemistry, Classic, Computer Science, Creative Writing, Criminal Justice, Education, Engineering, English, Finance, Geography, Geology, Geophysics, German, Greek, Journalism, Liberal Arts, Management, Marketing, Mathematics, Medical Technology, Music, Nursing, Pharmacy, Philosophy, Physical Education, Physics, Political Science, Psychology, Religion, Social Science

ATHLETIC PROFILE

Estimated Number of Baseball Scholarships: 11.7
Conference Affiliation: SouthEastern Conference
Program Profile: We have new clubhouse and locker rooms. Saze Fry Field is one of the top in the nation. It holds 4,500 with 1,400 stadium seats. We were ranked 15th in attendance in 1998 and 11th best recruiting class in 1998. We were 44-18 in 1997 which got us as high as 3rd in the nation. We have a huge indoor facility. Our field measures: 330, 360, 390, 360 and 320. It has natural grass. We offer great academics.
History: University of South Carolina baseball dates back to 1925 when games pitched by future major leaguer James McCutchen, were played against local teams. We have been to the College World Series 5 times.
Achievements: Qualified for post-season tournament 13 times and the College World Series five times. Ray Tanner was named 1998 SEC Coach of the Year; 7 players drafted by Boston Red Sox in 1998 including 1st round shortstop Adam Everett; 2 Freshmen All-American pitchers. In 1998, we had two All-American players.
Coaching: Ray Tanner, Head Coach, coached 9 years at North Carolina State. He was named Atlantic Coast Conference Coach of the Year and Region Coach of the Year in 1994. He was an assistant for team USA for 3 years. He was formerly an outfielder at NC State. Jim Toman, Assistant Coach, works with catchers and recruiting. He entered his 3rd year. He was formerly at NC State. Jerry Meyers, Assistant Coach, is responsible for the pitchers. He started his 3rd year with the program and was formerly at ODU.
Roster for 1998 team/In State: 18 **Out of State:** 16 **Out of Country:** 1
Total Number of Varsity/Jr. Varsity: 35 **Percent of Graduation:** 755
Number of Seniors on 1998 Team: 15 **Baseball Camp Dates:** Call (803) 777 7913
Freshmen Receiving Fin Aid/Athletic: 10 **Academic:** 4
Number of Fall Games: 20 **Number of Spring Games:** 56
Positions Needed for 1999/2000: All **Most Recent Record:** 44 - 18 - 0
Schedule: LSU, Alabama, Florida, Auburn, Mississippi State, Tennesse
Style of Play: Pitchers throw strikes, fielders make routine plays. Hitters do not get cheated. Play hard, have fun and win!!

University of South Carolina - Salkehatchie

P.O Box 617
Allendale, SC 29810
Coach: Joe Baxter

NJCAA
Indians/Maroon, Gold
Phone: (803) 584-3446
Fax: (803) 584-5038

ACADEMIC

Founded: 1965 **Type:** 4 Yr., Coed
Religion: Non-Affiliated **Campus Housing:** No
Undergraduate Enrollment: 820 **Graduate Enrollment:** None
Total Expenses by: Year **In State:** $ 1,840 **Out of State:** $ 4,614
Degrees Conferred: Associate
Programs of Study: Contact school for program of study.

University of South Carolina - Spartanburg

800 University Way
Spartanburg, SC 29303
Coach: Matt Fincher

NCAA II
Rifles/Black, Green
Phone: (864) 503-5135
Fax: (864) 503-5130

ACADEMIC

Founded: 1967 **Type:** 4 Yr., Public, Liberal Arts, Coed
Religion: Non-Affiliated **Campus Housing:** Yes

Web-site: http://www.uscsu.sc.edu/
SAT/ACT/GPA: Varies
Student/Faculty Ratio: 20:1
Male/Female Ratio: 40:60
Undergraduate Enrollment: 3,500
Graduate Enrollment: 500
Scholarships/Academic: Yes **Athletic:** Yes **Fin Aid:** Yes
Total Expenses by: Year **In State:** $ 7,700 **Out of State:** $ 11,000
Degrees Conferred: AA, BS, Masters
Programs of Study: More than 30 Fields of Study in Liberal Arts, Sciences, Business Administration, Nursing and Teacher Education, plus Associate Degree in Nursing. Master's degree programs are offered in Early Childhood Education and Elementary Education. Other graduate courses are offered at USCS through the Graduate Regional Studies program of the USCS system.

ATHLETIC PROFILE

Estimated Number of Baseball Scholarships: 4
Conference Affiliation: Peach Belth Athletic Conference
Program Profile: We have a 56 game season and an on-campus practice field. Games are played at Duncan Park, former home of the Spartanburg Phillies. It has a seating capacity for 3,500.
History: Our program was established in 1987 and has an overall record of 218-138.
Coaching: Matt Fincher, Head Coach, entered his 2nd year with the program. He was an assistant coach with the Chatham A's in CapeCod League during the Summer. David Dart - Assistant Coach.
Roster for 1998 team/In State: 14 **Out of State:** 15 **Out of Country:** 0
Number of Seniors on 1998 Team: 5 **Number of Sophomores on 1998 Team:** 7
Freshmen Receiving Fin Aid/Athletic: 6 **Academic:** 0
Positions Needed for 1999/2000: Pitchers, Outfielder
Schedule: Kennesaw, North Florida, Georgia College and State, Columbia, Wingate, Armstrong
Style of Play: We try to develop solid defense and manufacture runs.

Voorhees College

1 Voorhees Road
Denmark, SC 29042
Coach: Adrian West

NAIA
Tigers/Blue, White
Phone: (803) 793-3351
Fax: (803) 793-4584

ACADEMIC

Founded: 1897
Type: 4 Yr., Private, Liberal Arts, Coed
Religion: Episcopal
Campus Housing: No
Web-site: Not Available
SAT/ACT/GPA: 720 avg
Student/Faculty Ratio: 17:1
Male/Female Ratio: 1:3
Undergraduate Enrollment: 800
Graduate Enrollment: None
Scholarships/Academic: Yes **Athletic:** Yes **Fin Aid:** Yes
Total Expenses by: Year **In State:** $ 7,500 **Out of State:** $ 7,400
Degrees Conferred: BS, BA
Programs of Study: Accounting, Biology, Business Administration, Computer Science, Criminal Science, Early Childhood Education, Elementary Education, English, Health and Recreation, Mathematics, Physical Education, Political Science, Government, Sociology

ATHLETIC PROFILE

Conference Affiliation: EIAC

Winthrop University

Eden Terrace Road
Rock Hill, SC 29733
Coach: Joe Hudak

NCAA I
Eagles/Garnet, Gold
Phone: (803) 323-2129
Fax: (803) 323-2433

ACADEMIC

Founded: 1886
Type: 4 Yr., Public, Coed
Religion: Non-Affiliated
Campus Housing: Yes
SAT/ACT/GPA: 700/17 min (sliding scale)/
Web-site: http://www.winthorp.edu/
Student/Faculty Ratio: 17:1
Male/Female Ratio: 37:67
Undergraduate Enrollment: 4,133
Graduate Enrollment: 1,175
Scholarships/Academic: Yes **Athletic:** Yes **Fin Aid:** Yes
Total Expenses by: Year **In State:** $ 7,837 **Out of State:** $ 10,793
Degrees Conferred: BA, BS, BFA, MA, MS, MBA, MFA, Med
Programs of Study: Art, Art History, Biology, Business Administration, Business Education, Chemistry, Education, Computer Science, Dance, Distributive Education, Early Childhood Education, Elementary Education, English, History, Home Economics Education, Mass Communications, Mathematics, Medical Technology, Music, Music Education, Philosophy and Religion, Physical

ATHLETIC PROFILE

Conference Affiliation: Big South Conference
Program Profile: We are a young Division I program in a young Division Conference. We have an excellent schedule and great weather.
History: Baseball started in 1980 at the NAIA level, with very good success. We went Division I in 1987 with a very marginal success. We have improved greatly in the past 3 years.
Achievements: Coach Hudak was a 1992 and 1995 Big South Coach of the Year. Carl Dale was drafted by the Cardinals, 1994 2nd round.
Coaching: Joe hudak, Head Coach, just finished his 6th year at Winthrop after serving as a pitching coach at Division I Power, in Mississippi State. He was named Coach of the Year.
Style of Play: Win with pitching and defense. Aggressive offensively with base stealing, and with hit and run.

Wofford College

429 North Church Street
Spartanburg, SC 29303-3663
Coach: Ernie May
Email: mayed@wofford.edu
NCAA I
Terriers/Black, Old Gold
Phone: (864) 597-4126
Fax: (864) 597-4112

ACADEMIC

Founded: 1854
Type: 4 Yr., Private, Liberal Arts, Coed
Religion: Non-Affiliated
Campus Housing: Yes
Web-site: http://www.wofford.edu
SAT/ACT/GPA: Varies
Student/Faculty Ratio: 14:1
Male/Female Ratio: 50:50
Undergraduate Enrollment: 1,100
Graduate Enrollment: None
Scholarships/Academic: Yes **Athletic:** Yes **Fin Aid:** Yes
Total Expenses by: Year **In State:** $ 15,000 **Out of State:** $ 18,000
Degrees Conferred: BA, BS
Programs of Study: Accounting, Biology, Business, Chemistry, Computer Science, Education, Engineering, Finance, English, History, Humanities, Life Science, Mathematics, Physics, Physical Sciences, Political Science, Prelaw, Premed, Psychology, Religion, Science, Sociology

ATHLETIC PROFILE

Estimated Number of Baseball Scholarships: 3+
Conference Affiliation: Southern Conference
Program Profile: We are a fourth year Division I program. We have a 5 week Fall program and a 17 week Spring season. Duncan Park has a grass surface and seats 3,500.
History: Our program has developed from NAIA to Division II to Division I in the past twelve years. It is the oldest program in the state of South Carolina. The frst game of the program was in 1896.
Achievements: NAIA District II Coach of the Year in 1988; 1997 Anthony Salley was 24th round pick by Toronto as a left handed pitcher.

Coaching: Ernie May, Head Coach, started with the program in 1995-1996 as a head coach at Division I with an overall record of 37-99. He was the pitching coach at the University of Massachusetts where he led the team to a 1995 Atlantic Conference Championship. He was a pitching coach Division II at Springfield College for 4 consecutive Conference Championships Andy Kiah and Branden Mckillop - Assistant Coaches.

Roster for 1998 team/In State: 12 **Out of State:** 18 **Out of Country:** 0
Total Number of Varsity/Jr. Varsity: 30 **Percent of Graduation:** 90%
Number of Seniors on 1998 Team: 7 **Number of Sophomores on 1998 Team:** 6
Freshmen Receiving Fin Aid/Athletic: 8 **Academic:** 12
Number of Fall Games: 3 **Number of Spring Games:** 52
Positions Needed for 1999/2000: Pitchers, Catcher, 3rd Base, Middle Infielder, OF
Most Recent Record: 15 - 31 - 0
Baseball Camp Dates: 1999 - weeks of June 7,14,21; Overnight 9/1-5
Schedule: Auburn, Clemson, Georgia, South Carolina, UNC-Greensboro, Citadel
Style of Play: Extremely hard working group, an abundance of talent for the smallest Division I school with I-AA football.

SOUTH DAKOTA

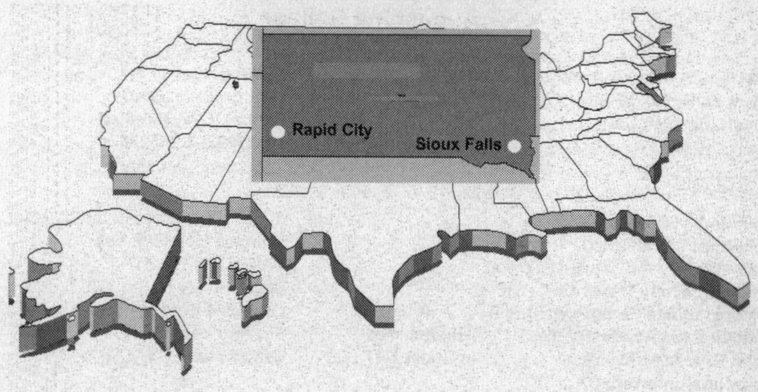

SCHOOL	CITY	AFFILIATION 99	PAGE
Augustana College	Sioux Falls	NCAA II	784
Dakota State University	Madison	NAIA	784
Dakota Wesleyan University	Mitchell	NAIA	785
Huron University	Huron	NAIA	785
Mount Marty College	Yankton	NAIA	786
Northern State University	Aberdeen	NCAA II	786
South Dakota State University	Brookings	NCAA II	787
University of South Dakota	Vermillion	NCAA II	787

Augustana College

2001 South Summit Avenue
Sioux Falls, SD 57197
Coach: Brett McCabe

NCAA II
Vikings/Navy, Gold
Phone: (605) 336-5541
Fax: (605) 336-5298

ACADEMIC

Founded: 1865
Religion: Non-Affiliated
Web-site: http://www.mst.angie.edu
Student/Faculty Ratio: 14:1
Undergraduate Enrollment: 1,550
Scholarships/Academic: Yes **Athletic:** Yes
Total Expenses by: Year **In State:** $ 17,000 **Out of State:** $ 17,000
Degrees Conferred: BA
Programs of Study: Business, Prelaw, Premed, Psychology, English, Communications, Art, Graphic Arts, Athletic Training, Geography, Sciences, Education

Type: 4 Yr., Private, Liberal Arts, Coed
Campus Housing: Yes
SAT/ACT/GPA: 17
Male/Female Ratio: 37:63
Graduate Enrollment: 200
Fin Aid: Yes

ATHLETIC PROFILE

Estimated Number of Baseball Scholarships: 3.8
Conference Affiliation: North Central Athletic Conference
Program Profile: Our program is designed to provide the student/athlete with a great baseball experience while obtaining an outstanding degree. We play home games on Ronker Field which is turf and has a seating capacity of approximately 200.
History: The baseball program started in 1915 at Augustana. In its 58th year history, the program has had 15 different head coaches. Brett McCabe, in his 2nd season, became the 16th coach in the history of the program.
Achievements: The Augustana Vikings baseball team has never won the North Central Conference.
Coaching: Brett McCabe, Head Coach, entered his 2nd year with the program. Benny Castello, Assistant Coach, entered his 2nd year with the program.
Roster for 1998 team/In State: 7 **Out of State:** 16 **Out of Country:** 0
Total Number of Varsity/Jr. Varsity: 25 **Percent of Graduation:** 95%
Number of Seniors on 1998 Team: 2 **Number of Sophomores on 1998 Team:** 6
Freshmen Receiving Fin Aid/Athletic: 8 **Academic:** 10
Number of Fall Games: 6 **Number of Spring Games:** 50
Positions Needed for 1999/2000: Pitchers, Catcher, Centerfield
Most Recent Record: 14 - 25 - 0
Schedule: University of Northern Colorado, NorthWest Missouri State, Missouri Western, Mankato State University, South Dakota State University, University of North Dakota
Style of Play: We will play to our strengths. We are looking for consistent pitching with a good defense to compliment a mix of speed and power on the offense.

Dakota State University

820 N Washington
Madison, SD 57042
Coach: Brad Doss

NAIA
Trojans/Reflex Blue, Pantone Yellow
Phone: (605) 256-5139
Fax: (605) 256-5138

ACADEMIC

Founded: 1881
Religion: Non-Affiliated
Web-site: http://www.dsu.edu
Student/Faculty Ratio: 15:1
Undergraduate Enrollment: 1,300

Type: 4 Yr., Public, Coed
Campus Housing: Yes
SAT/ACT/GPA: 18
Male/Female Ratio: 1:1.2
Graduate Enrollment:

Scholarships/Academic: Yes **Athletic:** Yes **Fin Aid:** Yes
Total Expenses by: Year **In State:** $ 3,312 **Out of State:** $ 5,102
Degrees Conferred: Bachelors Degree
Programs of Study: Elementary Education, Secondary Education, Information Systems, Computer Science, Business Administration, Computer Education, English for Information Systems, Health Information Management, Respiratory Care Administration, Fitness Wellness Management, Physical Education

ATHLETIC PROFILE

Conference Affiliation: South Dakota - Iowa Conference
Program Profile: We are a non-scholarship sport and games are played at Flynn Field in Madison. Flynn is a community stadium with natural grass and a capacity of 1,000. Playing season runs from mid-March through May. We have indoor facilities for hitting. Fielding at the fieldhouse is available.
History: After a 10 year hiatus, baseball was reintroduced to Dakota State in 1995. Conference championships were earned in 1983, 1984 & 1985. DSU competes in the South Dakota Iowa Conf.
Coaching: Brad Doss, Head Coach, played two years with team Canada. He was drafted by the Texas Rangers and directed free-agent tryouts for Torono and Atlanta. Aaron Arbogast, Assistant Coach, played collegiately at DSU. He coached the Madison Traveling teeners. Mike Mutziger, Assistant Coach, was head coach of the Madison Traveling Teeners and Legion teams.
Style of Play: Young team that is very aggressive, but makes some mistakes along the way. Like to manufacture runs as often as possible. Team is headed in the right direction going into its third year of existence.

Dakota Wesleyan University

1200 W University Avenue
Mitchell, SD 57301
Coach: Adam Neisius

NAIA
Tigers/Blue, White
Phone: (605) 995-2853
Fax: (605) 995-2150

ACADEMIC

Founded: 1885
Type: 4 Yr., Private, Liberal Arts, Coed
Religion: Methodist
SAT/ACT/GPA: 18 avg
Student/Faculty Ratio: 15:1
Male/Female Ratio: 40:60
Undergraduate Enrollment: 700
Graduate Enrollment: None
Scholarships/Academic: Yes **Athletic:** Yes **Fin Aid:** Yes
Total Expenses by: Year **In State:** $ 10,900 **Out of State:** $ 10,900
Degrees Conferred: AA, BA, MA
Programs of Study: Contact school for program of study.

ATHLETIC PROFILE

Conference Affiliation: (SDIC) South Dakota Iowa Conference
Program Profile: Our baseball park is called Caldwell Park and is in Mitchell,South Dakota . It has natural turf. Our playing season consists of a 50 game season. It starts the 1st of March with a tournament beginning in mid-May.
History: Our program began in the early 1980's and we have been a member of the SDEC since the conference began.
Style of Play: We are a fundamentally sound defensive team. We play with a lot of enthusiasm and will play hard every time out. We like to be aggressive at the plate and on the base paths.

Huron University

333 9th Street SW
Huron, SD 57350
Coach: Nolan Lane

NAIA
Tribe/Purple, Gold
Phone: (605) 352-8721
Fax: (605) 352-7421

ACADEMIC

Founded: 1883
Religion: Non-Affiliated
Web-site: http://www.huron.edu
Student/Faculty Ratio: 15:1
Undergraduate Enrollment: 500
Scholarships/Academic: Yes **Athletic:** Yes
Total Expenses by: Year **In State:** $ 11,300
Type: 4 Yr., Private, Liberal Arts, Coed
Campus Housing: Yes
SAT/ACT/GPA: 870/18
Male/Female Ratio: 55:45
Graduate Enrollment: 100
Fin Aid: Yes
Out of State: $ 11,300
Degrees Conferred: AA, AS, BA, BS, MBA
Programs of Study: Physical Education, Nursing, Criminal Justice, Secondary Education, Elementary Education, Business Administration, Psychology

ATHLETIC PROFILE

Conference Affiliation: South Dakota-Iowa Athletic Conference
Program Profile: We have a 55-game baseball schedule and a Spring trip. Our home field is a lighted. It is a former minor league ball park, with natural grass and a seating capacity of 5,000. We are one of the quickest rising programs in the Midwest.
History: Our program began in 1972.
Style of Play: Very aggressive running game (198-225). SB's last 2 years. Sound fundamentally on defense. Throw strikes, make plays. Line-drive hitters.

Mount Marty College

1105 West 8th
Yankton, SD 57078
Coach: Bob Tereshinski
NAIA
Lancers/Gold, Blue
Phone: (605) 668-1264
Fax: (605) 668-1357

ACADEMIC

Founded: 1936
Religion: Non-Affiliated
Web-site: Not-Available
Student/Faculty Ratio: 12:1
Undergraduate Enrollment: 990
Scholarships/Academic: Yes **Athletic:** Yes
Total Expenses by: Year **In State:** $ 11,100
Type: 4 Yr., Private, Coed
Campus Housing: Yes
SAT/ACT/GPA: 900avg/18avg
Male/Female Ratio: 33:67
Graduate Enrollment: 40
Fin Aid: Yes
Out of State: $ 11,100
Degrees Conferred: AA, AS, BA, BS, BSED, MED
Programs of Study: Accounting, Athletic Training, Behavioral Science, Biology, Biological Science, Business Administration, Commerce, Management, Chemistry, Communications, Computer Science, Criminal Justice, Predentistry, Elementary Education, Music, Music Education, Nursing, Radiological Technology

ATHLETIC PROFILE

Conference Affiliation: Independent

Northern State University

1200 South Jay Street
Aberdeen, SD 57401
Coach: Nate Gibbs
NCAA II
Wolves/Maroon, Gold
Phone: (605) 626-2488
Fax: (605) 626-2238

ACADEMIC

Founded: 1901
Religion: Non-Affiliated
Type: 4 Yr., Public, Liberal Arts, Coed
Campus Housing: No

Web-site: Not Available
Student/Faculty Ratio: 19:1
Undergraduate Enrollment: 3,150
Scholarships/Academic: Yes **Athletic:** Yes
Total Expenses by: Year **In State:** $ 5,000
SAT/ACT/GPA: 20 avg
Male/Female Ratio: 40:60
Graduate Enrollment: 210
Fin Aid: Yes
Out of State: $ 7,200
Degrees Conferred: AA, AS, BA, BSED, Med
Programs of Study: Contact school for program of study.

ATHLETIC PROFILE

Conference Affiliation: NSIC

South Dakota State University

Box 2820, Department of HPER
Brookings, SD 57007
Coach: Mark Ekeland
NCAA II
Jackrabbits/Royal, Yellow
Phone: (605) 688-5027
Fax: (605) 688-5999

ACADEMIC

Founded: 1881
Web-site: Not Available
Student/Faculty Ratio: 17:1
Undergraduate Enrollment: 8,100
Scholarships/Academic: Yes **Athletic:** Yes
Total Expenses by: Year **In State:** $ 5,250
Type: 4 Yr., Public, Liberal Arts, Coed
SAT/ACT/GPA: 22 avg
Male/Female Ratio: 52:48
Graduate Enrollment: 1,075
Fin Aid: Yes
Out of State: $ 7,650
Degrees Conferred: AS, BA, BS, BSN, MA, MS, PhD
Programs of Study: Agricultural, Animal, Biological Science, Botany, Broadcasting, Chemistry, Engineering, Computer, Design, Dietetics, Economics, Education, Geography, Journalism, Medical, Preprofessional Programs, Parks/Recreation, Psychology

ATHLETIC PROFILE

Conference Affiliation: North Central Intercollegiate Athletic Conference
Program Profile: We are one of the best baseball programs in the upper Midwest. We have a long and proud history and tradition of winning! We have great facilities on-campus. We play a Fall and a Spring season. We have indoor facilities for practice during the Winter. Yes, we do have Winter!
History: The baseball program dates back to 1902.
Achievements: 9 Conference Titles, 1 Regional Title, 1 Division II World Series appearance in 1984. Mark Ekeland named Conference Coach of the Year 1984, 1992, 1993 and Regional Coach of the Year 1984.
Coaching: We have 1 graduate assistant coach assigned to our program for a 2-year period. We usually have at least 2 senior assistant student coaches.
Style of Play: Aggressive both offensively and defensively! Find a way to win!

University of South Dakota

414 East Clark Street
Vermillion, SD 57069
Coach: Bryan Atchison
NCAA II
Coyotes/Red, White
Phone: (605) 677-5333
Fax: (605) 677-5073

ACADEMIC

Founded: 1862
Religion: Non-Affiliated
Web-site: Not Available
Student/Faculty Ratio: 17:1
Undergraduate Enrollment: 6,025
Type: 4 Yr., Public, Liberal Arts, Coed
Campus Housing: No
SAT/ACT/GPA:/20 avg
Male/Female Ratio: 45:55
Graduate Enrollment: 1,710

Scholarships/Academic: Yes **Athletic:** Yes **Fin Aid:** Yes
Total Expenses by: Year **In State:** $ 6,000 **Out of State:** $ 8,450
Degrees Conferred: AA, BA, BFA, MA, MBA, MFA, MD
Programs of Study: Contact school for program of study.

ATHLETIC PROFILE

Conference Affiliation: North Central Conference

TENNESSEE

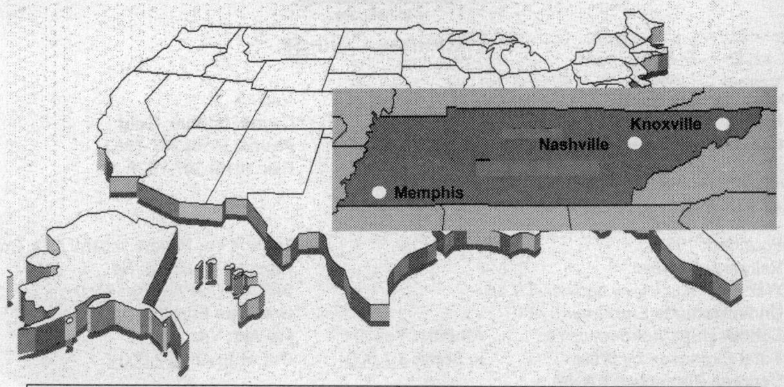

SCHOOL	CITY	AFILIATION 99	PAGE
Aquinas College	Nashville	NJCAA	790
Austin Peay State University	Clarksville	NCAA I	790
Belmont University	Nashville	NCAA I	791
Bethel College	McKenzie	NAIA	792
Carson - Newman College	Jefferson City	NCAA III	792
Chattanooga State Technical Community	Chattanooga	NJCAA	793
Christian Brothers University	Memphis	NCAA II/NAIA	794
Cleveland State Community College	Cleveland	NJCAA	794
Columbia State Community College	Columbia	NJCAA	794
Cumberland University	Lebanon	NAIA	795
Dyersburg State Community College	Dyersburg	NJCAA I	796
East Tennessee State University	Johnson City	NCAA I	797
Fisk University	Nashville	NCAA III	797
Freed - Hardeman University	Henderson	NAIA	798
Hiwassee College	Madisonville	NJCAA	798
Jackson State Community College	Jackson	NJCAA	799
King College	Bristol	NAIA	799
Lambuth University	Jackson	NCAA II/NAIA	800
Lane College	Jackson	NCAA II	801
Le Moyne - Owen College	Memphis	NCAA II	801
Lee University	Cleveland	NCCAA	802
Lincoln Memorial University	Harrogate	NCAA II	802
Martin Methodist College	Pulaski	NAIA	803
Maryville College	Maryville	NCAA III	804
Middle Tennessee State University	Murfreesboro	NCAA	804
Milligan College	Milligan College	NAIA	805
Motlow State Community College	Tullahoma	NJCAA	806
Rhodes College	Memphis	NCAA III	806
Roane State Community College	Harriman	NJCAA	807
Shelby State Community College	Memphis	NJCAA	807
Tennessee Technological University	Cookeville	NCAA I	808
Tennessee Wesleyan College	Athens	NAIA	808
Trevecca Nazarene College	Nashville	NAIA	809
Tusculum College	Greenville	NCAA II/NAIA	809
Union University	Jackson	NAIA	810
University of Memphis	Memphis	NCAA I	811
University of Tennessee - Knoxville	Knoxville	NCAA I	811
University of Tennessee - Martin	Martin	NCAA I	812
University of the South	Sewanee	NCAA III	813
Vanderbilt University	Nashville	NCAA I	813
Volunteer State Community College	Gallatin	NJCAA	814
Walters State Community College	Morristown	NJCAA	815

Aquinas College

4210 Harding Road
Nashville, TN 37205
Coach: Chuck Anderson

NJCAA
Cavaliers/Blue, Gold
Phone: (615) 297-7653
Fax: (615) 297-7970

ACADEMIC

Founded: 1961
Religion: Catholic
Web-site: http://www.aquinas-TN.edu
Undergraduate Enrollment: 400
Scholarships/Academic: Yes **Athletic:** Yes
Total Expenses by: Year **In State:** $ 7,000+
Degrees Conferred: AA, BA
Programs of Study: Nursing, Teacher Education, Liberal Arts

Type: 4 Yr., Private, Liberal Arts, Coed
Campus Housing: No
SAT/ACT/GPA: 870/18/2.0
Graduate Enrollment: None
Fin Aid: Yes
Out of State: $ 7,000+

ATHLETIC PROFILE

Conference Affiliation: TJCCAA
Coaching: Chuck Anderson - Head Coach.
Roster for 1998 team/In State: 6 **Out of State:** 15 **Out of Country:** 0
Total Number of Varsity/Jr. Varsity: 21 **Percent of Graduation:** 0
Number of Seniors on 1998 Team: 15 **Positions Needed for 1999/2000:** All
Freshmen Receiving Fin Aid/Athletic: 6 **Most Recent Record:** 19 - 19 - 1
Number of Fall Games: 0 **Number of Spring Games:** 56

Austin Peay State University

College Street
Clarksville, TN 37044
Coach: Gary McClure

NCAA I
Governors/Red, White
Phone: (931) 648-6266
Fax: (931) 648-7562

ACADEMIC

Founded: 1927
Web-site: Not Available
Student/Faculty Ratio: Unknown
Undergraduate Enrollment: 7,800
Scholarships/Academic: Yes **Athletic:** Yes
Total Expenses by: Year **In State:** $ 2,498

Type: 4 Yr., Public, Liberal arts, Coed
SAT/ACT/GPA: 19
Male/Female Ratio: Unknown
Graduate Enrollment: None
Fin Aid: Yes
Out of State: $ 4,563

Degrees Conferred: AS, BA, BBA, MA, MS
Programs of Study: Agriculture, Banking/Finance, Biological Science, Business Administration, Communications, Earth Science, Economics, Engineering, Technology, Forestry, Geography, Geology, History, Language, Latin, Management, Marketing, Mathematics, Microbiology, Optometry, Philosophy, Physical Education, Physical Therapy, Political Science, Preprofessional Programs

ATHLETIC PROFILE

Conference Affiliation: Ohio Valley Conference
Program Profile: Governors compete in ten-team Ohio Valley Conference, 56-game NCAA Schedule; annual Spring Break trip to Jacksonville, FL; schedule from Mid-February to early May; new permanent concession stands installed along with additional seating. Bringing total capacity to 1800; more improvements, including coaches offices and locker rooms, expected next year.
History: Program began in 1931. Two major leaguers Jim Stewart (sp.) and Greg Tubbs, Govs won school record 44 games in 1996; also won OVC regular season and tournament titles; advanced to first-ever NCAA regional at LSU; team ranked 36th nationally bry USA Today/Baseball Weekly.

Achievements: 4 OVC Coach of the Year awards; OVC champions in 1971, 1994, 1996; since 1987, several players have signed pro contracts, include four in 1996; 58 first-team All-OVC since 1963; APSU has had five OVC Player of the Year since 1971 and three Pitcher of the Year since 1992; four Academic All-Americans.
Coaching: Gary McClure, Head Coach, 255-249-3 in nine seasons; APSU all-time winningest baseball coach; two-time OVC Coach of the Year (1992, 1994). McClure became head coach while serving as graduate assistant at age 23. Brian Hetland, Assistant Coach, nine years at APSU. Steve Cornelison, Assistant Coach, two years.
Style of Play: Austin Peay baseball is noted for its aggressive style. We like to steal bases, hit and run, move runners, and play good, solid defense. We rely heavily on our starting pitchers. Our versatility and bench are also keys to our success.

Belmont University

1900 Bemont Boulevard
Nashville, TN 37212-3757
Coach: Dave Jarvis

NCAA I
Bruins/Red, White, Navy
Phone: (615) 640-6166
Fax: (615) 640-5584

ACADEMIC

Founded: 1951
Type: 4 Yr., Private, Liberal Arts, Coed
Religion: Christian
Campus Housing: Yes
Web-site: http://www.belmont.edu/athletics/athletic.htm
SAT/ACT/GPA: 1000/21/2.5
Student/Faculty Ratio: 14:1
Male/Female Ratio: 45:55
Undergraduate Enrollment: 3,000
Graduate Enrollment: 400
Scholarships/Academic: Yes **Athletic:** Yes **Fin Aid:** Yes
Total Expenses by: Year **In State:** $ 15,500 **Out of State:** $ 15,500
Degrees Conferred: BA, BS, BBA, BM, BMEd, BSN, BFA, MA, MSN, MS, MBA, Med
Programs of Study: Accounting, Art, Biology, Communications, Broadcasting, Chemistry, Child Care Administration, Church Music, Commercial Music, Computer Science, Ecionomics, Elementary Education, English, Exercise Science, Finance, French, Graphic Design, Health, History, Hospitality Management, Marketing, Mathematics, Medical Technology, Music, Music Business

ATHLETIC PROFILE

Estimated Number of Baseball Scholarships: 10
Conference Affiliation: Independent
Program Profile: With move from NAIA to NCAA I, the program has been upgraded. The primary practice field is at Shelby Park, city owned park. A working agreement has been reached to play 95% of games at Greer Stadium, home to the Seunds.
History: First year of the program was in 1952. The team was competitive in the early days of NCAA, but rose to prominence under Dave Whitten. He compiled a record of 661-452 with 8 Volunteer State Athletic Conference/Tennessee Collegiate Athletic Conference Titles.
Achievements: Dave Jarvis was name MidWest Community College Athletic Conference Coach of the Year in 1990-1992; Dave Whitten was named VSAC Coach of the Year in 1974. Jarvis MLB players: Chuck Malon by Phil; Jimmy Hurst by Boston, Bart Evans by KC, Whitten by Bernard - Mil.
Coaching: Dave Jarvis, Head Coach, began tenure in 1998. Came to Belmont University after stint as head assistant at Murray State; 324-152 record in nine years as JUCO head coach. Chris Moddelmog, Assistant Coach, former assistant coach at Murray State and is in-charge of recruiting. Dave Whitten returned as an assistant coach in-charge of pitching.
Roster for 1998 team/In State: 16 **Out of State:** 14 **Out of Country:** 0
Total Number of Varsity/Jr. Varsity: 30
Percent of Graduation: 80%
Number of Seniors on 1998 Team: 1
Number of Sophomores on 1998 Team: 6
Freshmen Receiving Fin Aid/Athletic: 9
Academic: 5
Baseball Camp Dates: TBA
Number of Spring Games: 56
Positions Needed for 1999/2000: All
Most Recent Record: 23 - 21 - 1
Schedule: Alabama-Birmingham, Kentucky, Vanderbilt, Middle Tennessee, Butler, Western
Style of Play: We like to play great defense and have quality pitching first offensively. We like to be very aggressive and put pressure on our opponent.

Bethel College

Cherry Street
McKenzie, TN 38201
Coach: Glenn Hayes

NAIA
Wildcats/Purple, Gold
Phone: (901) 352-4206
Fax: (901) 352-4069

ACADEMIC

Founded: 1842
Type: 4 Yr., Private, Liberal Arts, Coed
Religion: Presbyterian
Campus Housing: No
Web-site: http://www.bethel-college.edu
SAT/ACT/GPA: 700/17/2.0
Student/Faculty Ratio: 15:1
Male/Female Ratio: 43:57
Undergraduate Enrollment: 420
Graduate Enrollment: 40
Scholarships/Academic: Yes **Athletic:** Yes **Fin Aid:** Yes
Total Expenses by: Year **In State:** $ 12,000 **Out of State:** $ 12,000
Degrees Conferred: AA, BA, BS, MA, MED
Programs of Study: Accounting, Applied Mathematics, Biological Science, Business Administration, Chemistry, Elementary Education, English, Health Education, History, Music, Physical Education, Psychology, Religion, Social Science

ATHLETIC PROFILE

Estimated Number of Baseball Scholarships: 3
Conference Affiliation: KIAC
Program Profile: We have a two campus fields located off campus with natural grass. Indoor hitting cage. Playing season is from February to early March.
History: The program began in 1934, won National Conference titles, always a competitive team.
Achievements: Coach of the Year Awards; 5 Conference Titles (none in recent years); 8 All-Conference players.
Coaching: Glenn Hayes, Head Coach.
Roster for 1998 team/In State: 23 **Out of State:** 5 **Out of Country:** 0
Total Number of Varsity/Jr. Varsity: 28 **Percent of Graduation:** 80%
Number of Seniors on 1998 Team: 6 **Number of Sophomores on 1998 Team:** 5
Freshmen Receiving Fin Aid/Athletic: 10 **Academic:** 5
Number of Fall Games: 0 **Number of Spring Games:** 40
Positions Needed for 1999/2000: Catcher, Pitchers, Middle Infielders, 1st Base, 3rd Base
Baseball Camp Dates: May 27-29; June 1-4 **Most Recent Record:** 15 - 31 - 0
Schedule: Lambuth University, Freed-Hardeman University, Christian Brothers University, Lindsey Wilson College, Mount St. Mary, Illinois University South East
Style of Play: Good pitching, good defense, clutch hitting, play against base running and bunting.

Carson - Newman College

1646 Russell Avenue
Jefferson City, TN 37760
Coach: Gary Rundles

NCAA III
Eagles/Navy, Orange
Phone: (423) 471-3465
Fax: (423) 471-3514

ACADEMIC

Founded: 1851
Type: 4 Yr., Private, Liberal Arts, Coed
Religion: Southern Baptist
Campus Housing: Yes
Web-site: http://www.cn.edu/
SAT/ACT/GPA: 880/21
Student/Faculty Ratio: 12:1
Male/Female Ratio: 3:1
Undergraduate Enrollment: 2,200
Graduate Enrollment: 200
Scholarships/Academic: Yes **Athletic:** Yes **Fin Aid:** Yes
Total Expenses by: Year **In State:** $ 14,400 **Out of State:** $ 14,400
Degrees Conferred: BA, BS

Programs of Study: All Sciences, Humanities, Mathematics, Art, Athletic Training, Nursing, Business, Premed, Prelaw, Communication Arts, Computer Science, Education, English, Family and Consumer Services, Foreign Languages, General Studies, History, Human Studies, Math, Music, Natural and Physical Science

ATHLETIC PROFILE

Conference Affiliation: South Atlantic Conference
Program Profile: NCAA II program that plays a great schedule. We have one of the best on campus facilities in the NCAA II. Our season starts in February (6th) and will continue until first of May. We have a natural playing surface and can seat around 250 with a playing of other places to watch from.
History: Baseball started in CNC in 1929. Coach Frosey Holt coached for 35 years. 1965 Coach Bobby Wilson replaced him and Coach Wilson. Only 3 head coaches in the history of the school.
Achievements: SAC Coach of the Year in 1991 and 1996; Conference Champs in 1991 and 1993; Conference Tournament Champs in 1992, 1993, 1997; second in the conference in 1992, 1996, and 1997; 1992 Mike Brady players drafted ; 1988 David Owens and Deren Hodged; 1989 Rusty Bryan; 1990 Bob Badacoun and Chad Silver in 1991; Mike Thees; 1992 Todd Henderson, 1993 Jim Franklin, 1996 Scott May, 1997 Derick Henderson and Julio Guzman - a total of 11 players.
Coaching: Gary Rundles, Head Coach, entering 12 years as a head coach. He compiled a record of 249-187-3. Joey Seaver, Pitching Coach, entering 8th year. Denon Walraven, Graduate Assistant, entering one year. Tom Gretton , Graduate Assistant, entering second year.
Roster for 1998 team/In State: 12 **Out of State:** 18 **Out of Country:** 0
Total Number of Varsity/Jr. Varsity: 30/32 **Percent of Graduation:**
Number of Fall Games: 5-10 **Number of Spring Games:** 56
Positions Needed for 1999/2000: Outfielder, Pitcher, Middle-Infielder
Baseball Camp Dates: June 14-18; June 21-25
Most Recent Record: 26 - 32 - 0
Schedule: University of Tennessee, Tennessee Tech, Wingate University, Lincoln Memorial
Style of Play: We try to use our off to divert the attention of the pitcher. We are very aggressive on the bases and will run at will. We try to have sound pitching and defense and do the basics. We try to be very fundamentals.

Chattanooga State Technical Community College

4501 Amnicola Highway
Chattanooga, TN 37406
Coach: Bob Brotherton

NJCAA
Tigers/Royal, Orange
Phone: (423) 697-4707
Fax: (615) 634-3070

ACADEMIC

Founded: 1965 **Type:** 2 Yr., Jr. College, Coed
Student/Faculty Ratio: 16:1 **Male/Female Ratio:** 43:57
Undergraduate Enrollment: 8,750 **Graduate Enrollment:** None
Scholarships/Academic: No **Athletic:** Yes **Fin Aid:** Yes
Total Expenses by: Year **In State:** $ 1,000 **Out of State:** $ 3,700
Degrees Conferred: Associate
Programs of Study: Accounting, Advertising, Applied Art, Automotive Technology, Aviation Administration and Technology, Banking/Finance, Biological Science, Broadcasting, Business Adminstration, Communications, Computer Science and Technology, Criminal Justice, Deaf Interpreter Training, Drafting/Design Engineering and Technology, Fire Science, Flight Science

ATHLETIC PROFILE

Conference Affiliation: TJCCAA

Christian Brothers University

650 E Parkway S
Memphis, TN 38104
Coach: Joe Nadicksbernd

NCAA II/NAIA
Buccaneers/Scarlet, Grey
Phone: (901) 321-3370
Fax: (901) 321-3570

ACADEMIC

Type: 4 Yr., Private, Liberal Arts, Coed, Engineering
Founded: 1871
Religion: Catholic
Campus Housing: Yes
Web-site: http://www.cbu.edu
SAT/ACT/GPA: 930/20/2.5
Student/Faculty Ratio: 15:1
Male/Female Ratio: 51:49
Undergraduate Enrollment: 1,500
Graduate Enrollment: 300
Scholarships/Academic: Yes **Athletic:** Yes **Fin Aid:** Yes
Total Expenses by: Year **In State:** $ 16,180 **Out of State:** $ 16,180
Degrees Conferred: Bachelors, Masters
Programs of Study: Biology, Business Administration, Accounting, Economics-Finance, Management, Marketing, Telecommunications, Chemical Engineering, Chemistry, Computer Science, Engineering, Physics, English, History, Human Development, Liberal Studies, Mathematics

ATHLETIC PROFILE

Conference Affiliation: Tennessee Collegiate Athletic Conference
Program Profile: Small college program that plays a good schedule. Have own field on campus. Play both Fall and Spring in a very competitive NAIA conference. Good situation for a person who is academically oriented.
History: There have been 29 years of CBU baseball; have a reputation for hard-nosed team that has a winning tradition.
Achievements: Tradition of winning season; 3 players drafted over the recent years, several Academic All-Americans.
Coaching: Joe Nadicksbernd, Head Coach, 22 years of coaching experience, over 500 wins.
Style of Play: Fundamental - throw strikes - sound defense - make it happen offense.

Cleveland State Community College

PO Box 3570
Cleveland, TN 37320
Coach: Mike Policastro

NJCAA
Cougars/Columbia Blue
Phone: (423) 478-6219
Fax: (423) 614-8724

ACADEMIC

Founded: 1967
Type: 2 Yr., Jr. College, Coed
Student/Faculty Ratio: 19:1
Male/Female Ratio: 32:68
Undergraduate Enrollment: 3,500
Graduate Enrollment: None
Scholarships/Academic: No **Athletic:** Yes **Fin Aid:** Yes
Total Expenses by: Year **In State:** $ 950 **Out of State:** $ 3,600
Degrees Conferred: Associate
Programs of Study: Business Administration, Electrical/Electronic Technology, Human Services, Industrial Engineering Technology, Liberal Arts, Medical Laboratory Technology, Nursing

Columbia State Community College

PO Box 1315
Columbia, TN 38402-1315
Coach: Jim Painter

NJCAA
Chargers/Hunter Green, White
Phone: (931) 540-2633
Fax: (931) 540-2630

ACADEMIC

Founded: 1966
Type: 2 Yr., Jr. College, Coed
Student/Faculty Ratio: 20:1
Male/Female Ratio: 34:66
Undergraduate Enrollment: 3,465
Graduate Enrollment: None
Scholarships/Academic: No **Athletic:** Yes **Fin Aid:** Yes
Total Expenses by: Year **In State:** $ 950 **Out of State:** $ 3,600
Degrees Conferred: Associate
Programs of Study: Agriculture, Biological Science, Business Administration, Chemistry, Communications, Computer Information Systems, Dental Services, Economics, Electrical/Electronics Technology, Engineering Technology, Geography, History, Liberal Arts, Marketing, Mathematics

ATHLETIC PROFILE

Conference Affiliation: TJCAA
Program Profile: One of the top field in the South.
History: Columbia State Baseball was started by Dave Hall one year after the college opened. He coached 5 years from 1968-1972 and his record was 130-25. Won the state and region 5 times; attended the JUCO World Series in 1970 and 1972. Jim Painter assisted from 1970-1972 and became a head coach in 1973 in 23 years; since then Columbia is 831-330 with 4 years to the JUCO World Series.
Achievements: Jim Painter was named Coach of the Year five times; Region 19 Coach of the Year nine times; Eastern District titles 4 times; 10 Conference titles; 9 Region IV titles; 4 Eastern District titles; 35-40 drafted players; 22 All-Americans in 30 years; 15 in the past 25 years.
Coaching: Jim Painter, Head Coach, responsible with the infielding coach. Mike McLaury, Assistant Coach, responsible with the pitchers. Wayne Roberts, Assistant Coach, outfielder coach.
Style of Play: We are usually known as a hitting school. With Mike McLaury coming aboard as one pitching coach in 1997, we will be known for our pitching as well. We feel we are a well-rounded "fundamentals" team. And we act right on the field, too.

Cumberland University

One Cumberland Square
Lebanon, TN 37087
Coach: Woody Hunt

NAIA
Bulldogs/Maroon, White
Phone: (615) 444-2562
Fax: (615) 444-2569

ACADEMIC

Founded: 1842
Type: 4 Yr., Private, Liberal Arts, Coed
Religion: Non-Affiliated
Campus Housing: Yes
Web-site: http://www.cumberland.edu
SAT/ACT/GPA: 850/18/2.0
Student/Faculty Ratio: 12:1
Male/Female Ratio: 60:40
Undergraduate Enrollment: 1,206
Graduate Enrollment: 177
Scholarships/Academic: Yes **Athletic:** Yes **Fin Aid:** Yes
Total Expenses by: Year **In State:** $ 9,000 **Out of State:** $ 10,300
Degrees Conferred: Associates, Bachelors, Masters
Programs of Study: Art, Science, Biology, Criminal Justice, English, History, Mathematics, Natural Science, Psychology, Social Science, Sociology, Business Administration and Economics (General Business, Economics, Marketing, Management), Nursing, Education, Physical Education and Fine Arts, Elementary Education, Secondary Education, Graduate Studies (Arts in Education, Science, Business Administration)

ATHLETIC PROFILE

Estimated Number of Baseball Scholarships: 10
Conference Affiliation: Mid-South Conference
Program Profile: Cumberland is an NAIA program; play on natural grass playing surface called Ernest L. Stockton Field. Stadium size is 800; play Spring season with approximately 65 games.

History: Became a four year institution in 1983 after several years as a Junior College. The program has been around for several decades, but has been dropped & started back several times.
Achievements: 11 Conference Titles; 35 drafted players; 20 All-Americans; Coach of the Year in 1986, 1988, 1993, and 1997.
Coaching: Woody Hunt, Head Coach, was a finalist for National Coach of the Year in 1986, 1988, and 1993. Scott Corman, Assistant Coach, played at Cumberland University and was named All-Conference, All-Region player in 1993. Bart Carney, Assistant Coach, started in 1998; was a player at Cumberland University; signed with Baltimore Orioles. Kevin Hits, Assistant Coach, started with the program in 1997; played at Cumberland; was All-American in 1996; plays for San Diego Padres.
Roster for 1998 team/In State: 18 **Out of State:** 17 **Out of Country:** 2
Total Number of Varsity/Jr. Varsity: 0 **Percent of Graduation:** 75%
Number of Seniors on 1998 Team: 9 **Number of Sophomores on 1998 Team:** 0
Freshmen Receiving Fin Aid/Athletic: 8 **Academic:** 4
Most Recent Record: 51 - 14 - 0 **Number of Spring Games:** 65
Positions Needed for 1999/2000: Pitchers, Catchers, Outfielders
Baseball Camp Dates: June 1st for three weeks
Schedule: Florida Southern, North Alabama, Austin Peay, Birmingham Southern, Delta State
Style of Play: Cumberland is a program that usually has a good hitters with power; like to blend speed with power throughout the lineup. Pitching is usually sound and defense has been a strength in the past several years.

Dyersburg State Community College

1510 Lake Road
Dyersburg, TN 38024-0648
Coach: Jamie Frakes
Email: jfrakes@dscc.cc.tn.us

NJCAA I
Eagles/Navy Blue, Scarlet, White
Phone: (901) 286-3385
Fax: (901) 286-3333

ACADEMIC

Founded: 1969 **Type:** 2 Yr., Public, Jr. College, Coed
Religion: Non-Affiliated **Campus Housing:** No
Undergraduate Enrollment: 3,175 **Graduate Enrollment:** None
Scholarships/Academic: Yes **Athletic:** Yes **Fin Aid:** Yes
Total Expenses by: Year **In State:** $ 775 **Out of State:** $ 2,403
Degrees Conferred: Associates
Programs of Study: Liberal Arts, Nursing, Business and Technology, University Parallel

ATHLETIC PROFILE

Estimated Number of Baseball Scholarships: 8
Conference Affiliation: Western Division of the Tennessee Junior/Community C A A
Program Profile: DSCC plays ten baseball games during the Fall semester. We have an indoor workout and training regimen that utilizes many different baseball drills. We complement our training with weight circuit training, weight lifting, and aerobics during the off-season. We attempt to play a 56 game schedule in the Spring, which includes a Florida trip.
History: The program began in 1970. In the past three years the program has had three NCAA Academic All-Americans. Nine players in the last three years have advanced to higher college affiliated programs. In 1997 season record was 12 wins with 33 losses. Coach Frakes is in his fourth year of coaching the program. Assistant Coach Jamie Johnson is in his first season as an assistant. Most of the players come from the Tri-State service area which include Tennessee, Arkansas, and Missouri.
Achievements: We have had three NJCAA Academic All-Americans; Edward Sutton - transferred to St. Louis University; Brandon Lane - transferred to the University of Memphis (will attend med-school); John Gamble - transferred to the University of Missouri (Is currently playing).
Coaching: Jamie Frakes, Head Coach, entering his 4th year as a head coach. He played at Arkansas State University. Jamie Johnson, Assistant Coach, entering his first season as an assistant coach. He played at Murray State in Kentucky.
Roster for 1998 team/In State: 11 **Out of State:** 9 **Out of Country:** 0
Total Number of Varsity/Jr. Varsity: 22 **Percent of Graduation:** 55%

Number of Seniors on 1998 Team:
Number of Sophomores on 1998 Team: 4
Freshmen Receiving Fin Aid/Athletic: 5
Academic: 3
Number of Fall Games: 10
Number of Spring Games: 56
Positions Needed for 1999/2000: Pitchers, Outfielder
Most Recent Record: 19 - 28 - 0
Schedule: Volunteer State, Columbia State, Jackson State, John A. Logan
Style of Play: Usually we are small and quick. We play solid defense. Our offense is not powered by the long ball. We usually manufacture runs by getting basehits from the top and middle of the line-up.

East Tennessee State University

Box 70705, Memorial Ctr
Johnson City, TN 37614
Coach: Ken Campbell

NCAA I
Buccaneers/Navy, Old Gold
Phone: (423) 439-4496
Fax: (423) 439-6138

ACADEMIC

Founded: 1909
Type: 4 Yr., Public, , Coed,
Religion: Non-Affiliated
Campus Housing: Yes
Web-site: Not-Available
SAT/ACT/GPA: NCAA Requirements/
Student/Faculty Ratio: 20:1
Male/Female Ratio: 1:3
Undergraduate Enrollment: 12,000
Graduate Enrollment: 1,000
Scholarships/Academic: Yes
Athletic: Yes
Fin Aid: Yes
Total Expenses by: Year
In State: $ 6,482
Out of State: $ 11,308
Degrees Conferred: Bs, MA
Programs of Study: All

ATHLETIC PROFILE

Estimated Number of Baseball Scholarships: 7
Conference Affiliation: Southern Conference
Program Profile: We have practice field on campus. Play games in a minor league pro park which has seating capacity of 3,000.
History: ETSU became a member of the Southern Conference on July 1, 1978, after 21 years as a member of the Ohio Valley Conference.
Achievements: 6 players drafted over the past four years.
Coaching: Ken Campbell, Head Coach, high school coach to Tim Wakefield who played with the Pittsburgh Pirates. He compiled a record of 176-193. John Cloud, Assistant Coach.
Roster for 1998 team/In State: 20
Out of State: 10
Out of Country: 0
Total Number of Varsity/Jr. Varsity: 30
Percent of Graduation: 90%
Number of Seniors on 1998 Team: 5
Number of Sophomores on 1998 Team: 4
Freshmen Receiving Fin Aid/Athletic: 7
Academic: 3
Baseball Camp Dates: June 8-26
Number of Spring Games: 56
Positions Needed for 1999/2000: Pitchers, 3rd Base
Most Recent Record: 18 - 31 - 0
Schedule: Clemson, Tennessee, Wake Forest, Citadel, Georgia Southern, Western Carolina
Style of Play: Speed, defense, and hitting for average.

Fisk University

1000 - 17th Avenue North
Nashville, TN 37208
Coach: Phillip Kimbro

NCAA III
Bulldogs/Blue, Gold
Phone: (615) 329-8782
Fax: (615) 329-8782

ACADEMIC

Founded: 1867
Type: 4 Yr., Coed
Student/Faculty Ratio: 13:1
Male/Female Ratio: None
Undergraduate Enrollment: 900
Graduate Enrollment: 60
Scholarships/Academic: Yes **Athletic:** No **Fin Aid:** Yes
Total Expenses by: Year **In State:** $ 10,900 **Out of State:** $ 10,900
Degrees Conferred: Associate
Programs of Study: Art Education, Biological Science, Business Administration, Chemistry, Dramatic Arts, Economics, English, Fine Arts, French, History, Mathematics, Music, Music Education, Philosophy, Physics, Political Science, Preprofessional Programs, Psychology, Religion, Social Science, Spanish, Speech

ATHLETIC PROFILE

Conference Affiliation: CAC

Freed - Hardeman University

Box 178, FHU
Henderson, TN 38340
Coach: Joel Goss

NAIA
Lions/Maroon, White, Gold
Phone: (901) 989-6904
Fax: (901) 989-6910

ACADEMIC

Founded: 1869
Type: 4 Yr., Private, Liberal Arts, Coed
Religion: Church of Christ
Campus Housing: No
Web-site: Not Available
SAT/ACT/GPA: 18
Student/Faculty Ratio: 15:1
Male/Female Ratio: 47:53
Undergraduate Enrollment: 1,253
Graduate Enrollment: 252
Scholarships/Academic: Yes **Athletic:** Yes **Fin Aid:** Yes
Total Expenses by: Year **In State:** $ 10,500 **Out of State:** $ 10,500
Degrees Conferred: BA, BS, BSA, BSE, BSW, MED
Programs of Study: Accounting, Agricultural Business Management, Banking/Finance, Biological Science, Broadcasting, Business Administration, Chemistry, Communications, Computer Science, Dramatic Arts, Education, English, Fine Arts, History, Marketing, Mathematics, Medical Laboratory Technology, Psychology, Public Relations, Religion, Social Science

ATHLETIC PROFILE

Conference Affiliation: Trans South Conference
Program Profile: Play on Carnes Field which has a seating capacity of 500. It is natural grass field.
History: The program has record of 44-10 in 1997; won Trans South Conference; went to mid-South Regional; finished 7th nationally; 2 All-Americans and 12 All-Conference players in the past four years.
Achievements: 1996 and 1997 Conference Coach of the Year.

Hiwassee College

Hiwassee Road
Madisonville, TN 37354
Coach: Derek Wolfe

NJCAA
Tigers/Maroon, Gold
Phone: (423) 442-2001
Fax: (423) 442-3520

ACADEMIC

Founded: 1849
Type: 2 Yr.,Coed
Religion: Non-Affiliated
Campus Housing: No
Student/Faculty Ratio: 16:1
Male/Female Ratio: 45:55

Undergraduate Enrollment: 520 **Graduate Enrollment:** None
Scholarships/Academic: No **Athletic:** Yes **Fin Aid:** Yes
Total Expenses by: Year **In State:** $ 9,000 **Out of State:** $ 9,000
Degrees Conferred: Associate
Programs of Study: Accounting, Aerospace Science, Agriculture, Animal Scinece, Architectural Technology, Aviation Administration and Technology, Biblical Studies, Biological Science, Business Administration, Communications Equipment Technology, Communications, Computer Science, and Technology, Conservation, Drafting/Design, Engineering Technology, Equestrian Studies, Farm and Ranch Management

Jackson State Community College

2046 N Parkway
Jackson, TN 38301
Coach: Steve Corneliston

NJCAA
Generals/Kelly, Gold
Phone: (901) 424-3520
Fax: (901) 425-2647

ACADEMIC

Founded: 1967 **Type:** 2 Yr., Public, Jr. College, Coed
Student/Faculty Ratio: 20:1 **Male/Female Ratio:** 1:1.75
Undergraduate Enrollment: 3,000 **Graduate Enrollment:** None
Scholarships/Academic: Yes **Athletic:** Yes **Fin Aid:** Yes
Total Expenses by: Year **In State:** $ 3,400 **Out of State:** $ 6,500
Degrees Conferred: Associates
Programs of Study: Contact school for programs of study.

ATHLETIC PROFILE

Estimated Number of Baseball Scholarships: 13
Conference Affiliation: Tennessee Junior and Community College Athletic Association
Program Profile: Total year-round program, good outdoor stadium, inside hitting facilities/weight room, Fall season is in September-October with 12-15 games versus outside competition. Nov.-Dec. off-season conditioning. Spring season, play 50 games; natural turf, 200-seating capacity.
History: Program began in 1968 and produced many college and pro players, including Ross Grimsley (former National League Rookie of the Year). 1996 team finished 38-20, NJCAA Region VII Tournament Champions, NJCAA Eastern District Champions, sixth place in NJCAA Division I World Series.
Achievements: One of only three Junior Colleges to have an All-American each year since 1993; 3 players drafted since 1990; Conference Championships in 1996.
Roster for 1998 team/In State: 24 **Out of State:** 0 **Out of Country:** 0
Total Number of Varsity/Jr. Varsity: 24 **Percent of Graduation:** 55%
Number of Seniors on 1998 Team: 0 **Number of Sophomores on 1998 Team:** 10
Freshmen Receiving Fin Aid/Athletic: 6 **Academic:** 3
Number of Fall Games: 15 **Number of Spring Games:** 0
Positions Needed for 1999/2000: Pitchers, Infielders
Schedule: Volunteer State, Columbia State, Mississippi Gulf Coast, Lake Land Community College, East Central Mississippi, Mississippi Delta Community College

King College

1350 King College Road
Bristol, TN 37620
Coach: Craig Kleinmann
Email: cjkleinm@king.edu

NAIA
Tornado/Navy Blue, White, Red
Phone: (423) 652-6017
Fax: (423) 652-6041

ACADEMIC

Type: 4 Yr., Private, Liberal Arts, Coed, Preengineering **Founded:** 1867
Religion: Presbyterian **Campus Housing:** Yes
Web-site: http://www.king.edu **SAT/ACT/GPA:** 1100/24/2.4
Student/Faculty Ratio: 13:1 **Male/Female Ratio:** 1:3
Undergraduate Enrollment: 500 **Graduate Enrollment:** N/A
Scholarships/Academic: Yes **Athletic:** Yes **Fin Aid:** Yes
Total Expenses by: Year **In State:** $ 14,594 **Out of State:** $ 14,594
Degrees Conferred: BA, BS
Programs of Study: Applied Science, Mathematics, American Studies, Bible and Religion, Economics, Business Administration, Chemistry, English, Fine Arts, French, History, Mathematics, Medical Technology, Modern Foreign Languages, Political Science, Psychology, Preprofessional Programs

ATHLETIC PROFILE

Estimated Number of Baseball Scholarships: 12
Conference Affiliation: Tennessee - Virginia Athletic Conference
Program Profile: Play at Frazier Field located on campus with a seating capacity of 500. Natural grass, indoor and outdoor hitting facilities.
Achievements: TVAC Coach of the Year in 1995. NCCAA National Champs in 1988.
Coaching: Craig Kleinmann, Head Coach, entering first year with the program, played at Edison Community College and at King College; former assistant coach at King College in 1995 and 1997. Tom Woodley, Assistant Coach, entering first season with the program.
Roster for 1998 team/In State: 10 **Out of State:** 15 **Out of Country:** 0
Total Number of Varsity/Jr. Varsity: 25 **Percent of Graduation:** 90%
Number of Seniors on 1998 Team: 4 **Number of Sophomores on 1998 Team:** 6
Freshmen Receiving Fin Aid/Athletic: 5 **Academic:** 5
Number of Fall Games: 12 **Number of Spring Games:** 48
Positions Needed for 1999/2000: Pitchers, Catchers, Outfielder
Most Recent Record: 6 - 23 - 0 **Baseball Camp Dates:** June, December
Schedule: Lincoln Memorial, Tusculum, Carson Newman, Montreat, Tennessee Wesleyan College
Style of Play: Aggressive running and hitting, stress fundamentals.

Knoxville College

(Program Discontinued)

Lambuth University

705 Lambuth Boulevard
Jackson, TN 38301
Coach: Wayne Albury

NCAA II/NAIA
Eagles/Blue, White
Phone: (901) 425-3366
Fax: (901) 425-3231

ACADEMIC

Founded: 1843 **Type:** 4 Yr., Private, Liberal Arts, Coed
Religion: Methodist **Campus Housing:** Yes
Undergraduate Enrollment: 1,250 **SAT/ACT/GPA:** 18+
Student/Faculty Ratio: 20:1 **Male/Female Ratio:** 50:50
Scholarships/Academic: Yes **Athletic:** Yes **Fin Aid:** Yes
Total Expenses by: Year **In State:** $ 9,700 **Out of State:** $ 9,700
Degrees Conferred: BA, BS

Programs of Study: Accounting, Art, Applied Arts, Biblical Studies, Biology, Broadcasting, Business and Mangement, Chemistry, Communications, Computer Information Systems, Computer Science, Economics, Education, Elementary Education, English, Fashion, Merchandising, History, Interior Design, International Studies, Management, Marketing, Mathematics, Modern Languages, Music, Nutrition, Physical Education, Political Science, Predentistry, Premed, Prevet, Psychology, Religion, Science, Secondary Education, Social Science, Sociology, Spanish, Special Education, Speech Pathology, Speech Theraphy, Theatre

ATHLETIC PROFILE

Conference Affiliation: TCAC

Lane College

545 Lane Avenue
Jackson, TN 38301
Coach: Leonard Anderson

NCAA II
Dragons/Red, Blue
Phone: (901) 426-7568
Fax: (901) 423-7101

ACADEMIC

Founded: 1882
Religion: Non-Affiliated
Student/Faculty Ratio: 16:1
Undergraduate Enrollment: 670
Scholarships/Academic: Yes
Athletic: No
Total Expenses by: Year
In State: $ 8,350
Degrees Conferred: BA, BS

Type: 4 Yr., Coed
Campus Housing: No
Male/Female Ratio: 51:49
Graduate Enrollment: None
Fin Aid: Yes
Out of State: $ 8,350

Programs of Study: Biological Science, Business Administration, Chemistry, Civil Engineering, Communications, Computer Science, Education, Electrical Engineering, Elementary Education, English, History, Mathematics, Music, Nursing, Physical Education, Preprofessional Programs

ATHLETIC PROFILE

Conference Affiliation: Independent

Le Moyne - Owen College

807 Walker Avenue
Memphis, TN 38126
Coach: Randle Jennings

NCAA II
Magicians/Purple, Gold
Phone: (901) 942-7325
Fax: (901) 942-6273

ACADEMIC

Founded: 1862
Student/Faculty Ratio: 16:1
Undergraduate Enrollment: 1,340
Scholarships/Academic: No
Athletic: Yes
Total Expenses by: Year
In State: $ 9,100
Degrees Conferred: BBA, BA, BS

Type: 2 Yr., Coed
Male/Female Ratio: 41:59
Graduate Enrollment: 150
Fin Aid: Yes
Out of State: $ 9,100

Programs of Study: Accounting, Biological Science, Business Administration, Chemistry, Economics, Education, Engineering, English, Fine Arts, Health Education, History, Humanities, Mathematics, Natural Science, Physical Education, Political Science, Social Sciences

ATHLETIC PROFILE

Conference Affiliation: SIAC

Lee University

1120 Ocee Street
Cleveland, TN 37311
Coach: Dr. Dave Altopp
Email: daltopp@leeuniversity.edu

NCCAA
Flames/Maroon, White
Phone: (423) 614-8445
Fax: (423) 614-8443

ACADEMIC

Founded: 1918
Religion: Church of God
Web-site: http://www.leeuniversity.edu/
Student/Faculty Ratio: 19:1
Undergraduate Enrollment: 2,652
Scholarships/Academic: Yes **Athletic:** Yes
Total Expenses by: Year **In State:** $ 9,600
Degrees Conferred: BA, BS

Type: 4 Yr., Private, Liberal Arts, Coed
Campus Housing: No
SAT/ACT/GPA: 860/18
Male/Female Ratio: 49:51
Graduate Enrollment: None
Fin Aid: Yes
Out of State: $ 9,600

Programs of Study: Behavioral and Social Sciences, Education, Business, Bible and Christian Ministries, Language Arts, Accounting, Education, Elementary and Secondary Education, Physical Education, Secretarial and Related Programs

ATHLETIC PROFILE

Estimated Number of Baseball Scholarships: 9
Conference Affiliation: Tran South Athletic Conference
Program Profile: The program is three years old; started in 1996. Has combined record of 53-58 in first two years of program. First class playing facility with natural Bermuda turf double A specification lighting and inning by inning scoreboard. Dimensions of field are 330 left field line, 375 in both power alleys, 400 to center field with 14 ft. wall and 320 to right field line. Construction on a stadium is expected in the future. 10 game Fall schedule with 60 game Spring schedule.
History: The program began in 1996. Lee had a team in the late 1920's but discontinued it.
Achievements: 1993 Tennessee Collegiate Athletic Conference Coach of the Year; 1998 NCCAA South Regional Coach of the Year; 1995 NAIA representative at USA Olympic Baseball Trials; 1998 achieved 500th coach victory; several players drafted; one as high as the 7th round.
Coaching: Dr. Dave Altopp, Head Coach, entering as a head coach with a several players drafted; one drafted in the 7th round. He compiled a record of 503-606 record. Mark Brew, Assistant Coach, entering seven years as an assistant coach with Altopp.
Roster for 1998 team/In State: 6 **Out of State:** 16 **Out of Country:** 5
Total Number of Varsity/Jr. Varsity: 28 **Percent of Graduation:** 95%
Freshmen Receiving Fin Aid/Athletic: 3 **Academic:** 1
Number of Fall Games: 8 **Number of Spring Games:** 60
Positions Needed for 1999/2000: LHP, Catcher, Outfielder, RHP
Most Recent Record: 25 - 30 - 0
Schedule: Birmingham Southern, Kennesaw State University, Berry, Union, Lipscomb, Freed-Hardeman, University of Montevallo, Lincoln Memorial, Carson Newman, Cumberland University
Style of Play: Aggressive style of play offensively; like to steal, hit and run. Want to build team around good pitching and good defense.

Lincoln Memorial University

P.O. Box 2028
Harrogate, TN 37752
Coach: Tony Skole

NCAA II
Railsplitters/Navy, White
Phone: (423) 869-6345
Fax: (423) 869-6382

ACADEMIC

Founded: 1897
Religion: Non-Affiliated

Type: 4 Yr., Private, Liberal Arts, Coed
Campus Housing: Yes

Web-site: http://www.lmunet.edu
SAT/ACT/GPA: 910/19/2.3
Student/Faculty Ratio: 13:1
Male/Female Ratio: 1:3
Undergraduate Enrollment: 1,800
Graduate Enrollment: 200
Scholarships/Academic: Yes **Athletic:** Yes **Fin Aid:** Yes
Total Expenses by: Year **In State:** $ 11,500 **Out of State:** $ 11,500
Degrees Conferred: AA, AS, BA, BS, MED, MBA
Programs of Study: Majors: Accounting, Athletic Training, Biology, Chemistry, Communication Arts, Computer and Information Systems, Liberal Studies and Learning, Economics, English, Environmental Science, General Business, Health, History, Humanities, Management, Marketing, Mathematics, Medical Technology, Nursing, Physcial Education, Psychology, Social Science, Social Work, Sports Management, Veterinary Science, Visual Art, Wildlife and Fisheries Management; Preprofessional Programs: Dentistry, Engineering, Law, Medicine, Optometry, Pharmacy, Physical Therapy, Veterinary Medicine; Associates: Banking, Computer and Information Systems, Nursing, Veterinary Technology; Certifications: Athletic Coaching, K-12 Certification in 3 areas, Secondary in 10 areas; Graduate: Master of Education, Education Administration and Sup., Curriculum and Instruction, Guidance and Counseling, Master of Business Administration, Educational Specialist

ATHLETIC PROFILE

Conference Affiliation: Gulf South Conference
Program Profile: NCAA Division II, play in one of the top conferences in all conference baseball - GSC. Lamar Hennon Stadium seats 2,500. Natural playing surface, indoor facility for wet days, 2 full tunnels, pitching mounds. Have six weeks Fall schedule concluding with a Fall World Series. Spring games start in early February and runs throwing May and June.
History: The program began in 1938.
Achievements: Consistent top 25 program with a high outfielder which 13th in the country in 1997. Finished in the top 20 three times in 1990's; 7 players drafted in the last five years; 4 All-Americans; Jeremy Bales was a Freshman of the Year in GSC in 1997; 1st team All-Conference and 1st team All-Region.
Coaching: Tony Skole, Head Coach, works with the hitting and fielding. Eddie Graham, Assistant Coach, works with the pitching. Scott Arthur, Graduate Assistant, works with the outfielders and hitters. Naye Goucet, Graduate Assistant, works with the infielder and hitting.
Style of Play: Solid pitching, make the routine plays under pressure, aggressive base running. Make things happen and put pressure on the defense by bunting, stealing, hit and run. We are aggressive and well disciplined. Want players that will compete.

Martin Methodist College

433 West Madison Street
Pulaski, TN 38478
Coach: Jeff Dodson

NAIA
Indians/Red, White
Phone: (931) 363-9827
Fax: (931) 363-9873

ACADEMIC

Founded: 1870
Type: 2 Yr., Private, Jr. College, Coed
Religion: United Methodist
Campus Housing: Yes
Web-site: Not Available
SAT/ACT/GPA: 860/18
Student/Faculty Ratio: 13:1
Male/Female Ratio: 49:51
Undergraduate Enrollment: 500
Graduate Enrollment: None
Scholarships/Academic: Yes **Athletic:** Yes **Fin Aid:** Yes
Total Expenses by: Year **In State:** $ 9,585 **Out of State:** $ 9,585
Degrees Conferred: Associate
Programs of Study: Business, Elementary Education, Church Vocations, Human Services

ATHLETIC PROFILE

Conference Affiliation: Tran South Conference

Maryville College

502 E Lamar Alexander Parkway
Maryville, TN 37804
Coach: Eric Etchison

NCAA III
Fighting Scots/Orange, Garnet
Phone: (423) 981-8283
Fax: (423) 981-8285

ACADEMIC

Founded: 1819
Type: 4 Yr., Private, Liberal Arts, Coed
Religion: Presbyterian
Campus Housing: No
Web-site: http://www.maryvillecollege.edu/
SAT/ACT/GPA: 900/20
Student/Faculty Ratio: 14:1
Male/Female Ratio: 2.5:1
Undergraduate Enrollment: 900
Graduate Enrollment: N/A
Scholarships/Academic: Yes **Athletic:** No **Fin Aid:** Yes
Total Expenses by: Year **In State:** $ 17,000 **Out of State:** $ 17,000
Degrees Conferred: BA, Bmus, BSN, Certification in Elementary and Secondary Education.
Programs of Study: Art Education, Biology, Business Administration, Chemistry, Computer Science, Economics, Education, English, Fine Arts, Health Science, History, International Relations, Journalism, Management, Mathematics, Music, Music Education, Nursing, Physical Therapy, Political Science, Predental, Preengineering, Prelaw, Premed, Psychology, Religion, Science Education, Secondary Education, Social Science, Spanish, Speech

ATHLETIC PROFILE

Conference Affiliation: Independent Conference
Program Profile: 3,000 sq ft weight room; indoor pool, cage and training facility. One of the best Division III fields in the country.
History: Program began in 1876. Went to NCAA tournament 1974, 1977.
Achievements: 1991-1995 has 12 All-South Region USA Performers; 3 All-Americans; latest pro signed in 1991 Glen Cullop for the Reds; 2 NCAA National Tournament Appearances.
Coaching: Eric Etchison, Head Coach, fifth season as a head coach.
Style of Play: Aggressive, fundamental baseball; speed and quality, defense are our first objectives.

Middle Tennessee State University

P.O. Box 90 MTSU
Murfreesboro, TN 37132
Coach: Steve Peterson

NCAA
Blue Raiders/Royal Blue, White
Phone: (615) 898-2120
Fax: (615) 904-8285

ACADEMIC

Founded: 1911
Type: 4 Yr., Public, Liberal Arts, Coed
Religion: Non-Affiliated
Campus Housing: Yes
Web-site: http://www.mtsu.edu
SAT/ACT/GPA: 950/20/2.8
Student/Faculty Ratio: 21:1
Male/Female Ratio: 1:1.2
Undergraduate Enrollment: 15,415
Graduate Enrollment: 2,009
Scholarships/Academic: Yes **Athletic:** Yes **Fin Aid:** Yes
Total Expenses by: Year **In State:** $ 2,500 **Out of State:** $ 5,500
Degrees Conferred: AAS, BA, BS, BFA, BBA, BSW, MA, MS, MBA
Programs of Study: Aerospace, Art, Biology, Business, Computer, Criminal Justice, Economics, Environmental, Fashion, Finance, International, Interdisciplinary, Medical, Preprofessional Programs

ATHLETIC PROFILE

Estimated Number of Baseball Scholarships: 11.7
Conference Affiliation: Ohio Valley Conference
Program Profile: Has a natural playing surface that measures 330-365-390, lights, capacity is 2,000 at Reese Smith Field. Has a clubhouse and indoor training facility (10,000 sq. ft.).

History: Baseball, a part of campus life since 1912. In 1971, Lefty Solomar became the first full-time baseball coach. He inherited field that was of its present location and had dugouts established. In 1979, the field acquired lighting. Steve Peterson spearheaded the fundraising effort that has landed the fabulous new clubhouse. Conference; Tournament Champions last 10 out of 12 years; 8 NCAA Regionals.

Achievements: 1998: 2 players drafted and signed were Jeremy Owens with Padres and Randy Woodrun with Reds. Coach Peterson was named Coach of the Year in 1990 and 1995; Regular Season OVC Champions in 1997, 1996, 1995, 1993, 1992, 1991, 1990, 1988, 1987, 1982, 1981, 1976, 1968, 1959; Tournament OVC Champions in 1995, 1994, 1992, 1991,1990, 1988, 1987, 1982, 1981, 1976; NCAA Tournament Appearances in 1995, 1991, 1990, 1988, 1987, 1982, 1981, 1976; 1997 Brad Howard - Freshman All-American team; Since Coach Peterson has been here (1988), 23 players drafted professionally; 5 players still active - Jason Maxwell (1993/Cubs), J. Owens (1990/Rocky), George Ohkoek (1996/Diamondbacks), Danny Barner (1996/Pearl Rays), Clay Smellgrove (1997/Padres).

Coaching: Steve Peterson, Head Coach, beginning his 11th season at MTSU, for ten years compiled a record of 317-243-2. In ten years, he has guided MTSU to 7 regular season championships, 5 Tournament Championships; and four NCAA Regional. He has 2 Coach of the Year honors, has coached 3 OVC Player of the Year; 2 OVC Pitcher of the Year, and 23 first team All-Conference performers. Jim McGuire, Assistant Coach, been at MTSU since 1992 - recruiting coordinator, and works primarily with the infielders and hitters. Buddy Custer, Assistant Coach, been at MTSU since 1994 - focusing on coaching the pitchers and recruiting as well as the outfielders.

Roster for 1998 team/In State: 21 **Out of State:** 6 **Out of Country:** 3
Total Number of Varsity/Jr. Varsity: 30 **Percent of Graduation:** 0
Number of Seniors on 1998 Team: 6 **Number of Sophomores on 1998 Team:** 8
Freshmen Receiving Fin Aid/Athletic: 6 **Academic:** 0
Most Recent Record: 17 - 33.- 0 **Number of Spring Games:** 56
Positions Needed for 1999/2000: Pitcher-L, Middle Infielder, Catcher
Schedule: Auburn, Tennessee, Southern Mississippi, SW Missouri, Vanderbilt, Eastern Illinois
Style of Play: Solid pitching and defense, with the ability to score runs. Look for corner men who hit for power and a catcher that is very solid defensively. Want our middle infielders to be able to play all the infield positions. We recruit only starting pitchers that can come in and fill a need immediately.

Milligan College

P.O. Box 9
Milligan College, TN 37682-0009
Coach: Tom Phillips

NAIA
Buffaloes/Orange, Black, White
Phone: (423) 461-8722
Fax: (423) 461-8738

ACADEMIC

Founded: 1881
Religion: Christian Church
Web-site: http://www.milligan.edu/
Student/Faculty Ratio: 15:1
Undergraduate Enrollment: 850
Type: 4 Yr., Private, Liberal Arts, Coed
Campus Housing: Yes
SAT/ACT/GPA: 800+/19+
Male/Female Ratio: 50:50
Graduate Enrollment: 100
Scholarships/Academic: Yes **Athletic:** Yes **Fin Aid:** Yes
Total Expenses by: Year **In State:** $ 14,600 **Out of State:** $ 14,600
Degrees Conferred: AS, BA, BS, MED, MOT
Programs of Study: Accounting, Advertising, Art, Biblical Studies, Biology, Broadcasting, Business Administration, Chemistry, Communications, Computer Science, Education, Health Music, Religious Science, English, General Engineering, History, Humanities, Human Services, Liberal Arts, Management, Mathematics, Ministries, Music, Nursing, Predental, Premed, Prevet, Psychology, Radio and Television, Religion, Science, Social Work, Sociology, Theatre

ATHLETIC PROFILE

Estimated Number of Baseball Scholarships: 8 Full
Conference Affiliation: Tennessee - Virginia Athletic Conference

Program Profile: We have a Fall and Spring season; Junior program total of 100 games between all; 1,000 seat stadium in shadow mountains and willow trees.
History: Began near turn of century; historically in top 1/2 of conference.
Achievements: 9 players in the last 8 years have gone pro.
Coaching: Tom Phillips, Head Coach, entering first year as a head coach of the program. Ray Smith, Assistant Coach, coach in Minnesota Twin Organization during Summer.
Roster for 1998 team/In State: 15 **Out of State:** 19 **Out of Country:** 0
Total Number of Varsity/Jr. Varsity: 34 **Percent of Graduation:** 0
Number of Seniors on 1998 Team: 4 **Most Recent Record:** 19 - 20 - 0
Freshmen Receiving Fin Aid/Athletic: 18 **Academic:** 10
Number of Fall Games: 25 **Number of Spring Games:** 60
Positions Needed for 1999/2000: Pitcher, Catcher, 1st Base, Centerfielder, SS
Baseball Camp Dates: 1st - 3 weeks of June
Schedule: Montreat, Virginia Intermont, Carson - Newman, Shorter, Eckerd, Lindsey Wilson
Style of Play: Scratch for runs; aggressive on bases; pitch and play "D".

Motlow State Community College

PO Box 88100
Tullahoma, TN 37388
Coach: Don Rhoton

NJCAA
Bucks/Green, Gold
Phone: (931) 393-1615
Fax: (931) 393-1991

ACADEMIC

Founded: 1969 **Type:** 2 Yr., Jr. College, Coed
Undergraduate Enrollment: 3,300 **Student/Faculty Ratio:** 15:1
Scholarships/Academic: No **Athletic:** No **Fin Aid:** Yes
Total Expenses by: Year **In State:** $ 1,000 **Out of State:** $ 3,700
Degrees Conferred: Associate
Programs of Study: Accounting, Biological Science, Biomedical Technology, Business, Computer Information Systems, Computer Programming, Economics, Education, Engineering Technology, English, General Engineering, Georgraphy, History, Insurance, Liberal Arts, Mathematics, Occupational Therapy, Office Management

ATHLETIC PROFILE

Conference Affiliation: Tennessee JCCAA

Rhodes College

2000 N Parkway
Memphis, TN 38112
Coach: Jim Elgin

NCAA III
Lynx/Black, Red, White
Phone: (901) 843-3940
Fax: (901) 843-3749

ACADEMIC

Founded: 1848 **Type:** 4 Yr., Private, Liberal Arts, Coed
Religion: Presbyterian **Campus Housing:** Yes
Web-site: http://www.rhodes.edu/ **SAT/ACT/GPA:** 1150+/25+
Student/Faculty Ratio: 12:1 **Male/Female Ratio:** 45:55
Undergraduate Enrollment: 1,500 **Graduate Enrollment:** None
Scholarships/Academic: Yes **Athletic:** No **Fin Aid:** Yes
Total Expenses by: Year **In State:** $ 23,528 **Out of State:** $ 23,528
Degrees Conferred: BA, BS
Programs of Study: Art, Biology, Chemistry, English, History, Business and Management, International Studies, Philosophy, Political Science, Psychology, Religion

ATHLETIC PROFILE

Conference Affiliation: Southern Collegiate Athletic Conference
Program Profile: Rhodes runs an NCAA Division III program with an expanded 6-week Fall program (9 games) and a full Spring season, with the maximum number of games allowed by the NCAA. The Lynx play in the Reebok and Rhodes Invitational Tournaments. New stadium and playng facilities in the Fall of 1995.
History: Rhodes annually competes for the conference championship and increasing interest in NCAA selection committees.
Achievements: Numerous All-Conference, All-Region, Academic All-American; 4 SCAC Titles in the last 10 years.
Coaching: Jim Elgin, Head Coach, 1998 is his sixth years; two years as a head coach at Haywood County High School in Browsville, Tennessee; He graduated from Thodes in 1986.
Style of Play: Rhodes continues its strong hitting tradition and up tempo style of play with an emphasis on pitching and strong defense.

Roane State Community College

276 Patton Ln
Harriman, TN 37748
Coach: Larry Works

NJCAA
Raiders/Red, White, Blue
Phone: (423) 354-4538
Fax: (423) 882-4537

ACADEMIC

Founded: 1971
Type: 2 Yr., Jr. College, Coed
Web-site: Not-Available
SAT/ACT/GPA: 19
Undergraduate Enrollment: 5,000
Graduate Enrollment: None
Scholarships/Academic: Yes **Athletic:** Yes **Fin Aid:** Yes
Total Expenses by: Year **In State:** $ 2,100 **Out of State:** $ 2,800
Degrees Conferred: AS, AA
Programs of Study: Accounting, Biological Science, Business Administration, Chemistry, Computer Science and Technology, Corrections, Criminal Justice, Environmental Health Science, Law Enforcement, Liberal Arts, Mathematics, Optical Technology, Physical Education, Physical Therapy

ATHLETIC PROFILE

Estimated Number of Baseball Scholarships: 7-10
Conference Affiliation: Tennessess Junior and Community College Athletic Association
Program Profile: We play a 50-56 games in the Spring, one field is a natural Bermuda grass with measurements of 330 down the lines, 400 to the center, and excellent playing facility.
History: The program began in 1972-1973.
Achievements: Coach of the Year in 1997; Regional Runner-Up in 1997; 2 players currently in the Major Leagues; 1 currently in the AA.
Coaching: Larry Works, Head Coach.
Roster for 1998 team/In State: 22 **Out of State:** 2 **Out of Country:** 0
Total Number of Varsity/Jr. Varsity: 35 **Percent of Graduation:** 85%
Number of Seniors on 1998 Team: **Number of Sophomores on 1998 Team:** 14
Freshmen Receiving Fin Aid/Athletic: 10 **Most Recent Record:** 13 - 37 - 0
Number of Fall Games: 22 **Number of Spring Games:** 56
Positions Needed for 1999/2000: 2nd Base, Pitcher
Style of Play: Aggressive.

Shelby State Community College

PO Box 40568
Memphis, TN 38174-0568
Coach: Doug Darnall

NJCAA
Saluqis/Red, Black
Phone: (901) 544-5143
Fax: (901) 544-5970

ACADEMIC

Founded: 1970
Type: 2 Yr., Jr. College, Coed
Religion: Non-Affiliated
Campus Housing: No
Student/Faculty Ratio: 21:1
Male/Female Ratio: None
Undergraduate Enrollment: 5,862
Graduate Enrollment: None
Total Expenses by: Year **In State:** $ 1,024 **Out of State:** $ 4,096
Degrees Conferred: Associate
Programs of Study: Contact school for program of study.

ATHLETIC PROFILE

Conference Affiliation: TJCCAA
History: Shelby State CC's Baseball program began in 1971.
Style of Play: Hard nosed - aggressive offense and solid defense.

Tennessee Technological University

Athletics Box 5057
Cookeville, TN 38505
Coach: Mike Mack

NCAA I
Golden Eagles/Purple, Gold
Phone: (931) 372-3925
Fax: (931) 372-5724

ACADEMIC

Founded: 1915
Type: 2 Yr., Coed
Student/Faculty Ratio: 20:1
Male/Female Ratio: 53:47
Undergraduate Enrollment: 7,261
Graduate Enrollment: None
Scholarships/Academic: Yes **Athletic:** Yes **Fin Aid:** Yes
Total Expenses by: Year **In State:** $ 4,222+ **Out of State:** $ 10,286
Degrees Conferred: AA, BA, BS, BFA, MA, MS, MBA
Programs of Study: Business and Management, Education, Engineering, Home Economics, Parks/Recreation, Physical Science, Protective Services, Public Affairs

ATHLETIC PROFILE

Conference Affiliation: Ohio Valley Conference (OVC)
Program Profile: We have a new baseball club house. The lighted field was installed in 1997 with a new press box. Playing field is a natural turf which has a dimensions of 330 down lines, and 400 at the center.
History: Baseball won OVC championship in 1949, 1954, 1955 and won division titles in 1974, 1988. Was second in 1996. Has produced two All-Americans, 4 All-Region & 6 Academic All-Americans.
Achievements: Coach of the Year five times for Mays. In the last two years 1997 OVC Tournament and League Champs. Mark Maberry was All-American; 3 Players signed pro contracts while two others signed Independent contracts in the two years.

Tennessee Wesleyan College

210 College
Athens, TN 37371-0040
Coach: Jeff Smith

NAIA
Bulldogs/Royal, Gold
Phone: (423) 745-7504
Fax: (423) 744-9968

ACADEMIC

Founded: 1857
Type: 4 Yr., Private, Liberal Arts, Coed
Religion: Methodist-Holstein Conference
Campus Housing: Yes
Web-site: Not Available
SAT/ACT/GPA: 860/18/2.0
Student/Faculty Ratio: 4:1
Male/Female Ratio: 1:2
Undergraduate Enrollment: 750
Graduate Enrollment: None

Scholarships/Academic: Yes **Athletic:** Yes **Fin Aid:** Yes
Total Expenses by: Year **In State:** $ 11,690 **Out of State:**
Degrees Conferred: BA, BS
Programs of Study: Bachelor of Arts, Bachelor of Applied Science, Bachelor of Music, Bachelor of Education, Bachelor of Science, Preprofessional Preparations

ATHLETIC PROFILE

Conference Affiliation: Tennessee Collegiate Athletic Conference

Trevecca Nazarene College

333 Murfreesboro Road
Nashville, TN 37210
Coach: Ryan Gray
Email: rgray@trevecca.edu

NAIA
Trojans/Purple, White, Gold
Phone: (615) 248-1276
Fax: (615) 248-7798

ACADEMIC
Founded: 1901
Type: 4 Yr., Private, Liberal Arts, Coed
Religion: Nazarene
Campus Housing: Yes
Web-site: http://www.trevecca.edu
SAT/ACT/GPA: 860/18/2.5
Student/Faculty Ratio: 26:1
Male/Female Ratio:
Undergraduate Enrollment: 1,066
Graduate Enrollment: 515
Scholarships/Academic: Yes **Athletic:** Yes **Fin Aid:** Yes
Total Expenses by: Semester **In State:** $ 6,010 **Out of State:** $ 6,010
Degrees Conferred: 43 Bachelors, 6 Associates, 5 Masters
Programs of Study: Allied Health, Behavioral Science, Biological Science, Business Administration, Communications, Education, History, Information Science, Management, Mathematics, Miniseries, Philosophy, Psychology, Physician's Assistant, Prelaw, Religion, Science, Social Science, Speech

ATHLETIC PROFILE

Conference Affiliation: Tran South Athletic Conference
Program Profile: Has two tunnel indoor hitting facility with gold ball iron Mike Fitching Machine; 1st rate playing surface that is natural grass; owns a golf course reel mower; John deer Gator; tarp; state of the art conditioning and strength facility; state of the art sound system (stadium click effect).
History: Program began around 1970 and did not take long to build winning tradition. Have won 5 Conference Championships and 2 District Championships. Have been ranked as high as 8th in the Nation (1989). Have been in post-season play in 1993 and 1994.
Achievements: Volunteer State Athletic Conference Champs in 1979, 1980, 1985; NAIA District 24 baseball champs in 1982 and 1989; Tennessee Collegiate Athletic Conference Champs in 1987; Head Coach Ryan Gray has 4 Professional pieces of baseball Literature published in Coaching Digest.
Coaching: Dr. Ryan Gray, Head Coach, graduate of Union University in 1989. Brad Twigg, Assistant Coach, graduate of Trevecca in 1992. Dave Daniels, Assistant Coach, graduate of Tevecca 1998. Billy Aviles, Assistant Coach, graduate of Trevecca 1998.
Style of Play: Very aggressive base running; fundamentally sound defensively.

Tusculum College

60 Shiloh Road
Greenville, TN 37743
Coach: Doug Jones

NCAA II/NAIA
Pioneers/Black, Orange
Phone: (423) 636-7322
Fax: (423) 636-7370

ACADEMIC

Founded: 1794
Type: 4 Yr., Private, Liberal Arts, Coed
Religion: Presbyterian
Campus Housing: Yes

Web-site: http://www.tusculum.edu/ **SAT/ACT/GPA:** 860/18
Student/Faculty Ratio: 12:1 **Male/Female Ratio:** 1:1
Undergraduate Enrollment: 500 **Graduate Enrollment:** 1,000
Scholarships/Academic: Yes **Athletic:** Yes **Fin Aid:** Yes
Total Expenses by: Year **In State:** $ 14,850 **Out of State:** $ 14,850
Degrees Conferred: BS, BA, MA, MAEd
Programs of Study: Arts, Athletic Training, Biology, Business and Management, Computer Science, Education, English, Physical Education, Prelaw, Premed, Psychology, Sport Management

ATHLETIC PROFILE

Estimated Number of Baseball Scholarships: 5
Conference Affiliation: South Atlantic Conference
Program Profile: Play both Fall & Spring schedule. The playing surface is natural turf, four batting cages, practice infield. Stadium holds 1,000 spectators; dimensions are 330, 350, 380, 360, & 330.
History: The Pioneers have had a strong tradition in baseball. Formerly a member of the NAIA, have moved to NCAA II; 1999 will be first season in the South Atlantic Conference.
Achievements: 1998 SouthEast Independent Sub-Regional Champs; NAIA All-Americans in 1995 and 1996 Chad Busch, NAIA All-American Honorable Mention in 1998-Ryan Baker.
Coaching: Doug Jones, Head Coach, 1997 record was 29-17 lead the Pioneers to the NAIA Independent Sub-regional Championships; Appearances in SouthEast Regional Tournament.
Roster for 1998 team/In State: 11 **Out of State:** 28 **Out of Country:** 3
Total Number of Varsity/Jr. Varsity: 15 **Percent of Graduation:** 100%
Number of Seniors on 1998 Team: 6 **Number of Sophomores on 1998 Team:** 27
Freshmen Receiving Fin Aid/Athletic: 9 **Academic:** 15
Number of Fall Games: 6 **Number of Spring Games:** 50
Positions Needed for 1999/2000: Hitters, Pitcher, Catcher
Most Recent Record: 29 - 17 - 0 **Baseball Camp Dates:** Middle of June
Schedule: Lincoln Memorial, Catawba, Carson - Newmann, Anderson, Bluefield, Tampa
Style of Play: Put pressure on the opposition; aggressive on the basepath; sound fundamental baseball.

Union University

1050 Union University Drive
Jackson, TN 38305
Coach: Andy Rushing

NAIA
Bulldogs/Red, White
Phone: (901) 661-5333
Fax: (901) 661-5182

ACADEMIC

Founded: 1820 **Type:** 4 Yr., Private, Liberal Arts, Coed
Religion: Southern Baptist **Campus Housing:** Yes
Web-site: Not Available **SAT/ACT/GPA:** 820/20
Student/Faculty Ratio: 12:1 **Male/Female Ratio:** 40:60
Undergraduate Enrollment: 2,000 **Graduate Enrollment:** 250
Scholarships/Academic: Yes **Athletic:** Yes **Fin Aid:** Yes
Total Expenses by: Year **In State:** $ 9,750 **Out of State:** $ 9,750
Degrees Conferred: BA, BM, BS
Programs of Study: Accounting, Biological, Chemistry, Communications, Computer, Economics, Education, English, French, History, Journalism, Marketing, Mathematics, Medical, Ministiries, Music, Nursing, Physics, Preprofessional Programs, Psychology, Religion, Social Science, Spanish

ATHLETIC PROFILE

Estimated Number of Baseball Scholarships: 10
Conference Affiliation: Tran South Conference
Program Profile: Perennial top 20 NAIA. New facility in 1999 season; natural grass, lights, 850 permanent seats.

History: Long tradition of winning teams: NCAA small college National Champions in 1963 and NAIA World Series 3rd place in 1983; numerous conference championships; most recent 1996 Tennessee Collegiate Athletic Conference regular season champs.
Achievements: Conference Coach of the Year in 1987 and 1995; NCCAA Mid-East Region Coach of the Year in 1998; 9 NAIA All-Americans at Union; 4 Academic All-Americans; 6 drafted players.
Coaching: Andy Rushing, Head Coach, has 14 years as a college head coach, ten years at Union . He compiled a record of 412-301, at Union his record is 328-211. Brent Fronabarger, Assistant Coach, entering first year with the program; he was named All-American in 1996; holds 4 Union pitching records.
Roster for 1998 team/In State: 20 **Out of State:** 6 **Out of Country:** 0
Total Number of Varsity/Jr. Varsity: 26 **Percent of Graduation:** 95%
Number of Seniors on 1998 Team: 3 **Most Recent Record:** 42 - 20 - 0
Freshmen Receiving Fin Aid/Athletic: 3 **Academic:** 3
Number of Fall Games: 10 **Number of Spring Games:** 60
Positions Needed for 1999/2000: Pitcher, Middle Infielder
Schedule: Birmingham Southern, Auburn University, Berry, Lipscomb, Oklahoma City, Delta State
Style of Play: Emphasis on pitching, defense and speed.

University of Memphis

570 Normal
Memphis, TN 38152
Coach: Jeff Hopkins

NCAA I
Tigers/Blue, Grey
Phone: (901) 678-2452
Fax: (901) 678-4134

ACADEMIC

Founded: 1912 **Type:** 4 Yr., Public, Coed
Religion: Non-Affiliated **Campus Housing:** Yes
Web-site: http://www.memphis.edu/ **SAT/ACT/GPA:** 19
Student/Faculty Ratio: 18:1 **Male/Female Ratio:** 4:6
Undergraduate Enrollment: 20,000 **Graduate Enrollment:** 0
Scholarships/Academic: Yes **Athletic:** Yes **Fin Aid:** Yes
Total Expenses by: Year **In State:** $ 6,430 **Out of State:** $ 10,766
Degrees Conferred: BA, BS, MA, MS, PhD, EdD
Programs of Study: Accounting, Anthropology, Applied Mathematics, Art, Biology, Business and Management, Chemistry, Communications, Computer Science, Criminal Justice, Education, Economics, Geography, Geology,History, Journalism, Liberal Arts, Medical Technology, Marketing, Psychology, Physics, Physical Education, Political Science

ATHLETIC PROFILE

Conference Affiliation: Conference USA
Program Profile: The Tigers play their home games at Nat Buring Field. The stadium seats 2,000 and was renovated in 1992. The U of M season opens with the prestigious Service Acadamies Spring Classic, featuring such national powers as Arkansas and Kentucky.
History: The U of M program began in 1948 and has built a .629 winning percentage since then. The Tigers annually play one of the region's best schedules within Conference USA (South Florida, Tulane, Southern Miss) and outside the conference (Ole Miss, Miss State, Arkansas, Baylor).
Achievements: Won the Service Academy Spring Classic with defeat of #24 Notre Dame. Won the final Great MidWest Tournament and were one game from the College World Series in 1994.

University of Tennessee - Knoxville

P.O. Box 15016
Knoxville, TN 37901
Coach: Rod Delmonico

NCAA I
Volunteers/Orange, White
Phone: (423) 974-1223
Fax: (423) 974-5393

ACADEMIC

Founded: 1794
Religion: Non-Affiliated
Web-site: http://ath.utk.edu/womens/wsb/wsb.htm
Student/Faculty Ratio: 17:1
Undergraduate Enrollment: 19,017
Scholarships/Academic: Yes **Athletic:** Yes
Total Expenses by: Year **In State:** $ 7,094
Type: 4 Yr., Public, Coed
Campus Housing: Yes
SAT/ACT/GPA: 820/18/2.0
Male/Female Ratio: 1:1
Graduate Enrollment: 6,022
Fin Aid: Yes
Out of State: $ 12,150
Degrees Conferred: Offered 100 degrees
Programs of Study: Agricultural Sciences, Natural Resources, Education, Social Work, Architecture and Planning, Art and Sciences, Biomedical Science, Business Administration, Communications, Engineering, Human Ecology, Information Science, Nursing, Veterinary Medicine

ATHLETIC PROFILE

Estimated Number of Baseball Scholarships: 6
Conference Affiliation: SouthEastern Conference
Program Profile: Lindsey Nelson Stadium seats 4,500 and is natural grass. It was ranked 14th best collegiate stadium by Baseball America in 1998. Ranked Top 15 in the national attendance the past six years. State of the art scoreboard and message center installed in 1997 with chairback seating.
History: Program dates back to 1897, recording a record of 1,421-1,079 in 90 years of play. Made two College World Series Appearances, won three conference titles, sent 26 players to a major leagues. Currently have eight players in the major leagues and 18 playing minor league baseball.
Achievements: Over the past nine years, UT has reached the College World Series (1995); won two SEC Titles, four SEC Eastern Division titles, three SEC Eastern Division Tournaments, made five NCAA Regional Appearances, had 13 All-Americans, 3 Academic All-Americans, 55 players sign pro.
Coaching: Rod Delmonico, Head Coach, began coaching in 1990 and has compiled a 376-179 record in nine years. Led UT to 1995 College World Series where he was named National Coach of the Year. Had 43 players drafted & 12 sign professionally while at UT, including 2 first round picks.
Roster for 1998 team/In State: 20 **Out of State:** 8 **Out of Country:** 0
Total Number of Varsity/Jr. Varsity: 28 **Percent of Graduation:** 50%
Number of Seniors on 1998 Team: 4 **Number of Sophomores on 1998 Team:** 7
Freshmen Receiving Fin Aid/Athletic: 1 **Most Recent Record:** 36 - 20 - 0
Number of Fall Games: 0 **Number of Spring Games:** 56
Positions Needed for 1999/2000: Pitchers, 1st Base, 3rd Base, Outfielder
Baseball Camp Dates: June 7-11,14-18, 19-20; July 11-16, 18-23, 25-30
Schedule: LSU, Alabama, Florida, Mississippi State, Auburn, South Carolina
Style of Play: A strong defensive club that relys on a strong starting rotation. Uses a lot of team speed to put pressure on defense while utilizing the hit and run. Steps up with a power hitters in the middle of the line up.

University of Tennessee - Martin

1037 Elam Center
Martin, TN 38238
Coach: Bubba Cates
Email: vcates@utm.edu
NCAA I
Skyhawks/Royal, Orange
Phone: (901) 587-7337
Fax: (901) 587-7962

ACADEMIC

Founded: 1927
Religion: Non-Affiliated
Web-site: http://www.utm.edu
Student/Faculty Ratio: 20:1
Undergraduate Enrollment: 5,400
Scholarships/Academic: Yes **Athletic:** Yes
Total Expenses by: Year **In State:** $ 6,538
Type: 4 Yr., Public, Coed
Campus Housing: Yes
SAT/ACT/GPA: 910/19/2.25
Male/Female Ratio: 45:55
Graduate Enrollment: 400
Fin Aid: Yes
Out of State: $ 11,364
Degrees Conferred: BA, BS, MBUs, Med, MH

Programs of Study: Agricultural, Animal, Biological, Broadcasting, Chemistry, Civil Engineering, Criminal Justice, Dental Science, Earth Space, Economics, Finance, Geoscience, History, Management, Parks/Recreation, Pharmacy, Preprofessional Programs

ATHLETIC PROFILE

Estimated Number of Baseball Scholarships: 4
Conference Affiliation: Ohio Valley Conference
Program Profile: Moved from Division II to Division I in 1993. Year-round program with a natural grass field; stadium seating capacity is 500. Playing season runs from early February to mid-May.
Achievements: Jody Fuller in 1998 was drafted by Arizona Backs. UTM graduates Donnie Mitchell (Diamondbacks) and Paul Tinnell (Pirates) Directors of scouting for major league team.
Coaching: Bubba Cates, Head Coach.
Roster for 1998 team/In State: 28 **Out of State:** 6 **Out of Country:** 0
Total Number of Varsity/Jr. Varsity: 34 **Percent of Graduation:** 0
Number of Seniors on 1998 Team: 9 **Number of Sophomores on 1998 Team:** 0
Freshmen Receiving Fin Aid/Athletic: 3 **Academic:** 2
Most Recent Record: 15 - 31 - 0 **Number of Spring Games:** 56
Positions Needed for 1999/2000: 4-Pitchers, Catcher, Shortstop, Outfielder
Schedule: Tennessee, Vanderbilt, Memphis, Arkansas State, OVC Conference
Style of Play: Prepared to play with an intense desire to compete.

University of the South

735 University Avenue
Sewanee, TN 37375
Coach: Tom Flynn

NCAA III
Tigers/Purple, White
Phone: (931) 598-1455
Fax: (931) 598-1673

ACADEMIC

Founded: 1857 **Type:** 4 Yr., Private, Liberal Arts, Coed
Religion: Episcopal **Campus Housing:** Yes
Web-site: http://www.sewanee.edu **SAT/ACT/GPA:** 1180/25
Student/Faculty Ratio: 11:1 **Male/Female Ratio:** 1:1
Undergraduate Enrollment: 1,300 **Graduate Enrollment:** 100
Scholarships/Academic: Yes **Athletic:** No **Fin Aid:** Yes
Total Expenses by: Year **In State:** $ 21,425 **Out of State:** $ 21,425
Degrees Conferred: BA, BS
Programs of Study: American Studies, Anthropolgy, Biology, Chemistry, Comparative Literature, Economics, English, Fine Arts, French, Geology, German, German Studies, Greek, History, Latin, Mathematics, Mathematics and Computer Science, Medieval Studies, Music, Natural Resources, Emphasis on Forestry, Philosophy, Physics, Political Science, Psychology, Religion, Russian, Russian Area Studies, Social Science, Foreign Language, Spanish, Theatre Arts

ATHLETIC PROFILE

Conference Affiliation: SCAC

Vanderbilt University

Box 120158
Nashville, TN 37212
Coach: Roy Mewbourne

NCAA I
Commodores/Black, Gold
Phone: (615) 322-4727
Fax: (615) 343-8123

ACADEMIC

Type: 4 Yr., Private, Liberal Arts, Coed, Engineering **Founded:** 1873
Religion: Non-Affiliated **Campus Housing:** Yes

Web-site: http://www.vanderbilt.edu/
SAT/ACT/GPA: 1150/26
Student/Faculty Ratio: 8:1
Male/Female Ratio: 52:48
Undergraduate Enrollment: 5,500
Graduate Enrollment: 3,500
Scholarships/Academic: Yes **Athletic:** Yes **Fin Aid:** Yes
Total Expenses by: Year **In State:** $ 29,700 **Out of State:** $ 29,700
Degrees Conferred: BA, BS, MA, MS, MBA, MED, PhD, MD, JD
Programs of Study: Education, Engineering, Human Development, Literature, Liberal Arts and Sciences, Life Sciences, Mathematics, Music, Psychology, Social Sciences plus a full range of graduate and professional degree.

ATHLETIC PROFILE

Conference Affiliation: SouthEastern Conference
Program Profile: The addition of lights last March has increased attendance!
Achievements: 1995 MVP; Cape Cod League - Josh Paul (Junior).
Coaching: Roy Mewbourne, Head Coach.

Volunteer State Community College

1480 Nashville Pike
Gallatin, TN 37066
Coach: Kenny Thomas
NJCAA
Pioneers/Red, Royal Blue
Phone: (615) 452-8600
Fax: (615) 230-3629

ACADEMIC

Founded: 1970
Type: 2 Yr., Jr. College, Coed
Student/Faculty Ratio: 19:1
Male/Female Ratio: 35:65
Undergraduate Enrollment: 5,900
Graduate Enrollment:
Scholarships/Academic: No **Athletic:** Yes **Fin Aid:** Yes
Total Expenses by: Year **In State:** $ 1,000 **Out of State:** $ 3,700
Degrees Conferred: Associate
Programs of Study: Business Administration, Dental Services, Education, Emergency Medical Technology, Interdisciplinary Studies, Liberal Arts, Paralegal Studies, Physical Therapy, Radiological Technology, Respiratory Therapy

ATHLETIC PROFILE

Estimated Number of Baseball Scholarships: 16
Conference Affiliation: TJCCAA
Program Profile: Rank in the top 10 in the last five years, including #1 in 1998 (nationally); has 56 game season on natural turf with 1,500 seat stadium. We have indoor and outdoor hitting facilities.
History: Program began back in 1987-1988, after 10 year lay off. Ranked in the Top 10 of the NJCAA in the last three years (1997, 1996, and 1995); Ranked in the Top 20 of the NJCAA in the last five years; appeared in JUCO World Series in 1995.
Achievements: Coach of the Year in 1998, 1996, 1995, 1994, 1993 and 1989; Conference Titles; TJCCAA Western Division in 1998, 1996, 1994, 1990 and 1989.
Coaching: Kenny Thomas, Head Coach, compiled a record of 468-205. He was named Coach of the Year in 1998. Jackie Holt, Craig Mullins, and Caleb Slaughter, Assistant Coaches.
Roster for 1998 team/In State: 27 **Out of State:** 10 **Out of Country:** 0
Total Number of Varsity/Jr. Varsity: 37 **Percent of Graduation:** 75%
Number of Seniors on 1998 Team: 18 **Most Recent Record:** 50 - 10 - 0
Freshmen Receiving Fin Aid/Athletic: 10 **Academic:** 4
Number of Fall Games: 20 **Number of Spring Games:** 56
Positions Needed for 1999/2000: Catcher, Pitcher, Outfielder, Shortstop
Baseball Camp Dates: September - February
Schedule: Oklaoosa Walton CC, South Suburban College, Panola College, Wallace State - Hanceville, Columbia State, Motlow State
Style of Play: Likes to run, good pitching.

Walters State Community College

500 South Davy Crockett Pkwy
Morristown, TN 37813
Coach: Adam Cross

NJCAA
Senators/Navy, White, Red
Phone: (423) 585-6754
Fax: (423) 585-6853

ACADEMIC

Founded: 1970
Type: 2 Yr., Jr. College, Coed
Student/Faculty Ratio: 25:1
Male/Female Ratio: 37:63
Undergraduate Enrollment: 5,550
Graduate Enrollment: None
Scholarships/Academic: No **Athletic:** Yes **Fin Aid:** Yes
Total Expenses by: Year **In State:** $ 938 **Out of State:** $ 3,621
Degrees Conferred: Associate
Programs of Study: Agricultural Business. Computer, Criminal Education, Interdisciplinary, Liberal Arts, Paralegal, Radiological, Physical Respiratory Therapy

ATHLETIC PROFILE

Conference Affiliation: TNJCAA

TEXAS

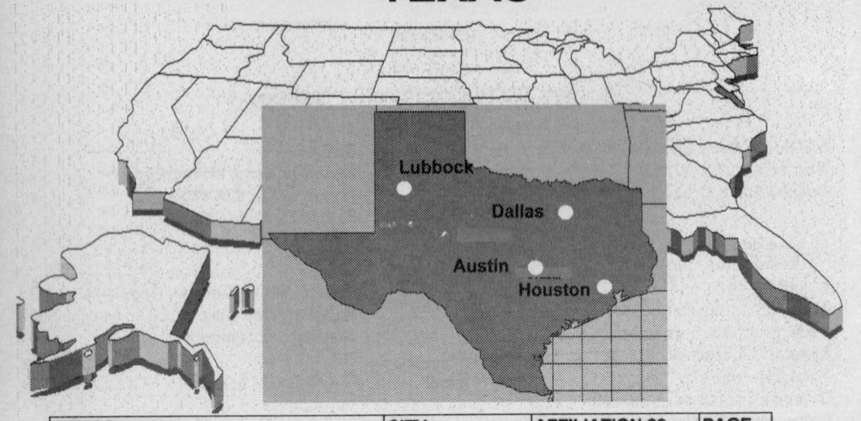

SCHOOL	CITY	AFFILIATION 99	PAGE
Abilene Christian University	Abilene	NCAA II	818
Alvin Community College	Alvin	NJCAA	818
Angelina College	Lufkin	NJCAA	819
Austin College	Sherman	NCAA III	819
Baylor University	Waco	NCAA I	820
Blinn College	Brenham	NJCAA	821
Brookhaven College	Farmers Branch	NJCAA	821
Cedar Valley College	Lancaster	NJCAA	822
Collin County Community College	Plano	NJCAA	822
Concordia University - Austin	Austin	NCAA II/NAIA	823
Dallas Baptist University	Dallas	NCAA I/NAIA	823
East Texas Baptist University	Marshall	NCAA II/NAIA	824
Eastfield College	Mesquite	NJCAA	824
Frank Phillips College	Borger	NJCAA	825
Galveston College	Galveston	NJCAA	826
Hardin - Simmons University	Abilene	NCAA II/NAIA	826
Hill Junior College	Hillsboro	NJCAA	827
Houston Baptist University	Houston	NCAA II	828
Howard County Junior College	Big Spring	NJCAA	828
Howard Payne University	Brownwood	NCAA III	828
Huston - Tillotson College	Austin	NAIA	829
Jarvis Christian College	Hawkins	NCAA I	829
Lamar University	Beaumont	NCAA I	830
Laredo Community College	Laredo	NJCAA	830
Le Tourneau University	Longview	NCAA III	831
Lon Morris College	Jacksonville	NJCAA	832
Lubbock Christian University	Lubbock	NAIA	832
McLennan Community College	Waco	NJCAA	833
McMurry University	Abilene	NCAA III	833
Navarro College	Corsicana	NJCAA	834
North Central Texas College	Gainesville	NJCAA I	835
North Lake College	Irving	NJCAA	835
Northeast Texas Community College	Mt Pleasant	NJCAA	836
Northwood University - Texas	Cedar Hill	NAIA	836
Odessa College	Odessa	NJCAA	836
Panola College	Carthage	NJCAA	837
Paris Junior College	Paris	NJCAA	838
Prairie View A & M University	Prairie View	NCAA I	838
Ranger College	Ranger	NJCAA	839
Rice University	Houston	NCAA I	839
Richland Community College	Dallas	NJCAA	840
Saint Edward's College	Austin	NCAA II/NAIA	840
Saint Mary's University	San Antonio	NCAA II/NAIA	841
Sam Houston State University	Huntsville	NCAA I	842
San Jacinto College - North	Houston	NJCAA	842

SCHOOL	CITY	AFFILIATION 99	PAGE
Schreiner College	Kerrville	NCAA III	843
Southwest Texas State University	San Marcos	NCAA I	844
Southwestern Adventist College	Keene	NAIA	844
Southwestern University	Georgetown	NCAA III	845
Sul Ross State University	Alpine	NCAA III	846
Tarleton State University	Stephenville	NCAA II	846
Texarkana College	Texarkana	NJCAA	847
Texas A & M University	College Station	NCAA I	848
Texas A & M U - Kingsville	Kingsville	NCAA II	848
Texas Christian University	Forth Worth	NCAA I	849
Texas College	Tyler	NAIA	850
Texas Lutheran College	Seguin	NCAA II/NAIA	850
Texas Southern University	Houston	NCAA I	851
Texas Tech University	Lubbock	NCAA I	852
Texas Wesleyan University	Forth Worth	NCAA II/NAIA	852
Trinity University	San Antonio	NCAA III	853
Tyler Junior College	Tyler	NJCAA	854
University of Dallas	Irving	NCAA III	854
University of Houston	Houston	NCAA	855
University of Mary Hardin - Baylor	Belton	NCAA III	856
University of Texas - Arlington	Arlington	NCAA I	856
University of Texas - Austin	Austin	NCAA I	857
University of Texas - Brownsville	Brownsville	NJCAA	858
University of Texas - Pan American	Edinburg	NCAA I	858
University of Texas - San Antonio	San Antonio	NCAA I	859
University of the Incarnate Word	San Antonio	NCAA II/NAIA	859
Vernon Regional Junior College	Vernon	NJCAA	860
Wayland Baptist University	Plainview	NAIA	860
West Texas A & M University	Canyon	NCAA II	861
Wharton County Junior College	Wharton	NJCAA	861
Wiley College	Marshall	NAIA	862

Abilene Christian University

Station ACU, Box 7916
Abilene, TX 79699
Coach: Brett Bonneau

NCAA II
Wildcats/Purple, White
Phone: (915) 674-2108
Fax: (915) 674-6904

ACADEMIC

Founded: 1906
Religion: Church of Christ
Web-site: Not Available
Student/Faculty Ratio: 18:1
Undergraduate Enrollment: 3,385
Scholarships/Academic: Yes **Athletic:** No
Total Expenses by: Year **In State:** $ 10,900

Type: 4 Yr., Private, Liberal Arts, Coed
Campus Housing: No
SAT/ACT/GPA: 700/17
Male/Female Ratio: 49:51
Graduate Enrollment: 685
Fin Aid: No
Out of State: $ 10,900

Degrees Conferred: AA, AS, BA, BS, BBA, BFA, BM, BSN, MA, MS
Programs of Study: Accounting, Advertising, Animal Science, Biochemistry, Biological Science, Communications, Computer Science, Education, French, German, Greek, Information Science, Journalism, Management, Microbiology, Physics, Political Science, Preprofessional Programs, Pscyhology, Religion, Social Sciences

ATHLETIC PROFILE

Conference Affiliation: Lone Star Conference

Alvin Community College

3110 Mustang Road
Alvin, TX 77511
Coach: Bryan Alexander

NJCAA
Dolphins/Red, White, Black
Phone: (281) 338-4710
Fax: (281) 585-5897

ACADEMIC

Founded: 1949
Religion: Non-Affiliated
Student/Faculty Ratio: 29:1
Undergraduate Enrollment: 4,085
Scholarships/Academic: No **Athletic:** Yes
Total Expenses by: Year **In State:** $ 850

Type: 2 Yr., Jr. College, Coed
Campus Housing: No
Male/Female Ratio: 45:55
Graduate Enrollment: None
Fin Aid: Yes
Out of State: $ 1,600

Degrees Conferred: Associate
Programs of Study: Aerospace Science, Automotive Technology, Biological Science, Business Administration, Computer Programming, Corrections, Heating, Refrigeration, Air Conditioning, Liberal Arts, Management, Paralegal Studies, Physical Education, Physical Science, Radio/Television, Respiratory Therapy, Retail Management

ATHLETIC PROFILE

Conference Affiliation: Region XIV
Program Profile: Our facilities include two cages and a field which has natural grass. Playing season is in the Fall and in the Spring.
History: Our program began in early 1970's.
Achievements: 1997 Karl Rijden drafted by San Diego Padres.
Coaching: Bryan Alexander, Head Coach, started in 1996-1997. His team was 2nd in the Division. Oscar Rivas - Assistant Coach.
Style of Play: Aggressive and like to run and make things happen.

Angelina College

P.O. Box 1768
Lufkin, TX 75902-1768
Coach: Jeff Livin

NJCAA
Roadrunners/Blue, Orange
Phone: (409) 633-5282
Fax: (409) 633-5438

ACADEMIC

Founded: 1968
Type: 2 Yr., Public, Coed
Religion: Non-Affiliated
Campus Housing: Yes
Student/Faculty Ratio: 17:1
Male/Female Ratio: 39:61
Undergraduate Enrollment: 4,000
Graduate Enrollment: None
Scholarships/Academic: Yes **Athletic:** Yes **Fin Aid:** No
Total Expenses by: Year **In State:** $ 3,900 **Out of State:** $ 3,900
Degrees Conferred: Associate
Programs of Study: Agriculture, Automotive Technology, Biological Science, Business Administration, Computer Science and Technology, Engineering, History, Humanities, Journalism, Liberal Arts, Mathematics, Medical Technology, Pharmacy, Physical Education, Physical Science, Physical Therapy, Radiological Technology, Real Estate, Science

ATHLETIC PROFILE

Estimated Number of Baseball Scholarships: 12
Conference Affiliation: Texas Eastern Athletic Conference
Program Profile: We have an 800 seat stadium. Our field has measurements of 330 down the lines and 400 to the center. It has a solid fence grass field.
Achievements: Sooner Athletic Conference Coach of the Year in 1995 (NAIA).
Roster for 1998 team/In State: 0 **Out of State:** 5 **Out of Country:** 0
Total Number of Varsity/Jr. Varsity: 26 **Freshmen Receiving Fin Aid/Athletic:** 16
Most Recent Record: 23 - 29 - 0 **Number of Sophomores on 1998 Team:** 7
Number of Fall Games: 16 **Number of Spring Games:** 56
Positions Needed for 1999/2000: Catcher, Pitcher, Shortstop, 3rd Base, 1st Base
Schedule: Galveston, San Jacinto College, Blinn, Northeast, Navarro

Austin College

900 Grand Avenue, Suite 6A
Sherman, TX 75090-4440
Coach: Bruce Mauppin

NCAA III
Kangaroos/Cardinal, Gold
Phone: (903) 813-2400
Fax: (903) 813-3196

ACADEMIC

Founded: 1849
Type: 4 Yr., Private, Liberal Arts, Coed
Religion: Presbyterian
Campus Housing: Yes
Web-site: http://www.austinc.edu/
SAT/ACT/GPA: 1000+/24
Student/Faculty Ratio: 15:1
Male/Female Ratio: 50:50
Undergraduate Enrollment: 1,200
Graduate Enrollment: 20
Scholarships/Academic: Yes **Athletic:** No **Fin Aid:** Yes
Total Expenses by: Year **In State:** $ 16,000 **Out of State:** $ 16,000
Degrees Conferred: BA, MAT
Programs of Study: American Studies, Art, Biochemistry (as an interdisciplinary major using Special Program Option), Biology, Business Administration, Chemistry, Classics, Communication Arts (Speech-Theatre-Media), Computer Science (as an interdisciplinary major using Special Program Option), Economics, English, French, German, History, International Studies, Latin, Latin American Studies, Mathematics, Music, Philosophy, Physical Education, Physics, Political Science, Psychology, Religion, Sociology, Spanish, Teacher Education (Austin Teacher Program - graduate level only)

ATHLETIC PROFILE

Conference Affiliation: American Southwest Conference
Program Profile: We are in a competitive NCAA III. The Fall schedule consists of 9 games and the Spring schedule consists of 36 games. Our natural grass stadium seats 350.
History: We started rebuilding the program in 1997. We will be very competitive in 1999.
Achievements: 2 All-Conference players since 1997.
Coaching: Bruce Mauppin, Head Coach, entered his 1st year with an overall record of 9-62-1.
Roster for 1998 team/In State: 32 **Out of State:** 0 **Out of Country:** 0
Total Number of Varsity/Jr. Varsity: 32 **Most Recent Record:** 5 - 28 - 1
Number of Seniors on 1998 Team: 2 **Number of Sophomores on 1998 Team:**
Freshmen Receiving Fin Aid/Athletic: 0 **Academic:** 12
Number of Fall Games: 9 **Number of Spring Games:** 36
Positions Needed for 1999/2000: Pitcher
Schedule: Southeastern Oklahoma State, Southwestern, Trinity, McMurry University, Howard Payne
Style of Play: Emphasize pitching, defense and situational hitting.

Baylor University

150 Bear Run
Waco, TX 76711
Coach: Steve Smith

NCAA I
Bears/Dark Green, Gold
Phone: (254) 710-3041
Fax: (254) 710-3008

ACADEMIC

Type: 4 Yr., Private, Liberal Arts, Coed, Engineering **Founded:** 1845
Religion: Baptist **Campus Housing:** Yes
Web-site: http://www.baylor.edu/ **SAT/ACT/GPA:** 700/17
Student/Faculty Ratio: 14:1 **Male/Female Ratio:** 45:55
Undergraduate Enrollment: 12,000 **Graduate Enrollment:** 1,800
Scholarships/Academic: Yes **Athletic:** Yes **Fin Aid:** Yes
Total Expenses by: Year **In State:** $ 15,500 **Out of State:** $ 15,500
Degrees Conferred: BA, BS, BFA, BBA, BME, BSAC, BSN, MA, MS, MBA, PhD, JD
Programs of Study: Anthropology, Biological Science, Business Administration, Chemistry, Communications, Computer Science, Computer Engineering, Design, Earth Science, Economics, Education, Geology, History, Information Studies, International Business, Journalism, Languages, Marketing, Mathematics, Mechanical Engineering, Preprofessional Programs

ATHLETIC PROFILE

Estimated Number of Baseball Scholarships: 11.7
Conference Affiliation: Big Twelve Conference
Program Profile: Our program has 13 designs to provide the student/athlete with a great baseball experience while obtaining an outstanding degree. Ferrel Field has natural grass and was named 1997 Turface ABCA College Field of the Year. It has 8,100 sq. foot covered and a hitting pavillion. We have first class locker room facilities. We put strong emphasis on success both on the field and in the classroom.
History: The first year of baseball at Baylor was1902. We are one of the strongest private schools in the South. The Bears have participated in 2 College World Series in 1977 and 1978. They were in 5 NCAA Regionals. Coach Mickey Sullivan retired in 1993, after a 21-year career at Baylor.
Achievements: 21 players were drafted since 1991; 1998 had 3 All-Americans; 1998 had 3 Academic All-Americans; 7 players Academic All-Big 12.
Coaching: Steve Smith, Head Coach, is a 1986 graduate. He was Mississippi State pitching coach for five years and a former BU player. He is in his 4th year as head coach after being assistant at Texas AandM and Mississippi State. He was 1998 Austin American Statesmen Big XII Conference Coach of the Year. Mitch Thompson, Assistant Coach, was former assistant at Auburn. Steve Johnigan - Assistant Coach.
Roster for 1998 team/In State: 29 **Out of State:** 12 **Out of Country:** 0
Total Number of Varsity/Jr. Varsity: 41 **Number of Spring Games:** 56

Number of Seniors on 1998 Team: 4 **Number of Sophomores on 1998 Team:** 7
Positions Needed for 1999/2000: Pitcher, Outfielder
Most Recent Record: 41 - 20 - 0
Baseball Camp Dates: June 14-18; 21-25; July 5-9; 9-11; 11-15
Schedule: Texas AandM, Texas Tech, Oklahoma State, Long Beach State, Rice, Texas
Style of Play: Offensively, we believe in a mix of speed and power. We stress good fundamental baseball with strong team defense and pitching that throw strikes.

Blinn College

902 College Avenue
Brenham, TX 77833-4098
Coach: Ty Harrington

NJCAA
Buccaneers/Royal Blue, White
Phone: (409) 830-4278
Fax: (409) 830-4030

ACADEMIC

Founded: 1883
Type: 2 Yr., Public, Coed
Religion: Non-Affiliated
Campus Housing: Yes
Web-site: http://www.blinncol.edu
SAT/ACT/GPA: Not Required
Student/Faculty Ratio: 25:1
Male/Female Ratio: 1:1
Undergraduate Enrollment: 9,200
Graduate Enrollment: None
Scholarships/Academic: Yes **Athletic:** Yes **Fin Aid:** Yes
Total Expenses by: Year **In State:** $ 4,740 **Out of State:** $ 6,640
Degrees Conferred: AA, AS, AAS
Programs of Study: Agricultural Science, Biological Science, Science, Business, Chemistry, Communications, Computer Science, Criminal Justice, Education, English, History, Management

ATHLETIC PROFILE

Conference Affiliation: Texas Junior College Athletic Conference
Program Profile: Our 56-game schedule goes from February into mid-May. We play at Leroy Dreyer Field (named for former Buc skipper and NJCAA Baseball Hall of Fame inductee). It was built in 1988 and is the annual site of Texas-New Mexico Junior College Baseball Coaches Association All-Star Game. It is a natural grass playing field and has 665 covered grandstand seats.
History: Baseball first began in 1903. Our modern day program began in 1945. Our first conference championship was 12 years later in '93. Coach Van Hook was named TJCAC and TJCBCA Coach of the Year. He coached the USA to a Silver medal in Junior Pan American Games in Guatemala in '91.
Achievements: 1992 NJCAA World Series 3rd place; 1993 and 1996 conference champs; 22 former Bucs' currently playing in the pros; 24 All-Americans since 1959; 96 players sign pro contracts in the history of the program.

Brookhaven College

3939 Valley View Lane
Farmers Branch, TX 75244-4997
Coach: Denny Dixon

NJCAA
Bears/Green, White, Gold
Phone: (214) 620-4121#
Fax: (214) 620-4897

ACADEMIC

Founded: 1978
Type: 2 Yr., Public, Coed
Undergraduate Enrollment: 9,060
Student/Faculty Ratio: 17:1
Total Expenses by: Year **In State:** $ 520+ **Out of State:** $ 900+
Degrees Conferred: Associate
Programs of Study: Accounting, Automotive Technology, Business Administration, Commerce, Management, Child Care/Child and Family Studies, Child Psychology, Commercial Art, Computer Information System, Electromechanical Technology, Engineering Technology, Fashion Merchandising, Liberal Arts, General Studies

Cedar Valley College

3030 North Dallas Avenue
Lancaster, TX 75134
Coach: Russell Stockton

NJCAA
Suns/Black, Orange, White
Phone: (972) 372-8008
Fax: (972) 860-8207

ACADEMIC

Founded: 1977
Type: 2 Yr., Public, Coed
Undergraduate Enrollment: 3,136
Student/Faculty Ratio: 25:1
Total Expenses by: Year **In State:** $ 520+ **Out of State:** $ 2,010+
Degrees Conferred: Associate
Programs of Study: Accounting, Automotive Technology, Fashion Merchandising, Legal Secretarial Studies, Liberal Arts, General Studies, Marketing, Retailing, Merchandising, Music, Veterinary Technology

ATHLETIC PROFILE

Conference Affiliation: Metro Athletic Conference

Collin County Community College

2800 E Spring Creek Pkwy
Plano, TX 75074
Coach: Greg Dennis

NJCAA
Express/Royal Blue, Grey
Phone: (972) 881-5927
Fax: (972) 881-5796

ACADEMIC

Founded: 1985
Type: 2 Yr., Jr. College, Coed
Student/Faculty Ratio: 20:1
Male/Female Ratio: 43:57
Undergraduate Enrollment: 10,100
Graduate Enrollment: None
Scholarships/Academic: Yes **Athletic:** Yes **Fin Aid:** Yes
Total Expenses by: Year **In State:** $ 2,750 **Out of State:** $ 3,750
Degrees Conferred: Associate
Programs of Study: Accounting, Advertising, Art, Biology, Business, Commercial, Computer Science, Economics, Education, Emergency Medical, Engineering, Horticulture, Philosophy

ATHLETIC PROFILE

Conference Affiliation: Region V, East Conference
Program Profile: Sewell Field is one of the nicest and fastest growing facilities in the metroplex.
History: Our program began in 1990 and has grown competitively for 6 years. The team has finished anywhere from 3rd to 6th in the previous seasons. Many former players have graduated and went on to Division I schools.
Achievements: 2 Academic All-Americans, 1 preseason All-American, first player, Willie Jackson, from program drafted last year in the 10th round by Cleveland
Coaching: Greg Dennis, Head Coach,was a two- year starter at McLennan CC. His teams finished 3rd and 1st nationally. He was first Team All-American Shortstop (1983). He played at Florida State (All Metro Conference) , at Baylor (All-SWC) and in the Toronto Bluejay organization. Tim Peters, Assistant Coach, was the pitching coach at Texarkana JC and University of Houston. He played Division I ball at the University of Arkansas. He played four years of pro ball. Jeff Bowling, Assistant Coach, has coached here 3 years. He played at Lon Morris and UNT. He is a super offensive coach and teacher.
Style of Play: Wide open offensive style, emphasis on aggressive base running and hitting. Team philosophy is consistent for everyone.

Concordia University - Austin

3400 IH - 35 North
Austin, TX 78705
Coach: Jeff Daley

NCAA II/NAIA
Tornados/Purple, White
Phone: (512) 452-7661x1120
Fax: (512) 459-8517

ACADEMIC

Founded: 1947
Type: 4 Yr., Private, Liberal Arts, Coed
Religion: Lutheran
Campus Housing: Yes
Web-site: http://www.austin.concordia.edu
SAT/ACT/GPA: 800/2.0
Student/Faculty Ratio: 12:1
Male/Female Ratio: 1:3
Undergraduate Enrollment: 500
Graduate Enrollment: 100
Scholarships/Academic: Yes **Athletic:** No **Fin Aid:** Yes
Total Expenses by: Year **In State:** $ 14,200 **Out of State:** $ 14,200
Degrees Conferred: Contact school
Programs of Study: Computer Science, Secondary Education, Business, Lutheran Ministry, Math, English, Premed

ATHLETIC PROFILE

Conference Affiliation: Heart of Texas Conference
Program Profile: We have a beautiful field in the heart of Austin in the shadow of Vermont. It measures 305 left, 310 right and 380 center . It seats 250.
History: Jeff Daley took over the program from James Keller who is in last stages of Lou Gehrig's desease. We hope to continue a tradition of never having a losing season.
Achievements: In the past 10 years we had 12 players playing in minor leagues and pro ball.
Coaching: Jeff Daley - Head Coach. Jeff Myer - Assistant Coach.
Roster for 1998 team/In State: 19 **Out of State:** 2 **Out of Country:** 0
Total Number of Varsity/Jr. Varsity: 21 **Percent of Graduation:** 95%
Number of Seniors on 1998 Team: 4 **Most Recent Record:** 11 - 31 - 0
Number of Fall Games: 3 **Number of Spring Games:** 36
Positions Needed for 1999/2000: Pitchers, Catchers
Style of Play: We want to be aggressive on offense and put pressure on opponent's defense. Will build club with a speed and improve defense to better pitching.

Dallas Baptist University

3000 Mountain Creek Parkway
Dallas, TX 75211
Coach: Jim Harp
Email: sports@bdu.edu

NCAA I/NAIA
Patriots/Red, White, Navy
Phone: (214) 333-5340
Fax: (214) 333-5306

ACADEMIC

Founded: 1965
Type: 4 Yr., Private, Coed
Religion: Southern Baptist
Campus Housing: Yes
Web-site: http://www.dbu.edu/
SAT/ACT/GPA: 710+/17+
Student/Faculty Ratio: 14:1
Male/Female Ratio: 50:50
Undergraduate Enrollment: 3,700
Graduate Enrollment: 307
Scholarships/Academic: Yes **Athletic:** Yes **Fin Aid:** Yes
Total Expenses by: Year **In State:** $ 10,000+appr. **Out of State:** $10,000+appr.
Degrees Conferred: BA, BS, BBA, BM, BCM, BLA, Med, MA, MS, MBA
Programs of Study: Accounting, Allied Health, Aviation Management, Banking and Finance, Biblical Studies, Biology, Broadcasting, Commuications, Computer Science, Criminal Justice, Dramatic Arts, Economics, English, Fine Arts, History, Marketing, Mathematics, Music, Music Performance, Nursing, Pastoral Studies, Physical Education, Political Science, Psychology, Real Estate, Religious Education, Social Science

ATHLETIC PROFILE

Estimated Number of Baseball Scholarships: 11.7
Conference Affiliation: Independent Conference
History: The program began in 1970. We have ranked in the NAIA top 10 for 15 consecutive years.
Achievements: 85 players drafted or signed as a free-agent; 41 All-Americans; 10 NAIA Sectional Championships; Jim Harp was named National Coach of the Year in 1985; SW Region Coach of the Year in 1984, 1985, 1989, 1994 and 1997.
Coaching: Jim Harp, Head Coach, has 26 years of coaching experience. He compiled a record of 1,973-1,052-530. He was inducted to NAIA Hall of Fame in 1997 and Texas Baseball Hall of Fame in 1997. He was NAIA Rawling NTL Coach of the Year in 1995 and Southwest Regional National Coach of the Year in 1984, 1985, 1989, 1994 and 1997. Brian Strickland - Assistant Coach.
Roster for 1998 team/In State: 24 **Out of State:** 8 **Out of Country:** 0
Total Number of Varsity/Jr. Varsity: 32 **Percent of Graduation:** 60%
Number of Seniors on 1998 Team: 5 **Most Recent Record:** 48 - 17 - 0
Freshmen Receiving Fin Aid/Athletic: 4 **Academic:** 1
Baseball Camp Dates: June 1-21 **Number of Spring Games:** 56
Positions Needed for 1999/2000: Pitchers, Catcher, 3rd Base, Shortstop
Schedule: Arkansas, Rice. Southwestern Louisiana, Baylor, LSU, Arkansas
Style of Play: Power hitters; solid defense and power.

East Texas Baptist University

1209 North Grove Street
Marshall, TX 75670
Coach: Jim Kneipp

NCAA II/NAIA
Tigers/Blue, Gold
Phone: (903) 935-7963x327
Fax: (903) 927-4488

ACADEMIC

Founded: 1912 **Type:** 4 Yr., Private, Liberal Arts, Coed
Religion: Baptist General Convention of Texas **Campus Housing:** Yes
Web-site: http://www.etbu.edu/ **SAT/ACT/GPA:** 860/18
Student/Faculty Ratio: 16:1 **Male/Female Ratio:** 40:60
Undergraduate Enrollment: 5,000 **Graduate Enrollment:** 1,400
Scholarships/Academic: Yes **Athletic:** Yes **Fin Aid:** Yes
Total Expenses by: Year **In State:** $ 10,350 **Out of State:** $ 10,350
Degrees Conferred: AA, AAS, ABA, BA, BS, BBA, BSEd, BM, BSM, MBA
Programs of Study: Applied Health and Preprofessional Programs, Biology, Business, Chemistry and Physics, Communication, English, Mathematics, Computer Science, Nursing, Religion, Teacher

ATHLETIC PROFILE

Conference Affiliation: Independent Conference

Eastfield College

3737 Motley Drive
Mesquite, TX 75150
Coach: Jeff Lightfoot
Email: jxl445@dccd.edu

NJCAA
Harvesters/Orange, Navy
Phone: (972) 860-7643
Fax: (972) 860-8374

ACADEMIC

Founded: 1970 **Type:** 2 Yr., Public, Coed
Religion: Non-Affiliated **Campus Housing:** No
Undergraduate Enrollment: 8,500 **Student/Faculty Ratio:** 25:1
Scholarships/Academic: No **Athletic:** No **Fin Aid:** Yes
Total Expenses by: Year **In State:** $ 1,500 **Out of State:** $ 2,200

Degrees Conferred: All transferred credit to 4-year school
Programs of Study: Associate degrees available.

ATHLETIC PROFILE

Conference Affiliation: Metro Athletic Conference
Program Profile: We play on a grass field with measurements of 320-400-320. It has a seating capacity of 200 and a great playing surface with constant upgrades. We play a 56 game schedule in Spring and 20 home games in the Fall. We have a strong weight and conditioning program and we focus on the fundamentals.
History: We began in 1970 and won over ten conference titles since that time. On his first year (1988), Head Coach Jeff Lightfoot lead the Harvesters to a school record 33-15 and a first conference title in 10 years.
Achievements: Conference Champions in 1972 through 1983 and 1985; Matt Jolls was named All-American in 1991; Junior Gorden was named All-American in 1996; Moose Coack - drafted by the Rangers in 1970's.
Coaching: Jeff Lightfoot, Head Coach, started in 1988 as a head coach. He compiled a record of 33-18. His team ranked 34th in the nation in the JUCO Division III. His team took a World Series trip May 14-22. He got his Masters at Texas A & M Commerce. Billy Tankalez, Assistant Coach, played at NE Texas CC and Louisiana Tech.
Roster for 1998 team/In State: 21 **Out of State:** 2 **Out of Country:** 1
Number of Seniors on 1998 Team: 10 **Most Recent Record:** 33 - 15 - 0
Freshmen Receiving Fin Aid/Athletic: 0 **Academic:** 40%
Number of Fall Games: 20 **Number of Spring Games:** 56
Positions Needed for 1999/2000: 1st Base, 3rd Base, Catcher, Pitcher
Schedule: San Jacinto Junior College, Northeast Texas JC, Panola JC, Tyler JC
Style of Play: Offensive - minded, with good speed and solid defense.

Frank Phillips College

PO Box 5118
Borger, TX 79008-5118
Coach: Dave Langen
Email: jgreen@fpc.cc.tx.us

NJCAA
Plainsmen/Royal, Gold
Phone: (806) 274-5311
Fax: (806) 274-6835

ACADEMIC

Founded: 1948 **Type:** 2 Yr., Public, Coed
Religion: Non-Affiliated **Campus Housing:** Yes
Web-site: http://www.fpc.cc.tx.us **Undergraduate Enrollment:** 1,100
Student/Faculty Ratio: 13:1 **Male/Female Ratio:** 1:1
Scholarships/Academic: Yes **Athletic:** Yes **Fin Aid:** Yes
Total Expenses by: Year **In State:** $ 3,230 **Out of State:** $ 3,230
Degrees Conferred: Certificates, AA, AS
Programs of Study: Liberal and Fine Arts, Math, Science, Physical Education, Computers, Business, Accounting, Nursing, Cosmetology, Agriculture, Music, Legal Assistant, Workforce Development, Air Conditioning/Heating, Welding, Developmental Education

ATHLETIC PROFILE

Estimated Number of Baseball Scholarships: 10
Conference Affiliation: WJCAC
Program Profile: We play on a natural grass field . It seats 200 and measures: 330 ft. left, 330 right field and 40 in the center. We play 20 Fall games and 56 Spring games.
Coaching: Dave Langen, Head Coach, started Spring of 1996 with a record of 60-52. Rex Threatt - Assistant Coach.
Roster for 1998 team/In State: 11 **Out of State:** 13 **Out of Country:** 0
Total Number of Varsity/Jr. Varsity: 24 **Percent of Graduation:** 0
Number of Seniors on 1998 Team: **Number of Sophomores on 1998 Team:** 6
Freshmen Receiving Fin Aid/Athletic: 7 **Most Recent Record:** 28 - 28 - 0

Number of Fall Games: 20 **Number of Spring Games:** 56
Positions Needed for 1999/2000: Shortstop, 3rd Base, Catcher, Pitcher
Schedule: Grayson Community, Hill Community, Trinidad State, Odessa, Howard, Seward CC

Galveston College

4015 Ave Q
Galveston, TX 77550
Coach: Charles Corbell

NJCAA
Whitecaps/Rust, Royal Blue
Phone: (409) 763-6551x316
Fax: (409) 762-9367

ACADEMIC

Founded: 1967
Type: 2 Yr., Public, Liberal Arts, Coed
Undergraduate Enrollment: 2,222
SAT/ACT/GPA: Open Admission Policy
Student/Faculty Ratio: 12:1
Male/Female Ratio: 50:50
Scholarships/Academic: Yes **Athletic:** Yes **Fin Aid:** Yes
Total Expenses by: Year **In State:** $ 7,000 **Out of State:** $ 7,700
Degrees Conferred: AA
Programs of Study: Accounting, Prebusiness, Premed, Preengineering, Nursing, General Studies, Radiology, Health Care Administration, Nuclear Medicine

ATHLETIC PROFILE

Estimated Number of Baseball Scholarships: 14
Conference Affiliation: NJCAA Region XIV
Program Profile: Our baseball stadium seats 800 and features natural grass. We play outside year-round.
History: The program started in 1992 when National Junior College Athletic Association affiliation began.
Achievements: National Champs in 1994, 8 All-Americans; Distinguished alumni; played Division I or minor league ball; 2 Big Leaguers; 50 drafted players.
Coaching: Charles Corbell, Head Coach, entered his 1st year with the program. He is a 9 year pro. Mike Taylor - Assistant Coach, San Jacinto - Toronto Organization. Allan Matt - Assistant Coach.
Roster for 1998 team/In State: 18 **Out of State:** 1 **Out of Country:** 3
Total Number of Varsity/Jr. Varsity: 22 **Percent of Graduation:** 5%
Number of Seniors on 1998 Team: 6 **Baseball Camp Dates:** 4 weeks in June
Freshmen Receiving Fin Aid/Athletic: 12 **Most Recent Record:** 47 - 11 - 0
Number of Fall Games: 20 **Number of Spring Games:** 56
Schedule: Meridian, San Jacinto College, Blinn College, Northeast Texas CC, Hill, Navarro
Style of Play: Aggressive pitching; hit and run offense, aggressive base running fundamental defense.

Hardin - Simmons University

Box 16185
Abilene, TX 79698-6185
Coach: Steve Coleman

NCAA II/NAIA
Cowboys/Purple, Gold
Phone: (915) 670-1493
Fax: (915) 670-1572

ACADEMIC

Founded: 1891
Type: 4 Yr., Private, Liberal Arts, Coed
Religion: Baptist
Campus Housing: Yes
Web-site: http://www.hsutx.edu/
SAT/ACT/GPA: 840
Student/Faculty Ratio: 17:1
Male/Female Ratio: 5:8
Undergraduate Enrollment: 1,671
Graduate Enrollment: 130
Scholarships/Academic: Yes **Athletic:** No **Fin Aid:** Yes
Total Expenses by: Year **In State:** $ 9,000-$11,000 **Out of State:** $ 9,000-$11,000

Degrees Conferred: AS, BA, BS, BFA, Bmus, BSN, MA, MBA, MED
Programs of Study: Accounting, Banking/Finance, Biology, Business Administration, Chemistry, Communications, Computer Science, Criminal Justice, Education, English, Fine Arts, History

ATHLETIC PROFILE

Conference Affiliation: TIAA
Program Profile: We have a natural grass (Bermuda and rye) field. It wraps-around the stands and seats 1400. We have major league facilities: lights, a carpeted dressing room,2 indoor batting tunnels and a weight room. We play in the Fall and in the Spring.
History: HSU won several division titles while a member of Division I TAAC and lost to National Champion Texas in the 1st round of the Midwest Regionals in 1982. We joined the nonscholarship TIAA in 1991. We earned 4 straight invitationals to the NAIA District VIII Tournament and a Conference Championship in 1995.
Achievements: James King Conference coach of the Year in 1995 and TIAA Conference Champs; 1982 TAAC Conference Champs; 3 All-Americans; 5 players drafted.
Style of Play: Aggressive and lots of hustle and work on fundamentals of the game.

Hill Junior College

112 Lamar Drive
Hillsboro, TX 76645
Coach: Gary Benton

NJCAA
Rebels/Red, White
Phone: (254) 582-2555
Fax: (254) 582-7591

ACADEMIC

Founded: 1923
Type: 2 Yr., Public, Jr. College, Coed
Student/Faculty Ratio: 25:1
Male/Female Ratio: 40:60
Undergraduate Enrollment: 2,200
Graduate Enrollment: None
Scholarships/Academic: None **Athletic:** Yes **Fin Aid:** Yes
Total Expenses by: Year **In State:** $ 4,200 **Out of State:** $ 4,600
Degrees Conferred: Associate
Programs of Study: Accounting, Agriculture, Animal Science, Applied Art, Art, Automotive Technology, Banking/Finance, Behavioral Science, Biological Science, Botany, Business Administration, Chemistry, Commercial Art, Communications, Computer Science, Cosmetology, Criminal Justice, Drafting/Design, Economics, Education, Electrical/Electronics Technology, Engineering and Applied Science, Engineering Science, and Technology, English, Farm/Ranch Management, Geography, Health Science, History, Horticulture, Humanities, Journalism, Law Enforcement, Liberal Arts, Machine/Tool Technology, Mathematics, Music, Music Education, Music Therapy, Nursing, Photography, Physical Education, Physical Science, Physics, Political Science

ATHLETIC PROFILE

Estimated Number of Baseball Scholarships: 12
Conference Affiliation: North Texas Junior College Athletic Conference
Program Profile: Since 1988, the baseball program has emerged as one of the top programs in the state of Texas. The Rebels have claimed five Region V Championships including four of the last five. 1997 proved to be a banner season for the Rebels as they advanced to the Junior College World Series in Grand Junction, CO. They won 47 games while leading the nation with 111 home runs. In the past ten years Hill has had thirty five players go on and play professional baseball. We had five All-Americans and over 80 players progressed to four-year universities. During the same time Hill baseball facilities have received over $ 350,000 worth of improvements. Included are: a clubhouse ,a dressing room, a prime star satellite, a stereo, a laundry facility a rest room and a shower. There is also a 2,500 sq. ft. weigth room and an indoor work-out available for a player to use day or night.
Achievements: 5 Region V Championships; advanced to the Junior College World Series
Coaching: Gary Benton, Head Coach, entered eleven years with the program. Trent Petrie - Assistant Coach, entered his 2nd year with the program.
Roster for 1998 team/In State: 80% **Out of State:** 18% **Out of Country:** 5%

Total Number of Varsity/Jr. Varsity: 30 **Number of Fall Games:** 20
Number of Seniors on 1998 Team: 0 **Number of Sophomores on 1998 Team:** 25%

Houston Baptist University

7502 Fondren Road
Houston, TX 77074
Coach: Brian Huddleston

NCAA II
Huskies/Blue, Orange
Phone: (281) 649-3332
Fax: (281) 649-3496

ACADEMIC

Founded: 1960
Religion: Southern Baptist
Web-site: Not Available
Student/Faculty Ratio: 17:1
Undergraduate Enrollment: 1,700
Scholarships/Academic: Yes **Athletic:** Yes
Total Expenses by: Year **In State:** $ 10,700
Degrees Conferred: A, BA, BS, BBA, BM, MA, MS, MBA
Programs of Study: Contact school for program of study.

Type: 4 Yr., Private, Liberal Arts, Coed
Campus Housing: No
SAT/ACT/GPA: 950 avg
Male/Female Ratio: 35:65
Graduate Enrollment: 500
Fin Aid: Yes
Out of State: $ 10,700

Howard County Junior College

1001 N Birdwell Lane
Big Spring, TX 79720
Coach: Brian Roper

NJCAA
Hawks/Red, Grey
Phone: (915) 264-5042
Fax: (915) 264-5170

ACADEMIC

Founded: 1945
Student/Faculty Ratio: 10:1
Undergraduate Enrollment: 2,400
Total Expenses by: Year **In State:** $ 2,600
Degrees Conferred: Associate
Programs of Study: Contact school for programs of study.

Type: 2 Yr., Jr. College, Coed
Campus Housing: No
Graduate Enrollment: None
Out of State: $ 3,000

ATHLETIC PROFILE

Conference Affiliation: Western Junior College Athletic Conference

Howard Payne University

1000 Fisk Avenue
Brownwood, TX 76801
Coach: Mike Kennemer

NCAA III
Yellow Jackets/Gold, Navy
Phone: (915) 649-8117
Fax: (915) 649-8920

ACADEMIC

Founded: 1889
Religion: Non-Affiliated
Web-site: http://www.hputx.edu
Student/Faculty Ratio: 18:1
Undergraduate Enrollment: 1,500
Scholarships/Academic: Yes **Athletic:** No
Total Expenses by: Year **In State:** $ 10,000

Type: 4 Yr., Private, Liberal Arts, Coed
Campus Housing: Yes
SAT/ACT/GPA: 830/19/80%
Male/Female Ratio: 50:50
Graduate Enrollment: None
Fin Aid: Yes
Out of State: $ 10,000

Degrees Conferred: BA, BS, BBA, BAAS, BM
Programs of Study: Accounting, Art, Biology, Business, Christian Studies, Communications, Computer, Education, History, Music, Medical Technology, Political Science, Psychology, Sociology, Social Work, Prelaw, Exercise and Sports Science

ATHLETIC PROFILE

Conference Affiliation: American Southwest Conference
Program Profile: The team plays on Don Sheperd Park which opened in February of 1995 and has natural turf. We play Fall and Spring seasons.The HPU clubhouse and office building opened in August 1997.
History: Began in 1988 and went to NAIA playoffs in 1991-1997. We were Conference Champions in 1992, 1993, 1994 and 1997. We nationally ranked NAIA in 1992 and in 1997. We also nationally ranked NCAA III in 1998 (as high as 23rd).
Achievements: Coach of the Year in 1992, 1993, 1994 and 1997; 4 Conference Titles; 4 All-Americans; 7 professional players since 1993.
Coaching: Mike Kennemer, Head Coach, has a BS and an MED. He started his 4th year. He compiled a record of 99-77 and was named Coach of the Year in 1997.
Roster for 1998 team/In State: 25 **Out of State:** 0 **Out of Country:** 1
Total Number of Varsity/Jr. Varsity: 8 /45 **Percent of Graduation:** 35%
Number of Seniors on 1998 Team: 7 **Number of Sophomores on 1998 Team:** 8
Freshmen Receiving Fin Aid/Athletic: 75% **Academic:** 25%
Number of Fall Games: 9 **Number of Spring Games:** 42
Most Recent Record: 32 - 13 - 0 **Baseball Camp Dates:** June
Positions Needed for 1999/2000: Pitcher, Corners
Schedule: Tarleton State, Abilene Christian, Southwestern, McMurray, Houston Baptist, Wisconsin
Style of Play: Whatever it takes to win!

Huston - Tillotson College

900 Chicon
Austin, TX 78702
Coach: Alvin Moore

NAIA
Rams/Maroon, Gold
Phone: (512) 505-3052
Fax: (512) 474-0762

ACADEMIC

Founded: 1875 **Type:** 4 Yr., Private, Coed
SAT/ACT/GPA: 700avg/16avg **Campus Housing:** Yes
Student/Faculty Ratio: 13:1 **Male/Female Ratio:** 46:54
Undergraduate Enrollment: 610 **Graduate Enrollment:** None
Scholarships/Academic: Yes **Athletic:** No **Fin Aid:** Yes
Total Expenses by: Year **In State:** $ 10,100 **Out of State:** $ 10,100
Degrees Conferred: BA, BS
Programs of Study: Accounting, Afro-American Studies, Banking/Finance, Biological Science, Business Administration, Chemistry, Personnel Management, Physical Education, Political Science, Preprofessional Programs, Social Science

ATHLETIC PROFILE

Conference Affiliation: Big State Conference

Jarvis Christian College

Hwy 80, P. O. Drawer G
Hawkins, TX 75765
Coach: Robert Thomas

NCAA I
Bulldogs/Royal Blue, Gold
Phone: (903) 769-2174
Fax: (903) 769-5882

ACADEMIC

Founded: 1913
Religion: Disciples of Christ
Undergraduate Enrollment: 497
Student/Faculty Ratio: 14:1
Scholarships/Academic: Yes **Athletic:** No
Total Expenses by: Year **In State:** $ 7,500
Degrees Conferred: BA, BS, BBA
Programs of Study: Contact school for program ofb study.

Type: 4 Yr., Private, Liberal Arts, Coed,
Campus Housing: No
SAT/ACT/GPA: 800+/18+
Male/Female Ratio: 43:57
Fin Aid: Yes
Out of State: $ 7,500

Lamar University

P. O. Box 10066
Beaumont, TX 77710
Coach: Jim Gilligan

NCAA I
Cardinals/Red, White
Phone: (409) 880-8315
Fax: (409) 880-2338

ACADEMIC

Founded: 1923
Religion: Non-Affiliated
Undergraduate Enrollment: 8,000
Student/Faculty Ratio: 17:1
Scholarships/Academic: Yes **Athletic:** Yes
Total Expenses by: Year **In State:** $ 6,214
Degrees Conferred: BA, BS, BAAS, BFA, MA,MS
Programs of Study: Advertising, Biological Science, Business, Engineering, Design, Dramatic Arts, Economics, Geology, History, Marketing, Math, Medical Nursing, Therapy, Technology, Speech, Pharmacy, Special Education

Type: 4 Yr., Public, Coed
Campus Housing: Yes
SAT/ACT/GPA: NCAA Requirements
Male/Female Ratio: 48:52
Fin Aid: Yes
Out of State: $ Varies

ATHLETIC PROFILE

Estimated Number of Baseball Scholarships: 11.7
Conference Affiliation: Southland Conference
Program Profile: We play at Vincent Beck Stadium on campus with a seating capacity of 3,500. Facilities include: lights, 6 batting cages, a 9x54 foot scoreboard ,6 bullpen mounds and grass surfaced with an astro turf baselines. There is a VIP lounge down on the right field line. Our weight room is down on the right field line.
History: We began in 1967 and have had 25 winning seasons. In 30 years of the program: we have 12 conference championships, 8 NCAA Regional Appearances and one 1995 Midwest Regional Wichita-KS where we finished 3rd .
Achievements: Coach of the Year 1976, 1977 and 1993. Over 700 wins, 12 Conference Titles, 56-All-Americans Performers; over 6 dozen players into pro-ball. Manager in Pioneer League (Class A) Salt Lake City, set record with 29 game winning streak.
Coaching: Jim Gilligan, Head Coach, is in his 21st season. He has more than a 664-393 record, eight NCAA tournaments and seven conference championships. Brian Briggers, Assistant Coach, was an assistant at Connors State. Jim Ricklefsond - Assistant Coach.
Style of Play: Aggressive, sound defensively (6th in NCAA 1994), strong pitching (outstanding depth).

Laredo Community College

West End Washington Street
Laredo, TX 78040
Coach: Ricardo Cuevas

NJCAA
Palominos/Green, Gold
Phone: (956) 721-5326
Fax: (956) 721-5877

ACADEMIC

Founded: 1946
Type: 2 Yr., Jr. College, Coed
Religion: Non-Affiliated
Campus Housing: No
Student/Faculty Ratio: 30:1
Male/Female Ratio: 42:58
Undergraduate Enrollment: 6,700
Graduate Enrollment: None
Scholarships/Academic: No **Athletic:** Yes **Fin Aid:** Yes
Total Expenses by: Year **In State:** $ 2,193 **Out of State:** $ 2,583
Degrees Conferred: AA, AAS
Programs of Study: Child Care, Computer, Construction, Data Processing, Electrical/Electronics Technology, Medical, Fashion, Fire Science, Hotel/Restaurant Management, International Law, Marketing, Science, Real Estate

ATHLETIC PROFILE

Conference Affiliation: TJCAC
Program Profile: The home playing field has natural grass and seats 750. We are the fastest growing city in the US. The climate is warm year round. We are on the border to Mexico. That offers an insight to Mexican culture and traditions. We have beautiful palm trees and friendly people.
History: The program began in 1986. We were State Runnerup twice (1990, 1992). We were ranked 1st by NJCAA Polls 1992. We were Conference Champions in 1992 and finished 5th in the Texas State tournament and Conference Runnerup of 1994.
Achievements: All-American David Chisum and over twenty players drafted to the pros. 1996 ranked 19th by NJCAA first poll.
Coaching: Troy Van Brunt - Head Coach. Ricardo Cuevas, Assistant Coach, played in the Mexican League and works with the infielders.
Style of Play: Hard, aggressive baseball.

Le Tourneau University

2100 S. Mobberly
Longview, TX 75605
Coach: Elliot Johnson

NCAA III
Yellow Jackets/Blue, Gold
Phone: (903) 233-3370
Fax: (903) 233-3822

ACADEMIC

Type: 4 Yr., Private, Liberal Arts, Coed, Engineering
Founded: 1946
Religion: Non-Denominational
Campus Housing: Yes
Web-site: http://www.letu.edu/
SAT/ACT/GPA: 900
Student/Faculty Ratio: 12:1
Male/Female Ratio: 4:1
Undergraduate Enrollment: 850
Graduate Enrollment: 0
Scholarships/Academic: Yes **Athletic:** Yes **Fin Aid:** Yes
Total Expenses by: Year **In State:** $ 16,00 **Out of State:** $ 16,000
Degrees Conferred: BS, BA
Programs of Study: Engineering, Aviation, Liberal Arts, Natural Science, Business Administration: Nearly 40 associates and bachelors programs.

ATHLETIC PROFILE

Conference Affiliation: American Southwest Conference
Program Profile: The program has five weeks of Fall practice with 10 playing dates against outside competition. We have an excellent Bermuda playing surface and off wall, portable bleachers.We do an off-season weight, plyometric and swimming program. We have a 48 game regular season (We made 5 consecutive winning seasons).
History: We began in the 1970's and had minimal success until 1993. We had ,back to back,25 victory seasons in 1993 and 1994. We have 24 wins or more in five consecutive seasons.
Coaching: Elliot Johnson - Head Coach, compiled a record of 457-257 in 16 years of college coaching. In five years of coaching compiled a record of 135 wins. Greg Johnston - Assistant Coach.

Roster for 1998 team/In State: 17 **Out of State:** 0 **Out of Country:** 0
Number of Seniors on 1998 Team: 4 **Number of Sophomores on 1998 Team:** 3
Number of Fall Games: 0 **Number of Spring Games:** 36
Positions Needed for 1999/2000: Most positions **Most Recent Record:** 30 - 17 - 1
Baseball Camp Dates: 1st week of June **Schedule:** McMurry University
Style of Play: Aggressive.

Lon Morris College

906 College AVenue
Jacksonville, TX 75766
Coach: Barry Hoffpauir

NJCAA
Bearcats/Green, White
Phone: (903) 589-4073
Fax: (903) 586-8562

ACADEMIC

Type: 2 Yr., Public, Coed
Degrees Conferred: Associate
Programs of Study: Accounting, Applied Science, Applied Arts, Art/Fine Arts, history, Biblical Studies, Business, Machine Technology, Chemistry, Commercial Art, Communications, Computer Science, Creative Writing, Dance, Economics, Education, Elementary Education, Physics, Religious

ATHLETIC PROFILE

Conference Affiliation: Texas Eastern Conference

Lubbock Christian University

5601 - 19th Street
Lubbock, TX 79407
Coach: Daren Hays
Email: chasport@juno.com

NAIA
Chaparrals/Blue, White, Red
Phone: (806) 796-8800
Fax: (806) 796-8934

ACADEMIC

Founded: 1957 **Type:** 4 Yr., Public, Coed
Undergraduate Enrollment: 1,100 **SAT/ACT/GPA:** 21avg
Student/Faculty Ratio: 15:1 **Male/Female Ratio:** 44:56
Scholarships/Academic: Yes **Athletic:** Yes **Fin Aid:** Yes
Total Expenses by: Year **In State:** $ 10,000 **Out of State:** $ 10,000
Degrees Conferred: AA, AS, BA, BS, BSED, MA, MS, MBA
Programs of Study: Accounting, Agricultural Business Management, Animal Science, Banking/Finance, Biblical Studies, Biological Science, Business Administration, Chemistry, Communications, Education, Foreign Languages, History, Journalism, Kinesiology, Mathematics, Physical Education, Physics, Political Science, Preprofessional Programs, Psychology

ATHLETIC PROFILE

Conference Affiliation: Sooner Athletic Conference
Program Profile: For the 8th time in school history, the 1998 Chaps earned more than 50 victories. The Chaps finished the season with a 52-18 record, making it the Southwest Regional in Mobile, Alabama where all 8 teams were ranked in the top 25 nationally, and where the season ended for the Chaps. The home field is an astro-turf infield with a grass outfield. It measures 345 feet down the lines, 385 feet to the power alleys and 410 feet to straight away center field. The stadium seats 750 in permanent seating and has room for approximately 1,000 more in bleacher seating.
History: LCU baseball began in 1971 and has gained a great reputation as a force in NAIA baseball. LCU won the NAIA World Series in 1983 and many players have gone on to play professional baseball. The program has seen three head coaches: Larry Hays (currently head coach at Texas Tech University), Jimmy Shankle and Daren Hays (son of Larry Hays). The Chaparrals wins/loss record of 1,248-647.

Achievements: Won Texoma Conference five times; won District VIII eleven times; won Area II three times; won Sooner Athletic Conference twice; has 6 World Series Appearances - place 5th , 3rd and 1st in 1983. Had the NAIA Player of the Year in 1986; 46 All-Americans; 10 All-American Scholar Athletes; 17 players drafted and 19 signed free-agent. This year (1998) Keith Hart was named NAIA Player of the Year; 3 more All-Americans

Coaching: Daren Hays, Head Coach, was a 4-year letterman at Lubbock Christian. He was drafted and signed by Texas Rangers. He has 2 years experience pro ball. He is in his 5th year as head coach. He compiled a record of 309-146 for seven years. He was named NAIA National Pitcher of the Week (March 19-25, 1989).

Roster for 1998 team/In State: 23 **Out of State:** 7 **Out of Country:** 1
Total Number of Varsity/Jr. Varsity: 23 **Percent of Graduation:** 83.3%
Number of Seniors on 1998 Team: 9 **Number of Sophomores on 1998 Team:** 3
Most Recent Record: 52 - 18 - 0 **Number of Spring Games:** 70
Schedule: Oklahoma City University, Oklahoma Baptist University, Southwest Texas State
Style of Play: The style of play of the 1998 team: "Offense and team speed will be the keys to our success this season. We have some power, speed, depth in pitching and defensive talent on the field. This should be a really fun year".

McLennan Community College

1400 College Drive
Waco, TX 76708
Coach: Paul Miller

NJCAA
Highlanders/Orange, Black, White
Phone: (254) 299-8847
Fax: (254) 299-8814

ACADEMIC

Founded: 1965
Religion: Non-Affiliated
Undergraduate Enrollment: 5,700
Type: 2 Yr., Jr. College, Coed
Campus Housing: No
Student/Faculty Ratio: 22:1
Scholarships/Academic: Yes **Athletic:** No **Fin Aid:** Yes
Total Expenses by: Year **In State:** $ 700 **Out of State:** $ 2,700
Degrees Conferred: Associate
Programs of Study: Accounting, Agricultural Science, Banking/Finance, Biological Science, Business, History, Journalism, Law Enforcement, Liberal Arts, Mathematics, Medical Secretary, Office Management, Philosophy, Physical Education, Physical Education, Preengineering, Real Estate, Relious Studies, Science, Social Science, Spanish

ATHLETIC PROFILE

Conference Affiliation: NTJCAA, NJCAA Region V

McMurry University

14th and Sayles, Box 938
Abilene, TX 79697
Coach: Lee Driggers

NCAA III
Indians/Maroon
Phone: (915) 793-4650
Fax: (915) 793-4659

ACADEMIC

Founded: 1923
Religion: Methodist
Web-site: http://www.mcm.edu
Student/Faculty Ratio: 15:1
Type: 4 Yr., Private, Liberal Arts, Coed
Campus Housing: Yes
Undergraduate Enrollment: 1,410
Male/Female Ratio: 1:1
Scholarships/Academic: Yes **Athletic:** No **Fin Aid:** Yes
Total Expenses by: Year **In State:** $ 14,802 **Out of State:** $ Varies
Degrees Conferred: BA, BFA, BS, BMEd, BBA, BSN, BS

Programs of Study: Accounting, Art Education, Art/Fine Arts, Athletic Training, Biology, Biological Science, Business Administration, Commerce, Management, Ceramic Art and Design, Chemistry, Communications, Computer Information System, Computer Science, Criminal Justice, English

ATHLETIC PROFILE

Conference Affiliation: American Southwest Conference
Program Profile: We are a third year program with 2 winning seasons. Walt Driggers Field is our $1,000,000 plus stadium with Tiff infield, triple-A lights and a 1,000 seating capacity. There are also: a full tarp, a ground level press box, a locker room with office space, two indoor cages and 2 outdoor cages. We have a 42- game schedule and we field a junior varsity team. The Fall season consists of 16 games. We have an extensive off-season program.
History: The program began in 1996 and has had five coaches. The 1996 season had a record of 27-19 and the 1997 season hada record of 26-20-1. We finished 2nd place in each of the first 2 seasons at McMurry.
Achievements: 1996 Ken Edwards and 1997 Mike Marton were Academic All-Americans; all five coaches either played at the Division I level or in the professional baseball.
Coaching: Lee Driggers - Head Coach. Marvin Stringfellow - Assistant Coach. Shane Shewmake - Assistant Coach. Jason Marshall - Assistant Coach. Scott Malone - Student Assistant Coach.
Style of Play: Well-coached; hustle and fundamentally sound.

Navarro College

3200 West 7th Avenue
Corsicana, TX 75110
Coach: Skip Johnson

NJCAA
Bulldogs/Red, White
Phone: (903) 874-6501
Fax: (903) 874-9651

ACADEMIC

Founded: 1947
Religion: Non-Affiliated
Web-site: http://www.navarro.com
Type: 2 Yr., Coed
Campus Housing: Yes
Undergraduate Enrollment: 3,300
Scholarships/Academic: No **Athletic:** Yes **Fin Aid:** Yes
Total Expenses by: Year **In State:** $ 4,400 **Out of State:** $ Varies
Degrees Conferred: Associates
Programs of Study: Accounting, Agricultural, Aviation, Biological Science, Broadcasting, Business, Chemistry, Computer Graphics, Criminal Justice, Drafting/Design, Electrical/Electronics Technology, Fire Science, Flight Training, General Engineering, Journalism, Law Enforcement, Marketing, Math

ATHLETIC PROFILE

Estimated Number of Baseball Scholarships: 15 Full
Conference Affiliation: TEAC
Program Profile: Our baseball program is built around a solid education and a fundamental knowledge of the game. We have excellent facilities that include a large ball yard with a natural grass in/outfield. There are also: complete indoor and outdoor hitting and throwing areas, complete weights and a conditioning room. We send kids to play pro ball or Division I every year.
History: The program has been in existence for ten years.
Achievements: Coach of the Year five times in a row; have won the conference five years in a row; had 2 All-Americans in 1997 with Brian Cole being named National Junior College Player of the Year; 10 drafted players.
Coaching: Skip Johnson, Head Coach, played for legendary Al Oglethorpe at UT Pan Am. He has been with Navarro since 1990 and became head coach in the Spring of 1995. He won the conference five years in a row with a record of 161-41. Heath Autrey - Assistant Coach.
Roster for 1998 team/In State: 30 **Out of State:** 5 **Out of Country:** 1
Most Recent Record: 44 - 13 - 0 **Percent of Graduation:** 99%
Number of Fall Games: 20 **Number of Spring Games:** 56
Positions Needed for 1999/2000: Pitcher, Catcher
Style of Play: Aggressive.

North Central Texas College

1525 West California Street
Gainesville, TX 76240
Coach: Kevin Darwin
Email: k.darwin@nctc.cc.tx.us

NJCAA I
Lions/Royal, White
Phone: (940) 668-7731
Fax: (940) 668-6049

ACADEMIC

Founded: 1924
Type: 2 Yr., Public, , Coed,
Undergraduate Enrollment: 4,500
Campus Housing: Yes
Student/Faculty Ratio: 30:1
Male/Female Ratio: 50:50
Scholarships/Academic: Yes **Athletic:** Yes **Fin Aid:** Yes
Total Expenses by: Year **In State:** $ 1,350 **Out of State:** $ 1,450
Degrees Conferred: Associate
Programs of Study: Agricultural, Automotive Technology, Business, Computer Science, Computer Technology, Criminal Justice, Drafting/Design, Liberal Arts, Electrical/Electronics Technology, Equestrian, Farm/Ranch Management, Law, Liberal Arts, Occupational Therapy

ATHLETIC PROFILE

Conference Affiliation: NJCAA Region V
Program Profile: We play all home in an old Minor League (AA) ball park. Have a 100'x50' indoor workout facility, three tunnels, a weight room and indoor pitching mounds. We play a competitive Fall schedule through November and a 56-game (+) Spring schedule.
History: We began playing baseball in the Spring of 1992. We have made two state tournament appearances. Our program has an average 30 wins a season. We have placed over 85% of the players at four-year universities. In the Spring of 1993, North Central Texas College fielded its first varsity intercollegiate baseball team, and with an all-freshman team, the Lions posted a very respectable 19-win season. That early success was an indicator of bigger and better things to come for the NCTC baseball over the next two seasons. In only their 2nd season of competition, the NCTC Lions went 33-13, coming up just short of a trip to the 1st round of the National junior College Athletic Association Championship play. Our team is posting an impressive record of 36-13 and is on its way to earning its 1st ever trip to the Texas/New Mexico State Tournament.
Achievements: Earned first trip to the Texas/New Mexico State Tournament. The Lions captured second place in Region V.
Coaching: Kevin Darwin, Head Coach, compiled a respectable 22-23 record during its first season. He was varsity letterman in baseball all four years in high school, an All-District pitcher and an MVP for two years. He was named to the All-Conference. Van Hendrick, Assistant Coach, was sport letterman in football, basketball and baseball . He received All-District honors in each sport. In his senior year, he was All-Conference and was maned "Come Back Player of the Year". He is completing his Master's in Education.
Style of Play: Aggressive fundamental baseball.

North Lake College

5001 N MacArthur Blvd
Irving, TX 75038-3899
Coach: Steve Cummings

NJCAA
Blazers/Blue, Green
Phone: (214) 659-5357#
Fax: (214) 659-5219

ACADEMIC

Founded: 1977
Type: 2 Yr., Jr. College, Coed
Religion: Non-Affiliated
Campus Housing: No
Undergraduate Enrollment: 6,233
Male/Female Ratio: 18:1
Total Expenses by: Year **In State:** $ 650+ **Out of State:** $ 2,140+
Degrees Conferred: Associate

Programs of Study: Accounting, Business Administration, Commerce, Management, Carpentry, Communications Equipment Technology, Computer Information Systems, Computer Programming, Construction Technology, Data Processing, Electrical/Electronics Technology, Engineering Technology, Liberal Arts, General Studies, Office Management

Northeast Texas Community College

PO Box 1307
Mt Pleasant, TX 75456
Coach: Chad Henry
Email: nmcnutt@ntcc.cc.tx.us

NJCAA
Eagles/Red, White, Blue
Phone: (903) 572-1911
Fax: (903) 575-0317

ACADEMIC

Founded: 1984
Type: 2 Yr., Public, Jr. College, Coed
SAT/ACT/GPA: Texas Academic Skill Program Test/
Web-site: http://www.ntcc.tx.us
Undergraduate Enrollment: 2,100
Graduate Enrollment: None
Scholarships/Academic: Yes **Athletic:** Yes
Fin Aid: Yes
Total Expenses by: Semester **In State:** $ 2,102
Out of State: $ 2,306
Degrees Conferred: Special courses fees may also apply
Programs of Study: Accounting, Agriculture, Banking, Business Administration, Computer Science, Cosmetology, Criminal Justice, Journalism, Management, Nursing, Physics, Engineering, Professional Office Services, Psychology, Sociology, Speech, Communications, Theatre

ATHLETIC PROFILE

Estimated Number of Baseball Scholarships: 15
Conference Affiliation: Texas Eastern Athletic Conference
Program Profile: The program has a very nice playing field that has a seating capacity of 1,500 and has a dimensions of 309 LF, 400 center and 325 Center.
History: The program began in 1993. We were 1993 Conference Champions; 1993 Conference Champs; 1996 National Champs and 1997 Regional Finalist.
Achievements: Coach of the Year NSCAA in 1996; Region 14 Coach of the Year in 1996; over 20 players drafted.

Northwood University - Texas

PO Box 58, 1114 W FM 1382
Cedar Hill, TX 75104
Coach: Pat Malcheski

NAIA
Knights/Blue, White
Phone: (972) 291-1541
Fax: (972) 293-6521

ACADEMIC

Founded: 1959
Type: 4 Yr., Private, Coed
Web-site: Not Available
SAT/ACT/GPA: 850/18
Student/Faculty Ratio: 17:1
Male/Female Ratio: 57:43
Undergraduate Enrollment: 290
Graduate Enrollment: None
Scholarships/Academic: Yes **Athletic:** Yes
Fin Aid: Yes
Total Expenses by: Year **In State:** $ 14,650
Out of State: $ 14,650
Degrees Conferred: A, BA
Programs of Study: Automotive, Marketing, Business Management, Management

Odessa College

201 West University
Odessa, TX 79764
Coach: Rick Zimmerman

NJCAA
Wranglers/Blue, White
Phone: (915) 335-6850
Fax: (915) 335-6304

ACADEMIC

Founded: 1946 **Type:** 2 Yr., Jr. College, Coed
Religion: Non-Affiliated **Campus Housing:** Yes
Undergraduate Enrollment: 5,000 **Student/Faculty Ratio:** 19:1
Scholarships/Academic: No **Athletic:** No **Fin Aid:** No
Total Expenses by: Year **In State:** $ 2,500 **Out of State:** $ 3,000
Degrees Conferred: Associate
Programs of Study: Accounting, Applied Art, Art/Fine Arts, Athletic Training, Automotive Technology, Biology, Biological Science, Business Administration, Commerce, Management, Computer Information Systems, Computer Science, Construction tEchnology, Cosmetology, Criminal Justice, Culinary Arts, Data Processing, Drafting/Design, Fashion Merchandising, Fire Science

ATHLETIC PROFILE

Estimated Number of Baseball Scholarships: 10
Conference Affiliation: Western Junior College Athletic Conference
Program Profile: Our American Legion Stadium has a seating capacity of 2,000. It has natural turf with a dimensions of 347-LF, 382-LCF, 396 LF, 380 RCF and 345-RCF. September to November iis our Fall season. Our Spring season goes from February to May.
History: Our program started in 1991. We had league champs 4 times, got 2nd place 4 times, got 1995 State Champs and made 3rd place finish in JUCO World Series (319-143) in 8 years.
Achievements: Conference Coach of the Year in 1991-1993-1995; Region District in 1995; Conference Titles in 1992, 1993, 1996 and '197; Region Champs in 1995; 4 All-Americans; 35 drafted players.
Coaching: Rick Zimmerman, Head Coach, compiled an overall record of 886-391 in twenty-one years. He is 7th on active all-time win list and 12th on all-time win list. He was named Region Coach of the Year 11 times, Conference Coach of the Year 15 times and District Coach of the Year 3 times. He was head coach of NJCAA all-star team - Mexico and got 3rd place finish in the American Games. Sean Parker, Assistant Coach, entered his 2nd season.
Roster for 1998 team/In State: 18 **Out of State:** 6 **Out of Country:** 0
Total Number of Varsity/Jr. Varsity: 24 **Percent of Graduation:** 75%
Baseball Camp Dates: June 2-5 **Number of Sophomores on 1998 Team:** 9
Freshmen Receiving Fin Aid/Athletic: 15 **Most Recent Record:** 39 - 16 - 0
Number of Fall Games: 20 **Number of Spring Games:** 56
Positions Needed for 1999/2000: Pitchers, Shortstop, Catcher, 3rd Base, 3-OF
Schedule: New Mexico Junior, Howard Junior, McClennan Junior, Trinidad State Junior, Pima
Style of Play: Very good pitching - strong hitting group in 2-3-4-5-6 holes. Average defense - average speed.

Panola College

1109 W Panola St
Carthage, TX 75633
Coach: Don Clinton
NJCAA
Ponies/Dk Green, White
Phone: (903) 693-2062
Fax: (903) 693-2018

ACADEMIC

Founded: 1947 **Type:** 2 Yr., Public, Coed
Undergraduate Enrollment: 2,500 **Campus Housing:** Yes
Student/Faculty Ratio: 25:1 **Male/Female Ratio:** 40:60
Scholarships/Academic: Yes **Athletic:** Yes **Fin Aid:** Yes
Total Expenses by: Year **In State:** $ 3,500 **Out of State:** $ 3,500
Degrees Conferred: AA, AAS
Programs of Study: Computer Information Systems, Cosmetology, Forest Technology, Nursing, Secretarial Studies, Office Management

ATHLETIC PROFILE

Conference Affiliation: TEAC
Program Profile: We are one of the top Junior Colleges in the South. We have a good playing field. It has natural turf and measures 330' down lines and 400' center.
History: We began in 1948. We won National Championship in 1969. We were runner-up in 1979 and won 40 conference championships.
Coaching: Don Clinton - Head Coach.
Style of Play: Solid pitching combined with team speed and timely hitting. We do not strive for homeruns, or just depend on having big innings -- we try to make things happen.

Paris Junior College

2400 Clarksville Street
Paris, TX 75460-6298
Coach: Deron Clark
NJCAA
Dragons/Dk Green, Gold
Phone: (903) 782-0218
Fax: (903) 782-0730

ACADEMIC

Founded: 1924
Type: 2 Yr., Public, Coed
Undergraduate Enrollment: 2,450
Campus Housing: Yes
Web-site: http://www.paris.cc.tx.us
Student/Faculty Ratio: 20:1
Total Expenses by: Year **In State:** $ 672+ **Out of State:** $ 1,056+
Degrees Conferred: Associate
Programs of Study: Agricultural Technology, Art/Fine Arts, Business Administration, Commerce, Management, Business Education, Computer Information Systems, Computer Technology, Construction Management, Cosmetology, Drafting/Design, Electrical/Electronics Technology, Elementary Education, Engineering Technology, Mathematics, Nursing, Real Estate, Science

Prairie View A & M University

PO Box 097
Prairie View, TX 77446-0097
Coach: John Tankersly
NCAA I
Panthers/Purple, Gold
Phone: (409) 857-4290
Fax: (409) 857-2408

ACADEMIC

Founded: 1876
Type: 4 Yr., Public, Liberal Arts, Coed
Religion: Non-Affiliated
Campus Housing: No
Web-site: Not Available
SAT/ACT/GPA: 750/15
Student/Faculty Ratio: 25:1
Male/Female Ratio: 48:52
Undergraduate Enrollment: 6,425
Graduate Enrollment: 740
Scholarships/Academic: Yes **Athletic:** No **Fin Aid:** Yes
Total Expenses by: Year **In State:** $ 6,450 **Out of State:** $ 9,100
Degrees Conferred: BA, BS, MA, MS, MBA, MED
Programs of Study: Accounting, Agricultural Economics, Agricultural Education, Agricultural Engineering, Agronomy, Animal Science, Architecture, Biology, Broadcasting, Business Administration, Civil Engineering, Computer Engineering, Engineering Technology, Finance/Banking

ATHLETIC PROFILE

Conference Affiliation: Southwestern Athletic Conference
Program Profile: The Panthers play in a stadium of natural grass that seats 1,500. There is both a Fall and Spring baseball program. There is an emphasis on academics: 'Students first, athletes second'.
History: The 1994 record for conference games was 8-12.
Achievements: There have been several players drafted into the pros in recent years.

Coaching: John Tankersly - Head Coach. Ray Burgess - Assistant Coach.
Style of Play: Concentrate on defense. We like to make things happen with speed; hit and run, bunt and run, steal.

Ranger College

College Circle
Ranger, TX 76470
Coach: Don Flowers

NJCAA
Rangers/Purple, White
Phone: (254) 647-3234
Fax: (254) 647-1656

ACADEMIC

Founded: 1926
Type: 2 Yr., Public, Coed
Undergraduate Enrollment: 725
Campus Housing: Yes
Student/Faculty Ratio: 15:1
Male/Female Ratio: 48:52
Scholarships/Academic: No **Athletic:** Yes **Fin Aid:** Yes
Total Expenses by: Year **In State:** $ 3,500 **Out of State:** $ 3,600
Degrees Conferred: Associate
Programs of Study: Automotive Technology, Computer Technology, Liberal Arts, Office Management, Science Education, Welding

Rice University

6100 Main -- MS 548
Houston, TX 77005-1892
Coach: Wayne Graham

NCAA I
Owls/Blue, Grey
Phone: (713) 527-6022
Fax: (713) 527-6019

ACADEMIC

Founded: 1892
Type: 4 Yr., Private, Coed
Student/Faculty Ratio: 9:1
Male/Female Ratio: 15:1
Undergraduate Enrollment: 2,600
Graduate Enrollment: 1,400
Scholarships/Academic: Yes **Athletic:** Yes **Fin Aid:** Yes
Total Expenses by: Year **In State:** $ 19,206 **Out of State:** $ 19,206
Degrees Conferred: BA, BS, MA, MS, MBA
Programs of Study: Anthropology, Architectural Behavioral Science, Biological Science, Chemistry, Chemical/Civil/Computer Engineering, Cognitive Science, Electrical Engineering, Environemental, Geology, Linguistics, Management, Material Science, Mathematics, Mechanical Engineering, Physical Fitness and Movement, Physical, Political Science, Pscyhology, Religion, Russian

ATHLETIC PROFILE

Conference Affiliation: Western Athletic Conference
Program Profile: We play at Cameron Field which has a 2,000 seat facility. It is a natural grass stadium with the Houston Medical Center as a backdrop. The Owls have had 155 wins in the past 4 years and are just 1 of 8 schools nationally (along with Miami, Florida State, USC, Oklahoma State, Alabama, Clemson and Tennessee) to have made it to the NCAA Regional Finals each of the last 2 years. Our team is generally recognized as the top athletic/academic institution for baseball in the South. Our team plays 56 games in the warm Houston climate.
History: Our baseball team has been in existence since 1913. Rice qualified for its first-ever NCAA regional in 1995, finishing 2nd at the South Regional.
Achievements: 1996 - Rice won its first-ever SWC postseason tournament, qualifying for the NCAA Midwest Regional where it finished second to Wichita State. The Owls eliminated defending national champions California State - Fullerton in the semifinals before losing to host Wichita State in the regional final. 1995 - Qualified for first-ever NCAA Regional, beating host LSU twice at the NCAA South Regional before losing to eventual national champions California State - Fullerton in the final. 4 All-America players in last 2 years (Jose Cruz Jr., Mark Quinn, Lance Berkman, Matt Anderson).

Coaching: Wayne Graham, Head Coach, has best win-loss percentage in school's history (184-107, .632). Twice he has been named SWC Coach of the Year and was named Collegiate Baseball Coach of the Decade in 1980's after winning an unprecedented 5 national championships at San Jacinto Junior College. Jon Prather - Assistant Coach. Chris Feris - Assistant Coach.
Style of Play: Fundamentally strong, tenacious, power baseball.

Richland Community College

12800 Abrams Road
Dallas, TX 75243
Coach: Joe Wharton

NJCAA
Thunderducks/Purple, Kelly Green
Phone: (972) 238-6260
Fax: (972) 238-3736

ACADEMIC

Founded: 1972
Type: 2 Yr., Public, , Coed,
Web-site: http://www.rlc.edu
Campus Housing: No
Student/Faculty Ratio: 30:1
Male/Female Ratio: 46:54
Undergraduate Enrollment: 12,000
Graduate Enrollment: None
Scholarships/Academic: Yes **Athletic:** No **Fin Aid:** Yes
Total Expenses by: Year **In State:** $ 251-$441 **Out of State:** $ 843
Degrees Conferred: Associates
Programs of Study: Accounting, Advertising, Agriculture, American Studies, Anthropology, Architecture, Art, Biological Sciences, Botany, Business Administration, Chemistry, Computer Science, Dance, Drama, Economics, Engineering, English, Entomology, Finance, Fine Arts, Geography, Geology, Health Sciences, History, Interior Design, Journalism, Legal Science, Liberal Arts, Life Sciences, Management, Marine Biology, Marketing, Mathematics, Management, Medical Technology, Microbiology, Music, Nursing, Pharmacy, Philosophy, Photojournalism, Physical Education, Physical Science, Physical Therapy, Pathology, Political Science, Psychology, Telecommunications, Theatre, Zoology

ATHLETIC PROFILE

Conference Affiliation: Metro Athletic Conference
Program Profile: The Thunderducks play 20 Fall games and 58 Spring games. Their home playing field has natural grass, with new dugouts, concession stands and restrooms.
History: Richland has been a member of the NJCAA since 1986, sending over 50 players to four-year colleges or the pros. We won 4 conference titles and went to the NJCAA World Series in 1995-1996.
Coaching: Joe Wharton, Head Coach, graduated from Baylor University in 1993. He was in the Yankee Organization for 3 years. Brad Croneth ,Assistant, was a former Big Leugers in Toronto. He was in the Big in 1994.
Style of Play: We play a very aggressive game.

Saint Edward's College

300 S Congress Avenue
Austin, TX 78704
Coach: Gene Salazar

NCAA II/NAIA
Hilltoppers/Navy, Gold
Phone: (512) 488-8497
Fax: (512) 416-5834

ACADEMIC

Founded: 1879
Type: 4 Yr., Public, Liberal Arts, Coed
Religion: Catholic
Campus Housing: No
Web-site: http://www.shsu.edu/
SAT/ACT/GPA: 1020
Student/Faculty Ratio: 22:1
Male/Female Ratio: 1:1
Undergraduate Enrollment: 10,500
Graduate Enrollment: 2,500
Scholarships/Academic: Yes **Athletic:** Yes **Fin Aid:** Yes

Total Expenses by: Year **In State:** $ 14,000 **Out of State:** $ 14,000
Degrees Conferred: BBA, BS, BA, BFA, BM, BACJ, BDJC, BAAS, MD
Programs of Study: Accounting, Art, Biology, Business Administration, Chemistry, Communications, Computer Information Systems, Computer Science, Creative Writing, English, Finance, Criminal Justice, Economics, Education, Elementary Education, English, History, Mathematics, Management, Marketing, Philosophy, Photography, Physical Education, Political Science, Psychology, Religion

ATHLETIC PROFILE

Conference Affiliation: Heart of Texas Conference
Program Profile: We play on a natural grass field located on campus. Our official season is in the Spring. St. Edward's sits on a hilltop overlooking Austin, is very scenic and has excellent weather year round.
Achievements: Last Heart of Texas Championships in 1990; had 5 players sign professional contracts in the last six seasons.

Saint Mary's University

One Camino Santa Maria
San Antonio, TX 78228
Coach: Charlie Migl

NCAA II/NAIA
Rattlers/Blue, Gold
Phone: (210) 436-3034
Fax: (210) 436-4272

ACADEMIC

Type: 4 Yr., Private, Liberal Arts, Coed, Engineering
Founded: 1852
Religion: Roman Catholic
Campus Housing: Yes
Web-site: http://www.stmarytx.edu/
SAT/ACT/GPA: 950/22
Student/Faculty Ratio: 18:1
Male/Female Ratio: 45:55
Undergraduate Enrollment: 2,575
Graduate Enrollment: 1,560
Scholarships/Academic: Yes **Athletic:** Yes **Fin Aid:** Yes
Total Expenses by: Year **In State:** $ 15,500 **Out of State:** $ 15,500
Degrees Conferred: BA, BS, BAS, BBA, MA, MS, MBA, PhD,JD
Programs of Study: Accounting, Banking/Finance, Biology, Chemistry, Business Education, Business Administration, Communications, Computer Engineering, Compuetr Science, Criminal Justice, Earth Science, Economics, Education, International Relations, Management, Marketing, Mathematics, Music, Philosophy, Physics, Political Science, Psychology, Social Sciences

ATHLETIC PROFILE

Conference Affiliation: Heart of Texas Conference
Program Profile: Our home facility is V.J. Keefe Memorial Stadium. It has a natural turf and a seating capacity for 3,500 people It is has 2 levels, offices, a meeting room, 2 clubhouse locker rooms, lights, a fully functioning press box and facilities. We are one of the nation's top programs since 1950's. Pitchers work on (Dr.) Mike Marshall's (Dodgers) system of Mechanics.
History: The original program began around 1910, but the modern program began in 1957 with ABCA Hall of Fame Coach Elmer Kosub. Present Head Coach Charlie Migl took over the program in 1987. Since 1957, St. Mary's is 902-519 (,635) overall and 351-124 (.739) in the conference.
Achievements: In 41 seasons (recorded), St. Mary's has won 23 Conference Titles and made 4 NAIA College World Series Appearances (1976, 1993, 1995 and 1996). We have had 33 All-Americans and produced 25 pro players, inlcluding major leaguer Bill Grabarkewitz and Danny Heep, and dogers top prospect Jeff Kubenka.
Coaching: Charlie Migl, Head Coach, has compiled a 397-167 record in 11 seasons. He has won 7 Conference Titles and made 3 NAIA World Series Appearances. He has been a Conference (and Region) Coach of the Year numerous times. He was All-American 3rd baseman in the late 1970's at St. Mary's (1978 grad.). Our Pitching Coach is John Maley (SW Texas in 1986). Our 1st base Coach is Jack Ard (UTSA in 1979).
Style of Play: Aggressive style of play with an emphasis on the defensive aspect of the game, along with fundamental development of the pitching staff.

Sam Houston State University

Box 2268, SHSU
Huntsville, TX 77341
Coach: John Skeeters

NCAA I
Bearkats/Orange, White
Phone: (409) 294-1731
Fax: (409) 294-3538

ACADEMIC

Founded: 1868
Type: 4 Yr., Public, Coed
Web-site: http://www.shsu.eduath
SAT/ACT/GPA: 1020/20
Student/Faculty Ratio: 22:1
Male/Female Ratio: 1:1
Undergraduate Enrollment: 12,000
Graduate Enrollment: 500
Scholarships/Academic: Yes **Athletic:** Yes **Fin Aid:** Yes
Total Expenses by: Semester **In State:** $ 3,000 **Out of State:** $ 5,500
Degrees Conferred: BBA, BS, BA, BFA, BM, BAAS, MD
Programs of Study: Agriculture, Business and Management, Communications, Education, Social Sciences, Visual and Performing Arts

ATHLETIC PROFILE

Estimated Number of Baseball Scholarships: 11.7
Conference Affiliation: Southland Conference
Program Profile: We have a year-round very competitive non-conference schedule beginning early February. Our conference has 10 baseball members (5 in Texas and 5 in Louisiana). We have very good facilities: a grass turf that has a seating capacity of 2,000 and indoor mounds and cages. We had one losing season in a long, long time.
History: Our program went through 1929 and was inactive until 1948. We were NAIA until 1983 and Division II until 1987. We had only four coaches since 1948. Skeeters,in his 24th year, won Conference Champs in 1985, 1986, 1987, 1989 and 1996.
Achievements: NAIA Champions in 1963; 9 trips to NAIA World Series; 3 NCAA II Regionals; 3 NCAA DI Regionals; Southland Champs in 1989 and1996; numerous All-Americans and professional players.
Coaching: John Skeeters - Head Coach, 24 years, .625 win %, hitting coach. Carlo Gott - Defense.
Roster for 1998 team/In State: 30 **Out of State:** 2 **Out of Country:** 0
Total Number of Varsity/Jr. Varsity: 30 **Percent of Graduation:** 85%
Number of Seniors on 1998 Team: 8 **Number of Sophomores on 1998 Team:** 8
Freshmen Receiving Fin Aid/Athletic: 8 **Academic:** 0
Most Recent Record: 28 - 28 - 0 **Number of Spring Games:** 56
Positions Needed for 1999/2000: Centerfielder, Shortstop
Schedule: Texas AandM, Baylor, Rice, Oklahoma, University of Houston
Style of Play: Solid defense - quality pitching, and pressure offense.

San Jacinto College - North

5800 Uvalde Rd
Houston, TX 77049
Coach: Chris Rupp

NJCAA
Gators/Green, Gold
Phone: (281) 459-7613
Fax: (281) 459-7606

ACADEMIC

Founded: 1975
Type: 2 Yr., Public, Coed
Undergraduate Enrollment: 4,080
Campus Housing: No
Student/Faculty Ratio: 20:1
Male/Female Ratio: 47:53
Scholarships/Academic: No **Athletic:** Yes **Fin Aid:** No
Total Expenses by: Hour **In State:** $ 12/hr **Out of State:** $ 22/hr
Degrees Conferred: AA, AAS

Programs of Study: Art, Behavioral Science, Biology, Business Administration, Chemistry, Computer Science, Drama, English, Foreign Languages, History, Journalism, mathematics, Music, Physics, Psychology, Social Science, Sociology, Speech

ATHLETIC PROFILE

Estimated Number of Baseball Scholarships: 18
Conference Affiliation: Texas Junior College Athletic Conference
Program Profile: We have 56 games per year from February through May. We have a natural grass playing field with measurements of 325 down the lines, 385 alleys and 400 center. There are on sight dressing rooms, a concession and approximately 400 seats
History: Our beginning date was in 1961. We took 12 trips to NJCAA National Tourney and won 5 National Championships. We were 3rd Runner-Up and got 2-3rd place finishes. We are the winningest team in the history of the NJCAA National Tournament. Former players include Roger Clemens, Andy Pettitte and Jeff McCurry.
Achievements: Chris Rupp was 1997 and 1998 Region XIV Coach of the Year and Southeastern District NICAA Coach of the Year in 1997 and 1998; Region XIV Champions 3rd and 2nd respectively in 1997 and 1998 World Series.
Coaching: Chris Rupp, Head Coach, stands 134-74 after five seasons at San Jacinto College North. He was a former star at Texas A&M University and coached North Shore High School (Houston) to a 134-59 record and 3 district titles. He was named 1997 and 1998 Region XIV Coach of the Year. Danny Watkins ,Assistant Coach, coached for 10 years at Vernon Regional College in Vernon Texas. DJ Wilson , Assistant Coach, entered his 2nd year with the program.
Roster for 1998 team/In State: 25 **Out of State:** 5 **Out of Country:** 0
Total Number of Varsity/Jr. Varsity: 30 **Percent of Graduation:** 50%
Number of Seniors on 1998 Team: 12 **Number of Sophomores on 1998 Team:** 0
Freshmen Receiving Fin Aid/Athletic: 15 **Most Recent Record:** 49 - 15 - 0
Number of Fall Games: 20 **Number of Spring Games:** 56
Positions Needed for 1999/2000: Pitchers, Outfielders, Corners
Schedule: Galveston College, Texarkana CC, Northeast Community College
Style of Play: Aggressive, fundamental baseball.

Schreiner College

2100 Memorial Boulevard
Kerrville, TX 78028-5697
Coach: Rusty Richards

NCAA III
Mountaineers/Maroon, White
Phone: (830) 792-7292
Fax: (830) 792-7310

ACADEMIC

Founded: 1932 **Type:** 4 Yr., Private, Liberal Arts, Coed
Religion: Presbyterian **Campus Housing:** Yes
Web-site: Not Available **SAT/ACT/GPA:** 860/18
Student/Faculty Ratio: 16:1 **Male/Female Ratio:** 1:1
Undergraduate Enrollment: 700 **Graduate Enrollment:** 750
Scholarships/Academic: Yes **Athletic:** No **Fin Aid:** Yes
Total Expenses by: Year **In State:** $ 16,000 **Out of State:** $ 24,000
Degrees Conferred: AA, AAS, BA
Programs of Study: Accounting, Art Education, Biochemistry, Biology, Business Administration, Chemistry, Communications, Computer Studies, English, Exercise Science, French, German, Fine Arts, History, Humanities, Management, Marketing, Mathematics, Philosophy

ATHLETIC PROFILE

Conference Affiliation: American Southwest Conference
Program Profile: The Mountaineers play on a beautiful natural surface with facility improvements on the way.
History: Several players were drafted: David Hulse by Texas Rangers, Eric Jupe by Florida Marlins on the 14th round in 1998.

Achievements: No conference titles; David Hulse - Big Leagues Texas Rangers.
Coaching: Rusty Richards, Head Coach, is in his 2nd year. He played at University of Texas pro ball for Atlanta Organization. He was head assistant at Arkansas State in 1995 and 1996.
Roster for 1998 team/In State: 30 **Positions Needed for 1999/2000:** Pitcher
Total Number of Varsity/Jr. Varsity: 24 **Most Recent Record:** 23 - 25 - 0
Number of Seniors on 1998 Team: 1 **Baseball Camp Dates:** Month of June
Freshmen Receiving Fin Aid/Athletic: 0 **Academic:** 15
Number of Fall Games: 9 **Number of Spring Games:** 42
Schedule: Nothwood, McMurry, Howard Payne, Trinity, Southwestern, Hardin Simmons
Style of Play: Aggressive and fundamentally sound.

Southwest Texas State University

601 University
San Marcos, TX 78666
Coach: Howard Bushong

NCAA I
Bobcats/Maroon, Gold
Phone: (512) 245-3586
Fax: (512) 245-2967

ACADEMIC

Founded: 1899 **Type:** 4 Yr., Public, Coed
Religion: Non-Affiliated **Campus Housing:** Yes
Web-site: http://www.swt.edu **SAT/ACT/GPA:** 920/20
Student/Faculty Ratio: 22:1 **Male/Female Ratio:** 44:56
Undergraduate Enrollment: 21,000 **Graduate Enrollment:** 5,000
Scholarships/Academic: Yes **Athletic:** Yes **Fin Aid:** Yes
Total Expenses by: Year **In State:** $ 3,552.50 **Out of State:** $ 6,120.50
Degrees Conferred: BA, BS
Programs of Study: Applied Arts, Sciences, International Studies, Business Administration, Exercise and Sports Science, Fine Arts, Music, Agriculture, Applied Sociology, Clinical Lab Science, Communication Disorders, Criminal Justice, Health Wellness Promotion, Health Professions, Family and Consumer Sciences, Health Information Management, Radiation Therapy, Recreational Administration, Social Work, Anthropology, Art, Biology, Chemistry, Computer Science, Economics, Mathematics, Physics, Philosophy, Theatre Arts, Communication, Geography, Education

ATHLETIC PROFILE

Conference Affiliation: Southland Conference
Program Profile: Our field dimensions are 330 line, 375 left-alley, 410 center-field and 330 UNE. We play on a grass field that has a 10 foot fence.
History: The program began in 1985 which was our first year in the NCAA Regional Tournament. We won 2 Texas Division Titles and 1 Conference Title.
Achievements: Howard Bushong - 1996 Coach of the Year in SLC; Will Brunson - LA Dodgers; Jack Ford-Chicago White Sox; Stephen Smith-Reds; Bryan Williams - Blue Jays.
Coaching: Howard Bushong, Head Coach, is in his 4th year. He was pit coach at the University of Texas for 3 years. His team made the College World Series 1992 and1993. He was 12 years at Westlake High School. They went to 6 state tournaments and got two State Championships. Tim Doherty, Assistant Coach,is in his 4th year. He was at USL one year three years at Seminole JC. He went three times to the UCO World Series.
Style of Play: Pitching and defense; offense runs and hit and runs.

Southwestern Adventist College

PO Box 567
Keene, TX 76059
Coach: Bruce Norman

NAIA
Knights/Gold, Maroon
Phone: (817) 645-3921
Fax: (817) 556-4744

ACADEMIC

Founded: 1840
Type: 4 Yr., Private, Coed
Undergraduate Enrollment: 1,251
Campus Housing: Yes
Student/Faculty Ratio: 12:1
Male/Female Ratio: 2:3
Scholarships/Academic: Yes **Athletic:** No
Fin Aid: Yes
Total Expenses by: Year **In State:** $ 20,200 **Out of State:** $ 20,200
Degrees Conferred: BA, BS, BFA
Programs of Study: Accounting, Biology, Biological Science, Broadcasting, Business Administration, Commerce, Management, Chemistry, Communications, Computer Programming, Computer Information Systems, Elementary Education, Emglish, Health Services Administration, History, International Relations, Journalism, Mathematics, Medical Technology, Nursing, Physical Fitness and Exercise Science, Physics, Psychology, Religious Studies, Office Management

Southwestern University

1001 East University
Georgetown, TX 78627
Coach: Jim Mallon
Email: sheltonj@Southwestern.edu
NCAA III
Pirates/Black, Gold
Phone: (512) 863-1381
Fax: (512) 863-1393

ACADEMIC

Founded: 1840
Type: 4 Yr., Private, Liberal Arts, Coed
Religion: Methodist
Campus Housing: Yes
Web-site: http://www.Southwestern.edu/
SAT/ACT/GPA: 1000/23+
Student/Faculty Ratio: 12:1
Male/Female Ratio: 49:51
Undergraduate Enrollment: 1,240
Graduate Enrollment: None
Scholarships/Academic: Yes **Athletic:** No
Fin Aid: Yes
Total Expenses by: Year **In State:** $ 19,869 **Out of State:** $ 19,869
Degrees Conferred: BS, BA, BFA, BM
Programs of Study: Accounting, American Studies, Animal Behavior, Art, Biology, Business, Chemistry, Child Study and Language Development, Communications, Computer Science, Economics, English, French, German, History, International Studies, Kinesiology, Math, Music, Philosophy, Physical Science, Physics, Political Science, Psychology, Religion, Sociology, Theatre

ATHLETIC PROFILE

Conference Affiliation: Southern Collegiate Athletic Conference
Program Profile: We have an all grass field with a measurements of 330-375-403-375-335. Rockwell Field has a seating capacity of 150. We do a 42 game season with 2 tournaments hosted by SU. If we qualify, we have a conference tournament.
History: The program began in the 1960's. Jim Mallon started here as a head coach in 1971. He compiled a record of 951-509. His teams finished 3rd in the nation in 1984 and 8th in 1983. We play at Rockwell Field
Achievements: Jim Mallon was named 5 times NAIA District Coach of the Year; 2 Conference Titles in 1996 and 1997; we are an Independent as NAIA school - Mallon was elected to the NAIA Hall of Fame in 1992; Mallon 3rd winningest coach in the NAIA history, 2nd winningest coach in the NCAA Division III; several Academics and athletics All-Americans.
Coaching: Jim Mallon, Head Coach, graduated from Baylor in 1967. He is in his 28th season at SU. He was NAIA District Coach of the Year. He is the third winningest coach in NAIA history and the second winningest coach in NCAA Division III history. He played college ball at Baylor University and was named All-SWC. He was 5 years with the Giants Organization up to AAR. He managed in professional baseball for Pittsburgh Pirates. Jim Shelton, Assistant Coach, graduated from St. Edward's in 1985. He is in his 10th season coaching. He has been five years at SU.
Roster for 1998 team/In State: 27 **Out of State:** 1 **Out of Country:** 0
Total Number of Varsity/Jr. Varsity: 30
Percent of Graduation: 95%
Number of Seniors on 1998 Team: 3
Most Recent Record: 31 - 10 - 0
Freshmen Receiving Fin Aid/Athletic: 0
Academic: 80%
Number of Fall Games: 9
Number of Spring Games: 41

Positions Needed for 1999/2000: Pitchers, Middle Infielders
Baseball Camp Dates: 1st week of June
Style of Play: Aggressive, solid pitching and defense.

Sul Ross State University

Box C-17
Alpine, TX 79832
Coach: Donnie Randall

NCAA III
Lobos/Scarlet, Grey
Phone: (915) 837-8226
Fax: (915) 837-8234

ACADEMIC

Founded: 1920
Type: 4 Yr., Public, Coed
Religion: Non-Affiliated
Campus Housing: Yes
Student/Faculty Ratio: 13:1
Male/Female Ratio: 60:40
Undergraduate Enrollment: 2,000
Graduate Enrollment: 500
Scholarships/Academic: Yes **Athletic:** No **Fin Aid:** Yes
Total Expenses by: Year **In State:** $ 5,500 **Out of State:** $ 7,500
Degrees Conferred: AAS, BA, BS, BBA, BM, MA, MS, MED, MBA
Programs of Study: Education, Animal Science, Agriculture, Biological Science, Business Administration, Communications, Criminal Justice, Fine Arts, Geology, Mathematics

ATHLETIC PROFILE

Conference Affiliation: American Southwest Conference
Program Profile: Our first year in the Division III was 1998. We are making transition from successful history at NAIA level. We are located in Alpine, TX, a rural community of 6,000 people. We play home games at historic Kokerndt Field, built in 1946. It was the featured in a 1989 article in Sports Illustrated where it was called "The Best Little Ballpark in Texas". It seats 1,100 with lights.
History: Our program began in 1921. In 1956 we were NAIA National Champs. The former Detroit Tiger Norm Cash is an alumni. Recent successes include 1990 and 1996 Conference Championships and 1997 American Southwest Conference Tournament Champions.
Achievements: Head Coach Donnie Randell was selected Conference Coach of the Year in 1996. Program has had four consecutive winning seasons in 1994-1997.
Coaching: Donnie Randell, Head Coach, graduated and played at University of Houston. He got MVP Southwest. He was Conference Playoffs Coach of the Year 1996. He has a record of 87-71. Milan Rasic ,Assistant Coach, played at the College of Southwest for 4 years where he was also an assistant coach for two years. Ivan Snively, Assistant Coach, is in his 1st year with the program. He is a former All-Conference catcher at Sul Ross.
Roster for 1998 team/In State: 23 **Out of State:** 1 **Out of Country:** 0
Total Number of Varsity/Jr. Varsity: 24 **Percent of Graduation:** 95%
Number of Seniors on 1998 Team: 11 **Number of Sophomores on 1998 Team:** 8
Freshmen Receiving Fin Aid/Athletic: 0 **Academic:** 4
Baseball Camp Dates: June **Number of Spring Games:** 39
Positions Needed for 1999/2000: Pitcher, Catcher
Most Recent Record: 17 - 21 - 0
Schedule: Texas Tech University, McMurry, Howard Payne, Southwestern, Texas Wesleyan
Style of Play: Hit with power, force the issue on the bases. Leader in conference with a 41 HR in 38 games. Play for big inning!

Tarleton State University

Box T-80
Stephenville, TX 76402
Coach: Jack Allen

NCAA II
Texans/Purple, White
Phone: (254) 968-9182
Fax: (254) 968-9831

ACADEMIC

Founded: 1899
Type: 4 Yr., Public, Coed
Religion: Non-Affiliated
Campus Housing: Yes
Undergraduate Enrollment: 6,500
SAT/ACT/GPA: 930/20
Student/Faculty Ratio: 20:1
Male/Female Ratio: 50:50
Scholarships/Academic: Yes **Athletic:** Yes **Fin Aid:** Yes
Total Expenses by: Year **In State:** $ 5,500 **Out of State:** $ 7,000
Degrees Conferred: BAAS, BA, BBA, BFA, BM, BS, BSW, MS, MBA, MA, MED
Programs of Study: Business/Office and Marketing/Distribution, Business Management, Communications, Computer, Education, Health

ATHLETIC PROFILE

Conference Affiliation: Lone Star Conference
Program Profile: Cecil Ballow Baseball Complex is on campus and has lights and natural grass field. It also has: a locker room, a weight room,an outdoor infield practice field and indoor and outdoor batting cages. It is located beside the Tarleton Horticultural Building on the South side of West Washington Street. The dimensions of the field are 320 feet down the lines, 365 feet in the alleys and 400 feet to center.
History: Our basebal programl started at Tarleton almost from the beginning of the college in 1899. Records indicate that Tarleton was playing intercollegiate baseball as early as 1904. Donnie Campbell coached Texas during the difficult transition in the early years in 1961 and 1962 when Tarleton became a senior college.We still managed a 10-11 record in Tarleton's first full season playing senior college teams.
Achievements: 1973 - 1978 NJCAA National Coach of the Year; 1973 Texans Sports Writer Coach of the Year, AACBC Coach of the Year in 1973-1978, TIAA Coach of the Year in 1991; Lone Star Conference Coach of the Year; 1998 has 25 All-Americans; 165 drafted players.
Coaching: Jack Allen, Head Coach, attended Sam Houston State. He has 32 years coaching experience. He compiled a record of 1,115-609-3. Trey Felan - Infield and Hitting Coach, 1989. Bryan Conger - Pitching Coach, 1996.
Roster for 1998 team/In State: 24 **Out of State:** 6 **Out of Country:** 2
Total Number of Varsity/Jr. Varsity: 45 **Most Recent Record:** 35 - 21 - 0
Number of Seniors on 1998 Team: 10 **Number of Sophomores on 1998 Team:** 0
Freshmen Receiving Fin Aid/Athletic: 3 **Academic:** 4
Positions Needed for 1999/2000: Pitcher **Number of Spring Games:** 56
Schedule: Texas A&M, University of Texas-Arlington, Mankato State, College of St. Francis
Style of Play: Pitching, speed and defense.

Texarkana College

2500 North Robison Road
Texarkana, TX 75599
Coach: Matt Deggs
NJCAA
Bulldogs/Navy, White
Phone: (903) 838-4541
Fax: (903) 832-5030

ACADEMIC

Founded: 1927
Type: 2 Yr., Public, Coed
Undergraduate Enrollment: 4,500
Campus Housing: No
Student/Faculty Ratio: 25:1
Male/Female Ratio: 1:3
Scholarships/Academic: Yes **Athletic:** Yes **Fin Aid:** Yes
Total Expenses by: Year **In State:** $ 3,000 **Out of State:** $ 3,400
Degrees Conferred: AA, AS
Programs of Study: Accounting, Business Administration, Electrical/Electronics Technology, Emergency Medical technology, Law Enforcement, Liberal Arts, Music, Natural Science, Nursing, Printing Technology, Real Estate

ATHLETIC PROFILE

Estimated Number of Baseball Scholarships: 15 Full
Conference Affiliation: Texas Eastern Athletic Conference
Program Profile: We play Fall and Spring schedules. Our Spring schedule is one of the toughest in the country. Our school enrollment is approximately 4,000. George Dabson Field is natural grass and has a seating capacity of 1,000.
Achievements: Over 50 players drafted since 1989.
Coaching: Matt Deggs, Head Coach, iss in his 1st year with the program and his overall record is 39-20.His conference record if 21-7. He got 2nd place in TEAC. His 1998 team broke 2 conference and 10 school records. Fourteen sophomores received 4 year scholarships. Scott Minnie - Assistant Coach.
Total Number of Varsity/Jr. Varsity: 27 **Most Recent Record:** 39 - 20 - 0
Number of Seniors on 1998 Team: **Number of Sophomores on 1998 Team:** 6
Number of Fall Games: 20 **Number of Spring Games:** 56
Positions Needed for 1999/2000: Catcher, 3-OF, 3rd Base, 2-Shortstops, 5-Pitchers
Schedule: San Jacinto, Seminole, Grayson College, Navarro, North East Texas, Conners State
Style of Play: Good pitching, strong up the middle defense and aggressive base running.

Texas A & M University

P.O. Box 30017
College Station, TX 77842
Coach: Mark Johnson

NCAA I
Aggies/Maroon, White
Phone: (409) 845-1991
Fax: (409) 862-1618

ACADEMIC

Founded: 1876 **Type:** 4 Yr., Public, Liberal Arts, Coed
Religion: Non-Affiliated **Campus Housing:** Yes
Web-site: http://sports.tamu.edu/sports/soccer/ **SAT/ACT/GPA:** 1100
Student/Faculty Ratio: 18:1 **Male/Female Ratio:** 49:51
Undergraduate Enrollment: 33,945 **Graduate Enrollment:** 6,774
Scholarships/Academic: Yes **Athletic:** Yes **Fin Aid:** Yes
Total Expenses by: Year **In State:** $ 7,725 **Out of State:** $ 14,145
Degrees Conferred: BA, BS, MA, MS, MBA, MD
Programs of Study: Agriculture, Life Sciences, Architecture, Business Administration, Education, Engineering, Geology, Sciences, Maritime Studies, Liberal Arts, Medicine, Science

ATHLETIC PROFILE

Conference Affiliation: Big Twelve Conference
Program Profile: Our top 25 program stadium seats 7,000 and has natural grass playing surface.
History: We have a highly successful program . We have been to regionals 10 of the past 14 years. Won College World Series in 1993. We ranked in the top 25.
Achievements: Coach of the Year in 1989; National Coach of the Year in 1993; Big 12 Coach of the Year in 1998.
Coaching: Mark Johnson, Head Coach, in his 15th year & is the 8th winningest active Div. I Coach with a record of 538-220. Jim Lawler, Assistant Coach. Both spoke at National ABCA Convention.
Baseball Camp Dates: June 1 - July 7
Schedule: Arizona, Oklahoma State, Michigan, California State-Northridge, University of Las Vegas
Style of Play: Outstanding pitching with a balance hitting attack.

Texas A&M University - Kingsville

Campus Box 202
Kingsville, TX 78363
Coach: Hector Salinas

NCAA II
Javelinas/Blue, Gold
Phone: (512) 593-3487
Fax: (512) 593-3587

ACADEMIC

Founded: 1925
Religion: Non-Affiliated
Student/Faculty Ratio: 17:1
Undergraduate Enrollment: 6,600
Scholarships/Academic: Yes **Athletic:** Yes
Total Expenses by: Year **In State:** $ 5,818
Type: 4 Yr., Public, Coed
Campus Housing: No
Male/Female Ratio: 52:48
Graduate Enrollment: 1,190
Fin Aid: Yes
Out of State: $ 10,378
Degrees Conferred: BA, BS
Programs of Study: Accounting, Agricultural Business Management, Animal Science, Biological Science, Business Administration, Chemical Engineering, Communications, Engineering, Management, Mathematics, Petroleum Engineering, Plant Science, Preprofessional Programs

ATHLETIC PROFILE

Conference Affiliation: Lone Star Conference
Program Profile: We have a very competitive program. We play home games on Nolan Ryan Field. We have a Fall ball that consist of four weeks. Our field is a natural grass with dimensions of 330 foul lines, 400 straight center and 385 in the alleys.
History: The program began in 1993. We finished with a record of 26-24 (no scholarship),2nd place finish in the Lone Star Conference. Our second year record is 26-24 and we finished 3rd in the LSC. In 1995, we won the Lone Star Conference and ranked 4th in the NCAA .In 1996, we finished 2nd 33-23 and in 1997 we finished 3rd with a record of 31-23.
Achievements: 1995 Coach of the Year in the Lone Star Conference; 1 All-American - Juan Sanchez in 1995; also slugging; National Champ; 5 players have gone on to play pro ball; 3 drafted players.
Coaching: Hector Salinas - Head Coach. The coaching staff is composed of volunteer and student assistants. Orlando Salina's son played here now he helps graduates here. Joe Cruise, Assistant Coach, helps as the Spring volunteer. Mario Flores Student Assistant. Roel Garcia - Student Assistant Coach.
Style of Play: A very offensively minded, try to be very sound defensively, especially up the middle. Pitching will try to to stay ahead of the batters, mostly try to pay sound baseball in all aspects of the game. We have good success and have been competitive every year.

Texas Christian University

2800 South University Drive
Forth Worth, TX 76129
Coach: Lance Brown
NCAA I
Horned Frogs/Purple, White
Phone: (817) 921-7985
Fax: (817) 921-7656

ACADEMIC

Founded: 1873
Religion: Disciple of Christ
Web-site: http://www.tcu.edu/
Student/Faculty Ratio: 15:1
Undergraduate Enrollment: 6,100
Scholarships/Academic: Yes **Athletic:** Yes
Total Expenses by: Year **In State:** $ 16,850
Type: 4 Yr., Private, Liberal Arts, Coed
Campus Housing: Yes
SAT/ACT/GPA: 1050/25/3.0
Male/Female Ratio: 40:60
Graduate Enrollment: 1,110
Fin Aid: Yes
Out of State: $ 16,850
Degrees Conferred: BA, BS, BFA, BBA, Bmus, Bmed, BSN, MA, MS, MFA, MED, PhD
Programs of Study: Business, Communication, Marketing, Criminal Justice, Nursing, Radio/Television Film, Computer Science, Journalism, Dance, Music, Art, Languages, Premed, Speech Communication, Education, Nutrition and Dietetics, Engineering, Kinesiology, Physical Education, Prelaw

ATHLETIC PROFILE

Conference Affiliation: Southwest Conference

Program Profile: TCU's Baseball Diamond is located on campus, less than a block from all student housing. It is a beautiful and functional facility offering optimum playing and wind conditions. Batters face a large, concrete retaining wall in center and left center. Dressing facilities are located nearby in Amon Carter Stadium. Bleachers seat 1,500. Infield is natural grass. Batting cages have artificial turf.
History: The TCU baseball program dates back to 1923 and has earned a career record of 1059-1080-16. In 1994, the Frogs were ranked for 8 consecutive weeks with the highest ranking of 14. TCU is excited that Hall-of-Famer, Nolan Ryan, is now the restricted earnings coach.
Achievements: 1994 was first trip to NCAA Regional Tournament in 38 years, Conference Championships; 5 TCU players drafted in 1994; 2 All-Americans; 1 named SWC All-Tournament Team, 1 named to District VI Baseball All-American ; 12 All-Americans; 1 Academic All-American; 98 All-Conference; 3 SWC Player of the Year.
Coaching: Lance Brown, Head Caoch, is a 1967 graduate of TCU.He was 1963 Southwest Conference Player of the Year and All-American. He has been 10 ten years at TCU. He was 1991 SWC Coach of the Year.

Texas College
(New Program)

2404 N. Grand Avenue
Tyler, TX 75072
Coach: Dr. Lucious Daily

NAIA
Steers/Purple, Gold
Phone: (903) 593-8311x67
Fax: (903) 593-0588

ACADEMIC

Type: 4 Yr., Private, Coed
Religion: Christian
Campus Housing: Yes
Total Expenses by: Year **In State:** $ 8,050 **Out of State:** $ 8,050
Degrees Conferred: BA, BS
Programs of Study: Arts, Biology, Business Administration, Computer Science, English, Elementary Education, History, Mathematics, Music, Physical Education, Political Science, Social Science, Social Work, Sociology

ATHLETIC PROFILE

Conference Affiliation: Red River Athletic Conference
Program Profile: Our field house has 900 capacity. Our baseball field is grass and has 200 seating capacity.
Coaching: Dr. Lucious Daily, Head Coach, compiled a record of 15-69.
Roster for 1998 team/In State: 6 **Out of State:** 17 **Out of Country:** 0
Total Number of Varsity/Jr. Varsity: 23 **Percent of Graduation:** 75%
Number of Seniors on 1998 Team: **Number of Spring Games:** 35
Freshmen Receiving Fin Aid/Athletic: 100% **Most Recent Record:** 5 - 30 - 0
Positions Needed for 1999/2000: Catcher, Pitchers
Schedule: Grambling State University, Prairie View, Northeast State University, Le Tourneu

Texas Lutheran College

1000 West Court Street
Seguin, TX 78155
Coach: Bill Miller
Email: miller _b@txlutheran.edu

NCAA II/NAIA
Bulldogs/Black, Gold
Phone: (830) 372-8124
Fax: (830) 372-8135

ACADEMIC

Founded: 1891
Type: 4 Yr., Private, Liberal Arts, Coed
Religion: Lutheran
Campus Housing: Yes
Web-site: http://www.txlutheran.edu/
SAT/ACT/GPA: 800+/18+
Student/Faculty Ratio: 15:1
Male/Female Ratio: 1:2

Undergraduate Enrollment: 1,100 **Graduate Enrollment:** None
Scholarships/Academic: Yes **Athletic:** Yes **Fin Aid:** Yes
Total Expenses by: Year **In State:** $ 14,042 **Out of State:** $ 14,042
Degrees Conferred: BBA, BA, BS
Programs of Study: Accounting, Applied Science, Arts, Biology, Business Administration, Chemistry, Communications, German, History, Computer Science, Economics, Education, English, Finance, Mathematics, Music, Philosophy, Physical Education, Physics, Political Science, Premed, Psychology, Social Science, Spanish, Theology, International Studies, Kinesiology, Management

ATHLETIC PROFILE

Conference Affiliation: Heart of Texas Conference
Program Profile: The TLU baseball program is constructed around discipline, players of good character that are fundametally sound and can compete at a championship level. Facilities include Mark Isbel Field on TLU campus that seats approximately 300 spectators. Playing season consists of 6 weeks in the Fall and 16 weeks during the Spring.
History: Baseball at Texas Lutheran began in 1949. Since that time TLU has won the Big State Conference Championship in 1975, 1979 and 1985. The Bulldogs were co-champions in 1965, 1969, 1971, 1974 1984 and 1997. TLU won NAIA District IV titles in 1971, 1986, 1988 and 1989 and advanced to the Southwest Regional Tournament in 1996 and 1997.
Achievements: Head Baseball Coach Bill Miller Coached at Judson High School in 1985-1992 where he compiled a record of 127 wins, 50 losses. District Champions in 1987, 1988, 1989; Bi - District Champions in 1987, 1988, 1989; Regional Champions in 1989; State Quarterfinalist in 1989; Coach of the Year in 1989. 1997 HOTC Tournament Runner-Up; 1997 HOTC co-champions; 1996, 1997 Southwest Regional. Seven All-Conference players; 2 Academic All-Americans, tournament qualifier; Dax Kiefer - drafted by Chicago Cubs in 1996.
Coaching: Bill Miller, Head Coach, compiled a record of 173 wins - 87 losses. He coached at Judson High School from 1985-1992 and compiled a record of 127 wins, 50 losses. Danny Banks - Student Assistant Coach, is in his 2nd year. He started at 2 base at Texas Lutheran University. Cody Farr ,Assistant Coach, graduated from and pitched at UTA. He played in Independent League for three years. Dax Kiefer,Assistant Coach, graduated from TLU in 1996 and was also drafted by Chicago Cubs minoerleague organization.
Style of Play: Aggressive, disciplined, fundamentally sound, practice and play at championship level.

Texas Southern University

3100 Cleburne Street
Houston, TX 77004
Coach: Candy Robinson

NCAA I
Fighting Tigers/Maroon, Grey, Black
Phone: (713) 313-7993
Fax: (713) 313-7273

ACADEMIC

Founded: 1947 **Type:** 4 Yr., Public, Coed
Religion: Non-Affiliated **Campus Housing:** Yes
Web-site: http://www.tsu.edu **SAT/ACT/GPA:** Open Admission
Student/Faculty Ratio: 7:1 **Male/Female Ratio:** 1:12
Undergraduate Enrollment: 7,895 **Graduate Enrollment:** 1,959
Scholarships/Academic: Yes **Athletic:** Yes **Fin Aid:** Yes
Total Expenses by: Year **In State:** $ 5,900 **Out of State:** $ 8,100
Degrees Conferred: BS, BA, MBA, MS, MA, PhD, JhD
Programs of Study: Biology, Chemistry, Physics, Sociology, Art, Music, History, English, Spanish, French, Political Science, Public Administration, Communications, Computer Science, Psychology, Social Work, Accounting, Marketing, General Business, Elementary and Secondary Education

ATHLETIC PROFILE

Estimated Number of Baseball Scholarships: 8.2
Conference Affiliation: Southwestern Athletic Conference

Program Profile: MacGregor Park is the homefield with a seating capacity of 950, natural field. Built in 1972, left 317, left center 365, center field 382, right field 317; 25 feet green monster in centerfield, and 2 batting cages.
History: The program began in 1950.
Achievements: 1991 SWAC Runner-Up in post-season tourney; Sunny Garcia in 1997 ERA Champion in Division I (1.66); drafted players since 1989-1989; Avery Johnson, in 1990 Divan Campbell and Arthur Ginnins in 1995; 1998 Sonny Garcia, Arthur Ginnins; Sonny Garcia was named 1997 All-South Region Selection.
Coaching: Candy Robinson, Head Coach, started 1991 to the present and compiled 194-255 record. He is a 1969 graduate of Grambling State BSE. Arthur Reggins, Assistant Coach, ia 1996 graduate of Texas Southern with a BS in Human Performance and was drafted in 1995. Brian White, Assistant Coach, is a 1996 and 1998 graduate of Texas Southern with a BS and a MS in Health. Ken Mack - Assistant Coach, 1998 co-captain.
Roster for 1998 team/In State: 18 **Out of State:** 15 **Out of Country:** 0
Total Number of Varsity/Jr. Varsity: 32 **Percent of Graduation:** 73%
Number of Seniors on 1998 Team: 8 **Most Recent Record:** 19 - 28 - 0
Freshmen Receiving Fin Aid/Athletic: 21 **Academic:** 19
Number of Fall Games: 0 **Number of Spring Games:** 56
Positions Needed for 1999/2000: Pitchers, 3rd Baseman, Shortstop
Schedule: NorthWestern State, Nicholls State, Southern University, Lamar University, Sam Houston
Style of Play: Team is a running team because we have tremendous team speed with a power hitters. Also we have great starting pitching with great closer in our bull pen. Stresses hard work with fundamental play on the field.

Texas Tech University

6th and Boston, Box 43021
Lubbock, TX 79409
Coach: Larry Hays

NCAA I
Red Raiders/Scarlet, Black
Phone: (806) 742-3355
Fax: (806) 742-1970

ACADEMIC

Founded: 1929 **Type:** 4 Yr., Public, Coed, Engineering
Religion: Non-Affiliated **Campus Housing:** Yes
Web-site: http://www.texastcch.com **SAT/ACT/GPA:** 1140/25
Student/Faculty Ratio: 18:1 **Male/Female Ratio:** 1.5:1
Undergraduate Enrollment: 20,806 **Graduate Enrollment:** 3,580
Scholarships/Academic: Yes **Athletic:** Yes **Fin Aid:** Yes
Total Expenses by: Year **In State:** $ 7,340 **Out of State:** $ Varies
Degrees Conferred: Bachelors, Masters
Programs of Study: Agricultural Science, Natural Resources, Architecture, Arts and Sciences, Business Administration, Education, Engineering, Human Science, Graduate School and Law

ATHLETIC PROFILE

Conference Affiliation: Southwest Conference

Texas Wesleyan University

1201 Wesleyan
Forth Worth, TX 76105-1536
Coach: Willie Gawlick
Email: gawlikw@hotmail.com

NCAA II/NAIA
Rams/Royal Blue, Gold
Phone: (817) 531-4212
Fax: (817) 531-4208

ACADEMIC

Founded: 1890 **Type:** 4 Yr., Private, Coed
Religion: Methodist **Campus Housing:** Yes

Web-site: http://www.txwesleyan.edu/ **SAT/ACT/GPA:** 950/18
Student/Faculty Ratio: 17:1 **Male/Female Ratio:** 45:55
Undergraduate Enrollment: 2,000 **Graduate Enrollment:** 850
Scholarships/Academic: Yes **Athletic:** Yes **Fin Aid:** Yes
Total Expenses by: Year **In State:** $ 11,600 **Out of State:** $ 11,600
Degrees Conferred: BA, BS, BME, BBA, MBA, MAT, ME, MHS, DJ
Programs of Study: Accounting, Business Administration, Finance, Management, Marketing, Sports Management, Business Education, Business Psychology, Mass Communication, Human Learning and Devleopment, Exercise and Sport Studies, Psychology, Reading, Biligual Education, Art, Music, Theatre Arts, Biology, Chemistry, English, Computer Science, Spanish, History, Mathematics, Political Science, Religion

ATHLETIC PROFILE

Conference Affiliation: Heart of Texas Conference
Program Profile: We are a NCAA Division II program and scholarships are available. Walk ons are invited. We play on a natural turf at Sycamore Park which has a seating capacity of 500. A new stadium is to be built within the next year with a seating capacity of 3,500.
History: Our program started in 1985 after having been dropped in 1981. We raised funds to establish the program. Former coaches were Frank Fultz ,Larry Smith and Brad Bass .Bass was Coach of the Year.
Achievements: Several Texas Wesleyan players have signed pro contracts, Texas Wesleyan has made several playoffs Appearances, Regional Finalist in 1995; Host of Baseball in January of each year with a several current and former major league in attendance. Past players Tommy Lasonda, Bobby Richardson, Duke Snider, Sparky Anderson and others.
Coaching: Willie Gawlik, Head Coach, coaches infielders, catchers and hitters. John Steel - Pitching Coach. John Johnson - Outfield Coach.
Style of Play: Aggressive style of play.

Trinity University

715 Stadium Drive
San Antonio, TX 78212
Coach: Tim Scannell

NCAA III
Tigers/Maroon, White
Phone: (210) 736-8287
Fax: (210) 736-8292

ACADEMIC

Founded: 1869 **Type:** 4 Yr., Private, Liberal Arts, Coed
Religion: Non-Affiliated **Campus Housing:** Yes
Web-site: http://www.trinity.edu/ **SAT/ACT/GPA:** 1100/25
Student/Faculty Ratio: 12:1 **Male/Female Ratio:** 50:50
Undergraduate Enrollment: 2,300 **Graduate Enrollment:** 200
Scholarships/Academic: Yes **Athletic:** No **Fin Aid:** Yes
Total Expenses by: Year **In State:** $ 19,000 **Out of State:** $ 19,000
Degrees Conferred: BA, BS, MA
Programs of Study: Anthropology, Art, Art History, Biology, Business Administration, Chemistry, Computer Science, Drama, Economics, English, Geoscience, History, International Studies, Mathematics, Modern Language and Literature, Music, Philosophy, Physics, Political Science

ATHLETIC PROFILE

Conference Affiliation: Southern Collegiate Athletic Conference
Program Profile: Bell Center is a $14 million facility, E M Stevens Field is an $800,000 facility built in 1992. E M Stevens Field was voted the 1st collegiate field in the nation. We play 36 games, 26 of which are home dates. Our all red brick, 117-acre campus sits on the San Antonio skyline.We play an all-season baseball program.
History: A one-time member of NCAA Division I, Trinity now is currently a member of NCAA Division III and a member of the SCAC since 1989.

Achievements: 1990 and 1995 SCAC Champions, Runner-Up in 1992 - 1994; 9 All-Conference players on the 1995 team; 4 first team selections and 5 2nd team selections.

Tyler Junior College

P.O. Box 9020
Tyler, TX 75711
Coach: Jon Groth

NJCAA
Apaches/Black, Gold
Phone: (903) 510-2865
Fax: (903) 510-2434

ACADEMIC

Founded: 1926
Undergraduate Enrollment: 8,000
Web-site: http://www.tyler.cc.tx.us/
Student/Faculty Ratio: 25:1
Scholarships/Academic: Yes **Athletic:** Yes
Total Expenses by: Year **In State:** $ 3,044
Degrees Conferred: AA, AS

Type: 2 Yr., Public, Jr. College, Coed
Campus Housing: No
SAT/ACT/GPA: None
Male/Female Ratio: 3:4
Fin Aid: Yes
Out of State: $ 3,644

Programs of Study: Business Management, Commercial Art, Computer Science, Criminal Justice, Electronics Technology, Emergency Medical Technology, Graphics Arts, Medical Laboratory Technician, Microcomputer Service, Horticulture Science, Radiologic Technology

ATHLETIC PROFILE

Conference Affiliation: Texas Eastern Athletic Conference
Program Profile: Home games are played at Mike Carter Field--one of the premier JC baseball facilities in the nation--4,000 seats, 3 artificial turf batting cages, 4 bullpen mounds, computerized scoreboard, locker room, laundry and showers, professional level lighting, infield tarp, concession, restrooms. Indoor facility include pitching mounds, batting cages, full infield area, weight room, track, computerized fitness assessment equipment and aerobic training equipment.
History: 1993 was the first year to field a team in 18 years. We are in the 6th season of NJCAA competition.
Achievements: 8 players on the TX-NM JUCO All-Star team; 12 All-TEAC Conference, more 3 of every 4 players move to four-year baseball programs; 27 moved to a four-year school such as Baylor, Texas A&M, Texas, Texas Tech, Houston, Arkansas, Etc..
Coaching: Jon Grot, Head Coach, has a Ph. D. He has been head coach 7 years. He was an assistant coach at Texas A&M, Gerogia Southern and University of New Orleans.
Style of Play: Solid fundamental baseball - aggressive. We keep a low number on our proster and try to go on war with a said group of athletic baseball players. We teach quality effort, in practice and in games, and in quality attitude at all times will help lead to success on the field. We also emphasize that each player do his best to reach his potential in the classroom.

University of Dallas

1845 East Nortgate Drive
Irving, TX 75062
Coach: James Vilade
Email: vilade@acue.udallas.edu

NCAA III
Crusaders/Navy, White
Phone: (972) 721-5117
Fax: (972) 721-5208

ACADEMIC

Founded: 1955
Religion: Catholic
Web-site: http://www.acad.udallas.edu/
Student/Faculty Ratio: 12:1
Undergraduate Enrollment: 1,500
Scholarships/Academic: Yes **Athletic:** No
Total Expenses by: Year **In State:** $ 17,000

Type: 4 Yr., Private, Liberal Arts, Coed
Campus Housing: Yes
SAT/ACT/GPA: 1100
Male/Female Ratio: 65:45
Graduate Enrollment: 400
Fin Aid: Yes
Out of State: $ 17,000

Degrees Conferred: Contact school
Programs of Study: Contact school for program of study.

ATHLETIC PROFILE

Conference Affiliation: American Southwest Conference
Program Profile: We have a newly built $300,000 complex with: natural grass, a state of the art field with astro-turf cages and a stadium that holds 300 people.
History: Our program started back-up in 1998, after 18 years of not having a team. Last season before 1998 was 1981.
Achievements: NAIA District 8 Champions in 1963; Central Zone Champions in 1974-1975; All-Americans are Smitty Duke, Jerry Grambley, and Gerald Turner; drafted player was Jerry Grambley by the Philadelphia.
Coaching: James Vilade, Head Coach, compiled a record of 25-17 and played at Baylor. Darrell Richardson, Assistant Coach, is responsible for the pitchers. He played at Rice.
Roster for 1998 team/In State: 16 **Out of State:** 12 **Out of Country:** 0
Total Number of Varsity/Jr. Varsity: 27 **Most Recent Record:** 25 - 17 - 0
Number of Seniors on 1998 Team: 10 **Number of Sophomores on 1998 Team:** 17
Number of Fall Games: 6 **Number of Spring Games:** 38
Positions Needed for 1999/2000: Shortstop, Catcher, Centerfield, 1st Base
Baseball Camp Dates: January 1999; June, July
Schedule: Notre Dame, Trinity, McMurray, Southwestern, Howard Payne
Style of Play: The University of Dallas style of play is aggressive with a concentration on fundamentals.

University of Houston

3100 Cullen
Houston, TX 77204
Coach: Rayner Noble

NCAA
Cougars/Red, White
Phone: (713) 743-9396
Fax: (713) 743-9488

ACADEMIC

Founded: 1927 **Type:** 4 Yr., Coed
Web-site: http://www.uh.edu **Campus Housing:** No
Student/Faculty Ratio: 19:1 **Male/Female Ratio:** 48:52
Undergraduate Enrollment: 21,426 **Graduate Enrollment:** 9,331
Scholarships/Academic: Yes **Athletic:** Yes **Fin Aid:** Yes
Total Expenses by: Year **In State:** $ 6,841 **Out of State:** $ 11,977
Degrees Conferred: BA, BS, BFA, MBA, MS
Programs of Study: Accounting, Anthropology, Architectural Engineering, Biochemistry, Biological Science, Chemical Engineering, Chemistry, Communications, Drafting/Design Technology, Economics, Education, English, French, Geology, German, History, Humanities, Information Science, Journalism, Mathematics, Natural Science, Optometry, Pharmacy, Preprofessional Programs

ATHLETIC PROFILE

Conference Affiliation: Conference USA
Program Profile: Our program is four years old with a $ 3.75 million dollar stadium. We play on a natural surface. Our field's dimensions are 330 lines and 400 in the center.
History: The University of Houston will celebrate 50 years of baseball next Spring. The Cougars have a new coach who is continuing to improve the program by bringing in top players. Cougars have been in nine NCAA regionals and two College World Series.
Achievements: 1997 Conference USA Tournament Champions; 1997 South 1 Regional; Dustin Carr All-American in 1997; 21st t Ro; Geoffrey Tomlisen was All-American in 1997 4th Ro; Shank Nance Fresh All-American.

Coaching: Rayner Noble, Head Coach, is In his 3rd year at Houston. He was a 5th -round draft pick by the Astros in 1983. He went on to pitch 5 years in the Astros organization reaching as high as Triple A. He has 8 years of experience with a Division I program. He was a high school teammate of Roger Clemens. Trip Coach - Assistant Coach. Todd Whitting - Assistant Coach.
Style of Play: Built on pitching and defense. Offensively aggressive and quick.

University of Mary Hardin - Baylor

900 College Street
Belton, TX 76513
Coach: Mickey Kerr
Email: mkerr@umhb.edu

NCAA III
Crusaders/Purple, Gold
Phone: (254) 295-4619
Fax: (254) 295-4614

ACADEMIC

Founded: 1845
Type: 4 Yr., Public, Liberal Arts, Coed
Religion: Southern Baptist
Campus Housing: Yes
Web-site: http://www.umhb.edu/
SAT/ACT/GPA: 900/19
Student/Faculty Ratio: 20:1
Male/Female Ratio: 1:1
Undergraduate Enrollment: 2,500
Graduate Enrollment: 240
Scholarships/Academic: Yes **Athletic:** Yes **Fin Aid:** Yes
Total Expenses by: Year **In State:** $ 10,400 **Out of State:** $ 10,400
Degrees Conferred: BA, BS, BBA, BFA, BM, BSN, MBA, MED
Programs of Study: Accounting, Art, Business Administration, Biology, Chemistry, Computer Information Systems, Computer Science, Economics, English, History, Finance, Mathematics, Management, Marketing, Medical Technology, Music Education, Nursing, Physical Education

ATHLETIC PROFILE

Estimated Number of Baseball Scholarships: 0
Conference Affiliation: American Southwest Conference
Program Profile: We play home games at Red Murff Field which has a seating capacity for 500 and is a natural grass. Playing season is in Fall and in Spring.
History: The program began in 1974. We affiliated with NAIA in 1979 and NCAA in 1998.
Achievements: Big State Conference Coach of the Year in 1983; Conference Champs; NAIA District 4 Coach of the Year in 1983.
Coaching: Mickey Kerr, Head Coach, started coaching at UMHB from 1981-1983 and 1997 to the present. He compiled a record of 80-101 at UMHB and overall record if 122-139. Micah Wells - Graduate Assistant Coach. Tyson Tidwell - Student Assistant Coach.
Roster for 1998 team/In State: 40 **Out of State:** 0 **Out of Country:** 0
Total Number of Varsity/Jr. Varsity: 40 **Percent of Graduation:** 75%
Number of Seniors on 1998 Team: 5 **Most Recent Record:** 26 - 10 - 0
Number of Fall Games: 9 **Number of Spring Games:** 36
Positions Needed for 1999/2000: Pitcher, Outfielder
Schedule: Southwestern, McMurray, Howard Payne, Sul Ross State, Hardin-Simmons, Mississippi
Style of Play: Strive to be disciplined and fundamentally sound.

University of Texas - Arlington

Box 19079
Arlington, TX 76019
Coach: Marvin 'Butch' McBroom

NCAA I
Mavericks/Royal Blue, White
Phone: (817) 272-2032
Fax: (817) 272-5037

ACADEMIC

Founded: 1895
Type: 4 Yr., Coed
Religion: Non-Affiliated
Campus Housing: Yes
Web-site: http://www.uta.edu/athletics
SAT/ACT/GPA: 700-1000/18-25/

Undergraduate Enrollment: 12,000 **Graduate Enrollment:** 8,000
Scholarships/Academic: Yes **Athletic:** Yes **Fin Aid:** Yes
Total Expenses by: Year **In State:** $ 7,500 **Out of State:** $ 14,200
Programs of Study: Architecture, Business Administration, Engineering, Liberal Arts, Nursing, Science, Social Work, Professional Teacher Education

ATHLETIC PROFILE

Conference Affiliation: Southland Conference
Program Profile: We recently remodeled Allan Saxe Stadium it seats 1,250. The field is one of the finest natural grass playing surfaces in Southwest USA. Our season opens in early February and concludes with an NCAA tournament in May.
History: 14 consecutive years with at I East 30 victories. We were conference champions and NCAA tournament participants in 1990 and 1992. The Mavericks have sent 56 players into professional baseball and produced 1995 and 1996 GTE Academic All-American B G Wilson, and 1996 Selection John Karant.
Achievements: Butch McBroom won Southland Conference Coach of the Year honors 4 times (1981, 1984, 1990, 1992). Won his 700th game in 1995. Team won SLC title in 1990 and 1992. Mavericks have produced 5 conference batting champions, 4 outstanding pitcher award winners and the league's Player of the Year.
Coaching: Butch McBroom, Head Coach, entered his 27th year overall, 24th year at UTA, 736-602 overall, 688-587 at UTA. Assistant Coaches - John Mocek (15th year), Ron Liggett (10th).

University of Texas - Austin

P.O. Box 7399
Austin, TX 78713
Coach: Augie Garrido
Email: www@www.utexas.edu

NCAA I
Longhorns/Burnt Orange, White
Phone: (512) 471-5732
Fax: (512) 471-5516

ACADEMIC

Founded: 1883 **Type:** 4 Yr., Public, Coed
Religion: Non-Affiliated **Campus Housing:** Yes
Web-site: http://www.utexas.edu **SAT/ACT/GPA:** 1110-1310
Student/Faculty Ratio: 18:1 **Male/Female Ratio:** 50:50
Undergraduate Enrollment: 35,861 **Graduate Enrollment:** 11,996
Scholarships/Academic: Yes **Athletic:** Yes **Fin Aid:** Yes
Total Expenses by: Year **In State:** $ 8,354 **Out of State:** $ 13,918
Degrees Conferred: BA, BS, MA, MS
Programs of Study: Business and Management, Communications, Education, Engineering, Letters/Literature, Life Sciences, Psychology, Social Sciences

ATHLETIC PROFILE

Estimated Number of Baseball Scholarships: TBA
Conference Affiliation: Big Twelve Conference
Program Profile: UT led Division I schools in attendance with 173,372, averaging 4,816 fans per game during the 1995 season.
History: The program's inception was in either the last 1800's or the early 1900's.
Coaching: Augie Garrido - Head Coach, first year.
Roster for 1998 team/In State: 25 **Out of State:** 10 **Out of Country:** 0
Total Number of Varsity/Jr. Varsity: 35 **Number of Spring Games:** 56
Number of Seniors on 1998 Team: 7 **Number of Sophomores on 1998 Team:** 6
Baseball Camp Dates: 6/1-5; 6/8-10; 6/15-19; 6/22-24; 7/6-10, etc
Schedule: Miami, University of Southern California, Stanford, LSU, Oklahoma, Oklahoma State, Texas Tech, Texas A &M, Baylor

University of Texas - Brownsville

80 Fort Brown
Brownsville, TX 78520
Coach: Eric Gonzales

NJCAA
Scorpion/Orange, Navy, White
Phone: (956) 544-8293
Fax: (956) 548-6568

ACADEMIC

Founded: 1973
Type: 4 Yr., Coed
Student/Faculty Ratio: 6:1
Campus Housing: No
Undergraduate Enrollment: 2,081
Graduate Enrollment: 671
Scholarships/Academic: Yes **Athletic:** Yes **Fin Aid:** Yes
Total Expenses by: Year **In State:** $ 1,024+ **Out of State:** $ 7,872+
Degrees Conferred: Bachelors
Programs of Study: Contact school for program of study.

ATHLETIC PROFILE

Program Profile: We have a new baseball field which is a natural grass and our playing season extends for a while due our beautiful weather here in South Texas.
History: In the past, our baseball team was doing well until the baseball field was torn down in 1987. Since then, the record has suffered a lot. This year (1997), we anticipate a great season, along with a beautiful brand new baseball field to back up our great team. We are looking forward to good things to come.
Coaching: Eric Gonzales - Head Coach. Omar Ramirez - Assistant Coach. Our coaching staff consists of two coaches that played Division I baseball and three coaches that played minor league.
Style of Play: Play a confident aggressive style of play of baseball. We play to win.

University of Texas - Pan American

1201 W University Drive
Edinburg, TX 78539
Coach: Reggie Tradeway

NCAA I
Broncos/Forest Green, White
Phone: (956) 381-2234
Fax: (956) 381-2882

ACADEMIC

Founded: 1927
Type: 4 Yr., Public, Coed
Undergraduate Enrollment: 11,800
Campus Housing: No
Web-site: http://panam.edu/
SAT/ACT/GPA: 700/17
Student/Faculty Ratio: 26:1
Male/Female Ratio: 45:55
Scholarships/Academic: Yes **Athletic:** Yes **Fin Aid:** Yes
Total Expenses by: Year **In State:** $ 6,495 **Out of State:** $ 10,874
Degrees Conferred: BA, BS, BFA, BSN, Masters
Programs of Study: Accounting, Banking and Finance, Business Administration, Communications, Dietetics, Economics, Elementary Education, English, Fine Arts, Health Education, History, Managment, Marketing, Medical Laboratory Technology, Nursing, Philosophy, Physical Fitness

ATHLETIC PROFILE

Conference Affiliation: Sun Belt Conference
History: Our program started in 1927. The school started as a Junior College, played in the NAIA, and now plays in NCAA Division I. Coach Ogletree has taken the Broncs to both the NAIA and NCAA College World Series, 13 NCAA Playoffs and has posted 24 winning seasons in the Valley.
Achievements: 1971 National Coach of the Year; 13 NCAA playoffs; 1 NCAA and 1 NAIA College World Series Appearance.
Coaching: Al Ogletree, Head Coach, was All-Southwest Conference catcher at Texas A&M.
Style of Play: "I like to let the kids play... It's their game and they ouht to play it. You've got to have fun, you've got to be loose'. Al Ogletree, Bronc Baseball '95.

University of Texas - San Antonio

6900 Loop 1604 West
San Antonio, TX 78249-0691
Coach: Mickey Lashley

NCAA I
Roadrunners/Orange, Navy, White
Phone: (210) 458-4805
Fax: (210) 458-4569

ACADEMIC

Founded: 1969
Type: 4 Yr., Public, Coed
Religion: Non-Affiliated
Campus Housing: Dorms/Apartments
Web-site: http://www.utsa.edu. sports
SAT/ACT/GPA: 900/86/2.0
Undergraduate Enrollment: 18,000
Graduate Enrollment: None
Scholarships/Academic: Yes **Athletic:** Yes **Fin Aid:** Yes
Total Expenses by: Year **In State:** $ 1,055/12 hrs. **Out of State:** $ 3,623/12 hrs.
Programs of Study: Anthropology, Architecture, Art, Biology, Chemistry, Civil Engineering, Communications, Computer Science, Criminal Justice, Economics, Electrical Enginerring, English, Finance, French, Geography, Geology, German, Health, History, Humanities, Information Systems, IDS, Interior Design, Kinesiology, Management, Management Science, Marketing, Mathematics, Mechanical Engineering, Mexican-American Studies, Music, Etc..

ATHLETIC PROFILE

Conference Affiliation: Southland Conference
Program Profile: Our program is only six years old. Home games are played in 1,000-seat stadium with grass field. We have good weather in the Spring, which means an exciting schedule.
History: Our program began in 1992. This is a young program which set a school record in 1994 with a 39-16 record.
Achievements: 6 seniors in 1995 are playing with the pros, 2 for the Reds, 1 for the Giants, 2 for the Cubs and 1 for the Brewers. 3 players from earlier classes have gone on to professional baseball.
Coaching: Mickey Lashley, Head Coach, was a former assistant at UT-San Antonio. David Coleman.
Style of Play: We play a contact game -- run and hit with major emphasis on pitching and defense. Rebuilding...lost ten varsity players at graduation.

University of the Incarnate Word

4301 Broadway
San Antonio, TX 78209-6397
Coach: Danny Heep

NCAA II/NAIA
Crusaders/Crimson, Grey
Phone: (210) 829-3830
Fax: (210) 805-3574

ACADEMIC

Founded: 1881
Type: 4 Yr., Private, Liberal Arts, Coed
Religion: Catholic
Campus Housing: Yes
Web-site: http://www.viwtx.edu
SAT/ACT/GPA: 840/18
Student/Faculty Ratio: 12:1
Male/Female Ratio: 1:3
Undergraduate Enrollment: 2,500
Graduate Enrollment: 500
Scholarships/Academic: Yes **Athletic:** Yes **Fin Aid:** Yes
Total Expenses by: Year **In State:** $ 15,997 **Out of State:** $ 15,997
Degrees Conferred: BA, BS, MA, MS, MBA, MED
Programs of Study: 40 undergraduate degrees in Applied Arts, Business Administration, Education, Fine Arts, Humanities, Social Sciences, Natural Science, Mathematics, Nursing

ATHLETIC PROFILE

Conference Affiliation: Heart of Texas Conference
Program Profile: We have a natural field. Spring season is in February. We play 50-game season. We do scrimmages in the Fall. We have indoor batting cage for off-season conditioning.

History: Our program dates from 1987. Our team record in 9 years has been 266-191-2. We have had only 2 losing seasons. Our best year was 1993 when went 37-13-2 and we won conference with 14-1 record. Our only other conference championship was in 1990.
Achievements: Steve Heying was named Coach of the Year in 1993; Eddie Ramon was All-American Honorable Mention; 1996 GTE All-District; Fred Lopze was named All-American; 2 Conference Titles; 4 players have been to pros.
Style of Play: Good defense, aggressive on base paths, play hit and run.

Vernon Regional Junior College

4400 College Drive
Vernon, TX 76384
Coach: Travis Walden

NJCAA
Chaparrals/Royal, White
Phone: (940) 553-1289
Fax: (940) 553-3902

ACADEMIC

Founded: 1973
Type: 2 Yr., Coed
Undergraduate Enrollment: 1,800
Campus Housing: No
Student/Faculty Ratio: 14:1
Male/Female Ratio: 15:1
Scholarships/Academic: Yes **Athletic:** Yes **Fin Aid:** Yes
Total Expenses by: Year **In State:** $ 3,200 **Out of State:** $ 3,500
Degrees Conferred: Associate
Programs of Study: Accounting, Banking/Finance, Business Administration, Communications, Dietetics, Economics, Elementary Education, English, Fine Arts, Health Education, history, Management, Marketing, Medical Therapy, Psychology, Secondary Education, Social Science

ATHLETIC PROFILE

Conference Affiliation: Region 5
Program Profile: Our facility has a lighted batting tunnel, a practice infield andcovered stands. The stadium has seating capacity of 750 and there is a dorm on site.
History: Our program began in 1987. We have been to state tournaments 4 of 8 years. Only twice have we not entered post season play.
Achievements: 24 players in NCAA Division I baseball; 10 players drafted or signed in 10 years; 12 players in Southwest Conference in 10 years.
Style of Play: Stress fundamentals, hard work, goal setting and achievement.

Wayland Baptist University

1900 W 7th St
Plainview, TX 79072
Coach: Brad Bass

NAIA
Pioneers/Blue, Gold
Phone: (806) 651-5033
Fax: (806) 651-4595

ACADEMIC

Founded: 1906
Type: 4 Yr., Private, Liberal Arts, Coed
Religion: Baptist
Campus Housing: Yes
Web-site: Not-Available
SAT/ACT/GPA: 8500/18
Student/Faculty Ratio: 13:1
Male/Female Ratio: 60:40
Undergraduate Enrollment: 1,000
Graduate Enrollment: 100
Scholarships/Academic: Yes **Athletic:** Yes **Fin Aid:** Yes
Total Expenses by: Year **In State:** $ 4,898 **Out of State:** $ 4,898
Degrees Conferred: BA, BBA, BS, MA, MBA, MB, MS
Programs of Study: Biology, Business Administration, Chemistry, Christian Studies, Composite Science, English, History, Human Services, Interdisciplinary Studies, Mass Communications

ATHLETIC PROFILE

Estimated Number of Baseball Scholarships: 3 1/2
Program Profile: Our new field should be completed for the Spring 1999 season. We are currently playing on a former minor league park. We play a 9 week Fall season and a 15 week Spring season. Our schedule includes a competition versus all levels of intercollegiate athletics. Varsity wil play approximately 60 games. Junior varsity will play approximately 30 games
History: Our program started in 1991. Jeff Livin coached for four years. The 1996 and 1997 season was coached by Bass. The program in the last two years has gone from no honored athletes to an All-American, 3 1st team All-Conference, 2 2nd team All-Conference, 1 signed with a major league (Padres), and a Coach of the Year Honors.
Achievements: The Pioneers finished 4th in the Conference in 1994. There have been 3 All-District players, 1 NAIA All-American and 1 player drafted into the major leagues. Two-time Coach of the Year 1995 and 1997, 2 former All-Americans, 1 Academic All-Americans, 2 drafted players.
Coaching: Brad Bass, Head Coach, compiled a record of 261-184 at Texas Wesleyan and also lead five teams in nine years to post-season play including Heart of Texas Conference Championship and second in Southwest Region. Terry Wiley - Assistant Coach.
Roster for 1998 team/In State: 48 **Out of State:** 18 **Out of Country:** 0
Total Number of Varsity/Jr. Varsity: 66 **Percent of Graduation:** 100%
Number of Seniors on 1998 Team: 2 **Most Recent Record:** 34 - 27 - 0
Freshmen Receiving Fin Aid/Athletic: 3 **Academic:** 10
Number of Fall Games: 0 **Number of Spring Games:** 60
Schedule: Oklahoma City State, Oklahoma Baptist, Oklahoma Christian, Southern Nazarene
Style of Play: Team is vey competitive and play hard.

West Texas A&M University

P.O. Box 49
Canyon, TX 79015
Coach: Todd Howey

NCAA II
Buffaloes/Maroon, White
Phone: (806) 656-2069
Fax: (806) 656-2688

ACADEMIC

Founded: 1910 **Type:** 4 Yr., Public, Liberal Arts, Coed
SAT/ACT/GPA: 950/20 **Campus Housing:** Yes
Student/Faculty Ratio: 18:1 **Male/Female Ratio:** 46:54
Undergraduate Enrollment: 6,600 **Graduate Enrollment:** 1,229
Scholarships/Academic: Yes **Athletic:** Yes **Fin Aid:** Yes
Total Expenses by: Year **In State:** $ 5,500 **Out of State:** $ 8,500
Degrees Conferred: BA, BS, BFA, MA, MBA, MFA, MED
Programs of Study: Accounting, Agribusiness, Communications, Computer/Information Science, Education, Egnlish, Finance, History, Marketing, Music, Nursing, Prelaw, Premed, Psychology

ATHLETIC PROFILE

Conference Affiliation: Lone Star Conference

Wharton County Junior College

911 Boling Highway
Wharton, TX 77488
Coach: Bob Nottebart

NJCAA
Pioneers/Scarlet, Grey
Phone: (409) 532-6369
Fax: (409) 532-6584

ACADEMIC

Founded: 1946 **Type:** 2 Yr., Jr. College, Coed
Religion: Non-Affiliated **Campus Housing:** No

Undergraduate Enrollment: 3,958
Student/Faculty Ratio: 17:1
Total Expenses by: Year **In State:** $ 884+ **Out of State:** $ 2,682+
Degrees Conferred: Associate
Programs of Study: Contact school for program of study.

ATHLETIC PROFILE

Conference Affiliation: Inter-Regional

Wiley College

711 Wiley Avenue
Marshall, TX 75670
Coach: Eddie Watson

NAIA
Wildcats/Purple, White
Phone: (903) 927-3292
Fax: (903) 938-8100

ACADEMIC

Founded: 1873
Type: 4 Yr., Private, Liberal Arts, Coed
Religion: Methodist
Campus Housing: No
Total Expenses by: Year **In State:** $ 7,694 **Out of State:** $ 7,694
Degrees Conferred: AA, BA, BS
Programs of Study: Biological Science, Business Administration, Chemistry, Communications, Cxomputer Science, Education, English, Hotel/RestaurantManagement, Music, Music Performance, Office Management, Phiolosophy, Physics, Religion, Social Science, Special Education

ATHLETIC PROFILE

Conference Affiliation: Interregional Conference

UTAH

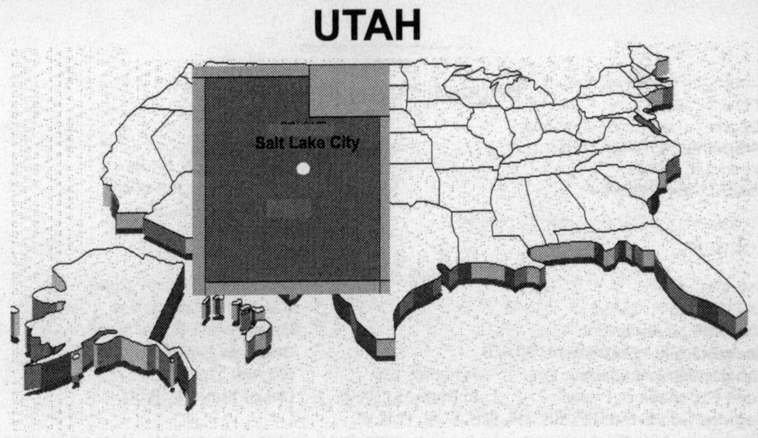

SCHOOL	CITY	AFFILIATION 99	PAGE
Brigham Young University	Provo	NCAA	864
College of Eastern Utah	Price	NJCAA	864
Dixie College	St George	NJCAA	865
Snow College	Ephraim	NJCAA	865
Southern Utah University	Cedar City	NCAA I	865
University of Utah	Salt Lake City	NCAA I	866
Utah Valley State College	Orem	NJCAA	867

Brigham Young University

54 Smithfield House BYU
Provo, UT 84602
Coach: Gary Pullins

NCAA
Cougars/Blue, White
Phone: (801) 378-5049
Fax: (801) 378-5656

ACADEMIC

Founded: 1876
Type: 4 Yr., Private, Coed
SAT/ACT/GPA: 26/3.3
Campus Housing: Yes
Student/Faculty Ratio:
Male/Female Ratio: 50:50
Undergraduate Enrollment: 30,000
Graduate Enrollment: 2,500
Scholarships/Academic: Yes **Athletic:** Yes **Fin Aid:** Yes
Total Expenses by: Year **In State:** $ 10,000 **Out of State:** $ 10,000
Degrees Conferred: BA, BS, MA, MS, EDD, PhD, JD
Programs of Study: Accounting, Advertising, Agriculture, Animal, Anthropology, Banking/Finance, Biology, Botany, Broadcasting, Manufacturing, Medical, Cartography, Ceramic, Engineering, Clothing/Textiles, Geography, Entomology, Fashion, Food, Humanities, International, Nursing, Nutrition, Philosophy, Psychology, Natural Resources, Special Education, Speech, Sports Medicine

ATHLETIC PROFILE

Estimated Number of Baseball Scholarships: 11.7
Conference Affiliation: Western Athletic Conference
Program Profile: Fall program for tryouts, indoor astroturf field, hitting cages, pitching mounds, stadium seats 2,500, strength training complex.
History: Long standing since the 1920's. BYU has been a major college program since 1942.
Achievements: CWS Appearances in 1968 and 1971; Regionals in 1974, 1981, 1983, 1985, 1988, 1991, and 1994. WAC Champions in 1968, 1971, 1979, 1981, 1983, 1985, 1988, and 1994; Divisional Champs in 1967- 1985, 1987, 1993, 1994, 1995, and 1996.
Coaching: Gary Pullins, Head Coach, has been at BYU 19 years. Bob Noel, Pitching Coach, full-time pitching coach since 1980.
Roster for 1998 team/In State: 10 **Out of State:** 12 **Out of Country:**
Total Number of Varsity/Jr. Varsity: 35 **Percent of Graduation:** 75%
Number of Seniors on 1998 Team: 4 **Number of Sophomores on 1998 Team:** 12
Freshmen Receiving Fin Aid/Athletic: 12 **Academic:** 3
Number of Fall Games: 0 **Number of Spring Games:** 56+
Schedule: ASU, Oklahoma, Rice, Fresno State, Hawaii, TCU
Style of Play: Uptempo - power game.

College of Eastern Utah

451 East 400 North
Price, UT 84501
Coach: Erik Madsen

NJCAA
Golden Eagles/Navy, Gold
Phone: (435) 637-2120
Fax: (435) 637-4102

ACADEMIC

Founded: 1937
Type: 2 Yr., Public, Coed
Undergraduate Enrollment: 2,850
Campus Housing: Yes
Student/Faculty Ratio: 23:1
Male/Female Ratio: 52:48
Scholarships/Academic: No **Athletic:** Yes **Fin Aid:** Yes
Total Expenses by: Year **In State:** $ 3,800 **Out of State:** $ 6,000
Degrees Conferred: Associate
Programs of Study: Business Administration, Cosmetology, Liberal Arts, Machine/Tool Technology, Mining Technology, Nursing, Office Management, Automotive Technology, Computer Graphics, Construction Technology, Early Childhood Education, Preengineering, Liberal Arts, General Studies

Dixie College

225 South 700 East
St George, UT 84770
Coach: Mike Littlewood

NJCAA
Rebels/Red, Grey
Phone: (435) 652-7530
Fax: (435) 673-8552

ACADEMIC

Founded: 1911
Type: 2 Yr., Public, , Coed,
Student/Faculty Ratio: 16:2
Campus Housing: Yes
Undergraduate Enrollment: 2,550
Graduate Enrollment: None
Scholarships/Academic: No **Athletic:** Yes **Fin Aid:** Yes
Total Expenses by: Year **In State:** $ 5,000 **Out of State:** $ 8,500
Degrees Conferred: Associate
Programs of Study: Accounting, Aircraft/Missile Maintenance, Architectural, Automotive Technology, Aviation, Biological Science, Computer Construction, Criminal Justice, Technology, Dental Services, Drafting/Design, Economics, Education, Medical Flight Training, Food Services, Forestry, Geography, Geology, Health, History, Humanities, Range Management, Speech, Travel

ATHLETIC PROFILE

Conference Affiliation: SWAC

Snow College

150 College Avenue
Ephraim, UT 84627
Coach: Robert Andersen

NJCAA
Badgers/Blue, White
Phone: (801) 283-4021
Fax: (801) 283-7429

ACADEMIC

Founded: 1888
Type: 2 Yr., Public, Coed
Student/Faculty Ratio: 20:1
Campus Housing: Yes
Undergraduate Enrollment: 2,400
Graduate Enrollment: None
Scholarships/Academic: No **Athletic:** No **Fin Aid:** Yes
Total Expenses by: Year **In State:** $ 4,500 **Out of State:** $ 7,900
Degrees Conferred: Associate
Programs of Study: Accounting, Agricultural, Agronomy, Animal, Automotive Technology, Biological Science, Botany, Business, Chemistry, Child Care/Family Studies, Communications, Computer, Construction, Criminal Justice, Earth Science, Economics, Entomology, Farm/Ranch, Forestry, Geography, Geology, Humanities, Natural Resources, Physics, Range, Social Science, Soil Consevation, Theatre, Voice, Wildlife

ATHLETIC PROFILE

Conference Affiliation: ICAC

Southern Utah University

351 West Center
Cedar City, UT 84720
Coach: DeLynn Corry

NCAA I
Thunderbirds/Red, Royal, White
Phone: (435) 586-1937
Fax: (435) 586-5444

ACADEMIC

Founded: 1897
Type: 4 Yr., Public, Liberal Arts, Coed
Religion: Non-Affiliated
Campus Housing: No

Web-site: Not Available
SAT/ACT/GPA: 21 avg
Student/Faculty Ratio: 22:1
Male/Female Ratio: 45:55
Undergraduate Enrollment: 4,985
Graduate Enrollment: 35
Scholarships/Academic: Yes **Athletic:** Yes **Fin Aid:** Yes
Total Expenses by: Year **In State:** $ 3,300 **Out of State:** $ 7,152
Degrees Conferred: AA, AS, AAS, BA, BS, MED
Programs of Study: Accounting, Agricultural Science, Art, Automotive, Biological, Botany, Business, Carpentry, Chemistry, Child Care, Communications, Computer, Constructions, Criminal, Dance, Drafting/Design, Economics, Education, English, Family, Geology, Geography, History, Interior, Math, Music, Physical Education, Political Science, Psychology, Secondary Education, Social Science, Sociology, Spanish, Special Education, Speech, Theatre, Zoology

ATHLETIC PROFILE

Conference Affiliation: Independent
History: The program was killed in 1989. This is our first year with double digits since reinstatement.
Achievements: Bill Groves was RMAC Coach of the Year in 1985-1986; 15 players drafted; most recent was Ryan Sensen, taken by San Francisco in the 8th round of the 1996 draft; 5 RMAC Titles.

University of Utah

Jon M Huntsman Ctr
Salt Lake City, UT 84112
Coach: Tim Esmay
NCAA I
Utes/Red, White
Phone: (801) 581-3526
Fax: (801) 585-6453

ACADEMIC

Founded: 1850
Type: 4 Yr., Public, Liberal Arts, Coed
Religion: Non-Affiliated
Campus Housing: Yes
Web-site: http://www.utah.edu
SAT/ACT/GPA: 700/23
Student/Faculty Ratio: 21:1
Male/Female Ratio: 54:46
Undergraduate Enrollment: 26,359
Graduate Enrollment: $ 4,800
Scholarships/Academic: Yes **Athletic:** Yes **Fin Aid:** Yes
Total Expenses by: Year **In State:** $ 7,937 **Out of State:** $ 13,334
Degrees Conferred: BA, BS, MS, MBA, MFA
Programs of Study: Accounting, Anthropology, Architecture, Art, Atmospheric Science, Meteorology, Banking/Finance, Biological Science, Chemistry, Classics, Communications, Computer, Geological, Geology, Linguistics, Medical, Mining, Nursing, Pharmacy, Physics, Psychology

ATHLETIC PROFILE

Conference Affiliation: Western Athletics Conference
Program Profile: Program is on the rise, set school record for win last season. Won North Division of WAC 1st place for the first time in 32 years. Have indoor football field and cages in PE Complex. Season begins in January 30th in Los Angeles and Loyola Marymount. Have on campus practice field. Play home games in four year AAA Minnesota Twins Park (Franklin Quostfield) that has a seating capacity of 16,000 people. One of the best college baseball fields in America.
History: Began in 1962 - had only one first place finish untill 1997.
Achievements: Conference (North-Davis) WAC Champions; 7 all was play in the last two years; 2 All-Americans in 1997 (1 freshman), 4 All-Americans on 1998 squad (2 Juco AM).
Coaching: Tim Esmay, Head Coach, played Arizona State, coached ASU and Grand Canyon University. Played twice in College World Series and coached in College World Series. John Flores, Pitching Coach, played at Grand Canyon, coached at Grand Canyon University. Todd Ddnuce, played at Arizona State, played in two CWS's, coached at Arizona State.
Style of Play: Very aggressive, hit the ball in the gaps. Had two sac bunts in 1997. Play hard; run through the walls. Work harder than everyone else.

Utah Valley State College

1200 South 800 West
Orem, UT 84058
Coach: Steve Gardner

NJCAA
Wolverines/Dk Green, Gold, White
Phone: (801) 222-8647
Fax: (801) 222-8813

ACADEMIC

Founded: 1941
Type: 2 Yr., Public, Coed
Web-site: http://www.uvsc.edu
Campus Housing: No
Undergraduate Enrollment: 14,756
Student/Faculty Ratio: 22:1
Total Expenses by: Year **In State:** $ 1,194 **Out of State:** $ 4,329+
Degrees Conferred: Associate
Programs of Study: Computer Graphics, Computer Informations Systems, Construction Management, Construction Technology, Hotel and Restaurant Management, Music, Nursing, Retail Management, Office Management

VERMONT

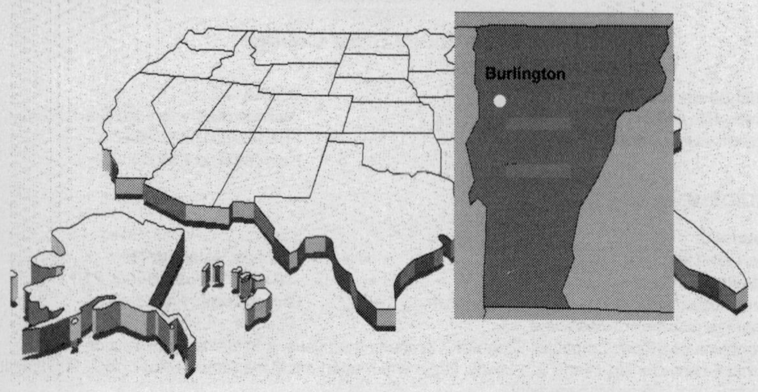

SCHOOL	CITY	AFFILIATION 99	PAGE
Castleton State College	Castleton	NCAA III\NAIA	869
Lyndon State College	Lyndonville	NAIA	869
Middlebury College	Middlebury	NCAA III	869
Norwich University	Northfield	NCAA III	870
Saint Michael's College	Colchester	NCAA II	871
Southern Vermont College	Bennington	NCAA III	871
University of Vermont	Burlington	NCAA I	872
Vermont Technical College	Randolph Center	NJCAA/NSCAA	872

Castleton State College

1 Seminary Street
Castleton, VT 05735
Coach: Jeff Lusk

NCAA III\NAIA
Spartans/Green, White
Phone: (802) 468-5611
Fax: (802) 468-2189

ACADEMIC

Founded: 1787
Type: 4 Yr., Public, Liberal Arts, Coed
Religion: Non-Affiliated
Campus Housing: Yes
Web-site: http://www.csc.vsc.edu/
SAT/ACT/GPA: 860/18
Student/Faculty Ratio: 18:1
Male/Female Ratio: 48:52
Undergraduate Enrollment: 1,543
Graduate Enrollment: 193
Scholarships/Academic: Yes **Athletic:** No **Fin Aid:** Yes
Total Expenses by: Year **In State:** $ 8,946+ **Out of State:** $ 13,458+
Degrees Conferred: AA, AS, ASN, BA, BS, BSW, MA
Programs of Study: Art, Business Administration, Accounting, Finance, Management, Marketing, Communications, Journalism, Mass Media, Computer Information Systems, Criminal Justice, Education, History, Literature, Math, Music, Biology, Geology, General Science, Physical Education, Psychology, Social Work, Sociology, Theatre Arts

ATHLETIC PROFILE

Conference Affiliation: Mayflower Conference

Lyndon State College

55 Vail Hill
Lyndonville, VT 05851
Coach: Darrell Pound

NAIA
Hornets/Green, White, Gold
Phone: (802) 626-9371
Fax: (802) 626-9770

ACADEMIC

Founded: 1911
Type: 4 Yr., Public, Liberal Arts, Coed
Religion: Non-Affiliated
Campus Housing: No
Web-site: http://www.lsc.vsc.edu/
SAT/ACT/GPA: 800+
Student/Faculty Ratio: 17:1
Male/Female Ratio: 55:45
Undergraduate Enrollment: 1,100
Graduate Enrollment: 70
Scholarships/Academic: Yes **Athletic:** No **Fin Aid:** Yes
Total Expenses by: Year **In State:** $ 9,000 **Out of State:** $ 12,900
Degrees Conferred: AA, AS, BA, BS, Med
Programs of Study: Accounting, Atmospheric Science, Behavioral Science, Biology, Business Administration, Communications, Computer Science, Education, English, Environmental Science, Humanities, Interdisciplinary Studies, Journalism, Liberal Arts, Managment, Mathematics, Meteorology, Natural Science, Parks, Physical Education, Psychology, Radio and Television, Recreation and Leisure, Social Science, Spanish, Special Education, Sports Management

ATHLETIC PROFILE

Conference Affiliation: Mayflower Conference

Middlebury College

Memorial Fieldhouse
Middlebury, VT 05753
Coach: Bob Smith

NCAA III
Panthers/Maroon, White
Phone: (802) 443-5364
Fax: (802) 443-2073

ACADEMIC

Founded: 1800
Type: 4 Yr., Private, Liberal Arts, Coed,
Religion: Non-Affiliated
Campus Housing: Yes
Web-site: http://www.middlebury.edu/
SAT/ACT/GPA: 1200+
Student/Faculty Ratio: 11:1
Male/Female Ratio: 50:50
Undergraduate Enrollment: 2,000
Graduate Enrollment: None
Scholarships/Academic: Yes **Athletic:** No **Fin Aid:** Yes
Total Expenses by: Year **In State:** $ 27,500 **Out of State:** $ 27,500
Degrees Conferred: BA, BS
Programs of Study: American Civilization, American Literature, Art, Biology, Chemistry and Biochemistry, Chinese, Classical Studies, French, Geography, Geology, German, History, Independent Scholar, International Studies, Japanese, Literary Studies, Mathematics, Molecular Biology and Biochemistry, Music, Philosophy, Physics, Political Science, Prelaw, Premed, Sociology-Anthropology, Spanish, Theatre-Dance and Film/Video, Women's Studies

ATHLETIC PROFILE

Estimated Number of Baseball Scholarships: 12
Conference Affiliation: New England Small College Athletic Conference
Program Profile: Our stadium has lights, natural surface field. Our team plays a 55 game schedule, NAIA-NCAA II opponents; season runs from mid-February through May.
History: Started in 1967 with a record of 607-468; 12 Conference Champions; playoffs 18 times.
Achievements: District Coach of the Year in 1984, Conference Coach of the Year 12 times; 12 Conference Titles; four draftees, 1 All-American; 1 Academic All-American.
Coaching: Bob Smith, Head Coach, enters his 20th season on the Middlebury staff and his 15th season at the helm of the baseball program. He also served as an assistant football coach at the college from 1979 to 1994, and he currently director of the physical education, club sports, and intramural programs at Middlebury. In 1998 he received the "Edward P. Markey Award" given by St. Michael's College to the person who has made outstanding contributions to Vermont collegiate baseball.
Roster for 1998 team/In State: 16 **Out of State:** 8 **Out of Country:** 1
Total Number of Varsity/Jr. Varsity: 25 **Percent of Graduation:** 78%
Number of Seniors on 1998 Team: 9 **Most Recent Record:** 24 - 23 - 0
Freshmen Receiving Fin Aid/Athletic: 10 **Academic:** 4
Number of Fall Games: 6 **Number of Spring Games:** 54
Positions Needed for 1999/2000: Catcher, Shortstop, Pitcher, Center Field
Schedule: Bellevue, Kansas Newman, Avila, Lindenwood, Harding, Mid-America Nazarene
Style of Play: Steal, hit and run, double steal, and bunt. Aggressive on the bases, capitalized on defensive. Lapses - get on base anyway you can, move into scoring position and get the run in.

Norwich University

Main Street
Northfield, VT 05663
Coach: Paul Booth

NCAA III
Cadets/Maroon, White
Phone: (802) 485-2230
Fax: (802) 485-2234

ACADEMIC

Founded: 1819
Type: 4 Yr., Private, Coed, Engineering
Religion: Non-Affiliated
Campus Housing: Yes
Web-site: http://www.norwich.edu/
SAT/ACT/GPA: 2.0
Student/Faculty Ratio: 14:1
Male/Female Ratio: 65:35
Undergraduate Enrollment: 1,400
Graduate Enrollment: 800
Scholarships/Academic: Yes **Athletic:** No **Fin Aid:** Yes
Total Expenses by: Year **In State:** **Out of State:** $ 20,773
Degrees Conferred: AA, AS, BA, BS, MA, MFA

Programs of Study: Accounting, Architecture, Biology, Business and Management, Chemistry, Civil Engineering, Communications, Computer Engineering, Computer Science, Criminal Justice, Earth Science, Economics, Electrical Engineering, English, Environmental Engineering, Environmental Science, History, Management, Mathematics, Medical Technology, Military Science, History, Naval Science, Nursing, Physical Education, Physics, Political Science, Premed, Psychology, Secondary Education, Sports Medicine

ATHLETIC PROFILE

Program Profile: Play home games at Garrity Field, capacity 500.
Achievements: Coach Booth guided the Cadets to a 12-10 mark in his initial season, the most victories by a Cadet baseball team in nine years.
Coaching: Paul Booth, Head Coach, since 1993 to the present, led Norwich to a 12-10 mark in his initail season, serves as a head coach at Thomas College.
Style of Play: We'd like to improve on what we did last year; we've got off to a slow start; we want to start strong and finish strong.

Saint Michael's College

Winooski Park
Colchester, VT 05439
Coach: Perry Bove

NCAA II
Knights/Purple, Gold
Phone: (802) 654-2500
Fax: (802) 654-2497

ACADEMIC

Founded: 1904
Type: 4 Yr., Private, Liberal Arts, Coed
Religion: Catholic
Campus Housing: Yes
Web-site: http://www.smcvt.edu/
SAT/ACT/GPA: 1000+
Student/Faculty Ratio: 14:1
Male/Female Ratio: 50:50
Undergraduate Enrollment: 1,700
Graduate Enrollment: 200
Scholarships/Academic: No **Athletic:** No **Fin Aid:** 60% student pop. rec
Total Expenses by: Year **In State:** $ 21,160 **Out of State:** $ 21,160
Degrees Conferred: BA, BS, MA, MS, MED
Programs of Study: Accounting, American Studies, Biochemistry, Biology, Business Administration, Chemistry , Computer Science, Economics, Elementary Education, Engineering

ATHLETIC PROFILE

Conference Affiliation: ECAC, NorthEast 10 Conference

Southern Vermont College

Monument Avenue Ext
Bennington, VT 05201
Coach: Scott McKenzie

NCAA III
Mountaineers/Dk Green, White
Phone: (802) 422-5427
Fax: (802) 442-5529

ACADEMIC

Founded: 1926
Type: 4 Yr., Private, Liberal Arts, Coed
Undergraduate Enrollment: 641
Campus Housing: Yes
Student/Faculty Ratio: 16:1
Male/Female Ratio: 1:1
Scholarships/Academic: No **Athletic:** No **Fin Aid:** Yes
Total Expenses by: Year **In State:** $ 16,100 **Out of State:** $ 16,100
Degrees Conferred: AA, BA, BS, AS, AND
Programs of Study: Accounting, Business Management, Communications, Criminal Justice, Child Development, Child Care Management, English, Environmental Studies, Gerontology

University of Vermont

194 S Prospect Street
Burlington, VT 05401
Coach: Bill Currier

NCAA I
Catamounts/Green, Gold
Phone: (802) 656-7701
Fax: (802) 656-0949

ACADEMIC

Founded: 1791
Religion: Non-Affiliated
Web-site: http://www.uvm.edu/
Student/Faculty Ratio: 15:1
Undergraduate Enrollment: 7,500
Scholarships/Academic: Yes **Athletic:** Yes
Total Expenses by: Year **In State:** $ 12,491

Type: 4 Yr., Public, Liberal Arts, Coed
Campus Housing: Yes
SAT/ACT/GPA: 1050+
Male/Female Ratio: 48:52
Graduate Enrollment: 2,000
Fin Aid: Yes
Out of State: $ 22,187

Degrees Conferred: AS, BA, BS, MA, MS, MBA, MED, PhD, MD
Programs of Study: Business, Computer Science, Accounting, Art, Biology, Agriculture, Anthropology, Botany, Broadcasting, Ecology, Chemistry, Engineering, Geography, Geology

ATHLETIC PROFILE

Conference Affiliation: America East Conference
Program Profile: Centennial Field has been upgraded and is now greatly improved.
Achievements: 1995 ranked third in the nation and third in the NorthEast.
Coaching: Bill Currier, Head Coach, tenth year at Vermont.

Vermont Technical College

Baseball Office
Randolph Center, VT 05061
Coach: Ted Shipley
Email: tshipley@night.vtc.vsc.edu

NJCAA/NSCAA
Knights/Green, Grey
Phone: (802) 728-1382
Fax: (802) 728-1390

ACADEMIC

Founded: 1866
Undergraduate Enrollment: 855
Web-site: http://www.vtc.vsc.edu
Student/Faculty Ratio: 10:1
Scholarships/Academic: Yes **Athletic:** No
Total Expenses by: Year **In State:** $ 10,833

Type: 2 Yr., Public, Coed, Engineering
Campus Housing: Yes
SAT/ACT/GPA: No minimum/
Male/Female Ratio: 2:1
Fin Aid: Yes
Out of State: $ 15,194

Degrees Conferred: AS, AAS, AE, BA, Certificate Programs
Programs of Study: Accounting, Agribusiness Management, Architectural and Building Engineering, Automotive Technology, Biotechnology, Business Technology, Civil and Environmental Engineering, Computer Engineering, Construction Practice and Management, Dairy Farm Management, Electrical

ATHLETIC PROFILE

Conference Affiliation: Nothern New England Small College Conference
Program Profile: "NSCAA" fall baseball program with 20 games in the fall and 10-15 in the spring. Natural grass diamond, outdoor bullpens and batting cages.
Achievements: Conference Champs in 1996; Regular Season Champs in 1997; Coach of the Year in 1996 and 1997.
Coaching: Ted Shipley, Head Coach, Lyndon State College (1986), All-Conference player; Athlete of the Year. Also was a player and a coach in semi pro league which enable Coach Shipley to work with many Division I players. In addition, coached at the Maine, high school and college level. John Scoskie, Assistant Coach, graduate of Maine, Orono in 1991, works with the pitchers. He is young and energetic staff that focused on positively teaching quality baseball.
Roster for 1998 team/In State: 11 **Out of State:** 4 **Out of Country:** 0

Total Number of Varsity/Jr. Varsity: 15
Percent of Graduation: 100%
Number of Seniors on 1998 Team: 5
Most Recent Record: 35 - 5 - 0
Freshmen Receiving Fin Aid/Athletic: 0
Academic: 8
Number of Fall Games: 20
Number of Spring Games: 10
Positions Needed for 1999/2000: Shortstop, Catcher, Pitchers
Schedule: St. Michael's, Castleton, Fulton Montgomey, Southern Maine, Colby Sawyer, Bunker Hill
Style of Play: Basic fundamentals, aggressive offensively, power hitting.

VIRGINIA

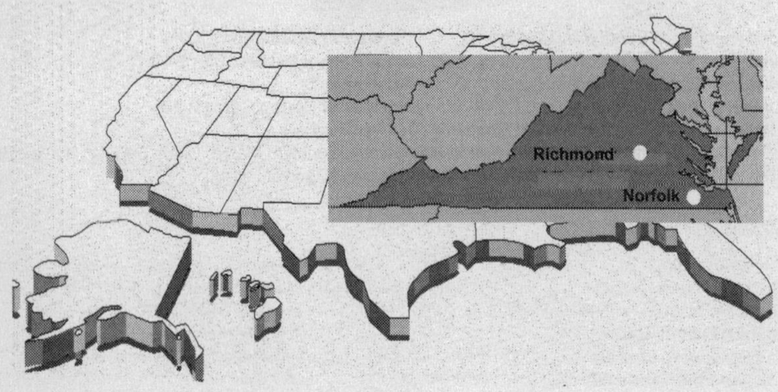

SCHOOL	CITY	AFFILIATION 99	PAGE
Averett College	Danville	NCAA III	875
Bluefield College	Bluefield	NAIA	875
Bridgewater College	Bridgewater	NCAA III	876
Christopher Newport University	Newport News	NCAA III	876
Clinch Valley College	Wise	NAIA	877
College of William and Mary	Williamsburg	NCAA I	877
Eastern Mennonite College	Harrisonburg	NCAA III	878
Emory and Henry College	Emory	NCAA III	879
Ferrum University	Ferrum	NCAA III	879
George Mason University	Fairfax	NCAA I	880
Hampden - Sydney College	Hampden-Sydney	NCAA III	880
James Madison University	Harrisonburg	NCAA I	881
Liberty University	Lynchburg	NCAA I	882
Longwood College	Farmville	NCAA II	883
Lynchburg College	Lynchburg	NCAA III	883
Mary Washington College	Fredericksburg	NCAA III	884
Norfolk State University	Norfolk	NCAA I	884
Old Dominion University	Norfolk	NCAA I	885
Radford University	Radford	NCAA I	886
Randolp - Macon College	Ashland	NCAA III	887
Saint Paul's College	Lawrenceville	NCAA II	887
Shenandoah University	Winchester	NCAA III	887
University of Richmond	Richmond	NCAA I	888
University of Virginia	Charlottesville	NCAA I	889
Virginia Commonwealth University	Richmond	NCAA I	890
Virginia Intermont College	Bristol	NAIA	890
Virginia Military Institute	Lexington	NCAA I	891
Virginia State University	Petersburg	NCAA II	891
VA Poly Institute & State University	Blacksburg	NCAA I	892
Virginia Wesleyan College	Norfolk	NCAA III	892
Washington and Lee University	Lexington	NCAA III	893

Averett College

420 W Main Street
Danville, VA 24541
Coach: Edward Fulton

NCAA III
Cougars/Blue, Gold
Phone: (804) 791-5759
Fax: (804) 791-5740

ACADEMIC

Founded: 1859
Religion: Virginia Baptist
Web-site: http://www.averett.edu/
Student/Faculty Ratio: 14:1
Undergraduate Enrollment: 1,000
Scholarships/Academic: Yes **Athletic:** No
Total Expenses by: Year **In State:** $ 16,800
Type: 4 Yr., Private, Liberal Arts, Coed
Campus Housing: Yes
SAT/ACT/GPA: 800
Male/Female Ratio: 1:3
Graduate Enrollment: 100
Fin Aid: Yes
Out of State: Varies
Degrees Conferred: AS, AA, BA, BS, BAS, BBA, MAT
Programs of Study: Accounting, Art, Art Education, Art History, Athletic Training, Aviation Administration, Biblical Studies, Biochemistry, Biological Science, Business, Chemistry

ATHLETIC PROFILE

Conference Affiliation: Dixie Conference
Program Profile: We began our fourth season in 1998 and play in one of the strongest Division III conferences in America, the Dixie Conference. Our home games next season will be played at Legion Field, home of the Appalachian League Danville Braves, which won the minor league award in 1995 for have the best rookie league park in America.
History: 1995 marked the beginning of Averett College baseball. The Cougars started by playing a junior college schedule. In 1996 we will play a complete Division III schedule and will enter conference play in the Dixie Conference.
Style of Play: We play an aggressive game and stress team offense advancing runners with the stolen bases and hit and run.

Bluefield College

3000 College Drive
Bluefield, VA 24605
Coach: Ashley Lawson

NAIA
Ramblin' Rams/Royal, Red, White
Phone: (540) 326-3682
Fax: (540) 326-4288

ACADEMIC

Founded: 1919
Web-site: http://www.bluefield.edu
Student/Faculty Ratio: 16:1
Undergraduate Enrollment: 725
Scholarships/Academic: Yes **Athletic:** Yes
Total Expenses by: Year **In State:** $ 13,810
Type: 4 Yr., Private, Liberal Arts, Coed
SAT/ACT/GPA: 860/18
Male/Female Ratio: 50:50
Religion: Baptist
Fin Aid: Yes
Out of State: $ 13,810
Degrees Conferred: Baccalaureate and Associate Degrees
Programs of Study: Business, Education, Fine Arts, Health, Physical Education, Recreation, Humanities, Science, Social Sciences, Art, Biological Science, Mathematics, Music, Ministries

ATHLETIC PROFILE

Conference Affiliation: Tennesse - Virginia Athletic Conference
Program Profile: NAIA 58-game schedule from the last week of February to the middle of May. Play at Bowen Field, home of the Bluefield Orioles, rookie league team of the Baltimore Orioles. The field is natural grass and the stadium seats 4000, has professional quality scoreboard, bullpens, clubhouses and other facilities.

History: The current program was started in 1978. The Rams have won over 100 games in the '90s, including a conference championship. In 1990 and 1991, they won more games than any other Virginia college, including Division I universities.
Achievements: Won the TVAC Title in 1990; in the 1990's have several All-Conference and All-Region players with 1 player being drafted by the Chicago Cubs.

Bridgewater College

404 East College Street
Bridgewater, VA 22812
Coach: Curt Kendall

NCAA III
Eagles/Red, Gold
Phone: (540) 828-5407
Fax: (540) 828-5484

ACADEMIC

Founded: 1880
Type: 4 Yr., Private, Liberal Arts, Coed
Religion: Church of the Brethren
Campus Housing: Yes
Web-site: http://www.bridgewater.edu/
Undergraduate Enrollment: 1,050
Student/Faculty Ratio: 15:1
Male/Female Ratio: 45:55
Scholarships/Academic: Yes **Athletic:** No **Fin Aid:** Yes
Total Expenses by: Year **In State:** $ 19,980 **Out of State:** $ 19,980
Degrees Conferred: BA, BS
Programs of Study: Accounting, Art, Athletic Training, Biological Science, Business Administration, Chemistry, Computer Science, Early Childhood Education, Economics, Elementary Education, English, French, German, Health Science, History, International Studies, Management, Mathematics, Medical Technology, Music, Music Education, Philosophy, Physical Education, Physical Science, Physics, Political Science, Predental, Prelaw, Premed, Prevet, Psychology, Religion, Science

ATHLETIC PROFILE

Conference Affiliation: Old Dominion Athletic Conference

Christopher Newport University

50 Shoe Lane
Newport News, VA 23606-2998
Coach: Curt Long

NCAA III
Captains/Royal, Silver
Phone: (757) 594-7054
Fax: (757) 594-7839

ACADEMIC

Founded: 1960
Type: 4 Yr., Public, Liberal Arts, Coed
Web-site: http://www.cnu.edu/
SAT/ACT/GPA: 480v/440m
Student/Faculty Ratio: 18:1
Male/Female Ratio: 41:51
Undergraduate Enrollment: 4,500
Graduate Enrollment: 100
Scholarships/Academic: Yes **Athletic:** No **Fin Aid:** Yes
Total Expenses by: Year **In State:** $ 8,516 **Out of State:** $ 13,136
Degrees Conferred: BA, BS, BM, BSA, BSBA, BSGA, BSIS, BSN, MAT, MS, MSN
Programs of Study: Accounting, Applied Physics, Art, Biology, Computer Engineering, Computer Science, Criminal Justice Administration, Economics, English, Finance, Fitness Management, French, German, History, Horticulture, Psychology, International Administration, International Culture and Commerce, International Relations, Japanese, Latin American Studies, Legal Studies, Managment, Marketing, Mathematics, Music, Music Composition, Music History, Music Theatre, Nursing, Philosophy, Political Science, Psychological Technology, Public Management, Recreation and Liesure Studies, Religious Studies, Social Work, Sociology, Spanish, Theatre Arts, Writing

ATHLETIC PROFILE

Conference Affiliation: DIAC

Clinch Valley College

1 College Avenue
Wise, VA 24293
Coach: Hank Banner

NAIA
Cavaliers/Red, Grey
Phone: (540) 328-0206
Fax: (540) 376-1023

ACADEMIC

Founded: 1954
Type: 4 Yr., Public, Liberal Arts, Coed
Web-site: Not Available
SAT/ACT/GPA: 1000+
Student/Faculty Ratio: 17:1
Male/Female Ratio: 2:3
Undergraduate Enrollment: Unknown
Graduate Enrollment: $ 1,200
Scholarships/Academic: Yes **Athletic:** Yes **Fin Aid:** Yes
Total Expenses by: Year **In State:** $ 7,952 **Out of State:** $ 7,952
Degrees Conferred: BA, BS
Programs of Study: Accounting, Biological, Communications, Dramatic Arts, Economics, Education, Information Science, Marketing, Mathematics, Medical, Music, Political Science, Prelaw

ATHLETIC PROFILE

Estimated Number of Baseball Scholarships: 4.5
Conference Affiliation: Tennessee - Virginia Athletic Conference
Program Profile: Solid small college program. Play a 40 game Spring season with a Florida Spring trip. Six week Fall program; natural turf playing field. Very nice indoor facilities and weight rooms.
History: Been very competitive for the past 15 years. CVU won 2 Championships in 1989 and 1990.
Achievements: Ray Spenilla Coach of the Year in 1989 & 1990; KIAC Champions in '89 & '90; All-Americans - Bill Higgins and Mike White; drafted were Bill Higgins, Nelson Metheney & Sean Brown.
Style of Play: We are a fundamental sound team that likes to manufacture runs. Rely on sound defense and good pitching. Good team speed and players who play extremely hard and have good baseball swing.

College of William and Mary

P.O. Box 399
Williamsburg, VA 23187
Coach: Jim Farr

NCAA I
Tribe/Green
Phone: (757) 221-3399
Fax: (757) 221-3412

ACADEMIC

Founded: 1693
Type: 4 Yr., Public, Liberal Arts, Coed
Religion: Multi-Denominational
Campus Housing: Yes
Web-site: http://www.wm.edu/
SAT/ACT/GPA: Varies
Student/Faculty Ratio: 12:1
Male/Female Ratio: 46:54
Undergraduate Enrollment: 5,300
Graduate Enrollment: 1,000
Scholarships/Academic: Few **Athletic:** Yes **Fin Aid:** Limited
Total Expenses by: Year **In State:** $ 9,750 **Out of State:** $ 19,500
Degrees Conferred: BA, BSC, BBA
Programs of Study: American Studies, Anthropology, Art Administration, Art History, Biology, Business, Chemistry, Computer Science, Economics, English, Geology, Kinesiology, Mathematics, Music, Philosophy, Physics, Psychology, Public Policy, Religion, Sociology, Theatre

ATHLETIC PROFILE

Conference Affiliation: Colonial Athletic Association

Program Profile: Stadium has a seating capacity of 1,200 will be ready in the Fall of 1998 and is a natural grass. Rising program under Coach Jim Farr. Located in SouthEastern Virginia, the climate is conducive to year-round play. For inclement weather, the Tribe has excellent facilities, including covered mound, batting cages, as well as an enclosed practice facility. Play 50-game plus season in the tough CAA conference.
History: 1997 record was 30 wins surpassed school record of 24 which had been tied 3 of the past 4 years.
Achievements: Coach of the Year in 1993; Rookie of the Year in 1997 - Catcher Brian Robers; All-Conference - Randy Lee - LHP/OF.
Coaching: Jim Farr, Head Coach, graduate of Penn State in 1978. John Cole, Assistant Coach, graduate of Ithaca College in 1986. Marlin Ikenberry,Assistant Coach, VMI in 1995.
Style of Play: Pitching - defense oriented; aggressive on the bases.

Eastern Mennonite College

1200 Park Road
Harrisonburg, VA 22802
Coach: Rob Roeschley
Email: roeschrd@emu.edu

NCAA III
Royals/Royal Blue, White
Phone: (540) 432-4333
Fax: (540) 432-4443

ACADEMIC

Founded: 1917
Type: 4 Yr., Private, Liberal Arts, Coed
Religion: Mennonite
Campus Housing: Yes
Web-site: http://www.emu.edu/
SAT/ACT/GPA: 880/19/2.0
Student/Faculty Ratio: 13:1
Male/Female Ratio: 40:60
Undergraduate Enrollment: 970
Graduate Enrollment: 290
Scholarships/Academic: Yes **Athletic:** No **Fin Aid:** Yes
Total Expenses by: Year **In State:** $ 17,700 **Out of State:** $ 17,700
Degrees Conferred: BA, BS, MA, Mdiv
Programs of Study: Accounting, Biology, Business and Management, Chemistry, Computer Science, Education, Health Sciences, Psychology, Letters/Literature, Life Sciences, Multi/Interdisciplinary Studies, Nursing, Philosophy, Premed, Protective Services, Public Affairs

ATHLETIC PROFILE

Conference Affiliation: Old Dominion Athletic Conference
Program Profile: We have a natural grass field with an asto-turf field used for practice during bad weather. We intend to build a program that consistently challenges for conference championships.
History: Program began in 1972 and has featured several winning seasons and 1 Conference Runner-Up season in 1983. More recently, the Royals have managed five winning seasons in the 1990's and set a school record for wins with 18 in 1996.
Achievements: Conference Runner-Up in 1983, two-time defending champion of the Saratosa Spring Break Classic.
Coaching: Rob Roeschley, Head Coach, 6th year, compiled a record of 60-100; played four years at Bluffton College. Own the school record for RBI and double in a season. Gary Messinger, Assistant Coach, entering second year with the program. Played at James Madison. Tony Veney, Assistant, entering fifth year with the program, former high school head coach, focuses on defense.
Roster for 1998 team/In State: 11 **Out of State:** 10 **Out of Country:** 0
Total Number of Varsity/Jr. Varsity: 21 **Percent of Graduation:** 90%
Number of Seniors on 1998 Team: 9 **Most Recent Record:** 13 - 19 - 0
Number of Fall Games: 4 **Number of Spring Games:** 32
Positions Needed for 1999/2000: Pitchers, Catcher, Outfielder, Middle Infielders
Schedule: Greensboro, Virginia Wesleyan, Guilford, Ferrum, Chowan, Bridgewater
Style of Play: We emphasize fundamentals and the mental part of baseball. We have a very "scrappy" team that never quits and takes advantage of opponent's mistakes.

Emory and Henry College

Baseball Office
Emory, VA 24327
Coach: Dewey Lusk

NCAA III
Wasps/Blue, Gold
Phone: (540) 944-4121
Fax: (540) 944-3673

ACADEMIC

Founded: 1836
Type: 4 Yr., Private, Liberal Arts, Coed
Religion: United Methodist
Campus Housing: Yes
Web-site: http://www.emory-henry.emory.va.us/
SAT/ACT/GPA: 930/19/2.5
Student/Faculty Ratio: 12:!
Male/Female Ratio: 1:1
Undergraduate Enrollment: 900
Graduate Enrollment: None
Scholarships/Academic: Yes **Athletic:** No **Fin Aid:** Yes
Total Expenses by: Year **In State:** $ 16,972 **Out of State:** $ 16,972
Degrees Conferred: BA, BS
Programs of Study: Accounting, Anthropology, Applied Mathematics, Art, Art Education, Biology, Business, Chemistry, Classics, Communications, Computer Information Systems, Computer Science, Creative Writing, Economics, Education, English, French, Geography, German, History, Human Services, Liberal Arts, Music, Philosophy, Physical Education, Physics, Political Science, Prelaw

ATHLETIC PROFILE

Conference Affiliation: Old Dominion Athletic Conference
Program Profile: Play 36 games in the Spring season (March-April). Devault Field (on campus) is home for the Wasps; 2 brick dugouts with bathroom facilities, outdoor batting cage, electronic scoreboard and completely fenced in (336 down the lines, 377 Center); Fall practice includes 4 weeks of practice with 8 games.
Coaching: Dewey Lusk, Head Coach, entering his 7th year as a head coach; BA from Emory and Henry in 1985 and MA from Gardner Webb in 1987.
Style of Play: Emory and Henry is known for its hitting.

Ferrum University

Route 40 West
Ferrum, VA 24088
Coach: Abe Naff

NCAA III
Panthers/Black, Gold
Phone: (540) 365-4488
Fax: (540) 365-4472

ACADEMIC

Founded: 1913
Type: 4 Yr., Private, Liberal Arts, Coed
Religion: Methodist
Campus Housing: Yes
Web-site: http://www.ferrum.edu/
SAT/ACT/GPA: 820/17
Student/Faculty Ratio: 14:1
Male/Female Ratio: 5:4
Undergraduate Enrollment: 1,100
Graduate Enrollment: None
Scholarships/Academic: Yes **Athletic:** No **Fin Aid:** Yes
Total Expenses by: Year **In State:** $ 15,600 **Out of State:** $ 15,600
Degrees Conferred: BA, BS, BSW
Programs of Study: Accounting, Agriculture, Art, Biology, Business Administration, Chemistry, Computer Science, Criminal Justice, Environmental Science, Fine Arts, French, Liberal Arts, Physical Education, Mathematical Science, Medical Technology, Philosophy, Psychology, Religion,

ATHLETIC PROFILE

Conference Affiliation: Dixie Intercollegiate Athletic Conference
Program Profile: NCAA Division III. The Panthers play a 36-game schedule from February through May. Games are played at Adams Field on campus.

History: Division III play began in 1986. Panthers have been to regional play seven times. Ferrum has had numerous All-Americans and drafted players.
Achievements: Won DIAC Crowns in 1990, 1992, and 1993; had 15 All-Americans; 34 All-Region; 42 All-Conference players; Coach Abe Naff was State Coach of the Year in 1990, 1992, and 1996
Coaching: Abe Naff, Head Coach, 14 years; 5 times Coach of the Year.
Style of Play: Offensive oriented - very aggressive on basepaths. Use of speed in the outfield, some power at the plate.

George Mason University

MS 3A5/Athletics, GMU
Fairfax, VA 22030-4444
Coach: Bill Brown

NCAA I
Patriots/Green, Gold
Phone: (703) 993-3221
Fax: (703) 993-3239

ACADEMIC

Founded: 1972
Type: 4 Yr., Public, Liberal Arts, Coed
Religion: Non-Affiliated
Campus Housing: Yes
Web-site: http://www.pubs.gmu.edu/sports
SAT/ACT/GPA: 1000/25/3.0
Student/Faculty Ratio: 17:1
Male/Female Ratio: 55:45
Undergraduate Enrollment: 13,831
Graduate Enrollment: 9,866
Scholarships/Academic: Yes **Athletic:** Full **Fin Aid:** Yes
Total Expenses by: Year **In State:** $ Varies **Out of State:** $ Varies
Degrees Conferred: Bachelors, Professional Masters, Doctoral
Programs of Study: 104 areas of study including: Accounting, Anthropology, Banking/Finance, Biology, Business, Chemistry, Computer, International, Journalism, Management, Marketing, Parks and Recreation, Preprofessional Programs

ATHLETIC PROFILE

Conference Affiliation: Colonial Athletic Conference
Program Profile: Home field is Raymond H. 'Hap' Spuhler Field-seats 900, natural grass. Program traditionally one of the best in CAA, and Mid-Atlantic region, competing with likes of VA Tech, Old Dominion, James Madison, Richmond, and East Carolina. Year-round program, with playing season in Spring. Travel to Southern sites early in season to play top teams.
History: Program began in 1968. Reached NAIA World Series in 1976. Made 4 NCAA Division I tournament appearances (1985, 1988, 1992, 1993). Won 3 conference championships (1985, 1988, 1992, 1993). 29 year all time record of 764-576-4, Division I record of 446-399-4 in 17 years.
Achievements: Coach Bill Brown was named CAA Coach of the Year three times; won CAA Title in 1988 and 1992; won ECAC South Title in 1985; 14 players drafted; 2 players reached the major league; All-American - Lonnie Goldberg.
Coaching: Bill Brown, Head Coach, all time leader in coaching victories; named Coach of the Year.
Style of Play: Emphasis on pitching and defense. Offensively, play style best suited to ball club.

Hampden - Sydney College

P.O. Box 698
Hampden-Sydney, VA 23943
Coach: Bob Humphreys

NCAA III
Tigers/Garnet, Grey
Phone: (804) 223-6981
Fax: (804) 223-6843

ACADEMIC

Type: 4 Yr., Private, Liberal Arts, All Male, Preengineering
Founded: 1776
Religion: Presbyterian
Campus Housing: Yes
Web-site: http://www.hsc.edu/
SAT/ACT/GPA: 950
Student/Faculty Ratio: 13:1
Male/Female Ratio: All Male

Undergraduate Enrollment: 950 **Graduate Enrollment:** None
Scholarships/Academic: Yes **Athletic:** No **Fin Aid:** Yes
Total Expenses by: Year **In State:** $ 21,000 **Out of State:** $ 21,000
Degrees Conferred: BA, BS
Programs of Study: Biology, Biochemistry, Biophysics, Chemistry, Physics, Economics, History, Mathematics, Computer Science, Philosophy, Physics, Political Science, Psychology, Religion

ATHLETIC PROFILE

Conference Affiliation: Old Dominion Athletic Conference
Program Profile: Excellent field-scenic setting; Fall and Spring schedule. The Tigers are in a rebuilding process in second season under Phil Culicerto. Play exciting Division III schedule with tough out of conference competition to go with ODAC slate. Team plays home games on nice grass field with dugout area modeled after Wrigley Field.
History: Baseball has been a varsity sport at HSC since 1880's. The team has enjoyed several very successful periods and players. Former Tiger, Bobby Humphrey, pitched in major leagues for Senators and Cardinals. HSC claimed the ODAC Championship in 1989 and reached NCAA Tournament in 1991.
Achievements: 1969 - Coach Louis Miller was named ODAC Coach of the Year; 1991 Coach Frank Fulton was named ODAC Coach of the Year; 1989 ODAC Champions; 1991 NCAA Division III Tournament participant.
Coaching: Bob Humphreys, Head Coach, member of the Hampden-Sydney Athletic Hall of Fame, and major league pitcher from 1962 to 1971, begins his first season as the skipper for the Hampden-Sydney baseball team. He brings over 30 years of major-league playing and coaching experience to the Tiger program, where he starred as a pitcher and third baseman from 1954 to 1958. He was a member of St. Louis Cardinal's 1964 World Series team and played for the Chicago Cubs and Washington Senators before concluding his career with the Milwaukee Brewers in 1971. Billy Carwile, Assistant Coach, former Prince Edward Academy standout, enters his first season with the program. He was a lettered four years and was a three-year starter.
Roster for 1998 team/In State: 19 **Out of State:** 1 **Out of Country:** 0
Total Number of Varsity/Jr. Varsity: 20 **Percent of Graduation:** 100%
Number of Seniors on 1998 Team: 2 **Number of Sophomores on 1998 Team:** 8
Number of Fall Games: 7 **Number of Spring Games:** 30
Positions Needed for 1999/2000: All **Most Recent Record:** 6 - 18 - 0
Schedule: Virginia Wesleyan, Mary Washington, Ferrum, Concord
Style of Play: Aggressive base running, solid pitching, manufacturing runs and solid defense. Utilized team's speed by hit and run and base stealing.

James Madison University

South Main Street **NCAA I**
Harrisonburg, VA 22807 **Dukes/Purple, Gold**
Coach: Spanky McFarland **Phone: (540) 568-6167**
Email: gotojmu@jmu.edu **Fax: (540) 568-6065**

ACADEMIC

Founded: 1908 **Type:** 4 Yr., Public, Coed
Religion: Non-Affiliated **Campus Housing:** Yes
Web-site: http://www.jmu.edu/ **SAT/ACT/GPA:** 1172
Student/Faculty Ratio: 18:1 **Male/Female Ratio:** 44:56
Undergraduate Enrollment: 11,643 **Graduate Enrollment:** 759
Scholarships/Academic: No **Athletic:** Yes **Fin Aid:** Yes
Total Expenses by: Year **In State:** $ 8,994 **Out of State:** $ 13,662
Degrees Conferred: BS, BA, MS, MA, MBA, MFA, EED
Programs of Study: Art, Biology, Chemistry, Sciences and Disorders, Computer, Geology, Health, Business, Kinesiology, Management, Marketing, Medical, Languages, Philosophy, Religion, Preprofessional Programs

ATHLETIC PROFILE

Estimated Number of Baseball Scholarships: 3-4
Conference Affiliation: Colonial Athletic Association
Program Profile: James Madison University baseball program boasts one of the attractive and modern facilities in the East. The J. Ward Longfield/Maw Stadium complex features one of the few artificially - surface fields in college baseball, permanent seating for 1,200, an electronic scoreboard, a permanent press box complete with broadcasting facilities and a grand level "VIP" box. There are also 2 permanent batting cages on the field.
History: 1997 registered program's 16th season with 30 or more wins, four straight year 31 or more wins. Marked the 25th consecutive season in which the program posted a non-losing season. Remains the only Virginia Division I program to advance to the College World Series in 1983. The last three season's JMU has led the CAA in hitting.
Achievements: In 1997, with the signing of Ray Baksh, Travic Harper and Eric Parker the program has had a player sign a pro contract for 22 straight seasons. During the Summer of 1997, there were 16 former Dukes playing professional baseball, 2 former Dukes coaching in the minor leagues and third in scouting.
Coaching: Spanky McFarland, Head Coach, former assistant coach at Florida State, South Florida and Georgia Tech; former head coach at Northern Illinois (started program - 6 years to NCAA tournament); named head baseball coach in October of 1997, which was a very unusual time of the year to take the reigns of a Division I baseball program.
Roster for 1998 team/In State: 17 **Out of State:** 15 **Out of Country:** 0
Total Number of Varsity/Jr. Varsity: 32 **Percent of Graduation:** 100%
Number of Seniors on 1998 Team: 4 **Number of Spring Games:** 56
Freshmen Receiving Fin Aid/Athletic: 8 **Most Recent Record:** 26 - 26 - 0
Positions Needed for 1999/2000: Catcher, LHP, Pitcher
Baseball Camp Dates: June 13; August 2; July 10-12; July 13-17, etc
Schedule: Miami, Georgia Southern, Virginia Commonwealth, Virginia, Virginia Tech, Maryland
Style of Play: Pitching, defense and aggressive offense.

Liberty University

1971 University Boulevard
Lynchburg, VA 24502
Coach: Dave Pastors
Email: dapastor@liberty.edu

NCAA I
Flames/Red, White, Blue
Phone: (804) 582-2103
Fax: (804) 582-2076

ACADEMIC

Founded: 1971 **Type:** 4 Yr., Private, Liberal Arts, Coed
Religion: Christian **Campus Housing:** Yes
Web-site: http://www.liberty.edu/ **SAT/ACT/GPA:** 800/17/2.0
Student/Faculty Ratio: 25:1 **Male/Female Ratio:** 2:3
Undergraduate Enrollment: 5,000 **Graduate Enrollment:** 400
Scholarships/Academic: Yes **Athletic:** Yes **Fin Aid:** Yes
Total Expenses by: Year **In State:** $ 13,200 **Out of State:** $ 13,200
Degrees Conferred: BA, MS, PhD, Religion
Programs of Study: Accounting, Biology, Communication, Journalism, Media Graphic, Advertising, Community Health Promotion, English, Exercise Science, General Studies, Mathematics, Music

ATHLETIC PROFILE

Estimated Number of Baseball Scholarships: 3.5
Conference Affiliation: Big South Conference
Program Profile: Al Worthington Baseball Stadium received 1998 Sports Turf Magazine Collegiate "Diamond of the Year", adding 13,000 sq. ft. baseball fieldhouse on third base side of field.

History: 1974/1975 was first year of the program. 1980, 1981, and 1982 competed in NAIA World Series. Became Div. I Independent Division I in 1985. Joined Big South Conference in 1992; won titles in 1993 & 1998; going to NCAA Regionals at Georgia Tech in 1993 & Florida State in 1998.
Achievements: Has 5 players drafted in 1998; 4 alumni played in major leagues: Sid Bream, Lee Guetterman, Randy Tomlin and Doug Grady, two pitchers drafted in 1998
Coaching: Dave Pastors, Head Coach, completed first year; was named Big South Coach of the Year. Jeff Edwards, completed first year at Liberty University, broken many offensive records. Randy Tomlin - five years in league.
Roster for 1998 team/In State: 10 **Out of State:** 22 **Out of Country:** 0
Total Number of Varsity/Jr. Varsity: 32 /12 **Percent of Graduation:** 95%
Number of Seniors on 1998 Team: 8 **Baseball Camp Dates:** 12/26-30; July
Freshmen Receiving Fin Aid/Athletic: 13 **Academic:** 13
Most Recent Record: 32 - 29 - 0 **Number of Spring Games:** 61
Positions Needed for 1999/2000: RHP, LHP
Schedule: Clemson, Oklahoma State, Florida State, Auburn, Wake Forest, Duke
Style of Play: Shattered school record for stolen bases (142) up from 39 the previous year (85) up from 51 previous year. Very up-tempo, pressure oriented.

Longwood College

201 High Street
Farmville, VA 23909
Coach: Buddy Bolding

NCAA II
Lancers/Blue, White
Phone: (804) 395-2352
Fax: (804) 395-2568

ACADEMIC

Founded: 1839
Type: 4 Yr., Public, Liberal Arts, Coed
Religion: Non-Affiliated
Campus Housing: Yes
Web-site: http://www.lwc.edu/
SAT/ACT/GPA: 1000
Student/Faculty Ratio: 1:23
Male/Female Ratio: 1:2
Undergraduate Enrollment: 3,300
Graduate Enrollment: 150
Scholarships/Academic: Varies **Athletic:** 1.75 **Fin Aid:** Varies
Total Expenses by: Year **In State:** $ 8,200 **Out of State:** $ 14,200
Degrees Conferred: BA, BS, BFA, BM, MA, MS
Programs of Study: Anthropology, Art, Biology, Business Administration, Chemistry, Computer Science, Elementary Education, Economics, English, History, Liberal Arts, Math, Modern Languages, Music, Physical Education, Physics, Political Science, Preengineering, Social Work, Sociology

Lynchburg College

1501 Lakeside Drive
Lynchburg, VA 24501-3199
Coach: Percy Abell

NCAA III
Hornets/Crimson, Grey
Phone: (804) 544-8496
Fax: (804) 544-8365

ACADEMIC

Founded: 1903
Type: 4 Yr., Private, Liberal Arts, Coed
Religion: Disciple of Christ
Campus Housing: Yes
Web-site: http://www.lynchburg.edu/
SAT/ACT/GPA: 900+
Student/Faculty Ratio: 12:1
Male/Female Ratio: 30:70
Undergraduate Enrollment: 1,500
Graduate Enrollment: 450
Scholarships/Academic: Yes **Athletic:** No **Fin Aid:** Yes
Total Expenses by: Year **In State:** $ 19,500 **Out of State:** $ 19,500
Degrees Conferred: BS, BA, MBA, MED

Programs of Study: Accounting, American Studies, Biology, Chemistry, Communications, Computer Science, English, Environmetal Science, German, History, International Business, Marketing, Mathematics, Medical Laboratory Technology, Music, Nursing, Philosophy, Physics, Political Science, Psychology, Religion, Secondary Education, Social Science, Spanish, Special Education

ATHLETIC PROFILE

Conference Affiliation: ODAC
Program Profile: Lynchburg Baseball program is a traditionally strong NCAA Division III program. The Hornets have garnered over 500 victories since 1970, making 7 NCAA Tournament Appearances since 1977, LC sports 14 All-Americans, including 3 who were 2-time All-Americans Selection. LC has had 51 1st team All-ODAC selections, including 6 Players of the Year choices. LC plays its home games at Fox Field, a natural grass surface with a dimensions of 320-L, 440-C, 325-R. The facility featured tiered bleachers with a capacity of 500, and include fences, backstop, dugouts, batting cage, and a prominent scoreboard.
History: The program began in 1907.
Achievements: 7 NCAA Tournaments, 6 ODAC Runner-Up, 3 All-Americans.

Mary Washington College

1301 College Avenue
Fredericksburg, VA 22401
Coach: Tom Sheridan

NCAA III
Eagles/Navy, Grey, White
Phone: (540) 654-1882
Fax: (540) 654-1892

ACADEMIC

Founded: 1908
Religion: Non-Affiliated
Web-site: http://www.mwc.edu/
Student/Faculty Ratio: 17:1
Scholarships/Academic: Yes **Athletic:** No
Total Expenses by: Year **In State:** $ 9,346

Type: 4 Yr., Public, Liberal Arts, Coed
Campus Housing: Yes
Undergraduate Enrollment: 3,000
Male/Female Ratio: 1:2
Fin Aid: Yes
Out of State: $ 14,306

Degrees Conferred: BA, BS, MFA
Programs of Study: American Studies, Art, Biology, Business Administration, Chemistry, Classics, Computer Science, Dance, Dramatic Arts, Economics, English, Environmental Science, French, Earth Science, Geography, Geology, Historic Preservation, International Affairs, Mathematics, Music

ATHLETIC PROFILE

Conference Affiliation: Capital Athletic Conference (CAC)
Program Profile: NCAA Division III Tournament four of last five years; CAC Champs (1992-1994); one of the finest Division III facilities in the nation, Battleground Stadium, grass, seats 1,000 (was completed in 1995).
History: 1988 was the first year and has had winning seasons from 1989-1995. This is one of the premier programs in NCAA South Region.
Achievements: Tom Sheridan named CAC Coach of the Year in 1991, 1992, 1993, and 1994; 3 pitchers are now in major league.
Style of Play: Aggressive, hit and run. Outstanding fundamentals stressed, especially on defense.

Norfolk State University

2401 Corprew Ave
Norfolk, VA 23504
Coach: Marty Miller

NCAA I
Spartans/Green, Gold
Phone: (757) 683-9539
Fax: (757) 683-8199

ACADEMIC

Founded: 1935
Type: 4 Yr., Public, Liberal Arts, Coed
Web-site: Not Available
SAT/ACT/GPA: 700/17
Student/Faculty Ratio: 22:1
Male/Female Ratio: 39:61
Undergraduate Enrollment: 7,600
Graduate Enrollment: 1,040
Scholarships/Academic: Yes **Athletic:** Yes **Fin Aid:** Yes
Total Expenses by: Year **In State:** $ 6,700 **Out of State:** $ 9,950
Degrees Conferred: AS, BS, BA, BIM, BSW, MA
Programs of Study: Accounting, Allied Health, Banking/Finance, Biological Science, Business Administration, Chemistry, Arts, Geography, History, Hotel/Restaurant Management, Journalism

ATHLETIC PROFILE

Conference Affiliation: Mid-Eastern Athletic Conference
Program Profile: The Spartans began playing in its new Marty Miller Field last season. It is the largest facility in the MEAC and it features a grass turf, lights for the night games and seating capacity is for 3,600 fans. The Spartans were one of the winningest program in Division II, capturing seven Central Intercollegiate Athletic Association Titles in the past 10 years.
History: The baseball program began in 1973 at Norfolk State University, with Marty Miller being the head coach since then. In that time span, NSU has gone 580-342-3 and has captured 17 conference championships.
Achievements: Marty Miller has won 15 CIAA Coach of the Year in his career. He was also the recipient of the Louisville Slugger Award in 1993 , 1994, and 1995. The most recent draftee was Deon Eaddy, selected in the 17th round of the last year's draft by the Chicago Cubs. Prior to Eaddy, 17 of Miller's players have been drafted.
Coaching: Marty Miller, Head Coach, won 15 CIAA Coach of the Year. Anthony Jones, Assistant.
Style of Play: Team has a great speed and a good hitters. A very aggressive with a number of upper classman.

Old Dominion University

5115 Hampton Boulevard
Norfolk, VA 23529
Coach: Tony Guzzo

NCAA I
Monarchs/Slate Blue, Silver
Phone: (757) 683-3375
Fax: (757) 683-3119

ACADEMIC

Type: 4 Yr., Public, Liberal Arts, Coed, Engineering
Founded: 1962
Religion: Non-Affiliated
Campus Housing: Yes
Web-site: http://www.odu.edu/
SAT/ACT/GPA: 850
Student/Faculty Ratio: 15:1
Male/Female Ratio: 51:49
Undergraduate Enrollment: 12,200
Graduate Enrollment: 5,800
Scholarships/Academic: Yes **Athletic:** Yes **Fin Aid:** Yes
Total Expenses by: Year **In State:** $ Depends on # of credits **Out of State:** $ Same
Degrees Conferred: BA, BS
Programs of Study: Accounting, Allied Health, Banking/Finance, Biology, Business Education, Business Administration, Chemistry, Communications, Community Planning, Computer Science, Construction Technology, Consumer Service, Economics, Education, Electrical Engineering, English, Fine Arts, Geography, Health Education, History, Home Economics, Journalism, Management, Marketing, Math, Medical Laboratory Technology, Medical Records Administration

ATHLETIC PROFILE

Estimated Number of Baseball Scholarships: 11.7
Conference Affiliation: Celenial Conference
Program Profile: The Old Dominion Monarchs play in the Bud Metheney Baseball Complex - a natural grass playing surface with a 2,500 seat stadium and lights. The "Bud" is also the only facility in the state with a dressing room on-site to the dugout.

History: The Old Dominion Baseball program began in 1981 and in 66 years has been successful in 58 percent of their games and in 22 years of Division I play ODU has won 63 percent of their games. ODU has been to four NCAA Tournaments in the 1990's and two players have been drafted in the first round this decade.
Achievements: Monarchs' coaches have won Coach of the Year honors six times. The school has won 16 Conference Titles since 1932; 14 Monarchs have earned All-American honors; 6 of the 14 Academic All-Americans; 8 ODU freshmen were named All-Americans; 35 players have been drafted, three in the 1st round.
Coaching: Tony Guzzo, Head Coach, has a record of 543-423-2; 140-86 at Old Dominion. In 20 years, he has earned 7 Coach of the Year awards; 2 Virginia State Coach of the Year & twice was a finalist for National Coach of the Year; Juan Ranero, Dan Nellum & Ryan Morris, Assistant Coaches.
Roster for 1998 team/In State: 10 **Out of State:** 15 **Out of Country:** 1
Total Number of Varsity/Jr. Varsity: 28 **Most Recent Record:** 28 - 29 - 0
Number of Seniors on 1998 Team: 8 **Number of Spring Games:** 56
Freshmen Receiving Fin Aid/Athletic: 5 **Academic:** 1
Positions Needed for 1999/2000: Pitcher, Catcher, Outfielder
Schedule: North Carolina, South Carolina, Wake Forest, North Carolina State, Richmond, Virginia

Radford University

P.O. Box 6913
Radford, VA 24142
Coach: Lew Kent
Email: lokent@runet.edu

NCAA I
Highlanders/Red, White, Navy
Phone: (540) 831-5881
Fax: (540) 831-6095

ACADEMIC

Founded: 1910 **Type:** 4 Yr., Public, Liberal Arts, Coed
Religion: Non-Affiliated **Campus Housing:** Yes
Web-site: http://www.runet.edu/ **SAT/ACT/GPA:** 850
Student/Faculty Ratio: 16:1 **Male/Female Ratio:** 45:55
Undergraduate Enrollment: 8,146 **Graduate Enrollment:** 959
Scholarships/Academic: Yes **Athletic:** Yes **Fin Aid:** Yes
Total Expenses by: Year **In State:** $ 7,458 **Out of State:** $ 12,032
Degrees Conferred: BA, BS, Masters
Programs of Study: Business and Economics, Education and Human Development, Arts and Science, Nursing and Health Services, Visual and Performing Arts

ATHLETIC PROFILE

Conference Affiliation: Big South Conference
Program Profile: Division I team, in Big South Conference. Play a great schedule. Facilities are among the best in the Region. Dedmon Center Park is natural grass surface with a capacity of 2,500. Play & travel over Spring break. Beautiful campus! We draw most players from Virginia & NE.
History: Program began in 1985, young program. 1995 was the first 30 win season, have placed 10 players in pro ball; 1 in the Big Leagues.
Achievements: In 1997 there were 3 drafted players; in 1996 freshman All-American; in 1994 freshman All-American; 1995 Coach of the Year; 1995 player drafted; 1994 player drafted; numerous All-Conference and All-Region and State Selections.
Coaching: Lew Kent, Head Coach, entering his fourth season as a head coach. He was an assistant coach at Radford and North Carolina State. Played in Cleveland Organization. Wayne Smith, Assistant, third season as an assistant. He was an assistant at University of Richmond.
Style of Play: Up and coming program; aggressive offense at the plate and on the basepaths. Sound pitching and defense. Fundamentally sound team.

Randolp - Macon College

P.O. Box 5005
Ashland, VA 23005
Coach: Gregg Waters

NCAA III
Yellow Jackets/Black, Yellow
Phone: (804) 752-7223
Fax: (804) 752-3748

ACADEMIC

Founded: 1830
Type: 4 Yr., Private, Liberal Arts, Coed
Religion: Methodist
Campus Housing: Yes
Web-site: http://www.rmc.edu
SAT/ACT/GPA: 1000/2.5
Student/Faculty Ratio: 11:1
Male/Female Ratio: 50:50
Undergraduate Enrollment: 1,200
Graduate Enrollment:
Scholarships/Academic: Yes **Athletic:** No **Fin Aid:** Yes
Total Expenses by: Year **In State:** $ 21,345 **Out of State:** $ 21,345
Degrees Conferred: BA, BS
Programs of Study: Liberal Arts, Business and Management, Languages, Letters/Literature, Life Sciences, Psychology, Social Sciences

ATHLETIC PROFILE

Conference Affiliation: ODAC

Saint Paul's College

406 Windsor Avenue
Lawrenceville, VA 23868
Coach: Oliver Harrison

NCAA II
Tigers/Black, Orange
Phone: (804) 848-2001
Fax: (804) 848-2001

ACADEMIC

Founded: 1888
Type: 4 Yr., Private, Liberal Arts, Coed
Religion: Episcopal
Campus Housing: No
Web-site: Not Available
SAT/ACT/GPA: 820 avg
Student/Faculty Ratio: 17:1
Male/Female Ratio: 1:2
Undergraduate Enrollment: 700
Graduate Enrollment: None
Scholarships/Academic: Yes **Athletic:** Yes **Fin Aid:** Yes
Total Expenses by: Year **In State:** $ 11,200 **Out of State:** $ 11,200
Degrees Conferred: BA, BS, BSED
Programs of Study: Biological Science, Business Administration, Business Education, Elementary Education, English, Mathematics, Political Science, Secondary Education, Social Science

ATHLETIC PROFILE

Conference Affiliation: CIAA
Achievements: Numerous All-Conference players.
Style of Play: We have a defensive team.

Shenandoah University

1460 University Drive
Winchester, VA 22601
Coach: Paul O'Neil
Email: poneil@su.edu

NCAA III
Hornets/White, Blue
Phone: (540) 665-4531
Fax: (540) 665-4934

ACADEMIC

Founded: 1875
Religion: United Methodist
Web-site: http://www.su.edu/
Student/Faculty Ratio: 10:1
Undergraduate Enrollment: 1,600
Scholarships/Academic: Yes **Athletic:**]No
Total Expenses by: Year **In State:** $ 11,200
Type: 4 Yr., Private, Liberal Arts, Coed
Campus Housing: Yes
SAT/ACT/GPA: 900
Male/Female Ratio: 40:60
Graduate Enrollment: 200
Fin Aid: Yes
Out of State: $ 12,700
Degrees Conferred: AS, BA, BS, BFA, BSM, MA, MS, MFA, MBA
Programs of Study: Accounting, Business Administration, Biology, Chemistry, Mass Communications, Computer Information Systems, Music, Theatre, Dance, Education, English, History, Business Management, Mathematics, Nursing, Philosophy, Psychology, Religion

ATHLETIC PROFILE

Conference Affiliation: Dixie Intercollegiate Athletic Conference
Program Profile: A relatively young program that has gained regional recognition and is now competing in the strongest Division III conference in the country. We have beautiful Bridgeforth Field, which is a natural grass, 2500-seat stadium where Winchester Royals of Valley League play. Facilities include press box, lights, bath rooms, grass field, concession stands, bull pens, cage, etc.. Playing season is in the Fall and in the Spring.
History: Program began in 1960 as JUCO, been varsity since 1984. Tod Held started the program from its grass roots in 1987-88. In just 3 years, the team won its 1st conference title and finished 6th in the South Region.
Style of Play: Extremely aggressive, fundamentally sound.

University of Richmond

28 West Hampton Way
Richmond, VA 23173
Coach: Ron Atkins
Email: ratkins@richmond.edu
NCAA I
Spiders/Red, Blue
Phone: (804) 289-8391
Fax: (804) 289-8820

ACADEMIC

Founded: 1830
Web-site: http://www.richmond.edu/
Student/Faculty Ratio: 10:1
Undergraduate Enrollment: 3,000
Scholarships/Academic: Yes **Athletic:** Yes
Total Expenses by: Year **In State:** $ 22,300
Type: 4 Yr., Private, Liberal Arts, Coed
Campus Housing: Yes
Male/Female Ratio: 51:49
Graduate Enrollment: None
Fin Aid: Yes
Out of State: $ 22,300
Degrees Conferred: BA, BS, MA, MBA, JD
Programs of Study: Accounting, Arts, Biology, Business, Chemistry, Classics, Computer Science, Criminal Justice, Economics, Education, English, Finance, French, German, Journalism, Management, Mathematics, Music, Philosophy, Physical Education, Physics, Political Education, Psychology, Religion, Social Science

ATHLETIC PROFILE

Estimated Number of Baseball Scholarships: 9
Conference Affiliation: Colonial Athletic Association
Program Profile: Top notch Division I conference (CAA). 1998 team RPI ranking 21. Play at Pitt Field which is natural grass, seats 600 with a dimensions of 328-350-380-350-328. Also have indoor cases and mounds; 5 week Fall program - Spring season is in February 15-May 15.
History: Began in 1915, 5 trips to the Regional in 1972, 1986, 1995, 1997, and 1998; CAA Champions in 1986, 1997 and 1998.
Achievements: Ron Atkins was named CAA Coach of the Year in 1991; All-Americans were Matt Pusey in 1997; Sean Casey in 1995, Tom Scioscia in 1994; 2 current major league players were Sean Casey (Cincinnati Reds) and Brian Jordan (St. Louis Cardinals).

Coaching: Ron Atkins, Head Coach, entering 14th season as a head coach. Compiled a record of 414-320, led team to 4 regional and 10 consecutive winning seasons. Mark McQueen - 11th year UR, pitched at Sam Houston State, Detroit Tigers Organization. Tag Montague, Assistant Coach, played at Virginia Commonwealth, 1 year at Randolph Macon College.
Roster for 1998 team/In State: 3 **Out of State:** 33 **Out of Country:** 0
Total Number of Varsity/Jr. Varsity: 36 **Percent of Graduation:** 98%
Number of Seniors on 1998 Team: 5 **Most Recent Record:** 41 - 17 - 0
Freshmen Receiving Fin Aid/Athletic: 9 **Academic:** 2
Number of Fall Games: 0 **Number of Spring Games:** 56
Positions Needed for 1999/2000: Catcher, Middle Infielder, Pitchers
Baseball Camp Dates: June 21-26; July 11-16
Schedule: Tennessee, South Carolina, Kentucky, Virginia Commonwealth University, Old Dominion
Style of Play: Types of play depends on the talent level for that year.

University of Virginia

P.O. Box 3785
Charlottesville, VA 22903
Coach: Dennis Womack
Email: snh5y@virgina.edu

NCAA I
Cavaliers/Blue, Orange
Phone: (804) 982-5776
Fax: (804) 982-4926

ACADEMIC

Founded: 1819 **Type:** 4 Yr., Public, Coed
Religion: Non-Affiliated **Campus Housing:** Yes
Web-site: http://www.virginia.edu/ **SAT/ACT/GPA:** 1150/3.5
Student/Faculty Ratio: 11:1 **Male/Female Ratio:** 48:52
Undergraduate Enrollment: 18,279 **Graduate Enrollment:**
Scholarships/Academic: Yes **Athletic:** Yes **Fin Aid:** Yes
Total Expenses by: Year **In State:** $ 10,500 **Out of State:** $ 21,000
Degrees Conferred: BA, BS, Masters, PhD, MD
Programs of Study: Many

ATHLETIC PROFILE

Estimated Number of Baseball Scholarships: 11
Conference Affiliation: Atlantic Coast Conference
Program Profile: Intense academic and athletic program that pushes the limits of the young men who choose our institution. We play on a natural grass field constructed in 1997. We play a full schedule that is among the most difficult in the country. Home field seats 2,300 and facilities includes all necessary equipment to assist in players' development.
History: Program was founded in 1889. We won the ACC in 1985 and 1996. We've had ten players drafted in the last five years including 2 in the 1st round and 1 each in the 2nd through fifth rounds.
Achievements: 1997 achievements were: 32-22 record and was fifth in the ACC; Final RPI ranking 30. 1996 achievements were: ACC Champs; Regional Runner-Up.
Coaching: Dennis Womack, Head Coach, entering his 19th year as a head coach. Steve Heon , Associate Coach, entering his 4th season, has an 11 years of coaching career. Steve Whitmyer , Pitching Coach. Aaron Weintraub, Volunteer Coach.
Roster for 1998 team/In State: 19 **Out of State:** 9 **Out of Country:** 0
Total Number of Varsity/Jr. Varsity: 28 **Percent of Graduation:** 90%
Number of Seniors on 1998 Team: 6 **Most Recent Record:** 21 - 16 - 1
Number of Spring Games: 56 **Baseball Camp Dates:** July 18-22; July 25-29
Positions Needed for 1999/2000: Catcher, Infielder, Pitcher
Schedule: Clemson, Florida State, Georgia Tech, NC State, Rice, South Alabama, Oklahoma State
Style of Play: Aggressiveness is under control. In the recruitment of position players, we look for competitiveness and mental toughness and speed.

Virginia Commonwealth University

819 W Franklin Street
Richmond, VA 23284-2003
Coach: Paul Keyes

NCAA I
Rams/Black, Gold
Phone: (804) 828-4820
Fax: (804) 828-9428

ACADEMIC

Founded: 1838
Type: 4 Yr., Public, Coed
Web-site: http://www.vcu.edu/
Campus Housing: Yes
Student/Faculty Ratio: 13:1
Male/Female Ratio: 40:60
Undergraduate Enrollment: 12,527
Graduate Enrollment: 4,177
Scholarships/Academic: Yes **Athletic:** Yes **Fin Aid:** Yes
Total Expenses by: Year **In State:** $ 9,057 **Out of State:** $ 17,219
Degrees Conferred: As, BA, BS, BFA, BSN, MA, MS, MBA, MFA, PhD
Programs of Study: Accounting, Biology, Chemistry, Economics, Engineering, Finance, Marketing, Health, Occupational, Physical, Radiation, Real Estate, Safety and Risk, Science, Sociology, Urban, Anthropology, Art Education, Nursing, Criminal Justice, Dance, Design, Music, Psychology, Religion

ATHLETIC PROFILE

Conference Affiliation: Colonial Athletic Association
Program Profile: VCU plays its home games at the Diamond, a 12,500 seat stadium that serves as their official home. The Rams have appeared in two NCAA Regionals (1988, 1992).
History: The program began playing in 1971 and did not become big until the mid-1980's when head coach Tony Guzzo moved the program into The Diamond. Guzzo led the Rams to two (1988, 1992) NCAA Regionals, while losing in the 1992 Central Regional Championship game to Texas.
Achievements: Brandon Inge was a freshman All-American in 1996; both in Collegiate Baseball and Baseball America as a utility player, while being named the CAA Newcomer of the Year.
Coaching: Paul Keyes, Head Coach, since 1994, former assistant coach at VCU, and Vanderbilt.
Style of Play: Rely on good pitching and defense, while using gap power and sluggers in the middle of the lineup to take advantage of good team speed.

Virginia Intermont College

PO Box 199
Bristol, VA 24201-4298
Coach: Ken Bowman

NAIA
Cobras/Black, Gold
Phone: (703) 466-7944
Fax: (703) 669-5763

ACADEMIC

Founded: 1884
Type: 4 Yr., Private, Liberal Arts, Coed
Religion: Baptist
Campus Housing: No
Student/Faculty Ratio: 12:1
SAT/ACT/GPA: 850/20
Undergraduate Enrollment: 635
Male/Female Ratio: 32:68
Scholarships/Academic: Yes **Athletic:** Yes **Fin Aid:** Yes
Total Expenses by: Year **In State:** $ 14,100 **Out of State:** $ 14,100
Degrees Conferred: AA, BA, BS
Programs of Study: Art Education, Biological Science, Business Administration, Dance, Elementary Education, English, Equestrian, Fine Arts, History, Marketing, Medical Laboratory Technology, Music, Office Management, Paralegal Studies, Photography, Political Science, Preprofessional Programs, Psychology, Secondary Education, Social Science

ATHLETIC PROFILE

Conference Affiliation: TVAC

Virginia Military Institute

Baseball Office
Lexington, VA 24450
Coach: Scott Gines
Email: giness@vmi.edu

NCAA I
Keydets/Red, White, Yellow
Phone: (540) 464-7609
Fax: (540) 464-7790

ACADEMIC

Type: 4 Yr., Public, Liberal Arts, Coed, Engineering
Founded: 1839
Religion: Non-Affiliated
Campus Housing: Yes
Web-site: http://www.vmi.edu/
SAT/ACT/GPA: 1160/3.0
Student/Faculty Ratio: 11:1
Male/Female Ratio: 50:1
Undergraduate Enrollment: 1,285
Graduate Enrollment: None
Scholarships/Academic: Yes **Athletic:** Yes **Fin Aid:** Yes
Total Expenses by: Year **In State:** $ 10,075 **Out of State:** $ 17,100
Degrees Conferred: BA, BS
Programs of Study: Mechanical Engineering, Civil Engineering, Electrical Engineering, Chemistry, Physics, Biology, Psychology, Modern Languages, English, History, Business and Economics

ATHLETIC PROFILE

Estimated Number of Baseball Scholarships: 11.7
Conference Affiliation: Southern Conference
Program Profile: Play on natural field; club house has 1,000 capacity, 4 cages, moderate climate.
History: Has a 113 years history. Full time staff; national recruiting; all players return for 1999; program on quick rise.
Achievements: Gines was named 1989 Big South Coach of the Year; 31 draft pick; free agent signs; 9 Academic All-Americans; 3 major leagues.
Coaching: Scott Gines, Head Coach, compiled a record of 83-87 for four years; was an assistant coach at University of Virginia; has a 17 years head coaching experience at Radford University; started coaching at Virginia Military from 1994 to the present.
Roster for 1998 team/In State: 18 **Out of State:** 12 **Out of Country:** 0
Total Number of Varsity/Jr. Varsity: 30 **Percent of Graduation:** 100%
Number of Seniors on 1998 Team: 9 **Most Recent Record:** 14 - 32 - 0
Freshmen Receiving Fin Aid/Athletic: 7 **Academic:** 1
Number of Fall Games: 0 **Number of Spring Games:** 56
Positions Needed for 1999/2000: Pitcher, Middle-infielder
Baseball Camp Dates: 6/15-19; 7/18-22; 25-29; 7/31-9/2; 9/7-9
Schedule: South Carolina, Duke, Auburn, Georgia Southern, Virginia, Western Carolina, Troy State
Style of Play: Running game based - aggressive offensive, fundamental defense with pitchers who dump strikes.

Virginia State University

P.O. Box 9058
Petersburg, VA 23806
Coach: Terrence Wittle

NCAA II
Trojans/Blue, Orange
Phone: (804) 524-5030
Fax: (804) 524-5763

ACADEMIC

Founded: 1882
Type: 4 Yr., Public, Coed
SAT/ACT/GPA: 700avg
Campus Housing: Yes
Student/Faculty Ratio: 24:1
Male/Female Ratio: 45:55
Undergraduate Enrollment: 3,250
Graduate Enrollment: 691
Scholarships/Academic: Yes **Athletic:** Yes **Fin Aid:** Yes
Total Expenses by: Year **In State:** $ 8,600 **Out of State:** $ 12,500

Degrees Conferred: AA, AS, BA, BS, MA, MS
Programs of Study: Accounting, Agricultural Business Management, Biological Science, Business Administration, Chemistry, Earth Science, Economics, Education, Engineering Technology, English, Geology, History, Home Economics, International Relations, Languages, Mathematics, Physical Education, Physics, Political Science, Psychology, Public Administration, Social Science

Virginia Poly Institute and State University

210 Cassell Coliseum
Blacksburg, VA 24061-0502
Coach: Chuck Hartman

NCAA I
Hokies/Maroon, Orange
Phone: (540) 231-9974
Fax: (540) 231-3060

ACADEMIC

Type: 4 Yr., Public, Liberla Arts, Coed, Engineering
Founded: 1872
Religion: Non-Affiliated
Campus Housing: Yes
Web-site: http://www.vt.edu/
SAT/ACT/GPA: No minimum
Student/Faculty Ratio: 17:1
Male/Female Ratio: 59:41
Undergraduate Enrollment: 19,496
Graduate Enrollment: 3,088
Scholarships/Academic: Yes **Athletic:** Yes **Fin Aid:** Yes
Total Expenses by: Year **In State:** $ 7,407 **Out of State:** $ 14,059
Degrees Conferred: BA, BS, MS, MED, PhD, Eed
Programs of Study: Agronomy, Animal Husbandry, Business Management, Education, Home Economics, Engineering, Forestry and Wildlife, Physical Science, Social Science, Veterinary

ATHLETIC PROFILE

Conference Affiliation: Atlantic Ten Conference
Program Profile: Virginia Tech has a highly-competitive program set on one of the nation's most beautiful campuses. English Field is a new baseball facility, features a natural grass field with a dimensions of 300-375-400. Stadium capacity is 1,500 with a nearly 800 theatre seats and a grassy hill that preserves a student tradition for gathering at the game. New pressbox and lights is next.
History: Baseball was the first varsity sport in Virginia Tech, making its debut in April of 1892. In 103 seasons the Hokies have won over 1,500 games. Program has just 2 losing seasons over the last 35 years. Tech has an average 36 wins a year during Chuck Hartman's 18 years at the helm.
Achievements: The program has been to the NCAA Tournament five times, most recently in 1994. Hokies won Metro Conference Tournament Championship in 1994, tied for Metro Regional Season Title in 1995 and were the Atlantic Ten Regular Season Champions in 1996.
Coaching: Chuck Hartman, Head Coach, since 1992, the ninth coach in the Division I history to win 1,000 games, currently ranks among the top six active coach in Division I coaches in wins with 1,138; named Metro Conference Coach of the Year in 1989, 1994 and Virginia Coach of the Year in 1986, 1992, and 1993.
Style of Play: Pitch it and catch it - three run homer, open offense - like to swing the bat.

Virginia Wesleyan College

1584 Wesleyan Drive
Norfolk, VA 23502
Coach: Nick Boothe
Email: nboothe@wvc.edu

NCAA III
Marlins/Blue, White, Grey
Phone: (757) 455-3200
Fax: (757) 461-2262

ACADEMIC

Founded: 1961
Type: 4 Yr., Private, Liberal Arts, Coed
Religion: Methodist
Campus Housing: Yes
Web-site: http://www.vwc.edu/
SAT/ACT/GPA: 900/19
Student/Faculty Ratio: 16:1
Male/Female Ratio: 1:3

Undergraduate Enrollment: 1,650 **Graduate Enrollment:** None
Scholarships/Academic: Yes **Athletic:** No **Fin Aid:** Yes
Total Expenses by: Year **In State:** $ 16,900 **Out of State:** $ 18,900
Degrees Conferred: BA, BS
Programs of Study: 35 different majors: Most popular are Business, Communications, Education, Biology and Liberal Arts

ATHLETIC PROFILE

Conference Affiliation: ODAC
Program Profile: Family oriented program, where everyone gets along with each other. Our facility is natural grass, which is open to the public with bleachers on both sides, and stadium bleachers
Achievements: Conference Champions in 1997 and 1997; Runner-Up to North Carolina Wesleyan in South Regional in 1997; Nick Boothe was named Coach of the Year in 1993, 1994 and 1997; players signed/drafted were Chris Detolo in 1991 with the Giants, Ryan Casey in 1995 with Cubs, Fella Dulby in 1997 with Broncos, and Brett Craun in 1998.
Coaching: Nick Boothe, Head Coach, entering 13th year with the porgam. Mike Lloyd, Assistant Coach, entering second year with the program. Dwayne Purger, Assistant Coach, entering second year with the program. Bobby Hoeft, Assistant Coach, entering second year with the program. St. Clair Jones, Assistant Coach, entering first year with the program.
Roster for 1998 team/In State: 3 **Most Recent Record:** 22 - 19 - 0
Baseball Camp Dates: 11/13-15; 6/21-25; 7/19-23; 7/11-15; 9/2-6
Schedule: North Carolina Wesleyan, Methodist, Mary Washington, Greensboro, Tufts, Bridgewater
Style of Play: Very aggresssive, we do not play station to station.

Washington and Lee University

P.O. Drawer 928
Lexington, VA 24450
Coach: Jeff Stickley

NCAA III
Generals/Royal Blue, White
Phone: (540) 463-8680
Fax: (540) 463-8173

ACADEMIC

Founded: 1749 **Type:** 4 Yr., Private, Coed
Religion: Non-Affiliated **Campus Housing:** Yes
Web-site: http://www.wlu.edu/ **SAT/ACT/GPA:** 1200
Student/Faculty Ratio: 12:1 **Male/Female Ratio:** 60:40
Undergraduate Enrollment: 1,600 **Graduate Enrollment:** 300
Scholarships/Academic: Yes **Athletic:** No **Fin Aid:** Yes
Total Expenses by: Year **In State:** $ 15,280 **Out of State:** $ 15,280
Degrees Conferred: BA, BS, JD
Programs of Study: 40+ majors icluding Business and Management, Communications, Languages, Life Science, Physical Sciences, Psychology, Social Sciences

ATHLETIC PROFILE

Conference Affiliation: Old Dominion Athletic Conference
Program Profile: Typical Division II program. Looking for students with 1200 SAT top 10% of class.
Achievements: Coach of the Year in 1996; 1 Player was named Honorable Mention All-American.
Coaching: Jeff Stickley, Head Coach. Jack Baizley, Assistant Coach.
Roster for 1998 team/In State: 20 **Out of State:** 1 **Out of Country:** 0
Total Number of Varsity/Jr. Varsity: 27 **Percent of Graduation:** 100%
Number of Seniors on 1998 Team: 1 **Number of Sophomores on 1998 Team:** 0

WASHINGTON

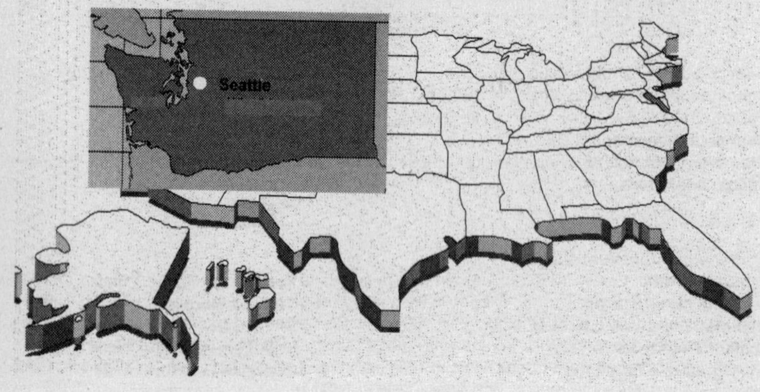

SCHOOL	CITY	AFFILIATION 99	PAGE
Central Washington University	Ellensburg	NCAA II/NAIA	895
Gonzaga University	Spokane	NCAA I	895
Pacific Lutheran University	Tacoma	NCAA III\NAIA	895
St. Martin's College	Lacey	NCAA II/NAIA	896
University of Puget Sound	Tacoma	NCAA III\NAIA	897
University of Washington	Seattle	NCAA I	897
Washington State University	Pullman	NCAA I	897
Whitman College	Walla Walla	NCAA III\NAIA	898
Whitworth College	Spokane	NCAA III\NAIA	899

Central Washington University

400 East 8th Avenue
Ellensburg, WA 98926
Coach: Desi Storey

NCAA II/NAIA
Wildcats/Red, Black
Phone: (509) 963-3018
Fax: (509) 963-1914

ACADEMIC

Founded: 1890
Type: 4 Yr., Public, Coed
Religion: Non-Affiliated
Campus Housing: Yes
Web-site: http://www.cwu.edu/
SAT/ACT/GPA: 820/17
Student/Faculty Ratio: 22:1
Male/Female Ratio: 49:51
Undergraduate Enrollment: 8,304
Graduate Enrollment: 281
Scholarships/Academic: Yes **Athletic:** Tuition waiver **Fin Aid:** Yes
Total Expenses by: Year **In State:** $ 10,018 **Out of State:** $ 16,204
Degrees Conferred: BA, BS, MA, MS
Programs of Study: Accounting, Actuarial Science, Anthropology, Banking and Finance, Biology, Broadcasting, Business Adminstration, Chemistry, Commmunications, Computer Science, Criminal Justice, Earth Science, Economics, Education, Engineering, Fine Arts, Geography, Geology, History

ATHLETIC PROFILE

Conference Affiliation: Independent Conference
Achievements: Twice qualified for NAIA World Series in 1970 and 1988.
Coaching: Desi Storey, Head Coach, sixth years as a head coach.

Gonzaga University

502 E Boone Avenue
Spokane, WA 99258
Coach: Steve Hertz

NCAA I
Bulldogs/Blue, Red, White
Phone: (509) 328-4220
Fax: (509) 323-5787

ACADEMIC

Type: 4 Yr., Private, Liberal Arts, Coed, Engineering
Founded: 1887
Religion: Catholic, Jesuit Indentity
Campus Housing: Yes
Web-site: http://www.gonzaga.edu/
SAT/ACT/GPA: Contact Admission
Student/Faculty Ratio: 14:1
Male/Female Ratio: 47:53
Undergraduate Enrollment: 3,000
Graduate Enrollment: 1,700
Scholarships/Academic: Yes **Athletic:** Yes **Fin Aid:** Yes
Total Expenses by: Year **In State:** $ 21,500 **Out of State:** $ 21,500
Degrees Conferred: BA,BS,MA,MBA,MEd, EdD, JD, MDiv
Programs of Study: Accounting, Arts, Biology, Broadcasting, Chemistry, Civil Engineering, Classics, Communications, Computer Information Systems, Computer Science, Criminal Justice, Economics, Electrical Engineering, Elementary Education, English, Finance, French, German, International Business, Italian, Journalism, Latin, Liberal Arts, Literature, Mathematics, Mechanical

ATHLETIC PROFILE

Conference Affiliation: West Coast Conference

Pacific Lutheran University

12180 Park Avenue
Tacoma, WA 98447
Coach: Larry Marshall

NCAA III\NAIA
Lutes/Black, Gold
Phone: (206) 535-8789

ACADEMIC

Founded: 1934
Religion: Assemblies of God
Web-site: http://www.nwcollege.edu/
Student/Faculty Ratio: 20:1
Scholarships/Academic: Yes **Athletic:** Yes
Total Expenses by: Year **In State:** $ 12,500
Type: 4 Yr., Private, Liberal Arts, Coed
Campus Housing: Yes
Undergraduate Enrollment: 800
Male/Female Ratio: None
Fin Aid: Yes
Out of State:
Degrees Conferred: BA, AA
Programs of Study: Behavioral Sciences, Business, Interdisciplinary Studies, Teacher Education, Religion and Philosophy, Church Ministries

ATHLETIC PROFILE

Conference Affiliation: Northwest of Independent
Achievements: The pitchers were drafted in 1995 by the Braves.
Coaching: Larry Marshall, Head Coach, 14 years at PLU, winningest coach in school's history.

St. Martin's College

(New Program)

5300 Pacific Avenue, SE
Lacey, WA 98503
Coach: Joe Dominiak
Email: athletics@crc.stmartin.edu
NCAA II/NAIA
Saints/Red, White, Black
Phone: (360) 438-4531
Fax: (360) 412-6191

ACADEMIC

Founded: 1895
Religion: Catholic
Web-site: http://www.stmartin.edu/
Student/Faculty Ratio: 12:1
Undergraduate Enrollment: 1,200
Scholarships/Academic: Yes **Athletic:** Yes
Total Expenses by: Year **In State:** $ 19,000
Type: 4 Yr., Private, Coed
Campus Housing: Yes
SAT/ACT/GPA: 860+
Male/Female Ratio: 50:50
Graduate Enrollment: 600
Fin Aid: Yes
Out of State: $ 19,000
Degrees Conferred: AA, AS, BA, BS, MA, MBA, MEd
Programs of Study: Business, Engineering, Education, Psychology, Community Services, Humanities, Science, Math, Social Science

ATHLETIC PROFILE

Estimated Number of Baseball Scholarships: 11
Program Profile: New Program just starting its third year; great facilities with a brand new field 1999, natural grass with 1,200 seat stadium.
History: Started three years ago; first year record was 7-28; second year 18-28. We play a very tough schedule with many Division I schools on it.
Achievements: In 1998 we had two sign professional contracts.
Coaching: Joe Dominiak, Head Coach, in his first year as a head coach @ St. Martin's. He came from a very successful program (community college) in Oregon winning the NWAAC his first year.
Roster for 1998 team/In State: 19 **Out of State:** 9 **Out of Country:** 0
Total Number of Varsity/Jr. Varsity: 28 **Percent of Graduation:** 88%
Number of Seniors on 1998 Team: 5 **Number of Sophomores on 1998 Team:** 4
Freshmen Receiving Fin Aid/Athletic: 4 **Academic:** 5
Number of Fall Games: 10 **Number of Spring Games:** 46
Most Recent Record: 18 - 28 - 0 **Baseball Camp Dates:** July
Positions Needed for 1999/2000: Catcher, LHP, Shortstop, 2nd Base
Schedule: University of Washington, Oregon State University, Lewis and Clark State, Willamette
Style of Play: Very aggressive, style of baseball with good fundamentals. Aggressive at the plate and bases. Very well conditioned pitchers. Have fun!!!

University of Puget Sound

1500 North Warner
Tacoma, WA 98416
Coach: Ken Garland

NCAA III\NAIA
Loggers/Green, Gold
Phone: (206) 756-3265
Fax: (253) 756-3634

ACADEMIC

Founded: 1888
Type: 4 Yr., Private, Liberal Arts, Coed
Web-site: http://www.ups.edu.com
Campus Housing: Yes
Student/Faculty Ratio: 12:1
Male/Female Ratio: 3:2
Undergraduate Enrollment: 2,800
Graduate Enrollment: 244
Scholarships/Academic: Yes **Athletic:** No **Fin Aid:** Yes
Total Expenses by: Year **In State:** $ 22,500 **Out of State:** $ 22,500
Degrees Conferred: BA, BS, MAT, MED, MPT, MDT
Programs of Study: Art, Asian Studies, Biology, Business Administration, Chemistry, Communications, Geology, History, International Political Economy, Math, Music, Natural Science

University of Washington

Box 354080
Seattle, WA 98195
Coach: Ken Knutson

NCAA I
Huskies/Purple, Gold
Phone: (206) 616-4335
Fax: (206) 865-7016

ACADEMIC

Type: 4 Yr., Public, Liberal Arts, Coed, Engineering
Founded: 1861
Web-site: http://www.washington.edu
SAT/ACT/GPA: 1058/3.6
Student/Faculty Ratio: 9:1
Male/Female Ratio: 50:50
Undergraduate Enrollment: 25,000
Graduate Enrollment: 10,000
Scholarships/Academic: Yes **Athletic:** Yes **Fin Aid:** Yes
Total Expenses by: Year **In State:** $ 3,300 **Out of State:** $ 6,000
Degrees Conferred: BA, BS, BFA, MS, MA, MBA, MFA, PhD
Programs of Study: Art and Sciences, Architecture, Urban Planning, Business, Law Medicine, Education, Engineering, Forestry, Nursing, Ocean and Fishery Sciences, Social Work, Psychology

ATHLETIC PROFILE

Conference Affiliation: Pacific - 10 North Conference
Program Profile: Building a new stadium. We will play on the new field in 1998; articial infield/grass outfield; will seat 3,500 with a lights - on the shore of Lake Washington; view of Mt. Rainer.
History: Has a 100+ years of baseball program.
Achievements: Won 4 of the past 6 Pacific 10 Championships; Pacific 10 Champions in 1997; ranked 13th last year which is 1996; Lost in the Midwest Regional Final in 1997 to Mississippi State; Coach Knutson Pacific National Coach of the Year in 1996 and 1997; freshman All-American in 1997 was Chris MacGrindell; freshman All-American in 1996 team USA in 1997; 12 time team MVP; Regional Participants in 1992, 1994, and 1997.
Coaching: Ken Knutson, Head Coach, Coach of the Year. Joe Ross andKevin Johnson, Assistants.
Style of Play: Aggressive, running and power.

Washington State University

Bohler Gym 113
Pullman, WA 99164
Coach: Steve Farrington

NCAA I
Cougars/Crimson, Grey
Phone: (509) 335-0310
Fax: (509) 335-0267

ACADEMIC

Founded: 1890
Type: 4 Yr., Public, Coed
Web-site: http://www.wsu.edu
SAT/ACT/GPA: 700avg/17avg
Student/Faculty Ratio: 16:1
Male/Female Ratio: 53:47
Undergraduate Enrollment: 16,000
Graduate Enrollment: 3,100
Scholarships/Academic: Yes **Athletic:** Yes
Fin Aid: Yes
Total Expenses by: Year **In State:** $ 7,900 **Out of State:** $ 13,000
Degrees Conferred: BA, BS, MA, MS, MBA
Programs of Study: Advertising, Animal, Anthropology, Banking/Finance, Biology, Chemistry, Communications, Computer, Criminal Justice, Food, French, Geology, German, History, Horticulture, Hotel/Restaurant Management, Nursing, International, Parks/Recreation Management, Preprofessional Programs, Psychology, Pharmacy, Philosophy, Soil, Speech, Wildlife, Biology

ATHLETIC PROFILE

Conference Affiliation: Pacific - 10 North Conference
Program Profile: Our program plays under NCAA Division I leadership in the Pacific 10 Northern Conference. We play our conference games against the University of Washington, Oregon State University, and Portland State University. We also play three teams every year from the Pacific 10 South Conference. Our program is one that is in a rebuilding status, but where we have been in the past should show where we will be in the future. Some of our famous alumni are John Olerud of the New York Mets, Aaron Sele of the Texas Rangers, Scott Hatteburg of the Boston Red Sox, Ron Cey, and Tom Niedenfuer. We play our home games at Arthur "Buck" Bailey Field. The stadium has a seating capacity of 3,500 and it is lighted and is a natural turf. The outfield is recently re-seeded to handle the drainage problem of the past years' weather. The field was completed in 1980, and a $25,000 lighting project was completed for the 1984 season.
History: The Cougar baseball program began its illustrious career in the year 1892 when it garnished a record of 11-1. Since then the Cougars baseball program has compiled a record of 2177-1146, with 41 Pacific 10 and Pacific North Cahmpionships. In 1988 the team set record of 52 wins. That same year John Olerud was also named the Baseball America Collegiate Baseball Player of the Year. John is now playing first base for the New York Mets. For 32 years (1962-1994) the baseball program was ran by Chuck "Bobo" Brayton. Over that stretch of 32 years he compiled 1,162 victories, which is the fourth winningest baseball coach in the history of NCAA Division I play. Brayton retired in 1994, giving way to long time junior coach Steve Farrington.
Achievements: WSU has 41 league titles and has appeared in the College World Series 4 times. The Cougars baseball program has produced 33 minor league ball players over the years. Some notable are John Olerud, Ron Cey, Scott Hatteburg, Aaron Sele, Tom Niedenfuer, Wes Stock, David Wainhouse, Doug Sisk, Ken Phelps, and numerous others that are still in the minor league. Current Coach Steve Farrington captured the Pacific 10 North Coach of the Year in his Rookies season in 1995. That same year he also led the squad to the program's 41st conference title. John Olerud was named 1988 College Baseball Player of the Year with a stats of 15-0 on the mound, and a .464 batting average. He also had 23 home runs that same season. He later went on to win the American League batting in 1993 while playing with the Toronto Blue Jays.
Coaching: Steve Farrington, Head Coach (Eastern Washington 1974), WSU record 28-30-0, second year at WSU, 1995 Pacific 10 Coach of the Year. Tom Chamberlain, Assistant Coach (OSU 1977). Buzzy Verduzco,Assistant (WSU 1985). Corky Franklin, Assistant Coach (WSU 1993).
Style of Play: Coach chose not to comment on this subject.

Whitman College

345 Boyers Street
Walla Walla, WA 99362
Coach: Travis Feezell

NCAA III\NAIA
Missionaries/Maize, Blue
Phone: (509) 527-5288
Fax: (509) 527-5960

ACADEMIC

Founded: 1859
Type: 4 Yr., Private, Liberal Arts, Coed
SAT/ACT/GPA: SAT I or ACT are required/
Web-site: http://www.whitman.edu/

Student/Faculty Ratio: 11:1 **Male/Female Ratio:** 48:52
Undergraduate Enrollment: 1,300 **Graduate Enrollment:** None
Scholarships/Academic: Yes **Athletic:** No **Fin Aid:** Yes
Total Expenses by: Year **In State:** $ 22,781 **Out of State:** $ 22,781
Degrees Conferred: BA
Programs of Study: Anthropology, Asian Studies, Art, Biology, Chemistry, Computer Science, Dramatic Arts, Economics, English, Environmental Studies, Fine Arts, French, Geology, German, History, Mathematics, Music, Philosophy, Physics, Political Science, Prelaw, Premed, Psychology

ATHLETIC PROFILE

Conference Affiliation: PNIAC

Whitworth College

300 West Hawthorne Road
Spokane, WA 99251-2101
Coach: Keith Ward

NCAA III\NAIA
Pirates/Crimson, Black
Phone: (509) 777-4394
Fax: (509) 777-3790

ACADEMIC

Founded: 1890 **Type:** 4 Yr., Private, Liberal Arts, Coed
Religion: Presbyterian **Campus Housing:** Yes
Web-site: http://www.whitworth.edu/ **SAT/ACT/GPA:** 1160 avg
Student/Faculty Ratio: 16.5:1 **Male/Female Ratio:** 40:60
Undergraduate Enrollment: 1,500 **Graduate Enrollment:** 300
Scholarships/Academic: Yes **Athletic:** Yes **Fin Aid:** Yes
Total Expenses by: Year **In State:** $ 19,824 **Out of State:** $ 19,824
Degrees Conferred: BS, BA, MEd, MIT, MIM
Programs of Study: Accounting, Art, Liberal Studies, Biology, Business, Chemistry, Communications, Computer Science, Cross-Cultural Studies, Economics, Education, Engineering, English, French, History, Journalism, Math, Music, Philosophy, P.E., Physics, Political Studies

ATHLETIC PROFILE

Conference Affiliation: Northwest of Independent Colleges
Program Profile: The Whitworth Fieldhouse has the full-length batting cages, a screen, a locker room, and a room for an entire infield. Merkle Field is located behind the fieldhouse. The natural grass field is the best in the area. The dimensions are 325' left, 400' to center, 325' to the right with a 20' high fence and 350' in the alleys.
History: The Whitworth baseball program has been around since 1893. Pirates have won 9 NCIC Titles, 7 District Titles and 1 National Championship.
Achievements: 4 Coaches over the years have won Coach of the Year; all 4 have won at least twice and one three-times; won 9 Conference Titles; 7 District Titles; 1 National Title; 5 All-Americans; 17 players have turned professional from our program.
Coaching: Keith Ward, Head Coach, Whitworth College alumni, entering his first season as a head coach. Bob Downs, Assistant Coach, graduate of San Diego State, entering fourth year as an assistant coach, has one year professional coaching career. Bob Moore, Pitching Coach, graduate of University of Hawaii, entering third year, has two years professional experience.
Style of Play: This year's team (1997) has both power and speed. We will utilize our power as in the past, but we will not rely on power alone , we will become know also for speed moving. The runners along, bunts, hit runners, stolen bases. Team averaged 7 runs per game in 1997 - should be there again or more.

WEST VIRGINIA

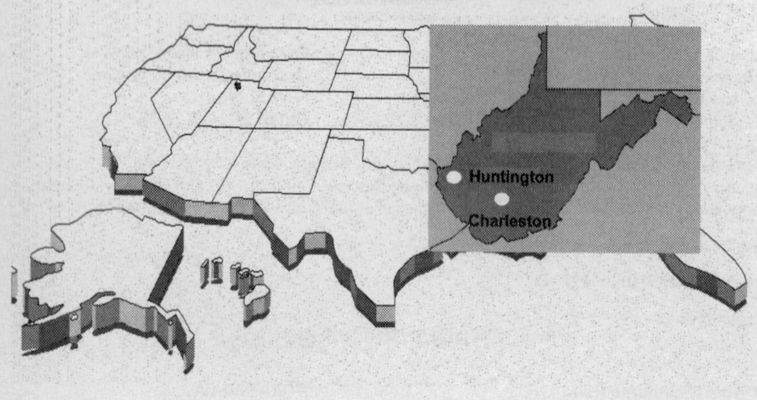

SCHOOL	CITY	AFFILIATION 99	PAGE
Alderson Broddus College	Phillippi	NCAA II	901
Bethany College	Bethany	NCAA III	901
Bluefield State College	Bluefield	NCAA II	902
Concord College	Athens	NCAA II	902
Davis and Elkins College	Elkins	NCAA II	903
Fairmont State College	Fairmont	NCAA II	903
Marshall University	Huntington	NCAA I	904
Potomac State College	Keyser	NJCAA	904
Salem - Teikyo University	Salem	NCAA II	905
Shepherd College	Shepherdstown	NCAA II	906
University of Charleston	Charleston	NCAA II	906
West Liberty State College	West Liberty	NCAA II	907
West Virginia State College	Institute	NCAA II	908
WV Institute of Technology	Montgomery	NCAA II	908
West Virginia University	Morgantown	NCAA I	909
West Virginia Wesleyan College	Buckhannon	NCAA II	909

Alderson Broddus College

I College Hill
Phillippi, WV 26416
Coach: Chad Hefner

NCAA II
Battlers/Blue, Grey, Gold
Phone: (304) 457-6265
Fax: (304) 457-6291

ACADEMIC

Founded: 1871
Religion: American Baptist
Web-site: Not Available
Student/Faculty Ratio: 13:1
Undergraduate Enrollment: 760
Scholarships/Academic: Yes **Athletic:** Yes
Total Expenses by: Year **In State:** $ 16,316

Type: 4 Yr., Private, Liberal Arts, Coed
Campus Housing: Yes
SAT/ACT/GPA: 820/17
Male/Female Ratio: 40:60
Graduate Enrollment: 40
Fin Aid: Yes
Out of State: $ 16,316

Degrees Conferred: Associate, Bachelors
Programs of Study: Accounting, Applied Music, Biology, Business Administration, Christian Studies, Church Music, Communications, Computer Science, General Science, Education, Social Studies, Medical Technology, Environmental Science, History, Liberal Arts, Literature, Languages, Art, Mathematics, Music Education, Political Science, Psychology, Nursing, Radiography, Secondary Education, Elementary Education, Biology, Chemistry, Physical Education, Sociology, Speech

ATHLETIC PROFILE

Conference Affiliation: WVIAC

Bethany College

Hummel Fieldhouse
Bethany, WV 26032
Coach: Rick Carver

NCAA III
Bisons/Kelly Green, White
Phone: (304) 829-7246
Fax: (304) 829-7290

ACADEMIC

Founded: 1840
Religion: Disciple of Christ
Web-site: http://www.bethanywvnet.edu/
Student/Faculty Ratio: 12:1
Undergraduate Enrollment: 800
Scholarships/Academic: Yes **Athletic:** No
Total Expenses by: Year **In State:** $ 24,000

Type: 4 Yr., Private, Liberal Arts, Coed
Campus Housing: Yes
SAT/ACT/GPA: 1000/23/2.8
Male/Female Ratio: 55:45
Graduate Enrollment: 1-12
Fin Aid: Yes
Out of State: $ 24,000

Degrees Conferred: BA, BS
Programs of Study: Biology, Chemistry, Business and Management, Chemistry, Communications, Computer Science, Economics, Education, Engineering, Environmental Science, Fine Arts, French, German, History, Journalism, Languages, Life Science, Math Philosphy, Physical Education, Physics, Political Science, Predentistry, Prelaw, Premed, Psychology, Public Administration

ATHLETIC PROFILE

Conference Affiliation: President's Athletic Conference
Program Profile: Division III program on the rise. Facilities improving each year. Offer varsity and junior varsity competition. Annual Spring trip - normally Florida and in 1999 California.
History: The program began in 1902 - since Carver took the program in 1991 we have led the nation in hitting. 1998 played 12 times ranked in top 35; extremely competitive schedule.
Achievements: Coach of the Year in 1991 and 1996; Louisville Slugger in 1994, 1995 and 1996; Dapper Dan in 1992, 1995 and 1997; 1 All-American in 1995.

Coaching: Rick Carver, Head Coach, compiled a record of 145-135; PAC record is 78-42. He was named Coach of the Year in 1991 and 1996. Tony Magnone, Assistant Coach.
Roster for 1998 team/In State: 5 **Out of State:** 28 **Out of Country:** 0
Total Number of Varsity/Jr. Varsity: 33 /18 **Percent of Graduation:** 100%
Number of Seniors on 1998 Team: 4 **Most Recent Record:** 17 - 23 - 0
Freshmen Receiving Fin Aid/Athletic: 0 **Academic:** 33
Number of Fall Games: 9 **Number of Spring Games:** 40
Positions Needed for 1999/2000: Left-handed pitcher, Catcher, Power Hitter
Schedule: Ohio Wesleyan, Marietta, West Virginia State, North Central, McMurray, Claremont
Style of Play: Aggressive base running - love to hit and run. Solid fundamental defense. Pitching philosophy is to mix up pitchers and throw strikes. Looking for fun, hard-nosed, scrappy players.

Bluefield State College

219 Rock Street
Bluefield, WV 24701
Coach: Geoff Hunter

NCAA II
Big Blues/Blue, Gold
Phone: (304) 327-4084
Fax: (304) 327-4179

ACADEMIC

Founded: 1895 **Type:** 4 Yr., Public, Coed
Religion: Non-Affiliated **Campus Housing:** No
Web-site: Not Available **SAT/ACT/GPA:** 700/17
Student/Faculty Ratio: 23:1 **Male/Female Ratio:** 41:59
Undergraduate Enrollment: 2,600 **Graduate Enrollment:** None
Scholarships/Academic: Yes **Athletic:** Yes **Fin Aid:** Yes
Total Expenses by: Year **In State:** $ 1,850 **Out of State:** $ 4,200
Degrees Conferred: AA, AAS, BA, BS, BSE, BSET, BBA
Programs of Study: Accounting, Biological, Business, Computer, Criminal Justice, Education, Engineering, English, Mathematics, Nursing, Physical Education, Science Education

ATHLETIC PROFILE

Conference Affiliation: WVIAC

Concord College

Athletics - PO Box 1000
Athens, WV 24712-1000
Coach: Kevin Garrett

NCAA II
Mountain Lions/Maroon, Grey
Phone: (304) 384-5347
Fax: (304) 384-5117

ACADEMIC

Founded: 1872 **Type:** 4 Yr., Public, Liberal Arts, Coed
Web-site: Not Available **SAT/ACT/GPA:** 700/17
Student/Faculty Ratio: 20:1 **Male/Female Ratio:** 40:60
Undergraduate Enrollment: 2,700 **Graduate Enrollment:** None
Scholarships/Academic: Yes **Athletic:** Yes **Fin Aid:** Yes
Total Expenses by: Year **In State:** $ 5,532 **Out of State:** $ 8,042
Degrees Conferred: A, BA, BBA, BSCIS, BSED, BSW
Programs of Study: Accounting, Banking and Finance, Broadcasting, Chemistry, Communications, Community Services, Computer Education, English, Geography, History, Hotel/Restaurant Management, Information Science, Marketing, Mathematics, Medical, Office Parks/Recreation

ATHLETIC PROFILE

Conference Affiliation: WVIAC

Davis and Elkins College

100 Campus Drive
Elkins, WV 26241
Coach: Lawrence Nesselrodt
Email: pri@dne.wvnet.edu

NCAA II
Senators/Scarlet, White
Phone: (304) 637-1342
Fax: (304) 637-1414

ACADEMIC

Founded: 1904
Religion: Presbyterian
Web-site: http://www.dne.wvnet.edu/
Student/Faculty Ratio: 15:1
Undergraduate Enrollment: 1,200
Scholarships/Academic: Yes **Athletic:** Yes
Total Expenses by: Year **In State:** $ 17,500
Degrees Conferred: AB, BS

Type: 4 Yr., Private, Liberal Arts, Coed
Campus Housing: Yes
SAT/ACT/GPA: 820/18
Male/Female Ratio: 50:50
Graduate Enrollment:
Fin Aid: Yes
Out of State: $ 17,500

Programs of Study: Arts, Fine Art, Biology, Environmental Science, Chemistry, Computer Science, Education, Nursing, Business Administration, Accounting, Management, Marketing, Communications, Political Science, Religion, Philosophy, Social Science, History, Prelaw, Premed

ATHLETIC PROFILE

Estimated Number of Baseball Scholarships: 7
Conference Affiliation: West Virginia Intercollegiate Athletic Conference, WVIAC
Program Profile: Philosphy is based on "academics, social conduct, and athletic committment". Facility includes indoor cage, year-round option. Breaking-ground on a new gym (1998); field is a natural turf infield, beam clay infield surface (dirt), new dugouts, rest rooms, storage building, open seating (plans for team rooms, concession, seating).
History: Began in 1951; won state championships in 1980; have won Northern Division of WVIAC in 1991, 1993, and 1995.
Achievements: WVIAC Coach of the Year in 1995; 10 drafted players; 3 All-Americans.
Coaching: Lawrence Nesselrodt, Head Coach, entering five years, compiled a record of 59-89; coached nine years at Garrett CC, MD and compiled a record of 201-179. Returned to alma mater in Spring of 1994 after coaching at JC alma mater (Garrett CC, Maryland). Deven Majkowski, Assistant Coach, entering first year with the program.
Roster for 1998 team/In State: 7 **Out of State:** 16 **Out of Country:** 1
Total Number of Varsity/Jr. Varsity: 22 **Percent of Graduation:** 60%
Number of Seniors on 1998 Team: 3 **Number of Sophomores on 1998 Team:** 11
Freshmen Receiving Fin Aid/Athletic: 2 **Academic:** 5
Baseball Camp Dates: 6/21-25 **Number of Spring Games:** 46
Positions Needed for 1999/2000: 1st Base, 3rd Base, Shortstop, Pitcher
Most Recent Record: 22 - 16 - 1
Schedule: West Virginia State, Slippery Rock, West Liberty, Bloomsburg, Mansfield, Shepherd
Style of Play: We stress fundamentals in all areas of play. We want to be smart and aggressive in our approach.

Fairmont State College

1201 Locust Avenue
Fairmont, WV 26554
Coach: Donnie Retton

NCAA II
Falcons/Maroon, White
Phone: (304) 367-4220
Fax: (304) 367-0202

ACADEMIC

Founded: 1867
SAT/ACT/GPA: 900/17/2.25
Student/Faculty Ratio: 22:1

Type: 4 Yr., Public, Coed
Campus Housing: Yes
Male/Female Ratio: 45:55

Undergraduate Enrollment: 6,700 **Graduate Enrollment:** None
Scholarships/Academic: Yes **Athletic:** Yes **Fin Aid:** Yes
Total Expenses by: Year **In State:** $ 5,878 **Out of State:** $ 7,946
Programs of Study: Elementary Education, Secondary Education, Business Administration, Criminal justice, Nursing, Psychology, History, Speech, Physical Education, Health Technology

ATHLETIC PROFILE

Estimated Number of Baseball Scholarships: 1
Conference Affiliation: WVIAC
Program Profile: Year-round program - instruction and repetitions in the Fall; weight lifting and conditioning program in the Fall and Winter. Play 45 plus games a year - week long Southern trip; astro-turf infielder. Rosier field with seating capacity of 200.
Achievements: Fairmont State has 14 players drafted since 1960; one drafted player on team for the 1998 season; drafted by CUBS in 37th round.
Coaching: Donnie Retton, Head Coach, compiled a record of 33-34-2; 1997 All-Conference catcher; made playoffs first year; 6 year assistant coach. Ronnie Retton & Charles Amett, Assistant Coaches.
Roster for 1998 team/In State: 23 **Out of State:** 7 **Out of Country:** 0
Total Number of Varsity/Jr. Varsity: 30 **Percent of Graduation:** 90%
Number of Seniors on 1998 Team: 6 **Number of Sophomores on 1998 Team:** 7
Freshmen Receiving Fin Aid/Athletic: 3 **Number of Spring Games:** 38
Most Recent Record: 13 - 16 - 1 **Baseball Camp Dates:** June 9-13
Positions Needed for 1999/2000: Pitchers, Catchers, Shortstop
Schedule: Kennesaw, West Georgia, Lock Haven, Slippery Rock, West Virginia, West Virginia
Style of Play: Aggressive, fundamentally sound, good pitching, and strong defense.

Marshall University

P.O. Box 1360
Huntington, WV 25715
Coach: David Piepenbrink

NCAA I
Thundering/Green, White
Phone: (304) 696-6454
Fax: (304)-696-6448

ACADEMIC

Founded: 1837 **Type:** 4 Yr., Public, Coed
Religion: Non-Affiliated **Campus Housing:** Yes
Web-site: http://www.marshall.edu/ **SAT/ACT/GPA:** 810/17
Student/Faculty Ratio: 18:1 **Male/Female Ratio:** 48:52
Undergraduate Enrollment: 10,800 **Graduate Enrollment:** 2,300
Scholarships/Academic: Yes **Athletic:** Yes **Fin Aid:** Yes
Total Expenses by: Year **In State:** $ 6,370 **Out of State:** $ 10,376
Degrees Conferred: AA, AAS, BA, BS, BFA, MA, MS, MBA
Programs of Study: Business/Office and Marketing/Distribution, Business and Management, Communications, Education, Health Science, Engineering, Parks/Recreation, Protective Services, Public Affairs, Fine Arts, Nursing, School of Medicine, Community and Technical College, Education

ATHLETIC PROFILE

Conference Affiliation: Southern Conference

Potomac State College

Fort Avenue
Keyser, WV 26726
Coach: TBA

NJCAA
Catamounts/Royal Blue, Gold
Phone: (304) 788-6880
Fax: (304) 788-6871

ACADEMIC

Founded: 1901 **Type:** 2 Yr., Public, , Coed,
Undergraduate Enrollment: 1,108 **Campus Housing:** Yes
Student/Faculty Ratio: 19:1 **Male/Female Ratio:**
Total Expenses by: Year **In State:** $ 1,866+ **Out of State:** $ 6,056+
Degrees Conferred: Associate
Programs of Study: Contact school for program of study.

ATHLETIC PROFILE

Program Profile: Play a year round program , 25 Fall games, and approximately 50 Spring (12 Spring games in Florida). Fall/Winter conditioning-strength program. The home playing field (Stayman Field) has natural grass, two indoor batting cages, two indoor mounds. State-of-the-art weight room. Last two years team GPA 2.5.
History: The program began year round in the mid-1970's. Last five years have had a .768 winning percentage. Since 1992 every sophomore has had scholarship offers from four year schools or have been drafted. Former alumnus John Kruk formerly with the Philadelphia Phillies and Chicago White Sox, now our Hitting Instructor. Former head coach was Jack Reynolds from 1973-1980.
Achievements: 1995 National Championship, 1993 National Runner-ups; Former Head Coach, Coach Rotruck 1995 NJCAA Coach of the Year; since 1991 3 All-Americans, 6 players drafted last 4 years never ranked lower than #5 Nationally.

Salem - Teikyo University

223 West Main Street
Salem, WV 26426
Coach: Brad Warnimont
NCAA II
Fighting Tigers/Green, Black, White
Phone: (304) 782-5632
Fax: (304) 782-5516

ACADEMIC

Founded: 1888 **Type:** 4 Yr., Private, Liberal Arts, Coed
Religion: Non-Affiliated **Campus Housing:** Yes
Web-site: http://www.stulib.salem-teikyo.wvnet.edu/ **SAT/ACT/GPA:** 17/2.0
Student/Faculty Ratio: 12:1 **Male/Female Ratio:** 60:40
Undergraduate Enrollment: 650 **Graduate Enrollment:** 50
Scholarships/Academic: Yes **Athletic:** Yes **Fin Aid:** Yes
Total Expenses by: Year **In State:** $ 17,049 **Out of State:** $ 17,049
Degrees Conferred: AA, AS, BA, AAS, BS, MA
Programs of Study: Accounting, Aeronautical Science, Airline Piloting Navigation, Biology, Equistrian Science, Broadcasting, Business Administration, Communications, Computer Science, Criminal Justice, Elementary Education, Engineering Technology, Industrial Engineering, Management, Marketing, Mathematics, Medical Laboratory Technology, Secondary Education

ATHLETIC PROFILE

Estimated Number of Baseball Scholarships: Several
Conference Affiliation: West Virginia Intercollegiate Athletic Conference
Program Profile: Game field is called Frank Loma Field at Clarksburg; facilities includes press box with a seating capacity of 1,200 enclosed, practice field in Salem, practice infield, three bull pen mounds, and two hitting cages with soft toss station.
History: Since 1940 - 7 conference championships, the last was in 1977. 1998 season had a record of 22-24 overall, 6th in conference. Qualified for conference tournament. In 1997 we went 12th place to 6th place.
Achievements: LHP drafted in 1994 with Baltimore. Coach of the Year; 1998 finished 8th in nation in stolen bases.
Coaching: Brad Warnimont, Head Coach, first year with the program was in 1998 with a record of 22-24; 1995 at Ashland took team to Division II World Series.
Roster for 1998 team/In State: 16 **Out of State:** 20 **Out of Country:** 1

Most Recent Record: 22 - 24 - 0
Percent of Graduation: 80%
Number of Seniors on 1998 Team: 5
Number of Sophomores on 1998 Team: 1
Freshmen Receiving Fin Aid/Athletic: 6
Academic: 15
Number of Fall Games: 0
Number of Spring Games: 56
Positions Needed for 1999/2000: Catcher, Middle Infielder
Schedule: Mercyhurst, West Virginia, Slippery Rock, Florida Southern, West Virginia Wesleyan
Style of Play: Very aggressive, very disciplined, great team speed.

Shepherd College

James Butcher Athletic Center
Shepherdstown, WV 25443-1569
Coach: Wayne Riser
NCAA II
Rams/Blue, Gold
Phone: (304) 876-5472
Fax: (304) 876-3267

ACADEMIC

Founded: 1871
Type: 4 Yr., Public, Coed
Undergraduate Enrollment: 3,600
Campus Housing: Yes
Web-site: http://www.shepherd.wvnet.edu/
SAT/ACT/GPA: 700
Student/Faculty Ratio: 18:1
Male/Female Ratio: 1:2
Scholarships/Academic: Yes **Athletic:** Yes
Fin Aid: Yes
Total Expenses by: Year **In State:** $ 5,500 **Out of State:** $ 9,500
Degrees Conferred: AA, AS, AAS, BA, BS, BFA
Programs of Study: Accounting, Applied Mathematics, Arts, Athletic Training, Biochemistry, Biology, Botany, Broadcasting, Business, Chemistry, Communications, Computer Informations Systems, Computer Science, Earth Science, Economics, Education, Engineering, English, Fine Art, History, International Studies, Liberal Arts, Literature, Mathematics, Music, Nursing, Occupational Safety and Health, Physical Education, Physical Fitness/Exercise Science, Physical Science, Plant Science, Political Science, Predentistry, Preengineering, Prelaw, Premed, Prevet, Psychology, Recreational and Leisure, Science, Sports Management, Theatre, Zoology

ATHLETIC PROFILE

Conference Affiliation: WVIAC
Program Profile: Shepherd College is located in the Shenandoah Valley on the banks of the Potomac River, Shepherdstown is the oldest town in the state, 1 mile from Maryland, 20 miles from Pennsylvania and Virginia, 65 miles from Washington DC and Baltimore. Fairfax Field recently upgraded, now has new dugouts, electronic scoreboard, press box for print and electronic media, outfield fence meshing, making it the leading on-campus baseball facility in the WVIAC.
Achievements: Coach Wayne Riser has led the Rams to the top of the WVIAC in the last three years, winning the 1994 WVIAC Northern Division Title and posting the first back-to-back 20 wins seasons in school history; was nationally ranked in 1996 for the first time in the school's history.
Coaching: Wayne Riser, Head Coach, was named 1994 WVIAC Coach of the Year. He develped the Sheperd College Instructional Baseball School for Youths and serve as a hitting Instructor at the Cal Ripken Sr. Baseball School in Emmitsburg, MD each Summer.

University of Charleston

2300 McCorke Avenue, SE
Charleston, WV 25304
Coach: Tom Nozica
Email: kjordan@uchaswv.edu
NCAA II
Golden Eagles/Maroon, Gold
Phone: (304) 357-4823
Fax: (304) 357-4989

ACADEMIC

Founded: 1888
Type: 4 Yr., Private, Liberal Arts, Coed
Web-site: http://www.uchaswv.edu/
SAT/ACT/GPA: 820/18

Student/Faculty Ratio: 14:1 **Male/Female Ratio:** 1:3
Undergraduate Enrollment: 1,500 **Graduate Enrollment:** 100
Scholarships/Academic: Yes **Athletic:** Yes **Fin Aid:** Yes
Total Expenses by: Year **In State:** $ 16,000 **Out of State:** $ 16,000
Degrees Conferred: AA, AS, BA, BS, MBA, MHRM
Programs of Study: Art, Biology, Chemistry, Education, English, Environmental Science, History, Mathematics, Music, Mass Communication, Political Science, Psychology, Social Science, Sports Science, Sports Medicine, Paralegal Studies, Accounting, Business Administration, Computer

ATHLETIC PROFILE

Estimated Number of Baseball Scholarships: 6
Conference Affiliation: West Virginia Intercollegiate Athletic Conference
Program Profile: Has a Fall playing program; strength program; Spring playing season; Spring tour (15 games). Indoor facillity includes cages, mounds, machines, etc., on campus practice facility (national) minor league stadium for games with a natural grass and seating for 4,500.
Achievements: Several division, conference championships, several players drafted or signed.
Coaching: Tom Nozica, Head Coach, started coaching with the program in 1969. Steve Crosier, Assistant Coach, entering second season with the program. Brian Mallory, Assistant Coach, started in 1997 and Greg Keaton, started in 1998.
Roster for 1998 team/In State: 10 **Out of State:** 18 **Out of Country:** 0
Total Number of Varsity/Jr. Varsity: 28 **Percent of Graduation:** 90%
Number of Seniors on 1998 Team: 1 **Most Recent Record:** 19 - 18 - 0
Freshmen Receiving Fin Aid/Athletic: 12 **Academic:** 4
Positions Needed for 1999/2000: Pitcher **Number of Spring Games:** 47
Baseball Camp Dates: TBA (3-January; 3-February; 1-June)
Schedule: Mobile, Ohio Dominican, Marietta, Pittsburgh - Johnstown, California-Pennsylvania
Style of Play: Aggressive, dictate game tempo; generate runs - run an inning "take what we want".

West Liberty State College

Bartell Fieldhouse
West Liberty, WV 26074
Coach: Robert McConnaughy

NCAA II
Hilltoppers/Gold, Black
Phone: (304) 336-8235
Fax: (304) 336-8304

ACADEMIC

Founded: 1837 **Type:** 4 Yr., Public, Liberal Arts, Coed
Web-site: http://www.wlsc.wvnet.edu/ **SAT/ACT/GPA:** 750/18/2.0
Student/Faculty Ratio: 19:1 **Male/Female Ratio:** 45:55
Undergraduate Enrollment: 2,500 **Graduate Enrollment:** 200
Scholarships/Academic: Yes **Athletic:** Yes **Fin Aid:** Yes
Total Expenses by: Year **In State:** $ 5,220 **Out of State:** $ 8,660
Degrees Conferred: AA, AS, BA, BS, MA, MS, MBA, PHd, JD
Programs of Study: Accounting, Banking/Finance, Biological, Business, Chemistry, Communications, Computer, Criminal, Dental, Nursing, Office, Economics, Education, English, Fashion, Geography, History, Interdisciplinary, Management, Marketing, Mathematics, Medical

ATHLETIC PROFILE

Conference Affiliation: WVIAC
Program Profile: School located in Northern arm of WV. Campus stretches over a wide hilltop, thus the name "Hilltoppers". Baseball program is perennial contender for Conference. It has been rebuilding for the past 2 years.
Achievements: Since 1986 - in playoffs every year, 4 conference titles, 6 district titles, in 6 Area 7 playoffs 6 straight years. 2-time participant NAIA World Series.
Coaching: Bo McConnaughy, Head Coach since 1983, played 3 years in the minor leagues.
Style of Play: We make the best of our mistakes and take advantage of other team's mistakes.

West Virginia Institute of Technology

405 Fayette Pike
Montgomery, WV 25136
Coach: Bill Briggs

NCAA II
Golden Bears/Gold, Blue
Phone: (304) 442-3144
Fax: (304) 442-3499

ACADEMIC

Founded: 1895
Type: 4 Yr., Public, Coed
SAT/ACT/GPA: 19avg
Campus Housing: Yes
Student/Faculty Ratio: 18:1
Male/Female Ratio: 64:36
Undergraduate Enrollment: 2,650
Graduate Enrollment: 20
Scholarships/Academic: Yes **Athletic:** Yes **Fin Aid:** Yes
Total Expenses by: Year **In State:** $ 4,240 **Out of State:** $ 8,410
Degrees Conferred: AA, AS, BA, BS
Programs of Study: Accounting, Banking/Finance, Biological Science, Business, Chemistry, City/Community/Regional Planning, Computer, Education, Engineering, English, Health, History, Industrial, Music, Management, Nursing, Paper and Pulp Science, Public Administration

ATHLETIC PROFILE

Conference Affiliation: WVIAC

West Virginia State College

CB 181, PO Box 1000
Institute, WV 25112-1000
Coach: Calvin Bailey

NCAA II
Yellow Jackets/Old Gold, Black
Phone: (304) 766-3208
Fax: (304) 766-3364

ACADEMIC

Founded: 1891
Type: 4 Yr., Public, Coed
Web-site: Not Available
SAT/ACT/GPA: 700/17
Student/Faculty Ratio: 19:1
Male/Female Ratio: 1:1
Undergraduate Enrollment: 4,500
Graduate Enrollment: None
Scholarships/Academic: Yes **Athletic:** Yes **Fin Aid:** Yes
Total Expenses by: Year **In State:** $ 4,240 **Out of State:** $ 8,410
Degrees Conferred: AA, AS, AAS, BA, BS
Programs of Study: 17 Bachelors Degrees offered.

ATHLETIC PROFILE

Conference Affiliation: West Virginia Intercollegiate Athletic Conference
Program Profile: Yellow Jacket Field is natural grass. Playing season is in the Spring.
History: Program began in 1954. In 18 years, the Yellow Jackets have not had a losing season.
Achievements: Coach Calvin Bailey just won his 9th WVIC title in twenty years. Won career victory number 500-current record is 506-241-2. Has had 17 players drafted and one every year in the 90's.
Coaching: Calvin Bailey, Head Coach, WVSC alumni, 18th year at the helm (442-216-2 record), guided WVSC to 7 WVIAC championships and 6 NAIA District 28 championships. Cal's winning percentage is .669. He spent 6.5 years with the Pirates and Padres Organizations' coaches, played 6.5 seasons with both the Pirates and Padres Organizations. Sean Lloyd, Assistant Coach.
Style of Play: Hitting and pitching.

West Virginia University

P.O. Box 0877
Morgantown, WV 26507
Coach: Greg Van Zant
Email: gvanzant@wvu.edu

NCAA I
Mountaineers/Old Gold, Blue
Phone: (304) 293-2308
Fax: (304) 293-2525

ACADEMIC

Founded: 1867
Type: 4 Yr., Public, Coed
Web-site: http://www.wvu.edu
Campus Housing: Yes
Student/Faculty Ratio: 15:1
Male/Female Ratio: 40:60
Scholarships/Academic: Yes **Athletic:** Yes **Fin Aid:** Yes
Total Expenses by: Year **In State:** $ 7,568 **Out of State:** $ 12,588
Degrees Conferred: BA, BS, several graduate degrees
Programs of Study: Over 130 programs of study.

ATHLETIC PROFILE

Estimated Number of Baseball Scholarships: 11.7
Conference Affiliation: Big East Conference
Program Profile: Hawley Field has a seating capacity of 1,500, natural grass with measurements of LF-325, CF-390, and RF-325. Eight 100 feet light poles, two lighted hitting tunnels, Shell Building which has a 54 sq. ft. indoor practice facility. The team has 56 game schedule versus all Division I opponents. Major League caliber strength and conditioning program.
History: 1892 was the first season of the program; 6 All-Americans; 38 players drafted; 56 players have played professionally, including 1997-first round draft pick Chris Enochs; 10 players currently in the pro ball. 12 NCAA Regional Tournament Appearances in 1996, 1994, 1987, 1985, 1982, 1967, 1964, 1963, 1962, 1961, 1955 and 1948.
Achievements: Coach Van Zant was named 1997 Big East Coach of the Year; 1996 ABCA East Region Coach of the Year; Big East Conference Champs in 1996; Big East Regular Season Champs in 1996 and 1997; All-Americans were Chris Enochs in 1997, Mark Landers in 1994, Joe Hatalla in 1962, Bill Moravic in 1964; drafted players were Chris Enochs in 1997 (1), Steve Beller in 1997 (24), Scott Seaboll in 1996, Mike Riley in 1996, Mark Lander in 1994, Steve Kline in 1993, Dan Barry in 1993, David Demoss in 1992, Joe Hudson in 1992, and Darrell Whitmore in 1990.
Coaching: Greg Van Zant, Head Coach, 1997 Big East Coach of the Year, entering fourth year at WVU. Graduate of WVU in 1983. Doug Little, Assistant Coach, entering fourth year. He was an Alderson-Broaddus graduate in 1988. Ron Moore,Assistant Coach, entering second year, graduate of Arkansas in 1991. Bruce Cameron,Assistant Coach, entering his second season, graduate of Concordia-NY in 1993. Doug Little, Assistant Coach.
Total Number of Varsity/Jr. Varsity: 29 **Percent of Graduation:** 90%
Most Recent Record: 37 - 17 - 1 **Number of Spring Games:** 56
Positions Needed for 1999/2000: Pitcher, Catcher, Infielder, Outfielder
Baseball Camp Dates: June, July, December
Schedule: Georgia Tech, Notre Dame, Rutgers, St. John's, North Carolina, State
Style of Play: Stress discipline and fundamentals.

West Virginia Wesleyan College

Box 92
Buckhannon, WV 26201
Coach: Randy Tenney

NCAA II
Bobcats/Orange, Black
Phone: (304) 473-8054
Fax: (304) 472-2571

ACADEMIC

Founded: 1890
Type: 4 Yr., Private, Liberal Arts, Coed
Religion: Methodist
Campus Housing: Yes
Web-site: http://www.wvwc.edu
SAT/ACT/GPA: NCAA standards

Student/Faculty Ratio: 14:1 **Male/Female Ratio:** 1:2
Undergraduate Enrollment: 1,600 **Graduate Enrollment:** 50
Scholarships/Academic: Yes **Athletic:** Yes **Fin Aid:** Yes
Total Expenses by: Year **In State:** $ 21,250 **Out of State:** $ 21,250
Degrees Conferred: BA, MS, MBA,
Programs of Study: Art, Accounting, Biology, Business Administration, Chemistry, Computer Information Systems, Computer Science, Communications Studies, Economics, Education, English, Engineering, Physics, Environmental Science, Finance, History, International Studies, Management, Marketing, Mathematics, Music, Physical Education, Sports Medicine, Philosophy, Physics, Political Science, Psychology, Public Relations, Religion, Sociology, Nursing

ATHLETIC PROFILE

Conference Affiliation: WVIAC
Program Profile: NCAA Division II, record in 1994 was 33-7. Play 40 games in Spring, 18 games in Fall, off-season strength and conditioning program. Turf indoor practice area, 3 indoor batting tunnel, 2 indoor mounds.
Achievements: Conference Champs in 1991, 1992, 1995, and 1996; District Champs in 1992 and 1993; Conference Coach of the Year in 1991 and 1992; District Coach of the Year in 1992; 9 All-Americans in the last three years; third in NCAA Division II Regional Tournament in 1996.
Coaching: Randy Tenney, Head Coach, 12 years as a head coach, two-time Coach of the Year.
Style of Play: Solid defense, aggressive offense, and consistent defense.

WISCONSIN

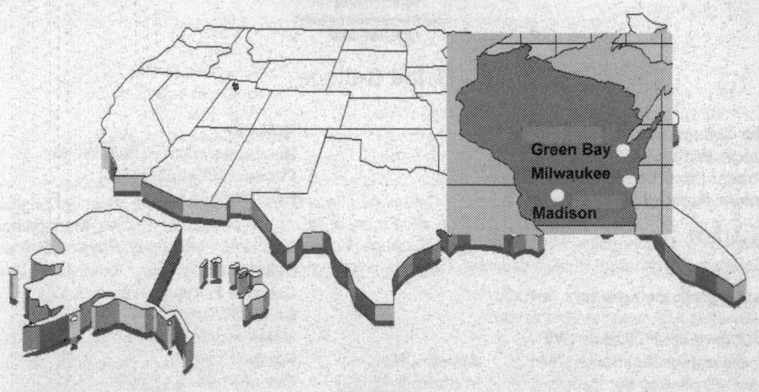

SCHOOL	CITY	AFFILIATION 99	PAGE
Beloit College	Beloit	NCAA III	912
Cardinal Stritch College	Milwaukee	NCAA III\NAIA	912
Carroll College	Waukesha	NCAA III	913
Carthage College	Kenosha	NCAA III	913
Concordia University	Mequon	NCAA III\NAIA	914
Edgewood College	Madison	NCAA	914
Lakeland College	Sheboygan	NCAA III	915
Lawrence University	Appleton	NCAA III	916
Madison Area Technical College	Madison	NJCAA III	917
Maranatha Baptist Bible College	Watertown	NCAA III	917
Marian College - Fond du Lac	Fond du Lac	NCAA III\NAIA	918
Milwaukee School of Engineering	Milwaukee	NCAA III	918
Ripon College	Ripon	NCAA III	919
Saint Norbert College	De Pere	NCAA III	920
University of Wisconsin - La Crosse	La Crosse	NCAA III	920
University of Wisconsin - Milwaukee	Milwaukee	NCAA I	921
University of Wisconsin - Oshkosh	Oshkosh	NCAA III	922
University of Wisconsin - Parkside	Kenosha	NCAA II	922
University of Wisconsin - Platteville	Platteville	NCAA III	923
University of Wisconsin - River Falls	River Falls	NCAA III	923
University of Wisconsin - Stevens Point	Stevens Point	NCAA III	924
University of Wisconsin - Stout	Menomonie	NCAA III	924
University of Wisconsin - Superior	Superior	NCAA III	925
University of Wisconsin - Whitewater	Whitewater	NCAA III	925
Viterbo College	La Crosse	NAIA	926
Waukesha County Technical College	Pewaukee	NJCAA	927
Western Wisconsin Technical College	La Crosse	NJCAA	927
Wisconsin Lutheran College	Milwaukee	NCAA III\NAIA	928

Beloit College

700 College Street
Beloit, WI 53511
Coach: Dave Degeorge
Email: degeorge@beloit.edu

NCAA III
Buccaneers/Navy Blue, White
Phone: (608) 363-2039
Fax: (608) 363-2044

ACADEMIC

Founded: 1846
Type: 4 Yr., Private, Liberal Arts, Coed
Undergraduate Enrollment: 1,200
Campus Housing: Yes
Web-site: http://www.stu.beloit.edu.
SAT/ACT/GPA: 22+
Student/Faculty Ratio: 12:1
Male/Female Ratio: 45:55
Scholarships/Academic: Yes **Athletic:** No **Fin Aid:** Yes
Total Expenses by: Year **In State:** $ 12,000 **Out of State:** $ 12,000
Degrees Conferred: BA, BS, MAT
Programs of Study: Art, Art History, Asian Studies, Biochemistry, Biology, Business and Management, Cell Biology, Chemistry, Communications, Comparative Literature, Computer Science, Creative Writing, Economics, Education, English, Environmental Biology, German, Journalism, Mathematics, Molecular Biology, Music, Philosophy, Physics, Political Science, Predentistry, Prelaw

ATHLETIC PROFILE

Conference Affiliation: Midwest Conference
Program Profile: The, Sports Center dedicated in 1987, contains Flood Arena, fully-equipped weight room, state-of-the-art fitness equipment, indoor track, indoor tennis courts, pitching and batting cages, racquetball courts, indoor pool and 2600 ft. dance room. Newly renovated, 3000-seat Tefler Park one of Division III best baseball fields (Summer home of Class A Beloit Snappers), covered grandstand, expansive dugouts, grass infield, batting cages, large bullpens.
History: Program began in late 1800's (reinstated in 1986 after 18 year layoff), has included 2 Hall of Famers, Lee MacPhail and Larry Hulbert, founder of the National League.
Achievements: John Rodgers was named Rookie of the Year in 1996; Brian Chesick was All-MWC; Defensive Player of the Year; All-Midwest Conference.
Coaching: Dave DeGeorge, Head Coach, is in his 8th season as Beloit College's head coach. He has guided the Buccaneers to the Midwest Conference Championship Tournament four of the last six seasons. Recorded more victories than any other coach in Beloit's 130-year baseball history. Graduated from Beloit in 1989 after a successful career as a middle infielder for the Bucs. Kerry Michaels, Assistant Coach, back for a third season as the Buccaneers defensive coach. Has been an amateur baseball coach for 22 years and has extensive experience with the Janesville Craig High School and Janesville Legion Squads.
Roster for 1998 team/In State: 10 **Out of State:** 16 **Out of Country:** 0
Total Number of Varsity/Jr. Varsity: 26 **Percent of Graduation:** 100%
Number of Seniors on 1998 Team: 6 **Most Recent Record:** 9 - 23 - 0
Freshmen Receiving Fin Aid/Athletic: 0 **Academic:** 11
Number of Fall Games: 0 **Number of Spring Games:** 34
Positions Needed for 1999/2000: Pitcher, Shortstop, Catcher, Pitcher,Outfielder
Baseball Camp Dates: December 28 and 29

Cardinal Stritch College

6801 North Yates Road
Milwaukee, WI 53217-3985
Coach: Chuck Mumfrey

NCAA III\NAIA
Crusaders/Red, White, Silver
Phone: (414) 352-5400
Fax: (414) 351-7516

ACADEMIC

Founded: 1937
Type: 4 Yr., Private, Liberal Arts, Coed
Religion: Roman Catholic
Campus Housing: Yes

Web-site: http://www.stritch.edu/ **SAT/ACT/GPA:** 980
Student/Faculty Ratio: 17:1 **Male/Female Ratio:** 40:60
Undergraduate Enrollment: 1,300 **Graduate Enrollment:** 1,800
Scholarships/Academic: Yes **Athletic:** Yes **Fin Aid:** Yes
Total Expenses by: Year **In State:** $ 15,000 **Out of State:** $ 15,000
Degrees Conferred: AA, AS, BA, MA, MS, MBA
Programs of Study: Accounting, Art, Biology, Business, Chemistry, Computer Science, Education, English, French, History, Communication, Mathematics, Music, Nursing, Psychology, Public Relations, Sociology, Spanish, Special Education, Theatre

ATHLETIC PROFILE

Conference Affiliation: Lake Michigan Conference

Carroll College

100 N East Avenue
Waukesha, WI 53186
Coach: Gary Richert

NCAA III
Pioneers/Orange, Navy
Phone: (414) 524-7322
Fax: (414) 524-7376

ACADEMIC

Founded: 1841 **Type:** 4 Yr., Private, Liberal Arts, Coed
Religion: Presbyterian **Campus Housing:** Yes
Web-site: http://www.carroll.cc.edu/ **SAT/ACT/GPA:** 20 average
Student/Faculty Ratio: 14:1 **Male/Female Ratio:** 1:2
Undergraduate Enrollment: 1,600 **Graduate Enrollment:** None
Scholarships/Academic: Yes **Athletic:** No **Fin Aid:** Yes
Total Expenses by: Year **In State:** $ 16,000 **Out of State:** $ 16,000
Degrees Conferred: BA, BS, BSMT, BSN, BSPT, MED
Programs of Study: Accounting, Art, Artificial Intelligence, Biology, Business Administration, Chemistry, Communications, Computer Science, Criminal Justice, Economics, Elementary Education, Environmental Science, Nursing, Medical Technology, Physical Education, Philosolphy, Psychology, Religious Studies, Social Work, Sociology Theater Art

ATHLETIC PROFILE

Conference Affiliation: Midwest Conference
Program Profile: A 30-game schedule from 1st week of March to end of April. Play at Frame Park in Waukesha right next to the Fox River and home of Waukesha's annual River Fest.
History: Carroll has played NCAA-sanctioned baseball since 1926.
Coaching: Gary Ritchert, Head Coach, graduated from Lake Land College in 1966.
Style of Play: Aggressive - running style, stress defense.

Carthage College

2001 Alford Park Drive
Kenosha, WI 53140
Coach: Augie Schmidt, Jr.

NCAA III
Redmen/Red, White, Black
Phone: (414) 551-5935
Fax: (414) 551-5995

ACADEMIC

Founded: 1847 **Type:** 4 Yr., Private, Liberal Arts, Coed
Web-site: Not Available **SAT/ACT/GPA:** 900/18
Student/Faculty Ratio: 15:1 **Male/Female Ratio:** 44:56
Undergraduate Enrollment: 1,990 **Graduate Enrollment:** 60
Scholarships/Academic: Yes **Athletic:** No **Fin Aid:** Yes

Total Expenses by: Year **In State:** $ 17,000 **Out of State:** $ 17,000
Degrees Conferred: BA, MED
Programs of Study: Accounting, Art, Athletic Training, Biological Science, Business, Chemistry, Conservatory, Criminal Justice, Design, Economics, Education, English, Languages, Geography, Health, History, International, Marketing, Math, Music, Natural Science, Pharmacy, Religion

ATHLETIC PROFILE

Conference Affiliation: CCIW
Program Profile: Two indoor batting cages in a separate upper gym; 1 batting cage indoors. New infield (natural grass), dugouts, scoreboard. A grandstand with pressbox will be under construction in late Summer - early Fall.
History: Baseball started in 1910. Current Head Coach, Augie Schmidt, started in 1988. Program has gone from a 4 win season to 39 win season and into the national rankings. Schmidt's record is 200-130-2.
Achievements: Nine All-Americans, 5 players drafted or signed as free agents. 1992 Midwest Region Runner-Up. 1993, 1994 and 1995 Central Region Champs. CCIS Champs 1992, 1993 and 1995. 3 consecutive 3rd place finishes at Div. III World Series 1993, 1994, 1995.
Coaching: Augie Schmidt, Head Coach, started in 1988. Record is 200-130-2. Regional Coach of the Year 1992, 1993, 1994. Conference Coach of the Year 1989, 1990, 1992, 1994, 1995. Golden Spike Award winner 1982. Toronto 1982 number one first draft pick. Brian Mosher - Pitching Coach. 7 years as assist at Carthage. Pitching staff has led CCIW in ERA 6 years & 6 pitchers All-American.
Total Number of Varsity/Jr. Varsity: 31/10-12 **Percent of Graduation:** 90%
Style of Play: Aggressive, hit and run. Combination of speed and power.

Concordia University

12800 North Lake Shore Drive
Mequon, WI 53092-9652
Coach: Val Keiper

NCAA III\NAIA
Falcons/Blue, White
Phone: (414) 243-4385
Fax: (414) 243-4475

ACADEMIC

Founded: 1881
Type: 4 Yr., Private, Liberal Arts, Coed
Religion: Lutheran-Missouri Synod
Campus Housing: Yes
Web-site: Not Available
SAT/ACT/GPA: 21+
Student/Faculty Ratio: 19:1
Male/Female Ratio: 42:58
Undergraduate Enrollment: 3,659
Graduate Enrollment: 478
Scholarships/Academic: Yes **Athletic:** No **Fin Aid:** Yes
Total Expenses by: Year **In State:** $ 7,100 **Out of State:** $ 7,100
Degrees Conferred: Associates, Masters, Bachelor
Programs of Study: Education, Business, Liberal Arts Majors, Occupational Therapy, Physical Therapy, Social Work, Criminal Justice,Communications, Nursing, Sport Medicine

ATHLETIC PROFILE

Conference Affiliation: Lake Michigan Conference
Program Profile: Play on a field that sits on a bluff overlooking Lake Michigan.
History: Program began in 1981.

Edgewood College

855 Woodrow Street
Madison, WI 53711
Coach: John Vodenlich
Email: jvodenlich@edgewood.edu

NCAA
Eagles/Red, Black, White
Phone: (608) 633-3289
Fax: (608) 633-3291

ACADEMIC

Founded: 1927
Type: 4 Yr., Private, Liberal Arts, Coed
Religion: Catholic
Campus Housing: Yes
Web-site: http://www.edgewood.edu
SAT/ACT/GPA: 860/18/2.5
Student/Faculty Ratio: 17:1
Male/Female Ratio: 1:2.5
Undergraduate Enrollment: 1,500
Graduate Enrollment: 500
Scholarships/Academic: Yes **Athletic:** No **Fin Aid:** Yes
Total Expenses by: Year **In State:** $ 14,000 **Out of State:** $ 14,000
Degrees Conferred: BS, BS, MBA, AA, MAE, MARS, MANA
Programs of Study: Accounting, Art, Art Therapy, Biology, Broad Fields Science, Business, Chemistry, Child Life, Computer Information Systems, Criminal Justice, Cytotechnology, Economics, Elementary Education, English, Graphic Design, History, International Relations, Mathematics, Music, Medical Technology, Nursing, Political Science, Psychology, Public Policy and Administration, Religion, Sociology, Predentistry, Prelaw, Premed, Prepharmacy, Preengineering

ATHLETIC PROFILE

Conference Affiliation: Lake Michigan Conference
Program Profile: The baseball field is a natural turf with a batting cage and a lights (Stample Field); indoor facilities include Edgedone which is on campus and McLain Center which is off-campus.
History: Last year was the most successful season in the ten year history of the program; 1997 season included the most conference wins; best finished in conference is 3rd place; most players selected to All-Conference team were four players.
Achievements: Finished 3rd place in the conference; several players selected to All-Conference.
Coaching: John Vodenlich, Head Coach, is in his second year as a head coach. He earned All-American honors twice as a player and spent the five years prior as an assistant at University of Wisconsin-Whitewater. John Fetherston - Assistant Coach.
Roster for 1998 team/In State: 17 **Out of State:** 2 **Out of Country:** 0
Total Number of Varsity/Jr. Varsity: 22 **Most Recent Record:** 11 - 23 - 0
Number of Seniors on 1998 Team: 2 **Number of Sophomores on 1998 Team:** 0
Freshmen Receiving Fin Aid/Athletic: 0 **Academic:** 100%
Number of Fall Games: 5 **Number of Spring Games:** 36
Positions Needed for 1999/2000: Catcher, 2-Pitchers, Power Hitter, Outfielder
Schedule: University of Wisconsin - Whitewater, Lewis University
Style of Play: We play fundamentally sound with an aggressive offensive approach.

Lakeland College

P.O. Box 359
Sheboygan, WI 53082-0359
Coach: John Weber
Email: weberjj@lakeland.edu
NCAA III
Muskies/Blue, Gold
Phone: (920) 565-1411
Fax: (920) 565-1399

ACADEMIC

Founded: 1862
Type: 4 Yr., Private, Coed
Religion: Non-Affiliated
Campus Housing: Yes
Web-site: http://www.lakeland.com
SAT/ACT/GPA: 19/2.0
Student/Faculty Ratio: 16:1
Male/Female Ratio: 45:55
Undergraduate Enrollment: 750
Graduate Enrollment: 50
Scholarships/Academic: Yes **Athletic:** No **Fin Aid:** Yes
Total Expenses by: Year **In State:** $ 16,100 **Out of State:** $ 16,100
Degrees Conferred: BA, MA
Programs of Study: 40 majors: Business, Education, Computer Science, Exercise Science, Social and Natural Sciences, Creative Arts

ATHLETIC PROFILE

Conference Affiliation: Lake Michigan Conference

Program Profile: Outstanding indoor facilities with batting cage and modern weight facility new on campus field, spacious, locker room, dug-outs, Spring trip to Florida for 11 days. We have a Fall schedule.
History: Program began in 1950; has two pro players. Program just beginning to come into own with on campus field and new facility.
Achievements: 1 Academic All-American; 1 All-American; 5 Conference Championships.
Coaching: John Weber, Head Coach, entering first year with the program, known for his ability of coaching pitchers; 1995 staff led nation in ERA for Division III. Has had 5 pitchers either drafted or signed in his four year coaching. Played on two teams that made Final Four of Division II College World Series while at Lewis University. Jason Bartelt , Assistant Coach, holds numerous career hitting records at Lakeland, excellent hitting instructor, played on team that holds record for most wins in a season. Damon Day, Assistant Coach.
Roster for 1998 team/In State: 18 **Out of State:** 9 **Out of Country:** 0
Total Number of Varsity/Jr. Varsity: 27 **Percent of Graduation:** 95%
Number of Seniors on 1998 Team: 2 **Baseball Camp Dates:** Summer 1999
Freshmen Receiving Fin Aid/Athletic: 0 **Academic:** 100%
Most Recent Record: 15 - 22 - 0 **Number of Spring Games:** 45
Positions Needed for 1999/2000: Pitcher, LHP, RHP, Shortstop, Outfielder
Schedule: Wisconsin-Oshkosh, Bethune-Cookman, Embry-Riddle, Wisconsin-Stevens Point, West Virginia Wesleyan, Wisconsin-Lacrosse, Manchester, Wisconsin-Parkside, Marian, Concordia
Style of Play: Aggressive pressure ball. Offense hits and hits with power. Aggressive on the basepaths. Put up big offensive numbers combined with solid pitching.

Lawrence University

P.O. Box 599
Appleton, WI 54912
Coach: Korey Krueger
Email: korey.j.krueger@lawrence.edu

NCAA III
Vikings/Blue
Phone: (920) 832-6760
Fax: (920) 832-7349

ACADEMIC

Founded: 1847
Undergraduate Enrollment: 1,225
Web-site: http://www.lawrence.edu/
Student/Faculty Ratio: 11:1
Scholarships/Academic: Yes **Athletic:** No
Degrees Conferred: BA, BM

Type: 4 Yr., Private, Liberal Arts, Coed
Campus Housing: Yes
SAT/ACT/GPA: 1020+/24+
Male/Female Ratio: 50:50
Fin Aid: Yes

Programs of Study: Anthropology, Biology, Geology, Mathematics, Physics, Psychology, Theatre and Drama, Biomedical Ethic, Environmental Studies, Neuroscience, Education, Life Sciences, Social

ATHLETIC PROFILE

Conference Affiliation: Midwest Conference
Program Profile: Lawrence University plays in the Midwest Conference. The season begins on February 1 and turns till mid-May. We play a Southern schedule every other year in Florida and a Western schedule in California. Our field is called Whiting Field and has unique dimensions for a college park. Left field is 315 feet, right field is 250 feet, and center is 415 feet.
History: Baseball began at Lawrence in 1958. Overall record is 327-482-10; pitching most wins in a season John Bill-8 in 1976-1979-slugging percentage is .620 in 1986-1989; career John Bill-23 in 1976-1979 career home runs is 14 in 1986-1989; batting average season Korey Krueger is .508 in 1993 - career Bill Simon is .374 in 1977-1980; Career hits - Bill Simon (120) in 1977-1980.
Achievements: We have not won the conference in the last 15 years. We have had a dry spell. No drafted players in the last decades. Brand new coach!!
Coaching: Korey Krueger, Head Coach, Lawrence University graduate in 1995. He is entering his second year with the program. Chad Boeker, Assistant Coach, 4th year, starting shortstop for UW-Platteville (1996 graduate), works with the infielders. Jon Arendt, Assistant Coach.
Roster for 1998 team/In State: 22 **Out of State:** 8 **Out of Country:** 0

Total Number of Varsity/Jr. Varsity: 30
Percent of Graduation: 100%
Number of Seniors on 1998 Team: 3
Number of Sophomores on 1998 Team: 0
Most Recent Record: 23 - 1 - 0
Number of Spring Games: 34
Positions Needed for 1999/2000: Pitchers/especially LHP, Shortstops
Baseball Camp Dates: March 5-7
Schedule: University of Wisconsin-Whitewater, Bethany, Chapman, Pacific University, LaVerne
Style of Play: We are a team that will be aggressive on the bases. We emphasize defense and unselfish play. Our players are smart individuals that concentrate on fundamental baseball.

Madison Area Technical College

3550 Anderson Street, Room #200
Madison, WI 53704
Coach: Leo Kalinowski
Email: lallen@madison.tec.wi.us

NJCAA III
Trojans/Royal Blue, White
Phone: (608) 246-6098
Fax: (608) 243-4385

ACADEMIC

Founded: 1965
Type: 4 Yr., Public, Coed
Religion: Non-Affiliated
Campus Housing: No
Undergraduate Enrollment: 9,000
Graduate Enrollment: None
Scholarships/Academic: Yes **Athletic:** No **Fin Aid:** Yes
Total Expenses by: Year **In State:** $ Varies **Out of State:** $ Varies
Degrees Conferred: Two-year associate degrees
Programs of Study: MATC Boasts a college parallel program with an emphasis on credits that will transfer to four year schools.

ATHLETIC PROFILE

Conference Affiliation: Wisconsin Technical College Conference
Program Profile: Completing brand new stadium hopefully by Spring of 1999, natural grass field. Program is 27 year old; excellent weight room and fitness facility, including swimming; 20 scrimmages in the Fall; 56 regular game schedule; recruit to walk-on ratio 75% to 25%.
History: The MATC baseball program began in 1971; 3 National titles (NJCAA Division III) in 1995, 1996, and 1997; 4 Region XIII Titles in 1994-1997; 3rd place NJCAA Division III in 1994; 18 WICC Conference Titles; 16 WJCAA State Titles.
Achievements: Coach Kalinowski was the NJCAA Division III Coach of the Year in 1995, 1996 & the NJCAA Region Coach of the Year in 1994, 1995, and 1996; 6 All-Americans & 8 drafted players.
Coaching: Leo Kalinowski, Head Coach, entering his 7th season in 1998, career record of 203-61; played at the University of Massachusetts. Lyle Hanson, Assistant Coach, has been an assistant for 20 season of 1997 as a full time assistant. Dave Schwei, Assistant Coach, entering second season, former pitcher.
Roster for 1998 team/In State: 88 **Out of State:** 12 **Out of Country:** 0
Total Number of Varsity/Jr. Varsity: 24
Most Recent Record: 35 - 15 - 0
Number of Seniors on 1998 Team: 8
Number of Sophomores on 1998 Team: 0
Number of Fall Games: 20
Number of Spring Games: 56
Positions Needed for 1999/2000: Best player available
Schedule: Triton, Seminole, Joliet, College of DuPage, Polk, Central Florida, Blackhawk
Style of Play: Very aggressive "put the ball in play" offense. Developing a fundamentally sound pitching staff of good depth of at least 8 pitchers and to relies to pitchers. Big emphasis on mental approach in all phases of games.

Maranatha Baptist Bible College

745 W Main Street
Watertown, WI 53094
Coach: Jerry Terrill

NCAA III
Crusaders/Royal, Gold
Phone: (920) 261-9300x2380
Fax: (414) 261-9109

ACADEMIC

Founded: 1968
Religion: Non-Affiliated
Student/Faculty Ratio: 20:1
Undergraduate Enrollment: 475
Scholarships/Academic: **Athletic:**
Total Expenses by: Year **In State:** $ 8,000
Type: 4 Yr., Private, Coed
Campus Housing: Yes
Male/Female Ratio: 50:50
Graduate Enrollment: 20
Fin Aid:
Out of State: $ 8,000
Degrees Conferred: Bachelors, Masters
Programs of Study: Biblical Studies, Biblical Languages, Business, Early Childhood Education, Education, Elementary Education, Humanities, Liberal Arts, Management, Ministries, Music, Nursing, Physical Education, Religion, Secondary Education, Speech, Sports Administration, Theology

Marian College - Fond du Lac

45 South National Avenue
Fond du Lac, WI 54935
Coach: Brian Gillogly
NCAA III\NAIA
Sabres/White, Red, Blue
Phone: (920) 923-7625
Fax: (920) 923-7625

ACADEMIC

Founded: 1936
Religion: Catholic
Web-site: Not Available
Student/Faculty Ratio: 15:1
Undergraduate Enrollment: 1,800
Scholarships/Academic: Yes **Athletic:** No
Total Expenses by: Year **In State:** $ 13,000
Type: 4 Yr., Private, Liberal Arts, Coed
Campus Housing: Yes
SAT/ACT/GPA: 20
Male/Female Ratio: 40:60
Graduate Enrollment: 600
Fin Aid: Yes
Out of State: $ 13,000
Degrees Conferred: BA, BS, BBA, BSEd, BSN, MA
Programs of Study: Accounting, Art, Biology, Business Administration, Chemistry, Communications, Criminal Justice, Cytotechnology, Education, English, Environmental Science, History, Human Development, Human Services, Liberal Arts, Management, Marketing, Mathematics, Medical Technology, Music, Nursing, Predentistry, Prelaw, Premed, Prevet, Psychology, Radiological

ATHLETIC PROFILE

Conference Affiliation: Lake Michigan Conference

Milwaukee School of Engineering

1025 North Broadway
Milwaukee, WI 53202
Coach: Leonard Vanden Boom
Email: vandenbo@msoe.edu
NCAA III
Raiders/Red, White
Phone: (414) 277-7219
Fax: (414) 277-6926

ACADEMIC

Founded: 1903
Web-site: http://www.msoe.edu/
Student/Faculty Ratio: 15:1
Undergraduate Enrollment: 2,500
Scholarships/Academic: Yes **Athletic:** No
Total Expenses by: Year **In State:** $ 18,000
Type: 4 Yr., Private, Coed, Engineering
Campus Housing: Yes
Male/Female Ratio: 5:1
Graduate Enrollment: 500
Fin Aid: Yes
Out of State: $ 18,000
Degrees Conferred: 10 Engineering Majors, Business, Nursing
Programs of Study: Business and Management, Engineering, Engineering Technology, Nursing

ATHLETIC PROFILE

Conference Affiliation: Lake Michigan Conference
Program Profile: We begin our play and practice in Fall (September and October); start Spring in February 1 through May 15. Field is natural grass.
History: The program began in 1974.
Achievements: Numerous Coach of the Year honors; Conference and State; 8 Conference Titles.
Coaching: Leonard Vanden Boom, Head Coach, also Dean of Academic Services, started coaching in 1974 to 1982 and 1995 to the present with a record of 144-124. Larry Madsen, Assistant Coach.
Roster for 1998 team/In State: 75% **Out of State:** 25% **Out of Country:** 0
Total Number of Varsity/Jr. Varsity: 26 /22 **Percent of Graduation:** 95%
Number of Seniors on 1998 Team: 5 **Number of Sophomores on 1998 Team:** 6
Freshmen Receiving Fin Aid/Athletic: 0 **Academic:** 85%
Number of Fall Games: 9 **Number of Spring Games:** 40+
Positions Needed for 1999/2000: Pitcher, Infielder, SS, 2nd Base
Most Recent Record: 20 - 20 - 0
Schedule: Wardberg, Fontbonne, Washington, DePauw, Chicago, Concordia, Rose Hulman
Style of Play: Solid defense - aggressive running offense.

Ripon College

300 Seward Street
Ripon, WI 54971
Coach: Gordon Gillespie
Email: graham@mac.ripon.edu

NCAA III
Red Hawks/Red, White
Phone: (920) 748-8776
Fax: (920) 748-1386

ACADEMIC

Founded: 1851 **Type:** 4 Yr., Private, Liberal Arts, Coed
Religion: Non-Affiliated **Campus Housing:** Yes
Web-site: http://www.ripon.edu/ **Student/Faculty Ratio:** 12:1
Scholarships/Academic: Yes **Athletic:** No **Fin Aid:** Yes
Total Expenses by: Year **In State:** $ 22,000 **Out of State:** $ 22,000
Degrees Conferred: BA
Programs of Study: Anthropology, Biology, Business and Management, Chemistry, Computer Science, Economics, English, History, Letters/Literature, Life Sciences, Math, Music, Physical Education, Philosophy, Physical Sciences, Physics, Political Science, Psychology, Social Science

ATHLETIC PROFILE

Conference Affiliation: Midwest Conference
Program Profile: The Ripon's Baseball has been the strongest in the conference as we normally appear in post-season play. 1997 was another strong season as the Red Hawks finished 22-13-1, and 14-2 in conference play. They were regular season champs and returned to the conference tournament for the second conference season. Brand new field built in 1996, natural grass, one of the state finest facilities.
History: Ripon is a personal contender for the Conference Championships boasting 9 Championships since 1962, 3 of those in the past 10 years. Ripon baseball began in 1953.
Achievements: Gordon Gillespie was recently named NAIA's Man of the Country, he is college baseball winningest coach (1,387-712). He has signed 56 players to major league contract.
Coaching: Gordon Gillespie, Head Coach, was named Conference Coach of the Year. Bob Gillespie, Assistant Coach, former head coach for 15 years.
Roster for 1998 team/In State: 23 **Out of State:** 2 **Out of Country:** 0
Total Number of Varsity/Jr. Varsity: 0 **Percent of Graduation:** 80%
Number of Seniors on 1998 Team: 4 **Number of Sophomores on 1998 Team:** 3
Most Recent Record: 14 - 15 - 0 **Number of Spring Games:** 35
Positions Needed for 1999/2000: Outfielder, Catcher, 2nd Base, Shortstop, Pitcher, 3rd Base

Schedule: University of Wisconsin-Oshkosh, Wooster, Aurora, Carthage, Allegheny, McMurray, Illinois Benedictine, Nova SouthEastern, St. Norbert, Monmouth
Style of Play: Great defense, base to base baseball; bunting; hit and run; slash; pitching.

Saint Norbert College

100 Grant Street
De Pere, WI 54115-2099
Coach: Tom Winske

NCAA III
Green Knights/Green, Gold
Phone: (920) 403-3530
Fax: (920) 403-3128

ACADEMIC

Founded: 1898
Religion: Roman Catholic
Web-site: http://www.snc.edu/
Student/Faculty Ratio: 15:1
Undergraduate Enrollment: 2,050
Scholarships/Academic: Yes **Athletic:** No
Total Expenses by: Year **In State:** $ 19,700
Degrees Conferred: BA, BS

Type: 4 Yr., Private, Coed
Campus Housing: No
SAT/ACT/GPA: No requirements/
Male/Female Ratio: 45:55
Graduate Enrollment: N/A
Fin Aid: Yes
Out of State: $ 19,700

Programs of Study: Biology, Business, Chemistry, Communications, International Studies, Business, Mathematics, Predentistry, Prelaw, Premed, Psychology, plus the usual Liberal Arts majors

ATHLETIC PROFILE

Conference Affiliation: Midwest Conference
Program Profile: Spring season includes Southern trip. College-owned field has natural grass. Average 28 to 30 games per season.
History: Began in 1958. 6 Division championships in last 13 years.
Achievements: 2 Midwest Conference North Division Titles; Coach of the Year in 1995 and 1996.
Coaching: Tom Winske, Head Coach, begins his first season this Spring. He is a well-recognized figure in Green Bay area baseball after coaching Green Bay Billy's to a 53-15 record during the Summer time of 1997 and starting the baseball program at Green Bay East High School. He coached the Green Bluejays American Legion team for eight seasons and De Pere Abbot Penning High School for two years. He played collegiately at Fort Hays State University, Kansas. He also was an assistant coach for one season at the NAIA school, helping the team to a No. 3 national ranking.

University of Wisconsin - La Crosse

1725 State Street
La Crosse, WI 54601
Coach: Mike Stuhr
Email: stuhr_md@mail.uwlax.edu

NCAA III
Eagles/Maroon, Grey
Phone: (608) 785-6540
Fax: (608) 785-6539

ACADEMIC

Founded: 1909
Religion: Non-Affiliated
Web-site: Not Available
Student/Faculty Ratio: 20:1
Undergraduate Enrollment: 8,000
Scholarships/Academic: Yes **Athletic:** No
Total Expenses by: Year **In State:** $ 5,173
Degrees Conferred: AA, AS, BA, BS, MS, MBA, MED

Type: 4 Yr., Public, Coed
Campus Housing: No
SAT/ACT/GPA: 21
Male/Female Ratio: 45:55
Graduate Enrollment: 650
Fin Aid: Yes
Out of State: $ 10,308

Programs of Study: Accounting, Archaeology, Art, Athletic Training, Biology, Business, Chemistry, Communications, Computer, Education, Finance, Georgraphy, History, Liberal Arts, Marketing, Math, Medical, Philosophy, Physics, Political science

ATHLETIC PROFILE

Conference Affiliation: Wisconsin Intercollegiate Athletic Conference
Program Profile: Has 36-45 game schedule; on campus facilities, 1998 NCAA Regional Participant; has 10-12 game Spring trip.
History: The program began in 1939. The last World Series Appearance was in 1979 (NAIA).
Achievements: 11 Conference Titles since 1958 (2nd highest total among conference team); 3 graduates have reached major league level; 1997 Northern Division Champs. 1998 - Joe Ohm was 19th round selection by Chicago Cubs.
Coaching: Mike Stuhr, Head Coach, entering fourth season. Gregg Langbean, Assistant Coach, responsible for pitchers, was 8 years as a professional pitcher. Steve Dannaho, Assistant Coach.
Roster for 1998 team/In State: 22 **Out of State:** 8 **Out of Country:** 0
Total Number of Varsity/Jr. Varsity: 30 **Percent of Graduation:** 79%
Number of Seniors on 1998 Team: 7 **Most Recent Record:** 25 - 18 - 0
Number of Fall Games: 0 **Number of Spring Games:** 36
Positions Needed for 1999/2000: Pitcher, Middle Infielder, Outfielder
Baseball Camp Dates: December 26, 28 and 29
Schedule: Wisconsin - Milwaukee, Winona State, Wisconsin - Oshkosh, Wisconsin - Stevens Point, University of Massachusetts - Dartmouth, California Lutheran, Chapman
Style of Play: We have built our team around strong pitching and solid defense. Overall aggressive style of offensively play.

University of Wisconsin - Milwaukee

North Building
Milwaukee, WI 53201
Coach: Jerry Augustine

NCAA I
Panthers/Black, Gold
Phone: (414) 229-5670

ACADEMIC

Founded: 1956 **Type:** 4 Yr., Public, Liberal Arts, Coed
Web-site: http://www.uwm.edu/ **SAT/ACT/GPA:** 21
Student/Faculty Ratio: 18:1 **Male/Female Ratio:** 1:1.2
Undergraduate Enrollment: 16,500 **Graduate Enrollment:** 5,500
Scholarships/Academic: Yes **Athletic:** Yes **Fin Aid:** Yes
Total Expenses by: Year **In State:** $ 8,179 **Out of State:** $ 15,420
Degrees Conferred: BA, BS, BFA, MA, MS, MBA, MFA, PhD
Programs of Study: Clinical Laboratory Sciences, Communication Science and Disorders, Health Information Administration, Health Science, Kinesiology, Occupational Therapy, Recreation, Architectural Studies, Accounting, Finance, Human Resources, Community Marketing, Civil Engineering, Computer Science, Art, Art Education, Dance, Film, Music, Music Education, Theatre, Africology, Anthropology, Art History, Biological Science, Chemistry, Classics, Communications, Comparative Literature, Economics, English, Film Studies, French, Geography, Geoscience, German, Political Science, Psychology, Russian, Sociology, Spanish, Nursing, Criminal Justice

ATHLETIC PROFILE

Conference Affiliation: Midwestern Collegiate Conference
Program Profile: UWM plays at Lincoln Park Field. Playing season consists of 56 games, 53 of which are played against Division I schools. Play in the South over Easter Break against some of the finest teams in the country.
History: The program has come a long way. Recently went to NCAA Division I (1990) where we are starting to show some success.
Achievements: 1993 Craig Scheffler (Pitcher) was selected in the 12th round by the LA Dodgers; 1995 Cory Bigler (Pitcher) selected in the 23rd round by the Pittsburgh Pirates.
Coaching: Jerry Augustine - Head Coach, third year as a head coach, played nine seasons in the major leagues, mostly with the Milwaukee Brewers.
Style of Play: We are aggressive hitters and baserunners with a well rounded defense. Looking to get a lot of production out of our people in the power slots.

University of Wisconsin - Oshkosh

800 Algoma Boulevard
Oshkosh, WI 54901
Coach: Tom Lechnir

NCAA III
Titans/Gold, Black, White
Phone: (920) 424-0374
Fax: (920) 424-7445

ACADEMIC

Founded: 1871
Type: 4 Yr., Public, Liberal Arts, Coed
Web-site: http://www.uwosh.edu/
SAT/ACT/GPA: 22 avg
Student/Faculty Ratio: 19:1
Male/Female Ratio: 43:57
Undergraduate Enrollment: 10,300
Graduate Enrollment: 2,000
Scholarships/Academic: Yes **Athletic:** No **Fin Aid:** Yes
Total Expenses by: Year **In State:** $ 4,800 **Out of State:** $ 8,700
Degrees Conferred: AA, AS, BA, BS, BFA, BSN, MA, MS, MBA, MEd
Programs of Study: 41 Majors, 15 Preprofessional programs, 24 additional Minors; Art, Business and Management, Communications, Computer Science, Education, Health Sciences, Journalism

ATHLETIC PROFILE

Conference Affiliation: Wisconsin State University Conference
Program Profile: One of the top NCAA Division III programs in the country. NCAA Division III champion in 1985 and 1994. Competed in the NCAA Division III World Series 11 times in the past 12 years. Finished 2nd at the NCAA Division III World Series in 1987, 1988 and 1993. Has compiled a 40-year record of 849-315-3, including an 80-9 mark the past 2 years.
History: Posted a 39-5 record in 1995 with a 3rd-place finish at the NCAA Division III World Series. Has won the Wisconsin State University Conference Championship 16 times in the past 17 years; 3 NCAA Division III Player of the Year honorees and 29 NCAA DIII All-American selections since 1956.
Achievements: 40 players signed professional contracts; 2 players have gained NCAA Division III Player of the Year honors a total of three times; 29 players have received NCAA Division III All-Americans honors; 2 NCAA Division III Coach of the Year Recepients.
Coaching: Tom Lechnir, Head Coach, 1 NCAA Division III Championship; 7 NCAA Division III World Series Appearances and 7 Conference Championships.
Style of Play: Aggressive, sound fundamental baseball. The tradition of winning and laying sent on to the next level speaks for itself.

University of Wisconsin - Parkside

P. O. Box 2000
Kenosha, WI 53141
Coach: Sal Bando, Jr.

NCAA II
Rangers/Forest Green, Black
Phone: (414) 595-2317
Fax: (414) 595-2225

ACADEMIC

Founded: 1960
Type: 4 Yr., Public, Liberal Arts, Coed
Web-site: http://www.uwp.edu/
Campus Housing: Yes
Student/Faculty Ratio: 20:1
Male/Female Ratio: 40:60
Undergraduate Enrollment: 4,000
Graduate Enrollment: 100
Scholarships/Academic: Yes **Athletic:** Yes **Fin Aid:** Yes
Total Expenses by: Year **In State:** $ 3,300 **Out of State:** $ 5,600
Degrees Conferred: BS, BA, MBA, MA
Programs of Study: Business, Computer, Pre- Health, Biological Science, Management, Communications, Education, Letters/Literature, Life Sciences, Nursing, Premed, Psychology

ATHLETIC PROFILE

Conference Affiliation: Great Lakes Valley Conference

Program Profile: Up and coming. Play in 2nd to 3rd best conference in all of Division II. New head coach with a big time Division I and professional experience. Field is on campus. An $11 million fieldhouse is under construction, will enhance indoor facility greatly. Team of the future, program is on the rise.
History: The program began in 1978. Sal Bando took over the program this year.
Achievements: 12 consecutive post-season appearances throughout the 1980's; 11 All-Americans and 8 gone to the major league baseball draft.
Coaching: Sal Bando, Jr., Head Coach. Kevin Bowers, Assistant. Mike Schuberts, Pitching.
Style of Play: ABC baseball. Lead off hitter on, bunt him over, etc..Do not have the team power to depend on the home run.

University of Wisconsin - Platteville

1 University Plaza
Platteville, WI 53818
Coach: Rich Duncan

NCAA III
Pioneers/Orange, Black
Phone: (608) 342-1567
Fax: (608) 342-1576

ACADEMIC

Founded: 1866
Religion: Non-Affiliated
Web-site: http://www.uwplatt.edu/
Student/Faculty Ratio: 15:1
Undergraduate Enrollment: 4,800
Scholarships/Academic: Yes **Athletic:** No
Total Expenses by: Year **In State:** $ 5,500

Type: 4 Yr., Public, Coed
Campus Housing: Yes
SAT/ACT/GPA: 21
Male/Female Ratio: 3:1
Graduate Enrollment: 500
Fin Aid: Yes
Out of State: $ 11,000

Degrees Conferred: BA, MS, AS, BS
Programs of Study: Accounting, Agriculture, Art, Biology, Botany, Broadcasting, Business, Chemistry, Communications, Computer Science, Criminal Justice, Liberal Arts, Marketing, Mathematics, Economics, Education, Engineering, Geology, Geography, Philosophy

ATHLETIC PROFILE

Conference Affiliation: Wisconsin State University Conference

University of Wisconsin - River Falls

410 S Third St.
River Falls, WI 54022-5001
Coach: Steve Block

NCAA III
Falcons/Red, Black
Phone: (715) 425-0746
Fax: (715) 425-3696

ACADEMIC

Founded: 1874
Web-site: Not Available
Student/Faculty Ratio: 18:1
Undergraduate Enrollment: 4,800
Scholarships/Academic: Yes **Athletic:** No
Total Expenses by: Year **In State:** $ 5,200

Type: 4 Yr., Public, Coed
SAT/ACT/GPA: 900/22
Male/Female Ratio: 45:55
Graduate Enrollment: 400
Fin Aid: Yes
Out of State: $ 9,900

Degrees Conferred: BA, BS, BFA, BME, BSW, MA
Programs of Study: Accounting, Agricultural, American Studies, Animal Science, Biological Science, Chemistry, Computer Science, Conservation, Early Childhood Education, Economics, Education, English, Food Services, Languages, Geology, Geography, History, Horticulture, Journalism, Land Use, Math, Music, Physical Science, Physics, Political Science, Preprofessional

ATHLETIC PROFILE

Conference Affiliation: WSUC
Program Profile: One of the best Division III schools in Wisconsin for baseball and academics. The facilities are top of the line indoor and outdoor. Playing season runs through March -May. Playing 36 games plus post-season. A natural grass infield with very good dimensions for a college field.
History: Program began in 1958.
Achievements: 4 Conference Titles with one drafted player in 1996 - Randy Sterns.

University of Wisconsin - Stevens Point

109 HEC
Stevens Point, WI 54481
Coach: Scott Pritchard

NCAA III
Pointers/Purple, Gold
Phone: (715) 346-4412
Fax: (715) 346-4655

ACADEMIC

Founded: 1894
Type: 4 Yr., Public, Coed
Religion: Non-Affiliated
Campus Housing: No
Web-site: Not Available
SAT/ACT/GPA: 24
Student/Faculty Ratio: 20:1
Male/Female Ratio: 49:51
Undergraduate Enrollment: 8,000
Graduate Enrollment: 500
Scholarships/Academic: Yes **Athletic:** No **Fin Aid:** Yes
Total Expenses by: Year **In State:** $ 5,000 **Out of State:** $ 7,500
Degrees Conferred: AA, AS, BA, BS, MA, MS, MBA, PhD, JD
Programs of Study: Accounting, Anthropology, Art, Biology, Broadcasting, Business, Chemistry, Communications, Computer, Education, English, Fashion Merchandising, Fish/Game, Forestry, History, International, Liberal Arts, Math, Medical, Music, Natural Resources, Preprofessional Program, Psychology, Social Science, Speech, Theatre, Wildlife

ATHLETIC PROFILE

Conference Affiliation: WAC
Program Profile: Has an indoor facility which has dimensions of 55,000 square feet, two full length batting cages. Field is natural grass. It was resurfaced in the Fall of 1996. Facilities include new scoreboard, press box which is under constructions.
History: Coming off best season ever. Finished season #6 in the nation (Division III) Program started in 1955. 1997 was first World Series appearance, second Midwest Regional. Finished 31-13 under first year Coach Scott Pretchard.
Achievements: Gary Kaluchowski, third team All-American in 1997.
Coaching: Scott Pritchard, Head Coach, entering third year as a head coach. Led Pointers to a 31-13 in 1997. Steve Foster, Pitching Coach, former Cincinnati Red. Andy Augustine, Assistant Coach, former catcher in Mariners Forms System.
Style of Play: Aggressive will fit style of play to the team's ability. Team showed ability to drive ball in 97, added speed in some positions, have also added quality depth.

University of Wisconsin - Stout

Johnson Fieldhouse
Menomonie, WI 54751
Coach: Terry Petrie

NCAA III
Blue Devils/Navy, White
Phone: (715) 232-1459
Fax: (715) 232-1684

ACADEMIC

Founded: 1891
Type: 4 Yr., Public, Coed, Engineering
Religion: Non-Affiliated
Campus Housing: No
Web-site: http://www.stout.edu
SAT/ACT/GPA: 1020/22/50%

Student/Faculty Ratio: 21:1
Male/Female Ratio: 51:49
Undergraduate Enrollment: 7,000
Graduate Enrollment: 600
Scholarships/Academic: Yes **Athletic:** No
Fin Aid: Yes
Total Expenses by: Year **In State:** $ 5,867
Out of State: $ 11,812
Degrees Conferred: BA, BS, MS, MA
Programs of Study: Apparel Design/Manufacturing, Applied Math, Art, Construction, Dietetics, Early Childhood Education, General Business, Graphic, Commercial, Communications, Packaging, Psychology, Retail, Technology, Telecommunications, Vocational

ATHLETIC PROFILE

Conference Affiliation: Wisconsin Intercollegiate Athletic Conference
Program Profile: Teams play a Fall intrasquad season, practice begins again in January. Plays doubleheader in Metrodome in Minneapolis, Minn., in February before playing Spring break schedule of 12 games in Ft. Myers, Fl. Bulk of Northern Division title in 1997 and advanced to both the conference tournament.
History: Stout baseball began in 1909. In the past 25 years, Stout has won two conference crowns and five division titles.
Achievements: Coach Petrie has been the Wisconsin College Coach of the Year in 1989; Conference Titles in 1982 and 1990; Northern Division Titles in 1983, 1987, 1989, 1993, and 1997; former Blue Devil Joe Vavra is presently a coach in Los Angeles Dodgers farm system and is a hitting coach for the Dodgers during training camp.
Coaching: Terry Petrie, Head Coach and Hitting Coach. Bob Thomas, Outfield; Mark Thomas, Pitchers; Larry Kuester, Infield.
Style of Play: Aggressive -- base running, makes things happen; hard hitting team; work hard in practice.

University of Wisconsin - Superior

1800 Grand Avenue
Superior, WI 54880
Coach: Jim Stukel

NCAA III
Yellowjackets/Old Gold, Black
Phone: (715) 394-8193
Fax: (715) 394-8110

ACADEMIC

Founded: 1893
Type: 4 Yr., Public, Liberal Arts, Coed
Web-site: Not Available
SAT/ACT/GPA: 21
Student/Faculty Ratio: 15:1
Male/Female Ratio: 50:50
Undergraduate Enrollment: 2,200
Graduate Enrollment: 250
Scholarships/Academic: Yes **Athletic:** No
Fin Aid: Yes
Total Expenses by: Year **In State:** $ 6,000
Out of State: $ 10,900
Degrees Conferred: AA, BA, BFA, BM, BME, MA
Programs of Study: Contact school for program of study.

ATHLETIC PROFILE

Conference Affiliation: WSUC

University of Wisconsin - Whitewater

800 West Main
Whitewater, WI 53190
Coach: Jim Miller
Email: miller@uwwwuax.uww.edu

NCAA III
Warhawks/Purple, White
Phone: (414) 472-5649
Fax: (414) 472-2791

ACADEMIC

Founded: 1868
Type: 4 Yr., Public, Coed
Religion: Non-Affiliated
Campus Housing: Yes

Web-site: http://www.uww.edu/ **SAT/ACT/GPA:** required
Undergraduate Enrollment: 8,500 **Graduate Enrollment:** 1,500
Scholarships/Academic: Yes **Athletic:** No **Fin Aid:** Yes
Total Expenses by: Year **In State:** $ 12,110 **Out of State:** $ 5,828
Degrees Conferred: BFA; BM; BS in Arts and Communication, Liberal Arts, Education, BSE
Programs of Study: Accounting, Art, Art Education, Biology, Business Education, Chemistry, Communicative Disorders, Economics, Elementary Education, English, Finance, French, General Business, General Science, Geography, German, History, Human Resources Managerment, International Studies, Journalism, Management, Management Computer Systems, Marketing

ATHLETIC PROFILE

Conference Affiliation: Wisconsin State University Conference
Program Profile: Facilities include 2 fields, dugouts, building with locker rooms and a press box. Always a top 20 team; 40 game schedule in the Spring. 4 games Metrodome in Minnesota and 14 games in Ft. Myers and 22 in Wisconsin.
History: Program began in 1956 - solid program; top 20 ranking for the last 11 years, World Series (5th in 1989); 7 All-Americans; 7 pitchers drafted. Bob Wickman is 88-89 is the best set up man in the major with the Milwaukee Brewers.
Achievements: State Coach of the Year in 1988-1990; 1989 Midwest Regional NCAA II Coach of the Year; Bob Wickman draft between 1st and 2nd round; 44 players overall in five years in the major league by the Yankees and Brewers. Kris Hanson 5th round by the Cleveland; 5 others pitcher late rounds or free-agent; 7 All-Americans
Coaching: Jim Miller, Head Coach, entering his 30th year as a head coach. He compiled a record of 274-159. Stan Zwellfel, Assistant Coach, entering his 8th season. Armando Hernandez ,Assistant Coach, entering 4th year. Steve Pease, Assistant Coach, entering 8th season. Sean Smith, entering 2nd season, played with the Atlanta Braves.
Roster for 1998 team/In State: 22 **Out of State:** 3 **Out of Country:** 0
Total Number of Varsity/Jr. Varsity: 43 **Percent of Graduation:** 98%
Number of Seniors on 1998 Team: 5 **Most Recent Record:** 22-16 -0
Positions Needed for 1999/2000: Pitchers, Outfielders
Baseball Camp Dates: December 27-30
Style of Play: Good pitching, great defense. Like to play for the big inning. We have hit 124 home runs in the last two years and could hit a 100 home runs this year. Power hitters at all nine positions.

Viterbo College

815 South 9th Street
La Crosse, WI 54601
Coach: Dale Varsho

NAIA
V-Hawks/Cardinal, Silver
Phone: (608) 796-3000
Fax: (608) 796-0367

ACADEMIC

Founded: 1890 **Type:** 4 Yr., Private, Liberal Arts, Coed
Religion: Catholic **Campus Housing:** Yes
Web-site: http://www.viterbo.edu/ **SAT/ACT/GPA:** 860/18
Student/Faculty Ratio: 14:1 **Male/Female Ratio:** 1:3
Undergraduate Enrollment: 1,600 **Graduate Enrollment:** 100
Scholarships/Academic: Yes **Athletic:** Yes **Fin Aid:** Yes
Total Expenses by: Year **In State:** $ 15,000 **Out of State:** $ 15,000
Programs of Study: Business, Computer, Education Fine Arts, Humanities, English, Biology, Chemistry, Mathematics, Nursing, Psychology, Religious Studies, Sociology, Preprofessional

ATHLETIC PROFILE

Conference Affiliation: Midwestern Classic Conference
Program Profile: Home games are played at the Dairyland Athletic Complex.

Achievements: 1988 and 1989 NAIA District finalist; 1990 NAIA District Coach of the Year; Player of the Year awards; 1990 Damian Miller drafted by the Minnesota Twins; 1991 Conference Champions.

Waukesha County Technical College

800 Main Street
Pewaukee, WI 53702
Coach: Steven J. Bochat

NJCAA
Owls/Blue, Gold
Phone: (414) 691-5453
Fax: (414) 691-5090

ACADEMIC

Founded: 1923
Web-site: http://www.waukesha.tec.wi.us
Student/Faculty Ratio: 23:1
Scholarships/Academic: No **Athletic:** No
Total Expenses by: Year **In State:** $ 1,534

Type: 2 Yr., Public, Jr. College, Coed
Campus Housing: Yes
Male/Female Ratio: 1:2
Fin Aid: Yes
Out of State: $ Varies

Degrees Conferred: Associate Degrees, Vocational, Advanced Technical Certificates
Programs of Study: Nursing, Political Science, Fire Science, Marketing, Business, Automotive, Construction, Electrical, Accounting, Health Coordinator, Medical Assistant, Real Estate

ATHLETIC PROFILE

Program Profile: Our program is a year-round sport. We have an indoor practice facility and are in the process of building a new outdoor baseball facility in the Summer of 1998.
History: Our baseball program has won four conference championships in the late 1980's and early 1990's. We've had ten players drafted and have a commitment to team unity.
Achievements: This is Steven Bochat's third season of building a program. We have to first established a consistent turnover of athletes before we can build a championship.
Coaching: Steven J Bochat, Head Coach (Pitchers, Catchers, Infielders), third season with his first year of 2 complete recruiting seasons. Randy Villerical, Assistant ,Infield, entering his 3rd season. Lee Monterz, assistant, Outfield, entering his 3rd year. Andy Harley, Assistant.
Style of Play: Our style of play is very conservative, we like to hit and run because of our player's speed. We basically try to play error free baseball and let our starting pitchers get through the fifth. Our relievers usually can carry us for two innings.

Western Wisconsin Technical College

6th and Vine St. K-100
La Crosse, WI 54601
Coach: David Lee

NJCAA
Cavaliers/Royal Blue, Vegas Gold
Phone: (608) 791-9902

ACADEMIC

Founded: 1911
Student/Faculty Ratio: 24:1
Scholarships/Academic: Yes **Athletic:** No
Total Expenses by: Year **In State:** $ 3,000

Type: 2 Yr., Public, Coed
Undergraduate Enrollment: 3,500
Fin Aid: Yes
Out of State: $ 9,000

Degrees Conferred: Associate
Programs of Study: Business, Health, Industrial, Home Economics

ATHLETIC PROFILE

Conference Affiliation: Wisconsin Junior College Association
Program Profile: Play 55 game Spring schedule on a new field in 1998. Program is designed for players to play as freshman and sophomores to educate them for a four-year institution. Playing on a new stadium in 1998. All players through program have the opportunity to better themselves and showcase talents to four-year schools.

History: This was third year of the program and have had made positive steps every year. Several years in three years have gone on to accept positions at area four-year institutions. Program was considered a club sport prior to 1995.
Achievements: Won 16 straight games in 1996, 1 All-Region player, 5 All-Conference selections, and hit .332 as a team.
Coaching: David Lee, Head Coach, graduate of Viterbo College, four years at WWTC, associate scout of the Tampa Bay Devil Rays, coached high school and played four years in college and semi-pro baseball. Greg Rediske, Assistant Coach, three years at WWTC. Kevin Wozney, Pitching Coach, second year as Pitching Coach, three years at Mankato State University (player), three years as a player in Texas Rangers Organization.
Style of Play: We adjust to team player's strengths every year, but we are aggressive on the field and at the plate. Our mental state is always in the game until the last out is made.

Wisconsin Lutheran College

8800 W Bluemound Road
Milwaukee, WI 53226-4626
Coach: Joel Mischke

NCAA III\NAIA
Warriors/Green, White
Phone: (414) 774-1695
Fax: (414) 259-0636

ACADEMIC

Founded: 1973
Religion: Lutheran
Web-site: http://www.wlc.edu
Student/Faculty Ratio: 12:1
Undergraduate Enrollment: 400
Scholarships/Academic: Yes **Athletic:** No
Total Expenses by: Year **In State:** $ 5,500
Degrees Conferred: BA, BS

Type: 4 Yr., Private, Liberal Arts, Coed
Campus Housing: Yes
SAT/ACT/GPA: 20+
Male/Female Ratio: 3:4
Graduate Enrollment:
Fin Aid: Yes
Out of State: $ 5,500

Programs of Study: Business and Management, Chemistry, Communications, Elementary Education, English, History, Liberal Arts, Mathematics, Music, Psychology, Secondary Education, Theology

ATHLETIC PROFILE

Conference Affiliation: Lake Michigan Conference
Program Profile: We utilize city parks in the area (Simmons Field, Lincoln Park and Zirkel Field). Practices are also conducted at one of these three fields. Our recreation center is large, making it unique for a school our size.
History: From the start of our baseball program until now outsiders can notice a change -- the sport of baseball is up and coming. by excessive recruiting and a full time coach, we are being put on the baseball map in the Midwest.
Achievements: 1995 won its first non-conference game in the school's history.
Style of Play: Hard-nosed, aggressive baseball. Execution is our strong point.

OTHER MEN'S BASEBALL PROGRAMS
(Not Listed in the *1999 College Guide)*

The following college Baseball programs did not submit profiles prior to publication of the 1999 edition of the ***Official Athletic College Guide: BASEBALL***. THE SPORT SOURCE regrets these omissions and will continue to encourage 100% participation by member colleges and universities. Please contact the National Collegiate Athletic Association (NCAA) for more information regarding their member institutions at (913)339-1906, or visit the NCAA website at **http://www.ncaa.org**. You may contact the National Association of Intercollegiate Athletics (NAIA) for more information regarding their member institutions at (918)494-8824, or visit the NAIA website at **http://www.naia.org**. For more information on the National Christian College Athletic Association (NCCAA) and their member institutions please call (765)674-8401, or visit their website at **http://www.bright.net/~nccaa**.

COLLEGE	ASSN	COACH	TELEPHONE
Allen University (SC)	NAIA	TBA	(803) 376-5745
Apprentice School (VA)	IND	Bryan Cave	(757) 380-3525
Arkansas Baptist College (AR)	NCCAA	Brian Rhees	(501) 374-4570
Bartlesville Wesleyan College (OK)	NCCAA	Marty Carver	(918) 335-6259
Circleville Bible College (OH)	NCCAA	Larry Olson	(740) 477-7702
Claflin College (SC)	NAIA	TBA	(803) 534-2710
Clearwater Christian (FL)	NCCAA	Jack Hughes	(727) 726-1153
Crown College (MN)	NCCAA	Mark McKeaver	(612) 446-4170
Faith Baptist College (LA)	NCCAA	TBA	(318) 684-6383
Great Lakes Christian College (MI)	NCCAA	Ron Klepal	(517) 321-0242
Hillsdale Freewill Baptist (OK)	IND	Tim Lesenbee	(405) 912-9000
Kansas Wesleyan University (KS)	NAIA	Tim Bellew	(785) 827-5541
Lancaster Bible College (PA)	NCCAA	Mark Heckerman	(717) 560-8267
Lipscomb University (TN)	NAIA	Mel Brown	(615) 269-1795
Martin Luther College (MN)	NCAA III	Drew Buck	(507) 354-8221
Misericordia College (PA)	NCAA III	Chas Edkins	(717) 674-6374
Morris Brown College (GA)	NAIA	Jim Mitchell	(404) 220-3615
Mount Senario College (WI)	NAIA	Vanderheyden	(715) 532-5511
Northwestern College (MN)	NCCAA	Dave Hieb	(651) 631-5345
Ohio Valley College (WVA)	IND	Bob Crawford	(304) 485-7384
Panhandle State University (TX)	NCAA II	TBA	(580) 349-2611
Patten College (CA)	NAIA	Alvin Moore	(510) 533-8300
Paul Quinn College (TX)	NSCAA	TBA	(214) 302-3567
Pillsbury Baptist Bible College (MN)	NCCAA	Matt McLachlan	(507) 451-2710
Saint Gregory's University (OK)	NAIA	Brian Leaver	(405) 878-5151
Saint Joseph's College (ME)	NAIA	Wil Sanborn	(207) 893-6675
Saint Martin's College (WA)	NAIA	Joe Dominiak	(360) 438-4531
Saint Rose, College of (NY)	NCAA II	Bob Bellizzi	(518) 454-5252
Saint Scholastica, College of (MN)	NCAA III	John Baggs	(218) 723-6555
Sioux Falls, University of (SD)	NAIA	Jim Denevan	(605) 331-6638
Southern Nazarene University (OK)	NAIA	Scott Shelby	(405) 491-6630
Southern Polytechnic State Univ. (GA)	IND	Charles Lumsden	(770) 528-5445
Tennessee Temple University (TN)	NCCAA	Kevin Templeton	(423) 493-4220
Thomas College (GA)	NAIA	Mike Lee	(912) 226-1621
Thomas College (ME)	NAIA	Greg King	(207) 873-0771
Toccoa Falls College (GA)	NCCAA	TBA	(706) 886-6831
Transylvania University (KY)	NAIA	Erik Hagen	(606) 233-8270
Trinity International University (IL)	NAIA	Mark Lundwick	(847) 317-7093
Warner Pacific College (OR)	NAIA	Mike Booth	(503) 775-4366
William Woods University (MO)	NAIA	Tom Vodnansky	(573) 592-1187

NCAA DIVISION I PROGRAMS

Listed in *The College Athletic Guide*

SCHOOL	ST
Alabama State University	AL
Alcorn State University	MS
Appalachian State University	NC
Arizona State University	AZ
Arkansas State University	AR
Auburn University	AL
Austin Peay State University	TN
Ball State University	IN
Baylor University	TX
Belmont University	TN
Bethune - Cookman College	FL
Boston College	MA
Bowling Green State University	OH
Bradley University	IL
Brown University	RI
Bucknell University	PA
Butler University	IN
California State Poly University - SLO	CA
California State University - Fresno	CA
California State University - Fullerton	CA
California State University - Long Beach	CA
California State University - Sacramento	CA
California State University - Northridge	CA
Campbell University	NC
Canisius College	NY
Carl Sandburg College	IL
Centenary College	LA
Central Connecticut State University	CT
Central Michigan University	MI
Charleston Southern University	SC
Chicago State University	IL
Citadel	SC
Clemson University	SC
Cleveland State University	OH
Coastal Carolina University	SC
College of Charleston	SC
College of the Holy Cross	MA
College of William and Mary	VA
Columbia University	NY
Coppin State College	MD
Cornell University	NY
Cowley County Community College	KS
Creighton University	NE
Dartmouth College	NH
Davidson College	NC
Delaware State University	DE
Drexel University	PA
Duke University	NC
Duquesne University	PA
East Carolina University	NC
East Tennessee State University	TN
Eastern Illinois University	IL
Eastern Kentucky University	KY
Eastern Michigan University	MI
Elon College	NC
Fairleigh Dickinson University-Teaneck	NJ
Florida A & M University	FL
Florida Atlantic College	FL
Florida International University	FL
Florida State University	FL

SCHOOL	ST
Fordham University	NY
Furman University	SC
George Mason University	VA
George Washington University	DC
Georgetown University	DC
Georgia Institute of Technology	GA
Georgia Southern University	GA
Georgia State University	GA
Gonzaga University	WA
Grambling State University	LA
Grand Canyon University	AZ
Harvard University	MA
High Point University	NC
Hofstra University	NY
Howard University	DC
Illinois State University	IL
Indiana State University	IN
Indiana University	IN
Iowa State University	IA
Jackson State University	MS
Jacksonville State University	AL
Jacksonville University	FL
James Madison University	VA
Jarvis Christian College	TX
Kansas State University	KS
Kaskaskia College	IL
La Salle University	PA
Lafayette College	PA
Lamar University	TX
Le Moyne College	NY
Lehigh University	PA
Lewis-Clark State College	ID
Liberty University	VA
Long Island University - Brooklyn	NY
Long Island University - C.W. Post	NY
Louisiana State Univ and A & M C	LA
Louisiana Tech University	LA
Loyola Marymount University	CA
Manhattan College	NY
Marist College	NY
Marshall University	WV
McNeese State University	LA
Mercer University	GA
Miami University - Ohio	OH
Michigan State University	MI
Mississippi State University	MS
Mississippi Valley State University	MS
Monmouth University	NJ
Morehead State U - Kentucky	KY
Mount Saint Mary's College	MD
Murray State University	KY
New Mexico State University	NM
New York Institute of Technology	NY
Niagara University	NY
Nicholls State University	LA
Norfolk State Univ	VA
North Carolina A & T State University	NC
North Carolina State University	NC
Northeast Louisiana University	LA
Northeastern University	MA

NCAA DIVISION I PROGRAMS

Listed in *The College Athletic Guide*

SCHOOL	ST
Northern Illinois University	IL
Northwestern State University - Louisiana	LA
Northwestern University	IL
Ohio State University	OH
Ohio University	OH
Oklahoma State University	OK
Old Dominion University	VA
Oral Roberts University	OK
Oregon State University	OR
Parkland College	IL
Pennsylvania State University	PA
Pepperdine University	CA
Prairie View A & M University	TX
Princeton University	NJ
Providence College	RI
Purdue University	IN
Radford University	VA
Rice University	TX
Rider University	NJ
Rutgers University - University of New	NJ
Sacred Heart University	CT
Saint Bonaventura University	NY
Saint Francis College - New York	NY
Saint John's University - New York	NY
Saint Joseph's University	PA
Saint Louis University	MO
Saint Mary's College - California	CA
Saint Peter's College	NJ
Sam Houston State University	TX
Samford University	AL
San Diego State University	CA
San Jose State University	CA
Santa Clara University	CA
Seton Hall University	NJ
Siena College	NY
Southeast Missouri State University	MO
Southeastern Louisiana University	LA
Southern Illinois University - Carbondale	IL
Southern University	LA
Southern Utah University	UT
Southwest Missouri State University	MO
Southwest Texas State University	TX
Stanford University	CA
Stetson University	FL
Temple University	PA
Tennessee Technological University	TN
Texas A & M University	TX
Texas Christian University	TX
Texas Southern University	TX
Texas Tech University	TX
Towson State University	MD
Troy State University	AL
Tulane University	LA
Univ of Southern California	CA
University of Akron	OH
University of Alabama	AL
University of Alabama - Birmingham	AL
University of Arizona	AZ
University of Arkansas	AR
University of Arkansas - Little Rock	AR

SCHOOL	ST
University of California - Berkeley	CA
University of California - Los Angeles	CA
University of California - Riverside	CA
University of California - Santa Barbara	CA
University of Central Florida	FL
University of Cincinnati	OH
University of Dayton	OH
University of Delaware	DE
University of Detroit Mercy	MI
University of Evansville	IN
University of Florida	FL
University of Georgia	GA
University of Hartford	CT
University of Hawaii - Hilo	HI
University of Hawaii - Manoa	HI
University of Illinois - Chicago	IL
University of Illinois - Urbana/Champaign	IL
University of Iowa	IA
University of Kansas	KS
University of Kentucky	KY
University of Las Vegas - Nevada	NV
University of Louisville	KY
University of Maine	ME
University of Maryland	MD
University of Maryland - Baltimore County	MD
University of Maryland - Eastern Shore	MD
University of Massachusetts - Amherst	MA
University of Memphis	TN
University of Miami	FL
University of Michigan - Ann Arbor	MI
University of Minnesota	MN
University of Mississippi (Ole Miss.)	MS
University of Missouri - Columbia	MO
University of Nebraska	NE
University of Nevada - Reno	NV
University of New Mexico	NM
University of New Orleans	LA
University of North Carolina - Asheville	NC
University of North Carolina - Chapel Hill	NC
University of North Carolina - Charlotte	NC
University of N Carolina - Greensboro	NC
University of North Carolina - Wilmington	NC
University of Northern Iowa	IA
University of Notre Dame	IN
University of Oklahoma	OK
University of Pennsylvania	PA
University of Pittsburgh	PA
University of Portland	OR
University of Rhode Island	RI
University of Richmond	VA
University of San Diego	CA
University of San Francisco	CA
University of South Alabama	AL
University of South Carolina - Columbia	SC
University of South Florida	FL
University of Southern Mississippi	MS
University of Southwestern Louisiana	LA
University of Tennessee - Knoxville	TN
University of Tennessee - Martin	TN
University of Texas - Arlington	TX

NCAA DIVISION I PROGRAMS

Listed in *The College Athletic Guide*

SCHOOL	ST
University of Texas - Austin	TX
University of Texas - Pan American	TX
University of Texas - San Antonio	TX
University of the Pacific	CA
University of Toledo	OH
University of Utah	UT
University of Vermont	VT
University of Virginia	VA
University of Washington	WA
University of Wisconsin - Milwaukee	WI
US Air Force Academy	CO
US Military Academy	NY
US Naval Academy	MD
VA Poly Institute & State University	VA
Valparaiso University	IN
Vanderbilt University	TN
Villanova University	PA
Virginia Commonwealth University	VA
Virginia Military Institute	VA
Wagner College	NY
Wake Forest University	NC
Washington State University	WA
West Virginia University	WV
Western Carolina University	NC
Western Illinois University	IL
Western Kentucky University	KY
Western Michigan University	MI
Wichita State University	KS
Winthrop University	SC
Wofford College	SC
Wright State University	OH
Xavier University	OH
Yale University	CT
Youngstown State University	OH

NCAA DIVISION II PROGRAMS

Listed in *The College Athletic Guide*

SCHOOL	ST
Abilene Christian University	TX
Adelphi University	NY
Alabama A & M University	AL
Albany State College	GA
Alderson Broddus College	WV
American International College	MA
Arkansas Tech University	AR
Armstrong Atlantic State University	GA
Ashland University	OH
Assumption College	MA
Augusta State University	GA
Augustana College	SD
Barry University	FL
Barton College	NC
Bellarmine College	KY
Belmont Abbey College	NC
Bemidji State University	MN
Bentley College	MA
Bloomsburg University	PA
Bluefield State College	WV
Bowie State University	MD
Bryant College	RI
California State Poly University - Pomona	CA
California State University - Chico	CA
California State University - Dominguez	CA
California State University - Hayward	CA
California State University - Los Angeles	CA
California State University - San	CA
California State University - Stanislaus	CA
California University - Pennsylvania	PA
Cameron University	OK
Catawba College	NC
Central Missouri State University	MO
Clarion University	PA
Clark Atlanta University	GA
Coker College	SC
College of Saint Rose	NY
Colorado School of Mines	CO
Columbia Union College	MD
Columbus State University	GA
Concord College	WV
Concordia College - New York	NY
CUNY - Queens College	NY
Davis and Elkins College	WV
Delta State University	MS
Dowling College	NY
East Central University	OK
East Stroudsburg University	PA
Eastern New Mexico University	NM
Edinboro University	PA
Elizabeth City State University	NC
Emporia State University	KS
Erskine College	SC
Fairmont State College	WV
Florida Institute of Technology	FL
Florida Southern College	FL
Fort Hays State University	KS
Francis Marion College	SC
Franklin Pierce College	NH
Gannon University	PA

SCHOOL	ST
Gardner - Webb University	NC
Georgia College	GA
Grand Valley State University	MI
Harding University	AR
Henderson State Univ.	AR
Houston Baptist University	TX
Indiana University - Pennsylvania	PA
Indiana University - Purdue U at FW	IN
Indiana Univ. - Purdue U - Indianapolis	IN
Keene State College	NH
Kennesaw State College	GA
Kentucky State University	KY
Kentucky Wesleyan College	KY
Kutztown University	PA
Lander University	SC
Lane College	TN
Le Moyne - Owen College	TN
Lenoire - Rhyne College	NC
Lewis and Clark Community College	IL
Lewis University	IL
Lincoln Memorial University	TN
Lincoln University	MO
Lock Haven Univ	PA
Longwood College	VA
Mankato State University	MN
Mansfield University	PA
Mars Hill College	NC
Mercy College	NY
Mercyhurst College	PA
Merrimack College	MA
Mesa State College	CO
Metropolitan State College - Denver	CO
Miles College	AL
Millersville University - Pennsylvania	PA
Mississippi College	MS
Missouri Southern State College	MO
Missouri Western State College	MO
Molloy College	NY
Morningside College	IA
Mount Olive College	NC
New Hampshire College	NH
New Mexico Highlands University	NM
Newberry College	SC
NJ Institute of Technology	NJ
North Dakota State University - Fargo	ND
Northern Kentucky University	KY
Northern State University	SD
Northwest Missouri State University	MO
Northwood University	MI
Oakland City College	IN
Oakland University	MI
Ouachita Baptist University	AR
Paine College	GA
Pfeiffer University	NC
Phila C of Textiles/Science	PA
Pittsburgh State University	KS
Presbyterian College	SC
Quincy University	IL
Quinnipiac College	CT
Regis University	CO

NCAA DIVISION II PROGRAMS

Listed in *The College Athletic Guide*

SCHOOL	ST
Rockhurst College	MO
Rollins College	FL
Saginaw Valley State University	MI
Saint Andrews College	NC
Saint Anselm College	NH
Saint Augustine's College	NC
Saint Cloud State Univ.	MN
Saint Joseph's College	IN
Saint Leo College	FL
Saint Michael's College	VT
Saint Paul's College	VA
Salem - Teikyo University	WV
San Francisco State University	CA
Savannah State College	GA
Shaw University	NC
Shepherd College	WV
Shippensburg University	PA
Slippery Rock University	PA
Sonoma State University	CA
South Dakota State University	SD
Southeastern Oklahoma State University	OK
Southern Arkansas University	AR
Southern Connecticut State University	CT
Southern Illinois University - Edwardsville	IL
Southwest Baptist University	MO
Southwest State University	MN
Southwestern Oklahoma State University	OK
Spoon River College	IL
State University of New York - Stony	NY
State University of West Georgia	GA
Stonehill College	MA
Tarleton State University	TX
Texas A & M U - Kingsville	TX
Truman State University	MO
Tuskegee University	AL
University of Alabama - Huntsville	AL
University of Albany	NY
University of Arkansas - Monticello	AR
University of Bridgeport	CT
University of California - Davis	CA
University of Central Arkansas	AR
University of Central Oklahoma	OK
University of Charleston	WV
University of Indianapolis	IN
University of Massachusetts - Lowell	MA
University of Minnesota - Duluth	MN
University of Missouri - Rolla	MO
University of Missouri - Saint Louis	MO
University of Montevallo	AL
University of Nebraska - Kearney	NE
University of Nebraska - Omaha	NE
University of New Haven	CT
University of North Alabama	AL
University of North Carolina - Pembroke	NC
University of North Dakota	ND
University of North Florida	FL
University of Northern Colorado	CO
University of Pittsburg - Johnstown	PA
University of South Carolina - Aiken	SC
University of South Carolina -	SC

SCHOOL	ST
University of South Dakota	SD
University of Southern Colorado	CO
University of Southern Indiana	IN
University of Tampa	FL
University of West Alabama	AL
University of Wisconsin - Parkside	WI
Valdosta State College	GA
Washburn University	KS
Wayne State College	NE
Wayne State University	MI
West Chester University	PA
West Liberty State College	WV
West Texas A & M University	TX
West Virginia State College	WV
West Virginia Wesleyan College	WV
Westminster College	PA
Wingate University	NC
Winona State University	MN
WV Institute of Technology	WV

NCAA III PROGRAMS

Listed in *The College Athletic Guide*

SCHOOL	ST
Adrian College	MI
Albertus Magnus College	CT
Albion College	MI
Albright College	PA
Alleghany College	PA
Allentown College St. Francis De Sales	PA
Alma College	MI
Alvernia College	PA
Amherst College	MA
Anderson University	IN
Anna Maria College	MA
Augsburg College	MN
Augustana College	IL
Aurora University	IL
Austin College	TX
Averett College	VA
Babson College	MA
Baldwin - Wallace College	OH
Baruch College	NY
Bates College	ME
Beaver College	PA
Becker College - Leicester Campus	MA
Beloit College	WI
Benedictine University	IL
Bethany College	WV
Bethel College	MN
Blackburn College	IL
Bluffton College	OH
Bowdoin College	ME
Brandies University	MA
Bridgewater College	VA
Bridgewater State College	MA
Buena Vista College	IA
California Institute of Technology	CA
California Lutheran University	CA
Calvin College	MI
Capital University	OH
Carleton College	MN
Carroll College	WI
Carson - Newman College	TN
Carthage College	WI
Case Western Reserve University	OH
Catholic University of America	DC
Central College	IA
Centre College	KY
Chapman University	CA
Chowan College	NC
Christopher Newport University	VA
Claremont - Mudds - Scrips College	CA
Clark University	MA
Clarkson University	NY
Coe College	IA
Colby - Sawyer College	NH
Colby College	ME
College Misericordia	PA
College of Mount Saint Joseph	OH
College of New Jersey	NJ
College of Staten Island	NY
College of Wooster	OH
Concordia College - Moorhead	MN

SCHOOL	ST
Concordia University	IL
Cornell College	IA
CUNY - John Jay College of Criminal	NY
CUNY - Lehman College	NY
Curry College	MA
Daniel Webster College	NH
De Pauw University	IN
Defiance College	OH
Delaware Valley College	PA
Denison University	OH
Dickinson College	PA
Drew University	NJ
Earlham College	IN
Eastern College	PA
Eastern Connecticut State University	CT
Eastern Mennonite College	VA
Eastern Nazarene College	MA
Eastern Oregon State College	OR
Elizabethtown College	PA
Elmhurst College	IL
Emerson College	MA
Emory and Henry College	VA
Emory University	GA
Endicott College	MA
Erie Community College	NY
Eureka College	IL
Fairleigh Dickinson Univ. - Madison	NJ
Ferrum University	VA
Fisk University	TN
Fitchburg State College	MA
Fontbonne College	MO
Framingham State College	MA
Franklin and Marshall College	PA
Franklin College	IN
Frostburg State University	MD
Gallaudet University	DC
Gettysburg College	PA
Gordon College	MA
Greensboro College	NC
Greenville College	IL
Grinnell College	IA
Grove City College	PA
Guilford College	NC
Gustavus Adolphos College	MN
Hamilton College	NY
Hamline University	MN
Hampden - Sydney College	VA
Hanover College	IN
Hartwick College	NY
Haverford College	PA
Heidelberg College	OH
Hendrix College	AR
Hilbert College	NY
Hiram College	OH
Hope College	MI
Howard Payne University	TX
Illinois College	IL
Illinois Wesleyan University	IL
Iona College	NY
Ithaca College	NY

NCAA III PROGRAMS

Listed in *The College Athletic Guide*

SCHOOL	ST
Jersey City State College	NJ
John Carroll University	OH
John Hopkins University	MD
Johnson & Wales University	RI
Juniata College	PA
Kalamazoo College	MI
Kean College - New Jersey	NJ
Kenyon College	OH
King's College - Pennsylvania	PA
Knox College	IL
La Roche College	PA
Lakeland College	WI
Lawrence University	WI
Le Tourneau University	TX
Lebanon Valley College	PA
Lincoln University - Pennsylvania	PA
Loras College	IA
Luther College	IA
Lynchburg College	VA
MA Maritime Academy	MA
Macalester College	MN
MacMurray College	IL
Manchester College	IN
Manhattanville College	NY
Maranatha Baptist Bible College	WI
Marietta College	OH
Mary Washington College	VA
Maryville College	TN
Maryville University - Saint Louis	MO
Marywood College	PA
Massachusetts College (N Adams State)	MA
Massachusetts Institute of Technology	MA
McMurry University	TX
Menlo College	CA
Messiah College	PA
Methodist College	NC
Middlebury College	VT
Millikin University	IL
Millsaps College	MS
Milwaukee School of Engineering	WI
Monmouth College	IL
Montclair State College	NJ
Moravian College	PA
Mount Saint Mary College	NY
Mount Union College	OH
Muhlenberg College	PA
Muskingum College	OH
Nebraska Wesleyan University	NE
Neumann College	PA
New England College	NH
Nichols College	MA
North Carolina Wesleyan College	NC
North Central College	IL
North Park University	IL
Northwestern College - Wisconsin	WI
Northwestern Oklahoma State University	OK
Norwich University	VT
Occidental College	CA
Ohio Dominican College	OH
Ohio Northern University	OH

SCHOOL	ST
Ohio Wesleyan University	OH
Olivet College	MI
Orange County Community College	NY
Otterbein College	OH
Pennsylvania State University - Behrend	PA
Plymouth State College	NH
Polytechnic University	NY
Pomona - Pitzer College	CA
Principia College	IL
Ramapo College of New Jersey	NJ
Randolp - Macon College	VA
Rensselaer Poly Institute	NY
Rhode Island College	RI
Rhodes College	TN
Richard Stockton College	NJ
Ripon College	WI
Rochester Inst of Technology	NY
Rockford College	IL
Roger Williams University	RI
Rose-Hulman Inst of Technology	IN
Rowan University	NJ
Rust College	MS
Rutgers University - Camden	NJ
Rutgers University - Newark	NJ
Saint John Fisher College	NY
Saint John's University	MN
Saint Joseph's College - New York	NY
Saint Lawrence University	NY
Saint Mary's University - Minnesota	MN
Saint Norbert College	WI
Saint Olaf College	MN
Salem State College	MA
Salve Regina University	RI
Savannah College of Arts & Design	GA
Schreiner College	TX
Shenandoah University	VA
Simpson College	IA
Skidmore College	NY
Southern Vermont College	VT
Southwestern University	TX
Springfield College	MA
State University of New York-	NY
State University of New York-Brockport	NY
State University of New York-Cortland	NY
State University of New York-Fredonia	NY
State University of New York-Maritime	NY
State University of New York-New Paltz	NY
State University of New York-Old	NY
State University of New York-Oneonta	NY
State University of New York-Oswego	NY
Stevens Institute of Technology	NJ
Stillman College	AL
Suffolk University	MA
Sul Ross State University	TX
Susquehanna University	PA
Swarthmore College	PA
Thiel College	PA
Thomas More College	KY
Trinity College - Connecticut	CT
Trinity University	TX

NCAA III PROGRAMS

Listed in *The College Athletic Guide*

SCHOOL	ST
Tufts University	MA
Union College	NY
University of California - San Diego	CA
University of Chicago	IL
University of Dallas	TX
University of Dubuque	IA
University of La Verne	CA
University of Mary Hardin - Baylor	TX
University of Massachusetts - Boston	MA
University of Massachusetts - Dartmouth	MA
University of Redlands	CA
University of Rochester	NY
University of Saint Thomas	MN
University of Scranton	PA
University of Southern Maine	ME
University of the South	TN
University of Wisconsin - La Crosse	WI
University of Wisconsin - Oshkosh	WI
University of Wisconsin - Platteville	WI
University of Wisconsin - River Falls	WI
University of Wisconsin - Stevens Point	WI
University of Wisconsin - Stout	WI
University of Wisconsin - Superior	WI
University of Wisconsin - Whitewater	WI
Upper Iowa University	IA
Ursinus College	PA
US Coast Guard Academy	CT
US Merchant Marine Academy	NY
Utica College - Syracuse University	NY
Vassar College	NY
Virginia Wesleyan College	VA
Wabash College	IN
Wartburg College	IA
Washington and Jefferson College	PA
Washington and Lee University	VA
Washington College	MD
Washington University - Saint Louis	MO
Waynesburg College	PA
Webster University	MO
Wentworth Institute of Technology	MA
Wesley College	DE
Wesleyan University	CT
Western Connecticut State University	CT
Western Maryland College	MD
Western New England College	MA
Westfield State College	MA
Westminster College	MO
Wheaton College	IL
Whittier College	CA
Widener University	PA
Wilkes University	PA
Willamette University	OR
William Paterson College	NJ
William Penn College	IA
Williams College	MA
Wilmington College	OH
Wittenberg University	OH
Worcester Polytechnic College	MA
Worcester State College	MA
York College- Pennsylvania	PA

NAIA PROGRAMS

Listed in *The College Athletic Guide*

SCHOOL	ST
Albertson College	ID
Alice Lloyd College	KY
Anderson College	SC
Aquinas College	MI
Asbury College	KY
Auburn University - Montgomery	AL
Avila College	MO
Azusa Pacific University	CA
Baker University	KS
Belhaven College	MS
Bellevue College	NE
Benedict College	SC
Benedictine College	KS
Berea College	KY
Berry College	GA
Bethany College	KS
Bethel College	IN
Bethel College	TN
Biola University	CA
Birmingham Southern College	AL
Bloomfield College	NJ
Bluefield College	VA
Brewton - Parker College	GA
Briar Cliff College	IA
Caldwell College	NJ
California Baptist College	CA
Campbellsville College	KY
Cedarville College	OH
Central Methodist College	MO
Central State University	OH
Clinch Valley College	VA
College of the Ozarks	MO
College of the Southwest	NM
Concordia College - Ann Arbor	MI
Concordia College - Nebraska	NE
Concordia College - Portland	OR
Concordia College - St. Paul	MN
Concordia University - Irvine	CA
Culver - Stockton College	MO
Cumberland College	KY
Cumberland University	TN
Dakota State University	SD
Dakota Wesleyan University	SD
Dana College	NE
Dickinson State University	ND
Doane College	NE
Dort College	IA
Edward Waters College	FL
Embry-Riddle Aeronautical	FL
Emmanuel College	GA
Evangel College	MO
Faulkner University	AL
Flagler College	FL
Florida Memorial College	FL
Freed - Hardeman University	TN
Friends University	KS
Geneva College	PA
Georgetown College	KY
Georgia Southwestern State University	GA
Goshen College	IN

SCHOOL	ST
Grace College	IN
Graceland College	IA
Grand View College	IA
Hannibal - LaGrange College	MO
Harris - Stowe State College	MO
Hastings College	NE
Huntingdon College	IN
Huntington College	AL
Huron University	SD
Husson College	ME
Huston - Tillotson College	TX
Illinois Inst of Technology	IL
Indiana Institute of Technology	IN
Indiana University Southeast	IN
Indiana Wesleyan University	IN
Iowa Wesleyan College	IA
Jamestown College	ND
Judson College	IL
Kansas Newman College	KS
King College	TN
LaGrange College	GA
Lindenwood College	MO
Lindsey Wilson College	KY
Louisiana College	LA
Louisiana State University-Shreveport	LA
Loyola University - New Orleans	LA
Lubbock Christian University	TX
Lyndon State College	VT
Lyon College	AR
Madonna University	MI
Malone College	OH
Marian College	IN
Martin Methodist College	TN
Master's College	CA
Mayville State University	ND
McKendree College	IL
Mid-America Nazarene University	KS
Midland Lutheran College	NE
Milligan College	TN
Minot State University	ND
Missouri Baptist College	MO
Missouri Valley College	MO
Montreat College	NC
Morris College	SC
Mount Marty College	SD
Mount Mercy College	IA
Mount Saint Clare College	IA
Mount Vernon Nazarene College	OH
Newman U (Kansas Newman U)	KS
North Greenville College	SC
Northwestern College - Iowa	IA
Northwood University	FL
Northwood University - Texas	TX
Nova Southeastern University	FL
Nyack College	NY
OK Christian U of Science & Arts	OK
Oklahoma Baptist University	OK
Oklahoma City University	OK
Olivet Nazarene University	IL
Ottawa University	KS

NAIA PROGRAMS

Listed in *The College Athletic Guide*

SCHOOL	ST
Palm Beach Atlantic College	FL
Peru State College	NE
Phila Cof Pharmacy & Science	PA
Piedmont College	GA
Pikeville College	KY
Point Loma Nazarene College	CA
Point Park College	PA
Robert Morris-Chicago Campus	IL
Saint Ambrose University	IA
Saint Francis College	IN
Saint Joseph's College	ME
Saint Thomas Aquinas College	NY
Saint Thomas University	FL
Saint Vincent College	PA
Saint Xavier University	IL
Selma University	AL
Shawnee State University	OH
Shorter College	GA
Siena Heights College	MI
Southern California College	CA
Southern College of Technology	GA
Southern Nazarene University	OK
Southern Wesleyan University	SC
Southwestern Adventist College	TX
Spring Arbor College	MI
Spring Hill College	AL
Sterling College	KS
Tabor College	KS
Talladega College	AL
Taylor University	IN
Teikyo Post University	CT
Tennessee Wesleyan College	TN
Texas College/New Program	TX
Tiffin University	OH
Trevecca Nazarene College	TN
Tri - State University	IN
Trinity Christian College	IL
Union College	KY
Union University	TN
University of Findlay	OH
University of Maine - Presque Isle	ME
University of Mary	ND
University of Mobile	AL
University of Rio Grande	OH
University of Saint Francis	IL
University of Science & Arts of OK	OK
Urbana University	OH
Valley City State University	ND
Virginia Intermont College	VA
Viterbo College	WI
Voorhees College	SC
Walsh University	OH
Warner Southern College	FL
Wayland Baptist University	TX
Webber College	FL
Western Baptist College	OR
Westmont College	CA
Wiley College	TX
William Carey College	MS
William Jewell College	MO

SCHOOL	ST
Williams Baptist College	AR
Wilmington College - Delaware	DE
York College - Nebraska	NE

NJCAA PROGRAMS

Listed in *The College Athletic Guide*

SCHOOL	ST
Abraham Baldwin College	GA
Alabama Southern Community College	AL
Allegany Community College	MD
Allen County Community College	KS
Alvin Community College	TX
Andrew College	GA
Angelina College	TX
Anne Arundel Community College	MD
Anoka - Ramsey Community College	MN
Aquinas College	TN
Arizona Western College	AZ
Baltimore City Community College	MD
Barton County Community College	KS
Belleville Area College	IL
Bergen Community College	NJ
Bethany Lutheran College	MN
Bevill State Community C - Fayette	AL
Bevill State Community C - Sumiton	AL
Bishop State Community College	AL
Black Hawk College	IL
Blinn College	TX
Bossier Parish Community College	LA
Brainerd Community College	MN
Brevard College	NC
Brevard Community College	FL
Brookdale Community College	NJ
Brookhaven College	TX
Broome Community College	NY
Broward Community College	FL
Bucks County Community College	PA
Bunker Hill Community College	MA
Burlington County College	NJ
Butler County Community College	PA
Butler County Community College	KS
Butte Community College	CA
Calhoun Community College	AL
Camden County College	NJ
Carl Albert State College	OK
Catonsville Community College	MD
Cecil Community College	MD
Cedar Valley College	TX
Central Alabama Community College	AL
Central Arizona College	AZ
Central College of Kansas	KS
Central Florida Community College	FL
Charles County Community College	MD
Chattahoochee Valley State Community	AL
Chattanooga State Technical Community	TN
Chesapeake College	MD
Chipola Junior College	FL
Cleveland State Community College	TN
Clinton Community College	NY
Cloud County Community College	KS
Coahoma Community College	MS
Cochise College	AZ
Coffeyville Community College	KS
Colby Community College	KS
College of DuPage	IL
College of Eastern Utah	UT
College of Lake County	IL

SCHOOL	ST
Collin County Community College	TX
Colorado Northwestern Community C	CO
Columbia - Greene Community College	NY
Columbia State Community College	TN
Columbus State Community College	OH
Community C of Allegheny C - Allegheny	PA
Community C of Allegheny C - South	PA
Community College of Rhode Island	RI
Connors State College	OK
Copiah - Lincoln Community College	MS
Corning Community College	NY
County College of Morris	NJ
Crowder College	MO
CUNY - Bronx Community College	NY
CUNY - Manhattan Community College	NY
CUNY - Queensborough Community	NY
Cuyahoga Community College	OH
Cypress College	CA
De Kalb College	GA
Dean College	MA
Delaware County Community College	PA
Delaware Tech Owens Campus	DE
Delgado Community College	LA
Des Moines Area Community College	IA
Dixie College	UT
Dodge City Community College	KS
Dundalk Community College	MD
Dutchess Community College	NY
East Central College	MO
East Central Community College	MS
East Mississippi Community College	MS
Eastern Oklahoma State College	OK
Eastfield College	TX
Eckerd College	FL
Elgin Community College	IL
Ellsworth Community College	IA
Enterprise State Junior Community	AL
Erie CC - North Campus	NY
Fairfield University	CT
Faulkner State Community College	AL
Fergus Falls Community College	MN
Finger Lakes Community College	NY
Florida Community College - Jacksonville	FL
Fort Scott Community College	KS
Frank Phillips College	TX
Frederick Community College	MD
Fulton - Montgomery Community C	NY
Gadsden State Community College	AL
Galveston College	TX
Garden City Community College	KS
Garrett Community College	MD
Gateway College - Technical College	CT
Genesee Community College	NY
Glen Oaks Community College	MI
Glendale Community College	AZ
Gordon College	GA
Grand Rapids Community College	MI
Gulf Coast Community College	FL
Hagerstown Junior College	MD
Henry Ford Community College	MI

NJCAA PROGRAMS

Listed in *The College Athletic Guide*

SCHOOL	ST
Herkimer County Community College	NY
Hibbing Community College	MN
Highland Community College	IL
Highland Community College	KS
Hill Junior College	TX
Hillsborough Community College - Dale	FL
Hinds Community College	MS
Hiwassee College	TN
Holmes Community College	MS
Holyoke Community College	MA
Howard County Junior College	TX
Hudson Valley Community College	NY
Hutchison Community College	KS
Illinois Central College	IL
Illinois Valley Community College	IL
Independence Community College	KS
Indian Hills Community College	IA
Indian River Community College	FL
Iowa Central Community College	IA
Iowa Lakes Community College	IA
Iowa Western Community College	IA
Itasca Community College	MN
Itawamba Community College	MS
Jackson State Community College	TN
Jamestown Community College	NY
Jefferson College	MO
Jefferson Community College	NY
Jefferson Davis Community College	AL
Jefferson State Community College	AL
John A. Logan Community College	IL
John Wood Community College	IL
Johnson County Community College	KS
Joliet Junior College	IL
Jones County Junior College	MS
Kankakee Community College	IL
Kansas City Kansas Community College	KS
Kellogg Community College	MI
Kemper Military College	MO
Keystone College	PA
Kingsborough Community College	NY
Kirkwood Community College	IA
Kishwaukee College	IL
Labette Community College	KS
Lackawanna Junior College	PA
Lake City Community College	FL
Lake Land College	IL
Lake Michigan College	MI
Lakeland Community College	OH
Lamar Community College	CO
Laredo Community College	TX
Lenoir Community College	NC
Lincoln College	IL
Lincoln Land Community College	IL
Lincoln Trail College	IL
Lon Morris College	TX
Longview Community College	MO
Louisburg College	NC
Lurleen B. Wallace State J C	AL
Luzerne County Community College	PA
Macomb Community College	MI

SCHOOL	ST
Manatee Community College	FL
Manchester College Technical College	CT
Maple Woods Community College	MO
Marshalltown Community College	IA
Massasoit Community College	MA
McHenry County College	IL
McLennan Community College	TX
Mercer County Community College	NJ
Meridian Community College	MS
Mesa Community College	AZ
Mesabi Range Community College	MN
Miami - Dade Community College	FL
Middle Georgia College	GA
Middlesex County College	NJ
Mineral Area College	MO
Mississippi Delta Community College	MS
Mississippi Gulf Coast Community	MS
Mitchell College	CT
Mohawk Valley Community College	NY
Montgomery College - Germantown	MD
Montgomery College-Rockville College	MD
Morton College	IL
Motlow State Community College	TN
Mott Community College	MI
Murray State College	OK
Muskegon Community College	MI
Nassau Community College	NY
Naugatuck Valley Community Technical	CT
Navarro College	TX
Neosho County Community College	KS
New Mexico Junior College	NM
New Mexico Military Institute	NM
Newbury College	MA
Niagara County Community College	NY
North Arkansas College - Technical	AR
North Central Missouri College	MO
North Dakota State Univ. - Bottineau	ND
North Florida Junior College	FL
North Hennepin Community College	MN
North Idaho College	ID
North Iowa Area Community College	IA
North Lake College	TX
North Shore Community College	MA
Northeast Mississippi Community College	MS
Northeast Texas Community College	TX
Northeastern OK A & M JC	OK
Northern Essex Community College	MA
Northland Community College	MN
Northwest Mississippi Community	MS
Northwest Nazarene College	ID
Northwest Shoals-Phil Campbell	AL
Norwalk Community Technical College	CT
Oakton Community College	IL
Odessa College	TX
Okaloosa - Walton Community College	FL
Olney Central College	IL
Otero Junior College	CO
Owens Community College	OH
PA State University - Beaver Campus	PA
Palm Beach Community College	FL

NJCAA PROGRAMS

Listed in *The College Athletic Guide*

SCHOOL	ST
Panola College	TX
Paris Junior College	TX
Pasco Hernando Community College	FL
Pearl River Community College	MS
Pensacola Junior College	FL
Phoenix College	AZ
Pima Community College	AZ
Polk Community College	FL
Potomac State College	WV
Prairie State College	IL
Pratt Community College	KS
Prince George's Community College	MD
Quinsigamond Community College	MA
Ranger College	TX
Raritan Valley Community College	NJ
Rend Lake Community College	IL
Richland Community College	TX
Ricks College	ID
Roane State Community College	TN
Rochester Community College	MN
Rock Valley College	IL
Rockland Community College	NY
Rose State College	OK
Roxbury Community College	MA
Saddleback College	CA
Saint Catharine College	KY
Saint Clair County Community College	MI
Saint John's River Community College	FL
Saint Louis Community College -	MO
Saint Louis Community College - Forest	MO
Saint Louis Community College -	MO
Saint Petersburg J C	FL
Salem Community College	NJ
San Jacinto College - North	TX
Santa Fe Community College	FL
Sauk Valley Community College	IL
Schenectady County Community College	NY
Scottsdale Community College	AZ
Seminole Community College	FL
Seminole State College	OK
Seward County Community College	KS
Shawnee Community College	IL
Shelby State Community College	TN
Shelton State Community College	AL
Sinclair Community College	OH
Snead State Community College	AL
Snow College	UT
South Georgia College	GA
South Mountain Community College	AZ
South Suburban College	IL
Southeastern Community College	NC
Southeastern Community College-North	IA
Southeastern Illinois College	IL
Southern Union State College	AL
Southwest Mississippi Community	MS
Southwestern Community College	IA
Spartanburg Methodist College	SC
Springfield Technical Community College	MA
State University of New York - Cobleskill	NY
SUNY C of Tech - Farmingdale	NY

SCHOOL	ST
Suffolk County Community College	NY
Suffolk-West Community College	NY
Surry Community College	NC
Sussex County Community College	NJ
Tallahassee Community College	FL
Texarkana College	TX
Three Rivers Community College	MO
Treasure Valley Community College	OR
Trinidad State Junior College	CO
Triton College	IL
Truett - McConnell College	GA
Tyler Junior College	TX
Ulster County Community College	NY
Union County College	NJ
University of Connecticut - Avery Point	CT
University of North Dakota - Williston	ND
University of S Carolina - Salkehatchie	SC
University of Texas - Brownsville	TX
Utah Valley State College	UT
Vermilion Community College	MN
Vernon Regional Junior College	TX
Vincennes University	IN
Volunteer State Community College	TN
Wabash Valley College	IL
Waldorf Junior College	IA
Wallace State C - Hanceville	AL
Wallace State Community C - Dothan	AL
Walters State Community College	TN
Waubonsee Community College	IL
Waukesha County Technical College	WI
Westark Community College	AR
Westchester Community College	NY
Western Oklahoma State College	OK
Western Wisconsin Technical College	WI
Westmoreland County Community	PA
Wharton County Junior College	TX
William Rainey Harper College	IL
Willmar Community College	MN
Yavapai College	AZ
Young Harris College	GA

DUAL AFFILIATION & OTHER PROGRAMS

Listed in *The Athletic College Guide*

SCHOOL	ST
DUAL AFFILIATIONS	
Central Washington University	WA
Christian Brothers University	TN
Concordia University - Austin	TX
Dominican College	NY
East Texas Baptist University	TX
Hardin - Simmons University	TX
Hawaii Pacific University	HI
Hillsdale College	MI
Lambuth University	TN
Limestone College	SC
Lynn University	FL
Northeastern State University	OK
Saint Edward's College	TX
Saint Mary's University	TX
St. Martin's College	WA
Texas Lutheran College	TX
Texas Wesleyan University	TX
Tusculum College	TN
University of the Incarnate Word	TX
University of West Florida	FL
Western Oregon University	OR
OTHERS	
Alabama A & M University	AL
Allan Hancock College	CA
Antelope Valley Community College	CA
Canada College	CA
Cerritos Community College	CA
Chaffey College	CA
Citrus Community College	CA
College of Marin	CA
College of St. Scholastica	MN
College of the Sequoias	CA
Contra Costa College	CA
De Anza College	CA
Lassen College	CA
Los Medanos College	CA
Long Beach City College	CA
Los Angeles Pierce College	CA
Santa Rosa Junior College	CA
Vermont Technical College	VT
West Valley College	CA

INDEX

www.thesportsource.com
1-800-862-3092

INDEX

www.thesportsource.com
1-800-862-3092

INDEX

www.thesportsource.com
1-800-862-3092

INDEX

www.thesportsource.com
1-800-862-3092

There are many Christmas and Summer baseball camps available to boys of all ages. Some camps are sponsored by college coaches, and others conducted by independent organizations. The staff of a number of these camps consist of college coaches, professional players and scouts.

The curriculum of these camps is designed to improve the serious baseball player's skills. They also provide the attending college coaches with the opportunity to take a personal look at high school players -- this may be the only chance the coaches will have to see these young men. This helps both the coach and player during the recruiting process.

The following directory lists a few of these camps and "Showcase" tournaments affiliated with the ***Athletic College Guide for Baseball.***

The Sport Source's

CAMP AND COLLEGE SHOWCASE TOURNAMENT DIRECTORY

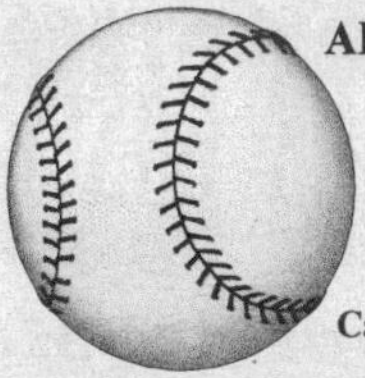

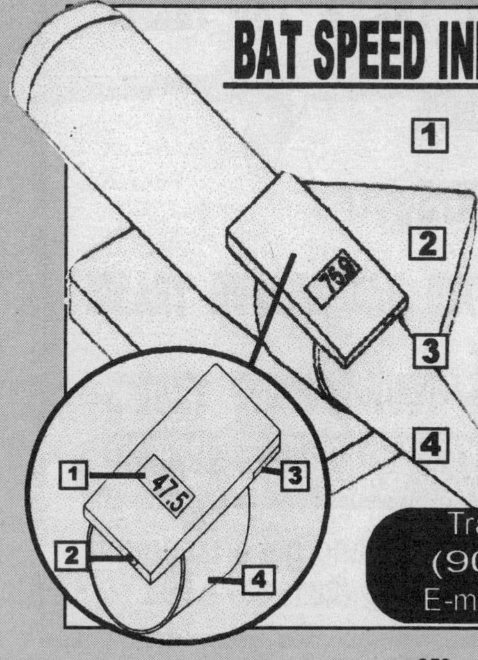

MickeyOwen
BASEBALL SCHOOL
LIVE IT • LOVE IT • LEARN IT
SUMMER ♦ MISSOURI ♦ May – August Ages 8-19
6 Sessions - Play 15-20 games on lighted professinally groomed fields. 4 lighted batting cages. Improve your skills with veteran instructors and games each night.
WINTER ♦ FLORIDA and ARIZONA
Ages 13-20 December 18-23 and 26-31
Ages 8-12 Dec. 26-31
Write or Call for Free Brochure or visit our website at www.mickeyowen.com
MickeyOwen
BASEBALL SCHOOL
Dept. SS • Miller, MO 65707
1-800-999-8369

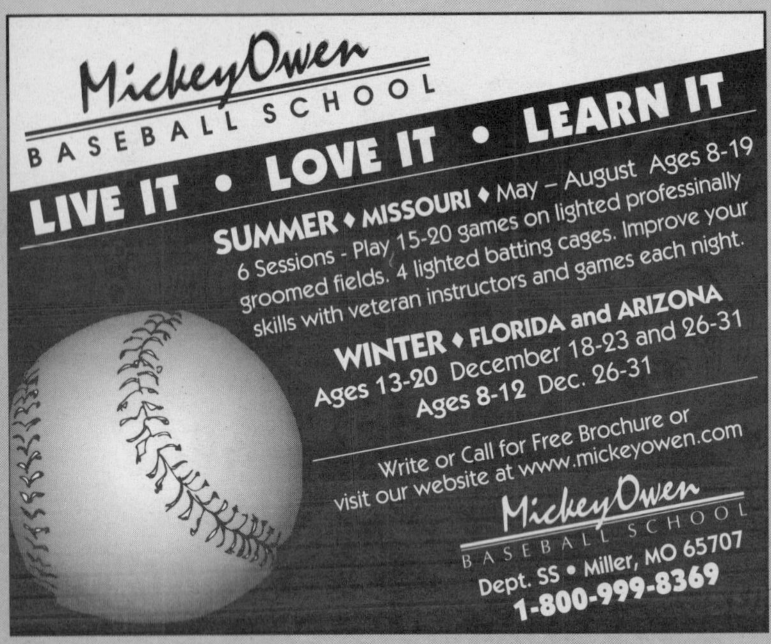

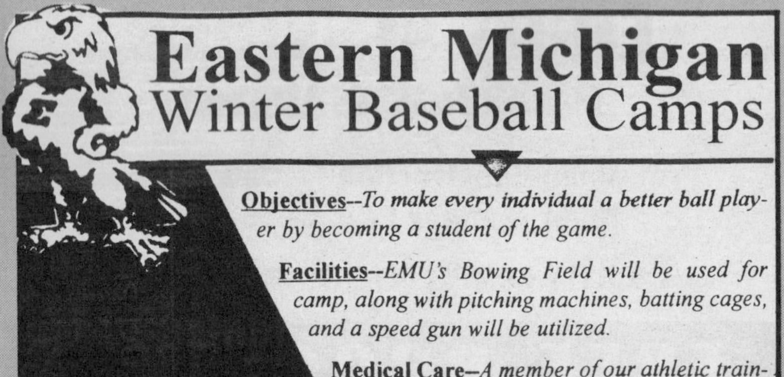
Eastern Michigan
Winter Baseball Camps
Objectives--To make every individual a better ball player by becoming a student of the game.
Facilities--EMU's Bowing Field will be used for camp, along with pitching machines, batting cages, and a speed gun will be utilized.
Medical Care--A member of our athletic training staff will be present during each session.
Camp Enrollment--Applications will be processed on a first-come, first-serve basis. A one time EMU baseball hat is included in the cost for each camper.
For more info:
Baseball Office
Bowen Field House
Eastern Michigan University
Ypsilanti, Michigan 48197
Phone: (734) 487-4568
Fax:(734) 487-4568

FIELD OF DREAMS

N.L.B.A.

(NEXT LEVEL BASEBALL ASSOCIATION)

BASEBALL CAMP 1999-2000

1984 All-Metro and Semi-Pro Star Outfielder, UMES
Andre' Stover, St.Louis Cards Scout

*"I would like to extend to you an invitation to attend the FIELD OF DREAMS baseball camp located on the beautiful campus of the University of Maryland, Eastern Shore. Our school will give you personalized training on all aspects of the game. Emphasis is placed on skill and knowledge, as well as game situations. Everyday is fully planned to best help maximize each person's full potential. The instructors are ex-college and professional scouts and players(*based on availablility) who will help instruct the fundamentals of succeeding to the next level. Come be a part of the successful hands-on training that will give you the winning formula to succeed."*

BASEBALL CAMP AGE

7-13 and 13-18 years of age

Delino DeShields

FEES

Overnight Campers: $325-$595
4 Day - 1 Week
Includes: Lodging, T-shirt, Transportation & Meals
Satelite Weekend Camps: $175-$250
Day Camps/Clinics: $75

For more information contact:

FIELD OF DREAMS
N.L.B.A.
P.O. BOX 11862
BALTIMORE, MD 21207
(410) 488-3362

Ira Smith
1997 Las Vegas Star Outfielder
1998 Future Major Leaguer

MIKE MARTIN BASEBALL SCHOOL

AT

FLORIDA STATE UNIVERSITY

MIKE MARTIN BASEBALL SCHOOL

JUNE 20 - 25; JULY 11-16; JULY 18 - 23; AUGUST 1- 6

AGES: 10 YRS -HIGH SCHOOL

A complete week of baseball which includes individual & group instruction, controlled games, & drills in a fun atmosphere. Campers will be grouped according to grade & ability.

COSTS: $215/DAY $335/OVERNIGHT W/ MEALS

SEMINOLE ADVANCED BASEBALL SCHOOL

JUNE 27- JULY 2 & JULY 25 - 30

1999, 2000, 2001 & 2002 HS GRADS

The most important week in a high school player's career. A very intense week of baseball instruction, games, & evaluation by a staff of college & junior college coaches. Thirteen first round draft picks have attended past schools.

COSTS: $315/DAY $435/OVERNIGHT W/ MEALS

SUPER SKILLS ACADEMY

JULY 4- 9

YEAR 2000 HIGH SCHOOL GRADUATES ONLY

An exclusive week of baseball for a limited number *(40)* of rising seniors (*YEAR 2000 GRADUATES ONLY*). The **Florida State** coaching staff will teach fundamentals, drills, & strategies with a "hands on" approach. The staff will utilize the latest teaching methods including the use of individual video taping, along with individual sessions evaluating form & mechanics on each aspect of a player's position, hitting, & base running.

COST: $795/OVERNIGHT ONLY W/ MEALS

1999 CHRISTMAS CAMPS

PLEASE CALL FOR INFORMATION

FOR A DETAILED BROCHURE WRITE:

FLORIDA STATE BASEBALL
PO BOX 2195
TALLAHASSEE FL 32316

CALL: 850-644-1073
FAX: 850-644-7213
E-MAIL: shough@mailer.fsu.edu

WOULD YOU SPEND $25
TO SAVE $25,000?
Official Athletic College Guide
THE SPORT SOURCE
Over 1600 Men's and Women's Scholarship Programs Listed
1999 SOCCER
Compiled and Edited by Charlie Kadupski
Official Athletic College Guide
THE SPORT SOURCE
Over 1400 Men's Scholarship Programs Listed
1999 BASEBALL
Edited And Compiled By Charlie Kadupski
Official Athletic College Guide
THE SPORT SOURCE
1999 SOFTBALL
Edited And Compiled By Charlie Kadupski
Over 880 Women's Scholarship Programs Listed
Official Athletic College Guide
THE
1999 VOLLEYBALL
Over 600 Men's and Women's Scholarship Programs Listed
THE DEFINITIVE GUIDES TO COLLEGE
ATHLETIC SCHOLARSHIP PROGRAMS!

Champion
DIAMONDS
MIDWEST COLLEGE
SHOWCASE
TOURNAMENTS
- June 4 thru 6
- July 2 thru 4
- August 6 thru 8
3 game tournaments
Individual Perfomance
Ratings Package
for more information
417-667-4993
www.championdiamonds.com
Nevada, MO

BASEBALL SHOWCASE

EXPOSURE IS AT YOUR FINGERTIPS.

"We'll build your Academic and Athletic Profile for you."

Show your skills to hundreds of college coaches at one of our national talent showcase events!

WHAT AWAITS YOU:

- The most accurate evaluation of your athletic ability
- A professional baseball service to represent you and provide a support system to help aggressively expose your abilities
- The right questions to ask recruiters and yourself
- Ways to narrow your college choices
- Directions on how to contact schools and coaches as needed.

CALL:(850) 914-2045

"You'll never be a good coach until you take your ego out of the game. You have to understand that learning is more important than winning.Once your players know how to play the game - winning will take care of itself."

Tony Lucadello
Former Scout for Philidephia Phillies
(Signed more major league players than any scout in the history of the game.)

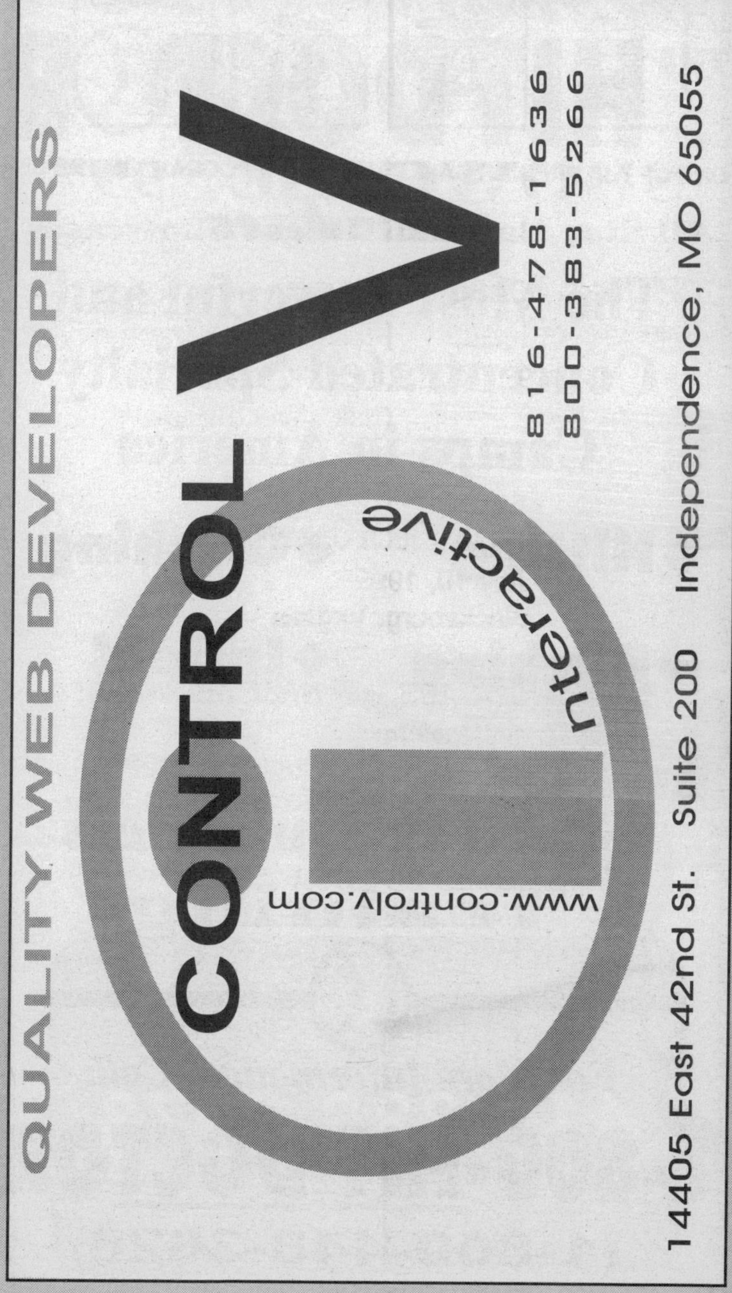
QUALITY WEB DEVELOPERS
CONTROL V
Interactive
www.controlv.com
816-478-1636
800-383-5266
14405 East 42nd St. Suite 200 Independence, MO 65055